*The impressive Diego Rivera murals at the Palacio National in Mexico City depict Mexico's tumultuous history. See chapter 3.* © Hollenbeck Photo.

*The planned resort town of Ixtapa boasts a pristine beach. See chapter 9.* © Hollenbeck Photo.

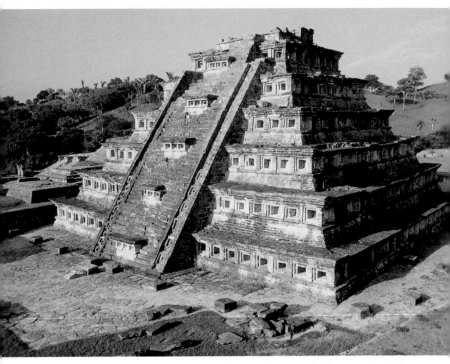

*The unique pre-Columbian Pyramid of the Niches at El Tajín, north of Veracruz, has 365 recesses extending to all four sides of the building. See chapter 11.* © Robert Frerck/Tony Stone Images.

*La Parroquia, in San Miguel de Allende, owes more to its builder's imagination and fancy than to the Gothic churches that were its inspiration. See chapter 5.* © Hollenbeck Photo.

*A market in Guadalajara, possibly the most quintessentially Mexican of cities. See chapter 7.*
*© Hollenbeck Photo.*

*Puerto Vallarta's Church of Nuestra Señora de Guadalupe is topped by a crown held up by a ring of angels. See chapter 8.* © *Joseph Nettis/Tony Stone Images.*

*Despite its sophisticated hotels, restaurants, nightlife, and growing number of eco-tourism attractions, Puerto Vallarta maintains a small-town charm. See chapter 8.* © *Steve Blyl Dave G. Houser Photography.*

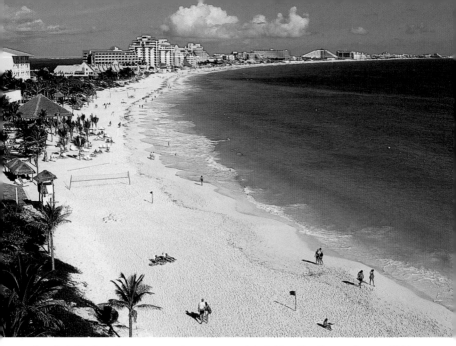

*Cancún is Mexico's showcase, a modern megaresort, but rich with a thousand years of history. See chapter 12.* *Top photo © Robert Frerck/Odyssey; bottom photo © Cosmo Condina/Tony Stone Images.*

*The reefs off Cozumel, one of the world's top dive destinations and a busy port of call for cruise ships. See chapter 13.* © M. Timothy O'Keefe Photography.

*The Temple of the Warriors at Chichén-Itzá is named for the carvings of soldiers that march along its walls. See chapter 14.* © Chris Cheadle/Tony Stone Images.

*The scenery is stunning at Urique Canyon, one of several that make up the region known as the Copper Canyon. See chapter 15.* © Jack Dykinga/Tony Stone Images.

*Land's End is where the Pacific meets the Sea of Cortez; the famous El Arco rock formation makes for a stunning backdrop. See chapter 16.* © Hollenbeck Photo.

# A New Star-Rating System & Other Exciting News from Frommer's!

In our continuing effort to publish the savviest, most up-to-date, and most appealing travel guides available, we've added some great new features.

Frommer's guides now include a new **star-rating system.** Every hotel, restaurant, and attraction is rated from 0 to 3 stars to help you set priorities and organize your time.

We've also added **seven brand-new features** that point you to the great deals, in-the-know advice, and unique experiences that separate travelers from tourists. Throughout the guide, look for:

***Finds*** Special finds—those places only insiders know about

***Fun Fact*** Fun facts—details that make travelers more informed and their trips more fun

***Kids*** Best bets for kids—advice for the whole family

***Moments*** Special moments—those experiences that memories are made of

***Overrated*** Places or experiences not worth your time or money

***Tips*** Insider tips—some great ways to save time and money

***Value*** Great values—where to get the best deals

We've also added a **"What's New"** section in every guide—a timely crash course in what's hot and what's not in every destination we cover.

## Here's what the critics say about Frommer's:

**"Amazingly easy to use. Very portable, very complete."**

—*Booklist*

**"Detailed, accurate, and easy-to-read information for all price ranges."**

—*Glamour Magazine*

**"Hotel information is close to encyclopedic."**

—*Des Moines Sunday Register*

**"Frommer's Guides have a way of giving you a real feel for a place."**

—*Knight Ridder Newspapers*

Frommer's®

# Mexico 2003

by David Baird and Lynne Bairstow

Wiley Publishing, Inc.

Published by:

**Wiley Publishing, Inc.**

909 Third Ave.
New York, NY 10022



ISBN 0-7645-6658-X
ISSN 1042-8399

Editors: Marie Morris, Kelly Regan
Production Editor: Heather Wilcox
Cartographer: Roberta Stockwell
Photo Editor: Richard Fox
Production by Wiley Indianapolis Composition Services

Front cover photo: Chaac-Mool statue at Chichén-Itzá, Yucatán peninsula
Back cover photo: The golf course at Cabo Real, Los Cabos

For information on our other products and services or to obtain technical support, please contact our Customer Care Department within the U.S. at 800-762-2974, outside the U.S. at 317-572-3993 or fax 317-572-4002.

Wiley also publishes its books in a variety of electronic formats. Some content that appears in print may not be available in electronic formats.

Manufactured in the United States of America

5 4 3 2

# Contents

## 13 Isla Mujeres, Cozumel & the Riviera Maya 525



## 14 Mérida, Chichén-Itzá & the Maya Interior 595



## 15 The Copper Canyon 640



## 16 Los Cabos & Baja California 661

# List of Maps

## About the Authors

**David Baird** (chapters 1, 5, 6, 7, 10, 11, 13, 14, and 15, and appendix A) is a writer, editor, and translator based in Austin, Texas. He spent part of his childhood in Morelia, Mexico, and later lived for 2 years among the Mazatec Indians in Oaxaca while he was doing graduate fieldwork.

**Lynne Bairstow** (chapters 1, 2, 3, 4, 8, 9, 12, 13, and 16) is a writer specializing in travel and the Internet who has lived in Puerto Vallarta, Mexico, at least part time for the past 9 years. She now lives there year-round and was assisted in her research for this book by Claudia Velo. In a previous professional life, Lynne was a vice-president for Merrill Lynch in Chicago and New York.

They are also the authors of *Frommer's Cancún, Cozumel & the Yucatán; Frommer's Portable Acapulco; Ixtapa & Zihuatanejo; Frommer's Portable Cancún; Frommer's Portable Los Cabos & Baja;* and *Frommer's Portable Puerto Vallarta, Manzanillo & Guadalajara,* which won Mexico's Pluma de Plata (Silver Quill) award, given for excellence in foreign travel writing about Mexico.

## An Invitation to the Reader

In researching this book, we discovered many wonderful places—hotels, restaurants, shops, and more. We're sure you'll find others. Please tell us about them, so we can share the information with your fellow travelers in upcoming editions. If you were disappointed with a recommendation, we'd love to know that, too. Please write to:

*Frommer's Mexico 2003*
Wiley Publishing, Inc. • 909 Third Ave. • New York, NY 10022

## An Additional Note

Please be advised that travel information is subject to change at any time—and this is especially true of prices. We therefore suggest that you write or call ahead for confirmation when making your travel plans. The authors, editors, and publisher cannot be held responsible for the experiences of readers while traveling. Your safety is important to us, however, so we encourage you to stay alert and be aware of your surroundings. Keep a close eye on cameras, purses, and wallets, all favorite targets of thieves and pickpockets.

### New! Frommer's Star Ratings & Icons

Every hotel, restaurant, and attraction listing in this guide has been ranked for quality, value, service, amenities, and special features using a star-rating scale. In country, state, and regional guides, we also rate towns and regions to help you narrow down your choices and budget your time accordingly. Hotels and restaurants in the Very Expensive and Expensive categories are rated on a scale of one (highly recommended) to three stars (exceptional). Those in the Moderate and Inexpensive categories rate from zero (recommended) to two stars (very highly recommended). Attractions, towns, and regions are rated according to the following scale: zero stars (recommended), one star (highly recommended), two stars (very highly recommended), and three stars (must-see).

In addition to the rating system, we also use seven icons to highlight insider information, useful tips, special bargains, hidden gems, memorable experiences, kid-friendly venues, places to avoid, and other useful information:

*Finds* *Fun Fact* *Kids* *Moments* *Overrated* *Tips* *Value*

The following abbreviations are used for credit cards:

| | | | | | |
|---|---|---|---|---|---|
| AE | American Express | DISC | Discover | V | Visa |
| DC | Diners Club | MC | MasterCard | | |

## FROMMERS.COM

Now that you have the guidebook to a great trip, visit our website at **www.frommers.com** for travel information on nearly 2,500 destinations. With features updated regularly, we give you instant access to the most current trip-planning information available. At Frommers.com, you'll also find the best prices on airfares, accommodations, and car rentals—and you can even book travel online through our travel booking partners. At Frommers.com, you'll also find the following:

- Online updates to our most popular guidebooks
- Vacation sweepstakes and contest giveaways
- Newsletter highlighting the hottest travel trends
- Online travel message boards with featured travel discussions

# What's New in Mexico

The decline in air travel that followed the September 11, 2001, terrorist attacks prompted airlines to reduce the number of flights to Mexico from the U.S. and Canada. Although the number of visitors to resort areas declined only slightly, the total number of tourists coming into the country fell substantially. Add the peso's status as one of the strongest currencies relative to the U.S. dollar (thus making Mexico more expensive for foreigners), and you can see that the Mexican tourism industry has cause for concern. Because the strong peso also is weakening the country's exports, look for Mexico to put downward pressure on its currency, which is the good news. The bad news is that the government's new fiscal reform package will make visiting Mexico a little more expensive: It includes higher consumption taxes for hotels and restaurants, especially for certain foods and alcoholic beverages.

On the political front, Mexico has shown great stability, managing to avoid crises in its transition from one-party rule to pluralism. President Vicente Fox's popularity declined over the last year, but his administration is doing better at working with the legislature.

A practical matter is the radical change in Mexico's telephone system, which created some confusion before the changeover was complete. All phone numbers now conform to the international standard of 10-digit numbers (a 2- or 3-digit area code and an 8- or 7-digit local number).

Here is a quick rundown on what else is new and noteworthy in Mexico:

**MEXICO CITY** For complete information, see chapter 3. Increased security and measures taken to counter police corruption have paid off—crime is down. Although visitors should still exercise prudence and common sense, they are finding Mexico City a much safer place. As part of this effort to continue to improve security and visitor services, an elite police force will be stationed along Avenida Reforma. These English-speaking officers have been trained to assist tourists and provide security.

Also along Reforma, a beautification project has installed new landscaping, planters, and benches, as well as 16 outdoor cafes. Monuments, sculptures, and traffic circles are also being restored; by late 2002, Reforma will have new lighting and news kiosks. Mexico City celebrates its 675th anniversary in 2003.

**Accommodations** Latin America's first **W Hotel,** in Mexico City's posh Polanco neighborhood, will open in late 2002. The 239-room hotel will include a business center, meeting spaces, a spa, and a restaurant.

**Casa Vieja,** a former private mansion in Polanco, is now a hacienda-style hotel. The 10 rooms and suites have fully equipped kitchens, digital TVs and VCRs, a host of special amenities, and the services of a 24-hour concierge.

The **Habita** hotel has quickly become one of the hippest spots to stay. Also in the Polanco district, it features a bi-level rooftop terrace with a heated lap pool, wall-to-wall fireplaces, bar, spa, and expansive views of the city. All of the 36 rooms are minimalist in design, but feature special services and sophisticated amenities.

A **Le Cirque** restaurant is slated to open at the Hotel Camino Real in summer 2002. Mexico City will be Le Cirque's third location since the world-famous restaurant opened in New York in 1974.

**Attractions** Following the completion of a rescue operation, the Catedral Metropolitan, the largest, oldest, and one of the most beautiful in the Americas, has been removed from the World Monuments Fund's list of endangered historic buildings. Its history comes to life in "Voices of the Cathedral," a new sound-and-light show. Period music accompanies the candlelit tour. Tickets ($25) are available through Ticketmaster (✆ **55/5325-9000**). The schedule for English-language performances was being finalized at press time; call ✆ **55/5512-7096** for details.

**MICHOACAN** **Morelia** has a new central *camionera* (bus station) on the northwest side of downtown. Visitors no longer arrive at the downtown bus station. Morelia has also been hard at work on an intensive beautification program for its historic center. For complete information, see chapter 6.

**PUERTO VALLARTA & THE CENTRAL PACIFIC COAST** For complete information, see chapter 8.

**Accommodations** Among the most intriguing of Mexico's unique inns is the newly opened **Verana** (✆ **800/677-5156;** www.verana.com), in Yelapa, a funky village 45 minutes south of Puerto Vallarta. In a palm jungle on a mountain overlooking a tranquil bay, it's a stylish place, with color-washed walls, open-air showers, and one-of-a-kind touches added by the owners, a former film design duo with European roots. A magical infinity pool that seems to drop off the edge of the mountain, well-stocked library, massage hut, and open-air restaurant and bar complement the magnificent setting.

**Attractions** Puerto Vallarta's leading tour operator, **Vallarta Adventures** (✆ **866/256-2739** toll-free from the U.S. or 322/291-1212; www.vallarta-adventures.com), was to unveil its newest adventure-tour offering in summer 2002. The "Tree-top Canopy" tour takes guests swinging from platform to platform at the tops of towering jungle palms. It's affiliated with the group that has made a similar tour among the most popular in Costa Rica.

**Vista Vallarta Golf Club** (✆ **322/290-0030**), opened its second course, a Tom Weiskopf design, adjacent to the existing Jack Nicklaus Signature course. Vista Vallarta will play host to the World Golf Championships in December 2002. This renowned event, which brings together the year's top golfers, is certain to place the Puerto Vallarta region squarely on the map of world-class golf destinations. The Banderas Bay area now has a total of seven courses; five of them opened in the past 2 years. The two newest opened in 2002 at the Paradise Village and Mayan Palace resorts.

**ACAPULCO & THE SOUTHERN PACIFIC COAST** For complete information, see chapter 9.

**Ixtapa/Zihuatanejo** A highway is under construction between Ixtapa/Zihuatanejo and Morelia, capital of Michoacán state. The Ixtapa/Zihuatanejo Convention & Visitors Bureau hopes to promote visits to the region that combine beach and colonial themes, starting in one place and departing from the other.

**OAXACA & CHIAPAS** For complete information, see chapter 10.

**Oaxaca** Tombs 7 and 104 in Monte Albán remain closed to the public until earthquake damage can be repaired.

The **Viajes Atlántida** agency, La Noria 101, near Armenta y López (✆ **951/514-7077**), offers daily service in Suburbans to **Puerto Escondido** and Pochutla. Seven daily trips go to Pochutla, four of which continue to Puerto Escondido. From Pochutla you can catch a *colectivo* to Huatulco or Puerto Angel. Service to Puerto Escondido costs $18 and takes 5 hours, which is much faster than the bus. The trip to Pochutla costs $13.50 and takes 4 hours. Buy tickets in advance. The agency is open from 5:30am to 11:30pm daily.

**San Cristóbal de las Casas** This remains one of the bargain spots of Mexico, and though the conflict with the Zapatistas hasn't been resolved to anyone's satisfaction, the situation remains peaceful.

**VERACRUZ & PUEBLA** Veracruz's aquarium has a new shark tank that practically doubles the site's tank volume. In Puebla, the Museo Bello will reopen after renovations. This attractive, fascinating colonial city also has several new dining options. For complete information, see chapter 11.

**CANCUN** For complete information, see chapter 12.

**Accommodations** **Blue Bay Getaway** is expanding, thanks to its acquisition of the adjacent Plaza Las Glorias hotel. The 175-room Plaza Las Glorias will be integrated with a $6 million renovation, and a common lobby will connect the hotels. The all-inclusive resort now has a total of 385 rooms and a new full-service spa.

The **JW Marriott Cancún Resort & Spa** recently opened adjacent to its sister hotel, the **Marriott Casa Magna** (a skywalk connects them). The new resort features five restaurants and bars, a freshwater lagoon, a free-form pool, a children's club, meeting space, and the region's largest spa, with over 30,000 square feet of pampering space. The hotel's 450 rooms and 79 suites all have private balconies.

**Beaches, Watersports & Boat Tours** The popular AquaWorld (✆ **998/848-8300;** www.aquaworld.com.mx) has added an adventure. The Skyrider is a custom-built double-seat parachair that takes twosomes high into the sky for an incredible view of the Cancún peninsula. The Skyrider departs from and returns to the Aquaworld boat, meaning a comfortable, safe descent.

**ISLA MUJERES, COZUMEL & THE RIVIERA MAYA** For complete information on this region, see chapter 13.

**Cozumel** The 18-hole course designed by Jack Nicklaus at the new Cozumel Country Club (north of the town, across the road from the seaside hotels) has finally been completed. A few island hotels offer guests discounts at the club.

**Puerto Morelos & Environs** Ceiba Del Mar, a medium-size spa resort, has opened on the northern edge of Puerto Morelos. It offers a full range of spa treatments in a tropical beach setting and lots of personal service.

**Playa del Carmen** New restaurants and new hotels add variety to this destination, which keeps growing at an astonishing rate.

**Tulum** Tulum now has a bank and three cash machines. The hotel zone remains exclusively the domain of small bungalow hotels, allowing Tulum to retain the feel of an escape from the outside world.

**MERIDA, CHICHEN-ITZA & THE MAYAN INTERIOR** For complete information on this region, see chapter 14.

**Mérida** The Izamal Express, a train that used to run excursions to Izamal from Mérida, is no longer operating, but you might want to ask about it when you're in town. For the last year there has been word of the imminent establishment of a luxury train between Mérida and Palenque, but there are no definite dates.

**LOS CABOS & BAJA CALIFORNIA** For complete information, see chapter 16.

Continental Airlines now flies nonstop to Los Cabos from Newark, N.J., and Atlanta. Alaska Airlines continues to expand service to Baja, and has added seats to flights from San Francisco, Los Angeles, and Seattle.

During the summer, many Los Cabos hotels offer reduced rates for midweek stays. Details appear on the official website, **www.visitcabo.com**.

**Accommodations** The 180-suite Marquis Los Cabos is slated to open by spring 2003.

**Attractions** In Cabo del Sol, the newest of Los Cabos' championship golf courses, an 18-hole Tom Weiskopf design, has opened. Cabo now offers a total of eight world-class golf course options.

1

# The Best of Mexico

Across Mexico, in villages and cities, in mountains, tropical coasts, and jungle settings, enchanting surprises await travelers. These might take the form of a fantastic small-town festival, delightful dining in a memorable restaurant, or even a stretch of road through heavenly countryside. Below is a starter list of our favorites, to which you'll have the pleasure of adding your own discoveries.

## 1 The Best Beach Vacations

- **Puerto Vallarta:** Spectacularly wide Banderas Bay offers 42km (26 miles) of beaches in various shapes, sizes, and appeal. Some, like Playa Los Muertos—the popular public beach in town—abound with *palapa* restaurants, beach volleyball, and parasailing. The beaches of Punta Mita, the exclusive development north of Vallarta, are of the white-sand variety, with crystalline waters and coral reefs just offshore. Others around the bay nestle in coves, accessible only by boat. Puerto Vallarta itself is the only place where an authentic colonial ambience mixes with true resort amenities. See "Puerto Vallarta," in chapter 8.
- **Puerto Escondido:** The best overall beach value in Mexico is principally known for its world-class surfing beach, Playa Zicatela. The surrounding beaches all have their own appeal; colorful fishing *pangas* dot the central town beach, parked under the shade of palms leaning so far over they almost touch the ground. Puerto Escondido offers unique accommodations at excellent prices, with exceptional budget dining and nightlife. See "Puerto Escondido," in chapter 9.
- **Ixtapa/Zihuatanejo:** These side-by-side resorts offer beach-goers the best of both worlds: serene simplicity and resort comforts. For those in search of a back-to-basics beach, the best and most beautiful is Playa La Ropa, close to Zihuatanejo. The wide beach at Playa Las Gatas, with its restaurants and snorkeling sites, is also a great place to play. The luxury hotels in Ixtapa, on the next bay over from Zihuatanejo, front Playa Palmar, a fine, wide swath of beach. See "Northward to Zihuatanejo & Ixtapa," in chapter 9.
- **Cancún:** In terms of sheer beauty, Mexico's best beaches are in Cancún and along the Yucatán's Quintana Roo coast, extending almost all the way to the Belizean border. The powdery, white-sand beaches front water the color of a Technicolor dream; it's so clear you can see through to the coral reefs below. Cancún offers the widest assortment of luxury beachfront hotels, with more restaurants, nightlife, and activities than any other resort destination in the country. See chapter 12.
- **Isla Mujeres:** There's only one small beach here—Playa Norte—but it's superb. From this island, you can dive El Garrafón reef,

# Mexico

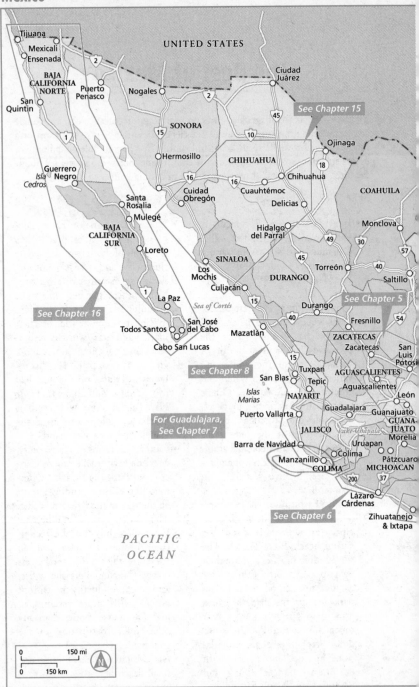

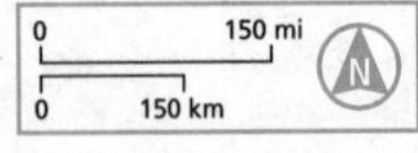
0
150 mi
0
150 km
N
UNITED STATES
Tijuana
Mexicali
Ensenada
BAJA CALIFORNIA NORTE
Puerto Penasco
San Quintin
Nogales
Ciudad Juárez
See Chapter 15
SONORA
Hermosillo
CHIHUAHUA
Ojinaga
Chihuahua
Guerrero Negro
Isla Cedros
Cuidad Obregón
Cuauhtémoc
COAHUILA
Santa Rosalia
Delicias
Mulegé
BAJA CALIFORNIA SUR
Hidalgo del Parral
Monclova
Loreto
SINALOA
Los Mochis
Torreón
DURANGO
Saltillo
Culiacán
La Paz
Sea of Cortés
See Chapter 16
Durango
See Chapter 5
Todos Santos
San José del Cabo
Mazatlán
Fresnillo
ZACATECAS
Cabo San Lucas
Zacatecas
San Luis Potosí
See Chapter 8
Tuxpan
San Blas
Tepic
AGUASCALIENTES
Aguascalientes
Islas Marias
NAYARIT
León
Puerto Vallarta
Guadalajara
Guanajuato
For Guadalajara, See Chapter 7
JALISCO
Lake Chapala
GUANAJUATO
Morelia
Barra de Navidad
Uruapan
Colima
Manzanillo
Pátzcuaro
COLIMA
MICHOACAN
Lázaro Cárdenas
See Chapter 6
Zihuatanejo & Ixtapa
PACIFIC OCEAN

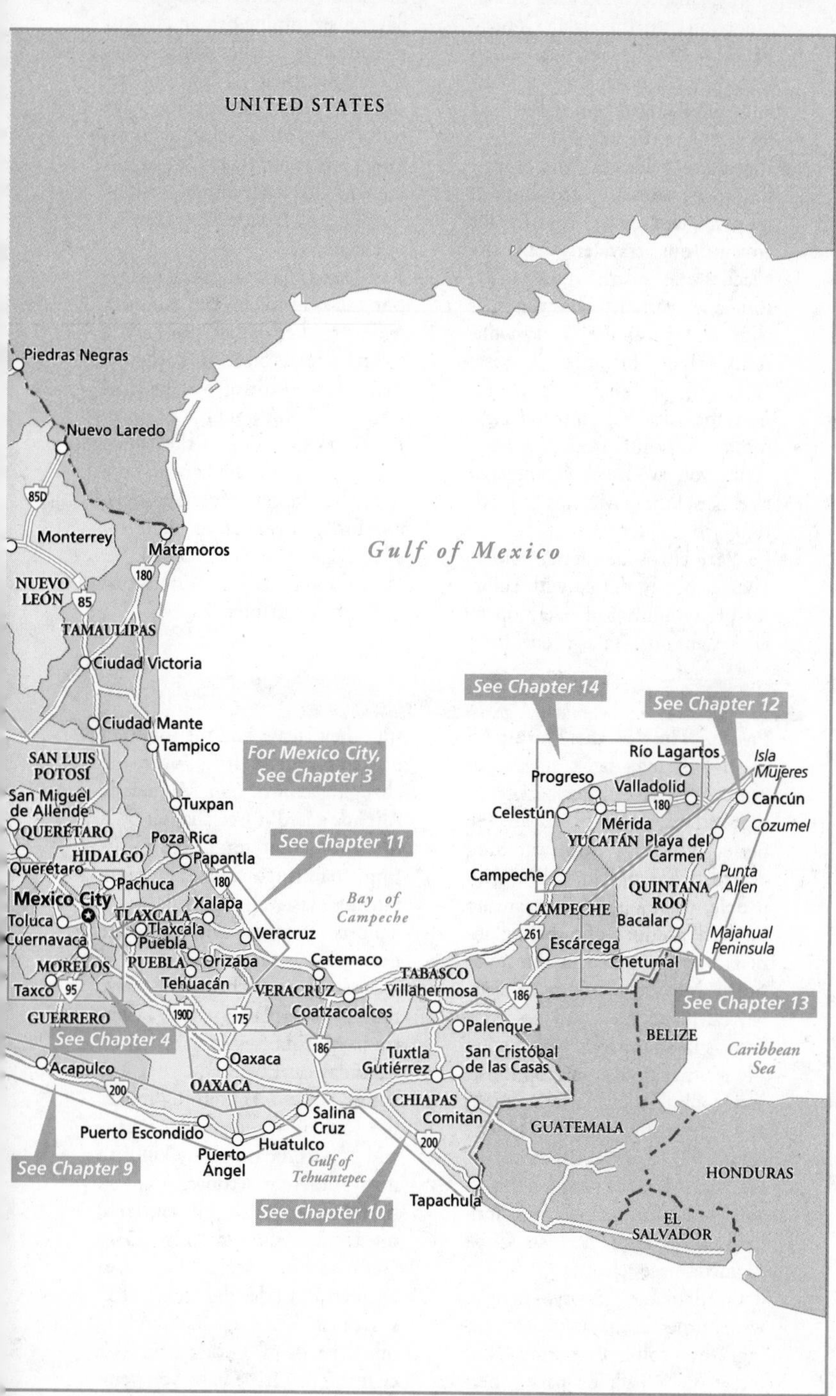
UNITED STATES
Gulf of Mexico
Piedras Negras
Nuevo Laredo
Monterrey
Matamoros
NUEVO LEÓN
TAMAULIPAS
Ciudad Victoria
Ciudad Mante
Tampico
SAN LUIS POTOSÍ
San Miguel de Allende
QUERÉTARO
Querétaro
HIDALGO
Tuxpan
Poza Rica
Papantla
Pachuca
Mexico City
Toluca
Cuernavaca
TLAXCALA
Tlaxcala
Puebla
Xalapa
Veracruz
PUEBLA
Orizaba
Tehuacán
MORELOS
Taxco
GUERRERO
Acapulco
VERACRUZ
Catemaco
Coatzacoalcos
TABASCO
Villahermosa
Palenque
Oaxaca
OAXACA
Puerto Escondido
Puerto Ángel
Huatulco
Salina Cruz
Gulf of Tehuantepec
Tuxtla Gutiérrez
San Cristóbal de las Casas
CHIAPAS
Comitan
Tapachula
GUATEMALA
BELIZE
HONDURAS
EL SALVADOR
Caribbean Sea
Bay of Campeche
For Mexico City, See Chapter 3
See Chapter 4
See Chapter 9
See Chapter 10
See Chapter 11
See Chapter 12
See Chapter 13
See Chapter 14
Progreso
Río Lagartos
Valladolid
Celestún
Mérida
YUCATÁN
Playa del Carmen
Campeche
CAMPECHE
Escárcega
QUINTANA ROO
Bacalar
Chetumal
Isla Mujeres
Cancún
Cozumel
Punta Allen
Majahual Peninsula
85D
85
180
95
190D
175
186
200
261

snorkel offshore, and take a boat excursion to the Isla Contoy national wildlife reserve, which features great birding and a fabulous, uninhabited beach. See "Isla Mujeres," in chapter 13.

- **Playa del Carmen:** Not only is the town currently the hottest, hippest place in the country for adventurous travelers, but the beaches are of the pure-white, soft-sand variety. The water is clear and turquoise, and swimming right offshore is safe. "Playa," as it's known, is not far from the ruins of Tulum and a 45-minute ferry ride from Cozumel, giving you two beach vacations in one. See "Puerto Morelos & Environs," in chapter 13.
- **La Paz:** This state capital borders a lovely beach, dotted with colorful playgrounds and lively open-air restaurants. Take a cue from the local residents, though, and pass on swimming here in favor of the exquisite beaches just minutes from downtown. La Paz's beaches and the islets just offshore have transformed this tranquil town into a center for diving, sea kayaking, and other adventure pursuits. See "La Paz: Peaceful Port Town," in chapter 16.
- **Los Cabos:** Dramatic rock formations and crashing waves mix with wide stretches of soft sand and a rolling break. Start at Pueblo la Playa, just north of San José del Cabo, and work your way down the Cabo Corridor to the famed Playa de Amor at Land's End. Some beaches are more appropriate for contemplation than for swimming, which isn't all bad. See "Los Cabos: Resorts, Watersports & Golf," in chapter 16.

## 2 The Best Cultural Experiences

- **Passing Time in the Plazas:** All the world may be a stage, but some parts have richer backdrops than others. Town plazas are the perfect settings for watching everyday life unfold. Alive with people, these open spaces are no modern product of urban planners, but are rooted in the traditional Mexican view of society. Several plazas are standouts: **Veracruz**'s famous *zócalo* (see chapter 11) features nearly nonstop music and tropical gaiety. One look tells you how important **Oaxaca**'s *zócalo* (see chapter 10) is to the local citizenry; the plaza is remarkably beautiful, grand, and intimate all at once. **Mexico City**'s Alameda (see chapter 3) has a dark, dramatic history—heretics were burned at the stake here during the colonial period—but today it's a people's park where lovers sit, cotton-candy vendors spin their treats, and the sound of organ grinders drifts over the changing crowd. **San Miguel de Allende**'s Jardín (see chapter 5) is the focal point for meeting, sitting, painting, and sketching. During festivals, it fills with dancers, parades, and elaborate fireworks. **Guanajuato** and **Querétaro** (see chapter 5) have the coziest of plazas, while El Centro in **Mérida** (see chapter 14) on a Sunday can't be beat.
- ***Música Popular:*** Nothing reveals the soul of a people like music, and Mexico boasts many kinds in many different settings. You can find brassy, belt-it-out **mariachi** music in the famous Plaza Garibaldi in Mexico City (see chapter 3), under the arches of El Parián in Tlaquepaque, and in other parts of Guadalajara (see chapter 7). Or perhaps you want to hear romantic **boleros** about

love's betrayal sung to the strumming of a Spanish guitar, or what Mexicans call ***música tropical*** and related cumbias, mambos, and cha-cha-chas (see chapters 12 and 14).

- **Regional Folk Dancing:** Whether it's the Ballet Folklórico in Mexico City or Guadalajara (see chapters 3 and 7), the almost-nightly park performances in Mérida (see chapter 14), or celebrations countrywide, these performances are diverse and colorful expressions of Mexican traditions.
- **Fireworks:** Mexicans have such a passion for fireworks and such a cavalier attitude toward them that it's a good thing the buildings are stone and cement, or the whole country would have burned down long ago. Many local traditions surround fireworks, and every festival includes some sort of display. The most lavish are the large constructions known as *castillos,* and the wildest are the *toros* that men carry over their shoulders while running through the streets, causing festival-goers to dive for cover.
- **Strolling el Malecón:** Wherever there's a seafront road, you'll find *el malecón* bordering it. This is generally a wide sidewalk for strolling, complete with vendors selling pinwheels and cotton candy. In some places, it has supplanted the plaza as a centerpiece of town life. The best examples are in **Puerto Vallarta, Mazatlán** (see chapter 8), **La Paz** (see chapter 16), **Cozumel** (see chapter 13), and **Veracruz** (see chapter 11).
- **Regional Fairs:** Almost every city and town has its regional fair, or *Feria Regional.* These fairs showcase the best products of the region—tequila or fruit liquors, livestock, intricately carved silver, or clay handicrafts. One of the most notable regional fairs is La Feria del Caballo in Texcoco, which takes place in late March or early April.

## 3 The Best Festivals & Celebrations

- **Festival de Nuestra Señora de Guadalupe:** This annual celebration leads up to Día de Nuestra Señora de Guadalupe, celebrated throughout Mexico on December 12. The Virgin of Guadalupe is the patron saint of Mexico, and is also identified with the Aztec earth goddess and mother of humankind. The basilica just outside of **Mexico City** features the largest celebration and the most impressive crowd of impassioned believers, but perhaps the best place to view the festivities is in **Puerto Vallarta,** where they continue around the clock for 12 days. It is a visual delight, especially for photographers. See "Exploring Mexico City," in chapter 3, and "Puerto Vallarta," in chapter 8.
- **Days of the Dead:** People across the country celebrate *Los Días de los Muertos* (Oct 31–Nov 2); they erect altars for the dead, with marigolds (the flower of the dead) and offerings of food and drink. The most popular celebrations happen in the villages around **Pátzcuaro** (see chapter 6) and in the valley of **Oaxaca** (see chapter 10). People head out to the cemetery for all-night vigils and sing and pray for the souls of the dearly departed. During the day, markets sell crafts and special items made just for the festival.
- **Carnaval:** Mexico has two particularly notable celebrations. Festivities in **Veracruz** fill the 3 days before Ash Wednesday, with fabulous floats, dancing in the plaza, and live entertainment.

**Mazatlán**'s party lasts a full week before Lent, with parades, strolling musicians, and crowds of revelers along the entire length of the *malecón*. See "Veracruz City," in chapter 11, and "Mazatlán," in chapter 8.

- **Holy Week:** The silver city of **Taxco** hosts one of the most compelling Holy Week commemorations in the country, beginning the Friday before Palm Sunday with nightly processions (and several during the day). On the evening of Holy Thursday, villagers carrying saints from the surrounding area are followed by hooded members of a society of self-flagellating penitents. On the Saturday morning before Easter, the Plaza Borda fills for the Procession of Three Falls, which reenacts the three times Christ stumbled and fell while carrying the cross. See chapter 4. In **San Miguel de Allende, Pátzcuaro** and surrounding communities, and **Oaxaca,** the solemn weeklong commemoration involves nightly candlelit processions through the streets and other religious events. See chapters 5, 6, and 10.
- **La Fiesta de los Locos:** In **San Miguel de Allende,** a town known for celebrating holidays, this one is the most fun for visitors. Young and old alike dress in grotesque costumes and parade around the center of town, or in dressed-up carts, to musical accompaniment. Keep an eye open for practical jokes. See "San Miguel de Allende," in chapter 5.
- **Guelaguetza:** On the last 2 Mondays in July, **Oaxaca** puts on a big show. Dance groups from communities across the state perform in the amphitheater on the hillside above the city. See "Oaxaca City," in chapter 10.
- **"Night of the Radishes":** Unique in the country, December 23 in **Oaxaca** is when the Oaxaqueños build fantastic sculptures out of radishes (the most prized vegetable cultivated during the colonial period), flowers, and dried cornhusks. They go on display on the *zócalo.* On December 24, each Oaxacan church organizes a procession with music, floats, and crowds bearing candles. See "Oaxaca City," in chapter 10.

## 4 The Best Archaeological Sites

- **Teotihuacán:** So close to Mexico City, yet centuries away. You can feel the majesty of the past in a stroll down the pyramid-lined Avenue of the Dead, from the Pyramid of the Sun to the Pyramid of the Moon. Imagine what a fabulous place this must have been when the walls were stuccoed and painted brilliant colors. See "A Side Trip to the Pyramids of San Juan Teotihuacán," in chapter 3.
- **Monte Albán:** A grand ceremonial city built on a mountaintop overlooking the valley of Oaxaca, Monte Albán offers the visitor panoramic vistas; a fascinating view of a society in transition, reflected in the contrasting methods of pyramid construction; and intriguing details in ornamentation. See "Oaxaca City," in chapter 10.
- **Palenque:** Like the ancient pharaohs, the rulers of this city built their tombs deep within their pyramids. Imagine the magnificent ceremony in A.D. 683 when King Pacal was entombed in his magnificent burial chamber, which lay unspoiled until its discovery in 1952. See "Palenque," in chapter 10.

- **Uxmal:** No matter how many times you see Uxmal, the splendor of its stone carvings is awe-inspiring. A stone rattlesnake undulates across the façade of the Nunnery complex, and 103 masks of Chaac—the rain god—project from the Governor's Palace. See "The Ruins of Uxmal," in chapter 14.
- **Chichén-Itzá:** Stand beside the giant serpent head at the foot of El Castillo pyramid and marvel at the architects and astronomers who positioned the building so precisely that shadow and sunlight form a serpent's body slithering from the peak to the earth at each equinox (Mar 21 and Sept 21). See "The Ruins of Chichén-Itzá," in chapter 14.

## 5 The Best Active Vacations

- **Biking in the Sierra Madre Foothills:** From Puerto Vallarta, professional mountain-bike trips venture into the mountains surrounding the picturesque village. Trips range from half-day excursions up the Río Cuale canyon to overnight visits to Yelapa. See "Puerto Vallarta," in chapter 8.
- **Scuba Diving in Cozumel:** The coral reefs off the island, Mexico's premier diving destination, are among the top 10 dive spots in the world. An easy journey to the Yucatán mainland offers a completely different experience in deep, clear *cenotes* (sinkholes, or natural wells). See chapter 13. Other excellent dive sites are in and around **Puerto Vallarta** and off **Los Cabos.** See chapters 8 and 16.
- **Fly-fishing off the Punta Allen Peninsula:** Serious anglers will enjoy the challenge of fly-fishing the saltwater flats and lagoons of Ascención Bay, near Punta Allen. See "Tulum, Punta Allen & Sian Ka'an," in chapter 13.
- **Hiking and Mountaineering in the Copper Canyon:** Miles and miles of beautiful, remote, challenging canyon lands are paradise for the serious hiker or rider. **Columbus Travel** (**© 800/843-1060**) can set hikers up with a Tarahumara Indian guide, who can take you deep into the canyons to places rarely viewed by tourists. Doug Rhodes of the **Paraíso del Oso** (**© 614/421-3372**) leads tours of experienced horseback riders on a 12-day ride that tests a rider's skill in mountainous terrain. It has to be the most challenging ride in North America. See "The Copper Canyon Train and Stops Along the Way," in chapter 15.
- **Golf in Los Cabos & Puerto Vallarta:** Puerto Vallarta, with its six championship designer courses, is *the* new destination for golfers to keep their eyes on. Added to the appeal of golf here are courses within easy driving distance along the Pacific Coast at El Tamarindo, Isla Navidad, and Manzanillo. See chapter 8. The Corridor between San José del Cabo and Cabo San Lucas is one of the world's premier golf destinations, with five championship courses open and a total of 207 holes slated for the area. See chapter 16.
- **Surfing Zicatela Beach in Puerto Escondido:** This world-class break is a lure for surfers around the globe. It challenges the best in the sport each September and October, when the waves peak and the annual surf competitions take place. See chapter 9. Other noted surf breaks in Mexico include Sayulita and Las Islitas Beach near **San Blas** (both north of Puerto Vallarta), and Playa

Costa Azul, on the outskirts of **San José del Cabo.** See chapters 8 and 16.

- **Sportfishing in La Paz:** Billfishing for magnificent marlin and sailfish is a popular sport throughout southern Baja, and La Paz pulls in the most consistent share. See chapter 16. Fishing is also excellent in Los Cabos, Mazatlán, Manzanillo, and Zihuatanejo. See chapters 8 and 9.
- **Sea Kayaking in the Sea of Cortez:** From Cabo San Lucas to La Paz, and continuing north, the Sea of Cortez is a sea kayaker's dream. It has dozens of tiny coves and impressive inlets to pull into and explore, under the watchful gaze of sea lions and dolphins. Professional outfitters provide gear, guides, and instruction for novices. See chapter 16.

## 6 The Best of Natural Mexico

- **Michoacán's Million Monarch March:** Mexico is an exotic land, and no place drives this home more forcefully than a mountain forest where you stand surrounded by the fluttering wings of millions of monarch butterflies—it's like being in a fairy tale. The setting is the rugged highlands of Michoacán, from mid-November through March. See "Morelia," in chapter 6.
- **Whale-watching:** Each winter, between December and April, magnificent humpback and gray whales return to breed and instruct their young in the waters offshore in Banderas Bay, fronting **Puerto Vallarta,** and in **Los Cabos.** See "Puerto Vallarta," in chapter 8, and "Los Cabos: Resorts, Watersports & Golf," in chapter 16.
- **Sea-Turtle Nesting Beaches:** Between June and November, sea turtles return to the beaches of their birth to lay their eggs in nests on the sand. With poaching and natural predators threatening these species, communities along Mexico's Pacific coast have established protected nesting areas. Many are open for public viewing and participation in the egg collection and baby-turtle release processes. Turtles are found along the Yucatán coast, in Baja Sur, on the Oaxaca coast, in Puerto Vallarta, and on Costa Alegre. See chapters 8, 10, 13, and 16.
- **Lago Bacalar** (Yucatán Peninsula): The waters of this crystal-clear, spring-fed lake—Mexico's second largest—are noted for their vibrant color variations, from pale blue to deep blue-green and turquoise. The area surrounding the lake is known for birding, with over 130 species identified. See "Lago Bacalar," in chapter 13.
- **The Rugged Copper Canyon:** The canyons known collectively as the Copper Canyon are beautiful, remote, and unspoiled. The entire network is larger than the Grand Canyon; it incorporates high waterfalls, vertical canyon walls, mountain forests in the canyon-rim country, and semiarid desert inside the canyons. This is the land of the Tarahumara Indians, who gained their legendary endurance from adapting to this wilderness. See chapter 15.
- **Desert Landscapes in Baja Sur:** The painted-desert colors and unique plant life are a natural curiosity in **Los Cabos,** where horseback, hiking, and ATV trips explore the area. The arid desert contrasts sharply with the intense blue of the strong sea surrounding the peninsula. See "Los Cabos: Resorts, Watersports & Golf," in chapter 16.

## 7 The Best Places to Get Away from It All

- **Costa Alegre:** Between Puerto Vallarta and Manzanillo, a number of superexclusive hotels cater to those with both time and money. These resorts—Las Alamandas, Hotel Careyes, and El Tamarindo—are miles from civilization and boast private beaches. See "Costa Alegre: Puerto Vallarta to Barra de Navidad," in chapter 8.
- **San Sebastián:** A 15-minute flight from Puerto Vallarta takes you a century back in time. The colonial mountain town of San Sebastián used to be the center of Mexico's mining operations; today, it's simply a place of delicious seclusion in a magical mountain setting. See "Puerto Vallarta," in chapter 8.
- **Punta Mita:** Its ancestral inhabitants considered the northern tip of the Bay of Banderas sacred ground. Today, the point where the Sea of Cortez, Pacific Ocean, and Banderas Bay meet is evolving into Mexico's most exclusive residential resort development. The beaches are white and the waters crystalline. See "Puerto Vallarta," in chapter 8.
- **Riviera Maya & Punta Allen Peninsula:** Away from the popular resort of Cancún, the Riviera Maya's heavenly quiet getaways offer tranquility at low prices on beautiful palm-lined beaches. South of the Tulum ruins, Punta Allen's beachside budget inns offer some of the most peaceful getaways in the country. See chapter 13.
- **Lago Bacalar:** The spring-fed waters of Lake Bacalar—Mexico's second-largest lake—make an ideal place to unwind. South of Cancún, near Chetumal, there's nothing around for miles. If you want adventure, you can take a kayak out on the lake, follow a birding trail, or venture to Belize or the nearby Maya ruins. See "Lago Bacalar," in chapter 13.
- **Cerocahui:** Up in the high Sierra Tarahumara, far from where the large tours stop, you'll find a peaceful little town surrounding a former mission. Nearby are two small hotels that are even more peaceful—no phones, no crowds, no traffic, just beautiful mountains and canyons clothed in pine forest. See "The Copper Canyon Train and Stops Along the Way," in chapter 15.
- **Todos Santos:** Purportedly home of the original Hotel California: You can check out any time, but you may not want to leave once you unwind for a while in this artists' outpost, also known as "Bohemian Baja." But come soon, because it's gaining the attention of like-minded adventurers. See "Todos Santos: A Creative Oasis," in chapter 16.

## 8 The Best Art, Architecture & Museums

- **Museo Nacional de Antropología:** Among the world's most outstanding museums, the Museum of Anthropology in Mexico City contains riches representing 3,000 years of the country's past. Also on view are fabulous artifacts of still-thriving indigenous cultures. The building, designed by architect Pedro Ramírez Vázquez, is stunning, too. See p. 98.
- **Museo Frida Kahlo (Frida Kahlo House and Museum):** While perhaps not a world-class collection of works by Mexico's

first couple of art, Frida Kahlo and Diego Rivera, this museum does contain a strong sampling of their works, plus their fascinating private collection. With rooms arranged as they were when the couple lived here, in the Mexico City suburb of Coyoacán, it also allows visitors to peek into the lives of these creative masters. See p. 98.

- **Palacio Nacional:** Mexico's center of government and presidential office was originally built in 1692 on the site of Moctezuma's "new" palace, to be the home of Hernán Cortez. The top floor, added in the late 1920s, holds a series of stunning Diego Rivera murals depicting the history of Mexico. See p. 100.
- **Palacio de Bellas Artes in Mexico City:** The country's premier venue for the performing arts, this fabulous building is the combined work of several masters, including the Italian architect Adamo Boari. The theater's exterior is turn-of-the-century Art Nouveau, covered in marble, while the interior is 1930s Art Deco. See p. 103.
- **The Templo Mayor's Aztec Splendor:** The Templo Mayor and Museo del Templo Mayor, in Mexico City, are an archaeological excavation and a museum with 6,000 objects on display. They showcase the variety and splendor of the Aztec Empire as it existed in the center of what is now Mexico City. See p. 102.
- **Catedral Metropolitana:** This towering cathedral, begun in 1573 and finished in 1788, blends baroque, neoclassic, and Mexican churrigueresque architecture, and was constructed primarily from the stones of destroyed Aztec temples. See p. 106.
- **Santa Prisca y San Sebastián Church:** One of Mexico's most impressive baroque churches, completed in 1758, this church in Taxco has an intricately carved façade, an interior decorated with gold-leafed saints and angels, as well as paintings by Miguel Cabrera, one of Mexico's most famous colonial-era artists. See p. 137.
- **Mexican Masks in Zacatecas:** Masks are a ubiquitous feature in Mexican festivals and folk art, and the Museo Rafael Coronel in Zacatecas has the greatest collection in the country. See p. 202.
- **Museo Virreinal de Guadalupe:** Six kilometers (4 miles) southeast of Zacatecas in the small town of Guadalupe, this Franciscan convent and art museum holds a striking collection of 17th- and 18th-century paintings by such masters as Miguel Cabrera and Cristóbal de Villalpando. The expressive, dramatic works will fascinate art lovers. See p. 203.
- **Morelia's Cathedral:** Sober lines, balanced proportions, a deft blending of architectural styles, and monumental height—Morelia's cathedral is the most beautiful in the country. It's built of brownish-pink stone that turns fiery rose in the late afternoon sun. See p. 218.
- **Puebla's Capilla del Rosario:** Located in the church of Santo Domingo, this chapel is a tour de force of baroque expression, executed in molded plaster, carved wood, Talavera tile, and gold leaf. The overall effect is to overpower the senses. See p. 480.
- **Puebla's Museo Amparo:** A magnificent collection of pre-Columbian and colonial art, beautifully displayed. See p. 482.

## 9 The Best Shopping

- **Bazar del Sábado in San Angel:** This festive weekly market in a colonial neighborhood south of Mexico City offers exceptional crafts, of a more sophisticated nature than you'll see in most *mercados.* Furnishings, antiques, and collectibles are also easy to find in surrounding garages and street plazas. See p. 119.
- **Polanco, Mexico City:** This fashionable neighborhood is noted for its designer boutiques, cigar shops, fine jewelers, and leather-goods offerings. See "Shopping," in chapter 3.
- **Contemporary Art:** Latin American art is surging in popularity and recognition. Galleries in Mexico City feature Mexico's masters and emerging stars, with Oaxaca, Puerto Vallarta and San Miguel de Allende galleries also offering excellent selections. See chapters 3, 5, 8, and 10.
- **Taxco Silver:** Mexico's silver capital, Taxco has hundreds of stores featuring fine jewelry and decorative objects. See "Taxco: Cobblestones & Silver," in chapter 4.
- **Talavera Pottery in Puebla & Dolores Hidalgo:** An inheritor of the Moorish legacy of ceramics, Puebla produces some of the most sought-after dinnerware in the world. The tiles produced there adorn building façades and church domes throughout the area. See chapter 11. Dolores Hidalgo, 40km (25 miles) northwest of San Miguel de Allende, produces attractive, inexpensive Talavera of less traditional design. Almost every block has a factory or store outlet. See "San Miguel de Allende," in chapter 5.
- **San Miguel de Allende's Diverse Crafts:** Perhaps it's the influence of the Instituto Allende art school, but something has given storekeepers here real savvy about choosing their merchandise. The stores have fewer typical articles of Mexican handicrafts and more interesting and eye-catching works than you'll find in other towns. And the shopping experience is low-key. See "San Miguel de Allende," in chapter 5.
- **Pátzcuaro's Fine Crafts:** Michoacán is known for its crafts, and Pátzcuaro is at the center of it all. You can find beautiful cotton textiles, woodcarvings, pottery, lacquerware, woven straw pieces, and copper items in the market, or you can track the object to its source in one of the nearby villages. See "Pátzcuaro," in chapter 6.
- **Decorative Arts in Tlaquepaque and Tonalá:** These two neighborhoods of Guadalajara offer perhaps the most enjoyable shopping in Mexico. Tlaquepaque has attracted many sophisticated and wide-ranging shops selling an incredible variety of decorative art. In Tonalá, more than 400 artisans have workshops, and you can visit many of them on regular days; on market days, wander through blocks and blocks of market stalls seeking that one perfect piece. See "Shopping," in chapter 7.
- **Huichol Art in Puerto Vallarta:** One of the last indigenous cultures to remain faithful to their customs, language, and traditions, the Huichol Indians come down from the Sierra Madre mountains to sell their unusual art to Puerto Vallarta galleries. Inspired by visions received during spiritual ceremonies, the Huichol create their art with colorful yarn or beads pressed into wax. See "Shopping," in chapter 8.
- **Oaxacan Textiles:** This area has the best weavings and naturally dyed textiles in Mexico; it's also

famous for its pottery (especially the black pottery), and colorful, imaginative woodcarvings. See "Oaxaca City," in chapter 10.

- **The Markets of San Cristóbal de las Casas:** This city, deep in the heart of the Maya highlands, has shops, open plazas, and markets featuring distinctive waist-loomed wool and cotton textiles, as well as leather shoes, handsomely crude pottery, genre dolls, and Guatemalan textiles. See "San Cristóbal de las Casas," in chapter 10.

## 10 The Hottest Nightlife

- **Polanco, Mexico City:** Mexico City, like any world capital, has sizzling nightlife. Latin, Cuban, and alternative music rock in the Polanco neighborhood. The club scene evokes the culture's roots in Madrid and Barcelona. Arrive fashionably late—the party doesn't think of getting started before midnight. See "Mexico City After Dark," in chapter 3.
- **Guadalajara's Sophisticated Scene:** Nightlife here extends to theater, classical music, jazz, and salsa, never forgetting mariachi music—which, when done properly, requires vocalists to really flaunt their talent. See "Guadalajara After Dark," in chapter 7.
- **Puerto Vallarta's Live Music:** Puerto Vallarta has an excellent selection of small clubs featuring jazz, blues, salsa, and good old rock 'n' roll. Still notable is Club Roxy, with an excellent house band. A new crop of salsa clubs feature bands direct from Cuba. You'll also find mariachi, pre-Columbian, and traditional Mexican ballads—along with DJs spinning house and hip-hop. See "Puerto Vallarta," in chapter 8.
- **Acapulco Discos:** Nightlife can't possibly get more lavish, extravagant, or flashy than it is in Acapulco, Mexico's hands-down diva. This city's main cultural attractions are the clubs that jam until sunrise, several of which have walls of windows overlooking the bay. See "Acapulco," in chapter 9.
- **The Lively Offerings of San Cristóbal de las Casas:** Small though it may be, this city has a live-music scene that can't be beat for fun and atmosphere. It's inexpensive, too. This is the perfect place to do some barhopping: It offers variety, convenience (everything is within walking distance), and no cover charges. See "San Cristóbal de las Casas," in chapter 10.
- **Cancún's Clubs in Malls:** Cancún's wide-ranging hot spots include most of the name-brand nightlife destinations, concentrated in entertainment malls and festival shopping centers, as well as hotel-lobby bars with live music, and sophisticated discos. Popular nightlife tours allow you to bypass lines and sample various clubs in a single night. The clubs here can accommodate up to 3,000, and there are plenty of options for staying out until the sun comes up. See "Cancún After Dark," in chapter 12.
- **Cabo San Lucas Beach Bars:** In the nightlife capital of Baja California, after-dark fun centers on the casual bars and restaurants that line the main drag, as well as those on the town's public Medano Beach. There's still a rowdy, outlaw feel to the place, despite the influx of tony hotels nearby. See "Los Cabos: Resorts, Watersports & Golf," in chapter 16.

## 11 The Best Luxury Hotels

- **Hotel Four Seasons** (Mexico City; ✆ **800/332-3442**): The standard of excellence in Mexico, and the most stylish choice in Mexico City, this hotel captures both serenity and elegance in a hacienda-style building that surrounds a picturesque courtyard. The gracious staff and offerings of unique cultural tours are bonuses. See p. 85.
- **Casa de Sierra Nevada** (San Miguel de Allende; ✆ **415/152-7040**): This luxury hotel has all the flavor of colonial Mexico; it's a collection of eight elegant colonial houses in one of the country's most appealing colonial towns. The owner keeps a stable of horses and a large ranch for guests' use. See p. 169.
- **Villa Montaña** (Morelia; ✆ **800/223-6510** in the U.S., or 800/448-8355 in Canada): The Villa Montaña defines perfection. From the layout of the grounds to the decoration of the rooms, every detail has been skillfully handled. The hotel perches on a ridge overlooking Morelia; from its terraces, guests can survey the city below. The restaurant is one of the city's best. See p. 221.
- **Four Seasons Resort Punta Mita** (✆ **800/332-3442**): The newest luxury resort in Mexico has already soared in popularity and is hailed for its unrivaled location (on a remote, pristine stretch of beach) and the stellar service characteristic of the Four Seasons chain. Also on site are an expansive spa and a private Jack Nicklaus Signature golf course. Located 30 minutes north of Puerto Vallarta's airport. See p. 302.
- **El Tamarindo** (between Manzanillo and Puerto Vallarta; ✆ **315/351-5032**): The most exclusive remote resort in Mexico, this stylish place combines large private *casitas* facing the Pacific with a stunning private oceanfront golf course. Fellow guests are likely to be Hollywood celebrities and the well-to-do from around the world. It's about an hour north of Manzanillo along Costa Alegre. See p. 326.
- **Villa del Sol** (Playa La Ropa, Zihuatanejo; ✆ **888/223-6510** in the U.S., or 755/554-2239): Few hotels meet the demanding standards of luxury and attention to detail required to be a member of the French Relais and Châteax, but this small beachfront inn does. It's also a member of the Small Luxury Hotels of the World. See p. 381.
- **Hotel Camino Real** (Oaxaca; ✆ **800/722-6466** in the U.S.): No other hotel in Mexico captures the sense of antiquity as well as this one. A magnificent hotel inside a 16th-century convent, it's in the middle of the best part of Oaxaca City. The spacious hotel has several beautiful, tranquil courtyards where renovation efforts have carefully preserved the marks of time. See p. 424.
- **Ritz-Carlton Hotel** (Cancún; ✆ **800/241-3333** in the U.S. and Canada): In a resort known for high-rise luxury, this hotel is in a class of its own, with spectacular facilities fronting a perfect beach. You'll find spacious, beautifully furnished rooms, elegant dining, and exceptional service. See p. 502.
- **Las Ventanas al Paraíso** (Los Cabos; ✆ **888/525-0483** in the U.S.): Easily one of Mexico's most popular luxury resorts, Las Ventanas comes complete with a deluxe European spa, excellent gourmet restaurant, and elegantly

appointed rooms and suites. From fireplaces and telescopes to private pools and rooftop terraces, each suite is a private slice of heaven. See p. 674.

- **Hotel Palmilla** (San José del Cabo; ✆ **800/637-2226** in the U.S.): Perched on a cliff above the sea, Baja's original luxury lodging is one of the most luxurious yet relaxed hotels in Mexico, with a championship golf course and a collection of room amenities designed for every imaginable comfort. See p. 673.

## 12 The Best Unique Inns

- **Casa de los Espíritus Alegres** (Guanajuato; ✆ **473/733-1013**): Folk art and atmosphere abound in this idiosyncratic "house of happy spirits," just outside the lovely mining town of Guanajuato. It's surely the quirkiest 16th-century hacienda you'll ever see. The individually named rooms are all uniquely and colorfully decorated, and each has its own fireplace. See p. 184.
- **Verana** (Yelapa; ✆ **800/677-5156** or 322/227-5420): The stylish Verana adds a dash of sophistication to funky Yelapa—a remote village accessible only by boat, about 45 minutes from Puerto Vallarta. Each of the five handcrafted *casas* has a unique architectural style that complements the expanse of vistas to the surrounding jungle and ocean. It's a perfect blend of style, romance, and nature. See p. 299.
- **Quinta María Cortez** (Puerto Vallarta; ✆ **888/640-8100** or 801/536-5850 in the U.S.): This is one of the country's most original places to stay; it's an eclectic B&B uniquely decorated with antiques, curios, and original art. It sits on a beautiful cove on Conchas Chinas beach. See p. 287.
- **La Casa Que Canta** (Zihuatanejo; ✆ **888/523-5050** in the U.S.): This architecturally dramatic hotel incorporates wonderful Mexican adobe and folk art in grandly scaled rooms. It's a delightful place to unwind, read on the terrace overlooking the bay, and order room service. See p. 380.
- **Hotel Santa Fe** (Puerto Escondido; ✆ **954/582-0170**): This Spanish-colonial-style inn has a welcoming staff and comfortable rooms appointed with rustic wood furnishings. The hacienda-style buildings, splashed with bougainvillea, surround two courtyard swimming pools. Across the street is the famed surfing beach, Zicatela. The restaurant is one of the best on the Pacific coast. See p. 393.
- **La Casa de los Sueños** (Isla Mujeres; ✆ **800/551-2558** in the U.S.): A private home turned upscale B&B, this stunning inn offers complete relaxation and luxury amenities. A large interior courtyard, tropical gardens, infinity pool, small beach, and *palapa*-shaded lounge area are just a few of the "un-common" areas guests share. See p. 538.
- **Hotel Jungla Caribe** (Playa del Carmen; ✆ **984/873-0650**): In the heart of Playa's pedestrian-only 5th Avenue, this inventive inn has high-style decor that mixes neoclassical with Robinson Crusoe. All rooms are spacious, with whimsical touches. It's 2 blocks from the beach and in the heart of the ultrahip town's action. See p. 570.
- **Casa Mexilio Guest House** (Mérida; ✆ **800/538-6802** in the U.S., or 999/928-2505): An

imaginative arrangement of rooms around a courtyard features a pool surrounded by a riot of tropical vegetation. The rooms are on different levels, connected by stairs and catwalks. Breakfast here provides extra incentive for getting out of bed. See p. 611.

- **Casa Natalia** (San José del Cabo; ✆ **888/277-3814** in the U.S.): This renovated historic home, now a charming inn, is an oasis of palms, waterfalls, and flowers against the desert landscape. Each room and suite is an artful combination of modern architecture and traditional Mexican touches. The restaurant is the hottest in town. See p. 669.
- **Mesón de la Sacristía de la Compañía** (Puebla; ✆ **222/232-4513**): No other place captures the feel of colonial Mexico, or does it with as much fun, as this small hotel that doubles as a popular nightspot and antique store. See p. 484.

## 13 The Best Inexpensive Inns

- **Best Western Hotel de Cortés** (Mexico City; ✆ **800/528-1234** in the U.S.): A historic building and former home of Augustinian friars offers exceptionally clean, comfortable, value-priced accommodations. It's on La Alameda park, near the Palace of Fine Arts and the Franz Mayer Museum. See p. 88.
- **Hotel Rancho Taxco Victoria** (Taxco; ✆ **762/622-0004**): With its pristine 1940s decor and fabulous hillside setting overlooking all of Taxco, this hotel gets special marks as an inexpensive inn that exudes all the charm of old-fashioned Mexico. See p. 139.
- **Hotel San Francisco Plaza** (Guadalajara; ✆ **33/3613-8954**): This two-story colonial-style hotel is a more agreeable place to stay than lodgings charging twice as much, and it's every bit as comfortable. It's in the downtown area, near the main plaza and several good restaurants and nightspots. See p. 246.
- **Los Cuatro Vientos** (Puerto Vallarta; ✆ **322/222-0161**): A quiet, cozy inn on a hillside overlooking Banderas Bay, it features colorfully decorated rooms built around a small pool and central patio, a daily continental breakfast, and the absolute best venue for sunsets in Puerto Vallarta. See p. 286.
- **Hotel Flor de María** (Puerto Escondido; ✆ **954/582-0536**): This hotel is charming in every way, from the hospitable owners, Lino and María Francato, to the guest rooms individually decorated with Lino's fine artistic touches. The restaurant is the best in town. See p. 395.
- **Misión de los Arcos** (Huatulco; ✆ **958/587-0165**): This new hotel, just a block from the central plaza, has a similar style to the elegant Quinta Real, at a fraction of the cost. An all-white façade and intriguing decorative touches give it an inviting feel. There's shuttle service to the Huatulco beaches. See p. 407.
- **Las Golondrinas** (Oaxaca; ✆ **951/514-3298**): We receive more favorable letters about this hotel than about any other in the country. It's small, simple, and colorful, with homey touches of folk art and pathways lined with abundant foliage. See p. 426.
- **Villa Catarina Rooms & Cabañas** (Playa del Carmen; ✆ **984/873-0970**): Here you'll find budget prices for stylishly rustic rooms and cabañas, with high-quality furnishings and folk-art

accents, that are nestled in a grove of palms and fruit trees. It's located 1 block from Playa del Carmen's exquisite beach. See p. 571.

- **Cuzan Guest House** (Punta Allen; ✆ **983/834-0358** in Felipe Carrillo Puerto): Getting to the isolated lobster-fishing village is half the adventure. You nest in a hammock, dine on lobster and stone crabs, and absolutely forget the outside world: There are no phones, TVs, or newspapers, and "town" is 56km (35 miles) away. Nature trips and bonefishing are the activities of choice. See p. 584.
- **Cabo Inn** (Cabo San Lucas; ✆ **624/143-0819**): This former bordello is the best budget inn in the area. Rooms are small but extra-clean and invitingly decorated, amenities are generous, and the owner-managers are friendly and helpful. Ideally located, close to town and near the marina, the inn caters to sportfishers. See p. 684.

## 14 The Best Spa Resorts

- **Hotel Spa Ixtapan** (Ixtapan; ✆ **800/638-7950** in the U.S.): In operation since 1939, this resort is a classic, traditional spa with consistently upgraded amenities and services. It's also close to the region's renowned thermal baths. See p. 142.
- **Misión Del Sol Resort & Spa** (Cuernavaca; ✆ **800/448-8355** in the U.S. and Canada): Mexico's finest spa resort, with every architectural and functional detail designed to soothe body and soul—from meditation rooms to reflexology showers to magnets under your mattress. The sumptuous, full-service spa and fitness center and delicious vegetarian cuisine make this a heavenly base for personal renewal. See p. 153.
- **Four Seasons Resort Punta Mita** (Punta Mita; ✆ **800/332-3442**): The enticing spa at this posh resort is one of its principal appeals. The menu of spa services based on native Mexican therapies is an intriguing complement to the modern facilities and amenities. Located north of Puerto Vallarta. See p. 302.
- **Paradise Village** (Nuevo Vallarta; ✆ **800/995-5714**): Excellent fitness facilities combined with pampering yet affordable spa services make this one of the best all-around spas in Mexico. Spa director Diana Mestre is a leading expert—and living proof—of the beneficial properties of indigenous Mexican spa therapies and natural treatments. See p. 300.
- **Le Méridien Cancún** (Cancún; ✆ **800/543-4300** in the U.S.): The Spa del Mar is a state-of-the-art, 1,394-square-m (15,000-sq.-ft.) facility bordering the brilliant Caribbean. It boasts the most complete spa in the area, with inhalation rooms, saunas, steam, Jacuzzis, cold plunges, Swiss showers, a cascading waterfall whirlpool, and 14 treatment rooms. There's also an expansive fitness center and salon services. See p. 500.
- **Las Ventanas al Paraíso** (Los Cabos; ✆ **888/525-0483** in the U.S.): This is an elegant and highly professional spa in the area's most exclusive resort. See "The Best Luxury Hotels," above, and p. 674.
- **Rancho La Puerta** (Baja Norte; ✆ **800/443-7565** in the U.S.): One of Mexico's best-known spas, Rancho La Puerta is a spa-vacation pioneer, having opened its doors—at the time, tent flaps—in 1940. A steady stream of guests returns to this pristine countryside for the constantly expanding facilities, spa services, and outdoor opportunities. See p. 709.

## 15 The Best Mexican Food & Drink

- **Fonda El Refugio, for Traditional Mexican Food** (Mexico City; ✆ **55/5207-2732**): This elegantly casual place prepares specialties from all over the country, including *manchamanteles* ("tablecloth stainers") on Tuesday and *albóndigas en chile chipotle* (meatballs in chipotle sauce) on Saturday. See p. 92.
- **El Estribo, for Premium Tequilas** (Mexico City; ✆ **55/5281-4554**): No longer is tequila relegated to salt-and-lime shooters; it's being recognized for its unique properties and subtle taste variations. Premium-tequila tastings are the rage; El Estribo is among the best of places for sampling. It offers more than 480 types, most of which are 100% blue agave, the mark of a fine tequila. See p. 124.
- **El Sacromonte, for artful *alta cocina*** (Guadalajara; ✆ **33/3825-5447**): Various dishes delight the senses with novel tastes and textures and skillful presentation. The menu describes each dish in Spanish haiku—a fun topic for conversation over an aperitif. See p. 248.
- **El Mirador, for Margaritas** (Acapulco; in the Hotel Plaza Las Glorias; ✆ **800/342-AMIGO** in the U.S.): You can enjoy a great margarita at many places in Mexico, but this is the only one that serves them with a view of the spectacular La Quebrada cliff divers. See p. 361.
- **El Naranjo, for Oaxacan Cuisine** (Oaxaca; ✆ **961/514-1878**): Oaxacan cooking is a wonderful regional variety, and I am delighted by what El Naranjo does with it. Each day offers a different *mole* in addition to several uncommon dishes. This is a wonderful place for throwing caution to the wind—the owner is meticulous about cleaning and sterilizing foods. See p. 427.
- **100% Natural, for Licuados:** *Licuados,* drinks made from fresh fruit mixed with water or milk, are much more popular than soft drinks. This restaurant chain offers the widest selection, including innovative mixtures like the Cozumel (spinach, pineapple, and orange) and the Caligula (orange, pineapple, beet, celery, parsley, carrot, and lime juices), a healthy indulgence. Branches in Puerto Vallarta, Acapulco, and Cancún.
- **Mariscos Villa Rica Mocambo** (Veracruz; ✆ **229/922-2113**), for fresh seafood, Veracruz style: Nobody does seafood the way Veracruz does seafood, and this restaurant captures the character of the region's cooking. See p. 469.

2

# Planning Your Trip to Mexico

A little planning can make the difference between a good trip and a great trip. When should you go? What's the best way to get there? How much should you plan on spending? What festivals or special events will occur during your visit? What safety or health precautions should you take? We'll answer these and other questions in this chapter. In addition to these basics, I highly recommend taking a little time to learn about the culture and traditions of Mexico. It can make the difference between simply getting away for a few days and truly adding cultural understanding to your trip. See appendix A for more details.

## 1 The Regions in Brief

**BAJA CALIFORNIA** A peninsula longer than Italy, Baja stretches 1,402km (876 miles) from its border with California at Mexico's northernmost city of **Tijuana** to **Cabo San Lucas** at its southern tip. On one side is the Pacific Ocean, on the other, the **Sea of Cortez.** Volcanic uplifting created the craggy desert-scape you see today. Culturally and geographically, Baja sits apart from mainland Mexico, and it remained isolated for centuries. Now the state of Baja California del Sur, it has developed into a vacation haven that offers golf, fishing, diving, and whale-watching in beautiful settings and at posh resorts.

**THE COPPER CANYON** The Copper Canyon is the common name for a region of roughly 16,835 square km (6,500 sq. miles) in the northern state of Chihuahua, midway between the state's capital city and the Pacific coast. Here you'll find a network of canyons deeply etched into the volcanic rock of the **Sierra Tarahumara.** The dramatic canyons are one of those rare places where one can sense the earth's creation. To get there, you ride the famous *Chihuahua al Pacífico* railroad. It starts at the seaport of Topolobampo, outside **Los Mochis,** and runs 624km (390 miles) to **Chihuahua City,** climbing to 2,121m (7,000 ft.) above sea level in the process. The train skirts the edge of more than 20 canyons, and the vistas are beautiful. To really get a feel for the canyon area, you have to stay in one of the towns along the way. Tours can accommodate any kind of traveler, from primitive camper to modern hotel patron.

**THE PACIFIC COAST** The Pacific coast has virtually every kind of beach and landscape imaginable. You can stay in modern resorts that offer inexhaustible arrays of amenities and activities, from sailing to scuba diving to golf, capped off by exuberant nightlife. Or you could stay in a sleepy coastal town where the scenery

**Map Pointer**

To locate these regions, please turn to the map of Mexico in chapter 1.

abounds with rustic charm, life is slower, and the beaches are quieter. By **Mazatlán,** the northern desert disappears, replaced by tropical vegetation and plantations of coconut and other fruit. At **Puerto Vallarta,** mountains covered in tropical forests meet the sea. For many, this is the most appealing place on the coast; the town is a wonderful combination of natural beauty, modern sophistication, and small-town charm. From here, it's a 5-hour car ride inland to **Guadalajara,** the most Mexican of cities and a wonderful place to shop, especially for decorative arts. Tropical forests interspersed with banana, mango, and coconut palm plantations cover the coast from Puerto Vallarta to **Manzanillo.** Well south of Manzanillo, in the state of Guerrero, are the beach towns **Zihuatanejo** and **Ixtapa.** Tree-covered mountains remain around **Acapulco,** though hillside development has marred them. From Acapulco, a road leads inland to **Taxco,** a mountainside colonial city famed for its hundreds of silver shops. Farther south along the coast are the beach villages of **Puerto Escondido** and **Puerto Angel,** and, beyond them, the nine gorgeous bays of **Huatulco.**

**THE NORTH-CENTRAL REGION** This funnel-shaped region stretches from the northern border with Texas and New Mexico to **Mexico City** and includes the beautiful colonial **silver cities.** The majority of this territory lies in the vast Chihuahua/Coahuila desert of the north between the two great **Sierra Madre ranges,** which meet in the south to form the central valley of Mexico. The colonial cities nestle in the mountains not far north and west of Mexico City. Here, in the cool mountain air against an elegant backdrop of cut stone and wrought iron, people go about their business and pleasure at a relaxed pace that gently induces the visitor to kick back and slow down.

**THE GULF COAST** Of all Mexico, this region is probably the least known, yet the whole coast, which includes the long, skinny state of Veracruz, holds marvelous pockets of scenery and culture. Highway 180 leads from **Matamoros** at the Texas border and offers a few glimpses of the Gulf, which in some places is the same cerulean blue as the Caribbean. Highlights of this region are the ruins of **El Tajín,** near the mountain village of Papantla; the mountain town of **Xalapa,** Veracruz's capital and home of the magnificent Museo de Antropología; and the lively, colorful port of **Veracruz.** This is a good region to visit if you're longing for the Mexico of yesteryear.

**TARASCAN COUNTRY** This region, in the state of Michoacán, presents two distinct visions of colonial architecture: **Pátzcuaro,** a town of tile roofs and adobe walls painted traditional white with dark red borders; and **Morelia,** a stately city of stone mansions, broad plazas, and a monumental cathedral. Many consider Michoacán the most beautiful state in the country. The eastern part of the state consists of high mountains with large tracts of pine and fir forests. Every year, millions of **monarch butterflies** make the long journey to congregate in a small part of the forest here. The central part of the state, a land of lakes, is the homeland of the Purépecha or Tarascan Indians. The villages throughout this area specialize in crafts for which the region is well known. Farther west lie the hotlands and the coast. Tourists largely neglect Michoacán, except during the Days of the Dead.

**OAXACA & CHIAPAS** This is the southern land of the Zapotec, Mixtec, and Maya cultures. Most people fly around this region, but a toll highway from near Puebla to **Oaxaca City** makes the area more accessible by car.

## Destination: Mexico—Red Alert Checklist

- Has the **U.S. State Department** (http://travel.state.gov/travel_warnings.html) issued any travel advisories regarding Mexico?
- Do you have your passport or official I.D.? If traveling in a coastal area, did you pack insect repellent? Sunblock? A hat? A sweater or jacket?
- Do you need to book tour, restaurant, or travel reservations in advance?
- Did you make sure attractions and activities that interest you are operating? Some attractions, such as seasonal nature tours, sell out quickly. (Mexico is considered at low risk for a terrorist attack; few event schedule changes or building closings have been instituted.)
- If you purchased traveler's checks, have you recorded the check numbers, and stored the documentation separately from the checks?
- Do you have your credit card personal identification numbers (PINs)?
- If you have an E-ticket, do you have documentation?
- Do you know the address and phone number of your country's embassy?

The valley of Oaxaca is one of the grandest places in Mexico: fascinating Indian villages everywhere, beautiful ruins, and a wonderful colonial city. **San Cristóbal de las Casas,** in Chiapas, is harder to get to, but definitely worth the effort. Entirely different from Oaxaca City, it inhabits cooler, greener mountains, and is more in the mold of a provincial, colonial town. Approaching San Cristóbal from any direction, you see small plots of corn tended by colorfully clad Maya. Oaxaca and Chiapas are rich in craftspeople, from woodcarvers to potters to weavers.

**THE YUCATAN PENINSULA** Travelers to the peninsula have an opportunity to see pre-Hispanic ruins—such as **Chichén-Itzá, Uxmal,** and **Tulum**—and the living descendants of the cultures that built them, as well as the ultimate in resort Mexico: **Cancún.** The peninsula borders the dull aquamarine Gulf of Mexico on the west and north, and the clear blue Caribbean on the east. It covers almost 217,559 square km (84,000 sq. miles), with nearly 1,600km (1,000 miles) of shoreline.

Lovely rock-walled Maya villages and crumbling *henequén* haciendas dot the interior of the peninsula. The placid interior contrasts with the hubbub of the Caribbean coast. From Cancún south to **Chetumal,** the jungle coastline is spotted with all kinds of development, from posh to budget. It also boasts an enormous array of wildlife, including hundreds of species of birds. The Gulf Coast beaches, while good enough, don't compare to those on the the Caribbean. National parks near **Celestún** and **Río Lagartos** on the Gulf Coast are home to amazing flocks of flamingos.

## 2 Visitor Information

The **Mexico Hotline** (© **800/44-MEXICO**) is an excellent source for general information; you can request brochures on the country and get answers to the most common questions.

More information (15,000 pages worth) about Mexico is available on the Ministry of Tourism's website, **www.mexico-travel.com**. Another excellent official source is the site of Mexico's Tourism Promotion Council, **www.visitmexico.com**.

The **U.S. State Department** (✆ **202/647-5225;** http://travel.state.gov/) offers a **Consular Information Sheet** on Mexico (http://travel.state.gov/mexico.html), with safety, medical, driving, and general travel information gleaned from reports by its offices in Mexico. You can also request the Consular Information Sheet by fax (✆ **202/647-3000**). Visit **http://travel.state.gov/travel_warnings.html** for other Consular Information sheets and warnings; and **http://travel.state.gov/tips_mexico.html** for *Tips for Travelers to Mexico.*

Another source is the Department of State's background notes series. Visit the State Department home page (www.state.gov/) for information.

The **Centers for Disease Control Hotline** (✆ **800/311-3435** or 404/639-3534; www.cdc.gov) is a source of medical information for travelers to Mexico and elsewhere. For travelers to Mexico and Central America, the number with recorded messages is ✆ **877/FYI-TRIP.** The toll-free fax number for requesting information is ✆ 888/232-3299. Information available by fax is also available at **www.cdc.gov/travel**. The U.S. State Department offers medical information for Americans traveling abroad and a list of air ambulance services at **http://travel.state.gov/medical.html**.

**MEXICAN GOVERNMENT TOURIST BOARD** The board has offices in major North American cities, in addition to the main office in Mexico City (✆ **55/5203-1103**).

**United States:** Chicago (✆ **312/606-9252**); Houston (✆ **713/772-2581,** ext.105, or 713/772-3819); Los Angeles (✆ **213/351-2069;** fax 213/351-2074); Miami (✆ **305/718-4095**); and New York (✆ **212/821-0304,** or 212/821-0322). The Mexican Embassy is at 1911 Pennsylvania Ave. N.W., Washington, DC 20005 (✆ **202/728-1750**).

**Canada:** 1 Place Ville-Marie, Suite 1931, Montréal, QUE, H3B 2C3 (✆ **514/871-1052**); 2 Bloor St. W., Suite 1502, Toronto, ON, M4W 3E2 (✆ **416/925-0704**); 999 W. Hastings, Suite 1110, Vancouver, BC, V6C 2W2 (✆ **604/669-2845**). Embassy office: 1500-45 O'Connor St., Ottawa, ON, K1P 1A4 (✆ **613/233-8988;** fax 613/235-9123).

## 3 Entry Requirements & Customs

### ENTRY REQUIREMENTS

All travelers to Mexico are required to present **proof of citizenship,** such as an original birth certificate with a raised seal, a valid passport, or naturalization papers. Those using a birth certificate should also have current photo identification, such as a driver's license or official ID. If the last name on the birth certificate is different from your current name, bring a photo identification card *and* legal proof of the name change, such as the original marriage license or certificate. *Note:* Photocopies are *not* acceptable.

The best ID is a passport. Safeguard your passport in an inconspicuous, inaccessible place like a money belt, and keep a copy of the critical pages with your passport number in a separate place. If you lose your passport, visit the nearest consulate of your native country as soon as possible for a replacement.

You must carry a **Mexican Tourist Permit (FMT),** the equivalent of a tourist visa, which Mexican border officials issue, free of charge, after proof of citizenship is accepted. Airlines generally provide the necessary forms aboard your flight to Mexico. The FMT is more important than a passport, so guard it carefully. If you lose it, you may not be permitted to leave the country until you can replace it—a bureaucratic hassle that can take anywhere from a few hours to a week.

The FMT can be issued for up to 180 days. Sometimes officials don't ask but just stamp a time limit, so be sure to say "6 months," or at least twice as long as you intend to stay. If you decide to extend your stay, you may request that additional time be added to your FMT from an official immigration office in Mexico.

In **Baja California,** immigration laws have changed; they allow FMTs for a maximum of 180 days per year, with a maximum of 30 days per visit. This is to encourage regular visitors, or those who spend longer periods in Mexico, to obtain immigration documents that denote partial residency.

For travelers entering Mexico by car at the border of Baja California, note that FMTs are issued only in Tijuana, Tecate, and Mexicali, as well as in Ensenada and Guerrero Negro. If you travel anywhere beyond the frontier zone without the FMT, you will be fined $40. Permits for driving a foreign-plated car in Mexico are available only in Tijuana, Ensenada, Tecate, Mexicali, and La Paz.

*Note:* Children under age 18 traveling without parents or with only one parent must have a notarized letter from the absent parent(s) authorizing the travel.

**Lost Documents** To replace a **lost passport,** contact your embassy or nearest consular agent. You must establish a record of your citizenship and also fill out a form requesting another FMT (tourist permit) if it, too, was lost. If your documents are stolen, get a police report from local authorities; having one *might* lessen the hassle of exiting the country without all your identification. Without the FMT, you can't leave the country, and without an affidavit affirming your passport request and citizenship, you may have problems at U.S. Customs when you get home. It's important to clear everything up *before* trying to leave. Mexican Customs may, however, accept the police report of the loss of the FMT and allow you to leave.

## CUSTOMS

### WHAT YOU CAN BRING INTO MEXICO

When you enter Mexico, Customs officials will be tolerant as long as you have no illegal drugs or firearms. You're allowed to bring in two cartons of cigarettes or 50 cigars, plus a kilogram (2.2 lbs.) of smoking tobacco; two 1-liter bottles of wine or hard liquor, and 12 rolls of film. A laptop computer, camera equipment, and sports equipment that could feasibly be used during your stay are also allowed. The underlying guideline is: Don't bring anything that looks as if it's meant to be resold in Mexico.

### WHAT YOU CAN TAKE HOME

Returning **U.S. citizens** who have been away for at least 48 hours are allowed to bring back, once every 30 days, $400 worth of merchandise duty-free. You'll be charged a flat rate of 4% duty on the next $1,000 worth of purchases. Be sure to have your receipts. On mailed gifts, the duty-free limit is $100. You cannot bring fresh foodstuffs into the United States; tinned foods are allowed. For more information, contact the **U.S. Customs Service,** 1300 Pennsylvania

Ave., NW, Washington, DC 20229 (© **877/287-8867;** www.customs.gov) and request the free pamphlet *Know Before You Go.*

For a clear summary of **Canadian** rules, request the booklet *I Declare* from the **Canada Customs and Revenue Agency** (© **800/461-9999** in Canada, or 204/983-3500; www.ccra-adrc.gc.ca). Canada allows citizens a $750 exemption, and you're allowed to bring back duty-free one carton of cigarettes, 1 can of tobacco, 40 imperial ounces of liquor, and 50 cigars. In addition, you're allowed to mail gifts to Canada valued at less than $60 a day, provided they're unsolicited and don't contain alcohol or tobacco (write on the package "Unsolicited gift, under $60 value"). Declare all valuables on the Y-38 form before departure from Canada, including serial numbers of items you already own, such as expensive cameras. *Note:* The $750 exemption can only be used once a year and only after an absence of 7 days.

**U.K. citizens returning from a non-EC country** have a customs allowance of 200 cigarettes; 50 cigars; 250g of smoking tobacco; 2 liters of still table wine; 1 liter of spirits or strong liqueurs (over 22% volume); 2 liters of fortified wine, sparkling wine or other liqueurs; 60cc (ml) perfume; 250cc (ml) of toilet water; and £145 worth of all other goods, including gifts and souvenirs. (People under 17 cannot have the tobacco or alcohol allowance.) For more information, contact **HM Customs & Excise,** Passenger Enquiry Point, 2nd Floor Wayfarer House, Great South West Road, Feltham, Middlesex, TW14 8NP (© **0181/910-3744,** or 44/181-910-3744 from outside the U.K.; www.open.gov.uk).

The duty-free allowance in **Australia** is $400 or, for those under 18, $200. Personal property mailed back from Mexico should be marked "Australian goods returned" to avoid payment of duty. Upon returning to Australia, citizens can bring in 250 cigarettes or 250 grams of loose tobacco, and 1,125ml of alcohol. If you're returning with valuable goods you already own, such as cameras, file form B263. A helpful brochure, available from Australian consulates or Customs offices, is *Know Before You Go.* For more information, contact **Australian Customs Services,** GPO Box 8, Sydney NSW 2001 (© **02/9213-2000**).

The duty-free allowance for **New Zealand** is $700. Citizens over 17 can bring in 200 cigarettes, or 50 cigars, or 250 grams of tobacco (or a mixture if their combined weight doesn't exceed 250g); plus 4.5 liters of wine and beer, or 1.125 liters of liquor. New Zealand currency does not carry import or export restrictions. Fill out a certificate of export, listing the valuables you are taking out of the country; that way, you can bring them back without paying duty. Most questions are answered in a free pamphlet available at New Zealand consulates and Customs offices: *New Zealand Customs Guide for Travellers, Notice no. 4.* For more information, contact **New Zealand Customs,** 50 Anzac Ave., P.O. Box 29, Auckland (© **09/359-6655**).

## GOING THROUGH CUSTOMS

Mexican Customs inspection has been streamlined. At most points of entry, tourists are requested to press a button in front of what looks like a traffic signal, which alternates on touch between red and green. Green light and you go through without inspection; red light and your luggage or car may be inspected. If you have an unusual amount of luggage or an oversized piece, you may be subject to inspection anyway.

## 4 Money

### CURRENCY

The currency in Mexico is the Mexican **peso.** Paper currency comes in denominations of 20, 50, 100, 200, and 500 pesos. Coins come in denominations of 1, 2, 5, 10, and 20 pesos, and 20 and 50 **centavos** (100 centavos equal 1 peso). The current exchange rate for the U.S. dollar, and the one used in this book, is around 9 pesos; at that rate, an item that costs 9 pesos would be equivalent to US$1.

Getting **change** is a problem. Small-denomination bills and coins are hard to come by, so start collecting them early in your trip. Shopkeepers everywhere always seem to be out of change and small bills; that's doubly true in markets.

Many establishments that deal with tourists, especially in coastal resort areas, quote prices in dollars. To avoid confusion, they use the abbreviations "Dlls." for dollars and "M.N." (*moneda nacional,* or national currency) for pesos.

The rate of exchange fluctuates daily, so you probably are better off not exchanging too much currency at once. Don't forget to have enough pesos to carry you over a weekend or Mexican holiday, when banks are closed. In general, avoid carrying the U.S. $100 bill, the bill most commonly counterfeited in Mexico and therefore the most difficult to exchange, especially in smaller towns. Since small bills and coins in pesos are hard to come by in Mexico, the $1 bill is very useful for tipping. A tip of U.S. coins, which cannot be exchanged into Mexican currency, is of no value to the service provider.

The bottom line on exchanging money: Ask first, and shop around. Banks generally pay the top rates.

Exchange houses (*casas de cambio*) are generally more convenient than banks because they have more locations and longer hours; the rate of exchange may be the same as at a bank or slightly lower. Before leaving a bank or exchange-house window, count your change in front of the teller before the next client steps up.

Large airports have currency-exchange counters that often stay open whenever flights are operating. Though convenient, they generally do not offer the most favorable rates.

A hotel's exchange desk commonly pays less favorable rates than banks; however, when the currency is in a state of flux, higher-priced hotels are known to pay higher rates than banks, in an effort to attract dollars. It pays to shop around, but in almost all cases, you receive a better rate by changing money first, then paying, rather than by paying with dollars.

### BANKS & ATMS

Banks in Mexico are rapidly expanding and improving services. They tend to be open weekdays from 9am until 5pm, and often for at least a half day on Saturday. The exchange of dollars, which used to stop at noon, can now be accommodated anytime during business hours in larger resorts and cities. Some, but not all, banks charge a service fee of about 1% to exchange traveler's checks. However, most purchases can be paid for directly with traveler's checks at the establishment's stated exchange rate. Don't even bother with personal checks drawn on

---

**Money Matters**

The **universal currency sign ($)** is used to indicate pesos in Mexico. The use of this symbol in this book, however, denotes U.S. currency.

---

### Tips A Few Words About Prices

The peso's value continues to fluctuate—at press time, it was roughly 9 pesos to the dollar. Prices in this book (which are always given in U.S. dollars) have been converted to U.S. dollars at 9 pesos to the dollar. Most hotels in Mexico—with the exception of places that receive little foreign tourism—quote prices in U.S. dollars. Thus, currency fluctuations are unlikely to affect the prices charged by most hotels.

Mexico has a **value-added tax** of 15% (*Impuesto de Valor Agregado,* or IVA; pronounced "ee-bah") on most everything, including restaurant meals, bus tickets, and souvenirs. (Exceptions are Cancún, Cozumel, and Los Cabos, where the IVA is 10%; as ports of entry, they receive a special 5% break on taxes.) Hotels charge the usual 15% IVA, plus a locally administered bed tax of 2% (in many but not all areas), for a total of 17%. In Cancún, Los Cabos, and Cozumel, hotels charge the 10% IVA plus 2% room tax. IVA will not necessarily be included in the prices quoted by hotels and restaurants. You may find that upper-end properties (three or more stars) quote prices without IVA included, while lower-priced hotels include IVA in their quotes. Always ask to see a printed price sheet and always ask if the tax is included.

a U.S. bank—the bank will wait for your check to clear, which can take weeks, before giving you your money.

Travelers to Mexico can easily withdraw money from **ATMs** in most major cities and resort areas. The U.S. State Department has an advisory against using ATMs in Mexico for safety reasons, stating that they should only be used during business hours, but this pertains primarily to Mexico City, where crime remains a significant problem. In most resorts in Mexico, the use of ATMs is perfectly safe—just use the same precautions you would at any ATM. Universal bank cards (such as the Cirrus and PLUS systems) can be used. This is a convenient way to withdraw money and avoid carrying too much with you at any time. The exchange rate is generally more favorable than that at a currency house. Most machines offer Spanish/English menus and dispense pesos, but some offer the option of withdrawing dollars. Be sure to check the daily withdrawal limit before you depart. For Cirrus locations abroad, check ✆ **800/424-7787** or **www.mastercard.com**. For PLUS outlets abroad, check ✆ **800/843-7587** or **www.visa.com**. Before you leave home, check your daily withdrawal limit, and make sure that your personal identification number (PIN) works in international destinations.

## TRAVELER'S CHECKS

Traveler's checks denominated in dollars are readily accepted nearly everywhere, but they can be difficult to cash on a weekend or holiday or in an out-of-the-way place. Banks and other establishments in Mexico frequently charge a small commission when traveler's checks are used.

You can get American Express traveler's checks over the phone by calling ✆ **800/221-7282;** Amex gold and platinum cardholders who use this number are exempt from the 1% fee. AAA members can obtain checks without a fee at most AAA offices. **Visa** offers traveler's checks at Citibank locations nationwide, as well as at several other banks. The service charge ranges between 1.5% and 2%. Call ✆ **800/732-1322** for information. **MasterCard** also offers traveler's checks. Call ✆ **800/223-9920** for a location near you.

### CREDIT CARDS

Visa, MasterCard, and American Express are the most accepted cards. You'll be able to charge most hotel, restaurant, and store purchases, as well as almost all airline tickets, on your credit card. You can get cash advances of several hundred dollars on your card, but there may be a wait of 20 minutes to 2 hours. You generally can't charge gasoline purchases in Mexico.

Charges will be made in pesos, then converted into dollars by the bank issuing the credit card. Generally you receive the favorable bank rate when paying by credit card. However, be aware that some establishments in Mexico add a 5% to 7% surcharge when you pay with a credit card. This is especially true when using American Express. Many times, advertised discounts will not apply if you pay with a credit card.

### WHAT TO DO IF YOUR WALLET GETS STOLEN

Almost every credit card company has an emergency 800 number to call if your card is stolen. These numbers are not toll-free within Mexico (see "Telephone/Fax" under "Fast Facts: Mexico," later in this chapter, for instructions on calling U.S. toll-free numbers). The company may be able to wire you a cash advance off your credit card immediately, and, in many places, can deliver an emergency credit card in a day or two. The issuing bank's toll-free number is usually on the back of the credit card—which doesn't help you much if the card was stolen. From within Mexico, dial ✆ **001-880555-1212** (a toll call) to gain access to the toll-free directory. Citicorp Visa's U.S. emergency number is ✆ **800/336-8472.** American Express cardholders and traveler's check holders should call ✆ **800/221-7282.** MasterCard holders should call ✆ **800/307-7309.**

If you carry traveler's checks, keep a record of their serial numbers, separately from the checks, so you're ensured a refund in just such an emergency.

Odds are that if your wallet is gone, the police won't be able to recover it for you. However, after you realize that it's gone and you cancel your credit cards, it is still worth informing them. Your credit card company or insurer may require a police report number. If you lose your wallet anywhere outside of Mexico City, before panicking, retrace your steps—you'll be surprised at how honest people are, and it is likely that you'll find someone trying to find you to return your wallet.

## 5 When to Go

### SEASONS

Mexico has two principal travel seasons. **High season** begins around December 20 and continues to Easter; in some places it begins as early as mid-November. **Low season** is from the day after Easter to mid-December; during low season, prices may drop 20% to 50%. In beach destinations popular with Mexican travelers, such as Veracruz and Acapulco, prices will revert to high season during July and August, the traditional national summer vacation period. Prices in inland cities seldom fluctuate from high to low season, but may rise dramatically during the weeks of **Easter** and **Christmas.** Taxco and Pátzcuaro raise prices during their popular Easter-week celebrations. In Isla Mujeres and Playa del Carmen, on the Yucatán Peninsula, high season starts earlier

**Moments** **Our Favorite Mexico Events**

All of the activities mentioned in the "Mexico Calendar of Events," below, are worth checking out. But several unforgettable festivals and celebrations deserve special mention. They are: Carnaval, Holy Week, Assumption of the Virgin Mary, Festival Cervantino, and the Feast of the Virgin of Guadalupe. Consult the calendar for more information.

than in the rest of the country and includes the month of August, when many European visitors arrive. All of these exceptions and others are mentioned in the chapters that follow.

Mexico has two main climate seasons: **rainy** (May to mid-Oct) and **dry** (mid-Oct through Apr). The rainy season can be of little consequence in the dry, northern region of the country. Southern regions typically receive tropical showers, which begin around 4 or 5pm and last a few hours. Though these rains can come on suddenly and be quite strong, they usually end just as quickly and cool off the air for the evening. **Hurricane season** particularly affects the Yucatán Peninsula and the southern Pacific coast, especially from June through October. However, if no hurricanes strike, the light, cooling winds, especially from September through November, can make it a perfect time to tackle the pre-Hispanic ruins that dot the interior of the peninsula.

***Norte* (northern) season** runs from late November through mid-January, when the jet stream dips far south and creates northerly winds and showers in many resort areas. These showers usually only last for a couple of days.

June, July, and August are unrelentingly hot on the Yucatán Peninsula and in most coastal areas, though temperatures rise only into the mid-80s to 90°F. Most of coastal Mexico experiences temperatures in the 80s in the hottest months. The northern states that border the United States experience very high summer temperatures.

**Elevation** is another important factor. High-elevation cities such as Mexico City and San Cristóbal de las Casas can be surprisingly cold. Temperatures can drop close to freezing at night in winter even in San Miguel de Allende and Guanajuato, which are at lower elevations.

## MEXICO CALENDAR OF EVENTS

During national holidays, Mexican banks and governmental offices—including immigration—are closed.

### January

**New Year's Day** (Año Nuevo). This national holiday is perhaps the quietest day in all of Mexico. Most people stay home or attend church. All businesses are closed. In traditional indigenous communities, new tribal leaders are inaugurated with colorful ceremonies rooted in the pre-Hispanic past. January 1.

**Three Kings Day** (Día de Reyes), nationwide. This day commemorates the Three Kings' bringing of gifts to the Christ Child. On this day, children receive gifts, much like the traditional Christmas gift-giving in the United States. Friends and families gather to share the *Rosca de Reyes*, a special cake. Inside the cake is a small doll representing the Christ Child; whoever receives the doll must host a tamales-and-*atole* party on February 2. January 6.

**Regional Fair,** León, Guanajuato. One of Mexico's largest fairs celebrates the founding of this shoemaking and leather-craft city. There are parades, theater, craft exhibits, music, and dance. January 9 to February 5.

**Feast of San Antonio Abad,** Mexico City. This feast is celebrated through the Blessing of the Animals at the Santiago Tlatelolco Church on the Plaza of Three Cultures, at San Juan Bautista Church in Coyoacán, and at the Church of San Fernando, 2 blocks north of the Juárez-Reforma intersection. January 17.

### February

**Candlemas** (Día de la Candelaria), nationwide. Music, dances, processions, food, and other festivities lead up to a blessing of seed and candles in a ceremony that mixes pre-Hispanic and European traditions marking the end of winter. Those who attended the Three Kings celebration reunite to share *atole* and tamales at a party hosted by the recipient of the doll found in the Rosca. February 2.

**Constitution Day** (Día de la Constitución). This national holiday is in honor of the current Mexican constitution, signed in 1917 as a result of the revolutionary war of 1910. It's celebrated through small parades. February 5.

**Carnaval.** Carnaval takes place the 3 days preceding Ash Wednesday and the beginning of Lent. The cities of Tepoztlán, Huejotzingo, Chamula, Veracruz, Cozumel, and Mazatlán celebrate with special gusto. In some places, such as Veracruz, Mazatlán, and Cozumel, the celebration resembles New Orleans's Mardi Gras, with a festive atmosphere and parades. In Chamula, the event harks back to pre-Hispanic times, with ritualistic running on flaming branches. On Shrove Tuesday in Tepoztlán and Huejotzingo, brilliantly clad masked dancers fill the streets. Transportation and hotels are packed, so it's best to make reservations 6 months in advance and arrive a couple of days ahead of the beginning of celebrations.

**Ash Wednesday.** The start of Lent and time of abstinence, this is a day of reverence nationwide; some towns honor it with folk dancing and fairs.

### March

**Annual Witches Conference,** Lake Catemaco, Veracruz. Shamans, white witches, black witches, and practitioners of macumba, Caribbean, Afro, and Antillean ritualistic practices gather on the shores of the lake. Tourists can witness the spectacle and pick up a good-luck charm. First weekend in March.

**Benito Juárez's Birthday.** This national holiday is observed through small hometown celebrations countrywide, especially in Juárez's birthplace, Guelatao, Oaxaca. March 21.

**Spring Equinox,** Chichén-Itzá. On the first day of spring, the Temple of Kukulkán—Chichén-Itzá's main pyramid—aligns with the sun, and the shadow of the plumed serpent moves slowly from the top of the building down. When the shadow reaches the bottom, the body joins the carved stone snake's head at the base of the pyramid. According to ancient legend, at the moment that the serpent is whole, the earth is fertilized. Visitors come from around the world to marvel at this sight, so advance arrangements are advisable. March 21. (The shadow appears Mar 19–Mar 23.) Elsewhere, equinox festivals and celebrations welcome spring, in the custom of the ancient Mexicans, with dances and prayers to the elements and the four cardinal points. It's customary to wear white with a red ribbon.

**Holy Week.** Mexico celebrates the last week in the life of Christ, from Palm Sunday through Easter Sunday, with somber religious processions almost nightly, spoofing of Judas, and reenactments of biblical events, plus food and craft fairs. Among the Tarahumara in the Copper Canyon, celebrations have pre-Hispanic overtones. Pátzcuaro, Taxco, and Malinalco hold special celebrations. Businesses close during this traditional week of Mexican national vacations.

If you plan on traveling to or around Mexico during Holy Week, make your reservations early. Airline seats on flights into and out of the country will be reserved months in advance. Buses to these towns and to almost anywhere else in Mexico will be full, so try arriving on the Wednesday or Thursday before Good Friday. Easter Sunday is quiet, and the week following is a traditional vacation period.

### April

**Cuernavaca Flower Fair.** You'll find exhibits and competition in floriculture and gardening, plus a sound-and-light show. April 3 to 7.

**San Marcos National Fair,** Aguascalientes. Mexico's largest fair, first held in 1604, lasts 22 days. About a million visitors come for bullfights and rodeos as well as *ranchera* music and mariachis. There are craft and industrial exhibits, markets, fireworks, and folk dancing. April 12 to May 4.

### May

**Labor Day.** National holiday. Workers' parades countrywide; everything closes. May 1.

**Cinco de Mayo,** Puebla and nationwide. This national holiday celebrates the defeat of the French at the Battle of Puebla. May 5.

**Feast of San Isidro.** A blessing of seeds and work animals honors the patron saint of farmers. May 15.

**Cancún Jazz Festival.** For dates and schedule information, call **© 800/44-MEXICO.**

### June

**Navy Day** (Día de la Marina). It's celebrated in all coastal towns, with naval parades and fireworks. June 1.

**Corpus Christi,** nationwide. This day honors the Body of Christ (the Eucharist) with processions, Masses, and food. Festivities include performances of *voladores* (flying pole dancers) beside the church and at the ruins of El Tajín. In Mexico City, children dressed as Indians and carrying decorated baskets of fruit for the priest's blessing gather with their parents before the National Cathedral. *Mulitas* (mules), handmade from dried cornhusks and painted, are traditionally sold there on that day. Dates vary.

**National Ceramics Fair and Fiesta,** Tlaquepaque, Jalisco. This pottery center on the outskirts of Guadalajara offers craft demonstrations and competitions as well as mariachis, dancers, and colorful parades. June 14.

**Día de San Pedro** (St. Peter and St. Paul's Day), nationwide. This feast day is celebrated wherever St. Peter is the patron saint; it also honors anyone named Pedro or Peter. It's especially festive at San Pedro Tlaquepaque, near Guadalajara, with numerous mariachi bands, folk dancers, and parades with floats. June 29.

### July

**Guelaguetza Dance Festival,** Oaxaca. This is one of Mexico's most popular events. Villagers from the seven regions around Oaxaca gather in the city's amphitheater. They dress in traditional costumes, and many wear colorful "dancing" masks. The celebration dates to pre-Hispanic times. Make advance reservations, as this festival attracts visitors from around the world. June 21 to 28.

### August

**International Chamber Music Festival,** San Miguel de Allende. Held for the last 20 years in this beautiful town, the festival features international award-winning classical music ensembles. August 1 to 15.

**Fall of Tenochtitlán,** Mexico City. The last battle of the Spanish Conquest took place at Tlatelolco, ruins that are now part of the Plaza of Three Cultures. Wreath-laying ceremonies there and at the Cuauhtémoc monument on Reforma commemorate the surrender of the last Aztec king, Cuauhtémoc, to Cortez, and the loss of thousands of lives. August 13.

**Assumption of the Virgin Mary.** This day is celebrated throughout the country with special Masses, and in some places with processions. In Huamantla, flower petals and colored sawdust carpet the streets. At midnight on August 15, a statue of the Virgin is carried through the streets; on August 16 there is a running of the bulls. On August 15 in Santa Clara del Cobre, near Pátzcuaro, Our Lady of Santa Clara de Asis and the Virgen de la Sagrado Patrona are honored with a parade of floats, dancers on the main square, and an exposition of regional crafts. Buses to Huamantla from Puebla and Mexico City will be full, and there are few hotels in Huamantla. Plan to stay in Puebla and commute to the festivities. August 15 to 17.

### September

**Mariachi Festival.** Guadalajara, Jalisco. These public concerts of mariachi music include visiting mariachi groups from around the world (even Japan!). Workshops and lectures focus on the history, culture, and music of the mariachi in Mexico. Call ✆ **800/44-MEXICO** to confirm dates and schedule of performances. September 1 to 15.

**Independence Day.** This national holiday (Sept 16) celebrates Mexico's independence from Spain with parades, picnics, and family reunions. At 11pm on September 15, the president gives the famous independence *grito* (shout) from the National Palace in Mexico City. At least half a million people crowd into the *zócalo,* and the rest of the country watches on TV or participates in local celebrations. Tall buildings downtown are draped in the national colors (red, green, and white), and the *zócalo* is ablaze with lights. Many people drive downtown at night to see the lights. Querétaro and San Miguel de Allende, where Independence conspirators lived and met, also celebrate elaborately; the schedule of events is exactly the same in every village, town, and city across Mexico. September 15 and 16.

**Fall Equinox,** Chichén-Itzá. The same shadow play that occurs during the spring equinox repeats. September 21 and 22.

### October

**Festival Cervantino,** Guanajuato. This festival began in the 1970s as a cultural event bringing performing artists from all over the world to this picturesque village northeast of Mexico City. Now the artists travel all over the republic after appearing in Guanajuato. Check local calendars for details. Early to mid-October.

**Fiestas de Octubre** (Oct Festivals), Guadalajara. This "most Mexican of cities" celebrates for a month with its trademark mariachi music. It's a bountiful display of popular culture and fine arts, and a spectacular spread of traditional food, Mexican beer, and wine. All month.

**Día de la Raza** ("Ethnicity Day," or Columbus Day). This day commemorates the fusion of the Spanish and Mexican peoples. October 12.

### November

**Day of the Dead.** This national holiday (Nov 1) actually lasts for 2 days: All Saints' Day—honoring saints and deceased children—and All Souls' Day, honoring deceased adults. Relatives gather at cemeteries countrywide, carrying candles and food, and often spend the night beside graves of loved ones. Weeks before, bakers begin producing bread in the shape of mummies or round loaves decorated with bread "bones." Sugar skulls emblazoned with glittery names are sold everywhere. Many days ahead, homes and churches erect altars laden with bread, fruit, flowers, candles, favorite foods, and photographs of saints and of the deceased. On both nights, costumed children walk through the streets, often carrying mock coffins and pumpkin lanterns, into which they expect money will be dropped.

The most famous celebration—which has become almost too well known—is on Janitzio, an island on Lake Pátzcuaro, Michoacán, west of Mexico City. Mixquic, a mountain village south of Mexico City, hosts an elaborate street fair, and around 11pm on both nights solemn processions lead to the cemetery in the center of town. Cemeteries around Oaxaca are well known for their solemn vigils, and some for their Carnaval-like atmosphere. November 1 and 2.

**Fiestas del Mar,** Puerto Vallarta. This celebration has a month-long calendar of activities, including art festivals, sports competitions, the Governor's Cup golf tournament, and an outstanding gourmet dining festival. Among the sporting events are sailing regattas, windsurfing exhibitions, and beach volleyball competitions. November 5 to 25.

**Revolution Day.** This national holiday commemorates the start of the Mexican Revolution in 1910 with parades, speeches, rodeos, and patriotic events. November 20.

**National Silver Fair,** Taxco. A competition of Mexico's best silversmiths and some of the world's finest artisans. There are exhibits, concerts, dances, and fireworks. November 29 to December 6.

### December

**Feast of the Virgin of Guadalupe,** nationwide. Religious processions, street fairs, dancing, fireworks, and Masses honor the patroness of Mexico. It is one of Mexico's most moving and beautiful displays of traditional culture. The Virgin of Guadalupe appeared to a young man, Juan Diego, in December 1531 on a hill near Mexico City. It's customary for children to dress up as Juan Diego, wearing mustaches and red bandanas. One of the most famous and elaborate celebrations takes place at the Basílica of Guadalupe, north of Mexico City, where the Virgin appeared. But every village celebrates this day, often with processions of children carrying banners, and with *charreadas* (rodeos), bicycle races, dancing, and fireworks. In Puerto Vallarta, the celebration begins on December 1 and extends through December 12, with traditional processions to the church for a brief Mass and blessing. In the final days, the processions and festivities take place around the clock. There's a major fireworks exhibition on the feast day at 11pm. December 12.

**Christmas Posadas.** On each of the 9 nights before Christmas, it's customary to reenact the Holy Family's search for an inn. Door-to-door candlelit processions pass through cities and villages nationwide, especially Querétaro and Taxco. Hosted by businesses and community organizations, these take the place of the northern tradition of a Christmas party. December 15 to 24.

**Christmas.** Mexicans often extend this national holiday and leave their jobs up to 2 weeks before Christmas, returning after New Year's. Many businesses close, and resorts and hotels fill up. Significant celebrations take place on December 23. Querétaro has a huge parade. In Oaxaca, you'll experience the "Night of the Radishes," with displays of huge carved radishes, as well as elaborate figures made of cornhusks and dried flowers. On the evening of December 24 in Oaxaca, processions culminate on the central plaza. On the same night, Santiago Tuxtla in Veracruz celebrates by dancing the *huapango* and with *jarocho* bands in the beautiful town square. December 24 and 25.

**New Year's Eve.** Like the rest of the world, Mexico celebrates New Year's Eve with parties, fireworks, and plenty of noise. Special festivities take place at Santa Clara del Cobre, near Pátzcuaro, with a candlelit procession of Christ, and at Tlacolula, near Oaxaca, with commemorative mock battles. December 31.

## 6 Insurance, Health & Safety

### TRAVEL INSURANCE AT A GLANCE

Check your existing insurance policies before you buy travel insurance to cover trip cancellation, lost luggage, medical expenses, or car rental insurance. You're likely to have partial or complete coverage. If you need some, ask your travel agent about a comprehensive package. The cost of travel insurance varies widely, depending on the cost and length of your trip, your age and overall health, and the type of trip you're taking.

Keep in mind that in the aftermath of the World Trade Center attacks, insurers no longer cover some airlines, cruise lines, and tour operators. *The bottom line:* Always, always check the fine print before you sign; more and more policies have built-in exclusions and restrictions that may leave you out in the cold if something goes awry.

For information, contact one of the following popular insurers: **Access America** (© 800/284-8300; www.accessamerica.com); **Travel Guard International** (© 800/826-1300; www.travelguard.com); **Travel Insured International** (© 800/243-3174; www.travelinsured.com); **Travelex Insurance Services** (© 800/228-9792; www.travelex-insurance.com).

### TRIP-CANCELLATION INSURANCE

**Trip cancellation insurance** is a good idea if you have paid a large portion of your vacation expenses up front.

Don't buy insurance from the tour operator that may be responsible for the cancellation; buy it only from a reputable travel insurance agency. Always check the fine print before signing on, and don't overbuy. You won't be reimbursed for more than the cost of your trip.

### MEDICAL INSURANCE

Your existing **health insurance** should cover you if you get sick while on vacation—but check to see whether you are fully covered when away from home, particularly if you belong to an HMO. With the exception of certain HMOs and Medicare/Medicaid, your medical insurance should cover medical treatment—even hospital care—overseas. Most hospitals make you pay up front at the time of care and send you a refund after you've returned home and filed all the paperwork. Members of **Blue Cross/Blue Shield** (© **800/810-BLUE** or www.bluecares.com) can use their cards at select hospitals in most major cities worldwide.

The cost of travel medical insurance varies widely. Check your existing policies before you buy additional coverage. Also, check to see if your medical insurance covers you for emergency medical evacuation: If you have to buy a one-way same-day ticket home and forfeit your nonrefundable ticket, you may be out big bucks.

If you require more insurance, try one of the following: **MEDEX International** (© 888/MEDEX-00 or 410/453-6300; www.medexassist.com); **Travel Assistance International** (© **800/821-2828** or 800/777-8710; www.travelassistance.com); or the **Divers Alert Network** (© **800/446-2671** or 919/684-8181; www.diversalertnetwork.org)

### LOST-LUGGAGE INSURANCE

Your homeowner's insurance should cover **stolen luggage.** The airlines are responsible for $2,500 on domestic flights if they lose your luggage. On international flights (including US portions of international trips), the limit is approximately $9.07 per pound, up to approximately $635 per checked bag. If you plan to check items more valuable than the standard liability, you may purchase "excess valuation" coverage from the airline, up to $5,000. Be sure to take any valuables or irreplaceable items with you in your carry-on luggage.

If you'll be driving in Mexico, see "Getting There: By Car" and "Getting Around: By Car," later in this chapter, for information on **collision** and **damage** and **personal accident insurance.**

## THE HEALTHY TRAVELER

### COMMON AILMENTS

Travelers to certain regions of Mexico occasionally experience **elevation sickness,** which results from the relative lack of oxygen and the decrease in barometric pressure that characterizes high elevations (over 1,515m/5,000 ft.). Symptoms include shortness of breath, fatigue, headache, insomnia, and even nausea. Mexico City is at 2,121m (7,000 ft.) above sea level, as are a number of other central and southern cities, such as San Cristóbal de las Casas (more than 2,121m/7,000 ft.). At high elevations, it takes about 10 days to acquire the extra red blood corpuscles you need to adjust to the scarcity of oxygen. To help your body acclimate, drink plenty of fluids, avoid alcoholic beverages, and don't overexert yourself during the first few days. If you have heart or lung problems, talk to your doctor before going above 2,424m (8,000 ft.).

---

*Tips* **Over-the-Counter Drugs in Mexico**

Antibiotics and other drugs that you'd need a prescription to buy in the States are available over the counter in Mexican pharmacies. Mexican pharmacies also carry a limited selection of common over-the-counter cold, sinus, and allergy remedies.

---

## *Tips* Treating & Avoiding Digestive Trouble

It's called "travelers' diarrhea" or *turista*, the Spanish word for "tourist": persistent diarrhea, often accompanied by fever, nausea, and vomiting, that used to attack many travelers to Mexico. (Some in the United States call this "Montezuma's revenge," but you won't hear it called that in Mexico.) Widespread improvements in infrastructure, sanitation, and education have practically eliminated this ailment, especially in well-developed resort areas. Most travelers make a habit of drinking only bottled water, which also helps to protect against unfamiliar bacteria. In resort areas, and generally throughout Mexico, only purified ice is used. If you do come down with this ailment, nothing beats Pepto Bismol, readily available in Mexico. A good high-potency (or "therapeutic") vitamin supplement and even extra vitamin C can help; yogurt is good for healthy digestion.

Since dehydration can quickly become life-threatening, the Public Health Service advises that you be careful to replace fluids and electrolytes (potassium, sodium, and the like) during a bout of diarrhea. Drink Pedialyte, a rehydration solution available at most Mexican pharmacies, or natural fruit juice (high in potassium) with a pinch of salt added.

**How to Prevent It:** The U.S. Public Health Service recommends the following measures for preventing travelers' diarrhea: **Drink only purified water** (boiled water, canned or bottled beverages, beer, or wine). **Choose food carefully.** In general, avoid salads (except in first-class restaurants), uncooked vegetables, undercooked protein, and unpasteurized milk or milk products, including cheese. Choose food that is freshly cooked and still hot. In addition, something as simple as **clean hands** can go a long way toward preventing *turista*.

**Mosquitoes** and **gnats** are prevalent along the coast and in the Yucatán lowlands. Insect repellent (*repelente contra insectos*) is a must, and it's not always available in Mexico. If you'll be in these areas and are prone to bites, bring along a repellent that contains the active ingredient DEET. Avon's Skin So Soft also works extremely well. If you're sensitive to bites, pick up some antihistamine cream from a drugstore at home.

Most readers won't ever see a scorpion (*alacrán*). But if one stings you, go immediately to a doctor.

### MORE SERIOUS DISEASES

You shouldn't be overly concerned about tropical diseases if you stay on the normal tourist routes and don't eat street food. However, both dengue fever and cholera have appeared in Mexico in recent years. Talk to your doctor or to a medical specialist in tropical diseases about precautions you should take. You can also get medical bulletins from the U.S. State Department and the Centers for Disease Control (see "Visitor Information," earlier). You can protect yourself by taking some simple precautions: Watch what you eat and drink; don't swim in stagnant water (ponds, slow-moving rivers, or wells); and avoid mosquito bites by covering up, using repellent, and sleeping under netting. The most dangerous areas seem to be on Mexico's west coast, away from the big resorts, which are relatively safe.

### EMERGENCY EVACUATION

In extreme medical emergencies, a service from the United States will fly people to American hospitals. **Global Lifeline** (✆ **888/554-9729,** or 01-800/305-9400 in Mexico) is a 24-hour air ambulance. Other companies also offer air evacuation service; for a list, refer to the U.S. State Department website, http://travel.state.gov/medical.html.

## THE SAFE TRAVELER

### CRIME

I have lived and traveled in Mexico for over a decade, have never had any serious trouble, and rarely feel suspicious of anyone or any situation. You will probably feel physically safer in most Mexican cities and villages than in any comparable place at home. However, crime in Mexico has received much attention in the North American press over the past several years. Many feel this unfairly exaggerates the real dangers, but it should be noted that crime, including taxi robberies, kidnappings, and highway carjackings, is on the rise. The most severe problems have been concentrated in Mexico City, where even long-time foreign residents will attest to the overall lack of security. Isolated incidents have also occurred in Ixtapa, Baja, and even traditionally tranquil Puerto Escondido. See "Visitor Information," earlier, for information on the latest **U.S. State Department advisories.**

Precautions are necessary, but travelers should be realistic. Common sense is essential. You can generally trust people whom you approach for help or directions—but be wary of anyone who approaches you offering the same. The more insistent the person is, the more cautious you should be. The crime rate is, on the whole, much lower in Mexico than in most parts of the United States, and the nature of crimes in general is less violent—most crime is motivated by robbery or jealousy. Random, violent, or serial crime is essentially unheard of in Mexico. You are much more likely to meet kind and helpful Mexicans than you are to encounter those set on thievery and deceit.

Although these general comments on crime are basically true throughout Mexico, the one notable exception is in **Mexico City,** where violent crime is serious. Do not wear fine jewelry, expensive watches, or any other obvious displays of wealth. Muggings—day and night—are common. Avoid the use of the **green Volkswagen taxis,** many of which have been involved in "pirate" robberies, muggings, and even kidnappings. Car theft and carjackings are also a common occurrence. Despite the rise in Mexico City's crime, you should be fine if you avoid ostentatious displays of wealth, follow common-sense precautions, and take taxis dispatched from official sites (*sitios*). More specific precautions can be found in chapter 3. (See also "Emergencies" under "Fast Facts: Mexico," later in this chapter.)

### BRIBES & SCAMS

As is the case around the world, there are the occasional bribes and scams in Mexico, targeted at people believed to be naive—i.e., the telltale tourist. For years Mexico was known as a place where bribes—called *mordidas* ("bites")—were expected; however, the country is rapidly changing. Frequently, offering a bribe today, especially to a police officer, is considered an insult, and it can land you in deeper trouble.

If you believe a **bribe** is being requested, here are a few tips on dealing with the situation. Even if you speak Spanish, don't utter a word of it to Mexican officials. That way you'll appear innocent, all the while understanding every word.

When you are crossing the border, should the person who inspects your car ask for a tip, you can ignore this request—but understand that the official may suddenly decide that a complete search of your belongings is in order. If faced with a situation where you feel you're being asked for a *propina* (literally, "tip"; colloquially, "bribe"), how much should you offer? Usually $3 to $5 or the equivalent in pesos will do the trick. Many tourists have the impression that everything works better in Mexico if you "tip," however, in reality, this only perpetuates the *mordida* attitude. If you are pleased with a service, feel free to tip, but you shouldn't tip simply to attempt to get away with something illegal or inappropriate, whether it is crossing the border without having your car inspected or not getting a ticket that's deserved. There's a number to **report irregularities with Customs officials** (© **800/001-4800** in Mexico). Your call will go to the office of the Comptroller and Administrative Development Secretariat (SECODAM); most employees there do not speak English. Be sure you have some basic information—such as the name of the person who requested a bribe or acted in a rude manner, as well as the place, time, and day of the event.

Whatever you do, **avoid impoliteness;** under no circumstances should you insult a Latin American official. Extreme politeness, even in the face of adversity, rules Mexico. In Mexico, *gringos* have a reputation for being loud and demanding. By adopting the local custom of excessive courtesy, you'll have greater success in negotiations of any kind. Stand your ground, but do it politely.

As you travel in Mexico, you may encounter several types of **scams,** which are typical throughout the world. One involves some kind of a **distraction** or feigned commotion. While your attention is diverted, a pickpocket makes a grab for your wallet. In another common scam, an **unaccompanied child** pretends to be lost and frightened and takes your hand for safety. Meanwhile the child or an accomplice plunders your pockets. A third involves **confusing currency.** A shoeshine boy, street musician, guide, or other individual might offer you a service for a price that seems reasonable—in pesos. When it comes time to pay, he or she tells you the price is in dollars, not pesos, and becomes very hostile if payment is not made. Be very clear on the price and currency when services are involved.

## 7 Tips for Travelers with Special Needs

### FAMILY TRAVEL

Children are considered the national treasure of Mexico, and Mexicans will warmly welcome and cater to your children. Many parents were reluctant to bring young children into Mexico in the past, primarily due to health concerns, but I can't think of a better place to introduce children to the exciting adventure of exploring a different culture. Some of the best destinations for children include Puerto Vallarta, Cancún, and La Paz. Hotels can often arrange for a baby-sitter.

Before leaving, ask your doctor which medications to take along. Disposable diapers cost about the same in Mexico but are of poorer quality. You can get Huggies Supreme and Pampers identical to the ones sold in the United States, but at a higher price. Many stores sell Gerber's baby foods. Dry cereals, powdered formulas, baby bottles, and purified water are easily available in midsize and large cities or resorts.

Cribs may present a problem; only the largest and most luxurious hotels provide them. However, rollaway beds are often available. Child seats or high chairs at restaurants are common.

Consider bringing your own car seat, as they are not readily available for rent in Mexico.

For more resources, check the following websites:

- **Family Travel Network** (www.familytravelnetwork.com).
- **Travel with Your Children** (www.travelwithyourkids.com).
- **The Busy Person's Guide to Travel with Children** (http://wz.com/travel/TravelingWithChildren.html).

## TRAVELERS WITH DISABILITIES

Mexico may seem like one giant obstacle course to travelers in wheelchairs or on crutches. At airports, you may encounter steep stairs before finding a well-hidden elevator or escalator—if one exists. Airlines will often arrange wheelchair assistance to the baggage area. Porters are generally available to help with luggage at airports and large bus stations, once you've cleared baggage claim.

Few airports allow boarding an airplane from the waiting room. You either descend stairs to a bus that ferries you to the plane, which you board by climbing stairs, or you walk across the tarmac to your plane and ascend the stairs. Deplaning presents the same problem in reverse.

Escalators (and there aren't many in the country) are often out of order. Stairs without handrails abound. Few rest rooms are equipped for travelers with disabilities; when one is available, access to it may be through a narrow passage that won't accommodate a wheelchair or a person on crutches. Many deluxe hotels (the most expensive) now have rooms with bathrooms for people with disabilities. Those traveling on a budget should stick with one-story hotels or hotels with elevators. Even so, there will probably still be obstacles somewhere. Generally speaking, no matter where you are, someone will lend a hand, although you may have to ask for it.

Mexico can offer many exciting experiences if you plan your itinerary with the help of the following resources:

- **Access Adventures** (**© 716/889-9096**).
- **Accessible Journeys** (**© 800/TINGLES** or 610/521-0339; www.disabilitytravel.com).
- **The Moss Rehab Hospital** (**© 215/456-9603;** www.mossresourcenet.org).
- **The Society for Accessible Travel and Hospitality** (**© 212/447-7284;** www.sath.org). Annual membership costs $45 for adults, $30 for seniors and students.

## SENIOR TRAVEL

Mexico is a popular country for retirees. For decades, North Americans have been living indefinitely in Mexico by returning to the border and re-crossing with a new tourist permit every 6 months. Mexican immigration officials have caught on, and now limit the maximum time in the country to 6 months within any year. This is to encourage even partial residents to acquire proper documentation.

Some of the most popular places for long-term stays are Guadalajara, Lake Chapala, Ajijic, and Puerto Vallarta, all in the state of Jalisco; San Miguel de Allende and Guanajuato in the state of Guanajuato; Cuernavaca in Morelos; Alamos in Sinaloa; and to a lesser extent Manzanillo in Colima and Morelia in Michoacán. But crowds don't necessarily indicate the only good places: Oaxaca, Querétaro, Puebla, Tepoztlán, and Valle de Bravo have much to offer, even though

Americans have yet to collect there in large numbers.

***AIM,*** Apdo. Postal 31–70, 45050 Guadalajara, Jal., is a well-written, informative newsletter for prospective retirees. Issues have evaluated retirement in Aguascalientes, Puebla, San Cristóbal de las Casas, Puerto Angel, Puerto Escondido and Huatulco, Oaxaca, Taxco, Tepic, Manzanillo, Melaque, and Barra de Navidad. Subscriptions are $18 to the United States and $21 to Canada. Back issues are three for $5.

**Sanborn Tours,** 2015 South 10th St., Post Office Drawer 519, McAllen, TX 78505-0519 (✆ **800/395-8482**), offers a "Retire in Mexico" orientation tour.

## GAY & LESBIAN TRAVELERS

Mexico is a conservative country, with deeply rooted Catholic religious traditions. Public displays of same-sex affection are rare and still considered shocking for men, especially outside of urban or resort areas. Women in Mexico frequently walk hand in hand, but anything more would cross the boundary of acceptability. However, gay and lesbian travelers are generally treated with respect and should not experience any harassment, assuming they give the appropriate regard to local culture and customs.

Puerto Vallarta is perhaps the most welcoming and accepting destination in Mexico, with a selection of accommodations and entertainment oriented especially toward gay and lesbian travelers. Vicki Skinner's **Doin' It Right in Puerto Vallarta** is a travel service that rents gay-friendly condos and villas for individuals and groups of up to 75. Her newsletter, the *PV Purple Pages,* offers travel specials and features tips, special events, and activities. (Subscriptions: 1010 University Ave., #C113-741, San Diego, CA 92103; ✆ **800/936-3646** or 619/297-3642; www.DoinItRight.com.)

## FEMALE TRAVELERS

As a female traveling alone, I can tell you firsthand that I feel safer traveling in Mexico than in the United States. But I use the same common-sense precautions I use anywhere else in the world and am alert to what's going on around me.

Mexicans in general, and men in particular, are nosy about single travelers, especially women. If a taxi driver or anyone else with whom you don't want to become friendly asks about your marital status, family, and so forth, my advice is to make up a set of answers (regardless of the truth): "I'm married, traveling with friends, and I have three children." Saying you are single and traveling alone may send the wrong message.

## STUDENT TRAVEL

Because Mexicans consider higher education more a luxury than a birthright, there is no formal network of student discounts and programs. Most Mexican students travel with their families rather than with other students, so student discount cards are not commonly recognized.

However, more hostels have entered the student travel scene. The **Mexican Youth Hostel Network,** or Red Mexicana de Albergues Juveniles (www.remaj.com) offers a list of hostels that meet international standards in Mexico City, Cuernavaca and surrounding areas, Oaxaca and Veracruz. The **Mexican Youth Hostel Association,** or Asociación Mexicana de Albergues Juveniles (www.hostels.com.mx) offers a list of hostels in Mexico City, Zacatecas, Guanajuato, Puerto Escondido, Uxmal, Palenque, Tulum, Cancún, and Playa del Carmen.

## 8 Getting There

### BY PLANE

The airline situation in Mexico is rapidly improving, with many new regional carriers offering scheduled service to areas previously not served. In addition to regularly scheduled service, charter service direct from U.S. cities to resorts is making Mexico more accessible. For information about saving money on airfares using the Internet, see "Planning Your Trip Online," later in this chapter.

**THE MAJOR INTERNATIONAL AIRLINES** The main airlines operating direct or nonstop flights from the United States to Mexico include **Aerocalifornia** (© 800/237-6225), **Aeromexico** (© 800/237-6639; www.aeromexico.com), **Air France** (© 800/237-2747; www.airfrance.com), **Alaska Airlines** (© 800/426-0333; www.alaskaair.com), **America West** (© 800/235-9292; www.americawest.com), **American Airlines** (© 800/433-7300; www.im.aa.com), **Continental** (© 800/525-0280; www.continental.com), **Mexicana** (© 800/531-7921; www.mexicana.com), **Northwest/KLM** (© 800/225-2525; www.nwa.com), **Taca** (© 800/225-2272; www.taca.com), **United** (© 800/241-6522; www.ual. com), and **USAirways** (© 800/428- 4322; www.usairways.com). **Southwest Airlines** (© 800/435-9792; www.iflyswa.com) serves the U.S. border.

The main departure points in North America for international airlines are Atlanta, Chicago, Dallas/Fort Worth, Denver, Houston, Los Angeles, Miami, New Orleans, New York, Orlando, Philadelphia, Raleigh/Durham, San Antonio, San Francisco, Seattle, Toronto, Tucson, and Washington, D.C.

**NEW AIR TRAVEL SECURITY MEASURES** In the wake of the terrorist attacks of September 2001, the airline industry began implementing sweeping security measures. Expect a lengthy check-in process and extensive delays. Although regulations vary from airline to airline, you can expedite the process by taking the following steps:

### *Tips* Luxury Bus Service from the Mexico City Airport

An airport-to-destination service to a number of cities in central Mexico takes the hassle out of travel. The deluxe buses serving these routes are air-conditioned and have video movies and a rest room. The price usually includes soft drinks (and passengers tend to stock up when they board).

If you're going to Puebla (see chapter 11), Estrella Roja buses ($10) depart hourly beginning at 6 or 7:30am from in front of the airport's Gate D (Sala D) exit. The bus runs every hour until midnight. Buses for Querétaro, Toluca, Pachuca, and Cuernavaca are in front of the covered concourse outside the terminal between exit doors for Gate D. If you have trouble locating them, ask for help at an information desk on the main concourse.

If precise scheduling is essential, call the **Airport Information Office** (© **55/5786-9341,** 55/5786-9342, 55/5786-9358, or 55/5571-3600) to verify names of buses, where to find them, and current schedules.

### *Tips* All About E-Ticketing

Only yesterday, **electronic tickets (E-tickets)** were the fast and easy alternative to paper tickets. They allowed passengers to avoid long lines at check-in, and saved airlines money on postage and labor. With increased security, however, an E-ticket no longer guarantees accelerated check-in. You often can't go straight to the gate, even if you have no bags to check. You'll probably need to show your printed receipt or confirmation of purchase, as well as a photo ID, and sometimes even the credit card with which you purchased your E-ticket. That said, an E-ticket is still fast and convenient. In addition, airlines often offer frequent flier miles as incentive for electronic bookings.

- **Arrive early.** Be at the airport at least 2 hours before your scheduled flight.
- **Try not to drive your car to the airport.** Parking and curbside access to the terminal may be limited. Call ahead and check.
- **Don't count on curbside check-in.** Some airlines and airports have altogether stopped curbside check-in. For up-to-date information, check with your airline.
- **Be sure to carry plenty of documentation.** A valid government-issued photo ID (federal, state, or local) is required. With an E-ticket, carry printed confirmation of purchase, and be ready to show the credit card with which you bought your ticket (see "All About E-Ticketing," above). This varies from airline to airline, so call ahead to make sure you have the proper documentation.
- **Know what you can carry on—and what you can't.** Travelers in the United States are limited to one carry-on bag, plus one personal bag (such as a purse or a briefcase). The Transportation Security Administration (TSA) restricts carry-on items; generally, anything that might be used as a weapon, from a corkscrew to a golf club, must be checked. For up-to-date information, go to the TSA's website (**www.tsa.gov**). Your airline may have additional restrictions. Call ahead to avoid problems.
- **Prepare to be searched.** Expect spot checks. Electronic items, such as laptops and cell phones, should be ready for additional screening. Limit the metal items you wear.
- **It's no joke.** When a check-in agent asks if someone other than you packed your bag, don't decide that this is the time to be funny.
- **No ticket, no gate access.** Only ticketed passengers will be allowed beyond screening checkpoints, except for those people with specific medical or parental needs.

## BY CAR

Driving is not the cheapest way to get to Mexico, but it is the best way to see the country. Even so, you may think twice about taking your own car south of the border once you've pondered the bureaucracy involved. One option is to rent a car once you arrive and tour around a specific region. Rental cars in Mexico are generally new, clean, and well maintained. Although they're pricier than in the United States, discounts are often available for rentals of a week or longer, especially when arrangements are made in advance from the United States. (See "Car Rentals," below, for more details.)

If, after reading the section that follows, you have additional questions or you want to confirm the current rules, call your nearest Mexican consulate or the Mexican Government Tourist Office. Although travel insurance companies are generally helpful, they may not have the most accurate information. To check on road conditions or to get help with any travel emergency while in Mexico, call ✆ **01-800/903-9200,** or 55/5250-0151 in Mexico City. English-speaking operators staff both numbers.

In addition, check with the **U.S. State Department** (see "Visitor Information," at the beginning of this chapter) for warnings about dangerous driving areas.

### CAR DOCUMENTS

To drive your car into Mexico, you'll need a **temporary car-importation permit,** which is granted after you provide a required list of documents (see below). The permit can be obtained through Banco del Ejército (*Banjercito*) officials, who have a desk, booth, or office at the Mexican Customs (*Aduana*) building after you cross the border into Mexico.

The following strict requirements for border crossing were accurate at press time:

- **A valid driver's license,** issued outside of Mexico.
- **Current, original car registration and a copy of the original car title.** If the registration or title is in more than one name and not all the named people are traveling with you, a notarized letter from the absent person(s) authorizing use of the vehicle for the trip is required; have it ready just in case. The registration and your credit card (see below) must be in the same name.
- **A valid international major credit card.** With a credit card, you are required to pay only a $22.50 car-importation fee. The credit card must be in the same name as the car registration. If you do not have a major credit card (American Express, Diners Club, MasterCard, or Visa), you must post a bond or make a deposit equal to the value of the vehicle. Check cards are not accepted.
- **Original immigration documentation.** This is either your tourist permit (FMT) or the original immigration booklet, FM2 or FM3, if you hold more permanent status.
- **A signed declaration promising to return to your country of origin with the vehicle.** Obtain this form (*Carta Promesa de Retorno*)

---

**Tips Carrying Car Documents**

You must carry your temporary car-importation permit, tourist permit (see "Entry Requirements," earlier), and, if you purchased it, your proof of Mexican car insurance (see below) in the car at all times. The temporary car-importation permit papers are valid for 6 months to a year, while the tourist permit is usually issued for 30 days. It's a good idea to overestimate the time you'll spend in Mexico, so that if you have to (or want to) stay longer, you'll avoid the hassle of getting your papers extended. Whatever you do, don't overstay either permit. Doing so invites heavy fines, confiscation of your vehicle (which will not be returned), or both. Also remember that 6 months does not necessarily equal 180 days—be sure that you return before the earlier expiration date.

---

from AAA or Sanborn's before you go, or from Banjercito officials at the border. There's no charge. The form does not stipulate that you must return by the same border entry through which you entered.

- **Temporary Importation Application.** By signing this form, you state that you are only temporarily importing the car for your personal use and will not be selling it. This is to help regulate the entry and restrict the resale of unauthorized cars and trucks. Vehicles in the U.S. are much less expensive and for years were brought into Mexico for resale. Make sure the permit is cancelled when you return to the U.S.

If you receive your documentation at the border, Mexican officials will make two copies of everything and charge you for the copies. For up-to-the-minute information, a great source is the Customs office in Nuevo Laredo, or *Módulo de Importación Temporal de Automóviles, Aduana Nuevo Laredo* (© **867/712-2071**).

*Important reminder:* Someone else may drive, but the person (or relative of the person) whose name appears on the car-importation permit must *always* be in the car. (If stopped by police, a non-registered family member driving without the registered driver must be prepared to prove familial relationship to the registered driver—no joke.) Violation of this rule subjects the car to impoundment and the driver to imprisonment, a fine, or both. You can drive a car with foreign license plates only if you have a foreign (non-Mexican) driver's license. You do not need an international driver's license in Mexico.

## MEXICAN AUTO INSURANCE

Liability auto insurance is legally required in Mexico. U.S. insurance is invalid; to be insured in Mexico, you must purchase Mexican insurance. Any party involved in an accident who has no insurance may be sent to jail and have his or her car impounded until all claims are settled. This is true even if you just drive across the border to spend the day. U.S. companies that broker Mexican insurance are commonly found at the border crossing, and several quote daily rates.

You can also buy car insurance through **Sanborn's Mexico Insurance,** P.O. Box 52840, 2009 S. 10th, McAllen, TX 78505-2840 (© **956/686-3601;** fax 800/222-0158 or 956/686-0732; www.sanbornsinsurance.com). The company has offices at all U.S. border crossings. Its policies cost the same as the competition's do, but you get legal coverage (attorney and bail bonds if needed) and a detailed mile-by-mile guide for your proposed route. Most of Sanborn's border offices are open Monday through Friday, and a few are staffed on Saturday and Sunday. **AAA** auto club also sells insurance.

## RETURNING TO THE UNITED STATES WITH YOUR CAR

You *must* return the car documents you obtained when you entered Mexico when you cross back with your car, or at some point within 180 days. (You can cross as many times as you wish within the 180 days.) If the documents aren't returned, heavy fines are imposed ($250 for each 15 days late), your car may be impounded and confiscated, or you may be jailed if you return to Mexico. You can only return the car documents to a Banjercito official on duty at the Mexican Customs (*Aduana*) building *before* you cross back into the United States. Some border cities have Banjercito officials on duty 24 hours a day, but others do not; some do not have Sunday hours. On the U.S. side, Customs agents may or may not inspect your car from stem to stern.

### BY SHIP

Numerous cruise lines serve Mexico. Some (including whale-watching trips) cruise from California to the Baja Peninsula and ports of call on the Pacific coast, or from Houston or Miami to the Caribbean (which often includes stops in Cancún, Playa del Carmen, and Cozumel). Several cruise-tour specialists offer substantial discounts on unsold cabins if you're willing to take off at the last minute. One such company is **The Cruise Line,** 150 NW 168 St., North Miami Beach, FL 33169 (© **800/777-0707** or 305/521-2200).

### BY BUS

Greyhound-Trailways (or its affiliates) offers service from around the United States to the Mexican border, where passengers disembark, cross the border, and buy a ticket for travel into the interior of Mexico. Many border crossings have scheduled buses from the U.S. bus station to the Mexican bus station.

## 9 The Pros & Cons of Package Tours

Say the words "package tour" and many people automatically feel as though they're being forced to choose: your money or your lifestyle. This isn't necessarily the case. Most Mexico packages let you have both your independence *and* your positive bank-account balance. Package tours are not the same thing as escorted tours. They are simply a way of buying airfare, accommodations, and other pieces of your trip (usually airport transfers, and sometimes meals and activities) at the same time.

For popular destinations like Mexico's beach resorts, they're often the smart way to go, because they can save you a ton of money. In many cases, a package that includes airfare, hotel, and transportation to and from the airport will cost you less than the hotel alone if you booked it yourself. That's because tour operators buy packages in bulk and then resell them to the public.

You can buy a package at any time of the year, but the best deals usually coincide with high season—mid-December through April—when demand is at its peak, and companies are more confident about filling planes. This may run contrary to common sense—you might think that package rates would be better during low season, when room rates and airfares plunge. But the key is air access, which is much easier during the winter. Packages vary widely, with some companies offering a better class of hotels than others. Some offer the same hotels for lower prices. Some offer flights on scheduled airlines, while others book charters. In some packages, your choices of accommodations and travel days may be limited. Each destination usually has some packagers that are better than the rest because they buy in even bigger bulk. Not only can that mean better prices, it can mean more choices.

### WARNINGS

- **Read the fine print.** Make sure you know *exactly* what's included in the price you're being quoted, and what's not.
- **Don't compare Mayas and Aztecs.** When evaluating different packagers, compare the deals they offer on similar properties. Most packagers can offer bigger savings on some hotels than others.
- **Know what you're getting yourself into—and if you can get yourself out of it.** Before you commit to a package, make sure you know how much flexibility you have. Often, packagers will

offer trip cancellation insurance (for around $25–$30), which will return your payment if you need to change your plans.

- **Use your best judgment.** Stay away from fly-by-nights and shady packagers. Go with a reputable firm with a proven track record. This is where your travel agent can come in handy.

## WHERE TO BROWSE

- For one-stop shopping on the web, go to **www.vacationpackager.com**, an extensive search engine that links you up with more than 30 packagers offering Mexican beach vacations—and even lets you custom design your package.
- Check out **www.2travel.com** and find a page with links to a number of the big-name Mexico packagers, including several of those listed here.
- For last-minute air-only or package bargains, check out **Vacation Hotline** (www.vacationhotline.net). Once you find your deal, you'll need to call to make booking arrangements. This service offers packages from the popular Apple and Funjet vacation wholesalers.

## RECOMMENDED PACKAGERS

- **Aeromexico Vacations** (**© 800/245-8585;** www.aeromexico.com) offers year-round packages to almost every destination it serves, including Acapulco, Cancún, Cozumel, Ixtapa/Zihuatanejo, Los Cabos, and Puerto Vallarta. Aeromexico has a large (over 100) selection of resorts in these destinations and more, in a variety of price ranges. The best deals are from Houston, Dallas, San Diego, Los Angeles, Miami, and New York, in that order.
- **Alaska Airlines Vacations** (**© 800/468-2248;** www.alaskaair.com) sells packages to Ixtapa/Zihuatanejo, Los Cabos, Manzanillo/Costa Alegre, Mazatlán, and Puerto Vallarta. Alaska flies direct from Los Angeles, San Diego, San Jose, San Francisco, Seattle, Vancouver, Anchorage, and Fairbanks. The website offers unpublished discounts that are not available through the phone operators.
- **American Airlines Vacations** (**© 800/321-2121;** http://aav1.aavacations.com) has year-round deals to Acapulco, Cancún, the Riviera Maya, Guadalajara, Los Cabos, Mexico City, and Puerto Vallarta. You don't have to fly with American if you can get a better deal on another airline; land-only packages include hotel, hotel tax, and airport transfers. American's hubs to Mexico are Dallas/Fort Worth, Chicago, and Miami. The website offers unpublished discounts that are not available through the operators.
- **America West Vacations** (**© 800/356-6611;** www.americawestvacations.com) has deals to Acapulco, Guadalajara, Ixtapa, Mazatlán, Manzanillo, Mexico City, Los Cabos, and Puerto Vallarta, mostly from its Phoenix gateway. Many packages to Los Cabos include car rentals. The website offers discounted featured specials that are not available through the operators. You can also book hotels without air by calling the toll-free number. Book golf vacations to Los Cabos through www.awagolf.com or **© 888/AWA-GOLF.**
- **Apple Vacations** (**© 800/365-2775;** www.applevacations.com) offers inclusive packages to all the beach resorts, and has the largest choice of hotels in Acapulco, Cancún, Cozumel, Huatulco, Ixtapa, Loreto, Los Cabos, Manzanillo, Mazatlán, Puerto Vallarta, and the

Riviera Maya. Scheduled carriers for the air portion include American, United, Mexicana, Delta, TWA, US Airways, Reno Air, Alaska Airlines, AeroCalifornia, and Aeromexico. Apple perks include baggage handling and the services of a company representative at major hotels.

- **Classic Custom Vacations** (✆ **800/221-3949** or 800/344-5687; www.classiccustomvacations.com) specializes in package vacations to Mexico's finest luxury resorts. It combines discounted first-class and economy airfare on American, Continental, Mexicana, Alaska, America West, and Delta with stays at the most exclusive hotels in Cancún, the Riviera Maya, Mérida, Oaxaca, Guadalajara, Mexico City, Puerto Vallarta, Mazatlán, Costa Alegre, Manzanillo, Ixtapa/Zihuatanejo, Acapulco, Huatulco, and Los Cabos. In many cases, packages also include meals, airport transfers, and upgrades.
- **Continental Vacations** (✆ **800/634-5555** and 888/989-9255; www.continental.com) has year-round packages to Cancún, Cozumel, Puerto Vallarta, Cabo San Lucas, Acapulco, Ixtapa, Mazatlán, Mexico City, and Guadalajara, The best deals are from Houston; Newark, N.J.; and Cleveland. You have to fly Continental. The Internet deals offer savings not available elsewhere.
- **Delta Vacations** (✆ **800/872-7786;** www.deltavacations.com) has year-round packages to Acapulco, Puerto Vallarta, Los Cabos, Cozumel, and Cancún. Atlanta is the hub, so expect the best prices from there.
- **Funjet Vacations** (book through any travel agent; www.funjet.com for general information) is one of the largest vacation packagers in the United States. Funjet has packages to Acapulco, Cancún, Cozumel, the Riviera Maya, Huatulco, Los Cabos, Mazatlán, Ixtapa, and Puerto Vallarta. You can choose a charter or fly on American, Continental, Delta, Aeromexico, US Airways, Alaska Air, TWA, or United.
- **GOGO Worldwide Vacations** (✆ **888/636-3942;** www.gogowwv.com) has trips to all the major beach destinations, including Acapulco, Cancún, Mazatlán, Puerto Vallarta, and Los Cabos. It offers several exclusive deals from higher-end hotels. Book through any travel agent.
- **Mexicana Vacations,** or MexSea-Sun Vacations (✆ **800/531-9321;** www.mexicana.com) offers getaways to all the resorts. Mexicana operates daily direct flights from Los Angeles to Los Cabos, Mazatlán, Cancún, Puerto Vallarta, Manzanillo, and Ixtapa/Zihuatanejo.
- **Online Vacation Mall** (✆ **800/839-9851;** www.onlinevacationmall.com) allows you to search for and book packages offered by a number of tour operators and airlines to Acapulco, Cancún, Cozumel, Guaymas, Huatulco, Ixtapa/Zihuatanejo, La Paz, Los Cabos, Puerto Vallarta, the Riviera Maya, Mazatlán, and Mexico City.
- **Pleasant Mexico Holidays** (✆ **800/448-3333;** www.pleasantholidays.com) is one of the largest vacation packagers in the United States, with hotels in Acapulco, Cancún, Cozumel, Ixtapa/Zihuatanejo, Los Cabos, Mazatlán, and Puerto Vallarta.

## REGIONAL PACKAGERS

**From the East Coast: Liberty Travel** (✆ **888/271-1584;** www.libertytravel.com), one of the biggest packagers in the Northeast, often runs a

### *Finds* Out-of-the-Ordinary Places to Stay

Mexico lends itself beautifully to the concept of small, private hotels in idyllic settings. They vary in style from grandiose estate to palm-thatched bungalow. **Mexico Boutique Hotels** (www.MexicoBoutiqueHotels.com) specializes in smaller places to stay with a high level of personal attention and service. Most options have less than 50 rooms, and the accommodations consist of entire villas, *casitas,* bungalows, or a combination. The Yucatán is especially noted for the luxury haciendas throughout the peninsula.

full-page ad in the Sunday papers, with frequent Mexico specials. You won't get much in the way of service, but you will get a good deal.

**From the West: Suntrips** (✆ **800/357-2400,** or 888/888-5028 for departures within 14 days; www.suntrips.com) is one of the largest West Coast packagers for Mexico, with departures from San Francisco and Denver; regular charters to Cancún, Cozumel, Los Cabos and Puerto Vallarta; and a large selection of hotels.

**From the Southwest:** Town and Country (book through travel agents) packages regular deals to Los Cabos, Mazatlán, Puerto Vallarta, Ixtapa, Manzanillo, Cancún, Cozumel, and Acapulco with America West from the airline's Phoenix and Las Vegas gateways.

## 10 Active Vacations in Mexico

Mexico has more than 120 **golf** courses, concentrated in the resort areas, with excellent options in Mexico City and Guadalajara. Los Cabos, in Baja Sur, has become the country's preeminent golf destination; the Puerto Vallarta area enjoys a growing reputation. For details on courses and events, see chapters 16 and 8. Visitors to Mexico can also enjoy **tennis, racquetball, squash, water-skiing, surfing, bicycling,** and **horseback riding. Scuba diving** is excellent, not only off the Yucatán's Caribbean coast (especially Cozumel), but also on the Pacific coast at Puerto Vallarta and Manzanillo, and off Baja in the Sea of Cortez. **Mountain and volcano climbing** is a rugged sport that allows you to meet like-minded folks from around the world. The top peaks are just 80km (50 miles) south of Mexico City—the snowcapped volcanoes Popocatépetl (5,420m/17,887 ft.) and Ixtaccihuatl (5,255m/17,342 ft.). For information on visiting and climbing the volcanoes, contact the **Club de Exploraciones de México** in Mexico City (✆ **55/5740-8032**).

**PARKS** Most national parks and nature reserves are understaffed or unstaffed. Reliable Mexican companies (such as AMTAVE members; see below) and many U.S.-based companies offer adventure trips.

**OUTDOORS ORGANIZATIONS & TOUR OPERATORS** **AMTAVE** (Asociación Mexicana de Turismo de Aventura y Ecoturismo, A.C.) is an active association of eco- and adventure tour operators. It publishes an annual catalog of participating firms and their offerings, all of which must meet certain criteria for security, quality, and training of the guides, as well as for sustainability of natural and cultural environments. For more information, contact AMTAVE in Cancun (✆ **800/509-7678** or 998/884-9580;

fax 998/884-3667; www.amtave.com).

The **Archaeological Conservancy,** 5301 Central Ave. NE, Suite 402, Albuquerque, NM 87108 (© **505/266-1540;** www.americanarchaeology.org), presents one trip per year led by an expert, usually an archaeologist. The trips change from year to year and space is limited; make reservations early.

**ATC Tours and Travel,** Calle 16 de Septiembre 16, 29200 San Cristóbal de las Casas, Chi. (© **967/67-82550** or 967/67-82557; fax 967/67-83145; www.atctours.com.mx), a Mexico-based tour operator with an excellent reputation, offers specialist-led trips, primarily in southern Mexico. In addition to trips to the ruins of Palenque and Yaxchilán (extending into Belize and Guatemala by river, plane, and bus if desired), ATC offers horseback tours to Chamula or Zinacantán, and day trips to the ruins of Toniná around San Cristóbal de las Casas; birding in the rain forests of Chiapas and Guatemala (including in the El Triunfo Reserve of Chiapas); hikes to the shops and homes of native textile artists of the Chiapas highlands; and walks from the Lagos de Montebello in the Montes Azules Biosphere Reserve, with camping and canoeing. The company can also prepare custom itineraries.

**Baja Expeditions,** 2625 Garnet Ave., San Diego, CA 92109 (© **800/843-6967** or 858/581-3311; fax 858/581-6542; www.bajaex.com), offers natural-history cruises, whale-watching, sea kayaking, camping, scuba diving, resort and day trips out of Loreto or La Paz, Baja California, and San Diego, California. Small groups and special itineraries are Baja Expeditions' specialty.

**Bike Mex,** Calle Guerrero 361, 48300 Puerto Vallarta, Jal. (© **322/223-1680** or 322/223-1834; www.bikemex.com), offers day or overnight mountain-biking excursions in the Sierra Madre foothills near Puerto Vallarta. One excellent overnight trip travels to the old mountain mining towns of Mascota, Talpa de Allende, and San Sebastián, with a combination of van transport and biking between towns, and stays in old haciendas.

The **California Native,** 6701 W. 87th Place, Los Angeles, CA 90045 (© **800/926-1140** or 310/642-1140; www.calnative.com), offers small-group deluxe 7-, 8-, 9-, and 11-day escorted tours through the Copper Canyon. Many trips visit the towns of Batopilas, Urique, and Tejeban as well as the customary destinations of Creel, El Fuerte, Divisadero, Chihuahua, and Cerocahui. The guides are known throughout the area for their work with the Tarahumara Indians. In addition to escorted trips, the company offers a full range of custom itineraries.

**Columbus Travel,** 900 Rich Creek Lane, Bulverde, TX 78163-2872 (© **800/843-1060** in the U.S. and Canada, or 830/885-2000; fax 830/885-2010; www.canyontravel.com), specializes in the Copper Canyon and has a variety of adventures, from easy to challenging. It designs trips for special-interest groups of agriculturists, geologists, rock hounds, and bird-watchers, and custom trips to the Copper Canyon. The owner works with the Tarahumara Indians.

**Culinary Adventures,** 6023 Reid Dr. NW, Gig Harbor, WA 98335 (© **253/851-7676;** fax 253/851-9532), specializes in a short but select list of cooking tours in Mexico. They feature well-known cooks and travel to regions known for excellent cuisine. The owner, Marilyn Tausend, is the co-author of *Mexico the Beautiful Cookbook* and *Cocinas de la Familia* (Family Kitchens).

**Far Flung Adventures,** P.O. Box 377, Terlingua, TX 79852 (✆ **800/359-4138** or 915/371-2489; www.farflung.com), organizes specialist-led river trips to the Antigua, Actopan, and Filobobo rivers, in Veracruz.

**Gorgas Science Foundation,** 510 E. St. Charles, Brownsville TX 78520 (✆ **956/504-6862**), offers weeklong trips once or twice a year (usually in June) to the northernmost tropical cloud forest in the Americas, and to the Rancho El Cielo in the remote El Cielo Biosphere Reserve, 80km (50 miles) south of Ciudad Victoria, Tamaulipas, in northern Mexico. The Gorgas Science Foundation of Texas Southmost College sponsors the trips. The area is rich in birds, orchids, and bromeliads and is home to endangered black bear, jaguar, and ocelot.

**Expediciones México Verde,** Homero 526-801, 11510 México, D.F. (✆ **555/255-4400;** www.rafting-mexico.com.mx), under the leadership of Agustín Arroyo, offers a tour covering the original route of Cortez—though unlike Cortez and his henchmen, you're not on horseback or on foot. Highlights include the ruins of Zempoala; the cities of Veracruz (where you learn the local dance, *danzón*), Xalapa and its excellent Museo de Antropología, Puebla, Tlaxcala, and Mexico City; river rafting (if you desire); plus cultural experiences in food, history, and literature. Trips can be customized.

**Mexico Travel Link Ltd.,** 300-3665 Kingsway, Vancouver, BC V5R 5W2 Canada (✆ **604/454-9044;** fax 604/454-9088; www.mexicotravel.net), offers cultural, sports, and adventure tours to Mexico City and surrounding areas, Baja, Veracruz, the Copper Canyon, the Mayan Route, and other destinations.

**Mexico Motorcycle Adventures, Inc.,** 697 18th St., Beaumont, Texas 77706 (✆ **409/838-9983;** fax 409/833-2550; mexicocycles.com), offers off-road motorcycle tours to the Copper Canyon, Baja, and La Cola de Caballo, outside Monterrey.

**Mountain Travel Sobek,** 6420 Fairmount Ave., El Cerrito, CA 94530 (✆ **800/227-2384,** 888/687-6235, or 510/527-8100; www.mtsobek.com), takes groups kayaking in the Sea of Cortez, whale-watching in Baja, and kayaking, hiking, and camping in Veracruz. Sobek is one of the world's leading ecotour outfitters.

**Natural Habitat Adventures,** 2945 Center Green Court, Suite H, Boulder, CO 80301 (✆ **800/543-8917** or 303/449-3711; www.nathab.com), offers naturalist-led natural history and adventure travel. Expeditions focus on monarch butterfly watching in Michoacán and gray whale-watching in Baja.

**Naturequest,** 30872 South Coast Hwy, Suite PMB, Laguna Beach, CA 92651 (✆ **800/369-3033** or 949/499-9561; www.naturequesttours.com), specializes in the natural history, culture, and wildlife of the Copper Canyon and the remote lagoons and waterways off Baja California. A 10-day hiking trip ventures into rugged areas of the canyon; a less strenuous trip goes to Creel and Batopilas, in the same area. Baja trips get close to nature, with special permits for venturing by two-person kayak into sanctuaries for whales and birds.

**North Star** (✆ **800/258-8434** or 520/773-9917; fax 520/773-9965; www.adventuretrip.com), guides 6-day sea-kayaking trips in the Sea of Cortez, with boat support, from October to May. Several routes are available. No prior kayaking experience is necessary, but you have to be in good physical condition. Custom trips for groups of 10 or more can be arranged.

**Oaxaca Reservations/Zapotec Tours,** 4955 North Claremont Ave., Suite B, Chicago, IL 60625

(© **800/44-OAXACA** outside Illinois, or 773/506-2444; fax 773/506-2445; www.oaxacainfo.com), offers a variety of tours to Oaxaca City and the Oaxaca coast (including Puerto Escondido and Huatulco). Its specialty trips include Day of the Dead in Oaxaca and the Food of the Gods Tour of Oaxaca. The coastal trips emphasize nature, while the Oaxaca City tours focus on the immediate area, with visits to weavers, potters, markets, and archaeological sites. This is also the U.S. contact for several hotels in Oaxaca City, which offer a 10% discount for reserving online.

**One World Workforce,** P.O. Box 3188, La Mesa, CA 91944 (© **800/451-9564**), arranges 1-week "hands-on conservation" trips that offer working volunteers a chance to help with sea-turtle conservation at Bahía de Los Angeles, in Baja (spring, summer, and fall), and along the Majahuas beach 96km (60 miles) south of Puerto Vallarta (summer and fall).

**Tour Baja,** P.O. Box 827, Calistoga, CA 94515 (© **800/398-6200** or 707/942-4550; fax 707/942-8017; www.tourbaja.com), offers sea-kayaking tours in the Loreto area. For over 20 years, owner Trudi Angell has been guiding these trips. She and her guides offer first-hand knowledge of the area. Kayaking, mountain biking, and pack trips, and sailing charters combine these elements with outdoor adventures.

**Sea Trek Sea Kayaking Center,** P.O. Box 561, Woodacre, CA 94973 (© **415/488-1000;** fax 415/488-1707; www.SeaTrekKayak.com). Alternating sea-kayaking trips between Alaska and Baja for 19 years has given Sea Trek an intimate knowledge of the peninsula's coastline. Eight-day trips depart from and return to Loreto, and a 12-day expedition travels from Loreto to La Paz. An optional day excursion to Bahía Magdalena for gray whale-watching is available. Full boat support is provided, and no previous paddling experience is necessary.

**Trek America,** P.O. Box 189, Rockaway, NJ 07866 (© **800/221-0596** or 973/983-1144; fax 973/983-8551; www.trekamerica. com), organizes lengthy, active trips that combine trekking, hiking, van transportation, and camping in the Yucatán, Chiapas, Oaxaca, the Copper Canyon, and Mexico's Pacific coast, and a trip that covers Mexico City, Teotihuacán, Taxco, Guadalajara, Puerto Vallarta, and Acapulco.

**Veraventuras,** Santos Degollado 81-8, 91000 Xalapa, Ver. (© **228/818-9579,** or 01-800/712-6572 in Mexico; fax 228/818-9680; www.veraventuras.com.mx), uses specially trained leaders on well-organized and -outfitted adventures into the state of Veracruz, including rafting the rapids of the Antigua, Actopán, Barranca, and Filobobos rivers.

## 11 Planning Your Trip Online

With a mouse, a modem, and a certain do-it-yourself determination, Internet users can tap into the same travel-planning databases that were once accessible only to travel agents. Sites such as **Frommers.com, Travelocity.com, Expedia.com,** and **Orbitz.com** allow consumers to comparison shop for airfares, book flights, find last-minute bargains, and reserve hotel rooms and rental cars.

But don't fire your travel agent just yet. Although online booking sites offer tips and hard data to help you bargain shop, they cannot offer the hard-earned experience that makes a seasoned, reliable travel agent an invaluable resource. And for consumers with complex itineraries, a trusty travel agent is still the best way to arrange the most direct flights to and from the best airports.

The benefits of researching your trip online can be well worth the effort:

- **Last-minute specials,** known as "E-savers," such as weekend deals or Internet-only fares, are offered by airlines to fill empty seats. Most of these are announced on Tuesday or Wednesday and must be purchased online. Sign up for weekly e-mail alerts at airline websites (see below) or check megasites that compile comprehensive lists, such as Smarter Living (http://smarterliving.com) or WebFlyer (www.webflyer.com).
- The best of the travel-planning sites are now **highly personalized;** they track your frequent-flier miles, and store your seating and meal preferences, tentative itineraries, and credit-card information.
- All major airlines offer **incentives**—bonus frequent-flier miles, Internet-only discounts, sometimes even free cell-phone rentals—when you purchase online or buy an E-ticket.

## TRAVEL-PLANNING & BOOKING SITES

The best travel-planning and booking sites cast a wide net, offering domestic and international flights, hotel and rental-car bookings, plus news, destination information, and deals on cruises and vacation packages. Free (one-time) registration is often required for booking. Because several airlines no longer pay commissions on tickets sold by online travel agencies, be aware that these online agencies will either impose a $10 surcharge if you book a ticket on that carrier—or neglect to offer those air carriers' offerings.

The sites in this section are not a comprehensive list, but a discriminating selection to get you started. Recognition is given to sites based on their content value and ease of use and is not paid for—unlike some website rankings, which are based on payment. This is a press-time snapshot of leading websites—some undoubtedly will have evolved or moved by the time you read this.

- **Travelocity** (www.travelocity.com or www.frommers.travelocity.com) and **Expedia** (www.expedia.com) are the most popular sites, each offering an excellent range of options.
- **Orbitz** (www.orbitz.com) is a popular site launched by United, Delta, Northwest, American, and

### *Tips* Frommers.com: The Complete Travel Resource

For an excellent travel-planning resource, we highly recommend **Frommers.com** (www.frommers.com). You'll find the travel tips, reviews, monthly vacation giveaways, and online-booking capabilities thoroughly indispensable. Among the special features are our popular **Message Boards,** where Frommer's readers post queries and share advice (sometimes even our authors show up to answer questions); **Frommers.com Newsletter,** for the latest travel bargains and inside travel secrets; and Frommer's **Destinations Section,** where you'll get expert travel tips, hotel and dining recommendations, and advice on the sights to see for more than 2,500 destinations around the globe. When your research is done, the **Online Reservation System** (www.frommers.com/booktravelnow) takes you to Frommer's favorite sites for booking your vacation at affordable prices.

Continental airlines. At press time, travel-agency associations were waging an antitrust battle against this site.

- **Qixo** (www.qixo.com) is another powerful search engine. It allows you to search for flights and hotel rooms on 20 other travel-planning sites (such as Travelocity) at once, and sorts results by price.
- **Priceline** (www.priceline.com) lets you "name your price" for airline tickets, hotel rooms, and rental cars. For tickets, you have to accept any flight between 6am and 10pm on the dates you've selected, and you may have to make one or more stops. Tickets are nonrefundable, and no frequent-flyer miles are awarded.

### ONLINE TRAVELER'S TOOLBOX

- **Foreign Languages for Travelers** (www.travlang.com). Learn basic terms in more than 70 languages and click on any underlined phrase to hear what it sounds like. *Note:* Free audio software and speakers are required.
- **Intellicast** (www.intellicast.com). Weather forecasts for all 50 states and cities around the world. *Note:* temperatures are in Celsius for many international destinations.
- **Cybercafes.com** (www.cybercafes.com). Locate Internet cafes at hundreds of locations around the globe.
- **Universal Currency Converter** (www.xe.net/currency). See what your dollar or pound is worth in more than 100 other countries.
- **U.S. State Department Travel Warnings** (http://travel.state.gov/travel_warnings.html). Reports on places where health concerns or unrest might threaten U.S. travelers. It also lists the locations of U.S. embassies around the world.

## 12 Getting Around

*An important note:* If your travel schedule depends on a vital connection—say, a plane trip or a ferry or bus connection—use the telephone numbers in this book or other resources to find out if the connection you are depending on is still available. Although we've done our best to provide accurate information, transportation schedules can and do change.

### BY PLANE

To fly from point to point within Mexico, you'll rely on Mexican airlines. Mexico has two large private national carriers: **Mexicana** (✆ **800/366-5400** toll-free in Mexico), and **Aeromexico** (✆ **800/021-4000** toll-free in Mexico), in addition to several up-and-coming regional carriers. Mexicana and Aeromexico offer extensive connections to the United States as well as within Mexico.

Several new regional carriers are operated by or can be booked through Mexicana or Aeromexico. Regional carriers are Mexicana's **Aerocaribe** and **Aero Mar,** and Aeromexico's **Aerolitoral.** For points inside the state of Oaxaca only—Oaxaca City, Puerto Escondido, and Huatulco—contact **Zapotec Tours** (✆ **800/44-OAXACA,** or 773/506-2444 in Illinois). The regional carriers are expensive, but they go to difficult-to-reach places. In each applicable section of this book, we've mentioned regional carriers with all pertinent telephone numbers.

Because major airlines can book some regional carriers, read your ticket carefully to see if your connecting flight is on one of these smaller carriers—they may use a different airport or a different counter.

**AIRPORT TAXES** Mexico charges an airport tax on all departures. Passengers leaving the country on international flights pay $18—in dollars or the peso equivalent. It has become a common practice to include this departure tax in your ticket price, but double-check to make sure so you're not caught by surprise at the airport. Taxes on each domestic departure within Mexico are around $12.50, unless you're on a connecting flight and have already paid at the start of the flight, in which case you shouldn't be charged again.

Mexico charges an $18 "tourism tax," the proceeds of which go into a tourism promotional fund. Your ticket price may not include it, so be sure to have enough money to pay it at the airport upon departure.

**RECONFIRMING FLIGHTS** Although Mexican airlines say it's not necessary to reconfirm a flight, it's still a good idea. To avoid getting bumped on popular, possibly overbooked flights, check in for an international flight 1½ hours in advance of travel.

## BY CAR

Most Mexican roads are not up to U.S. standards of smoothness, hardness, width of curve, grade of hill, or safety markings. Driving at night is dangerous—the roads are rarely lit; trucks, carts, pedestrians, and bicycles usually have no lights; and you can hit potholes, animals, rocks, dead ends, or uncrossable bridges without warning.

The spirited style of Mexican driving sometimes requires super vision and reflexes. Be prepared for new customs, as when a truck driver flips on his left turn signal when there's not a crossroad for miles. He's probably telling you the road's clear ahead for you to pass. Another custom that's very important to respect is turning left. Never turn left by stopping in the middle of a highway with your left signal on. Instead, pull onto the right shoulder, wait for traffic to clear, then proceed across the road.

**GASOLINE** There's one government-owned brand of gas and one gasoline station name throughout the country—**Pemex** (Petroleras Mexicanas). There are two types of gas in Mexico: *magna,* 87-octane unleaded gas, and premium 93 octane. In Mexico, fuel and oil are sold by the liter, which is slightly more than a quart (40l equals about 10½ gal.). Many franchise Pemex stations have bathroom facilities and convenience stores—a great improvement over the old ones. *Important note:* No credit cards are accepted for gas purchases.

**TOLL ROADS** Mexico charges some of the highest tolls in the world for its network of new toll roads; as a result, they are rarely used. Generally speaking though, using the toll roads will cut your travel time. Older toll-free roads are generally in good condition, but travel times tend to be longer.

**BREAKDOWNS** If your car breaks down on the road, help might already be on the way. Radio-equipped green repair trucks operated by uniformed English-speaking officers patrol major highways during daylight hours to aid motorists in trouble. These **"Green Angels"** perform minor repairs and adjustments free, but you pay for parts and materials.

Your best guide to repair shops is the Yellow Pages. For repairs, look under "Automóviles y Camiones: Talleres de Reparación y Servicio"; auto-parts stores are under "Refacciones y Accesorios para Automoviles." To find a mechanic on the road, look for a sign that says TALLER MECANICO.

Places called *Vulcanizadora* or *Llantera* repair flat tires, and it is common to find them open 24 hours a day on the most traveled highways. Even if the place looks empty, chances are you will find someone who can help you fix a flat.

**MINOR ACCIDENTS** When possible, many Mexicans drive away from minor accidents, or try to make an immediate settlement, to avoid involving the police. If the police arrive while the involved persons are still at the scene, everyone may be locked in jail until blame is assessed. In any case, you have to settle up immediately, which may take days. Foreigners who don't speak fluent Spanish are at a distinct disadvantage when trying to explain their version of the event. Three steps may help the foreigner who doesn't wish to do as the Mexicans do: If you were in your own car, notify your Mexican insurance company, whose job it is to intervene on your behalf. If you were in a rental car, notify the rental company immediately and ask how to contact the nearest adjuster. (You did buy insurance with the rental, right?) Finally, if all else fails, ask to contact the nearest Green Angel, who may be able to explain to officials that you are covered by insurance. See also "Mexican Auto Insurance" in "Getting There," earlier.

**CAR RENTALS** You'll get the best price if you reserve a car at least a week in advance in the United States. U.S. car-rental firms include **Advantage** (✆ 800/777-5500 in the U.S. and Canada), **Avis** (✆ 800/331-1212 in the U.S., 800/TRY-AVIS in Canada), **Budget** (✆ 800/527-0700 in the U.S. and Canada), **Hertz** (✆ 800/654-3131 in the U.S. and Canada), **National** (✆ 800/CAR-RENT in the U.S. and Canada), and **Thrifty** (✆ 800/367-2277 in the U.S. and Canada; www.thrifty.com), which often offers discounts for rentals in Mexico. For European travelers, **Kemwel Holiday Auto** (✆ 800/678-0678) and **Auto Europe** (✆ 800/223-5555) can arrange Mexican rentals, sometimes through other agencies. These and some local firms have offices in Mexico City and most other large Mexican cities. You'll find rental desks at airports, all major hotels, and many travel agencies.

Cars are easy to rent if you are 25 or over, and have a major credit card, valid driver's license, and passport with you. Without a credit card you must leave a cash deposit, usually a big one. One-way rentals are usually simple to arrange but more costly.

Car-rental costs are high in Mexico because cars are more expensive. The condition of rental cars has improved greatly over the years, and clean new cars are the norm. The basic cost of the 1-day rental of a Volkswagen Beetle at press time, with unlimited mileage (but before 15% tax and $15 daily insurance), was $44 in Cancún, $48 in Mexico City, $40 in Puerto Vallarta, $48 in Oaxaca, and $35 in Mérida. Renting by the week gives you a lower daily rate. Avis was offering a basic 7-day rate for a VW Beetle (before tax or insurance) of $220 in Cancún and Puerto Vallarta, $180 in Mérida, and $250 in Mexico City. Prices may be considerably higher if you rent around a major holiday. Also double-check charges for insurance—some companies will increase the insurance rate after several days. Always ask for detailed information about all charges you will be responsible for.

Car-rental companies usually write credit-card charges in U.S. dollars.

**Deductibles** Be careful—these vary greatly in Mexico; some are as high as $2,500, which comes out of your pocket immediately in case of damage. On a VW Beetle, Hertz's deductible is $1,000 and Avis's is $500.

**Insurance** Insurance is offered in two parts: **Collision and damage** insurance covers your car and others if the accident is your fault, and **personal accident** insurance covers you

**Bus Hijackings**

The U.S. State Department notes that bandits target long-distance buses traveling at night, but there have been daylight robberies as well. Buses are more common targets than individual cars—they offer thieves more bucks for the bang.

and anyone in your car. Read the fine print on the back of your rental agreement and note that insurance may be invalid if you have an accident while driving on an unpaved road.

**Damage** Always inspect your car carefully and note every damaged or missing item, no matter how minute, on your rental agreement, or you may be charged.

### BY TAXI

Taxis are the preferred way to get around almost all of Mexico's resort areas, and around Mexico City. Fares for short trips within towns are generally preset by zone, and are quite reasonable compared with U.S. rates. (Los Cabos is one exception. Another is taxi service to the north side of the bay from Puerto Vallarta. Travelers are better off renting a car than paying these exorbitant taxi fares—$80 for a one-way trip to Punta Mita.) For longer trips, or excursions to nearby cities, taxis can generally be hired for around $10 to $15 per hour, or for a negotiated daily rate. One-way trips, say, between Cancún and Playa del Carmen, or Huatulco and Puerto Escondido, can be arranged. A negotiated one-way price is usually much less than the cost of a rental car for a day, and a taxi travels much faster than a bus. For anyone who is uncomfortable driving in Mexico, this is a convenient, comfortable alternative. A bonus is that you have a Spanish-speaking person with you in case you run into trouble. Many taxi drivers speak at least some English. Your hotel can assist you with the arrangements.

### BY BUS

Except for the Baja peninsula, where bus service is not well developed, Mexican buses run frequently, are readily accessible, and can get you to almost anywhere you want to go. They're often the only way to get from large cities to other nearby cities and small villages. Don't hesitate to ask questions if you're confused about anything, but note that little English is spoken in bus stations.

Dozens of Mexican companies operate large, air-conditioned, Greyhound-type buses between most cities. Classes are second (*segunda*), first (*primera*), and deluxe (*ejecutiva*), which goes by a variety of names. Deluxe buses often have fewer seats than regular buses, show video movies, are air-conditioned, and make few stops. Many run express from point to point. They are well worth the few dollars more. In rural areas, buses are often of the school-bus variety, with lots of local color.

Whenever possible, it's best to buy your reserved-seat ticket, often using a computerized system, a day in advance on long-distance routes and especially before holidays. Schedules are fairly dependable, so be at the terminal on time. Current information may be obtained from local bus stations. See appendix B for a list of helpful bus terms in Spanish.

## 13 Recommended Books

**HISTORY & CULTURE** For an overview of pre-Hispanic cultures, pick up a copy of Michael D. Coe's *Mexico: From the Olmecs to the Aztecs* or Nigel Davies's *Ancient Kingdoms of Mexico.* Richard Townsend's *The Aztecs* is a thorough, well-researched examination of the Aztec and the Spanish conquest. *The Hummingbird and the Hawk,* by R. C. Padden, gives a briefer, more vivid account of the Aztec and the Conquest of Mexico. It's out of print, but worth a trip to the library. For the Maya, Michael Coe's *The Maya* is probably the best general account. For a survey of Mexican history through modern times, *The Course of Mexican History* by Michael C. Meyer, et al., is rather lengthy, but well written and organized. *The Wind That Swept Mexico,* by Anita Brenner, is an illustrated account of the Mexican Revolution and a good read. For contemporary culture, start with Octavio Paz's classic, *The Labyrinth of Solitude,* which still generates controversy among Mexicans. For a recent collection of writings by Subcomandante Marcos, leader of the Zapatista movement, try *Our Word is Our Weapon* (Seven Stories Press, 2000). Another source would be *Basta! Land and the Zapatista Rebellion* (LPC, 1999) by George Collier, et. al. Finally, for those already familiar with Mexico and its culture, Guillermo Bonfil's *Mexico Profundo: Reclaiming a Civilization* is a rare bottom-up view of Mexico today.

**ART & ARCHITECTURE** *Mexico: A History in Art* by Bradley Smith is out of print, but you can still find it in used bookstores. It is an oversized book with beautiful photos and great explanatory text. *Art and Time in Mexico: From the Conquest to the Revolution,* by Elizabeth Wilder Weismann, covers Mexican religious, public, and private architecture. *Casa Mexicana,* by Tim Street-Porter, takes readers through the interiors of some of Mexico's finest homes-turned-museums, public buildings, and private homes.

*Folk Treasures of Mexico,* by Marion Oettinger, is the fascinating story behind the 3,000-piece Mexican folk-art collection amassed by Nelson Rockefeller over a 50-year period.

**NATURE** *A Naturalist's Mexico,* by Roland H. Wauer, is a fabulous guide to birding in Mexico. *A Hiker's Guide to Mexico's Natural History,* by Jim Conrad, covers Mexican flora and fauna and tells how to find the easy-to-reach as well as out-of-the-way spots he describes. *Peterson Field Guides: Mexican Birds,* by Roger Tory Peterson and Edward L. Chalif, is an excellent guide.

## *FAST FACTS:* Mexico

*Abbreviations* Dept. (apartments); Apdo. (post office box); Av. (*Avenida;* avenue); c/ (*Calle;* street); Calz. (*Calzada;* boulevard). "C" on faucets stands for *caliente* (hot), "F" for *fría* (cold). PB (*planta baja*) means ground floor; in most buildings the next floor up is the first floor (1).

*Business Hours* In general, businesses in larger cities are open between 9am and 7pm; in smaller towns many close between 2 and 4pm. Most close on Sunday. In resort areas it is common to find more stores open on Sundays, and for shops to stay open late, often until 8pm or even 10pm. Bank hours are Monday to Friday from 9 or 9:30am to anywhere between 3 and 7 pm. Increasingly, banks open on Saturday for at least a half-day.

*Cameras/Film* Film costs about the same as in the United States. Tourists wishing to use a video or still camera at any archaeological site in Mexico or at many museums operated by the Instituto de Antropología e Historia (INAH) must pay $4 per camera at each site visited. (Listings for specific sites and museums note this fee.) Also, use of a tripod at any archaeological site requires a permit from INAH. It's courteous to ask permission before photographing anyone. It is never considered polite to take photos inside a church in Mexico. In some areas, such as around San Cristóbal de las Casas (see chapter 10), there are other restrictions on photographing people and villages.

*Car Rentals* See "Getting Around," earlier in this chapter.

*Climate* See "When to Go," earlier in this chapter.

*Currency* See "Money," earlier in this chapter.

*Customs* See "Entry Requirements & Customs," earlier in this chapter.

*Doctors/Dentists* Every embassy and consulate can recommend local doctors and dentists with good training and modern equipment; some of the doctors and dentists speak English. See the list of embassies and consulates under "Embassies/Consulates," below. Hotels with a large foreign clientele can often recommend English-speaking doctors.

*Documents* See "Entry Requirements & Customs," earlier in this chapter.

*Driving Rules* See "Getting Around," earlier in this chapter.

*Drug Laws* It may sound obvious, but don't use or possess illegal drugs in Mexico. Mexican officials have no tolerance for drug users, and jail is their solution, with very little hope of getting out until the sentence (usually a long one) is completed or heavy fines or bribes are paid. Remember, in Mexico the legal system assumes you are guilty until proven innocent. *Note:* It isn't uncommon to be befriended by a fellow user, only to be turned in by that "friend," who collects a bounty. Bring prescription drugs in their original containers. If possible, pack a copy of the original prescription with the generic name of the drug.

U.S. Customs officials are on the lookout for diet drugs that are sold in Mexico but illegal in the U.S. Possession could land you in a U.S. jail. If you buy antibiotics over the counter (which you can do in Mexico) and still have some left, U.S. Customs probably won't hassle you.

*Drugstores* *Farmacias* (pharmacies) will sell you just about anything, with or without a prescription. Most pharmacies are open Monday to Saturday from 8am to 8pm. The major resort areas generally have one or two 24-hour pharmacies. Pharmacies take turns staying open during off hours, so if you are in a smaller town and need to buy medicine during off hours, ask for the *farmacia de turno.*

*Electricity* The electrical system in Mexico is 110 volts AC (60 cycles), as in the United States and Canada. In reality, however, it may cycle more slowly and overheat your appliances. To compensate, select a medium or low speed on hair dryers. Many older hotels still have electrical outlets for flat two-prong plugs; you'll need an adapter for any plug with an enlarged end on one prong or with three prongs. Many better hotels have three-hole outlets (*trifásicos* in Spanish). Those that don't may have loan adapters, but to be sure, it's always better to carry your own.

*Embassies and Consulates* They provide valuable lists of doctors and lawyers, as well as regulations concerning marriages in Mexico. Contrary to popular belief, your embassy cannot get you out of jail, provide postal or banking services, or fly you home when you run out of money. Consular officers can provide advice on most matters and problems, however. Most countries have an embassy in Mexico City, and many have consular offices or representatives in the provinces.

The Embassy of the **United States** in Mexico City is at Paseo de la Reforma 305, next to the Hotel María Isabel Sheraton at the corner of Río Danubio (© **55/5209-9100**); hours are Monday to Friday from 8:30am to 5:30pm. Visit www.usembassy-mexico.gov for addresses of the U.S. consulates inside Mexico. There are U.S. Consulates General at López Matéos 924-N, Ciudad Juárez (© **656/611-3000**); Progreso 175, Guadalajara (© **33/3825-2700**); Av. Constitución 411 Pte., Monterrey (© **81/8345-2120**); and Tapachula 96, Tijuana (© **664/622-7400**). In addition, there are consular agencies in Acapulco (© **744/469-0556**); Cabo San Lucas (© **624/143-3566**); Cancún (© **998/883-0272**); Cozumel (© **987/872-4574**); Hermosillo (© **662/217-2375**); Ixtapa/Zihuatanejo (© **755/553-2100**); Matamoros (© **868/812-4402**); Mazatlán (© **669/916-5889**); Mérida (© **999/925-5011**); Nogales (© **631/313-4820**); Nuevo Laredo (© **867/714-0512**); Oaxaca (© **951/514-3054**); Puerto Vallarta (© **322/222-0069**); San Luis Potosí (© **444/811-7802**); and San Miguel de Allende (© **415/152-2357**).

The Embassy of **Australia** in Mexico City is at Rubén Darío 55, Col. Polanco (© **55/5531-5225**; fax 55/5531-9552). It's open Monday to Thursday from 8:30am to 2pm and 3 to 5pm, and Friday from 8:30am to 2pm.

The Embassy of **Canada** in Mexico City is at Schiller 529, Col. Polanco (© **55/5724-7900**); it's open Monday through Friday from 9am to 1pm and 2 to 5pm. At other times, the name of a duty officer is posted on the door. Visit **www.canada.org.mx** for addresses of consular agencies in Mexico. There are Canadian consulates in Acapulco (© **744/484-1305**); Cancún (© **998/883-3360**); Guadalajara (© **33/3615-6215**); Mazatlán (© **669/913-7320**); Monterrey (© **81/8344-2753**); Oaxaca (© **951/513-3777**); Puerto Vallarta (© **322/222-5398**); San José del Cabo (© **624/142-4333**); and Tijuana (© **664/684-0461**)

The Embassy of **New Zealand** in Mexico City is at José Luis Lagrange 103, 10th Floor, Col. Los Morales Polanco (© **55/5283-9460;** kiwimexico@compuserve.com.mx). It's open Monday to Thursday from 8:30am to 2pm and 3 to 5:30pm, Friday from 8:30am to 2pm.

The Embassy of the **United Kingdom** in Mexico City is at Río Lerma 71, Col. Cuauhtémoc (© **55/5207-2089;** www.embajadabritanica.com.mx). It's open Monday to Friday from 8:30am to 3:30pm.

The Embassy of **Ireland** in Mexico City is at Cerrada Blvd. Avila Camacho 76, 3rd floor, Col. Lomas de Chapultepec (© **55/5520-5803**). It's open Monday to Friday from 9am to 5pm.

The **South African** Embassy is at Andres Bello 10, 9th floor, Col. Polanco (© **55/5282-9260**). It's open Monday to Friday from 8am to 3:30pm.

*Emergencies* The 24-hour **Tourist Help Line** in Mexico City is © **800/903-9200** or 55/5250-0151. A tourist legal assistance office (Procuraduría del Turista) is in Mexico City (© **55/5625-8153** or 55/5625-8154). Though the phones are frequently busy, they operate 24 hours, and there is always an English-speaking person available.

*Holidays* See "When to Go," earlier in this chapter.

*Information* See "Visitor Information," earlier in this chapter.

*Internet Access* In large cities and resort areas, a growing number of top hotels offer business centers with Internet access. You'll also find cyber-cafes in destinations that are popular with ex-pats and business travelers. Even in remote spots, Internet access is common. Note that many ISPs automatically cut off your Internet connection after a specified period of time (say, 10 min.), because telephone lines are at a premium. Some Telmex offices also have free Internet kiosks in their reception areas.

*Language* Spanish is the official language in Mexico. English is spoken and understood to some degree in most tourist areas. Furthermore, you will find that Mexicans are very accommodating with foreigners who try to speak Spanish, even in broken sentences. For basic vocabulary, refer to appendix B.

*Legal Aid* International Legal Defense Counsel, 111 S. 15th St., 24th Floor, Packard Building, Philadelphia, PA 19102 (✆ **215/977-9982**), is a law firm specializing in legal difficulties of Americans abroad. See also "Embassies/Consulates" and "Emergencies," above.

*Liquor Laws* The legal drinking age in Mexico is 18; however, asking for ID or denying purchase is extremely rare. Grocery stores sell everything from beer and wine to national and imported liquors. You can buy liquor 24 hours a day, but during major elections, dry laws often are enacted for as much as 72 hours in advance of the election—and they apply to tourists as well as local residents. Mexico does not have laws that apply to transporting liquor in cars, but authorities are beginning to target drunk drivers more aggressively. It's a good idea to drive defensively.

It is not legal to drink in the street; however, many tourists do so. Use your judgment—if you are getting drunk, you shouldn't drink in the street, because you are more likely to get stopped by the police. As is the custom in Mexico, it is not so much what you do, but how you do it.

*Mail* Postage for a postcard or letter is 1 peso; it may arrive anywhere from 1 to 6 weeks later. A registered letter costs $1.90. Sending a package can be quite expensive—the Mexican postal service charges $8 per kilo (2.20 lbs.)—and unreliable; it takes 2 to 6 weeks, if it arrives at all. Packages are frequently lost within the Mexican postal system, although the situation has improved in recent years. The recommended way to send a package or important mail is through FedEx, DHL, UPS, or another reputable international mail service.

*Newspapers and Magazines* The English-language newspaper, the *News,* is published in Mexico City and distributed nationally. It carries world news and commentary, plus a calendar of the day's events, including concerts, art shows, and plays. Newspaper kiosks in larger Mexican cities carry a selection of English-language magazines.

*Pets* Taking a pet into Mexico is easy but requires a little planning. Animals coming from the United States and Canada need to be checked for health within 30 days before arrival in Mexico. Most veterinarians in major cities have the appropriate paperwork—an official health certificate, to be presented to Mexican Customs officials, that ensures the pet's vaccinations are up-to-date. When you and your pet return from Mexico, U.S. Customs officials will require the same type of paperwork. If your stay extends beyond the 30-day time frame of your U.S.-issued certificate, you'll need an updated Certificate of Health issued by a veterinarian in Mexico that states the condition of your pet and the status of its vaccinations. To check last-minute changes in requirements, consult the Mexican Government Tourist Office nearest you (see "Visitor Information," earlier in this chapter).

*Police* In Mexico City, police are to be suspected as frequently as they are to be trusted; however, you'll find many who are quite honest and helpful. In the rest of the country, especially in the tourist areas, most are very protective of international visitors. Several cities, including Puerto Vallarta, Mazatlán, Cancún, and Acapulco, have a special corps of English-speaking Tourist Police to assist with directions, guidance, and more.

*Safety* See "Insurance, Health & Safety," earlier in this chapter.

*Smoking* Smoking is permitted and generally accepted in most public places, including restaurants, bars, and hotel lobbies. Nonsmoking areas and hotel rooms for nonsmokers are becoming more common in higher-end establishments, but they tend to be the exception rather than the rule.

*Taxes* There's a 15% IVA (value-added) tax on goods and services in most of Mexico, and it's supposed to be included in the posted price. This tax is 10% in Cancún, Cozumel, and Los Cabos. There is a 5% tax on food and drinks when they are consumed in restaurants that sell alcoholic beverages with an alcohol content of more than 10%, and this tax applies whether you drink alcohol or not. Tequila is subject to a new 25% luxury tax. Mexico imposes an exit tax of around $18 on every foreigner leaving the country (see "Airport Taxes" under "Getting Around: By Plane," earlier).

*Telephone/Fax* Mexico's telephone system is slowly but surely catching up with modern times. All telephone numbers have 10 digits. Every city and town that has telephone access has a 2-digit (Mexico City, Monterrey, and Guadalajara) or 3-digit (everywhere else) area code. In Mexico City, Monterrey, and Guadalajara, local numbers have 8 digits; elsewhere, local numbers have 7 digits. To place a local call, you do not need to dial the area code. Many fax numbers are also regular telephone numbers; ask whoever answers for the fax tone (*"me da tono de fax, por favor"*). Cellular phones are very popular for small businesses in resort areas and smaller communities. To call a cellular number inside the same area code, dial 044 and then the number. To dial the cellular phone from anywhere else in Mexico, first dial 01, and then the 3-digit area code and the 7-digit number. To dial it from the U.S., dial 011-52, plus the 3-digit area code and the 7-digit number.

The **country code** for Mexico is **52.**

**To call Mexico:** If you're calling Mexico from the United States:

1. Dial the international access code: 011
2. Dial the country code: 52
3. Dial the 2- or 3-digit area code, then the 8- or 7-digit number. For example, if you wanted to call the U.S. consulate in Acapulco, the

whole number would be 011-52-744-469-0556. If you wanted to dial the U.S. embassy in Mexico City, the whole number would be 011-52-55-5209-9100.

**To make international calls:** To make international calls from Mexico, first dial 00, then the country code (U.S. or Canada 1, U.K. 44, Ireland 353, Australia 61, New Zealand 64). Next, dial the area code and number. For example, to call the British Embassy in Washington, you would dial 00-1-202-588-7800.

**For directory assistance:** Dial ✆ **040** if you're looking for a number inside Mexico. *Note:* Listings usually appear under the owner's name, not the name of the business, and your chances to find an English-speaking operator are slim to none.

**For operator assistance:** If you need operator assistance in making a call, dial 090 to make an international call, and 020 to call a number in Mexico.

**Toll-free numbers:** Numbers beginning with 800 within Mexico are toll-free, but calling a U.S. toll-free number from Mexico costs the same as an overseas call. To call an 800 number in the U.S., dial 001-880 and the last 7 digits of the toll-free number. To call an 888 number in the U.S., dial 001-881 and the last 7 digits of the toll-free number.

*Time Zone* Central Standard Time prevails throughout most of Mexico. The states of Sonora, Sinaloa, and parts of Nayarit are on Mountain Standard Time. The state of Baja California Norte is on Pacific Time, but Baja California Sur is on Mountain Time. Most of Mexico observes **daylight saving time.**

*Tipping* Most service employees in Mexico count on tips for the majority of their income—this is especially true for bellboys and waiters. Bellboys should receive the equivalent of 50¢ to $1US per bag; waiters generally receive 10% to 20%, depending on the level of service. It is not customary to tip taxi drivers, unless they are hired by the hour or provide touring or other special services.

*Toilets* Public toilets are not common in Mexico, but an increasing number are available, especially at fast-food restaurants and Pemex gas stations. These facilities and restaurant and club restrooms commonly have attendants, who expect a small tip (about 25¢).

*Useful Phone Numbers* **Tourist Help Line,** available 24 hours (✆ **800/903-9200** toll-free inside Mexico). **Mexico Hotline** (✆ **800/44-MEXICO**). **U.S. Dept. of State Travel Advisory,** staffed 24 hours (✆ **202/647-5225**). **U.S. Passport Agency** (✆ **202/647-0518**). **U.S. Centers for Disease Control International Traveler's Hotline** (✆ **404/332-4559**).

*Water* Most hotels have decanters or bottles of purified water in the rooms, and the better hotels have either purified water from regular taps or special taps marked *agua purificada.* Some hotels charge for in-room bottled water. Virtually any hotel, restaurant, or bar will bring you purified water if you specifically request it but will usually charge you for it. Drugstores and grocery stores sell bottled purified water. Some popular brands are Santa María, Ciel, and Bonafont. Evian and other imported brands are also widely available.

3

# Mexico City

For me, Mexico City is the only place where you can find insight into this captivating country—veiled in mysticism, infused with an appreciation of the moment, and proud of its heritage. Founded over 675 years ago as the ancient city of Tenochtitlán and capital of the Aztec Empire, today it is has some 22 million inhabitants.

You only need to stand in the center of the Plaza of Three Cultures to visually comprehend the undisputed significance of this city. Here, the remains of an Aztec pyramid, a colonial church, and a towering modern office building face one another, a testament to the city's prominence in ancient and contemporary history. Located at the heart of the Americas, Mexico City has been a center of life and commerce for over 2,000 years. Teotihuacans, Toltecs, Aztecs, and European conquistadors all contributed to the city's fascinating evolution, art, and heritage. Although residents refer to their city as simply México (*Meh*-hee-koh), its multitude of ancient ruins, colonial masterpieces, and modern architecture has prompted others to call it "The City of Palaces."

The central downtown area resembles a European city, dominated by ornate buildings and broad boulevards, and interspersed with public art, parks, and gardens. This sprawling city is thoroughly modern and, in places, unsightly and chaotic, but it never strays far from its historical roots. In the center are the partially excavated ruins of the main Aztec temple; pyramids rise just beyond the city. The geography of Mexico City is as impressive as its history. Surrounded by towering mountains, the city sits on an enormous dry lakebed in a highland valley, at an elevation of 2,242m (7,400 ft.).

The sheer number of residents trying to exist here, combined with economic malaise, high unemployment, and government corruption, has created an environment where petty crime (principally robberies) is common. A few years ago, Mexico City's notoriety came from its rising crime rate, a trend that—thankfully—is in reverse. Over the past several years, the city has achieved admirable progress in making visitors feel more secure, with special safety programs, faster response to reports of crime, programs that are effectively combating corruption, and a vastly increased police presence.

Violent crime in Mexico is largely concentrated among drug traffickers and politicians, but kidnappings and murders of businesspeople, both Mexican and foreign, are numerous. Mexico City has many treasures to enjoy, but safety concerns demand that you dress and behave modestly as you explore the city.

Technically, Mexico City is a "Federal District" (similar to Washington, D.C.), called the *Distrito Federal,* or D.F. One finds here a microcosm of all that is happening in the rest of the country—it's not only the seat of government, but in every way the dominant center of Mexican life.

All-important government and private business flows through the capital; in the streets, coffeehouses, and executive suites of Mexico City, the nation's political and economic directions are set.

You've undoubtedly heard about Mexico City's pollution. Major steps to improve the air quality (restricted driving, factory closings, emission-controlled buses and taxis) have worked wonders, but the problem persists. On some days you won't notice it; on other days it will make your nose run, your eyes water, and your throat rasp. If you have respiratory problems, be very careful; the city's elevation makes matters even worse. Minimize your exposure to the fumes by refraining from walking busy streets during rush hour. Sunday, when many factories are closed and many cars escape the city, should be your prime outdoor day. One positive note: In the evenings the air is usually deliciously cool and relatively clean. (See also "Pollution," under "Fast Facts: Mexico City.")

Mexico City is a feast of urban energy, culture, dining, and shopping. The city has sidewalk cafes and cantinas; bazaars and boutiques; pyramids, monuments, and museums; and a multitude of entertainment options. And when you've had your fill of the city, memorable towns and historic national landmarks are only a couple of hours away in any direction.

## 1 Orientation

The thought of tackling the world's most enormous city is enough to daunt even the most experienced traveler, but fortunately Mexico City is quite well organized. Almost all the important sites are in several key areas that are easily walkable and easy to reach.

### ARRIVING & DEPARTING

**BY PLANE** For information on carriers serving Mexico City from the United States, see chapter 2.

Mexico City's **Benito Juárez International Airport** is something of a small city, where you can grab a bite, have an espresso, or buy clothes, books, gifts, and insurance, as well as exchange money or stay in a hotel room.

Near Gate A is a guarded **baggage-storage area** (another is near Gate F). The key-locked metal lockers measure about 2 feet by 2 feet by 18 inches and cost $3 daily. Larger items are stored in a warehouse, which costs $3.50 to $8.50 for each 24 hours, depending on the size. You may leave your items for up to a month.

The Mexico City Hotel and Motel Association offers a **hotel-reservation service** for its member hotels. Look for its booths before you leave the baggage-claim area, or near Gate A on the concourse. Representatives will make the call according to your specifications for location and price. If they book the hotel, they require 1 night's advance payment and will give you a voucher, which you must present at the hotel. Ask about hotels with special deals. **Telephones** (Ladatel) are all along the public concourse; for instructions on how to use them, see chapter 2 and appendix B.

When you're getting ready to leave Mexico City and need local information on flights, times, and prices, contact the airlines directly. Although airline numbers change frequently, the following may be useful: **Aerocalifornia** (**© 55/5207-1392**), serving Culiacán, Durango, Hermosillo, Matamoros, Mérida, Puebla, Puerto Vallarta, Torreón, Veracruz Villa Hermosa, Guadalajara, Monterrey, Tijuana, Chihuahua, Ciudad Juarez, La Paz, Los Cabos, Loreto,

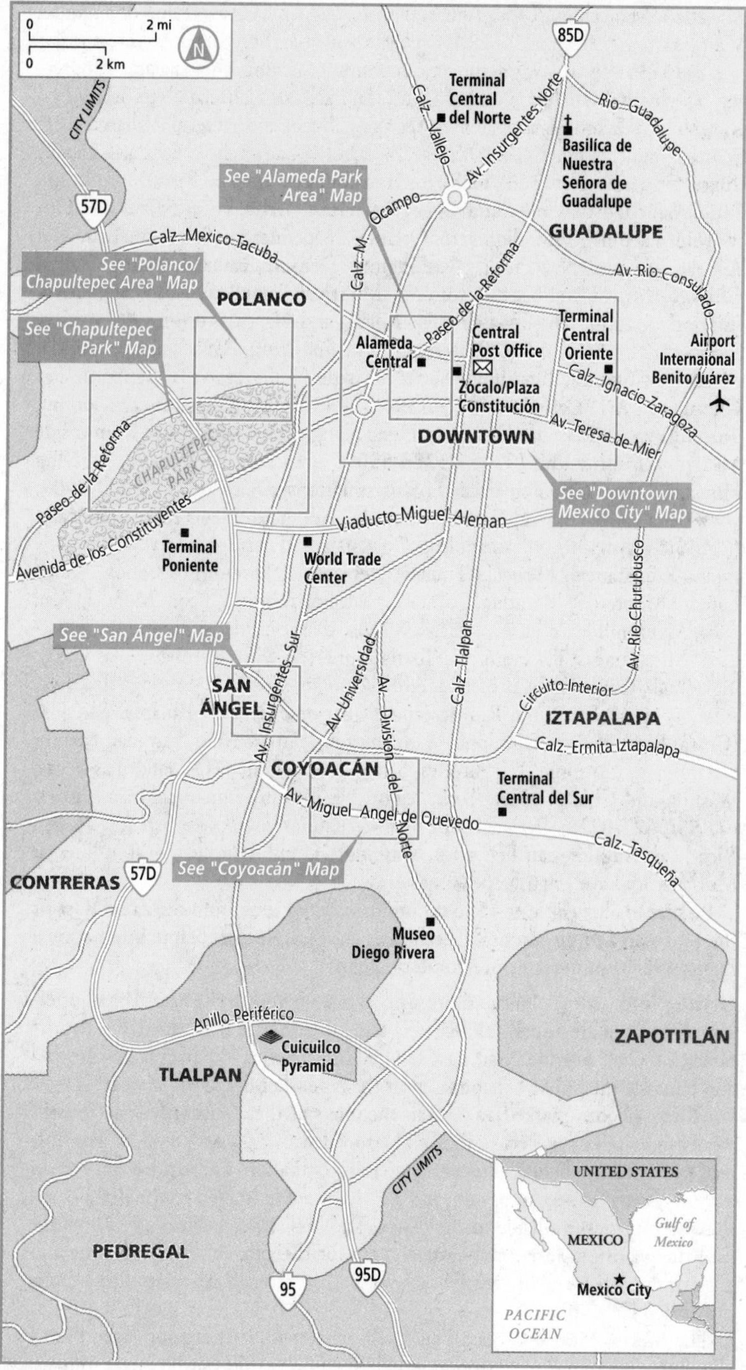
0 2 mi
0 2 km
N
CITY LIMITS
85D
57D
Terminal Central del Norte
Calz. Vallejo
Av. Insurgentes Norte
Rio Guadalupe
Basilíca de Nuestra Señora de Guadalupe
See "Alameda Park Area" Map
Ocampo
GUADALUPE
Calz. Mexico-Tacuba
Calz. M.
Paseo de la Reforma
Av. Rio Consulado
See "Polanco/ Chapultepec Area" Map
POLANCO
See "Chapultepec Park" Map
Alameda Central
Central Post Office
Zócalo/Plaza Constitución
Terminal Central Oriente
Calz. Ignacio Zaragoza
Airport Internaional Benito Juárez
Av. Teresa de Mier
DOWNTOWN
CHAPULTEPEC PARK
Paseo de la Reforma
See "Downtown Mexico City" Map
Avenida de los Constituyentes
Viaducto Miguel Aleman
Terminal Poniente
World Trade Center
Av. Rio Churubusco
See "San Ángel" Map
Av. Universidad
Av. División del Norte
Calz. Tlalpan
Circuito Interior
SAN ÁNGEL
Av. Insurgentes Sur
IZTAPALAPA
Calz. Ermita Iztapalapa
COYOACÁN
Terminal Central del Sur
Av. Miguel Angel de Quevedo
Calz. Tasqueña
CONTRERAS
57D
See "Coyoacán" Map
Museo Diego Rivera
Anillo Periférico
Cuicuilco Pyramid
TLALPAN
ZAPOTITLÁN
CITY LIMITS
UNITED STATES
Gulf of Mexico
MEXICO
PEDREGAL
Mexico City
95
95D
PACIFIC OCEAN

Mazatlán, Manzanillo, León, Aguascalientes, San Luis Potosí, Tampico, Ciudad Victoria, Tepic, Colima, Los Mochis, Tucson, and Los Angeles. **Aeromexico** (✆ **55/5133-4000;** www.aeromexico.com.mx), serving Guadalajara, Monterrey, Tijuana, Chihuahua, Ciudad Juarez, La Paz, Los Cabos, Loreto, Mazatlán, Manzanillo, Leon, Aguascalientes, Ixtapa-Zihuatanejo, Puerto Vallarta, Veracruz, Acapulco, Huatulco, Oaxaca, Tapachula, Campeche, Mérida, Cancún, Tuxtla Gutierrez, New York, Chicago, Houston, Los Angeles, Paris, Madrid, São Paulo, Santiago de Chile, and Lima. **American Airlines** (✆ **55/5209-1400;** www.im.aa.com), with flights to Orlando, Sacramento, San Francisco, Los Angeles, Seattle, New York, Washington, Denver, Salt Lake City, Dallas, Chicago, Miami, Vancouver, Toronto, Montreal, Sao Paulo, Rio de Janeiro, London, Madrid, Paris, Manchester, Milan, and Narita, from inside Mexico. **Aviacsa** (✆ **55/5716-9005**), serving Cancún, León, Guadalajara, Mérida, Monterrey, Oaxaca, Tapachula, Tijuana, Tuxtla Gutierrez, Villa Hermosa, and Chetumal. **Air Canada** (✆ **55/5208-1883;** www.aircanada.ca), serving Toronto, Vancouver, London, Paris, Hong Kong, Taipei, and Tokyo from inside Mexico. **Continental** (✆ **55/5283-5500;** www.continental.com), serving Houston, New York, and other U.S. destinations. **Delta** (✆ **55/5279-0909;** www.delta.com), serving Atlanta, Los Angeles, and New York. **Mexicana** (✆ **55/5448-0990**), to Acapulco, Guadalajara, Puerto Vallarta, Monterrey, Ixtapa-Zihuatanejo, Mexicali, Tijuana, Hermosillo, Loreto, Los Cabos, Nuevo Laredo, Monterrey, Mazatlan, Zacatecas, Saltillo, Tampico, Leon, Morelia, Poza Rica, Manzanillo, Colima, Veracruz, Xalapa, Oaxaca, Puerto Escondido, Huatulco, Minatitlan, Villa Hermosa, Tuxtla Gutierrez, San Cristóbal de las Casas, Tapachula, Ciudad del Carmen, Mérida, Cancun, Cozumel, Santiago de Chile, Buenos Aires, Sao Paulo, Rio de Janeiro, Bogotá, Caracas, Panama, San Jose (Costa Rica), Santo Domingo, San Salvador, Guatemala, Havana, Miami, Orlando, San Antonio, Los Angeles, San Jose (California), Oakland, Las Vegas, Washington, Chicago, New York, Montreal, Toronto, and Frankfurt. **United** (✆ **55/5627-0222;** www.ual.com or www.ualmexico.mx), to San Jose (Costa Rica), Los Angeles, San Francisco, Washington, and Chicago. Most airlines in Mexico City have English-speaking personnel.

Be sure to allow at least 45 to 60 minutes' travel time from the Zona Rosa or the *zócalo* area to the airport. Check in at least 90 minutes before international flights and 60 minutes before domestic flights.

**Getting into Town** Ignore those who approach you in the arrivals hall offering taxis; they are usually unlicensed and unauthorized. **Authorized airport taxis,** however, provide good, fast service. After exiting the baggage-claim area and entering the public concourse, near the far end of the terminal near Gate A, you'll see a booth marked TAXI. Staff members at these authorized taxi booths wear bright-yellow jackets or bibs emblazoned with TAXI AUTORIZADO (authorized taxi). Tell the ticket-seller your hotel or destination, as the price is based on a zone system. Expect to pay around $17 for a *boleto* (ticket) to the Zona Rosa. Present your ticket outside to the driver. Taxi "assistants" who lift your luggage into the waiting taxi naturally expect a tip for their trouble. Putting your luggage in the taxi is the driver's job. (See also "Important Taxi Safety Precautions in Mexico City," below.)

The **Metro,** Mexico City's modern subway system, is cheap and faster than a taxi, but it seems to be growing in popularity among thieves who target tourists. If you try it, be forewarned: As a new arrival, you'll stand out. If you are carrying a suitcase, or anything much larger than a briefcase, don't even bother going to the station—they won't let you on with it. For Metro information, see "Getting Around," later in this chapter.

Here's how to find the Metro at the airport: As you come from your plane into the arrivals hall, turn left toward Gate A and walk all the way through the long terminal, out the doors, and along a covered sidewalk. Soon, you'll see the distinctive Metro logo that identifies the Terminal Aérea station, down a flight of stairs. The station is on Metro Line 5. Follow the signs for trains to Pantitlán. At Pantitlán, change for Line 1 ("Observatorio"), which takes you to stations that are just a few blocks south of the *zócalo* and La Alameda park: Pino Suárez, Isabel la Católica, Salto del Agua, and Balderas.

**BY CAR** Driving in Mexico City is as much a challenge and an adventure as driving in any major metropolis. Here are a few tips. First, check whether your license-plate number permits you to drive in the city that day (break the rule, and the fine can be as much as $1,600). Traffic runs the course of the usual rush hours—to avoid getting tangled in traffic, plan to travel before dawn. Park the car in a guarded lot whenever possible.

Here are the chief thoroughfares for getting out of the city: Insurgentes Sur becomes Highway 95 to Taxco and Cuernavaca. Insurgentes Norte leads to Teotihuacán and Pachuca. Highway 57, the Periférico (loop around the city), is also known as Bulevard Manuel Avila Camacho, to denote street addresses; it goes north and leads out of the city to Tula and Querétaro. Constituyentes leads west out of the city past Chapultepec Park and connects with Highway 15 to Toluca, Morelia, and Pátzcuaro. (Reforma also connects with Highway 15.) Zaragoza leads east to Highway 150 to Puebla and Veracruz.

**BY BUS** Mexico City has a bus terminal for each of the four points of the compass: north, east, south, and west. You can't necessarily tell which terminal serves which area of the country by looking at a map, however.

Some buses leave directly from the **Mexico City airport.** Departures are from a booth located outside **Gate D** (Sala D), and buses also park there. Tickets to Cuernavaca and Puebla each run about $7, with departures every 45 minutes. Other destinations include Querétaro, Pátzcuaro, and Toluca.

If you're in doubt about which station serves your destination, ask any taxi driver—they know the stations and the routes they serve. All stations have restaurants, money-exchange booths or banks, post offices, luggage storage, and long-distance telephone booths where you can also send a fax.

*Taxis from bus stations:* Each station has a taxi system based on fixed-price tickets to various zones within the city, operated from a booth or kiosk in or near the entry foyer of the terminal. Locate your destination on a zone map or tell the seller where you want to go, and buy a *boleto* (ticket). See also the "Important Taxi Safety Precautions in Mexico City" box, below.

For bus riders' terms and translations, see appendix B.

**Terminal Central de Autobuses del Norte** Called "Terminal Norte," "Central Norte" (© **55/5133-2444**) is Mexico's largest bus station, on Avenida de los 100 ("Cien") Metros. It handles most buses coming from the U.S.–Mexico border. It also handles service to and from the Pacific Coast as far south as Puerto Vallarta and Manzanillo; the Gulf Coast as far south as Tampico and Veracruz; and such cities as Guadalajara, San Luis Potosí, Durango, Zacatecas, Morelia, and Colima. You can also get to the pyramids of San Juan Teotihuacán and Tula from here. By calling the above number, you can purchase tickets over the

### Tips: Important Taxi Safety Precautions in Mexico City

There has been a marked increase in violent crime against both residents and tourists using taxis for transportation in Mexico City, concentrated among users of Volkswagen "bug" taxis. Robberies of taxi passengers have become increasingly violent, with beatings and even murders not uncommon. Victims have included U.S. citizens. These occurrences have become so common and so severe that, as of the time of this update, the U.S. State Department had issued a standing **travelers' advisory** concerning taxi travel in Mexico City.

If you plan to use a **taxi from the airport or bus stations,** use only an authorized airport cab with all the familiar markings: yellow car, white taxi light on the roof, and TRANSPORTACION TERRESTRE painted on the doors. Buy your ticket from the clearly marked taxi booth inside the terminal—nowhere else. After purchasing your ticket, go outside to the line of taxis, where an official taxi chief will direct you to the next taxi in line. Don't follow anyone else.

In Mexico City, *do not hail a passing taxi on the street.* Most hotels have official taxi drivers who are recognized and regulated by the terminal and city; they are considered safe taxis to use. These are known as authorized or *sitio* taxis. Hotels and restaurants can call the radio-dispatched taxis. **Official Radio Taxis (© 55/5271-9146,** 55/5271-9058, or 55/5273-6125) are also considered safe. You can hire one of these taxis from your hotel; the driver will frequently act as your personal driver and escort you through your travels in the city. This is a particularly advisable option at night.

phone, charging them to a credit card. The operators can also provide exact information about prices and schedules, but few speak English.

**To get downtown** from the Terminal Norte, you have a choice: The **Metro** has a station (Terminal de Autobuses del Norte, or **TAN**) right here, so it's easy to hop a train and connect to all points. Walk to the center of the terminal, go out the front door and down the steps, and go to the Metro station. This is Línea 5. Follow the signs that say DIRECCION PANTITLAN. For downtown, you can change trains at La Raza or Consulado (see the Mexico City Metro map on the inside back cover). Be aware that if you change at La Raza, you'll have to walk for 10 to 15 minutes and will encounter stairs. The walk is through a marble-lined underground corridor, but it's a long way with heavy luggage. If you have heavy luggage, you most likely won't be allowed into the Metro in the first place.

Another way to get downtown is by **trolleybus.** The stop is on Avenida de los Cien Metros, in front of the terminal. The trolleybus runs down Avenida Lázaro Cárdenas, the "Eje Central" (Central Artery). Or try the "Central Camionera del Norte–Villa Olímpica" buses, which go down Avenida Insurgentes, past the university. Just like the Metro, the trolley will not let you board if you are carrying anything larger than a small carry-on suitcase. Backpacks seem to be an exception, but not large ones with frames.

**Terminal de Autobuses de Pasajeros de Oriente (© 55/5762-5210)** The terminal is known as **TAPO.** Buses going east (Puebla, Amecameca, the Yucatán

All official taxis, except the expensive "Turismo" cars, are painted predominantly yellow, orange, or green, have white plastic roof signs bearing the word *Taxi,* have TAXI or SITIO painted on the doors, and are equipped with meters. Look for all these indications, not just one or two of them. Even then, be cautious. The safest cars to use are sedan taxis (luxury cars without markings) dispatched from four- and five-star hotels. They are the most expensive, but worth it—taxi crime in Mexico City is very real.

**Do not use VW Beetle taxis,** which are frequently involved in robberies of tourists. Even though they are the least expensive taxis, you could be taking your life into your hands should you opt to use one. In any case, never get in a taxi that does not display a large 5-by-7-inch laminated **license card** with a picture of the driver on it; it's usually hanging from the door chain or glove box, or stuck behind the sun visor. *If there is no license, or if the photo doesn't match the driver, don't get in.* It's illegal for a taxi to operate without the license in view. No matter what vehicle you use for transportation, lock the doors as soon as you get in. Do not carry credit cards, your passport, or large sums of cash, or wear expensive jewelry when taking taxis.

The U.S. State Department advisory also specifies that taxis parked in front of the **Bellas Artes Theater** and in front of nightclubs, restaurants, or cruising tourist areas should be avoided.

Peninsula, Veracruz, Xalapa, San Cristóbal de las Casas, and others) arrive and depart from here. Oaxaca buses, which pass through Puebla, arrive and depart from here as well.

To get to TAPO, take a HIPODROMO–PANTITLAN bus east along Alvarado, Hidalgo, or Donceles; if you take the Metro, go to the San Lázaro station on the eastern portion of Line 1 (DIRECCION PANTITLAN).

**Terminal Central de Autobuses del Sur** (© **55/5689-4987** or 55/5689-9745) Mexico City's southern bus terminal is at Avenida Taxqueña 1320, right next to the Taxqueña Metro stop, the last stop on Line 2. The Central del Sur handles buses to and from Cuernavaca, Taxco, Acapulco, Zihuatanejo, and intermediate points. The easiest way to get to or from the Central del Sur is on the Metro. To get downtown from the Taxqueña Metro station, look for signs that say DIRECCION CUATRO CAMINOS. Or take a trolleybus on Avenida Lázaro Cárdenas.

**Terminal Poniente de Autobuses** (© **55/5271-0038**) The western bus terminal is conveniently located right next to the Observatorio Metro station, at Sur 122 and Tacubaya.

This is the smallest terminal; it mainly serves the route between Mexico City and Toluca. It also handles buses to and from Ixtapan de la Sal, Valle de Bravo, Morelia, Uruapan, Querétaro, Colima, Ixtapa-Zihuatanejo, Acapulco, and Guadalajara. In general, if the Terminal Norte also serves your destination, you'd be better off going there. It has more buses and better bus lines.

## VISITOR INFORMATION

The Federal District Department provides several information services for visitors. **Infotur** offices offer information in English and Spanish, including maps, a wide selection of brochures, and access to information from the Mexico Secretary of Tourism website. The most convenient office is in the Zona Rosa at Amberes 54, at the corner of Londres (✆ **55/5525-9380**). Others are at the TAPO bus terminal and at the airport. They're open daily from 9am to 7pm.

**SECTUR,** Mexico's Secretary of Tourism, has developed a website to address safety concerns about travel to this city and other areas in Mexico. The website, www.safemexico.com, offers perhaps not-so-objective assessments of destinations, as well as travel safety tips. **The Mexico City Secretary of Tourism** has also launched a website, www.mexicocity.gob.mx, which includes details on safety precautions and a variety of other topics.

The **Mexico City Chamber of Commerce** (✆ **55/5592-2665**) maintains an information office with a very friendly, helpful staff that can sell you detailed maps of the city or country and answer questions. It's conveniently located at Reforma 42—look for the Cámara Nacional de Comercio de la Ciudad de México. It's open Monday through Thursday from 9am to 2pm and 3 to 6pm; Friday from 9am to 2pm and 3 to 5:30pm.

## CITY LAYOUT

**FINDING AN ADDRESS** Despite its size, Mexico City is not hard to get a feel for. The city is divided into 350 *colonias,* or neighborhoods. Taxi drivers are notoriously ignorant of the city, including the major tourist sights and popular restaurants. Before getting into a taxi, always give a street address, *colonia,* and cross streets as a reference, and show the driver your destination on a map that you carry with you. Some of the most important colonias are *Colonia Centro* (historic city center); Zona Rosa (*Colonia Juárez*); Polanco (*Colonia Polanco*), a fashionable neighborhood immediately north of Chapultepec Park; *colonias Condesa* and *Roma,* south of the Zona Rosa, where there are many restaurants in quiet neighborhoods; and all the Lomas—including Lomas de Chapultepec and Lomas Tecamachalco—which are exclusive neighborhoods west of Chapultepec Park. In addresses, the word is abbreviated *Col.,* although the full *colonia* name is vital in addressing correspondence.

**STREET MAPS** Should you want more detailed maps of Mexico City than the ones included in this guide, you can get them easily. The **Infotur** office (see "Visitor Information," above) generally has several free maps available. Bookstores carry several local map-guides, with greater detail. The best-detailed map is the *Guia Roji,* available at bookstores in Mexico City. It features all the streets in Mexico City and is updated annually.

## MEXICO CITY NEIGHBORHOODS IN BRIEF

**Centro Histórico** Centro Histórico refers to the heart of Mexico City, its business, banking, and historic center, including the areas in and around La Alameda and the *zócalo.* The Spaniards built their new capital city on top of the destroyed capital of the conquered Aztec, and today, it is home to over 1,500 buildings. This is where you'll find the historic landmarks, the most important public buildings, the partially unearthed Aztec ruins of the Great Temple, and numerous museums. There are restaurants, shops, and hotels in this area as well. In the past few years, the nightlife has really picked up, with some exquisite bars and clubs in historic buildings.

A $300 million face-lift is being completed this year (2003), in honor of the city's 675th anniversary. In addition to a beautification program for the *zócalo*—including the addition of a grassy knoll—other elements of the program include the restoration and conversion of more than 80 18th- and 19th-century buildings. The city has committed an additional 400 police officers to regularly patrol the district.

**Chapultepec Park and Polanco** A large residential area west of the city center and Zona Rosa, it centers on Chapultepec Park. The largest green area in Mexico City, it was dedicated as a park in the 15th century by the Aztec ruler Netzahualcoyotl. Together with the neighboring *colonia* of Polanco (north of the park), this is currently Mexico City's most exclusive address. With its zoo, many notable museums, antiques shops, stylish shopping and dining, and upscale hotels, it's an ideal place for discovering contemporary Mexican culture. **Presidente Masaryk** is the main artery.

**Coyoacán** Eight kilometers (5 miles) from the city center, east of San Angel and north of the Ciudad Universitaria, Coyoacán (Koh-yoh-ah-*kahn*) is an attractive, colonial-era suburb noted for its beautiful town square, cobblestone streets, fine old mansions, and several of the city's most interesting museums. This was the home of Frida Kahlo and Diego Rivera, and of Leon Trotsky after his exile from Stalin's USSR. It's a wonderful place to spend the day, but overnight accommodations are limited. Attractions in Coyoacán are listed in the section "Southern Neighborhoods," later in this chapter.

From downtown, the Metro Line 3 can take you to the Coyoacán or Viveros station, within walking distance of Coyoacán's museums. IZTACALA–COYOACAN buses run from the center to this suburb. If you're coming from San Angel, the quickest and easiest way is to take a cab for the 15-minute ride to the Plaza Hidalgo. Sosa, a pretty street, is the main artery into Coyoacán from San Angel. Or you can catch the "Alcantarilla–Col. Agrarista" bus heading east along the Camino al Desierto de los Leones or Avenida Altavista, near the San Angel Inn. Get off when the bus gets to the corner of Avenida Mexico and Xicoténcatl in Coyoacán.

**San Angel** Eight kilometers (5 miles) south of the city center, San Angel (Sahn *Ahn*-hail) was once a village but has been absorbed by the city. It's a beautiful neighborhood of cobblestone streets and colonial-era homes, with several worthwhile museums. This is where the renowned Bazar del Sábado (Sat Bazaar) is held. It's full of artistic and antique treasures, with excellent restaurants as well—a good place to spend a day. Other attractions in San Angel include a wonderful baroque fountain made of broken pieces of porcelain at the Centro Cultural Isidro Fabela, better known as the Casa del Risco (Plaza San Jacinto 15), and the ethereal Iglesia San Jacinto, a 16th-century church with an exquisite baroque altar, bordering the Plaza San Jacinto.

The nearest Metro station is M.A. Quevedo (Line 3). From downtown, take a *colectivo* (marked SAN ANGEL) or bus (marked INDIOS VERDES–TLALPAN or CENTRAL

NORTE–VILLA OLIMPICA) south along Insurgentes near the Zona Rosa. Ask to get off at La Paz. To the east is a pretty park, the Plaza del Carmen, and to the west is a Sanborn's, on the eastern side of Insurgentes.

**Xochimilco** Twenty-four kilometers (15 miles) south of the town center, Xochimilco (So-chee-*meel*-co) is noted for its famed canals and Floating Gardens, which have existed here since the time of the Aztec. Although the best-known attractions are the more than 80km (50 miles) of canals (see "Parks & Gardens," later, for details), Xochimilco itself is a colonial-era gem: It seems small, with its bricked streets, but they can become heavy with traffic—it has a sizable population of 300,000. Restaurants are at the edge of the canal and shopping area, and historically significant churches are within easy walking distance of the main square. In the town of Xochimilco, you'll find a busy market, specializing in rugs, ethnic clothing, and brightly decorated pottery.

Xochimilco hosts an amazing 422 festivals annually, the most famous of which celebrate the **Niñopa,** a figure of the Christ Child is believed to possess miraculous powers. The figure is venerated on January 6 (Three Kings Day), February 2 (annual changing of the Niñopa's custodian), April 30 (Day of the Child), and December 16 through 24 (*posadas* for the Niñopa). Caring for the Niñopa is a coveted privilege, and the schedule of approved caretakers is filled through 2031. March 28 through April 4 (it varies slightly) is the *Feria de la Flor Más Bella del Ejido,* a flower fair when the most beautiful girl with Indian features and costume is selected. For more information and exact dates, contact the **Xochimilco Tourist Office** (Subdirección de Turismo), Pino 36 (© **55/5676-8879;** fax 55/5676-0810), 2 blocks from the main square. It's open Monday through Saturday from 10am to 8pm. Attractions in Xochimilco are listed in the section "Southern Neighborhoods," later.

To reach Xochimilco, take the Metro to Taxqueña, then the *tren ligero* (light train), which stops at the main plaza of Xochimilco. From there, take a taxi to the main plaza of the town of Xochimilco. Buses run all the way across the city from north to south to end up at Xochimilco, but they take longer than the Metro. Of the buses coming from the center, the most convenient is LA VILLA–XOCHIMILCO, which you catch going south on Correo Mayor and Pino Suárez near the *zócalo,* or near Chapultepec on Avenida Vasconcelos, Avenida Nuevo León, and Avenida Division del Norte.

**Zona Rosa** West of the Centro, the "Pink Zone" was once the city's most exclusive residential neighborhood. It has given way to the countless tourists who visit, with a dazzling array of luxury hotels, designer boutiques, fine dining, and nightlife. Many of the streets are pedestrian-only, making it an inviting place for shopping or taking in the sights over a cappuccino or aperitif at one of the numerous cafes. It's the most popular place to stay, despite the fact that it has fewer real historic or cultural attractions than other parts of the city.

## 2 Getting Around

Mexico City has a highly developed and remarkably cheap public transportation system. It is a shame that the sharp increase in crime and resulting safety concerns have made these less comfortable options for travelers. The Metro, first- and second-class buses, minibuses (*colectivos*), and yellow or green VW taxis will take you anywhere you want to go for very little money—but the recent visitor warnings about the use of public transportation should be respected. Because even *sitio* taxis (official taxis registered to a specific locale or hotel) are relatively inexpensive, and are the safest way to travel today within the city, they are what I use when traveling solo in this city.

**BY TAXI** Taxis operate under several distinct sets of rules, established in early 1991. *Please read the cautionary box "Important Taxi Safety Precautions in Mexico City," earlier, before using any taxi.*

**Metered Taxis** Yellow or green VW Beetle and *sitio* (radio-dispatched) cabs provide low-cost service. Although you may encounter a gouging driver, or one who advances the meter or drives farther than necessary to run up the tab, most service is quick and adequate. These taxis operate strictly by the meter: If the driver says his meter isn't working, find another taxi. But then, you will be heeding the warnings, and won't be using one . . . now, will you?

**"Turismo" Taxis** These are by far *the safest way to travel* within Mexico City. The unmarked cabs, usually well-kept luxury cars assigned to specific hotels, have special license plates, and bags covering their meters. Although more expensive than the VW taxis, "turismo" taxis, along with radio-dispatched taxis, are the safest ones to use. The drivers negotiate rates with individual passengers for sightseeing, but rates to and from the airport are established. Ask the bell captain what the airport fare should be, and establish it before taking off. These drivers are often licensed English-speaking guides and can provide exceptional service. In general, expect to pay around $15 per hour for guided service, and about 15% more than metered rates for normal transportation. Often, these drivers will wait for you while you shop or dine to take you back to the hotel, or they can be called to come back and pick you up.

**BY METRO** The subway system in Mexico City offers a smooth ride for one of the lowest fares anywhere in the world (1.50 pesos, or 15¢ per ride). Ten lines crisscross the sprawling city. Each train usually has nine cars.

As you enter the station, buy a *boleto* (ticket) at the glass *taquilla* (ticket booth). Insert your ticket into the slot at the turnstile and pass through; inside, you'll see two large signs showing the line's destination (for example, for Line 1, it's OBSERVATORIO and PANTITLAN). Follow the signs in the direction you want and *know where you're going,* since there is usually only one map of the routes, at the entrance to the station. You'll see two signs everywhere: **SALIDA,** which means "exit," and **ANDENES,** which means "platforms." Once inside the train, you'll see above each door a map of the station stops for that line with symbols and names.

**CORRESPONDENCIAS** indicates transfer points. The ride is smooth, fast, and efficient (although hot and crowded during rush hours). The stations are clean and beautifully designed and have the added attraction of displaying archaeological ruins unearthed during construction. There is also a subterranean passage that goes between the Pino Suárez and Zócalo stations so you can avoid the crowds and the rain along Pino Suárez. The Zócalo station features dioramas and large photographs of the different periods in the history of the Valley of México. At Pino Suárez you'll find the foundation of a pyramid from the Aztec Empire.

# Downtown Mexico City

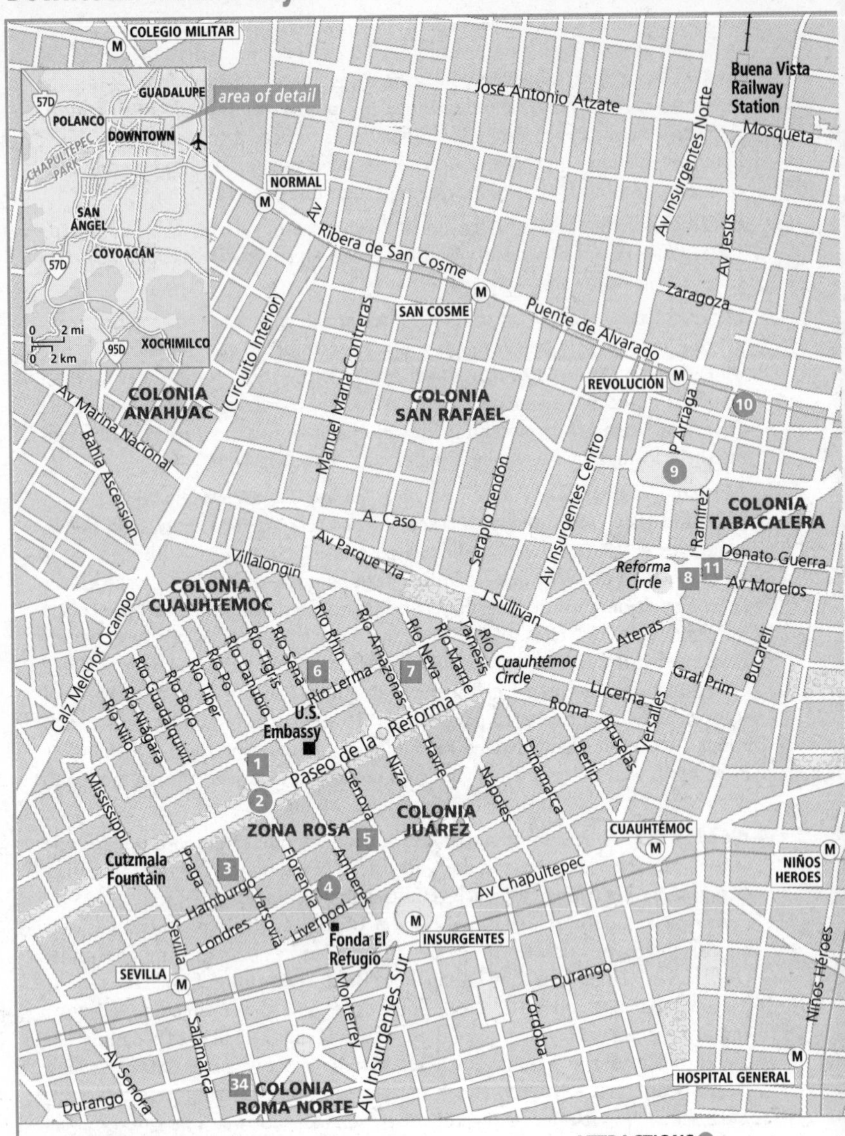


**ACCOMMODATIONS ■**

Best Western Hotel de Cortés **13**
Best Western Hotel Majestic **28**
Casa González **6**
Hotel Calinda Quality Geneve & Spa **5**
Hotel Gillow **24**
Hotel Imperial **11**
Hotel María Isabel Sheraton **1**
Hotel Sevilla Palace **8**
La Casona Hotel-Relais **34**
María Cristina **7**
Galería Plaza **3**

**ATTRACTIONS ●**

Casa de Azulejos **18**
Catedral Metropolitana **25**
FONART **14**
La Alameda **15**
Lagunilla Market **21**
La Torre Latinoamericana **17**
Mercado Insurgentes **4**

- Merced Market **31**
- Monumento a las Héroes de la Independencia **2**
- Museo de la Ciudad **30**
- Museo Nacional de Arte **19**
- Museo Nacional de San Carlos **10**
- Palacio de Bellas Artes **16**
- Palacio Nacional/ Diego Rivera murals **27**
- Plaza and Cemetery of San Fernando **12**
- Plaza de la República/ Monumento a la Revolución **9**
- Plaza de Garibaldi **20**
- Plaza de Santo Domingo **22**
- Secretaría de Educación Pública **23**
- Suprema Corte de Justicia **29**
- Templo Mayor **26**

### Tips The Subway Skinny

The Metro system runs workdays from 5am to midnight, Saturday from 6am to 1am, and Sunday and holidays from 7am to midnight. Baggage larger than a small carry-on is not allowed on the trains. In practice, this means that bulky suitcases or backpacks will make you persona non grata. On an average day, Mexico City's Metro handles more than five million riders—leaving little room for bags! But in effect, if no one stops you as you enter, you're in.

**Watch your bags and your pockets.** Metro pickpockets prey on the unwary (especially foreigners) and are very crafty—on a crowded train they've been known to empty a fanny pack from the front. Be careful, and carry valuables inside your clothing.

The Metro is crowded during daylight hours on weekdays and consequently pretty hot and muggy in summer. In fact, you may find it virtually unusable downtown between 4 and 7pm on weekdays, because of sardine-can conditions. At some stations, there are even separate lanes roped off for women and children; the press of the crowd is so great that someone might get molested. Buses, *colectivos,* and taxis are all heavily used during these hours. You can sometimes beat the mob scene by choosing one of the fore or aft cars—they seem to be less crowded. Or simply wait a few minutes for the next train.

**BY BUS** Moving millions of people through this sprawling urban mass is a gargantuan task, but the city officials do a pretty good job of it. Bus stops on the major tourist streets usually have a map posted with the full route description.

The large buses that used to run on the major tourist routes (**Reforma** and **Insurgentes**) tended to become overpacked and have been phased out in favor of smaller, more frequent buses. Crowding is now uncommon except perhaps during peak hours. The cost in pesos is the U.S. equivalent of 20¢ to 35¢. Although the driver usually has change, try to have exact fare or at least a few coins when you board.

One of the most important bus routes runs between the *zócalo* and the Auditorio (National Auditorium in Chapultepec Park) or the Observatorio Metro station. The route is Avenida Madero or Cinco (5) de Mayo, Avenida Juárez, and Paseo de la Reforma. Buses marked ZOCALO run this route.

Another important route is **INDIOS VERDES–TLALPAN,** which runs along Avenida Insurgentes, connecting the northern bus terminal (Terminal Norte), Buenavista railroad station, Reforma, the Zona Rosa, and, far to the south, San Angel and University City.

**BY COLECTIVO** Also called *peseros* or *combis,* these are sedans or minibuses, usually green and gray, that run along major arteries. They pick up and discharge passengers along the route, charge established fares, and provide more comfort and speed than the bus. Cards in the windshield display routes; often a Metro station is the destination. One of the most useful routes for tourists runs from the ***zócalo*** along **Avenida Juárez,** along **Reforma** to **Chapultepec,** and back again. Get a *colectivo* with a sign saying ZOCALO, not VILLA. A Villa bus or *pesero* goes to the Basílica de Guadalupe. Some of the minibuses on this route have automatic sliding doors—you don't have to shut them, a motor does.

As the driver approaches a stop, he may put his hand out the window and hold up one or more fingers. This is the number of passengers he's willing to take on (vacant seats are difficult to see if you're outside the car).

**RENTAL CARS** If you're planning on traveling to Puebla (see chapter 11) or a surrounding area, a rental car might come in handy. But using taxis and the Metro eliminates the risk of getting lost in an unsavory area. And due to high rates of auto theft, I don't recommend renting a car. But if you do, the least-expensive rental car is the (old-style) manual-shift Volkswagen Beetle, manufactured in Mexico. The price jump is considerable beyond the VW Beetle, and you pay more for automatic transmission and air-conditioning in any car. Hertz, Budget, National, and Avis, among other agencies, are represented at the airport, and each has several city offices as well. Daily rates and deductibles vary considerably. It's more economical to arrange the rental from your home country than to wait to rent one upon arrival. (See also "Getting Around," in chapter 2.)

## *FAST FACTS:* Mexico City

In "Fast Facts: Mexico," in chapter 2, you'll find the answers to all sorts of questions about daily life in Mexico City, but here are a few essentials:

*American Express* The Mexico City office is at Reforma 234 (✆ **55/5207-7282**), in the Zona Rosa. It's open for banking, the pickup of American Express clients' mail, and travel advice Monday through Friday from 9am to 6pm and Saturday from 9am to 1pm.

*Banks* Banks are usually open Monday through Friday from 9am to 5pm; many now offer Saturday and even Sunday business hours. Bank branches at the airport are open whenever the airport is busy, including weekends. They usually offer ATMs and good rates of exchange. Banks and money-exchange offices line Avenida Reforma. The Historic Center downtown also has banks and money-exchange booths on almost every block, as does the Zona Rosa.

*Bookstores* In Mexico City, **Sanborn's** always has a great selection of books in English, as well as magazines and newspapers.

About the most convenient foreign- and Spanish-language bookstore in Mexico City, with a good selection of guidebooks and texts on Mexico, is **Librería Gandhi,** Av. Juárez N. 4, near Avenida Lázaro Cárdenas (✆ **55/5510-4231;** www.gandhi.com.mx), right across from the Bellas Artes. It's open daily from 10am to 9pm. The **New Option,** Rosas Moreno 152 (✆ **55/5705-3332** or 55/5705-7368), is open Monday through Friday from 9am to 6pm and Saturday from 10am to 4pm. The **Museo Nacional de Antropología,** in Chapultepec Park (✆ **55/5553-1902** or 55/5211-0754), also has a fair selection of books on Mexico, particularly special-interest guides. It's open Tuesday to Sunday from 9am to 6pm. Also in Chapultepec, the bookstore **Otro Lugar de la Mancha,** Esopo 11 Chapultepec (✆ **55/5280-4826**), offers a small but outstanding collection of books, music, and art, plus an upstairs cafe in a historic home. It's open Monday to Friday from 8am to 10pm, Saturday and Sunday from 9am to 10pm.

*Currency Exchange* The alternative to a bank is a currency-exchange booth, or *casa de cambio*. These often offer extended hours, with greater convenience to hotels and shopping areas, and rates similar to bank exchange rates. Usually, their rates are much better than those offered by most hotels. Use caution when exiting both banks and currency exchanges, which are popular targets for muggings.

*Drugstores* The drug departments at Sanborn's stay open late. Check the phone directory for the location nearest you. After hours, check with your hotel staff, which can usually contact a 24-hour drugstore.

*Elevation* Remember, you are now at an elevation of 2,194km (7,240 ft.)—almost a kilometer in the sky. There's a lot less oxygen in the air than you're used to. If you run for a bus and feel dizzy when you sit down, it's the elevation. If you think you're in shape but huff and puff getting up Chapultepec Hill, it's the elevation. If you have trouble sleeping, it may be the elevation. If your food isn't digesting, again, it's the elevation. It takes about 10 days or so to adjust to the scarcity of oxygen. Go easy on food and alcohol the first few days in the city.

*Emergencies* The Mexico City government has an emergency number for visitors—dial ✆ **060** for assistance 24 hours a day. The number is hard to reach, so have a local or Spanish speaker help you. In case of a crime or accident, contact the Procuraduría del Turista (✆ **55/5625-8153,** 55/5625-8154, or 55/5625-8763). A government-operated service, **Locatel** (✆ **55/5658-1111;** www.df.gob.mx/servicios/locatel), is most often associated with finding missing persons anywhere in the country. With a good description of a car and its occupants, they'll search for motorists who have an emergency back home. **SECTUR,** or Secretaría de Turismo (✆ **55/5250-0123,** 55/5250-0493, 55/5250-0027, 55/5250-0151, 55/5250-0292, or 55/5250-0589; www.mexico-travel.com), staffs telephones 24 hours daily to help tourists in difficulty.

*Hospitals* The **American–British Cowdray (ABC) Hospital** is at Calle Sur 132 136, at the corner of Avenida Observatorio, Colonia las Américas (✆ **55/5230-8000**).

*Hot Lines* If you think you've been ripped off on a purchase, call the **consumer protection office,** the Procuraduría Nacional del Consumidor (✆ **55/5568-8722** or 55/5272-9847; www.profeco.gob.mx). SECTUR also sponsors Infotur, a 24-hour tourist-assistance line (✆ **55/5250-0123** or 55/5205-0493).

*Internet Access* Surprisingly enough, it is easier to find cybercafes in some resort areas than in Mexico City. However, most hotels that cater to business travelers offer Internet connections in their business centers. In the Zona Rosa there is the **Java Chat Café Internet,** Genova 44 (✆ **55/5525-6853**). It's open daily from 8am to 11:30pm. The price per hour of access is around $4.

*Pollution* September and October seem to be light months for pollution. Mid- to late November, December, and January are noted for heavy pollution. During January, schools may even close because of it, and restrictions on driving that are usually imposed only on weekdays may apply on weekends; be sure to check before driving into or around the city. (See "Rental Cars," under "Getting Around," earlier in this chapter.) Be careful if you have respiratory problems; being at an altitude of 2,194km (7,240 ft.) will make your problems even worse. Just before your visit, call the Mexican Government Tourist Office nearest you (see "Visitor Information, Entry Requirements & Money," in chapter 2, for the address) and ask for the latest information on pollution in the capital. Minimize your exposure to the fumes by refraining from walking busy streets during rush hour. Make Sunday, when many factories are closed and many cars escape the city, your prime sightseeing day.

*Post Office* The city's main post office, the ***Correo* Mayor**, is a block north of the Palacio de Bellas Artes on Avenida Lázaro Cárdenas, at the corner of Tacuba (✆ **55/5512-0091**). For general postal information, call **Fono-Post ✆ 55/5709-9600.**

If you need to mail a package in Mexico City, take it to the post office called Correos Internacional 2, Calle Dr. Andrade and Río de la Loza (Metro: Balderas or Salto del Agua). It's open Monday through Friday from 8am to noon. Don't wrap your package securely until an inspector examines it. Although postal service is improving, your package may take weeks, or even months, to arrive at its destination. (For a glossary of mail terms, see appendix B.)

Packages may be sent by UPS, FedEx, MexPost, or DHL for a greater assurance of making it to their destinations sooner rather than later.

*Restrooms* There are few public restrooms. Use those in the larger hotels and in cafes, restaurants, and museums. Seasoned travelers frequently carry their own toilet paper and hand soap. Many public restrooms at museums and parks have an attendant who dispenses toilet paper for a "tip" of 5 pesos, in lieu of a usage charge.

*Safety* Read the "Safety," "Crime," and "Bribes & Scams" sections under "Health, Safety & Insurance" in chapter 2, and the "Important Taxi Safety Precautions in Mexico City" box, earlier. In response to rising crime, Mexico City has added hundreds of new foot and mounted police officers, and there's a strong military presence. But they can't be everywhere. Watch out for pickpockets. Crowded subway cars and buses provide the perfect workplace for petty thieves, as do major museums (inside and out), crowded outdoor markets and bullfights, and indoor theaters. The "touch" can range from light-fingered wallet lifting or purse opening to a fairly rough shove by two or three petty thieves. Be extra careful anywhere that attracts a lot of tourists: on the Metro, in Reforma buses, in crowded hotel elevators and lobbies, at the Ballet Folklórico, and at the Museo de Antropología.

Robberies may occur in broad daylight on crowded streets in "good" parts of town, outside major tourist sights, and in front of posh hotels. The best way to avoid being mugged is to not wear any jewelry of value, especially expensive watches. If you find yourself up against a handful of these guys, the best thing to do is relinquish the demanded possession, flee, and then notify the police. (You'll need the police report to file an insurance claim.) If you're in a crowded place, you could try raising a fuss—whether you do it in Spanish or English doesn't matter. A few shouts of *"¡Ladrón!"* ("Thief!") might put them off, but that could also be risky. Overall, it's wise to leave valuables in the hotel safe and to take only the cash you'll need for the day, and no credit cards. Conceal a camera in a shoulder bag draped across your body and hanging in front of you, not on the side.

*Taxes* Posted prices generally include Mexico's 15% sales tax; however, it may be added. If in doubt, ask *"¿Más IVA?"* (Plus tax?) or *"¿Con IVA?"* (With tax?). There are also airport taxes for domestic and international flights, but the price of your ticket usually includes them. (See "Getting Around," in chapter 2.)

*Telephones* Telephone numbers within Mexico City are eight digits; the first digit of the local phone number is always 5. Generally speaking, Mexico City's telephone system is rapidly improving (with new digital lines replacing old ones), offering clear, efficient service. Some of this improvement is resulting in numbers changing. As elsewhere in the country, the telephone company changes numbers without informing the telephone owners or the information operators. Business telephone numbers may be registered in the name of the corporation, which may be different than the name of a hotel or restaurant owned by the corporation. Unless the corporation pays for a separate listing, the operator uses the corporate name to find the number. The local number for **information** is ✆ **040,** and you are allowed to request three numbers with each information call.

Coin-operated phones are prone to vandalism; most have been replaced by **card-only Ladatel phones.** Ladatel cards are usually available at pharmacies and newsstands near public phones. They come in denominations of 20, 50, and 100 pesos. **Long-distance calls** within Mexico and to foreign points can be surprisingly expensive. Consult "Fast Facts: Mexico" in chapter 2 and "Telephones & Mail" in appendix B for how to use phones. Hotels are beginning to charge for local calls, but budget-priced hotels are less likely to do this because they lack the equipment to track calls from individual rooms.

*Weather/Clothing* Mexico City's high altitude means you'll need a warm jacket and sweater in winter. The southern parts of the city, such as the university area and Xochimilco, are much colder than the central part. In summer, it gets warm during the day and cool, but not cold, at night. May to October is the rainy season (this is common all over Mexico)—take a raincoat or rain poncho. The showers may last all day or for only an hour or two.

## 3 Where to Stay

Not only is Mexico City one of the most exciting cities in the world, it can also be one of the most affordable when it comes to accommodations. For $20 to $40, you can find a double room in a fairly central hotel, complete with a bathroom and often such extras as air-conditioning and TV. Many hotels have their own garages where guests can park free.

The best hotel values are concentrated in the downtown **Historic District,** which has recently undergone a dining and nightlife renaissance. Luxury hotels are mostly in the two most popular areas for mainstream tourism: The **Zona Rosa** seems to attract predominantly those in the city for business or shopping,

**Finds** **Free Sunday Concerts**

Every Sunday, concerts organized by Mexico City's Cultural Institute take place at the *zócalo,* generally around 6pm. They feature a changing array of traditional and classical Mexican talent—and can draw crowds of 5,000 or more to the historic central plaza! For more information, call ✆ **55/5535-7704** or 55/5140-0945.

whereas the **Chapultepec/Polanco** neighborhood is ideally located near museums and other cultural attractions.

Hotels in these zones not only offer more deluxe accommodations and amenities, but also generally have their own fleets of taxis (see "Getting Around: By Taxi," earlier) and secured entrances for guests. The crime rate, though on the decline, is still quite high; given this unfortunate reality, visitors should consider staying in the most secure accommodations they can afford.

## CHAPULTEPEC PARK & POLANCO

### VERY EXPENSIVE

**Casa Vieja** ★★ Pure Mexican style and service are the hallmarks of this luxury boutique hotel, a true gem known more to locals than tourists. Once a private residence, Casa Vieja has 10 rooms and suites, all decorated with bold colors, unique handicrafts, exquisite antiques, and original furnishings. Each has a living and kitchen area, ample bedroom, and sizable bath with Jacuzzi tub. Notwithstanding the lovely decor, the real attraction here is the highly personalized, gracious service. A rooftop bar and terrace serves made-to-order breakfasts, included in the price of your stay. The only negative I can note is that in some rooms, you tend to overhear conversations in the halls and common areas, leading you to believe your own privacy may be compromised.

Eugenio Sue 45 (½ block from Av. Masaryk), Col. Polanco, 11560, Mexico D.F. ✆ **55/5282-0067** or 55/5281-4468. Fax 55/5281-3780. www.casavieja.com. 10 suites. $350 jr. suite, $550 master suite, $850 Presidential suite. Rates include American breakfast. AE, MC, V. Limited parking. Metro: Polanco. **Amenities:** Bar and cafe with light meal service; 24-hr. room service; laundry and dry cleaning; concierge. *In room:* A/C, TV, VCR, fax, dataport, minibar, kitchen, hair dryer, safe-deposit box.

**Habita** ★★ If you're into the hot and the hip, and don't mind attitude with your stay, this is your place in Mexico City. Although I feel this hotel takes minimalism to a stark extreme, I still give high points to Habita for changing the Mexico City hotel scene. A boutique hotel of modernist design and minimalist interiors—so much so that they border on a dorm room feel—it has quickly become the hot hotel in the city's most stylish neighborhood. The white and steel room decor is understated, and elegant gray Mexican marble lines the bathrooms from floor to ceiling. The city's current hot club, AREA, occupies a rooftop terrace. Adjacent to the lobby is an appropriately chic but otherwise unimpressive restaurant, AURA, and bar.

Av. Presidente Masaryk 201, Col. Polanco, 11560 México, D.F. ✆ **800/337-4685** in the U.S., or 55/5282-3100. Fax 55/5282-3101. www.hotelhabita.com. 36 units. $224 double; $275 jr. suite. AE, MC, V. Valet parking $3.50. Metro: Polanco. **Amenities:** Restaurant, 2 bars; 24-hr. room service; rooftop heated pool and solarium; small, well-equipped gym; sauna; steam room; Jacuzzi; massage; laundry and dry cleaning; concierge; tour services; business center. *In room:* A/C, TV, dataport, minibar, hair dryer, safe-deposit box.

**Hotel Camino Real** ★★★ Long one of the capital's leading hotels, the Camino Real is also a work of art itself, set amid Mexico's finest museums. A

## Polanco/Chapultepec Area

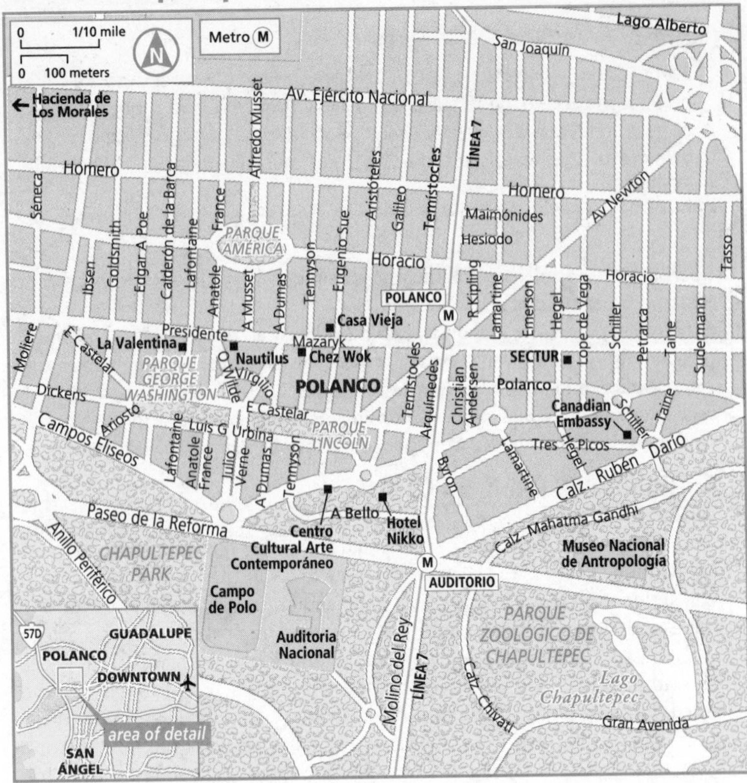


perennial favorite, it is one of the capital's hot spots for business and social entertaining, and frequently sells out. Designed by renowned architect Ricardo Legorreta, the building is a classic example of contemporary Mexican architecture; over 400 works of art by Mexican masters and other celebrated contemporary artists complement the design. A stunning Rufino Tamayo mural, *Man Facing Eternity,* greets visitors as they enter the front doors, a mural by José Luis Covarrubias graces the La Huerta restaurant, and an impressive sculpture by Alexander Calder dominates the foyer. The spacious rooms, all with brightly colored, modern decor and a sitting and desk area, contain armoires that conceal the TV and minibar. Executive Club rooms come with bathrobes; rates here include continental breakfast, evening cocktail hour, and daily newspaper. **Fouquet's de Paris** is the hotel's best restaurant and one of the capital's top dining establishments. The Lobby Bar occasionally features some of Latin America's finest performers. *Note:* In late 2001, Hilton took over the management of Camino Real hotels in Mexico; this property's public areas have been remodeled, and rooms are in the process of being upgraded.

Mariano Escobedo 700, 11590 Colonia Anzúrez México, D.F. ✆ **800/722-2646** in the U.S. and Canada, or 55/5263-8888. Fax 55/5250-6897. www.caminoreal.com/mexico/. 709 units. $270 double; $405 suite; $351 Executive Club. AE, DC, MC, V. Metro: Chapultepec. **Amenities:** 3 restaurants, popular bar with live entertainment; full-service business center; complete gym; massage; sauna; steam room; 4 tennis courts; pool; laundry and dry cleaning; car rental; travel agency; salon; concierge. *In room:* A/C, TV, minibar, dataport, hair dryer, safe-deposit box.

**Tips** **Festival del Centro Histórico**

In March of every year, a series of concerts, cultural events, art exhibits, and public performances take place in—and in honor of—Mexico City's historic downtown district. For more information or a calendar of events, call the **Delegacíon Cuauhtemoc** (✆ **55/5702-1205** or 55/5535-5343).

**Hotel Four Seasons** ★★★ One of the finest hotels in all of Mexico, and my personal favorite, the Four Seasons sets the standard for service with a staff noted for gracious manners. In the style of an elegant Mexican hacienda, the hotel's rooms surround a beautiful interior courtyard—a veritable sanctuary in this busy city. Although you're only steps from the busy Paseo de la Reforma, the grounds of the eight-story hotel seem more like the quiet countryside surrounding a gracious manor house. On one side of the large and inviting outdoor courtyard, there's umbrella-covered alfresco dining with colonnaded walkways all around; other dining rooms and bars face this pleasant scene.

The huge, airy rooms have high ceilings and are resolutely sumptuous. Each has plush bedspreads, beautiful Talavera lamps and bathroom accessories, Indonesian tapestries, and rich dark-wood furnishings, including a working desk. All rooms have twice-daily maid service (with ice refills), complimentary daily newspaper, and bathrooms with separate shower and tub, dual sinks, and illuminated makeup mirrors. Most rooms face the interior courtyard, two deluxe suites have patios facing the courtyard, and most Executive Suites (with one or two separate bedrooms) overlook Reforma. About 100 rooms are reserved for nonsmokers. Expert-led private tours to many of the city's historic sites and museums are a unique offering; weekend guests have the option of one or two tours included in the price of the room—a true value. The Four Seasons is at the western end of the Zona Rosa, near Chapultepec Park and Polanco and opposite the Hotel Marquís Reforma.

Reforma 500, Col. Juárez, 06600 México, D.F. ✆ **800/332-3442** in the U.S., 800/268-6282 in Canada, or 55/5230-1818. Fax 55/5230-1817. www.fourseasons.com. 240 units. $310 double; $400–$480 suite. Special weekend cultural packages generally available. 2 rooms for travelers with disabilities are available. AE, DC, MC, V. Free valet parking. Metro: Sevilla. **Amenities:** 2 restaurants, 2 bars; spa with completely equipped gym; massage; sauna; whirlpool; heated rooftop swimming pool; complete business center; laundry and dry cleaning; 1-hr. pressing service; room service; salon. *In room:* A/C, TV, dataport, minibar, bathrobes, hair dryer, iron, safe-deposit box.

**Hotel Marquís Reforma** ★ *Overrated* With a faux Art Deco exterior and an overdone combination of glass, marble, and dark mahogany within, the Marquís Reforma opened in 1991 and has been billed as one of the city's state-of-the-art luxury hotels. If superfluity is your style, you'll be thrilled here. If you prefer understated elegance, try another choice—you'll feel imposed upon here. It does have an excellent location, however, at the eastern end of Chapultepec Park opposite the Four Seasons at the western end of the Zona Rosa. Rooms vary in shape and size. Some have terraces; some separate living rooms, dining rooms, and bedrooms; some an attached meeting room. Standard double rooms have king-size beds and small sitting areas. The rooms billed as business rooms lack a suitable desk and are smaller than normal for the type and price. A piano player entertains nightly in the lobby **Caviar Bar,** the highlight of the hotel, which serves tea, drinks, and light meals.

Paseo Reforma 465, Col. Cuauhtémoc, 06500 México, D.F. ✆ **800/235-2387** in the U.S., 55/5229-1200. Fax 55/5229-1212. www.marquisreformahl.com.mx. 208 units. $310 double; $395–$575 suite. AE, DC, MC, V. Free parking adjacent to hotel. Metro: Sevilla. **Amenities:** Restaurant, coffee shop, lobby bar; room service; complete business center; fitness center with workout equipment, 3 whirlpools, sauna and steam rooms; massage; laundry; salon; car rental. *In room:* A/C, TV, dataport, minibar, hair dryer, safe-deposit box.

## ZONA ROSA & SURROUNDING AREAS

### VERY EXPENSIVE

**Galería Plaza** ★★★ Located in the heart of the Zona Rosa, the Galería Plaza has earned a reputation as one of the highest-quality hotels in Mexico City. It's immensely popular with business travelers. The large, bright rooms have light-colored wood and wicker furniture. All come with dual-line phones and purified tap water. Marble bathrooms have makeup mirrors and a telephone extension. Universal outlets accommodate a fax or computer, and electrical adapters are available from the concierge. Executive Floor rates include free local calls, parking privileges, continental breakfast, and afternoon cocktails served in the Executive Lounge. Guest Office rooms contain a nearly complete office, including printer/fax/copier, desk, speakerphone with dataport, and special telephone rates that include free local calls and long-distance access, plus in-room faxing without a surcharge. Nonsmoking floors are also available. The staff is professional, efficient, and accommodating.

> **Tips Weekend Deals**
>
> The top hotels often substantially lower rates Friday through Sunday, as most of their clientele is traveling business professionals.

Hamburgo 195, 06600 México, D.F. ✆ **55/5230-1717.** Fax 55/5207-5867. www.brisas.com.mx. 439 units. $238 double. Rooms for travelers with disabilities are available. AE, DC, MC, V. Free covered guarded parking. Metro: Insurgentes. **Amenities:** 3 restaurants, lobby bar; full-service business center; heated rooftop swimming pool; fully equipped fitness center; room service; laundry and dry cleaning; 24-hr. concierge; travel agency; car rental. *In room:* A/C, TV, dataport, minibar, coffeemaker, hair dryer, iron, safe-deposit boxes.

**Hotel María Isabel Sheraton** ★★ The María Isabel Sheraton's location in front of the *Monumento de la Independencia* is ideal: It's next to the U.S. Embassy and across Reforma from the heart of the Zona Rosa. A favorite for business travelers, the hotel offers premium amenities in all its rooms. Tower suites, the most deluxe, occupy the fourth floor and have private check-in, butler service, and continental breakfast and evening canapés. The **Jorongo Bar,** a Mexico City institution, offers live entertainment nightly from 7pm to 1am. (See "Mexico City After Dark," later.)

Paseo de la Reforma 325, at Río Tiber, 06500 México, D.F. ✆ **800/325-3535** in the U.S., or 55/5242-5555. Fax 55/5207-0684. www.sheraton.com. 755 units. $280 standard double; $325 Tower. AE, MC, V. Covered parking $5.50. Metro: Insurgentes (6 blocks away). **Amenities:** 3 restaurants, 2 bars; 24-hr. room service; complete business center; full-service fitness center; 2 tennis courts; open-air pool; privileges at nearby golf course; travel agency; salon; laundry and dry cleaning. *In room:* A/C, TV, dataport, minibar, hair dryer, safe.

### EXPENSIVE

**Hotel Calinda Quality Geneve & Spa** ★ One of the capital's most popular hotels, the Geneve has been receiving guests for more than 90 years. It's known for its comfort, convenience, and top-notch location just steps from the Zona Rosa restaurants and shops. Rooms are modern, with colonial-style furniture. You may want to request one on an upper floor; lobby noise has a way of traveling in this hotel. A third of the rooms have air-conditioning. Although business services are available, the hotel is especially popular with Zona Rosa shoppers and sightseers.

Londres 130 (between Génova and Amberes), 06600 México, D.F. ✆ **800/221-2222** in the U.S., or 55/55080-0800. Fax 55/5207-4160. www.hotelescalinda.com.mx. 320 units. $208 double. AE, DC, MC, V. Limited street parking; free parking next door. Metro: Insurgentes. **Amenities:** 2 restaurants (1 with bar); spa facilities, including fitness center and massage; babysitting; business center; laundry service; travel agency. *In room:* A/C, TV, hair dryer.

**La Casona Hotel-Relais** ★★★ *Finds* Reminiscent of a small European luxury hotel, this exquisite establishment opened in 1996 after restoration of a dilapidated 1923 building. It has since been designated an artistic monument by Mexico's National Institute of Fine Arts. Each luxuriously decorated room is unique; all have antique furniture. Tall interior shutter doors on windows in each room keep out sound and light at night, and thick window glass mutes street noise by day. Oriental-style rugs warm the hardwood floors throughout hallways and rooms. A small wine cellar and bar below the lobby is a popular gathering place for drinks and conversation. The hotel is 3 blocks south of the Diana Circle on Reforma, and 4 longish blocks west of the western edge of the Zona Rosa. Chapultepec Park is about a 20-minute walk to the northwest. More important than decor or location is the excellence of service here—truly capable of giving you a pampered feeling.

Durango 280 (corner of Cozumel), Col. Roma, 06700 México, D.F. ✆ **800/223-5652** in the U.S., or 55/5286-3001. Fax 55/5211-0871. www.lacasona.com.mx. 29 units. $184 double. Rates include American breakfast. AE, DC, MC, V. Gated parking $4 per day. Metro: Sevilla (4 blocks away). **Amenities:** Restaurant, bar; concierge; currency exchange; room service; laundry service; safe-deposit boxes (in lobby); small gym with steam room; solarium. *In room:* A/C, TV, dataport.

## MODERATE

**Hotel Imperial** ★ *Value* This classic hotel, which dates to 1904 and has been designated a historic monument, is one of the most memorable buildings along the Avenida Reforma. It has been the home of one Mexican president, the site of the assassination of a another, and, for years, the U.S. embassy. The Imperial changed hands several times before returning to its original name and status as a five-star hotel in 1989. Popular with foreign—especially European—guests, it's one of the best values in the area. Rooms are extra large, with high ceilings and carpeting, although the traditional-style furnishings are a bit dated. All have either a king or two double beds, plus desks and sitting areas. Bathrooms are very large, with tubs and separate vanities. Each Master Suite, at the tip of one of the five floors of the building, has a unique triangular bedroom overlooking Avenida Reforma, living/dining room, bar, and whirlpool in the bathroom. All rooms are entered from a central atrium with staircase (there's also an elevator).

Paseo de la Reforma 64 (at Morelos), Col. Juarez Cp., 06600 México, D.F. ✆ **55/5705-4911.** Fax 55/5703-3122. www.hotelimperial.com.mx. 65 units. $170 double; $233–$315 suite. AE, DC, MC, V. Free parking. Metro: Revolución or Juárez. **Amenities:** Noted Spanish restaurant and bar Gaudi, with live music nightly; business center; concierge; room service; laundry and dry cleaning. *In room:* A/C, TV, minibar, hair dryer, safe-deposit box.

**Hotel Sevilla Palace** Although the Sevilla Palace is top quality in every way, it's largely overlooked by foreigners. Contemporary in style, with a full array of services, it offers excellent value for the area. Rooms are large and handsomely furnished, and most have large showers and couches with sitting/table areas.

Paseo de la Reforma 105, Col. Revolución Cp., 06030 México, D.F. ✆ **800/732-9488** in the U.S., or 55/5566-8877. Fax 55/5703-1521. www.sevillapalace.com.mx. 414 units. $141 double; $202 suite. AE, MC, V. Free parking. Metro: Hidalgo or Revolución. **Amenities:** Restaurant, coffee shop, lobby bar with evening piano entertainment; business center; workout room with enclosed swimming pool and whirlpool; spa and gym; room service; shopping arcade; laundry service. *In room:* A/C, TV, dataport, minibar, hair dryer, safe-deposit box.

### INEXPENSIVE

**Casa González** Casa González is a two-story hostel made up of two converted mansions. The houses, with little grassy patios out back and a huge shade tree, contain rooms that are charming and homey—and heated for those chilly mornings. Each is unique, and some have a terrace or balcony. Meals (optional) are taken in a dining room brightened by stained glass and international conversation. Casa González is especially good for women traveling alone, although there are only three single rooms. The warm, caring management ensures that each guest feels more like part of a shifting, growing family than just a passing visitor. There's limited parking in the driveway, for an additional charge of $6 per day.

Río Sena 69 (Río Lerma and Río Panuco), 06500 México, D.F. ✆ **55/5514-3302.** Fax 55/5511-0702. 22 units. $38–$40 double; $65 suite for 4. No credit cards. Metro: Insurgentes (4 blocks away). **Amenities:** Dining room.

**María Cristina** ★ This classic choice for budget travelers is conveniently located just a 10-minute walk from the Zona Rosa. Rooms are bright and have one king or two double beds, ample closets, and modern bathrooms. The large lobby with overstuffed couches and a fireplace makes a comfortable meeting place. A grassy courtyard offers lounge chairs for reading or relaxing. The hotel is at Río Neva, on the north side of Reforma.

Río Lerma 31, 06030 México, D.F. ✆ **55/5703-1212** or 55/5566-9688. Fax 55/5566-9194. 150 units. $75 double; $105 suite. AE, DC, MC, V. Free guarded parking. **Amenities:** Coffee shop with bar service; safe-deposit box (in reception area). *In room:* TV.

## CENTRO HISTORICO & SURROUNDING AREAS

### MODERATE

**Best Western Hotel de Cortés** ★★ *Finds* This baroque-style hotel offers comfortable, modern accommodations in a fascinating historic building—a former home for Augustinian friars. The 18th-century stone structure features rooms on two floors surrounding a central colonial courtyard with a graceful fountain and Mexican restaurant. It's on La Alameda park, a short distance from the Palace of Fine Arts and the Franz Mayer Museum. Rooms vary in size and features, but all contain hand-woven bedspreads, carpeting, and a desk The modern bathrooms have three-prong plugs and tile accents. Security boxes are available in the reception area.

Av. Hidalgo 85, 06300 México, D.F. ✆ **800/528-1234** in the U.S., or 55/5518-2184. Fax 55/5521-0234. www.hoteldecortes.com.mx. 29 units. $150 double; $170 suite. AE, DC, MC, V. No parking available. Metro: Hidalgo. **Amenities:** Courtyard restaurant/bar. *In room:* TV, minibar.

**Best Western Hotel Majestic** ★★ This classic hotel's prime location—facing the *zócalo,* the impressive central plaza of Mexico City—is reason enough to stay here. The Majestic is somewhat of a Mexico City institution that visitors should experience at least once. The comfortable lobby has a glass ceiling that is also the floor of a sitting area surrounded by rooms. Rooms that don't look onto the *zócalo* overlook Avenida Madero or the hotel's inner court. The lobby and courtyard are decorated with stone arches, beautiful tiles, and stone fountains.

Furnishings in the rooms are rather dated, but are in the process of being upgraded. Tile bathrooms have tub/shower combos. In lower-floor rooms facing Avenida Madero, noise from the street may be a problem—quieter rooms look out onto the interior courtyard, which has its own aviary. Occupants of rooms facing the *zócalo* will get an unexpected jolt from the early-morning flag-raising ceremony, complete with marching feet, drums, and bugle. The popular rooftop cafe/restaurant with umbrella-shaded tables serves all three meals. You can save quite a few dollars by booking direct with the hotel and by asking for promotional rates or discounts.

Av. Madero 73, Col. Centro Cp., 06000 México, D.F. ✆ **800/528-1234** in the U.S., or 55/5521-8600. Fax 55/5512-6262. www.majestic.com.mx. 85 units. $85–$120 double; $200 suite. AE, MC, V. No parking. Metro: Zócalo. **Amenities:** Restaurant/bar; room service; travel agency; babysitting. *In room:* TV, minibar.

## INEXPENSIVE

**Hotel Catedral** *Value* This modern hotel in a stellar location is also an excellent value. One block north of Calle Tacuba is the tree-shaded Calle Donceles, where you'll find the eight-story (with elevator) Hotel Catedral, half a block from the Templo Mayor and a block from the Museo San Ildefonso. Rooms are modern; all have purified drinking water from a special tap, good over-bed reading lights, and TVs with U.S. cable channels. Some have tub/shower combinations, and some have whirlpool tubs. Rooms on the upper floors afford views of Mexico City's mammoth cathedral. On the seventh floor, a terrace with small tables and chairs offers great views. The Catedral's location is ideal for sightseeing, and the central downtown district is experiencing a revival. Because heavily trafficked streets surround the hotel, add 45 minutes to your departure time if you go to the airport from here. In front of the big, marble-embellished lobby is the bustling restaurant. The cozy bar beyond the reception desk also serves food.

Calle Donceles 95 (between Brasil and Argentina), 06020 México, D.F. ✆ **55/5521-6183.** Fax 55/5512-4344. www.hotelcatedral.com.mx. 116 units. $50 double. AE, MC, V, DISC. Free parking. Metro: Zócalo. **Amenities:** Restaurant, bar; room service. *In room:* TV, hair dryer, safe-deposit box.

**Hotel Gillow** The dignified-looking, seven-story Gillow is a modern hotel with six stories of rooms grouped around a long, glass-canopied, rectangular courtyard with a colonial fountain. Were it in the Zona Rosa, the Gillow could easily cost three times what it does. The well-kept, carpeted rooms have comfortable beds, tub/shower combinations, and excellent lighting. Some units are small, with one double bed and enough room for one person's luggage. Others are quite spacious, with a long carpeted bench for suitcases. Interior-room windows open to an airshaft; exterior rooms have small terraces with wrought-iron furniture. We have received reader complaints about loud music from a neighboring disco on weekend nights; request a room as far away from street noise as possible. The hotel is between Cinco de Mayo and Madero—a hard-to-beat downtown location.

Isabel la Católica 17, 06000 México, D.F. ✆ **55/5518-1440.** Fax 55/5512-2078. hgillow@prodigy.net.mx. 103 units. $42 double. AE, MC, V. No parking available. Metro: Zócalo. **Amenities:** Restaurant and bar; concierge; tour desk; laundry service. *In room:* TV.

## NEAR THE AIRPORT

**Hilton Airport Hotel** ★ This on-site hotel is the newest and nicest of the airport hotels in terms of service and facilities. The staff is attentive and the rooms are nicely furnished, though small. Each has color TV with U.S. channels, a nice-size work desk, and an ergonomic executive chair. It can't be beat for convenience and a guarantee of making an early-morning plane. To get there, exit the terminal near Gate A and walk right, down the corridor to Sala F and the international departure gates. You'll see the signs.

Carlos Capitán s/n (Sala F, 3rd floor), 15520 México, D.F. ✆ **800/228-9290** or 55/5133-0505. Fax 55/5133-0500. www.hilton.com.mx. 129 units. $190 double; $300 jr. suite. AE, DC, MC, V. Covered and uncovered parking $1 per hr. **Amenities:** Restaurant, lobby bar; business center; small health club; 24-hr. room service; 24-hr. concierge; laundry and pressing service. *In room:* A/C, TV with pay movies, dataport, minibar, coffeemaker, hair dryer, iron, safe-deposit box.

## 4 Where to Dine

As in most of the world's major cities, dining in Mexico City is sophisticated, with cuisine that spans the globe. From high chic to the Mexican standard of *comida corrida,* the capital offers something for every taste and budget. The **Polanco area** in particular has become a place of exquisite dining options, with new restaurants rediscovering and modernizing classic Mexican dishes. The **Centro Histórico** has seen a resurgence of ultrahip restaurants and clubs open for late-night dining and nightlife. Cantinas, until not so long ago the privilege of men only, offer some of the best food and colorful local atmosphere.

Everybody eats out in Mexico City, regardless of social class. Consequently, you can find restaurants of every type, size, and price range scattered across the city. Mexicans take their food and dining seriously, so if you see a full house, that's generally recommendation enough. But those same places may be entirely empty if you arrive early—remember, here, lunch is generally eaten at 3pm, with dinner not even considered before 9pm.

Although American-type chains such as McDonald's, Subway, Burger King, Pizza Hut, VIPS, Denny's, and the Hard Rock Cafe have affiliates in Mexico City, I feel no need to list them here. You'll run across them frequently, but with so many unique and wonderful choices at your disposal in every price range, why fall back on the familiar? Venture out, dig in, and enjoy!

### CHAPULTEPEC PARK & POLANCO

#### VERY EXPENSIVE

**Chez Wok** ★ HAUTE CHINESE Opened in the fashionable Polanco area in 1992 with five chefs from Hong Kong and their incredible recipes, Chez Wok immediately became *the* place to feast on Chinese food. It hasn't lost its popularity, especially for power lunches. It's generally packed and, although prices are high, most dishes serve two or three people. The dining area, with large and small sections, has a combination of booths and tables with an elegant but simple yellow, black, and beige decor. Main courses include steamed red snapper with white-wine sauce, chicken in shrimp paste with sesame and crab sauce, and the house specialty, Peking duck.

Tennyson 117, 2nd floor (at Masaryk), Col. Polanco. ✆ **55/5281-3410** or 55/5281-2921. Reservations recommended. Main courses $21–$55. AE, MC, V. Daily 1:30–4:45pm; Mon–Sat 7:30–11:45pm. Valet and free parking available. Metro: Polanco.

**La Galvia y Bar El Canto** ★ MEXICAN HAUTE CUISINE/INTERNATIONAL A top dining address, La Galvia seats its guests in a large window-framed room and treats them to impeccable service and refined food from a short but select menu. The appetizer menus (cold and hot) include black-bean soup with *nopalitos* (baby cactus). Entrees include salmon in soy sauce, and *róbalo* (sea bass) with sesame seeds and three-chile sauce. The menu changes every 3 months. For dessert, try the Helena chocolate torte. You'll find the restaurant in Polanco, immediately behind the Hotel Presidente Inter-Continental. The adjoining Bar El Canto offers live music and Cuban music shows every Saturday night. An upscale business crowd frequents this restaurant, which frowns on casual attire.

Campos Eliseos 247 (at Eugenio Sue), Col. Polanco. ✆ **55/5281-2310.** Reservations recommended. Main courses $30–$46. AE, DC, MC, V. Mon–Fri 1:30–11pm; Sat 2–11pm; Sun 2–5pm. Metro: Auditorio.

## EXPENSIVE

**Fonda Santa Clara** ★★★ TRADITIONAL MEXICAN/PUEBLA One of the city's fine dining establishments, this one presents the best of Puebla's cuisine to a full house daily. The menu lists a full range of daily and seasonal specialties. The large serving of *manchamantel* (literally, "tablecloth stainer") is a sweet, smooth *mole* made by blending chiles, apricots, pears, apples, and bananas, served over pork or chicken—it's fabulous. The *sartenada ranchera* is enough to fill two diners. The feast is a combination plate of superbly seasoned and grilled meats, sausage, and bacon served with onions, salsa, and avocado. Service is refined and attentive. Arrive early, because every seat in its several dining areas will be filled, especially at lunch. If you happen to be visiting between late July and September, you must try *chiles en nogada,* a delicious blend of hot chiles stuffed with meat and fruit and covered in walnut sauce. This is one of the most baroque dishes in Mexican cuisine. Fonda Santa Clara is a more expensive cousin of the Fonda de Santa Clara in Puebla, but the menus are almost identical. Mexico City has two branches: One is in Polanco, and the other is on the south side, in San Jerónimo—take a taxi to both.

Homero 1910 (between the Periférico Norte and Blas Pascal), Col. Polanco. ✆ **55/5557-6144.** Also at Av. San Jerónimo 775, Col. San Jerónimo Lídice. ✆ **55/5683-0730.** Reservations recommended. Main courses $20–$35. AE, DC, MC, V. Mon 7:30am–6pm; Tues–Fri 7:30am–midnight; Sat 8:30am–midnight; Sun 8:30am–6pm.

**La Fonda del Recuerdo** ★★ MEXICAN/SEAFOOD/VERACRUZ For an all-out good time, no other restaurant in the city compares to this one. Diners enjoy their platters of Mexican food amid a glorious din created by *jarocho* musicians from Veracruz (several groups rove around the restaurant at once). Come here if you want to immerse yourself in Mexico and join people eating, drinking, singing, and having the time of their lives. The menu is authentically Mexican, with an emphasis on seafood; specials match the culinary traditions of whichever Mexican holiday is closest. Arrive before 1:30pm for lunch or you'll have to wait in a long line, which nonetheless will be worth it if you have all afternoon. At night, it's just as festive, but try to make it before 9pm, if you care to avoid the crowd. It's near the corner of Bahía de Santa Bárbara—take a taxi.

Bahía de las Palmas 37, Col. Verónica Anzures, Delegación Miguel Hidalgo Cp. 11300. ✆ **55/5260-0545.** www.fondadelrecuerdo.com. Reservations recommended. Main courses $10–$20. AE, DC, MC, V. Mon–Sat 1pm–midnight; Sun 1–8pm.

**La Valentina** ★★ MEXICAN NOUVELLE CUISINE In the midst of posh Polanco, on the second floor of a small boutique-filled shopping center, is this dignified restaurant with an elegantly casual flair. Pale-apricot stucco walls, shiny wood floors, and wood-beamed ceilings set off the cozy nooks of immaculately set tables. The menu features specialties from some of the country's best Mexican cooks. For example, there's Marta Chapa's breaded shrimp with sesame, lettuce, herbs, and chiles; cilantro soup by Suzanna Palazuelos; and Patricia Quintana's fillet in butter and salsa. The bar is worth a visit on its own, with an impressive selection of premium tequilas, a selection of fine art, live trio music, and an upscale cantina-style atmosphere.

Presidente Masaryk 393 (near the corner of Lafontaine), Col. Polanco. ✆ **55/5282-2656** or 55/5282-2514. Reservations recommended. Main courses $20–$25. AE, DC, MC, V. Daily 2pm–2am. Valet parking $2.50. Metro: Polanco.

### MODERATE

**Le Olivier** ★★★ *Finds* COUNTRY FRENCH/BISTRO This bright, bustling bistro would be reminiscent of an authentic French cafe—were it not for the fact that its patrons tend to be business professionals rather than bohemians. Opened in 2000, this place packs in a crowd, and with good reason—the food is superb. Choices range from patés to soufflés (definitely plan ahead and save room for a chocolate soufflé for dessert!). There's an excellent representation of country French fare, including steak frites, cassoulets, and fricassees. The restaurant is 12 blocks from the Polanco station. You could venture in without reservations, but depending on the night, you might not get in without them. There is no bar to wait in.

Masaryk 69-C (at Torcuato Tasso). ✆ **55/5545-3133.** Main courses $15–$25. AE, MC, V. Daily 2pm–1am. Reservations strongly recommended. Valet parking $2.50. Metro: Polanco.

**Nautilus** SEAFOOD/INTERNATIONAL An outdoor restaurant on Polanco's main drag, this is a popular place to relax at an umbrella-shaded sidewalk table, dine, and watch the passing scene. The menu features seafood, pasta, and steak. Filet Moctezuma comes with *huitlacoche* and *flor de calabaza.* Plus, there's a full lineup of special tacos—try the lobster version.

Masaryk 360-4 (between Oscar Wilde and Muset). ✆ **55/5280-2283** or 55/5282-1320. www.nautilus.com.mx. Main courses $15–$25. AE, MC, V. Mon–Sat 8am–11pm; Sun 9am–9pm. Valet parking $1.50. Metro: Polanco or Auditorio.

## ZONA ROSA & SURROUNDING AREAS

### EXPENSIVE

**Cicero-Centenario** ★★★ INTERNATIONAL/NOUVELLE MEXICAN Cicero-Centenario is the epitome of Mexico's elegant cafe society and one of the most noted restaurants in the country. Stylish, eccentric, artistic, and whimsical all at once, this place offers not just excellent food but a complete dining experience *à la mexicana.* Tables in the intimate nooks of the restaurant's smart salons look out on a backdrop of stained glass, antiques, and flickering candlelight. Among the highlights on the menu are starters such as a delectable cream of cilantro soup or crêpes stuffed with squash flower blossoms and Gruyere cheese in a mild poblano chile sauce. Main dishes include recipes developed for the restaurant by noted chef and author Patricia Quintana, such as chicken in a rich almond sauce and her renowned *mole poblano.* There is another branch of the restaurant in the Historic Center of the city (see below).

Londres 195 (between Florencia and Amberes). ✆ **55/5533-3800** or 55/5533-4276. Reservations recommended. Main courses $10–$40. AE, DC, MC, V. Mon–Sat 1pm–1am. Valet parking available. Metro: Insurgentes.

**Restaurant Passy** ★ FRENCH/INTERNATIONAL The Restaurant Passy is an elegant old favorite of locals and tourists alike. The attractive, restrained decor features low lights, antiques, linen, and candles. The service is polished and polite, and the menu is traditional French: Oysters Rockefeller, onion or oyster soup, chicken cordon bleu, canard (duck) à l'orange, and coq au vin are among the Continental favorites. There's also a good selection of fish.

Amberes 10 (between Reforma and Hamburgo). ✆ **55/5208-2087.** Reservations recommended. Main courses $10–$25. AE, MC, V. Mon–Sat 1–11pm. Valet parking available. Metro: Insurgentes.

### MODERATE

**Fonda El Refugio** ★★ MEXICAN The service, food, and atmosphere at Fonda El Refugio have been shaped by more than 40 years of tradition, making it a very special place for authentic Mexican dining. Although small, it's unusually congenial, with a large fireplace decorated with gleaming copper pots and pans. Rows and rows of culinary awards and citations hang behind the desk. The restaurant manages the almost impossible task of being both elegant and informal. The menu runs the gamut of Mexican cuisine, from *arroz con plátanos* (rice with fried bananas) to *enchiladas con mole poblano,* topped with the rich, thick, spicy chocolate sauce of Puebla. There's a daily specialty. Try the chiles stuffed with ground beef or cheese, and for dessert have some coconut candy. Fonda El Refugio is very popular, especially on Saturday night, so get there early.

Liverpool 166 (between Florencia and Amberes), Col. Juarez Zona Rosa. ✆ **55/5207-2732** or 55/5525-8128. Main courses $7–$9. AE, MC, V. Mon–Sat 1pm–midnight; Sun 1–10pm. Valet parking $1. Metro: Insurgentes.

## CENTRO HISTORICO & SURROUNDING AREAS

### EXPENSIVE

**Cicero-Centenario** ★★★ INTERNATIONAL/NUEVA COCINA MEXICANA This Cicero-Centenario shares an ambience of magical realism with its sister restaurant in the Zona Rosa. Tucked in the historic zone in an elegant two-story 18th-century mansion, it is among the most popular eating establishments in the city. At every meal, all the tables have reservation cards. The menu is essentially the same as the other Cicero's—fish, beef, and chicken served with great sauces and seasonings. Each day there's a different special: on Friday, whitefish from Pátzcuaro; on Saturday, *manchamanteles*—both traditional Mexican fare transformed into gourmet delights. From June through September you'll see *chiles en nogada;* during April and May, *gusanos de maguey.* The latter is a seasonal worm dish: Worms that live on the maguey leaves (the tequila plant) are a regional delicacy. They're served fried, accompanied with guacamole and tortillas. The restaurant is 5 blocks northeast of La Alameda, not far from the Santo Domingo Plaza and Church.

República de Cuba 79 (between República de Chile and Palma), Delegación Cuauhtémoc Cp. ✆ **55/5521-7866.** Reservations recommended. Main courses $7–$30. AE, DC, MC, V. Mon–Sat 1pm–1am; Sun 1:30–7pm. Metro: Allende.

### MODERATE

**Café Tacuba** ★★ MEXICAN One of the city's most popular restaurants, Café Tacuba dates to 1912 and boasts a handsome colonial-era atmosphere. Guests are welcomed into one of two long dining rooms, with brass lamps, dark oil paintings, and a large mural of nuns working in a kitchen. The menu is authentic Mexican with traditional dishes, including tamales, enchiladas, chiles rellenos, *mole,* and *pozole.* Thursday through Sunday from 6pm until closing, a wonderful group of medieval-costumed singers entertains; their sound is like the melodious *estudiantina* groups of Guanajuato accompanied by mandolins and guitars. A trio plays on Mondays and Tuesdays from 8 to 10pm.

Tacuba 28 (between República de Chile and Bolívar), Col. Centro. ✆ **55/5512-8482.** Breakfast $4–$10; main courses $9–$13; *comida corrida* $10–$15. AE, MC, V. Daily 8am–11:30pm. Metro: Allende.

**Restaurant Danubio** SEAFOOD/SPANISH/INTERNATIONAL This place has been a Mexico City tradition since 1938, and it remains an excellent choice for lunch. Locals enjoy this restaurant on weekends with their families. The house specialty is *langostinos* (baby crayfish), and the menu offers a range of selections emphasizing seafood. Danubio is noted for its excellent wine cellar. The restaurant is south of La Alameda.

Uruguay 3 (near Lázaro Cárdenas). ✆ **55/5512-0912.** www.danubio.com. Main courses $15–$30. AE, DC, MC, V. Daily 1–10pm. Metro: Bellas Artes or Salto del Agua.

## INEXPENSIVE

**Café Cinco de Mayo** MEXICAN Less than a block west of the cathedral on the south side of the street, this Mexican-style lunchroom is bright with fluorescent lights and loud with conversation. Regulars take their places at the long counter. Waiters scurry here and there bearing enormous glasses of fresh orange juice, cups of hot coffee, baskets of *pan dulce,* sandwiches, pork chops—just about anything you can imagine. If you order *café con leche,* a waiter will approach with a big copper coffeepot, pour an inch of thick, bitter coffee into the bottom of your glass, and then fill it up with hot milk. The restaurant is between the *zócalo* and Palma.

Cinco de Mayo 57. No phone. Breakfast $1.75–$3; main courses $2.50–$6.50; *comida corrida* $2.75–$4. AE, DISC, MC, V. Daily 7am–11pm. Metro: Zócalo.

**Sanborn's Casa de Azulejos** MEXICAN/AMERICAN Known today as Sanborn's House of Tiles (for the tiles covering the outside walls), this gorgeous antique building was once the palace of the counts of the Valley of Orizaba. For many years it has housed a branch of the Sanborn's restaurant and variety-store chain. The food is good but standard fare, found throughout the Sanborn's chain everywhere in Mexico. You go to the House of Tiles for the building, not the food. Dining tables are set in an elaborate covered courtyard complete with carved pillars, tiles, and peacock frescoes. The second floor has lovely secluded dining areas and a handsome bar. It's directly across from the San Francisco church and diagonally across from the Latin American Tower.

Madero 4. ✆ **55/5518-6676.** Main courses $6–$8; dessert and coffee $3–$4. AE, DC, MC, V. Daily 7am–1am. Metro: Bellas Artes.

## CANTINAS

**Cantina La Guadalupana** ★★ *Finds* MEXICAN Opened in 1928, this cantina is in Coyoacán, the southern neighborhood that was once the home of the artists Diego Rivera and Frida Kahlo and the revolutionary Leon Trotsky. From the entrance—off a narrow, cobblestone, colonial street—to the antiquated bar, a sense of nostalgia permeates the comfortable, jovial cantina. The operation is as traditional as the menu. For those who are only drinking, waiters bring the customary small plates of complimentary snacks that range from crisp jícama slices with lime and chile to pigs' feet in a red sauce.

Higuera 14 (1 block from the central plaza), Coyoacán. ✆ **55/5554-6253.** Main courses $3.25–$5; mixed drinks $2.75–$6. AE, MC, V. Mon–Sat 1–11:30pm; Sun 1–6pm.

**La Nueva Opera Bar** ★★ *Moments* INTERNATIONAL La Opera Bar, 3 blocks east of La Alameda, is the most opulent of the city's cantinas. Slide into a dark wood booth below gilded baroque ceilings, patches of beveled mirror, and exquisite small oil paintings. Or opt for a linen-covered table with a basket of fresh bread. La Opera is the Mexican equivalent of a London gentlemen's club, although it has become so popular for dining that fewer and fewer men play dominoes. In fact, you see people enjoying romantic interludes in cavernous booths—but tables of any kind are hard to find. Service is best if you arrive for lunch when it opens or go after 5pm when the throngs have diminished; the jacketed waiters cater to regulars at the expense of unknown diners. The Spanish and Mexican menu is sophisticated and extensive, and the atmosphere for lunch and dinner is excellent. Try the incredible "Aperital Batido," the bartender's special aperitif. While you wait for your meal, look to the ceiling for the bullet hole that legend says Pancho Villa left when he galloped in on a horse. It's half a block toward the *zócalo* from Sanborn's House of Tiles.

### *Moments* Café, Por Favor!

If you think espresso bars are a recent phenomenon, or coffee drinks a development of the past decade, you may be intrigued to learn that in Mexico, drinking good coffee has been considered an art form for generations. Some of the best coffee can be found in small cafes that have a crowd of regulars who congregate to catch up the local *chisme,* or gossip.

**Café La Habana,** downtown on Bucareli and Morelos, is one of the most famous, a longstanding cafe with a rich history—and a reputation for strong coffee, all roasted and ground in-house. Ask the waiter and he'll tell you how Fidel Castro and the Ché Guevara planned the Cuban revolution while sipping an espresso *cortao.* It's open Monday through Saturday from 7:30am to 11pm.

More European-style coffeehouses are in the Zona Rosa, frequented by businesspeople and trendy urban residents. Some of the most popular are **Salón de Té Auseba** and **Duca d'Este,** both on Hamburgo near Florencia. They serve excellent coffee and scrumptious cakes, as well as a variety of herbal teas. The sidewalk cafe **Konditori,** Genova 61, is another good option, on a pedestrian-only street. Open daily 7am to midnight.

The Condesa neighborhood, east of Chapultepec Park, is another top cafe zone. **El Péndulo,** Nuevo León 115, close to Insurgentes, is a favorite. It combines its cafe setting with a book and music store, and so tends to draw intellectuals, writers, and students. It frequently hosts live music and poetry readings. It's open Monday through Friday from 8am to 11pm and weekends from 10am to 11pm.

Cinco de Mayo 10, Col. Centro. ✆ **55/5512-8959.** Reservations recommended at lunch. Main courses $4–$10; mixed drinks $3.50–$6. AE, MC, V. Mon–Sat 1pm–midnight. Metro: Bellas Artes.

## 5 Exploring Mexico City

The diverse attractions in Mexico City stem from its complex layers of history. From the simple pleasure of a stroll through a bustling *mercado* to museums filled with treasures of artistic and historic significance, Mexico City has much to explore.

Mexico City was built on the ruins of the ancient city of Tenochtitlán. A downtown portion of the city, comprising almost 700 blocks and 1,500 buildings, has been designated a Historical Zone (Centro Histórico). The area has surged in popularity, and neglected buildings are rapidly being converted into chic clubs and trendy restaurants, recalling its former colonial charm.

Remember that this is a city, and a major one at that; dress is more professional and formal here than in other parts of the country. The altitude makes temperatures much cooler, which is often a surprise for travelers with preconceptions of Mexico as perpetually hot. In summer, always be prepared for rain, which falls almost daily. In winter, carry a jacket or sweater—stone museums are cold inside, and when the sun goes down, the outside air gets quite cold.

# Historic Downtown (Centro Histórico)

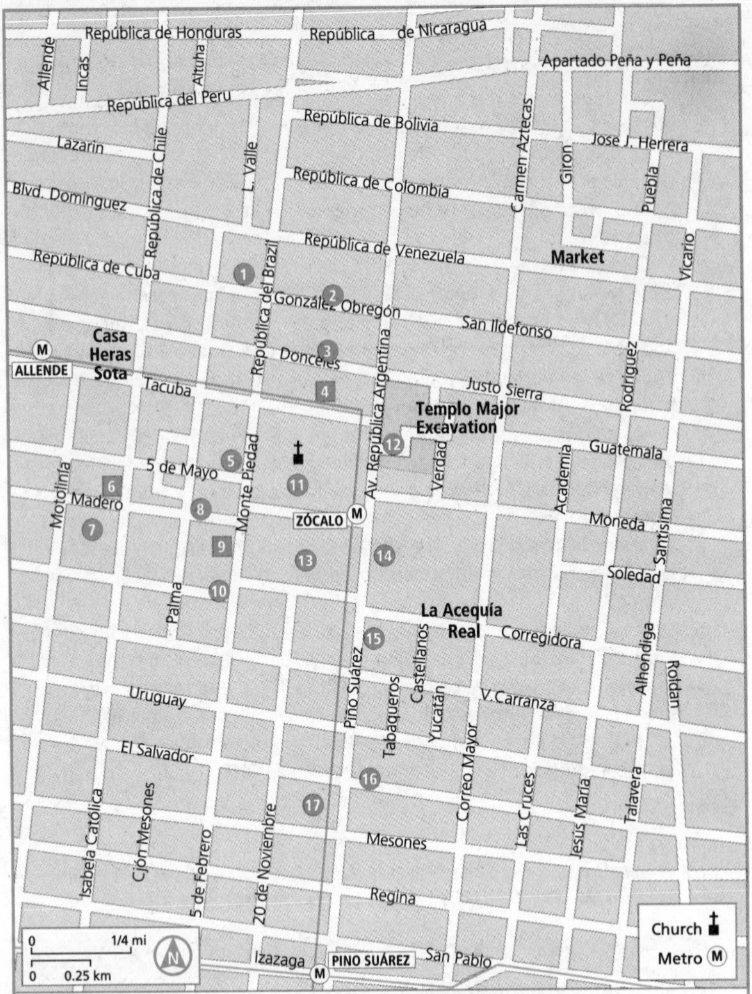

República de Honduras
República
de Nicaragua
Apartado Peña y Peña
Allende
Incas
Altuha
República del Peru
República de Bolivia
Lazarin
Jose J. Herrera
República de Chile
L. Valle
República de Colombia
Carmen Aztecas
Giron
Puebla
Blvd. Dominguez
República de Venezuela
Market
Vicario
República de Cuba
República del Brazil
González Obregón
San Ildefonso
Casa
Heras
Sota
ALLENDE
Donceles
Rodriguez
Tacuba
Justo Sierra
Templo Major
Excavation
Av. República Argentina
Guatemala
5 de Mayo
Monte Piedad
Verdad
Academia
Motolinia
Madero
ZÓCALO
Moneda
Santisima
Soledad
Palma
La Acequía
Real
Corregidora
Castellanos
Alhondiga
Roldan
Piño Suárez
Uruguay
Tabaqueros
Yucatán
V.Carranza
El Salvador
Correo Mayor
Isabela Católica
Cjón Mesones
Las Cruces
Jesús María
Talavera
5 de Febrero
20 de Noviembre
Mesones
Regina
Izazaga
PINO SUÁREZ
San Pablo
0
1/4 mi
0
0.25 km
N
Church
Metro
1
2
3
4
5
6
7
8
9
10
11
12
13
14
15
16
17

**ACCOMMODATIONS ■**

Hotel Catedral **4**
Hotel Gillow **6**
Hotel Majestic **9**

GUADALUPE
area of detail
57D
POLANCO
CHAPULTEPEC PARK
DOWNTOWN
SAN ÁNGEL
COYOCÁN
57D
0
2 mi
0
2 km

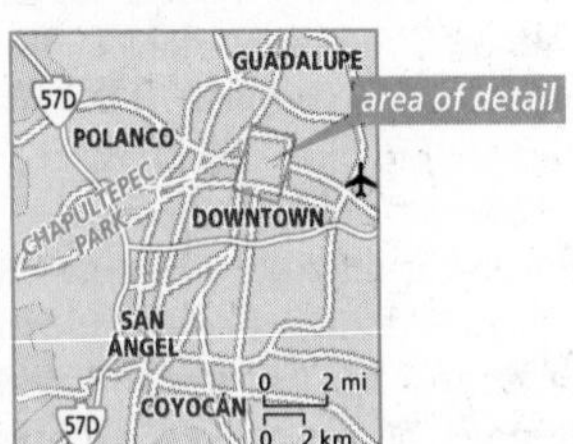

**ATTRACTIONS ●**

Catedral Metropolitana **11**
Gran Hotel Ciudad de México **10**
Iglesia y Hospital de Jesús Nazareno **17**
Nacional Monte de Piedad **5**
Museo de la Ciudad de México **16**
Museo del Templo Mayor **12**
Palacio de Iturbide **7**
Palacio de Mineria **8**
Palacio Nacional **14**
Plaza de Santo Domingo **1**
Secretaria de Educacíon Pública **2**
Suprema Corte de Justicia **15**
Teatro de la Ciudad **3**
Zócalo **13**

### Mexico City Neighborhoods

Several of Mexico City's outlying neighborhoods are worth a visit. Outside the Historic Center, San Angel, Coyoacán, and Xochimilco have developed their own unique appeal and attractions. For a more extensive description and directions, see "Mexico City Neighborhoods in Brief," earlier in this chapter, and the neighborhood maps on the following pages.

## THE TOP ATTRACTIONS

**Basílica de Nuestra Señora de Guadalupe** ★★ Within the northern city limits is the famous Basílica of Guadalupe—not just another church, but the central place of worship for Mexico's patron saint and the home of the image responsible for uniting pre-Hispanic Indian mysticism with Catholic beliefs. It is virtually impossible to understand Mexico and its culture without appreciating the national devotion for Our Lady of Guadalupe. The blue-mantled Virgin of Guadalupe is the most revered image in the country, and you will see her countenance wherever you travel.

The Basílica occupies the site where, on December 9, 1531, a poor Indian named Juan Diego reputedly saw a vision of a beautiful lady in a blue mantle. The local bishop, Zumarraga, was reluctant to confirm that Juan Diego had indeed seen the Virgin Mary, so he asked the peasant for evidence. Juan Diego saw the vision a second time, on December 12, and when he asked her for proof, she instructed him to collect the roses that began blooming in the rocky soil at his feet. He gathered the flowers in his cloak and returned to the bishop. When he unfurled his cloak, the flowers dropped to the ground and the image of the Virgin was miraculously emblazoned on the rough-hewn cloth. The bishop immediately ordered the building of a church on the spot, and upon its completion, the cloth with the Virgin's image was hung in a place of honor, framed in gold. Since that time, millions of the devout and the curious have come to view the miraculous image that experts, it is said, are at a loss to explain. So heavy was the flow of visitors—many approached for hundreds of yards on their knees—that the old church, already fragile, was insufficient to handle them. An audacious New Basílica, designed by Pedro Ramírez Vazquez, the same architect who did the breathtaking Museo Nacional de Antropología, opened in 1987.

The miracle cloak hangs behind bulletproof glass above the altar. Moving walkways going in two directions transport the crowds a distance below the cloak. If you want to see it again, take the people-mover going in the opposite direction; you can do it as many times as you want.

In 2002, the Pope was to declare Juan Diego a saint, a very big deal in this predominantly Catholic country—especially since he would be the first Mexican to achieve sainthood. The achievement was not, however, without controversy—Juan Diego's images are increasingly taking on a "European" appearance, and native Mexicans insist that Juan Diego be portrayed as the dark-skinned indigenous peasant he was.

To the right of the modern basilica is the Old Basílica, actually the second one built to house the cloak—the first one is higher up on the hill. Unfortunately, the Old Basílica is tilting precariously and is not open to visitors. Restoration has been ongoing for at least 10 years, but lately has moved more rapidly. To the back of it is the entrance to the Basílica Museum, with a very good display of religious art in restored rooms. One of the side chapels, with a silver altar, is adjacent to the museum.

Outside the museum is a garden commemorating the moment Juan Diego showed the cloak to the archbishop. Numerous photographers with colorful backdrops gather there to capture your visit on film. At the top of the hill, behind the basilica, is the **Panteón del Tepeyac,** a cemetery for Mexico's more infamous folk (Santa Anna among them), and several gift shops specializing in religious objects and other folk art. The steps up this hill are lined with flowers, shrubs, and waterfalls, and the climb, though tiring, is worthwhile for the view from the top.

If you visit Mexico City on **December 12,** you can witness the grand festival in honor of the **Virgin of Guadalupe.** The square in front of the basilica fills with the pious and the party-minded as prayers, dances, and a carnival atmosphere attract thousands of the devout. Many visitors combine a trip to the basilica with one to the **ruins of Teotihuacán,** since both are out of the city center in the same direction.

Villa de Guadalupe. ✆ **55/5577-6022.** Free admission; museum 55¢. Tues–Sun 10am–6pm. Free guided tours (in Spanish) Fri–Sat noon. Metro: Basílica or La Villa. From Basílica, take exit marked SALIDA AV. MONTIEL; walk a block or so north of the station to a major intersection (Montevideo; you'll know it by the VIPS and Denny's across the street to the left); turn right onto Av. Montevideo and cross the overpass; after about a 15-min. walk, you'll see the church ahead. From La Villa, walk north on Calzada de Guadalupe.

**Museo Frida Kahlo** ★★★ Although during her lifetime Frida Kahlo was known principally as the wife of muralist Diego Rivera, today her art surpasses his in popularity. Kahlo dedicated her life to both her painting and her passionate, tortured love for her husband. Her emotional and physical pain—her spine was pierced during a serious streetcar accident in her youth—were the primary subjects of her canvases, many of which are self-portraits. Her paintings are now acknowledged as not only exceptional works of Latin American art, but as some of the purest artistic representations of female strength and struggle ever created. As her paintings have surged in renown and price, so has interest in the life of this courageous, provocative, and revolutionary woman.

Kahlo was born in this house on July 7, 1910, and lived here with Rivera from 1929 to 1954. During the 1930s and 1940s it was a popular gathering place for intellectuals. As you wander through the rooms of the cornflower-blue house, you'll get a glimpse of the life they led. Most of the rooms remain in their original state, with mementos everywhere. Tiny clay pots hang about; the names Diego and Frida are painted on the walls of the kitchen. In the studio upstairs, a wheelchair sits next to the easel with a partially completed painting surrounded by brushes, palettes, books, photographs, and other intimate details of the couple's art-centered lives.

Frida and Diego collected pre-Columbian art, and many of the rooms contain jewelry and terracotta figurines from Teotihuacán and Tlatelolco. Kahlo even had a mock-up of a temple built in the garden to exhibit her numerous pots and statues. On the back side of the temple are several skulls from Chichén-Itzá. A cafe on the first floor serves light snacks, and the adjacent bookstore offers a full range of Kahlo and Rivera books and other commercialized memorabilia.

To learn more about their remarkable lives, I recommend Bertram D. Wolfe's *Diego Rivera: His Life and Times* and Hayden Herrara's *Frida: A Biography of Frida Kahlo.*

Londres 247, Coyoacán. ✆ **55/5554-5999.** Admission $2. No cameras allowed. Tues–Sun 10am–6pm. Metro: Coyoacán.

**Museo Nacional de Antropología** ★★★ Occupying 4,088 square m (44,000 sq. ft.), Mexico City's anthropology museum is regarded as one of the

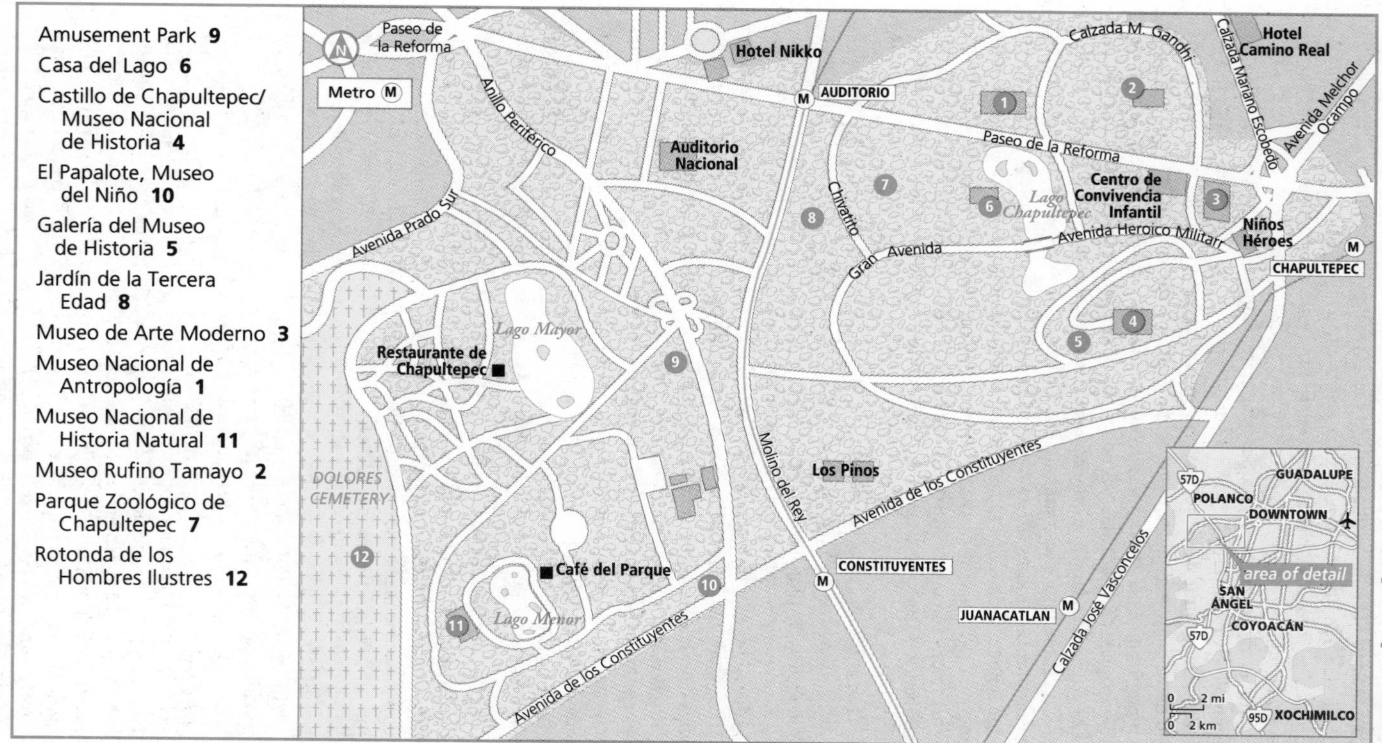

Amusement Park 9
Casa del Lago 6
Castillo de Chapultepec/ Museo Nacional de Historia 4
El Papalote, Museo del Niño 10
Galería del Museo de Historia 5
Jardín de la Tercera Edad 8
Museo de Arte Moderno 3
Museo Nacional de Antropología 1
Museo Nacional de Historia Natural 11
Museo Rufino Tamayo 2
Parque Zoológico de Chapultepec 7
Rotonda de los Hombres Ilustres 12
Metro
Paseo de la Reforma
Anillo Periférico
Avenida Prado Sur
Hotel Nikko
AUDITORIO
Auditorio Nacional
Chivatito
Gran Avenida
Paseo de la Reforma
Calzada M. Gandhi
Calzada Mariano Escobedo
Hotel Camino Real
Avenida Melchor Ocampo
Centro de Convivencia Infantil
Lago Chapultepec
Avenida Heroico Militarr
Niños Héroes
CHAPULTEPEC
Lago Mayor
Restaurante de Chapultepec
DOLORES CEMETERY
Café del Parque
Lago Menor
Avenida de los Constituyentes
Molino del Rey
Los Pinos
Avenida de los Constituyentes
CONSTITUYENTES
JUANACATLAN
Calzada José Vasconcelos
GUADALUPE
POLANCO
DOWNTOWN
area of detail
SAN ÁNGEL
COYOACÁN
XOCHIMILCO
57D
95D
0 2 mi
0 2 km

top museums in the world and offers the single best introduction to the culture of Mexico. First-floor rooms are devoted to the country's pre-Hispanic cultures. Second-floor rooms cover contemporary rural cultures through their crafts and everyday life.

Inside the museum is an open courtyard (containing the Chávez Morado fountain) with beautifully designed rooms running around three sides on two levels. The **ground-floor rooms** are devoted to history—from prehistoric days up to the most recently explored archaeological sites—and are the most popular among studious visitors. These rooms include dioramas of Mexico City when the Spaniards arrived, and reproductions of part of a pyramid at Teotihuacán. The Aztec calendar stone "wheel" occupies a proud place.

Save some time and energy for the livelier and more readily comprehensible **ethnographic rooms** upstairs. This section is devoted to the way people throughout Mexico live today, complete with straw-covered huts, tape recordings of songs and dances, crafts, clothing, and lifelike models of village activities. This floor, a living museum, strikes me as vital to the understanding of contemporary Mexico because of the importance of pre-Hispanic customs in Mexican village life.

The museum has a lovely, moderately priced restaurant with cheerful patio tables. *Note:* Most of the museum is wheelchair accessible; however, assistance will be needed in places.

A sweeping restoration of the museum took place during 2000 and 2001. The $13 million refurbishment project was the first since the museum opened in 1964. Over 2,000 new artifacts and information garnered from some 200 recent digs have been incorporated throughout the 23 rooms. In addition, new computerized touch-screen technology with video images and sound depicting rituals and customs are on display, providing visitors with a richer, more interactive experience. For the first time, exhibit signs are presented with English as well as Spanish explanations.

Chapultepec Park. ✆ **55/5553-6381.** www.sunsite.dcaa.unam.mx/antropol/. Admission $3; free Sun. Still camera $3, amateur video camera $4.50. No tripods or flash permitted. Tues–Sun 9am–7pm. Metro: Auditorio.

**Palacio Nacional and the Diego Rivera Murals** ★★ This complex of countless rooms, wide stone stairways, and numerous courtyards adorned with carved brass balconies is where the president of Mexico works. Even so, it's better known for the fabulous second-floor Diego Rivera murals depicting the history of Mexico. Begun in 1692 on the site of Moctezuma's "new" palace, this building became the site of Hernán Cortez's home and the residence of colonial viceroys. It has changed much in 300 years, taking on its present form in the late 1920s when the top floor was added. Just 30 minutes here with an English-speaking guide provides essential background for an understanding of Mexican history. The cost of a guide is negotiable: $8.25 or less, depending on your bargaining ability.

Enter by the central door, over which hangs the bell rung by Padre Miguel Hidalgo when he proclaimed Mexico's independence from Spain in 1810—the famous *grito.* Each September 15, Mexican Independence Day, the president of Mexico stands on the balcony above the door to echo Hidalgo's cry to the thousands of spectators who fill the *zócalo.* Take the stairs to the Rivera murals, which were painted over a 25-year period. The *Legend of Quetzalcoatl* depicts the famous tale of the feathered serpent bringing a blond-bearded white man to the

Coyoacán

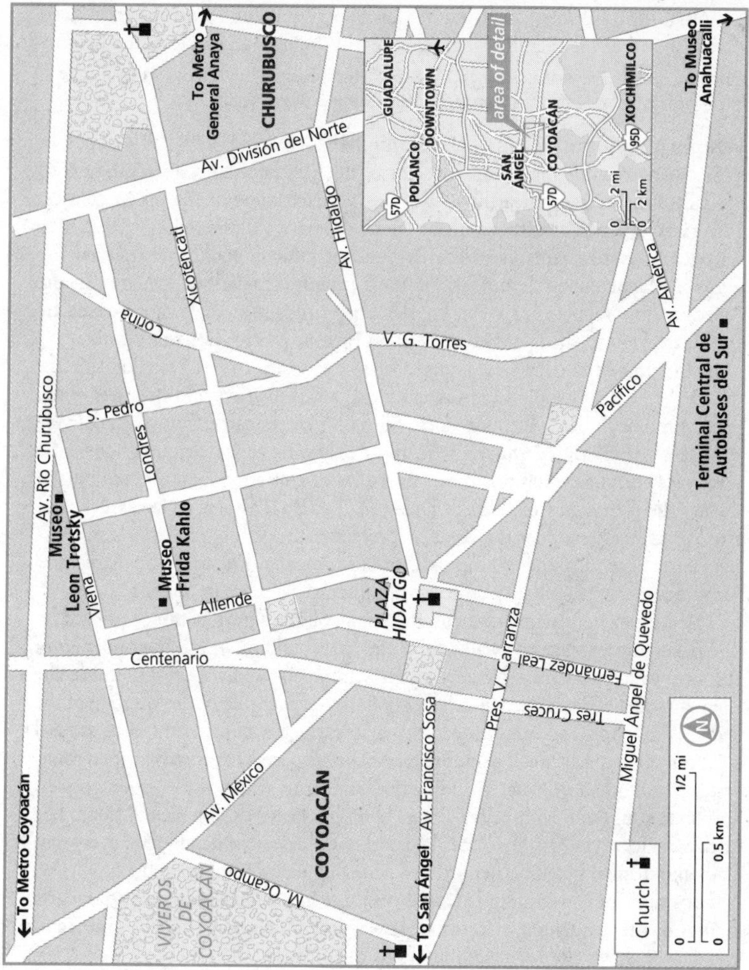


country. When Cortez arrived, many Aztecs, recalling this legend, believed him to be Quetzalcoatl. Another mural tells of the American Intervention when American invaders marched into Mexico City during the War of 1847. It was on this occasion that the military cadets of Chapultepec Castle (then a military school) fought bravely to the last man. The most notable of Rivera's murals is the *Great City of Tenochtitlán,* a study of the original settlement in the Valley of Mexico. The city is but a small part of the mural; the remainder is filled with what appear to be four million extras left over from a Hollywood epic, including the lovely Xochiquetzal, goddess of love, with her crown of flowers and tattooed legs. Diego Rivera, one of Mexico's legendary muralists, left an indelible stamp on Mexico City, his painted political themes affecting the way millions view Mexican history. Additional examples of Rivera's stunning and provocative interpretations are found at the Bellas Artes, the National Preparatory School, the Department of Public Education, the National School of Agriculture at

Chapingo, the National Institute of Cardiology, and the Museo Mural Diego Rivera (housing the mural formerly located in the now razed Hotel del Prado).

Palacio Nacional, Av. Pino Suárez, facing the *zócalo*. Free admission, but visitor tags required; be prepared to leave a form of photo identification in exchange. Mon–Sat 9am–5:30pm. Metro: Zócalo.

**Templo Mayor and Museo del Templo Mayor (Great Temple)** ★★★ In 1978, workmen digging on the east side of the Metropolitan Cathedral, next to the Palacio Nacional, unearthed an exquisite Aztec stone of the moon goddess Coyolxauhqui. Major excavations by Mexican archaeologists followed, and they uncovered interior remains of the Pyramid of Huitzilopochtli, also called the Templo Mayor (Great Temple)—the most important religious structure in the Aztec capital. What you see are the remains of pyramids that were covered by the great pyramid the Spaniards saw upon their arrival in the 16th century.

At the time of the 1521 Conquest, the site was the center of religious life for the city of 300,000. No other museum illustrates the variety and splendor of the Aztec Empire the way this one does. All 6,000 pieces came from the relatively small plot of excavated ruins just in front of the museum. Strolling along the walkways built over the site, visitors pass a water-collection conduit constructed during the presidency of Porfirio Díaz (1877–1911), as well as far earlier constructions. Shelters cover the ruins to protect traces of original paint and carving. Note especially the Tzompantli, or Altar of Skulls, a common Aztec and Maya design. Explanatory plaques with building dates are in Spanish.

The Museo del Templo Mayor (Museum of the Great Temple) opened in 1987. To enter it, take the walkway to the large building in the back portion of the site, which contains fabulous artifacts from on-site excavations. Inside the door, a model of Tenochtitlán gives a good idea of the scale of the vast city of the Aztec. The rooms and exhibits, organized by subject, occupy many levels around a central open space. You'll see some marvelous displays of masks, figurines, tools, jewelry, and other artifacts, including the huge stone wheel of the moon goddess Coyolxauhqui ("she with bells painted upon her face") on the second floor. The goddess ruled the night, the Aztec believed, but died at the dawning of every day, slain and dismembered by her brother, Huitzilopochtli, the sun god.

Look also for the striking jade-and-obsidian mask and the full-size terracotta figures of the *guerreros águilas,* or eagle warriors. A cutaway model of the Templo Mayor shows the layers and methods of construction.

Off the *zócalo*. © **55/5542-0606.** Fax 55/5542-1717. Admission (valid for museum and ruins) $3; free admission Sun. Video camera permit $3.50; no flash photos. Tues–Sun 9am–5:50pm (last ticket sold 5pm). Metro: Zócalo.

## ARCHITECTURAL HIGHLIGHTS

**Casa de los Azulejos** This "House of Tiles" is one of Mexico City's most precious colonial gems and popular meeting places. It's covered in gorgeous blue-and-white tiles, and dates from the end of the 1500s, when it was built for the count of the Valley of Orizaba. According to the oft-told story, during the count's defiant youth his father proclaimed: "You will never build a house of tiles." A tiled house was a sign of success, and the father was sure his son would amount to nothing. So when success came, the young count covered his house in tiles, a fine example of Puebla craftsmanship. The tiled murals in the covered courtyard, where the restaurant is located, were restored a few years back. Tile craftsmen from Arabia were brought in to ensure that the technique was true to the original 16th-century work. Today the tile-covered house is a branch of the Sanborn's restaurant/newsstand/gift shop/drugstore chain (see "Where to Dine,"

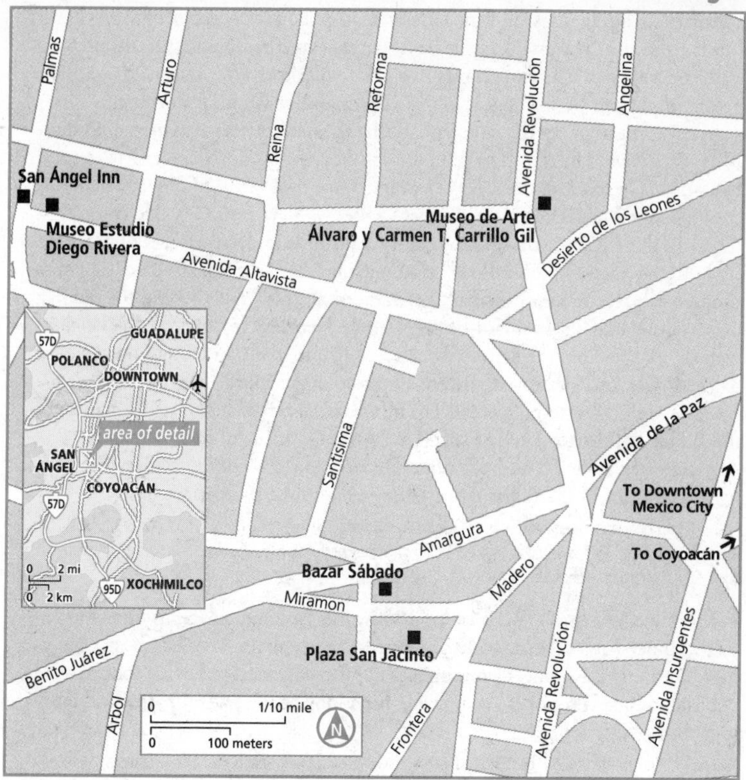


earlier). You can stroll through to admire the interior, or have a cool drink or a full meal. Pause to see the Orozco mural, *Omniscience,* on the landing leading to the second floor (where the restrooms are).

Madero 4, Centro Histórico. ✆ **55/5518-6676.** Daily 7am–1am. Metro: Bellas Artes.

**Gran Hotel Ciudad de México** Originally a department store, the Gran Hotel boasts one of the most splendid interiors of any downtown building. Step inside to see the lavish lobby with gilded open elevators on both sides, topped with a breathtaking 1908 stained-glass canopy by Jacques Graber.

On the fourth floor, overlooking the *zócalo,* El Mirador restaurant makes a great stop for a coffee or drink with a view.

Palma and Piedad, facing the *zócalo,* Centro Histórico. ✆ **55/5510-4042.** Fax 55/5512-6772. Free admission to view the lobby. Daily 24 hr. Metro: Zócalo.

**Palacio de Bellas Artes** ★★ The theater's exterior is turn-of-the-century Art Nouveau, built during the Porfiriato and covered in Italian Carrara marble. Inside, it's completely 1930s Art Deco. Since construction began in 1904, the theater (which opened in 1934) has sunk some 4m (12 ft.) into the soft belly of Lake Texcoco. The palacio is the work of several masters: Italian architect Adamo Boari, who made the original plans; Antonio Muñoz and Federico Mariscal, who modified his plans considerably; and Mexican painter Gerardo Murillo ("Doctor Atl"), who designed the fabulous Art Nouveau glass curtain that was constructed by Louis Comfort Tiffany in the Tiffany Studios of New York. Made from nearly a million iridescent pieces of colored glass, the curtain portrays the Valley of Mexico with its two great volcanoes. You can see the curtain before important performances at the theater and on Sunday mornings.

In addition to being the concert hall, the theater houses permanent and traveling art shows. On the third level are famous murals by Rivera, Orozco, and Siqueiros. The controversial Rivera mural *Man in Control of His Universe* was commissioned in 1933 for Rockefeller Center in New York City. He completed the work there just as you see it: A giant vacuum sucks up the riches of the earth to feed the factories of callous, card-playing, hard-drinking white capitalist thugs, while the noble workers of the earth, of all races, rally behind the red flag of socialism and its standard-bearer, Lenin. Needless to say, the Rockefellers weren't so keen on the new purchase. Much to their discredit, they had it painted over and destroyed. Rivera duplicated the mural here as *Man at the Crossing of the Ways* to preserve it. For information on tickets to performances of the **Ballet Folklórico,** see "Mexico City After Dark," later in this chapter.

*A note of caution:* The U.S. State Department advisory specifies that taxis parked in front of the Bellas Artes Theater should be avoided.

Calle Lopez Peralta, east end of La Alameda, Centro Histórico. © **55/5512-2593,** ext. 152. www.cnca.gob.mx. Free admission to view building, when performances are not in progress; museum $3. Tues–Sun 10am–6pm. Metro: Bellas Artes.

**Palacio de Minería** Built in the 1800s, this "mining palace" is one of architect Manuel Tolsá's finest works and one of the capital's most handsome buildings. Formerly the school of mining, it's occasionally used today for concerts and cultural events. If it's open, step inside for a look at the several patios and fabulous stonework.

Tacuba 5, Centro Histórico. © **55/5512-8094.** www.tolsa/mineria.unam.mx. Free admission. Mon–Fri 9am–8pm. Metro: Bellas Artes.

## CEMETERIES

**Plaza and Cemetery of San Fernando** At one end of the plaza is the 18th-century San Fernando Church; next to it, 2½ blocks west of La Alameda, is a small cemetery by the same name where a few of Mexico's elite families are buried. It's the only 19th-century cemetery remaining in the city. President Benito Juárez was the last person buried here, on July 23, 1872.

Puente de Alvarado and Vicente Guerrero, near La Alameda. Free admission. Daily 8am–3pm. Metro: Hidalgo.

**Rotonda de los Hombres Ilustres** The din of traffic recedes in the serene resting place where Mexico's military, political, and artistic elite are buried. It's more like an outdoor monument museum than a cemetery; the stone markers are grouped in a double circle around an eternal flame. A stroll here is a trip through Who's Who in Mexican history. Among the famous buried here are the artists Diego Rivera, David Alfaro Siqueiros, José Clemente Orozco, and Gerardo Murillo; presidents Sebastian Lerdo de Tejada, Valentín Gómez Farías, and Plutarco Calles; musicians Jaime Nuño (author of the Mexican national anthem), Juventino Rosas, and Agustín Lara; and outstanding citizens such as the philanthropist and writer Carlos Pellicer. Stop in the building at the entrance and the guard will give you a map with a list of those buried here, which includes biographical information.

Constituyentes and Av. Civil Dolores, Dolores Cemetery, Chapultepec Park. Free admission. Daily 6am–6pm. Metro: Constituyentes.

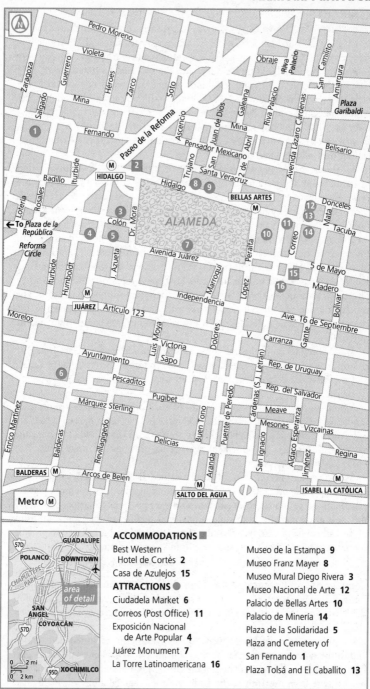

# Alameda Park Area

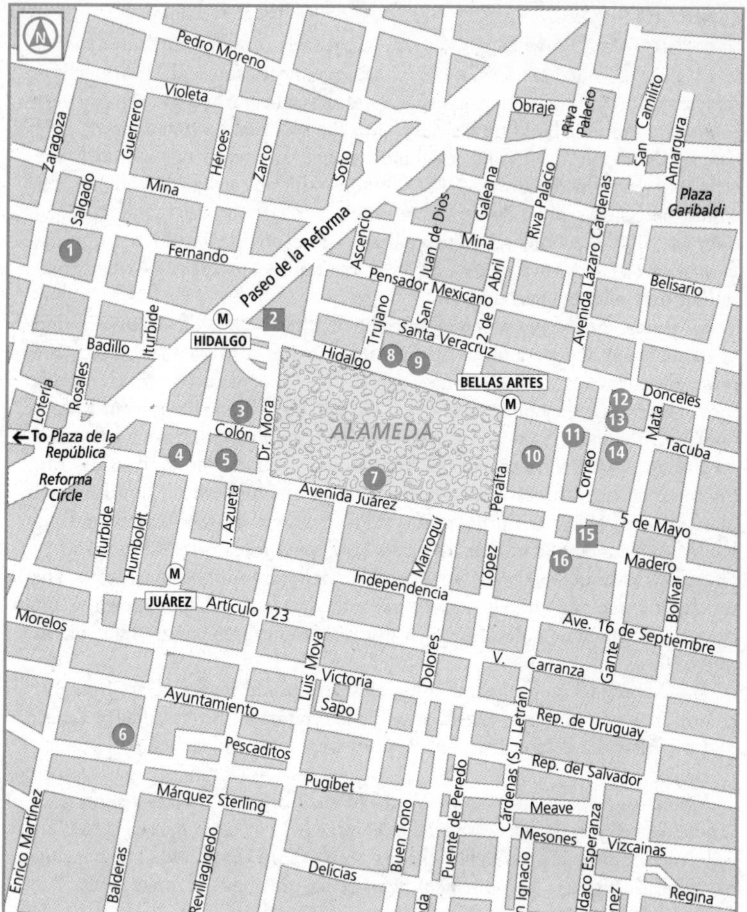

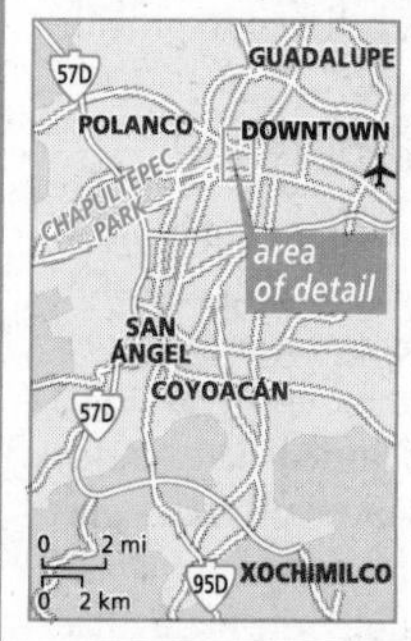


**ACCOMMODATIONS** ■

Best Western Hotel de Cortés **2**

Casa de Azulejos **15**

**ATTRACTIONS** ●

Ciudadela Market **6**

Correos (Post Office) **11**

Exposición Nacional de Arte Popular **4**

Juárez Monument **7**

La Torre Latinoamericana **16**

Museo de la Estampa **9**

Museo Franz Mayer **8**

Museo Mural Diego Rivera **3**

Museo Nacional de Arte **12**

Palacio de Bellas Artes **10**

Palacio de Minería **14**

Plaza de la Solidaridad **5**

Plaza and Cemetery of San Fernando **1**

Plaza Tolsá and El Caballito **13**

## CHURCHES

**Catedral Metropolitana** ★★★ An impressive, towering cathedral, begun in 1567 and finished in 1788, it blends baroque, neoclassic, and Mexican churrigueresque architecture. As you look around the cathedral and the Sagrario next to it, note how the building has sunk into the soft lake bottom beneath. The base of the façade is far from level and straight, and when one considers the weight of the immense towers—127,000 tons—it's no surprise. Scaffolding has almost become a part of the structure, in place to stabilize the building. However, in 2000 the Catedral Metropolitana came off the World Monuments Fund's list of 100 Most Endangered Sites, as a result of an extensive reconstruction of the building's foundation.

In Mexico, the sacred ground of one religion often becomes the sacred ground of its successor. Cortez and his Spanish missionaries converted the Aztec, tore down their temples, and used much of the stone to construct a church on this spot. The church they built was pulled down in 1628 while the present Metropolitan Cathedral was under construction. The building today has 5 naves and 14 chapels. As you wander past the small chapels, you may hear guides describing some of the cathedral's outstanding features: the tomb of Agustín Iturbide, placed here in 1838; a painting attributed to the Spanish artist Bartolomé Esteban Murillo; and the fact that the stone holy-water fonts ring like metal when tapped with a coin. Like many huge churches, it has catacombs underneath. The much older-looking church next to the cathedral is the chapel known as the Sagrario, another tour de force of Mexican baroque architecture built in the mid-1700s.

The Metropolitan Cathedral contains many prized works of art from the colonial era, of a variety of artistic styles. The Altar de los Reyes (Altar of Kings) and the Altar del Perdon (Altar of Pardon) were built and carved by Jerónimo de Balbas in 1737.

A new sound-and-light show, "Voices of the Cathedral," takes visitors on a candlelit stroll through the cathedral, accompanied by period music. Tickets are $25, and are available through Ticketmaster (✆ **55/5325-9000**). The schedule of English-language performances was being finalized at press time; call 55/5512-7096 for details.

As you walk around the outside of the cathedral, you will notice a reminder of medieval trade life. The west side is the gathering place of carpenters, plasterers, plumbers, painters, and electricians who have no shops. Craftspeople display the tools of their trades, sometimes along with pictures of their work. In front of the cathedral, you can buy crystals, gemstones, and herbs, believed to provide special qualities of protection and cure from various afflictions.

The *zócalo,* on Cinco de Mayo, Centro Histórico. Free admission. Daily 7am–7pm. Metro: Zócalo.

**Convent of San Bernardino de Siena** This 16th-century building is noted for its flower petals carved in stone—a signature of the Indians who did most of the work—on 16th-century *retablos,* including one of the country's three such altarpieces that has miraculously been preserved for more than 400 years. The last Indian governor of Xochimilco, Apoxquiyohuatzin, is buried here. Inside and to the right, the skull over the font is from a pre-Hispanic skull rack signifying an Indian/Christian mixture of the concept of life and death. Eight lateral *retablos* date from the 16th to the 18th centuries. The fabulous gilt main altar, also from the 16th century, is like an open book with sculpture and religious paintings. A profusion of cherubic angels decorates columns and borders. Some of the altar paintings are attributed to Baltasar Echave Orio the Elder. Over the altar, above the figure of Christ, is San Bernardino with the *caciques* (local authorities) dressed in clothing with Indian elements, and without shoes.

Pino and Hidalgo (facing the main square), Xochimilco. Free admission. Daily 8am–8pm. *Tren ligero* (light train): Xochimilco.

**Iglesia y Hospital de Jesús Nazareno** Hernán Cortez founded this church soon after the Conquest. A stone marker on Pino Suárez marks it as the spot where Cortez and Moctezuma reportedly met for the first time. Cortez died in Spain in 1547; his remains are in a vault inside the chapel (entered by a side door on República del Salvador). Vaults on the opposite wall store the remains of Cortez's relatives. Notice the Orozco mural, *The Apocalypse,* on the choir ceiling.

Pino Suárez and El Salvador, Centro Histórico. Free admission. Mon–Sat 7am–8pm; Sun 7am–1pm and 5–8pm. Metro: Zócalo.

## HISTORIC BUILDINGS & MONUMENTS

### CHAPULTEPEC PARK & POLANCO

**Castillo de Chapultepec/Museo Nacional de Historia** This site had been occupied by a fortress since the days of the Aztec, although the present palace wasn't built until the 1780s. The castle offers a beautiful view of Mexico City. During the French occupation of the 1860s, Carlota (who designed the lovely garden surrounding the palace) could sit up in bed and watch her husband, Maximilian, proceeding down Reforma on his way to work. Later, this was the official home of Mexico's president until 1939. Today, the castle houses a variety of historical artifacts covering the period between 1521 and 1917. You'll see murals by Orozco, Siqueiros, and others; elaborate European furnishings brought here by Maximilian and Carlota; and jewelry and colonial art.

Chapultepec Park and Polanco. ✆ **55/5553-6224,** 55/5553-6246, or 55/5553-6396. Admission $3; free admission Sun. Tues–Sun 9am–5pm (tickets sold until 4pm). Metro: Chapultepec.

### ZONA ROSA & SURROUNDING AREAS

**Monumento a los Héroes de la Independencia** ★ Without a doubt, the *Monument to the Heroes of Independence* is the most noted of Mexico City's exceptional public sculptures and monuments. The "Angel" is both a landmark and homage to those who lost their lives fighting for independence. Set upon a tall marble shaft, the golden angel is an important and easily discerned guidepost for travelers. A creation of Antonio Rivas Mercado, the 7m- (22-ft.-) high, gold-plated bronze angel, cast in Florence, Italy, was completed in 1906 at a cost of $2.5 million. With its base of marble and Italian granite, the monument's total height is 45m (150 ft.).

Paseo de la Reforma, Florencia, and Río Tiber intersection. Reforma/Zona Rosa. Metro: Insurgentes.

### CENTRO HISTORICO & SURROUNDING AREAS

**Monumento a la Revolución and Museo Nacional de la Revolución** The Art Deco *Monument to the Revolution,* in the large **Plaza de la República,** has a curious history. The government of Porfirio Díaz, who was perennially "reelected" president of Mexico, began construction of what was intended to be a new legislative chamber. However, only the dome was raised by the time the Mexican Revolution (1910) put an end to his plans, not to mention his dictatorship. In the 1930s, after the revolutionary turmoil had died down, the dome was finished as a monument. The remains of two revolutionary presidents, Francisco Madero and Venustiano Carranza, were entombed in two of its pillars, and it was dedicated to the Revolution. Later, the bodies of presidents Plutarco Elías Calles and Lázaro Cárdenas were also buried there.

Beneath the *Monument to the Revolution* is the **Museo Nacional de la Revolución** (entry directly across from the Frontón). It chronicles the tumultuous years from 1867 through 1917, when the present constitution was signed, in excellent exhibits of documents, newspaper stories, photographs, drawings, clothing, costumes, uniforms, weapons, and furnishings.

Av. Juárez and La Fragua. Plaza de la Republica s/n, Col. Tabacalera en el sotano del *Monumento a la Revolución*. ✆ **55/5546-2115** or 55/5566-1902. www.arts-history.mx/museorevolution//historia. Admission 60¢. Tues–Sat 9am–5pm; Sun 9am–3pm. From the Colón Monument on Reforma, walk 2 blocks north on I. Ramírez; the monument looms ahead. Metro: Revolución.

**Secretaría de Educación Pública** The Secretariat of Public Education was built in 1922 and decorated with a great series of more than 200 Diego Rivera murals dating from 1923 and 1928. Other artists did a panel here and there, but the Rivera murals are the most outstanding.

República de Cuba, between República de Brazil and República de Argentina. ✆ **55/5512-1707.** www.sep.gob.mx. Free admission. Daily 9am–6pm. Metro: Allende.

**Suprema Corte de Justicia** The Supreme Court of Justice, built between 1935 and 1941, is the highest court in the country. Inside, on the main staircase and its landings, are Orozco murals depicting a theme of justice.

Pino Suárez and Corregidora, Centro Histórico. No phone. Free admission. Mon–Fri 9am–5:30pm. Metro: Zócalo.

## OTHER MUSEUMS & GALLERIES

Mexico City boasts over 90 museums that celebrate its several thousand years as a hemispheric cultural center. Following is a selection of the most notable, listed by neighborhood.

### CHAPULTEPEC PARK/POLANCO

**El Papalote, Museo del Niño** *Kids* This interactive children's museum opened in 1993. The Building of the Pyramids holds most of the more than 350 exhibits, while two films alternate (10 shows daily) in the IMAX building. There's virtually nothing here that children can't touch; once they discover this, they'll want to stay a long time. As they say, adults must be accompanied by children, except on Thursday, when it remains open until 11pm to give "big kids" a chance to enjoy it themselves.

Av. de los Constituyentes 268, Chapultepec Park, Section 2. ✆ **55/5224-1260,** or 55/5237-1781. www.papalote.org.mx. Admission to museum $5 adults, $4 children; admission to museum and IMAX show $8 adults, $7 children. Mon–Fri 9am–1pm and 2–6pm; Sat–Sun and holidays 10am–2pm and 3–7pm; Thurs 7pm–11pm. Metro: Constituyentes.

**Galería del Museo de Historia** About 200 yards below Chapultepec Castle is this circular glass building, also known as the Museo Caracol (Snail Museum) for its spiral shape, and as the Museo de la Lucha del Pueblo Mexicano por su Libertad (Museum of the Mexican People's Fight for Their Liberty) for its content. It's a condensed chronological history of Mexico from 1800 to 1917, complete with portraits, reproductions of documents, and dramatic dioramas. The more recent years are also represented, with large photographic blowups. Some scenes, such as Maximilian's execution, are staged with great drama and imagination. In many ways, this museum is more riveting than the Museo Nacional de Historia on the hill above.

Chapultepec Park. ✆ **55/5553-6391.** www.cwnca.gob.mx. Admission $2.50; free admission Sun. Tues–Sun 9am–5:30pm. Metro: Chapultepec.

**Museo de Arte Moderno** ★ The Museum of Modern Art is known for having the best permanent exhibition of painters and sculptors from the modern Mexican art movement. It also features some of the most important temporary exhibitions of national and international modern art in the world. Representing the Mexican muralist movement are significant works by the three greats: Diego Rivera, José Clemente Orozco, and David Alfaro Siqueiros. The main building is a round, two-story structure with a central staircase. Two of the museum's four permanent spaces are dedicated to the permanent collection, which also contains works by Mexico's other modern masters—Tamayo, José Luis Cuevas, Alejandro Colunga, Francisco Toledo, and Vladamir Cora. The remaining two spaces house visiting exhibitions. The museum's surrounding gardens exhibit large-scale public sculptures.

Chapultepec Park. ✆ **55/5553-6233.** www.arts-history.mx/museo/mam/home.html. Admission $2; discounts for students and teachers with ID; free admission Sun. Tues–Sun 10am–5:30pm. Metro: Chapultepec.

**Museo Nacional de Historia Natural** The 10 interconnecting domes that form the Museum of Natural History contain stuffed and preserved animals and birds; tableaux of different natural environments with the appropriate wildlife; exhibits on geology, astronomy, biology, and the origin of life; and more. It's a fascinating place for anyone with the slightest curiosity about nature and is totally absorbing for youngsters.

Chapultepec Park, Section 2, s/n. Delegación, Miguel Hidalgo Cp. 11800. ✆ **55/5516-2848.** www.arts-history.mx/hnatural.html. Admission $1.50; free admission Tues. Tues–Sun 10am–5pm. Metro: Constituyentes.

**Museo Rufino Tamayo** ★ Oaxaca-born painter Rufino Tamayo not only contributed a great deal to modern Mexican painting, but also collected pre-Hispanic, Mexican, and foreign works, including pieces by de Kooning, Warhol, Dalí, and Magritte. Tamayo's pre-Hispanic collection is in Oaxaca, but here you can see a number of his works and the remainder of his collection (unless a special exhibit has temporarily displaced them).

Chapultepec Park. ✆ **55/5286-6529** or 55/5286-6599. mrtamayo@prodigy.net.mx. Admission $1.50; free admission Sun. Tues–Sun 10am–6pm. Free guided tours Sat–Sun 10am–2pm. Metro: Chapultepec.

## CENTRO HISTORICO & SURROUNDING AREAS

**Museo de la Ciudad de México** Before you enter the Museum of Mexico City, go to the corner of República del Salvador and look at the enormous stone serpent head, a corner support at the building's base. The stone was once part of an Aztec pyramid. At the entrance, a stone doorway opens to the courtyard of this mansion, built in 1778 as the House of the Counts of Santiago de Calimaya. This classic building was converted into the Museum of the City of Mexico in 1964 and should be visited by anyone interested in the country's past. Dealing solely with the Mexico Valley, where the first people arrived around 8000 B.C., the museum contains some fine maps and pictographic presentations of the initial settlements and outlines of the social organization as it developed, as well as models of several famous buildings. Upstairs is the studio of Mexican impressionist Joaquín Clausell (1866–1935). There's a good bookstore, to the left after you enter.

Pino Suárez 30, Centro Histórico. ✆ **55/5542-0487.** Admission $1. Tues–Sun 10am–6pm. Metro: Zócalo.

**Museo Franz Mayer** One of the capital's foremost museums, the Franz Mayer Museum opened in 1986 in a beautifully restored 16th-century building on Plaza de la Santa Veracruz on the north side of La Alameda. The extraordinary 10,000-piece collection of antiques, mostly Mexican objects from the 16th through 19th centuries, was amassed by one man: Franz Mayer. A German immigrant, he adopted Mexico as his home in 1905 and grew rich here. Before his death in 1975, Mayer bequeathed the collection to the country and arranged for its permanent display through a trust with the Banco Nacional. The pieces, mostly utilitarian objects (as opposed to pure art objects), include inlaid and richly carved furniture; an enormous collection of Talavera pottery; gold and silver religious pieces; sculptures; tapestries; rare watches and clocks (the oldest is a 1680 lantern clock); wrought iron; old-master paintings from Europe and Mexico; and 770 *Don Quixote* volumes, many of which are rare editions or typographically unique. There's so much here it may take two visits to absorb it. In the central courtyard, a very pleasant cafe serves coffee and light snacks.

Av. Hidalgo 45, facing La Alameda. ✆ **55/5518-2265.** www.art-history.mx/museos/franz/. Admission $1.50; free admission Tues. Tues–Sun 10am–5pm. Guided tours by appointment, Mon–Sat 10:30am, 11:30am, and 12:30pm. Metro: Hidalgo or Bellas Artes.

**Museo Mural Diego Rivera** This museum houses Diego Rivera's famous mural *Dream of a Sunday Afternoon in Alameda Park,* which was painted on a wall of the Hotel Prado in 1947. The hotel was demolished after the 1985 earthquake, but the precious mural, perhaps the best known of Rivera's works, was saved and transferred to its new location in 1986. The huge picture, 15m (50 ft.) long and 4m (13 ft.) high, chronicles the history of the park from the time of Cortez onward. Portrayed in the mural are numerous historical figures. More or less from left to right, but not in chronological order, they include: Cortez; a heretic suffering under the Spanish Inquisition; Sor Juana Inés de la Cruz, a brilliant and progressive woman who became a nun to continue her scholarly pursuits; Benito Juárez, seen putting forth the laws of Mexico's great Reforma; the conservative Gen. Antonio López de Santa Anna, handing the keys to Mexico to the invading American Gen. Winfield Scott; Emperor Maximilian and Empress Carlota; José Martí, the Cuban revolutionary; Death, with the plumed serpent (Quetzalcoatl) entwined about his neck; Gen. Porfirio Díaz, great with age and medals, asleep; a police officer keeping La Alameda free of "riffraff" by ordering a poor family out of the elitists' park; and Francisco Madero, the martyred democratic president who caused the downfall of Díaz, and whose betrayal and alleged murder by Gen. Victoriano Huerta (pictured on the right) resulted in years of civil turmoil.

Plaza de la Solidaridad, Balderas, and Colón, Centro Histórico–Alameda. ✆ **55/5510-2329** and 55/5512-0754. www.arts-history.mx/museomural/. Admission $1.50; free admission Sun. Tues–Sun 10am–6pm. Metro: Hidalgo.

**Museo Nacional de Arte** The National Art Museum's palacelike building, designed by Italian architect Silvio Contri and completed in 1911—a legacy of the years of Europe-loving Porfirio Díaz—was built to house the government's offices of Communications and Public Works. Díaz occupied the opulent second-floor salon, where he welcomed visiting dignitaries. The National Museum of Art took over the building in 1982. Wander through the immense rooms with polished wooden floors as you view the wealth of paintings showing Mexico's art development, primarily covering the period from 1810 to 1950. There's a nice cafe on the second floor.

Tacuba 8, Centro Histórico. ✆ **55/5512-3224** or 55/5510-8604. Fax 55/5521-7320. Admission varies depending upon exhibition and is occasionally free; free admission Sun. Tues–Sun 10am–5:30pm. Metro: Allende.

**Museo Nacional de la Estampa** *Estampa* means "engraving" or "printing," and this museum is devoted to understanding and preserving the graphic arts. Housed in a beautifully restored 16th-century building, the museum has both permanent and changing exhibits. Displays include those from pre-Hispanic times, when clay seals were used for designs on fabrics, ceramics, and other surfaces. But the most famous works here are probably those of José Guadalupe Posada, Mexico's famous printmaker, who poked fun at death and politicians through his skeleton figure drawings. If your interest in this subject is deep, ask to see the video programs on graphic techniques—woodcuts, lithography, etchings, and the like.

Av. Hidalgo 39 (next door to the Museo Franz Mayer), Centro Histórico–Alameda. ✆ **55/5521-2244.** Admission $1.50; free admission Sun. Tues–Sun 10am–5:30pm. Metro: Bellas Artes.

**Museo Nacional de San Carlos** The San Carlos Museum exhibits 15th- to 19th-century European paintings. The museum was once the Academy of San Carlos, an art school that some of the country's great painters—Rivera and Orozco among them—attended. The beautiful converted mansion was built in the early 1800s by architect Manuel Tolsá; it was later the home of the Marqués de Buenavista.

The rooms on the first and second floors hold some of Mexico's best paintings, by both Mexican and European artists. There is also a gallery with prints and engravings. In the mansion's elliptical court are displays of 19th-century Mexican statuary and busts by Manuel Vilar and his pupils, and off to one side is a pretty garden court shaded by rubber trees.

Puente de Alvarado 50 (at Arizpe). ✆ **55/5566-8522** or 55/5592-3721. www.mnsancarlos.com. Admission $2.50; free admission Sun. Wed–Mon 10am–6pm. English tours available by reservation for nominal charge. Walk 5½ blocks west of La Alameda (2½ blocks west of San Fernando Plaza). Metro: Revolución.

## SOUTHERN NEIGHBORHOODS

**Archaeological Museum of Xochimilco** The building dates from 1904, when it was the pump house for the springs. It houses artifacts from the area, many of them found when residents built their homes—10,000-year-old mammoth bones; figures dating from the Teotihuacán period, including figures of Tlaloc (god of water and life), Ehecatl (god of the wind), Xipe Totec (god of renewal and of plants), and Huehueteotl (god of fire); polychrome pottery; carved abalone; and tombs showing funerary practices. One unique piece is a clay figure of a child holding a bouquet of flowers.

Av. Tenochtitlán and Calle La Planta, Santa Cruz Acalpixcan. ✆ and fax **55/2157-1757.** Admission $1. Tues–Sun 10am–5pm. From Xochimilco (see "Mexico City Neighborhoods in Brief," earlier), take a cab or microbus to Tulyehualco. The museum is at Tenochtitlán and La Planta, on the left.

**Diego Rivera Anahuacalli Museum** ★ Not to be confused with the Museo Estudio Diego Rivera near the San Angel Inn (see below), this is probably the most unusual museum in the city. Designed by Rivera before his death in 1957, it's devoted to his works as well as his extensive collection of pre-Columbian art. With over 52,000 pieces, it is the largest private collection displayed in Mexico. Constructed of pedregal (the lava rock in which the area abounds), it resembles Maya and Aztec architecture. Anahuacalli means "House of Mexico"; *Anahuac* was the old name for the ancient Valley of Mexico.

In front of the museum is a reproduction of a Toltec ball court, and the entrance to the museum is a coffin-shaped door. Light filters in through translucent onyx slabs, supplemented by lights inside niches and wall cases containing the exhibits. Twenty-three display rooms are arranged in chronological order, with thousands of the pieces stashed on the shelves, tucked away in corners, and peeking out of glass cases.

Upstairs, in a replica of Rivera's studio, you'll find the original sketches for some of his murals and two in-progress canvases. There's a photo of his first sketch (of a train), done at the age of 3, plus a color photograph of him at work later in life. Rivera (1886–1957) studied in Europe for 15 years and spent much of his life as a devoted Marxist. Yet he came through political scrapes and personal tragedies with no apparent diminution of creative energy. A plaque in the museum proclaims him "a man of genius who is among the greatest painters of all time."

Calle Museo 150, Col. San Pedro Tepetapa. ✆ **55/5617-3797.** mudrivera@interflow.com.mx. Admission $2. Tues–Sun 10am–6pm. Metro: Taxqueña; then *tren ligero* (light train) to Xotepingo. Go west on Xotepingo (Museo) 3 short blocks; cross División del Norte and go another 6 blocks.

**Museo de Arte Alvar y Carmen T. Carrillo Gil** Sometimes called the Museo de la Esquina (Corner Museum)—it's at a major intersection on Avenida de la Revolución—this modern gallery features a collection that includes rooms dedicated to the works of José Clemente Orozco (1883–1949), Diego Rivera (1886–1957), David Alfaro Siqueiros (1896–1974), and other Mexican painters.

Revolución 1608 (at Desierto de los Leones). ✆ **55/5550-3983.** Admission $1.50; free admission Sun. Tues–Sun 10am–6pm. No Metro service.

**Museo Dolores Olmedo Patiño** ★ Art collector and philanthropist Olmedo left her former home, the grand Hacienda La Noria, as a museum featuring the works of her friend Diego Rivera. At least 137 of his works are displayed here, including his portrait of Olmedo, 25 paintings of Frida Kahlo, and 37 creations of Angelina Beloff (Rivera's first wife), many of them drawings and engravings. Besides the paintings, there are fine pre-Hispanic pieces on display, colonial furniture and other hacienda artifacts, and a collection of folk art. An excellent gift shop and a cafeteria are on the premises. Olmeda was the executor of both the Rivera and Kahlo estates.

Av. México 5843, Col. La Noria, Xochimilco. ✆ **55/5555-1016** or 55/5555-0891. Fax 55/5555-1642. www.art-history.mx/mdop/. Admission $2. Tues–Sun 10am–6pm. Metro: Taxqueña; then *tren ligero* (light train) to Xochimilco. Get off at the La Noria station.

**Museo Estudio Diego Rivera** Here, in the studio designed and built by Juan O'Gorman in 1928, Rivera drew sketches for his wonderful murals and painted smaller works. He died here in 1957. Now a museum, the Rivera studio holds some of the artist's personal effects and mementos, and there are changing exhibits relating to his life and work. (Don't confuse Rivera's studio with his museum, called the Anahuacalli; see above.)

Calle Diego Rivera and Av. Altavista (across from San Angel Inn), Col. San Angel. ✆ **55/5616-0996.** Admission $1; free admission Sun. Tues–Sun 10am–6pm. No Metro service. By taxi, go up Insurgentes Sur to Altavista and make a left.

**Museo Leon Trotsky** During Lenin's last days, Stalin and Trotsky fought a silent battle for leadership of the Communist Party in the Soviet Union. Trotsky stuck to ideology, while Stalin took control of the party mechanism. Stalin won, and Trotsky was exiled to continue his ideological struggle elsewhere. Invited by Diego Rivera, he settled here on the outskirts of Mexico City to continue his work and writing on political topics and Communist ideology. His ideas clashed with those of Stalin in many respects, and Stalin, wanting no opposition or dissension in world Communist ranks, set out to have Trotsky assassinated. A first attempt failed, but it served as a warning to Trotsky, his wife, Natalia, and their household. The house became a veritable fortress, with watchtowers, thick steel doors, and round-the-clock guards, several of whom were Americans who sympathized with Trotsky's philosophies. Finally, a man thought to have been paid, cajoled, or blackmailed by Stalin, directly or indirectly, was able to gain admittance to the house by posing as a friend of Trotsky's and of his political views. On August 20, 1940, he put an ice pick into the philosopher's head. The assailant was caught, and Trotsky died of his wounds shortly afterward. Because Trotsky and Rivera had previously had a falling out, both Rivera and Kahlo were suspects for a short time.

The home's furnishings are much more meager than you might expect for such a famous person. You can visit Natalia's study, the communal dining room, and Trotsky's study—with worksheets, newspaper clippings, books, and cylindrical wax dictating records still spread around—as well as the fortress-like bedroom. Closets still hold the couple's personal clothing. Some of the walls bear the bullet holes left from the first attempt on his life. Trotsky's tomb, designed by Juan O'Gorman, is in the garden. You will be able to recognize this house by the brick riflemen's watchtowers on top of the high stone walls.

Av. Río Churubusco 410 (between Gómez Farías and Morelos), Col. Del Carmen Coyoacán. ✆ **55/5658-8732** or 55/5554-0687. Admission $1.50. Tues–Sun 10am–5pm. Metro: Coyoacán. From Plaza Hidalgo, go east on Hidalgo 3 blocks to Morelos, then north 8 blocks to Churubusco. House is on the left.

## OUTDOOR ART/PLAZAS

**Plaza de las Tres Culturas** Three cultures converge here: Aztec, Spanish, and contemporary Mexican. Surrounded by modern office and apartment buildings are large remains of the **Aztec city of Tlatelolco,** site of the last battle of the Conquest of Mexico. Off to one side is the **Church of Santiago.** During the Aztec Empire, Tlatelolco was on the edge of Lake Texcoco, linked to the Aztec capital by a causeway. Bernal Díaz de Castillo, in his *True Story of the Conquest of New Spain,* described the roar from the dazzling market there, and the incredible scene after the last battle of the Conquest in Tlatelolco on August 13, 1521—the dead bodies were piled so deep that walking there was impossible. That night determined the fate of the country and completed the Spanish takeover of Mexico. It was also here, in October 1968, that government troops fired on thousands of protesters who had filled the square, killing hundreds—a dark, unforgotten day.

View the pyramidal remains from raised walkways over the site. The church, off to one side, was built in the 16th century entirely of volcanic stone. The interior has been tastefully restored, preserving little patches of fresco in stark-white plaster walls, with a few deep-blue stained-glass windows and an unadorned stone altar. Sunday is a good day to combine a visit here with one to the Lagunilla street market (for details, see "Shopping," later in this chapter), which is within walking distance, south across Reforma.

Lázaro Cárdenas and Flores Magón, Centro Histórico. Metro: Tlatelolco.

**Plaza de Santo Domingo** This fascinating plaza—and wonderful slice of Mexican life—has arcades on one side, a Dominican church on another. A statue of the Corregidora of Querétaro, Josefa Ortiz de Domínguez, dominates the plaza. The plaza is best known for the scribes who compose and type letters for clients unable to do so for themselves. Years ago, it was full of professional writers clacking away on ancient typewriters, and a few still ply their trade on ancient electric typewriters among a proliferation of small print shops and presses. Emperor Cuauhtémoc's palace once occupied this land, before Dominicans built their monastery here.

Bordered by República de Venezuela, República de Brazil, República de Cuba, and Palma sts., Centro Histórico. Metro: Tacuba.

**Plaza Tolsá and El Caballito** This plaza is known for the huge equestrian statue in front of the Museo Nacional de Arte. The gallant statue of King Carlos IV of Spain (1788–1808) atop a high-stepping horse was the work of Mexican sculptor Manuel Tolsá. Mexicans call the statue "El Caballito" ("The Little Horse"), and the name reveals a lot: They prefer not to mention Carlos, who was king shortly before the Mexican independence movement began in 1810. Despite the subject's unpopularity, the statue remains one of the largest and most finely crafted equestrian statues in the world. Erected first in the *zócalo,* it was moved in 1852 to a traffic circle in the Paseo de la Reforma. A few years ago El Caballito was shifted to this more dignified and appropriate position in front of the museum opposite the handsome **Palacio de Minería.**

Correo Mayor and Tacuba, near La Alameda, Centro Histórico. Metro: Bellas Artes.

**Zócalo** ★★ Every Spanish colonial city in North America was laid out according to a textbook plan, with a plaza at the center surrounded by a church, government buildings, and military headquarters. Because Mexico City was the capital of New Spain, its *zócalo* is one of the grandest, graced on all sides by stately 17th-century buildings.

*Zócalo* actually means "pedestal" or "plinth." A grand monument to Mexico's independence was planned and the pedestal built, but the project was never completed. Nevertheless, the pedestal became a landmark for visitors, and soon everyone was calling the square the *zócalo,* even after the pedestal was removed. (Its official name, which you will rarely hear, is Plaza de la Constitución.) It covers almost 10 acres and is bounded on the north by Cinco de Mayo, on the east by Piño Suárez, on the south by 16 de Septiembre, and on the west by Nacional Monte de Piedad. The downtown district, especially north of the Templo Mayor, one of the oldest archaeological sites in the city, has suffered long neglect, but a restoration project is slowly renewing much of its colonial charm. Occupying the entire east side of the *zócalo* is the majestic red tezontle stone Palacio National, seat of the Mexican national government.

Juárez and 20 de Noviembre, Centro Histórico. Metro: Zócalo.

## PARKS & GARDENS

**Alameda Park** Today the lovely tree-filled Alameda Park attracts pedestrians, cotton-candy vendors, strollers, lovers, and organ grinders. Long ago, the site was an Aztec marketplace. When the conquistadors took over in the mid-1500s, heretics were burned at the stake here under the Spanish Inquisition. In 1592, the governor of New Spain, Viceroy Luis de Velasco, converted it to a public park. Within the park, known as La Alameda, is the **Juárez Monument,** sometimes called the ***Hemiciclo*** (hemicycle or half-circle), facing Avenida Juárez. Enthroned as the hero he was, Juárez assumes his proper place here in the pantheon of Mexican patriots. European (particularly French) sculptors created most of the other statuary in the park in the late 19th and early 20th centuries.

Av. Juárez and Lázaro Cárdenas. Free admission. Metro: Belles Artes.

**Chapultepec Park** One of the biggest city parks in the world, 551-acre Chapultepec Park is more than a playground. Besides accommodating picnickers on worn-away grass under centuries-old trees, it has canoes on the lake; jogging and bridle paths; vendors selling balloons, souvenirs, and food; a miniature train; an auditorium; and **Los Pinos,** home of Mexico's president. The park is also home to the **City Zoo** and **La Feria** amusement park. Most important for tourists, it contains a number of interesting museums, including the Museo Nacional de Antropología.

Between Paseo de la Reforma, Circuito Interior, and Av. Constituyentes. Free admission. Daily 5am–5pm. Metro: Chapultepec.

**Floating Gardens of Xochimilco** ★ In the southern neighborhood of Xochimilco are more than 80km (50 miles) of canals known as the "Floating Gardens." They consist of two main parts. The first is the tourism-oriented area in the historic center of town, where colorful boats take loads of tourists (some of them picnicking along the way) through a portion of the canals. Lively music, some of it provided by mariachi and trio musicians for hire who board the boats, is a staple. Historic buildings, restaurants, souvenir stands, curio sellers, and boat vendors border this area. The other section, north of the center of town, is the ecology-oriented area: Parque Natural Xochimilco. On Sunday, Xochimilco (especially the tourist-oriented section) is jammed; on weekdays, it's nearly deserted. As you enter Xochimilco proper, you will see many places to board boats. Should you miss them, however, turn along Madero and follow signs that say LOS EMBARCADEROS (the piers).

Southern neighborhood of Xochimilco. © **55/5673-7890.** Admission to area $1.50. Boat rides $16.50 per boat, which 8–10 people may share. Mon–Fri 9am–6pm; Sat–Sun 9:30am–5pm.

### BEST VIEW

**La Torre Latinoamericana** From the observation deck on the 42nd floor of this soaring skyscraper, the Latin American Tower, you can take in fabulous views of the whole city. Buy a ticket for the deck at the booth as you approach the elevators. Tokens for the telescope are on sale here, too. You then take an elevator to the 37th floor, cross the hall, and take another elevator to the 42nd floor. An employee will ask for your ticket as you get off.

Madero and Lázaro Cárdenas, Centro Histórico. © **55/5521-0844.** Admission $3.50 adults, $3 children. Daily 9:30am–11pm. Metro: Bellas Artes.

## 6 Organized Tours

Mexico City is a great place for looking around on your own, and in general this is the easiest and least expensive way to see whatever you like. If your time is limited, you may want to acclimate yourself quickly by taking a tour or two.

Among the noncommercial offerings are **free guided tours** sponsored by the **Mexico City Historical Center** (© **55/5510-4737,** ext. 1499), which is housed in the 18th-century home of Don Manuel de Heras y Soto, at Donceles and República de Chile. Groups meet each Sunday at 10:45am at a central gathering place for that day's tour, which varies from week to week. These tours might explore a historic downtown street, cafes and theaters, cemeteries, or the

### Tips Tours: The Downside

Many readers have written to say they were unhappy with the sightseeing tours of this or that company. The reasons are myriad: The tour was too rushed; the guide knew nothing and made up stories about the sights; the tour group spent most of its time in a handcrafts shop (chosen by the tour company) rather than seeing the sights. Do tour companies get a kickback from souvenir shops? Of course! If you meet someone who has recently taken a guided tour and liked it, go with the same company. Otherwise, you might do well to see the sights on your own, following the detailed information in this book. Your hotel can arrange a private car by the hour or day—generally with a driver who is also an English-speaking guide. This can be less expensive or only slightly more than the cost of an organized tour, with greater flexibility and personalized service.

colonial churches of Xochimilco. Most tours, which last about 2 hours, are in Spanish; as many as 300 people may be divided among 10 guides. Visitors can ask a day in advance for a guide who speaks their language. Since the center's phone is almost always busy, you'll have to visit the office, in the far back of the building, on the right and up a spiral staircase, to get a list of upcoming tours and gathering locations. Office hours are Monday through Friday from 9am to 3pm and 6 to 9pm.

If you're a guest of the **Hotel Four Seasons,** be sure to take advantage of its excellent weekend cultural tours, led by noted experts. These highly recommendable tours are available only to Four Seasons guests and are included in the price of the room.

The many commercial tours include a 4-hour city tour of such sites as the **Metropolitan Cathedral,** the **Nacional Palace,** and **Chapultepec Park and Castle;** a longer tour to the **Shrine of Guadalupe** and nearby pyramids at **Teotihuacán;** and the Sunday tour that begins with the **Ballet Folklórico,** moves on to the **Floating Gardens of Xochimilco,** and may or may not include lunch and the afternoon bullfights. Almost as popular are 1-day and overnight tours to Puebla, Cuernavaca, Taxco, and Acapulco. There are also several nightclub tours.

## 7 Shopping

From handcrafts to the finest in designer apparel, Mexico City, like any major metropolitan area, is a marvelous place for shopping. From malls to *mercados,* numerous places display fascinating native products and sophisticated goods.

The two best districts for browsing are on and off **Avenida Presidente Masaryk,** in Polanco, and the **Zona Rosa.** Polanco's shops include Burberrys of London, Christian Dior, Gianni Versace, Gucci, Hermès, Luis Vuitton, Giorgio Armani, and Cartier. Think New York's Fifth Avenue or Chicago's Mag Mile, and you'll get the picture. The 12 square blocks at the heart of the Zona Rosa are home to antiques shops, boutiques, art galleries, silver shops, and fine jewelers. A few unique shops deserve particular mention.

Several government-run shops and a few excellent private shops have exceptionally good collections of Mexico's arts and crafts. Here's the rundown on the best places to shop, from small, selective crafts shops to vast general markets.

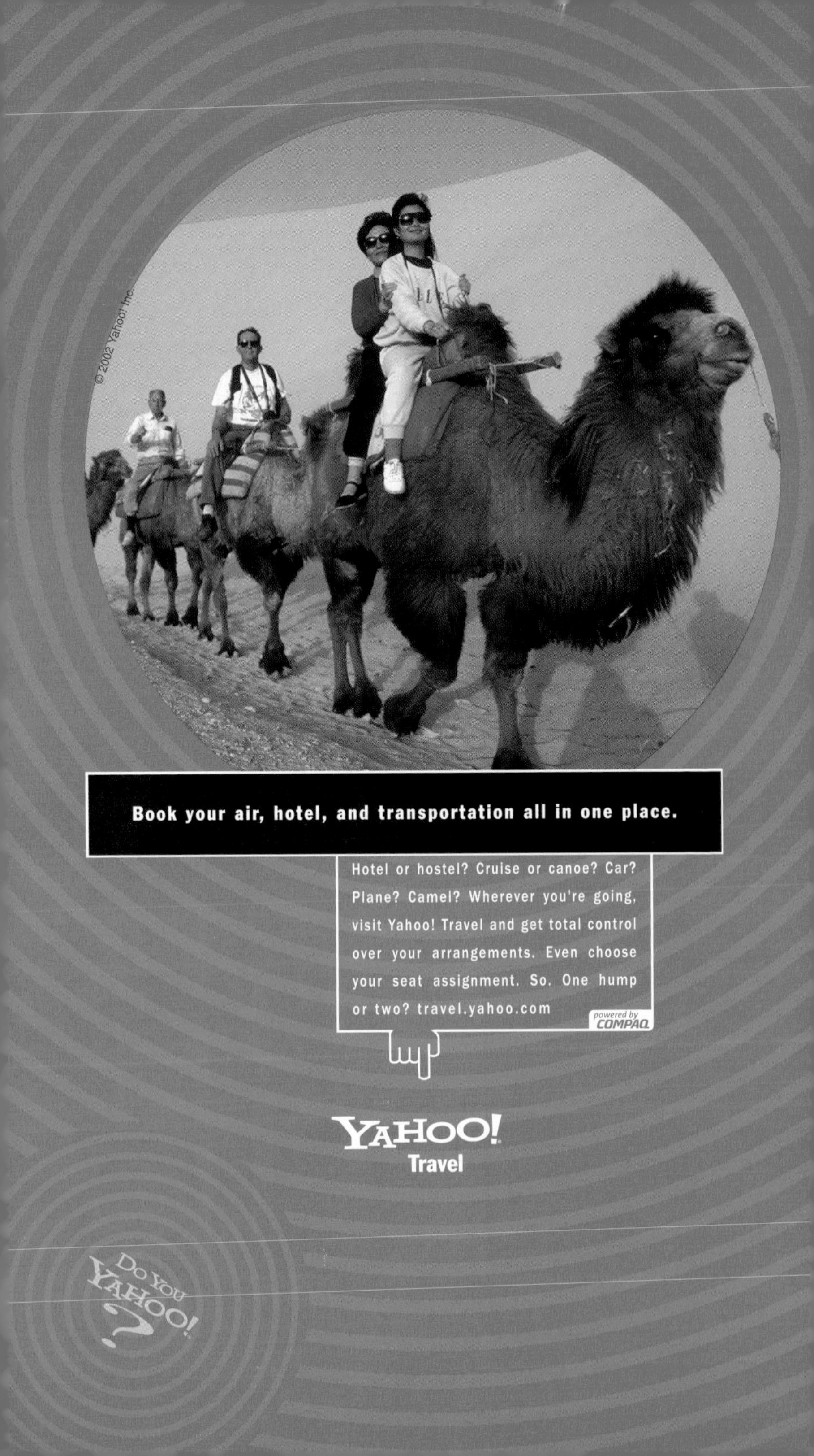
© 2002 Yahoo! Inc.
Book your air, hotel, and transportation all in one place.
Hotel or hostel? Cruise or canoe? Car? Plane? Camel? Wherever you're going, visit Yahoo! Travel and get total control over your arrangements. Even choose your seat assignment. So. One hump or two? travel.yahoo.com
powered by COMPAQ
YAHOO!
Travel
Do You Yahoo!?

## SHOPPING A TO Z

### ART

**Artesanos de México** This shop in the Zona Rosa sells crafts from all over Mexico. It isn't large, but it's a good place to see handsome displays of pottery, textiles, and original art. It's open Monday through Friday from 11am to 7pm. Londres 117, Zona Rosa. ✆ **55/5514-2025** or 55/5514-7455. AE. Metro: Insurgentes.

**Arvil. Galeria de Arte y Libros de Arte** Collectible works of art—auction-quality pieces—by Mexican masters. It's open Monday through Friday from 10am to 2:30pm and 4 to 7pm and Saturday from 10am to 3pm. Cerrada de Hamburgo 7 and 9, Reforma/Zona Rosa. ✆ **55/5207-2647.** Fax 55/5207-3994. By appointment only. AE, MC, V. Metro: Insurgentes.

**Exposición Nacional de Arte Popular (FONART)** This store is usually loaded with crafts: papier-mâché figurines, textiles, earthenware, colorful candelabra, hand-carved wooden masks, straw goods, beads, bangles, and glass. The Fonda Nacional para el Fomento de las Artes (FONART), a government organization that helps village craftspeople, operates the store. It's open daily from 10am to 7pm. Juárez 89, Centro Histórico. ✆ **55/5521-0171.** MC, V. Metro: Hidalgo or Juárez.

**FONART** Another branch of the government-operated store (see above) is in the heart of the Zona Rosa. Although it's in small, narrow, upstairs quarters, it is chock-full of folk art, much of it not duplicated at the larger store on Juárez. It's open Monday through Saturday from 10am to 7pm. Londres 136A, Zona Rosa. ✆ **55/5598-5552** or 55/5598-1666. MC, V. Metro: Insurgentes.

**López Quiroga Gallery** Auction-quality works of art by contemporary Latin American masters, including Toledo, Tamayo, and Siqueiros. It's open Monday through Friday from 10am to 8pm and Saturday from 10am to 2pm. Aristoteles 169, Polanco. ✆ **55/5280-1247.** Fax 55/5280-3960. www.arte-mexico.com. AE, DC, MC, V. No Metro station.

---

### *Kids* A Mexico City Just for Kids

The **Ciudad de los Niños** (City of Children) is a truly innovative attraction for youthful visitors to Mexico City. It is a comprehensive fantasy village where children interact as part of a "virtual" economy and have the chance to experience adult life—complete with working, then choosing whether to spend or save their earnings. They first board an American Airlines replica plane for the "trip" to Ciudad de los Niños. When they "arrive," they enter the airport, pass through immigration, and receive some "money." They can choose to put this in the bank, or spend it at various community establishments, which include restaurants, a gas station, a beauty shop, a racetrack, and other service providers. They can also choose to "work" at any of the above places and earn more "Niño money." Ciudad de los Niños is in the Santa Fé shopping mall, Vasco de Quiroga 3800 (✆ **55/5251-5006**), next to the Liverpool store. It's open Monday through Friday 9am to 7pm, and Saturday and Sunday from 10am to 3pm and 4 to 9pm. Admission is $6 for children 2 to 3 years old and adults, $12 for children ages 4 to 16. Free for travelers with disabilities and seniors. Visa and MasterCard are accepted. *Note:* It's mostly Spanish-speaking, but go anyway—children seem to quickly move beyond any language barriers.

**O.M.R. Gallery** This gallery has earned a reputation for discovering and introducing emerging talents and new artists from Latin America. It's open Monday through Friday from 10am to 3pm and 4 to 7pm, Saturday from 10am to 2pm. Plaza Río de Janeiro 54. Plaza Río de Janeiro, Col. Roma. © **55/5511-1179**, 55/5525-3095, or 55/5207-1080. Fax 55/5533-4244. AE, MC, V. Metro: Insurgentes.

**Victor Artes Populares Mexicanas** Owned by the Fosado family, which has been in the folk art business for more than 50 years, Victor, near La Alameda, is a shop for serious buyers and art collectors. The Fosados buy most of their crafts from Indian villages near and far, and supply various exhibits with native crafts. It's open Monday through Friday from 12:30 to 7pm. Fco. I. Madero 8 Y 10, 2nd floor, Room 305, Centro Histórico. © **55/5512-1263.** AE, MC, V. Metro: Bellas Artes or Allende.

## GLASS

**Avalos Brothers** *Finds* For more than 100 years, blown glass has come from this run-down location in the old section of town. You can watch men and women scurry around with red-hot glass in various stages of shaping until it cools. A showroom to the left of the entrance holds shelves full of glass objects—pitchers, vases, plates, glasses, flowers, cream and sugar containers, and the like—in different colors. Few tourists seem to find their way here, but among locals this is the store of choice for selection and price. It is near the La Merced market where Carretones dead-ends into Tapacio, a short block south of San Pablo. It's open Monday through Friday from 9am to 5:30pm and Saturday from 9am to 3pm. Carretones 5, Centro Histórico. © **55/5522-5311.** Fax 55/5522-6420. www.carretones.com.mx. Metro: La Merced.

## JEWELRY

Besides the shops mentioned below, dozens of jewelry stores and optical shops are on Madero from Motolinia to the *zócalo,* in the portals facing the National Palace. **Nacional Monte de Piedad/National Pawn Shop,** also opposite the National Palace, has an enormous jewelry selection. The first Latin American branch of **Tiffany's** is on Avenida Masaryk in Polanco.

**Bazar del Centro** Located between La Alameda and the *zócalo,* this colonial-era building was the palace of the Counts of Miravale. Now it houses shops selling jewelry, precious stones, and silver. It's open Monday through Friday from 10am to 7pm and Saturday from 10am to 3pm. Isabel la Católica 30, Centro Histórico. No phone. Metro: Zócalo.

**Los Castillo** This Zona Rosa branch of the famous Taxco silversmith family houses some of their best work—pieces you won't see at their shop in Taxco, for example. Besides handsome silver jewelry, you'll find decorative bowls made of porcelain fused with silver, napkin rings, and furniture with silver and porcelain tops. It's open Monday through Friday from 10am to 7pm and Saturday from 10am to 3pm. Amberes 41, Col. Juárez, Zona Rosa. © **55/5511-6198** or 55/5511-8396. AE, MC, V. Metro: Insurgentes.

**Tane** Tucked in the Zona Rosa, this is the original store of one of Mexico's top silver designers, with branches only in the best hotels and shopping centers. The quantity of good-quality silver work is enormous, from jewelry to platters, pitchers, plates, cutlery, frames, candlesticks, and even the signature china, by Limoges. There are also branches in the Hotel Presidente Inter-Continental, in the Polanco and San Angel neighborhoods, and at the airport. It's open Monday through Friday from 10am to 7pm and Saturday from 11am to 2:30pm. Amberes 70, Reforma/Zona Rosa. ✆ **55/5510-9429.** AE, MC, V. Metro: Insurgentes.

## MARKETS

**Bazar del Sábado** *Moments* A festive and unique shopping experience, the Bazar Sábado is held (as its name indicates) only on Saturday. Located in an expensive colonial-era suburb of cobblestone streets, mansions, and parks a few kilometers south of the city, it's my top recommendation for passing a Saturday afternoon in Mexico City. The actual bazaar building is an elegant two-story mansion built around a courtyard.

The central area houses an excellent, authentic, hectic Mexican cafe where waiters hustle to serve tacos hot off the grill and frosty margaritas, plus *antojitos* and traditional main dishes like enchiladas. Marimba music plays in the background. Dozens of small rooms surrounding the courtyard serve as permanent stalls featuring original works of high-quality decorative art. You'll find blown glass, original fine jewelry, papier-mâché figures, masks, and embroidered clothing. The prices are on the high side, but the quality is equally high, and the designs are sophisticated. On adjacent plazas, hundreds of easel artists display their paintings, and surrounding homes abound with antiques, fine rugs, and hand-carved furniture for sale. Members of indigenous groups from Puebla and elsewhere bring their folk art—baskets, masks, pottery, textiles, and so on—to display in the parks. Restaurants (some in mansions) lining the streets play host to leisurely diners seated at umbrella-shaded tables. Plan to spend Saturday touring the attractions on the southern outskirts of the city. (See also "San Angel," under "Mexico City Neighborhoods in Brief," earlier in this chapter.) It's open Saturday from 9am to 6pm. Plaza de San Jacinto, San Angel.

**Centro Artesanal (Mercado de Curiosidades)** This rather modern building set back off a plaza consists of a number of stalls on two levels, selling everything from leather to tiles. They have some lovely silver jewelry and, as in most non-fixed-price stores, the asking price is high but the bargained result is often very reasonable. It's open Monday through Saturday from 10am to 5:30pm. Corner of Ayuntamiento and Dolores, Reforma North. Metro: Guerrero.

**Lagunilla Market** This is one of the most interesting and unusual markets in Mexico—but watch out for pickpockets. The best day is Sunday, when the Lagunilla becomes a colorful outdoor market filling the streets for blocks. Arrive around 9am. Vendors sell everything from axes to antiques. The two enclosed sections, on either side of a short street, Calle Juan Salvages, are open all week. They have different specialties: The one to the north is noted for clothes, *rebozos,* and blankets; the one to the south for tools, pottery, and household goods, such as attractive hanging copper lamps. This is also the area to find old and rare books, many at a ridiculously low cost, if you're willing to hunt and bargain. It's open daily from 9am to 5pm. 3 blocks east of Plaza de Garibaldi. Metro: Allende.

**Mercado de La Ciudadela** An excellent place to get authentic arts and crafts, this market has hundreds of stalls with arts and crafts from all over Mexico. It's across from the Escuela Nacional de Artes. A few places take credit cards. It's open daily 7am to 8pm. Balderas, between Reforma and Chapultepec. Metro: Balderas.

**Mercado Insurgentes** Mercado Insurgentes is a full-fledged crafts market tucked into the Zona Rosa. Because of its address, you might expect exorbitant prices, but vendors in the maze of stalls are eager to bargain, and good buys aren't hard to come by. It's open Monday through Saturday from 9am to 5:30pm. Londres between Florencia and Amberes, Zona Rosa. Metro: Insurgentes.

**Merced Market** This is the city's biggest market and among the most fascinating in the country; the intense activity and energy level are akin to those at Oaxaca's Abastos Market (see chapter 10). Officially it's housed in several modern buildings, but shops line the tidy, crowded streets all the way to the *zócalo.*

The first building is mainly for fruits and vegetables; the others contain about what you'd find if a department store joined forces with a discount warehouse—especially housewares, such as hand-held citrus juicers of all sizes, tinware, colorful spoons, and decorative oilcloth. The main market, east of the *zócalo* on Circunvalación between General Anaya and Adolfo Gurrión, is the place to stock up on Mexican spices. The easy 13-block walk from the *zócalo* zigzags past many shops. Or take the Metro; the stop is right outside the market. It's open Monday through Friday from 8am to 4pm, Saturday from 8am to 2pm. Circunvalación between General Anaya and Adolfo Gurrión. Metro: Merced.

**Nacional Monte de Piedad (National Pawn Shop)** This building used to be a pawn shop for all sorts of items, but now is reserved for the more profitable and saleable jewelry, with a couple of small rooms set aside for art and antiques. The building is on the site of Moctezuma's old Axayácatl palace, where the captive emperor was accidentally killed. Cortez used the site to build a viceregal palace. Pedro Romero de Terreros, the Count of Regla, an 18th-century silver magnate from Pachuca, donated the present building so that Mexican people could get low-interest loans. It's open Monday through Friday from 8:30am to 6pm, Saturday from 8:30am to 3pm. Corner of Monte de Piedad and Cinco de Mayo, Centro Histórico. Metro: Zócalo.

### MUSIC

**Sanborn's,** the popular Mexican variety store, with locations throughout Mexico City, carries an excellent selection of traditional and popular Mexican music in most of its larger stores. In addition, consider this specialty shop if you want to get into a deeper Mexican groove:

**Mercado de Discos** This may not be the most upscale-looking place, but the selection of national and international records and tapes is immense. It's 2 blocks from the Palacio de Bellas Artes. It's open Monday through Saturday from 10am to 8pm, Sunday from 11am to 7pm. Eje Central/Cárdenas 10 (between Madero and 16 de Septiembre), Centro Histórico. ✆ **55/5521-5853.** AE, DC, MC, V. Metro: Lázaro Cárdenas.

## 8 Mexico City After Dark

From mariachis, reggae, and opera to folkloric dance, classical ballet, and dinner shows, the choice of nighttime entertainment in Mexico City is enormous and sophisticated. Prices are much lower than those for comparable entertainment in most of the world's major cities. If you're willing to let *la vida mexicana* put on its own fascinating show for you, the bill will be even less. People-watching, cafe-sitting, music, and even a dozen mariachi bands all playing at once can be yours for next to nothing.

### THE ENTERTAINMENT SCENE

Mexico City has a very impressive club scene, with great places for dancing to music ranging from salsa to techno. In recent years, the **Historic Center** downtown has earned a reputation for having the broadest range of hip clubs

**Tips** **Crime at Night**

Make sure to leave valuables—especially watches and jewelry—at your hotel, and bring only the cash or credit cards you will need. While I list Metro stops, these should probably be used only for orientation; take only authorized *sitio* taxis (see the advisory "Important Taxi Safety Precautions in Mexico City," at the beginning of this chapter) or hire a private taxi by the hour and have an escort waiting for you as you sample the festivities of the city. Your hotel can help with these arrangements.

concentrated within walking distance, but the action is shifting back to the posh **Polanco** neighborhood. The **Zona Rosa** remains highly popular, and may be a more comfortable place for tourists. There the music tends to be more English-language than Spanish, and the masses of people strolling the sidewalks give the area a festive, friendly feel. Clubs and dinner-dance establishments tend to get going around 10 or 11pm and stay open until at least 3am. Many clubs operate only Thursday through Saturday.

**Fiesta nights** give visitors a chance to dine on typical Mexican food and see wonderful regional dancing, which seems always to be a treat no matter how many times you've seen it.

For lower-key nightlife and people-watching, outdoor cafes remain a popular option. Those on **Copenhague Street,** in the thick of the Zona Rosa scene, are among the liveliest, but with one or two exceptions, they have become more expensive than they are good. Another tradition is **Garibaldi Square,** where mariachis tune up and wait to be hired, but *be especially careful*—it's now known as much for its chronic street crime as for the music.

Hotel lobby bars tend to have live entertainment of the low-key type in the late afternoon and into the evening. The exception is the lobby bar at the Camino Real, which occasionally books top-name Latin American talent.

## THE PERFORMING ARTS

Mexico City's performing arts scene is among the finest and most comprehensive in the world. It includes opera, theater, ballet, and dance, along with concerts of symphonic, rock, and popular music.

For current information on cultural offerings, the best source is the Sunday edition of the English-language daily newspaper, the ***News,*** which has full listings of cultural events. It lists a limited number of events on other days. ***Donde, Tiempo Libre,*** and ***Concierge,*** free magazines found in hotels, are other good sources for locating the newest places, but they don't have complete listings of changing entertainment or current exhibits. **Ticketmaster** (✆ **55/5325-9000**) usually handles ticket sales for major performances.

The **Folkloric Ballet of Mexico** is perhaps the city's most renowned entertainment for visitors here, with its stunning presentation of regional dance.

*Note:* The majority of the theatrical performances at the Palacio de Bellas Artes and in other theaters around the city are presented in Spanish.

### FOLKLORIC BALLET

**Palacio de Bellas Artes** Although various groups perform around the city, the finest offering is at the Palacio de Bellas Artes, where the famed **Ballet Folklórico de México** performs twice a week. The Ballet Folklórico is a celebration of pre- and post-Hispanic dancing. A typical program includes Aztec ritual dances, agricultural dances from Jalisco, a fiesta in Veracruz, a wedding celebration—all linked with mariachis, marimba players, singers, and dancers.

Because the Bellas Artes books many other events—visits by foreign opera companies, for instance—the Ballet Folklórico occasionally moves. In that case, it usually appears in the **National Auditorium** in Chapultepec Park. Check at the Bellas Artes box office. The show is popular and tickets sell rapidly (especially to tour agencies at twice the cost). The box office is on the ground floor of the Bellas Artes, main entrance. Ballet Folklórico performances are on Sunday at 9:30am and Wednesday at 8:30pm.

The Fine Arts theater not only offers the finest in performing arts, but is architecturally worth a visit (see "Exploring Mexico City," earlier). *Note:* The U.S. State Department advisory specifies that taxis parked in front of this theater should be avoided. Eje Central and Av. Juárez, Centro Histórico–Alameda. ✆ **55/5512-2593,** ext. 152. www.cnca.gob.mx. Box office Mon–Sat 11am–7pm; Sun 8:30am–7pm. Tickets $20–$30. Metro: Bellas Artes.

## THE CLUB & MUSIC SCENE

This warning can't be reiterated enough: *Take an authorized* sitio *taxi or hire a car for transportation to all nightspots.* Metro stops are given merely as a point of reference.

### MARIACHIS

Mariachis play the music of Mexico. Although the songs they play may be familiar—ranging from traditional *boleros* to Mozart to the Beatles—their style and presentation are unique to Mexico. Known for their distinctive dress, strolling presentation, and mix of brass and guitars, they epitomize the romance and tradition of the country. They look a little like Mexican cowboys dressed up for a special occasion—tight trousers studded with silver buttons down the outside of the legs, elaborate cropped jackets, embroidered shirts with big bow ties, and grandiose sombrero hats. The dress dates to the French occupation of Mexico in the mid–19th century, as does the name. *Mariachi* is believed to be an adaptation of the French word for marriage; this was the type of music commonly played at weddings in the 15th and 16th centuries. The music is a derivative of *fandango,* which was the most popular dance music of the elite classes in 16th-century Spain. In Mexico, fandango became the peasant's song and dance.

In Mexico City, the mariachis make their headquarters around the **Plaza de Garibaldi,** 5 blocks north of the Palacio de Bellas Artes—up Avenida Lázaro Cárdenas, at Avenida República de Honduras. Mariachi players are everywhere in the plaza. At every corner, guitars are stacked together like rifles in an army camp. Young musicians strut proudly in their outfits, on the lookout for señoritas to impress. They play when they feel like it, when there's a good chance to

---

**Tips** **A Note of Caution in Garibaldi Square**

Plaza de Garibaldi, *both day and night,* is increasingly populated by thieves looking to separate tourists from their valuables. Although the police presence has increased, it's still best to visit by private taxi. If you go, don't take credit cards or excess money with you. Go with a crowd of friends rather than alone, or take a tour that includes Garibaldi.

---

gather some tips, or when someone orders a song—the going rate is $1.50 to $3.25 per song.

Should you want to enjoy mariachi music in a more tourist-friendly venue, I can recommend:

**Jorongo Bar** For wonderful mariachi and trio music in plush surroundings, make your way to the Hotel María Isabel Sheraton, facing the Angel Monument. This bar has enjoyed a reputation for mariachi music for decades—it's an institution. Nightly from 7pm to midnight, you can enjoy the smooth and joyous sounds for the price of a drink ($5–$9) plus cover. Hotel María Isabel Sheraton, Reforma 325, Zona Rosa. ✆ **55/5242-5555.** Cover $7. AE, MC, V. Metro: Insurgentes.

## CLUBS & MUSIC BARS

**AREA Bar and Terrace, at the Habita** *Finds* The rooftop bar of this oh-so-chic boutique hotel is also Mexico City's hottest nightspot. Umbrellas top tables, but otherwise, you're under the stars—and likely, surrounded by a few—in an ultra-trendy crowd sipping tequila cocktails and Cosmopolitans. If there's a chill in the air, the fireplace or veiled space heaters will take care of it. Decor is minimalist, of course, with a few white couches. Barstools set along the railing look out over the city. If you can make it past the bouncer and down the circular stairway to the lower terrace and pool area, you've really arrived—that's the super VIP section. Music is mainly Euro, chill, and house. It's open nightly from 7pm to 4am, and packed from Thursday to Saturday. Habita hotel, Av. Presidente Masaryk 201, Polanco. ✆ **55/5282-3100.** No reservations. No cover. AE, MC. V. Metro: Polanco.

**Bar Fly** *Finds* The talented house band—direct from Cuba—makes this small but stylish bar sizzle. By midnight the tiny dance floor is overflowing. It's on the second floor of an upscale shopping center. It's open Wednesday to Saturday from 8pm to 2am; live music starts at 11pm. Masaryk 393, Polanco. ✆ **55/5282-2906.** No cover; 2-drink minimum. AE, MC, V. Metro: Polanco.

**Bar León** This is an outstanding choice for dancing merengue and salsa, with live groups frequently featured. It's open Monday through Saturday from 9pm to 3am. Brasil 5, Centro Histórico. ✆ **55/5510-3093.** Cover $5.50–$22.50. MC, V. Metro: Zócalo.

**Casa de Paquita la del Barrio** This nightclub features its namesake and star performer, Paquita la del Barrio, famous for her resonant voice, interpretation of traditional ballads, and feminist songs that bear witness to the macho attitude in Mexico. Paquita takes the stage each evening at 7:30, 9, and 11pm, solo or with other performers. This is a top choice for rousing Mexican music. It's open Thursday through Saturday from 3pm to 3am. Zarco 202, Col. Guerrero. ✆ **55/5583-8131.** Cover $5 and up. AE, MC, V. Metro: Guerrero.

**La Boom** This popular disco and dance club features mostly techno, with a dose of Mexican hip-hop added to the mix. It's open Wednesday through Saturday from 11pm to 4am. Rodolfo Gaona 3, Col. Lomas de Sotelo, Chapultepec/Polanco. ✆ **55/5580-6473.** www.laboom.com.mx. Cover $18; additional charge for concert performances. No credit cards. Metro: Toréo.

**La Llorona** On weekends there's often a line out the door and down the street at this trendy downtown club, where the cover charge entitles you to open bar service. You'll hear recorded techno, hip-hop, disco, and rock—with an emphasis on danceability. It's in an elegant 18th-century building. It's open Friday and Saturday from 10pm to 3:30am. Mesones 87, Centro Histórico. ✆ **55/5709-8361.** Cover $15 men, $3 women. AE, DC, MC, V. Metro: Zócalo.

**Luna Café** This bar and dance club is mostly noted for its location and view—it's between the terraces of the Majestic Hotel and Grand Hotel, facing the *zócalo*. It sports classical Mexican decor, has an ample dance floor, and serves a full menu. It's open Wednesday through Saturday from 9pm to 1am. Plaza Constitución (zócalo) 13, Centro Histórico. No phone. No cover. MC, V. Metro: Zócalo.

**Salon Tropicana** This dance club and bar features Mexican romantic, mariachi, and salsa music. It's open Tuesday through Sunday from 7:30pm to 5am. Eje Centro Lázaro Cárdenas 43, Centro Histórico. ✆ **55/5529-7316.** Cover $4. AE, DC, MC, V. Metro: Salto del Agua, Bellas Artes.

**Tropicoso** Transport yourself to the tropics! This dance club features hot rhythms for dancing to salsa, marimba, merengue, and other Afro-Caribbean beats. It also offers an excellent snack menu. It's open Wednesday through Saturday from 10pm to dawn. Paseo de la Reforma 169, Col. Guerrero. ✆ **55/5529-3495.** Cover $11.50; higher for special events. MC, V. Metro: Guerrero.

## BARS

**Bar Museo Frida** Capitalizing on the popularity of the Mexican artist, this bar allows you to indulge in Frida fantasies over a premium tequila or cold beer. It boasts a great location and wonderful ambience for Frida fans. It's open Monday through Thursday from 2pm to 2am, Friday from 2pm to 3am, and Saturday from 9pm to 3am. Hamburgo 32, Col. Juárez, Reforma/Zona Rosa. ✆ **55/5511-8353.** No cover. AE, DC, MC, V. Metro: Insurgentes.

**Caviar Bar** While guests enjoy light meals and drinks in this stylish hotel's lobby bar, a string quartet plays in the evening. It's elegant and wonderfully soothing. It's open daily from noon to 12:45am. Hotel Marquís Reforma, Reforma 465, Col. Cuauhtémoc. ✆ **55/5229-1200.** No cover. AE, DC, MC, V. Metro: Insurgentes.

**El Estribo** This small but swank bar serves premium tequilas, and a lot of 'em—some 480 in all, including very rare and collectible tequilas. Before you head there with a plan to try them all, you should know that nearly a third are so rare they're not even for sale. El Estribo, which occupies a corner of the elegant 16th-century mansion La Hacienda de los Morales, opened in 1995. As is the case with most of the moderate and finer tequilas sold in Mexico, the vast majority are fully distilled from blue agave (look for the wording "100% Agave Azul"). This denotes pure, high-quality tequila, not the inexpensive blend (like Cuervo Gold) that most U.S. consumers are used to. This is the perfect place to sample smooth, complex aged *reposado* and *añejo* tequilas—Mexico's answer to fine single-malt whisky. You can try some of the house specialties, including the tequila Estribo (with apple juice, cassis, and cream), or a perfect margarita. It's open daily from 1pm to 1am. La Hacienda de los Morales, Vazquez de Mella 525, Col. del Bosque, Cp. 11510 (Chapultepec). ✆ **55/5281-4554.** www.haciendalosmorales.com. No cover. AE, MC, V.

**La Casa de las Sirenas** This bar serves 146 types of tequila—one of the widest selections available anywhere—in a stylish atmosphere. Although it also serves food, it's best known for its bar crowd and ambience. It becomes a popular club, playing recorded rock music, Thursday through Saturday evenings. It's in a 17th-century colonial building, with a courtyard filled with flowering plants and trees, almost in front of the Templo Mayor in the Historic Centro. It's open Monday to Saturday from 8am to 11pm, Sunday from 8am to 6pm. Guatemala 32, Centro Histórico, behind the cathedral. ✆ **55/5704-3345** or 55/5704-3225. www.alacarta.com.mx/sirenas/. No cover. AE, MC, V. Metro: Zócalo.

**La Nueva Opera Bar** La Opera has been the classic cantina in Mexico City since 1870, with a magnificent bar. It's opulent in atmosphere and rich in historic significance. (See "Cantinas" under "Where to Dine," earlier). It's open Monday through Saturday from 1pm to midnight, Sunday (appetizer menu only) from 1 to 6pm. Cinco de Mayo 10, Centro Histórico. ✆ **55/5512-8959.** No cover. AE, MC, V. Metro: Bellas Artes.

**Museo El Bar** This is an elegant atmosphere for enjoying a cocktail, cognac, or premium tequila while listening to recorded Nuevo Mexican rock and Latin jazz. It has long hallways with connecting passages and small intimate rooms with chandeliers that blink to the beat of the music. It's open Thursday through Saturday from 10pm to 3am. Madero 6, 1st floor, Centro Histórico. ✆ **55/5510-4020.** No cover. MC, V. Metro: Zócalo.

### STRIP CLUBS

**The Men's Club Mexico City** Here you will find entertainment for men, including erotic shows and private dancing. Special parties are also featured; call for details. It's open Monday through Friday from 2pm to 2am, Saturday from 9:30pm to 2am. Varsovia 54, Col. Juárez, Zona Rosa. ✆ **55/5533-2224.** www.mensclub.com.mx. Cover $18 Mon–Tues and Thurs–Sat; $24 Wed (package includes buffet and national wine from 2–5pm). AE, MC, V. Metro: Insurgentes.

## 9 A Side Trip to the Pyramids of San Juan Teotihuacán ★★★

48km (30 miles) NE of Mexico City

The ruins of Teotihuacán are among the most remarkable in Mexico—indeed, they are among the most important ruins in the world. Mystery envelops this former city of 200,000; although it was the epicenter of culture and commerce for ancient Mesoamerica, its inhabitants vanished without a trace. *Teotihuacán* (pronounced Teh-oh-tee-wa-*khan*) means "place where gods were born," reflecting the Aztec belief that the gods created the universe here.

Occupation of the area began around 500 B.C., but it wasn't until after 100 B.C. that construction of the enormous Pyramid of the Sun commenced. Teotihuacán's rise coincided with the classical Romans' building of their great monuments, and with the beginning of cultures in Mexico's Yucatán Peninsula, Oaxaca, and Puebla. Teotihuacán's magnificent pyramids and palaces covered 31 square km (12 sq. miles). At its zenith around A.D. 500, the city counted more inhabitants than in contemporary Rome. Through trade and other contact, Teotihuacán's influence was known in other parts of Mexico and as far south as the Yucatán and Guatemala. Still, little is known about the city's inhabitants: what language they spoke, where they came from, or why they abandoned the place around A.D. 700. It is known, however, that at the beginning of the 1st century A.D., the Xitle volcano erupted near Cuicuilco (south of Mexico City) and decimated that city, which was the most prominent city of the time. Those inhabitants migrated to Teotihuacán. Scholars believe that Teotihuacán's decline, probably caused by overpopulation and depletion of natural resources, was gradual, perhaps occurring over a 250-year period. In the last years, it appears that the people were poorly nourished and that the city was deliberately burned.

Ongoing excavations have revealed something of the culture. According to archaeoastronomer John B. Carlson, the cult of the planet Venus that determined wars and human sacrifices elsewhere in Mesoamerica was prominent at Teotihuacán as well. (Archaeoastronomy is the study of the position of stars and planets in relation to archaeology.) Ceremonial rituals were timed with the appearance of Venus as the morning and evening star. The symbol of Venus at Teotihuacán (as at Cacaxtla, 80km/50 miles away, near Tlaxcala) appears as a star or half star with a full or half circle. Carlson also suggests the possibility that people from Cacaxtla conquered Teotihuacán, since name glyphs of conquered peoples at Cacaxtla show Teotihuacán-like pyramids. Numerous tombs with human remains (many of them either sacrificial inhabitants of the city or perhaps war captives) and objects of jewelry, pottery, and daily life have been uncovered along the foundations of buildings. It appears that the primary deity at Teotihuacán was a female, called "Great Goddess" for lack of any known name.

Today, what remains are the rough stone structures of the three pyramids and sacrificial altars, and some of the grand houses, all of which were once covered in stucco and painted with brilliant frescos (mainly in red). The Toltec, who rose in power after the city's decline, were fascinated with Teotihuacán and incorporated its symbols into their own cultural motifs. The Aztec, who followed the Toltec, were fascinated with the Toltec and with the ruins of Teotihuacán; they likewise adopted many of their symbols and motifs. For more information on Teotihuacán and its influence in Mesoamerica, see appendix A, "Mexico in Depth." Fascinating articles about the ruins have appeared in *National Geographic* (Dec 1995) and *Archeology* (Dec 1993). The murals of Teotihuacán are the focus of an article in *Arqueología* (vol. 3, no. 16, 1995), published in Spanish in Mexico by the Instituto Nacional de Antropología e Historia.

## ESSENTIALS

**GETTING THERE & DEPARTING** **By Car** Driving to San Juan Teotihuacán on the toll Highway 85D or the free Highway 132D takes about an hour. Head north on Insurgentes to leave the city. Highway 132D passes through picturesque villages but can be slow due to the surfeit of trucks and buses. Highway 85D, the toll road, is less attractive but faster.

**By Private Sedan or Taxi** If you prefer to explore solo or want more or less time than an organized tour allows, consider hiring a private car and driver for the trip. They can easily be arranged through your hotel or at the Secretary of Tourism (SECTUR) information module in the Zona Rosa and cost about $11 to $15 an hour. The higher price is generally for a sedan with an English-speaking driver who doubles as a tour guide. Rates can also be negotiated for the entire day.

**By Bus** Buses leave daily every half hour (from 5am–10pm) from the Terminal Central de Autobuses del Norte; the trip takes 1 hour. When you reach the Terminal Norte, look for the AUTOBUSES SAHAGUN sign at the far northwest end, all the way down to the sign 8 ESPERA. Be sure to ask the driver where you should wait for returning buses, how frequently buses run, and especially the time of the last bus back.

**ORIENTATION** The ruins of Teotihuacán (© **55/5956-0052**) are open daily from 7am to 6pm. Admission is $2.50; free on Sunday. Using a video camera costs $3.

A small trolley-train that takes visitors from the entry booths to various stops within the site, including the Teotihuacán museum and cultural center, runs only on weekends and costs 60¢ per person.

Keep in mind that you're likely to be doing a great deal of walking, and perhaps some climbing, at an altitude of more than 2,121m (7,000 ft.) Take it slow, bring sunblock and drinking water, and during the summer be prepared for almost daily afternoon showers.

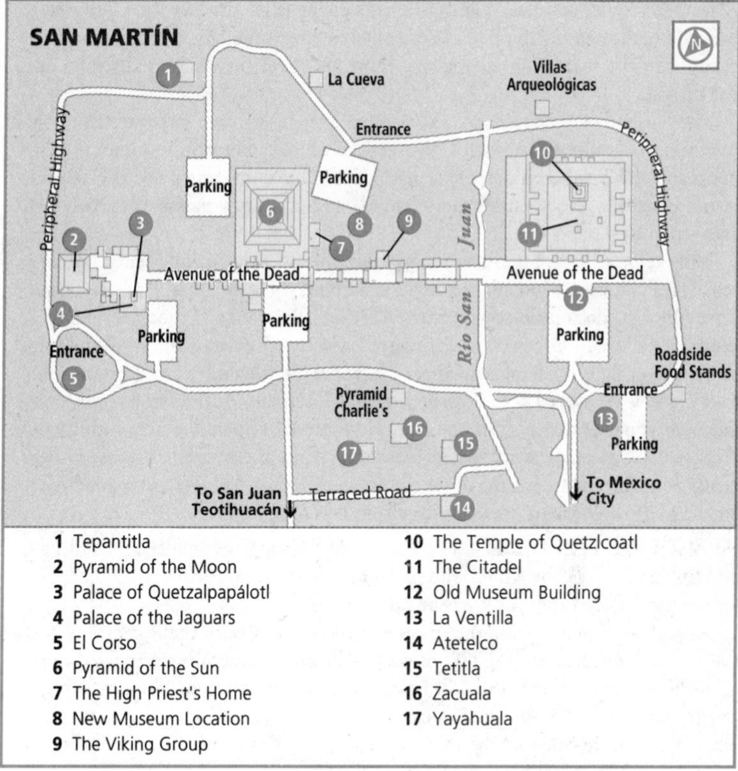


A good place to start is at the **Museo Teotihuacán** ★. This excellent museum is state-of-the-art, with interactive exhibits and, in one part, a glass floor on which visitors walk above mock-ups of the pyramids. On display are findings of recent digs, including several tombs, with skeletons wearing necklaces of human and simulated jawbones, and newly discovered sculptures.

**The Layout** The grand buildings of Teotihuacán were laid out in accordance with celestial movements. The front wall of the **Pyramid of the Sun** is exactly perpendicular to the point on the horizon where the sun sets twice annually (at the equinoxes). The rest of the ceremonial buildings were laid out at right angles to the Pyramid of the Sun.

The main thoroughfare, which archaeologists call the **Avenue of the Dead (Calzada de los Muertos),** runs roughly north-south. The **Pyramid of the Moon** is at the northern end, and the **Ciudadela (Citadel)** is on the southern part. The great street was several kilometers long in its prime, but only a kilometer or two has been uncovered and restored.

## EXPLORING THE TEOTIHUACAN ARCHAEOLOGICAL SITE

**THE CIUDADELA** The Ciudadela, or Citadel, was named by the Spaniards. This immense sunken square was not a fortress at all, although the impressive walls make it look like one. It was the grand setting for the Feathered Serpent Pyramid and the Temple of Quetzalcoatl. Scholars aren't certain that the Teotihuacán culture embraced the Quetzalcoatl deity so well known in the Toltec,

Aztec, and Maya cultures. The feathered serpent is featured in the Ciudadela, but whether it was worshipped as Quetzalcoatl or a similar god isn't known. Proceed down the steps into the massive court and head for the ruined temple in the middle.

The Temple of Quetzalcoatl was covered over by an even larger structure, a pyramid. As you walk toward the center of the Ciudadela's court, you'll approach the Feathered Serpent Pyramid. To the right, you'll see the reconstructed temple close behind the pyramid, with a narrow passage between the two structures.

Early temples were often covered by later ones in Mexico and Central America. The Pyramid of the Sun may have been built up in this way. Archaeologists have tunneled deep inside the Feathered Serpent Pyramid and found several ceremonially buried human remains, interred with precise detail and position, but as yet no royal personages. Drawings of how the building once looked show that every level was covered with faces of a feathered serpent. At the Temple of Quetzalcoatl, you'll notice at once the fine, large carved serpents' heads jutting out from collars of feathers carved in the stone walls; these weigh 4 tons. Other feathered serpents are carved in relief low on the walls. You can get a good idea of the glory of Mexico's ancient cities from this temple.

**AVENUE OF THE DEAD** The Avenue of the Dead got its strange and forbidding name from the Aztec, who mistook the little temples that line both sides of the avenue for tombs of kings or priests.

As you stroll north along the Avenue of the Dead toward the Pyramid of the Moon, look on the right for a bit of wall sheltered by a modern corrugated roof. Beneath the shelter, the wall still bears a painting of a jaguar. From this fragment, you might be able to reconstruct the breathtaking spectacle that must have been visible when all the paintings along the avenue were intact.

**PYRAMID OF THE SUN** The Pyramid of the Sun, on the east side of the Avenue of the Dead, is the third-largest pyramid in the world. The first and second are the Great Pyramid of Cholula, near Puebla, and the Pyramid of Cheops on the outskirts of Cairo, Egypt. Teotihuacán's Pyramid of the Sun is 221m (730 ft.) per side at its base—almost as large as Cheops. But at 64m (210 ft.) high, the Sun pyramid is only about half as high as its Egyptian rival. No matter—it's still the biggest restored pyramid in the Western Hemisphere, and an awesome sight. Although the Pyramid of the Sun was not built as a great king's tomb, it is built on top of a series of sacred caves, which aren't open to the public.

The first structure of the pyramid was probably built a century before Christ, and the temple that used to crown the pyramid was completed about 400 years later (A.D. 300). By the time the pyramid was discovered and restoration was begun (early in the 20th century), the temple had disappeared, and the pyramid was just a mass of rubble covered with bushes and trees.

It's a worthwhile 248-step climb to the top. The view is extraordinary and the sensation exhilarating.

**PYRAMID OF THE MOON** The Pyramid of the Moon faces a plaza at the northern end of the avenue. The plaza is surrounded by little temples and by the Palace of Quetzalpapalotl or Quetzal-Mariposa (Quetzal-Butterfly) on the left (west) side. You have about the same range of view from the top of the Pyramid of the Moon as you do from its larger neighbor, because the moon pyramid is built on higher ground. The perspective straight down the Avenue of the Dead is magnificent.

**PALACE OF QUETZALPAPALOTL** The Palace of Quetzalpapalotl lay in ruins until the 1960s, when restoration work began. Today, it reverberates with its former glory, as figures of Quetzal-Mariposa (a mythical, exotic bird-butterfly) appear painted on walls or carved in the pillars of the inner court.

Behind the Palace of Quetzalpapalotl is the Palace of the Jaguars, complete with murals showing jaguars and some frescoes.

## WHERE TO DINE

Vendors at the ruins sell drinks and snacks, but many visitors choose to carry a box lunch—almost any hotel or restaurant in the city can prepare one for you. A picnic in the shadow of this impressive ancient city allows extended time and perspective to take it all in. There is a **restaurant** in the new Museo Teotihuacán, which is the most convenient place for a snack or a meal.

**La Gruta** MEXICAN La Gruta is a huge, delightfully cool, natural grotto. You have the option of ordering a five-course set-price lunch or choosing your own combination—perhaps a plate of tostadas and a soft drink or beer—but its sole specialty is traditional Mexican food. It's a spirited place to end a day of exploration.

Peripheral Hwy. ✆ **55/5956-0127** or 55/5956-0104. www.lagruta.com.mx. Main courses $13–$19. AE, DISC, DC, MC, V. Daily 11am–7pm. Just northwest of Gate 5 on the Peripheral Hwy.

4

# Silver, Spas & Spiritual Centers: From Taxco to Tepoztlán

It may seem as if the small towns in this region of Mexico are trying to capitalize on recent trends in travel toward spas and self-exploration, but in reality, they've helped define them. From the restorative properties of thermal waters and earth-based spa treatments, to delving into the mystical and spiritual properties of gemstones and herbs, the treasures and knowledge in these towns have existed for years—and, in some cases, for centuries.

This is only a sampling of some of the more interesting towns south and west of Mexico City. They are fascinating in their diversity, history, and mystery, and make for a unique travel experience, either on their own or combined. They vary in character from mystical villages to sophisticated spa towns, with archaeological and colonial-era attractions in the mix. And with their proximity to Mexico City, the nation's busiest city and airport, all are within easy reach by private car or taxi—or by inexpensive bus—in under a few hours.

The legendary silver city of **Taxco,** on the road between Acapulco and Mexico City, is renowned for its museums, picturesque hillside colonial-era charm, and, of course, its silver shops. North of Taxco and southwest of Mexico City, over the mountains, are the venerable thermal spas at **Ixtapan de la Sal,** as well as their more modern counterparts in **Valle de Bravo.** Verdant **Cuernavaca,** known as the land of eternal spring, has gained a reputation for its exceptional spa facilities and its wealth of cultural and historic attractions. Finally, **Tepoztlán,** with its enigmatic charms and legendary pyramid, captivates the few travelers who find their way there.

## 1 Taxco: Cobblestones & Silver ★★

178km (111 miles) SW of Mexico City; 80km (50 miles) SW of Cuernavaca; 296km (185 miles) NE of Acapulco

In Mexico and around the world, the town of Taxco de Alarcón—most commonly known simply as Taxco (*tahs*-ko)—is synonymous with silver. Once here, you'll see that the town's geography and architecture are equally precious: Taxco sits at nearly 1,515m (5,000 ft.) on a hill among hills, and almost any point in the city offers fantastic views.

Hernán Cortez discovered Taxco as he combed the area for treasure, but its rich caches of silver weren't fully exploited for another 2 centuries. In 1751, the French prospector Joseph de la Borda commissioned the baroque Santa Prisca Church that dominates Taxco's *zócalo* (Plaza Borda) as a way of giving something back to the town.

The fact that Taxco has become Mexico's most renowned center for silver design, even though it now mines only a small amount of silver, is the work of an American, William Spratling. Spratling arrived in the late 1920s with the intention of writing a book. He soon noticed the skill of the local craftsmen and opened a workshop to produce handmade silver jewelry and tableware based on pre-Hispanic art, which he exported to the United States in bulk. The workshops flourished, and Taxco's reputation grew. Today, it is home to hundreds of silver shops.

The tiny one-man factories that line the cobbled streets all the way up into the hills supply most of Taxco's silverwork. "Bargains" are relative, but nowhere else will you find this combination of diversity, quality, and rock-bottom prices. Generally speaking, the larger shops that most obviously cater to a tourist trade will have the highest prices—but they may be the only ones to offer "that special something" you're looking for. For classic designs in jewelry or other silver items, shop around, and wander the back streets and smaller venues.

You can get an idea of what Taxco is like by spending an afternoon, but there's much more to this picturesque town of 87,000 than just the Plaza Borda and the shops surrounding it. Stay overnight, wander its steep cobblestone streets, and you'll discover little plazas, fine churches, and, of course, an abundance of silversmiths' shops.

The main part of town is relatively flat. It stretches up the hillside from the highway, and it's a steep but brief walk up. White VW minibuses, called *burritos,* make the circuit through and around town, picking up and dropping off passengers along the route, from about 7am until 9pm. These taxis are inexpensive (1 peso, or about 9¢), and you should use them even if you've arrived by car, because parking is practically impossible. Also, the streets are so narrow and steep that most visitors find them nerve-racking to navigate. Find a secured parking lot for your car, or leave it at your hotel, and forget about it until you leave.

*Warning:* Self-appointed guides will undoubtedly approach you in the *zócalo* (Plaza Borda) and offer their services—they get a cut (up to 25%) of all you buy in the shops they take you to. Before hiring a guide, ask to see his **Departamento de Turismo** credentials. The Department of Tourism office on the highway at the north end of town can recommend a licensed guide.

## ESSENTIALS

**GETTING THERE & DEPARTING** **By Car** From Mexico City, take Paseo de la Reforma to Chapultepec Park and merge with the Periférico, which will take you to Highway 95D on the south end of town. From the Periférico, take the Insurgentes exit and merge until you come to the sign for Cuernavaca/Tlalpan. Choose either CUERNAVACA CUOTA (toll) or CUERNAVACA LIBRE (free). Continue south around Cuernavaca to the Amacuzac interchange, and proceed straight ahead for Taxco. The drive from Mexico City takes about 3½ hours.

From Acapulco you have two options: Highway 95D is the toll road through Iguala to Taxco, or you can take the old two-lane road (95) that winds more slowly through villages; it's in good condition.

**By Bus** From Mexico City, buses depart from the Central de Autobuses del Sur station (Metro: Taxqueña) and take 2 to 3 hours, with frequent departures.

Taxco has two bus stations. Estrella de Oro buses arrive at their own station on the southern edge of town. Estrella Blanca service, including *Futura* executive-class buses, and Flecha Roja buses arrive at the station on the northeastern edge of town on Avenida Los Plateros (Ave. of the Silversmiths, formerly Av. Kennedy). Taxis to the *zócalo* cost around $1.

# Side Trips from Mexico City

To Querétaro
0
25 mi
0
25 km
Mountain
Ruins
MICHOACÁN
MEXICO
GUERRERO
Ruinas Tula
126
57D
55
55D
Presa Huapango
Villa del Carbon
Río Pearl
Atlacomulco
146
55D
To Guadalajara
15
55
Río Lerma
134
15
15
Zitacuaro
Ruinas Calixtlahuaca
Toluca
1
Valle de Bravo
Metepec
PARQUE NACIONAL DESIERTO DE LOS LEONES
PARQUE NACIONAL NEVADO DE TOLUCA
Avándaro
Nevado de Toluca (15,026')
PARQUE NACIONAL LAGUNAS DE ZEMPOALA
Temascaltepec
550
134
Ruinas Malinalco
Tenancingo
Ixtapan de la Sal
Tonatico
95
Taxco
95
95D
95D
To Chilpancingo & Acapulco
UNITED STATES
Gulf of Mexico
MEXICO
Mexico City
PACIFIC OCEAN

Pachuca
Tulancingo
130
130
HIDALGO
85
132
85D
PUEBLA
57D
Lago Zumpango
Teotihuacán
85D
Otumba
Tepotzotlán
Altatonga
132D
Acolman
PARQUE NACIONAL EL CONTADOR
119
Tlalnepantla
85
Texcoco
136
Chapingo
PARQUE NACIONAL MOLINO DE FLORES
MEXICO CITY, DF
TLAXCALA
Ruinas Tizatlan
Apizaco
Netzahualcóyotl
136
117
Los Reyes
150
190
Ruinas Cacaxtla
Humantla
Villa Alvaro Obregon
190D
Tlaxcala
Santa Ana Chiautempan
57
Xochimilco
Chalco
San Martín Texmelucan
Iztaccihuatl (17,331')
Mixquic
115
190
95
PARQUE NACIONAL IZTA-POPO
190D
Huejotzingo
Amacameca
95D
To Veracruz
Cholula
115
Popocatepetl (17,751')
Tonantzintla
Acatepec
Tepoztlán
Puebla
Ruinas Cholula
190D
Cuernavaca
Atlixco
Lago Valsequillo
190
Cuautla
160
MORELOS
PUEBLA
Izúcar de Matamoros
Río Amacuzac
To Oaxaca

## Taxco

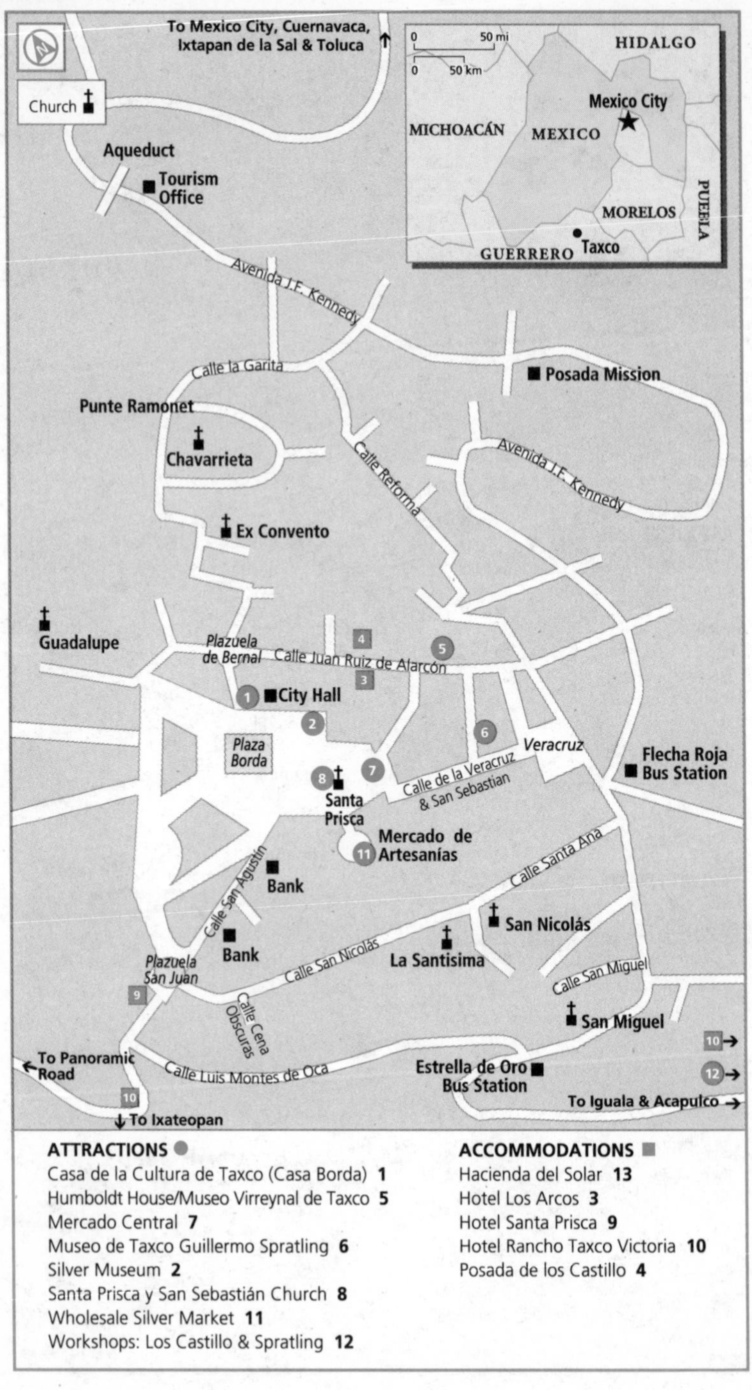


**ATTRACTIONS**

Casa de la Cultura de Taxco (Casa Borda) **1**
Humboldt House/Museo Virreynal de Taxco **5**
Mercado Central **7**
Museo de Taxco Guillermo Spratling **6**
Silver Museum **2**
Santa Prisca y San Sebastián Church **8**
Wholesale Silver Market **11**
Workshops: Los Castillo & Spratling **12**

**ACCOMMODATIONS**

Hacienda del Solar **13**
Hotel Los Arcos **3**
Hotel Santa Prisca **9**
Hotel Rancho Taxco Victoria **10**
Posada de los Castillo **4**

**VISITOR INFORMATION** The **State of Guerrero Dirección de Turismo** (✆ and fax **762/622-6616** or 762/622-2274) has offices at the arches on the main highway at the north end of town (Av. de los Plateros 1), which is useful if you're driving into town. The office is open daily 8am to 8pm. To get there from the Plaza Borda, take a *combi* ("Zócalo-Arcos") and get off at the arch over the highway. As you face the arches, the tourism office is on your right.

**CITY LAYOUT** The center of town is the tiny **Plaza Borda,** shaded by perfectly manicured Indian laurel trees. On one side is the imposing twin-towered, pink-stone **Santa Prisca Church;** whitewashed, red-tile buildings housing the famous silver shops and a restaurant or two line the other sides. Beside the church, deep in a crevice of the mountain, is the **wholesale silver market**—absolutely the best place to begin your silver shopping, to get an idea of prices for more standard designs. You'll be amazed at the low prices. Buying just one piece is perfectly acceptable, though buying in bulk can lower the per-piece price. One of the beauties of Taxco is that its brick-paved and cobblestone streets are completely asymmetrical, zigzagging up and down the hillsides. The plaza buzzes with vendors of everything from hammocks and cotton candy to bark paintings and balloons.

**FAST FACTS** The post office (✆ **762/622-0501**) is on the outskirts, on the highway to Acapulco. It's in a row of shops with a black-and-white CORREO sign. The telephone area code is **762.**

## EXPLORING TAXCO

Shopping for jewelry and other items is the major pastime for tourists. Prices for silver jewelry at Taxco's more than 300 shops are about the best in the world, and everything is available, from $1 trinkets to artistic pieces costing hundreds of dollars.

In addition, Taxco is the home of some of Mexico's finest stone sculptors and is also a good place to buy masks. However, beware of so-called "antiques"—there are virtually no real ones for sale.

### Spanish & Art Classes in Taxco

The Universidad Nacional Autónoma de México (UNAM) is on the grounds of the Hacienda del Chorrillo, formerly part of the Cortez land grant. Here, students learn silversmithing, Spanish, drawing, composition, and history under the supervision of UNAM instructors. Classes are small, and courses generally last 3 months. The school provides a list of prospective town accommodations that consist primarily of hotels—more reasonable accommodations for a lengthy stay are available, but best arranged once you're there. At many locations all over town, you'll find notices of furnished apartments or rooms for rent. For information about the school, contact either the **Dirección de Turismo** (tourist office) in Taxco (see "Information," above), or write the school directly: **UNAM,** Hacienda del Chorrillo, 40200 Taxco, Gro. (✆ **762/622-0124** for the Spanish school, 762/622-3690 for the art school).

Taxco also offers cultural attractions. Besides the opulent, world-renowned Santa Prisca y San Sebastián Church, you can visit the Spratling Archaeology Museum, the Silver Museum, and the Humboldt House/Museo Virreynal de Taxco.

**Malasia Tours,** Plazuela San Juan 5 (✆ and fax **762/622-7983** or 762/622-3808), offers daily tours to the Cacahuamilpa Caves and the ruins of Xochicalco for $59, including transportation, ticket, and the services of a guide. It also sells bus tickets to Acapulco, Chilpancingo, Iguala, and Cuernavaca. The agency is to the left of La Hamburguesa. Another agency offering similar services is **Turismo Garlum,** next to the Santa Prisca Church (✆ **762/622-3021** or 762/622-3037). It offers daily tours to the Cacahuamilpa Caves and the Santa Prisca Church for $14, which includes transportation, ticket, and the services of a guide. Both agencies are open daily from 10am to 2pm and 4 to 7pm.

**SPECIAL EVENTS & FESTIVALS** **January 18** marks the annual celebration in honor of Santa Prisca, with public festivities and fireworks displays. **Holy Week** ★★ in Taxco is one of the most poignant in the country, beginning the Friday a week before Easter with processions daily and nightly. The most riveting procession, on Thursday evening, lasts almost 4 hours and includes villagers from the surrounding area carrying statues of saints, followed by hooded members of a society of self-flagellating penitents, chained at the ankles and carrying huge wooden crosses and bundles of penetrating thorny branches. On Saturday morning, the Plaza Borda fills for the **Procession of Three Falls,** reenacting the three times Christ stumbled and fell while carrying the cross.

Taxco's **Silver Fair** starts the last week in November and continues through the first week in December. It includes a competition for silver works and sculptures among the top silversmiths. At the same time, **Jornadas Alarconianas** features plays and literary events in honor of Juan Ruíz de Alarcón (1572–1639), a world-famous dramatist who was born in Taxco—and for whom Taxco de Alarcón is named. Both the silver fair and these readings were traditionally held in the spring, but have been switched to the late fall. Art exhibits, street fairs, and other festivities are part of the dual celebration.

## SIGHTS IN TOWN

**Casa de la Cultura de Taxco (Casa Borda)** Diagonally across from the Santa Prisca Church and facing Plaza Borda is the home José de la Borda built for his son around 1759. It is now the Guerrero State Cultural Center, housing classrooms and exhibit halls where period clothing, engravings, paintings, and crafts are displayed. The center also books traveling exhibits.

Plaza Borda 1. ✆ **762/622-6617** or 762/622-6632. Fax 762/662-6634. Free admission. Tues–Sun 10am–9pm.

**Humboldt House/Museo Virreynal de Taxco** Stroll along Ruíz de Alarcón (the street behind the Casa Borda) and look for the richly decorated façade of the Humboldt House, where the renowned German scientist and explorer Baron Alexander von Humboldt (1769–1859) spent a night in 1803. The museum houses 18th-century memorabilia pertinent to Taxco, most of which came from a secret room discovered during the recent restoration of the Santa Prisca Church. Signs with detailed information are in Spanish and English. As you enter, to the right are two huge and very rare *tumelos* (three-tiered funerary paintings). The bottom two were painted in honor of Charles III of Spain; the top one, with a carved phoenix on top, was supposedly painted for the funeral of José de la Borda.

The three stories of the museum are divided by eras, and by persons famous in Taxco's history. Another section is devoted to historical information about Don Miguel Cabrera, Mexico's foremost 18th-century artist. Fine examples of clerical garments decorated with gold and silver thread hang in glass cases. Excellently restored Cabrera paintings hang throughout the museum; some were found in the displayed frames, others were haphazardly rolled up. And, of course, a small room is devoted to Humboldt and his sojourns through South America and Mexico.

Calle Juan Ruíz de Alarcón 12 ✆ **762/622-5501.** Admission $1.75, $1.15 for students and teachers with ID. Tues–Sat 10am–6:30pm; Sun 9am–3:30pm.

**Mercado Central** Located to the right of the Santa Prisca Church, behind and below Berta's, Taxco's central market meanders deep inside the mountain. Take the stairs off the street. In addition to a collection of wholesale silver shops, you'll find numerous food stands, always the best place for a cheap meal.

Plaza Borda. Restaurant daily 7am–6pm; shops daily 10am–8pm.

**Museo de Taxco Guillermo Spratling** A plaque in Spanish explains that most of the collection of pre-Columbian art displayed here, as well as the funds for the museum, came from William Spratling. You'd expect this to be a silver museum, but it's not—for Spratling silver, go to the Spratling Ranch Workshop (see "Nearby Attractions," below). The entrance floor of this museum and the one above display a good collection of pre-Columbian statues and implements in clay, stone, and jade. The lower floor has changing exhibits. To find the museum, turn right out of the Santa Prisca Church and right again at the corner; continue down the street, veer right, then immediately left. It will be facing you.

Calle Porfirio A. Delgado 1. ✆ **762/622-1660.** Admission $3.35 adults, free for children under 13; free admission Sun. Tues–Sat 9am–6pm; Sun 9am–3pm.

**Santa Prisca y San Sebastián Church** ★★ This is Taxco's centerpiece parish church; it faces the pleasant Plaza Borda. José de la Borda, a French miner who struck it rich in Taxco's silver mines, funded the construction. Completed in 1758 after eight years of labor, it's one of Mexico's most impressive baroque churches. The ultra-carved façade is eclipsed by the interior, where the intricacy of the gold-leafed saints and cherubic angels is positively breathtaking. The paintings by Miguel Cabrera, one of Mexico's most famous colonial-era artists, are the pride of Taxco. The sacristy (behind the high altar) contains more Cabrera paintings.

Guides, both children and adults, will approach you outside the church offering to give a tour, and it's worth the few pesos to get a full explanation of what you're seeing. Make sure the guide's English is passable, however, and establish whether the price is per person or per tour.

Plaza Borda. ✆ **762/622-0184.** Free admission. Daily 6:30am–8pm.

**Silver Museum** The Silver Museum, operated by a local silversmith, is a relatively recent addition to Taxco. After entering the building next to Santa Prisca (upstairs is Sr. Costilla's restaurant), look for a sign on the left; the museum is downstairs. It's not a traditional public museum; nevertheless, it does the much-needed job of describing the history of silver in Mexico and Taxco, as well as displaying some historic and contemporary award-winning pieces. Time spent here seeing quality silver work will make you a more discerning shopper in Taxco's silver shops.

Plaza Borda. ✆ **762/622-0658.** Admission $1.50 adults, $1 children. Daily 10am–5:30pm.

## NEARBY ATTRACTIONS

The impressive **Grutas de Cacahuamilpa** ★, known as the Cacahuamilpa Caves or Grottoes (✆ **555/150-5031**), are 20 minutes north of Taxco. There are hourly guided tours daily at the caverns, which are truly sensational and well worth the visit. To see them, you can join a tour from Taxco (see "Exploring Taxco," above) or take a *combi* from the Flecha Roja terminal in Taxco; the one-way fare is $2.50. The caves are open daily from 10am to 5pm. Admission is $3.50. For more information, see "Sights near Tepoztlán," later.

For a spectacular view of Taxco, ride the **gondola** to the Hotel Monte Taxco. Catch a ride across the street from the state tourism office, left of the arches, near the college campus. Take a taxi or the *combi* marked "LOS ARCOS" (exit just before the arches, turn left, and follow the signs to the gondola). The gondolas operate daily 8am to 6pm; the cost is $2.80 round-trip.

**Los Castillo** Don Antonio Castillo was one of hundreds of young men to whom William Spratling taught the silversmithing trade in the 1930s. He was also one of the first to branch out with his own shops and line of designs, which over the years have earned him a fine reputation. Castillo has shops in several Mexican cities. Now, his daughter Emilia creates her own noteworthy designs, including decorative pieces with silver fused onto porcelain. Emilia's work is for sale on the ground floor of the Posada de los Castillo, just below the Plazuela Bernal. Another store, featuring the designs of Don Antonio, is in Mexico City's Zona Rosa, at Amberes 41. The workshop is open by appointment only.

8km (5 miles) south of town on the Acapulco Hwy.Also at Plazuela Bernal, Taxco. ✆ **762/622-1016**, or 762/622-1988 (workshop and fax). Free admission. Workshop Mon–Fri 9am–2pm and 3–6pm.

**Spratling Ranch Workshop** William Spratling's hacienda-style home and workshop on the outskirts of Taxco still bustles with busy hands reproducing unique designs. A trip here will show you what distinctive Spratling work was all about, for the designs crafted today show the same fine work. Although the prices are higher than at other outlets, the designs are unusual and considered collectibles. There's no store in Taxco, and unfortunately, most of the display cases hold only samples. With the exception of a few jewelry pieces, most items are by order only. Ask about their U.S. outlets.

10km (6 miles) south of town on the Acapulco Hwy. No phone. Free admission. Mon–Sat 9am–5pm. The *combi* to Iguala stops at the ranch; fare is 70¢.

## WHERE TO STAY

Taxco is an overnight visitor's dream: charming and picturesque, with a respectable selection of pleasant, well-kept hotels. Hotel prices tend to rise at holiday times (especially Easter week).

### MODERATE

**Hacienda del Solar** ★★ This hotel comprises several Mexican-style cottages, all on a beautifully landscaped hilltop with magnificent views of the surrounding valleys and the town. The decor is slightly different in each cottage, but most contain lots of beautiful handcrafts, red-tile floors, and bathrooms with handmade tiles. Several rooms have vaulted tile ceilings and private terraces with panoramic views. Others come equipped with more modern amenities, televisions, or a minibar. Standard rooms have no terraces and only showers in the bathrooms; deluxe rooms have sunken tubs (with showers) and terraces. Junior suites are the largest and most luxurious accommodations. The hotel is 4km

(2½ miles) south of the town center off Highway 95 to Acapulco; look for signs on the left and go straight down a narrow road until you see the hotel entrance.

Paraje del Solar s/n (Apdo. Postal 96), 40200 Taxco, Gro. ✆ and fax **762/622-0323.** 22 units. $130 double; $130–$150 jr. or deluxe suite. **Amenities:** Restaurant (with spectacular city view; see "Where to Dine," below); heated outdoor pool; tennis court; travel desk; room service; laundry service.

### INEXPENSIVE

**Hotel los Arcos** ★ Los Arcos occupies a converted 1620 monastery. The handsome inner patio is bedecked with Puebla pottery and has a lively restaurant area, all around a central fountain. The rooms are nicely but sparsely appointed, with natural tile floors and colonial-style furniture. You'll feel immersed in colonial charm and blissful quiet. To find the hotel from the Plaza Borda, follow the hill down (with Hotel Agua Escondida on your left) and make an immediate right at the Plazuela Bernal; the hotel is a block down on the left, opposite the Posada de los Castillo (see below).

Juan Ruíz de Alarcón 4, 40200 Taxco, Gro. ✆ **762/622-1836.** Fax 762/622-7982. 21 units. $39 double. No credit cards. **Amenities:** Restaurant; tour desk.

**Hotel Rancho Taxco Victoria** ★★ The Rancho Taxco Victoria clings to the hillside above town, with stunning views from its flower-covered verandas. It exudes the charm of old-fashioned Mexico. The comfortable furnishings, though slightly run-down, evoke the hotel's 1940s heyday. In front of each standard room are a table and chairs set out on the tiled common walkway. Each deluxe room has a private terrace; each junior suite has a bedroom, a nicely furnished large living room, and a spacious private terrace overlooking the city. Some units have TVs. Even if you don't stay here, come for a drink in the comfortable bar and living room, or sit on the terrace to take in the fabulous view. To get here from the Plazuela San Juan, go up a narrow, winding cobbled street named Carlos J. Nibbi. The hotel is at the top of the hill.

Carlos J. Nibbi 5 and 7 (Apdo. Postal 83), 40200 Taxco, Gro. ✆ **762/622-0004.** Fax 762/622-0010. 63 units. $62 standard double, $89 deluxe double; $100 jr. suite. AE, MC, V. Free parking. **Amenities:** Restaurant, bar; small outdoor pool.

**Hotel Santa Prisca** ★★ *Value* The Santa Prisca, 1 block from the Plaza Borda on the Plazuela San Juan, is one of the older and nicer hotels in town. Rooms are small but comfortable, with standard bathrooms (showers only), tile floors, wood beams, and a colonial atmosphere. For longer stays, ask for a room in the adjacent new addition, where the rooms are sunnier, quieter, and more spacious. There is a reading area in an upstairs salon overlooking Taxco, as well as a lush patio with fountains.

Cenaobscuras 1, 40200 Taxco, Gro. ✆ **762/622-0080** or 762/622-0980. Fax 762/622-2938. 34 units. $46 double, $52 superior double; $64 suite. AE, MC, V. Limited free parking. **Amenities:** Dining-room-style restaurant and bar; money exchange; room service; laundry service; safe-deposit boxes.

**Posada de los Castillo** ★ Each room in this delightful small hotel is simply but beautifully appointed with handsome carved doors and furniture; bathrooms have either tubs or showers. The manager, Don Teodoro Contreras Galindo, is a true gentleman and a fountain of information about Taxco. To get here from the Plaza Borda, go downhill a short block to the Plazuela Bernal and make an immediate right; the hotel is a block farther on the right, opposite the Hotel los Arcos (see above).

Juan Ruíz de Alarcón 7, 40200 Taxco. Gro. ✆ and fax **762/622-1396.** 13 units. $33 double. No credit cards.

## WHERE TO DINE

Taxco gets a lot of day-trippers from the capital and Acapulco, most of whom choose to dine close to the Plaza Borda. Prices in this area are high for what you get. Just a few streets back, you'll find some excellent, simple *fondas* or restaurants.

### VERY EXPENSIVE

**Toni's** ★ STEAKS/SEAFOOD High on a mountaintop, Toni's is an intimate, classic restaurant enclosed in a huge, cone-shaped *palapa* with a panoramic view of the city. Eleven candlelit tables sparkle with crystal and crisp linen. The menu, mainly shrimp or beef, is limited, but the food is superior. Try tender, juicy prime roast beef, which comes with Yorkshire pudding, creamed spinach, and baked potato. Lobster is sometimes available. To reach Toni's, it's best to take a taxi. Note that it's open for dinner only.

In the Hotel Monte Taxco. ✆ **762/622-1300.** Reservations recommended. Main courses $13.50–$22. AE, MC, V. Tues–Sat 7pm–1am.

### MODERATE

**Cielito Lindo** MEXICAN/INTERNATIONAL Cielito Lindo is probably the most popular place on the plaza for lunch. The menu is ample—there's something for every taste—but the best choices are the classic Mexican dishes. Chicken *mole* is an excellent choice. The tables, laid with blue-and-white local crockery, are usually packed, and plates of food disappear as fast as the waiters can bring them. You can get anything from soup to roast chicken, enchiladas, tacos, steak, and dessert, as well as frosty margaritas.

Plaza Borda 14. ✆ **762/622-0603.** Breakfast $4.90–$7; main courses $7.50–$14. No credit cards. Daily 10am–11pm.

**La Ventana de Taxco** ★ ITALIAN The spectacular view of the city from this restaurant makes it one of the best places to dine in Taxco. The food—standard Italian fare—is also quite good, if not predictable. The pasta dishes are the most recommendable. Lasagna is a big favorite, and Sicilian steak is also popular.

In the Hacienda del Solar hotel, Paraje del Solar s/n. ✆ and fax **762/622-0323.** Breakfast $3–$7; main courses $10–$20. V, MC. Daily 8–11am and 1–10:30pm.

**Sotavento Restaurant Bar Galería** ★★ ITALIAN/INTERNATIONAL This stylish restaurant has paintings decorating the walls and a variety of linen colors on the table. The menu features many Italian specialties—try deliciously fresh spinach salad and large pepper steak for a hearty meal; or Spaghetti Barbara, with poblano peppers and avocado, for a vegetarian meal. To find this place from the Plaza Borda, walk downhill beside the Hotel Agua Escondida, then follow the street as it bears left (don't go right on Juan Ruíz de Alarcón) about a block. The restaurant is on the left just after the street bends left.

Juárez 8, next to City Hall. No phone. Main courses $3–$8. No credit cards. Tues–Sun 1pm–midnight.

**Sr. Costilla's** MEXICAN/INTERNATIONAL The offbeat decor at "Mr. Ribs" includes a ceiling decked out with an assortment of cultural curios. Several tiny balconies hold a few minuscule tables that afford a view of the plaza and church, and they fill up long before the large dining room does. The menu is typical of Carlos Anderson restaurants (you may have encountered them in your Mexican travels), with Spanglish sayings and a large selection of everything from soup, steaks, sandwiches, and spareribs to desserts and coffee. Wine, beer, and drinks are served.

Plaza Borda 1 (next to Santa Prisca, above Patio de las Artesanías). ✆ and fax **762/622-3215.** Main courses $8–$20. MC, V. Sun–Fri 1–11pm; Sat 1pm–midnight.

### INEXPENSIVE

**Restaurante Ethel** MEXICAN/INTERNATIONAL This family-run place is opposite the Hotel Santa Prisca, 1 block from the Plaza Borda. It has colorful cloths on the tables and a tidy, homey atmosphere. The hearty daily *comida corrida* consists of soup or pasta, meat (perhaps a small steak), dessert, and good coffee.

Plazuela San Juan 14. ✆ **762/622-0788.** Breakfast $4.45–$5.55; main courses $5.15–$6.30; *comida corrida* (served 1–5pm) $5.15. No credit cards. Daily 9am–9pm.

## TAXCO AFTER DARK

**Paco's** (no phone) is the most popular place overlooking the square for cocktails, conversation, and people-watching, all of which continue until midnight daily. Taxco's version of a disco, **Windows,** is high up the mountain in the **Hotel Monte Taxco** (✆ **762/622-1300**). The whole city is on view, and music runs the gamut from the hit parade to hard rock. For a cover of $6.70, you can dance away Saturday night from 10pm to 3am.

Completely different in tone is **Berta's** (no phone), next to the Santa Prisca Church. Opened in 1930 by a lady named Berta, who made her fame on a drink of the same name (tequila, soda, lime, and honey), it's the traditional gathering place of the local gentry and more than a few tourists. Spurs and old swords decorate the walls, and a saddle is casually slung over the banister on the stairs leading to the second-floor room, where tin masks leer from the walls. A Berta (the drink, of course) costs about $2; rum, the same. It's open daily from 11am to around 10pm.

National drinks (not beer) are two-for-one nightly between 6 and 8pm at the terrace bar of the **Hotel Rancho Taxco Victoria** (✆ **762/622-0004**), where you can also drink in the fabulous view.

# 2 Ixtapan de la Sal: A Thermal Spa Town

120km (75 miles) SW of Mexico City

The whitewashed town of Ixtapan de la Sal (not to be confused with Ixtapa, on the Pacific coast) is known for its thermal mud baths—this is an original spa town, with generations of healing traditions.

Hotels in Ixtapan de la Sal tend to be full on weekends and Mexican holidays, as the town is a popular retreat from Mexico City. There's little to do but relax. Cuernavaca, Taxco, and Toluca are all easy side trips.

## ESSENTIALS

**GETTING THERE & DEPARTING** **By Car** From Mexico City, take Highway 15 to Toluca. In Toluca, Highway 15 becomes Paseo Tollocan. Follow Tollocan south until you see signs pointing left to Ixtapan de la Sal. After the turn, continue straight for around 16km (10 miles). Just before the town of Tenango del Valle, you have a choice of the free road to Ixtapan de la Sal or the toll road. The free road winds through the mountains and takes 1½ hours. The inexpensive two-lane toll road has fewer mountain curves and takes around an hour—it's worth taking. The toll road stops about 16km (10 miles) before Ixtapan; the rest of the trip is on a curvy mountainous drive.

## Ixtapan de la Sal

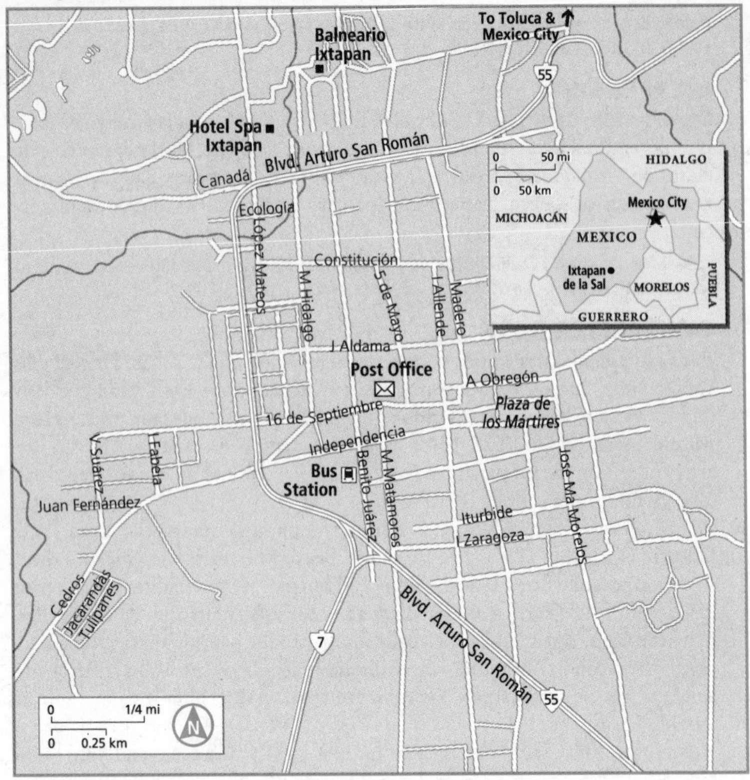


**By Bus** From Mexico City's Terminal Poniente, buses leave for Ixtapan de la Sal every few minutes. Request a bus that's taking the toll road, which cuts the travel time by 30 to 60 minutes, to about 2½ hours. To return, take a bus marked MEXICO DIRECTO, which leaves every 10 minutes and usually stops in Toluca. Buses from here also go to Cuernavaca and Taxco every 40 minutes.

### A PUBLIC SPA

The **Balneario Ixtapan** (**© 721/143-0331**), next to the Hotel Spa Ixtapan, is the town's public spa and bathhouse. It's not one of those modern, pampering spas, but a spa in the traditional manner—think Turkish baths. It aims to restore balance through age-old treatments involving the elements. You can take private thermal water baths or choose among massages, facials, hair treatments, paraffin wraps, pedicures, and manicures—all at prices ranging from $12 and $20 each. The spa is open daily from 8am to 6pm.

### WHERE TO STAY & DINE

**Hotel Spa Ixtapan** ★★ *Value* The town's only first-class hotel is on 35 manicured and flower-filled acres. It's been in operation since 1939, and though it's continually upgraded, some areas that have been left untouched provide guests with the nostalgic feel of the original resort. When you compare this spa's comfort, weight-loss programs, good food, and relaxing pace to the offering at other spas, you'll understand its continued popularity. It's one of the best spa values in Mexico, although very expensive for Ixtapan.

The resort offers golf, tennis, riding, swimming, and miles of trails for walking, jogging, or biking. It also has freshwater and thermal mineral swimming pools, an outdoor whirlpool, and a host of spa facilities for body treatments. The guest rooms are large, comfortable, and stylishly furnished. A business center and new pool, bar, and grill area were added recently. For dining, you have your choice of two areas. One serves a menu geared for weight loss, with vegetarian options; the other offers a more traditional international menu. The hotel offers first-run movies, classical concerts, and folkloric ballet and live musical performances. A sports casino has bowling, billiards, Ping-Pong, and other games.

The spa week goes from Monday through Friday, with Sunday arrival preferred. Spa facilities are closed on Sunday. Hotel guests not on the spa program can use the facilities on a per-treatment basis, and there's no daily admission charge. Round-trip taxi transportation from the Mexico City airport can be arranged at the time of reservation for around $220, which can be shared by up to four people.

Blvd. San Román s/n, Ixtapan de la Sal, 51900 Edo. de México. ✆ **800/638-7950** in the U.S., or 721/143-0021. Fax 721/143-0856. www.spamexico.com. 217 units, 45 villas. $289 double or villa. 4-day spa package $695 per person double; 7-day spa package $1,237 per person double; 21-day spa package $3,853 per person double; 28-day spa package $4,140 per person double. Rates include meals. AE, MC, V. **Amenities:** 2 dining rooms; disco (weekends only); private 9-hole golf course; 2 tennis courts; full-service spa with fully equipped gym, aerobics room and classes, steam room, solarium, 3 indoor whirlpools, 2 outdoor pools (1 thermal, 1 freshwater), sauna; horseback riding; mountain bikes; hiking trails; tour desk; laundry; room service. *In room:* TV, minibar.

## 3 Valle de Bravo & Avándaro: Mexico's Switzerland

152km (95 miles) SW of Mexico City

At 1,040m (6,070 ft.), Valle de Bravo has aptly been called the "Switzerland of Mexico." Ringed by pine-forested mountains and set beside a beautiful man-made lake, Valle de Bravo is a 16th-century village with cobblestone streets and colonial structures built around a town plaza. Like San Miguel de Allende, Taxco, and Puerto Vallarta, Valle de Bravo is a National Heritage village; new construction must conform to the colonial style of the original village.

The village's cobbled streets, small restaurants, hotels, spas, and shops are full on weekends—this is a very popular retreat from Mexico City. Some shops and restaurants may be closed weekdays. The crafts market, 3 blocks from the main square, is open daily from 10am to 5pm, and colorfully dressed Mazahua Indians sell their handmade tapestries daily around the town plaza.

Bass fishing, windsurfing, sailing, and water-skiing are popular on the lake. Excursions from here include a trip to the nesting grounds of the monarch butterfly between November and February. It can be very rainy and chilly from September through December, in addition to the summer rainy season.

The neighboring town of Avándaro (6km/4 miles away) is a popular place for weekend homes for well-to-do residents of Mexico City.

### ESSENTIALS

**GETTING THERE & DEPARTING By Car** From Mexico City, the quickest and most direct route is Highway 15 to Toluca. In Toluca, Highway 15 becomes Paseo Tollocan. Follow Tollocan south until you see signs pointing left to Highway 134 and Valle de Bravo, Francisco de los Ranchos, and Temascaltepec. After the turn, continue on Highway 142 until Francisco de los Ranchos, where you bear right, following signs to Valle de Bravo. The drive from this point takes about 1½ to 2 hours.

# Valle de Bravo & Avándaro

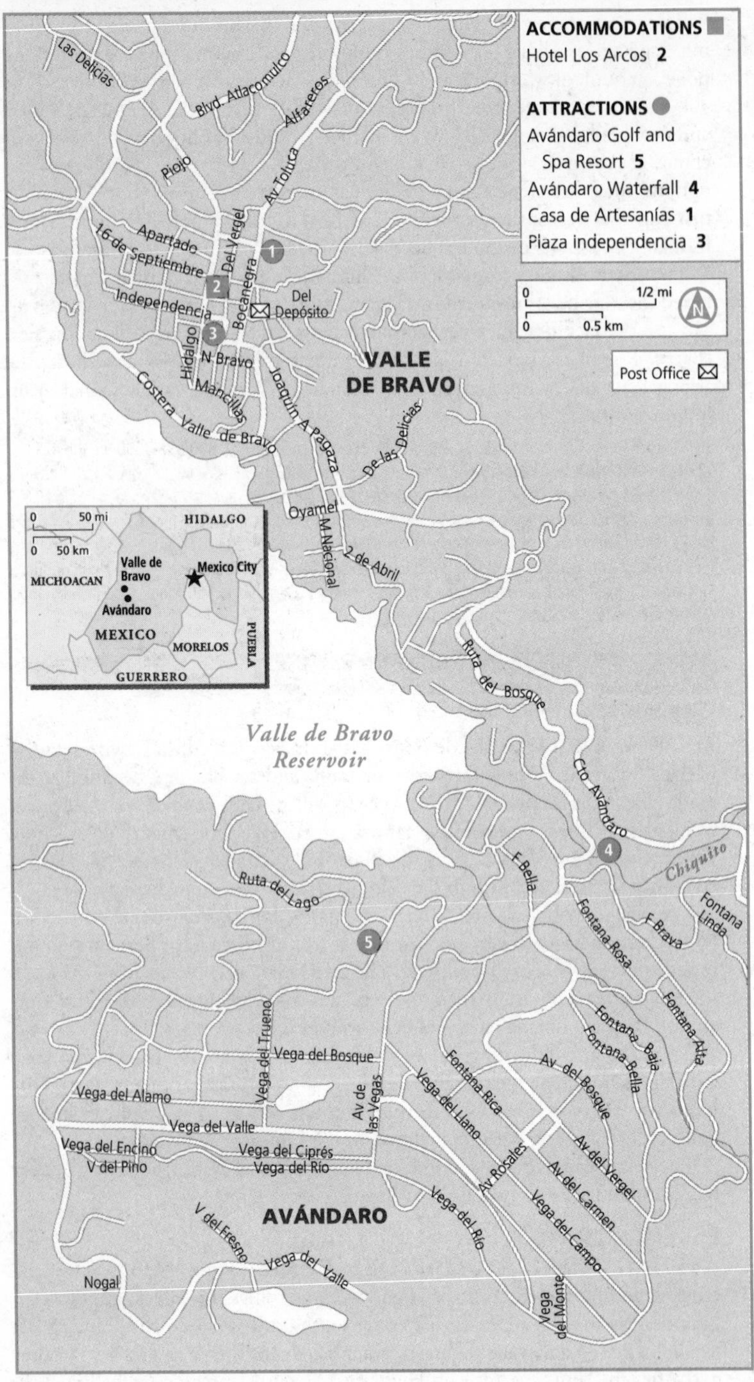

ACCOMMODATIONS
Hotel Los Arcos 2
ATTRACTIONS
Avándaro Golf and Spa Resort 5
Avándaro Waterfall 4
Casa de Artesanías 1
Plaza independencia 3
0 1/2 mi
0 0.5 km
Post Office
VALLE DE BRAVO
AVÁNDARO
Valle de Bravo Reservoir
Las Delicias
Blvd. Atlacomulco
Alfareros
Piojo
Av. Toluca
Apartado
16 de Septiembre
Del Vergel
Bocanegra
Independencia
Del Depósito
Hidalgo
N. Bravo
Mancillas
Joaquín A Pagaza
Costera Valle de Bravo
De las Delicias
Oyamel
M Nacional
2 de Abril
Ruta del Bosque
Cto Avándaro
Chiquito
F. Bella
Fontana Rosa
F. Brava
Fontana Linda
Fontana Alta
Fontana Baja
Fontana Bella
Ruta del Lago
Vega del Trueno
Vega del Bosque
Av de las Vegas
Vega del Llano
Fontana Rica
Av del Bosque
Vega del Alamo
Vega del Valle
Vega del Encino
V del Pino
Vega del Ciprés
Vega del Río
Av Rosales
Av del Vergel
Av del Carmen
Vega del Campo
Vega del Río
V del Fresno
Vega del Valle
Nogal
Vega del Monte
0 50 mi
0 50 km
HIDALGO
Valle de Bravo
Mexico City
MICHOACAN
Avándaro
MEXICO
MORELOS
PUEBLA
GUERRERO

**By Bus** From Mexico City's Terminal Poniente, buses leave every 20 minutes for the 3-hour journey. First-class buses depart hourly.

### WHERE TO STAY & DINE

In addition to the restaurants at the hotels listed here, there are several fine restaurants on or near Valle de Bravo's central square.

**Avándaro Golf and Spa Resort** ★★ Nestled on 296 acres amid large estates, lushly forested mountains, and a gorgeous, rolling 18-hole golf course, this resort has one of the loveliest settings in Mexico. Rooms come in two categories: large, beautifully furnished deluxe suites, and small, less luxurious cabañas. All have fireplaces and terraces or balconies overlooking the grounds, and all were upgraded recently. Transportation from Mexico City can be arranged.

Fracc. Avándaro, 51200 Valle de Bravo, Edo. de México. ✆ **726/266-1651.** www.grupoavandaro.com.mx. (Reservations ✆ 555/280-1532, 555/280-5532, or 555/282-0578, in Mexico City.) 82 units. $167 double cabaña; $400 deluxe suite. 7-day spa or golf package available. AE, MC, V. Free parking. **Amenities:** 2 restaurants; 25m junior Olympic-size pool; 18-hole golf course; 7 tennis courts; ultramodern spa with well-trained staff and full range of services, including massage, wraps, facials, aerobics, exercise classes, and body treatments; sauna; steam rooms; hot and cold whirlpools; weight-training equipment; room service. *In room:* TV, hair dryer, safe-deposit box.

**Hotel los Arcos** The Hotel los Arcos, close to the main square, has views of the village and mountains. Two stories of rooms on one side and three stories on the other surround a swimming pool. Nineteen rooms have fireplaces, an important feature in winter here. Some rooms have balconies, and most have glass walls with views.

Bocanegra 310, 51200 Valle de Bravo, Edo. de México. ✆ and fax **726/262-0042,** 726/262-0531 or 726/262-0168. 25 units. Mon–Thurs $71–$96 double; Fri–Sun $115–$135 double. AE, MC, V. **Amenities:** Restaurant/bar; outdoor pool. *In room:* TV.

## 4 Cuernavaca: Land of Eternal Spring ★★★

102km (64 miles) S of Mexico City; 80km (50 miles) N of Taxco

Often called the "land of eternal spring," Cuernavaca is known these days as much for its rejuvenating spas and spiritual sites as it is for its perfect climate and flowering landscapes. If springtime is when the earth experiences its annual rebirth, then what better setting for a personal renaissance? Spa services are easy to find, but more than that, Cuernavaca exudes a sense of deep connection with its historical and spiritual heritage. Cuernavaca's palaces, walled villas, and elaborate haciendas are home to museums, spas, and extraordinary guesthouses.

Wander the traditional markets and you'll see crystals, quartz, onyx, and tiger's eye, in addition to tourist trinkets. These stones come from the Tepozteco Mountains—for centuries considered an energy source—which cradle Cuernavaca to the north and east. This area is where Mexico begins to narrow, and several mountain ranges converge. East and southeast of Cuernavaca are two volcanoes, also potent symbols of earth energy, Ixaccihuatl (the Sleeping Woman) and the recently active Popocatépetl (the Smoking Mountain). The geography and the wisdom of the ancient inhabitants, passed down through the years, have given a restorative energy to this privileged place.

Cuernavaca, capital of the state of Morelos, is also a cultural treasure, with a past that closely follows the history of Mexico—it was always considered a sanctuary for residents of the capital city. So divine are the landscape and climate that both the Aztec ruler Moctezuma and colonial Emperor Maximilian built private retreats here. Today, the roads between Mexico City and Cuernavaca are jammed almost every weekend, as city residents seek the same respite. As a result, restaurants and hotels may be full as well. Cuernavaca even has a large American colony, plus many students attending the numerous language and cultural institutes.

Emperor Charles V gave Cuernavaca to Hernán Cortez as a fief, and in 1532 the conquistador built a palace (now the Museo de Cuauhnahuac), where he lived on and off for half a dozen years before returning to Spain. Cortez introduced sugarcane cultivation to the area, and African slaves were brought in to work in the cane fields, by way of Spain's Caribbean colonies. His sugar hacienda at the edge of town is now the impressive Hotel de Cortez. The economics of sugarcane production failed to serve the interests of the indigenous farmers, and there were numerous uprisings in colonial times.

After Mexico gained independence from Spain, powerful landowners from Mexico City gradually dispossessed the remaining small landholders, imposing virtual serfdom on them. This condition led to the rise of Emiliano Zapata, the great champion of agrarian reform, who battled the forces of wealth and power, defending the small farmer with the cry of "*¡Tierra y Libertad!*" (Land and Liberty!) during the Mexican Revolution following 1910.

Today, Cuernavaca's popularity has brought with it an influx of wealthy foreigners and industrial capital. With this commercial growth, the city has also acquired the less desirable by-products of increased traffic, noise, and air pollution.

## ESSENTIALS

**GETTING THERE & DEPARTING** **By Car** From Mexico City, take Paseo de la Reforma to Chapultepec Park and merge with the Periférico, which will take you to Highway 95D, the toll road on the far south of town that goes to Cuernavaca. From the Periférico, take the Insurgentes exit and continue until you come to signs for Cuernavaca/Tlalpan. Choose either the Cuernavaca Cuota (toll) or the old Cuernavaca Libre (free) road on the right. The free road is slower and very windy, but is more scenic.

**By Bus** *Important note:* Buses to Cuernavaca depart directly from the Mexico City airport. (See "Getting There," in chapter 3, for details.) The trip takes an hour. The Mexico City Central de Autobuses del Sur exists primarily to serve the Mexico City–Cuernavaca–Taxco–Acapulco–Zihuatanejo route, so you'll have little trouble getting a bus. Pullman has two stations in Cuernavaca: downtown, at the corner of Abasolo and Netzahualcoyotl (© **777/318-0907** and 777/312-6063), 4 blocks south of the center of town; and Casino de la Selva (© **777/312-9473**), less conveniently located near the railroad station.

**Líneas Unidas del Sur/Flecha Roja** (© **777/312-2626**), with 33 buses daily from Mexico City, has a new terminal in Cuernavaca at Morelos 329, between Arista and Victoria, 6 blocks north of the town center. Here, you'll find frequent buses to Toluca, Chalma, Ixtapan de la Sal, Taxco, Acapulco, the Cacahuamilpa Caves, Querétaro, and Nuevo Laredo.

**Estrella de Oro** (© **777/312-3055** or 777/312-8296), Morelos 900 in Las Palmas, serves Iguala, Chilpancingo, Acapulco, and Taxco.

**Autransportes Oro** (© **777/320-2748** or 777/320-2801), on Blvd. Cuauhnahuac Km 2.5 in Col. Buganvilias, serves Puebla and Izucar de Matamoros, among other destinations.

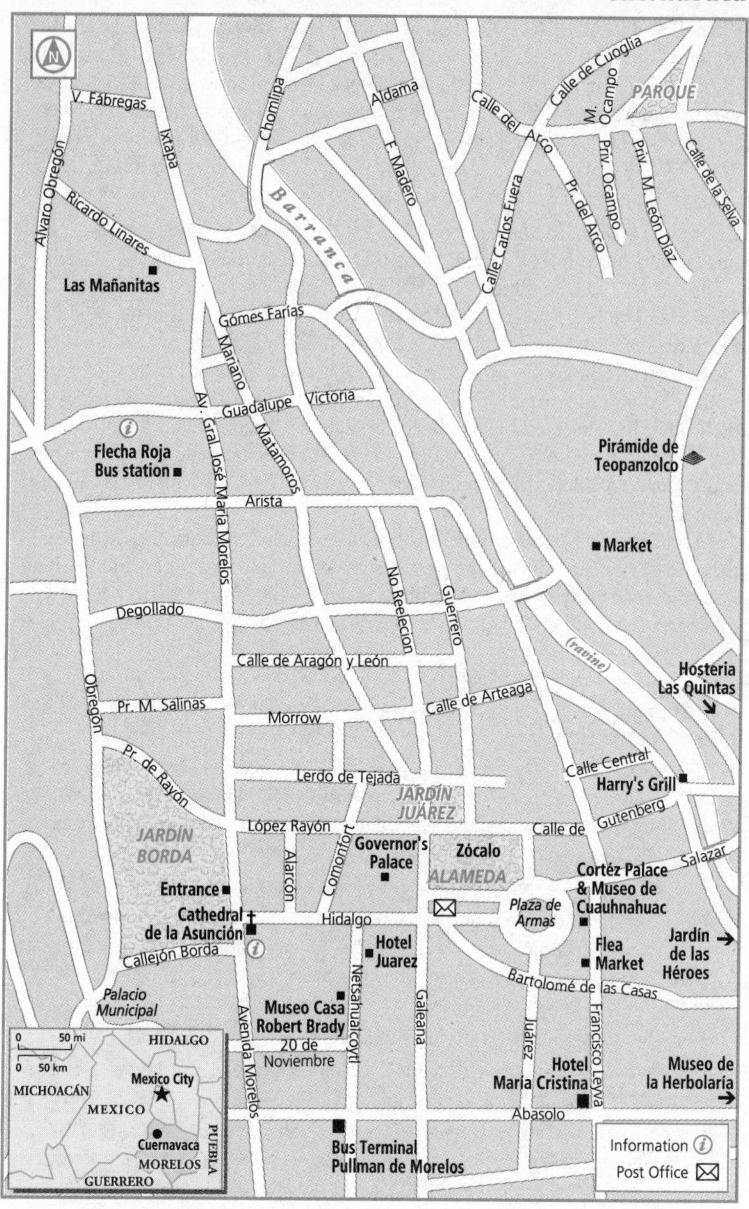


**Estrella Roja** (**© 777/318-5934**), a second-class station at Galeana and Cuauhtemotzin in Cuernavaca, about 8 blocks south of the town center, serves Cuautla, Yautepec, Oaxtepec, and Izúcar de Matamoros.

The **Autobuses Estrella Blanca** terminal in Cuernavaca is at Morelos Sur 503, serving Taxco.

**VISITOR INFORMATION** Cuernavaca's **State Tourist Office** is at Av. Morelos Sur 187, between Jalisco and Tabasco (© **777/314-3881,** or © and fax 777/314-3872 or 777/314-3920), half a block north of the Estrella de Oro bus station and about a 15- to 20-minute walk south of the cathedral. It's open Monday to Friday from 8am to 5pm. There's also a **City Tourism kiosk** (© **777/318-7561** or 777/318-6498), on Morelos beside the El Calvario Church. It's open daily from 8am to 5pm.

**CITY LAYOUT** In the center of the city are two contiguous plazas. The smaller and more formal, across from the post office, has a Victorian gazebo (designed by Gustave Eiffel, of Eiffel Tower fame) at its center. This is the **Alameda.** The larger, rectangular plaza with trees, shrubs, and benches is the **Plaza de Armas.** These two plazas are known collectively as the ***zócalo*** and form the hub for strolling vendors selling balloons, baskets, bracelets, and other crafts from surrounding villages. It's all easy-going, and one of the great pleasures of the town is hanging out at a park bench or table in a nearby restaurant. On Sunday afternoons, orchestras play in the gazebo. At the eastern end of the Alameda is the **Cortez Palace,** the conquistador's residence, now the Museo de Cuauhnahuac.

*Note:* The city's street-numbering system is extremely confusing. It appears that the city fathers, during the past century or so, imposed a new numbering system every 10 or 20 years. An address given as "no. 5" may be in a building that bears the number "506," or perhaps "Antes no. 5" (former no. 5).

## *FAST FACTS:* Cuernavaca

*American Express* The local representative is **Viajes Marín,** Edificio las Plazas, Loc. 13 (© **777/314-2266** or 777/318-9901; fax 777/312-9297; www.viajesmarin.com.mx). It's open daily from 9am to 2pm and 4 to 7pm.

*Area Code* The telephone area code is **777.**

*Banks* Bank tellers (from 9am to 3 or 5pm, depending on the bank), ATMs, and *casas de cambio* change money. The closest bank to the *zócalo* is **Bancomer,** Matamoros and Lerdo de Tejada, cater-corner to Jardín Juárez (across López Rayón from the Alameda). Most banks are open until 6pm Monday through Friday and half days on Saturday.

*Elevation* Cuernavaca sits at 1,533m (5,058 ft.).

*Hospital* **Hospital Cuernavaca,** Calle Cuauhtemoc 305, Col Lomas de la Selva (© **777/311-2482,** 777/311-2483, or 777/311-2484).

*Internet Access* **Café Internet,** in La Plazuela, Las Casas 8 (© **777/318-4330**), across from the Cortez Palace, offers access for $2.50 per hour, in addition to full computer services and monthly fee programs. It's open Monday to Saturday from 9am to 9pm, Sunday from 11am to 8pm.

*Pharmacy* **Farmacias del Ahorro,** Av Teopanzolco (© **777/316-5563**), is open daily from 9am to 8pm.

*Population* Cuernavaca has 400,000 residents.

*Post Office* The *correo* (© **777/312-4379**) is on the Plaza de Armas, next door to Café los Arcos. It's open Monday to Friday from 9am to 3pm, Saturday from 9am to 1pm.

*Spanish Lessons* Cuernavaca is known for its Spanish-language schools. Generally, the schools will help students find lodging with a family or provide a list of potential places to stay. Rather than make a long-term commitment in a family living situation, try it for a week, then decide. Contact the **Center for Bilingual Multicultural Studies,** San Jerónimo 304 (Apdo. Postal 1520), 62000 Cuernavaca, Morelos (© **777/317-1087** or 777/317-2488); **Instituto de Idioma y Cultura en Cuernavaca** (© **777/317-8947;** fax 777/317-0455; www.idiomaycultura.com or www.cuenavaca.inosel.com.mx/icc); or **Universal Centro de Lengua y Comunicación Social A.C.** (Universal Language School), J.H. Preciado 171 (Apdo. Postal 1-1826), 62000 Cuernavaca, Morelos (© **777/318-2904** or 777/312-4902; www.universal-spanish.com). Note that the whole experience, from classes to lodging, can be quite expensive; the school may accept credit cards for the class portion.

## EXPLORING CUERNAVACA

On weekends, the whole city (including the roads, hotels, and restaurants) fills with people from Mexico City. This makes weekends more hectic, but also more fun. You can spend 1 or 2 days sightseeing pleasantly enough. If you've come on a day trip, you may not have time to make all the excursions listed below, but you'll have enough time to see the sights in town. Also notable is the traditional public market, or ***mercado,*** adjacent to the Cortez Palace. It's open daily from 10am to 10pm, and the colorful rows of stands are a lively place for testing your bargaining skills as you purchase pottery, silver jewelry, crystals, and other trinkets. Note that the Cuauhnahuac museum, a key attraction, is closed on Monday.

**Catedral de la Asunción de María** ★ *Moments* As you enter the church precincts and pass down the walk, try to imagine what life in Mexico was like in the old days. Construction on the church began in 1529, a mere 8 years after Cortez conquered Tenochtitlán (Mexico City) from the Aztec, and was completed in 1552. The churchmen could hardly trust their safety to the tenuous allegiance of their new converts, so they built a fortress as a church. The skull and crossbones above the main door is a symbol of the Franciscan order, which had its monastery here. The monastery is still here, in fact, and open to the public; it's on the northwest corner of the church property. Also visible on the exterior walls of the main church are inlaid rocks, placed there in memory of the men who lost their lives during its construction.

Once inside, wander through the various sanctuaries and the courtyard, and pay special attention to the impressive frescos painted on the walls, in various states of restoration. The frescos date to the 1500s, and have a distinct Asian style.

The main church sanctuary is stark, even severe, with an incongruous modern feeling (it was refurbished in the 1960s). Frescos on these walls, discovered during the refurbishing, depict the persecution and martyrdom of St. Felipe de Jesús and his companions in Japan. No one is certain who painted them. In the churchyard, you'll see gravestones marking the tombs of the most devout—or wealthiest—of the parishioners. Being buried on the church grounds was believed to be the most direct route to heaven.

At the corner of Hidalgo and Morelos (3 blocks southwest of the Plaza de Armas). Free admission. Daily 8am–2pm and 4–10pm.

**Jardín Borda** Across Morelos Street from the cathedral is the Jardín Borda (Borda Gardens). José de la Borda, brother of the Taxco silver magnate, ordered a sumptuous vacation house built here in the late 1700s. When he died in 1778, his son Manuel inherited the land and transformed it into a botanical garden. The large enclosed garden next to the house was a huge private park, laid out in Andalusian style, with little kiosks and an artificial pond. Maximilian found it worthy of an emperor and took it over as his private summerhouse in 1865. He and Empress Carlota entertained lavishly in the gardens and held frequent concerts by the lake. After Maximilian, the Borda Gardens suffered decades of neglect.

The gardens were completely restored and reopened in October 1987 as the Jardín Borda Centro de Artes. In the gateway buildings, several galleries hold changing exhibits and large paintings showing scenes from the life of Maximilian and from the history of the Borda Gardens. One portrays the initial meeting between Maximilian and La India Bonita, who became his lover.

On your stroll through the gardens, you'll see the little man-made lake on which Austrian, French, and Mexican nobility rowed little boats in the moonlight. Ducks have taken the place of dukes, however. There are rowboats for rent. The lake is now artfully adapted as an outdoor theater, with seats for the audience on one side and the stage on the other. A cafe serves refreshments and light meals.

Morelos 271, at Hidalgo. ✆ **777/318-1038** or 777/318-1052. Fax 777/318-3706. Admission $1; free admission Sun. Tues–Sun 10am–5:30pm.

**Jardín Botánico y Museo de Medicina Tradicional y Herbolaría ★★** This museum of traditional herbal medicine, in the south Cuernavaca suburb of Acapantzingo, occupies a former resort residence built by Maximilian, the Casa del Olindo or Casa del Olvido. During his brief reign, the Austrian-born emperor came here for trysts with La India Bonita, his Cuernavacan lover. The building was restored in 1960, and the house and gardens now preserve the local wisdom of folk medicine. The shady gardens are lovely to wander through, and you shouldn't miss the 200 orchids growing near the rear of the property. However, the lovers' house, the little dark-pink building in the back, is closed. Take a taxi, or catch *combi* no. 6 at the mercado on Degollado. Ask to be dropped off at Matamoros near the museum. Turn right on Matamoros and walk 1½ blocks; the museum will be on your right.

Matamoros 14, Acapantzingo. ✆ **777/312-5955**, 777/312-3108, or 777/314-4046. www.cib.uaem.mx. Free admission. Daily 9am[nd)5:30pm.

**Museo Casa Robert Brady ★★** This museum in a private home contains more than 1,300 works of art. Among them are pre-Hispanic and colonial pieces; oil paintings by Frida Kahlo and Rufino Tamayo; and handcrafts from America, Africa, Asia, and India. Robert Brady, an Iowa native with a degree in fine arts from the Art Institute of Chicago, assembled the collections. He lived in Venice for 5 years before settling in Cuernavaca in 1960. Through his years and travels, he assembled this rich mosaic of contrasting styles and epochs. The wildly colorful rooms are exactly as Brady left them. Admission includes a guide in Spanish; English and French guides are available if requested in advance.

Calle Netzahualcoyotl 4 (between Hidalgo and Abasolo). ✆ **777/318-8554.** Fax 777/314-3529. www.geocities.com/thebradymuseum. Admission $2.50. Tues–Sun 10am–6pm.

**Museo de Cuauhnahuac** The museum is in the Cortez Palace, the former home of the greatest of the conquistadors, Hernán Cortez. Construction started in 1530 on the site of a Tlahuica Indian ceremonial center and was finished by the conquistador's son, Martín. The palace later served as the legislative headquarters for the state of Morelos. It's in the town center, at the eastern end of the Alameda/Plaza de Armas.

In the east portico on the upper floor, there's a large Diego Rivera mural commissioned by Dwight Morrow, U.S. ambassador to Mexico in the 1920s. It depicts the history of Cuernavaca from the coming of the Spaniards to the rise of Zapata (1910). On the lower level, there's an excellent bookstore with a selection of books on Mexican art, architecture, and literature (some English titles are available). It's open daily from 10am to 8pm.

Tour guides in front of the Palace offer their services in the museum and at other points of interest in Cuernavaca, for about $10 per hour. Make sure you see official credentials issued by SECTUR (the Tourism Secretariat) before hiring one of these guides. This is also a central point for taxis in the downtown area.

In the Cortez Palace, Leyva 100. ✆ **777/312-8171**. www.newton.net.mx/cuauhnahuac. Admission $3.30; free admission Sun. Tues–Sun 9am–6pm.

## ACTIVITIES AND EXCURSIONS

**GOLF** With its perpetually spring-like climate, Cuernavaca is an ideal place for golf. The **Tabachines Golf Club and Restaurant,** Km. 93.5 Carr. Mexico-Acapulco (✆ **777/314-3999**), is the city's most popular course, open for public play. Percy Clifford designed this 18-hole course, surrounded by beautifully manicured gardens blooming with bougainvillea, gardenias, and other flowers. The elegant restaurant is a popular place for breakfast, lunch, or the especially popular Sunday brunch. Greens fees are $84 during the week and $167 on weekends. American Express, Visa, and MasterCard are accepted. It's open Tuesday to Sunday from 7am to 6pm; tee times are available from 7am to 2pm.

Also in Cuernavaca is the **Club de Golf Hacienda San Gaspar,** Av. Emiliano Zapata Col. Cliserio Alanis (✆ **777/319-4424** or 777/319-0002), an 18-hole golf course designed by Joe Finger. It's surrounded by more than 3,000 trees and has two artificial lagoons, plus beautiful panoramic views of Cuernavaca, the Popocatepetl and Iztacihuatl volcanoes, and the Tepozteco Mountains. Greens fees are $45 on weekdays, $89 on weekends; carts cost an additional $28 for 18 holes, and a caddy is $17 plus tip. American Express, Visa, and MasterCard are accepted. Additional facilities include a gym with whirlpool and sauna, pool, four tennis courts, and a restaurant and snack bar. It's open Wednesday to Monday from 7am to 7pm.

**LAS ESTACAS** Either a side trip from Cuernavaca or a destination on its own, Las Estacas, Km. 6.5 Carretera Tlaltizapán–Cuautla, Morelos (✆ **777/312-4412** or 777/312-7610 in Cuernavaca, or 734/345-0077 or 734/345-0159; www.lasestacas.com) is a natural water park. Its clear spring waters are reputed to have healing properties. In addition to the crystal-clear rivers, Las Estacas has two pools, wading pools for children, horseback riding, and a traditional-style spa (or *balneario*), open daily from 8am to 6pm. Several restaurants serve simple food, such as quesadillas, fruit with yogurt, sandwiches, and *tortas.* Admission is $12 for adults, $7.50 for children under 4 feet tall. There is also a trailer park and a small, basic hotel that charges $91 to $114 for a double room; rates include the entrance fee to the *balneario* and breakfast. Cheaper lodging options are also available; you can rent an adobe or straw hut with two bunk beds for $13.50. Visit the Website for other options. MasterCard and Visa are accepted. On weekends, the place fills with families. Las Estacas is

36km (23 miles) east of Cuernavaca. To get there, take Highway 138 to Yautepec, then turn right on the first exit past Yautepec.

**PYRAMIDS OF XOCHICALCO** ★ This beautiful ceremonial center provides clues to the history of the whole region. Artifacts and inscriptions link the site to the mysterious cultures that built Teotihuacán and Tula, and some of the objects found here make it appear as though the residents were also in contact with the Mixtec, Aztec, Maya, and Zapotec. The most impressive building in Xochicalco is the *pirámide de la serpiente emplumada* (pyramid of the plumed serpent), with its magnificent reliefs of plumed serpents twisting around seated priests. Underneath the pyramid is a series of tunnels and chambers with murals on the walls. There is also an observatory, where from April 30 through August 15 you can follow the trajectory of the sun as it shines through a hexagonal opening. The pyramids (✆ **777/314-3920**) are 36km (23 miles) southwest of Cuernavaca. They're open Tuesday to Sunday from 10am to 6pm. Admission is $3.50.

## WHERE TO STAY

Because so many residents of Mexico City come down for a day or two, tourist traffic at the hotels may be heavy on weekends and holidays. Reservations during these times are recommended.

### EXPENSIVE

**Camino Real Sumiya** ★★ About 11km (7 miles) south of Cuernavaca, this unusual resort, whose name means "the place of peace, tranquility, and longevity," was once the home of Woolworth heiress Barbara Hutton. Using materials and craftsmen from Japan, she constructed the estate in 1959 for $3.2 million on 30 wooded acres. The main house, a series of large interconnected rooms and decks, overlooks the grounds and contains restaurants and the lobby. Sumiya's charm is in its relaxing atmosphere, which is best midweek (escapees from Mexico City tend to fill it on weekends). The guest rooms, which cluster in three-story buildings bordering manicured lawns, are simple in comparison to the striking Japanese architecture of the main house. Rooms have subtle Japanese accents, with austere but comfortable furnishings and scrolled wood doors. Hutton built a kabuki-style theater and exquisite Zen meditation garden, which are now used only for special events. The theater contains vividly colored silk curtains and gold-plated Temple paintings protected by folding cedar and mahogany screens. The garden has strategically placed rocks representing the *chakras,* or energetic points of the human body.

Cuernavaca is an inexpensive taxi ride away. Taxis to the Mexico City airport cost $112 one way. From the freeway, take the Atlacomulco exit and follow signs to Sumiya. Ask directions in Cuernavaca if you're coming from there; the route to the resort is complicated.

Interior Fracc. Sumiya s/n, Col. José Parres, 62550 Jiutepec, Mor. ✆ **800/7-CAMINO** in the U.S., or 777/320-9199. Fax 777/320-9142. www.caminoreal.com/sumiya/. 163 units. $248 double or single; $385 suite. Low-season packages and discounts available. AE, DC, MC, V. **Amenities:** 2 restaurants, poolside snack bar; outdoor pool; 10 tennis courts; golf privileges nearby; convention facilities with simultaneous translation capabilities; room service; business center. *In room:* A/C, TV, minibar, dual-line phones with dataport, ceiling fans, hair dryer, iron, safe.

**Las Mañanitas** *Overrated* This has been Cuernavaca's most renowned luxury lodging for years. Although it is impeccably maintained, Las Mañanitas has an overly formal feeling to it, which takes away from some guests' comfort. The rooms are formal in a style that was popular 15 years ago, with gleaming polished molding and brass accents, large bathrooms, and rich fabrics. There are several sections. Rooms in the original mansion, called terrace suites, overlook the restaurant and inner lawn; the large rooms in the patio section each have a secluded patio; and those in the luxurious, expensive garden section each have a patio overlooking the pool and emerald lawns. Thirteen rooms have fireplaces, and the hotel also has a heated pool in the private garden. The hotel is one of only two in Mexico associated with the prestigious Relais & Château chain. Transportation to and from the Mexico City airport can be arranged through the hotel for $268 round-trip. The restaurant overlooking the gardens is one of the country's premier dining places (see "Where to Dine," below). It's open to nonguests for lunch and dinner only.

Ricardo Linares 107 (5½ long blocks north of the Jardín Borda), 62000 Cuernavaca, Mor. ✆ **777/314-1466** or 777/312-4646. Fax 777/318-3672. www.lasmananitas.com.mx. 22 units. $140–$340 double; $348 suite. Rates include breakfast. AE. Free valet parking. **Amenities:** Restaurant; outdoor pool; concierge; room service; laundry service. *In room:* Safe-deposit box.

**Misión Del Sol Resort & Spa** ★★★ *Finds* This adults-only hotel and spa offers an experience that rivals any in North America or Europe—and is an exceptional value. You feel a sense of pure peace from the moment you enter the resort, which draws on the mystical wisdom of the ancient cultures of Mexico, Tibet, Egypt, and Asia. Guests and visitors are encouraged to wear light-hued clothes to contribute to the harmonious flow of energy.

The guest rooms, villas, and common areas are in architecturally stunning adobe buildings that meld with the natural environment. Streams border the extensive garden areas. Group activities such as reading discussions, chess club, and painting workshops take place in the Salon; films are shown here on weekend evenings. Rooms are large and peaceful; each looks onto its own garden or stream and has three channels of ambient music. Bathrooms are large, with sunken tubs; the dual-headed showers have river rocks set into the floor, as a type of reflexology treatment. Beds contain magnets for restoring proper energy flow; all linens are 100 percent cotton. A recessed seating area with a sofa offers a comfortable place for reading or relaxing. Villas have two separate bedrooms, plus a living/dining area and a meditation room. Airport transfers from Mexico City are available for $190 one-way.

The spa has a menu of 32 services, with an emphasis on water-based treatments. Elegant relaxation areas are interspersed among the treatment rooms and whirlpool. The Oratorium is a special structure (built with rounded corners and a domed ceiling with skylight) used for meditation: A flowing stream, bamboo, and verdant plants surround it.

Av. General Diego Díaz Gonzalez 31. Col. Parres. 62550, Cuernavaca, Mor. ✆ **800/448-8355,** from the U.S. and Canada, 800/999-9100 toll-free inside Mexico, or 777/321-0999. Fax 777/321-1195. www.misiondelsol.com.mx. 42 units, 10 villas. $276 deluxe double; $581 villa (up to 4 persons), $640 Villa Magnolia (up to 4 persons). Special spa and meal packages available. AE, MC, V. Free parking. Children under 15 not accepted. **Amenities:** Restaurant (creative vegetarian/international); spa services, including massages, body wraps, scrubs, facial treatments, *temazcal* (pre-Hispanic sweat lodge purification), Janzu, phototherapy; daily meditation, yoga, tai chi classes/sessions; 2 tennis courts; Ping-Pong table; well-equipped gym. *In room:* A/C, bathrobes, safe-deposit box.

## MODERATE

**Hotel Posada María Cristina** ★★ The María Cristina's high walls conceal many delights: a small swimming pool, lush gardens with fountains, a good restaurant, and patios. Guest rooms vary in size; all are exceptionally clean and comfortable, with firm beds and colonial-style furnishings. Bathrooms have inlaid Talavera tiles and skylights. Suites are only slightly larger than normal rooms. La Casona, the handsome little restaurant on the first floor, overlooks the gardens and serves excellent meals based on Mexican and international recipes. Even if you don't stay here, consider having a meal. The Sunday brunch ($13 per person) is especially popular. The hotel is half a block from the Palacio de Cortez.

Leyva 20, at Abasolo (Apdo. Postal 203), 62000 Cuernavaca, Mor. ✆ **777/318-6984** or 777/318-5767. Fax 777/312-9126. www.maria-cristina.com. 19 units. $200 double; $212–$300 suite or cabaña. AE, MC, V. Free parking. **Amenities:** Restaurant and bar; outdoor pool; concierge; tour desk. *In room:* A/C, TV, ceiling fans, hair dryers.

### INEXPENSIVE

**Hotel Juárez** Its rates and location (downtown, 1 block from the Casa Borda) make the Juárez a good choice for those intent on exploring the town's cultural charms. Each of the two-story hotel's simple rooms is old-fashioned but well kept. To get here from the Cathedral, go east on Hidalgo, then turn right on Netzahualcoyotl. The hotel is about a block down on the left.

Netzahualcoyotl 19, 62000 Cuernavaca, Mor. ✆ **777/314-0219.** 12 units. $28 double. No credit cards. Limited street parking. **Amenities:** Small outdoor pool; tour desk. *In room:* TV, fan.

## WHERE TO DINE

### EXPENSIVE

**Restaurant Las Mañanitas** *Overrated* MEXICAN/INTERNATIONAL Las Mañanitas has set the standard for sumptuous, leisurely dining in Cuernavaca, but it has reached the point where its reputation surpasses the reality. Though the setting is exquisite and the service superb, the food is not as noteworthy as one would expect. Tables are set on a shaded terrace with a view of gardens, strolling peacocks, and softly playing violinists or a romantic trio. The ambience is lovely, and the service extremely attentive. When you arrive, you can enjoy cocktails in the cozy *sala* or on lounge chairs on the lawn; when you're ready to dine, a waiter will present you with a large blackboard menu listing a dozen or more daily specials. The cuisine is Mexican with an international flair, drawing on seasonal fruits and vegetables and offering a full selection of fresh seafood, beef, pork, veal, and fowl, but in standard preparations. Try cream of watercress soup, filet of red snapper in cilantro sauce, and black-bottom pie, the house specialty. Las Mañanitas is 5½ long blocks north of the Jardín Borda.

In Las Mañanitas hotel, Ricardo Linares 107. ✆ **777/314-1466** or 777/312-4646. www.lasmananitas.com.mx. Reservations recommended. Main courses $16–$32. AE. Daily 1–5pm and 7–11pm.

### MODERATE

**Casa Hidalgo** ★★★ GOURMET MEXICAN/INTERNATIONAL Set in a beautifully restored colonial building across from the Palacio de Cortez, this is a recent addition to Cuernavaca dining. The food is more sophisticated and innovative than that at most places in town. Specialties include cream of Brie soup, smoked rainbow trout, and the exquisite Spanish-inspired filet Hidalgo—breaded and stuffed with *serrano* ham and *manchego* cheese. There are always daily specials, and bread is baked on the premises. Tables on the balcony afford a view of the action in the plaza below. The restaurant is accessible by wheelchair.

Calle Hidalgo 6. ✆ **777/312-2749.** Reservations recommended on weekends. Main courses $12.50–$19.50. AE, MC, V. Mon–Thurs 1:30–11pm; Fri–Sat 1:30pm–midnight; Sun 1:30–11:30pm. Valet parking available.

**Restaurant La India Bonita** ★★ MEXICAN Housed among the interior patios and portals of the restored home of former U.S. Ambassador Dwight Morrow, La India Bonita is a gracious haven where you can enjoy the setting as well as the food. Specialties include *mole poblano* (chicken with a sauce of bitter chocolate and fiery chiles) and *fillet a la parrilla* (charcoal-grilled steak). There are also several daily specials. A breakfast mainstay is *desayuno Maximiliano,* a gigantic platter featuring enchiladas. The restaurant is 2 blocks north of the Jardín Juárez.

Morrow 15 (between Morelos and Matamoros). Col. Centro. ✆ **777/318-6967** or 777/312-5021. Breakfast $4.15–$6.50; main courses $6.70–$13.50. AE, MC, V. Tues–Sat 8am–11pm; Sun 9am–6pm.

**Restaurant Vienés** ★ VIENNESE This tidy, somewhat Viennese-looking place, a block from the Jardín Juárez, is a legacy of this city's Viennese immigrant heritage. The menu has old-world specialties such as grilled trout with vegetables and German potato salad. For dessert there's apple strudel followed by Viennese coffee. A daily "executive menu" offers a complete fixed-priced meal for $8.50. Next door, the restaurant runs a pastry and coffee shop, **Los Pasteles del Vienés.** Although the menu is identical, the atmosphere in the coffee shop is much more leisurely, and the tempting pastries are on display in glass cases.

Lerdo de Tejada 12 (between Morelos and Morrow). ✆ **777/318-4044** or 777/314-3404. Breakfast $3–$5; main courses $6–$9. Daily 8am–10pm. AE, MC, V.

### INEXPENSIVE

**La Universal** ★★ *Value* MEXICAN/PASTRIES This is a busy place, partly because of its great location (overlooking both the Alameda and Plaza de Armas), partly because of its traditional Mexican specialties, and partly because of its reasonable prices. It's open to the street and has many outdoor tables, usually filled with older men discussing the day's events or playing chess. These tables are perfect for watching the parade of street vendors and park life. The specialty is a Mexican grilled sampler plate, including *carne asada,* enchilada, pork cutlet, and grilled green onions, beans and tortillas, for $10. A full breakfast special for $4 is served Monday to Friday from 9:30am to noon. There's also a popular happy hour on weekdays from 2 to 10pm.

Guerrero 2. ✆ **777/318-6732** or 777/318-5970. Breakfast $4–$7.50; main courses $4–$14.50; *comida corrida* $8.90. AE, MC, V. Daily 9:30am–midnight.

## CUERNAVACA AFTER DARK

Cuernavaca has a number of cafes right off the Jardín Juárez where people gather to sip coffee or drinks till the wee hours. The best are La Parroquia and La Universal (see "Where to Dine," above). There are band concerts in the Jardín Juárez on Thursday and Sunday evenings.

A recent—and welcome—addition is **La Plazuelo,** a short, pedestrian-only stretch of a bricked street across from the Cortez Palace. Here, coffee shops alternate with tattoo parlors and live-music bars—something is always going on. It's geared toward a 20-something, university crowd.

**Harry's Grill,** Gutenberg 5 at Salazar, just off the main square (✆ **777/312-7639**), is part of the Carlos Anderson chain, and dependable for nocturnal fun. It offers the chain's usual good food and craziness, with Mexican revolutionary posters and flirtatious waiters. Although it serves full dinners, I'd recommend you go for drinks. The restaurant is open daily from 1pm to 1am; the bar, Tuesday to Saturday from 9pm to 3am. Visa, MasterCard, and American Express are accepted.

## 5 Tepoztlán ★★

72km (45 miles) S of Mexico City; 45km (28 miles) NE of Cuernavaca

Tepoztlán is one of the strangest and most beautiful towns in Mexico. Largely undiscovered by foreign tourists, it occupies the floor of a broad, lush valley whose walls were formed by bizarrely shaped mountains that look like the work of some abstract expressionist giant. The mountains are visible from almost everywhere in town-even the municipal parking lot has a spectacular view.

Tepoztlán is small and steeped in legend and mystery—it is adjacent to the alleged birthplace of Quetzalcoatl, the Aztec serpent god—and comes about as close as you're going to get to an unspoiled, magical mountain hideaway. Though tranquil during the week, on the weekends (especially Sun), the town is overrun with escapees from Mexico City. Most Tepoztlán residents, whether foreigners or Mexicans, tend to be mystically or artistically oriented—although some also appear to be just plain disoriented.

Aside from soaking up the ambience, two things you must do are climbing up to the Tepozteco pyramid and hitting the weekend crafts market. In addition, for those interested in holistic medicine, Tepoztlán offers a variety of treatments, cures, diets, massages, and sweat lodges. Some of these are available at hotels; for some, you have to ask around. Many locals swear that the valley possesses mystical curative powers and is one of the world's most important centers of positive energy.

If you have a car, Tepoztlán provides a great starting point for traveling this region of Mexico. Within 90 minutes are Las Estacas, Taxco, las Grutas de Cacahuamilpa, and Xochicalco (some of the prettiest ruins in Mexico). Tepoztlán is 20 minutes from Cuernavaca and only an hour south of Mexico City, which—given its lost-in-time feel—seems hard to believe.

### ESSENTIALS

**GETTING THERE & DEPARTING** **By Car** From Mexico City, the quickest route is via 95 (the toll road) to Cuernavaca; just before the Cuernavaca city limits, you'll see the clearly marked turnoff to Tepoztlán on 95D and Highway 115. The slower, free federal highway 95D, direct from Mexico City, is also an option, and may be preferable if you're departing from the western part of the city. Take 95D south to Km. 71, where the exit to Tepoztlán on Highway 115 is clearly indicated.

**By Bus** From Mexico City, buses to Tepoztlán run regularly from the Terminal de Sur and the Terminal Poniente. The trip takes an hour.

In addition, you can book round-trip transportation to the Mexico City airport through **Marquez Sightseeing Tours** (✆ **777/320-9109** and 777/315-5875) and two hotels: the **Posada del Tepozteco** (✆ **739/395-0010**), and **Casa Iccemayan** (✆ **739/395-0899**). The round-trip cost varies between $125 and $200.

### EXPLORING TEPOZTLÁN

Tepoztlán's **weekend crafts market** is one of the best in central Mexico. More crafts are available on Sunday, but if you can't stand the multitudes, Saturday is quite good, too. Vendors sell all kinds of ceramics, from simple fired clay works resembling those made with pre-Hispanic techniques, to the more commercial versions of Majolica and pseudo-Talavera. There are also puppets, carved wood figures, and some textiles, especially thick wool Mexican sweaters and jackets made out of *jerga.* Very popular currently is the "hippie"-style jewelry that earned Tepoztlán its fame in the '60s and '70s. The market is also remarkable for its food stands, where you can get everything from *carne asada* to *sopes,* quesadillas, *caldos,* and much more.

The other primary activity is hiking up to **Tepozteco pyramid.** The climb is steep, but not difficult. The trail (actually a long natural staircase) is shaded by dense vegetation and is beautiful from bottom to top. Once you arrive at the pyramid you are treated to remarkable views and, if you are lucky, a great show by a family of *coatis* (tropical raccoons), who visit the pyramid most mornings to beg for food; they especially love bananas. The pyramid is a Tlahuica construction that pre-dates the Nahuatl (Aztec) domination of the area. It was the site of important celebrations in the 12th and 13th centuries. The main street in Tepoztlán, Avenida 5 de Mayo, takes you to the path that leads you to the top of the Tepozteco. The trail begins where Avenida 5 de Mayo changes its name to Camino del Tepozteco. The hike is about an hour each way, but if you stop and take in the scenery and really enjoy the trail, it can take up to 2 hours each way.

Also worth visiting is the **former convent Dominico de la Navidad,** just east of the main plaza. It was built between 1560 and 1588, and is now a museum.

## SIGHTS NEAR TEPOZTLAN

Many nearby places are easily accessible by car. Tour services also offer trips to these areas, and will provide pick-up service from your hotel. One good service is **Marquez Sightseeing Tours,** located in Cuernavaca (✆ **777/320-9109** or 777/315-5875). Marquez has both four- and seven-passenger vehicles, very reasonable prices, and a large variety of set tours. The utterly dependable owner, Arturo Marquez Diaz, speaks passable English and will allow you to design your own tour. He also offers transportation to and from Mexico City airport.

Two tiny, charming villages, **Santo Domingo Xocotitlán** and **Amatlán,** are only a 20-minute drive from Tepoztlán and can be reached by minibuses, which depart regularly from the center of town. There is nothing much to do in these places except wander around absorbing the marvelous views of the Tepozteco Mountains and drinking in the magical ambience.

**Las Grutas de Cacahuamilpa** ★, known as the Cacahuamilpa Caves or Grottoes (✆ **555/150-5031**), is an unforgettable system of caverns with a wooden walkway for easy access and viewing. You'll see spectacular rock formations, which are lit up as you pass from chamber to chamber. Admission for 2 hours is $3.50; a guide for groups, which can be assembled on the spot, costs an additional $8. The caverns are open daily from 10am to 5pm, and are 90 minutes from Tepoztlán.

Located 40 minutes southeast of Tepoztlán is **Las Estacas,** a small, lush, ecological resort with a cold-water spring that is reputed to have curative powers. The ruins of **Xochicalco** (see "Cuernavaca," earlier), and the colonial town of **Taxco** (see section 1 of this chapter) are easily accessible from Tepoztlán.

## WHERE TO STAY

The town gets very busy on the weekends, so if your stay will include Friday or Saturday night, make reservations well in advance. Unfortunately, though there are a number of places to stay in Tepoztlán, most are very basic, so-so accommodations. There are, however, a jewel of a small hotel and a good option for budget travelers.

**Casa Iccemayan** This small, friendly, family-operated spot offers eight small bungalows spaced around a beautiful garden. It's about 7 blocks downhill from the center of town. Special rates are available for those staying a week or more.

Calle Olvido 26, Tepoztlán, Mor. ✆ **739/395-0899** or 739/395-0096. Fax 739/395-2159. 8 bungalows. $40 double. No credit cards. Free parking. **Amenities:** Communal kitchen; small outdoor pool.

**Posada Tepozteco** ★★ This property looks out over the town and down the length of the spectacular valley; the views from just about anywhere are superb. Rooms are tastefully furnished in rustic Mexican style. All but the least expensive have terraces and views. All suites have small whirlpool tubs. The grounds are exquisitely landscaped, and the atmosphere intimate and romantic.

Paraíso 3 (2 blocks from the town center), Tepoztlán, Mor. ✆ **739/395-0010.** Fax 739/395-0323. www.mexicoglobal.com/tepozteco. 19 units. $145–$225 double. Rates include breakfast. AE, MC, V. Free parking. **Amenities:** Restaurant with stunning view; small outdoor pool.

## WHERE TO DINE

In addition to the two choices listed below, the **Hotel Tepoztlán,** Industrias 6 (✆ **739/395-2810**), offers some of the best vegetarian fare in the area. It's 3 blocks from the main square, and it's open daily for breakfast, lunch, and dinner, with main courses priced around $5.

**El Ciruelo Restaurant Bar** ★ MEXICAN GOURMET This picturesque restaurant, surrounded by beautiful flowering gardens and adobe walls, offers a sampling of Tepoztlán's essence in one place. The service is positively charming, and the food divine. House specialties include chalupas of goat cheese, chicken with *huitlacoche,* and a regional treat—milk candies.

Zaragoza 17, Barrio de la Santisima, in front of the church. ✆ **739/395-1203.** Dinner $7.50–$25. No credit cards. Sun–Thurs 1–7pm; Fri–Sat 1pm–midnight.

**Restaurant Axitla** ★★★ *Finds* GOURMET MEXICAN/INTERNATIONAL Axitla is not only the best restaurant in Tepoztlán, but also one of the finest in Mexico for showcasing this country's cuisine. Gourmet Mexican delicacies are all made from scratch using the freshest local ingredients. Specialties include chicken breast stuffed with wild mushrooms in a *chipotle chile* sauce, *chiles en nogada,* and exceptional *mole.* There are also excellent steaks and fresh seafood.

As if the food weren't enough—and believe me, it is—the setting will make your meal even more memorable. The restaurant is at the base of the Tepozteco Pyramid, surrounded by 3 acres of jungle-like gardens that encompass a creek and lily ponds. The views of the Tepozteco Mountains are magnificent. Memo and Laura, the gracious owners, speak excellent English and are marvelous sources of information about the town and the whole area.

Avenida del Tepozteco, at the foot of the trail to the pyramid. ✆ **739/395-0519.** Lunch $5–$10; dinner $5–$20. MC, V. Wed–Sun 10am–7pm.

# 5

# San Miguel de Allende & the Colonial Silver Cities

Mexico's colonial silver mining cities—San Miguel, Querétaro, San Luis Potosí, Guanajuato, and Zacatecas—lie northwest of Mexico City in the rugged mountains of the Sierra Madre Occidental. The towns, in colonial settings with backdrops of high mountains, feature an ideal climate, local handcrafts, good food, and many memorable sites to visit.

**San Miguel de Allende** is the smallest of the cities. Its cobblestone streets and fanciful church set it apart from the rest, as do its numerous restaurants and interesting shops. For many years it has supported a resident population of artists, writers, and expatriates. **Guanajuato** and **Zacatecas,** with their winding streets and alleys and diminutive plazas, seem more like medieval towns than colonial cities. In contrast, **Querétaro** and **San Luis Potosí** have stately colonial centers of broad plazas and monumental civil and religious architecture.

Travel through these parts is easy and relaxing; there is little crime, and the inhabitants are gracious. The region is a good introduction to Mexico's interior and is well suited for a family vacation. All Mexicans, but especially those in this region, are family-oriented and warm up quickly when they see a family traveling together. If you go, take your swimsuit—the region has many natural hot springs that have become popular bathing spots.

The colonial silver cities are close to the Mexican capital by modern standards, but at the time of their founding, this land was the frontier. In pre-Columbian times, the great civilizations of central Mexico never established more than a tenuous sway here. Mountainous and arid, this was the land of the Chichimeca, a large nation of nomadic tribes who would occasionally band together to make raids upon their civilized neighbors to the south. After the Spanish conquest of the Aztec empire in 1521, the conquistadors turned their attention to this region in search of precious metals. The Chichimecans resisted these encroachers, but epidemic diseases brought from Europe soon decimated the native population. The Spanish established mining cities in quick succession, stretching from Querétaro (established in 1531) north all the way to Zacatecas (1548) and beyond. They found considerable quantities of gold, but silver proved present in such vast amounts that it made Mexico world-famous as a land of riches.

For three centuries of colonial rule, much of the mines' great wealth went to build urban centers of impressive and lasting architecture. It's wonderful to walk leisurely through these cities and view them, not one building at a time, but in broad views of colonial cityscapes. Until recently, most of the region had been spared from overwhelming growth because many industries that otherwise would have sprung up here were drawn away by Mexico City's disproportionate influence.

Life remains very civilized here; it is savored and enjoyed at a relaxed pace and not lived at breakneck speed. Many people in these cities have ancestors who lived here at least a century ago. Residents maintain a broad network of kinfolk, friends, and acquaintances. I've walked down streets with locals who would give their warmest greeting to every third or fourth person we passed. Often, I've had conversations in which I mention someone from a completely different context, only to hear something like "Oh, he's married to my cousin." This is the kind of intimate and close-knit world you enter when visiting this part of Mexico.

## EXPLORING THE SILVER CITIES

The order in which you visit these cities depends on how you enter the region. The most common ways of getting here are flying into Mexico City and taking the bus that goes directly from the airport to Querétaro, or flying into the León/Guanajuato airport. Zacatecas and San Luis Potosí also have international airports that receive a few flights from the U.S. Or you can get to this region by car or bus from the U.S. border. Several superhighways connect the region to the U.S. From Texas, the first of the silver cities that you reach would most likely be San Luis Potosí (which bills itself as the "Gateway to the United States").

Once in the region, you'll find the roads are good and fairly well marked. Driving within these towns, however, can be maddening due to convoluted, narrow streets and bizarre traffic routing (especially in Guanajuato and Zacatecas). If you ever have difficulty navigating your way into the center of town, simply hail a cab to lead the way. Parking can also be a problem; we have included, when possible, good motels where you can park and leave your car for the length of your visit. If you prefer to travel by bus, by all means do so. This region is blessed with good bus stations, and frequent, inexpensive first-class buses connect all these cities, which tend to be only 2 to 3 hours apart from each other.

As to how you can best allot your time, much depends on your interests. At a bare minimum, I recommend 2 to 3 days each in San Miguel de Allende, Zacatecas, and Guanajuato. But these cities are best seen at a leisurely pace. Part of their considerable charm is their relaxed way of life.

## 1 San Miguel de Allende ★★★

288km (180 miles) NW of Mexico City; 120km (75 miles) E of Guanajuato; 64km (40 miles) NW of Querétaro

San Miguel de Allende mixes the best aspects of small-town life with the cosmopolitan pleasures of a big city. It is the smallest of the cities included in this chapter and perhaps the most relaxed, but it offers such a variety of restaurants, shops, and galleries that urbanites can find themselves quite at home—hence the town's lasting popularity. This explains, too, why hotel and restaurant prices in San Miguel are a little higher than in the other colonial cities.

Most of the buildings in the central part of the town date from the colonial era or the 19th century; the law requires newer buildings to conform to existing architecture, and the town has gone to some lengths to retain its cobblestone streets.

San Miguel has a large community of Americans: some retired, some attending art or language school, and some who have come here to live simply and follow their creative muses—painting, writing, and sculpting. The center of this

The Colonial Silver Cities

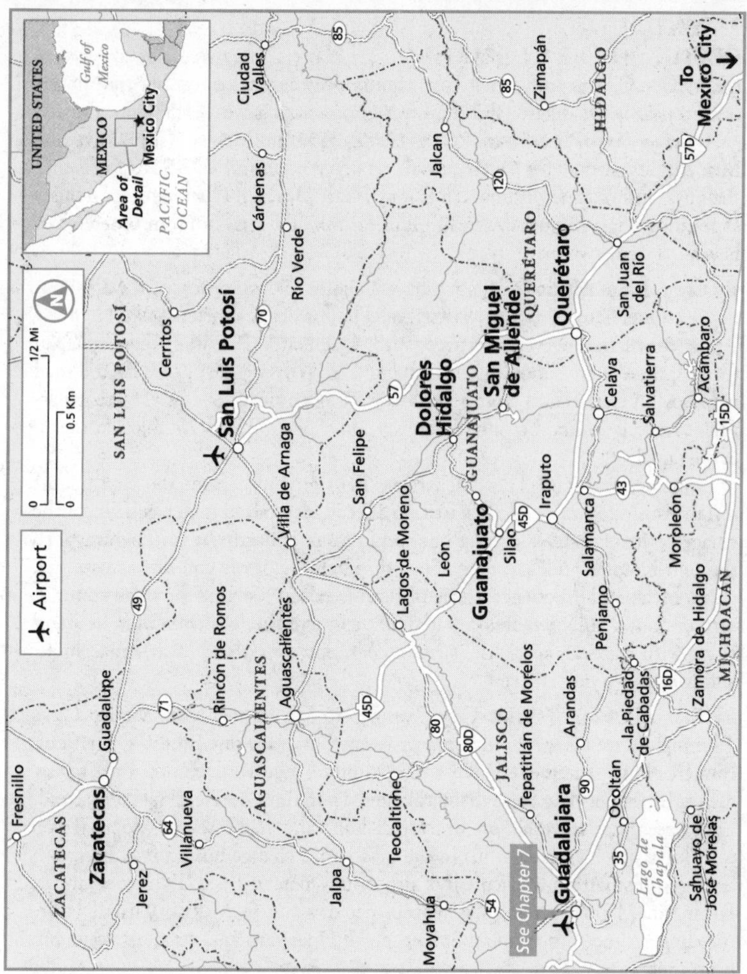


community is the public library in the former convent of Santa Ana. This is a good place to find information on San Miguel or just to sit on the patio and read a magazine or book. The little American colony gets along well with the townsfolk and has had surprisingly little effect on the way of life.

One of the most notable aspects of San Migueleña society is the number of festivals it celebrates; in a country that needs only the barest of excuses to hold a fiesta, it is known far and wide for them. The town celebrates so many festivals that the odds of coming upon one by accident are decidedly in the visitor's favor. Most of these celebrations are of a religious character and are meant to combine social activity with religious expression. People still practice Catholicism with great fervor here—going on religious pilgrimages, attending all-night vigils, ringing church bells at the oddest times throughout the night (something that some visitors admittedly might not find so amusing). See "Special Events & Festivals," below.

## ESSENTIALS

**GETTING THERE & DEPARTING** **By Plane** The two major airports are the Mexico City airport, which is 3½ hours away and has direct bus transportation to nearby Querétaro, and the León-Guanajuato airport, 1½ hours away.

*Arriving:* **AeroPlus** buses (✆ **55/5786-9357** in Mexico City) leave the Mexico City airport for Querétaro about every hour and cost $21. You'll find the buses just outside the doors in front of Gate D. From Querétaro, local buses ($4) run to San Miguel every 20 minutes. See "By Bus To/From Querétaro," below.

**By Car** **From Mexico City:** You have a choice of two routes for the 3½-hour trip—a Querétaro bypass or via Celaya. The former is shorter—take Highway 57, a four-lane freeway, north toward Querétaro. Past the Tequisquiapan turnoff, there is an exit on the right marked "A [TO] SAN MIGUEL." This toll road bypasses Querétaro and crosses Highway 57 again north of town. Here it narrows to two lanes and becomes Highway 111. Some 32 km (20 miles) farther is San Miguel.

**From Guanajuato:** The quick route is to go south from the city a short distance on Highway 110, then east on a secondary, paved road passing near the village of Joconoxtle. The long but scenic route is northeast on Highway 110 through Dolores Hidalgo, then south on Highway 51. If you drive this route, take a break and experience a slice of rural Mexican life near the small community of Santa Rosa, where a few restaurants serve the local *mezcal de la sierra* along with Mexican specialties such as *chorizo, cecina* (dried meat), guacamole, and Mexican-style barbecue.

**By Bus** **To/From Mexico City:** The trip to San Miguel from Mexico City's Terminal Norte takes 4 hours on a first-class bus (with one stop in Querétaro). Primera Plus, Satélite, ETN, and Omnibus de Mexico run one to six deluxe buses per day. Flecha Amarilla and Herradura de Plata operate second-class buses that leave almost every half-hour and make several stops. If you can't leave quickly, catch a bus to Querétaro and change buses there. For buses leaving directly from Mexico City's airport to Querétaro, see "By Plane," above. From San Miguel, a total of six buses per day run to Mexico City. If you're traveling on the spur of the moment, go to Querétaro and get a first-class bus from there.

**To/From Querétaro:** If you arrive in Querétaro by first-class bus, go out the front door and cross to the terminal in front. Buses for San Miguel leave about every 20 minutes, usually alternating between Flecha Amarilla and Herradura de Plata. The trip takes a little more than an hour and costs $4.

**To/From Guanajuato:** Primera Plus (Flecha Amarilla's first-class bus line) has five nonstop buses a day to and from San Miguel. ETN has one deluxe bus per day.

**To/From Nuevo Laredo:** A first-class Transportes del Norte/Estrella Blanca bus leaves Nuevo Laredo at 6:30pm, arriving in San Miguel de Allende between 7 and 8am the next day. The return bus leaves San Miguel at 7pm and arrives in Nuevo Laredo around 7am. Autobuses Americanos has a similar schedule. You have the option of buying a ticket all the way through Nuevo Laredo to any of several major Texas cities. This option entails changing buses in San Luis Potosí.

The **bus station** in San Miguel is 2km (1½ miles) west of town on the westward extension of Calle Canal. Taxis to town are cheap ($2) and available at all hours.

# San Miguel de Allende

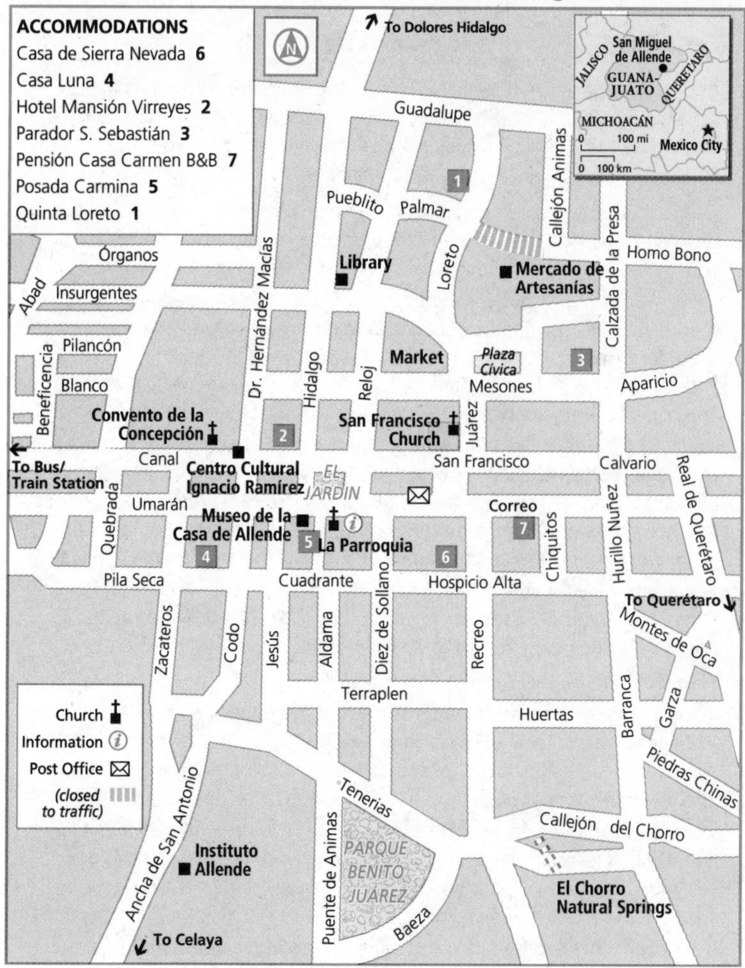


**VISITOR INFORMATION** The state **tourist information office** is in a small office to the left of the Parroquia (✆ **415/152-6565**). Office hours are Monday to Friday from 10:30am to 2:30pm and 5 to 7pm, weekends from 10am to noon. Also, look out for any of four different monthly publications for tourists. These are free and have a lot of advertising, but also some useful info and a calendar of events.

**CITY LAYOUT** San Miguel's central square, **El Jardín,** is shaded by groomed Indian laurel trees. The center of city life, El Jardín is the point of reference for just about all places in the middle of town and is bounded by Correo (Post Office St.), San Francisco, Hidalgo, and Reloj.

**GETTING AROUND** Buses to outlying villages (La Taboada thermal pool, for example) leave from the little plaza by the *mercado.* Taxis to places inside town should not cost more than $2 or $2.50, unless ordered from a hotel.

## *FAST FACTS:* San Miguel De Allende

*American Express* The local representative is **Viajes Vertiz,** Hidalgo 1 (✆ **415/152-1856;** fax 415/152-0499), open Monday to Friday from 9am to 2pm and 4 to 6:30pm, Saturday from 10am to 2pm.

*Area Code* The telephone area code is **415.**

*Climate* San Miguel can be warm in summer and cold enough for wool clothing in winter, especially at night or occasionally when a norther (a strong, sudden north wind) makes its way this far south.

*Communication & Shipping Services* Several services offer packing and shipping, mail boxes, telephone messages, long distance, faxes, and the like. One is **Border Crossings,** Correo 19, Int. 2 (✆ **415/152-2497;** fax 415/152-3672). **Pack 'n' Mail** has sizable space at Calle Jesús 2-A (✆ and fax **415/152-3191**). The hours for both are weekdays from 9am to 6pm, Saturday 10am to 3pm.

*Currency Exchange* Two convenient places near El Jardín change money. **Dicambio,** Correo 13, is open Monday to Friday from 8am to 4pm, Saturday and Sunday from 10am to 2pm. Next door is **DEAL,** open Monday to Friday from 9am to 6pm, Saturday 9am to 2pm. There are cash machines at several banks—one on the corner of the Jardín in the Casa del Conde, and a few on San Francisco Street.

*Drugstore* Try the **Farmacia Agundus** (✆ **415/152-1198**), Canal 26 at Macías. It's open daily from 10am to midnight.

*Elevation* San Miguel sits at 1,862m (6,143 ft.).

*Internet Access* Try **Estación Internet,** Portal Allende 4, 2nd floor (✆ **415/152-4465**). Hours are weekdays from 9am to 8pm, Saturday and Sunday from 10am to 2pm. Another office, at Recreo 13, 2nd floor, is open from 10am to 6pm weekdays.

*Library* The **Biblioteca Pública** (Public Library), Insurgentes 25 (✆ **415/152-0293**), is a social institution for the American community. It has a good selection of books in Spanish and English. Hours are Monday to Saturday from 10am to 2pm and 4 to 7pm.

*Newspaper* An English-language paper, ***Atención,*** carries local news as well as full listings of what to see and do.

*Parking* San Miguel is congested, and street parking is scarce. *Note:* White poles, signs, or both at the ends of streets mark the stopping point for parking (so that other cars can make a turn). Police are vigilant about parking and ticket with glee.

*Population* San Miguel has 70,000 residents.

*Post Office* The *correo,* Calle Correo 16, is open Monday to Friday from 9am to 3pm for all services (stamps are sold until 5pm), Saturday from 9am to 1pm.

*Seasons* Because of the fast freeway access from Mexico City, San Miguel is popular with weekenders from the capital. Arrive early on Friday or make a reservation ahead of time for weekends, especially long weekends. There's also a squeeze on rooms around the Christmas and Easter holidays and around the feast of San Miguel's patron saint, on September 29.

## SPECIAL EVENTS & FESTIVALS

San Miguel celebrates 30 to 40 festivals a year. These are just the standouts: January 17 is the **Blessing of the Animals.** In the morning, locals bring their decorated pets and farm animals to the town's churches to be doused with holy water. The first Friday in March celebrates **Our Lord of the Conquest,** and the day before is filled with music, fireworks, and decorated teams of oxen. After a celebratory mass, there is dancing by the *concheros.* Two weeks before Holy Week is the procession of **Our Lord of the Column.** Between then and Easter Sunday there are more processions, and altars are set up in honor of **La Virgen Dolorosa.** In May is the **Festival of the Holy Cross.** In June around Saint Anthony's Day is the **Fiesta de los Locos** ("The Madmen Festival") ★★, when many dress up in carnavalesque costumes and go cavorting about the center of town. August begins the preparatory festivals for September 29, the festival of San Miguel's **patron saint.** Parades, fireworks, and band concerts begin in August and continue throughout September. A *pamplonada* (running of the bulls) occurs during the third week of September. At the beginning of November is the **Day of the Dead,** followed by the **Christmas fiestas.** In addition to all of this, you have the **Chamber Music Festival** in summer, **Jazz Music Festival** in the fall, and a couple of arts fairs that occur on varying dates.

## EXPLORING SAN MIGUEL

It's difficult to be bored in San Miguel. The shopping is excellent, and you'll run out of time before you can try all the good restaurants. San Miguel is well situated for side trips to Dolores Hidalgo, Querétaro, Guanajuato, and San Luis Potosí. This is also one of Mexico's most popular towns for Spanish and art classes, just in case you find a lull during your vacation. Though San Miguel doesn't have the impressive colonial architecture of neighboring Querétaro or Guanajuato, it has much to catch the eye—fine courtyards, beautiful interiors, and small architectural details that easily escape notice.

### THE TOP ATTRACTIONS

**La Parroquia** ★★ Different from all other Mexican churches, la Parroquia has become the emblem of San Miguel. The church is an object of great pride to the citizenry and a source of great discomfort for architectural purists. Originally built in the colonial style, it was remade in the late 19th century by a local builder named Zeferino Gutiérrez, who reconstructed the towers and façade. Gutiérrez was supposedly unlettered, but he had seen pictures and postcards of European Gothic churches and worked from these alone, drawing his designs in the sand. I find the finished product fascinating—a very personal vision of the Gothic style that owes more to the builder's imagination and fancy than to the European churches that were its inspiration. The inside is not nearly as much fun as the outside; the church was looted on several occasions during times of social upheaval, and this kind of art criticism has put a damper on commissioning costly paintings and decoration. Still, there are things to see. My favorite, and one often missed, is the crypt beneath the altar. You get to it through a door on the right side. You'll have to seek out the caretaker, who can unlock the door (for a small tip).

South side of El Jardín. No phone. Free admission. Daily 7am–9pm.

**Museo de la Casa de Allende** ★ The house of San Miguel's most famous son and namesake, the independence leader Ignacio Allende, is now a museum.

It is of the genre known as "museos regionales" that you will find across Mexico in any city or town of considerable size. The objective of these museums is to present a view of the local area from prehistoric times to recent history; to explain what roles the region played in the context of national development; and to give some idea of how the great historical movements that swept across Mexico ran their courses at the local level—a micro-historical view. For the sake of context, this museum goes back a tad too far, starting with the creation of the solar system and the beginning of time, but from there it quickly moves to the meat of the matter—the way of life in the region during pre-Hispanic and colonial times.

Featured is a small biographical exhibit on Allende as one of the initiators of the independence movement, which began in nearby Dolores Hidalgo, and on what national independence meant for San Miguel and the local area. Explanations are in Spanish only, but the artifacts—including fossils, pre-Hispanic pottery, colonial-era furnishings, and articles of daily life—and the beauty of the house are worth the admission price.

Southwest corner of El Jardín. No phone. Admission $2. Tues–Sun 10am–4:30pm.

**Centro Cultural Ignacio Ramírez (Bellas Artes/El Nigromante)** Housed in the former Convento de la Concepción (1755), 2 blocks west of El Jardín, the Centro is a branch of the Palacio de Bellas Artes of Mexico City. The two-story cloister, surrounding an enormous courtyard with large trees and a gurgling fountain, houses art exhibits and classrooms for drawing, painting, sculpture, lithography, textiles, ceramics, dramatic arts, ballet, regional dance, piano, and guitar. A mural by David Alfaro Siqueiros and some of his memorabilia are worth seeing. A bulletin board lists concerts and lectures at this institute and elsewhere in the city. You can also dine in these pleasant surroundings at the restaurant **Las Musas,** which serves pasta dishes, salads, sandwiches, and desserts between 10am and 8pm (until 2pm Sun). Before you leave, take a look at the magnificent dome behind the convent. It belongs to the Iglesia de la Concepción and was designed by the same unschooled architect who designed the Parroquia (see above).

Hernández Macías 75 (between Canal and Insurgentes). © **415/152-0289.** Free admission. Mon–Fri 9am–9pm; Sat 10am–7pm; Sun 10am–2pm.

## MORE ATTRACTIONS

The **Centro de Crecimiento,** Zamora Ríos 6, a donation-supported school for children with disabilities, conducts regular Saturday tours (10am–1pm) to interesting places in the countryside around San Miguel. Donations are $15 per person; tickets are available at Casa Maxwell, a store at Canal 14.

The **House and Garden Tour** ★, sponsored by the Biblioteca Pública, is universally enjoyed. The tour opens the doors of some of the city's most interesting colonial and contemporary houses. Tours leave Sunday at 11:30am from the library, Insurgentes 25 (© **415/152-0293**), and last about two hours. A $15 donation goes to support various library projects benefiting the youth of San Miguel.

A couple of the most enjoyable walks in town are to the lookout point **El Mirador,** especially at sunset, which colors the whole town and the lake beyond, and to **Parque Juárez,** a large and shady park.

## NEARBY ATTRACTIONS

Just outside of San Miguel are several hot mineral springs that have been made into bathing spots. They're all just off the road leading to Dolores Hidalgo. La

## Learning at the Source: Going to School in San Miguel

San Miguel is known for its Spanish-language and art schools. These schools cater to English speakers and often provide a list of apartments for long-term stays. Rates for language classes are usually hourly and get lower the more hours you take. If your principal need is to practice conversation, it's best to look for small classes.

**Instituto Allende,** calle Ancha de San Antonio 20, 37700 San Miguel de Allende, Guanajuato (✆ **415/152-0190;** fax 415/152-4538; www.instituto-allende.edu.mx), put San Miguel on the map in the 1930s. Its founders were Enrique Fernández Martínez, the former governor of the state of Guanajuato, and Stirling Dickinson, an American. Today, it thrives in the 18th-century home of the former counts of Canal, a beautiful place with elegant patios and gardens, art exhibits, and murals. You can wander past classrooms where weavers, sculptors, painters, ceramists, photographers, and students are at work. Much of the craft work that San Miguel is known for sprang from this institute. The language office maintains a list of local families who rent rooms for stays of a month or more. The institute offers an MFA degree, and the school's credits are transferable to at least 300 colleges and universities in the United States and Canada; noncredit students are also welcome.

**Academia Hispano Americana,** Mesones 4 (Apdo. Postal 150), 37700 San Miguel de Allende, Guanajuato (✆ **415/152-0349;** fax 415/152-2333), has a reputation for being a comparatively tougher language school with an emphasis on grammar as well as conversation. Classes are limited to 12 people. The work is intensive, and the school is particularly interested in students who plan to use Spanish in their careers, and in North Americans who sincerely feel the need to communicate and understand the other Americas. The school has a continuous program of study of 12 4-week sessions for 35 hours a week. Private lessons cost $10 per hour. It's a member of the International Association of Language Centers. To request a brochure, write to the registrar. Office hours are Monday to Friday, 8am to 1pm and 3:30 to 6:30pm.

**Spanish4u,** 20 de Enero Sur 42, Col. San Antonio, 37750 San Miguel de Allende, Guanajuato (✆ **415/152-4115;** www.spanish4u.com), formerly Inter/Idiomas, primarily uses a conversational method. Classes are kept small, usually three students and a teacher. Each student's level of Spanish is evaluated before placement in a class. You can begin any time and pay by the hour or week or for private lessons.

Also see the **Centro Cultural Ignacio Ramírez,** in "The Top Attractions," above.

Taboada, the most popular of these springs, and La Gruta, the nicest, lie close to one another, just 8km (5 miles) outside San Miguel.

Near these hot springs is the sanctuary of **Atotonilco el Grande** (15km/9 miles away), a complex of chapels, dormitories, and dining rooms, and a fascinating church. World Monuments Watch has placed the church among the world's most important buildings meriting preservation. Father Luis Felipe Neri

Alfaro, an austere priest and mystic, founded the church in 1740. Alfaro thought the area in dire need of a religious presence, since many people would gather at the thermal springs to bathe publicly and immodestly—what he considered depraved behavior. He commissioned a local artist, Martínez Pocasangre, to paint murals illustrating the instructive verses that Alfaro wrote, with much emphasis on the dangers that lie in wait for the human soul. The murals and accompanying verses cover the entire ceiling and walls. They are vivid and moving, and add brightness and color to an otherwise dark and severe structure.

Alfaro chose this spot for his sanctuary because it was here that he was granted an ecstatic vision of Christ. The location proved propitious: At this church, 70 years later, the Virgin of Guadalupe first became the foremost symbol of Mexican identity. In 1810, when the Spanish authorities in Querétaro uncovered the conspiracy to liberate Mexico from Spanish rule, the leader, Father Miguel Hidalgo, was in the town of Dolores. Warned of the danger, he hastily declared independence and then marched his impromptu insurrectionist army toward San Miguel. En route, he passed through Atotonilco where he took the church's image of the Virgin of Guadalupe as his banner, declaring her the protector of the revolutionary forces.

The church and adjoining buildings still function throughout the year as a religious retreat for people who come from all over the country for a week of prayer, penance, and mortification. These spiritual exercises are conducted quietly with no public display. You can get to Atotonilco by cab or by taking the "El Santuario" bus at the market. It passes every hour on the hour, and goes through Taboada on its way to Atotonilco.

## SHOPPING

San Miguel is a town of artists; you'll find art for sale not only in galleries, but in restaurants, offices, and just about anywhere there's space in a public area. San Miguel is also a town of artisans working mainly with clay, iron, brass, tin, blown glass, and papier-mâché. And San Miguel is a town of shopkeepers who sell not only locally produced items, but folk art and decorative objects from across Mexico. There are so many stores, and they are so different from each other, that a list would not be helpful. The best advice I can give to shoppers is to explore the area around the main square; if you're looking for something in particular (say, gold-leaf candlesticks or a Huichol ceremonial mask), ask the shopkeepers you meet. Most of them have a good idea of what's out there. You just have to keep asking and looking.

That said, you should have some pertinent information about shopping in San Miguel. Stores are usually open Monday through Saturday 9am to 2pm and 4 to 7 or 8pm. Most stores close on Sunday. If you're interested in Talavera pottery, consider going to nearby Dolores Hidalgo (see the section "A Side Trip to Dolores Hidalgo," later). Most of the shops that deal with metal work are on and around Calle Zacateros. Also, a **handcrafts market** (Mercado de Artesanías) occupies a walkway 3 blocks long that descends from the municipal market past the Hotel Quinta Loreto.

## WHERE TO STAY

Lodging in San Miguel has become pricier than lodging in other nearby cities. For a long stay (a month or more), check at the instituto or the academia (see "Learning at the Source: Going to School in San Miguel," above) and other bulletin boards around town for lists of apartments or rooms to rent. Most apartments have kitchens and bedding; some come with maid service. San

Miguel is a popular weekend getaway for residents of the capital, and a few hotels raise rates on weekends. Secured parking is at a premium; if your hotel doesn't provide it, you'll pay around $12 to $15 daily in a guarded lot.

## VERY EXPENSIVE

**Casa de Sierra Nevada** ★★★ This handsome hotel occupies several 16th-century townhouses on a street just above El Jardín. With picturesque terraces and courtyards bedecked in flowers and plants, some with charming views and considerable privacy, this place feels like a true getaway from the modern world. Each room has its own design, and most have private patios or secluded entrances and working fireplaces. All have decorative antiques and tile floors with area rugs. Guests receive a fruit basket, flowers, and daily newspaper. The newest rooms are apart from the rest, down by the Parque Juárez, and have their own restaurant on the premises, which is less formal than the one in the main complex. The hotel, a member of the Small Luxury Hotels of the World, is 2 blocks southeast of El Jardín, between Diez de Sollano and Recreo. Transportation from either airport is available. The hotel also has an equestrian center a short distance from town on a 500-acre ranch. Balloon rides are also available.

Hospicio 35, 37700 San Miguel de Allende, Gto. ✆ **415/152-7040.** Fax 415/152-1436. www.quintareal.com. 33 units. $310 double; $380–$450 suite. AE, MC, V. Free valet parking. Children under 16 not accepted. **Amenities:** 2 restaurants (formal and informal, Continental and Mexican), 2 bars; large heated pool; golf at local club; horseback riding; spa; concierge; tour and activities desk; room service until 10pm; in-room massage; overnight laundry and dry cleaning. *In room:* TV, minibar, fridge, hair dryer, bathrobe, safe.

**La Puertecita Boutique Hotel** ★★ *Kids* This is a hotel especially appreciated by those who can't find the charm in church bells and firecrackers going off at odd hours of the night, and by those who seek a luxury hotel and are traveling with children. Set on the side of a narrow canyon (which it has all to itself), the peaceful hotel is above and a little removed from the central part of town. It has ample grounds surrounded by a fence, with terraced gardens and the ruined remains of an aqueduct for a touch of local character. Rooms, especially deluxe units and suites, are large; many have vaulted brick ceilings, small terraces, and beautifully tiled large bathrooms. They are furnished and decorated in a smart, modern Mexican style. The junior and one-bedroom suites have living areas and, in some cases, a dining area for four. Six suites have kitchenettes. Superior rooms and villas come with a king or a queen bed; the deluxe rooms and suites have a king or two queen beds. There are also two-bedroom suites, which are the equivalent of a one-bedroom suite with a deluxe room attached.

Santo Domingo 75, 37740 San Miguel de Allende, Gto. ✆ **415/152-5011.** Fax 415/152-5505. www.lapuertecita.com. 33 units. $230 double; $240–$270 suite. AE, MC, V. Free guarded parking. **Amenities:** Restaurant (international), bar; 2 small outdoor pools (1 heated); golf and tennis at local club; exercise equipment; outdoor whirlpool; game room; concierge; tour desk; courtesy car; room service until 9pm; in-room massage; babysitting; same-day laundry and dry cleaning; nonsmoking rooms. *In room:* TV, dataport, hair dryer, bathrobe, safe.

## EXPENSIVE

**Casa de la Cuesta** ★ In an upper *barrio* (neighborhood) of the town stands this magnificent house, a lovely example of how colonial architecture can be rethought in modern terms. The combined effect of architecture and location is dramatic. The entrance to the house is through a long tunnel-like passage that abruptly opens up to the first of two courtyards. On three sides are structures of different heights, which make use wherever possible of rooftop terraces. In one of these structures is a studio and gallery, which the owners (who are art dealers) use for shows or workspace. Guest rooms encircle the arcaded rear courtyard, with a lot of terraces and common space, much of which has a fine view of the central part of town. Rooms are large and comfortable; most contain king beds and have lots of color, detail, and a mix of modern and colonial furnishings that make them more interesting than a standard hotel room. Two suites have kitchens. The casa is about a 10-minute walk to the center of town.

Cuesta de San Jose 32. ✆ and fax **415/154-4324.** www.casadelacuesta.com. 6 units. $120 double. Rates include full breakfast. MC, V. **Amenities:** In-room massage; overnight laundry; nonsmoking rooms.

**Casa Luna B&B** ★★★ *Finds* What a visual treat this place is! The patio beyond the threshold looks like a set for a film version of *Tales of the Alhambra.* The rooms are done up to the max, but in a playful, untraditional manner with lots of local details. The colorful Frida Kahlo Blue Folk Art Room speaks for itself; the Calendar Room is decorated in old Mexican calendars; the Red Room has a canopy bed and large fireplace. All rooms are quite large and come with down comforters, gas fireplaces, and large bathrooms with shower/tub combinations. Most have private patios. The common areas of the house (including a rooftop terrace where you can order wine, beer, or a margarita in the evening) are beautiful places to relax. A small room is available for massages. Breakfasts are delicious, and the house offers cooking classes on Fridays. Transportation from the airport can be arranged. Casa Luna is 4 blocks southwest of the Jardín.

Pila Seca 11, 37700 San Miguel de Allende, Gto. ✆ and fax **415/152-1117.** www.casaluna.com. 9 units. $126–$136 double. Rates include full breakfast. Children under 17 not accepted. AE, MC, V (for deposits). **Amenities:** Bar; tour information; massage; nonsmoking rooms. *In room:* Safe.

## MODERATE

**Pensión Casa Carmen** ★ Every B&B has its own feel, and this one has that of a friendly Mexican household. Unlike some places where the sumptuous building and grounds can be off-putting, this place sets one at ease—a pretty little Mexican patio with orange trees and a fountain; large rooms that are comfortably but simply furnished; and a gracious, helpful landlady who speaks English. All rooms have gas heaters and come with either two twins or one queen-size bed. Of these, the penthouse is perhaps the most comfortable, but the ones in the first courtyard have the most character. Bathrooms vary in size. Breakfast (daily) and the afternoon meal (Mon–Sat) are served in a pleasant dining room; the cooking is good. You can reserve rooms by the day, week, or (at a discount) month. The pensión can arrange transportation from one of the airports. The hotel is 2½ blocks east of the Jardín.

Correo 31, near Recreo (Apdo. Postal 152), 37700 San Miguel de Allende, Gto. ✆ and fax **415/152-0844.** ccarmen@unisono.net.mx. 11 units. $83 double. Rates include breakfast and lunch. Children under 14 not accepted. No credit cards.

**Posada Carmina** ★ This centrally located hotel is comfortable, beautiful, and well managed. It's a half block south of the plaza, next to the Parroquia, in a large colonial mansion made from the same stone as the church. The two floors of rooms surround a stately courtyard with orange trees growing around a stone fountain, and bougainvillea and llamarada creeping up the walls. Rooms are ample and well furnished. There is one lovely suite with a large, roofed terrace that faces west, away from the Parroquia. Most of the bathrooms are comfortably sized but simple, with small mirrors (and, in some, little counter space) and plenty of hot water. Light sleepers may find that the bells of the Parroquia prove a nuisance in the front rooms.

Cuna de Allende 7, 37700 San Miguel de Allende, Gto. ✆ **415/152-0458.** Fax 415/152-1036. 23 units. $60–85 double; $120 suite. No credit cards. **Amenities:** Restaurant; room service until 7pm. *In room:* TV.

### INEXPENSIVE

**Hotel Mansión Virreyes** Judicious remodeling has raised the comfort level in this three-story colonial hotel a half block off the Jardín. Once a private home, it became the first hotel in San Miguel soon after the Mexican Revolution ended. The rooms are simple and comfortable but can be a little breezy. Almost all face the interior courtyard and come with two full beds and carpeted floors. Bathrooms are small to medium in size. As is the case with most other hotels in this price range, the TV adds little to the value of the room.

Canal 19, 37700 San Miguel de Allende, Gto. ✆ **415/152-3355** or 415/152-0851. Fax 415/152-3865. mansionvirreyes@prodigy.net.mx. 25 units. Fri–Sun $75 double; Mon–Thurs $60 double. AE, MC, V. Rates include full breakfast. **Amenities:** Restaurant; room service until 10pm. *In room:* TV.

**Parador San Sebastián** *Value* The San Sebastián is a modest colonial house turned hotel with surprisingly spacious, attractive rooms for the price. The rooms are simple, quiet, and comfortable; rates depend on the number and size of the beds. There are tables and chairs in the courtyard and on the rooftop terrace. This *parador* doesn't take reservations, so you have to try your luck. The hotel is 3½ blocks northeast of the Jardín between Colegio and Nuñez.

Mesones 7, 37700 San Miguel de Allende, Gto. ✆ **415/152-7084.** 27 units. $22–$29 double. No credit cards. Free parking.

**Quinta Loreto** *Value* This motel-like *quinta* is a good place to stay whether traveling by car or not. It has great rooms for the price, a lovely garden, and a friendly atmosphere. Rooms come with ceiling fans and heaters. The cheaper rooms, without phones or televisions, are almost as nice as the others. Most rooms contain one double and one twin bed. The food is good and the laundry service a bargain. Make reservations—the Loreto is very popular and often books up weeks in advance. Nonguests can come for breakfast ($3–$5) and for lunch ($7). The *quinta* is on a small street below the crafts market off Calle Loreto, about 7 blocks from the main square.

Calle Loreto 15, 37700 San Miguel de Allende, Gto. ✆ **415/152-0042.** Fax 415/152-3616. hqloreto@cybermatsa.com.mx. 40 units. $44–$50 double. Weekly and monthly discounts available. AE, MC, V. Free parking. **Amenities:** Restaurant; small pool; tour desk; overnight laundry. *In room:* TV.

## WHERE TO DINE

In Mexico, there is nothing else quite like San Miguel for the number, variety, and quality of its restaurants. The competition among restaurants is fierce; new places open all the time, while established restaurants close down or change ownership with unsettling frequency. Many of these restaurants have such elegant settings that you may become spoiled. Vegetarians will have no problem—most restaurants have legitimate vegetarian main courses. Reservations generally aren't necessary except during unusually crowded times. For the best baked goods (pastries, French bread, croissants, cakes), try **El Petit Four** on Calle Mesones 99-1, down the street from the Angela Peralta Theater. It's open Tuesday to Saturday from 8am to 8pm, Sunday from 9am to 6pm. There's a small seating area, or you can take your baked goods with you. The shop also sells coffee.

The restaurant in the main part of **Casa de Sierra Nevada** (see "Where to Stay," above) serves mostly continental cuisine (main courses are $15–$35), and reservations and a coat and tie are recommended; the restaurant in Parque Juárez is less formal and serves good Mexican food at reasonable prices. For a less expensive meal, I like the restaurant in the **Posada Carmina** (see above).

## MODERATE

**El Market Bistro** ★★ CLASSIC FRENCH Despite what the name might suggest, there is no postmodern jumble of cooking styles here—the food is traditional French. The main dining area is in a country-style courtyard just beyond the small, popular wine bar. Off the courtyard, there are interior dining rooms in case the night is chilly. The place has an informal feel, with none of the pretentiousness that often accompanies French food in Mexico. There are two menus: full and light. The full menu is full indeed; dishes include chateaubriand Béarnaise, tournedos montagnarde, braised sweetbreads, and salmon a la Provenzale.

Hernández Macías 95. [tel.] **415/152-3229.** Reservations recommended during high season. Main courses $7–$16. AE, MC, V. Daily 1–11pm.

**La Piazza** SOUTHERN ITALIAN Owner Omar Sereno learned to cook Italian food in Philadelphia and knows what pleases North American tastes. Specialties of the house include linguine pescatora and salmon Alcaperri. The restaurant has the perfect wood-burning oven for producing delicious pizzas. If weather permits, try dining on the rooftop terrace.

Hernández Macías 93. ✆ **415/152-7454.** Main courses $7–$15; pizzas $9–$13. AE, MC, V. Tues–Sat 1–11pm; Sun 1–10pm.

**L'Invito** ★★ ITALIAN Silvia Bernardini, the owner and chef, seems to prefer making dishes that rely upon their preparation rather than a liberal use of spices and herbs for their flavors. Good examples of this are *brasato* (beef cooked in a delicately flavored vegetable gravy) and chicken alla Rossini (which has a creamy lemon sauce). Her tastes run toward rich and subtle flavors and away from showiness. She offers a variety of salads and dishes with pasta, which she makes on the premises. For dessert, there's tiramisu.

Umarán 19. ✆ **415/152-7333.** Fixed-price menu $13–$17; main courses $8–$12. AE, MC, V. Mon–Sat 1pm–midnight.

**Mama Mía** ITALIAN An institution in San Miguel, this is a place one goes for dinner with entertainment and maybe even a good view. You can dine alfresco in a tree-shaded brick courtyard and enjoy live Latin American or flamenco music nightly. During the summer, the restaurant offers service on its rooftop terrace. In addition to the Italian specialties, there are Mexican and American specials and a large breakfast menu. There's also a nice selection of coffee-based drinks prepared with Kahlúa or brandy. At night, this is one of the most popular spots in town. The restaurant is 1 block southwest of El Jardín.

Umarán 8 (between Jesús and Hernández Macías). ✆ **415/152-2063.** Breakfast $2–$3; main courses $4–$15. AE, MC, V. Daily 9am–11:30pm (bar until 2am Thurs–Sat).

**Restaurant/Bar Bugambilia** ★★★ MEXICAN One can ask little more of a restaurant—delicious and attractive dishes, a large menu, good service, well-spaced tables, and a choice between dining in an elegant plant-filled courtyard and a large dining room, which in cool weather holds a roaring fire. This is fine dining *a la mexicana;* Sra. Arteaga offers a delicious variation on *chiles en nogada* (stuffed poblano chile with walnut cream sauce)—she marinates the pepper and serves it cold, not fried in batter. The *chile en nogada* has been the object of many "improvements," but most fail because they don't preserve the essence of this baroque dish, which balances opposites like the point and counterpoint of a fugue. Too spicy or too sweet, too strong a taste of meat or onions, and the magic is lost. Something simpler, perhaps? Start with the *caldo Xochitl* (the perfect soup for an irritable stomach), followed by traditional *enchiladas del portal* cooked in a *chile ancho* sauce.

Hidalgo 42. © **415/152-0127.** Main courses $8–$17. Reservations recommended during popular festivals. AE, MC, V. Mon–Sat noon–10:30pm; Sun noon–9:30pm. From the Jardín, walk 2½ blocks north on Hidalgo.

### INEXPENSIVE

**Cafe Santa Ana** ★ LIGHT MEALS/VEGETARIAN This is a cool, secluded spot where you can eat well for little money. The cafe specializes in light, but not plain, meals. The menu changes weekly; a couple of constant favorites include the *baguette de berenjena* (grilled eggplant and peppers with cheese on a baguette with pesto mayonnaise), and spinach salad with avocado, pralines, and cumin dressing. The menu always has chicken breast prepared in some fashion: A typical dish would be with green *pipián,* or with mushrooms and white-wine sauce. Did I mention the coffee?

Insurgentes 25 (rear patio of the library). © **415/152-7305.** Main courses $5–$10. No credit cards. Tues–Fri 9am–4pm and 6–11pm; Mon 9am–4pm.

**El Correo** AMERICAN/MEXICAN This restaurant has a comfortable, simple dining room in the traditional Mexican style, but the cooking transcends borders. For breakfast, try *migas natural* for a hearty breakfast with eggs, onions, tomatoes, and *chile* or *ranchero* sauce; or you can tank up on apple fritters, orange juice, or fruit with yogurt and granola. For homesick stomachs, at lunch there's fried chicken, stuffed baked potatoes, and soup. If you feel like Mexican fare, try the tortilla soup, for which the restaurant is well known, or the enchiladas. This restaurant is opposite the post office, half a block east of the Jardín.

Correo 23. © **415/152-0151.** Breakfast $3–$4; main courses $4–$6. AE, MC, V. Thurs–Tues 9am–10pm.

**El Pegaso Restaurant & Bar** INTERNATIONAL Decorated in a cheerful, colorful style, and with a friendly, helpful staff, this restaurant is popular with expatriates and visitors. It's particularly good for breakfast. The wide array of dishes includes eggs Benedict. For lunch or dinner you can order sandwiches, soups, salads, or the daily special, which is more complete and includes Asian dishes. The restaurant is 1 block east of the Jardín.

Corregidora 6 at Correo. © **415/152-13-51.** Reservations not accepted. Breakfast $2.50–$5; soups, salads, sandwiches $4–$7; main courses $5–$13. MC, V. Mon–Sat 8:30am–10pm.

**Olé Olé** MEXICAN Festive and friendly, this small restaurant is a riot of red and yellow streamers and bullfight memorabilia. The small menu specializes in grilled main courses—beef or chicken *fajitas,* shrimp brochettes, and *arrachera* (skirt steak). It also includes dishes such as *champiñones al ajillo* (mushrooms in garlic and *guajillo chile*) and *chistorra* (Spanish-style sausage). To find it, walk north from the San Francisco Plaza on Juárez and cross Mesones; jog left then right where the street becomes Loreto, and continue for 3 or 4 blocks. Look for a yellow building on the left with a small sign.

Loreto 66. © **415/152-0896.** Main courses $5–$10. No credit cards. Daily 1–9pm.

**Tío Lucas** STEAKS With probably the best steaks in town, Tío Lucas is popular with local residents. You can get a Chateaubriand here with any kind of sauce you like. All steaks are served with potatoes and vegetables. Make sure to arrive with an appetite because servings are large. Between 8:30pm and midnight, there's live jazz—some of the best live music in town.

Mesones 103 (at Hernández Macías). © **415/152-4996.** Main courses $7–$13. MC, V. Daily noon–midnight.

**Tips Recommended Day Trip Tours**

**Dolores Hidalgo** is the most popular destination for day-trippers from San Miguel. Some people make a day trip of Guanajuato and Querétaro. It's a hurried way of seeing them (especially Guanajuato), but it can be done.

Several tour guides and companies in San Miguel make trips to all of these places. **Leandro Delgado** (✆ **415/152-0155;** leandrotours@hotmail.com) is an independent tour guide who is well informed and conscientious. He speaks English, is a good driver, and is familiar with the artisans of Dolores Hidalgo and Guanajuato. The office at the **Travel Institute of San Miguel,** Cuna de Allende 11 (✆ **415/152-1630** or 415/152-0078, ext. 4; fax 415/152-0121), is open Monday to Saturday from 9am to 7pm. Both of these businesses offer trips to see the **monarch butterflies,** 5 hours away in the state of Michoacán (see chapter 6). This is an exhausting trip that should be done in 2 days, overnighting in the town of Angangueo, and can only be done in season (late Nov to late Mar).

## SAN MIGUEL AFTER DARK

To see a calendar of events, find a copy of the local paper, *Atención,* or one of the free monthly periodicals for visitors. Bellas Artes and the Angela Peralta Theater also post announcements of performances around town. Local regulations make existence easier for restaurant/bars than for simple bars, so many live-music acts perform in restaurants. Clubs and discos tend to spring up and then die off quickly. One club that has persisted is **La Cava de la Princesa,** Recreo 3 (✆ **415/152-1403**). It books a lot of live acts playing different kinds of music, as well as impersonators of Mexican pop stars. The cover charge is $3 to $8. A couple of the restaurants mentioned above are popular nightspots: **Tío Lucas** is a fun place to hear jazz, and **Mama Mía** has a bar area where salsa and jazz bands play on the weekends. There is a $4 cover. In the summer you can enjoy the late afternoon and early evening from its rooftop terrace. If you don't feel like hearing music, how about a drink and a movie? The **Cine Bar** at the Hotel Jacaranda (✆ **415/152-1015**), Calle Aldama 53, shows recently released American movies on a large screen and includes popcorn and a drink with the $6 price of admission. Waiters come to your table with drinks and will bring the dinner menu as well. The film starts rolling at 7:30pm. There are also a couple of bars near El Jardín that are good places if you just want to enjoy a drink with friends. One such place is **La Fragua,** next to Allende's house.

## A SIDE TRIP TO DOLORES HIDALGO: FINE POTTERY—AND SHRIMP ICE CREAM?

**Dolores Hidalgo** lies 40km (25 miles) northwest of San Miguel on Highway 35. Most people go there to shop in the factory warehouses of the Talavera companies, but the town itself merits a visit. It remains a quiet, provincial town with a lovely main square and parish church on whose steps Father Hidalgo proclaimed the independence of Mexico. The church has a charming façade that, if forced, I would label late Mexican baroque, but that doesn't do it justice. The interior of the church was plundered at various times but retains a couple of altarpieces that are worth a peek.

The main square has a quaint, small-town feel to it. Vendors sell ice cream in exotic flavors—tequila, shrimp, and *pulque* (beer) are just a few enticing examples—as well as mango, *guanábana,* and other more familiar standbys. It all started 30 years ago on a dare, and then caught on for the notoriety it gave the vendors. Ask for some impossibly bad flavor like cilantro-mezcal-chocolate-chip or chicken *mole* swirl, and, without batting an eye, they'll tell you they're fresh out and to come back tomorrow. Most of these ice creams are known as *nieves* and are low in fat; for a richer ice cream ask for a *mantecado.* If you're hungry, there is a restaurant on the east side of the square called El Patio.

Dolores has two small museums: The **Casa de Hidalgo** (admission $2), which is filled with letters and historical artifacts having to do with Father Hidalgo, will be of most interest to history buffs; the **Museo de la Independencia** (admission 50¢), a more dramatic approach to the theme of independence, also has a small collection of memorabilia of José Alfredo Jiménez, the king of ranchera music.

The **Talavera** pottery produced in Dolores is quite handsome and colorful, if somewhat less traditional than Talavera produced elsewhere. It is also cheaper and more plentiful. You can find all kinds of objects, from sink basins to napkin rings to hand-painted tiles. The pieces are formed with molds and then painted freehand. Prices here are considerably lower than what you'll pay in San Miguel. Below is a short list of Talavera, tile, and pottery factories. You'll come across the first two before you enter the town.

**Talavera San Gabriel** This store carries a large selection of ceramic-framed mirrors and drawer knobs, tiles, sinks, candelabra, casseroles, bowls, platters, anthropomorphic jars and candlesticks, ginger jars, and tissue holders. If the bus lets you off here, you'll need a taxi to continue into town. It's open Monday to Saturday from 8am to 5pm, Sunday from 8am to 2pm. Km 15 Carretera a San Miguel. ✆ and fax **418/182-0139.**

**Talavera A. Mora** On the highway after San Gabriel, you can't miss this store, which offers a lot of lead-free Talavera. Ask to see the production and you'll get a tour of the factory in back. Merchandise includes the popular dinnerware with a blue-and-yellow fish motif, zoomorphic planters, and much more. It's open Monday to Saturday from 9am to 6pm, Sunday from 10am to 6pm. Avenida del Salvador 5, Rancho Sta. Teresa. ✆ **418/182-1884.**

**Bazar El Portón** Located on the right side of the road as you enter Dolores, this is not a Talavera factory. It sells massive old (or just old-looking) doors and other architectural pieces, and new carved-wood furniture. Among the jumble are horse-head table pedestals, old wooden mining troughs, wagon wheels, rearing stallions, and carved sofas. It's open Monday to Friday from 8am to 6pm, Saturday from 8am to 5pm. Km 3 Avenida de los Héroes. ✆ **418/182-0894.** Fax 418/182-2229.

**Vajillas Fortino Guerrero** This store specializes in lead-free dinnerware. It has sets on display and carries about seven different patterns. The store is down a bit from Bazar El Portón, on the same side of the road. Hours are Monday to Friday from 9am to 2pm and 3 to 6pm, Saturday till noon. Calzada de los Héroes s/n. ✆ **418/182-2440.**

**Talavera Cortés** Homeowners in San Miguel frequent this store for Talavera tiles, sinks, towel racks, fancy wall-switch plates, knobs, and drawer pulls. You can watch craftspeople at work upstairs and browse the large warehouse downstairs. It's open Monday to Friday from 7am to 4:30pm, Saturday from 7am to 1pm. Distrito Federal 8, at Tabasco. ✆ **418/182-0900.**

**Azulejos Talavera Vázquez** This is a cornucopia of ceramics, from giant ginger jars to ashtrays and sinks. It has good prices on colorful ceramic picture frames in many sizes. It's 1 block south of the church with the gold and green tile dome. It's open Monday to Saturday from 8am to 7pm, Sunday from 10am to 3pm. Puebla at Tamaulipas. ✆ **418/182-0630.**

## 2 Guanajuato ★★

354km (221 miles) NW of Mexico City; 56km (35 miles) SE of León; 93km (58 miles) W of San Miguel de Allende; 208km (130 miles) SW of San Luis Potosí; 163km (102 miles) N of Morelia; 280km (175 miles) SE of Zacatecas

If you're going to Mexico to lose yourself, you'll have no problem doing so on the streets of Guanajuato (gwah-na-*whah*-toh). They seem designed for just such a purpose as they curl this way and that, becoming alleys or stairways, and intersecting each other at different angles. At times it can seem like the Twilight Zone; I've heard of people hurriedly passing by a curious-looking shop intending to return later, and then never being able to locate it again. To make matters worse, the streets are filled with things that can draw your attention away from the business of getting from one place to another. The town is so photogenic; everywhere you look is postcard material. Most buildings, like the streets, are irregular in shape, creating a jumble of walls, balconies and rooftops meeting each other in anything but a right angle. The churches are the exception, having regular floor plans, but even they show asymmetry—despite the best efforts of their builders, none has two matching towers, but this only adds to their considerable charm.

Founded in 1559, Guanajuato soon became a fabulously rich town, with world-famous mines (such as La Valenciana, Mineral de Cata, and Mineral de Rayas) that earned their owners titles of nobility. Guanajuato was one of Mexico's most important colonial mining cities (along with Zacatecas and San Luis Potosí) from the 16th through the 18th centuries. Their mines produced a third of all the silver in the world, and Guanajuato bloomed with elaborate churches and mansions. The city was plagued by floods until the citizenry finally diverted the river, leaving a bed for what has become a subterranean highway with cantilevered houses jutting out high above the roadway. To improve traffic flow, the city has opened an impressive network of tunnels (it is, after all, a mining town) that actually manages to increase a visitor's confusion but is quite handy once it's understood.

Still, on the surface Guanajuato seems like an old Spanish city that has been dumped into a Mexican highland valley. It's one of Mexico's hidden gems; although uncovered by relatively few foreign tourists, Guanajuato remains a popular weekend trip for people from Mexico City. Clean and beautifully preserved, Guanajuato should be high on your list of the finest places to visit in Mexico.

### ESSENTIALS

**GETTING THERE & DEPARTING** **By Plane** Air access is good, with frequent flights in and out of the León/Bajío airport, 27km (17 miles) from downtown Guanajuato ($27 for a taxi). The airport has an ATM, pharmacy, and gift store. **American Airlines'** local telephone number is ✆ **01-800/904-6000; Continental**'s is ✆ **01-800/900-5000; Delta**'s is ✆ **01-800/902-2100. Aeromexico** (✆ **01-800/021-4000**) and its affiliate, **Aerolitoral,** fly to and from Los Angeles, Tijuana, Mexico City, Puerto Vallarta, Monterrey, and Ciudad Juárez. **Mexicana** (✆ **01-800/502-2000**) flies to and from Chicago, Oakland, Los Angeles, Denver, San Jose, Guadalajara, Mexico City, and Tijuana. **Magnicharters** (✆ **477/717-5242**) flies to Ixtapa on Thursdays and Sundays. **AeroMar** (✆ **01-800/704-2900**) flies to and from Saltillo and Puebla.

## Guanajuato

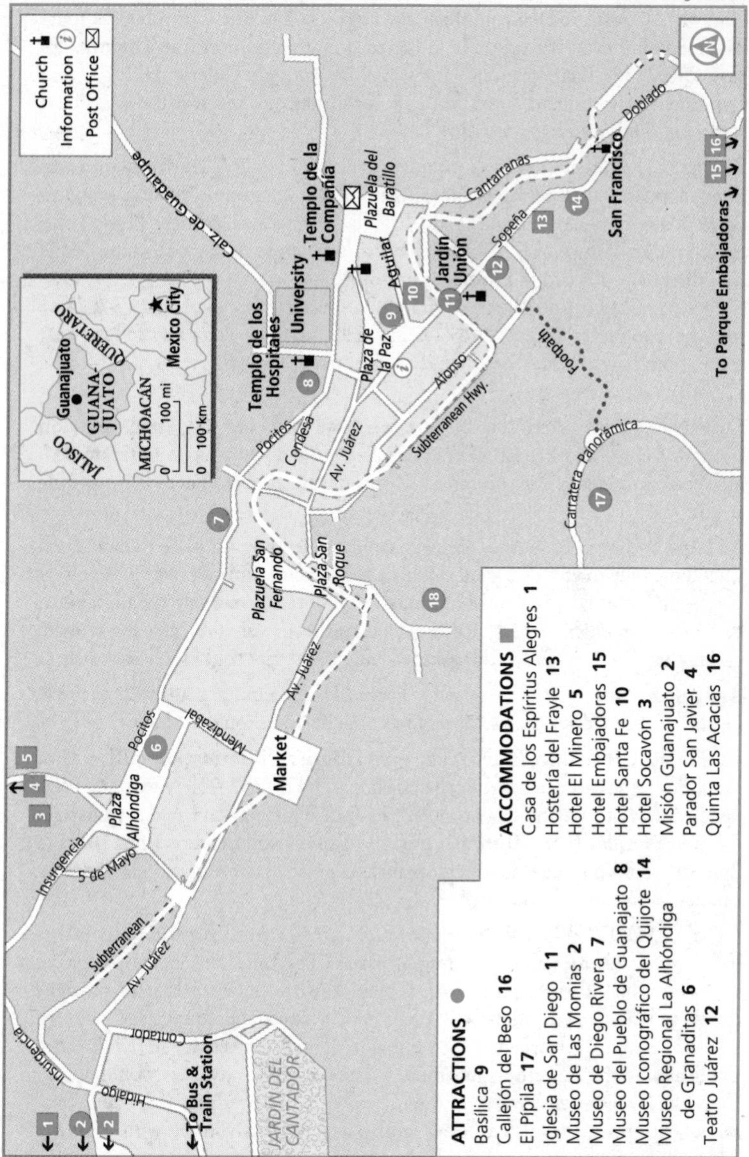


There are airline ticket offices in León and at the León/Bajío airport. In Guanajuato, travel agencies can arrange flights. One particularly helpful travel agent is María Teresa Gutiérrez of **Cambio 2000,** Paseo Madero 32 (© **473/731-1895**).

**By Car** From Mexico City there are two routes. The faster route (4½ hr.), although it may look longer, is Highway 57 north and northwest to Highway 45D at Querétaro, west through Salamanca to Irapuato, where you follow

Highway 45 north to Silao and then take Highway 110 east. The route is a four-lane road almost all the way. The other route continues north on Highway 57 past Querétaro, then west on Highway 110 through Dolores Hidalgo, and continues to Guanajuato. From San Luis Potosí, the quickest way to Guanajuato is through Dolores Hidalgo (3 hr.).

**By Bus** The bus station in Guanajuato is 6km (3½ miles) southwest of town. From Mexico City's Terminal Norte, you'll have no trouble finding a bus to Guanajuato. Servicios Coordinados, Estrella Blanca, and Primera Plus all run express buses (5 hr.). You shouldn't have to wait more than a half-hour. Make sure the bus you board is a *directo* (nonstop).

From San Miguel de Allende, Primera Plus has five first-class buses *Vía Presa* (the short route) to Guanajuato (1½ hr.). Herradura de Plata also follows that route. Both have service from the other silver cities, Guadalajara (4 hr.), Morelia (2½ hr.), and elsewhere.

**ORIENTATION** **Arriving by Plane** Note that the only transportation from the León/Bajío airport, 27km (17 miles) from downtown, is a **private taxi.** You arrange and pay for the cab ($27) inside the airport. There is no shuttle service.

**Arriving by Car** Try not to lose your sanity while finding a place to park. Such a winding, hilly town defies good verbal or written directions. Be alert for one-way streets, and after winding around through the subterranean highway a bit, you'll be oriented enough to park. Consider parking your car until you leave town, because the frustration of parking and driving in the city could spoil your visit.

**Arriving by Bus** The bus station is about 6km (3½ miles) southwest of town, on the road to Celaya. Cabs are easy to come by and should cost about $4.

**VISITOR INFORMATION** The state **tourism information office** is at Plaza de la Paz 14, across from the basilica (© **473/732-0397, ext. 107**). It's open Monday to Wednesday from 9am to 7pm, Thursday and Friday from 9am to 8pm, Saturday from 10am to 4 pm, and Sunday and holidays from 10am to 2pm. It has a knowledgeable English-speaking staff. Here you can get information and a free map of the city.

**CITY LAYOUT** Guanajuato is a town of narrow streets, alleys, and stairs that wend their way to small, picturesque plazas. The hilly terrain and tangle of streets are difficult to represent on a map. You'll soon learn that maps aren't drawn to scale, nor do they show every narrow street and connecting stairway. The best way to get oriented to the major sights is to get the *Mapa Turístico* published by the state tourism office. It represents the city as it would appear from the overlook at Pípila's statue. Then visit the overlook (see "El Pípila" among the attractions listed below) and compare what you see with the map. This will help you get your bearings.

The **Jardín Unión,** a small wedge-shaped plaza, is the center of the city—the place where students, locals, and visitors gather. Facing the Jardín from the direction of El Pípila are both the **Teatro Juárez** and **Templo de San Diego.** From this plaza, you are within walking distance of all the major sights.

**GETTING AROUND** Walking is the only way to get to know the historic district of this labyrinthine town. For longer stretches, taxis are reasonably priced and abundant, except between 2 and 4pm when office workers are trying to get home for the midafternoon meal. As usual, you should establish the price before setting out.

## *FAST FACTS:* Guanajuato

*Area Code* The telephone area code is **473.**

*Climate* The city has mild temperatures in summer, but in winter it can dip to freezing.

*Elevation* Guanajuato sits at 2,038m (6,724 ft.).

*Emergency/Police* Seguridad Pública (✆ **473/732-0266** or 473/732-0171).

*Hospital* You have two reasonable choices: **Centro Médico La Presa,** Paseo de la Presa 85 (✆ **473/731-1074**), and **Clínica Plaza Mayor,** in the western part of the city (✆ **473/732-2305**).

*Internet Access* There are several Internet cafes in the downtown area, with a lot of turnover. The best way to find one is to ask at the tourism office.

*Language School* There are five language schools in Guanajuato. The best known is **Instituto Falcón,** Callejón de la Mora 158, 36000 Guanajuato, Guanajuato (✆ **473/731-0745;** www.infonet.com.mx/falcon), which gets very high marks from its students. The institute provides skilled and dedicated tutors for those at all levels. It can also arrange boarding with local families.

*Pharmacy* **Farmacia Embajadoras,** Paseo Madero 10 (✆ **473/732-0996**), or **Farmacia La Perla,** Juárez 146 (✆ **473/732-1175**).

*Population* Guanajuato has 135,000 residents.

*Post Office* The *correo,* on the corner of Navarro and Carcamanes, near the Templo de la Compañía, is open Monday to Friday from 9am to 6pm.

*Seasons* Guanajuato has several high seasons during which hotel, and in some cases restaurant, prices go up, and unreserved rooms are hard to find. The high seasons are Christmas, Easter week, all of the Festival Cervantino (mid-Oct), and July and August.

## SPECIAL EVENTS & FESTIVALS

Every year, from about October 7 to 22, the state of Guanajuato sponsors the **Festival Cervantino** (International Cervantes Festival), two weeks of performing arts from all over the world. In recent years, the festival has featured marionettes from the Czech Republic, the Eliot Feld Ballet from New York, the Kiev Ballet, and a host of Mexican artists. The shows are held in open plazas and theaters all over town. Book rooms well in advance during the festival; if Guanajuato is full, consider staying in nearby San Miguel de Allende.

For ticket information and a schedule, contact Festival Cervantino, Plaza San Francisquito 1, 36000 Guanajuato, Gto. (✆ **473/731-1221**). Once you know the schedule, you can order tickets through **Ticketmaster** in Mexico City (✆ **55/5325-9000**). Keep your confirmation number; you'll need it to pick up your tickets in Guanajuato. The best time to be at the festival is during the week; on weekends it's absolute madness.

## EXPLORING GUANAJUATO

### THE TOP ATTRACTIONS

**El Pípila** This is the best vantage point in Guanajuato for photographs—the whole city unfolds below you, with great views in every direction. A new funicular railway runs up the hill from behind the church of San Diego. You can also climb the hill on foot up a rugged winding pathway. Just look for signs that read AL PIPILA ("To El Pípila").

The statue is the city's monument to José de los Reyes Martínez, better known as El Pípila. According to the story, El Pípila (if he existed) was a brave young miner in Father Hidalgo's ragtag army of peasants and workers fighting for Mexican independence. Guanajuato was the first real battle of the war. The Spanish forces took up their position inside the formidable Alhóndiga de Granaditas, which seemed an invincible fortress to Hidalgo's poorly armed forces. But El Pípila managed to breach the Spanish defenses by tying a flagstone to his back as protection, crawling to the fortress doors, and setting them ablaze. Today, El Pípila's statue raises a torch high over the city in everlasting vigilance; the inscription at his feet proclaims AUN HAY OTRAS ALHONDIGAS POR INCENDIAR ("There still remain other *alhóndigas* to burn").

Free admission. Daily 24 hr.

**Museo del Pueblo de Guanajuato** ★★ North of the Plaza de la Paz and before the Rivera Museum lies this 17th-century mansion that once belonged to the Marqués San Juan de Rayas. The first and third floors display traveling exhibits; the second holds a fascinating collection of colonial-era civil and religious pieces gathered by distinguished local muralist José Chávez Morado. As a collector, Chávez had an eye for the macabre, acquiring death portraits, some eerie portraits of the living, and religious paintings on the subject of mortality. Also in the collection are some paintings by Hermenegildo Bustos, a talented portrait artist of the mid-19th century. In addition, there is a small collection of pre-Hispanic artifacts and several folk-art testimonials dedicated to the miraculous powers of various saints. The museum contains a couple of Chávez's murals; other works can be found in La Alhóndiga down the street.

Calle Positos 7. ✆ **473/732-2990.** Admission $2. Tues–Sat 10am–6:30pm; Sun 10am–2:30pm.

**Museo Iconográfico del Quijote** ★ *Finds* There are only a few truly universal characters in the world of literature: Hamlet, Faust, Don Juan, and Don Quixote come to mind. Writers far and wide have taken up these characters and reworked their stories. But Don Quixote more than the others has become a favorite subject of artists. The list includes Dalí, Picasso, Miró, Raul Angiano, José Guadalupe Posada, Daumier, José Moreno Carbonero, and Pedro Coronel. This museum, a long block southeast of the Jardín Unión, past the Hostería del Frayle, holds a fascinating collection of art based upon Don Quixote—all Quixote, all the time! Particularly forceful are the sculptures and murals, but it is the sheer variety of forms that makes a stroll through this museum so entertaining.

Manuel Doblado 1. ✆ **473/732-6721.** Free admission. Tues–Sat 10am–6:30pm; Sun 10am–2:30pm.

**Museo Regional La Alhóndiga de Granaditas** ★ A long block away on the same street as the Rivera Museum, you'll see the huge Alhóndiga on the left (the entrance is on Positos).

The Alhóndiga de Granaditas was built between 1798 and 1809 as the town granary. The Spanish took refuge here in 1810 when El Pípila (see below) and company laid siege and finally took the building. A horrible slaughter ensued. This barbarous act convinced many people who had been leaning toward independence to remain loyal to Spain, although when the Spanish forces under Félix Calleja retook Guanajuato, they exacted an equally horrible revenge on the locals. (The exhibitions tell the story.) By the next year, the royal forces triumphed, and the heads of the insurrectionists Hidalgo, Allende, Aldama, and Jiménez adorned the four corners of the building, where they remained from 1811 to 1821 as a dissuasive reminder.

The old granary now houses a *museo regional.* Two floors of rooms surround a large courtyard. Part of the first floor is dedicated to the insurrectionist heroes, and another part has an exhibition of regional crafts. The second floor houses exhibits from pre-Hispanic to more recent times. Adorning the two stairways to the second floor are the vivid murals of José Chávez Morado, who donated his pre-Hispanic art collection to the museum (and whose colonial-era collection is in the Museo del Pueblo de Guanajuato). The exhibits that follow take you through the region's colonial era and its role in the struggle for independence, all the way up to the Mexican Revolution. Explanatory text is in Spanish only, but the artifacts are interesting and well displayed. Down the hill from the Alhóndiga is the Mercado Hidalgo, housed in a large, airy iron structure that dates from 1903 (see "Shopping," below).

Mendizabal 6. ✆ **473/732-1112.** Admission $2.75, free for students with ID; free for all Sun. Video camera $4. Tues–Sat 10am–2pm and 4–6pm; Sun 10am–3pm.

**Museum Birthplace of Diego Rivera** ★ From the Museo del Pueblo, walk 1½ blocks farther down the street, and you'll find the house where the artist Diego Rivera was born on December 8, 1886. It has been restored and converted into a museum. The first floor is furnished as it might have been in the era of Rivera's birth. Upstairs there's a pretty good collection of his early works. He began painting when he was 10 years old and eventually moved to Paris, where he became a Marxist during World War I. The house contains a few sketches of some of the earlier murals that made his reputation, and paintings from 1902 to 1956. The fourth floor holds a small auditorium where lectures and conferences take place.

Calle Positos 47. ✆ **473/732-1197.** Admission $2. Tues–Sat 10am–6:30pm; Sun 10am–2:30pm.

**Teatro Juárez** Built in 1903 during the opulent era of the Porfiriato, this theater is now the venue for many productions, especially during the Festival Cervantino. The exterior is starkly at odds with its surroundings—Greco-Roman columns and pediments adorned with fin-de-siècle bronze lions and lanterns. The interior is also lavishly decorated. Box seats rise up four stories along the walls of the theater, and there's not a bad seat in the house.

Jardín de la Unión. ✆ **473/732-0183.** Admission $1. Still camera $1, video camera $2. Tues–Sun 9am–1:45pm and 5–7:45pm.

## MORE ATTRACTIONS

The **Church of San Diego,** on the Jardín Unión, stands almost as it did in 1633, when it was built under the direction of Franciscan missionaries. After a 1760 flood that nearly destroyed it, reconstruction was completed in 1786; the Count of Valenciana gave half the funds. The pink cantera-stone façade is a fine example of the Mexican churrigueresque style.

The **Plazuela del Baratillo,** just behind the Jardín Unión, has a beautiful fountain (a gift from Emperor Maximilian) at its center. You'll always find people sitting around it peacefully, some in the shade and others in the sun. Its name derives from its former role as a weekly market (*tianguis*); vendors would yell *"¡barato!"* ("cheap"). The Plazuela San Fernando is larger and has a stone platform where there are local Mexican dances, with the younger generation decked out in bright costumes.

The **university** was founded in 1732, but its entrance was rebuilt in 1945 in imposing neoclassical style. The university is just behind Plaza de la Paz, and it's open every day. Visitors are welcome.

The **Church of the Compañía,** next to the university, was built in 1747 by the Jesuit order as the biggest of their churches at that time. It is distinctly churrigueresque on the outside, but the interior, which was restored in the 19th century, is not. This church was built as part of a Jesuit university, founded in 1732 on orders of Philip V on the site of the present university; it's the last of 23 universities the Jesuit order built in Mexico.

## NEARBY ATTRACTIONS

The following attractions are all a short distance above the city, and the best way to get to them is by taxi. You can hire one for $11 per hour. I would recommend taking the panoramic highway around the city, which allows you to pass by La Valenciana, La Cata, and La Raya; each place has a mine and a church. Tailings (gravel) mark the sites of the old mines. The highway winds around to El Pípila. The drive is enjoyable and lasts about an hour, with a couple of stops.

**Museo de Los Momias (Mummy Museum)** *Kids* First-time visitors find this museum grotesque or incredibly fascinating (or both): Mummified remains of Guanajuato's residents, some of whom wear tattered clothing from centuries past, are on display in tall showcases and glass caskets. Dryness and the earth's gases and minerals have caused decomposition to halt in certain sections of the *panteón* (cemetery). Because graveyards have limited space, bodies are exhumed to make room for newcomers. Those on display were exhumed between 1865 and 1985. The mummies stand or recline in glass cases, grinning, choking, or staring. It's impossible to resist the temptation to go up and look at them (everybody does), and this is the only graveyard I've seen with souvenir stands next to the main gate, selling sugar effigies of the mummies. If you catch a school group tour (and you know Spanish), you'll hear macabre discussions of the gruesome deaths more than a few of the residents suffered—much of which you should probably chalk up to haunted house hyperbole.

Museo de Los Momias. Esplanada del Panteón. ✆ **473/732-0639.** Admission $3. Still camera $1, video camera $2. Daily 9am–6pm. At the northwestern end of town, the steep Esplanada del Panteón leads up to the municipal cemetery.

**Iglesia de San Cayetano (La Valenciana)** ★★ The owner of the nearby La Valenciana mine built this magnificent church, completed toward the end of the colonial period. It is the finest example of the Mexican ultra-baroque style. The interior is a dazzling affair filled from floor to ceiling with gilded carvings and *retablos* (altarpieces). The best time to see it is midafternoon, when sunlight pours through the windows, illuminating the golden carvings. Across the road from the church is an *artesanía* store and wonderful restaurant, La Casa del Conde de la Valenciana (see "Shopping" and "Where to Dine," below). La Valenciana silver mine supposedly produced a fifth of the silver circulating in the world from 1558 to 1810 and is still in operation. The mining operations are above the church on the other side of the road at the top of the mountain. It's an eight-sided vertical shaft (500m/1,650 ft. deep) surrounded by a tall stone wall with large wooden doors and a miner's chapel at the entrance. The miners extract silver and about 50 other minerals and metals.

On the other side of the church and down below is a secondary shaft no longer in use, where a guide can take you into the mine and explain something of its operation for a $1 fee. There were only Spanish-speaking guides when I was there. To find it, look for a sign that says BOCAMINA–LA VALENCIANA. Templo de la Valenciana, Valenciana. Free admission. Daily 9am–6pm.

**Templo de Cata** Up above the city, perched on the mountain to the north, is this small, elaborate "miners' church." Cata is also the name of the mine nearby and the *barrio* that surrounds the church. A lovely baroque façade, with just one tower standing, decorates the outside. Until a couple of years ago, this church held an enormous number of personal testimonials that covered the walls from floor to ceiling. Most of these took the traditional form of small square sheets of metal with painted scenes (in a primitive folk style) and explanatory text describing the miracles performed by the church's Señor de Villaseca. "El Trigueñito" (roughly translated as "the olive-skinned one"), as he is affectionately called, is a popular figure in Guanajuato, especially with miners and truck and taxi drivers. And the testimonials were a touching display of the highly personal relationship these people have with El Trigueñito. What has become of all these testimonials is now the question. At first, the removal of the testimonials was supposed to be temporary, but, as time passes, I suspect they might not be coming back. Carretera Panorámica. Free admission. Daily 9am–5pm.

**A NEARBY MUSEUM** Surrounding Guanajuato were more than 150 haciendas of wealthy colonial mine owners. Most are now either in ruins or restored and privately owned, but one has been made into the **Museo Exhacienda San Gabriel de Barrera** ★. About 3km (2 miles) from town on the road to Marfil, it's a lovely place noted for its elaborate gardens in different styles (Arab, English, and Spanish, for example). The rest of the grounds are lovely. The hacienda house presents a good picture of 18th-century life in the grand style. As is often the case, the hacienda has its own chapel (baroque, of course), with a key identifying the various figures depicted in the *retablo.* There is also a state-run shop displaying all the handcrafts produced in the state. The grounds are open daily from 9am to 6pm; admission is $2.50, plus $1 for a still camera or $1.50 for a video camera. The store's hours are Wednesday to Sunday from 10am to 5pm.

The **Hotel Misión Guanajuato** is just across the road. See "Where to Stay," below, for information and directions.

## SHOPPING

Stores in Guanajuato keep the usual hours—10am to 2pm and 4 to 8pm. The **Mercado Hidalgo,** or municipal market, is one of the most orderly in Mexico, and it's a good place to browse or just watch from the raised walkway that encircles the main floor. Aside from food and vegetable stalls, there's lots of pottery and ceramic ware.

**Artesanías Vázquez** Outlet for a factory in Dolores Hidalgo, this place is small but loaded with the colorful Talavera-style pottery for which Dolores is famous. You'll see plates, ginger jars, frames, cups and saucers, serving bowls, and the like. Cantarranas 8. ✆ **473/732-5231.**

**Casa de Capelo** Famous ceramist Javier de Jesús Hernández, known simply as Capelo, has his workshop and showroom high above Guanajuato, past La Valenciana church. You'll see signs for the store, which point to a dirt road that climbs steeply to the left of the highway. Its hours are Monday to Friday from 10am to 6pm. Carretera a Dolores Hidalgo s/n. ✆ **473/732-8964.**

**The Gorky González Workshop** This prize-winning ceramist has dedicated himself to bringing back the traditional Talavera of Guanajuato. His work is lovely. The workshop is a short cab ride from the historic center. The showroom is open Monday to Friday from 10am to 2pm and 4 to 6pm, Saturday from 10am to 1pm. Call first. Calle Pastita Ex huerta de Montenegro (by the baseball field). ✆ **473/731-0389.**

**La Casa del Conde de la Valenciana** Though small, this shop carries a selection of the finest crafts from all over Mexico. It's open daily from 10am to 6pm. Across from the church of San Cayetano. ✆ **473/732-2550.**

**Rincón Artesanal** Objects in carved wood, wax, papier-mâché, pewter, and ceramic, produced in different workshops throughout the state of Guanajuato, stock this store. It also carries items from farther afield, including beautiful *catrina calaveras* (skeleton statues in fancy dress) from the state of Michoacán. The lovely mother and daughter who own and run the place are very helpful. It's open daily from 10am to 9pm. Sopeña 5 (1 block east of Jardín Unión). ✆ **473/732-8632.**

## WHERE TO STAY

During the International Cervantes Festival in mid-October, rooms are virtually impossible to find without a reservation, and even then it's good to claim your room early in the day. Some visitors have to stay as far away as Querétaro, León, or San Miguel de Allende and come to Guanajuato for the day. Many hotels offer discounts during low season.

### VERY EXPENSIVE

**Quinta Las Acacias** ★★ To stay here is to go back in time, not to the colonial period as with so many hotels, but to the late 19th century, when architecture and design in Mexico were borrowing heavily from French (called *afrancesado*) and Victorian architecture. This elegant house, like so many on the Paseo de la Presa, was built then and has been painstakingly remodeled. The rooms are decorated and furnished with period furniture, wallpaper, wainscoting, and nice little touches such as fresh-cut flowers. I prefer the three suites on the second floor (in Mexico, this is the first floor) to the two on the third floor. Behind the house are three larger, modern suites that have Jacuzzis. Rooms contain one king or two queen beds and have spacious, well-equipped bathrooms. Breakfast can be served in the dining room, on the terrace, or in the guest's room. The cocktail area serves drinks until 10pm.

Paseo de la Presa 168. 36000 Guanajuato, Gto. ✆ **888/497-4129** in the U.S. or ✆ 473/731-1517. Fax 473/731-1862. www.quintalasacacias.com.mx. 9 units. $210–$244 suite, $255–$300 suite with Jacuzzi. AE, MC, V. Rates include breakfast. Free limited parking. Children under 14 not accepted. **Amenities:** Bar; large outdoor Jacuzzi; tour desk; same-day laundry and dry cleaning. *In room:* A/C, TV, dataport, hair dryer, safe, robes, slippers.

### EXPENSIVE

**Casa de los Espíritus Alegres B&B** ★★★ *Moments* Folk art and atmosphere abound in this idiosyncratic "house of happy spirits." The house bursts with energy and vibrant folk art, incorporating 20th-century comfort in a 16th-century hacienda. All are uniquely and colorfully decorated, fulfilling the promise of "a skeleton in every closet," and each has its own fireplace.

Breakfast, served overlooking the garden, features Californian and Mexican food, with generous helpings of fresh fruit. Check out the hand-painted chairs (decorated by artist friends of the owners); one pays homage to Frida Kahlo. Guests have use of the folk-art-decorated living room, and may borrow history, travel, and art books as well as paperback novels. The efficient manager, Betsy McNair, can offer sound advice for guests visiting Guanajuato and the surrounding cities. The B&B is 3km (2 miles) from downtown (10 min. by taxi).

La Exhacienda la Trinidad 1, 36250 Marfil, Gto. ✆ and fax **473/733-1013.** casaspirit@aol.com. 8 units. $135–$158 double. Rates include breakfast. No credit cards. **Amenities:** Massage; nonsmoking rooms.

**Hotel Misión Guanajuato** ★ This three- to five-story hotel (without an elevator) is in a secluded spot next to the Hacienda San Gabriel Barrera. Much like a convent, most of the rooms have views of interior courtyards; unlike a convent, they offer all the creature comforts (except air-conditioning, which is rarely needed in this climate). The rooms are large, attractive, quiet, and come with two double beds and a terrace or balcony. Ten suites have minibars and coffeemakers. The grounds, pool, and tennis court are immaculately kept, and the staff is helpful. The hotel offers free transportation to and from town several times daily between 9am and 7pm. If you're driving, follow signs for the Convention Center and then look for HOTEL MISION signs.

Km 2.5 Camino Antiguo a Marfil, 36250 Guanajuato, Gto. ✆ **473/732-3980.** Fax 473/732-6092. 138 units. $140 double. AE, MC, V. Free parking. **Amenities:** Restaurant (Mexican/international), bar; large outdoor pool; tennis court; tour desk (Sat–Sun only); courtesy shuttle; business center; secretarial services; room service until 11pm; babysitting; overnight laundry and dry cleaning; nonsmoking rooms. *In room:* TV, dataport.

**Parador San Javier** ★★ *Kids* Created from a former silver-mining hacienda, the San Javier is built around lovely tree-shaded grounds (completely walled in) about 5 blocks above the Alhóndiga. Rooms in the six-story back section are large, carpeted, quiet, and comfortable. They've all been remodeled with the cheerful, contemporary Mexican colors and painted furniture. Four rooms in the older wing are slightly larger, with vaulted brick ceilings; they have more character and go for the same price. The suites are larger and have separate sitting rooms. A lovely pool is open during the season. Beneath the hotel bar is a cave with a natural spring that was the water source for the original hacienda.

Plaza Aldama 92, 36020 Guanajuato, Gto. ✆ **473/732-0650** or 473/732-0626. Fax 473/732-3114. www.hotelmex.com/paradorsanjavier. 114 units. $125 double; $145–$175 suite. Weekday discounts available. AE, MC, V. Free guarded parking. **Amenities:** Restaurant, bar; large heated pool (seasonal), wading pool; room service until 11:30pm; babysitting; same-day laundry and dry cleaning; nonsmoking rooms. *In room:* TV, dataport, safe.

## MODERATE

**Hostería del Frayle** This comfortable hotel located 1 block from the Jardín Unión offers quiet, albeit not the most attractive, rooms. The old part of the hotel in front is part of a colonial house and has three rooms that look out over the street; the rest of the rooms are in the newer part in back. The plumbing in the old part could be described as colonial—nothing major, just be prepared to run the hot water for up to 5 minutes before it gets hot. The rooms in back vary in size from large to medium, have carpeted floors, and one full bed or two twins (most with new mattresses). Bathrooms are medium in size, with limited counter space.

Sopeña 3, 36000 Guanajuato, Gto. ✆ and fax **473/732-1179.** 37 units. $95 double. MC, V. **Amenities:** Restaurant/bar; tour desk; room service until midnight; overnight laundry and dry cleaning; nonsmoking rooms. *In room:* TV, safe.

**Hotel Embajadoras** I liked this hotel a lot more before the owners raised the rates by about 40 percent. Still, you might want to call for a price check. The location is good—right on Parque Embajadoras, a tree-lined square that's a 10-minute walk east of the main square. The rooms border a pleasant central patio. All have carpeted floors and are comfortable, quiet, and plainly furnished.

Covered walkways with chairs link the rooms. A good, reasonably priced restaurant and bar takes care of meals.

Parque Embajadoras, 36000 Guanajuato, Gto. ✆ **473/731-0105** or 473/731-0084. Fax 473/731-0063. 27 units. $72 double. Promotional rates in low season. MC, V. Free parking. **Amenities:** Restaurant; tour info; room service until 9:30pm. *In room:* TV.

**Hotel Posada Santa Fe** ★ Right on the Jardín Unión, this hotel is for those who want to be in the thick of things from the moment they step out the door. It dates to the 1860s, having survived both the Reform wars and the Revolution, and the old lobby is a great place to have a drink. In the last few years, the hotel underwent extensive remodeling, and the wiring and plumbing in most of the building was replaced, which was money well spent. But the size of the rooms was one thing that couldn't be changed. They're small, except for the suites and some of the rooms with exterior views. They are, however, attractive and well kept, and I found them comfortable. Standard rooms hold either one double or two twin beds. Exterior-view rooms and suites have larger bathrooms and fancier furniture; most have king-size beds. The lower prices are for low season.

Jardín Unión, 36000 Guanajuato, Gto. ✆ **473/732-0084.** Fax 473/732-4653. santafe@int.com.mx. 48 units. $83–$112 double, $114–$200 exterior views and suites. AE, MC, V. Free limited valet parking. **Amenities:** Restaurant, 2 bars; whirlpool; room service until 10pm; overnight laundry. *In room:* TV.

### INEXPENSIVE

**Hotel El Minero** *Value* Only 2 blocks above the Museo Alhóndiga, this four-story (no elevator) hotel has that rare combination of cheap and cheerful rooms that are ample in size. They have newly installed tile floors, attractive paint jobs, ceiling fans, and small tile bathrooms with showers. Most have a double and a single bed. One drawback is that you have to walk a few blocks (to Hotel Socavón, which has the best restaurant in the neighborhood) to get a decent breakfast.

Alhóndiga 12-A, 36000 Guanajuato, Gto. ✆ **473/732-5251.** Fax 473/732-4739. 20 units. $30 double. MC, V. *In room:* TV.

**Hotel Socavón** *Socavón* means "mine shaft," and that's something of the feel you get when you walk from the door to the reception area. Farther back, up a couple of flights of stairs, are four floors of rooms (no elevator) around a small colonial-style courtyard. Rooms have tile floors, fans, cable TV with a few English channels, and small bathrooms. All rooms are quiet and have either two full beds or a full and a twin. This hotel never has rooms during the Festival Cervantino.

Alhóndiga 41, 36000 Guanajuato, Gto. ✆ **473/732-4845** or 473/732-7344. hotelsocavon@hotmail.com. 38 units. $42–$49 double. AE, MC, V. Free sheltered parking. **Amenities:** Restaurant/bar; room service until 11pm; babysitting; overnight laundry. *In room:* TV.

## WHERE TO DINE

The quality of restaurants in the downtown area is inexplicably poor. The only ones I like are **Truco 7** and **El Gallo Pitagórico** (as much for the view as for the food), listed below, and the restaurant of the **Hotel Posada Santa Fe** (see above), where you can dine reasonably well outside in the Jardín. A pretty place that has a different feel from the Jardín is the open Plaza de la Paz, a block away. Here you can sit down, have a drink, and perhaps nibble on an appetizer at one of the outdoor tables of **La Tasca de los Santos** in front of Guanajuato's cathedral. If you're in search of coffee, the best in town is at the **Café Dada** on the Plaza del Baratillo. It's open from 9am to 11pm daily; look for the small sign shaped like a coffee cup above the door.

### EXPENSIVE

**Casa del Conde de la Valenciana** ★★ MEXICAN/INTERNATIONAL Dine in the former home of the count of La Valenciana, across the street from his other creation, La Valenciana church. You can eat on the patio or in one of the dining rooms. The menu is a combination of old standards and original recipes. For an appetizer, try a fresh salad or refreshing *gazpacho* served in a vessel encased in ice. For a main course, you can choose one of Mexico's traditional dishes, such as chicken *mole* (or *enmoladas*), or perhaps chicken breast *a la flor de calabaza* (in a mild, satisfying cream sauce of blended squash flowers and poblano chile). For dessert, the ice creams are popular. The shady patio is so relaxing and the chairs so comfortable that most tourists linger over coffee and dessert far longer than they intend to. If you want to shop after eating, there's a wonderful furniture and decorative arts shop, with several rooms of merchandise.

Carretera, Guanajuato-Dolores km 5, opposite La Valenciana church. ✆ and fax **473/732-2550.** Main courses $7–$12. MC, V. Mon–Sat 10:30am–6pm.

**La Hacienda de Marfil** ★★ INTERNATIONAL In the Marfil area outside Guanajuato proper, next to the Casa de Espíritus Alegres (see "Where to Stay," above), this stylish, shady, outdoor restaurant attracts a clientele that comes for leisurely, unrushed dining. The menu changes every three months; typical dishes are trout in almond sauce, squash-blossom crepes, and fillet Roquefort. You can also order steaks and fine fresh salads with a choice of dressings. It's best to travel by cab.

Arcos de Guadalupe 3, Marfil. ✆ **473/733-1148.** Main courses $12–$18. AE, MC, V. Tues–Sun 1:20–6:30pm.

### MODERATE

**La Casona del Cielo** MEXICAN/INTERNATIONAL This beautiful second-floor restaurant is close to Gorky Gonzalez's workshop, and his Talavera decorates the tables and walls. Popular dishes include *arrachera Louraint* (beef in pastry with *huitlacoche*), *lomo Santo al Xoconoztle* (steak covered with prickly pear–orange sauce), and *pollo al pistache* (chicken sautéed with pistachio nuts). To get here, take a cab, but call first—it's often closed.

Pastita 76. ✆ **473/731-2000.** Main courses $6–$15. AE, MC, V. Tues–Sat 12:30–10pm; Sun–Mon 12:30–6pm.

### INEXPENSIVE

**El Gallo Pitagórico** ITALIAN Lasagna with a view—getting here from the main square is roughly the equivalent of climbing a few flights of stairs. Look for a deep blue house on the hill behind San Diego church, well below the statue of El Pípila. It's not hard to find. Dining on the upper terrace at night, with the city lights for a backdrop, is very romantic. Besides the lasagna, house specialties include a variety of pastas, *filetto alla italiana,* and crostini.

Constancia 10-A. ✆ **473/732-6758.** Reservations recommended. Main courses $5–$10. MC, V. Tues–Sun 2–11:30pm.

**Truco 7** ★ MEXICAN With its economical prices and warm atmosphere, this place is a solid choice for any meal. The three dining rooms are small and a bit crowded, yet nicely decorated with leather *equipal* tables and chairs and paintings by local artists. The restaurant occupies an 18th-century structure originally built for members of the Valenciana silver family. Calle Truco, a short street south of the basilica, runs between the Jardín Unión and the Plaza de la Paz.

Truco 7. ✆ **473/732-8374.** Reservations not accepted. Breakfast $2–$4; *comida corrida* (served 2–4pm) $3; main courses $5–$8. No credit cards. Daily 8:30am–11:30pm.

### Moments The Redolent Mexican Cantina

If you're curious about Mexican cantinas, swinging saloon doors and all, Guanajuato is a good place to do your fieldwork. You should know, however, that most of these are *men-only* drinking dives.

The town's favorite son is José Alfredo Jiménez, the undisputed master of *ranchera* music. This is the quintessential drinking music (one long lament punctuated by classic Mexican yelps) that drives most non-Mexicans screaming from the building. But after downing a few *copitas,* you may warm up to it, and after asking about Jiménez, you'll probably get a few more drinks on the house. Around the Jardín Unión are a couple of cantinas that aren't bad; I enjoyed a few shots at one called **El Incendio** ("Fire"), Cantarranas 15. Unlike most cantinas, this place welcomes women. The barkeep was a good talker, and the colorful wall murals held icons of Mexican popular culture—María Félix on one, opposite the lovesick Agustín Lara. We had our choice of beer, tequila, or mezcal, and all the good-natured conversation we could handle. El Incendio opens at 10am and closes at 4am.

You may be surprised to see an open urinal at the end of the bar. While this is a standard feature in cantinas and part of the, er, authentic flavor, you still may wish to opt for a seat at the opposite end.

### GUANAJUATO AFTER DARK

If city planners had known the **Jardín Unión** would be so popular, they might have made it larger. This tiny plaza, shaded by Indian laurel trees, is the heart of the city and the best hangout. No other spot in town rivals its benches and sidewalk restaurants.

You can catch some worthwhile free **theater** in Plazuela de San Roque at 8pm on Sundays when the university is in session. Students perform short theatrical pieces known as *entremeses* (literally, "intermissions"). These are usually costumed period pieces that rely more on action than dialogue, so you don't need to understand too much Spanish to get the point. The costumes are great and look curiously appropriate in this plazuela.

More conventional nightspots—i.e., discos—aren't difficult to find; ask at your hotel. A different kind of place is **La Dama de las Camelias,** Sopeña 32, an unpretentious second-floor bar that doesn't get going until late in the evening. The music is all classic recordings of *danzón, mambo, son cubano,* and *salsa.* It opens at 8pm, starts getting busy around midnight, and closes at 4am. Another salsa bar is behind the San Diego church at the foot of the hill where El Pípila stands.

## 3 Santiago de Querétaro ★★★

213km (133 miles) NW of Mexico City; 96km (60 miles) SE of San Miguel Allende; 200km (125 miles) S of San Luis Potosí

Querétaro is the oldest city in this chapter, and the most historic. During the colonial era, it played a central role in the conquest and evangelization of northern Mexico. In later times, it was at the center of events in the three wars that forged the Mexican nation: La Independencia, La Reforma, and La Revolución.

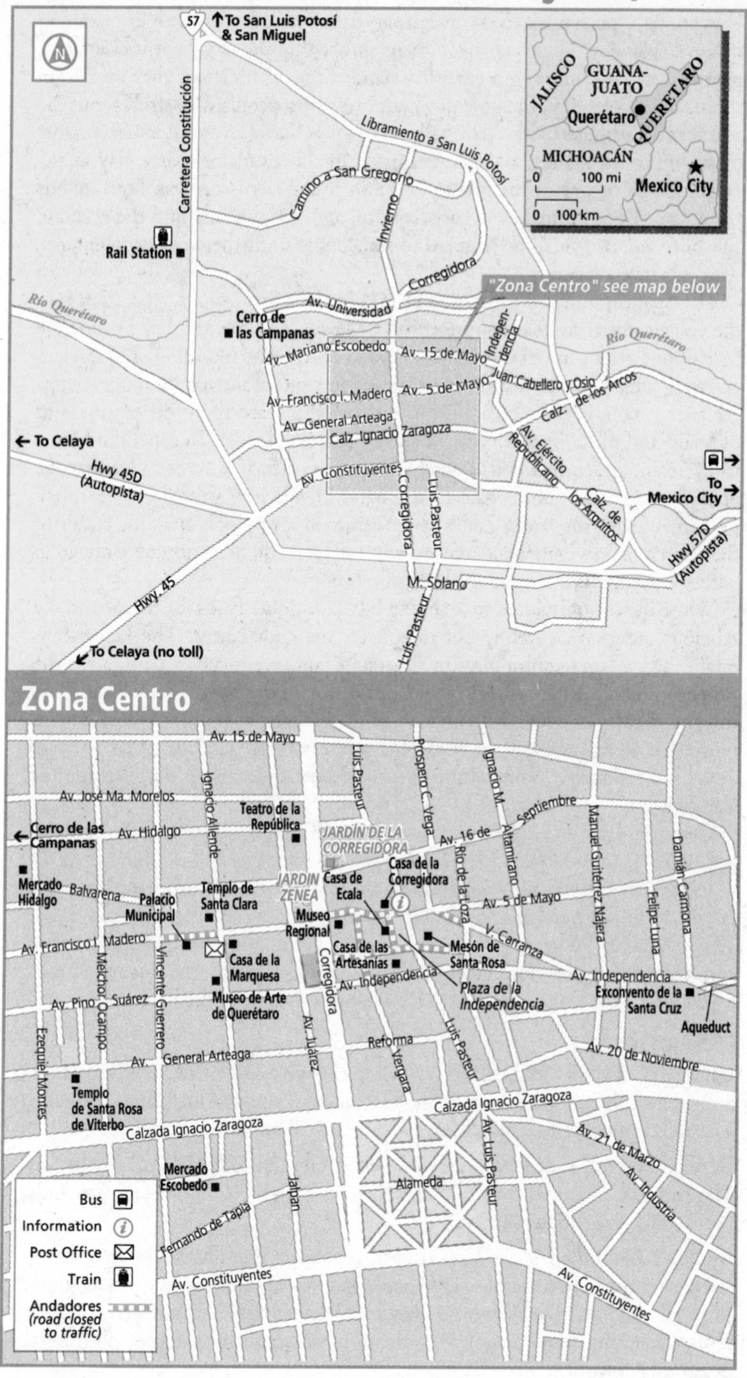
57
To San Luis Potosí & San Miguel
JALISCO
GUANAJUATO
QUERÉTARO
Querétaro
MICHOACÁN
Mexico City
0 100 mi
0 100 km
Carretera Constitución
Libramiento a San Luis Potosí
Camino a San Gregorio
Invierno
Rail Station
Corregidora
"Zona Centro" see map below
Río Querétaro
Av. Universidad
Cerro de las Campanas
Independencia
Av. Mariano Escobedo
Av. 15 de Mayo
Av. 5 de Mayo
Juan Caballero y Osio
Calz. de los Arcos
Av. Francisco I. Madero
Av. General Arteaga
Calz. Ignacio Zaragoza
To Celaya
Av. Ejército Republicano
Hwy 45D (Autopista)
Av. Constituyentes
Corregidora
Luis Pasteur
Calz. de los Arquitos
To Mexico City
Hwy 57D (Autopista)
M. Solano
Hwy. 45
Luis Pasteur
To Celaya (no toll)
Zona Centro
Av. 15 de Mayo
Luis Pasteur
Prospero C. Vega
Ignacio M. Altamirano
Av. José Ma. Morelos
Ignacio Allende
Teatro de la República
Cerro de las Campanas
Av. Hidalgo
JARDÍN DE LA CORREGIDORA
Av. 16 de Septiembre
Manuel Guitérrez Nájera
Damián Carmona
Mercado Hidalgo
Balvarena
Palacio Municipal
Templo de Santa Clara
JARDIN ZENEA
Casa de Ecala
Casa de la Corregidora
Río de la Loza
Av. 5 de Mayo
Felipe Luna
Museo Regional
V. Carranza
Av. Francisco I. Madero
Casa de la Marquesa
Casa de las Artesanías
Mesón de Santa Rosa
Melchor Ocampo
Vincente Guerrero
Corregidora
Av. Independencia
Plaza de la Independencia
Av. Independencia
Exconvento de la Santa Cruz
Aqueduct
Av. Pino Suárez
Museo de Arte de Querétaro
Ezequiel Montes
Av. Juárez
Reforma
Vergara
Luis Pasteur
Av. 20 de Noviembre
Av. General Arteaga
Templo de Santa Rosa de Viterbo
Calzada Ignacio Zaragoza
Calzada Ignacio Zaragoza
Av. Luis Pasteur
Av. 21 de Marzo
Mercado Escobedo
Jalpan
Alameda
Av. Industria
Bus
Information
Post Office
Train
Andadores (road closed to traffic)
Fernando de Tapia
Av. Constituyentes
Av. Constituyentes

Downtown Querétaro is lively, pedestrian-friendly, and filled with eye-opening colonial splendor. The local government spruced up the city, kept it clean, and provided street vendors with attractive stands (it regulates where they can set up shop). In the evenings, the downtown area fills with people who stroll about the plazas and *andadores* (pedestrian walkways), eat at one of the outdoor restaurants or at one of the stands, and perhaps listen to the municipal band play in the Jardín Zenea or one of the other plazas. Since the city is only an hour by bus from San Miguel, it makes an easy day trip, and you can stay into the evening. But once you do, you'll be tempted to stay longer to further your acquaintance with this lovely city.

The Spanish founded Querétaro (1531) in their first serious expedition into the vast northern stretches of present-day Mexico. In time, the city became the base of operations for all expeditions headed north. The founding of Querétaro occurred after a battle with the Chichimeca in which Santiago (St. James), now the patron saint of the city, appeared in the clouds. Santiago is the patron saint of Spain and of La Reconquista, the seven-century struggle to expel the Moors from Spain, which had ended barely 40 years earlier. It is no wonder that the Spanish hoped he would again lend a hand in this new struggle for territory. (When you visit the Jardín Zenea at the center of town, look up at the façade of the church of San Francisco, and you will see a forceful depiction of Santiago in battle, lopping off the turbaned head of a Moor.)

While the conquistadors were setting out to conquer lands for the crown, the religious orders were setting out to convert souls for Christ. The Franciscans established a large community in Querétaro and eventually a college for the propagation of the faith, the first such institution in the New World. From here, the Franciscans set out (always on foot, as the Franciscan Rule forbade riding on horseback or in carriages) to evangelize and establish missions as far away as Texas and California. Some of the history of these endeavors is nothing short of astounding.

Centuries later, Mexican independence began in Querétaro with the conspiracy of 1810 (of which Father Hidalgo was a member). A little more than 50 years after that, Querétaro was again in the thick of it when Emperor Maximilian made his last stand against the Liberal army (and was executed shortly thereafter). Another 50 years passed, and the city became the site of the laborious constitutional convention during the Mexican Revolution. The document that it produced, the Constitution of 1917, remains the law of the land.

## ESSENTIALS

**GETTING THERE & DEPARTING** **By Plane** Fly to Mexico City. At the airport, exit through the doors facing Gate D, and you will find direct bus service to Querétaro (4 hr.). Buses leave about every hour and cost $19.

**By Car** From Mexico City, take the super toll road 57D (2½ hr.). From San Miguel, take Highway 111 to 57D, then turn right (1 hr.). From San Luis Potosí, take 57D south (2½ hr.).

**By Bus** From the Mexico City airport, see above. From Mexico City's northern bus terminal, buses leave every 15 minutes. Make sure you get a *directo* (nonstop). From San Miguel, second-class buses leave every 15 minutes. The bus station is south of town. Look for a booth in the terminal that sells cab tickets. A cab ride downtown costs $2.50.

**VISITOR INFORMATION** There is a good **tourism information office** (© **442/238-5000,** ext. 5067 or 5212) at Pasteur Norte 4, just off the Plaza de la Independencia on the north side. It's open weekdays from 8am to 8pm, weekends from 9am to 8pm. The office conducts tours of the city ($3) in a trolley-style bus. Tours leave at 9, 10, and 11am, and 4, 5, and 6pm, and take about an hour. They are usually in Spanish unless there's a group of English speakers going. One tour covers the territory east of the plaza and drives by the impressive aqueduct. The other tour goes west, reaching the Cerro de Campanas, where Maximilian was executed. These are abbreviated trips that necessarily leave a lot unseen, but they're good for getting an idea of the city's layout. There are plans to organize a longer tour that visits sites just outside the city, but it is not finalized. Ask about walking tours, too.

**CITY LAYOUT** The heart of downtown is the Jardín Zenea, at the intersection of the main north-south and east-west streets, Corregidora and Madero. Just east is the Plaza de Armas, and farther east are the Convento de la Cruz and the famous aqueduct. West of Jardín Zenea are several plazas, churches, convents, museums, and, at the western boundary of the downtown area (a little too far to walk), the Cerro de Campanas.

### *FAST FACTS:* Querétaro

*American Express* The local representative is **Agencia Turismo Beverly,** Av. Tecnológico 118, Col. San Angel (© **442/216-1500**). Office hours are Monday to Friday from 9am to 2pm and 4 to 6pm, Saturday from 9am to noon.

*Area Code* The telephone area code is **442.**

*Climate* The average temperature in summer is 75°F (24°C), in winter 56°F (13°C).

*Elevation* Querétaro sits at 1,818m (6,000 ft.).

*Emergency* The central emergency number (similar to 911) is © **066.**

*Hospital* The local hospital is the **Hospital General de Querétaro** (© **442/216-2036**).

*Internet Access* Cybercafes are opening all the time, but if you can't find one, try **Inform@,** Hidalgo 75-B, between Ezequiel Montes and Ocampo streets. It's open Monday to Friday from 10am to 2pm and 4 to 8pm, Saturday from 10am to 2pm.

*Parking* To find parking in the downtown area, look for white square signs with the capital letter E in light blue. There are a couple of places at Pino Suárez 45 and 17. Rates run about $1 for the first hour, and 25¢ for every hour after that.

*Population* Querétaro has 640,000 residents.

*Post Office* The *correo,* Arteaga 5, is open Monday to Saturday from 9am to 2:30pm.

## A STROLL AROUND THE HISTORIC CENTER

In the center of Querétaro, you'll notice right away how many lovely plazas, churches, and convents there are. If you're really observant, you'll notice that the plazas are frequently located next to the churches. Most of these plazas were formed at the cost of the many convents in town, which lost much of their real estate to the government after the Reform Law. This is true of the town's most important plaza, **Jardín Zenea,** where we will begin. This plaza used to be part of the atrium of San Francisco Church and Convent, which you see facing the park across Corregidora Street. This park is popular every night but especially on Sunday, when the municipal band plays dance music of the '40s, '50s, and '60s. The old bandstand dates from the turn of the century.

Turn toward **San Francisco Church,** and you will see on the façade the depiction of St. James mentioned earlier. It's directly under the clock. From the beginning, this church was the most important in town and remains so today, the more recent cathedral notwithstanding. It and the attached cloister are all that remain of a large complex that included several chapels and beautiful orchards that extended a few blocks east and south. Inside the church, you will see a few interesting remains of baroque decoration. The main altar is a rather uninteresting piece of neoclassicism that replaced what reputedly was a masterpiece of baroque design. This is a common story with churches in Querétaro: Many of the beautiful baroque *retablos* managed to escape plunderers, only to fall prey to "improvers," as was the case here.

Next door to the church is the cloister, which is now the **Museo Regional** ★. Admission is $2; free on Tuesday. It's open Tuesday to Sunday from 10am to 7pm. Exhibits include artifacts from pre-Hispanic, colonial, and republican times. The architecture shows common traits of Franciscan design in the simplicity of its lines and paucity of decoration, which you can contrast with the rich decoration (caryatids and all) in the convent of San Agustín (see below), now a museum of colonial art.

Leaving the museum, turn left and then left again and you'll be on the pedestrians-only Andador Libertad. This leads to the small Plaza de Independencia or Plaza de Armas, with its carefully hedged Indian laurel trees, outdoor restaurants, and colonial mansions. Before you get to it, you'll pass the **Casa Queretana de Artesanía,** Andador Libertad 52 (✆ **442/214-1235**), a handcrafts store run by the state. It's on the right and has no sign. It sells weavings, regional clothing, pottery, hand-carved furniture, onyx, opals, and jewelry incorporating other semiprecious stones, all from Querétaro. It also carries a variety of items from other regions of Mexico. It's open Tuesday to Friday from 11:30am to 2pm and 4 to 8pm, Saturday from 11:30am to 9pm, and Sunday from 11:30am to 5pm.

At the opposite end of the Plaza de Independencia is the **Casa de la Corregidora,** a home of Doña Josefa Ortiz de Domínguez, a heroine of the War of Independence who is known as "La Corregidora" (the mayor's wife). Despite being under lock and key, she managed to warn Father Hidalgo that their conspiracy to liberate Mexico from Spain had been discovered. Hidalgo got the message and hurried to proclaim independence in Dolores. For her actions, Domínguez was imprisoned several times between 1810 and 1817. She died impoverished and forgotten, although today she is revered. She was the first woman to appear on a Mexican coin—the 5-centavo piece, minted from 1942 to 1946. Around the corner and across the street (Calle Pasteur) is the tourism office; you can inquire here about city tours.

As you walk toward the Casa de la Corregidora, you will pass the **Casa de Ecala** on your left. Built in a magisterial baroque style with beautiful balconies and wrought iron, it dates from the 18th century. The fountain in the middle of the plaza honors Querétaro's greatest benefactor, a Spanish grandee named Don Juan Antonio Urrutia y Arana, who built a large aqueduct to bring water to the city.

To view the aqueduct, continue east on Andador Libertad. It ends in 1 block, so you must dog-leg to the next eastbound street, either Independencia or

Carranza. In 3 blocks you will arrive at the plaza, church, and convent. This is the **Convento de La Santa Cruz** ★★, where missionaries were trained to evangelize the heathens as far away as California and Nicaragua. It is a simple monastery in the Franciscan style. You can take a short tour, which shows how the water from the aqueduct arrived here and how it fed a system of fountains known as *cajas de agua* that operated across the old city. From these, the citizens of Querétaro would fill their buckets. You will also be shown a thorn tree said to have grown from the walking stick of Friar Antonio Margil de Jesús, a famous missionary who covered vast territories on foot. This thorn tree is considered miraculous because its thorns grow in the shape of the cross.

Behind the church is a small plaza where the city's most illustrious are buried; it affords a good view of the 74 arches of the **aqueduct** that connects two prominences across an expanse of bottomland. This feat of engineering was begun in 1726 and finished in 1738.

To get back to the Jardín Zenea, you can work your way through some of the *andadores* around Plaza de la Independencia, or stay on Calle Independencia all the way to Calle Corregidora. If you go this way, you'll pass a small museum on your right after you cross Rio de la Losa. Called **La Casa de la Zacatecana** (no sign), it presents a vision of what many colonial mansions were like in Querétaro, with period furnishings and decor. Associated with this house (as with a couple of others in town) is a tale of illicit love, crime, and final retribution. Colonial Mexico is a fertile land for gothic tales, and in my travels I have heard many.

Back at Jardín Zenea, head west on Calle Madero. At the first corner, just before the street becomes an *andador,* is the opulent **La Casa de la Marquesa** ★, a colonial residence turned hotel. Walk in and check out the courtyard, which has elaborate *mudéjar*-style arches and patterned walls. Cater-corner from this hotel is a fountain of Neptune by one of Mexico's most famous architects, Eduardo Tresguerras, who is responsible for much of Querétaro's 19th-century neoclassical architecture.

The **church and former Convent of Santa Clara** ★★★ is behind the fountain. The church is a must-see; inside are five astonishing baroque *retablos* and a choir loft, all gilded and each a self-contained composition. In prominent positions are sculptures and paintings of saints; here and there, the faces of angels appear out of the enveloping, thickly textured ornament. Gazing upon these is like gazing upon a mandala. The juxtaposition of straight lines and multiple facets with overflowing curves that move inward and outward make the *retablos* appear fluid and structured at the same time. The key to enjoying these *retablos* is not to look for proportion, balance, or the underlying reason behind them, but to look at them as the exultant expression of a religious sentiment that defies these very concepts.

For a greater acquaintance with the colonial religious mind, walk south 1 block on Allende. On your right will be the **Museo de Arte** ★★ (**✆ 442/212-3523**) in the former **convent of San Agustín.** Admission is $2; free on Tuesday. The museum is open Tuesday to Sunday from 11am to 7pm. It contains one of the great collections of Mexican colonial art, but the architecture of the former convent alone is worth the price of admission. In contrast to the Franciscan convents, highly stylized human forms, complex geometric lines, and vegetal motifs are everywhere. The art is organized by century and style of painting. The collection has works by Europeans, but its focus is works by painters in New Spain, including the most famous of the land.

If you're still in the mood for colonial splendor, continue south 1 block to Arteaga Street, turn right, and head west for 3 blocks to the **church and former**

### Tips Shopping for Opals

The small state of Querétaro is one of the two principal places in the world that mine opals commercially (the other is southern Australia). The opal is a soft stone that is noted for its iridescent play of color. Prices vary depending on size, color, shape, and transparency. A few stores in Querétaro, usually called *lapidarias,* sell locally mined opals and other semiprecious stones. One is the **Lapidaria de Querétaro,** Corregidora Nte. 149-A, a few blocks north of Jardín Zenea (✆ **442/214-2140**). It's open Monday to Friday from 10am to 2pm and 5 to 7:30pm. Or stop by **El Artesano,** a little shop at Corregidora Nte. 42, near the Jardín Zenea and across from Sears. Owner Alfredo Vázquez, who carves miniatures out of opals and other semiprecious stones, speaks mostly Spanish, and is a fountain of information on opals and the trade. Another source is Lapidaria Ramírez, Pino Suárez 98.

**convent of Santa Rosa de Viterbo** ★★. Like Santa Clara, it is one of the masterpieces of colonial baroque architecture. On the outside, notice the fanciful flying buttresses (a style that as far as I know is unique to Querétaro) and the imaginative tower. Inside, the church is much like Santa Clara, with magnificent gilt *retablos* occupying all available wall space. Also like Santa Clara, the main altar failed to escape the "improvers."

Farther west is the **Cerro de las Campanas** (Hill of Bells), where Maximilian was executed. To get there you'll have to take a cab. You'll find a large but ugly statue of Juárez that was built to counter a small, sad memorial chapel for Maximilian built by his brother, Emperor Francis Joseph of Austria.

## WHERE TO STAY

Querétaro lacks the hotel selection of San Miguel. There are two beautiful luxury hotels, **La Casa de la Marquesa** and **Hotel Mesón de Santa Rosa.** To spend a night in either one, make reservations at least three weeks in advance.

**Hotel Mesón de Santa Rosa** ★★ With its large open courtyards, clean lines, and simple stone and ironwork, this hotel presents a colonial architecture that contrasts sharply with La Casa de la Marquesa. Of the two, I prefer the Santa Rosa for its large courtyards and simple elegance (and lower rates). Rooms surround courtyards that hold a heated pool, a fountain, and a stone trough for watering your horses (a vestige of the original tavern, which served wagon and mule drivers). Rooms are quiet, large, and comfortable, with colonial-style furniture, high ceilings, and carpeted floors. They have large bathrooms and come with either two doubles or a king-size bed. The hotel is on the southwest corner of the Plaza de Independencia—a perfect spot. The restaurant might be the best in town.

Pasteur 17 Sur, 76000 Querétaro, Qro. ✆ **442/224-2623.** Fax 442/212-5522. www.mesondesantarosa.com.mx. 21 units. $130 double; $208 suite. AE, MC, V. Valet parking $6. **Amenities:** Restaurant; bar; medium-size heated outdoor pool; room service until 11pm; same-day laundry and dry cleaning. *In room:* TV, dataport, minibar, coffeemaker, hair dryer, safe.

**Hotel Señorial** This is a simple hotel 4 blocks from the Jardín Zenea. Rooms are plainly furnished and carpeted. The beds (usually two twins or two doubles) are comfortable; rooms with air-conditioning are about $5 extra. The important thing is to get an even-numbered room. Odd-numbered rooms are in the south wing, which occasionally has unbelievably noisy plumbing.

Guerrero Nte. 10-A, 76000 Querétaro, Qro. ✆ and fax **442/214-3700.** 54 units. $43–$59 double. MC, V. Free parking. **Amenities:** Restaurant; room service. *In room:* TV.

**La Casa de la Marquesa** ★★ Few hotels in Mexico can match this one for sheer colonial opulence. Even if you don't stay here, make a point of walking into the courtyard lobby or dining here. Built for the wife of a Spanish marquis, the house, with its Moorish-inspired arches, tiles, and painted walls, has an Andalusian feel to it. Rooms are large, have all the amenities, and are beautifully furnished with period pieces and Persian rugs. Some rooms are across the street in another colonial house, La Casa Azul. The hotel, a member of the Small Luxury Hotels of the World, prides itself on the attention it gives its guests. The restaurant serves international and Mexican food and does a good job of it. The location is excellent.

Madero 41, 76000 Querétaro, Qro. ✆ **442/212-0092.** Fax 442/212-0098. www.marquesa.com. 25 units. $270 royal suite; $330 imperial suite. AE, MC, V. Free valet parking. **Amenities:** Restaurant (international), bar; membership at local golf club and local spa; concierge; tour desk; executive business services; room service until 11pm; in-room massage; overnight laundry and dry cleaning. *In room:* A/C, TV, dataport, hair dryer, bathrobes.

**Mesón de la Luna** This is a three-story hotel with quiet rooms removed from the street. The cheerful, mid-size rooms have tile floors and one or two double beds. Larger rooms come with carpeting and roomier bathrooms. The hotel is 7 blocks from the center of town.

Mariano Escobedo 104 (between Guerrero and Ocampo), 76000 Querétaro, Qro. ✆ **442/212-4378.** 40 units. $33–$47 double. No credit cards. Free parking. *In room:* TV.

## WHERE TO DINE

For fine dining, try the restaurants at either of the luxury hotels. The modern restaurant district is in the area surrounding the aqueduct, where you'll find just about anything. The restaurants listed below are in the downtown area.

**Cafetería Bisquets** MEXICAN This modest restaurant a couple of blocks south of Jardín Zenea serves inexpensive *comida casera* (home-cooking) on a lovely little patio. One of the specialties is paper-thin *milanesa* with green enchiladas on the side. For breakfast, the most popular item is the *bisquet*—something like an American biscuit, but larger and toasted. It comes with your choice of topping and is commonly accompanied by a *café con leche.*

Pino Suárez 7. ✆ **442/214-1481.** Main courses $2–$5. No credit cards. Daily 7:30am–11pm.

**Cafetería La Mariposa** MEXICAN Look for the wrought-iron butterfly sign when you turn left on Peralta (2 blocks north of Jardín Zenea) to find this popular coffee shop and restaurant. It's good for typical Mexican food such as enchiladas and breakfasts. It also sells sweets and pastries, which you see to your left when you enter. For something regional, try the *enchiladas queretanas.*

Ángela Peralta 7. ✆ **442/212-1166.** Main courses $3–$6. No credit cards. Daily 8am–9:30pm.

**Restaurante Bar 1810** MEXICAN/INTERNATIONAL This is one of the restaurants on the Plaza de Armas across from the house of La Corregidora. It has a large and varied menu, and is the perfect place to enjoy an afternoon or evening meal. There is indoor dining as well. Your best bet is to stick with traditional Mexican specialties, which are well prepared; the soups are wonderful. Sunday brunch is especially popular.

Andador Libertad 62. ✆ **442/212-3324.** Main courses $7–$12. MC, V. Daily 8am–midnight.

### SIDE TRIPS FROM QUERETARO

In the northern part of the small state of Querétaro is a mountain range known as the **Sierra Gorda.** It makes a lovely 2- or 3-day trip whether you're in the mood to see beautiful mountain landscapes with pine forests and old Spanish missions or to simply get away from all the people. There are some comfortable, inexpensive hotels in the towns of Jalpan and Concá, among others. Tours to the region from Querétaro are a bargain. A company called **Jocha** (**© 442/212-8940**) operates a recommended tour.

## 4 Zacatecas ★

627km (392 miles) NW of Mexico City; 198km (124 miles) NW of San Luis Potosí; 322km (201 miles) NE of Guadalajara; 298km (186 miles) SE of Durango

Zacatecas, like Guanajuato, owes its beauty to the wealth of silver extracted from its mines. The farthest flung of the silver cities, it is a jewel in the rough. High over the town center looms a steep mountain that's accessible by cable car. From there, you can gaze over the city and beyond to the wild and desolate surroundings. The scene makes you realize what a frontier town Zacatecas was, and after you have been in town for a few days, it makes you appreciate its present sophistication all the more. In this city out in the middle of nowhere, you will find startlingly good museums, beautiful architecture, and wonderful restaurants. There also seems to be a high degree of civic pride, judging from the fact that the city has gone to the enormous trouble of hiding all the power and telephone cables. This adds greatly to the beauty of the town and makes strolling along the streets a pleasure.

### ESSENTIALS

**GETTING THERE & DEPARTING By Plane Mexicana** (**© 800/531-7921** in the U.S., 01-800/502-2000 in Mexico, or 492/922-7429 locally) flies nonstop to and from Chicago, Denver, and Los Angeles. Seats are hard to come by around Christmas, when native Zacatecans fly home in large numbers. Within Mexico, Mexicana flies nonstop to and from Leon/Guanajuato, Mexico City, and Tijuana.

Transportation from the airport, 29km (18 miles) north of Zacatecas, is about $12 by taxi. **Aero Transportes** (**© 492/922-5946**) provides shuttle bus transportation to and from the airport ($4.50); allow 30 minutes for the ride.

**By Car** From the south, you can take Highway 45D, a toll road in various spots, from Querétaro through Irapuato, León, and Aguascalientes. At about $20, it's expensive but fast. Highway 54 heads northeast to Saltillo and Monterrey (a 5- to 6-hr. drive) and southeast to Guadalajara (a 4½-hr. drive). Highway 49 leads north to Torreón (4 hr.) and southeast to San Luis Potosí (2½ hr.). Highway 45 heads to Durango (4 hr.).

**By Bus Omnibus de México, Estrella Blanca,** and their many affiliates handle first-class bus travel to and from Zacatecas. Together, they operate 30 buses a day to Guadalajara and to San Luis Potosí, more than that to Mexico City (via Querétaro), and 10 per day to Guanajuato. I usually don't buy a ticket ahead of time unless I'm traveling during a national holiday or during December and August (vacation months), or I'm going all the way to the border. **The Central Camionera** (bus station) is on a hilltop a bit out of town. The taxi ride costs about $3.

# Zacatecas

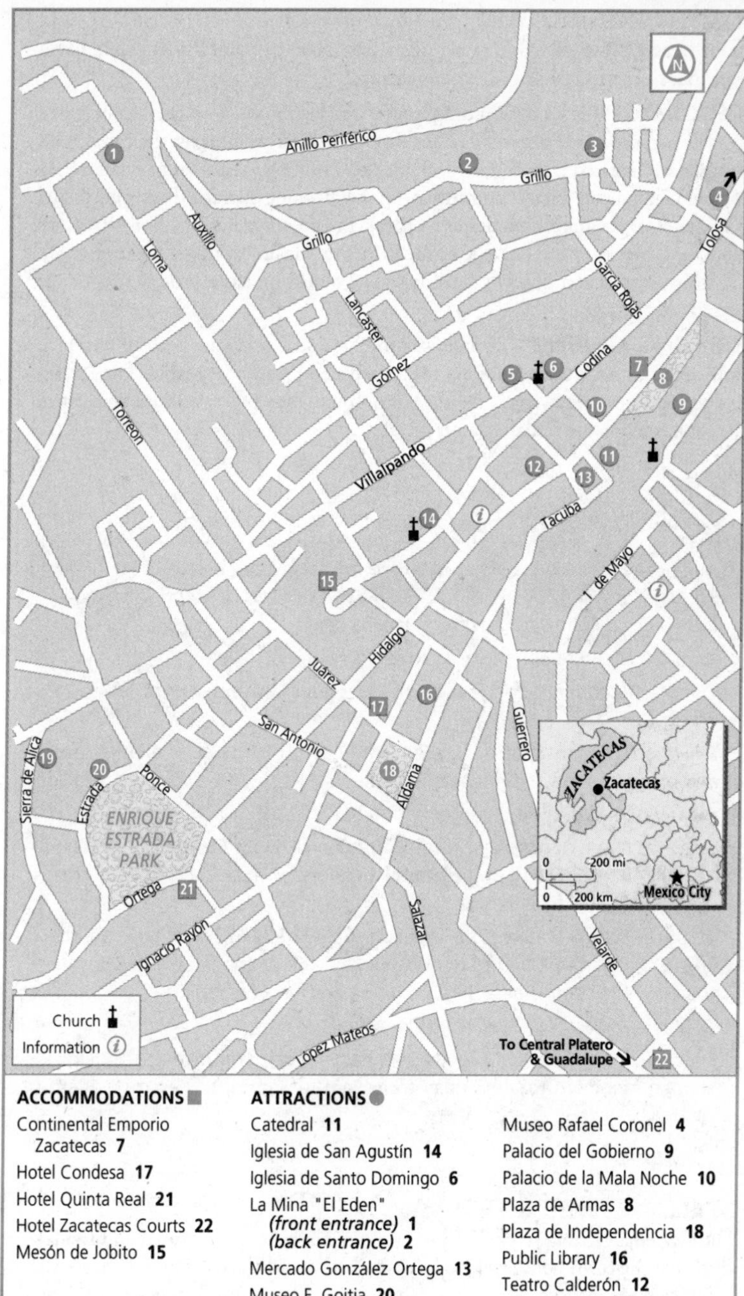


**ACCOMMODATIONS ■**

Continental Emporio Zacatecas **7**
Hotel Condesa **17**
Hotel Quinta Real **21**
Hotel Zacatecas Courts **22**
Mesón de Jobito **15**

**ATTRACTIONS ●**

Catedral **11**
Iglesia de San Agustín **14**
Iglesia de Santo Domingo **6**
La Mina "El Eden"
*(front entrance)* **1**
*(back entrance)* **2**
Mercado González Ortega **13**
Museo F. Goitia **20**
Museo Pedro Coronel **5**
Museo Rafael Coronel **4**
Palacio del Gobierno **9**
Palacio de la Mala Noche **10**
Plaza de Armas **8**
Plaza de Independencia **18**
Public Library **16**
Teatro Calderón **12**
Teleférico Station **3**
Viajes Mazzoco **19**

**VISITOR INFORMATION** The downtown office is at Hidalgo 403, 2nd floor (✆ **492/924-4047**); it's open daily from 8am to 8pm. If you would like a calendar of events, ask for an *agenda cultural.*

**CITY LAYOUT** Understanding traffic circulation in the middle of town requires an advanced degree in chaos theory. I either walk or let the cab drivers handle it. The city's main axis is Hidalgo. From the main square (**Plaza de Armas**), it goes 8 blocks southwest to the Enrique Estrada Park and Hotel Quinta Real (changing names as it goes); in the opposite direction it reaches another 8 blocks to the Rafael Coronel Museum (again making a name change). The historical center of town extends several blocks on either side of this 1-mile stretch of Hidalgo.

**GETTING AROUND** I enjoy walking around Zacatecas, but the terrain is hilly and the air is thin. Cabs are inexpensive and readily available. Their availability declines somewhat between 2 and 4pm, when office workers snag them to get home for the midafternoon meal.

## *FAST FACTS:* Zacatecas

*American Express* Visit **Viajes Mazzoco,** a travel agent, Enlace 115 (✆ **492/922-0859** or 492/922-5159; fax 492/924-0277). Hours are Monday to Friday from 9am to 6pm, Saturday from 9am to 2pm.

*Area Code* The telephone area code is **492.**

*Climate* It's cool enough year-round to require a sweater or other warm wrap.

*Elevation* The city is at a lofty 2,485m (8,200 ft.). The air is always crisp and cool but a tad thin for some people.

*Emergency/Police* The emergency number is ✆ **066.**

*Hospital* The two hospitals in town are **Clínica Santa Elena,** Av. Guerrero 143 (✆ **492/922-6861**), and **Hospital San José,** Cuevas Cancino 208, near the clinic (✆ **492/922-3892**).

*Internet Access* **Galaxy Café Internet** (✆ **492/924-4779**), Ignacio Hierro 502, is open from 10am to 9pm weekdays. Go up the alley between the tourism office and the Calderón theater, and turn right.

*Population* Zacatecas has 230,000 residents.

*Post Office* The *correo,* Allende 111, half a block from Avenida Hidalgo, is open Monday through Friday from 9am to 3pm, Saturday from 10am to 2pm.

## SPECIAL EVENTS & FESTIVALS

During Semana Santa (Holy Week), Zacatecas hosts an **international cultural festival** that the town hopes will rival the similar Festival Cervantino in Guanajuato. Painters, poets, dancers, musicians, actors, and other artists converge on the town.

The annual **Feria de Zacatecas,** which celebrates the founding of the city, begins the Friday before September 8 and lasts for three weeks, incorporating the national Fiestas Patrias (independence celebration). Cockfights, bullfights, sporting events, band concerts, and general hoopla prevail. Famous bullfighters appear, and the cheap bullfight tickets go for around $8.

## EXPLORING ZACATECAS

**SIGHTS** In town you can visit museums and churches, tour an **abandoned silver mine,** ride a cable car up to the **Cerro de la Bufa,** perhaps take in a concert, and partake of an old Saturday night tradition called *callejoneadas,* in which people go strolling and singing with tambourines, drums, and a burro laden with mezcal through the winding streets and alleyways (*callejones*) of the city. Zacatecas remains largely neglected by foreign tourists, though it is popular with Mexicans. Consequently, the various sights provide little descriptive material in English. If you don't speak Spanish, you might want to hire a bilingual tour guide. Try contacting **Viajes Mazzoco** (see American Express, above, in "Fast Facts"). It offers several tours that you can choose from for a fixed price. Some take you around the city; others take you to **nearby ruins** or to some of the old towns near Zacatecas, such as **Jerez** or **Fresnillo.**

**SHOPPING** **Zacatecan handcrafts** include stone and woodcarvings, leatherwork, and silver. Examples can be found in shops inside the old **Mercado González Ortega** on Hidalgo, next to the cathedral. A few other stores on Hidalgo and Tacuba sell crafts and antiques. Occasionally, Huichol Indians sell their crafts around the Plaza Independencia. Of all its handcrafts, Zacatecas is best known for its stone carvings. Many architects and builders from the United States come to Zacatecas when they need fancy stonework.

### A STROLL AROUND TOWN

The **Plaza de Armas,** the town's main square on avenida Hidalgo, is where you'll find the **cathedral** ★★★, with its famous façade. Nowhere else in Mexico is there anything like this; the depth of relief in the carving (4 in. and more) and sheer wealth of detail create the impression that the images are formed not in stone but in some softer material, such as cake icing. The cathedral took 23 years to build (1729–52), and the final tower wasn't completed until 1904.

To the left of the cathedral, on the Plaza de Armas, is the 18th-century **Palacio de Gobierno,** where viceregal-era governors lived. By the time of Mexico's revolt against Spain in 1810, Don Miguel de Rivera (Count of Santiago de la Laguna), owned it. Since 1834, it's been a government building. Inside is a modern **mural** (1970) by Antonio Pintor Rodríguez showing the history of Zacatecas. It is a fairly straightforward chronological presentation of history from left to right, except for the center panel, which represents prominent Zacatecans. Below it is a stone frieze depicting the economic underpinning that supports society and drives historical events. It flows into the mural's central panel, tying society's leaders to the soil of their motherland.

To the left of the Palacio de Gobierno is the **Residencia de Gobernadores,** with its multicolor stonework; the governor lived here until 1950. Across the street from the plaza are the **Palacio de la Mala Noche** ("Palace of the Bad Night") and the Continental Plaza Hotel. The palacio's name comes from the mine that brought great wealth to its original owner, Manuel de Rétegui, a philanthropic Spaniard. In case you're thinking that such fine stonework is becoming a lost art, look at the hotel's façade, which was done within the last 40 years.

Climb the small street next to the Palacio de la Mala Noche, and you'll face the massive walls of the church of **Santo Domingo,** which fronts an open space that it shares with the Museo Pedro Coronel (see "Museums," below). This church and the building that houses the museum belonged to the Jesuits until their expulsion in 1767. Afterward, the Dominicans occupied the church and convent. Inside are some lovely baroque gilt *retablos.*

**Moments** **A Tasty Drink to Try**

If in walking through the center of town you spot men with burros carrying clay jugs, you might want to flag them down. They sell *agua miel,* the unfermented juice of the maguey. It is a favorite drink with Zacatecans, many of whom think it has curative powers. It tastes good, too, and is very cheap. You need to be out early because they usually sell out by noon.

Two blocks south of Santo Domingo, on Calle Dr. Hierro (the mostly level street that parallels Hidalgo), is another grand church, **San Agustín.** This one is in partial ruins. During the Reform Wars, Zacatecas's liberal leaders kicked out the Augustinian friars, converted church and convent into a hotel and gambling casino, and destroyed the reportedly beautifully gilt altarpieces. The bishop of Zacatecas promptly excommunicated these Philistines. Twenty years later, a Presbyterian missionary society bought the property and dismantled the complex, ultrabaroque façade that decorated the east door. Again, excommunication of all involved quickly followed. Now the government owns the building, and some restoration has taken place. You'll see lots of odd bits of masonry crammed into any available niche, waiting for someone to figure out just where they go.

Turn and go downhill, and you'll be back on Avenida Hidalgo. Walk back toward the cathedral (right), and you'll pass on your left the **Teatro Calderón** (inaugurated first in 1836 and again in 1891 after a fire). A stately building with lovely stained-glass windows, it is also a favorite spot for people to sit and watch passers-by. The opera star Angela Peralta sang here several times in the 1800s. Zacatecas has a flourishing music school, and performers are always on tour; still, you might be able to catch a concert here. A little farther down Hidalgo, a block before the cathedral on the same side of the street, is the 19th-century **Mercado Jesús González Ortega,** which used to be the town's main market. A pleasant, old-fashioned market, it now holds small stores selling handicrafts and some of the region's wines.

Backtrack along Hidalgo, and over the next few blocks you will pass by some lovely buildings and climb up to **Enrique Estrada Park** (the street changes names and becomes Av. General Jesús González Ortega). The **equestrian statue** (1898) portrays none other than General González Ortega himself, hero of the Battle of Calpulalpan. Behind it are a gazebo with marvelous acoustics and a pleasant, shady park that is a romantic spot for young couples at night. Beginning at Estrada Park and extending southward are the lovely arches of the **Aqueduct of Zacatecas.** Two of these arches frame the doorway to the Quinta Real Hotel, which you can enter to see the town's old bull ring, a lovely sight. You can also have a drink in the hotel bar.

## A RIDE UP CERRO DE LA BUFA ★★

To get to the cable car station from the Plaza de Armas, you must climb one of the streets or alleys that lead up the hill that faces the cathedral. But first, glance up to see if the cars are running; if it's windy, they won't be. The first cross street will be Villalpando or Hierro; go right, and make a left when you get to the *Callejón* (alley) de García Roja. If you're unaccustomed to the thin air, this is quite a climb. An easier way to get there is to catch bus no. 7, which you can pick up along Juárez, or a cab. The cable car (✆ **492/922-5694**) is a great ride up to the Cerro de la Bufa. The view from the top is best in the late afternoon and early evening, when the sun is low in the sky, but if you intend to ride the cable car down, you can't stay too late. It operates only from 10am to 6pm, but the walk down is fairly easy if you want to stay later. The ride costs $2.25 one-way, $4.50 round-trip.

On Cerro de la Bufa is the Museo de la Toma de Zacatecas, which will be of most interest to Spanish-speaking history buffs. It displays artifacts and enlarged newspaper articles about the capture of Zacatecas by Pancho Villa. This was a decisive battle of the Revolución, and one of Villa's greatest victories. The museum is in need of investment; admission is $2. Beside the museum is the beautiful church **La Capilla de la Virgen del Patrocinio,** patroness of Zacatecas. Around the far side of the *cerro* is the **Mausoleo de los Hombres Ilustres de Zacatecas,** where many of the city's heroes are entombed.

## MUSEUMS

**La Mina "El Eden"** ★ This mine is a giant gash carved diagonally through the core of a mountain following the trail of a silver vein as it moved deeper and deeper underground. To see this gash and think that all the stone and ore that once occupied this space was mined and extracted by hand provokes a sense of wonder. The mine opened in 1586, using forced Indian labor. The Indians (mainly Caxcanes) began working in the mine at the age of 10 or 12 and lived to about 36 years of age. Accidents, tuberculosis, and silicosis caused their early deaths. The mine was extremely rich, yielding gold, copper, zinc, iron, and lead in addition to silver, but it eventually closed when an attempt to use explosives resulted in an inundation of water in the lower levels. Unfortunately, there are no English-speaking guides here, although the tour is eye-opening even for those who don't speak Spanish. Manikins illustrate some of the mining process, and the ropes and catwalks you see are what would have been in the mine originally. A visit also includes a short, unremarkable train ride.

The mine's back entrance is only a block from the cable-car terminal. I prefer this entrance because most people start at the main entrance, so you can avoid the crowds. When you get to the ticket office, buy your ticket right then. According to the rules, a tour must begin within 15 minutes after the first ticket is purchased. On my last two visits I've had the guide all to myself (a tip is appreciated). After the tour is over, you can exit by the front entrance, which puts you on Juárez, just a few blocks above Hidalgo.

For directions on getting to the front entrance, see "El Malacate," below, under "Zacatecas After Dark."

Cerro Grillo. ✆ **492/922-3002.** Admission $2 (includes train and tour). Daily 10am–6pm.

**Museo F. Goitia** ★★ These days, I don't expect anyone to believe what they read about modern art, and since my credentials as a critic are nil, I'll be brief. I was surprised by this small museum and the work of Goitia and his Zacatecan comrades. I walked in expecting it to be a display of regional chauvinism, but I found the works moving, serious, and meaningful. Francisco Goitia (1882–1960) is famous in Mexico, and the brothers Rafael and Pedro Coronel

---

*Tips* **Museum Admissions**

Unlike the rest of Mexico, where museum admission is usually free on Sunday, museums in Zacatecas are never free. Children 4 to 10 years old and adults over 65 pay half price.

---

amassed great collections that became the basis for two highly touted museums. The other artists are Julio Relas and José Kuri Brença.

Enrique Estrada 102, Col. Sierra de Alica. © **492/922-0211.** Admission $3. Tues–Sun 10am–5pm. Walk 7 short blocks south of the cathedral on Hidalgo, cross Juárez, and continue up the hill. Turn right on Manuel Ponce (look for the aqueduct) and walk 2 more short blocks. Look for the imposing white "palace" behind the park.

**Museo Pedro Coronel** ★★ Pedro Coronel, in addition to being an artist, was a collector of inspired tastes. He acquired works from all over the world, but the strongest parts of the collection are the works of European modern masters (Dalí, Picasso, Miró, Kandinsky, Braque, Rouault, and the gang), pre-Columbian Mesoamerica, and West Africa. All but a few of the pieces of modern art are illuminating. Many date from early in the artist's career, and some display a seminal character that points in the direction of later works. This museum is not large; after a while you drift into the Mesoamerican room. Beautiful stuff, and seeing it so quickly after the modern art gets your mind working out strange and improbable connections. There is no filler here; all of the pre-Columbian pieces are outstanding. The same can be said of the African material, but in this case the connections with modern art are tangible.

Plaza de Santo Domingo. © **492/922-8021.** Admission $3. Fri–Wed 10am–5pm. Facing the cathedral, walk left to the next street, De Veyna, turn left, and walk 1 block up to Plaza de Santo Domingo and the museum.

**Museo Rafael Coronel** ★★★ First stroll through the tranquil gardens and ruins of the former Franciscan convent, filled with trailing blossoms and framed by crumbling arches and the open sky. A small wing contains Coronel's drawings on paper. Once you step inside the mask museum, you'll be dazzled by the sheer number of fantastic masks. There are 4,500 of them from all over Mexico, and they're so exotic and dissimilar that you would think that they came from all over the world. There are entire walls filled with bizarre demons with curling 3-foot-long horns and noses; red devils; animals and unidentifiable creatures; spitting snakes, pigs, or rats; conquistadors—anything the mind can conjure. The masks, both antique and contemporary, are festooned with all manner of materials, from human hair, animal fur, fabric, plant fibers, and bones to metal screening, steel wool, sequins, plastic, and glitter.

One wing of the museum is dedicated to puppets. There are dioramas showing a bullfight, battling armies, and even a vision of hell. The puppets are some of the hundreds created during the last century by the famous Rosete-Aranda family of Huamantla, Tlaxcala, where there is also a puppet museum.

Also in the museum, to the left after you enter, is the Ruth Rivera room, where some of Diego Rivera's drawings are on display. Ruth Rivera is the daughter of Diego Rivera and the wife of Rafael Coronel. The museum also has a delightful ground-floor cafe that serves coffee and pastries and a small gift shop.

Calle Chevano, between Juan de Tolosa and Vergel Nuevo. © **492/922-8116.** Admission $3. Thurs–Tues 10am–5pm. Facing the cathedral, walk left up Hidalgo to the Founder's Fountain (about 2 blocks), then take the left fork (Calle Abasolo) 2 more short blocks; at the large yellow-ocher building and traffic triangle, take the right fork. You'll spot the large, old temple ahead.

### A SIDE TRIP TO NEARBY GUADALUPE

In the nearby town of Guadalupe, now almost a suburb of Zacatecas, is a large Franciscan convent and evangelical college founded by a famous member of the evangelical college of Querétaro, Fray Antonio Margil de Jesús. It remains an active monastery, but a large part of the convent houses a wonderful museum of colonial art, which will impress anyone interested in art and painting of any kind. Some people might skip this one because they suppose colonial art to be staid, scholastic, and full of arcane symbolism. Not true. The paintings, mostly from the 1700s, are by some of the greatest painters of New Spain—Cabrera, Villalpando, Correa, and others. They are detailed, expressive, dramatic, and eye-catching for their use of anachronisms and fantastical themes. There is also a smaller museum displaying antique carriages from colonial times and classic cars. Zacatecas had a lively carriage-building industry in the colonial era.

A taxi to Guadalupe runs about $8. Transportes de Guadalupe buses go to Guadalupe from the Central Camionera in Zacatecas. A Ruta 13 bus leaves for Guadalupe from López Mateos and Salazar, just up from the Hotel Gallery. The bus stops a block from the convent. It leaves about every 15 minutes or so and costs 50¢ for the 20-minute ride. If you're driving, take López Mateos east, and follow the signs. When you enter the town, ask anyone for directions to the convent. The convent's church has a lovely façade and holds the famous 19th-century Capilla de Nápoles, a chapel in the shape of a cross with lots of gilding and beautiful designs. You cannot enter the chapel, but you can see it from the ground floor of the church or from the organ loft, which is accessible from the museum. Between Guadalupe and Zacatecas is a school for silversmiths. Known as the **Centro Platero de Zacatecas,** it will most likely cease to operate in a couple of years. It is difficult to get to unless you take a taxi. If you decide to go, you'll find some workshops as well as people who will be happy to explain how they work with silver.

**Convento de Guadalupe/Museo Virreinal de Guadalupe** ★★★ To a dedicated museumgoer, seeing these paintings exhibited in galleries with open air circulation and no climate control is a little unsettling. But with Zacatecas's climate, there may not be much cause for concern. The museum has about 350 works. On the first floor are over 20 portraits depicting scenes of St. Francis's life. The stairway to the second floor has some large, striking paintings, including Cabrera's *Virgin of the Apocalypse,* and Arnáez's *The Triumph of the Sweet Light of Jesus,* which looks like a propagandistic work showing the victory of Rome over the pagans and the Reformation. Highlights on the second floor include the organ loft, 14 oval paintings by Cabrera, 4 by Villalpando, and the surprising work of a local artist named Gabriel José de Ovalle, who distorts space and deforms human features in a style that seems much more modern than the 1700s. Guides are available for a tour of the museum and to view the Capilla de Nápoles (if the resident monks aren't celebrating mass).

Jardín Juárez, Ote., Guadalupe. ✆ **492/923-2089** or 492/923-2386. Admission $3; free to all on Sun. Daily 10am–4:30pm.

**Museo Regional de la Historia** This museum, to the right of the convent, contains examples of carriages and antique cars. Collected from all over Mexico, they formerly belonged to ex-presidents and famous historical figures.

Jardín Juárez, Guadalupe. ✆ **492/923-2386** or 492/923-2089. Free admission. Tues–Sun 10am–4:30pm.

## WHERE TO STAY

Zacatecas has a great selection of hotels. In the fall and winter, heat can come in handy. Of the hotels listed here, all but the Condesa have heaters in the rooms, but many hotels in Zacatecas do not. Prices quoted here include the 17% tax.

### VERY EXPENSIVE

**Hotel Quinta Real** ★★★ Mexico is full of hotels made from converted colonial mansions, convents, and haciendas, but how many have risen from bullrings? And yet, it's the beauty, not the novelty, that makes this hotel so great. It has won several design awards, undoubtedly because the architects knew enough to leave the beautiful old bullring intact and keep the hotel small enough to be unobtrusive. A few of the graceful arches that remain from the town's colonial aqueduct frame the entrance. Inside the lobby, you can survey the whole arena, with its arches and stepped levels. On one side is the restaurant, below it a bar, and to the left are shops. The rooms were built along the outside of the bullring, and their windows open onto a small courtyard. Rooms are large, with spacious, well-equipped bathrooms, a writing desk, and a couch. Master suites are one room with a king or two double beds; *gran clase* suites are a good bit larger and have a sitting area and a whirlpool tub.

Av. Rayón 434, 98000 Zacatecas, Zac. ✆ **800/445-4565** in the U.S. and Canada or 492/922-9104. Fax 492/922-8440. www.quintareal.com. 49 suites. $225 master suite, $240 suite *gran clase*. AE, MC, V. Free guarded parking. **Amenities:** Restaurant (international), bar; golf and health club privileges at local club; concierge; tour desk; secretarial service; room service until 11pm; in-room massage; babysitting; overnight laundry and dry cleaning; nonsmoking rooms. *In room:* A/C, TV, hair dryer, iron.

## EXPENSIVE

**Continental Emporio Zacatecas** ★★ A comfortable colonial hotel in the best location in town, right on the Plaza de Armas, this is a popular choice with Mexican tourists and businesspeople. The spacious rooms on its six floors are carpeted and well furnished. Rooms in the back are quiet; the sunny front rooms, mostly junior suites, have balconies and good views of the cathedral and Cerro de la Bufa. Those on the fourth floor in front have the great view while being shielded from the street noise and also have enjoyable terraces. The rooms in back face the interior patio, complete with gurgling fountain, and contain one king or two double beds. Bathrooms are medium sized, with a decent amount of counter space. The tap water is purified.

Av. Hidalgo 703, Col. Centro, 98000 Zacatecas, Zac. ✆ **492/922-6183.** Fax 492/922-6245. www.hotelesemporio.com.mx. 113 units. $140 double; $160 jr. suite. AE, MC, V. Free secured parking. **Amenities:** Restaurant (international), bar; golf and tennis at local club; tour desk; car rental; secretarial services; room service until 11pm; massage; babysitting; overnight laundry and dry cleaning; nonsmoking rooms. *In room:* TV, hair dryer.

**Mesón de Jobito** ★★ This two-story modern hotel occupies a traditional *vecindad,* which was a common form of housing for the lower classes in olden days. The buildings ramble back from the entrance, forming private alleys decorated with ornamental plants and flowers and painted in traditional Mexican colors. The hotel has an intimate feel. The rooms are large, carpeted, and nicely furnished, with queen- or king-size beds and large bathrooms. The hotel is 5 blocks from the cathedral, off the street above Hidalgo. A couple of the junior suites are large and stylishly decorated. Rates vary seasonally and are highest from September to December.

Jardín Juárez 143, 98000 Zacatecas, Zac. ✆ and fax **492/924-1722,** or 01-800/021-0040 in Mexico. hmjobito@logicnet.com.mx. 53 units. $177–215 double; $200–$250 suite. AE, MC, V. Sheltered parking $7. **Amenities:** 2 restaurants (international, Spanish), 2 bars; golf at local club; tour desk; car rental; secretarial services; 24-hr. room service; babysitting; same day laundry and dry cleaning; nonsmoking rooms. *In room:* A/C, TV, hair dryer, safe.

## INEXPENSIVE

**Hotel Condesa** *Value* The good location, well-kept rooms, and economical price are the main attractions here. Many rooms, especially on the lower floors, have been remodeled and have modern furniture, cheerful paint, and new bathroom tile. These rooms have interior views. Rooms on the third floor haven't been remodeled, but those facing east overlook Cerro de la Bufa and the market below the hotel. Some remodeled rooms contain king-size beds; other units have a double or two twins.

Av. Juárez 102, 98000 Zacatecas, Zac. ✆ and fax **492/922-1160.** xepic@internet.zac.itesm. 60 units. $35–$39 double. AE, MC, V. **Amenities:** Restaurant, cafe/bar; room service; overnight laundry; tour desk. *In room:* TV.

**Motel Zacatecas Courts** This motel-style lodging has carpeting, hot water 24 hours a day, and comfortable beds. It is a 10-minute walk from the main square. Be sure to get a room in the back, away from the street. Also, you must ask to have the heat turned on in the room, and ask for extra blankets in winter.

López Velarde 602, 98000 Zacatecas, Zac. ✆ **492/922-0328.** Fax 492/922-1225. 92 units. $44 double. AE, MC, V. Free enclosed parking. **Amenities:** Restaurant; tour info; room service. *In room:* TV.

## WHERE TO DINE

The dining in Zacatecas is very good. In addition to the establishments listed below, the restaurants at the Quinta Real and Mesón del Jobito have good reputations. Gorditas might be considered the state food of Zacatecas, and the most popular gordita place is **Gorditas Doña Julia,** which operates three or four locations. The best coffee in town is at Café San Patricio, below the tourism office. It doesn't open until 9am.

**Café Nevería Acrópolis** MEXICAN This restaurant and coffee shop with a soda fountain is a popular meeting spot for breakfast, afternoon coffee, or dessert. The kitchen does itself credit with breakfast, enchiladas, and chile relleno zacatecas (a poblano chile stuffed with cheese sitting on top of a spicy *picadillo*). Behind the cash register are photos and signatures of famous patrons, including Gregory Peck and Jane Fonda.

Av. Hidalgo and Rinconada de Catedral. ✆ **492/922-1284.** Breakfast $4–$6; main courses $4–$8. MC, V. Daily 8am–10pm.

**La Cantera Musical Restaurant Bar** ★ MEXICAN/REGIONAL This restaurant is best known for its regional cooking, especially typical dishes such as *asado de bodas* (a pork dish made with cinnamon and ancho and guajillo chiles) and *mole zacatecano* (a sweet and spicy chicken dish). You can also get a number of Mexican standards. The dining room is attractive. The restaurant is below the Mercado González Ortega, by the cathedral.

Tacuba 2, Centro Comercial El Mercado. ✆ **492/922-8828.** Main courses $3–$8. AE, MC, V. Mon–Fri 1pm–midnight; Sat–Sun 9am–11pm.

**La Cuija** ★★ INTERNATIONAL/REGIONAL This stylish restaurant under the Centro Comercial has comfortable, attractively set tables in a heavily colonnaded room. Appetizers are referred to as "something to open the mouth," and the *quesadillas de flor de calabaza* (squash-blossom quesadillas) are especially good reasons for doing so. The restaurant has its own vineyards. The menu features a good selection of dishes, including *chile mestizo,* which is an ancho chile stuffed with huitlacoche, with a sauce of ground corn, cream, and a bit of aged cheese. Friday and Saturday nights, a guitar trio plays.

Tacuba T-5, Centro Comercial "El Mercado." ✆ **492/922-8275.** Reservation not accepted during Semana Santa. Main courses $7–$15. AE, MC, V. Daily 1pm–midnight.

**Los Dorados de Villa** ★★ MEXICAN If your grandmother were Mexican, this is how you would want her to cook. The green *pozole* (soup with chicken, hominy, lettuce, and radishes) is excellent, as are the enchiladas, which come in

*Moments* **A Nighttime Musical Stroll Through Town**

The **Callejoneada Zacatecana** could be the best way to tour the city's picturesque back streets and alleys. It is a traditional walk through the *callejones* (the little curving alleys, byways, and plazas), accompanied by music, dancing, and a burro carrying mezcal. It takes place on Saturdays beginning around 9pm (8pm in cold weather). Be sure to ask in the lobby of your hotel if there will be one while you're in town. If you want a free tour, tag along with a group as it marches through the streets—they're hard to miss, with the drums, horns, and flower-bedecked burro laden with barrels.

many varieties (I recommend the zacatecanas and the rojas). Other menu items include tostadas, tacos, soups, and guacamole. The name of the place refers to "the golden ones"—Pancho Villa's honor guard of fearless soldiers. The owner is a collector of memorabilia, and artifacts and reproductions from La Revolución cover the walls of the small dining room. Decorative paper cutouts hang from the ceiling, making the room feel even smaller, but festive, too. Los Dorados is not far from the Rafael Coronel Museum; walk north several blocks on Hidalgo, keeping to the left each time the street forks.

Plazuela de García 1314. ✆ **492/922-5722.** Reservations recommended on weekends. Main courses $4–$6. No credit cards. Daily 2:30pm–midnight.

### ZACATECAS AFTER DARK

**El Malacate** Disco music in a mine deep inside the earth—does "Disco Inferno" ring a bell? Whose life could be considered complete without having made the scene here? Call in advance if you want to reserve a table. The entrance is at the end of Calle Dovali. From Hidalgo, walk up Juárez, which turns into Torreón. Just past the Seguro Social building on Avenida Torreón, you'll find Dovali; turn right. Take a cab if you don't want to be so bushed that you can't boogie. The club is open Thursday to Sunday from 9:30pm to 2am. Mina El Eden, Calle Dovali. ✆ **492/922-3727.** Cover $10.

## 5 San Luis Potosí

418km (261 miles) N of Mexico City; 346km (216 miles) NE of Guadalajara; 202km (126 miles) N of Querétaro; 189km (118 miles) E of Zacatecas

San Luis Potosí, more than a mile high in central Mexico's high-plains region, was among the country's most picturesque and prosperous mining cities. It is now the largest and most industrial of the silver cities, with more than a half a million inhabitants, but you would never know it if you stayed in the historic central district. It has rich colonial architecture and is known for its great plazas. Capital of the state of the same name, San Luis Potosí was named for Louis IX, saintly king of France; *Potosí,* the Quechua word for richness, was borrowed from the incredibly rich Bolivian Potosí silver mines, which San Luis's mines were thought to rival.

### ESSENTIALS

**GETTING THERE & DEPARTING By Plane Aeromar** (✆ **888/627-0207** in the U.S., or 444/817-7936) offers a direct flight on Sunday to and from San Antonio; **Continental** (✆ **800/231-0856** in the U.S., or

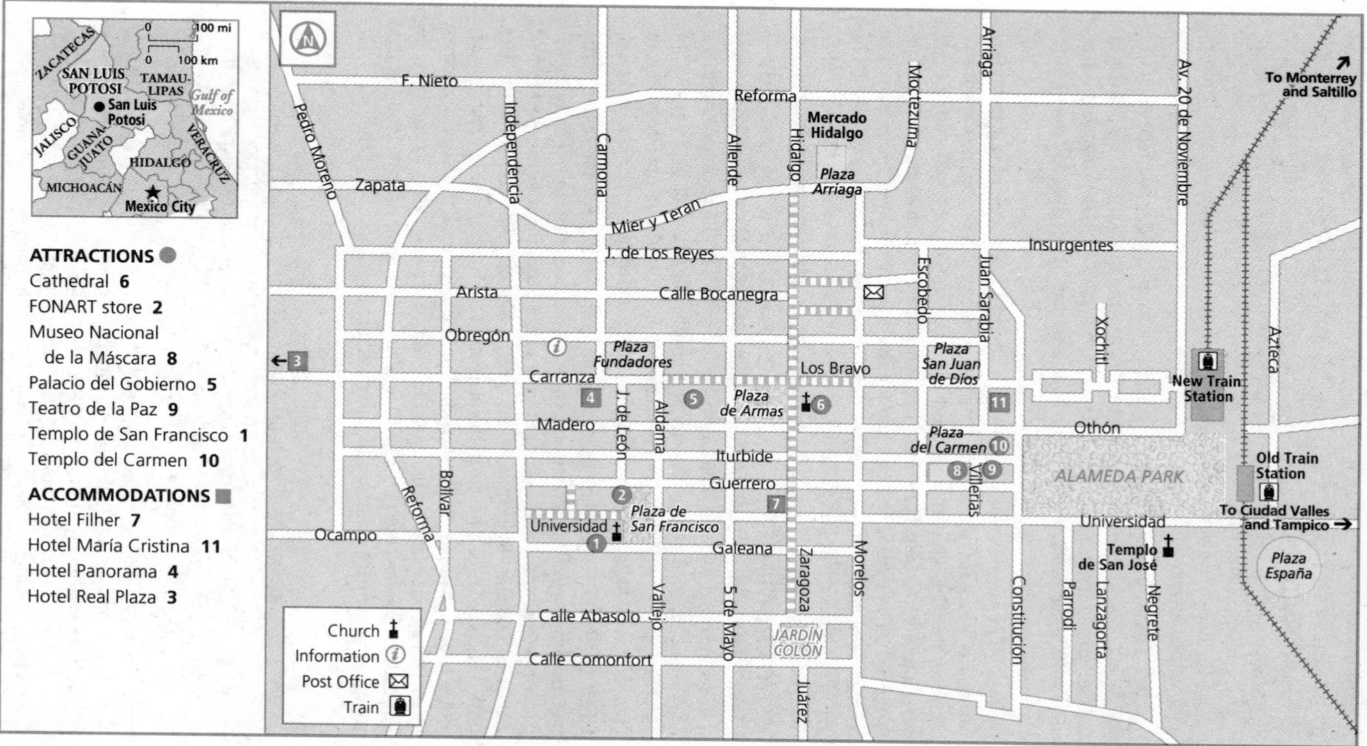
ZACATECAS
SAN LUIS POTOSI
TAMAULIPAS
Gulf of Mexico
San Luis Potosi
JALISCO
GUANAJUATO
HIDALGO
VERACRUZ
MICHOACÁN
Mexico City
0 100 mi
0 100 km
ATTRACTIONS
Cathedral 6
FONART store 2
Museo Nacional de la Máscara 8
Palacio del Gobierno 5
Teatro de la Paz 9
Templo de San Francisco 1
Templo del Carmen 10
ACCOMMODATIONS
Hotel Filher 7
Hotel María Cristina 11
Hotel Panorama 4
Hotel Real Plaza 3
F. Nieto
Pedro Moreno
Zapata
Independencia
Carmona
Reforma
Allende
Hidalgo
Mercado Hidalgo
Plaza Arriaga
Moctezuma
Arriaga
Av. 20 de Noviembre
To Monterrey and Saltillo
Mier y Teran
J. de Los Reyes
Insurgentes
Arista
Calle Bocanegra
Escobedo
Juan Sarabia
Xochitl
Azteca
Obregón
Plaza Fundadores
Carranza
Los Bravo
Plaza San Juan de Dios
New Train Station
J. de León
Aldama
Plaza de Armas
Madero
Othón
Iturbide
Plaza del Carmen
Villerias
ALAMEDA PARK
Old Train Station
Bolívar
Reforma
Guerrero
Plaza de San Francisco
Universidad
To Ciudad Valles and Tampico
Ocampo
Galeana
Zaragoza
Morelos
Templo de San José
Plaza España
Constitución
Parrodi
Lanzagorta
Negrete
Calle Abasolo
Vallejo
5 de Mayo
Jardín Colón
Calle Comonfort
Juárez
Church
Information
Post Office
Train

01-800/900-5000 in Mexico) flies to and from Houston. Aeromar, **Mexicana** (✆ **444/833-5326**), **Aero California** (✆ **444/811-8050**), and **Aerolitoral** (✆ **444/822-2229**) operate domestically. For transportation to the airport from all downtown hotels ($10), call **AeroTaxi** (✆ **444/811-0165** or 444/811-0167).

The **airport** is about 11km (7 miles) from downtown. A taxi to the city center is $10. A *colectivo* van is more economical, but don't tarry in the terminal, because they leave quickly.

**By Car** From Mexico City, take Highway 57; from Guadalajara, take Highway 80. There's dramatic scenery on the second half of the trip between Aguascalientes and San Luis Potosí—hair-raising hills and scenic *pueblitos* (little towns). If you're coming from the north, it takes 6 to 7 hours to drive the 536km (335 miles) from Monterrey.

**By Bus** The large Central Camionera is 3km (2 miles) east of downtown on Guadalupe Torres at Diagonal Sur. City buses marked CENTRAL go to the bus station from the Alameda park for around 25¢. Taxis cost about $3. Most of the bus travel is through **Estrella Blanca** and its many affiliates, which occupy the counters to the left as you enter. You can buy a ticket for any of the affiliates from any counter. To the right as you enter are three other first-class bus companies: ETN (mostly to Mexico City and Guadalajara), Primer Plus (to Mexico City and Querétaro), and Omnibus de Mexico (to Mexico City, Guadalajara, and Querétaro).

**VISITOR INFORMATION** The **State Tourism Office** (✆ **444/812-9939** or 444/812-9943; fax 444/812-6769) is at Obregón 520, a block west of Plaza Fundadores in an old mansion built in the French style. The information office has a helpful staff, a good map of the city and historic district, and, of course, lots of brochures. It's open Monday to Friday from 8am to 9pm, Saturday from 9am to 2pm. Plaza Fundadores is a block from the northwest corner of the Plaza de Armas.

**CITY LAYOUT** The Plaza de Armas (or Jardín Hidalgo) is the center of the historic district. All the streets bordering it are pedestrian only. The principle pedestrian street runs north-south in front of the plaza; the southern part (called Zaragoza) extends 8 blocks to the Jardín Colón, and the northern part (called Hidalgo) runs 5 blocks to the main market. The city also has many plazas and a large downtown park called the Alameda. Avenida Carranza is another important street; it heads east from the Plaza de Armas, passes by the Plaza de Fundadores, and extends to the fancy residential section of the city. Fronting this street are many banks, clubs, and fancy restaurants.

## *FAST FACTS:* San Luis Potosí

*American Express* The local representative is **Grandes Viajes,** Avenida Carranza 1077 (✆ **444/817-6004;** fax 444/811-1166). Hours are Monday to Friday from 9am to 2pm and 4 to 7pm, Saturday from 10am to 1pm.

*Area Code* The telephone area code is **444.**

*Climate* San Luis is on the high plateau more than a mile above sea level, but the weather can get hot during May, June, and sometimes July. In winter it occasionally drops to freezing at night. Rain is rare, with an average rainfall of 14 inches per year. It falls between May and November, mostly in August.

*Currency Exchange* Four *casas de cambios* near the main post office offer better rates and better service than the banks. Two are in the arcade on Julián de los Reyes, and two are on Mariano Escobedo. This is just a few blocks northeast of the Plaza de Armas. All are open Saturday. The historic district has a lot of *cajeros automáticos* (cash machines), usually located in glass cubicles beside the banks.

*Emergency* San Luis's central emergency number is © **060.**

*Hospital* The **Hospital Centro Médico,** Antonio Aguilar 155 (© **444/813-3797**), is one of the best hospitals in the country.

*Post Office* The *correo,* Morelos 235, 4 blocks north-northeast of the Plaza de Armas, is open Monday to Friday from 8am to 3 pm, Saturday 9am to 1pm. Look for a narrow one-story building made of gray stone.

*Population* San Luis Potosí has 850,000 residents.

## EXPLORING SAN LUIS POTOSI

### A STROLL AROUND THE HISTORIC CENTER

San Luis has more streets designated solely for pedestrian use than any of the other silver cities. The center of town is the **Plaza de Armas** or Jardín Hidalgo, dating from the mid-1700s and shaded by magnolia and flamboyant trees. The **bandstand** in the center of the plaza was built in 1947 (in colonial style), using pink volcanic stone. Free band concerts usually begin on Thursday and Sunday at around 7:30 or 8pm. On the west side of the plaza is the **Palacio de Gobierno.** It has been much repaired, restored, and added to through the centuries—the back and the south façade were redone as recently as 1973. The front of the building retains much of the original 18th-century decoration, at least on the lower floors. On the second floor, you'll find the rooms that Juárez occupied when he established his temporary capital here. It's worth a peek.

Across the plaza from the Government Palace is the **cathedral.** The original building had only a single bell tower; the one on the left was built in 1910 to match, although today the newer tower looks older. In design and construction, the cathedral does not compare favorably with several of the other churches in town. The Count of Monterrey built the **Palacio Municipal,** on the north side of the cathedral, in 1850. He filled it with paintings and sculptures, little of which survived the city's stormy history. When the count died in 1890, the palace was taken over by the bishop, and in 1921 by the city government. Since then, it has been San Luis's city hall, left undisturbed until January 1, 1986, when it was firebombed in a moment of social unrest. It was restored and functions again.

Southeast of the Jardín Hidalgo is one of the city's most famous squares, **Plazuela del Carmen,** named for the **Templo del Carmen** ★ church. From the jardín, walk east along Madero-Othón to Escobedo and the plazuela. The entire area you see was once part of the extensive grounds of the 18th-century Carmelite monastery. The church survives from that time and is perhaps the Potosinos' favorite place of worship. The **Teatro de la Paz** and the **Museo Nacional de la Máscara** also face the plaza. This mask museum is not particularly large, can be seen in less than an hour, and costs only 50¢. In addition to the masks, some of which are quite striking, you get to see the inside of an elegant 19th-century mansion.

Attached to the Teatro de la Paz (enter to the right of the theater's main entrance) is the **Sala German Gedovius** (✆ **444/812-2698**). It has four galleries for exhibitions of international and local art. It's open Tuesday to Sunday from 10am to 2pm and 4 to 6pm. Admission is free.

The square is a fine place to rest before heading a couple of blocks east to get to the shady, cool **Alameda,** the city's largest downtown park. Vendors sell handcrafts, fruits, and all manner of snacks. Just across Negrete is the magnificent **Templo de San José,** with lots of ornate gold decorations, huge religious paintings, and *El Señor de los Trabajos,* a miracle-working statue with many *retablos* testifying to the wonders it has performed.

### PLAZAS

San Luis Potosí has more plazas than any other colonial city in Mexico. The two most famous ones are mentioned above. **Plaza de San Francisco** is southeast of the Plaza de Armas along Aldama, between Guerrero and Galeana. This shady square takes its name from the Franciscan monastery on the south side of the plaza and the church on the west side. It holds some beautiful stained glass; many statues and paintings from the colonial era; and a crystal chandelier shaped like a sailing ship. This is San Luis society's favorite church for weddings.

Another square is **Plaza de los Fundadores** ("Founders' Square"), at the intersection of Obregón and Aldama (northwest of the Jardín Hidalgo). Facing it is the **Loreto Chapel,** with its exquisite baroque façade. The neighboring church of **El Sagrario** belonged to the Jesuits before the order was expelled from Mexico.

## SHOPPING

The best one-stop shopping in San Luis is at the government-operated **FONART** crafts store (✆ **444/812-7521**) on the Plaza de San Francisco. The building was originally part of the Convent of San Francisco, founded in 1590. Today it houses the offices of the Casa de la Cultura, and a branch of FONART on the ground floor. This one is especially well stocked with some of the country's best crafts. It's open Monday to Saturday from 10am to 2pm and 4 to 7pm. Another place to try is the state-run store **La Casa del Artesano,** Carranza 540 (no phone), 5 blocks west of Jardín Hidalgo. The store carries examples of every kind of craft made in the state. Each room in the store is dedicated to the crafts of one of the cultural or climatic zones of the state. The store is open Monday to Saturday from 10am to 2pm and 4 to 8pm.

Several blocks along the pedestrian Calle Hidalgo from the Jardín Hidalgo, you'll find the city's **Mercado Hidalgo,** a mammoth building devoted mostly to food, but also offering, among other things, baskets, *rebozos* (shawls), and straw furniture.

The walk along Hidalgo is an introduction to the city's commercial life. Hardware stores, craft shops, shoe stores, groceries, and taverns all crowd the street. Past the Mercado Hidalgo is another big market, the Mercado República.

A well-loved local chocolate factory is **Constanzo,** which has several outlets throughout the city, including three on Carranza. Most outlets are open Monday to Saturday from 10am to 1:30pm and 4 to 8:30pm.

## WHERE TO STAY

There are no luxury hotels in the historic center. Most of them (the María Dolores, Real de Minas, and Holiday Inn) are to the east, where the highway from Mexico City enters the town. The Westin is to the west, along the highway to Guadalajara. All rates listed below include the 17% tax.

### EXPENSIVE

**Westin San Luis Potosí** ★★ Certainly the loveliest hotel in San Luis, the Westin offers comfort and service in surroundings that exemplify how contemporary Mexican architects have worked the elements of colonial architecture to achieve an aesthetic that is new without being divorced from its past. The rooms are along a three-story stone arcade that surrounds a broad courtyard. All are large, carpeted, and decorated with flair. They come with either two full- or one king-size bed, a writing table, and a small dining table. Bathrooms are very large, with marble tiles, countertops, and shower/tub combinations. Suites are even larger and offer a stereo with a CD player, a large whirlpool tub, a safe, and bathrobes. I prefer the rooms that have an interior view of the courtyard. The center of town is 15 to 20 minutes away by car.

Real de Lomas 1000, 78210 San Luis Potosí, S.L.P. ✆ **800/228-3000** in the U.S. or 444/825-0125. Fax 444/825-0200. www.westin.com. 123 units. $230 double; $250 suite. Children under 12 stay free in parents' room. AE, MC, V. Free valet parking. **Amenities:** Restaurant, bar; heated small pool; access to nearby health club with tennis and racquetball; kid's club; concierge; tour desk; car rental; airport transportation; business center; executive business services; 24-hr. room service; babysitting; same-day laundry and dry cleaning; nonsmoking rooms. *In room:* A/C, TV, dataport, minibar, hair dryer, iron.

### MODERATE

**Hotel Panorama** ★ Aptly named, this hotel is in a 10-story glass building near the Plaza Fundadores. Many years ago, it was *the* hotel in San Luis, but newer, fancier hotels and a certain amount of decay changed that. Now the guest rooms are being completely remodeled, starting with the executive levels. I'm told that all rooms will be remodeled, but in Mexico one never knows. Rooms vary in size from medium to large; none feel cramped. Bathrooms are a little small. The difference in the remodeled rooms is amazing; they have air-conditioning, new carpet, lovely marble bathrooms with plenty of counter space, modern mahogany-stained furniture, and much better lighting. Most rooms come with two full-size beds, but some have a king. All rooms have an exterior view. Even if you don't stay here, visit the hotel's restaurant and bar in the evening (Mon–Sat 7pm–2am) and catch the view of the city.

Av. Carranza 315, 78000 San Luis Potosí, S.L.P. ✆ **444/812-1777.** Fax 444/812-4591. hpanorama@compaq.net.mx. 127 units. $65–$80 double. AE, MC, V. Free secured parking. **Amenities:** Restaurant, cafe, 2 bars (1 rooftop); disco; medium-size heated pool; Jacuzzi; tour desk; car rental; room service until 11pm; babysitting; same-day laundry and dry cleaning; nonsmoking rooms; executive-level rooms. *In room:* A/C, TV, dataport, minibar, iron.

**Hotel Real Plaza** ★ A modern nine-story hotel 8 blocks from the Plaza de Armas, the Real Plaza offers comfort and quiet at a good price. The medium-size rooms are carpeted and well lit but have no style. They are preferable, however, to the unremodeled rooms at the Panorama. Bathrooms are a little larger than at the Panorama, but some rooms have no view. It's probably worth doing a little price comparison, keeping in mind that you'll be doing a little more walking from here.

Av. Carranza 890, 78250 San Luis Potosí, S.L.P. ✆ **444/814-6969.** Fax 444/814-6639. www.realplaza.com.mx. 268 units. $72 double. MC, V. Free secured parking. **Amenities:** Restaurant (Mexican), bar; tour desk; room service until 11pm; babysitting; same-day laundry. *In room:* A/C, TV, dataport.

### INEXPENSIVE

**Hotel Filher** *Value* Good location and medium to large rooms painted in cheerful colors are the high points of this economical three-story hotel. If you want quiet, request a room on the third floor; if you want a window and a firm new mattress, book a room on the second. Rates are higher for second-floor rooms. Of these, I like the ones facing the pedestrian-only Zaragoza. They have balconies with a good view, and though there may be street noise, you don't get the noise that reverberates through the rather loud lobby. This hotel is a good choice in warm weather because the rooms are airy and have tile floors rather than carpeting. They also have ceiling fans. Hot water can take as long as 5 minutes to get to the rooms.

Av. Universidad 375 (at Zaragoza), 78000 San Luis Potosí, S.L.P. ✆ **444/812-1562.** Fax 444/812-1564. 50 units. $49 double. AE MC, V. Parking 1 block away. **Amenities:** Restaurant, bar; limited room service.

**Hotel María Cristina** The María Cristina is in a narrow nine-story building around the corner from the Plaza del Carmen. It's next door to (and often confused with) the Hotel Nápoles. Rooms have recently been refurnished with "French-style" side tables and headboards and new, comfortable mattresses. All rooms are small and have a ceiling fan, and most don't offer much of a view. The bathrooms are small, with little counter space, but they offer filtered water from the faucet (a rarity in this price range). More good news is that the rooms are quiet, carpeted, and warmer in the winter than the rooms at the Filher. Rooms contain one full or two twin beds.

Juan Sarabia 110, 78000 San Luis Potosí, S.L.P. ✆ **444/812-9408.** Fax 444/812-8823. 74 units. $59 double. AE, MC, V. Free guarded parking. **Amenities:** 2 restaurants, bar; tour info; room service until 11:30pm. *In room:* TV.

## WHERE TO DINE

San Luis has some good restaurants, both of the fine-dining variety and the local, good-eatin' variety. For the latter, try the **Posada del Virrey** on the Plaza de Armas, the large 24-hour **Café Pacífico** (not the small one) near the Plaza del Carmen on Constitución, or **La Parroquia** on the Plaza Fundadores. Below are a few restaurants where Potosinos go when they want something different.

### EXPENSIVE

**El Callejón de San Francisco** ★★ MEXICAN If the night air is comfortable, there's no lovelier place for dinner than this restaurant's rooftop terrace, with San Francisco's cupola and bell towers for a backdrop. Even if it's a tad too chilly, you can still enjoy yourself; just ask the waiter for a *jorongo* (ho-*rong*-o), a traditional woolen wrap for the shoulders. There's also a dining room downstairs. The menu has a number of Mexican standards at reasonable prices. The *enchiladas potosinas* (which are in the appetizer section) make a full meal. If you like sharp contrasts of bitter and sweet, try *chiles ventilla* (dried red chiles stuffed with cheese and bathed in a sweet sauce of cream and *cajeta*). More conventional dishes are *chiles en nogada* and *pechuga Doña Luz* (chicken breast in poblano cream sauce). The restaurant is on a pedestrian street beside San Francisco church and behind FONART.

Callejón de Lozada 1. ✆ **444/812-4508.** Reservations recommended on weekends. Main courses $4–$8. AE, MC, V. Tues–Sat 1:30pm–midnight; Sun 1:30–6pm.

**La Corriente Restaurant Bar** ★ REGIONAL It's hard to categorize this place because its specialties run in three directions: down-home country Mexican dishes, using mostly beef; a large selection of blended fruit and vegetable drinks, conventional and unconventional; and *antojitos* (Mexican supper foods served after 7pm). Of the main dishes, I liked *chamorro pibil* (pork cooked in a Huastecan mole) and *puntas al chipotle* (beef in a spicy chipotle sauce). The juices are filling—don't make the mistake of getting one and a main course or full breakfast; try an appetizer such as the *quesadillas de huitlacoche.*

The restaurant is in a large old house with a roofed patio and several dining rooms with high ceilings.

Carranza 700 (at Reforma). ✆ **444/812-9304.** Reservations accepted. Main courses $5–$10; blended juices $3. AE, MC, V. Mon–Sat 8am–midnight; Sun 10am–6pm.

**La Gran Vía** ★ SPANISH/INTERNATIONAL Ask any prosperous Potosino for the best restaurant in town, and he or she will tell you this place. On walking in, you certainly get the feel of a restaurant that's been around a long time and doesn't need to impress. It has polish, but nothing fancy in its decor (except some lovely Talavera pieces). Spanish specialties include *lechón asado* (roast suckling pig), *callos a la madrileña* (beef tripe cooked in a tomato sauce), and *cocido* (traditional Spanish potage made with garbanzo beans). I would go for any of these or the chef's special over the international menu, which seemed a little weak. The soups are also worthy—a mushroom and cilantro, and the classic Spanish garlic. In the afternoons and evenings, there's live piano music in the dining room to the left—choose your table accordingly.

Av. Carranza 560. ✆ **444/812-2899.** Reservations accepted. Main courses $7–$15. AE, MC, V. Mon–Sat 1pm–midnight; Sun 1–7pm.

**Restaurant Orizatlán** ★★ HUASTECAN This colorful restaurant specializes in the traditional Huastecan cooking of eastern San Luis Potosí. If you are hungry, try the *parrillada a la Huasteca* for two. A large sampling of typical dishes, it includes portions of the *zacahuil,* Mexico's largest *tamal.* The waiters will keep the Huastecan enchiladas coming until you beg them to stop. Less ambitious eaters can order a la carte. After dinner, the restaurant serves complimentary home-style cordials made from several fruits and puts on a mini Huastecan fandango, with music and dance.

Pascual M. Hernández 240. ✆ **444/814-6786.** Breakfast $4; main courses $5–$9. AE. Mon–Sat 8am–11pm; Sun 8am–7pm. Eight blocks south of Plaza de Armas on Zaragoza, turn left at Jardín Colón; restaurant is about 30m (100 ft.) down.

## SAN LUIS AFTER DARK

The most popular clubs in town are those where you can sit down to a late supper or drinks and hear guitarists and vocalists. Most of the music is romantic—*trova* or ballads. In the downtown area, a number of bars offer this kind of entertainment. They include **La Compañía,** Mariano Arista 350 (✆ **444/812-9693**); **Viejo San Luis,** Carranza 485-A (✆ **444/814-0801**); and **Restaurant Bar 1913,** Galeana 205 (✆ **444/812-8352**). **Staff,** 423 Carranza, is a popular discotheque for those in their 20s.

# 6

# Michoacán

West of Mexico City and southeast of Guadalajara lies the state of Michoacán (meech-oh-ah-*kahn*), the homeland of more than 200,000 Tarascan Indians, properly known as the Purépecha. The land is mountainous in the east, north, and center, but in the south and west it drops to a broad lowland plain that meets the Pacific. The state gets more rain and is consequently greener than its neighbors Jalisco and Guanajuato, and many Mexicans consider it the most beautiful state in their country. However, it remains relatively unvisited by foreign tourists.

Michoacán merits a visit for many reasons. High in the mountains, in the extreme northeastern part of the state, a small miracle occurs every year. An isolated patch of forest becomes the meeting place for millions of monarch butterflies, the final link in a migratory chain stretching from Mexico to as far away as Canada and back again. During peak season (Dec–Mar), the tree limbs bend under the weight of the monarchs, and the undulation of so many wings creates a dazzling spectacle. (See "Michoacán's Monarch Migration," later in this chapter.) Across the northern half of the state is a belt of geothermal energy that produces hot springs, many of which are bathing spots. In central Michoacán are highland lakes and colorful Indian towns that evoke the Mexico of old. These towns are well known for their handcrafts and the syncretic celebrations honoring their ancestors on the Day of the Dead. Farther west and south is the famous volcano Paricutín, the only major volcano born in modern times (1943).

The two most important cities in Michoacán, **Morelia** and **Pátzcuaro,** offer the visitor contrasting visions of the colonial past. Morelia is a city built of chiseled stone, planned with architectural considerations, and possessed of a clear-cut geometry and monumental proportions. In contrast, Pátzcuaro consists of undulating adobe walls, crooked red tile roofs, and narrow meandering streets. The former is proud of its Spanish heritage; the latter remains rooted in its Indian origins.

The first real city to be built in what is now Michoacán was most likely the one that left us the ruins at present-day Tingambato. This city was connected with the central Mexican cities of Teotihuacán and Tula, and was probably some kind of trading center. At some later date, the Purépecha arrived—we don't know from where. Their language is unlike any other in Mexico; the closest linguistic connection is with native peoples in Ecuador. They settled here, formed either an empire or a confederation of cities, and successfully defended their lands from the expansionist Aztec—the only highland civilization that managed to do so.

The Purépecha were not vassals of the Aztec, so they did not simply submit to Spanish rule after the collapse of the Aztec empire. In the history of the conquest and conversion of the Purépecha, two men represent the extremes of Spanish attitudes toward the Indians. One was the conquistador Nuño de Guzmán, whose rapaciousness and cruelty made him infamous even among fellow conquistadors, and eventually earned him a prison cell in Spain. The other was Vasco de Quiroga, a humanist who believed in the ideas of Erasmus and Thomas More. He joined the church late in life and came to Michoacán as the first bishop of the Purépecha, establishing his see in Pátzcuaro. He strove to build a utopian society of cooperative communities, organizing and instructing each village in the practice of a specific craft. To this day, the different villages largely follow his organization of crafts.

## EXPLORING MICHOACAN

Traveling from one major town to another takes only an hour or 2, and public transportation is frequent. You should plan 2 days in **Morelia** (more if you intend to see the butterflies) and a minimum of 2 days in **Pátzcuaro,** but more like a week if you're interested in taking day trips to the lakes and the villages in the region and want to look into the local handcrafts. **Uruapan,** another important town, is an easy day trip from either city, although you may want to stay longer to visit the **Paricutín volcano.** During Easter week or Day of the Dead observances (Nov 1–2), the Plazas Grandes in Pátzcuaro and Uruapan overflow with regional crafts. Reserve rooms well in advance for these holidays.

# 1 Morelia ★

312km (195 miles) NW of Mexico City; 365km (228 miles) SE of Guadalajara

The first Viceroy of Mexico ordered the founding of the city in 1541 under the name Valladolid. The name was later changed to honor the revolutionary hero José María Morelos, who was born here.

Morelia was intended as a bastion of Spanish culture for the region's large population of Indians. The adjective people most frequently use to describe Morelia is "aristocratic." And indeed, the city's greatest appeal lies in its grand colonial architecture.

## ESSENTIALS

**GETTING THERE & DEPARTING** **By Plane** **Mexicana** (© **800/531-7921** or 443/324-3808) has flights to and from the U.S. Flights from San Francisco, Oakland, San Jose, Los Angeles, and Chicago are either one-stop or nonstop, depending on the destination and day of the flight. Mexicana also flies direct to several destinations within Mexico. **Aeromexico/Aerolitoral** (© **800/237-6639,** 443/324-2424, or 443/324-3604) flies to and from Mexico City, Guadalajara, Querétaro, Tepic, and Tijuana, with connections to U.S. destinations.

Morelia's airport is **Aeropuerto Francisco J. Mújica,** a 45-minute drive from the city center on km 27 of the Carretera Morelia-Zinapécuaro. Taxis meet each flight. **Budget** has a car-rental office there (© **800/527-0700** in the U.S. and Canada, or 443/313-3399).

**By Car** With the **new toll highway** running between Mexico City and Guadalajara, the trip to Morelia from either city, formerly 6 hours, now takes only 4. **Highway 15** (the long route) runs west from Mexico City and east and south from Guadalajara. Both sections of Highway 15 are mountainous and slow, with beautiful vistas. From Mexico City, the toll highway goes to Toluca, then through Atlacomulco and Marvatío. From Guadalajara, it goes through La Barca (northeast of Lake Chapala). Tolls run close to $20. Coming from either direction, you will see the very large Lake Cuitzeo; then look for the intersection with Highway 43 and turn south. **Highway 43 North** is a fairly direct and straight route from Guanajuato (2½ hr.) and from San Miguel de Allende (3 hr.). Four-lane **Highway 120** connects Pátzcuaro and Morelia; the trip takes about 50 minutes. (Midway, you'll see a turnoff for Tupátaro and Cuanajo, covered in "Side Trips from Pátzcuaro," later.)

**By Bus** You will arrive at the new Central Camionera in the far northwest side of town, near the soccer stadium. First-class and deluxe bus service to and from Morelia is excellent, and regional service to Pátzcuaro is quite frequent.

**VISITOR INFORMATION** The **Tourist Information Office** is in a former Jesuit monastery, the Palacio Clavijero, at the corner of Madero and Nigromante (© **443/317-2371** or 443/312-8081). The office is open weekdays from 9am to 8pm, weekends from 9am to 2pm.

**CITY LAYOUT** The heart of the city is the **cathedral,** with the Plaza de Armas on its left and the Plaza Melchor Ocampo on its right. The two-way street running east-west in front of the cathedral is **Avenida Madero,** the city's main street. It meets the lovely colonial aqueduct and the modern fountain **Las Tarascas** a half-mile east of the cathedral. This segment of Madero, along with several blocks to either side, is the old part of town (see "Other Attractions," below.) From the fountain, the **aqueduct** heads southeast toward what has become the fashionable part of town.

**GETTING AROUND** Taxis are a bargain here. Still, you should settle the fare before you enter the cab.

## *FAST FACTS:* Morelia

*American Express* The local representative is **Gran Turismo Viajes,** Av. Camelinas 3233, Int. 102–103, Fracc. Las Américas (© **443/324-0484;** fax 443/324-0495). Hours are Monday to Saturday from 9am to 2pm and 4 to 6pm.

*Area Code* The telephone area code is **443.**

*Climate* Morelia can be a bit chilly in the morning and evening, especially from November through February.

*Elevation* Morelia sits at 1,930m (6,368 ft.).

*Emergencies* The local number for emergencies is © **443/312-2222.**

*Hospital* The best in town is the **Sanatorio de la Luz,** Calle Bravo 50, in the Chapultepec Norte neighborhood (© **443/314-4568,** 443/314-4464 or 443/315-2966).

*Internet Access* **Share Web Cyber Café,** Av. Madero Ote. 573-C (© **443/312-3312**), is open Monday to Saturday from 10am to 10pm, Sunday from 2 to 10pm.

*Newspapers* The local paper, *La Voz de Michoacán,* has an English-language "What's New in Morelia This Week" page that appears every Monday and lists cultural and artistic events.

*Population* Morelia has 520,000 residents.

*Post Office/Telegraph Office* Both are in the Palacio Federal, on the corner of Madero and Serapio Rendón, 5 blocks east of the cathedral.

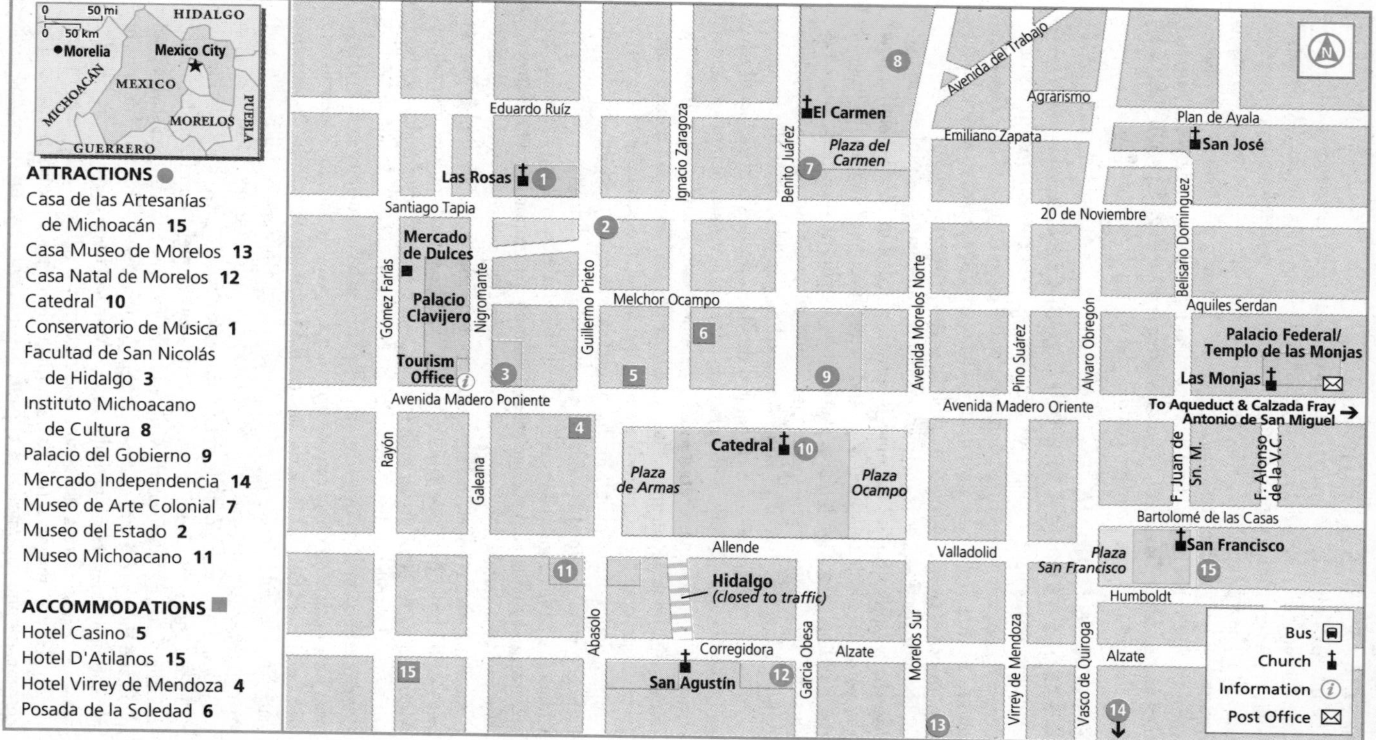
HIDALGO
0 50 mi
0 50 km
Morelia
Mexico City
MICHOACÁN
MEXICO
MORELOS
PUEBLA
GUERRERO
ATTRACTIONS
Casa de las Artesanías de Michoacán 15
Casa Museo de Morelos 13
Casa Natal de Morelos 12
Catedral 10
Conservatorio de Música 1
Facultad de San Nicolás de Hidalgo 3
Instituto Michoacano de Cultura 8
Palacio del Gobierno 9
Mercado Independencia 14
Museo de Arte Colonial 7
Museo del Estado 2
Museo Michoacano 11
ACCOMMODATIONS
Hotel Casino 5
Hotel D'Atilanos 15
Hotel Virrey de Mendoza 4
Posada de la Soledad 6
Eduardo Ruíz
Las Rosas
Santiago Tapia
Mercado de Dulces
Gómez Farías
Palacio Clavijero
Nigromante
Tourism Office
Guillermo Prieto
Melchor Ocampo
Ignacio Zaragoza
Benito Juárez
El Carmen
Plaza del Carmen
Avenida del Trabajo
Agrarismo
Emiliano Zapata
Plan de Ayala
San José
20 de Noviembre
Belisario Dominguez
Aquiles Serdan
Palacio Federal/ Templo de las Monjas
Las Monjas
Avenida Morelos Norte
Pino Suárez
Alvaro Obregón
Avenida Madero Poniente
Avenida Madero Oriente
To Aqueduct & Calzada Fray Antonio de San Miguel
Rayón
Galeana
Catedral
Plaza de Armas
Plaza Ocampo
F. Juan de Sn. M.
F. Alonso de la V.C.
Bartolomé de las Casas
San Francisco
Plaza San Francisco
Allende
Valladolid
Hidalgo (closed to traffic)
Humboldt
Abasolo
Corregidora
Garcia Obesa
Alzate
Morelos Sur
Virrey de Mendoza
Vasco de Quiroga
San Agustín
Bus
Church
Information
Post Office

## SPECIAL EVENTS & FESTIVALS

**The International Guitar Festival** attracts musicians from all over the world. The dates for the festival vary, but it usually takes place in early spring. In May, the city holds the **International Organ Festival** (linked to the variable feast day of Corpus Christi). The cathedral has what might be the largest pipe organ in this hemisphere—if you like organ music, consider attending this festival. The **International Festival of Music** is in July. September is the month of the *fiestas patrias;* on **Independence Day** (Sept 16) and **Morelos's Birthday** (Sept 30), there are large fireworks displays (*castillos*), parades, and a good deal of celebrating.

## EXPLORING MORELIA

### A STROLL THROUGH THE COLONIAL CENTER

Downtown Morelia is a good town for walking. One comes across interesting details on just about any street, and street crime poses little problem. The walk outlined below could take a whole day. The museums open at 9am; you'll find a lot of places closed on Mondays, holidays, and between 2 and 4pm.

The **cathedral** ★★★ is the place to begin. Built with the pink stone that Morelia is famous for, it's the most beautiful cathedral in Mexico. Notice how the main street widens in front of it, and a cross street lines up with the front of the building. The city builders consciously sought to accentuate the city's churches by creating open spaces that would allow distant perspectives. This cathedral took the place of an earlier one; construction began in 1640 and ended in 1745. The new cathedral incorporated the finest features of the styles of religious architecture already in the city, including plateresque, mannerist, and a native style of baroque characterized by sobriety and restraint—qualities that came naturally to Morelianos. The cathedral's impressive size and monumental proportions were necessary to place it at the top of the hierarchy of the city's temples, and to make plain Morelia's superiority to rival Pátzcuaro. The Italian architect who designed it worked closely with the different authorities of Morelia's sizable religious community, and he did a masterful job balancing the architectural elements in the façade and shaping the proportions of the towers. The inside is stately, but (as is often the case) the cathedral's most valuable possessions were plundered. Things to look for include the beautiful **organ** ★ with 4,600 pipes (see "Special Events," above); the silver baptismal font where Mexico's first emperor, Agustín de Iturbide, was baptized; and the elegant choir with carved wooden stalls.

Across the main street (Madero) from the cathedral is a two-story stone building with little decoration on its exterior walls, yet topped with fanciful, Oriental-style decorations and finials. This is the **Palacio del Gobierno,** built in 1732 as a seminary. It now holds sweeping murals depicting the history of Michoacán and Mexico. Some are the work of a well-known local artist, Alfredo Zalce.

As you leave the palacio, turn left and walk down Madero for 2 blocks. You will see a small church on your right with a tall wrought-iron fence; turn right at Calle Vasco de Quiroga and walk 1 block. To your left, you will see a broad plaza and the **church and convent of San Francisco** ★★. This and San Agustín are the two oldest religious buildings in Morelia. Both drew on the Spanish renaissance architectural style known as plateresque (already antiquated by that time) because they wanted to accentuate Morelia's Spanish heritage. The convent is quite striking; it has elegant, Moorish windows on the second floor, borrowed from Spanish Mudéjar architecture. The interior courtyard, unlike any other in Morelia, has a medieval feel. Instead of being broad and open with light arches, it is closed and heavily buttressed with columns set closely together. The former convent now houses a local **handcrafts museum** and the best shopping in Morelia (see "Shopping," below).

Morelia's **city market** is 5 blocks south of San Francisco in a plain, warehouse-like structure. It's much like other Mexican city markets and a good place to observe details of local life. If you're going to walk as far as the market, you should also visit the **church of the Capuchinas.** It's a precious little baroque church with a gilt, highly ornate *retablo* (altarpiece) inside. Unfortunately, it is often closed; the best time to try is from 8 to 9am and from 7 to 8pm, when the father opens the church for mass. To get there from San Francisco, continue along Calle Vasco de Quiroga. If you want to skip the market, go straight down the street that lines up with the front of San Francisco, and turn left at the second intersection on Calle Morelos Sur. One block down on your left is the Casa Museo de Morelos (see below). The **Templo de Capuchinas** is 5 blocks away from San Francisco, slightly downhill. You'll come across a shaded plaza that fronts a church. That's it. Beside the church is a pedestrian walkway crowded with vendors; this leads to the market, which is a good place to pick up sombreros, huaraches, and such.

From the market, backtrack to the church and turn left (west) on the street that runs in front of the church (Ortega y Montáñez). Walk 2 blocks to Morelos Sur. Turn right (uphill) and after 1 long block, look for the **Casa Museo de Morelos,** Morelos Sur 323 (© **443/313-2651**), on your right. This is where José María Morelos lived as an adult. It's a grand house, with furniture and personal effects that belonged to the independence leader, as well as a period kitchen. For history buffs, there is an exhibition of his four campaigns against Spanish royalist forces. The museum is open daily from 9am to 7pm; admission is $2.

The next place to see is the **Museo Regional Michoacano** ★, at the intersection of Allende and Abasolo (© **443/312-0407**). To get there, walk uphill toward Madero, turn left when you get to the plaza next to the cathedral (1 block before Madero), and walk through the stone arcades behind the cathedral. At the end of the arcades and across the street, cater-corner to the Plaza de Armas, is this museum. It provides a colorful view of the state from prehistoric times to Mexico's Cardenist period of the 1930s. Isidor Huarte, father of Ana Huarte (Emperor Iturbide's wife), originally owned the building, which was finished in 1775. The museum is open Tuesday through Saturday from 9am to 7pm, Sunday from 9am to 4pm. Admission is $2.

To take a break, sit at one of the outdoor cafes under the stone arches facing the front of the cathedral, order refreshments, and watch people pass by (a common pastime for Morelianos).

From there, go west on Madero for 1 block until you get to the corner of Nigromante. On the right corner, you'll find the **College of San Nicolás de Hidalgo,** a beautiful colonial-era building that claims to house the oldest university in the New World. Founded in Pátzcuaro in 1540, the university moved to Valladolid (present-day Morelia) in 1580 and became the University of Michoacán in 1917. On the other corner is another of Morelia's oldest church structures, the **Iglesia de la Compañía de Jesús,** built by the Jesuits. It is now a lovely library. Through a doorway to the right of the church is the **tourist information office.** Attached to the church is the former convent, now called the **Palacio Clavijero.** To see the graceful arches and rose-colored stone of its broad interior courtyard (the most photographed in Morelia), turn down Nigromante and follow it to the main entrance. The former convent now houses state government offices. Once you've seen the Palacio, continue down the street to the little park. Facing the park is the **Conservatorio de las Rosas,** a former Dominican convent. It became a music school in 1785 and is now the home of the internationally acclaimed **Morelia Boys Choir.** The choir practices on weekday afternoons. If you would like to attend a concert, ask for information inside.

Cater-corner from the conservatory, at the junction of Santiago Tapia and Guillermo Prieto, is the **Museo del Estado** (**© 443/313-0629**). Exhibits include a display on the archaeology and history of the area and a 19th-century apothecary shop. The museum is open Monday to Friday from 9am to 2pm and 4 to 8pm, Saturday and Sunday from 9am to 2pm and 4 to 7pm. Admission is free. Look for or ask about concerts and other goings-on.

To visit another interesting museum, continue east on Santiago Tapia 2 blocks to Benito Juárez and turn north (left). The **Museo de Arte Colonial** ★, Av. Benito Juárez 240 (**© 443/313-9260**), is a colonial mansion that houses a large collection of religious art from the 16th to the 18th centuries. One section displays Christ figures made from the paste of corn stalks. This was a pre-Columbian artistic technique among the Purépecha, and the missionaries soon had their Indian converts using it to create the Christ figures and saints that adorn many churches in Mexico. (La Parroquia in San Miguel de Allende contains another example of this craft.) The museum is open Tuesday through Sunday from 10am to 2pm and 5 to 7pm. Admission is free.

Just around the corner from this museum (turn right as you exit) is the colonial **Plaza del Carmen.** Snake-oil salesmen often perform to a crowd here. On the opposite side of the plaza, behind a heavy wrought-iron fence, is the church and former convent of **El Carmen.** The entrance is at the opposite end from the church, on Morelos Norte. The building is home to the state's **Instituto Michoacano de Cultura** (**© 443/313-1320**), which has made this a comfortable and utilitarian destination; you can examine the calendars posted at the entrance to see whether a concert, film, or exhibition is happening during your stay. You can also sit down and have coffee while viewing the large stone courtyard built in the style often used by the Carmelites (a religious order that included Saints Theresa of Ávila and John of the Cross). In and about the courtyard are a museum of native masks, a large bookstore, and a gallery. Entrance is free. The institute is open daily from 10am to 8pm.

## OTHER ATTRACTIONS

If you enjoy walks, try going east on Madero from the cathedral. After a couple of blocks, you'll reach the **Templo de las Monjas** ("Nuns' Temple"), a lovely old church with a unique twin façade and B-shaped floor plan. Beside it is the massive **Palacio Federal,** which houses, among many other official bureaus, the post and telegraph offices. Continue and you'll reach the colonial **aqueduct** and **Las Tarascas fountain.** The graceful arches of the aqueduct stretch from here more than a mile eastward. A beautiful stone walkway, lined with trees and long stone benches, starts from one of the arches in front of the fountain. This is **La Calzada Fray Antonio de San Miguel** ★, and it leads to the **church of San Diego** ★. The most ornate church in Morelia, San Diego is also known as **El Santuario de Guadalupe.** In early December, stands fill the entire plaza in front of it and the length of the calzada, and visitors celebrate the feast day of the Virgin of Guadalupe (Dec 12). Occasionally, you'll see people walking on their knees the entire length of the calzada. The distance from the cathedral to San Diego is a little more than a mile. You can take a taxi back or, if you still feel like walking, return by crossing the large plaza to the right of the church, passing by the equestrian statue of Morelos, going under the aqueduct, and entering the park known as **El Bosque** (the forest). Inside the park are a couple of grand fin-de-siècle mansions that are now museums. West of the park is a middle-class neighborhood. Continue west and work your way back to Madero. If you get turned around here, note that if you're walking on level ground, you're parallel to or heading toward Madero; if you're walking downhill, you're heading away from it.

## SHOPPING

**Casa de las Artesanías** ★★ This is both a museum and one of the best crafts shops in Mexico. In the showroom on the right as you enter, you'll find an array of objects produced in the Indian villages of Michoacán's central highlands, including carved-wood furniture from Cuanajo, pottery from Tzintzuntzan, wood masks from Tócuaro, lacquerware from Pátzcuaro and Uruapan, cross-stitch embroidery from Tarecuato, copperware from Santa Clara, guitars from Paracho, and close-woven hats from Jarácuaro. Straight ahead in the interior courtyard are showcases laden with the best regional crafts. Upstairs, individual villages have sales outlets. Sometimes you'll find artisans demonstrating their craft. The shop and museum are open daily from 9am to 8pm. Exconvento de San Francisco, Plaza Valladolid. ✆ **443/312-1248.**

**Mercado de Dulces** Occupying the back part of the former Jesuit convent is the sweets market—a collection of stalls selling the typical sweets that Morelia is famous for, such as *ates* (a thick fruit paste), candied fruit wedges, jelly candies, honey, strawberry jam, pralines, toasted coconut, and milk candies. A shop upstairs has all kinds of regional artesanías and hundreds of picture postcards from all over Michoacán. The mercado is open daily from 7am to 10pm. Behind the Palacio Clavijero, along Valentín Gómez Farías. No phone. From the cathedral, head west on Madero and turn right on Gómez Farías; entrance is half a block down on the right.

# WHERE TO STAY

Rates listed here assume double occupancy and include the 15% value-added tax.

## VERY EXPENSIVE

**Villa Montaña** ★★★ High above the city on the Santa María Ridge, this hotel radiates beauty and tranquility. Rooms are in a small complex of buildings on a hillside, separated by gardens and connected by footpaths. The buildings are at different levels; this, as well as the placement of the entrances, allows for privacy. Villa Montaña, a member of the Small Luxury Hotels of the World, has no rough edges. Rooms are large, impressively furnished, and have working fireplaces. Most come with two doubles or a king-size bed. Bathrooms are ample, with tub-shower combinations and lots of counter space. The restaurant does a great job with local dishes, and having a drink on the terrace overlooking the city is one of the delights of staying here.

Patzimba 201, Col. Vista Bella 58090 Morelia, Mich. ✆ **800/223-6510** in the U.S., 800/448-8355 in Canada, 443/314-0231, or 443/314-0179. Fax 443/314-9696. www.villamontana.com.mx. 38 units. $195 double; $250–$290 suite, $450 2-bedroom suite. Rates include 7.5% service charge. Weekend discounts available. AE, MC, V. Free secured parking. **Amenities:** Restaurant (international/regional), terrace bar; heated outdoor pool; golf and gym at local country club; lighted tennis court; concierge; tour desk; business center; executive business services; room service until 11pm; in-room massage; babysitting; same-day laundry and dry cleaning. *In room:* TV, dataport, hair dryer, safe, bathrobes.

## EXPENSIVE

**Hotel Virrey de Mendoza** ★★ This is one of the old-style grand hotels one often finds in Mexico's colonial cities. Unlike others, this one has no hint of decay; it is beautifully kept and most impressive. It's also right on the Plaza de Armas. Furnishings vary, but all rooms are comfortable. They have lots of character—wood floors with area rugs, period furniture, old-fashioned tile bathrooms with tub/shower combinations. Bed choices include two twins, one full, two queen-size, or one king-size. Standard rooms are medium size; of the eight exterior rooms, two have balconies. Suites are larger, and master suites have separate sitting rooms. The viceroy suite (*suite virreinal)* is really grand, with a large third-floor terrace that looks out over the Plaza de Armas to the cathedral. If you crave quiet, avoid a room facing Madero. Interior rooms are lovely, but I prefer the exterior rooms on the upper floors.

Av. Madero Pte. 310, 58000 Morelia, Mich. © **443/312-4940.** Fax 443/312-6719. www.hotelvirrey.com. 55 units. $120 double; $195 suite. Weekend discounts available. AE, MC, V. Free valet parking. **Amenities:** Restaurant, lobby bar; golf at local club; tour desk; car rental; room service until 11pm; in-room massage; babysitting; same-day laundry and dry cleaning. *In room:* TV, hair dryer.

### MODERATE

**Best Western Hotel Casino ★** A colonial hotel that's not as striking as the Posada de la Soledad, the Best Western should still be considered for its location—across the street from the cathedral—and for the comfort and quiet of its rooms. The medium-size rooms are simply furnished and carpeted. Some units in front have a balcony and view of the cathedral (but aren't as quiet as interior rooms). Many units have two doubles or one double and one twin.

Portal Hidalgo 229, 58000 Morelia, Mich. © **800/528-1234** in the U.S., or 443/313-1328. Fax 443/312-1252. www.hotelcasino.com.mx. 47 units. $80 double. AE, MC, V. Free valet parking. **Amenities:** Restaurant (Mexican/regional), bar; tour desk; car rental; business center; room service until 9:30pm; same-day laundry and dry cleaning; nonsmoking rooms. *In room:* TV, dataport, coffeemaker, hair dryer.

**Posada de la Soledad ★** Past the massive wooden doors of this colonial hotel is a large, beautiful courtyard with antique carriages parked beneath stone arches. Some rooms have fireplaces and small balconies. Standard rooms vary from small to medium. The price depends on whether the room faces the more elegant front courtyard (these rooms are generally bigger) or the rear courtyard. Rooms have rugs or carpeting, Spanish-style furniture, high ceilings, and one or two double beds. Bathrooms vary in size and quality; most are ample, and many contain tub/shower combinations. The location is great—1 block north of the cathedral on Zaragoza (across from Madero).

Ignacio Zaragoza 90, 58000 Morelia, Mich. © **443/312-1888** or 443/313-0627. www.hsoledad.com. 58 units. $86 double; $92–$105 suite. AE, DC, MC, V. **Amenities:** Restaurant, bar; tour desk; car rental; room service until 10pm; babysitting; same-day laundry and dry cleaning. *In room:* TV, safe.

### INEXPENSIVE

**Hotel D'Atilanos** This is the most comfortable inexpensive hotel in the downtown area. Two floors of rooms surround a simple, pleasant patio. The rooms are simply furnished, with one or two doubles, two twins, or one king bed. Most units are large, but bathrooms are small. I prefer the downstairs rooms for their high ceilings.

Corregidora 465, 58000 Morelia, Mich. © **443/313-3309** or 443/312-0121. 27 units. $36–$45 double. AE, MC, V. **Amenities:** Restaurant; limited room service; overnight laundry.

## WHERE TO DINE

**Casa de la Calzada ★** INTERNATIONAL This restaurant, in a relaxing setting that fronts the calzada, can be an enjoyable stop on a walking tour of the city. The menu includes several light dishes, making it ideal for when you're not terribly hungry or want just dessert and coffee. You can take a table on the pleasant patio or in one of the equally pleasant dining rooms; there's a bar in the rear, and sometimes management sets tables out in front. The salads are healthy and trustworthy; *cazuela San Miguel* comes in a toasted flour-tortilla bowl with raspberry vinaigrette and small chunks of breaded cheese. Pasta Citrus is vegetables and pasta stir-fried in olive oil, with ground macadamia nuts and lots of lime juice. For heavier meals, the restaurant offers *arrachera* (skirt steak) with a variety of sauces, and chicken breast stuffed with shrimp.

The dessert menu is tempting; one of the choices, a small chocolate cake with chocolate sauce in the middle, is actually called *tentación* (temptation).

Calzada Fray Antonio de San Miguel 344. ✆ **443/313-5319.** Main courses $8–$13. AE, MC, V. Tues–Sat 1:45–11pm; Sun 1:45–6pm.

**Cenaduría Lupita** ★ ANTOJITOS REGIONALES Translated literally, *antojitos* means "little cravings." This is the traditional supper food of most Mexicans, but they usually eat it at home or in greasy-spoon joints whose cleanliness is doubtful. A good-looking, comfortable restaurant that specializes in *antojitos* is a rarity; rarer still is one that does such a good job. Take your pick of tacos, quesadillas, tostadas, tamales, and such—all the food that was transformed beyond recognition into Tex-Mex—prepared Michoacán style. The restaurant is a half block off Avenida Lázaro Cárdenas; take a cab.

Sánchez de Tagle 1004. ✆ **443/312-1340.** Supper $3–$6. MC, V. Wed–Mon 7–11pm.

**El Anzuelo** SEAFOOD/STEAKS This simple outdoor restaurant in the modern part of town serves delicious food prepared with great care. It makes the perfect Mexican seafood cocktail and wonderful *ceviche*. After either of those as a starter, you might order a saltwater or freshwater fish dish (one specialty uses apple in a light curry sauce; another has a mild sauce of cream and poblano chiles), or filet mignon if you don't feel like fish. The owners are meticulous about food preparation. El Anzuelo is open only in the afternoon. On Sunday, it offers paella, and the restaurant gets very crowded. Take a taxi.

Av. Camelinas 3180. ✆ **443/314-8339** or 443/324-3237. Main courses $5–$9. MC, V. Tues–Sun noon–5:30pm.

**La Casa del Portal** ★ REGIONAL/INTERNATIONAL This upstairs restaurant is in a beautiful stone mansion facing the Plaza de Armas. The floors, walls, and ceilings of the old house have remained virtually intact, including the antique wallpaper and other details. There are several dining rooms, and on occasion the rooftop terrace is open for dining. Most of the furniture comes from the owner's workshop—his colorful designs make use of many furniture-making traditions of the region. The restaurant doubles as a sort of factory outlet, and all the furniture is for sale. What's for dinner? The menu includes several regional standards, such as *enchiladas portal* (Michoacán-style enchiladas) and *arrachera valladolid*, a skirt steak accompanied by a few standard Mexican sides. There are also a few international offerings.

Guillermo Prieto 30 (cater-corner from Virrey de Mendoza; entrance is on the side street). ✆ **443/313-4899.** Main courses $6–$12. AE, MC, V. Daily 8:30am–10pm.

**Las Mercedes Restaurant** INTERNATIONAL This is a downtown courtyard restaurant decorated with palms, flowers, succulents, and various architectural pieces obviously salvaged from other buildings (there is also a separate dining room). A plate of small tacos, homemade bread, and herb-flavored butter starts things off while you contemplate your choices. Specialties include *sopa milpera* (corn soup), *sopa mercedes* (with chipotle), beef brochette, chicken breast a la portuguesa (stuffed with cheese, wrapped in bacon, and covered in white wine and parsley sauce), and trout Florentine.

León Guzmán 47. ✆ **443/312-6113.** Fax 443/313-3222. Main courses $8–$14. AE, MC, V. Mon–Sat 1:30pm–midnight; Sun 1:30–6pm. From the cathedral, walk 4 short blocks west on Madero. Turn right on León Guzmán and look for a small sign on the left.

**Las Trojes** STEAKHOUSE/REGIONAL A *troje* (or *troxe*) is the traditional dwelling of the highland Purépecha Indians, constructed of rough-cut wood planks. They can vary in size, and some approach barn dimensions. This restaurant is made of seven connected *trojes,* with some large glass windows inserted. For starters, try *sopa tarasca* (a famous regional bean soup). Main courses include filet mignon, *cecina* (beef or pork sliced thin, spiced, and dried), chicken stuffed with cheese en brochette, and whitefish—the famous delicately flavored fish from the region's lakes. Vegetarians can try the *champiñones al ajillo* (mushrooms in garlic). You'll need a taxi to get here from the historic center.

Juan Sebastián Bach 51, Colonia La Loma. ✆ **443/314-7344.** Main courses $9–$16. AE, MC, V. Mon–Sat 1pm–midnight; Sun 1–6pm. Valet parking available.

**San Miguelito** ★ *Finds* MEXICAN An amusing restaurant with good food, San Miguelito tries to capture the real *mexicano* atmosphere—the place is loaded with icons of Mexican culture, many of them parodies. The bar and waiting area, for example, is a miniature bullring dedicated to the Silvetis, a Mexico *torero* dynasty. One part of the main dining room is the *Rincon de las Solteronas* (the bachelorette corner), where many images of Saint Anthony hang upside down—the custom in Mexico when a girl is petitioning him for a boyfriend or husband. Any guest is welcome to make a petition; the staff will be happy to show you how. Most of the dishes contain beef; the most popular is grilled filet served with a sauce, such as cream and poblano chile or a mesquite-flavored concoction. The menu also lists chicken dishes, including breast of chicken with a corn chowder sauce. Appetizers include breaded cheese; for dessert there's a delicious version of cherries jubilee. You'll probably want to take a cab—it's too far to walk, but too close to concern yourself with driving.

Av. Camelinas (cater-corner from the convention center). ✆ **443/324-2300.** Main courses $9–$13. AE, MC, V. Mon–Wed 2–11pm; Thurs–Sat 2pm–midnight; Sun 2–5pm.

## MORELIA AFTER DARK

For nighttime entertainment, be sure to check the calendar of events at the **Instituto Michoacano de Cultura** (see "A Stroll Through the Colonial Center," earlier). In addition, you can sit at one of the cafes under the stone arches across from the Plaza de Armas to do some people-watching (a very Moreliano thing to do). Aside from the discos that are mostly on the fashionable east side, there are few nightlife options. The following are my favorites. For dancing, go to **La Casa de la Salsa** (✆ **443/313-9362**), a large dance hall facing Plaza Morelos at the end of the calzada. It's open Tuesday through Saturday from 9pm to 3am. It books live music on Friday and Saturday ($4 cover). You can call ahead to reserve a table; the band plays a lot of salsa, merengue, and mambo.

If you want to hear live Latin American folk music (and eat something), try **Peña Colibrí** (✆ **443/312-2261**), Galeana 36, behind the Virrey de Mendoza. It opens daily at 8pm and closes around midnight.

A third option is **La Azotea,** the rooftop club of the Los Juaninos Hotel, on the corner of Madero and Morelos Sur, across from the plaza and east of the cathedral. A live band starts playing Wednesday through Saturday at

## *Moments* Michoacán's Monarch Migration

A visit to the winter nesting grounds of the monarch butterfly, high in the mountains of northeast Michoacán, is a stirring experience. It might be the highlight of your trip. The season lasts from mid- to late November through March. Tour operators in Morelia offer a day trip to see the butterflies for $50 to $60 per person. The tour takes 10 to 12 hours and involves hiking up a mountain at a high altitude. You shouldn't consider doing this if you're not in decent physical condition.

The best time to see the butterflies is on a sunny day, when they flutter through the air in a blizzard of orange and black. At the center of the group, the branches of the tall fir trees bow under their burden of butterflies, whose wings undulate softly as the wind blows through the forest; it's quite a spectacle.

From Morelia, you'll have no difficulty finding a tour; most hotels and all travel agencies can put you in contact with one. I particularly recommend guides **Luis Miguel López Alanís** (✆ **443/320-1157**) and **Alfredo de la Cruz Ibarra** (✆ **443/331-4473**). They speak English, are federally licensed, and belong to a small cooperative of guides called Mex Mich Guías (mexmich@prodigy.net.mx). Most tours provide transportation, guide, soft drinks, and usually lunch. Make sure that the tour includes transportation all the way to the trail head. A good guide is important, if only to answer all the questions that these butterflies and their strange migration provoke.

Two butterfly sanctuaries are open to the public. (The monarchs congregate at seven sites, but five are closed to visitors.) They are **El Rosario** (admission $3; open daily from 10am–5 or 6pm) and the newer **Chincua.** It is less of a drive, but usually more of a walk to the nucleus of the butterfly group—but not always. Throughout the season, the groups shift, moving up and down the mountains and making for a longer or shorter climb.

If you're driving, take the *autopista* to Mexico City, exit at Maravatio and go right. Keep right after going through Maravatio and take the narrow two-lane road towards Angangueo. When you get to a T-junction, go right, toward San Felipe. Go through Ocampo and continue until you get to Rosario, where you will find a parking lot near the trail head. If you want to make this a leisurely trip, spend the night in the nearby town of Angangueo at **Hotel Don Bruno** (✆ **715/156-0026;** $55 double). It's a pretty hotel, but you should still ask to see the room before you accept it.

Travel agencies from **San Miguel de Allende** also book monarch tours, which take 2 days. See the section on San Miguel de Allende in chapter 5 for details.

around 9:30pm. The music is best described as Latin lounge music—the cultural equivalent of Tony Bennett or Rosemary Clooney. You can also get a great view of the cathedral.

## 2 Pátzcuaro ★★★

370km (231 miles) NW of Mexico City; 285km (178 miles) SE of Guadalajara; 69km (43 miles) SW of Morelia

Pátzcuaro is perhaps the loveliest town in Mexico. Crooked cobblestone streets, smooth stucco walls painted white with dark red borders, blackened tile roofs that join to form ramshackle rooflines—it is a town meant to be photographed and painted. During the rainy season, when low clouds roll in and curl through the tall trees, and water drips from the low-slung overhangs, a sweet melancholy descends upon the town.

Pátzcuaro is in the heart of the Purépecha homeland. Beside it is Lake Pátzcuaro (one of the world's highest at 2,200m/7,250 ft.), whose shores border dozens of Indian villages. In these villages and in town, visitors frequently hear the soft sounds of the Purépechan language in the background as they take in the sights. Although distinct regional costumes are seldom seen today, Indian women still braid their hair with ribbons and wear the blue *rebozos* (long woolen wraps) that serve them in so many ways.

### ESSENTIALS

**GETTING THERE & DEPARTING** **By Car** See "Getting There & Departing" under "Morelia," earlier, for information from Mexico City, Guadalajara, San Miguel de Allende, and Morelia. From Morelia there are two routes to Pátzcuaro; the faster is the new four-lane **Highway 120,** which passes near Tiripetío and Tupátaro/Cuanajo (see "Side Trips from Pátzcuaro," later). The longer route, **Highway 15,** takes a little more than an hour and passes near the pottery-making village of Capula and then through Quiroga, where you follow signs to Pátzcuaro (see "Side Trips from Pátzcuaro," later).

**By Bus** The bus station is on the outskirts of Pátzcuaro, 5 minutes away by taxi ($2). If you're going anywhere outside of Michoacán, it's usually best to go to Morelia first. If you're going straight to Mexico City, the **Pegaso** bus company offers nonstop service. Buses between Morelia and Pátzcuaro run every 10 minutes. To visit any of the lakeside villages or nearby towns, public transportation is a viable option. From the Pátzcuaro bus station, there are buses to Tócuaro and Erongarícuaro every 20 minutes; to Tupátaro and Cuanajo every hour; to Tzintzuntzan and Quiroga every 40 minutes; and to Santa Clara del Cobre every hour. For Ihuatzio, you can pick up a minivan or a bus from the Plaza Chica.

**VISITOR INFORMATION** The **State Tourism Office,** Cuesta Buenavista 7 (© **434/342-1214**), near the basilica, is open Monday through Saturday from 9am to 3pm and 4 to 7pm, and Sunday 9am to 2pm. Although you might not find someone who speaks English, the staff will try to be helpful, and you can pick up useful maps and brochures.

**CITY LAYOUT** In a way, Pátzcuaro has two town centers, both plazas a block apart from each other. **Plaza Grande,** also called Plaza Principal or Plaza Don Vasco de Quiroga, is picturesque and tranquil, with a fountain and a statue of Vasco de Quiroga. Hotels, shops, and restaurants in colonial-era buildings flank this plaza. **Plaza Chica,** also known as Plaza Gertrudis Bocanegra, flows into the market, and around it swirls the commercial life of Pátzcuaro. Plaza Chica is north of Plaza Grande.

**GETTING AROUND** With the exception of Lake Pátzcuaro, the lookout, the bus station, and hotels on Lázaro Cárdenas, everything is within walking distance. Taxis are cheap. The lake is over a mile from town; buses make the run every 15 minutes from both the Plaza Grande and the Plaza Chica, going all the way to the pier (the *embarcadero* or *muelle*).

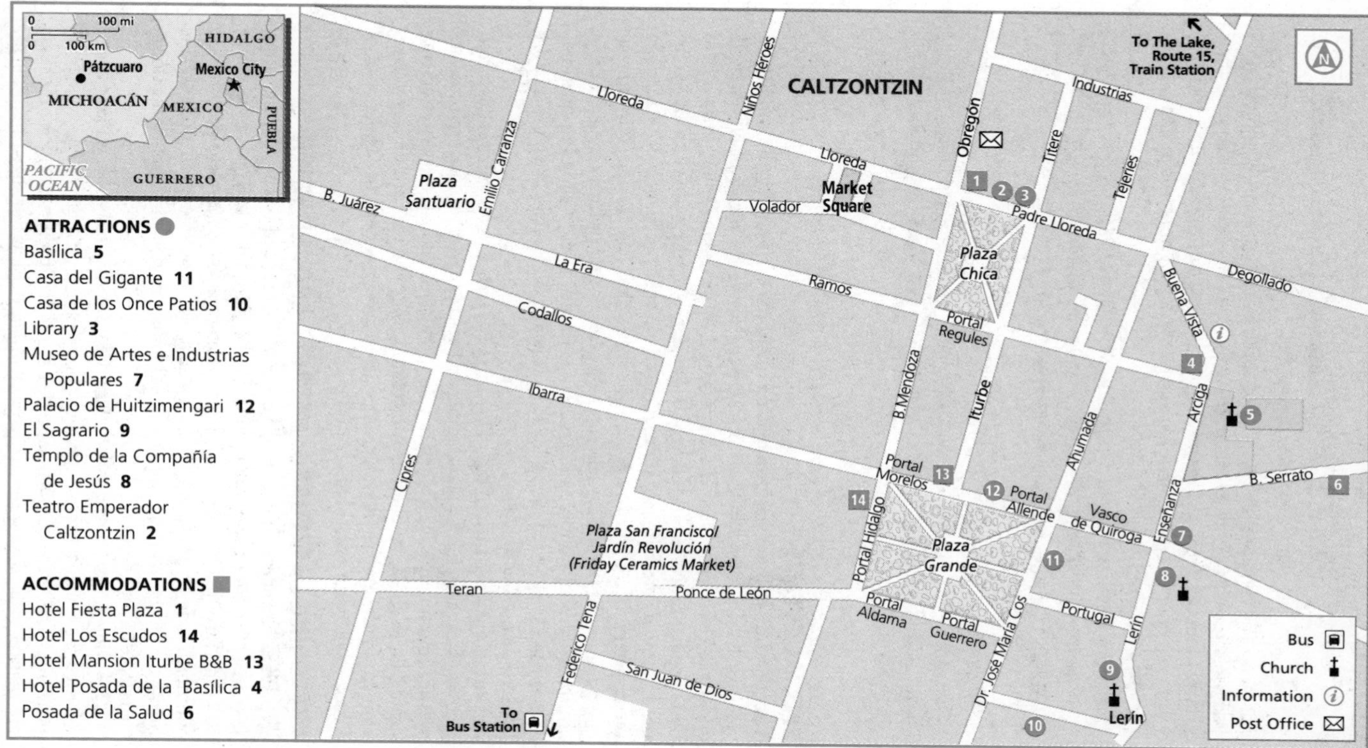
To The Lake, Route 15, Train Station
CALTZONTZIN
Market Square
Plaza Chica
Plaza Grande
Plaza Santuario
Plaza San Francisco
Jardín Revolución
(Friday Ceramics Market)
To Bus Station
Obregón
Títere
Tejerías
Industrias
Padre Lloreda
Lloreda
Volador
Niños Héroes
Ramos
La Era
Codallos
Ibarra
Emilio Carranza
B. Juárez
Cipres
Teran
Ponce de León
San Juan de Dios
Federico Tena
Degollado
Buena Vista
Arciga
B. Serrato
Enseñanza
Ahumada
Iturbe
B. Mendoza
Portal Regules
Portal Morelos
Portal Hidalgo
Portal Aldama
Portal Guerrero
Portal Allende
Vasco de Quiroga
Portugal
Lerín
Dr. José María Cos
Bus
Church
Information
Post Office
HIDALGO
PUEBLA
Mexico City
MEXICO
MICHOACÁN
GUERRERO
Pátzcuaro
PACIFIC OCEAN
0 100 mi
0 100 km
ATTRACTIONS
Basílica 5
Casa del Gigante 11
Casa de los Once Patios 10
Library 3
Museo de Artes e Industrias Populares 7
Palacio de Huitzimengari 12
El Sagrario 9
Templo de la Compañía de Jesús 8
Teatro Emperador Caltzontzin 2
ACCOMMODATIONS
Hotel Fiesta Plaza 1
Hotel Los Escudos 14
Hotel Mansion Iturbe B&B 13
Hotel Posada de la Basílica 4
Posada de la Salud 6

## FAST FACTS: Pátzcuaro

*Area Code* The telephone area code is **434.**

*Climate* The climate is delightful most of the year, but occasional blustery days bring swirls of chilled air from across the lake, causing everyone to retreat indoors. From October through April, it's cold enough for a heavy sweater, especially in the morning and evening. Few hotels have fireplaces or any source of heat in the rooms.

*Elevation* Pátzcuaro sits at an altitude of 2,200m (7,250 ft.).

*Emergency* Dial ✆ **434/349-0209** for emergency assistance.

*Hospital* The **Hospital Civil Dr. Gabriel García** is at Calle Romero 18 (✆ 434/342-0285).

*Population* Pátzcuaro has 70,000 residents.

*Post Office* The *correo,* located half a block north of Plaza Chica, on the right side of the street, is open Monday to Friday from 10am to 2pm and 4 to 8pm.

## SPECIAL EVENTS

The island of **Janitzio** has achieved international celebrity for the candlelight vigil that local residents hold at the cemetery during the nights of November 1 and 2, the Days of the Dead. **Tzintzuntzan,** a village 16km (10 miles) away, also hosts popular festivities, including folkloric dances in the main plaza and in the nearby *yácatas* (pre-Hispanic ruins), concerts in the church, and decorations in the cemetery. If you want to avoid the crowds, skip Janitzio and Tzintzuntzan and go to one of the smaller **lakeside villages or other islands** on the lake that also have extraordinary rituals. The tourism office (see "Visitor Information," above) has a schedule of events for the entire area and publishes an explanatory booklet, *Días de los Muertos.*

During the week surrounding **Day of the Dead,** artisans and vendors from all over Michoacán fill the Plaza Grande in Pátzcuaro with regional crafts**. Easter week,** beginning the Friday before Palm Sunday, is special, too. Most activity centers on the basilica. There are processions involving the surrounding villages almost nightly, and in Tzintzuntzan, there's a reenactment of the betrayal of Christ and a ceremonial washing of the feet.

## EXPLORING PÁTZCUARO: A STROLL AROUND TOWN

The **Plaza Grande** is in the middle of town, surrounded by colonial-era buildings. A **stone fountain** in the center of the plaza holds a large figure of the beloved Vasco de Quiroga, "Tata Vasco," depicted in a benevolent posture. On the north side of the plaza is the **Palacio de Huitziméngari,** built by the Spaniards for the Tarascan emperor. Local Indian artisans now occupy the slowly deteriorating building.

One long block north is the **Plaza Chica,** crisscrossed by walkways and adorned with the statue of Gertrudis Bocanegra, a heroine of Mexican independence. This is the commercial center of town. On the west side of the plaza are **market** stalls selling pottery, copper, *rebozos* (a kind of shawl traditionally worn by Indian women), serapes (a small woolen blanket that is sometimes carried over the shoulder), and food. On some days, the stalls extend a couple of blocks up the street. What was once San Agustín church is on the north side of the plaza. The cloister was remodeled in the 20th century and converted into the **Teatro Emperador Caltzontzin,** the municipal theater. The old church is now the public library; inside, all the way to the back, you'll find an early work of Juan O'Gorman—a large mural stretching the width and height of the nave.

Don Vasco built the **basilica,** on a hill just east of the Plaza Chica, although he died before it was inaugurated in 1554. It was designated a basilica by papal decree in 1907. Now reconstructed, it has survived many catastrophes, human and natural—from earthquakes to the civil war of the mid–19th century. Be sure to visit the main altar to see the **Virgin de la Salud.** She is a sacred figure to the Indians of this region, who come from the villages to pay homage to her and petition her healing power on the eighth day of each month.

Two blocks south of the basilica is the **Museo de Artes e Industrías Populares** ★★ (✆ **434/342-1029**). It occupies yet another beautiful colonial building (1540), originally Don Vasco's College of San Nicolás. The rooms, filled with fine examples of regional popular art such as crafts and costumes, open to a central courtyard. The museum guides are well informed about the various crafts—a good thing, because the works bring many questions to mind. The museum is open Tuesday through Saturday from 9am to 7pm, Sunday from 9am to 3pm. Admission is $3, free on Sunday. Behind the museum are some recent excavations of Purépechan ruins.

Of the many old churches in Pátzcuaro, one of the most interesting is the **Templo de la Compañía de Jesús,** just south of the museum. This church was Don Vasco's cathedral before the basilica; afterward, it was given to the Jesuits. The buildings across the street from the church were once part of the complex, containing the hospital, soup kitchen, and living quarters for religious scholars.

The **Casa de los Once Patios** (House of Eleven Patios) ★, between José María Cos and Enseñanza, is another achievement of the colonial period. Formerly a convent belonging to the Catherine nuns, today it houses the **Casa de las Artesanías de Michoacán,** with every type of local artistry for sale (see "Shopping," below).

## SHOPPING

Pátzcuaro is one of Mexico's best shopping towns: It has terrific textiles, copper, woodcarvings, lacquerwork, and straw weavings made in the region. Most shops are on the **Plaza Grande** and the streets leading from it to the **Plaza Chica,** the place of choice for copper vendors. There are also a couple of shops on the street facing the basilica. If you're interested in investigating a particular craft, you can find out which village or villages specialize in it, and if the villages have shops or a market. Tzintzuntzan, Ihuatzio, Cuanajo, Tupátaro, and Santa Clara del Cobre all have shops (see "Side Trips from Pátzcuaro," below).

**Casa de las Artesanías de Michoacán/House of Eleven Patios** This is the best one-stop shopping in the village. Small shops sell textile arts, pottery

---

*Tips* **Festival Hotel Crunch**

Make hotel reservations months in advance for Holy Week or Days of the Dead. Most hotels require a 3-night minimum stay during these events. There are some other, less popular festivals in Pátzcuaro and surrounding towns; check with the tourist office to see if any will occur during your visit.

---

and ceramic dishes, lacquerwork, paintings, woodcarvings, jewelry, copper work, and musical instruments (including the famous Paracho guitars). Much of the merchandise was produced in the region. Most shops are open daily from 9am to 2pm and 4 to 7pm. Calle Madrigal de las Altas Torres, between José Cos and Lerín. No phone.

**Comunidad de Santa Cruz** *Finds* Berta Servín Barriga is the powerhouse behind this cooperative. Women of the farming community of nearby Santa Cruz, where she lives, send their embroidery work here to be sold. They embroider scenes of village life on colorful cloth panels ranging from 3 by 5 inches to 20 by 40 inches, and on tablecloths and clothing. Ask Berta or her daughter Esther to explain the events in each festive scene. There's no sign; the shop is next to Mantas Típicas (see below), near the corner of Lerin. It's open Monday through Friday from 10am to 8pm, Saturday and Sunday from 10am to 5pm. José María Cos 3. No phone.

**Diseño Artesano** Owner Esperanza Sepúlveda designs one-of-a-kind clothing using locally made fabrics. Her shop, on the west side of the Plaza Grande, is open daily from 10am to 3pm and 4:30 to 8pm. José Cos 1. No phone.

**Friday Pottery Market** *Finds* Early each Friday morning this plaza, 1 block west of the Plaza Grande, fills with vendors of various styles of regionally made pottery, most of it not for sale in Pátzcuaro on other days. This is a market for locals that few tourists seem to hear about. Prices are *cheap*. Plaza San Francisco, Ponce de León at Federico Teña. No phone.

**Galería del Arcángel** Across from the Museo Regional, this store ("the Archangel's Gallery") offers a fine collection of quality regional pottery and hand-carved furniture, plus some of the best crafts from other parts of Mexico. It's open daily from 9am to 7pm. Arciga 30. ✆ and fax **434/342-1724.**

**Galeria Iturbe** Most of the artwork here is by local painters, mask makers, and other artists. You might also find a typical Day of the Dead altar. There's a small selection of books on Mexican art and culture. Enter through the Hotel Iturbe (go all the way to the back) or from Calle Iturbe, off the Plaza Grande. It's open daily from 10am to 8pm. Portal Morelos 59. ✆ **434/342-0368.**

**Mantas Típicas** *Value* A factory outlet for the company's textile mill, this is one of several textile outlets on the Plaza Grande. Colorful foot-loomed tablecloths, napkins, bedspreads, and bolts of fabric cover the shelves. It's open daily from 9am to 7pm. José Cos 5 (at the corner of Lerin). ✆ **434/342-1324.** Fax 434/342-0527.

**Market Plaza** The House of Eleven Patios (see above) should be your first stop and this your second. The entire plaza fronting the food market holds covered stalls selling crafts, clothing, rugs, rebozos, and more. Locally knitted sweaters are a good buy. Streets surrounding the plaza churn with exuberant sellers of fresh vegetables and caged birds. West of Plaza Chica. No phone.

**Palacio Huitziméngari** On the north side of the Plaza Grande, in a decaying building, are a few shops run by folk from neighboring towns. Most of the merchandise is pottery and woodcarvings. Plaza Grande. No phone.

## WHERE TO STAY

**Hotel Fiesta Plaza** Fiesta Plaza has three stories of rooms (no elevator) along three sides of an open courtyard that's furnished with tables and chairs. This is a new, attractive building with pine columns, wrought-iron banisters, and wide arcades that hold attractive sitting areas. The comfortable rooms have pine

**Tips** **If Pátzcuaro's Packed Solid . . .**

During Easter Week and Days of the Dead, Pátzcuaro's hotels fill up; visitors should be aware of three inexpensive hotels in the nearby town of Santa Clara. The **Hotel Oasis,** Portal Allende 144 (© **434/343-0040**), is the better of the two on the town's main plaza; **Hotel Real del Cobre,** Portal Hidalgo 19 (© **434/343-0205**), has a restaurant. The third hotel, **Camino Real** (© **434/343-0281**), is a few blocks away and is comparable to the Oasis. All three charge $25 to $40 for a double.

furniture, carpets, and small, tiled bathrooms. All have windows that open onto the courtyard. The hotel faces the north side of the Plaza Chica.

Plaza Bocanegra 24, 61600 Pátzcuaro, Mich. © **434/342-2515**, or © and fax 434/342-2516. mexitur@mail.ml.com.mx. 60 units. $75 double. MC, V. Free parking. **Amenities:** Restaurant, bar; room service until 10pm; overnight laundry. *In room:* Safe, hair dryer on request.

**Hotel Los Escudos** This hotel is in a mansion on the west side of Plaza Grande, the birthplace of Gertrudis Bocanegra. It's a great location, and the courtyard captures some of the house's colonial feel. Renovation, though it added to the hotel's comforts, has drained it of some of its original charm. The hotel is in the process of remodeling to correct the earlier mistakes. Rooms are decorated with red or blue carpeting, red drapes, and lace curtains, with scenes of historic Pátzcuaro painted on the walls. Some rooms have fireplaces; others have private balconies overlooking the plaza. A recently opened second section, a few doors down, has slightly cheaper rooms. There's a good restaurant off the lobby.

Portal Hidalgo 73, 61600 Pátzcuaro, Mich. © **434/342-0138** or 434/342-1290. Fax 434/342-0649. losescudos@yahoo.com. 45 units. $40–$55 double. MC, V. Free parking. **Amenities:** Restaurant. *In room:* TV.

**Hotel Mansión Iturbe Bed and Breakfast** ★★ Located on the north side of the Plaza Grande, this 17th-century mansion has kept more of its original character than any of the other colonial buildings-turned-hotels. You'll feel more like a guest in a large country house than a hotel patron. The owners have worked hard to keep the old local touches, such as raised thresholds. Rooms are on the second floor and have the original plank flooring, along with heavy, dark, Spanish-style wooden furniture and fresh-cut flowers. Most bathrooms are large. Rates include a welcome drink, full breakfast with cappuccino or coffee, and a 2-hour use of a bicycle. Instant coffee and hot water are available in the lobby in the morning before the restaurant opens. The hotel staff is helpful and can set you up with tour guides or recommend shopping places. For long-term guests, the fourth night is free (some restrictions apply).

Portal Morelos 59, 61600 Pátzcuaro, Mich. © **434/342-0368** or 434/342-3628. Fax (in Morelia for reservations) 443/313-4593. www.mexonline.com/iturbe.htm. 15 units. $85 double; $105 suite. Rates include full breakfast. 4th night free (some restrictions apply). Ask about special promotions. AE, MC, V. Free parking. **Amenities:** 2 restaurants, bar; bike rental; tour and activities desk. *In room:* TV.

**Hotel Posada de la Basílica** This colonial-style hotel in a great location across from the basilica has a lovely patio. The rooms, which border the patio on three sides, have tile floors and fireplaces. Seven have small balconies overlooking the street. Bathrooms are a little dark, and the rooms can be a bit chilly. The restaurant has a fabulous view of the mountains, the tile rooftops, and the lake.

Arciga 6 (at La Paz), 61600 Pátzcuaro, Mich. © **434/342-1108.** Fax 434/342-0659. 12 units. $130 double. MC, V. Free enclosed parking. **Amenities:** Restaurant; room service; laundry. *In room:* TV.

**Posada de la Salud** *Value* This *posada* offers two tiers of quiet rooms built around an attractive courtyard. All rooms have carved wooden headboards and matching desks. Two rooms have fireplaces. The inn is a good bargain. It's on the southeast side of the basilica, a long half block up on the right.

Serrato 9, 61600 Pátzcuaro, Mich. © **434/342-0058.** 15 units. $30 double. No credit cards. **Amenities:** Laundry service.

## WHERE TO DINE

Restaurants open late and close early; don't plan on hot coffee if you're up early, but do plan ahead for late-evening hunger pangs. For inexpensive eats, try the **tamal** and ***atole* vendors** in front of the basilica and by the market. Housewives also sell steamy cups of *atole,* hot *corundas* (triangular tamales), and tamales. The *corundas* are one street food you can eat safely, and they are fresher and more delicious than those served in restaurants. Breakfast costs $1 or less.

In the evenings at the Plaza Chica, you can get a meal of chicken with simple enchiladas and heaps of fried potatoes and carrots. Look for a stand called El Pollo Placentero. You can also get *buñuelos,* which drip with honey. **Café Botafumeiro,** a coffee shop on the southwest corner of Plaza Grande, offers a variety of excellent Uruapan coffees and hot chocolate by the cup or kilo.

**El Patio** MEXICAN/REGIONAL High ceilings, good lighting, and paintings of local scenes make this a pleasant place to dine. Specialties include *sopa tarasca* (a regional bean soup to which you add cheese, fried tortilla strips, and toasted chiles), *trucha salmonada al vino blanco* (farm-raised trout—fed on special foods that turn the flesh salmon-colored—cooked in white-wine sauce), and *pescado blanco* (the prized fish of the region, very mild, cooked the traditional way in a light batter). Standard Mexican dishes include enchiladas and more. El Patio is on the south side of Plaza Grande.

Plaza Grande 19. © **434/342-0484.** Breakfast $4–$5; main courses $7–$12. MC, V. Daily 8:30am–10:30pm.

**El Primer Piso** MEXICAN/INTERNATIONAL El Primer Piso, which means "The First Floor" (second floor in American usage), offers a bit of everything but focuses mostly on dishes of its own creation: *pechuga enogada* (chicken breast in walnut cream sauce) with cashews, for instance, and *pescado en salsa negra* (fish in a three-chile vinaigrette). These are good, as are the appetizers. The soups are more conventional—Tarascan, French onion, and Provençal. The restaurant is on the same block as El Patio, across from the southeast corner of the Plaza.

Vasco de Quiroga 29. © **434/342-0122.** Main courses $8–$10. AE. Mon and Wed–Sat 1–10pm; Sun 1–8pm.

**Restaurant Doña Paca** ★★ *Moments* MICHOACAN This is one of the best places for regional Michoacán cuisine. With leather *equipal* chairs, beamed ceilings, French doors facing the portals and Plaza Grande, and photos of old Pátzcuaro decorating the walls, it's a good place to linger. You can also eat outdoors under the arcade. Try trout served *al gusto* (as you like it) with a choice of cilantro (marvelous), garlic, or other herbs; or chicken in mango sauce. This is one of the few places featuring *churipo,* a regional beef and vegetable stew served with *corundas* (like *tamales,* without filling)—but make sure it's available. For a tasty dessert, try a *buñuelo* topped with coconut yogurt. Margarita Arriaga, the English-speaking owner, prides herself on her coffee, with good reason.

Hotel Iturbe, Portal Morelos 59. © **434/342-3628.** Breakfast $5–$10; main courses $8–$12. AE, MC, V. Daily 8:30–10:30am, 1:30–5:30pm, and 7–9pm.

## PATZCUARO AFTER DARK

Generally speaking, Pátzcuaro closes down before 10pm, so bring a good book or plan to rest up. Late-night music lovers can go to **Viejo Gaucho** to hear Mexican trios and soloists performing traditional and *nueva trova.* The small restaurant serves *empanadas,* pastas, pizza, steaks, and mixed drinks. It's in the Hotel Iturbe, Portal Morelos 59 (© **434/342-3627**); enter from Calle Iturbe. It's open Tuesday through Saturday from 6pm to midnight. Music starts between 8:30 and 9pm. After the music starts, there's a $2.50 cover charge. The Viejo Gaucho is also open for lunch on Sunday from 2 to 6pm.

## SIDE TRIPS FROM PATZCUARO

**EL ESTRIBO: A SCENIC OVERLOOK** For a good view of the town and the lake, head for the lookout at El Estribo, on the hill 3km (2 miles) west of town. Driving from the main square on Calle Ponce de León and following the signs takes 10 to 15 minutes. Walking up the steep hill will take about 45 minutes. Once you reach the gazebo, you can climb more than 400 steps to the summit of the hill for a bird's-eye view. The gazebo area is great for a picnic; there are barbecue pits and sometimes a couple selling soft drinks and beer.

**JANITZIO** No visit to Pátzcuaro would be complete without a trip on the lake, preferably across to the island village of **Janitzio** ★★, dominated by a hilltop statue of José María Morelos. The village church is famous for the annual **Day of the Dead** ceremony, held at midnight on November 1. Villagers climb to the churchyard carrying lit candles in memory of their dead relatives, then spend the night in graveside vigil. The long day begins October 30 and lasts through November 2.

The most economical way to get to Janitzio is by colectivo launch, which makes the trip when enough people have gathered to go, about every 20 to 30 minutes from about 7:30am to 6pm. Round-trip fare is $3 for those ages 5 and up; children under 5 ride free. A private boat costs $35 round-trip; a trip to three islands costs $50. The **ticket office** on the pier, or *embarcadero* (© **434/342-0681**), is open daily from 8am to 6pm. The pier is about a mile from the main square, and the 5-minute taxi ride costs less than $2.

At the ticket office, a map of the lake posted on the wall details boat trips to various islands and lakeshore towns. Launches will take you wherever you want to go. Up to 20 people can split the cost.

**TZINTZUNTZAN: RUINS & HANDCRAFTS** Tzintzuntzan (tzeen-*tzoon*-tzahn) is an ancient village 16km (10 miles) from Pátzcuaro on the road to Quiroga (see "By Bus" under "Getting There & Departing," earlier). In earlier centuries, Tzintzuntzan was the capital of the Purépechan empire (a confederation of more than 100 towns and villages). On a hill on the right before you enter town, pyramids upon pyramids remind visitors of the town's past. Today, the village is known for its straw handcrafts—mobiles, baskets, and figures (skeletons, airplanes, reindeer, turkeys, and the like)—as well as pottery and woven goods. Several open-air **woodcarving workshops,** full of life-size wooden saints and other figures, are across from the basket market.

During the week of February 1, the village honors **Nuestro Señor del Rescate** (Our Lord of the Rescue) with religious processions. The village also takes part in Holy Week celebrations.

**LAKESIDE VILLAGES: A PORTRAIT OF INDIAN LIFE** If you want an up-close view of the village life of the Purépecha, meet up with **Francisco Castilleja** (© **434/344-0167**), an English-speaking Mexican who lives in

Erongarícuaro. He conducts tours of the villages that explain their daily life, customs, and beliefs. He passes through the Restaurant Doña Paca in the Hotel Iturbe at 10am every day but Sunday and takes people to the villages of **Erongarícuaro, Uricho,** and **Tócuaro** to visit households, small workshops, and a well-known mask maker. The cost depends on the size of the group.

**SANTA CLARA DEL COBRE: COPPER SMITHERY** About 30 minutes away by car (a $10 taxi ride), **Santa Clara del Cobre** ★ is a good side trip if you want to purchase copper items or see how copper is worked. Although the copper mines of pre-Conquest times have disappeared, local artisans still make copper vessels using the age-old method of hammering pieces out by hand. They don't work on Sundays and are strict observers of "San Lunes" (taking Mon off to recover from the weekend), but on other days, the sound of hammering fills the air. If you want to see someone practicing the craft, go to one of the larger stores and ask if you can visit the *taller* (studio). You can also visit the **Museo del Cobre** (Copper Museum), half a block from the main plaza at Morelos and Pino Suárez. The museum section of the building displays copper pieces that date to pre-Columbian times. A sales showroom to the left of the entrance features the work of local craftsmen. Admission is 50¢; the museum is open Tuesday to Sunday from 10:30am to 3pm and 5 to 7pm.

The **National Copper Fair** is held here each August. It coincides with the **Festival de Nuestra Señora de Santa Clara de Asis** (Aug 12) and the **Festival of the Virgin of the Sacred Patroness** (Aug 15), with folk dancing and parades. For information, call the tourism office in Morelia.

Buses for Santa Clara leave every few minutes from the Pátzcuaro bus station. If you want to spend the night in town, see the box "If Pátzcuaro's Packed Solid," p. 231.

**TUPATARO & CUANAJO: A HISTORIC CHURCH & HAND-CARVED FURNITURE** The turn-off for these colonial-era villages is approximately 32km (20 miles) northwest of Pátzcuaro, off Highway 120 on the way to Morelia (see "Getting There & Departing," earlier). The narrow paved road passes first through tiny **Tupátaro** (pop. 600), which in Tarascan means "place of tule of Chuspata" (*tule* means "reed").

Just opposite the small main plaza is the **Templo del Señor Santiago Tupátaro,** unique in Mexico for its 18th-century painted ceiling. Restored in 1994, it's still the parish church but is overseen by the Institute of Anthropology and History. The church was built in 1775 after the miraculous discovery of a crucifix formed in a pine tree. Indian artists painted the entire wood-plank ceiling with scenes of the life and death of Christ and Mary. The magnificent gilt *retablo,* still intact behind the altar, features Solomonic columns and paintings. Santiago (St. James) is in the center of the *retablo,* and the face of the Eternal Father is above him. The sign of the dove crowns the *retablo.* There's no admission charge, and photography is not permitted. The church is open daily from 8am to 8pm. Days of religious significance include the Tuesday of Carnaval week and July 25, which honors Santiago (St. James).

**Cuanajo** (pop. 8,000) is 8km (5 miles) farther. It's a village devoted to hand-carved pine furniture and weaving. On the road as you enter, and around the pleasant, tree-shaded main plaza, you'll see storefronts with **colorful furniture** inside and on the street. Parrots, plants, the sun, the moon, and faces are carved on the furniture, which is painted in bright colors. Furniture is also sold at a **cooperative** on the main plaza. Here you'll also find soft-spoken women who weave tapestries and thin belts on waist looms. Everything is for sale. It's open daily from 9am to 6pm.

Festival days in Cuanajo include March 8 and September 8, both of which honor the patron saint Virgin María de la Natividad. These are solemn occasions when neighboring villages make processions carrying figures of the holy Virgin.

**IHUATZIO: TULE FIGURES & PRE-HISPANIC ARCHITECTURE** This little lakeside village is renowned for its **weavers of tule figures**—fanciful animals such as elephants, pigs, and bulls, made from a reed that grows on the edge of the lake—and for a rather spread-out assembly of pre-Hispanic buildings. The turnoff to Ihuatzio is a paved road a short distance from the outskirts of Pátzcuaro on the road to Tzintzuntzan.

**ZIRAHUEN: A PRISTINE LAKE** If you want to visit one of the few lakes in Mexico that remains more or less in its natural state, make the trip to **Zirahuén,** about 11km (7 miles) west of Pátzcuaro on the road to Uruapan. There's no regular bus service, so getting to Zirahuén without a car is difficult. Lakeside restaurants serve fish—but make sure it's fresh.

## 3 Uruapan: Handcrafts & Volcanoes

61km (38 miles) west of Pátzcuaro

Uruapan has long been a large commercial center for western Michoacán. It's a larger, busier town than Pátzcuaro. For tourists, the best feature is the **Parque Nacional Eduardo Ruíz,** a lovely botanical garden with flowing water everywhere you look. Uruapan is also useful as a base for several interesting side trips, the most famous of which is to the **Paricutín volcano** and the lava-covered church and village near **Angahuan.** See "Angahuan, Paricutín Volcano & a Church Buried in Lava," below.

### ESSENTIALS

The **tourist office** (✆ **452/524-7199**) is at Juan Ayala 16. It's open Monday through Saturday from 9am to 2pm and 4 to 7pm.

The main plaza, **Jardín Morelos/Plaza de los Mártires,** is actually a long, narrow rectangle running east to west, with the churches and La Huatápera Museum on the north side and a few hotels on the south. Everything you need is within a block or two of the square, including the market, which is behind the churches.

### WHERE TO STAY & DINE

The best hotel in town is the **Hotel Cupatitzio** (✆ **452/523-2022**), next to the national park. It has plenty of amenities, including a good restaurant, a large pool, and a lovely garden. A room for two people costs $97 (AE, MC, V). Also consider two inexpensive hotels by the main plaza: The comfortable **Hotel Villa de Flores,** Emiliano Carranza 15 (✆ **452/524-2800;** MC, V), and the slightly less desirable, slightly cheaper **Hotel Nuevo Alameda,** Av. 5 de Febrero 11 (✆ **452/523-3635;** MC, V). Rooms go for $30 to $40. Both have restaurants, and there are restaurants on or near the plaza.

### EXPLORING URUAPAN & BEYOND

Uruapan's main plaza fills with artisans and craft sellers from around the state before and during **Easter week.** There's an unbelievable array of wares, all neatly displayed.

**La Huatápera** ★, attached to the church on the main square, is a good museum of regional crafts. It occupies a former hospital built in 1533 by Fray Juan de San Miguel, a Franciscan. It's open daily from 9:30am to 1:30pm and 3:30 to 6pm. Admission is free.

For the finest in foot-loomed, brilliantly colored tablecloths, napkins, and other **textiles,** take a taxi to **Telares Uruapan** ★★ (© **452/524-0677** or 452/524-6135), in the **Antigua Fábrica de San Pedro,** Calle Miguel Treviño s/n. Call ahead, and the English-speaking owners may be able to give you a tour of the factory.

When you enter the **Parque Nacional Eduardo Ruíz,** a botanical garden 8 blocks west of the main plaza, you'll feel as if you're deep in the tropics. This semitropical paradise contains jungle paths, deep ravines, rushing water, and clear waterfalls. The garden is open daily from 8am to 6pm, and there is a small admission fee.

## A WATERFALL OUTSIDE OF URUAPAN

Eight kilometers (5 miles) outside of town is the **Tzaráracua** waterfall. It's easy to catch a bus from Uruapan's bus station; a cab costs $4. Either one will drop you off at the entrance to the park well above the falls.

From here you have a pretty view of the mountains, which are covered in pine trees. You have to descend quite a bit to get to the falls, but it seems quick and easy compared to the 40-minute climb back up. The trail is very good, and there are handrails almost everywhere. The vegetation changes quickly to subtropical plants and ferns as you get closer to the falls. Here, the Río Cupatitzio, which originates as a bubbling spring in the national park in Uruapan, forms a cascade on its way to the Pacific. The falls themselves are pretty but not spectacular. Still, it makes for a good walk through a lovely area.

## ANGAHUAN, PARICUTIN VOLCANO & A CHURCH BURIED IN LAVA

About 34km (21 miles) from Uruapan is **Angahuan,** a village and point of departure for trips to **Paricutín volcano** ★★, which began an extended eruption in 1943 that eventually buried portions of another village in lava. **Autotransportes Galeana** buses leave every 30 minutes from Uruapan's Central Camionera for the hour-long trip. To return, pick up the bus where it dropped you off. A taxi costs $12.

**THE ERUPTION STORY** If you don't know the tale of Paricutín's volcanic blast, stop by the plaza in Angahuan and look at the carved wooden door of a house that faces the church (around the stone fence to the right, two doors down). Etched in pictures and words, the story says that a local man was plowing his cornfield in the valley on February 20, 1943, when at 3pm the ground began to boil. At first, he tried to plug it up; when that proved impossible, he fled. By that evening, the earth was spitting fire and smoke. Some villagers fled that night; others, days later. The volcano remained active, continually spewing, until March 6, 1952, when it ceased as suddenly as it had begun.

**USING A GUIDE** Angahuan has a little tourist center that rents cabins and runs a small cafeteria (© **452/520-8786**). It allows a good view of the volcano and the tower of the **Church of San Juan Parangaricutiro** (try saying that five times fast), which is half-buried in lava. You will undoubtedly be offered a guide and horses for a trip to either or both places. Although a horse is not necessary, a guide is advisable.

**CLIMBING THE VOLCANO** Allow at least 8 hours from Angahuan. The round trip is about 22km (14 miles). *Take plenty of food and water—they are not available along the way.* The hike is mostly flat, with some steeper rises toward the end. Climbing the steep crater takes about 40 minutes for those who exercise regularly. Count on more time to walk around the crater's rim on top (1.5–3km/1–2 miles) and enjoy the spectacular view.

The trip to the volcano takes 6 to 7 hours on horseback, including the time spent climbing the crater, which you must do on foot. On the way, you can pass by the old church tower of Parangaricutiro. The asking price for a horse is around $20, and you'll need to pay for one for a guide. Don't be surprised when, a few kilometers into the ride, the guide asks for a tip to be paid at the end of the trip. A good guide will climb to the top of the crater with you and point out various interesting features, including steaming fumaroles. Acting as a volcano guide is one of the conspicuously poor Angahuan villagers' few opportunities to earn money. Just withhold payment until the ride is over, and services are delivered as promised. Plan to spend an entire day for the trip from Uruapan, the ride to the foot of the volcano, the short climb, and the return trip.

# 7

# Guadalajara

Guadalajara is the second largest city in Mexico (with 3½ million people, it's a very distant second to Mexico City), but because it's the homeland of *mariachi* music, the *jarabe tapatío* (the Mexican hat dance), and tequila, many consider it the most Mexican of cities. Despite its size, Guadalajara is easy to navigate, and the people are friendly and helpful. And unlike in Mexico City, visitors can enjoy big-city pleasures without big-city hassles.

Guadalajara is the capital of the state of Jalisco and, on occasion in Mexico's stormy history, has functioned as the nation's capital. The historic center of Guadalajara, especially the area around the cathedral, is a wonderful place to wander among colonial plazas, fountains, churches, and convents. On the relatively new Plaza Tapatía, you can enjoy a pleasant walk from the cathedral all the way to the impressive Hospicio Cabañas. With its shopping, restaurants, cultural life, history, architecture, and mild climate, Guadalajara is a great side trip into the interior from Puerto Vallarta or Manzanillo.

The handcrafts and decorative arts are perhaps the best in Mexico. Shoppers can browse through the sophisticated shops of **Tlaquepaque,** which offer an immense variety of merchandise. Or they can visit **Tonalá,** a bargain-hunter's paradise with hundreds of workshops.

While in Guadalajara, you will undoubtedly come across the word *tapatío* (or *tapatía*). In the early days, people from the area were known to trade in threes, called *tapatíos.* Gradually, the locals came to be called *tapatíos,* too, and the word now signifies Guadalajaran when referring to a thing, a person, or a manner of doing something.

## 1 Orientation

### GETTING THERE

**BY PLANE** Guadalajara's international airport is a 25- to 45-minute ride from the city. Taxi tickets to Guadalajara, priced by zone, are for sale in front of the airport. Taxis are the only transport from town to the airport (around $11 to the center of town; $9 returning).

**Major Airlines** See chapter 2 for a list of toll-free numbers for international airlines serving Mexico. Numbers in Guadalajara are: **Aeromar** (© 33/3615-8509), **Aeromexico** (© 33/3669-0202), **American** (© 01-800/904-6000), **Continental** (© 01-800/900-5000), **Delta** (© 33/3630-3530), **Mexicana** (© 01-800/502-2000), and **United** (© 33/3616-9489).

**Aero California** (© 33/3616-2525) serves Guadalajara from Tijuana, Mexico City, Los Mochis, La Paz, and Puebla; **Aeromexico** and **Mexicana** have flights and connections throughout Mexico, as does **Aviacsa** (© 33/3616-9706).

**BY CAR** Guadalajara is at the hub of several four-lane toll roads (called *cuotas* or *autopistas*), which can cut travel time considerably but are expensive. From

# Greater Guadalajara

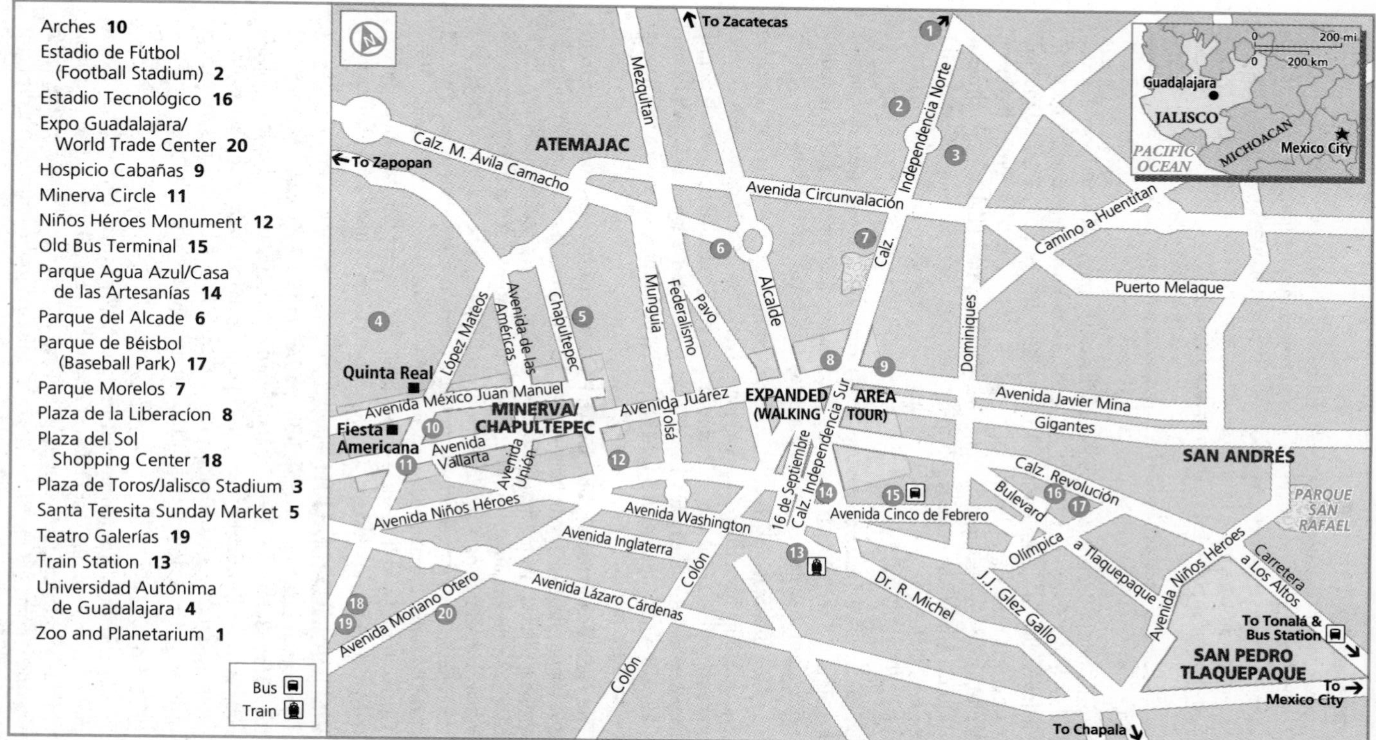

### Impressions

*The men [of Guadalajara] are handsome and cling to their attractive charro outfits and extremely large sombreros. At one time the brims of their hats were so wide that they were declared a public nuisance. Any man caught wearing a sombrero with a brim that extended much beyond his shoulders was arrested and fined.*

—Burton Holmes, Mexico, 1939

Nogales on the **U.S. border,** follow Highway 15 south (21 hr.). From **Tepic,** a quicker route is toll road 15D (5 hr., $30). From **Puerto Vallarta,** go north on Highway 200 to Compostela; toll road 68D heads east to join the Tepic toll road. Total time is 5½ hours, and the tolls add up to $25. From **Barra de Navidad,** on the coast southeast of Puerto Vallarta, take Highway 80 northeast (4½ hr.). From **Manzanillo,** you might also take this road, but toll road 54D through Colima to Guadalajara (3½ hr., $22) is faster. From **Mexico City,** take toll road 15D (7 hr., $43).

**BY BUS** Two bus stations serve Guadalajara. The old one, near downtown, has buses to Lake Chapala and other nearby areas; the new one, 10 km (6 miles) southeast of downtown, handles buses to more distant destinations.

**The Old Bus Station** For destinations within 96km (60 miles) of Guadalajara, including Lake Chapala, Ajijic, Jocotepec, Mazamitla, and San Juan Cosalá, go to the old bus terminal on Niños Héroes off Calzada Independencia Sur. If your destination is the Lake Chapala region, look for **Transportes Guadalajara-Chapala,** which operates frequent bus and *combi* (minivan) service to Chapala beginning at 6am.

**The New Bus Station** **The Central Camionera** is a 35-minute ride from downtown. Taxi fare for the trip is about $6. This bus station resembles an international airport, with seven terminals connected by a covered walkway. Each building contains different bus lines, offering first- and second-class service for different destinations, so it can be a little confusing. The best place to get bus information, make reservations, and buy tickets is downtown at the **Agencia Plaza Tapatía,** Calzada Independencia 254, a "bus-ticket agency" under Plaza Tapatía. It works with all six main bus lines that connect Guadalajara to the rest of Mexico. Many travel agencies also sell bus tickets to important destinations.

## VISITOR INFORMATION

The **State of Jalisco Tourist Information Office** is at Calle Morelos 102 (© **33/3668-1600** or 33/3668-1601) in the Plaza Tapatía, at Paseo Degollado and Paraje del Rincón del Diablo. It's open Monday to Friday from 9am to 8pm; Saturday, Sunday, and festival days from 9am to 1pm. The office has a supply of maps as well as a monthly calendar of cultural events in the city.

## CITY LAYOUT

The ***Centro Histórico*** (downtown area), with all its attractions, will be of great interest to the visitor. West of downtown is the fashionable hotel and restaurant district, with boutiques, shopping centers, and the like; to the northwest is **Zapopan,** home of Guadalajara's patron saint; and to the southeast are the crafts towns of **Tlaquepaque** and **Tonalá.**

The main artery for traffic from downtown to the hotel and restaurant district is **Avenida Vallarta.** It starts downtown as **Juárez.** The main arteries for returning to downtown are **Mexico** (called Juan Manuel downtown) and **Hidalgo,** both north of Vallarta. Vallarta heads due west, where it intersects another major artery, **Avenida Adolfo López Mateos,** at **Minerva Circle** (*Fuente Minerva* or simply *La Minerva*). Minerva Circle, a 15-minute drive from downtown, is the central point of reference for the west side. To go to Zapopan from downtown, take Avenida Avila Camacho, which you can pick up on Alcalde; it takes 20 minutes by car. To Tlaquepaque and Tonalá, take Calzada Revolución. Tlaquepaque is 8km (5 miles) from downtown and takes 15 to 20 minutes by car; Tonalá is 5 minutes farther. Another major thoroughfare, Calzada Lázaro Cárdenas, connects the west-side hotel district to Tlaquepaque and Tonalá, bypassing downtown; it cuts travel time considerably.

## GUADALAJARA NEIGHBORHOODS IN BRIEF

**Centro Histórico** The heart of the city contains the five main plazas, the cathedral, and several museums and public buildings. Two of those buildings hold spectacular murals by Orozco, in my opinion the best of the Mexican muralists. Theaters, restaurants, shops, and clubs dot the area, which also holds the largest covered market in Latin America. All of this is in a space roughly 12 blocks by 12 blocks, an easy area for a good walker to explore on foot. On the plazas and pedestrian-only streets, walking can be quite pleasant.

**Parque Agua Azul** This is a large inner-city green space 20 blocks south of the Centro Histórico. It has a children's area and miniature train. Nearby you'll find the state-run crafts shop (worth the short trip), theaters, and the anthropology museum.

**Chapultepec/Minerva Circle/ Plaza del Sol** These areas constitute the west side of the city. Chapultepec is the neighborhood between downtown and Minerva Circle. Surrounding Minerva are several malls. Southwest from Minerva Circle along Avenida López Mateos is the Plaza del Sol area. The west side holds most of the fine dining spots, luxury hotels, boutiques, and galleries, as well as the American, British, and Canadian consulates.

**Zapopan** Founded in 1542, Zapopan is a suburb of Guadalajara. It's noted for its 18th-century basilica, the home of Guadalajara's patron saint, the Virgin of Zapopan. Enormous throngs of people honor her every October 12. Zapopan's main square and basilica are worth seeing. Next to the basilica is a small museum about the life and customs of the Huichol Indians, who live in a remote region of the state. It has a museum shop whose proceeds go to aid the Indians.

**Tlaquepaque** This was a village of artisans (especially potters) that grew into a market center. In the last 30 years, it has attracted designers from all over Mexico. Every major form of art and craft is for sale here: furniture, pottery, glass, jewelry, woodcarvings, leather goods, sculptures, and paintings. The shops are sophisticated, yet Tlaquepaque's center has retained a small-town feel that makes door-to-door browsing enjoyable and relaxing.

**Tonalá** This has remained a town of artisans. Plenty of stores sell mostly local products from the town's more than 400 workshops. You'll see wrought iron, ceramics, blown glass, and papier-mâché. A busy street market operates each Thursday and Sunday.

## 2 Getting Around

**BY TAXI** Taxis are the best and easiest way to get around town. Almost all of them have meters, and though drivers are reluctant to use them, you can insist that they do. Cab fares for most of town run between $4 and $7. There are three fare structures: for day, night, and suburbia.

**BY CAR** Keep in mind the several main arteries (see "City Layout," above). The **Periférico** is a loop around the city that connects with most other highways entering the city. Traffic on the two-lane Periférico is slow and filled with trucks. Several important freeway-style thoroughfares crisscross the city. **González Gallo** leads south from the town center and connects with the road to Lake Chapala. **Avenida Vallarta** continues past La Minerva and eventually feeds onto **Highway 15,** bound for Tequila and on to Puerto Vallarta.

**BY BUS & COLECTIVO** The electric bus is quite handy for travel between downtown and the west side. It bears the sign PAR VIAL and runs east along Hidalgo and west along the next street to the north, Calle Independencia (not Calzada Independencia). Hidalgo passes along the north side of the cathedral. The Par Vial goes as far east as Mercado Libertad and as far west as Minerva Circle.

Six varieties of city buses run along many of the same routes but offer different grades of service. The best are **Línea Turquesa buses,** which have the letters TUR on the side. They are air-conditioned, have comfortable seats, and carry only as many passengers as there are seats; they are worth the price (about 60¢ for most destinations). The handiest route is the **706 TUR,** which runs from the Centro Histórico southeast to Tlaquepaque, the Central Camionera (the new bus station), and Tonalá. For more information on Tlaquepaque and Tonalá, see "Shopping," later. The same bus runs in the reverse direction, northwest to Zapopan. You can catch this bus on Av. 16 de Septiembre.

Many buses run north-south along the Calzada Independencia (not Calle Independencia), but the **"San Juan de Dios–Estación"** bus goes between the points you are likely to want—San Juan de Dios church, next to the Mercado Libertad, and the railroad station (*estación*) past Parque Agua Azul. Fares are generally 40¢; exact change is not necessary. The city also has a rapid-transit system, ***Tren Ligero,*** but it doesn't serve areas that are of interest to visitors.

### *FAST FACTS:* Guadalajara

*American Express* The local office is at Av. Vallarta 2440, Plaza los Arcos (© **33/3615-8910**); it's open Monday to Friday from 9am to 6pm, Saturday from 9am to noon.

*Area Code* The telephone area code is **33.**

*Books/Newspapers/Magazines* **Gonvil,** a popular bookstore chain, has a branch across from Plaza de los Hombres Ilustres on Avenida Hidalgo, and another a few blocks south at Avenida 16 de Septiembre 118 (Alcalde becomes 16 de Septiembre south of the cathedral). It carries few English selections. **Sanborn's,** at the corner of Juárez and 16 de Septiembre, does a good job of keeping English-language periodicals in stock, but most are specialty magazines. Many newsstands sell the two English local papers, the *Guadalajara Reporter* and the *Guadalajara Weekly.* For the widest selection of English-language books, try **Sandi Bookstore,** Av. Tepeyac 178 (✆ **33/3121-0863**), in the Chapalita neighborhood on the west side.

*Business Hours* Store hours are generally Monday to Saturday from 10am to 2pm and 4 to 8pm.

*Climate & Dress* Guadalajara is mild year-round, with the occasional freak cold spell. Generally, from November through March, you'll need a sweater in the evening. The warmest months, April and May, are hot and dry. From June through September, the city gets afternoon and evening showers that keep the temperature a bit cooler. Dress in Guadalajara is conservative; attention-getting sportswear (short shorts, halters, and the like) is out of place.

*Consulates* The largest **American consular offices** in the world are here, at Progreso 175 (✆ **33/3825-2998** or 33/3825-2700). Other consulates include the **Canadian consulate,** Hotel Fiesta Americana, Local 31 (✆ **33/3615-6215**); the **British consulate,** Eulogio Parra 2539, Oficina 12 (✆ **33/3616-0629**); and the **Australian consulate,** López Cotilla 2030 (✆ **33/3615-7418**). These offices all keep roughly the same hours: Monday to Friday 8am to 4pm.

*Currency Exchange* The best rates are found 3 blocks south of the cathedral on López Cotilla, between Corona and Degollado. There are more than 20 *casas de cambio* on these 2 blocks. Almost all post their rates, which are better than the banks' and are without the long lines.

*Emergencies* The emergency phone number for Guadalajara is ✆ **080.**

*Hospitals* For medical emergencies, visit the **Hospital México-Americano,** Cólomos 2110 (✆ **33/3642-7152**).

*Internet Access* Most of the big hotels have business centers that you can use. If you're downtown, **C.C.C.P.** is an Internet cafe at Avenida Alcalde 159-34, just north of the cathedral in a small shopping center called Plaza Alegria. Its hours are Monday to Saturday from 9am to 9pm.

*Language Classes* Foreigners can study Spanish at the **Foreign Student Study Center,** University of Guadalajara, Calle Tomás V. Gómez 125, 44100 Guadalajara, Jalisco (✆ **33/3616-4399**). **IMAC** is a private Spanish school at Donato Guerra 180 in the Centro Histórico (✆ **33/3613-1080**).

*Luggage Storage/Lockers* You can store luggage in the main bus station, the Central Camionera, and at the Guadalajara airport.

*Police* Tourists should first try to contact the Jalisco tourist information office in Plaza Tapatía (✆ **33/3658-1600**). If you can't reach the office, call the municipal police at ✆ **33/3617-6060.**

*Post Office* The *correo* is at the corner of Carranza and calle Independencia, about 4 blocks northeast of the cathedral. Standing in the plaza behind the cathedral, facing the Degollado Theater, walk to the left and turn left on Carranza; walk past the Hotel Mendoza, cross Calle Independencia, and look for the post office on the left. It's open Monday through Thursday 9am to 5pm, Saturday 10am to 2pm.

*Safety* Guadalajara doesn't have the violent crime that Mexico City does. Crimes against tourists and foreign students are infrequent and most often take the form of pickpocketing and purse snatching. Criminals usually work in teams and target travelers in busy places, such as outdoor restaurants: One will create a distraction while the other slips off with whatever the tourist has set down. Purse-snatchers usually target unaccompanied women at night and rarely in places with crowds. The same is true of necklace snatching (the assailant grabs a necklace, especially if it has a gold chain, and pulls hard, hoping it will break).

## 3 Where to Stay

Life has been good to Guadalajara's *hoteleros,* and prices have risen accordingly. Rates shown are the standard rack rates and include the 17% tax. In slow periods, look for discounts; the big hotels are also in the habit of giving business discounts.

Almost all of the luxury hotels in Guadalajara are on the west side, which has the majority of the shopping malls, boutiques, fashionable restaurants, and clubs. There is also a lot to do in the Centro Histórico, making it a good place to stay. Finally, Tlaquepaque is a comfortable suburb and is perfect for shoppers; the only drawback is that almost everything but the Parián shuts down very early. Chain hotels not included below are the Hilton, Camino Real, Howard Johnson, and Crowne Plaza.

### VERY EXPENSIVE

**Fiesta Americana** ★★ A dramatic 22-story luxury hotel, similar to the Presidente Intercontinental but less expensive and with fewer amenities, the Fiesta Americana caters mainly to business travelers. The location is excellent—in front of Minerva Circle, in western Guadalajara—and service is great. Request floors 4 through 10, which have been remodeled. Rooms are large and carpeted, with two doubles or one king and a soundproof door. The large, well-equipped bathrooms hold shower/tub combinations. The furniture is modern and understated. The executive-level Fiesta Club is on limited-access floors.

Aurelio Aceves 225, Glorieta Minerva, 44100 Guadalajara, Jal. © **800/FIESTA1** in the U.S. and Canada, or 33/3825-3434. Fax 33/3630-3671. www.fiestaamericana.com.mx. 391 units. $220–$244 double, $255 Fiesta Club double; $281–$624 suite. 1 room is equipped for guests with disabilities. AE, DC, MC, V. Free secured parking. **Amenities:** Restaurant, lobby bar; heated medium-size pool; golf privileges at local club; 2 lighted tennis courts; gym; children's activities (Fiesta kids' program on Sun); concierge; tour desk; car rental; business center; executive business services; 24-hr. room service; babysitting; same-day laundry and dry cleaning; nonsmoking rooms; executive-level rooms. *In room:* A/C, TV with pay movies, dataport, minibar, coffeemaker, hair dryer.

**Hotel Presidente Inter-Continental** ★★★ Housed in a 14-story glass building with an atrium lobby, this hotel offers top-quality services and amenities. There is little turnover in staff, and the concierge has proven more capable and knowledgeable than any other in the city. The recently remodeled rooms are comfortable and quiet, with modern furnishings that include a desk with a modem/phone outlet, and a small table with two chairs. Club rooms have discreet check-in and an elevator entrance, are on limited-access hallways; rates include continental breakfast, newspaper, and evening cocktails. The extra privacy and services are good for Mexican soap opera stars or repeat guests who like having their preferences known in advance. If you're neither of these, opt for one of the other rooms. The lobby bar is popular, and during the season, bullfighters relax here after the *corrida.* The hotel sits across from the Plaza del Sol shopping center in western Guadalajara.

Av. López Mateos Sur y Moctezuma, 45050 Guadalajara, Jal. ✆ **800/327-0200** in the U.S. and Canada, or 33/3678-1234. Fax 33/3678-1222. www.interconti.com. 409 units. $240–315 double, $320 club double; $395 club suite. Weekend packages available. AE, DC, MC, V. Free sheltered parking. **Amenities:** 2 restaurants, lobby bar; outdoor heated pool; golf at nearby clubs; health club with saunas, steam rooms, and whirlpools; concierge; tour desk; car rental; large business center; executive services; salon; 24-hr. room service; massage; babysitting; same-day laundry and dry cleaning; nonsmoking rooms; executive-level rooms. *In room:* A/C, TV with pay movies, dataport, minibar, coffeemaker, hair dryer, iron, safe.

**Quinta Real** ★★★ This chain of hotels specializes in building properties that are suggestive of Mexico's heritage, in contrast to the comfortable but generic luxury hotel. No glass skyscraper here—two four-story buildings made of stone, wood beam, plaster, and tile occupy lush grounds. Rooms vary quite a bit: Eight have brick cupolas, some have balconies, and four are equipped with a whirlpool tub in the bathroom. All are large, with a split-level layout and antique decorative touches. And all come with large, fully equipped bathrooms with tub/shower combinations and excellent water pressure. You can choose between two doubles or one king-size bed. The hotel is 2 blocks from Minerva Circle in western Guadalajara. Ask for a room that doesn't face López Mateos.

Av. Mexico 2727 (at López Mateos), 44680 Guadalajara, Jal. ✆ **800/445-4565** in the U.S. and Canada, or 33/3615-0000. Fax 33/3630-1797. www.quintareal.com. 78 suites. $310 master suite, $330 grand-class suite. AE, DC, MC, V. Free secured parking. **Amenities:** Restaurant, bar; small outdoor heated pool; golf at local club; access to nearby health club; concierge; tour desk; car rental; business center; executive business services; room service until midnight; babysitting; same-day laundry and dry cleaning; nonsmoking rooms. *In room:* A/C, TV, dataport, minibar, hair dryer, iron, safe.

## EXPENSIVE

**Holiday Inn Hotel and Suites Centro Histórico** ★ This hotel has the most comfortable lodging in the downtown area. Its location, a few blocks from the main square, is good, too. Standard rooms are carpeted and decorated in Mexican architectural colors. The furniture is modern Mexican with a few wrought-iron pieces—the overall effect is quite cheerful. The size and lighting are good; bathrooms are medium-size and well equipped, with ample counter space. The suites are larger, but otherwise not worth the extra cost.

Av. Juárez 211, 44100 Guadalajara. Jal. ✆ **800/HOLIDAY** in the U.S. or Canada or 33/3613-1763. www.holidayinn.com. 90 units. $165 double; $190 suite. AE, MC, V. Free secured parking. **Amenities:** Restaurant and bar; fitness room; business center; limited room service; same-day laundry and dry cleaning; nonsmoking rooms. *In room:* A/C, TV, dataport, minibar, coffeemaker, hair dryer, iron.

**Hotel de Mendoza** ★ On a quiet street next to the Degollado Theater and Plaza Tapatía, 2 blocks from the cathedral, the Mendoza has the best location of any downtown hotel. The decor would best be described as an attempt at old Spanish, with wood paneling and old-world accents. Standard rooms are medium size and comfortable. Bed choices are one queen, two full, or two queen size. Bathrooms are small but have enough counter space. Suites have an additional sitting area and larger bathrooms. Rooms face the street, an interior courtyard, or the pool. One note: The bath towels are the narrowest I've ever seen—obviously the brainchild of a demented cost-cutting expert. If the hotel hasn't changed these, ask for a couple extra when you check in.

Carranza 16, 44100 Guadalajara, Jal. ✆ **800/221-6509** in the U.S., or 33/3613-4646. Fax 33/3613-7310. www.demendoza.com.mx. 106 units. $134 double; $150 suite. AE, DC, MC, V. Secured parking $3.50. **Amenities:** Restaurant, bar; small pool; tour desk; room service until 10:30pm; same-day laundry and dry cleaning; nonsmoking rooms. *In room:* A/C, TV, dataport.

**Hotel Misión Carlton** ★ The Misión Carlton is a 20-story hotel near Parque Agua Azul, a short cab ride or good walk from the historic center. Remodeled last year, it offers spacious, well-furnished rooms with large writing tables and good closet areas. The large bathrooms have make-up mirrors and plenty of counter space. Despite the remodeling, the rooms seem dated, though comfortable. Rooms come with two full beds or one king. Mattresses are a little springier than the standard. Ask for a room with a view of the park.

Av. Niños Héroes 125, 44100 Guadalajara, Jal. ✆ **800/448-8355** in the U.S. and Canada, or 33/3614-7272. Fax 33/3613-5539. www.hotelesmision.com.mx. 193 units. $160 double. Weekend discounts available. AE, DC, MC, V. Free valet parking. **Amenities:** Restaurant, 2 bars; medium-size pool; children's activities on weekends; concierge; tour desk; car rental; business center; executive business services; salon; limited room service; babysitting; same-day laundry and dry cleaning; nonsmoking rooms. *In room:* A/C, TV, dataport, minibar, coffeemaker, hair dryer.

## MODERATE

**Calinda Roma** This comfortable, modestly priced hotel is in the Centro Histórico on busy Avenida Juárez, close to the main plazas. It seems to be perpetually under renovation; most rooms are decent, but a few are truly dismal yet go for the same price. Ask for a remodeled room that doesn't face Juárez. These are medium in size, well lit, with simple furniture and good mattresses. Bathrooms are medium to small in size, but they have good lighting and counter space. There's a small pool and sunning area on the roof.

Juárez 170, 44100 Guadalajara, Jal. ✆ **800/228-5151** in the U.S., 01-800/900-0000 in Mexico, or 33/3614-8650. Fax 33/3614-2629. 120 units. $105 double. AE, DC, MC, V. Free secured parking. **Amenities:** Restaurant, lobby bar; small pool; room service until 11pm; same-day laundry and dry cleaning; nonsmoking rooms. *In room:* A/C, TV, dataport, iron.

**Hotel Cervantes** ★ *Value* This six-story downtown hotel offers modern amenities at a great price. The rooms are attractive and medium size. They have wall-to-wall carpeting and tile bathrooms with ample sink areas and shower/tub combinations. The lower price is for one double bed; the higher price is for a king or two doubles. This is not a particularly noisy hotel, but if you require absolute quiet, request an interior room. The Cervantes is 6 blocks south and 3 blocks west of the cathedral.

Prisciliano Sánchez 442, Col. Centro Histórico, 44100 Guadalajara, Jal. ✆ and fax **33/3613-6686.** 100 units. $65–$75 double. AE, MC, V. Free secured parking. **Amenities:** Restaurant, lobby bar; small outdoor heated pool; tour desk; room service until 10pm; babysitting; same-day laundry and dry cleaning. *In room:* A/C, TV.

**La Villa del Ensueño** ★★ *Finds* This B&B in central Tlaquepaque is a lovely alternative to big-city hotels. A modern interpretation of traditional Mexican architecture, it is a delight to the eye—small courtyards and beautiful gardens bordered by old stucco walls, which have been painted in muted shades of orange oxide or covered in carefully trimmed ivy, with an occasional wrought-iron balcony or stone staircase. The rooms are individually decorated and have more character than most hotel rooms. All contain ceiling fans. Doubles have either two twin or two double beds. Guests receive a complimentary cocktail on arrival.

Florida 305, 45500 Tlaquepaque, Jal. ✆ **800/220-8689** in the U.S., or 33/3635-8792. Fax 818/597-0637 in the U.S. www.mexonline.com/ensueno.htm. 18 units. $95 double, $105 deluxe double; $117 2-bedroom unit; $140 suite. Rates include full breakfast, light laundry service. AE, MC, V. Free secured parking. **Amenities:** Bar; indoor and small outdoor pool.

## INEXPENSIVE

**Hotel San Francisco Plaza** ★★ *Value* This colonial-style downtown hotel is both pleasant and a bargain. Its rooms are big and comfortable, with attractive furnishings. All have rugs or carpeting, and most have tall ceilings (except in the remodeled area behind the reception desk). The hotel is built in colonial style around four courtyards, which contain fountains and potted plants. Rooms along the Sánchez Street side are much quieter now that the management has installed double windows. Some units along the back wall of the rear patio have small bathrooms. A small plaza out front gives the hotel its name. The San Francisco Plaza is 6 blocks south and 2 blocks east of the cathedral.

Degollado 267, 44100 Guadalajara, Jal. ✆ **33/3613-8954** or 33/3613-8971. Fax 33/3613-3257. 76 units. $47 double. AE, MC, V. Free parking. **Amenities:** Restaurant; limited room service; babysitting; same-day laundry and dry cleaning; ironing service. *In room:* A/C, TV.

## 4 Where to Dine

Guadalajara has many excellent restaurants for fine dining and for typical local fare. Most of the fine-dining spots are on the west side. Those in the Centro Histórico are uniformly bad, with two exceptions: **La Fonda de San Miguel** and **Siglo XV.** Tlaquepaque has some good choices, but they all close around 8pm. Popular eateries serving good local fare are abundant, especially in the Centro Histórico. Local dishes worth trying include *birria* (goat, lamb, or pork covered in maguey leaves and roasted). It comes in a tomato-based broth or with the broth on the side. To get it properly prepared, go to one of the many *birrierías.* There are about a half dozen in Las Nueve Esquinas neighborhood, downtown; in Tlaquepaque, try **Birriería El Sope.** Another local favorite is *torta ahogada,* similar to a sub sandwich with a spicy pork filling. Jalisco-style *pozole* is chicken-and-hominy soup to which you add lime juice, onion, Mexican oregano, and chiles.

For a quick meal, there are several **Sanborn's** in the city. This is a popular national chain of restaurants and coffee shops; the traditional dish is *enchiladas suizas.* It's a good idea to keep your guidebook handy when taking a taxi; I've found that many drivers are unfamiliar with even the most popular places and require an address. It's a good idea to make reservations in the evening, especially for restaurants on the west side.

### EXPENSIVE

**"Restaurant with No Name"** ★ ALTA COCINA Dine on a cool, shaded patio that has the informal feel of a Mexican country house. Vegetation grows pretty much at will and has been coaxed to form green canopies; peacocks strut around, unruffled by the goings-on. This place could also be called Restaurant with No Menu; the waiters recite the full list of dishes in English or Spanish, and you can interrupt with questions at any time. I don't feel comfortable without text on a page, but I was comforted by the waiter's ability to answer my questions and by how he rewound and fast-forwarded through his presentation. Many dishes are a bit underspiced. I did like the strong-flavored pork in a three-chile sauce (rich-flavored chiles, not hot ones). I also liked the seafood dishes. The restaurant is 1½ blocks north of Tlaquepaque's Parián.

Madero 80, Tlaquepaque. ✆ **33/3635-4520** or 33/3635-9677. Breakfast $4–$7; main courses $14–$25. AE, DISC, MC, V. Daily 8:30am–10pm.

### MODERATE

**Adobe Fonda** ★★ NUEVA COCINA This charming restaurant shares space with a large, attractive *artesanía* store on the pedestrian-only Independencia. The menu is highly inventive and thoughtfully designed. Homemade bread and tostadas come to the table with an olive oil-based chile sauce, pico de gallo, and *requezón de epazote* (herb-flavored fresh cheese). Among the soups are delicious *crema de cilantro* and an interesting mushroom soup with a dark beer broth. The main courses present some difficult decisions, with intriguing combinations of Mexican, Italian, and Argentine ingredients: shrimp quesadillas accompanied by *chimichurri* with *nopal;* filet in creamy ancho sauce; chicken breast in cashew and poblano chile sauce. The margaritas are noteworthy, too.

Francisco de Miranda 27, corner of Independencia, Tlaquepaque. ✆ **33/3657-2792.** Main courses $8–$17. AE, MC, V. Daily 12:30–6:30pm.

**Casa Fuerte** MEXICAN/INTERNATIONAL Clothing designer Irene Pulos has turned her former showroom into this popular, charming patio restaurant. The setting is colorfully Mexicano: pastel walls and waiters sporting bold Pulos-designed vests. Imaginatively prepared dishes include shrimp in tamarind, stuffed chicken in *guajillo* sauce, fresh vegetable salads, steaks, and fajitas.

224-A Independencia, Tlaquepaque. ✆ **33/3639-6481.** Reservations recommended. Main courses $7–$14. AE, DISC, MC, V. Daily noon–8pm.

**El Sacromonte** ★★★ ALTA COCINA The food here is so exquisite that I try to dine here every time I'm in Guadalajara. The restaurant places great emphasis on presentation and artful design, from the menu in verse (haikus in Spanish that lose a lot in translation) to "Queen Isabel's crown," a dish of shrimp woven together in the shape of a crown and covered in a divine lobster and orange sauce. The appetizers, such as quesadillas with rose petals, are also things of beauty. My favorite soup, *el viejo progreso,* is a cream soup of Roquefort and chipotle. The dining area is a pleasant, shaded, open-air patio. This place is popular, so make reservations or show up between meal times.

Pedro Moreno 1398, west side. ✆ **33/3825-5447** or 33/3827-0663. Reservations recommended. Main courses $9–$16. MC, V. Mon–Sat 1:30pm–midnight.

**Hostería del Angel** ★ TAPAS/SPANISH-ITALIAN DELI This is a difficult restaurant to categorize. The owner and chef cooked for years in Spain and Italy, where he became fascinated with the making of cheeses and deli meats such as prosciutto and Spanish *jamón serrano.* Now he has opened a restaurant where he can combine his specialties with Mexican ingredients. He serves different tapas every day, and a large variety of wines. This is a wonderful place to go in the evening for a glass of wine and some tapas, a sandwich, or a *rotalata* of cheese, meats, and vegetables. The restaurant is 4 blocks from the basilica of the Virgin of Zapopan, half a block off the *calzada* (promenade).

5 de Mayo 295, Zapopan, west side. ✆ and fax **33/3656-9516.** Reservations not accepted. *Comida corrida* $5–$6; deli specialties and tapas $4–$6. AE, MC, V. Tues–Sat 9am–midnight.

**La Destilería** ★★ MEXICAN You know that with a name like "The Distillery," tequila will somehow be involved. Although this museum-restaurant is filled with artifacts, photos, and curios depicting every stage of the tequila-making process, it's the food that really pulls in the tapatíos. This is one of those places almost sure to please everyone. Specialties include *molcajete de la casa*—steaming fajitas, *rajas* (chile strips), cheese, onion, and avocado in a large, sizzling *molcajete* (three-legged stone mortar). The spicy steak dish, *medallones Tenochtitlán,* is memorable, as is the delicately flavored fish in parsley sauce. You can order salads here without hesitation (all greens are washed in an antimicrobial solution), and the dessert menu includes such favorites as *pastel de tres leches.*

And, with its vast selection of tequilas, it's the perfect place to do a little tasting. It's 5 blocks northwest of Fuente Minerva.

Av. Mexico 2916 (corner of Nelson), Fracc. Terranova, west side. © **33/3640-3440** or 33/3640-3110. Main courses $9–$18. AE, DISC, MC, V. Mon–Sat 1pm–midnight; Sun 1–6pm.

**La Fonda de San Miguel** ★★ *Moments* MEXICAN My favorite way to enjoy a good meal in Mexico is to have it in an elegant colonial courtyard. I love the contrast between the bright, noisy street and the cool, serene courtyard. This restaurant is in a beautiful courtyard in the former convent of Santa Teresa de Jesús. (You can check out the shops and galleries as you enter.) While enjoying the stone arches and gurgling fountain, you are served little crisp tacos, pumpkin bread, and mildly spiced butter to awaken the appetite. For main courses, try *chiles en nogada* (a combination of spicy and sweet) if it's in season, or perhaps a traditional *mole poblano.* The restaurant is 4 blocks west and 1 block south of the cathedral.

Donato Guerra 25, downtown. © **33/3613-0809.** Reservations recommended. Breakfast $5; main courses $8–$16. AE, MC, V. Sun–Mon 9am–6pm; Tues–Sat 9am–midnight.

**La Trattoría Pomodoro Ristorante** ITALIAN Good food, a comfortable dining area, and fast and friendly service make this place popular. It has natural wood chairs, cushioned seats, linen tablecloths, and a large span of windows looking out onto Niños Héroes. There's separate seating for smokers and nonsmokers. For starters, you might want to sample the antipasto bar or shrimp in white-wine cream sauce with chiles. As a main course, the fettuccine Alfredo is excellent. The price of the main course includes the superb salad bar and garlic bread.

Niños Héroes 3051, west side. © **33/3122-1817.** Reservations recommended. Pasta $7–$14; chicken, beef, seafood $10–$15. AE, MC, V. Daily 1pm–midnight. Free parking.

**Mariscos Progreso** ★ SEAFOOD/MEXICAN On a large, open patio shaded by trees and tile roofs, waiters navigate among the tables carrying large platters of delicious seafood. Mexicans do a wonderful job with seafood, and this popular restaurant does the tradition proud. Charcoal-grilled, Mexican-style food is the specialty here, but the kitchen cooks in a variety of ways. For a sampling of grilled favorites, try the *parrillada* for two. Sometimes there's quite a bit of *ambiente,* with *mariachis* adding to the commotion. At other times, the crowd thins and one can rest peacefully from the exertions of shopping with a cold drink. It's half a block from the Parián.

Progreso 80, Tlaquepaque. © **33/3657-4995.** Reservations not accepted. Main courses $7–$14. AE, MC, V. Daily 11am–7pm.

**Siglo XV** SPANISH This restaurant goes to great lengths to create a dining hall suggestive of 15th-century Spain—stone walls, tables and benches made of thick wooden planks, torches, and the like. The end result is impressive, and the food is excellent, too. Popular favorites include scallops, *callos a la madrileña* (beef tripe cooked in tomato sauce), paella, and *cochinillo asado a la segoviana* (roasted pig). From Wednesday to Saturday, there are flamenco performances, and every night there is live acoustic music. The restaurant is in the downtown neighborhood known as Las Nueve Esquinas.

Colón 383, downtown. © **33/3614-4278.** Reservations recommended on weekends. Main courses $7–$15. AE, MC, V. Tues–Sat 2pm–1am. Valet parking available.

## INEXPENSIVE

**Café Madrid** MEXICAN This little coffee shop is like many coffee shops used to be—a social institution where people come in, greet each other and the staff by name, and chat over breakfast or coffee and cigarettes. Change comes slowly here. For example, despite the fact that it's an informal place, the waiters wear white jackets with black bow ties, as they did 20 years ago. The coffee and Mexican breakfasts are good, as is the standard Mexican fare served in the afternoon. The front room opens to the street, with a small lunch counter and another room in the back. From the Plaza de Armas, walk 1 block on Corona to Juárez and turn right; the cafe is on the right.

Juárez 264, downtown. ✆ **33/3614-9504.** Breakfast $2–$4; main courses $3–$6. No credit cards. Daily 7:30am–10:30pm.

**La Chata Restaurant** REGIONAL/MEXICAN This popular downtown spot offers tasty Mexican standards at reasonable prices. Aromas waft into the street from the kitchen in front, where women with their heads wrapped in bandanas busily stir, chop, and fry. Past this is a large dining area. Local dishes include *pozole* (chicken, pork, and hominy in a broth to which you add onions, radishes, chile, and oregano) and *torta ahogada* (a spicy pork sandwich). If you're very hungry, the sampler platter of *antojitos* for four people will fit the bill. To find La Chata from the Plaza de Armas, walk 1½ blocks south on Corona; it's on the right.

Corona 126 (between Juárez and López Cotilla), downtown. ✆ **33/3613-0588.** Reservations not accepted. Breakfast $3–$5; main courses $4–$7. AE, DC, MC, V. Daily 8am–11:30pm.

**Los Itacates Restaurant** ★★ *Value* MEXICAN This is the Mexican equivalent of down-home cooking—nothing exotic or unheard-of, just well-prepared traditional food. This place, very popular with office workers, is packed during the afternoon dinner hour (2–4pm), but at other times it's easy to find a table. The atmosphere is festive, with colorfully painted chairs and table coverings. You can dine outdoors at sidewalk tables or in one of the three interior rooms. Specialties include *pozole, lomo adobado* (baked pork in dark chile sauce), and chiles rellenos. *Pollo Itacates* is a quarter of a chicken, two cheese enchiladas, potatoes, and rice. Los Itacates is 5 blocks north of Avenida Vallarta.

Chapultepec Nte. 110, west side. ✆ **33/3825-1106** or 33/3825-9551. Breakfast buffet $4; tacos 50¢; main courses $3–$6. MC, V. Mon–Sat 8am–11pm; Sun 8am–7pm.

# 5 Exploring Guadalajara

## SPECIAL EVENTS

In September, when Mexicans celebrate independence from Spain, Guadalajara goes all out, with a full month of festivities. The celebrations kick off with the **Encuentro Internacional del Mariachi,** in which *mariachi* bands from around the world come to their mecca to play before knowledgeable audiences and rehearse with other mariachis. Bands come from as far as Japan and Russia, and the event takes on a curious postmodern hue. There are concerts in several venues. In the Degollado Theater, you can hear orchestral arrangements of classic *mariachi* songs with solos by famous *mariachis.* You might be acquainted with many of the classics without even knowing it. The culmination is a parade of thousands of *mariachis* and *charros* (Mexican cowboys) through downtown Guadalajara. Catch it if you're there during the first 10 days of September.

**Downtown Guadalajara**

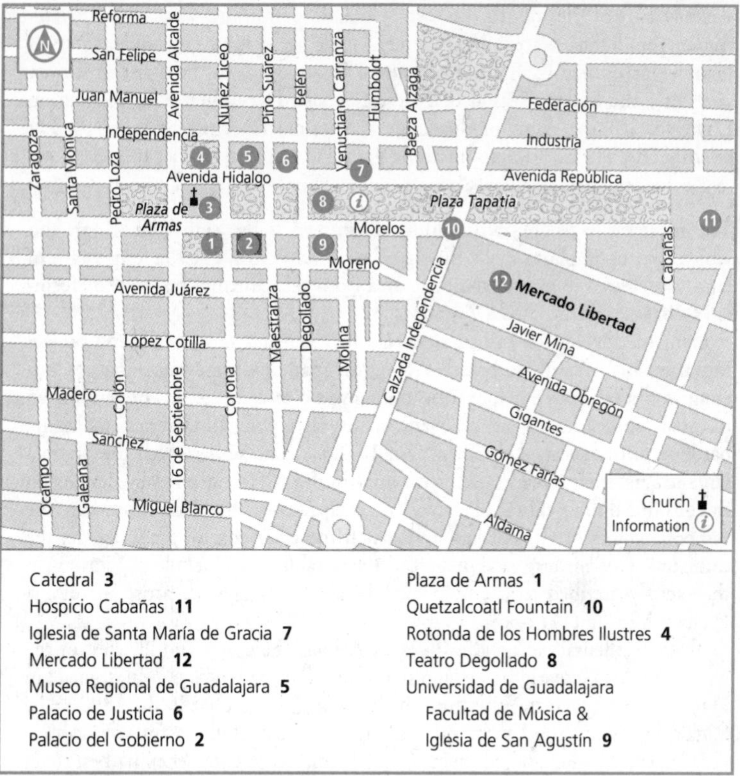


On **September 15,** a massive crowd assembles in front of the Governor's Palace to await the traditional *grito* (shout for independence) at 11pm. The grito commemorates Father Miguel Hidalgo de Costilla's cry for independence in 1810. The celebration features live music on a street stage, spontaneous dancing, fireworks, and shouts of "*¡Viva México!*" and "*¡Viva Hidalgo!*" The next day is the official Independence Day, with a traditional parade; the plazas downtown resemble a country fair and market, with booths, games of chance, stuffed-animal prizes, cotton candy, and candied apples. Live entertainment stretches well into the night.

On **October 12,** a **procession** ★★ honoring Our Lady of Zapopan celebrates the feast day of the Virgin of Zapopan. Around dawn, her small, dark figure begins the 5-hour ride from the Cathedral of Guadalajara to the suburban Basilica of Zapopan (see "Other Attractions," below). The original icon dates from the mid-1500s; the procession began 200 years later. Today, crowds spend the night along the route and vie for position as the Virgin approaches. She travels in a gleaming new car (virginal in that it must never have had the ignition turned on), which her caretakers pull through the streets. During the previous months, the figure visits churches all over the city. You will likely see neighborhoods decorated with paper streamers and banners honoring the Virgin's visit.

The celebration has grown into a month-long event, **Fiestas de Octubre,** which kicks off with an enormous parade, usually on the first Sunday (or possibly Sat) of the month. Festivities include performing arts, rodeos (*charreadas*), bullfights, art exhibits, regional dancing, a food fair, and a Day of Nations incorporating all the consulates in Guadalajara. By the time this is over, you enter the holiday season of **November and December,** with Revolution Day (Nov 20), the Virgin of Guadalupe's saint's day (Dec 12), and several other celebrations. There's always something going on from September to December.

## DOWNTOWN GUADALAJARA

The most easily recognized building downtown is the **cathedral** ★, around which four open plazas make the shape of a Latin cross. Later, a long swath of land was cleared to extend the open area from the cathedral east to the Hospicio Cabañas, creating **Plaza Tapatía.**

Construction on the cathedral started in 1561 and was an ongoing project into the 18th century. With such a long time span, it was inevitable that remodeling would take place before the building was ever completed. The result is an unusual façade that is an amalgam of several architectural styles, including baroque, neoclassical, and Gothic. An 1818 earthquake destroyed the original large towers; their replacements were built in the 1850s, inspired by designs on the bishop's dinner china. The colors on the towers—blue and yellow—are the symbolic colors of Guadalajara and match the city's coat of arms. Inside, the cathedral is open, airy, and majestic. Items of interest include a painting in the sacristy ascribed to the renowned 17th-century Spanish artist Bartolomé Estaban Murillo (1617–82).

To the cathedral's left is the **Plaza de Armas,** the oldest and loveliest of the plazas. An Art Nouveau bandstand stands in its center. The bandstand, made in France, was a gift to the city from the dictator Porfirio Díaz in the 1890s. The female figures on the bandstand exhibited too little clothing for conservative Guadalajarans, who clothed them. The dictator, recognizing when it's best to let the people have their way, said nothing.

Facing the plaza is the **Palacio del Gobierno** ★★. This handsome palace, built in 1774, blends Spanish and Moorish elements. Inside the central courtyard, above the staircase to the right, is a spectacular mural of Hidalgo by the modern Mexican master José Clemente Orozco (1883–1949). The Father of Independence appears high overhead, bearing directly down on the viewer and looking as implacable as a force of nature. Guadalajara's native son achieved this effect through the dramatic use of proportion and perspective that are the hallmarks of his work. On one of the adjacent walls is another mural, *The Carnival of Ideologies,* a dark satire on the prevailing fanaticisms of Orozco's day. Another mural by Orozco, inside the second-floor chamber of representatives, shows Hidalgo again, this time in a more conventional posture, writing the proclamation to end slavery in Mexico. The palacio is open from 10am to 8pm.

On the opposite side of the cathedral from the Plaza de Armas is the **Rotonda de los Hombres Ilustres.** Sixteen white columns, each supporting a bronze statue, stand as monuments to Guadalajara's and Jalisco's distinguished sons.

Facing the east side of the rotunda is the **Museo Regional de Guadalajara,** Liceo 60 (✆ **33/3614-9957**). Originally a convent, it was built in 1701 in the churrigueresque (Mexican baroque) style and contains some of the region's important archaeological finds, fossils, historic objects, and art. Among the highlights are a giant reconstructed mammoth's skeleton and a meteorite weighing 1,715 pounds, discovered in Zacatecas in 1792. On the first floor, there's a fascinating exhibit of pre-Hispanic pottery, and some exquisite pottery and clay figures recently unearthed near Tequila during the construction of the toll road.

On the second floor is a small but interesting ethnography exhibit of the contemporary dress of the state's indigenous peoples, including the Coras, Huicholes, Mexicaneros, Nahuas, and Tepehuanes. It's open Tuesday to Saturday from 9am to 6:45pm, Sunday from 9am to 2:45pm. Admission is $2.50 for adults, $1 for children (children enter free Sun). On Tuesday admission is free for all.

Behind the Cathedral is the Plaza de la Liberación, with the **Teatro Degollado** (deh-goh-*yah*-doh) on the opposite side. This neoclassical 19th-century opera house was named for Santos Degollado, a local patriot who fought with Juárez against Maximilian and the French. Apollo and the nine muses decorate the theater's pediment, and the interior is famous for both the acoustics and the rich decoration. It hosts a variety of performances during the year, including the Ballet Folclórico on Sunday at 10am. It's open Monday to Friday 10am to 2pm and during performances (see "Guadalajara After Dark," later, for more information).

To the right of the theater, across the street, is the sweet little **church of Santa María de Gracia,** built in 1573 as part of a convent for Dominican nuns. On the opposite side of the Teatro Degollado is the **church of San Agustín,** The former convent is now the **University of Guadalajara School of Music.**

Behind the Teatro Degollado begins the Plaza Tapatía, which leads to the Instituto Cabañas. It passes between a couple of low, modern office buildings. The Tourism Information Office is in a building on the right-hand side.

Beyond these office buildings, the plaza opens into a large expanse, now framed by department stores and offices and dominated by the abstract modern **Quetzalcoatl Fountain.** This fluid steel structure represents the mythical plumed serpent Quetzalcoatl, who figured so prominently in pre-Hispanic religion and culture, and exerts a presence even today.

At the far end of the plaza is the Hospicio Cabañas, formerly an orphanage and known today as the **Instituto Cultural Cabañas** ★★, Cabañas 8 (✆ **33/3617-4322**). This vast structure is impressive for both its size (more than 23 courtyards) and its grandiose architecture, especially the cupola. Created by the famous Mexican architect Manuel Tolsá, it housed homeless children from 1829 to 1980. Today, it's a thriving cultural center offering art shows and classes. The interior walls and ceiling of the main building display murals painted by Orozco in 1937, at the height of his powers. His *Man of Fire,* in the dome, is said to represent the spirit of humanity projecting itself toward the infinite. Other rooms hold additional Orozco works, as well as excellent contemporary art and temporary displays. The institute's own Ballet Folklórico performs here every Wednesday at 8:30pm (see "Guadalajara After Dark," below, for more info). Hours are Tuesday to Saturday from 10:30am to 6pm, Sunday from 10:30am to 3pm. Admission is $1.

Just south of the Hospicio Cabañas (to the left as you exit) is the **Mercado Libertad** ★, Guadalajara's gigantic covered central market, the largest in Latin America. This site has been a market plaza since the 1500s; the present buildings date from the early 1950s (see "Shopping," below).

## OTHER ATTRACTIONS

At **Parque Agua Azul** (Blue Water Park), plants, trees, shrubbery, statues, and fountains create a perfect refuge from the bustling city. Many people come here to exercise early in the morning. The park is open daily 7am to 6pm. Admission is $1 for adults, 50¢ for children.

Across Independencia from the park, cater-corner from a small flower market, is the **Museo de Arqueología del Occidente de Mexico,** Calzada Independencia con Av. del Campesino. It houses a fine collection of pre-Hispanic pottery from Jalisco, Nayarit, and Colima. The museum is open Tuesday to Sunday 10am to 2pm and 4 to 7pm. There's a small admission charge.

The state-run **Casa de las Artesanías** (© **33/3619-4664**) is just past the park entrance at Calzada Independencia and González Gallo (for details, see "Shopping," below).

**The Basílica of the Virgin of Zapopan** ★ A wide promenade several blocks long leads to a large, open plaza and the basilica. This is the religious center of Guadalajara, with the plaza holding hundreds of thousands of people on the Virgin's feast day (see "Special Events," above). The church dates from the 18th century and is a lovely (and somewhat anachronistic) combination of baroque and plateresque styles. The cult of the Virgin of Zapopan practically began with the foundation of Guadalajara itself. She is much revered and the object of many pilgrimages. In front of the church are several stands selling religious figures and paraphernalia. On one side of the church is a lovely museum and store dedicated to the betterment of the Huichol Indians. It is well worth a visit.

Main Plaza, Zapopan (10km/6 miles northwest of downtown), Jalisco. No phone. Free admission. Daily 7am–7pm; museum daily 10am–7pm.

**Museo de las Artes de la Universidad de Guadalajara** This museum books many important traveling exhibitions. An early show featured contemporary artists from all over the Americas. Several rooms house the university's permanent collection, consisting mainly of works by Mexican and Jaliscan artists. There are also some bold Orozco murals: On one wall of the auditorium and the cupola above are *Man, Creator and Rebel* and *The People and Their False Leaders.* The museum is a short ride west of downtown, across from the University of Guadalajara.

Juárez 975. © **33/3625-7553.** Admission $2. Tues–Sat 10am–8pm; Sun and holidays noon–8pm.

**Museo de la Ciudad** This fine museum, which opened in 1992 in a former convent, chronicles Guadalajara's fascinating past. The eight rooms, beginning on the right and proceeding in chronological order, cover the period from just before the city's founding to the present. Unusual artifacts, including rare Spanish armaments and equestrian paraphernalia, give a sense of what day-to-day life was like. As you browse, dust off your Spanish and read the explanations, which give details not otherwise noted in the displays.

Independencia 684 (at M. Barcena). © **33/3658-2531.** Admission 50¢. Wed–Sat 10am–5:30pm; Sun 10am–2:30pm.

## 6 Shopping

Many visitors to Guadalajara come specifically for the shopping in Tlaquepaque and Tonalá (see below). If you have little free time, try the government-run **Casa de las Artesanías** ★, González Gallo 20 at Calzada Independencia (© **33/3619-4664**), in Parque Agua Azul, just south of downtown. This place is perfect for one-stop shopping, with two floors of pottery, silver jewelry, dance masks, glassware, leather goods, and regional clothing from around the state and the country. As you enter, on the right are museum displays showing crafts and regional costumes from the state of Jalisco. The craft store is open Monday to Friday from 10am to 6pm, Saturday from 10am to 5pm, Sunday from 10am to 3pm.

Guadalajara is known for its shoe industry; if you're in the market for a pair, try the **Galería del Calzado,** a shopping center made up exclusively of shoe stores. It's on the west side, about 6 blocks from Minerva Circle, at Avenidas Mexico and Yaquis.

*Mariachis* and *charros* come to Guadalajara from all over Mexico to buy their highly worked belts and boots, wide-brimmed *sombreros,* and embroidered shirts. Several tailor shops and stores specialize in these outfits. One is **El Charro,** which has a store in the Plaza del Sol shopping center, across the street from the Hotel Presidente Intercontinental, and one downtown on Juárez.

To view a good slice of what constitutes the material world for most Mexicans, try the mammoth **Mercado Libertad** ★ downtown. Besides food and produce, there are crafts, household goods, clothing, magic preparations, and more. Although it opens at 7am, the market isn't in full swing until around 10am. Come prepared to haggle.

## SHOPPING IN TLAQUEPAQUE & TONALA

Almost everyone who comes to Guadalajara for the shopping has Tlaquepaque and Tonalá in mind. These two suburbs are traditional handcraft centers that produce and sell a wide variety of *artesanía.*

### TLAQUEPAQUE (TLAH-KEH-*PAH*-KEH)

Located about 20 minutes from downtown, **Tlaquepaque** ★★★ has the best shopping for handcrafts and decorative arts in all of Mexico. Over the years, it has become a fashionable place, attracting talented designers in a variety of fields. Even though it's a suburb of a large city, it has a cozy, small-town feel; it's a pleasure simply to stroll through the central streets from shop to shop. No one hassles you; no one does the hard sell. There are some excellent places to eat (see "Where to Dine," earlier), or you can grab some simple fare at **El Parián,** a building in the middle of town that houses a number of small eateries.

A taxi from downtown Guadalajara will cost you $5, or you can take one of the deluxe **Turquesa buses** that make a fairly quick run from downtown to Tlaquepaque and Tonalá (see "Getting Around," earlier).

The **Tlaquepaque Tourism Office,** Morelos 288 (© **33/3635-5756** or 33/3657-3846), has a helpful, English-speaking staff. It's open Monday to Friday from 9am to 3pm, Saturday from 9am to 1pm. Most stores in Tlaquepaque close between 2 and 4pm and stay open until 7 or 8pm. Most are closed or have reduced hours on Sunday.

If you are interested in pottery and ceramics, two museums are worth a visit. The **Regional Ceramics Museum,** Independencia 237 (© **33/3635-5404**), displays several aspects of traditional Jalisco pottery as produced in Tlaquepaque and Tonalá. The high-quality examples date back several generations. Note the cross-hatch design known as *petatillo* on some of the pieces; it's one of the region's oldest traditional motifs and is, like so many other motifs, a real pain to produce. Look for the wonderful old kitchen and dining room, complete with pots, utensils, and dishes. The museum is open Tuesday to Saturday from 10am to 4pm, Sunday from 10am to 1pm; admission is free. The **Museo Pantaleón Panduro** ★★, P. Sánchez 191 (© **33/3635-1089,** ext. 17), is named after a famous local 19th-century artisan. It displays prize-winning pieces from the national ceramics contest held each year in Tlaquepaque, many of which display astounding virtuosity. Categories include miniatures, traditional designs, and original designs. It's open Tuesday to Sunday from 10am to 6pm; admission is free. If you still haven't had your fill, the Museo Nacional de Cerámica is in Tonalá (see below).

### Tips Packing It In

If you need your purchases packed safely so that you can check them as extra baggage, or if you want them shipped, talk to **Margaret del Rio.** She is an American who runs a large packing and shipping company at Juárez 347, Tlaquepaque (✆ **33/3657-5652**). Paying the excess baggage fee usually is cheaper than shipping but less convenient.

A number of workshops permit visitors to watch artisans at work. A popular workshop is **La Rosa de Cristal,** Contreras Medillín 173, a glassblowing factory. It's open Monday to Saturday from 10am to 7pm. If you're interested in a particular craft, talk to the city tourism office; the staff can help locate workshops that are open to the public.

The following list of Tlaquepaque shops will give you an idea of what to expect. This is just a small fraction of what you'll find; the best approach might be to just follow your nose. The main shopping is along **Independencia,** a pedestrian-only street that starts at El Parián. You can go door to door visiting the shops until the street ends, then work your way back on Calle **Juárez,** the next street over, north of Independencia.

**Agustín Parra** So you bought an old hacienda and are trying to restore its chapel—where do you go to find traditional baroque sculpture, religious art, gold-leafed objects, and even entire *retablos?* Parra is famous for exactly this kind of work, and the store is lovely. It's open Monday to Saturday 10am to 7pm. Independencia 158. ✆ **33/3657-8530.**

**Bazar Hecht** One of the village's longtime favorites. Here you'll find wood objects, handmade furniture, and a few antiques. It's open Monday to Saturday from 10am to 2:30pm and 3:30 to 7pm. Juárez 162. ✆ **33/3657-0316.**

**Casa Canela** One of the most elegant stores in Tlaquepaque, this is a feast for the eyes. Browse through rooms full of furniture and decorative objects. It's open Monday to Friday from 10am to 2pm and 3 to 7pm, Saturday from 10am to 6pm, Sunday 11am to 3pm. Independencia 258, near Calle Cruz Verde. ✆ **33/3635-3717.**

**Ken Edwards** Ken Edwards was among the first artisans to produce high-fired, lead-free stoneware in Tonalá, and his blue-on-blue pottery is now sold all over Mexico. This showroom has a large selection of his work. There's a section of seconds for bargain hunters. The shop is next door to the "Restaurant With No Name" (the factory is in Tonalá). It's open Monday to Saturday from 10:30am to 7pm. Madero 70. ✆ **33/3635-5456.**

**Sergio Bustamante** Sergio Bustamante's imaginative, original bronze, ceramic, and papier-mâché sculptures are among the most sought after in Mexico—as well as the most copied. He also designs silver jewelry. This exquisite gallery showcases his work. It's open Monday to Saturday from 10am to 7pm, Sunday from 11am to 4pm. Independencia 236 at Cruz Verde. ✆ **33/3639-5519.**

**Tete Arte y Diseño** Architectural decorative objects are mixed in with pottery, antiques, glassware, and paintings at this shop. It's open Monday to Saturday from 10am to 7pm. Juárez 173. ✆ **33/3635-7347.**

**Tierra Tlaquepaque** Here you'll find unusual, rustic, and finely finished pottery, as well as wood sculptures, table textiles, and decorative objects. Open

Monday to Saturday 10am to 7pm, Sunday 11am to 5pm. Independencia 156. ✆ 33/3635-9770.

### TONALA: A TRADITION OF POTTERY MAKING

**Tonalá** ★★ is a pleasant, modest town not far from Tlaquepaque. The streets were paved only recently, and there aren't any fancy shops. You will find Tonalá easier on the wallet than Tlaquepaque. The village has been a center of pottery making since pre-Hispanic times; half of the more than 400 workshops here produce a wide variety of high- and low-temperature pottery. Other local artists work with forged iron, cantera stone, brass and copper, marble, miniatures, papier-mâché, textiles, blown glass, and gesso. This is a good place to look for custom work in any of these materials; a large pool of craftspeople can be located by just asking around a little.

Market days are Thursday and Sunday. Expect large crowds, and blocks and blocks of stalls displaying locally made pottery and glassware, as well as cheap manufactured goods, food, and all kinds of bric-a-brac. "Herb men" sell a rainbow selection of dried medicinal herbs from wheelbarrows; magicians entertain crowds with sleight-of-hand; and craftspeople spread their colorful wares on the plaza's sidewalks. I prefer to visit Tonalá on non-market days, when it's much easier to get around and see the glass and pottery stores. This is the place for buying sets of margarita glasses, the widely seen blue-rimmed rustic glassware, the pottery typically associated with Mexico, and finely painted *petatillo* ware.

The **Tonalá Tourism Office** (✆ **33/3683-1740;** fax 33/3683-0590) is in the Artesanos building, set back from the road at Atonaltecas 140 Sur (the main street leading into Tonalá) at Matamoros. Hours are Monday to Friday from 9am to 3pm, Saturday from 9am to 1pm. They offer free walking tours on Monday, Tuesday, Wednesday, and Friday at 9am and 2pm, Saturday at 9am and 1pm. They include visits to artisans' workshops (where you'll see ceramics, stoneware, blown glass, papier-mâché, and the like). Tours last 3 to 4 hours and require a minimum of five people. Visitors can request an English-speaking guide. Also in Tonalá, cater-corner from the church, you'll see a small tourism information kiosk that's staffed on market days and provides maps and useful information.

Tonalá is also the home of the **Museo Nacional de Cerámica,** Constitución 104, between Hidalgo and Morelos (✆ **33/3683-0494**). The museum occupies a two-story mansion and displays work from Jalisco and all over the country. There's a large shop in the front on the right as you enter. The museum is open Tuesday to Friday from 10am to 5pm, Saturday and Sunday from 10am to 2pm. Admission is free; the fee for using a video or still camera is $8.50 per camera.

## 7 Guadalajara After Dark

### FOLKLORIC BALLET

**Ballet Folclórico de la Universidad de Guadalajara** ★★ This dance company, acclaimed as the finest of its kind in Mexico, performs traditional dances from Jalisco and other parts of the country. For more than a decade, it has been performing at the Degollado Theater. Performances are on Sunday at 10am. Degollado Theater, Plaza Tapatía. ✆ **33/3614-4773** or 33/3613-1115. Tickets $3–$17. Ticket office daily 10am–1pm and 4–7pm.

**Ballet Folklórico Nacional del Instituto Cultural Cabañas** Performances are every Wednesday at 8:30pm at the theater of the Instituto Cultural

## Tequila: The Name Says It All

Tequila is an entertaining (and intoxicating) town, well worth a day trip from Guadalajara. Several taxi drivers charge about $55 to take you to the town, get you into a tour of a distillery, take you to a restaurant, and then haul you back to Guadalajara. A few of them speak English. One driver is José Gabriel Gómez (✆ **33/3649-0791** at home), who has a new car and drives carefully. Call him in the evening. Tour companies also arrange bus trips to Tequila; see a travel agency in Guadalajara.

Tequila has many distilleries, including the famous brands **Sauza** and **José Cuervo.** All the distilleries—the big, modern ones and the smaller, more traditional factories—offer tours. If you're on your own, a good place to hook up with a tour is at the little booth outside the city hall on the main square. Two young women who speak English run tours to any of the local factories. The tour costs only $3 and lasts about 2 hours. All tours show how tequila is made, what traditions are followed, and what differences exist between tequilas; they end, of course, with a tasting. Avenida Vallarta runs straight to the highway to Tequila, which is about an hour outside of Guadalajara.

Another way to learn about tequila is to take the **Tequila Express,** which leaves from the train station every Saturday at about 10am and goes to the town of Amatitán, home of the Herradura distillery. The Guadalajara Chamber of Commerce (*Cámara de Comercio*), at Vallarta and Niño Obrero (✆ **33/3122-7920**), organizes this trip. You can buy tickets there or at an office at Morelos 395, at Colón, in the Centro Histórico (✆ **33/3614-3145**). Office hours are Monday to Friday from 9am to 2 pm and 4 to 6pm. Tickets cost $58 for adults, $32 for children 6 to 12. The fare includes an open bar and tequila tasting that begins on the train, a variety show, a tour of a distillery and a maguey plantation, and dinner. It returns to Guadalajara at about 7:30pm.

Cabañas (see "Downtown Guadalajara," earlier). At the far end of the Plaza Tapatía. ✆ **33/3618-6003.** Tickets $6–$8.

### MARIACHIS

You can't go far in Guadalajara without coming across some *mariachis,* but seeing really talented performers takes some effort (see the listing for La Feria, below). If you're interested in the flavor and atmosphere of the music, try **El Parián** in Tlaquepaque, where *mariachis* serenade diners under the archways.

### THE CLUB & MUSIC SCENE

Tapatíos are notoriously fickle about clubs and discos. One moment a particular club is the place to be, the next moment, it's passé. At present, the disco of choice is **El Mito** (✆ **33/3615-7246**), in the popular shopping center Centro Magno on Avenida Vallarta. It plays mostly pop music from the '80s. Entrance is restricted to people over 25; the cover is $7.

**Bar Copenhagen 77** ★★ This dark, snug little den with upholstered walls and wood trim is the perfect setting for jazz. Pianist Carlos de la Torre, whose elegant, economic style infuses his interpretations of bebop, modern, and Latin jazz, leads the house band. This is the real stuff, a fact demonstrated by the number of jazz heavyweights who come to sit in with the band or just listen. The club faces the Parque de la Revolución (along Juárez, 9 blocks west of the Plaza de Armas), on your left as you walk down López Cotilla. You can just have drinks, or you can order from the small, well thought-out menu; the specialty is paella. Marcos Castellanos 140-Z. ✆ **33/3826-7306.** No cover. Restaurant Mon–Sat 2pm–1am; jazz begins at 8:30pm.

**El Cubilete** ★★ *El Cubilete* (the dice cup) is a small club tucked away in an old downtown neighborhood called Las Nueve Esquinas (the nine corners). This up-and-coming area has a couple of other clubs that are worth checking out, as well as the Siglo XV restaurant (see earlier). The house band at El Cubilete is very tight, and the club books excellent traveling Cuban bands. On weekends, the place really gets cooking when Rosalía takes the stage. The talented Cuban diva has an easy, natural stage presence and an ability to ad-lib that makes her a joy to watch. When Rosalía is singing, the club can get very crowded. El Cubilete serves drinks and Cuban and regional foods, including *birria, tortas ahogadas,* and *carne asada.* Gral. Río Seco 9. ✆ **33/3658-0406** or 33/3613-2096. Reservations recommended. $5 cover on weekends. Mon–Sat 2pm–1am; live salsa Tues–Sat 10pm–1am.

**La Feria** ★★ To get a good sampling of local color, try this multilevel restaurant and bar with a center stage. The afternoon and nighttime shows feature a variety of acts, including a great mariachi band, some very impressive (and expressive) singers, a *charro* who performs rope tricks, some *ballet folklórico* dancers, and a few games involving the audience. The owner promised a free drink to anyone who shows a Frommer's book—so hold him to it. You might want to try a *paloma,* the most popular tequila drink in Guadalajara. The menu is Mexican, with an emphasis on grilled meats. La Feria is downtown, 5 blocks south of the Plaza de Armas. Corona 291. ✆ **33/3613-7150** or 33/3613-1812. Reservations recommended. No cover. Daily noon–3am. Variety show at 3:30 and 10pm.

8

# Puerto Vallarta & the Central Pacific Coast

The Pacific coast of Mexico is known for its palm-studded jungles that sweep down to meet the deep blue of the Pacific Ocean. It's a spectacular backdrop for three modern resort cities and smaller coastal villages that border this stretch of coastline, from Mazatlán through Puerto Vallarta and curving down to Manzanillo. Collectively, it's known as the Mexican Riviera. Modern hotels, easy air access, and a growing array of activities and adventure tourism attractions have transformed this region of Mexico into one of the country's premier resort areas.

**Puerto Vallarta,** with its traditional Mexican architecture and gold-sand beaches bordered by jungle-covered mountains, is the second most visited resort in Mexico (trailing only Cancún). Vallarta maintains a small-town charm despite boasting sophisticated hotels, great restaurants, a thriving arts community, active nightlife, and a growing variety of ecotourism attractions. **Mazatlán** may be the greatest resort value in Mexico, luring visitors with its exceptional fishing, historic downtown, and new championship golf facilities. **Manzanillo** is surprisingly relaxed; even though it's one of Mexico's most active commercial ports, it also offers great fishing and golf. And along **Costa Alegre,** between Puerto Vallarta and Manzanillo, pristine coves are home to unique luxury and value-priced resorts that cater to travelers seeking seclusion and privacy. Just north of Puerto Vallarta is **Punta Mita,** home of the first Four Seasons resort in Latin America and a Jack Nicklaus golf course. With four more luxury resorts and two more golf courses on tap, it is emerging as Mexico's most exclusive luxury address.

Villages such as **Rincon de Guayabitos, Barra de Navidad,** and **Melaque** are laid-back and almost undiscovered. Starkly different from the spirited resort towns, they offer travelers a glimpse into local culture. Excursions to these smaller villages make easy day trips or extended stays.

## 1 Puerto Vallarta ★★★

885km (553 miles) NW of Mexico City; 339km (212 miles) W of Guadalajara; 285km (178 miles) NW of Manzanillo; 447km (278 miles) SE of Mazatlán; 239km (149 miles) SW of Tepic

No matter how extensively I travel in Mexico, Puerto Vallarta remains my absolute favorite part of this colorful country, for its unrivaled combination of simple pleasures and sophisticated charms. No other place in Mexico offers both the best of the country's natural beauty and an authentic dose of its vibrant culture.

Puerto Vallarta's seductive innocence captivates visitors, beckoning them to return—and to bring friends. Beyond the cobblestone streets, graceful cathedral,

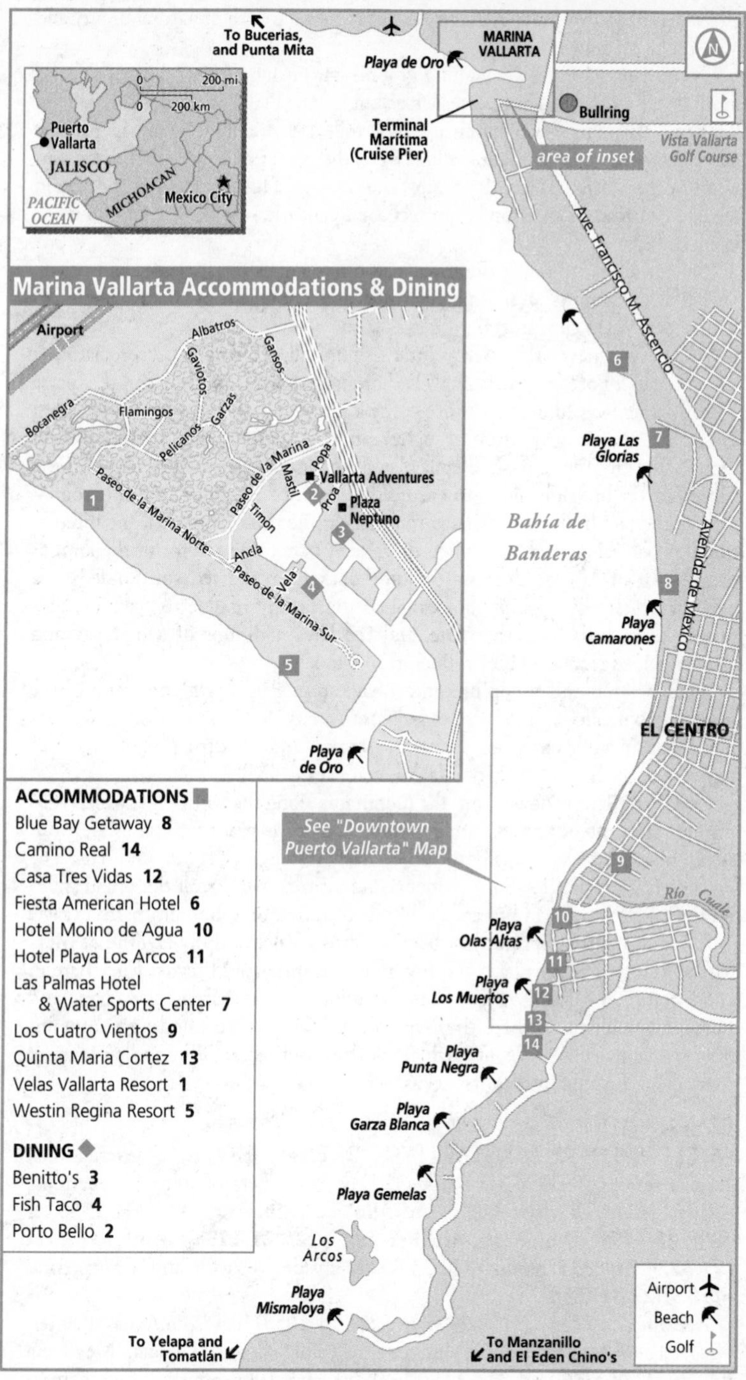

To Bucerias, and Punta Mita
Playa de Oro
MARINA VALLARTA
Terminal Marítima (Cruise Pier)
Bullring
area of inset
Vista Vallarta Golf Course
Puerto Vallarta
JALISCO
MICHOACAN
Mexico City
PACIFIC OCEAN
0 200 mi
0 200 km
Ave. Francisco M. Ascencio
Marina Vallarta Accommodations & Dining
Airport
Albatros
Gansos
Gaviotos
Bocanegra
Flamingos
Pelicanos
Garzas
Paseo de la Marina
Popa
Mastil
Vallarta Adventures
Proa
Plaza Neptuno
Timon
Paseo de la Marina Norte
Ancla
Vela
Paseo de la Marina Sur
Playa de Oro
Playa Las Glorias
Bahía de Banderas
Avenida de Mexico
Playa Camarones
EL CENTRO
See "Downtown Puerto Vallarta" Map
Río Cuale
Playa Olas Altas
Playa Los Muertos
Playa Punta Negra
Playa Garza Blanca
Playa Gemelas
Los Arcos
Playa Mismaloya
To Yelapa and Tomatlán
To Manzanillo and El Eden Chino's
Airport
Beach
Golf
ACCOMMODATIONS
Blue Bay Getaway 8
Camino Real 14
Casa Tres Vidas 12
Fiesta American Hotel 6
Hotel Molino de Agua 10
Hotel Playa Los Arcos 11
Las Palmas Hotel & Water Sports Center 7
Los Cuatro Vientos 9
Quinta Maria Cortez 13
Velas Vallarta Resort 1
Westin Regina Resort 5
DINING
Benitto's 3
Fish Taco 4
Porto Bello 2

and welcoming atmosphere, Puerto Vallarta offers a wealth of natural beauty and man-made pleasures.

Ecotourism activities are gaining ground—from mountain biking the Sierra foothills to whale-watching, ocean kayaking, and diving with giant mantas in Banderas Bay. Forty-two kilometers (26 miles) of beaches, many in pristine coves accessible only by boat, extend from the center of town around the bay. High in the Sierra Madre Mountains, the mystical Huichol Indians still live in relative isolation in an effort to protect their centuries-old culture from outside influences.

Its natural appeal aside, the town also offers hotels of all classes and prices, over 250 restaurants, a sizzling nightlife, and enough shops and galleries to tempt even jaded consumers.

Vallarta was never the "sleepy little fishing village" that many proclaim. It began life as a port for processing silver brought down from mines in the Sierra Madre—then was forever transformed by a movie director and two star-crossed lovers. In 1963 John Huston brought stars Ava Gardner and Richard Burton here to film the Tennessee Williams play *Night of the Iguana.* Burton's new love, Elizabeth Taylor, came along to ensure the romance remained in full bloom—despite the fact both were married to others at the time. Titillated, the international paparazzi arrived, and when they weren't shooting photos of the famous couple—or of Ava Gardner water-skiing back from the set, surrounded by a bevy of beach boys—they photographed the beauty of Puerto Vallarta. This seaside town was never the same, and the later additions of a highway and airport helped it mature into the resort it is today.

Luxury hotels and shopping centers have sprung up north and south of the original town, allowing Vallarta to grow into a city of 250,000 without sacrificing its considerable charms. It boasts the services and infrastructure of a modern city as well as the authenticity of a colonial Mexican village.

Cool breezes flow down from the mountains along the Río Cuale, which runs through the center of town. Fanciful public sculptures grace the main waterfront street, or *malecón,* which is bordered by lively restaurants, shops, and bars. The *malecón* is a magnet for both residents and visitors, who stroll the broad walkway to take in an ocean breeze, a multihued sunset, or a moonlit, perfect wave.

If I sound partial, it's not just because Puerto Vallarta is my favorite of Mexico's sunny resorts; this has been my home for the past 11 years. I live here in good company—there's a considerable colony of American, Canadian, and European residents. Perhaps they feel as I do: that the surrounding mountains offer the equivalent of a continual, comforting embrace, adding to that sense of welcome that so many visitors feel as well.

## ESSENTIALS

**GETTING THERE & DEPARTING** **By Plane** For a list of international carriers serving Mexico, see chapter 2. Local numbers of some international carriers serving Puerto Vallarta are **Alaska Airlines** (✆ **322/221-1350** or 322/221-1353), **American Airlines** (✆ **322/221-1799**), **America West** (✆ **322/221-1333** or 001/880-235-9292 inside Mexico), and **Continental** (✆ **322/221-1025**).

**Aeromexico** (✆ **322/224-2777** or 322/221-1055) flies from Aguascalientes, Guadalajara, La Paz, León, Mexico City, Morelia, and Tijuana. **Mexicana** (✆ **322/224-8900** or 322/221-1266) has direct or nonstop flights from Guadalajara, Mazatlán, and Mexico City.

**By Car** The coastal **Highway 200** is the only choice from Mazatlán (6 hr. north) or Manzanillo (3½–4 hr. south). Highway 15 from Guadalajara to Tepic takes 6 hours; to save as much as 2 hours, take Highway 15A from Chapalilla to Compostela, bypassing Tepic, then continue south on Highway 200 to Puerto Vallarta.

**By Bus** The bus station, **Central Camionera de Puerto Vallarta,** is just north of the airport, approximately 11km (7 miles) from downtown. It offers overnight guarded parking and baggage storage. Most major first-class bus lines operate from here, with transportation to points throughout Mexico, including Mazatlán, Tepic, Manzanillo, Guadalajara, and Mexico City. Taxis into town cost approximately $13.50 and are readily available; public buses operate from 7am to 11pm and regularly stop in front of the arrivals hall.

**ORIENTATION** **Arriving by Plane** The airport is close to the north end of town near the Marina Vallarta, about 10km (6 miles) from downtown. **Transportes Terrestres** minivans and **Aeromovil** taxis make the trip. They use a zone pricing system, with fares clearly posted at the respective ticket booths. Fares start at $10 for a ride to Marina Vallarta and go up to $30 for the south shore hotels. Federally licensed airport taxis exclusively provide transportation from the airport, and their fares are more than three times as high as city (yellow) taxi fares. A trip to downtown Puerto Vallarta costs $18, whereas a return trip using a city taxi costs only $5. Only airport cabs may pick up passengers leaving the airport. However, if you don't have too much baggage, you can cross the highway using the new overpass, and there you'll find yellow cabs lined up.

**VISITOR INFORMATION** The **Municipal Tourism Office,** Juárez and Independencia (✆ **322/223-2500,** ext. 230), is in a corner of the white Presidencia Municipal building (city hall) on the northwest end of the main square. In addition to offering a listing of current events and a collection of promotional brochures for local activities and services, the staff can also assist with specific questions—there's usually an English speaker on staff. This is also the office of the tourist police. It's open Monday to Friday from 9am to 8pm. During low season it may close for lunch between 1 and 3pm or 2 and 4pm.

The **State Tourism Office,** Plaza Marina L 144, 2nd floor (✆ **322/221-2676,** 322/221-2677, or 322/221-2678), also offers promotional brochures and can assist with specific questions about Puerto Vallarta and other points in the state of Jalisco, including Guadalajara, Costa Alegre, the town of Tequila, and the program that promotes stays in authentic rural haciendas. It's open Monday to Friday from 9am to 5pm.

**CITY LAYOUT** The seaside promenade, the *malecón,* is frequently used as a reference point for giving directions. It's next to **Paseo Díaz Ordaz** and runs north-south through the central downtown area. From the waterfront, the town stretches back into the hills a half-dozen blocks. The areas bordering the **Río Cuale** are the oldest parts of town—the original Puerto Vallarta. The area immediately south of the river, called **Olas Altas** after its main street (and sometimes Los Muertos after the beach of the same name), is home to a growing selection of sidewalk cafes, fine restaurants, espresso bars, and hip nightclubs. Once you're in the center of town, you'll find nearly everything within walking distance both north and south of the river. **Bridges** on Insurgentes (northbound traffic) and Ignacio Vallarta (southbound traffic) link the two sections of downtown.

**AREA LAYOUT** Beyond downtown, Puerto Vallarta has grown along the beach to the north and south. Linking downtown to the airport is **Avenida**

**Francisco Medina Ascencio** (sometimes known by its previous name, Av. de las Palmas). Along this main thoroughfare are many luxury hotels (in an area called the **Zona Hotelera,** or Hotel Zone), plus several shopping centers with casual restaurants.

**Marina Vallarta,** a resort city within a city, is at the northern edge of the Hotel Zone not far from the airport. It boasts the most modern luxury hotels, plus condominiums and homes, a huge marina with 450 yacht slips, a golf course, restaurants and bars, a water park, and several shopping plazas. Because the area was originally a swamp, the beaches are the least desirable in the area, with darker sand and seasonal inflows of cobblestones. (Exquisite pools at the oceanfront hotels more than make up for them.) The Marina Vallarta peninsula faces the bay and looks south to the town of Puerto Vallarta—yet feels like a world apart.

**Nuevo Vallarta** is a planned resort north of the airport, across the Ameca River in the state of Nayarit (about 13km/8 miles north of downtown). It also has hotels, condominiums, and a yacht marina, but very little in the way of restaurants, shopping (other than a relatively new mall), or other attractions. Most hotels there are all-inclusive, with some of the finest beaches in the bay, but guests usually travel into Puerto Vallarta (about a $13 cab ride) for anything other than poolside or beach action. Regularly scheduled public bus service costs about $1.55 and runs until 10pm.

**Bucerías,** a small beachfront village of cobblestone streets, villas, and small hotels, is farther north along Banderas Bay, 30km (19 miles) beyond the airport. Past Bucerías, following the curved coastline of Banderas Bay, is **Punta Mita.** Once a rustic fishing village, it is in the process of development as a luxury destination—in the works are a total of five super-exclusive luxury boutique resorts, private villas, and three golf courses. The site of an ancient celestial observatory, it is an exquisite setting, with white sand beaches and clear waters—a departure from other beaches in the area.

In the other direction from downtown is the southern coastal highway, home to more luxury hotels. Immediately south of town lies the exclusive residential and rental district of **Conchas Chinas.** Ten kilometers (6 miles) south, on **Playa Mismaloya** (where *Night of the Iguana* was filmed), lies the Jolla de Mismaloya Resort. There's no road on the southern shoreline of Banderas Bay, but three small coastal villages are popular attractions for visitors to Puerto Vallarta: **Las Animas, Quimixto,** and **Yelapa,** all accessible only by boat. Yelapa, on a beautiful sheltered cove, has been a popular haven for long-term ex-pat visitors and artists due to its seclusion, natural beauty, and simplicity of life. Offering a selection of primitive accommodations, Yelapa—which has only solar-powered electricity—also offers beachside restaurants and hikes to one of two jungle waterfalls. Quimixto and Las Animas are popular day excursions by tour boat or water taxi. The tiny, pristine cove of **Caletas,** site of John Huston's former home, is a popular day or nighttime excursion (see "Boat Tours," later).

---

### *Tips* Steer Clear of the Rambo Bus!

Buses in Vallarta tend to be rather aggressive, and some even sport names—including "Terminator," "Rambo," and "Tornado." Don't tempt fate by assuming these buses will stop for pedestrians. Although Vallarta has an extremely low crime rate, bus accidents are frequent—and frequently fatal.

---

**Tips Don't Let Taxi Drivers Steer You the Wrong Way**

Beware of restaurant recommendations offered by taxi drivers—many receive a commission from restaurants where they discharge passengers. Be especially wary if a driver tries to talk you out of a restaurant you've already selected.

**GETTING AROUND** **By Taxi** Taxis are plentiful and relatively inexpensive. Most trips from downtown to the northern Hotel Zone and Marina Vallarta cost $3.50 to $7; to or from Marina Vallarta to Mismaloya Beach (to the south) costs $10. Rates are charged by zone and are generally posted in the lobbies of hotels. Taxis can also be hired by the hour or day for longer trips. Rates run $10 to $15 per hour, with discounts available for full-day rates—consider this as an alternative to renting a car.

**By Car** Rental cars are available at the airport and through travel agencies, but unless you're planning a distant side trip, don't bother. Car rentals are expensive, averaging $66 per day, and parking around town is difficult. If you see a sign for a $10 jeep rental or $20 car rental, be aware that these are lures to get people to attend timeshare presentations. Unless you are interested in a timeshare, stopping to inquire will be a waste of your time.

**By Bus** City buses are easy to navigate and inexpensive. They run from the airport through the Hotel Zone along Morelos Street (1 block inland from the *malecón*), across the Río Cuale, and inland on Vallarta, looping back through the downtown hotel and restaurant districts on Insurgentes and several other downtown streets. To get to the northern hotel strip from old Puerto Vallarta, take the Zona Hoteles, Ixtapa, or Las Juntas bus. These buses may also post the names of hotels they pass, such as Krystal, Fiesta Americana, Sheraton, and others. Buses marked MARINA VALLARTA travel inside this area, stopping at the major hotels there. These buses, costing about 45¢, will serve just about all your transportation needs frequently and inexpensively.

Buses run generally from 6am to 11pm, and it's rare to wait more than a few minutes for one. Another bus route travels south every 10 to 15 minutes to either Mismaloya Beach or Boca de Tomatlán (the destination is indicated in the front window) from Plaza Lázaro Cárdenas, a few blocks south of the river at Cárdenas and Suárez, and along Basilio Badillo, between Piño Suárez and Insurgentes.

**By Boat** The cruise ship pier (*muelle*), also called Terminal Marítima, is where **excursion boats** to Yelapa, Las Animas, Quimixto, and the Marietas Islands depart. It's north of town near the airport and an inexpensive taxi or bus ride from town. Just take any bus marked IXTAPA, LAS JUNTAS, PITILLAL, or AURORA and tell the driver to let you off at the Terminal Marítima. *Note:* Odd though it may seem, you must pay a $1.50 fee to gain access to the pier—and your departing excursion boat.

**Water taxis** to Yelapa, Las Animas, and Quimixto leave at 10:30 and 11am from the pier at Los Muertos Beach (south of downtown), on Rodolfo Rodríguez next to the Hotel Marsol. Another water taxi departs at 11am from the beachfront pier at the northern edge of the *malecón.* A round-trip ticket to Yelapa (the farthest point) costs $25. Return trips usually depart between 3 and 4pm, but confirm the pickup time with your water taxi captain. Other water taxis depart from Boca de Tomatlán, located about 30 minutes south of town by public bus. These water taxis are the better option if you want more flexible departure and return times from the southern beaches. Generally, they leave on the hour for the southern shore destinations, or more frequently if there is traffic. Price is about $20 round-trip, with rates now clearly posted on a sign on the beach. A private boat taxi can be hired for $35 to $56 (depending on your destination), allowing you to choose your own return time. They'll take up to eight people for that price, so often people band together at the beach to hire one.

## *FAST FACTS:* Puerto Vallarta

*American Express* The local office is at Morelos 660, at the corner of Abasolo (© **01-800/504-0400** in Mexico, or 322/223-2955). It's open Monday to Friday from 9am to 6pm, Saturday 9am to 1pm. It offers excellent, efficient travel agency services in addition to money exchange and traveler's checks.

*Area Code* The telephone area code is **322.**

*Climate* It's warm all year, with tropical temperatures; however, evenings and early mornings in the winter can turn quite cool. Summers are sunny, but with an increase in humidity during the rainy season, between May and October. Rains come almost every afternoon in June and July, and are usually brief but strong—just enough to cool off the air for evening activities. In September, heat and humidity are least comfortable and rains heaviest.

*Consumer Assistance* Tourists with complaints about taxis, stores, abusive timeshare presentations, or other matters should contact **PROFECO,** the consumer protection office (© **322/225-0000** or 322/225-0018). The office is open Monday to Friday from 8:30am to 3:30pm.

*Currency Exchange* Banks are found throughout downtown and in the other prime shopping areas. Most banks are open Monday to Friday from 9am to 5pm, with shorter hours on Saturday. ATMs are common throughout Vallarta, including the central plaza downtown. They are becoming the most favorable way to exchange currency, with bank rates plus 24-hour convenience. Money exchange houses (*casas de cambio*), located throughout town, offer longer hours than the banks with only slightly lower exchange rates.

*Embassies/Consulates* The consulates are in a building on the southern border of the central plaza (you'll see the U.S. and Canadian flags). The **U.S. Consular Agency** office (© **322/222-0069;** fax 322/223-0074, 24 hours a day for emergencies) is open Monday to Friday from 10am to 2pm. The **Canadian Consulate** (© **322/222-5398** or 322/223-0858; 24-hr. emergency line 01-800/706-2900) is open Monday to Friday 9am to 4pm.

*Emergencies* **Police** emergency, © **060;** local police, © **322/221-2587** or 322/221-2588; intensive care **ambulance,** © **322/225-0386** (*Note:* English-speaking assistance is not always available at this number); **Red Cross,** © **322/222-1533.**

*Hospitals* The following offer U.S.-standards service and are available 24 hours: **Ameri-Med Urgent Care,** Francisco Medina Ascencio at Plaza

Neptuno, Local D-1, Marina Vallarta (✆ **322/221-0023;** fax 322/221-0026; www.amerimed-hospitals.com); and **San Javier Marina Hospital,** Francisco Medina Ascencio 2760, Zona Hotelera (✆ **322/226-1010**).

*Internet Access* Puerto Vallarta is probably the most wired destination in Mexico. **The Net House,** Ignacio L. Vallarta 232 (✆ **322/222-6953;** info@vallartacafes.com), 2 blocks past the southbound bridge, has 17 computers with fast connections and English keyboards. It's open daily from 8am to 2am and charges $4 per hour. **Café Net** (✆ **322/222-0092**), Olas Altas 250, at the corner of Basilio Badillo, charges $2 for 30 minutes. It offers complete computer services, a full bar, and food service. It's open daily from 8am to 2am. Some hotels have lobby e-mail kiosks, but they're more expensive than the Net cafes.

*Newspapers & Magazines* ***Vallarta Today,*** a daily English-language newspaper (✆ **322/225-3303** or 322/224-2829), is a good source for local information and upcoming events. The quarterly city magazine ***Vallarta Lifestyles*** (✆ **322/221-0106**) is also very popular but provides listings only of services that advertise. Both are for sale at area newsstands and hotel gift shops. The weekly ***P.V. Tribune*** (✆ **322/223-0585**) is distributed free throughout town and offers a more objective local viewpoint.

*Pharmacies* **CMQ Farmacia,** Basilio Badillo 365 (✆ **322/222-1330**), is open 24 hours and delivers to hotels free with a minimum purchase of $10. **Farmacia Guadalajara,** Emiliano Zapata 232 (✆ **322/224-1811**), is also open 24 hours a day.

*Post Office* The *correo* is at Mina 188 (✆ **322/222-1888**). It's open Monday to Friday from 8am to 7pm, Saturday from 9am to 1pm.

*Safety* Puerto Vallarta enjoys a very low crime rate. Public transportation is perfectly safe to use, and Tourist Police (dressed in white safari uniforms with white hats) are available to answer questions, give directions, and offer assistance. Most crime or encounters with the police are linked to using or purchasing drugs—so don't (see chapter 2). *Note:* The tourist police conduct random personal searches for drugs. Although there is some question about their right to do this, the best course of action if they want to frisk you is to comply—objecting will likely result in a free tour of the local jail. However, you are within your rights to request the name of the officer conducting the search. Report any unusual incidents to the local consular office.

## BEACHES, ACTIVITIES & EXCURSIONS

Travel agencies can provide information on what to see and do in Puerto Vallarta and can arrange tours, fishing trips, and other activities. Most hotels have a tour desk on-site. Of the many travel agencies in town, I highly recommend **Tukari Servicios Turísticos,** Av. España 316 (✆ **322/224-7177;** fax 322/224-2350), which specializes in ecological and cultural tours. Another source is **Xplora Adventours** (✆ **322/223-0661**), in the Sierra Madre shop on the *malecón.* It has listings of all locally available tours, with photos, explanations, and costs; however, be aware that a timeshare resort owns the company, so part of the information you receive will be an invitation to a presentation, which you may decline. **American Express Travel Services,** Morelos 660 (✆ **322/223-2955**),

**Moments** **Special Events in Puerto Vallarta**

Each November, **Fiestas del Mar** (SeaFest) includes a gourmet dining festival, cultural festival, art exhibitions, tennis tournaments, regattas, and more. Dates vary; call the Tourism Board (© **888/384-6822** from the U.S.) for dates and schedule. From December 1 through December 12, the **Festival of the Virgin of Guadalupe** ★—Mexico's patron saint—inspires one of the most authentic displays of culture and community in Mexico. Each business, neighborhood, association, or group makes a pilgrimage (called *peregrinaciones*) to the church, where they exchange offerings for a brief blessing by the priest. These processions, especially those created by hotels, often include floats, Aztec dancers, and mariachis, and are followed by fireworks. Hotels frequently invite guests to participate in the walk to the church. It's an event not to be missed.

also has a varied selection of high-quality, popular tours. One of the tour companies with the largest—and best quality—selection of boat cruises and land tours is **Vallarta Adventures** (© **866/256-2739** toll-free from the U.S., or 322/297-1212, ext. 3; www.vallarta-adventures.com). I can highly recommend any of their offerings. Book with them directly and get a 10% discount when you mention Frommer's.

### THE BEACHES

For years, beaches were Puerto Vallarta's main attraction. Although visitors today are exploring more of the surrounding geography, the sands are still a powerful draw. Over 42km (26 miles) of beaches extend around the broad Bay of Banderas, ranging from action-packed party spots to secluded coves accessible only by boat.

**IN TOWN** The easiest to reach is **Playa Los Muertos** (also known as Playa Olas Altas or Playa del Sol), just off Calle Olas Altas, south of the Río Cuale. The water can be rough, but the wide beach is home to a wide array of *palapa* restaurants that offer food, beverage, and beach-chair service. The two most popular are the adjacent El Dorado and La Palapa, at the end of Pulpito Street. On the southern end of this beach is a section known as "Blue Chairs"—the most popular gay beach. Vendors stroll the length of Los Muertos, and beach volleyball, parasailing, and jet skiing are all popular pastimes. The **Hotel Zone** is also known for its broad, smooth beaches, accessible primarily through the hotel lobbies.

**SOUTH OF TOWN** **Playa Mismaloya** is in a beautiful sheltered cove about 10km (6 miles) south of town along Highway 200. The water is clear and beautiful, ideal for snorkeling off the beach. Entrance to the public beach is just to the left of the Jolla de Mismaloya Hotel. Colorful *palapa* restaurants dot the small beach, and you can rent beach chairs for sunning. You can also stake out a table under a *palapa* for the day. Using a restaurant's table and *palapa* is a reciprocal arrangement—they let you be comfortable, and you buy your drinks, snacks, and lunch there. *Night of the Iguana* was filmed at Mismaloya. **La Jolla de Mismaloya Resort and Spa** (© **322/226-0600**) has a restaurant on the restored film set—**La Noche de la Iguana Set Restaurant,** open daily from noon to 11pm. The movie runs continuously in a room below the restaurant, and photo stills from the filming hang in the restaurant. The restaurant is accessible by land on the point framing the south side of the cove. Just below the restaurant is **John Huston's Bar & Grill,** serving drinks and light snacks 11am to 6pm.

La Jolla de Mismaloya Resort and Spa is to the right of the public beach, and restaurants there are open to nonguests. The beach at **Boca de Tomatlán,** just down the road, is similar in setup to Mismaloya, but without a large resort. The two are accessible by public buses, which depart from the corner of Basilio Badillo and Insurgentes every 15 minutes from 5:30am to 10pm and cost just 60¢.

**Las Animas, Quimixto,** and **Yelapa** beaches offer a true sense of seclusion; they are accessible only by boat (see "Getting Around," above, for information about water-taxi service). They are larger than Mismaloya, offer intriguing hikes to jungle waterfalls, and are similarly set up, with restaurants fronting a wide beach. Overnight stays are available only at Yelapa (see "Side Trips from Puerto Vallarta," later).

**NORTH OF TOWN** The beaches at **Marina Vallarta** are the least desirable in the area, with darker sand and seasonal inflows of stones.

The entire northern coastline from Bucerías to Punta Mita is a succession of sandy coves alternating with rocky inlets. For years the beaches to the north, with their long, clean breaks, have been the favored locale for surfers. The broad, sandy stretches at **Playa Anclote, Playa Piedras Blancas,** and **Playa Destiladeras,** which all have *palapa* restaurants, have made them favorites with local residents looking for a quick getaway. The stellar white sand beach at Punta Mita, home of the new Four Seasons, is closed to road access, except for guests of the hotel.

## ORGANIZED TOURS

**BOAT TOURS** Puerto Vallarta offers a number of boat trips, including sunset cruises and snorkeling, swimming, and diving excursions. They generally travel one of two routes: to the **Marietas Islands,** which are a 30- to 45-minute boat ride off the northern shore of Banderas Bay, or to **Yelapa, Las Animas,** or **Quimixto** along the southern shore. The trips to the southern beaches make a stop at **Los Arcos,** an island rock formation south of Puerto Vallarta, for snorkeling. Don't base your opinion of underwater Puerto Vallarta on this, though—with dozens of tour boats dumping quantities of snorkelers overboard at the same time each day, this is exactly when the fish know *not* to be there. It is, however, an excellent site for night diving. When comparing boat cruises, note that some include lunch, while most provide music and an open bar on board. Most leave around 9:30am, stop for 45 minutes of snorkeling, and arrive at the beach destination around noon for a 2½-hour stay before returning around 3pm. At Quimixto and Yelapa, visitors can take a half-hour hike to a jungle waterfall or rent a horse for the ride. Prices range from $45 for a sunset cruise or a trip to one of the beaches with open bar, to $85 for an all-day outing with open bar and meals.

One boat, the ***Marigalante*** (**© 322/223-0309**), is an exact replica of Columbus's ship the *Santa Maria,* built in honor of the 500-year anniversary of his voyage to the Americas. It features a daytime "pirate's cruise" ($62 per person), complete with picnic barbecue and treasure hunt, and a sunset dinner cruise ($73 per person) with folkloric dance and fireworks.

One of the best trips is a day trip to **Caletas** ★★, the cove where John Huston made his home for years. **Vallarta Adventures** (**© 866/256-2739** toll-free in the U.S., or 322/297-1212, ext. 3; www.vallarta-adventures.com) holds the exclusive lease on the private cove and has done an excellent job of restoring

### Moments Art Along the *Malecón*

One of the great pleasures of strolling Puerto Vallarta's *malecón* is taking in the fanciful sculptures that line the seaside promenade. Among the notable works on display is *Nostalgia,* across from Carlos O'Brian's restaurant. Created by Ramiz Barquett, it depicts a couple sharing a romantic moment while gazing out to the bay. Farther south is the sculpture group at the *Rotonda del Mar,* locally known as *Fantasy by the Sea.* It's an array of sculpture "chairs" by renowned Mexican artist Alejandro Colunga. This wildly creative series—a large octopus head tops one chair, and another bench has two giant ears for backrests—always seems to draw a crowd. Closer to the main square is the *Boy on the Seahorse* sculpture, an image that has come to represent Puerto Vallarta. Don't miss the fountain across from the main square; its three bronze dolphins seem ready to leap right into the bay. Other sculptures along the *malecón* include the controversial "ladder to heaven" by Sergio Bustamante, and Mathis Lidice's interpretation of the passage of time, across from Hotel Rosita at the northernmost edge of the *malecón.*

Huston's former home, adding exceptional day-spa facilities and landscaping the beach, which is wonderful for snorkeling. The quality facilities and relative privacy have made this excursion ($70 per person) one of the most popular. It also offers an evening cruise, complete with dinner and a spectacular contemporary dance show, "Rhythms of the Night" (see "Puerto Vallarta After Dark," later).

Travel agencies sell tickets and distribute information on all cruises. If you prefer to spend more time at Yelapa or Las Animas without snorkeling and cruise entertainment, see the information about travel by water taxis, earlier, under "Getting Around."

**Whale-watching tours** become more popular each year. Viewing humpback whales is almost a certainty from mid- to late November through March. The majestic whales have migrated to this bay for centuries (in the 1600s, it was called "Humpback Bay") to bear their calves. The noted local authority is **Open Air Expeditions,** Guerrero 339 (✆ and fax **322/222-3310;** openair@vivamexico.com), which offers ecologically oriented 4-hour tours in small boats for $80. Groups of up to 12 travel in specially designed soft boats, and the twice-daily tours (8:30am and 1:30pm) include a healthful snack and T-shirt. The company also spearheads a photo-ID project to track returning whales—each one has unique markings on its fluke, or tail. **Vallarta Adventures** (✆ **866/256-2739** toll-free in the U.S., or 322/297-1212, ext. 3; www.vallarta-adventures.com) offers whale-watching photo excursions in small boats for $80. The trip includes a predeparture briefing on whale behaviors. This company also features whale-watching on tours to the Marietas Islands. For $60 you get lunch, time at a private beach, and a more festive than educational ambience aboard large catamarans.

**LAND TOURS** **Tukari Servicios Turísticos** (see "Beaches, Activities & Excursions," above) can arrange trips to the fertile birding grounds near **San Blas,** 3 to 4 hours north of Puerto Vallarta in the state of Nayarit, and shopping trips to **Tlaquepaque and Tonalá** (6 hr. inland, near Guadalajara). A day trip to **Rancho Altamira,** a 50-acre working ranch, includes a barbecue lunch and horseback riding, then a stroll through **El Tuito,** a small nearby colonial-era village. The company can also arrange an unforgettable morning at **Terra Noble Art & Healing Center** (© **322/223-3530** or 322/222-5400), a mountaintop day spa and center for the arts where participants can get a massage or treatment, work in clay and paint, and have lunch in a heavenly setting overlooking the bay.

Hotel travel desks and travel agencies, including Tukari and American Express, can also book the ever-popular **Tropical Tour** or **Jungle Tour** ($25), a basic orientation to the area. These excursions are really expanded city tours that include a drive through the workers' village of Pitillal, the affluent neighborhood of Conchas Chinas, the cathedral, the market, the Taylor-Burton houses, and lunch at a jungle restaurant. Any stop for shopping usually means the driver picks up a commission for what you buy.

The **Sierra Madre Expedition** is another excellent tour offered by **Vallarta Adventures** (© **866/256-2739** toll-free from the U.S., or 322/297-1212, ext. 3; www.vallarta-adventures.com). The daily excursion travels in Mercedes all-terrain vehicles north of Puerto Vallarta through jungle trails, stopping at a small town, venturing into a forest for a brief nature walk, and winding up on a pristine secluded beach for lunch and swimming. The $70 outing is worthwhile because it takes tourists on exclusive trails into scenery that would otherwise be off-limits.

**AIR TOURS** Speaking of off-limits, you can explore some of the most remote and undiscovered reaches of the Sierra Madre mountains in Vallarta Adventures' **San Sebastián Air Adventure** (© **866/256-2739** toll-free from the U.S., or 322/297-1212, ext. 3; www.vallarta-adventures.com). A 15-minute flight aboard a 14-seat turbo-prop Cessna Caravan takes you into the heart of the Sierra Madre. The plane is equipped with raised wings, which allow you to admire—and photograph—the mountain scenery. The plane arrives on a gravel landing strip in the old mining town of San Sebastián, a beautiful village that dates to 1603. One of the oldest mining towns in Mexico, it reached its prosperous peak in the 1800s, with over 30,000 inhabitants. Today, San Sebastián remains an outstanding example of how people lived and worked in a remote Mexican mountain town—it's a living museum. The half-day adventure costs $130, and includes the flight, a walking tour of the town (including a stop at the old Hacienda Jalisco, a favored getaway of John Huston, Liz and Dick, and their friends), plus brunch in town. For those who would like to spend more time in San Sebastián, other excursions include overnight stays and return trips by bike or horseback. There's also a **Jeep tour** to San Sebastián. The cost of $84 per person, for up to four people per Jeep, includes a guide. This tour departs at 9am and returns at 5pm. Call Pacific Travel (© **322/225-2270**) to reserve.

Anyone for a taste of tequila? We're talking about the town, and a sampling of the best of the spirit of Mexico. Vallarta Adventures (see above) offers a half-day trip that takes you at a comfortable pace to the classic town, where you visit one of the original haciendas and tequila (agave) fields. A comfortable 35-minute flight aboard a private 16-passenger plane takes you to the town of Tequila. This is the only region in the world where this legendary spirit is distilled. The visit centers around Herradura Tequila's impressive 18th-century Hacienda San Jose, where you learn about the myth and the tradition of producing tequila from the stately plants that line the hillsides of the town—an experience comparable to California's winery tours. Departures are every

Thursday at 10am from the Aerotron private airport (adjacent to the Puerto Vallarta International Airport); the group returns to Puerto Vallarta by 8pm. Cost is $290, which includes all air and ground transportation, tours, lunch, and beverages.

**TOURS IN TOWN** Every Wednesday and Thursday in high season (late Nov through Easter), the **International Friendship Club** (✆ **322/222-5466**) offers a **private home tour** of four villas in town. It costs $30 per person, with proceeds donated to local charities. Arrive early because this tour sells out quickly! It starts at the Hotel Molino de Agua, Av. Ignacio L. Vallarta 130, adjacent to the southbound bridge over the Río Cuale. Get there at 10am, and you can buy breakfast while you wait for the group to gather. The tour departs at 11am and lasts approximately 2½ hours.

You can also tour the **Taylor/Burton villas** (Casa Kimberley; ✆ **322/222-1336**), at 445 Calle Zaragoza. Tours of the two houses owned by Elizabeth Taylor and Richard Burton cost $8. Call ahead daily between 9am and 6pm, and if the manager is available, he will take you through the house.

**A TASTY TOUR** Possibly the most spirited tour in town is the **Don Porfidio Tequila Distillery Tour** (✆ **322/221-2543,** 322/221-2547, or 322/221-2545), at Porfidio's facility 10 minutes north of town. It shows how agave plants are juiced, fermented, distilled, and bottled for shipping. The fee ($10) includes a glass of Porfidio—reputed to be one of Mexico's finest tequilas, but in reality is a blend of other premium tequilas with exceptional packaging and marketing. It doesn't quite compare to a visit to the tequila fields and traditional tequila-making haciendas, but if you don't have time for the half-day tour outlined above, this is an interesting, albeit abbreviated, glimpse at the tequila-making process.

## STAYING ACTIVE

**DIVING** Underwater enthusiasts from beginner to expert can arrange scuba diving through **Vallarta Adventures** (✆ **866/256-2739** toll-free from the U.S., or 322/297-1212, ext. 3; www.vallarta-adventures.com), a five-star PADI dive center. Dives take place at Los Arcos, a company-owned site at Caletas Cove, Quimixto Coves, the Marietas Islands, or the offshore La Corbeteña, Morro, and Chimo reefs. The company also offers a full range of certification courses (through Instructor). **Chico's Dive Shop,** Díaz Ordaz 772–5, near Carlos O'Brian's (✆ **322/222-1895;** www.chicos-diveshop.com), offers similar dive trips and is also a PADI five-star dive center. Chico's is open daily from 8am to 10pm and has branches at the Marriott, Las Palmas, Holiday Inn, Fiesta Americana, Krystal, San Marino, Villa del Palmar, Paradise Village, and Playa Los Arcos hotels.

**ECOTOURS & ACTIVITIES** **Open Air Expeditions** (✆ and fax **322/222-3310;** openair@vivamexico.com) offers nature-oriented trips, including birding and ocean kayaking in Punta Mita. **Ecotours de México,** Ignacio L. Vallarta 243 (✆ and fax **322/222-6606**), has eco-oriented tours, including seasonal (Aug–Nov) trips to a turtle preservation camp where you can witness hatching baby Olive Ridley turtles.

**FISHING** Arrange fishing trips through travel agencies or through the **Cooperativa de Pescadores** (Fishing Cooperative), on the *malecón* north of the Río Cuale, next door to the Rosita Hotel (✆ **322/222-1202** or 322/224-7886). Fishing charters cost $180 to $350 a day for four to eight people; price varies with the size of the boat. Although the posted price at the fishing cooperative is the same as what you'll find through travel agencies, you may be able to negotiate a lower price at the cooperative, which does not accept credit cards. It's open Monday to Saturday from 7am to 10pm, but make arrangements a day ahead. You can also arrange fishing trips at the Marina Vallarta docks, or by calling **Fishing with Carolina** (© **322/224-7250,** or cellular 044-322/292-2953; fishingwithcarolina@hotmail.com), which uses a 30-foot Unitlite sportsfisher, fully equipped with an English-speaking crew. Fishing trips generally include equipment and bait, but drinks, snacks, and lunch are optional, so check to see what the price includes.

**GOLF** Puerto Vallarta is an increasingly popular golf destination; five courses have opened in the past 3 years, bringing the total in the region to nine. The Joe Finger–designed course at the **Marina Vallarta Golf Club** (© **322/221-0073**) is an 18-hole, par-74, private course that winds through the Marina Vallarta peninsula and affords ocean views. It's for members only, but most luxury hotels in Puerto Vallarta have memberships for their guests. A bar, restaurant, golf pro, and pro shop are on the premises. Greens fees are $136 in high season, $115 in low season. Fees include golf cart, range balls, and tax. Hiring a caddy costs $8 to $10. Club rentals, lessons, and special packages are available.

North of town in the state of Nayarit, about 16km (10 miles) beyond Puerto Vallarta, is the 18-hole, par-72 **Los Flamingos Club de Golf** (© **329/296-5006**). Open to the public, it features beautiful jungle vegetation and has just undergone a renovation and upgrade of the course. It's open from 7am to 5pm daily, with a snack bar (but no restaurant) and full pro shop. The greens fee is $95 and includes the use of a golf cart; hiring a caddy costs $12 plus tip for a caddy, and club rental is $22 to $44. A free shuttle runs from downtown Puerto Vallarta; call for pickup times and locations.

The breathtaking new Jack Nicklaus Signature course at the **Four Seasons Punta Mita** (© **329/291-6000;** fax 329/291-6060) has eight oceanfront holes and an ocean view from every hole on the course. Its hallmark is Hole 3B, the "Tail of the Whale," with a long drive to a green on a natural island—the only natural-island green in the Americas. It requires an amphibious cart to take you over when the tide is high, and there's an alternate hole for when the ocean or tides are not accommodating. It's open only to guests of the Four Seasons resort or to members of other golf clubs with a letter of introduction from their pro. Selected other area hotels also have guest privileges—ask your concierge. Greens fees for nonguests are $260, including cart, with (Calloway) club rentals for $60. Lessons are available from PGA pro Rick Avina.

A second Jack Nicklaus course is at the new **Vista Vallarta Golf Club** (© **322/290-0030**), along with one designed by Tom Weiskopf. The course is slated to host the World Golf Championships in December 2002. It's in the foothills of the Sierra Madre, behind the bullring in Puerto Vallarta. A round costs $167 per person, including cart.

**American Golf Tours** (© **322/225-2056;** www.mexicogolftours.com) offers professionally guided golf tours to area courses and down Costa Alegre. Prices vary according to the number of golfers and whether you choose optional overnight stays. Personalized packages can be arranged, and club and shoe rentals are available.

**HORSEBACK-RIDING TOURS** Travel agents and local ranches can arrange guided horseback rides. **Rancho Palma Real,** Carretera Vallarta, Tepic 4766 (© **322/221-2120**), has an office 5 minutes north of the airport; the ranch is in Las Palmas, approximately 40 minutes northeast of Vallarta. It is by far the nicest horseback riding tour in the area. The horses are in excellent condition, and you enjoy a tour of local farms on your way to the ranch. The price ($62; AE only) includes breakfast and lunch.

**Rancho El Charro,** Av. Francisco Villa 895 (✆ **322/224-0114** or cellular 322/292-0122; www.ranchoelcharro.com), and **Rancho Ojo de Agua,** Cerrada de Cardenal 227, Fracciónamiento Las Aralias (✆ and fax **322/224-0607**), also offer high-quality tours. Both ranches are about a 10-minute taxi ride north of downtown toward the Sierra Madre foothills. The morning and sunset rides last 3 hours and take you up into the mountains overlooking the ocean and town. The cost is $39. The ranches have their own comfortable base camp for serious riders who want to stay out overnight.

Rancho El Charro offers an exclusive "Fly-away to a Hide-away in San Sebastián" day trip from 9:30am to 5pm. A 15-minute flight takes you to the 17th-century mining town (see "Side Trips from Puerto Vallarta," later). A bilingual guide meets you at the airstrip, well-tended horses in tow; after a short ride to the Hacienda Jalisco, you'll get a light breakfast and a tour of the hacienda. The ride continues into town along a riverside trail used by the locals since mining days. A thorough tour of the town touches on the historic buildings, church, carpenter shop, and coffee plantation, before heading back to the hacienda for a gourmet lunch. Overnight stays can be arranged. The cost is $278 per person, minimum four people, and advance reservations are required.

Rancho El Charro also organizes a "Horseback on Mexico's Hacienda Trail" tour. The 3- to 7-day journeys by horseback into the mountains are offered from November 1 through April 30. There's a four-person minimum and a 15-person maximum. The cost ($270 per person per day; no credit cards) includes food, horses, camping en route, and stays in centuries-old haciendas. The ranch can arrange hotels in Puerto Vallarta and provide complete details on the quality of horses and accommodations. For details, contact Pam Aguirre of Rancho El Charro (see above).

**MOUNTAIN BIKING & HIKING** **Bike Mex** ★, Calle Guerrero 361 (✆ **322/223-1834** or 322/223-1680; www.bikemex.com), offers expert guided biking and hiking tours up the Río Cuale canyon and to outlying areas. The popular Río Cuale bike trip costs $42 for 4 hours and includes bike, helmet, gloves, insurance, water, lunch, and an English-speaking guide. Trips take off at 9am or 2pm, but starting times are flexible; make arrangements a day ahead.

Who says Yelapa is accessible only by boat? I've traveled with Bike Mex on its all-day, advanced-level bike trip to this magical cove (see "Side Trips from Puerto Vallarta," later). Riders depart at 7:30am in a van, traveling to the starting point in the town of El Tuito. The 53km (33-mile) ride includes 30km (18½ miles) of climbs to a peak elevation of 1,091m (3,600 ft.). The journey consists of switchbacks, fire roads, single tracks, awesome climbs, and steep downhills before ending up at a beachfront *palapa* restaurant in Yelapa. You have the option of staying the night in Yelapa or returning that afternoon by small boat. This tour costs $160, takes 4 to 6 hours, includes all bike gear, drinks, lunch, boat and land transportation, guide, and *ample* encouragement. Other bicycle trips, such as those along the beachfront of Punta Mita, are also available. Bike Mex also arranges guided **hiking tours** along the same routes; prices start at $30, depending on the route.

**SAILING** **Sail Vallarta,** Club de Tenis Puesta del Sol, Local 7-B, Marina Vallarta (✆ **322/221-0096;** fax 322/221-0097; gallonavarro@aol.com), offers a

**Tips** **A Spectator Sport**

**Bullfights** are held from December through April beginning at 5pm on Wednesdays at the La Paloma bullring, across the highway from the town pier. Travel agencies can arrange tickets, which cost around $25.

variety of sailing vessels for hire. A group day sail, including crew, use of snorkeling equipment, drinks, food, and music, plus a stop at a beach for swimming and lunch, costs $82. Most trips include a crew, but you can make arrangements to sail yourself. Prices vary for full boat charters, depending on the vessel and amount of time. **Vallarta Adventures** (© **866/256-2739** toll-free from the U.S., or 322/297-1212, ext. 3; www.vallarta-adventures.com) offers two beautiful sailboats for charter or small-group sails (up to 12 people). Their service is superb, as is the quality of the food and beverages. These are known as the boats that are most frequently under sail—many other sailing charters prefer to motor around the bay.

**SWIMMING WITH DOLPHINS** Ever been kissed by a dolphin? Take advantage of a unique opportunity to swim with Pacific bottlenose dolphins in a clear lagoon. **Dolphin Adventure** ★★ (© **866/256-2739** toll-free from the U.S., or 322/297-1212, ext. 3; www.vallarta-adventures.com) operates an interactive dolphin-research facility—considered the finest in Latin America—that allows limited numbers of people to swim with dolphins Monday through Saturday at scheduled times. Cost for the swim is $130. Reservations are required, and they generally sell out at least a week in advance. You may prefer the **Dolphin Encounter** ($60), at the same facility, which allows you to touch and learn about the dolphins in smaller pools, so you're ensured up-close-and-personal time with them. Dolphin Adventures has two facilities—one in the lagoon of Nuevo Vallarta, and at the headquarters of Vallarta Adventures. I give this my highest recommendation. Not only does the experience leave you with an indescribable sensation, but it's a joy to see these dolphins—they are well cared for, happy, and spirited. The program is about education and interaction, not entertainment or amusement, and is especially popular with children 10 and older.

**TENNIS** Many hotels in Puerto Vallarta offer excellent tennis facilities; many have clay courts. The full-service **Continental Plaza Tennis Club** (© **322/224-0123**) is at the Continental Plaza hotel in the Hotel Zone. It offers indoor and outdoor courts (including a clay court), full pro shop, lessons, clinics, and partner matches.

**WATER-SKIING & PARASAILING** Water-skiing, parasailing, and other watersports are available at many beaches along the Bay of Banderas. The best known for watersports equipment rental is **Club Bananas Water Sports Center,** at the beach of the Las Palmas Hotel, Av. Francisco Medina Ascencio km 2.5, Hotel Zone (© **322/224-0650**). WaveRunners, banana boats, parasailing, and water-skiing are all available to rent by the hour, half day, or full day.

## A STROLL THROUGH TOWN

Puerto Vallarta's cobblestone streets are a pleasure to explore; they're full of tiny shops, rows of windows edged with curling wrought iron, and vistas of red-tile roofs and the sea. Start with a walk up and down the *malecón,* the seafront boulevard.

Among the sights you shouldn't miss is the **municipal building** on the main square (next to the tourism office), which has a large Manuel Lepe mural inside in its stairwell. Nearby, up Independencia, sits the **Parish of Nuestra Señora de Guadalupe church,** Hidalgo 370 (**© 322/222-1326**), topped with a curious crown held in place by angels—a replica of the one worn by Empress Carlota during her brief time in Mexico as Emperor Maximilian's wife. On its steps, women sell religious mementos; across the narrow street, stalls sell native herbs for curing common ailments. Services in English are held Sunday at 10am. Regular parish hours are Monday to Saturday from 7:30am to 8:30pm, Sunday from 6:30am to 8:30pm.

Three blocks south of the church, head east on Libertad, lined with small shops and pretty upper windows, to the **municipal market** by the river. After exploring the market, cross the bridge to the island in the river; sometimes a painter is at work on its banks. Walk down the center of the island toward the sea, and you'll come to the tiny **Museo Río Cuale** (no phone), which has a small but impressive permanent exhibit of pre-Columbian figurines. It's open Monday to Saturday from 10am to 4pm. Admission is free.

Retrace your steps to the market and Libertad, and follow Calle Miramar to the brightly colored steps up to Zaragoza. Midway is a magnificent view over rooftops to the sea, plus a cute cafe, **Graffiti** (no phone), where you can break for a cappuccino and a snack. Up Zaragoza to the right 1 block is the famous **pink arched bridge** that once connected Richard Burton's and Elizabeth Taylor's houses. In this area, known as **"Gringo Gulch,"** many Americans have houses.

## SHOPPING

Shopping in Puerto Vallarta is generally concentrated in small, eclectic, independent shops rather than impersonal malls. You can find excellent **folk art,** original **clothing** designs, and fine home accessories at great prices. Vallarta is known for having the most diverse and impressive selection of **contemporary Mexican fine art** outside Mexico City. It also has an abundance of tacky T-shirts and the ubiquitous **silver jewelry.**

### THE SHOPPING SCENE

There are a few key shopping areas: central downtown, the Marina Vallarta *malecón,* the popular *mercados,* and on the beach—where the merchandise comes to you. Some of the more attractive shops are found 1 to 2 blocks in **back of the *malecón.*** Start at the intersection of Corona and Morelos streets—interesting shops spread out in all directions from here. **Marina Vallarta** has two shopping plazas, Plaza Marina and Neptuno Plaza, both on the main highway coming from the airport into town, but both offer a limited selection of shops. **Neptuno Plaza,** anchored by a Radio Shack and Internet cafe, has recently become the better option. Although still home to a few interesting shops, the marina boardwalk (*marina malecón*) is dominated by real estate companies, timeshare vendors, restaurants, and boating services.

Puerto Vallarta's **municipal market** is just north of the Río Cuale, where Libertad and A. Rodríguez meet. The *mercado* sells clothes, jewelry, serapes, shawls, leather accessories and suitcases, papier-mâché parrots, stuffed frogs and armadillos, and, of course, T-shirts. Be sure to comparison-shop, and definitely bargain before buying. The market is open daily from 9am to 7pm. Upstairs, a **food market** serves inexpensive Mexican meals—for more adventurous diners,

# Downtown Puerto Vallarta

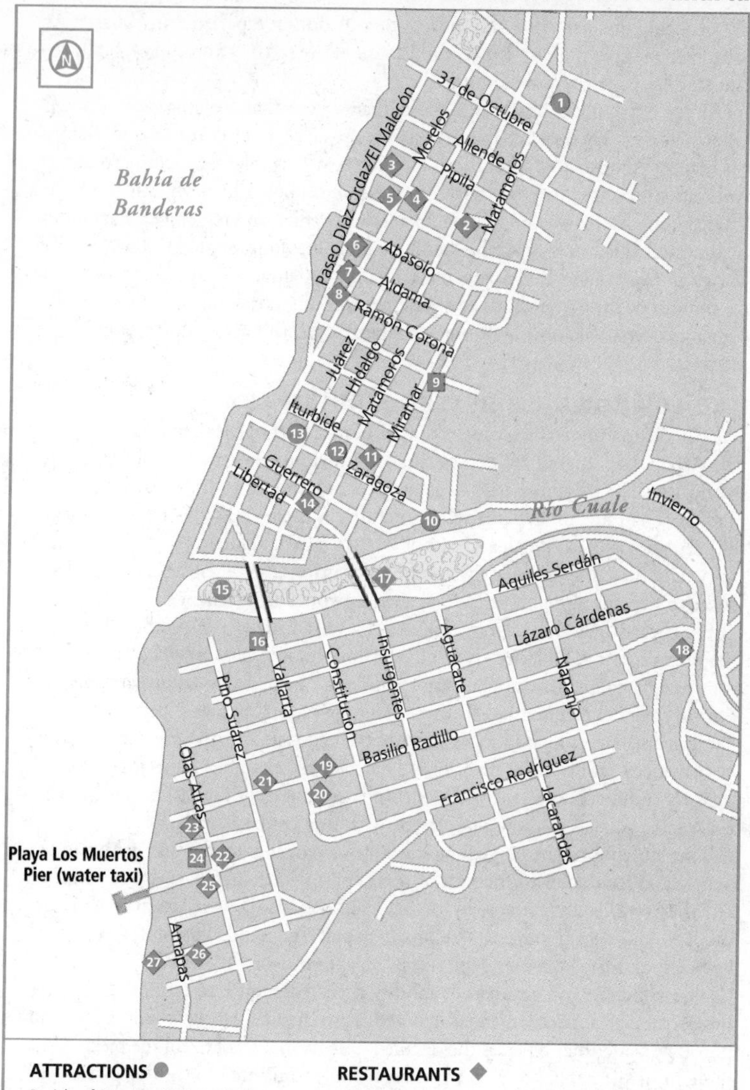


**ATTRACTIONS** ●

Parish of Nuestra Señora de Guadalupe **12**
Gringo Gulch (neighborhood) **10**
Main Square **13**
Isla del Río Cuale **15**
Terra Noble Center for the Arts **1**

**ACCOMMODATIONS** ■

Hotel Molino de Agua **16**
Hotel Playa Los Arcos **24**
Los Cuatro Vientos **9**

**RESTAURANTS** ◆

Adobe Café **20**
Archi's **3**
Archie's Wok **25**
Café des Artistes **2**
Café Kaiser Maximilian **23**
Café San Angel **22**
de Santos **5**
Fajita Republic **21**
Kit-Kat **26**
La Dolce Vita **6**
La Palapa **27**
Las Palomas **7**
Le Bistro **17**
Los Pibes **19**
Planet a Vegetariano **11**
Red Cabbage Café **18**
Rito's Baci **4**
Trio **14**
Tutifruti **8**

it's probably the best value and most authentic dining experience in Vallarta. An **outdoor market** is along Río Cuale Island, between the two bridges. Stalls sell crafts, gifts, folk art, and clothing.

Along any public beach, it's more than likely that walking **vendors** will approach you. Their merchandise ranges from silver jewelry to rugs and T-shirts to masks. "Almost free!" they'll call out, in seemingly relentless efforts to attract your attention. If you're too relaxed to think of shopping in town, this can be an entertaining alternative for picking up a few souvenirs, and remember: Bargaining is expected. The most reputable beach vendors are concentrated at Los Muertos Beach in front of the El Dorado and La Palapa restaurants (Calle Pulpito).

In most of the better shops and galleries, shipping, packing, and delivery services to Puerto Vallarta hotels are available. Some will also ship to your home address.

## THE LOWDOWN ON HUICHOL INDIAN ART

Puerto Vallarta offers the best selection of Huichol art in Mexico. Descendants of the Aztec, the Huichol are one of the last remaining indigenous cultures in the world that has remained true to its ancient traditions, customs, language, and habitat. The Huichol live in adobe structures in the high Sierras (at an elevation of 1,394m/4,600 ft.) north and east of Puerto Vallarta. Due to the decreasing fertility (and therefore productivity) of the land surrounding their villages, they have come to depend more on the sale of their artwork for sustenance.

Huichol art has always been cloaked in a veil of mysticism—probably one of the reasons serious collectors seek out this form of *artesanía.* Huichol art is characterized by colorful, symbolic yarn "paintings," inspired by visions experienced during spiritual ceremonies. In these ceremonies, artists ingest peyote, a hallucinogenic cactus, which induces brightly colored visions; these are considered to be messages from their ancestors. The visions' symbolic and mythological imagery influences the art, which encompasses not only yarn paintings but also fascinating masks and bowls decorated with tiny colored beads.

The Huichol might be geographically isolated, but they are savvy businesspeople and have adapted their art to meet consumer demand—original Huichol art, therefore, is not necessarily traditional. Iguanas, jaguars, sea turtles, frogs, eclipses, and eggs appear as a result of popular demand. For more traditional works, look for pieces that depict deer, scorpions, wolves, or snakes.

The Huichol have also had to modify their techniques to create more pieces in less time and meet increased demand. Patterned fill-work, which is faster to produce, sometimes replaces the detailed designs that used to fill the pieces. The same principle applies to yarn paintings. While some are beautiful depictions of landscapes and even abstract pieces, they are not traditional themes.

Huichol Indians may also be seen on the streets of Vallarta—they are easy to spot, dressed in white clothing embroidered with colorful designs. A number of

---

**Tips** **Beware the Silver Scam**

Much of the silver sold on the beach is actually alpaca, a lower-quality silver metal (even though many pieces are stamped with the designation ".925," supposedly indicating true silver). Prices for silver on the beach are much lower, as is the quality. If you're looking for a more lasting piece of jewelry, you're better off in a silver shop.

---

### Fun Fact A Huichol Art Primer: Tips for What to Buy

Huichol art falls into two main categories: yarn paintings and beaded pieces. All other items you might find in Huichol art galleries are either ceremonial objects or items used in everyday life.

**Yarn paintings** are made on a wood base covered with wax and meticulously overlaid with colored yarn. Designs represent the magical vision of the underworld, and each symbol gives meaning to the piece. Paintings made with wool yarn are more authentic than those made with acrylic; however, acrylic yarn paintings are usually brighter and have more detail because the threads are thinner. It is normal to find empty spaces where the wax base shows. Usually the artist starts with a central motif and works around it, but it's common to have several independent motifs that, when combined, take on a different meaning. A painting with many small designs tells a more complicated story than one with only one design and fill-work on the background. Look for the story of the piece on the back of the painting. Most Huichol artists write in pencil in Huichol and Spanish.

**Beaded pieces** are made on carved wooden shapes depicting different animals, wooden eggs, or small bowls made from gourds. The pieces are covered with wax and tiny *chaquira* beads are applied one by one to form designs. Usually the beaded designs represent animals; plants; the elements of fire, water, or air; and certain symbols that give a special meaning to the whole. Deer, snakes, wolves, and scorpions are traditional elements; other figures, such as iguanas, frogs, and any animals not indigenous to Huichol territory, are incorporated by popular demand. Beadwork with many small designs that do not exactly fit into one other is more time consuming and has a more complex symbolic meaning. This kind of work has empty spaces where the wax shows.

fine Huichol galleries are in downtown Puerto Vallarta (see individual listings under "Crafts & Gifts" and "Decorative & Folk Art," below).

A notable place for learning more about the Huichol is **Huichol Collection,** Morelos 490, across from the sea-horse statue on the *malecón* (**© 322/223-2141**). Not only does this shop offer an extensive selection of Huichol art in all price ranges, but it also has a replica of a Huichol adobe hut, informational displays explaining more about their fascinating way of life and beliefs, and usually a Huichol artist at work.

## CLOTHING

Vallarta's single true department store is **LANS,** with branches at Juárez 867 (**© 322/226-9100;** www.lans.com.mx), and in Plaza Caracol, next door to the supermarket Gigante, in the Hotel Zone (**© 322/226-9100**). Both offer a wide selection of name-brand clothing, accessories, footwear, cosmetics, and home furnishings. Along with the nationally popular **LOB, Carlos 'n' Charlie's,** and **Bye-Bye** brands, Vallarta offers a distinctive shop featuring original designs.

**Laura López Labra Designs** The most comfortable clothing you'll ever enjoy. LLL is renowned for her trademark all-white (or natural) designs in 100%

cotton or lace. Laura's fine gauze fabrics float in her designs of seductive skirts, romantic dresses, blouses, beachwear, and baby dolls. Men's offerings include cotton drawstring pants and lightweight shirts. Other designs include a line of precious children's clothing and some pieces with elaborate embroidery based on Huichol Indian designs. Personalized wedding dresses are also available. Open Monday to Saturday from 10am to 2pm and 5 to 9pm. Basilio Badillo 324. ✆ **322/222-3074.**

## CONTEMPORARY ART

Known for sustaining one of the stronger art communities in Latin America, Puerto Vallarta has an impressive selection of fine galleries featuring quality original works. The several dozen galleries get together to offer art walks almost every week between November and April, alternating between galleries in Marina Vallarta and downtown. These are a social highlight of Vallarta during high season.

**Galería AL (Arte Latinoamericano)** This gallery showcases contemporary works created by young, primarily Latin American artists, as well as Vallarta favorite Marta Gilbert. Feature exhibitions take place every two weeks during high season. The historic building (one of Vallarta's original structures) has exposed brick walls; small rooms of exhibition spaces on the second and third floors surround an open courtyard. It's also rumored to have a friendly resident ghost, who partner Susan Burger says has been quite welcoming. It's open Monday to Saturday from 10:30am to 9pm. Josefa Ortiz Dominguez 155. ✆ and fax **322/222-4406.**

**Galería Dante** This gallery-in-a-villa showcases contemporary sculptures and classical reproductions of Italian, Greek, and Art Deco bronzes—against a backdrop of gardens and fountains. Located on the "Calle de los cafés," the gallery is open during the winter Monday to Saturday from 10am to 5pm, and by appointment. Basilio Badillo 269. ✆ **322/222-2477.** Fax 322/222-6284. www.galleriadante.com.

**Galería Pacífico** Since opening in 1987, Galería Pacífico has been considered one of the finest galleries in Mexico. On display is a wide selection of sculptures and paintings in various media by midrange masters and up-and-comers alike. The gallery is 1½ blocks inland from the fantasy sculptures on the *malecón.* Among the artists whose careers Galería Pacifica has influenced are rising international sensation Rogelio Díaz, Ramiz Barquet, and Patrick Denoun. Open Monday to Saturday from 10am to 3pm and 5pm to 9pm, and Sunday by appointment. Between May and October, check for reduced hours or vacation closings. Aldama 174, 2nd floor. ✆ **322/222-5502.** www.artmexico.com.

**Galería Rosas Blancas** This notable member of Puerto Vallarta's gallery community features contemporary painters from throughout Mexico. The downstairs courtyard exhibition space showcases a featured artist, while the upstairs offers a sampling of the artists who regularly exhibit here. A shop next door sells art supplies and books on Mexican art in English and Spanish. Owner Marcella Alegría also runs the adjacent folk-art store, Querubines (see "Decorative & Folk Art," below). It's open Monday to Saturday from 9am to 9pm. Juárez 523. ✆ **322/222-1168.**

**Galería Uno** One of Vallarta's first galleries, the Galería Uno features an excellent selection of contemporary paintings by Latin American artists, plus a variety of posters and prints. During the high season, featured exhibitions change every two weeks. In a classic adobe building with open courtyard, it's also a casual, *salón*-style gathering place for friends of owner Jan Lavender. It's open

Monday to Saturday from 10am to 9pm. A branch, **Arte de las Americas** (✆ **322/221-1985**), is at Marina Vallarta between La Taberna and the Yacht Club. It exhibits some of the same artists but has a decidedly more abstract orientation. It's open Monday to Saturday 10am to 2pm and 5 to 9pm. Morelos 561 (at Corona). ✆ **322/222-0908.**

**Studio Cathy Von Rohr** This lovely studio showcases the work of Cathy Von Rohr, one of the most respected artists in the area. For years, Cathy lived in the secluded cove of Majahuitas, on the bay's southern shore, and much of her work reflects the tranquility and deep connection with the natural world that resulted. Paintings, prints, and sculptures are featured. It's open by appointment and does not accept credit cards. Manuel M. Dieguez 321. ✆ **866/256-2739** toll-free in the U.S., or **322/222-5875.** www.cathyvonrohr.com.

### CRAFTS & GIFTS

**Alfarería Tlaquepaque** Opened in 1953, this is Vallarta's original source for Mexican ceramics and decorative crafts, all at excellent prices. Talavera pottery and dishware, colored glassware, birdcages, baskets, and wood furniture are just a few of the many items in this warehouse-style store. It's open Monday to Sunday from 9am to 9pm. Av. México 1100. ✆ **322/223-2121.** www.at.com.mx.

**El Vuelo** Here you'll find ethnic and contemporary gifts, including world music (the Cuban selection is outstanding), books, woven fabrics, jewelry, and decorative objects for the home. It's open Monday to Friday from 9am to 9pm, Saturday from 9am to 3pm. Morelos 684, ½ block from American Express. ✆ **322/222-1822.**

**Safari Accents** Flickering candles glowing in colored-glass holders welcome you into this highly original shop overflowing with creative gifts, one-of-a-kind furnishings, and reproductions of paintings by Frida Kahlo and Botero. It's open daily from 9am to 11pm. Olas Altas 224, Local 5. ✆ **322/223-2660.**

### DECORATIVE & FOLK ART

**Azul Siempre Azul** Religious figurative pieces, antique *retablos* (painted scenes on tin backgrounds depicting the granting of a miracle), artistic jewelry, and beeswax candles in grand sizes all come together in this tiny store brimming with captivating treasures. It's open Monday to Saturday from 10am to 9pm. Ignacio L. Vallarta 228, across from Club Roxy, just over the southbound bridge. ✆ **322/223-0060.**

**La Tienda** Fine antiques and decorative objects for the home, including unique furniture, religious-themed items (including *retablos*), glassware, and pewter. There is also an outstanding selection of rustic candlesticks and beeswax candles, both in a variety of sizes. It's open Monday to Saturday from 10am to 2pm and 4 to 8pm. Rodolfo Gómez 122, near Los Muertos Beach. ✆ **322/222-1535.** latienda@pvnet.com.mx.

**Lucy's CuCu Cabaña and Zoo** *Finds* Owners Lucy and Gil Givens have assembled one of the most entertaining, eclectic, and memorable collections of Mexican folk art—about 70% of which is animal-themed. Each summer they travel and personally select the handmade works created by over 100 indigenous artists and artisans. Items include metal sculptures, Oaxacan wooden animals, *retablos* (commemorations of miracles), and fine Talavera ceramics. Five percent of all sales goes to benefit the Puerto Vallarta Animal Protection Association, organized by the Givenses. Hours are Monday to Saturday from 10am to 10pm. The store is closed May 15 to October 15. Basilio Badillo 295. No phone.

**Olinala** Two floors of fine indigenous Mexican crafts and folk art, including an impressive collection of museum-quality masks and original contemporary art by Brewster Brockman, the gallery owner. Hours are Monday to Friday from 10am to 2pm and 5 to 8pm, Saturday from 10am to 2pm. Cárdenas 274. ✆ 322/222-4995.

**Querubines** *Finds* This is my personal favorite for the finest-quality artisanal works from throughout Mexico. Owner Marcella García Alegría travels across the country to select the items, which include exceptional artistic silver jewelry, embroidered and hand-woven clothing, bolts of loomed fabrics, tin mirrors and lamps, glassware, pewter frames and trays, high-quality wool rugs, straw bags, and Panama hats. The store is open Monday to Saturday from 9am to 9pm. Under the same ownership and open the same hours, **Serafina,** Basilio Badillo 260 (✆ **322/223-4594**), features a more extensive selection of cotton clothing and one-of-a-kind handmade jewelry. Juárez 501A (corner of Galeana, behind Planet Hollywood). ✆ 322/223-1727.

## JEWELRY & ACCESSORIES

**Mosaiqe** It's a potpourri of global treasures—an extensive selection of silk, cotton, and cashmere pareos and shawls, plus resort bags, jewelry, and home décor items. There's a second location at Juarez 279 (✆ **322/223-3183**). It's open Monday to Saturday from 10am to 9pm, Sunday from noon to 8pm. Basilio Badillo 277. ✆ 322/223-3146.

**Viva** At Viva, both the shop and the jewelry are stunning. You enter through a long corridor lined with displays showcasing exquisite jewelry from 72 international designers. The main room has a large glass pyramid-shaped skylight as its roof, with comfy couches surrounded by memorable jewelry displays. Viva also features the largest selection of authentic French espadrilles and ballet slippers in Latin America. Hours are daily from 10am to 11pm. Basilio Badillo 274. ✆ 322/222-4078.

## TEQUILA & CIGARS

**La Casa del Habano** This fine tobacco shop has certified quality cigars from Cuba, Mexico, and the Dominican Republic, along with humidors, cutters, elegant lighters, and other smoking accessories. It's also a local cigar club, with a walk-in humidor for regular clients. In the back, you'll find comfy leather couches, TV sports, and full bar service—in other words, a manly place to take a break from shopping. It's open Monday to Saturday from 11am to 8pm. Aldama 170. ✆ 322/223-2758.

**La Casa del Tequila** Here you'll find an extensive selection of premium tequilas, plus information and tastings. Also available are cigars from Cuba and Veracruz, books, tequila glassware, humidors, and other tequila-drinking and cigar-smoking accessories. In the back, there's a garden patio with a bar that serves espresso drinks and tequila drinks, plus a taco bar that serves top-quality snacks with a terrific selection of salsas. It's open Monday to Saturday from 10am to 10pm. Morelos 589. ✆ 322/222-2000.

# WHERE TO STAY

Beyond a varied selection of hotels, Puerto Vallarta has many other types of accommodations. Oceanfront or marina-view condominiums and elegant private villas are also available; both can offer families and small groups a better value and more ample space than a hotel. For more information on short-term rentals, check out **www.virtualvallarta.com**, which lists a wide array of rental options. Prices start at $99 a night for non-beachfront condos and go to $1,000 for penthouse condos or private villas. One full-service travel agency that specializes in Puerto Vallarta villa rentals is **Holland's** (✆ **888/867-2723** or 618/236-2787; www.PuertoVallartaVillas.com). **Vicki Skinner's Doin' it Right in Puerto Vallarta** (✆ **800/936-3646** or 941/486-0505; www.DoinItRight.com) is a service that rents condos and villas for individuals and groups (up to 75 people), can package private chef and tour services with accommodations, and represents numerous gay-friendly properties.

This section lists hotels in directional order, moving south along Banderas Bay from the airport.

## MARINA VALLARTA

Marina Vallarta is the most modern and deluxe area of hotel development in Puerto Vallarta. Located immediately south of the airport and just north of the cruise-ship terminal, it's a planned development whose centerpiece is a 450-slip modern marina. The boardwalk surrounding the marina is filled with excellent restaurants, bars, galleries, and shops. A stay here is a world apart from the quaintness of downtown Puerto Vallarta.

The hotels reviewed below are on the beachfront of the peninsula. The beaches here are much less attractive than beaches in other parts of the bay; the sand is darker and firmly packed, and, during certain times of the year, quite rocky. These hotels compensate with oversized pool areas and exotic landscaping. Still, if you're longing for a beautiful beach, try one of the southern hotel options. This area is better for families and those looking for lots of centralized activity. Marina Vallarta is also home to an 18-hole **golf course** designed by Joe Finger. Also here, across from the Mayan Palace Resort, is the **Mayan Palace Aquapark** (✆ **322/226-6000,** ext. 824), with water slides and tubes, pools, an inner-tube canal, and snack-bar facilities. It's open to the public daily from 11am to 6pm and costs $15 for adults, $12 for kids.

In addition to the hotels reviewed below, another reliable choice is the **Hacienda Cora,** on the golf course at Pelicanos 311 (✆ **322/221-0800;** fax 322/221-0801). The elegant, boutique-style hotel has extra-large rooms, an onsite spa, and a lovely pool with shade cabañas. High season rates average $250.

Because of traffic more than distance, a taxi from the Marina to downtown takes 20 to 30 minutes.

**Velas Vallarta Grand Suite Resort** ★★★ *Kids* The beachfront Velas Vallarta is an excellent choice for families. Each suite offers a full-size, fully equipped kitchen, ample living and dining areas, separate bedroom or bedrooms, and a large balcony with seating. The apartments are tastefully decorated, with light wood furnishings, cool terrazzo floors, bright fabrics, and marble tub/shower combinations. This property is part hotel, part full-ownership condominiums, which means each suite is the size of a true residential unit, offering the feeling of a home away from home. The suites all have partial ocean views; they face a central area where three freeform swimming pools, complete with bridges and waterfalls, meander through tropical gardens. A full range of services—including restaurants, minimarket, deli, tennis courts, spa, and boutiques—means you'd never need to leave the place if you don't want to. The Marina Vallarta Golf Club is across the street, and special packages are available for Velas guests.

Paseo de la Marina 485, Marina Vallarta, Puerto Vallarta, Jal., 48354. ✆ **800/659-8477** in the U.S. and Canada, or 322/221-0091. Fax 322/221-0755. www.velasvallarta.com. 361 units. High season $258 double, $410–$760 suite; low season $211 double, $351–$700 suite. AE, DC, MC, V. Free indoor parking. **Amenities:** 2 restaurants, poolside snack bar, lobby bar; 3 pools; beach with watersports equipment rental; 3 lighted tennis courts; fitness center with spa and massage; minimarket; deli; salon; activities program for children and adults; bicycle rentals; golf privileges at Marina Vallarta Golf Club; laundry; car rental; concierge; room service; travel agency. *In room:* A/C, TV, dataport, full kitchen with coffeemaker, hair dryer, iron, safe.

**Westin Regina Resort** ★★★ Stunning architecture and vibrant colors are the hallmark of this award-winning property, considered Puerto Vallarta's finest. Although the grounds are large—over 21 acres with 258m (850 ft.) of beachfront—the warm service and gracious hospitality create the feeling of an intimate resort. Hundreds of tall palms surround the spectacular central freeform pool. Frequently you'll find hammocks strung between the palms closest to the beach, where there's a wooden playground for kids. Rooms are contemporary in style, brightly colored, with oversized wood furnishings, tile floors, original art, and tub/shower combinations. Balconies have panoramic views. Eight junior suites and selected double rooms have Jacuzzis, and the five grand suites and presidential suite are two-level, with ample living areas. Two floors of rooms make up the Royal Beach Club, with VIP services, including private concierge, plush bathrobes, continental breakfast, newspaper, cocktails, and canapés. The fitness center is one of the most modern, well-equipped facilities in Vallarta.

Paseo de la Marina Sur 205, Marina Vallarta, Puerto Vallarta, Jal., 48321. ✆ **800/228-3000** in the U.S., or 322/221-1100. Fax 322/221-1121. www.westinpv.com. 280 units. High season $258–$295 double, $585–$802 suite; low season $217–$234 double, $480–$600 suite. AE, DC, MC, V. Free parking. **Amenities:** 2 restaurants, 2 poolside bars, lobby bar; oceanside pool; 3 lighted grass tennis courts; full-service, state-of-the-art health club with treadmills, Stairmasters, resistance equipment, sauna, steam room, solarium, whirlpool, massage, and salon; golf privileges at Marina Vallarta Golf Club; Kid's Club; laundry; 24-hr. room service; travel agency; car rental; shopping arcade. *In room:* A/C, TV, dataport, minibar, coffeemaker, hair dryer, iron, safe-deposit box.

## THE HOTEL ZONE

The main street running between the airport and town is Avenida Francisco Medina Ascencio, commonly referred to as Avenida de las Palmas, for the stately palm trees that line the dividing strip. The hotels along this road were the result of the tourism boom that Vallarta enjoyed in the early 1980s, and most have been exceptionally well maintained. All offer excellent, wide beachfronts with generally tranquil waters for swimming. From here it's a quick taxi or bus ride to downtown.

**Blue Bay Getaway** ★ *Value* The newest hotel in Vallarta, this all-inclusive hotel caters to adults only and has an outstanding location just minutes from town on a wide, beautiful stretch of beach. It's also an exceptional value, with all meals, beverages, activities, and entertainment included in the price of your room. Blue Bay is becoming known for working to offer good value for all-inclusive stays—the buffets are varied, and you have the option of an a la carte restaurant.

Three types of rooms are available, all decorated in sunny golden and yellow hues with vibrant blue accents. The four-story Coral tower has the best rooms (double superior), with tile floors, small balconies with ocean or mountain views, and bathrooms with showers and tubs. The 11-story Arcos tower houses deluxe and standard rooms. Deluxe rooms are the most spacious, with private balconies and ocean views. Standard rooms are the least expensive and are smaller, do not have balconies, and have showers without tubs. These rooms offer mountain views only, through small, curtained windows, but are a great value, especially since you probably won't spend too much time in your room. The hotel is next door to the Sheraton Buganvilias, which is larger, offers family activities and a disco, but doesn't have as nice a beach. Guests at the Blue Bay Getaway may use the facilities at the Blue Bay Club, on the southern shore of Puerto Vallarta. Shuttles run between the two resorts every hour.

Av. Francisco Medina Ascencio km 1.5, Puerto Vallarta, Jal. ✆ **322/223-3600.** Fax 322/223-3601. www.bluebayresorts.com. 358 units. High season $92 per person standard double, $106 per person superior double, $114 per person deluxe double; low season $87 per person standard double, $93 per person superior double, $101 per person deluxe double. Rates are all-inclusive (food, drink, nightly entertainment, nonmotorized watersports). AE, MC, V. Free parking. Children not accepted. **Amenities:** 2 restaurants, snack bar, 5 bars; nightly entertainment and shows; large beachfront pool with activities; smaller, quieter pool with wet bar; tennis court; spa with sauna, whirlpool tub, massage; nonmotorized watersports equipment; bikes; salon; small shopping strip with art and crafts shops; tour desk; car rental desk; laundry and dry cleaning service; safe-deposit boxes in reception area. *In room:* A/C, TV, hair dryer, safe-deposit boxes ($2/day).

**Fiesta Americana Puerto Vallarta** ★ The Fiesta Americana's towering, three-story, thatched *palapa* lobby is a landmark in the Hotel Zone, and the hotel is known for its excellent beach and friendly service. An abundance of plants, splashing fountains, constant breezes, and comfortable seating areas in the lobby create a casual South Seas ambience. The nine-story terracotta-colored building embraces a large plaza with a pool facing the beach. Marble-trimmed rooms in neutral tones with pastel accents contain carved headboards and comfortable rattan and wicker furniture. All have private balconies with ocean and pool views.

Av. Francisco Medina Ascencio km 2.5, Puerto Vallarta, Jal., 48300. ✆ **322/224-2010.** Fax 322/224-2108. www.fiestaamericana.com. 291 units. High season $232 double, $256–$819 suite; low season $148 double, $256–$819 suite. AE, DC, MC, V. Limited free parking. **Amenities:** 3 restaurants, lobby bar with live music nightly; large pool with activities, and children's activities in high season; laundry; room service; travel agency; salon. *In room:* A/C, TV, minibar, hair dryer, safe.

## DOWNTOWN TO LOS MUERTOS BEACH

This part of town has recently undergone a renaissance; economical hotels and good-value guesthouses dominate the accommodations market. Several blocks off the beach, you can find numerous budget inns offering clean, simply furnished rooms; most offer discounts for long-term stays. The neighborhood is older, but very friendly and generally safe. Most of Vallarta's nightlife activity now centers in the areas south of the Río Cuale and along Olas Altas.

**Hotel Molino de Agua** ★ With an unrivaled location adjacent to both the Río Cuale and the ocean, this hotel is a mix of stone and stucco-walled bungalows and small beachfront buildings, spread out among winding walkways and lush tropical gardens. It's immediately past the Río Cuale—after crossing the southbound bridge, it's on your right. Although it's centrally located on a main street, open spaces, big trees, birds, and lyrical fountains lend it tranquility. The individual bungalows are in the gardens between the entrance and the ocean. They are well maintained and simply furnished, with a bed, wooden desk and chair, Mexican tile floors, beamed ceilings, and beautiful tile bathrooms. Wicker rocking chairs grace the private patios. Rooms and suites in the two small two- and three-story buildings on the beach have double beds, private terraces, and are decorated in rustic Mexican style.

Vallarta 130 (Apdo. Postal 54), Puerto Vallarta, Jal., 48380. ✆ **322/222-1957.** Fax 322/222-6056. www.molinodeagua.com. 58 units. High season garden bungalow $120 double, oceanfront room or suite $143–$195 double; low season bungalow $88 double, suite $106–$132 double. AE, MC, V. Free secured parking. **Amenities:** Restaurant and bar; beachside pool; pool with whirlpool; tour desk; car rental desk. *In room:* A/C.

**Hotel Playa Los Arcos** ★★ This is one of Vallarta's perennially popular hotels and a favorite of mine, with a stellar location in the heart of Los Muertos Beach, central to the Olas Altas sidewalk-cafe action and close to downtown. The four-story structure is U-shaped, facing the ocean, with a small swimming pool in the courtyard. Rooms with private balconies overlook the pool. The 10 suites have ocean views; 5 of these have kitchenettes. The standard rooms are small but pleasantly decorated and immaculate, with carved wooden furniture painted pale pink. On the premises are a *palapa* beachside bar with occasional live entertainment, a gourmet coffee shop, and the popular Maximilian's gourmet restaurant. It's 7 blocks south of the river.

Olas Altas 380, Puerto Vallarta, Jal., 48380. ✆ **800/648-2403** in the U.S., or 322/222-1583. Fax 322/222-2418. www.playalosarcos.com. 175 units. High season $116–$140 double, $166 suite; low season $91 double, $137 suite. AE, MC, V. Limited street parking. **Amenities:** 2 restaurants, lobby bar; pool; tour desk; car rental services; laundry; babysitting; safe-deposit boxes and money exchange at front desk. *In room:* A/C, TV.

**Los Cuatro Vientos** ★★ This quiet, secluded inn is in the center of downtown on a hillside overlooking Banderas Bay. Rooms surround a small central patio. A short flight of stairs takes you to the second-floor patio, which holds the pool, flowering trees, and the cozy Chez Elena restaurant. The cheerful, spotless, colorful rooms have fans, small tiled bathrooms, brick ceilings, red-tile floors, and glass-louvered windows. Each is decorated with simple Mexican furnishings, folk art, and antiques. The rooftop deck and El Nido bar have a panoramic view of the city; open from 3:30 to 10:30pm, it's great for late afternoon sunning, and the best place in the city for sunset drinks. The restaurant serves continental breakfast for guests only from 6 to 11am.

The hotel is a favorite with solo women travelers, and even offers weeklong "Women's Getaway" packages several times a year, with cultural discussions and recreational activities.

Matamoros 520, Puerto Vallarta, Jal., 48300. ✆ **322/222-0161.** Fax 322/222-2831. www.cuatrovientos.com. 14 units. High season $55 double, $69 suite (up to 4 people); low-season discounts available. Rates higher at Christmas and New Year's. Rates include continental breakfast. MC, V. Very limited street parking. **Amenities:** Restaurant (Mexican; open daily 6–11pm), rooftop bar; small courtyard pool.

### SOUTH TO MISMALOYA

**Camino Real** ★★★ The original luxury hotel in Puerto Vallarta, the Camino Real has retained its place as a premier property. Scores of loyal guests think only of staying here, and its free classical concerts (held the first Thurs of each month) occupy an integral place in the local community. It has unquestionably the nicest beach of any Vallarta hotel, with soft white sand in a private cove. Set apart from other properties, with a lush mountain backdrop, it retains the exclusivity that made it popular from the beginning—yet it's only a 5- to 10-minute ride to town. The hotel consists of two buildings: the 250-room main hotel, which curves gently with the shape of the Playa Las Estacas, and the newer 11-story Camino Real Club tower, also facing the beach and ocean. An ample pool fronts the main building, facing the beach. Standard rooms in the main building are large; some have sliding doors opening onto the beach, and others have balconies. A two-story Presidential suite in the main building has a large private pool. Royal Beach Club rooms (from the sixth floor up) feature balconies with whirlpool tubs. The top floor consists of six two-bedroom Fiesta Suites, each with a private swimming pool. All rooms have the signature vibrant colors of Camino Real hotels. Under new ownership, the already well-maintained hotel recently underwent renovations and upgrades.

Carretera Barra de Navidad km 3.5, Playa Las Estacas, Puerto Vallarta, Jal., 48300. ✆ **800/722-6466** in the U.S. and Canada, or 322/221-5000. Fax 322/221-6000. www.caminoreal.com. 337 units. High season $180–$410 double, $600–$1,000 suite; low season $166–$242 double, $570–$880 suite. AE, DC, MC, V. Free secured parking. **Amenities:** 4 restaurants, lobby bar, pool bar; swimming pool; beach *palapas* with chair, towel, and dining service; 2 lighted grass tennis courts; fitness room with weights; convenience store;

laundry; 24-hr. room service; travel agency; car rental; children's program (Easter and Christmas vacations). *In room:* A/C, TV, minibar, dataport, hair dryer, iron, safe-deposit box.

**Casa Tres Vidas** ★★ *Value* Terraced down a hillside to Conchas Chinas Beach, Casa Tres Vidas is three individual villas that make a great, affordable place to stay for families or groups of friends. Set on a stunning private cove, Tres Vidas gives you the experience of your own private villa, complete with service staff. It offers outstanding value for the location—close to town, with sweeping panoramic views from every room—as well as for the excellent personal service. Each villa has at least two levels and over 465 square m (5,000 sq. ft.) of mostly open living areas, plus a private swimming pool, heated whirlpool, and air-conditioned bedrooms. The Vida Alta penthouse villa has three bedrooms, plus a rooftop deck with pool and bar. Vida Sol villa has an 18-foot-high domed living room with fireplace. Its three bedrooms sleep 10 (two rooms have two king-size beds each). Directly on the ocean, Vida Mar is a four-bedroom villa, accommodating 8. A bonus is that the staff prepares gourmet meals in your villa twice a day—you choose the menu and pay only for the food.

Sagitario 134, Playa Conchas Chinas, Puerto Vallarta, Jal., 48300. ✆ **888/640-8100** or 801/531-8100 in the U.S., or 322/221-5317. Fax 322/221-53-27. www.casatresvidas.com. 3 villas. High season $568–$597 villa; low season $410–$439 villa. Rates include services. Special summer 1- or 2-bedroom rates available; minimum 3 nights. AE, MC, V. Very limited street parking. **Amenities:** 2 prepared daily meals; private pool; concierge; tour desk; car rental. *In room:* Kitchen facilities, safe-deposit boxes.

**Quinta María Cortez** ★★★ *Finds* A sophisticated, imaginative B&B on the beach, this is Puerto Vallarta's most original place to stay—and one of Mexico's most memorable inns. Most of the seven large suites, uniquely decorated with antiques, whimsical curios, and original art, have a kitchenette and balcony. Sunny terraces, a small pool, and a central gathering area with fireplace and *palapa*-topped dining area (where an excellent full breakfast is served) occupy different levels of this seven-story house. A rooftop terrace offers another sunbathing alternative—and is among the best sunset-watching spots in town. The *quinta* is on a beautiful cove on Conchas Chinas beach, and the rocks just offshore form tide pools, perfect for wading and snuggling. A terrace fronting the beach supports Roman columns and accommodates chairs for taking in the sunset.

The Quinta María wins my highest recommendation (in fact, I enjoyed living here for a few years when it still accepted long-term stays), but admittedly it's not for everyone. Air-conditioned areas are limited, due to the open nature of the suites and common areas, but then, that's a large part of the charm. Breakfast is served under a thatched-roof area, overlooking the pool and ocean below. Those who love it return year after year, charmed by this remarkable place, and by the consistently gracious service.

Sagitario 132, Playa Conchas Chinas, Puerto Vallarta, Jal., 48300. ✆ **888/640-8100** or 801/536-5850 in the U.S., or 322/221-5317. Fax 322/221-53-27. www.quinta-maria.com. 7 units. High season $150–$275 double; low season $106–$205 double. Rates include breakfast. AE, MC, V. Very limited street parking. Children not accepted. **Amenities:** Small pool; concierge. *In room:* CD players, dataport, mini-refrigerator, coffeemaker, hair dryer, safe-deposit box.

## WHERE TO DINE

Puerto Vallarta has the most exceptional dining scene of any resort town in Mexico. Over 250 restaurants serve cuisines from around the world in addition to fresh seafood and regional dishes. Chefs from France, Switzerland, Germany, Italy, and Argentina have come for visits and stayed to open restaurants. In celebration of this diversity, Vallarta's culinary community hosts a 2-week-long Gourmet Dining Festival as part of its annual SeaFest each November.

Dining is not limited to high-end options—there are plenty of small, family-owned restaurants, local Mexican kitchens, and vegetarian cafes. Vallarta also has its branches of the world food-and-fun chains: Hard Rock Cafe, Planet Hollywood, Outback Steakhouse, and even Hooters. I won't bother to review these restaurants, where the consistency and decor are so familiar.

Of the inexpensive local spots, one long-standing favorite for light meals and fresh fruit drinks is **Tutifruti,** Morelos 552 (© **322/222-1068**). It's open Monday to Saturday from 8am to 8pm. No credit cards. A favorite for cheap eats is **Archi's,** Morelos 799 at Pípila, behind Carlos O'Brian's (© **322/222-4383**). It serves only char-grilled hamburgers, chicken burgers, fish filet burgers, hot dogs, and homemade fries in a surfer-inspired atmosphere. It's open Tuesday to Sunday from 11am to 1am; cash only; delivery available. **El Planeta Vegetariano,** Iturbide 270, just down from the main church (© **322/222-3073**), serves an inexpensive, bountiful, and delicious vegetarian lunch buffet. It's available Monday to Saturday from 11am to 5:30pm, and costs $4.50 (no credit cards). The restaurant serves dinner a la carte from 6 to 10pm.

## MARINA VALLARTA

Contrary to conventional travel wisdom, most of the best restaurants in the Marina are in hotels. Especially notable are **Andrea** (fine Italian cuisine), at Velas Vallarta, and **Garibaldi** (exceptional seafood), on the beachfront of the Westin Regina Resort. (See "Where to Stay," earlier, for more information.) Other choices are along the boardwalk bordering the marina yacht harbor. My pick for the best "cheap eats" in the area are the fish tacos at **Marina Fish Taco,** in the Las Palmas II commercial center at the eastern entrance to the marina *malecón* (no phone). A variety of fish and seafood tacos cost just $1.50 per order. It's open Monday to Saturday from noon to 8pm. Also notable is the **Café Gourmet,** next to the Vallarta Adventures offices in Condominiums Marina Golf, Local 11 (© **322/221-0362**). It serves excellent coffee and espresso drinks. Hours are Monday to Saturday from 8am to 10pm, Sunday from 5pm to 10pm.

**Benitto's** ★★ CAFE Wow! What a sandwich! Benitto's food would be reason enough to come to this tiny, terrific cafe inside the Plaza Neptuno—but added to this are the original array of sauces and the very personable service. This place is popular with locals for light breakfasts, filling lunches, and fondue and wine in the evenings. It's the best place in town to find pastrami, corned beef, or other traditional (gringo!) sandwich fare, all served on your choice of gourmet bread. Draft beer and wine are available, as are Benitto's specialty infused waters. A new location is scheduled to open soon downtown, on Josefa Ortiz de Dominguez and Juarez, with the same menu in a larger location.

Inside Plaza Neptuno. © **322/209-0288** or 322/209-0287. benittosdeli@prodigy.net.mx. Breakfast $3–$6; main courses $5–$7. No credit cards. Daily 8:30am–10:30pm

**Porto Bello** ★ ITALIAN One of the first restaurants in the marina, this remains a favorite, serving authentically flavorful Italian dishes with exceptional service in your choice of an elegant interior or marina-front setting. For starters, fried calamari is delicately seasoned, and grilled vegetable antipasto could easily serve as a full meal. Signature dishes include fusilli prepared with artichokes, black olives, lemon juice, basil, olive oil, and Parmesan cheese, and sautéed fish filet with shrimp and clams in saffron tomato sauce. Indoor dining is air-conditioned, and there is occasionally live music in the evening.

Marina Sol, Local 7 (Marina Vallarta *malecón*). © **322/221-0003**. Main courses $7–$19. AE, MC, V. Daily noon–11pm.

## DOWNTOWN

It's not that I'm particularly partial to Italian or Continental cuisine; it just happens that the best restaurants here happen to fall into these categories. Although Vallarta has over 250 restaurants, it lacks in the categories of Mexican cuisine and seafood. It does boast an exceptional community of European chefs—our good fortune!

### Expensive

**Café des Artistes** ★★ FRENCH/INTERNATIONAL This sophisticated restaurant is known as the place in town for that very special evening. Located in a restored house that resembles a castle, with an interior that combines murals, lush fabrics and an array of original works of art, Café des Artistes is the creation of award-winning Chef Thierry Blouet, a member of the French Academie Culinaire and Maitre Cuisinier de France. The Nobel Prize–winning Mexican novelist Carlos Fuentes wrote of this restaurant, "At Café des Artistes, there is no dish that is not a work of art, nor a work of art that does not feed the spirit."

There are three dining areas—the streetside balcony, the interior dining rooms, and my personal favorite, the terraced garden. Despite the decorative setting, the real star here is the food. The menu is highly original, with dishes drawing heavily on chef Blouet's French training, yet using regional specialty ingredients. Noteworthy entrees include shrimp sautéed with mushrooms, *guajillo chile* and *raicilla* sauce, and the renowned roasted duck glazed with honey, soy, ginger, and lime sauce, served with pumpkin risotto. And speaking of pumpkin, don't miss the signature starter, pumpkin and prawn soup served from a carved gourd. Chef Blouet started his culinary career as a pastry chef, so be sure to save room for one of his desserts, which are as lovely to look at as they are to savor. The only downside here is that it is easily the most expensive meal in town, but it's worth the splurge.

Guadalupe Sanchez 740. ✆ **322/222-3228,** 322/222-3229, or 322/222-3230. www.cafedesartistes.com. Main courses $17–$31. AE, MC, V. Daily 6–11:30pm.

### Moderate

**de Santos** ★★ MEDITERRANEAN After opening a couple of years ago, de Santos quickly became the hot spot in town for late-night dining and bar action. Although the food initially didn't live up to the atmosphere and music, now it absolutely does. It's Mediterranean-inspired; best bets include lightly breaded calamari, paella Valenciana, and excellent thin-crust pizzas. Also ask about nightly specials. The cool, refined interior feels more urban than resort, and it boasts the most sophisticated sound system in town—including a DJ who spins to match the mood of the crowd. It probably helps that one of the partners is also a member of the wildly popular Latin group Mana. Prices are extremely reasonable for the quality and overall experience of an evening here.

Morelos 771, Centro. ✆ **322/223-3052.** Main courses $5–$20. AE, MC, V. Daily 5pm–1am; bar closes at 4am on weekends.

**La Dolce Vita** ★★ ITALIAN This popular eatery combines good food, a casually upbeat atmosphere, attentive service, and great entertainment. Overlooking the *malecón,* La Dolce Vita offers excellent views and prime people-watching through its oversized windows and from the second-floor balcony. Despite its choice location and superb food, prices remain more than reasonable. The food is authentic in preparation and flavor, from thin-crust, brick-oven pizzas to savory homemade pastas—my favorite is "Braccio de Fiero," topped with spinach, black olives, and fresh tomatoes. The Sweet Life, the house band, plays sultry jazz Thursday and Friday evenings.

Paseo Díaz Ordaz 674, Centro. ✆ **322/222-3852.** Main courses $6.50–$17. AE, MC, V. Mon–Sat noon–2am; Sun 6pm–1am.

**Las Palomas** MEXICAN One of Puerto Vallarta's first restaurants, this is the power-breakfast place of choice—and a popular hangout for everyone else throughout the day. Authentic in atmosphere and menu, it's one of Puerto Vallarta's few genuine Mexican restaurants, with the atmosphere of a gracious home. Breakfast is the best value, with mugs of steaming coffee spiced with cinnamon poured as soon as you're seated. Try classic *huevos rancheros* or *chilaquiles* (tortilla strips, fried and topped with red or green spicy sauce, cream, cheese, and fried eggs). Lunch and dinner offer traditional Mexican specialties, plus a selection of stuffed crêpes. The best places for checking out the *malecón* and watching the sun set while sipping an icy margarita are the spacious bar and upstairs terrace.

Paseo Díaz Ordaz 594. ✆ **322/222-3675.** Breakfast $8–$12; lunch $8.50–$22; main courses $8.50–$22. AE, MC, V. Daily 8am–midnight.

**Rito's Baci** ★★ ITALIAN If the food weren't reason enough to come here (and it definitely is!), then Rito himself would be, with his gentle, devoted attention to every detail of this cozy *trattoria.* His grandfather emigrated from Italy, so the recipes and tradition of Italian food come naturally to him. So does his passion for food—it's obvious as he describes the specialties, which include lasagna (vegetarian, *verde,* or meat-filled); ravioli stuffed with spinach and ricotta; spaghetti with garlic, anchovy, and lemon zest; or a side of homemade Italian sausage. Everything is made by hand from fresh ingredients. Pizza-lovers favor the Piedmonte, with that famous sausage and mushrooms, and the Horacio, a cheeseless pizza with tomatoes, oregano, and basil. Sandwiches come hot or cold; arrive hungry, as they're a two-handed operation. Because Rito offers home and hotel delivery, I enjoy his food more than any other restaurant's! It's 1½ blocks off the *malecón.*

Domínguez 181 (between Morelos and Juárez). ✆ **322/222-6448.** Pasta $8–$17.25; salads and sandwiches $3.50–$7; pizza $13–$17.25. MC, V. Daily 1–11:30pm.

**Trio** ★★★ *Finds* INTERNATIONAL Trio is the current darling of Vallarta restaurants, with diners beating a path to the modest but stylish cafe where chef/owner Bernhard Güth's undeniable passion for food imbues each dish. Chef Güth combines local ingredients with impressive culinary experience; memorable entrees include San Blas shrimp in roasted red pepper and mango sauce, risotto with wild mushrooms, ricotta ravioli with sun-dried tomatoes, and grilled sea bass with vegetables, served in black olive salsa. These dishes may not be on the menu when you arrive, though—it's a constantly changing work of art. Trio is noted for the perfected melding of Mexican and Mediterranean flavors. Despite the sophisticated menu, the atmosphere is always comfortable and welcoming, and Bernhard is regularly seen chatting with guests at the end of the evening. There is also a rooftop bar area for a more comfortable wait for a table or for after-dinner coffee. A real treat!

Guerrero 264. ✆ **322/222-2196.** Reservations recommended. Main courses $13.50–$25.50. AE, MC, V. Year-round daily 6pm–midnight; high season Mon–Fri noon–3:30pm.

### SOUTH OF THE RÍO CUALE TO OLAS ALTAS

South of the river is the densest restaurant area, where you'll find the street Basilio Badillo, nicknamed "Restaurant Row." A second main dining drag has emerged along Calle Olas Altas, with a variety of cuisines and price categories. Its wide sidewalks are lined with cafes and espresso bars, generally open from 7am to midnight.

### Expensive

**Café Kaiser Maximilian** ★★ INTERNATIONAL This bistro-style cafe has a casually elegant atmosphere with a genuinely European feel. It's the prime place to go if you want to combine exceptional food with great people-watching. Austrian-born owner Andreas Rupprechter is always on hand to ensure that the service is as impeccable as the food is delicious. Indoor, air-conditioned dining is at cozy tables; sidewalk tables are larger and great for groups of friends. The cuisine merges old-world European preparations with regional fresh ingredients. My favorite is filet of trout with almonds and white-wine sauce, served on a bed of spinach—so much so that I've never tried any other dish, although friends tell me mustard chicken with mashed potatoes is excellent, and braised baby lamb with rosemary and poblano peppers is simply divine. The restaurant also offers northern European classics like *Rahmschnitzel* (sautéed pork loin and homemade noodles in creamy mushroom sauce). Desserts are especially tempting, as are gourmet coffees—Maximilian has an Austrian cafe and pastry shop next door.

Olas Altas 380-B (at Basilio Badillo, in front of the Hotel Playa Los Arcos), Zona Romantica. ✆ **322/223-0760.** Reservations recommended in high season. Main courses $16–$26. AE, MC, V. Mon–Sat 6–11pm.

**Le Bistro** ★★ MEXICAN/INTERNATIONAL A long-standing favorite for dining, Le Bistro is especially enjoyable for breakfast. I consider a morning meal here one of Vallarta's best values. Le Bistro is known for its elegant décor, great recorded jazz music, and open-air setting on the island in the midst of the Río Cuale—all creating a singular experience that blends sophistication in a typically Vallarta atmosphere. Favorite choices at breakfast are eggs Benedict and eggs *motuleño* style (sunny side up, smothered in tomato-based sauce and served with cheese, peas, and fried plantains). The specialty is crêpes, which come in a variety of flavors for breakfast, lunch, or dinner. Especially scrumptious are those filled with chicken breast and squash blossoms (a Mexican delicacy) in hollandaise sauce. The menu also has an excellent selection of innovative Mexican cuisine, including duck in Oaxacan black *mole,* and rock Cornish hen stuffed with herbed rice, dried tropical fruits, and nuts, finished in mango cilantro sauce. The vegetarian offerings are more creative than most. An impressive wine list and ample selection of specialty coffees complements the menu.

Isla Rio Cuale 16-A (just east of northbound Cuale bridge). ✆ **322/222-2083.** www.lebistro.com. Reservations recommended in high season. Breakfast $5–$8; main courses $18.50–$24.50. AE, MC, V. Mon–Sat 9am–midnight.

**Los Pibes** ★★ ARGENTINEAN/STEAKS You won't find a better steak anywhere in Vallarta—or many other places. Los Pibes offers signature thick cuts, exceptional quality, and a variety of preparations. Argentinean Cristina Juhas opened this restaurant in 1994 for her *pibes* (children), and the rave reviews have grown over the years. You select your huge portion of steak from a tray of fresh meat (all imported from the U.S.). While it's being prepared, try a wonderful *empanada* filled with meat or corn and cheese, or savor an order of *alubias,* marinated beans served with bread. The homemade sausage is also delicious, and you won't find a better *chimichurri* sauce. In addition to beef, Los Pibes has an ample selection of salads, side dishes, chicken, and pastas, as well as an excellent wine list. A second location, equally delicious, is on the Marina Vallarta *malecón* (✆ **322/221-0669**).

Basilio Badillo 261 (at Ignacio Vallarta). ✆ **322/223-1557.** Reservations recommended in high season. Main courses $18.50–$24.50. AE, MC, V. Mon–Sat 5pm–11:30pm.

## Moderate

**Adobe Café** ★★ INTERNATIONAL Adobe Café offers a classically chic atmosphere in which to enjoy innovative cuisine based on traditional Mexican specialties. Santa Fe–style decor with rustic wood accents provides a serene backdrop, and tables are comfortably large for enjoying a leisurely meal. Waiters are attentive without being intrusive. The menu features imaginative dishes, including grilled jumbo shrimp battered in coconut and served with homemade apple sauce, penne pasta with Italian sausage in creamy tequila sauce, and tenderloin of beef stuffed with *huitlacoche* in cheese sauce—to name just a few specialties. Owner Rodolfo Choperena is almost always on hand, which accounts for the consistently fine food and service.

Basilio Badillo 252 (at Ignacio Vallarta). ✆ **322/222-6720** or 322/223-1925. www.adobecafe.com.mx. Reservations recommended in high season. Main courses $12–$22. MC, V. Wed–Mon 6–11pm. Closed Aug–Sept.

**Archie's Wok** ★★★ *Finds* ASIAN/SEAFOOD Since 1986, Archie's has been legendary in Puerto Vallarta for serving original cuisine influenced by the intriguing flavors of Thailand, China, and the Philippines. Archie was Hollywood director John Huston's private chef during the years he spent in the area. Today his wife Cindy upholds his legacy at this tranquil retreat. The Thai Mai Tai and other tropical drinks, made from only fresh fruit and juices, are a good way to kick off a meal, as are the consistently crispy and delicious Filipino spring rolls. The popular Singapore fish filet features lightly battered filet strips in sweet-and-sour sauce; Thai garlic shrimp are prepared with fresh garlic, ginger, cilantro, and black pepper. Vegetarians have plenty of options, including broccoli, tofu, mushroom, and cashew stir-fry in a black bean and sherry sauce. Finish with the signature Spice Islands coffee, or a slice of lime cheese pie. Thursday to Saturday from 8 to 11pm, there's live classical harp and flute in Archie's Oriental garden.

Francisco Rodríguez 130 (½ block from the Los Muertos pier). ✆ **322/222-0411.** awok@pvnet.com.mx. Main courses $6–$21. AE, MC, V. Mon–Sat 2–11pm. Closed Sept–Oct.

**La Palapa** ★ SEAFOOD/MEXICAN This colorful, open-air, *palapa*-roofed restaurant on the beach is a decades-old local favorite, but with each recent visit, I have found the quality of both the food and service keeps improving—it's an exceptional dining experience, day or night. Enjoy a tropical breakfast by the sea, lunch on the beach, cocktails at sunset, or a romantic dinner (on a cloth-covered table in the sand). For lunch and dinner, seafood is the specialty; featured dishes include grilled shrimp in a *guajillo* (chile) and mango sauce, and poached red snapper with fresh cilantro sauce. Its location in the heart of Los Muertos Beach makes it an excellent place to start or end the day; I favor it for breakfast or, even better, a late-night sweet temptation and specialty coffee, while watching the moon over the bay. A particular draw is the all-you-can-eat Sunday brunch, which entitles you to a spot on popular Los Muertos beach for the day. There are acoustic guitars and vocals nightly from 8 to 11pm, generally performed by the owner Alberto himself.

Pulpito 103. ✆ **322/222-5225.** Reservations recommended for dinner in high season. Breakfast $2.50–$10; main courses $9.50–$25; salad or sandwiches $6.70–$10. AE, MC, V. Daily 9am–11:30pm.

### Inexpensive

**Café San Angel** CAFE This comfortable, classic sidewalk cafe is a local gathering place from sunrise to sunset. For breakfast, choose a *burrito* stuffed with eggs and *chorizo* sausage, a three-egg Western omelet, crêpes filled with mushrooms, or a tropical fruit plate. Deli sandwiches, crêpes, and pastries round out the small but ample menu. It also has exceptional fruit smoothies, like the Yelapa—a blend of mango, banana, and orange juice—and perfectly made espresso drinks. Note that the service is reliably slow and frequently frustrating, so choose this place if you have time on your side. Bar service and Internet access are available.

Olas Altas 449 (at Francisco Rodríguez). ✆ **322/223-2160.** Breakfast $3.50–$5; main courses $3.50–$6. Daily 7am–2am.

**Fajita Republic** ★★ MEXICAN/SEAFOOD/STEAKS Fajita Republic is consistently popular—and deservedly so. It has hit on a winning recipe: delicious food, ample portions, welcoming atmosphere, and low prices. The specialty is, of course, *fajitas,* grilled to perfection in every variety: steak, chicken, shrimp, combo, and vegetarian. All come with a generous tray of salsas and toppings. This "tropical grill" also serves sumptuous barbecued ribs, Mexican *molcajetes* with incredibly tender strips of marinated beef filet, and grilled shrimp. Starters include fresh guacamole served in a giant spoon and the ever-popular Mayan cheese sticks (breaded and deep-fried). Try an oversized mug or pitcher of Fajita Rita Mango Margaritas—or another spirited temptation. This is a casual, fun, festive place in a garden of mango and palm trees.

Pino Suárez 321 (at Basilio Badillo), 1 block north of Olas Altas. ✆ **322/222-3131.** Breakfast $3.60–$4.70; main courses $9–$17. MC, V. Daily 9am–midnight.

**Red Cabbage Café (El Repollo Rojo)** ★★ *Finds* MEXICAN The tiny, hard-to-find cafe is worth the effort—a visit here will reward you with exceptional traditional Mexican cuisine and a whimsical crash course in contemporary culture. The small room is covered wall to wall and table to table with photographs, paintings, movie posters, and news clippings about the cultural icons of Mexico. Frida Kahlo figures prominently in the decor, and a special menu duplicates dishes she and husband Diego Rivera prepared for guests.

Specialties from all over Mexico include divine *chiles en nogada* (poblanos stuffed with ground beef, pine nuts, and raisins, topped with sweet cream sauce and served cold), intricate chicken *mole* from Puebla, and hearty *carne en su jugo* (steak in its juice). In addition, this is probably the most diverse, tasty vegetarian menu in town (the owner offers cooking classes for groups of four or more). This is not the place for an intimate conversation, however—the poor acoustics cause everyone's conversations to blend together, although generally what you're hearing from adjacent tables are raves about the food.

Calle Rivera del Río 204A (across from Río Cuale). ✆ **322/223-0411.** Main courses $8–$19.50. No credit cards. Daily 5–10:30pm.

## JUNGLE RESTAURANTS

One of the unique attractions of Puerto Vallarta is its "jungle restaurants," south of town toward Mismaloya. They offer open-air dining in a tropical setting by the sea or beside a mountain river. The many varieties of "jungle" and "tropical" tours (see "Organized Tours," earlier) include a stop for swimming and lunch. If you travel on your own, a taxi is the best transportation—the restaurants are quite a distance from the main highway. Taxis are usually waiting for return patrons.

The newest and most recommendable of the jungle restaurants is **El Nogalito** ★ (✆ and fax **322/221-5225**). Located beside a clear jungle stream, the exceptionally clean, beautifully landscaped ranch serves lunch, beverages, and snacks on a shady, relaxing terrace. Several hiking routes depart from the grounds, and the restaurant provides a guide (whom you tip) to point out the native plants, birds, and wildlife. It's much closer to town than the other jungle restaurants: To find it, travel to Punta Negra, about 8km (5 miles) south of downtown Puerto Vallarta. A well-marked sign points up Calzada del Cedro, a dirt road, to the ranch. It's open daily from 11am to 5:30pm; no credit cards are accepted.

Just past Boca de Tomatlán, at Highway 200 km 20, is **Chico's Paradise** (✆ **322/222-0747** or 322/223-0413; chicos@prodigy.net), offering spectacular views of massive rocks—some marked with petroglyphs—and the surrounding jungle and mountains. There are natural pools and waterfalls for swimming, plus a small *mercado* selling pricey trinkets. The menu features excellent seafood as well as Mexican dishes. The quality is quite good, and the portions are generous, although prices are higher than in town—remember, you're paying for the setting. It's open daily from 10am to7pm; no credit cards are accepted.

The mediocre, somewhat unkempt restaurants up the hill from the entrance to Mismaloya, at Highway 200 km 6.5, are **Chino's Paraíso** and **El Edén** (no phones). El Nogalito and Chico's Paradise are better options.

## PUERTO VALLARTA AFTER DARK

Puerto Vallarta's spirited nightlife reflects the town's dual nature: part resort, part colonial Mexican town. In the past few years, Vallarta has seen an expansion of live music, especially in clubs along Calle Ignacio L. Vallarta (the extension of the main southbound road) after it crosses the Río Cuale. Along one 3-block stretch you'll find a live blues club, sports bar, Harley Davidson–themed bar with live rock, live mariachi music, gay dance club, steamy live salsa dance club, and the obligatory **Señor Frog's.** Walk from place to place and take in a bit of it all!

The ***malecón,*** which used to be lined with restaurants, is now known more for hip dance clubs and a few more relaxed options, all of which look out over the ocean. You can first stroll the broad walkway by the water's edge and check out the action at the various clubs, which extend from **Bodeguita del Medio** on the north end to **Hooters** just off the central plaza.

**Marina Vallarta's** clubs offer a more upscale, indoor, air-conditioned atmosphere. Also south of the Río Cuale, the Olas Altas zone's small cafes and martini bars buzz with action. In this zone, there's also an active gay and lesbian club scene.

### PERFORMING ARTS & CULTURAL EVENTS

Truth be told, cultural nightlife beyond the **Mexican Fiesta** is limited. Culture in Vallarta centers on the visual arts; the opening of an exhibition has great social and artistic significance. Puerto Vallarta's gallery community comes together to present almost weekly **art walks,** where new exhibits are presented, featured artists are in attendance, and complimentary cocktails are served. These social events alternate between the galleries along the Marina Vallarta *malecón* and those in the central downtown area. Check listings in the daily English-language newspaper, *Vallarta Today,* to see what's on the schedule during your stay.

### FIESTA NIGHTS

Major hotels in Puerto Vallarta feature frequent fiestas for tourists—extravaganzas with open bars, Mexican buffet dinners, and live entertainment. Some are fairly authentic and make a good introduction for first-time travelers to Mexico; others can be a bit cheesy. Shows are usually held outdoors but move indoors when necessary. Reservations are recommended.

**Krystal Vallarta Hotel** One of the best fiesta nights is here on Tuesday and Saturday at 7pm. These things are difficult to quantify, but Krystal's program is probably less tacky than those at most of its counterparts. Av. de las Palmas, north of downtown off the airport road. ✆ **322/224-1041.** kvallart@krystal.com.mx. Cover $48.

**Rhythms of the Night (Cruise to Caletas)** ★★★ *Moments* This is an unforgettable evening under the stars at John Huston's former home at the pristine cove called Las Caletas. The smooth, fast Vallarta Adventures catamaran travels here, entertaining guests along the way. Tiki torches and native drummers greet you at the dock. There's no electricity—you dine by the light of candles, the stars, and the moon. The buffet dinner is delicious—steak, seafood, and generous vegetarian options. Everything is first class. The show, set to the music of native bamboo flutes and guitars, showcases indigenous dances in contemporary style. The cruise departs at 6pm and returns by 11pm. Departs from Terminal Marítima. ✆ **866/256-2739** toll-free from the U.S. or 322/297-1212, ext 3. www.vallarta-adventures.com. Cost $75 (includes cruise, dinner, open bar, entertainment).

## THE CLUB & MUSIC SCENE

### Restaurant/Bars

**Carlos O'Brian's** Vallarta's original nightspot, this was once the only place for an evening of revelry. Although the competition is stiffer nowadays, COB's still packs them in—especially the 20-something set. Late at night the scene resembles a college party. It's open daily from noon to 2am. Happy hour is noon to 6pm. Paseo Díaz Ordaz (malecón) 786, at Pípila. ✆ **322/222-1444** or 322/222-4065. Weekend cover $11 (includes 2 drinks); no cover weekdays.

**de Santos** ★★★ Vallarta's chicest dining spot is known more for the urban, hip crowd the bar draws. The atmosphere really rocks, and it's a great place for a late drink. The decor is minimalist, with exposed-brick walls, high ceilings, and, in the back, an open-air patio (the interior is air-conditioned). The owners obviously put the bulk of their investment into the elegant lighting and outstanding sound system. One partner is a member of the super-hot Latin rock group Mana, who uses Vallarta as a home base for writing new songs. As the hour grows late, the music volume increases. The DJ matches the music to the crowd, which varies in age from 20s on up, but shares a common denominator of cool style. The place is so popular that plans are in place to open a club next door by winter 2002-2003. It's open weekdays from 5pm to 2am, weekends from 5pm to 4am. Morelos 771. ✆ **322/223-3052** or 322/223-3053. No cover.

**Kit Kat Club** ★★ It's swank and sleek and reminiscent of a New York club, but don't be fooled—the Kit Kat Club also has a terrific sense of humor. In the golden glow of candlelight, lounge around in cushy, leopard-patterned chairs or cream-colored, overstuffed banquettes, listening to swinging tunes while you sip a martini. Not only is the place very hip, it also serves good food, with especially tasty appetizers—that can double as light meals—and scrumptious desserts. Michael, the owner, describes his air-conditioned lounge and cafe as cool, crazy, wild, jazzy, and sexy. I agree. It's open daily from 6pm to 2am. Martini "T" dances daily from 5 to 7pm. Pulpito 120, Playas Los Muertos. ✆ **322/223-0093.** No cover.

**La Bodeguita del Medio** ★ This authentic Cuban restaurant and bar has quickly become a local favorite for its casual energy, terrific live music, and *mojitos*—stiff rum-based drinks with fresh mint and lime juice. It is a branch of the original Bodeguita in Havana (reputedly Hemingway's favorite restaurant there), which opened in 1942. If you can't get to that one, the Vallarta version has successfully imported the essence—plus, there's a small souvenir shop that sells Cuban cigars, rum, and other items. The downstairs has large wooden windows that open up to the *malecón* street action, while the upstairs offers terrific views of the bay. Walls throughout are decorated with old photographs and patrons' signatures—if you can, find a spot and add yours! I feel the food is less memorable here then the music and atmosphere, so I suggest drinks and dancing, nothing more. Malecón (at Allende). ✆ **322/223-1585.** No cover. Daily 11:30am–2am.

**La Cantina** ★★ It's a Mexican classic gone contemporary. *Cantinas* are a centuries-old tradition, and this one has retained the fundamentals while updating the concept to a hip club. Cantinas serve little complimentary plates of food as your table orders drinks. La Cantina does this from 1pm to 5pm; dishes might include *carne con chile* (meat in chile sauce), soup of the day, or *quesadillas.* In the evenings, recorded music alternates between sultry boleros and the hottest in Mexican rock, at levels that permit conversation, creating a romantic, clubby atmosphere. If you require more stimulation, play a board game in one of the smaller rooms or on the larger open-air patio. Beers cost $1.50, bar drinks $2.50. No credit cards. It's open Sunday to Wednesday from noon to 2am, Thursday to Saturday from noon to 4am. Morelos 709, downtown. ✆ **322/222-7701.** No cover.

### Rock, Jazz & Blues

**Club Roxy** ★★ Currently the most popular live-music club in Vallarta, Club Roxy features a hot house band led by club owner Pico, playing a mix of reggae, blues, rock, and anything by Santana. Live music jams between 10pm and 2am Monday to Saturday nights. It's open daily from 6pm to 2am. Ignacio L. Vallarta 217 (between Madero and Cárdenas, south of the river). No cover. ✆ **322/223-2402.**

**El Faro Lighthouse Bar** ★ A circular cocktail lounge at the top of the Marina lighthouse, El Faro is one of Vallarta's most romantic nightspots. Live or recorded jazz plays, and conversation is manageable. Drop by at twilight for the magnificent panoramic views. It's open daily from 5pm to 2am. Royal Pacific Yacht Club, Marina Vallarta. ✆ **322/221-0541** or 322/221-0542. elfaropv@pvnet.com.mx. No cover.

**Mariachi Loco** This live and lively mariachi club features singers belting out boleros and ranchero classics. The mariachi show begins at 9pm—the mariachis stroll and play as guests join in impromptu singing—and by 10pm it gets going. After midnight the mariachis play for pay, which is around $11 for each song played at your table. There's Mexican food until 1am. It's open daily from 1pm to 4am. Lázaro Cárdenas 254 (at Ignacio Vallarta). ✆ **322/223-2205.** No cover.

## DANCE CLUBS & DISCOS

A few of Vallarta's clubs or discos charge admission, but generally you pay just for drinks—$3.90 for a margarita, $2.80 for a beer, more for whiskey and mixed drinks. Keep an eye out for discount passes frequently available in hotels, restaurants, and other tourist spots. Most clubs are open from 10pm to 4am.

**Christine** Proving that disco is alive and well, this dazzling club draws a crowd with an opening laser-light show, pumped-in dry ice and oxygen, flashing lights, and a dozen large-screen video panels. The sound system is truly amazing, and the mix of music can get almost anyone dancing. Dress code: No shorts for men, tennis shoes, or thongs. Open daily 10pm to 4am, the light show begins at 11pm. In the Krystal Vallarta Hotel, north of downtown off Av. Francisco Medina Ascencio. ✆ **322/224-0202.** Cover free to $6.

**Emporium by Collage** A multilevel monster of nighttime entertainment, Emporium includes a pool salon, video arcade, bowling alley, and the always-packed Disco Bar, with frequent live entertainment. It's just past the entrance to Marina Vallarta, air-conditioned, and very popular with a young, mainly local crowd. It's open daily from 10am to 6am. Calle Proa s/n, Marina Vallarta. ✆ **322/221-0505** or 322/221-0861. Cover $5.50–$22.

**J & B Salsa Club** This is the locally popular place to go for dancing to Latin music—from salsa to samba, the dancing here is hot! Fridays, Saturdays, and holidays the air-conditioned club features live bands. It's open Monday to Saturday from 10pm to 6am. Av. Francisco Medina Ascencio, km 2.5 (Hotel Zone). ✆ **322/224-4616.** Cover $9.

**The Palm Video & Show Bar** The big screen above the dance floor of this colorful, lively club plays the most danceable videos in town—certain to get you moving. The pool table is regularly in play, and the air-conditioned club frequently books live shows featuring female impersonators. This is a gay-friendly but not exclusively gay club, with a spirited, festive atmosphere. It's open daily from 7pm to 2am. Olas Altas 508. ✆ **322/223-4817.** www.thepalmbar.com. Cover $3 show nights only.

**Señor Frog's** The sheer size of this hot new outpost of the famed Carlos 'n' Charlie's chain is daunting, but it fills up and rocks until the early morning hours. Cute waiters are a signature of the chain, and one never knows when they'll assemble on stage and call on a bevy of beauties to join them in a tequila-drinking contest. Occasionally live bands appear. Although mainly popular with the 20s set, all ages will find the air-conditioned club fun. There's food service, but it's better known for its dance-club atmosphere. It's open daily from 11am to 4am. Ignacio L. Vallarta and Venustiano Carranza. ✆ **322/222-5171** or 322/222-5177. Cover free – $11 (includes 2 drinks).

**Zoo** Your chance to be an animal and get wild in the night. The Zoo even has cages to dance in if you're feeling unleashed. This popular club has a terrific sound system and a great variety of dance music, including techno, reggae, and rap. Every hour's happy hour, with two-for-one drinks. It opens daily at noon and closes in the wee hours. Paseo Díaz Ordaz 630 (the malecón).✆ **322/222-4945.** Cover $11 (includes 2 drinks).

### A SPORTS BAR & A STRIP JOINT

**Micky's No Name Cafe** With a multitude of TVs and enough sports memorabilia to start a mini-museum, Micky's is a great venue for catching your favorite game. It shows all NBA, NHL, NFL, and MLB broadcast events, plus pay-per-view. Mickey's also serves great barbecued ribs and USDA imported steaks. It's open daily from 9am to midnight. Morelos (malecón) 460, at Mina. ✆ **322/223-2508.** No cover.

**Q'eros** This air-conditioned adult nightclub features exotic dancers, private shows, and stripteases. It's open nightly from 9pm to 6am. Av. Francisco Medina Ascencio, in front of Plaza Genovesa. ✆ **322/222-4367.** Cover $5.

## GAY & LESBIAN CLUBS

Vallarta has a vibrant gay community with a wide variety of clubs and nightlife options, including special bay cruises and evening excursions to nearby ranches. The free ***Southside PV Guide,*** Amapas 325 (✆ **322/222-2517;** pvguide@hotmail.com), specializes in gay-friendly listings.

**Club Paco Paco** This combination disco, cantina, and rooftop bar stages a spectacular "Trasvesty" transvestite show every Thursday, Friday, Saturday, and Sunday night at 1:30am. It's open daily from 1pm to 6am and is air-conditioned. Ignacio L. Vallarta 278. ✆ **322/222-1899.** www.pacopaco.com. Cover $6 (includes 1 drink) after 10pm or start of first show, whichever is earlier.

**Los Balcones** One of the original gay clubs in town, this bi-level space with several dance floors and an excellent sound system earned a few chuckles when *Brides* magazine listed it as one of the most romantic spots in Vallarta. Air-conditioned, it's open from 9pm to 4am and posts nightly specials, including exotic male dancers. Juárez 182. ✆ **322/222-4671.** No cover.

**Ranch Disco Bar** This place is known for the nightly "Ranch Hand's Show," at 11:30pm and 2am. The club also has a new dance floor. It's open daily from 9pm to 6am. Venustiano Carranza 239 (around the corner from Paco Paco). ✆ **322/223-0537.** Cover $4.50 (includes 1 drink).

# SIDE TRIPS FROM PUERTO VALLARTA

**YELAPA: ROBINSON CRUSOE MEETS JACK KEROUAC** ★ It's a cove straight out of a tropical fantasy, and only a 45-minute trip by boat from Puerto Vallarta. Yelapa has no electricity or cars, and just one paved (pedestrian-only) road. It's accessible only by boat. Its tranquility, natural beauty, and seclusion have made it a popular home for hippies, hipsters, artists, writers, and a few ex-pats (looking to escape the stress of the world, or perhaps the law). A seemingly strange mix, but you're unlikely to ever meet a stranger there—Yelapa remains casual and friendly.

To get there, travel by excursion boat or inexpensive water taxi (see "Getting Around," earlier). There's also a challenging mountain bike trip with Bike Mex (see "Mountain Biking & Hiking" under "Staying Active," earlier). You can spend an enjoyable day, but I recommend a longer stay—it provides a completely different perspective.

Once you're in Yelapa, you can lie in the sun, swim, snorkel, eat fresh grilled seafood at a beachfront restaurant, or sample the local moonshine, *raicilla.* The local beach vendors specialize in the most amazing pies you've ever tasted (coconut, lemon, or chocolate). Equally amazing is how the pie ladies walk the beach while balancing the pie plates on their heads; they sell crocheted swimsuits, too. You can also tour this tiny town or hike up a river to see one of two waterfalls. The closest to town is about a 30-minute walk from the beach. *Note:* If you use a local guide, agree on a price before you start out. Horseback riding, guided bird-watching, fishing trips, and paragliding are also available.

For overnight accommodations, local residents frequently rent rooms, and there's also the rustic **Hotel Lagunita** (✆ **329/298-0554;** www.hotel-lagunita.com). Its 27 cabañas have private bathrooms, and the hotel has electricity, a salt-water pool, massage, and an amiable restaurant and bar. This is the most accommodating place for most visitors—although you may need to bring your own towels, which are known to be in short supply. It's quite popular for yoga students and other groups. Rooms are in the process of being remodeled. Rates run $78 during the season and $55 in the off-season (MC, V).

An elegant new alternative is the **Verana** (✆ **800/677-5156** or 322/227-5420; www.verana.com), a stylish enclave in this remote village. The five *casas* sit high above Yelapa's bay, on the western edge, with views from every angle. Rooms, the work of film production designer Heinz Leger and prop stylist Veronique Lieve, have an eclectic style that blends rustic with sophisticated. Electricity is limited, which seems to add to the pervasive sense of romance. Rates are $750 double for the three-night minimum stay, including breakfast and dinner.

If you stay over on a Wednesday or Saturday during the winter, don't miss the regular dance at the **Yelapa Yacht Club** ★ (no phone). Typically tongue-in-cheek for Yelapa, the "yacht club" consists of a cement dance floor and a disco ball, but the DJ spins a great range of tunes, from Glenn Miller to N*Sync, attracting all ages and types to the dance. Dinner ($5–$12) is a bonus—the food may be the best anywhere in the bay. The menu changes depending on what's fresh. Ask for directions; it's located in the main village, on the beach.

### NUEVO VALLARTA & NORTH OF VALLARTA: ALL-INCLUSIVE

Many people assume Nuevo Vallarta is a suburb of Puerto Vallarta, but it's a stand-alone destination over the state border in Nayarit. Original plans called for a mega-resort development—complete with marina, golf course, and luxury hotels. Although it got off to a slow start, it is finally being built. Currently, it's a collection of mostly all-inclusive hotels, located on one of the widest, most attractive beaches in the bay. The biggest resort, Paradise Village, has a growing marina and just opened an 18-hole golf course inland from the beachfront strip of hotels. The recently opened Paradise Plaza shopping center, next to Paradise Village, adds much to the area in terms of shopping, dining, and services. It's open from 10am to 10pm. To get to the beach here, you travel down a lengthy entrance road from the highway, passing by fields that are great for birding, and nearby lagoons that are great for kayaking.

Also worthwhile is a day spent at the **Etc. Beach Club,** Paseo de los Cocoteros 38, Nuevo Vallarta (✆ **322/297-0174**). This beach club has a volleyball net, showers, restroom facilities, and food and drink service on the beach, both day and night. To get there, take the second entrance to Nuevo Vallarta coming from Puerto Vallarta and turn right on Paseo de los Cocoteros; it is past the Vista Bahia hotel. It's open daily during the winter from 11am to 10:30pm, summer from 11am to 7pm. Drinks cost $2.50 to $7, entrees $4.50 to $17; cash only.

A trip into downtown Puerto Vallarta takes about 30 minutes by taxi, costs about $15, and is available 24 hours a day. The ride is slightly longer by public bus, which costs $1.20 and operates from 7am to 11pm.

**Hotel Club Marival** This all-inclusive hotel sits almost by itself at the northernmost end of Nuevo Vallarta. Done in Mediterranean style, it's a refreshing alternative to the mega-resorts that tend to dominate the area. This smaller property has a large variety of rooms, ranging from standard units with no balconies to large master suites with whirlpools. The master suites have minibars and hair dryers. The broad white-sand beach is one of the real assets here—it stretches over 500 yards. There is also an extensive activities program, including fun for children. Coming from the Puerto Vallarta airport, Club Marival is the first resort to your right on Cocoteros Avenue when you enter Nuevo Vallarta from the second entrance.

Paseo de los Cocoteros y Blvd. Nuevo Vallarta s/n, Nuevo Vallarta, Nayarit 63735. ✆ **322/297-0100**. Fax 322/297-0160. www.clubmarival.com. 646 units. High season $123 per person double; low season $115 per person double. Upgrade to Jr. suite $50 per day, to Master suite with whirlpool $300 per day. Request your upgrade when making reservations. Rates are all-inclusive. Ask for seasonal specials. AE, MC, V. **Amenities:** 6 restaurants, 8 bars; 3 pools and a whirlpool for adults; 2 pools and a water park for children; 4 lighted tennis courts; business center; spa; beauty shop. *In room:* A/C, TV, safe-deposit boxes.

**Paradise Village** ★★ Truly a village, this self-contained resort on an exquisite stretch of beach has a full array of guest services, from an on-site disco to a full-service European spa and health club. The collection of pyramid-shaped buildings, designed in Maya-influenced style, houses well-designed all-suite accommodations in studio, one-bedroom, and two-bedroom configurations. All have sitting areas and kitchenettes, making the resort ideal for families or groups of friends. The Maya theme extends to both oceanfront pools, with mythical creatures forming water slides and waterfalls. The exceptional spa is reason enough to book a vacation here, with treatments, hydrotherapy, massage (including massage on the beach), and fitness and yoga classes. Special spa packages are always available.

Paseo de los Cocoteros 001, Nuevo Vallarta, Nay. 63731. ✆ **800/995-5714** or 322/226-6770. Fax 322/226-6713. www.paradisemexico.com. 490 units. High season $225–$433 double, 2-bedroom suite $334, 3-bedroom suite $581; low season $151–$292 double, 2-bedroom suite $280, 3-bedroom suite $435. AE, DC, MC, V. **Amenities:** 2 restaurants, 2 beachfront snack bars; theme nights; nightclub; 4 tennis courts; 2 oceanfront swimming pools; lap pool; European spa and complete fitness center; basketball court; beach volleyball; watersports center; petting zoo; full marina; championship golf club with 18-hole course; Kid's Club; travel services desk; guests-only rental car fleet. *In room:* A/C, TV, dataport, minibar, coffeemaker, hair dryer, iron, safe-deposit box.

**BUCERIAS: A COASTAL VILLAGE** ★ Only 18km (11 miles) north of the Puerto Vallarta airport, Bucerías (Boo-sayr-*ee*-ahs, meaning "place of the divers") is a small coastal fishing village of 10,000 people in Nayarit state on Banderas Bay. It's caught on as an alternative to Puerto Vallarta for those who find the pace of life there too invasive. Bucerías offers a seemingly contradictory mix of accommodations—trailer-park spaces and exclusive villa rentals tend to dominate, although there's a small selection of hotels as well.

To reach the town center by car, take the exit road from the highway and drive down the shaded, divided street that leads to the beach. Turn left when you see a line of minivans and taxis (which serve Bucerías and Vallarta). Go straight ahead 1 block to the main plaza. The beach, with a lineup of restaurants, is half a block farther. You'll see cobblestone streets leading from the highway to the beach, and hints of villas and town homes behind high walls. Second-home owners and about 1,500 transplanted Americans have already sought out this peaceful getaway; tourists have discovered its relaxed pace as well.

If you take the bus to Bucerías, exit when you see the minivans and taxis to and from Bucerías line up on the street that leads to the beach. To get here from Puerto Vallarta via public transportation, take a minivan or bus marked BUCERIAS (they run from 6am–9pm). The last minivan stop is Bucerías's town square. There's also 24-hour taxi service.

**Exploring Bucerías** Come here for a day trip from Puerto Vallarta just to enjoy the long, wide, uncrowded beach, along with the fresh seafood served at the beachfront restaurants or at one of the unusually great cafes listed below. If you are inclined to stay a few days, you can relax inexpensively and explore more of Bucerías. Sunday is street-market day, but it doesn't get going until around noon, in keeping with the town's casual pace.

The **Coral Reef Surf Shop,** Heroe de Nacozari 114-F (✆ **329/298-0261**), carries a great selection of surfboards and gear for sale, and offers surfboard and boogie board rentals, surf lessons, and ATV and other adventure tours to surrounding areas.

**Where to Stay** Unfortunately, I cannot recommend any of the hotels in Bucerías; they're run-down, and most people who choose to stay here opt for a private home rental. For advance planning, check out the villa rental bulletin board at **www.sunworx.com**. **Las Palmas** in Bucerías (✆ **329/298-0060;** fax 329/298-1100) will book accommodations, including villas, houses, and condos. Call ahead, or ask for directions to the office, when you get to Bucerías. It's open Monday to Friday from 9am to 2pm and 4 to 6pm, Saturday from 9am to 2pm.

**Where to Dine** Besides those mentioned below, there are many seafood restaurants fronting the beach. The local specialty is *pescado sarandeado,* a whole fish smothered in tasty sauce and slow-grilled.

**Cafe Magaña** BARBECUED RIBS Famous for its ribs and chicken, Cafe Magaña gives you a choice of 10 original homemade sauces. Flavors have mythological names and contain creative ingredients like ginger, garlic, oranges, apples, cinnamon, and chiles. The sauces have been such a hit that British owner Jeff Rafferty also offers them bottled and for sale—and says to look for them available commercially soon. This casual, colorful cafe and take-out restaurant also features TV sports and an occasional live band.

Lázaro Cárdenas 40. ✆ **329/298-1091.** www.sunworx.com/salsa/. Main courses $7–$12. No credit cards. Fri–Wed 5–11pm.

**Karen's Place** ★ INTERNATIONAL/MEXICAN This casual oceanside restaurant offers classic cuisine, plus Mexican favorites in a style that appeals to North American appetites. Known for Sunday brunch (9am–3pm), it also is a great place to spend the day on the beach while enjoying a light lunch, and makes a romantic dining spot. Their best-selling dinner is a Parmesan herb-crusted fish filet, with a salad of baby greens. This casual, comfortable restaurant also features live music every evening.

On the beach at the Costa Dorada, Calle Lazaro Cardenas. ✆ **329/298-1499.** Breakfast $4.50–$5.50; Sun brunch (9am–3pm) $12; main courses $5.50–$13. No credit cards. Tues–Sun 9am–10pm.

**Mark's** ★★ *Finds* ITALIAN/STEAK/SEAFOOD It's worth a special trip to Bucerías just to eat at this covered-patio restaurant. The most popular American hangout in town, Mark's offers a great assortment of thin-crust pizzas and flatbread, baked in its brick oven and seasoned with fresh herbs grown in the garden. Everything has exquisite flavorings—some favorites include shrimp in angel-hair pasta, pesto-crusted fish fillet, ahi tuna served rare, and filet mignon with bleu-cheese ravioli. Multitalented chef Jan Marie (Mark's charming wife and partner) runs an adjacent boutique, with the nicest selection of women's resort wear in town. The bar televises all major sporting events. Mark's is half a block from the beach.

Lázaro Cárdenas 56. ✆ **329/298-0303.** Pasta $8.70–$18.50; main courses $13–$22. MC, V. High season daily noon–11pm; low season Wed–Mon 5:30–11pm. From the highway, turn left just after bridge, where there's a small sign for Mark's. Double back left at next street (immediately after you turn left) and turn right at next corner. Mark's is on the right.

**PUNTA MITA: EXCLUSIVE SECLUSION** ★★★ At the northern tip of the bay is an arrowhead-shaped piece of land called Punta Mita. Considered a sacred place by the Indians, this is the point where Banderas Bay, the Pacific Ocean, and the Sea of Cortez come together. The natural beauty here is magnificent, with white-sand beaches and coral reefs just offshore. Stately rocks jut out along the shoreline, and the water is a dreamy translucent blue. Punta Mita is evolving into one of Mexico's most exclusive developments. The master plan calls for a total of five luxury hotels, plus several high-end residential communities interspersed among three championship golf courses. It is the first luxury residential development in Mexico intended for the foreign market. Today, all you'll find is the elegant Four Seasons Resort and its Jack Nicklaus Signature golf course.

**Four Seasons Resort Punta Mita** ★★★ *Finds* The Four Seasons Resort has brought a new standard of luxury to Mexico's Pacific Coast. This boutique hotel, situated on 1,000 acres of land bordered on three sides by the ocean, artfully combines seclusion and pampering service with a welcoming sense of comfort. Accommodations are in three-story *casitas,* which surround the main building where the lobby, cultural center, restaurants, and pool are located.

Every guest room offers breathtaking views of the ocean from a large terrace or balcony. Most suites also offer a private plunge pool, as well as a separate sitting room, bar, and powder room. Two- and three-bedroom suites are available. Room interiors are typical Four Seasons—plush and spacious, with a king or two double beds, plus a seating area and oversized bathroom with a deep soaking tub, separate glass-enclosed shower, and dual vanity sink.

More than the stylish luxury, this hotel boasts unerring service that is both warm and unobtrusive. It's a place to completely get away—bear in mind that you are at least 45 minutes from Puerto Vallarta's activities—but then, most guests feel so relaxed and at ease here, it's hard to think of places beyond the resort. The centerpiece is the 19-hole (1 hole is on a natural island) Jack Nicklaus Signature golf course. It has ocean views from every hole and eight holes that border the ocean (see "Golf," under "Staying Active," earlier, for complete details). A full-service spa, tennis center, and private championship golf course are options enough, it seems.

Bahía de Banderas, Nay. 63734. ✆ **800/332-3442** or 329/291-6000. Fax 329/291-6060. www.fourseasons.com. 140 units. High season $691–$796 double, $1,814–$2,048 suite; low season $457–$656 double, $1,170–$1,287 suite. AE, DC, MC, V. Valet parking. **Amenities:** 2 restaurants, lobby bar; 24-hr. room service; heated infinity pool surrounded by private cabañas; watersports equipment including sea kayaks, Windsurfers, surfboards, and sunfish sailboats; daily activity agenda; tour desk; cultural center with lectures and activities; full-service fitness center; European-style spa; tennis center with 4 courts of various surfaces; Kids for All Seasons children's activity program; 24-hr. concierge service; complimentary video library. *In room:* A/C, TV/VCR, dataport, minibar, coffeemaker, hair dryer, iron, safe-deposit box.

**SAYULITA: MUCH MORE THAN A GREAT SURF SPOT** Sayulita is only 40km (25 miles) northwest of Puerto Vallarta, on Highway 200 to Tepic, yet it feels worlds away. It captures the simplicity and tranquility of beach life that has long since left Vallarta. For years, Sayulita has been principally a surfers' destination—the main beach in town is known for its consistent break and long, ridable waves. Recently, visitors and locals who find Vallarta becoming too cosmopolitan have started to flock to Sayulita.

An easygoing attitude seems to permeate the air in this true beach town. Yet despite its simplicity, a few niceties are popping up among the basic accommodations, inexpensive Mexican food stands, and hand-made, hippie-style baubles.

Sayulita is a popular stage for surfing tournaments and raves; on any given weekend you might encounter a flock of techno-beat-loving ravers or perfect-swell-seeking surfers—or a Huichol Indian family that has come down to sell their wares. It's this eclectic mix of the cool, the unusual, and the authentic Mexican that makes Sayulita such a special place.

To get to Sayulita, you can rent a car, or take a taxi from the airport or downtown Vallarta. The rate is about $50 to get to the town plaza. You can also take a taxi back to Vallarta. Agustín (© **327/275-0234**) has the best local service, making trips to the Puerto Vallarta airport for $44 and to downtown for $50. The stand is on the main square, or you can call for pickup at your hotel. Another option is to contact the professional, bilingual tour guide service run by Mónico and Pedro (© **311/258-4024** or 311/258-4151). They can pick you up at the airport and drive you to Sayulita for $55. They also lead tours to Vallarta, Punta Mita, and other surrounding areas, including a Huichol Indian community.

One of the nicest selections of authentic fine crafts from all over Mexico is at **La Lupita Artesanías,** Av. Revolución and Playa Azul (© **327/275-0484**), which also serves as Sayulita's informal information center. Owner Upi Viteri has been dealing with fine arts, crafts, and Mexican culture in general for the last 15 years, and selects every article in her store. She seeks out the works of innovative artisans who show at national arts and crafts contests. At La Lupita you will find one-of-a-kind pieces, from masks to ceremonial drums, and decorative accents made of tin, carved wood, and papier-mâché. Open Monday to Saturday from 9am to 2pm and 4 to 8pm. MC and V are accepted. The store is on the access road to Sayulita, 2 blocks before the bridge that takes you to the center of town.

**Where to Stay** Sayulita offers several private homes for rent. Your best option is to contact **Upi Viteri** (© **327/275-0484;** upiviteri@prodigy.net.mx), who has access to some of the nicest rental properties.

**Aurinko Bungalows** ★ Located half a block from the beach, these are classic beach accommodations—quiet, rustic, and casual. With tall palms all around, you may feel as if you're on a South Sea island. The rooms are impeccably clean, with cotton linens and fluffy white towels. Each room has a ceiling fan, open-air seating area, and fully equipped kitchenette.

Calle Marlín 7 Centro, Sayulita, Nay., 63732, © **327/275-0010.** www.sayulita-vacations.com, 6 units. $57–$67 1-bedroom suite, $88–$103 2-bedroom suite. 20% low-season discount. MC, V. *In room:* Kitchenette, coffeemaker.

**Villa Amor** ★★★ *Finds* A personal favorite, Villa Amor is a collection of inviting, airy, perfectly appointed guest rooms—think of it as your private villa by the sea. Owner Rod Ingram and his design team have carefully crafted each space and individual suite into something truly special. The exterior walls curve invitingly and open up to breathtaking views all around. The one- and two-bedroom suites have fully equipped kitchenettes, plus open-air seating or dining areas (or both), and some have plunge pools. TVs are available on request.

Camino Playa a Los Muertos s/n, Sayulita, Nay., 63732. © **327/275-0196.** Fax 327/275-0263. www.villaamor.com. 21 units. $50–$75 double; $85–$125 1-bedroom villa, $180–$250 2-bedroom villa. No credit cards. **Amenities:** Restaurant; room service; concierge; massage; kayaks; bicycles; boogie boards; surfboards; tour desk. *In room:* Fan.

**Where to Dine** If you are in Sayulita, chances are you heard about it because of **Don Pedro's,** the most popular restaurant in town, in the heart of the town's main beach.

**El Tigre** MEXICAN El Tigre is the local favorite for real Mexican food at real Mexican prices. The place is basic-except for the two huge-screen TVs that broadcast every sporting event of any relevance, from the Super Bowl to

Mexican soccer. Dishes include smoked fish, chiles rellenos, and fresh fish and seafood cooked in a variety of ways.

East side of the main square, next to the church. No phone. Main courses $4–$14. No credit cards. High season daily 5–11pm; low season hours vary. From Av. Revolución, go left on pedestrian street by Choco-Banana.

**L'Ultima Spiaggia** ITALIAN Paolo, an Italian chef, runs this tiny restaurant by the seashore. The menu is simple and classic, with salads, pizzas and pastas. Start with dorado carpaccio. Paolo picks the freshest ingredients at the market every morning for his daily specials. They usually include fresh fish and seafood pasta dishes. The pizzas, baked in a wood-burning oven, have thin, crispy crusts. Don't miss the gnocchi, homemade fresh every day. The restaurant has a table out by the sea, which is perfect for romantic dinners. Breakfast features more European-style offerings, including light omelets and fresh fruit. The espressos and cappuccinos are by far the best in Sayulita.

Camino Playa a los Muertos s/n, downstairs from Villa Amor. ✆ **322/100-6879.** Breakfast $3–$8; pizza $7–$11; main courses $8–$17. No credit cards. Tues–Sun 8:30–11am and 6–11pm.

**Rollie's** BREAKFAST Breakfast heaven! This family restaurant emanates a happy aura that puts its patrons in a good mood. The menu reflects the tone of the place, with options such as Rollie's Delight (blended fresh orange and banana), Adriana's Rainbow (an omelet with cheese, tomatoes, green peppers, and onions), and my personal favorite, Indian Pipe Pancakes. All dishes come with Rollie's famous potatoes (lightly seasoned pan-fried new potatoes). The place tends to be very crowded on weekends, so be prepared to sit and wait—the wait is worthwhile.

Av. Revolución, 2 blocks west of the main square. ✆ **327/275-0235.** Breakfast $3–$8. No credit cards. Daily Nov–Apr 8am–noon. Closed May–Oct.

**SAN SEBASTIAN: AN AUTHENTIC MOUNTAIN HIDEAWAY** ★★★ If you haven't heard about San Sebastián yet, it probably won't be long—its remote location and historic appeal have made it the media's new darling destination in Mexico. Originally discovered in the late 1500s and settled in 1603, the town peaked as a center of mining operations, swelling to a population of over 30,000 by the mid-1800s. Today, with roughly 600 year-round residents, San Sebastián retains all the charm of a village locked in time, with an old church, a coffee plantation, an underground tunnel system—and without a T-shirt shop.

**Getting There** By car, it's a 2½-hour drive up the Sierra Madre from Puerto Vallarta on an improved road, but it can be difficult during the summer rainy season, when the road washes out frequently. **Vallarta Adventures** (✆ **866/256-2739** toll-free from the U.S., or 322/297-1212, ext. 3; www.vallarta-adventures.com) runs a daily plane service for half-day tours and can occasionally accommodate overnight visitors. The small private airport can arrange flights. **Aerotron** (✆ **322/221-1921**) charges about $130 round-trip, **Taxis Aereos de Nayarit** (✆ **322/221-1990**) about $88 round-trip, depending on the type of plane and number of passengers.

**Where to Stay** There are two places to stay in San Sebastián. The first is the very basic **El Pabellon de San Sebastián,** which faces the town square. Its nine simply furnished rooms surround a central patio. Don't expect extras here; rates run $40 per double. The town's central phone lines handle reservations—you call (✆ **322/297-0200**) and leave a message or send a fax, and hopefully the hotel will receive it. More secure is e-mail: ssb@pvnet.com.mx. Except on holidays, there is generally room at this inn. No credit cards.

A more enjoyable option is the stately **Hacienda Jalisco,** built in 1850 and once the center of mining operations in this mining town. The beautifully landscaped, rambling old hacienda is near the airstrip a 15-minute walk from town. Proprietor Bud Acord has welcomed John Huston, Liz Taylor, Richard Burton, Peter O'Toole, and a cast of local characters over the years.

The 10 extra-clean rooms have wood floors, rustic furnishings and antiques, and working fireplaces; some are decorated with pre-Columbian reproductions. The ample bathrooms are beautifully tiled and have skylights. Hammocks grace the upstairs terrace, while a sort-of museum on the lower level attests to the celebrity guests and importance the hacienda has enjoyed over the years. Because of its remote location, all meals are included. Rates are $120 per couple per night, including meals; alcoholic beverages are extra. Reserve through e-mail (ssb@pvnet.com.mx), or through the town telephones listed above. Group rates and discounts for longer stays are available. No credit cards accepted. Guided horseback, walking, or mine tours can be arranged through the Hacienda.

## 2 Mazatlán ★

1,078km (674 miles) NW of Mexico City; 502km (314 miles) NW of Guadalajara; 1,561km (976 miles) SE of Mexicali

Mazatlán is comfortable, casual, value-packed Mexico at its best. More than any other beach resort in the country, it probably best represents the golden beaches, fresh seafood, and inexpensive vacation accommodations that typified Mexico's appeal to travelers in the first place. Although some developments are edging Mazatlán into the golf-playing, manicured resort that typifies most of Mexico today, it is going there grudgingly—most of Mazatlán remains refreshingly simplistic.

Mazatlán's lures continue to be its expansive beaches and renowned sportfishing. The evolving golf scene, luxury yacht harbor, and growing selection of accommodations have yet to catch the attention of enough tourists to drive prices to the levels of other Mexican resorts—good news for travelers looking for economy in a beach resort.

Mazatlán is a city with a population of nearly 500,000, and is the largest port between Los Angeles and the Panama Canal. Elegant reminders of its history, 27km (17 miles) of sandy beaches, and a geographically diverse environment to explore are all added attractions in Mazatlán's efforts to become a premier beach resort.

Limited flight availability is the principle factor holding back Mazatlán's growth. Charter operators have picked up some of the slack and are the predominant means of arrival here.

Once known as a spring break haven and a place to party, Mazatlán is now attracting more families, mature travelers, and other tourists with an eye for value. It enjoys strong repeat business and positive word of mouth, as it continues to offer exceptional vacation values.

### ESSENTIALS

#### GETTING THERE

**BY PLANE** There are numerous direct or nonstop flights to Mazatlán. From the United States, **Aeromexico** (✆ **800/237-6639** in the U.S., and 800/021-4000 in Mexico) flies from Los Angeles, Atlanta, Phoenix, and Tucson, via Mexico City. **Mexicana** (✆ **800/531-7921** in the U.S.) has direct service from Denver, Chicago, Los Angeles, Miami, and San Antonio, most connecting through Mexico City. **Aero California** (✆ **800/237-6225** in the U.S.) flies from Los Angeles. **Alaska Airlines** (✆ **800/426-0333** or 669/985-2730) serves Vancouver, Seattle, Portland, San Francisco, and Los Angeles. Within Mexico, **Aero California** (✆ **669/985-2557,** 669/981-5970, or 669/985-3434 at the airport) flies from La Paz, Guadalajara, and Mexico City. **Aeromexico** (✆ **669/914-1111**) has flights from Hermosillo, Durango, Monterrey, Puerto Vallarta, Tijuana, and León, all via Guadalajara or Mexico City. **Mexicana** (✆ **669/982-2888**) offers service from Mexico City and Los Cabos. Check with a travel agent for the latest **charter flights.**

**BY BUS** First-class and deluxe buses depart almost hourly for Guadalajara (7 hr., $35 first-class one-way) and Mexico City (14½ hr., $67 first-class one-way), and less often to other points within Mexico.

**BY CAR** To reach Mazatlán from the United States, take **International Highway 15** from Nogales, Arizona, to Culiacán. At Culiacán, change to the four-lane **tollway**—it costs about $40 but is really the only road considered safe and in drivable condition. On the tollway, total trip time from the United States to Mazatlán is about 10 hours. Consider an overnight stop, because driving at night in Mexico can be dangerous. From Puerto Vallarta, the 560km (350-mile) drive is not easy—the road winds through the mountains, but is in generally good condition. Take Highway 200 north to Las Varas. There it becomes four-lane Highway 68; follow that until you see a detour for Highway 15. Take 15 north to Mazatlán.

**BY FERRY** **Passenger ferries** operated by SEMATUR run between Mazatlán and La Paz, Baja California. The ferry leaves daily at 3pm and carries cars, with Thursdays reserved for only cargo and seated passengers (no cabins). The trip takes 18 hours. Seats cost $52, tourist-class service with two beds $116, cabin class with two beds and a private bath $142, and special class $167. Prices for cars vary, depending on the size of the car. For example, a Volkswagen Golf costs $230. For information, call ✆ **629/981-7020;** toll-free within Mexico, 01-800/696-9600. Tickets for the ferry must be purchased in advance at the ferry office on Carnaval Street or through travel agents; MasterCard and Visa are accepted. To find the ferry office, go south on Olas Altas and turn left on Alemán; Carnaval is the second street. Turn right and you'll find the office in the middle of the block. Ferries return from La Paz to Mazatlán daily.

## ORIENTATION

**ARRIVING** The Rafael Buelna International Airport (airport code: MZT) is 27km (17 miles) southeast of the hotel-and-resort area of town. The following rental-car companies have counters in the airport, open during flight arrivals and departures: **Hertz** (✆ **800/623-3650** in the U.S., or 669/985-0845), **Budget** (✆ **800/322-9976** in the U.S., or 669/982-6363), and **National** (✆ **800/227-7368** in the U.S., or 669/982-4000). Daily rates run $55 to $145. A car is desirable if you want to explore the surrounding coastline and villages, but it is not essential.

Taxis and *colectivo* minivans run from the airport to hotels; taxis cost about twice as much as the *colectivo,* which runs $23 to $28, depending on the location of your hotel. Only taxis make the return trip to the airport; they cost $25 to $30. The **Central de Autobuses** (main bus terminal) is at Río Tamazula and Chachalacas. To get there from Avenida del Mar, walk 3 blocks inland on Río Tamazula; the station is on your right. Taxis line up in front of the bus station.

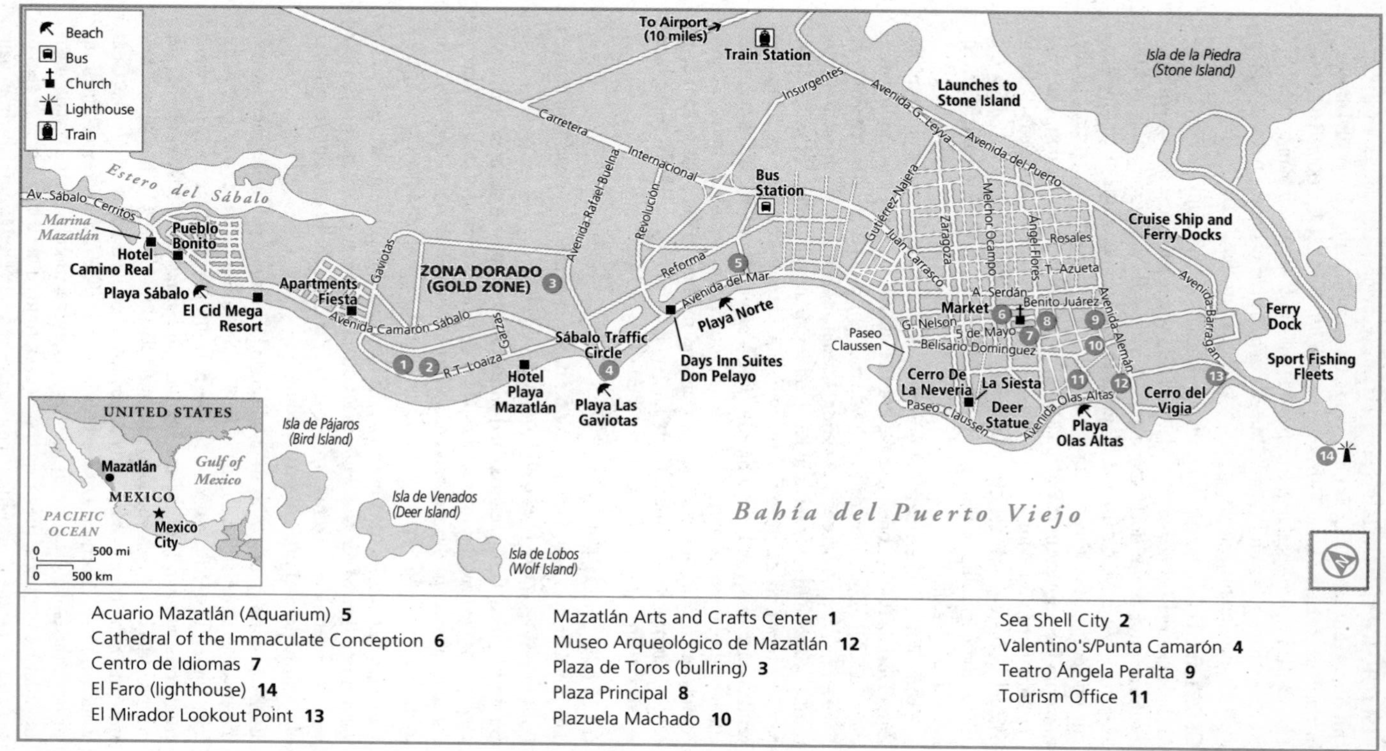

Beach
Bus
Church
Lighthouse
Train
To Airport (10 miles)
Train Station
Insurgentes
Avenida G. Leyva
Launches to Stone Island
Isla de la Piedra (Stone Island)
Avenida del Puerto
Carretera
Internacional
Bus Station
Estero del Sábalo
Av. Sábalo-Cerritos
Marina Mazatlán
Hotel Camino Real
Pueblo Bonito
Playa Sábalo
El Cid Mega Resort
Apartments Fiesta
Gaviotas
ZONA DORADO (GOLD ZONE)
Avenida Rafael Buelna
Revolución
Reforma
Avenida del Mar
Avenida Camarón Sábalo
Garzas
R.T. Loaiza
Hotel Playa Mazatlán
Sábalo Traffic Circle
Playa Las Gaviotas
Playa Norte
Days Inn Suites Don Pelayo
Gutiérrez Nájera
Juan Carrasco
Zaragoza
Melchor Ocampo
Ángel Flores
Rosales
T. Azueta
A. Serdán
Benito Juárez
Avenida Alemán
Market
G. Nelson
5 de Mayo
Belisario Domínguez
Paseo Claussen
Cerro De La Nevería
La Siesta
Deer Statue
Avenida Olas Altas
Playa Olas Altas
Cerro del Vigía
Cruise Ship and Ferry Docks
Avenida Barragán
Ferry Dock
Sport Fishing Fleets
UNITED STATES
Mazatlán
MEXICO
Gulf of Mexico
PACIFIC OCEAN
Mexico City
0 500 mi
0 500 km
Isla de Pájaros (Bird Island)
Isla de Venados (Deer Island)
Isla de Lobos (Wolf Island)
Bahía del Puerto Viejo
Acuario Mazatlán (Aquarium) 5
Cathedral of the Immaculate Conception 6
Centro de Idiomas 7
El Faro (lighthouse) 14
El Mirador Lookout Point 13
Mazatlán Arts and Crafts Center 1
Museo Arqueológico de Mazatlán 12
Plaza de Toros (bullring) 3
Plaza Principal 8
Plazuela Machado 10
Sea Shell City 2
Valentino's/Punta Camarón 4
Teatro Ángela Peralta 9
Tourism Office 11

**VISITOR INFORMATION** The extremely helpful and professional **City and State Tourism Office** is on Avenida Camarón Sábalo (corner of Tiburón) in the Ban Rural building, 4th floor (✆ **669/916-5160;** fax 669/916-5166). The staff is English-speaking. It's open Monday to Friday from 8am to 5pm. To preview what's going on in Mazatlán before you arrive, check the website for the local English-language newspaper; www.pacificPearl.com.

**CITY LAYOUT** Mazatlán extends north from the peninsula port area along Avenida Gabriel Leyva and Avenida Barragan, where the cruise ships, sportfishing boats, and ferries dock. Downtown begins with the historic area of **Old Mazatlán** (Viejo Mazatlán) and **Playa Olas Altas** to the south. A curving seaside boulevard, or ***malecón,*** runs 27km (17 miles) along the waterfront, all the way from Playa Olas Altas to **Playa Norte,** changing names often along the way. Traveling north, it begins as Paseo Olas Altas and then becomes Paseo Claussen parallel to the commercial downtown area. The name changes to Avenida del Mar at the beginning of the Playa Norte area, where several moderately priced hotels are located.

About 6km (4 miles) north of downtown lies the Sábalo traffic circle in the **Zona Dorada** (Gold Zone) near the **Punta Camarón,** a rocky outcropping over the water. The Zona Dorada begins where Avenida del Mar intersects Avenida Rafael Buelna and becomes **Avenida Camarón Sábalo,** which leads north through the abundant hotels and fast-food restaurants of the tourist zone. From here, the resort hotels, including the huge El Cid resort complex, spread northward along and beyond **Playa Sábalo.** The **Marina Mazatlán** development has changed the landscape north of the Zona Dorada considerably, as hotels, condo complexes, and private residences rise around the new marina. This area north of the Marina El Cid is increasingly known as Nuevo Mazatlán. North of here is **Los Cerritos** (Little Hills), the northern limit of Mazatlán.

## GETTING AROUND

The downtown transportation center for buses, taxis, and *pulmonías* (see below) is on the central Plaza Principal, facing the cathedral.

**BY TAXI** **Eco Taxis** are green-and-white cabs with posted set fares. Taxis can easily be flagged around town and can also be rented by the day or by the hour. Agree on a price in advance. Fares between the Zona Dorada and Old Mazatlán average $4.50 to $6.50; within the Zona Dorada, you should pay about $3.50.

**BY *PULMONIA*** These open-air vehicles resembling overgrown golf carts carry up to three passengers. ***Pulmonías*** (literally "pneumonias") have surreylike tops and open sides. As a rule, they're slightly cheaper than taxis, but you should also still settle on a price before boarding.

**BY BUS** Buses, some with air-conditioning, cover most of the city and are relatively easy to use, although knowing some Spanish is helpful. Fares are 80¢ for local routes. The "Sábalo Centro" line runs from the Gold Zone along the waterfront to downtown near the market and the central plaza; at Avenida Miguel Alemán, the buses turn and head south to Olas Altas. The "Cerritos-Juárez" line starts near the train station, cuts across town to the *malecón* beside the Gold Zone, and heads north to Los Cerritos and back. The "Sábalo Cocos" line runs through the Gold Zone, heads inland to the bus station, and goes on to downtown (also stopping at the market) by a back route. The "Playa Sur" line goes to the area where the sportfishing and tour boats depart. Buses run daily from 6am to 10:30pm.

## *FAST FACTS:* Mazatlán

*American Express* The office is on Avenida Camarón Sábalo in the Centro Comercial Balboa shopping center, Loc. 15 and 16 (✆ **669/913-0600;** fax 669/916-5908), between the traffic circle and the El Cid resort. It's open Monday to Friday from 9am to 6pm, Saturday from 9am to 1pm.

*Area Code* The telephone area code for Mazatlán is **669.**

*Banks* Most banks exchange foreign currency Monday to Friday from 9am to noon. Banks are generally open until 6pm, and some have limited hours on Saturday.

*Climate* As the northernmost major beach resort on the mainland, Mazatlán can be cooler in summer than the resorts farther south. The wettest month is September.

*Emergencies* Dial ✆ **060.** For medical emergencies, contact the **Sharp Hospital,** Rafael Buelna and Las Cruces (✆ **669/986-5676**).

*Internet Access* Numerous places offer access. The fastest service in town is at the **Cyber Café Mazatlán,** in the Centro Comercial Lomas, Av. Camarón Sábalo 204 (✆ **669/914-0008**). It offers cable access rather than dial-up, and charges $2.50 per half hour, $4 per hour. It's open daily 9am to 10pm. **Mailboxes Etc.,** Avenida Camarón Sábalo 202 local 4 esq. Sierra de Venados (✆ **669/916-4010;** fax 669/916-4011; mbe15@mzt.megared.net.mx), charges $3 for 30 minutes and $1 per printed page. It's open Monday to Friday from 9am to 7pm, Saturday and Sunday from 9am to 3pm.

*Language Classes* Spanish-language classes begin every Monday at the **Centro de Idiomas** (✆ **669/985-5606;** fax 669/982-2053; www.spanish-link.org), 3 blocks west of the cathedral near 21 de Marzo and Canizales. In addition to small-group (maximum 10 students) and individual instruction, the language center offers a homestay program and a person-to-person program that matches students with local people. On Friday at 7pm, the center holds free Spanish and English conversation groups open to both visitors and locals. For more information, call or write Dixie Davis, Belisario Domínguez 1908, Mazatlán, Sin.

*Pharmacy* **Farmacias Hidalgo,** Herman R. Hidalgo s/n (✆ **669/985-4545** or 669/94646), is open 24 hours.

*Police* The local police number is ✆ **669/983-4510.**

*Post Office* The *correo* is downtown on Benito Juárez just off Angel Flores, on the east side of the main plaza (✆ **669/981-2121**). Hours are Monday to Friday from 8am to 5pm, Saturday from 9am to 1pm.

## ACTIVITIES ON & OFF THE BEACH

To orient yourself, walk up and enjoy the panoramic view from **El Faro,** the famous lighthouse on the point at the south end of town. It's the second-highest lighthouse in the world (only Gibraltar's is higher), towering 135m (447 ft.) over the harbor. Begin at the end of Paseo Centenario, near the sportfishing docks. There's a refreshment stand at the foot of the hill. Allow about 45 minutes for the climb. The view is nearly as spectacular from the top of **Cerro del Vigía** (Lookout Hill), which is accessible by car from Paseo Olas Altas.

**BEACHES** At the western edge of downtown is rocky, pebbly **Playa Olas Altas,** a lovely stretch of pounding surf, but not suitable for swimming. Around a rocky promontory north of Olas Altas is **Playa Norte,** which offers several kilometers of good sand beach.

At the Sábalo traffic circle, Punta Camarón juts into the water, and on either side of the point is **Playa Las Gaviotas.** Farther north, **Playa Sábalo** is perhaps the best beach in Mazatlán. The next point jutting into the water is Punta Sábalo, beyond which you'll find a bridge over a channel that flows in and out of a lagoon. Beyond the marina, more beaches stretch all the way to Los Cerritos. Remember that all beaches in Mexico are public property, so you have the right to enjoy the beach of your choice.

Mazatlán is one of only a few resorts in Mexico where surfing is common on central town beaches. The waves are best at **Los Pinos,** north of the fort—known in surfing circles as "the Cannon"—and at Playa Los Gaviotas and Playa Los Sábalos.

A good beach that makes a great day trip, is on the ocean side of **Isla de la Piedra** (Stone Island). From the center of town, board a "Circunvalación" or "Playa Sur" bus from the north side of the Plaza Principal for the ride to the boat landing, Embarcadero–Isla de la Piedra. Small motorboats make the 5-minute trip to the island every 15 minutes or so from 7am to 6pm for a modest price. When you arrive on the island, walk through the rustic little village to the ocean side, where the pale-sand beaches, bordered by coconut groves, stretch for miles. On Sunday afternoons, the *palapa* restaurants on the shore have music and dancing, attracting mainly Mexican families; on other days the beach is almost empty. **Carmelita's** has delicious fish called *lisamacho;* it's grilled over an open fire and served slightly blackened with fresh, hot corn tortillas and salsa. It's open daily from 10am to 6pm and doesn't accept credit cards.

The local gay beach is on **Isla de las Chivas.** Transportation to the island is by launches, which you can catch at the Muelle Puntilla, located next to the docks where the ferry to La Paz departs.

**CRUISES & BOAT RENTALS** The **Fiesta Cruise** runs a large double-decker boat Tuesday to Sunday at 10:30am, leaving from the south beach near the lighthouse. The 3-hour cruise takes in the harbor and bay; bilingual guides explain the marine life while recorded music alternates between mariachi and rock. Tickets cost $20 per person, $31 with open bar, $10 for children 5 to 10. Purchase tickets through a major hotel or travel agency, or call ✆ **669/913-0623** or 669/985-2237. The **Kolonahe Sailing Adventure** departs for Isla de Venados (Deer Island) Tuesday through Sunday from Marina El Cid. Reserve through any travel agent or through El Cid directly (see below). This excursion sails aboard a 50-foot trimaran to the island, where guests enjoy a picnic lunch and beverages, plus the use of snorkel equipment, boogie boards, kayaks, and canoes for a cost of $45 per person. Departure is at 9:15am, with the boat returning at 3:30pm.

*Anfibios,* amphibious vehicles that operate on land and in the water, head for Isla de Venados (Deer Island), one of three big islands off the coast. Trips last 2 to 2½ hours; they leave from the beaches of the **El Cid resort** (✆ **669/913-3333,** ext. 3341) daily at 10am, noon, and 2pm. Round-trip tickets cost $15, plus $15 for snorkeling gear.

**DEEP-SEA FISHING** Mazatlán claims to be the billfish and shrimp capital of the world, and whether or not it's a valid claim, deep-sea fishing in Mazatlán is generally less expensive than in other parts of Mexico. If you request it (please do!), your captain will practice "catch and release." Rates are around $240 per day for a 24-foot *lancha* for up to three persons, $350 per day for a 38-foot cruiser for up to four persons, and $430 per day for a 36-foot cruiser for up to four passengers; rates do not include fishing licenses, drinks, or gratuities. Try the **Flota Estrella** (© **669/982-2665** or 669/982-3878; fax 669/982-5155) or the **Aries Fleet** (© **669/916-3468**). Locals suggest making fishing reservations for October through January at least a month in advance; at the very least, do it the minute you arrive in town. You may also choose to rent a *panga* (a small, uncovered, fiberglass boat with outboard motor) at a rate of $40 per hour, with a minimum of 4 hours—it's the way the locals fish.

**OTHER WATERSPORTS** Among the best places to rent watersports equipment, from snorkeling gear to Hobie Cats, are the Aqua Sport Center at the **El Cid resort** (© **669/913-3333**) and the Ocean Sport Center at the **Hotel Camino Real** (© **669/913-1111**).

**SPECIAL EVENTS IN NEARBY VILLAGES** On the weekend of the first Sunday in October, **Rosario,** a small town 45 minutes south on Highway 15, holds a **festival honoring Our Lady of the Rosary.** Games, music, dances, processions, and festive foods mark the event. From May 1 to 10, Rosario holds its **Spring Festival.**

In mid-October, the village of **Escuinapa,** south of Rosario on Highway 15, holds a **Mango Festival.**

For more information, call the State Tourism Office at © **669/916-5160.**

**SPECTATOR SPORTS** There's a bullring (Plaza de Toros) on Rafael Buelna about a mile from the Golden Zone. From December through early April, **bullfights** are held every Sunday and on holidays at 4pm; locals recommend arriving by 2pm. Tickets range from $12 for general admission (ask for the shady side—*la sombra*) to $30 for the front of the shaded section; most travel agencies and tour desks sell advance tickets.

Mexican **rodeos,** or *charreadas,* take place at the Lienzo Charro (bullring) of the Asociación de Charros de Mazatlán (© **669/986-3510**) on Saturdays or Sundays beginning at 4pm. Tickets (around $5) are available through local travel agents and hotel concierge desks, who will have the current schedule.

At Playa Olas Altas, daring **cliff divers** take to the rock ledges of **El Mirador** and plunge into the shallow, pounding surf below, a la Acapulco. The divers perform sporadically during the day as tour buses arrive near their perch, sometimes diving with torches at 7pm. After the dive, they collect donations from spectators. Follow the *malecón* to the esplanade and look for the mermaid statue to find El Mirador.

**TENNIS, GOLF & OTHER OUTDOOR SPORTS** Mazatlán has more than 100 tennis courts. Try the **El Cid resort,** on Camarón Sábalo (© **669/913-3333**), although hotel guests have priority, or the **Racquet Club Gaviotas, Ibis,** and **Río Bravo** in the Golden Zone (© **669/913-5939**). Many larger hotels in Mazatlán also have courts.

As for **golf,** Mazatlán is probably the best golf value in Mexico. Try the 27-hole course at the **El Cid resort** (© **669/913-3333**). Nine holes designed by Lee Trevino complement the 18 holes designed by Robert Trent Jones, Jr. It's open to the public, with preference given to hotel guests. Tee times book up quickly. Greens fees for nonguests range from $58 for 9 holes, plus $17 for the caddy, to $73 for 18 holes, plus $17 for the caddy. El Cid's guests get a discount of 15%. El Cid's facilities include a John Jacobs golf school, the only one in Mexico.

Another option is the 9-hole course at the **Club Campestre Mazatlán** (✆ **669/980-1570**), which is open to the public. Greens fees are $20 for 9 holes, $34 for 18 holes; a caddy costs an extra $8 and $15, a cart $12 and $22, respectively. It's on Highway 15 on the outskirts of downtown.

Mazatlán's newest course is at the **Estrella del Mar Golf Club** (✆ **669/982-3300**). The 18-hole, 7,004-yard course, also designed by Robert Trent Jones, Jr., stretches along 3km (2 miles) of coastline on Isla de la Piedra, a peninsula just south of downtown Mazatlán. There's a PGA pro on staff, and daily clinics. Greens fees run $103 ($59 after 1pm), including cart, but no caddies are available at present. It's open daily from 7:30am to sunset. Also on site are a golf shop, restaurant, and bar. Clubs are available for rent for $30 plus tax.

You can rent horses for **horseback riding** on Isla de la Piedra for $6 per hour. Ask your hotel's travel agent to arrange a **kayaking excursion** on El Verde Comacho Ecological Lagoon, or take a trip to Teacapán for **birding** in one of Mexico's largest estuaries (see "Road Trips from Mazatlán," later).

**Kelly's Bicycle Shop,** Av. Camarón Sábalo 204 L-10 (no phone), in the Zona Dorada, arranges mountain-bike tours and rentals of aluminum-frame bikes with full suspension. A half-day guided tour costs $25; rentals are $5 per half-day and $10 per full day. Bike rentals include water bottle, snack, map, and general information on routes.

## EXPLORING MAZATLAN

Mazatlán may be best known for its wide, sandy beaches and sporting activities, but visitors who neglect to sample the city's cultural events and attractions are missing out on a multidimensional destination.

### MUSEUMS

**Acuario Mazatlán** *Kids* Children and adults interested in the sea will love the Mazatlán Aquarium. With over 200 species of fish, including sharks, eels, and sea horses, it is one of the largest and best in Mexico. Next to the aquarium are a playground and a botanical garden, with an aviary and crocodile exhibit. Staff members feed the sea lions, birds, and fish at shows almost hourly.

Av. de los Deportes 111, ½ block off Av. del Mar. ✆ **669/981-7815** or 669/981-7817. www.pacificpearl.com/acuario. Admission $5.50 adults, $3 children 3–11. Daily 9:30am–6pm.

**Museo Arqueológico de Mazatlán** This small, attractive archaeological museum displays both pre-Hispanic artifacts and a permanent contemporary art exhibit. From Olas Altas, walk inland on Sixto Osuna 1½ blocks; the museum is on your right. Art exhibits are sometimes held in the Casa de la Cultura across the street from the museum.

Sixto Osuna 76, 1½ blocks in from Paseo Olas Altas. ✆ **669/981-1455.** Free admission. Mon–Fri 8am–3pm.

### ARCHITECTURAL HIGHLIGHTS

Two blocks south of the central plaza stands the lovely **Teatro Angela Peralta** (✆ **669/982-4447**), a national historic monument. Built between 1869 and 1874, it most recently underwent renovations in 1998. The 841-seat Italian-style theater has three levels of balconies, two fąades, and, in true tropical style, a lobby with no roof. The theater was named for one of the world's great divas, who, along with the director and 30 members of the opera, died in Mazatlán of

### *Moments* Mazatlán's Carnaval: A Weeklong Party

The week before Lent (usually in Feb) is Mazatlán's famous Carnaval, or Mardi Gras. People come from all over the country and abroad for this flamboyant celebration, topped in size and revelry only by those held in Río de Janeiro and New Orleans. Highlights of the event include parades, special shows, the coronation of the Carnaval queen, outdoor concerts, more than 150 food and beverage vendors, all-night parties, and extravaganzas all over town. For event information, check at major hotels or the tourism office and look for posters. Every night during Carnaval week, all along the Olas Altas oceanfront drive in the southern part of town, the streets fill with music from roving mariachi groups, local traditional *bandas sinaloenses* (sporting lots of brass instruments), and electrified bands under tarpaulin shades. The crowd increases each day until the last night (Shrove Tues), when musicians, dancers, and people out for a good time pack the *malecón.* The following day, Ash Wednesday, the party is over. People receive crosses of ashes on their foreheads at church, and Lent begins.

cholera in an 1863 epidemic. Some city tours stop at the theater; if you're visiting on your own, the theater is open daily from 9am to 6pm. The fee for touring the building is $1. It regularly schedules folkloric ballets, along with periodic performances of classical ballet, symphony concerts, opera, and jazz. For information, call or check at the theater box office.

The 20-block historic area near the theater, including the small square **Plazuela Machado** (bordered by Frías, Constitución, Carnaval, and Sixto Osuna), abounds with beautiful old buildings and rows of colorful townhouses trimmed with wrought iron and carved stone; many buildings were restored as part of the 1998–1999 downtown beautification program—although much remains to be done. Small galleries are beginning to move into the area as the neighborhood becomes the center of Mazatlán's artistic community. Check out the **townhouses** on Libertad between Domínguez and Carnaval and the two lavish **mansions** on Ocampo at Domínguez and at Carnaval. For a rest stop, try the **Café Pacífico** (decorated with historic pictures of Mazatlán) on the Plazuela Machado.

The **Plaza Principal,** also called Plaza Revolución, is the heart of the city, filled with vendors, shoeshine stands, and people of all ages out for a stroll. At its center is a Victorian-style, wrought-iron bandstand with a diner-type restaurant underneath. Be sure to take in the **Cathedral of the Immaculate Conception,** built in the 1800s, with its unusual yellow-tiled twin steeples and partially tiled façade. It's on the corner of Calle 21 de Marzo and Nelson.

## ORGANIZED TOURS

In addition to 3-hour **city tours** ($20), there are excursions to many colorful and interesting villages nearby, such as Concordia and Copala (see below). Some towns date from the 16th-century Spanish Conquest; others are modest farming or fishing villages. Information and reservations are available at any travel agency or major hotel, and all accept American Express, MasterCard, and Visa. Two recommended tour agencies are **Marlin Tours** (✆ **669/913-5301**) and **Ole Tours** (✆ **669/916-6287**).

**COPALA-CONCORDIA** This popular countryside tour stops at several mountain villages where artisans craft furniture and other items. Copala is a historic mining village with a Spanish-colonial church. The tour ($45), also known as the "Mountain Tour," includes lunch and soft drinks. For more about Copala, see "Road Trips from Mazatlán," later.

**MAZATLAN JUNGLE TOUR** Some might say that David Pérez's **"Jungle Tour"** (© and fax **669/914-1444** or 669/914-0451) is misnamed, but it's still worthwhile. It consists of a 1½-hour boat ride past a Mexican navy base, Mazatlán's shrimp fleet and packing plants, and into the mangrove swamps to Isla de la Piedra (Stone Island). There's a 3-hour stop at a pristine beach that has what could be the world's largest sand dollars. Horseback rides on the beach are $6 for a half-hour. After the beach stop, feast on *pescado zarandeado* (fish cooked over coconut husks, green mangrove, and charcoal). Tours run from 9am to 3pm and cost $42 per person. Days vary, so call for dates and reservations. MasterCard and Visa are accepted.

## WHERE TO STAY

The hotels in downtown Mazatlán are generally older and less expensive than those along the beachfront heading north. As a rule, room rates rise the farther north you go from downtown. The three major areas to stay are Olas Altas and downtown, the Playa Norte (North Beach), and the Zona Dorada.

### THE ZONA DORADA

The Gold Zone is an elegant arc of gold sand linked by a palm-lined boulevard and bordered by the most deluxe hotels and a sprinkling of elaborate beach houses. A bonus here is the sunset view: The three islands just offshore seem to melt gradually into the fading colors. Many hotels along this beach cut their prices from May through September, making a good deal even that much better.

**El Cid Mega Resort** ★★★ El Cid Mega Resort is as much a destination as it is a hotel—with *mega* being the operative word. Although it is large—bordering on imposing—El Cid offers every service and convenience you can think of, from deluxe rooms to eco-tours. Both a hotel and a residential development, El Cid has three beachfront buildings, private villas, and a 27-hole golf course on 900 acres. The main 17-story beachfront tower, **Castilla,** was renovated in 1999; there's also the 28-story, all-suite **El Moro Tower** and the lower-rise, lower-priced **Granada,** near the golf course. Although room layouts vary, most are heavily detailed in marble and feature private balconies and contemporary, upscale furnishings. *Mega* also applies to extra services at El Cid, where a program called "Active Learning Vacations" is encouraging more involved vacations, priced as special packages. There are opportunities to improve your golf, tennis, or sailing skills or indulge in a Fit for Life program through the on-site spa. All-inclusive options are also available; ask for special deals. This resort has

---

*Tips* **Mazatlán Hotel Crunch**

Mazatlán hotels fill up quickly during Carnaval, Easter week, and spring break; some of the choicest rooms are reserved a year in advance, and room rates generally rise 30% to 40%. High season in Mazatlán, as in the rest of Mexico, is December 20 to Easter; low season begins the day after Easter and extends to December 19.

---

something for every type of traveler and is especially ideal for those to whom "size matters."

Camarón Sábalo s/n (between Rodolfo T. Loaiza and Circuito Campeador), 82110 Mazatlán, Sin. ✆ **800/525-1925** in the U.S., or 669/913-3333. Fax 669/914-1311. www.elcid.com. 1,320 units. High season $106–$281 double, $281 jr. suite, $396–$536 suite; low season $89–$244 double, $244 jr. suite, $343–$465 suite. AE, DC, MC, V. Free guarded parking. **Amenities:** 11 restaurants, 8 bars; glitzy disco; 8 swimming pools (including 1 saltwater pool); 9 tennis courts and tennis academy; marina; sailing school; complete spa and fitness center; watersports equipment; "Mega Kids Club"; concierge; tour desk; car rental desk; business center; shopping arcade; salon; room service; babysitting; laundry and dry cleaning. *In room:* A/C, TV, hair dryer, iron, safe-deposit box.

**Hotel Camino Real** ★★ The grande dame of Mazatlán's hotels, the Camino Real continues to be the most sophisticated in town, and the best choice for those seeking seclusion. It's considered to have the best location in Mazatlán, on a rocky cliff overlooking the sea, and the beach edges a small cove that's perfect for swimming. The hallmark purple-and-pink color scheme decorates the marble-floored hallways and rooms, which have bathtubs and showers, large closets, and vanity tables. Junior suites have king-size beds and comfy couches. Last year's renovations have made the rooms the most contemporary in Mazatlán. The hotel is about a 10-minute drive from the heart of the Gold Zone. Higher rates are for rooms with an ocean view; other rooms have a marina view.

Punta de Sábalo s/n, 82100 Mazatlán, Sin. ✆ **800/716-9757** or 669/913-1111. Fax 669/914-0311. 169 units. High season $104–$195 double, $260 jr. suite; low-season discounts and special packages available. AE, DC, MC, V. Free guarded parking. **Amenities:** 2 restaurants, lobby bar; small heated pool; 2 tennis courts; room service; travel agency. *In room:* A/C, TV, minibar.

**Pueblo Bonito** ★★ The all-suite Pueblo Bonito continues to be a favored place to stay in Mazatlán. The kitchenettes and ample seating areas, along with architectural touches that include curved ceilings, arched windows, and tiled floors, make you feel more at home than in traditional hotels. The extra space means it's a good choice for families or friends traveling together. The grounds are gorgeous—peacocks and flamingos stroll over lush lawns, a waterfall cascades into a large pool, and a row of *palapas* lines the beachfront. A second Pueblo Bonito resort, Emerald Bay (✆ **669/989-0525**), mirrors the refined style and all-suite concept of this resort. It's about 15 minutes north of town at Av. Ernesto Coppel Campaña s/n, Camino al Delfín, Zona Nuevo Mazatlán. It has 60 units and a luxury spa.

Av. Camarón Sábalo 2121 (Apdo. Postal 6), 82110 Mazatlán, Sinaloa. ✆ **800/699-9000** in Mexico, or 669/914-3700. Fax 669/914-1723. www.pueblobonito.com. 250 units. $202 jr. suite, $240 1-bedroom suite for 2 adults and 2 children. AE, MC, V. Free guarded parking. **Amenities:** 3 restaurants, 1 with popular Sun brunch; 2 large pools; gym; sauna; massage; whirlpool; room service; concierge; sightseeing desk; valet parking; babysitting; tour desk; car rental desk; laundry service. *In room:* A/C, TV.

## PLAYA NORTE

The waterfront between downtown and the Gold Zone is Mazatlán's original tourist hotel zone. Moderately priced hotels and motels line the street across from the beach, where taco and souvenir vendors set up shop on weekends. Señor Frog's, Mazatlán's most famous restaurant, is in this neighborhood, as is the bus station. From May through September, many hotels cut their prices.

**Apartments Fiesta** *Value* A good value for long-term stays, the bright-blue-and-orange Fiesta is 3 blocks inland from Camarón Sábalo, an easy walk from the beach. Accommodations are one-bedroom apartments, all with kitchens, clustered around a small courtyard. Each apartment is decorated differently, with a variety of wooden tables, chairs, and beds. There are no TVs or telephones, but calls can be made through the main office, and rental TVs can be arranged. The proprietors, Yolanda and Francisco Olivera, are very accommodating hosts. They don't take reservations far in advance and prefer that you call a week before you plan to visit.

Ibis 502 at Río de la Plata, 82110 Mazatlán, Sin. ✆ **669/913-5355;** ✆ and fax 669/913-1764. www.hudsontours.com. 8 units. $25–$72 double per night, $150–$425 double per week, $238–$910 double per month. No credit cards. Free parking. **Amenities:** Sundeck; barbecue pit. *In room:* A/C.

**Hotel Playa Mazatlán** ★★ *Kids* The most happening place on this stretch of the Gold Zone, the Hotel Playa Mazatlán is enduringly popular with families, tour groups, and regulars who return annually for winter vacations or spring break. The quietest rooms are in the three-story section surrounding the well-tended interior gardens; those by the terrace restaurant and beach can be noisy. The beach is one of the liveliest in town. The hotel hosts popular Mexican fiestas on Tuesdays, Thursdays, and Saturdays, and a fireworks display on Sundays.

Av. Rodolfo T. Loaiza 202, 82000 Mazatlán, Sin. ✆ **800/762-5816** in the U.S., or 669/913-4455. Fax 669/914-0366. www.playamazatlan.com 423 units. $119 garden-view double, $142 oceanview double. AE, MC, V. Free guarded parking. **Amenities:** 2 restaurants, bar; 3 pools; 2 outdoor whirlpools; gym; watersports rental equipment; laundry service; room service; in-house doctor; small gift shop/pharmacy; tour desk. *In room:* A/C, TV.

**Howard Johnson Don Pelayo** The Don Pelayo remains a top choice among budget inns. It's on the North Beach at the edge of the *malecón.* The very clean, regularly updated waterfront rooms have small balconies; all rooms have satellite TV, a king-size bed or two double beds, and central air-conditioning (without individual controls). Lighting and furnishings are gradually being improved. Suites have minibars. The hotel is very popular with families and has ample RV parking.

Av. del Mar 1111 (Apdo. Postal 1088), 82000 Mazatlán, Sin. ✆ **669/983-2221** or 669/983-1888. Fax 669/984-0799. 165 units. $91 double, $104 jr. suite. AE, MC, V. Free enclosed parking. **Amenities:** Restaurant, bar; swimming pool; whirlpool; wading pool with slide. *In room:* A/C, TV.

## DOWNTOWN SEAFRONT/PLAYA OLAS ALTAS

The old section of Mazatlán spreads around a picturesque beach a short walk from downtown. Movie stars of the '50s and '60s came here for sun and surf, and the hotels where they stayed are still here. These hotels are right on the waterfront, and their seaside rooms have private balconies with views of the cove and the sunset. There are a few seafront restaurants along here, making it easy to dine near your hotel.

**Hotel La Siesta** ★ The historic La Siesta occupies a well-maintained building surrounded by the old mansions of Mazatlán. Inside, three levels encircle a central courtyard; rooms facing the ocean have balconies opening to sea breezes and pounding waves. Guest rooms at the back of the hotel are quieter but less charming; all have two beds, a small table and chair, good lighting, and dependably hot water. For such functional accommodations, there's a surprising array of guest services. A bonus is the popular **El Shrimp Bucket** restaurant, in the courtyard, where live marimbas and recorded music play until 11pm. This is one of the most popular hotels in Old Mazatlán and fills up quickly. Reservations are strongly advised. To get here from the deer statue on Olas Altas, go right 1 block.

Av. Olas Altas 11 Sur, 82000 Mazatlán, Sin. ✆ **669/981-2640** or 669/981-2334. Fax 669/982-2633. www.lasiesta.com.mx. 57 units. $51 oceanview double, $45 interior double. AE, MC, V. Street parking. **Amenities:** Restaurant and bar; concierge; room service; laundry; in-room massage; money exchange; safe-deposit boxes. *In room:* A/C, TV.

## WHERE TO DINE

Mazatlán boasts one of the largest shrimp fleets in the world, so it's no surprise that shrimp and seafood are the specialties. Most restaurants are very casual and moderately priced, offering good value. A cheap-eats treat is to stop in one of the many *loncherías* scattered throughout the downtown area. Here you can get a *torta* (a sandwich on a small French roll) stuffed with a variety of meats, cheeses, tomatoes, onions, and chiles for around $2.

### THE ZONA DORADA

#### Expensive

**Angelo's** ★ ITALIAN/SEAFOOD Even locals consider this hotel restaurant one of the best in town, as much for its ambience as for its food. Beveled glass doors reveal a dining room gleaming with brass, polished wood, and crystal chandeliers. A pianist plays in the background as formally dressed waiters present menus featuring homemade pastas; shrimp dishes, including superb scampi; and a large selection of imported wines.

In the Pueblo Bonito hotel, Camarón Sábalo 2121. ✆ **669/914-3700,** ext. 8608. Reservations required. Main courses $8–$24. AE, MC, V. Daily 6–11:30pm.

**Papagayo Restaurant** ★ INTERNATIONAL Nestled on the beach at the Inn at Mazatlán, diners at Papagayo enjoy the natural beauty of the beachfront, with a choice of beach or open-air patio seating, and a view across the water to Las Tres Islas, the three imposing islands just offshore. The food is consistent and elegantly presented, with an extensive menu of international fare; favorites are shrimp CocoLoco, and tournedos Rossini in wild mushroom sauce.

The Inn at Mazatlán, Camarón Sábalo 6291. ✆ **669/913-4151.** Main courses $9.50–$28. AE, MC, V. Daily 7am–11:30am and 7–10pm.

**Señor Pepper's** ★★ INTERNATIONAL Managing to be both elegant and comfortable, this restaurant is known for serving the best steaks in Mazatlán. Potted plants, candlelight, and lots of polished crystal, silver, and brass give the dining room a romantic feeling, and some nights it seems as if all the diners are old friends. The enormous Sonoran beef steaks are grilled over mesquite; lobster and shrimp are also big hits. The nightly special includes appetizer, steak or seafood, vegetables, and soup or salad; there is a complimentary appetizer for those having only drinks at the bar. It's located across from the Camino Real Hotel.

Av. Camarón Sábalo s/n. ✆ **669/914-0101.** Main courses $20–$39. AE, MC, V. Daily 6pm–11pm; bar daily 5pm–2am.

#### Moderate

**No Name Café** ★★ INTERNATIONAL The 30 TVs are one of the main attractions of this restaurant and sports bar, the best place in town to watch your favorite sporting events. Sports memorabilia, including pennants, posters, team photos, and baseball card collections, covers every square inch of the place. Between games, rousing rock 'n' roll and country music will lure you onto the dance floor. Renowned for having the best barbecue ribs in town, the cafe also has seating on a tree-covered courtyard surrounded by *palapas.*

The menu is as oriented to the good ol' USA as the setting, with outdoor-grilled steaks, spare ribs, pork chops, thick hamburgers, and barbecued chicken—plus grilled shrimp, for a touch of Mazatlán. For dessert, the homemade banana-coconut cream pie is sumptuous.

Rodolfo T. Loaiza 4178, Zona Dorada. ✆ **669/913-2031.** Main courses $5.50–$19.88. AE, MC, V. Daily noon–12:30am.

**Terraza Playa** MEXICAN/INTERNATIONAL During the day, diners enjoy the action on the beach plus a view across to Isla de Venados (Deer Island). After sundown, the stars overhead (in the open terrace) and the sound of the surging waves are a backdrop to live music and dancing from 7pm to midnight. The menu is standard international fare, well prepared, with excellent, friendly service. Especially popular is the breakfast buffet.

In the Hotel Playa Mazatlán, Rodolfo T. Loaiza 202. ✆ **669/913-4455.** Breakfast $3.50–$7; Mexican plates $4.50–$9.50; seafood and meat $7.50–$14.50. AE, MC, V. Daily 6am–midnight.

### Inexpensive

**Jungle Juice** ★★ *Finds* MEXICAN/STEAKS/SEAFOOD This comfortable patio and upstairs bar has a definite Mexican flair that gives the partially open-air restaurant a festive touch. Grilled meats and lobster are the specialties at this juice-and-smoothie joint, which has evolved into a full-fledged grill and bar. Smoothies and juices are still the specialties, as are vegetarian plates and meat dishes grilled over mesquite on the patio. This casual spot also serves good breakfasts and makes a nice stop after shopping in the Gold Zone. Look for daily specials on the blackboard. To get here from Pastelería Panamá, take Sábalo and turn right on Las Garzas; it's a block down on your right. Heading north on Loaiza, Las Garzas and the Pastelería Panamá are on the right after the Sábalo traffic circle, before the Mazatlán Arts and Crafts Center.

Las Garzas 101. ✆ **669/913-3315.** Main courses $5–$20. MC, V. Daily 8am–10pm; bar daily 6pm–2am.

**Pura Vida I** ★ VEGETARIAN/HEALTH FOOD Nearly hidden behind thick plants, Pura Vida has several small seating sections with wood picnic tables and white canvas umbrellas. The specialty at this perfect morning spot is an extensive selection of juices and smoothies, from kelp to papaya. The energetic staff serves omelets and whole-wheat pancakes for breakfast, and burgers, purified salads, soups, and Mexican specialties for lunch. There are plenty of vegetarian dishes, like soy burgers. The veggie and white-chicken sandwiches served on whole-wheat rolls are fabulous. To get here from Pastelería Panamá on Sábalo, turn right on Las Garzas, then left 1 block down onto Laguna. The cafe is on your right. There's a second location at Camarón Sábalo 777, in the Costa de Oro (✆ **669/916-6600;** open daily from 8am–3pm).

Calle Laguna 777. ✆ **669/916-5815.** Main courses $2–$6. No credit cards. Daily 8am–10pm.

## DOWNTOWN & PLAYA NORTE

### Moderate

**Bahía Mariscos** SEAFOOD A historic townhouse in Olas Altas has been transformed into a charming restaurant specializing in bountiful seafood lunches. The *campechana bahía* is a delicious medley of shrimp, octopus, oysters, and calamari, and the fried whole fish is one of the best you'll find in the city. The owner also offers tours of the house, which dates to the turn of the 20th century. To get here from El Shrimp Bucket (at Mariano Escobedo and Olas Altas), walk south 1 block and turn left on Escobedo; the restaurant is on your left—it's the bright spot on an avenue of deserted houses.

Mariano Escobedo 203. ✆ **669/981-2645.** Main courses $9–$22. MC, V. Daily 10am–8pm. Closed 1 week in Oct.

**Copa de Leche** ★★ *Moments* MEXICAN This shaded sidewalk cafe on the waterfront at Playa Olas Altas feels the way Mazatlán must have in the 1930s, and the food is consistently as good as the ocean view. The menu includes *pechugas en nogada* (chicken breast in pecan-and-pomegranate sauce); shrimp in tamarind sauce; traditional *alambre* barbecue (beef cooked with onion, peppers, mushrooms, ham, and bacon); wonderful seafood soup loaded with squid, shrimp, and chunks of fish; and great shrimp with *chipotle* sauce. Inside, the decor is updated Mexican, the bar is an old wooden boat, and the dining tables are covered with linen cloths. To get here from El Shrimp Bucket (at Mariano Escobedo and Olas Altas), turn south and walk half a block down Olas Altas; the cafe is on your left.

Av. Olas Altas 1220 A Sur. © **669/982-5753.** Fax 669/981-3897. Breakfast $4–$8; main courses $5.50–$17. AE, MC, V. Daily 7am–11pm.

**El Shrimp Bucket** ★ MEXICAN/SEAFOOD El Shrimp Bucket is among the most popular restaurants in town. The specialty is Mazatlán's famous shrimp, in the air-conditioned dining room or under umbrellas in the center courtyard. For wining, dining, and dancing, this is a great place for a rousing time, another proof of the success of the Anderson chain formula. El Shrimp Bucket is on Olas Altas at the corner of Mariano Escobedo.

In the Hotel La Siesta, Av. Olas Altas 111 (at Mariano Escobedo). © **669/981-6350** or 669/982-8019. Mexican plates $4.50–$10; seafood and steak $9–$22. AE, DISC, MC, V. Daily 7am–11pm.

**Señor Frog's** INTERNATIONAL A sign over the door says JUST ANOTHER BAR AND GRILL, but once inside you'll know that's just another of the Anderson chain's infamous understatements. The decor is delightfully wacky, the food consistently tasty, and the loud music extremely danceable. With an atmosphere this friendly and lively, revelers have been known to dance on the tables late into the night. Try the tasty ribs, Caesar salad, or caramel crêpes. The restaurant is on the waterfront drive at Playa Norte next to the Frankie Oh! disco.

North Beach *malecón,* Av. del Mar s/n. © **669/985-1110** or 669/982-1925. Main courses $7–$22. AE, MC, V. Daily noon–1:30am.

## SHOPPING

Mazatlán shopping runs the gamut from precious stones to seashells—with plenty of T-shirts in between! Most stores are open Monday to Saturday 9 or 10am to 6 or 8pm. Very few close for lunch, and many stores are open on Sunday afternoon.

**La Zona Dorada** is the best area for shopping. For a huge selection of handcrafts from all over Mexico, visit the **Mazatlán Arts and Crafts Center,** Calle Gaviotas and Loaiza (© **669/913-5022**). It accepts cash only. Nearby **Sea Shell City,** Avenida Rodolfo T. Loaiza between Las Garzas and Avenida del Mar (© **669/913-1301;** AE, MC, V) is exactly what the name implies(more shell-covered decorative items than you ever dreamed could exist, from the tacky to the sublime. **Gallery Michael,** Avenida Las Garzas 18, off Avenida Camarón Sábalo (no phone), has an excellent selection of Tlaquepaque crafts and fine silver jewelry. It is near the Dairy Queen and does not accept credit cards.

For fine jewelry, seek out **Pardo Jewellers,** Avenida Rodolfo T. Loaiza 411 (© **669/914-3354;** AE, MC, V), and **Rubio Jewellers,** in the Costa de Oro Hotel, Avenida Camarón Sábalo (© **669/914-3167;** AE, MC, V). Shops throughout the Gold Zone have a good selection of name-brand clothing, fabrics, silver jewelry, leather, art, and Mexican crafts.

The **Centro Mercado** in Old Mazatlán is another kind of shopping experience. Here you'll find women selling fresh shrimp under colorful umbrellas; open-air food stalls; and indoor shops stacked with pottery, clothing, and crafts (mostly of lesser quality). Small galleries and shops are beginning to appear in Old Mazatlán; one of the nicest is **NidArt Galería,** Avenida Libertad and Carnaval (© **669/981-0002**), next to the Angela Peralta Theater. It's open Monday to Saturday from 10am to 2pm, it features changing exhibits of contemporary art.

**La Gran Plaza** is a large shopping mall 3 blocks from the waterfront on Avenida de los Deportes. The plaza has a large supermarket, department stores, and specialty shops. A good place for buying basic items, it's open daily from 10am to 9pm.

## MAZATLAN AFTER DARK

Mazatlán is known for its vibrant Mexican fiestas and equally colorful local bar scene, where dancing on bars, atop tables, and inside cages can be a nightly event. Traditional mariachi groups, *tambora* bands, and live romantic music create a festive mood in many local restaurants and hotel bars.

**Happy hour specials** abound in value-oriented Mazatlán. One particular favorite is **El Adobe,** in the Costa de Oro hotel (© **669/913-5344** or 669/913-5043). This three-level restaurant and bar has views to the Pacific, overlooking the cascading waterfalls and hotel gardens. From 5 to 10pm, El Adobe serves two-for-one tropical drinks in oversized brandy snifters.

A free **fireworks** show takes place every Sunday at 8pm on the beach fronting the Hotel Playa Mazatlán, Rodolfo T. Loaiza 202, in the Golden Zone (© **669/913-5320** or 669/989-0555). The display is visible from the beach and from the hotel's Terraza Playa restaurant.

The same hotel also presents Mazatlán's most popular **Fiesta Mexicana,** complete with buffet, open bar, folkloric dancing, and live music. Fiestas begin at 7pm on Tuesday, Thursday, and Saturday year-round; try to arrive by 6pm to get a good table. Tickets are $32.

### CLUBS & BARS

**Café Pacífico** If you're staying downtown or prefer a quiet atmosphere, this bodega-like bar in a restored historic building on Plazuela Machado is a pleasant place to spend some time. The thick roof beams and walls are decorated with braided garlic, dried peppers, and old photographs. It's open daily from 11am to 1am. Heriberto Frías 501. © **669/981-3972.** No cover.

**Joe's Oyster Bar** Beer, burgers, fresh oysters, and high-volume dance music are the house specialties at this casual, *palapa*-topped, open-air disco. It's open daily from 11am to 2am. On the beachfront at Los Sábalos Hotel, Rodolfo T. Loaiza 100. © **669/983-5333.** No cover.

**Valentino's** Dramatically perched on a rocky outcropping overlooking the sea, this all-white, Moorish-looking building houses one of the area's most popular discos. There's a good high-tech light show complete with green laser beams. For a break from the pulsating dance floor, there are pool tables in another room, and some (relatively) quiet areas for talking. Part of this disco complex is the Bora Bora, a pub-style bar complete with volleyball court and surfing simulator. It's open daily from 9pm to 4am. Punta Camarón, near the Camarón Sábalo traffic circle. © **669/984-1666.** Cover $5–$10.

## ROAD TRIPS FROM MAZATLAN

### TEACAPAN: ABUNDANT WILDLIFE & A RUSTIC VILLAGE

Just 2 hours (131km/82 miles) south of Mazatlán is the fishing village of Teacapán, at the tip of an isolated peninsula that extends 29km (18 miles) down a coastline of pristine beaches. Mangrove lagoons and canals border its other side. Palm and mango groves, cattle ranches, and an occasional cluster of houses dot the peninsula, which ends at the Boca de Teacapán, a natural marina separating the states of Sinaloa and Nayarit. Shrimping boats line the beach at the edge of the marina, which backs up to the worn houses and dirt streets of town. A ragged place, it's recommended for those interested in birding, but probably not of much interest to other travelers.

Birders hire local fishermen to take them out around the lagoons, where they can see herons, flamingos, Canadian ducks, and countless other species. Inland, the sparsely populated land is a haven for deer, ocelot, and wild boars. There's talk of making the entire peninsula into an ecological preserve, and thus far, residents have resisted attempts by developers to turn the area into a large-scale resort. For now, visitors find the ultimate peaceful refuge.

**GETTING THERE** **By Car** Drive south from Mazatlán on the highway to Escuinapa. There are no signs marking the right turn for the road to Teacapán; ask for directions in Escuinapa. If you're arriving from the south, turn left at the Bancomer building.

**By Bus** **Autotransportes Escuinapa** runs several second-class buses daily to Escuinapa (the fare is about $5); from there you can transfer to Teacapán (about $3). The second-class bus station is behind the first-class station, across the lot where the buses park.

#### Where to Stay

**Rancho Los Angeles** The Rivera family has created this small resort amid coconut groves at the edge of the sea. The best rooms are in the hacienda-style building, with terraces beside a long beach, and in the single rustic bungalow a few feet from the main building. Other rooms are in a motel-like structure beside the main road to town and are not recommended if you have a choice(they are small, noisy, and oddly furnished. There are newer cabins on the beach and a trailer park for 40 trailers. Boat tours and horseback riding are available. The hotel's small restaurant serves meals on the patio by the pool.

Km 25 Carretera Escuinapa–Teacapán. ✆ **669/953-1344** (leave a message for Mr. Rivera). Reservations Palmas 1-B, Col. Los Pinos, 82000 Mazatlán, Sin; ✆ and fax **669/981-7867.** 20 units. $35 streetside double, $45 waterfront double; $60 suite; $150 3-bedroom bungalow; $120 4-bedroom *casa.* AE. **Amenities:** Restaurant; pool. *In room:* A/C.

### COPALA: AN OLD SILVER TOWN

Popular tours from Mazatlán stop here for lunch only, but Copala is well worth an overnight stay. The town was founded in 1565, and from the late 1880s to the early 1900s it was the center of the region's silver-mining boom. When the mines closed, the town was nearly deserted. Today, it's a National Historic Landmark with 600 full-time residents and a part-time community of retired Canadian and U.S. citizens devoted to Copala's picturesque solitude.

Every building in town is painted white, and most have red-tile roofs splashed with bougainvillea. Cobblestone streets wind from the entrance to town up slight hills to the main plaza and the 1610 Cathedral of San José. The town kicks into high gear (relatively speaking) around noon, when tour buses arrive and visitors stroll the streets surrounded by small boys selling geodes extracted from the local hills. By 3pm, most of the outsiders have left. You can wander the streets in peace and visit the century-old cemetery, the ruins of old haciendas, and the neighborhoods of white villas. The town's burros, roosters, and dogs provide the main background noise, and few cars clutter the streets.

**GETTING THERE** Tours go to Copala and Concordia (see "Organized Tours," earlier). Copala is an easy 2-hour drive from Mazatlán; drive south for about 25 minutes until you get to the detour for Durango, then turn west and drive to Concordia. From there, follow the signs for Copala; it's about 22km (14 miles). The Autotransportes Concordia bus service runs four buses daily from the second-class bus station, behind the first-class bus station. The fare is $4; check the schedule carefully before departing so you don't get stranded in Copala, where there are few places to spend the night.

### Where to Stay & Dine

**Daniel's** ★ Daniel's restaurant is Copala's best-known landmark, revered for the superb banana-cream-coconut pie served with nearly every meal. Owner Daniel Garrison restored his uncle's turn-of-the-century home into the restaurant, which is set against a backdrop of the Sierra Madre foothills. The restaurant fills with guests at lunch, and later in the day it becomes the favorite hangout of local expatriates. To the side of the restaurant is a small hotel offering large guest rooms with bathrooms, comfortable beds, fans, and windows looking out to the countryside. Daniel's also offers Copala tours for visitors driving down from Mazatlán. The restaurant is less than a 10-minute walk from town. Contacting Daniel's by phone is a little complicated, but doable: Place a call to the town's public phone (© **669/985-4225**). The person who answers will send for someone from Daniel's, and you can call back in 5 minutes.
At the entrance to town. No phone. 10 units. $42 double. Rates include breakfast. No credit cards.

## 3 Costa Alegre: Puerto Vallarta to Barra de Navidad ★★★

Costa Alegre is one of Mexico's most spectacular coastal areas, a 232km (145-mile) stretch that connects tropical forests with a series of dramatic cliff-lined coves. Tiny outpost towns line the route, while dirt roads trail down to a succession of magical coves with pristine beaches, most of them steeped in privileged exclusivity. Considered one of Mexico's greatest undiscovered treasures, this area is becoming a favored hideaway for publicity-fatigued celebrities and those in search of natural seclusion.

The area is referred to as **Costa Alegre** (Happy Coast)—the marketer's term for the area—and **Costa Careyes** (Turtle Coast), after the many sea turtles that nest here annually. It is home to an eclectic array of the most captivating and exclusive places to stay in Mexico, with a selective roster of activities that includes championship golf and polo. Along the line, however, you will encounter the funky beach towns that were the original lure for travelers who discovered the area.

Stops along Highway 200, as it meanders between Puerto Vallarta to the north and Manzanillo to the south, can be an enjoyable day trip, but travelers usually make the drive en route to a destination along the coast.

**EXPLORING COSTA ALEGRE** Costa Alegre is more an ultimate destination than a place to rent a car and take a drive. Most of the beaches are tucked into coves accessed by dirt roads that can extend for miles inland. If you do drive along this coast, Highway 200 is safe, but it's not lit and it curves through the

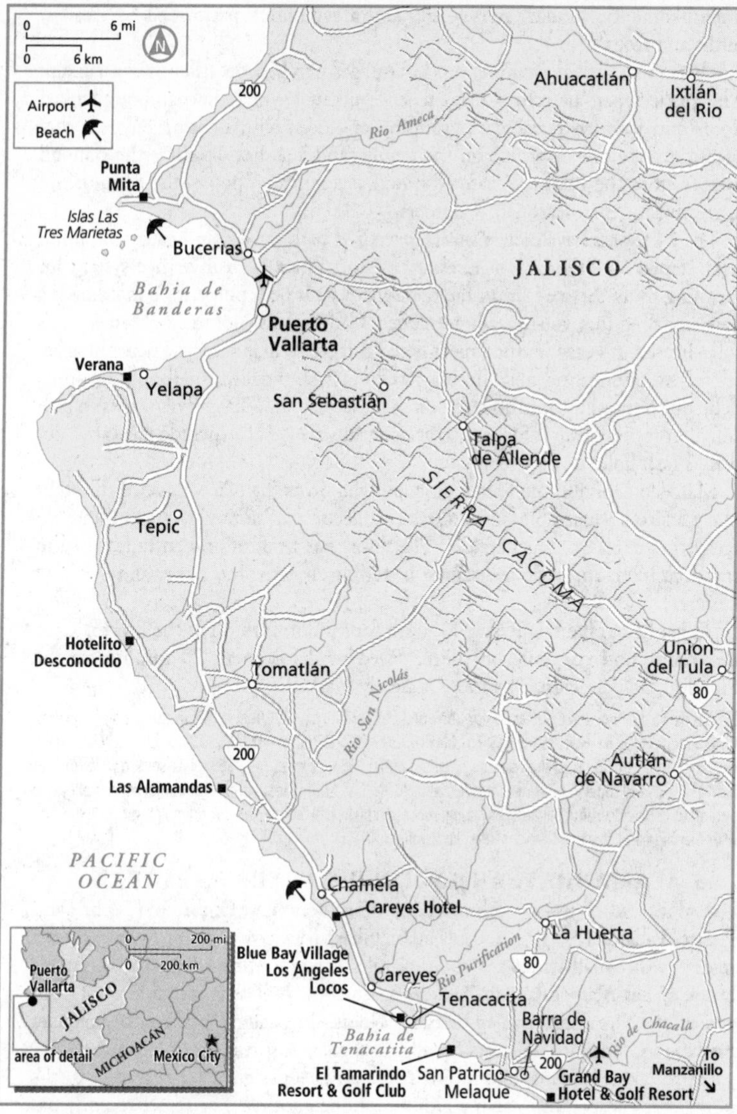


mountains, so travel only during the day. A few buses travel this route, but stop only at the towns that line the highway; many of them are several kilometers inland from the resorts tucked in along the coast.

## ALONG COSTA ALEGRE (NORTH TO SOUTH)

### CRUZ DE LORETO & ITS LUXURY ECO-RETREAT

**Hotelito Desconocido** ★★★ *Moments* The fact that the Hotelito Desconocido ("little unknown hotel") is ecologically minded is a bonus in my opinion, but it's not the principal appeal. A cross between *Out of Africa* and *Blue Lagoon,* it is among my favorite places to stay in Mexico. Think camping out with luxury linens, romantic candles everywhere, and a symphony performed by cicadas, birds, and frogs.

The rooms, called *palafitos,* are in cottages perched on stilts over a lagoon. The rustic, open-air rooms seem to extend out beyond the bamboo-planked doors and wooden terraces. A grouping of suites, with inviting daybeds that practically cry out *siesta,* are on the ample sand bar that separates the tranquil estuary from the Pacific Ocean. Also here is a saltwater pool—the ocean is too aggressive for even seasoned swimmers.

The 24 rooms have cotton sheets, oversized bath towels, and gauzy mosquito nets draped over the beds—necessary or not. There is an inventive system for morning room service—from the comfort of your bed, pull a rope that hoists a flag, signaling that you're ready for coffee. Ceiling fans cool the air, and water is solar-heated. It's easy to disconnect here. In fact, it's mandatory: There's no electricity, no phones, no neighboring restaurants, nightclubs, or shopping—only delicious tranquility for those in search of seclusion. What service lacks in polished professionalism it makes up for in enthusiasm. Rates include meals but not drinks (alcoholic or nonalcoholic).

Marcello Murzilli, the Italian designer who owns the place, traveled throughout Mexico to assemble an admirable collection of antiques, curios, and "so tacky they're classy" knickknacks. The resort has been prominently featured in travel, fashion, and style magazines, including *Architectural Digest* and *Travel & Leisure.*

To get here, take Highway 200 south for 1 hour, turn off at the exit for Cruz de Loreto, and continue on the unpaved road for about 25 minutes to the Hotelito Desconocido. The route is clearly marked.

Playón de Mismaloya s/n, Cruz de Loreto, Tomatlán, Jal. 48360. ✆ **800/851-1143** in the U.S. and Canada. Reservations ✆ **01-800/851-1143** in Mexico, 322/222-2526, or 322/222-2546; fax 322/223-0293. www.hotelito.com. 30 units. High season *palafito* double $580, *palafito* suite $660; low season *palafito* double $430, *palafito* suite $520. Rates include meals. AE, MC, V. **Amenities:** 2 restaurant/bars; beach volleyball; birding tours; windsurfing; billiards; kayaking; mountain biking; hiking; horseback riding; primitive-luxury spa with massage and spa treatments, sauna, and whirlpool.

## LAS ALAMANDAS: AN EXCLUSIVE LUXURY RESORT

**Las Alamandas** ★★★ Almost equidistant between Manzanillo (1½ hr.) and Puerto Vallarta (1¾ hr.) lies Las Alamandas, Mexico's premier ultra-exclusive resort. A dirt road winds for about a mile through a tiny village to the guardhouse of Las Alamandas, on 70 acres against low hills that are part of a 1,500-acre estate. The resort, owned by Isabel Goldsmith, daughter of British financier Sir James Goldsmith, consists of villas and *palapas* spread among four beaches, gardens, lakes, lagoons, and a bird sanctuary. It's designed for privacy—to the point that guests rarely catch a glimpse of one another. The resort recently has air-conditioning and telephones, yet manages to keep the experience as natural as possible. Its architecture is a mix of Mediterranean, Mexican, and southwestern United States; furnishings are a stunning blend of Mexican handcrafted furniture, pottery, folk art, and bright textiles from Mexico and Guatemala. Although exquisite, the furnishings exude a relaxed feel. The resort accommodates only 22 guests.

The six spacious villas have high-pitched tiled roofs, cool tiled floors, and tiled verandas with ocean views. They have several bedrooms (each with its own bathroom) and can be rented separately or as a whole house; guests who rent whole villas have preference for reservations. Some villas are on the beach, others are across a cobblestone plaza. TVs with VCRs are available on request, but there's no reception from the outside. Transportation in the hotel's van to and from Manzanillo ($225 one-way) and Puerto Vallarta ($225 one-way) can be arranged when you reserve your room. Air transport from Puerto Vallarta is also available; call for details and prices.

Hwy. 200, Manzanillo–Puerto Vallarta, Jal. 48800. Mailing address Domicilio Conocido Costa Alegre QUEMARO Jalisco, Apdo. Postal 201, San Patricio Melaque, Jal. CP 48980. ✆ **888/882-9616** in the U.S. and Canada, or 322/285-5500. Fax 322/285-5027. www.alamandas.com. 11 units. High season $504–$1,545 unit, $1,896–$3,674 villa; low season $375–$1,007 unit, $1,180–$2,340 villa. Meal plans available. AE, MC, V. **Amenities:** Restaurant; 60-ft. pool; lighted tennis court; weight room; horses; hiking trails; birding boat tours; mountain bikes; boogie boards; concierge; tour desk; book and video library; room service; landing strip (make advance arrangements). *In room:* A/C, dataport, minibar.

## CAREYES

**The Careyes Hotel** ★★ The Careyes is a gem of a resort nestled on a small, pristine cove between dramatic cliffs that are home to the super-exclusive villas of Careyes. This area has practically defined the architectural style that defines Mexico beach chic—bold washes of vibrant colors, open spaces, and gardens that showcase the tropical flowers and palms indigenous to the area.

The hotel, a Starwood Luxury Collection Property, and has just completed significant upgrades in services and facilities. The pampering accommodations all face the ocean and are stylishly simplistic. Although guests come here for isolation, you can enjoy many services, including a full European spa and polo. It's both rustic and sophisticated, with the room façades awash in scrubbed pastels forming a U around the center lawn and freeform pool. Earthy, elegant Mexican tiles and decorative accents give each room a dramatic feel, from the colony shutters and white-tile floors to the handsome loomed bedspreads and colorful pillows. Some rooms have balconies; all have ocean views. Twenty rooms have private pools, and villas are also available for rent through the hotel. The hotel is popular for weddings and small corporate retreats.

The hotel offers a number of special-interest activities for guests. Named after the hawksbill turtle (*carey* in Spanish), the hotel sponsors a Save the Turtle program in which guests can participate between July and December.

The hotel is roughly 160km (100 miles) south of Puerto Vallarta. It's about a 2-hour drive north of Manzanillo on Highway 200, and about a 1-hour drive from the Manzanillo airport. Taxis from the Manzanillo airport charge around $100 one way. There are car-rental counters at the Manzanillo and Puerto Vallarta airports. A car would be useful only for exploring the coast—Barra de Navidad and other resorts, for example—and the hotel can also make touring arrangements.

Km 53.5 Hwy. 200, Careyes, Jal. CP 48970. Mailing address Apdo. Postal 24, Cihuatlán, Jal. CP 48970. ✆ **800/525-4800** in the U.S. and Canada, or 315/351-0000. Fax 315/351-0100. www.grupoplan.com. 48 units. High season $250 double, $395–$460 suite; low season $225 double, $350–$450 suite. AE, MC, V. **Amenities:** Restaurant and bar, deli; large oceanfront pool; fully equipped, state-of-the-art spa with massage, hot and cold plunge pools, steam, sauna, weight equipment; 2 tennis courts; paddle court; kayaks; windsurf boards; Aquafins; privileges at super-exclusive El Tamarindo resort (40km/25 miles south), with 18-hole mountaintop golf course; "Just for Kids" children's activity program (during Christmas and Easter vacation); book and video library; laundry; room service. *In room:* A/C, TV, minibar, small refrigerator, robes, hair dryer.

## TENACATITA BAY

Located 60 minutes (53km/33 miles) north of the Manzanillo airport, this jewel of a bay is accessible by an 8km (5-mile) dirt road that passes through a small village set among banana plants and coconut palms. Sandy, serene beaches are tucked into coves around the bay (frolicking dolphins along the beachfront are a common sight), and exotic birds fill a coastal lagoon. Swimming and snorkeling are good here, and the bay is a popular stop for luxury yachts cruising down the coast. Just south of the entrance to Tenacatita is a sign for the all-inclusive **Blue Bay Los Angeles Locos,** as well as the exclusive **El Tamarindo** resort and golf club. There is no commercial or shopping area, and dining options outside your hotel are limited to a restaurant or two that may emerge during the winter months (high season). Relax—that's what you're here for.

**Blue Bay Village Los Angeles Locos** ★ On a 3-mile stretch of sandy beach, Blue Bay Village Los Angeles Locos offers an abundance of activities and entertainment. An extensive activities program and an ample selection of dining and entertainment options offer guests excellent value. It's a good choice for families and groups of friends. All rooms have ocean views, with either balconies or terraces. The three-story hotel is basic in decor and amenities, but comfortable. The attraction here is the wide array of on-site activities, plus a "Jungle River" cruise excursion (included in the room rate). **La Largata Disco** is a little on the dark and smoky side but can really rock, depending on the crowd—it's basically the only option on the bay.

Km 20 Carretera Federal 200, Tenacatita 48989, Municipio de la Huerta, Jal. ✆ **800/BLUE BAY** in the U.S., 315/351-5020, or 315/351-5100. Fax 315/351-5050. www.bluebayresorts.com. 204 units. High season $101 double; low season $87 double. Rates are all-inclusive. AE, MC, V. **Amenities:** 2 restaurants and snack (with buffets and a la carte dining), 3 bars; disco; nightly shows and entertainment; adult pool; kids' pool adjacent to the beach; 3 tennis courts; windsurfing; kayaks; Hobie cats; pool tables; horseback riding; basketball court; exercise room; massage; laundry; Kid's Club; babysitting. *In room:* A/C, TV.

**El Tamarindo** ★★★ *Finds* Currently my favorite resort in all of Mexico, El Tamarindo is a gem that combines stunning jungle surroundings with exquisite facilities, gracious service, and absolute tranquility. The area's most luxurious resort, it comes complete with its own golf course. For years, it was invitation only, to accommodate guests of the development's owner or those interested in buying surrounding real estate. Now part of Starwood Hotels' Luxury Collection, it may finally gain the recognition it deserves.

The bungalows exude an air of exclusivity—guests each have their own thatched-roof villa complete with splash pool and whirlpool, plus lounging and dining areas that complement the stunning bedrooms. Details like bouquets of tropical flowers, fresh plums, and a basket filled with rolled white towels are standard here. At check-in, you're assigned a personal "butler," who is on call to meet your every need. The bedrooms—with dark hardwood floors and furnishings—can be closed off for air-conditioned comfort, but the remaining areas are open to the sea breezes and heady tropical air.

The different categories of bungalows denote their location—Beachfront (on a calm, private cove), Palm Tree, Garden, and Forest. The non-beachfront bungalows all have the same quality decor and amenities but feature more closed-in areas—after all, you are in the tropical jungle. Anyone squeamish about creepy-crawlies may be uncomfortable in the beginning, as the rainforest brings in the occasional land crab or bug, but listening to the life around you is a spectacular sensation. On 2,000 acres of tropical rainforest bordering the Pacific Ocean, you'll feel as if you've found your own personal, tropical bit of heaven.

El Tamarindo has a championship 18-hole golf course; the approach to the first hole is through a forest of palms so tall they block the sun. The course has seven oceanside holes and dramatic views. It's heavenly, and you'll often be the only one on the course.

Despite the fact that the resort restaurant is the only dining option, you won't be disappointed. Noted chef and author Patricia Quintana created the divine menu, which changes daily, based on her book, *The Food of the Water Gods.*

El Tamarindo is about 3 hours south of Puerto Vallarta and 40 minutes north of the Manzanillo airport. To get there, take Highway 200, then turn west at the clearly marked exit for El Tamarindo. Follow the clear signs down the smoothly paved, winding road for about 25 minutes to the resort.

Km 7.5 Carretera Melaque–Puerto Vallarta, Cihuatlan, Jal. CP 48970. ✆ **315/351-5032.** Fax 315/351-5070. www.starwood.com. 28 bungalows. High season Beachfront bungalow $669, 2-bedroom Palm Tree bungalow $550, Forest bungalow $437; low season Beachfront bungalow $617, 2-bedroom Palm Tree bungalow $525, Forest bungalow $385. AE, MC, V. **Amenities:** Restaurant and bar; large beachfront pool with whirlpool; 2 clay tennis courts; estuary bird-watching tours; windsurfing; kayaking; aquafin sailboats; horseback riding; mountain biking; hiking; en-suite dining; spa services; yoga classes; *temazcal* (Aztec steam hut). *In room:* A/C, dataport, bathrobes, hair dryer, safe.

## BARRA DE NAVIDAD & MELAQUE

This pair of rustic beach villages (only 5km/3 miles apart) has been attracting long-time travelers to Mexico for decades. Only 30 minutes north of Manzanillo's airport, or 104km (65 miles) north of downtown, Barra has a few brick or cobblestone streets, good budget hotels and restaurants, and funky beach charm. All of this lies incongruously next to the super-luxurious Grand Bay Hotel, which sits on a bluff across the inlet from Barra. Melaque offers budget hotels on and off the beach, fewer restaurants, and little in the way of funky charm, although the beach is as wide as and more beautiful than Barra's. Both villages appeal to those looking for a quaint, quiet, inexpensive retreat rather than a modern, sophisticated destination. The Grand Bay Hotel, with its five-star quality and 27-hole golf course, provides a whole new dimension to vacationing in Barra—just as Barra adds a whole new dimension to vacationing in a luxury resort.

In the 17th century, Barra de Navidad was a harbor for the Spanish fleet; from here, galleons first set off in 1564 to find China. Located on a crescent-shaped bay with curious rock outcroppings, Barra de Navidad and neighboring Melaque are connected by a continuous beach on the same wide bay, and they revel in their relaxed pace. It's safe to say that the only time Barra and Melaque hotels are full is during Easter and Christmas weeks. **Barra de Navidad** has more charm, more tree-shaded streets, better restaurants, more stores, and more conviviality between locals and tourists. Barra is very laid-back; faithful returnees adore its lack of flash. Other than the Grand Bay Hotel, on the cliff across the waterway in what is called Isla Navidad (although it's not on an island), nothing is new or modern. But there's a bright edge to Barra now, with more good restaurants and limited—but existent—nightlife.

**Melaque,** on the other hand, is larger, rather sun-baked, treeless, and lacking in attractions. It does, however, have plenty of cheap hotels available for longer stays and a few restaurants. Although the beach between the two is continuous, Melaque's beach, with deep sand, is more beautiful than Barra's, where wave action packs down the sand.

Although **Isla Navidad Resort** has a manicured 27-hole golf course and the super-luxurious Grand Bay Hotel, the area's pace hasn't quickened as fast as expected. The golf is challenging and delightfully uncrowded, with another exceptional course at nearby El Tamarindo. Simply put, it's become a serious golfer's dream.

## ESSENTIALS

**GETTING THERE** Buses from Manzanillo frequently run up the coast along Highway 200 on their way to Puerto Vallarta and Guadalajara (for about $3.50). Most stop in the central villages of Barra de Navidad and Melaque. From the Manzanillo airport, it's only around 30 minutes to Barra, and taxis are available. Puerto Vallarta is a 3-hour (by car) to 5-hour (by bus) ride north on Highway 200 from Barra. From Manzanillo, the highway twists through some of the Pacific Coast's most beautiful mountains.

**VISITOR INFORMATION** The **tourism office** for both villages is at Jalisco 67 (between Veracruz and Mazatlán), Barra (✆ and fax **315/355-5100**). The office is open Monday to Friday from 9am to 5pm. The **Travel Agency Isla Navidad Tours,** Veracruz 204-A, Barra de Navidad (✆ **315/355-5666** or 315/355-5667) can handle arrangements for plane tickets and sells bus tickets from Manzanillo to Puerto Vallarta and Guadalajara. It's open Monday to Saturday from 10am to 8pm. American Express, MasterCard, and Visa are accepted.

**ORIENTATION** In Barra, hotels and restaurants line the main beachfront street, **Legazpi.** From the bus station, beachfront hotels are 2 blocks straight ahead, across the central plaza. Two blocks behind the bus station and to the right is the lagoon side. More hotels and restaurants are on its main street, **Morelos/Veracruz.** Few streets are marked, but 10 minutes of wandering will acquaint you with the village's entire layout. There's a taxi stand at the intersection of Legazpi and Sinaloa streets. The posted rate for trips to Manzanillo is $30. Legazpi, Jalisco, Sinaloa, and Veracruz streets border Barra's **central plaza.** It seems active with playing kids, and an occasional market sells fresh flowers.

## ACTIVITIES ON & OFF THE BEACH

Swimming and enjoying the attractive beach and views of the bay take up most tourists' time. You can hire a small boat for a coastal ride or fishing in two ways. Go toward the *malecón* on Calle Veracruz until you reach the tiny boatmen's cooperative, with fixed prices posted on the wall, or walk two buildings farther to the water taxi ramp. The inexpensive ($2) water taxi is the best option for going to Colimilla (5 min. away) or across the inlet (3 min., $1) to the Grand Bay Hotel. Water taxis make the rounds regularly, so if you're at Colimilla, wait, and a water taxi will be along shortly. At the cooperative, a 30-minute **lagoon tour** costs $20, and a **sea tour** costs $25. **Sportfishing** is $80 for up to four people for half a day in a small *panga* (open fiberglass boat, like the ones used for water taxis).

To arrange unusual **area tours, real estate rentals,** and **sports-equipment rental,** contact **The Crazy Cactus,** Jalisco 8, half a block inland from the town church on Legazpi (✆ and fax **315/355-6099;** crazycactusmx@yahoo.com). It's operated by Trayce Ross, who also rents cars and handles real estate sales. Her daughter, who does custom building, runs the adjoining gift shop. The store may be closed from May through October.

The Grand Bay Hotel's beautiful and challenging 27-hole, 7,053-yard, par-72 **golf course** is open to the public. Hotel guests pay greens fees of $166 for 18 holes, $192 for 27 holes, while nonguests pay $216 and $240, respectively; prices include a motorized cart. Caddies are available, as are rental clubs. The Crazy Cactus (see above) can arrange golf at El Tamarindo's gorgeous mountaintop course about 32km (20 miles) north of Barra.

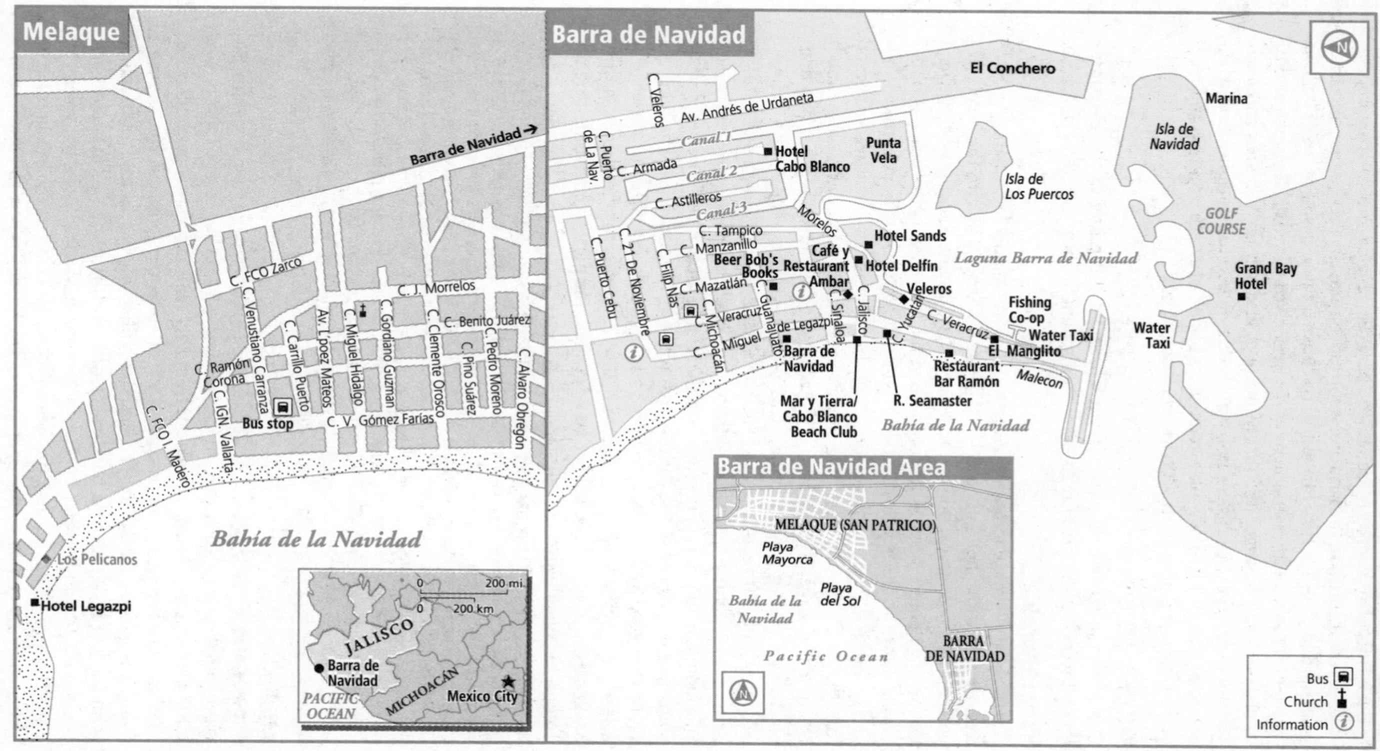

Melaque
Barra de Navidad
Barra de Navidad →
C. FCO Zarco
C. J. Morrelos
C. Benito Juárez
C. Venustiano Carranza
C. Carrillo Puerto
Av. L'poez Mateos
C. Miguel Hidalgo
C. Gordiano Guzman
C. Clemente Orosco
C. Pino Suárez
C. Pedro Moreno
C. Alvaro Obregón
C. Ramón Corona
C. IGN. Vallarta
Bus stop
C. V. Gómez Farías
C. FCO I. Madero
Bahía de la Navidad
Los Pelicanos
Hotel Legazpi
0
200 mi
0
200 km
JALISCO
Barra de Navidad
MICHOACÁN
Mexico City
PACIFIC OCEAN
El Conchero
C. Veleros
Av. Andrés de Urdaneta
C. Puerto de La Nav.
Canal 1
C. Armada
Canal 2
Hotel Cabo Blanco
Punta Vela
C. Astilleros
Canal 3
Morelos
C. Tampico
C. Manzanillo
Hotel Sands
C. Puerto Cebu
C. 21 De Noviembre
C. Filip Nas
Beer Bob's Books
Café y Restaurant Ambar
Hotel Delfín
C. Mazatlán
C. Guanajuato
C. Sinaloa
C. Jalisco
C. Yucatán
Veleros
C. Veracruz de Legazpi
C. Michoacán
C. Miguel
Barra de Navidad
C. Veracruz
Isla de Los Puercos
Laguna Barra de Navidad
Fishing Co-op
Water Taxi
El Manglito
Restaurant Bar Ramón
Malecon
Mar y Tierra/ Cabo Blanco Beach Club
R. Seamaster
Bahía de la Navidad
Marina
Isla de Navidad
GOLF COURSE
Grand Bay Hotel
Water Taxi
Barra de Navidad Area
MELAQUE (SAN PATRICIO)
Playa Mayorca
Playa del Sol
Bahía de la Navidad
Pacific Ocean
BARRA DE NAVIDAD
Bus
Church
Information

**Beer Bob's Books,** Av. Mazatlán 61, between Sinaloa and Guanajuato, is a book-lover's institution in Barra and a sort of community service that the rather grouchy Bob does for fun. His policy of "leave a book if you take one" allows vacationers to select from hundreds of neatly shelved paperbacks, as long as they leave a book in exchange. It's open Monday to Friday from 1 to 4pm and occasionally in the evenings. "Beer Bob" got his name because in earlier days when beer was cheap, he kept a cooler stocked, and book browsers could sip and read. (When beer prices went up, Bob put the cooler away.)

## WHERE TO STAY

Low season in Barra is any time except Christmas and Easter weeks. Except for those 2 weeks, it doesn't hurt to ask for a discount at the inexpensive hotels.

### Very Expensive

**Grand Bay Hotel** ★ *Overrated* Across the yacht channel from Barra de Navidad, this luxurious hotel opened in 1997 on 1,200 acres next to the hotel's 27-hole golf course. It overlooks the village, bay, Pacific Ocean, and Navidad lagoon. The hotel's beach is narrow and on the lagoon. A better beach is opposite the hotel on the bay in Barra de Navidad. The spacious rooms are sumptuously outfitted with marble floors, large bathrooms, and hand-carved wood furnishings. Prices vary according to view and size of room, but even the modest rooms are large; all have cable TV. Each comes with a king-size or two double beds, a glass-top desk, ceiling fans plus air-conditioning, and a balcony. Executive suites are enormous and include a separate glass shower and bathtub, living room, dining table, bar with butler's kitchen and separate entry, and enormous bedroom. Junior suites lack the dining area. All suites have a steam sauna and telephones in the bathroom as well as a sound system. The hotel is a short water-taxi ride across the inlet from Barra de Navidad; it can also be reached by paved road from Highway 200. Although the hotel bills itself as being on the Island of Navidad at Port Navidad, the port is the marina, and the hotel is on a peninsula, not an island.

Isla Navidad, Col. 45110. ✆ **888/GRANBAY** in the U.S., 315/355-5050, or 315/331-0500. Fax 315/355-6070. www.grandbay.com. 199 units. High season $381–$460 double, $550–$680 suite; low season $275–$321 double, $468–$614 suite. Ask about tennis, golf, fishing, and honeymoon packages. Rates include round-trip transportation to and from Manzanillo airport. AE, DC, DISC, MC, V. **Amenities:** 2 restaurants, 2 bars; golf club with food and bar service; swimming pool with water slides and swim-up bar; 27-hole, par-72 golf course designed by Robert Von Hagge; golf club with pro shop and driving range; 150-slip marina with private yacht club; 3 lighted grass tennis courts with stadium seating; small but sufficient workout room; 24-hr. concierge; room service; laundry and dry cleaning; business center; salon; Kid's Club with activity program; babysitting. Fishing, boat tours, and other excursions can be arranged. *In room:* A/C, TV, dataport, minibar, hair dryer, bathrobes, magnified makeup mirrors, iron, security box.

### Moderate

**Hotel Cabo Blanco** ★★ Located on the point where you cross over to Isla Navidad, the Cabo Blanco is an outstanding option for family vacations or longer-term stays. Rooms are pleasantly rustic, with tile floors, large tile tubs, separate dressing areas, and stucco walls. The hotel overlooks the bay, but it's a 5-minute walk to the beach. The beamed-ceiling lobby is in its own building; rooms are in hacienda-style buildings surrounded by gardens. The atmosphere is generally tranquil, except during weekends and Mexican holidays, when this hotel tends to fill up. Because the Cabo Blanco doesn't front the beach, it has an affiliated beach club and restaurant, Mar y Tierra (see "Where to Dine," below).

Armada y Bahía de la Navidad s/n, 48987 Barra de Navidad, Jal. ✆ **315/355-5103** or 315/355-5136. Fax 315/355-6494. 101 units. $75 double; $256 suite with kitchenette. All-inclusive option $72 per person. AE,

MC, V. **Amenities:** 2 restaurants; 4 pools (2 adults only); 2 tennis courts; concierge; tour desk; car-rental desk; laundry service. *In room:* A/C, TV.

## Inexpensive

**Hotel Barra de Navidad** ★ At the northern end of Legazpi, this popular, comfortable beachfront hotel has friendly management and some rooms with balconies overlooking the beach and bay. Other, less expensive rooms afford only a street view. Only the oceanview rooms have air-conditioning. A nice swimming pool is on the street level to the right of the lobby.

Legazpi 250, 48987 Barra de Navidad, Jal. ✆ **315/355-5122.** Fax 315/355-5303. 59 units. $53–$75 double. MC, V.

**Hotel Delfín** One of Barra's better-maintained hotels, the four-story (no elevator) Delfín is on the landward side of the lagoon. It offers pleasant, basic, well-maintained, well-lit rooms. Each has red-tile floors and a double, two double, or two single beds. The tiny courtyard, with a small pool and lounge chairs, sits in the shade of an enormous rubber tree. From the fourth floor, there's a view of the lagoon. A breakfast buffet is served from 8:30 to 10:30am (see "Where to Dine," below).

Morelos 23, 48987 Barra de Navidad, Jal. ✆ **315/355-5068.** Fax 315/355-6020. 24 units. $36–$45 double; ask about low-season discounts. MC, V. Free parking. **Amenities:** Restaurant; pool.

**Hotel Sands** The colonial-style Sands, across from the Hotel Delfín (see above) on the lagoon side at Jalisco, offers small but homey rooms with red-tile floors and windows with both screens and glass. The recently remodeled bathrooms have new tiles and fixtures. Lower rooms look onto a public walkway and wide courtyard filled with greenery and singing birds; upstairs rooms are brighter. Twelve rooms (suites or bungalows) have air-conditioning and kitchenette facilities. The hotel is known for its warm hospitality and high-season happy hour (2–6pm) at the pool terrace bar beside the lagoon. On weekends from 9pm to 4am, an adjacent patio "disco" plays recorded music for dancing. Breakfast is served from 7:30am to noon. Fishing trips can be arranged, and tours to nearby beaches are available.

Morelos 24, 48987 Barra de Navidad, Jal. ✆ and fax **315/355-5018** or ✆ 315/616-2859. 42 units. High season $61 double; low season $42 double. Rates include breakfast. Discounts for stays of 1 week or more. MC, V (6% surcharge). **Amenities:** Restaurant and bar; pool with whirlpool overlooking lagoon beach; children's play area; tour desk.

## WHERE TO DINE

**El Manglito** ★ SEAFOOD/INTERNATIONAL Located on the placid lagoon, with a view of the palatial Grand Bay Hotel, El Manglito serves home-style Mexican food to a growing number of repeat diners. The whole fried fish accompanied by drawn garlic butter, boiled vegetables, rice, and French fries, is a crowd-pleaser. Other enticements include boiled shrimp, chicken in orange sauce, and shrimp salad.

Veracruz, near the boatmen's cooperative. No phone. Main courses $5–$10. No credit cards. Daily 9am–11pm.

**Hotel Delfín** INTERNATIONAL The second-story terrace of this small hotel is a pleasant place to begin the day. The self-serve buffet offers an assortment of fresh fruit, juice, granola, yogurt, milk, pastries, and unlimited coffee. The price includes made-to-order eggs and delicious banana pancakes—for which the restaurant is known.

Morelos 23. ✆ **315/355-5068.** Breakfast buffet $4. No credit cards. Daily 8:30am–noon.

**Mar y Tierra** INTERNATIONAL Hotel Cabo Blanco's beach club is also a popular restaurant and bar, and a great place to spend a day at the beach. On the beach, there are shade *palapas* and beach chairs, and a game of volleyball seems constantly in progress. The colorful restaurant is decorated with murals of mermaids. Perfectly seasoned shrimp fajitas come in plentiful portions.

Legazpi s/n (at Jalisco). ✆ **315/355-5028.** Main courses $10–$17. AE, MC, V. Wed–Sun 2–10pm (opens at 10am for hotel guests).

**Restaurant Bar Ambar** CREPES/SPANISH/FRENCH This cozy, thatched-roof, upstairs restaurant is open to the breezes. The crêpes are named after towns in France; the delicious crêpe Paris, for example, is filled with chicken, potatoes, spinach, and green sauce. Sweet dessert crêpes are also available. International main dishes include imported rib-eye steak in Dijon mustard sauce, mixed brochettes, quiche, and Caesar salad. Ambar serves Spanish-style tapas from noon until 6pm, and adds French specialties during dinner.

Av. Veracruz 101-A (at Jalisco). No phone. Crêpes $5–$13; main courses $5–$15. No credit cards. Daily noon–midnight (happy hour 1pm–midnight). Closed July–Oct.

**Restaurant Bar Ramón** ★ *Value* SEAFOOD/MEXICAN It seems that everybody eats at Ramón's, where the chips and fresh salsa arrive unbidden, and service is prompt and friendly. The food is especially good—however, most options are fried. Try fresh fried shrimp with French fries, or any daily special that features vegetable soup or chicken fried steak. Great value!

Legazpi 260. ✆ **315/355-6435.** Main courses $6–$10. MC, V. Daily 7am–11pm.

**Seamaster** SEAFOOD/INTERNATIONAL This cheery, colorful restaurant on the beach facing the ocean is a great place for sunsets and margaritas, or a meal anytime. Specialties include steamed shrimp (peeled or unpeeled), fried calamari, barbecue chicken, ribs, steak, chicken wings, hamburgers, and other sandwiches. During high season, it turns into a popular disco at night.

Legazpi (at Yucatán). No phone. Main courses $5–$15. No credit cards. Daily noon–midnight.

### BARRA DE NAVIDAD AFTER DARK

When dusk arrives, visitors and locals alike find a cool spot to sit outside, sip cocktails, and chat. Many outdoor restaurants and stores in Barra accommodate this relaxing way to end the day, adding extra tables and chairs for drop-ins. It's very friendly.

During high season, the **Hotel Sands** poolside and lagoon-side bar has happy hour from 2 to 6pm. The colorful **Sunset Bar and Restaurant,** facing the bay at the corner of Legazpi and Jalisco, is a favorite for sunset watching, and then a game of oceanside pool or dancing to live or taped music. It's most popular with travelers ages 20 to 30. In the same vein, **Chips Restaurant,** on the second floor facing the ocean at the corner of Yucatán and Legazpi near the southern end of the *malecón,* has an excellent sunset vista. Live music follows the last rays of light, and patrons stay for hours. **Piper's Lover Bar & Restaurant,** on Legazpi, is done in the style of the Anderson's chain—but it's not one of them. Still, it is lively, with pool tables and occasional live music.

At the **Disco El Galeón,** in the Hotel Sands on Calle Morelos, cushioned benches and cement tables encircle the round dance floor. It's all open-air, and about as stylish as you'll find in Barra. It serves drinks only. Admission is $6, and it's open Friday and Saturday from 9pm to 4am.

### A VISIT TO MELAQUE (SAN PATRICIO)

For a change of scenery, you may want to wander over to Melaque (also known as San Patricio), 5km (3 miles) from Barra on the same bay. You can walk on the beach from Barra or take one of the frequent local buses from the bus station near the main square in Barra. The bus is marked MELAQUE. To return to Barra, take the bus marked CIHUATLAN.

Melaque's pace is even more laid-back than Barra's, and though it's a larger village, it seems smaller. It has fewer restaurants and less to do. Although there are more hotels or "bungalows," as they are usually called, few manage the charm of those in Barra. If Barra hotels are full on a holiday weekend, Melaque would be a second choice for accommodations. The paved road ends where the town begins. A few yachts bob in the harbor, and the palm-lined beach is gorgeous.

If you come by bus from Barra, you can exit the bus anywhere in town or stay on until the last stop, which is the bus station in the middle of town a block from the beach. Restaurants and hotels line the beach; it's impossible to get lost, but some orientation will help. Coming into town from the main road, you'll be on the town's main street, **Avenida López Matéos.** You'll pass the main square on the way to the waterfront, where there's a trailer park. The street going left (southeast) along the bay is **Avenida Gómez Farías;** the one going right (northwest) is **Avenida Miguel Ochoa López.**

**WHERE TO DINE** At the north end of Melaque beach is **Los Pelicanos** (**© 315/355-5415**). It serves the usual seafood specialties; the tender fried squid is delectable. In addition, you can find burritos, nachos, and hamburgers. Many Barra guests come here to stake a place on the beach and use the restaurant as headquarters for sipping and nipping. It's peaceful to watch the pelicans bobbing. It's open daily from 9am to 10pm. The restaurant is at the far end of the bay before the **Hotel Legazpi** (**© 315/355-5397**), a pleasant place to stay. It has 20 rooms, charges $40 for a double, and doesn't accept credit cards.

In addition to the Los Pelicanos, there are many rustic ***palapa* restaurants** in town on the beach and farther along the bay at the end of the beach. You can settle in on the beach and use one of the restaurants as your base for drinking and dining.

## 4 Manzanillo ★

256km (160 miles) SE of Puerto Vallarta; 267km (167 miles) SW of Guadalajara; 64km (40 miles) SE of Barra de Navidad

Manzanillo has long been known as a resort town with wide, curving beaches, legendary sportfishing, and a highly praised diversity of dive sites. Now, however, it is emerging as a key golf destination, with two courses listed in the top 10 of *Golf Digest*'s 2000 Mexico Golf rankings.

One reason could be Manzanillo's enticingly tropical geography—vast groves of tall palms, abundant mango trees, and successive coves graced with smooth sand beaches. To the north, mountains blanketed with palms rise alongside the shoreline. And over it all lies the veneer of perfect weather, with balmy temperatures and year-round sea breezes. Even the approach by plane into Manzanillo showcases the promise—you fly in over the beach and golf course. Once on the ground, you exit the airport through a palm grove to reach the main highway into town.

Manzanillo is a dichotomous place—it is both Mexico's busiest commercial seaport and a tranquil, traditional town of multicolor houses cascading down the hillsides to meet the central commercial area of simple seafood restaurants, shell shops, and a few salsa clubs. The activity in Manzanillo can be neatly divided into two zones: the downtown commercial port and the luxury Santiago Peninsula resort zone to the north. The busy harbor and rail connections to Mexico's interior dominate the downtown zone. A visit to the town's waterfront *zócalo,* a shady plaza teeming with birds and anchored by twin gazebos, provides a glimpse into local life. The exclusive Santiago Peninsula, home to the resorts and golf course, separates Manzanillo's two golden sand bays.

## ESSENTIALS

**GETTING THERE & DEPARTING** **By Plane** **Aeromexico,** its sister airline, **Aerolitoral** (© **800/237-6639** in the U.S., 314/334-1226 at the airport), and **Mexicana** (© **800/531-7921** in the U.S., 314/333-2323 at the airport) offer flights to and from Mexico City, Durango, Chihuahua, and Mazatlán and to cities in the United States and Canada. **Alaska Airlines** (© **800/426-0333** in Mexico, or 314/334-2211) offers service from Los Angeles; **America West** (© **800/235-9292**) flies from Phoenix; and **Aero California** (© **800/237-6225** in the U.S. and Canada, or 314/334-1414) has flights from Los Angeles. Ask a travel agent about the numerous charters from the States in the winter.

The **Playa de Oro International Airport** is 40km (25 miles; 45 min.) northwest of town. *Colectivo* (minivan) airport service is available from the airport; hotels arrange returns. Make reservations for return trips 1 day in advance. The *colectivo* fare is based on zones and runs $8 to $10 for most hotels. Private taxi service between the airport and downtown area is around $25. **Budget** (© **800/527-0700** or 314/333-1445) and **AutoRentas** (© **314/333-2580**) have counters in the airport open during flight arrivals; they will also deliver a car to your hotel. Daily rates run $56 to $78. You need a car only if you plan to explore surrounding cities and the Costa Alegre beaches.

**By Car** **Coastal Highway 200** leads from Acapulco (south) and Puerto Vallarta (north). From Guadalajara, take Highway 54 through Colima into Manzanillo. Outside Colima you can switch to a toll road, which is faster but less scenic.

**By Bus** Buses run to Barra de Navidad (1½ hr. north), Puerto Vallarta (5 hr. north), Colima (1½ hr. east), and Guadalajara (4½ hr. north), with deluxe service and numerous daily departures. Manzanillo's **Central Camionera** (bus station) is about 12 long blocks east of town. If you follow Hidalgo east, the Camionera will be on your right.

**VISITOR INFORMATION** The **tourism office** (© **314/333-2277** or 314/333-2264; fax 314/333-1426) is on the Costera Miguel de la Madrid 4960, km 8.5. It's open Monday to Friday from 9am to 3pm and 5 to 7pm.

**CITY LAYOUT** The town lies at one end of a 7-mile-long beach facing Manzanillo Bay and its commercial harbor. The beach has four sections—**Playa Las Brisas, Playa Azul, Playa Salahua,** and **Playa Las Hadas.** At the other end of the beaches is the high, rocky **Santiago Peninsula.** Santiago is 11km (7 miles) from downtown; it's the site of many beautiful homes and the best hotel in the area, Camino Real Las Hadas, as well as the hotel's Mantarraya Golf Course. The peninsula juts out into the bay, separating Manzanillo Bay from Santiago Bay. Playa Las Hadas is on the south side of the peninsula, facing Manzanillo Bay, and **Playa Audiencia** is on the north side, facing Santiago Bay. The inland town of **Santiago** is opposite the turnoff to Las Hadas.

Activity in downtown Manzanillo centers on the **central plaza,** officially known as the Jardín Alvaro Obregón, which is separated from the waterfront by

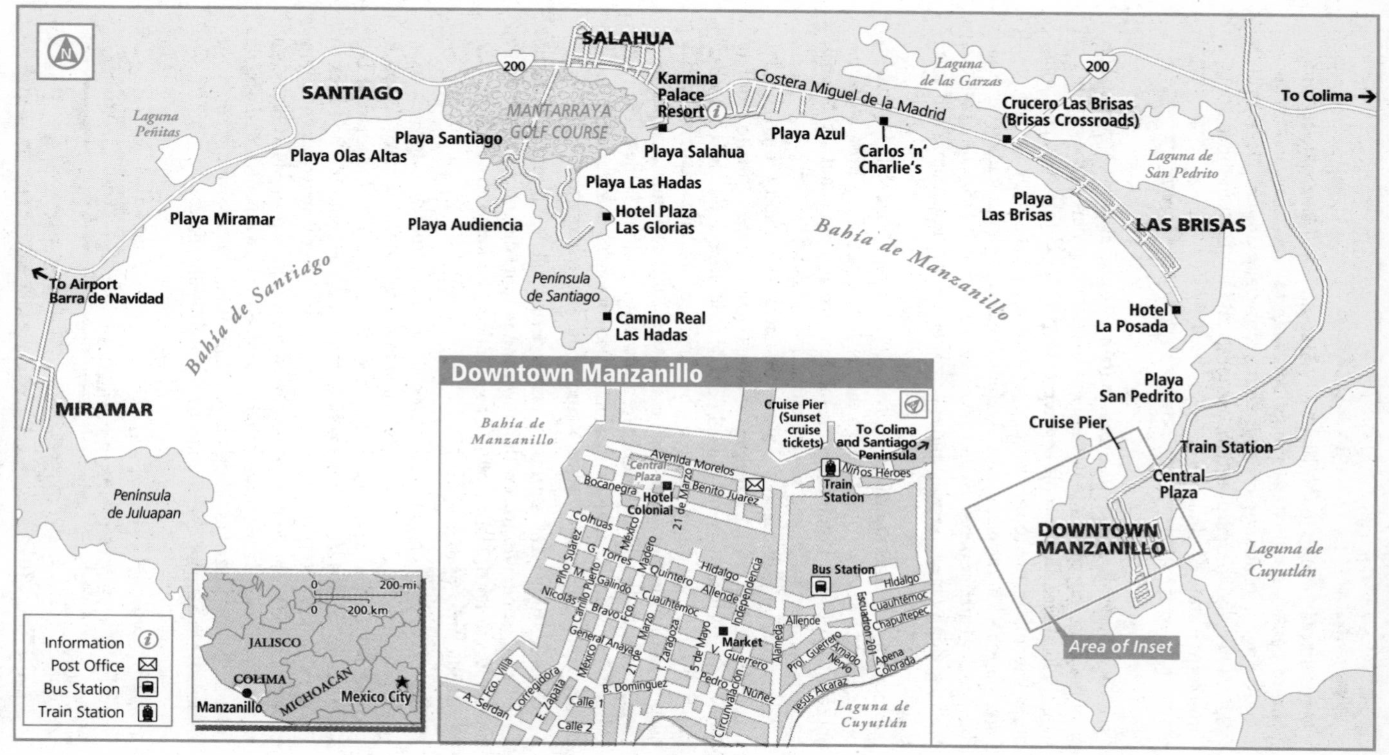
SALAHUA
200
SANTIAGO
Laguna Peñitas
MANTARRAYA GOLF COURSE
Playa Santiago
Playa Olas Altas
Karmina Palace Resort
Costera Miguel de la Madrid
Laguna de las Garzas
Crucero Las Brisas (Brisas Crossroads)
To Colima
Playa Azul
Carlos 'n' Charlie's
Playa Salahua
Playa Las Hadas
Laguna de San Pedrito
Playa Las Brisas
LAS BRISAS
Playa Miramar
Playa Audiencia
Hotel Plaza Las Glorias
Bahía de Manzanillo
To Airport Barra de Navidad
Bahía de Santiago
Península de Santiago
Camino Real Las Hadas
Hotel La Posada
MIRAMAR
Playa San Pedrito
Cruise Pier
Train Station
Central Plaza
DOWNTOWN MANZANILLO
Laguna de Cuyutlán
Area of Inset
Península de Juluapan
Downtown Manzanillo
Bahía de Manzanillo
Cruise Pier (Sunset cruise tickets)
To Colima and Santiago Peninsula
Avenida Morelos
Central Plaza
Niños Héroes
Bocanegra
Hotel Colonial
21 de Marzo
Benito Juárez
Train Station
Colhuas
Pino Suárez
G. Torres
México
Madero
Hidalgo
Quintero
Independencia
Bus Station
M. Galindo
Carrillo Puerto
Nicolás Bravo
Fco. I.
Cuauhtémoc
Allende
Escuadron 201
Cuauhtémoc
Chapultepec
General Anaya
21 de Marzo
I. Zaragoza
5 de Mayo
Market
Alameda
Prol. Guerrero
Amado Nervo
Apena Colorada
V. Guerrero
Fco. Villa
Corregidora
E. Zapata
México
B. Domínguez
Pedro Núñez
Circunvalación
Jesús Alcaraz
A. Serdán
Calle 1
Calle 2
Laguna de Cuyutlán
0 200 mi
0 200 km
JALISCO
COLIMA
Manzanillo
MICHOACÁN
Mexico City
Information
Post Office
Bus Station
Train Station

### *Tips* Motorist Advisory: Carjackings

Motorists planning to follow Highway 200 south from Manzanillo toward Lázaro Cárdenas and Ixtapa should be aware of reports of random bus and motorist hijackings on that route, especially around Playa Azul. Before heading in that direction, ask locals and the tourism office about the current state of affairs.

a railroad, shipyards, and a basketball court with constant pick-up games. The plaza has flowering trees, a fountain, twin kiosks, and a view of the bay. It is a staple of local life, where people congregate on park benches to swap gossip and throw handfuls of rice to the ever-present *palomas* (doves—really just pigeons). Large ships dock at the pier nearby. **Avenida México,** the street leading out from the plaza's central gazebo, is the town's principal commercial thoroughfare. Walking along here, you will find a few shops, small restaurants, and juice stands.

Once you leave downtown, the highway (the **Costera Miguel de la Madrid,** or the Costera Madrid) runs through the neighborhoods of Las Brisas, Salahua, and Santiago to the **hotel zones** on the Santiago Peninsula and at Miramar. Shell shops, mini-malls, and several restaurants are along the way.

There are two main lagoons. **Laguna de Cuyutlán,** almost behind the city, stretches south for miles, paralleling the coast. **Laguna de San Pedrito,** north of the city, parallels the Costera Miguel de la Madrid; it's behind Playa Las Brisas beach. Both are good birding sites. There are also two bays. **Manzanillo Bay** encompasses the harbor, town, and beaches. The Santiago Peninsula separates it from the second bay, **Santiago.** Between downtown and the Santiago Peninsula is **Las Brisas,** a flat peninsula with a long stretch of sandy golden beach, a lineup of inexpensive but run-down hotels, and a few good restaurants.

**GETTING AROUND By Taxi** Taxis in Manzanillo are plentiful. Fares are fixed by zones; rates for trips within town and to more distant points should be posted at your hotel. Daily rates can be negotiated for longer drives outside the Manzanillo area.

**By Bus** The local buses (*camionetas*) make a circuit from downtown in front of the train station, along the Bay of Manzanillo, and to the Santiago Peninsula and the Bay of Santiago to the north; the fare is 30¢. The ones marked LAS BRISAS go to the Las Brisas crossroads, to the Las Brisas Peninsula, and back to town; MIRAMAR, SANTIAGO, and SALAHUA buses go to outlying settlements along the bays and to most restaurants mentioned below. Buses marked LAS HADAS go to Santiago Peninsula and make a circuit past the Las Hadas resort and the Sierra Manzanillo and Plaza Las Glorias hotels. This is an inexpensive way to see the coast as far as Santiago and to tour the Santiago Peninsula.

## *FAST FACTS:* Manzanillo

*American Express* The local representative is **Bahías Gemelas Travel Agency,** km 10, Costera Miguel de la Madrid (✆ **314/333-1000** or 314/333-1053; fax 314/333-0649). It's open Monday to Friday from 10am to 2pm and 4 to 6pm, Saturday from 10am to 2pm.

*Area Code* The telephone area code is **314.**

*Bank* **Banamex,** just off the plaza on Avenida México, downtown (✆ **314/332-0115**), is open from Monday to Friday 9am to 4pm, but changes foreign currency only until 12:30pm.

*Internet Access* The air-conditioned **Net Café,** Calle Benito Juárez 115, Int. 7-B (✆ **314/332-2660;** mayocomp@bay.net.mx) is half a block from the central plaza. It charges $3 per hour. It's open Monday to Friday from 10am to 2pm and 4:30 to 8:30pm, Saturday from 10am to 2pm.

*Post Office* The *correo,* Dr. Miguel Galindo 30, opposite Farmacia de Guadalajara, downtown (✆ **314/332-0022**), is open Monday to Saturday from 9am to 1pm.

## ACTIVITIES ON & OFF THE BEACH

Activities in Manzanillo revolve around its golden sand beaches, which frequently accumulate a film of black mineral residue from nearby rivers. Most of the resort hotels are completely self-contained, with restaurants and sports on the premises. Manzanillo's public beaches provide an opportunity to see more local color and scenery. They are the daytime playground for those staying off the beach or at places without pools.

**BEACHES** **Playa Audiencia,** on the Santiago Peninsula, offers the best swimming as well as snorkeling, but **Playa San Pedrito,** shallow for a long way out, is the most popular beach for its proximity to downtown. **Playa Las Brisas** offers an optimal combination of location and good swimming. **Playa Miramar,** on the Bahía de Santiago past the Santiago Peninsula, is popular with bodysurfers, windsurfers, and boogie boarders. It's accessible by local bus from town. The major part of **Playa Azul** drops off sharply but is noted for its wide stretch of golden sand.

**BIRDING** Several lagoons along the coast offer good birding. As you go from Manzanillo past Las Brisas to Santiago, you'll pass **Laguna de Las Garzas** (Lagoon of the Herons), also known as Laguna de San Pedrito, where you can see many white pelicans and huge herons fishing in the water. They nest here in December and January. Directly behind downtown is the **Laguna de Cuyutlán** (follow the signs to Cuyutlán), where you'll usually find birds in abundance; species vary between summer and winter.

**DIVING** **Underworld Scuba** (✆ and fax **314/333-0642;** cellular 314/358-0327; www.gomanzanillo.com), owned by longtime resident and local diving expert Susan Dearing, conducts highly professional diving expeditions and classes. Many locations are so close to shore that there's no need for a boat. Close-in dives include the jetty with coral growing on the rocks at 14m (45 ft.), and a nearby sunken frigate downed in 1959 at 8m (28 ft.). Divers can see abundant sea life, including coral reefs, seahorses, giant puffer fish, and moray eels. A one-tank dive requiring a boat costs $50 per person (with a three-person minimum), or two tanks for $80 ($10 discount if you have your own equipment). A three-stop snorkel trip costs $35. All guides are certified divemasters, and the shop also offers diver certification classes (PADI, YMCA, and CMAS) in very intensive courses of various durations. The owner offers a 10% discount on your certification when you mention you read about her in a Frommer's guide. MasterCard and Visa are accepted.

**ESCORTED TOURS** Because Manzanillo is so spread out, you might consider a city tour. Reputable local tour companies include **Hectours** (✆ **314/333-1707**) and **Bahías Gemelas Travel Agency,** the American Express representative (✆ **314/333-1000;** fax 314/333-0649). Schedules are flexible; a half-day city tour costs around $25. Other tours include the daylong Colima Colonial Tour ($67), which stops at a sugarcane plantation, Colima's Archeological Museum, and principle colonial buildings, and passes the active volcano. Offerings change regularly, so ask about new tours.

**FISHING** Manzanillo is famous for its fishing, particularly sailfish. Marlin and sailfish are abundant year-round. Winter is best for dolphin fish and dorado (mahimahi); in summer, wahoo and rooster fish are in greater supply. The international sailfish competition is held around the November 20 Revolution Day holiday, and the national sailfish competition is in February. You can arrange fishing through travel agencies or directly at the fishermen's cooperative (✆ **314/332-1031**), located downtown where the fishing boats are moored. Call from 7am to 7pm. A fishing boat is approximately $39 to $57 per hour, with most trips lasting about 5 hours.

**GOLF** The 18-hole **La Mantarraya Golf Course** (✆ **314/331-0101**) is open to nonguests as well as guests of Camino Real Las Hadas. At one time, La Mantarraya was among the top 100 courses in the world, but it's been passed by newer entries. Still, the compact, challenging 18-hole course designed by Roy and Pete Dye is a beauty, endearingly tropical with banana trees, blooming bougainvillea, and coconut palms at every turn. A lush and verdant place (12 of the 18 holes are played over water), it remains in the top 10 of Mexico's 125 courses.

When the course was under construction, workers dug up pre-Hispanic ceramic figurines, idols, and beads at the site where the 14th hole now lies. It is believed to have been an important ancient burial site. The course culminates with its signature 18th hole, with a drive to the island green off El Tesoro (the treasure) beach and directly in front of the new Karminda Palace Resort. Local lore says this beach still may hold buried treasure from Spanish galleons, whose crews were the first to recognize the perfection of this natural harbor, and who used it during the 16th century as their starting point for voyages to the Pacific Rim. Greens fees are $110 for 18 holes, $50 for a cart.

The fabulous 27-hole golf course associated with the **Grand Bay Hotel** in Barra de Navidad, an easy distance from Manzanillo, is also open to the public. The Robert Von Hagge design is long and lovely, with each hole along rolling, tropical landscapes. It is wide open, with big fairways and big greens, and features plenty of water (2 lagoon holes, 13 lakeside holes, and 8 holes along the Pacific). The greens fees are $166 for 18 holes, $192 for 27 holes for hotel guests, $216 and $240, respectively, for nonguests, including a motorized cart. Barra is about a 1- to 1½-hour drive north of Manzanillo on Highway 200. (See "Activities On & Off the Beach" under "Barra de Navidad & Melaque," earlier.)

**A MUSEUM** The **Museum of Archeology and History** (✆ **314/332-2256**) is a small but impressive structure that houses exhibits depicting the region's history, plus rotating exhibitions of contemporary Mexican art. It's on Avenida Niños Heroes where it intersects with Avenida Teniente Azueta, on the road leading between the downtown and Las Brisas areas. Every Friday evening, the museum hosts free cultural events, which might be a trio playing romantic ballads or a chamber music ensemble. Performances begin at 8pm. Hours are Tuesday to Saturday from 10am to 2pm and 5 to 8pm, Sunday from 10am to 1pm.

**SHOPPING** Manzanillo has a selection of shops carrying Mexican crafts and clothing, mainly from nearby Guadalajara, one of Mexico's artisan centers. Almost all are downtown on the streets near the central plaza. Shopping downtown is an experience—for example, you won't want to miss the shop bordering the plaza that sells a combination of shells, religious items (including shell-framed Virgin of Guadalupe nightlights), and orthopedic supplies. The Plaza Manzanillo is an American-style mall on the road to Santiago, and there's a traditional *tianguis* (outdoor) market in front of the entrance to Club Maeva, with touristy items from around Mexico. Most resort hotels also have boutiques or shopping arcades.

**SUNSET CRUISES** To participate in this popular activity, buy tickets from a travel agent or downtown at La Perlita Dock (across from the train station) fronting the harbor. Tickets are on sale at La Perlita daily 8:30am to 2pm and cost around $25. The trips vary in their combinations of drinks, music, and entertainment and last 1½ to 2 hours.

## WHERE TO STAY

Manzanillo's strip of coastline consists of three areas: **downtown,** with its shops, markets, and commercial activity; **Las Brisas,** the hotel-lined beach area immediately north of the city; and **Santiago,** the town and peninsula, now virtually a suburb to the north at the end of Playa Azul. Transportation by bus or taxi makes all three areas fairly convenient to each other. Reservations are recommended for hotels during the Easter, Christmas, and New Year's holidays.

### DOWNTOWN

**Hotel Colonial** ★ An old favorite, this three-story colonial-style hotel in the central downtown district added five new units in 2000. Popular for its consistent quality, ambience, and service, it has beautiful blue-and-yellow tile, colonial-style carved doors and windows in the lobby and restaurant. Rooms are decorated with minimal furniture, red-tile floors, and basic comforts. The hotel is 1 block inland from the main plaza at the corner of Juárez and Galindo.

Av. México 100 and González Bocanegra, 28200 Manzanillo, Col. ✆ **314/332-1080,** 314/332-0668, 314/332-1230, or 314/332-1134. 42 units. $37 double. AE, MC, V. **Amenities:** Restaurant and bar; tour desk. *In room:* A/C, TV.

### LAS BRISAS

Earthquake damage Las Brisas suffered in 1995 has yet to be repaired. The area looks run-down, with numerous buildings in various states of disrepair. However, it still lays claim to one of the best beaches in the area and is known for its constant gentle sea breezes—a true pleasure in the summer months.

**Hotel La Posada** This small inn has a bright-pink stucco facade with a large arch that leads to a broad tiled patio right on the beach. The rooms have exposed brick walls and simple furnishings with Mexican decorative accents. Mattresses are beginning to sag, and the place could use some upkeep, but it remains popular with longtime travelers to Manzanillo. The atmosphere is casual and informal—help yourself to beer and soft drinks, and at the end of your stay, owner Bart Varelmann (a native of Ohio) counts the bottle caps you deposited in a bowl labeled with your room number. The restaurant, which is open to nonguests, serves daily during high season 8 to 11am and 1:30 to 8pm. A meal costs around $7. During low season, the restaurant is open 8am to 3pm. Stop by for a drink at sunset; the bar's open until 9pm all year. It's located at the end of Las Brisas Peninsula, closest to downtown, and is on the local Las Brisas bus route.

Av. Lázaro Cárdenas 201, Las Brisas (Apdo. Postal 135), 28200 Manzanillo, Col. ✆ and fax **314/333-1899.** www.mexonline/laposada.htm. 24 units. High season $72 double; low season $48 double. Rates include breakfast. AE, MC, V. **Amenities:** Restaurant and bar; money exchange; laundry service; safe-deposit boxes.

## SANTIAGO

Five kilometers (3 miles) north of Las Brisas is the wide Santiago Peninsula. The settlement of Salahua is on the highway where you enter the peninsula to reach the hotels Las Hadas, Plaza Las Glorias, and Sierra Manzanillo, as well as the Mantarraya Golf Course. Buses from town marked LAS HADAS pass by these hotels every 20 minutes. Past the Salahua turnoff, at the end of the settlement of Santiago, an obscure road on the left is marked ZONA DE PLAYAS and leads to the hotels on the other side of the peninsula and Playa de Santiago.

### Film Fact

The movie *10* featured Manzanillo's signature property, Las Hadas—along with Bo Derek.

**Camino Real Las Hadas** ★★★ For me, Las Hadas is the most compelling reason to visit Manzanillo. This elegant, white, beachfront resort, a member of the Leading Hotels of the World, is built in Moorish style into the side of the rocky peninsula. The service is gracious, warm, and unobtrusive. Rooms spread out over meticulously landscaped grounds and overlook the bay; cobbled lanes lined with colorful flowers and palms connect them. The resort is large but maintains an air of seclusion. (Motorized carts are on call for transportation within the property.)

Views, room size, and amenities differentiate the six types of accommodations, which can vary greatly. If you're not satisfied with your room, ask to be moved. Understated and spacious, the better units have white-marble floors, sitting areas, and large, comfortably furnished balconies. Camino Real Club rooms on the upper tier have upgraded amenities and great bay views; nine Club rooms have private pools. The lobby is a popular place for curling up in one of the overstuffed seating areas or, at night, for enjoying a drink and live music. La Mantarraya, the hotel's 18-hole, par-71 golf course, was designed by Pete and Roy Dye.

Av. de los Riscos s/n, Santiago Peninsula, 28200 Manzanillo, Col. ✆ **800/722-6466** in the U.S. and Canada, or 314/334-0000. 233 units. High season $250–$300 double, $462–$557 Fantasy Suite, $629–$972 Camino Real Club; low season $190–$232 double, $386–$477 Fantasy Suite, $557–$630 Camino Real Club. AE, DC, MC, V. Free guarded parking. **Amenities:** 4 restaurants, including the elegant Legazpi (see "Where to Dine," below), 4 lounges and bars; theme nights ($50 per person); 2 pools; shade tents on the beach; 10 tennis courts (8 hard-surface, 2 clay); marina for 70 vessels; scuba diving, snorkeling, sailing, and trimaran cruises; concierge; tour desk; car rental; shopping arcade; travel agency; small workout room; in-room massage; babysitting; laundry and dry cleaning. *In room:* A/C, TV, dataport, minibar, hair dryer, robes, safe-deposit box.

**Hotel Plaza Las Glorias** ★★ The sunset-colored walls of this pueblo-like hotel ramble over a hillside on Santiago Peninsula. The restaurant on top and most rooms afford a broad vista of other red-tiled rooftops and either the palm-filled golf course or the bay. It's one of Manzanillo's undiscovered resorts, known more to wealthy Mexicans than to Americans. Originally conceived as private condominiums, the accommodations were designed for living; each unit is spacious, stylishly furnished, and very comfortable. Each has a huge living room; a small kitchen/bar; one, two, or three large bedrooms with tile or brick floors; large Mexican-tiled bathrooms; huge closets; and large furnished private patios with views. Some units contain whirlpool tubs, and a few rooms can be partitioned off and rented by the bedroom only. Rooms can be a long walk from the main entrance, through a succession of stairways and paths. If stair climbing bothers you, try to get a room by the restaurant and pool—you'll have a great view, and a hillside rail elevator goes straight from top to bottom.

Av. de Tesoro s/n, Santiago Peninsula. 28200 Manzanillo, Col. © **314/334-1098.** Fax 314/333-1395. lasglorias@delfin.colimanet.com. 103 units. $110 double. Packages available. AE, MC, V. **Amenities:** Restaurant (with occasional live music); pool; game area; beach club on Las Brisas beach, with pool and small restaurant; transportation to and from beach club (once daily in each direction); room service; babysitting (with advance notice); laundry service. *In room:* A/C, TV, security box.

**Hotel Sierra Manzanillo** ★ This all-inclusive hotel has 21 floors overlooking La Audiencia beach, and a full program of activities, dining, and entertainment. Its excellent kids' program makes it a top choice for families. Architecturally, it mimics the white Moorish style of Las Hadas that has become so popular in Manzanillo. Inside, it's palatial in scale and awash in pale-gray marble. Room decor picks up the pale-gray theme with armoires that conceal the TV and minibar. Most standard rooms have two double beds or a king-size bed, plus a small table, chairs, and desk. Several rooms at the end of most floors are small, with one double bed, small porthole-size windows, no balcony, and no view. Most rooms, however, have balconies and ocean or hillside views. The 10 honeymoon suites are carpeted and have sculpted shell-shaped headboards, king-size beds, and chaises. Junior suites have a sitting area with couch, and large bathrooms. Scuba-diving lessons take place in the pool, and excellent scuba-diving sites are within swimming distance of the shore.

Av. La Audiencia 1, Los Riscos, 28200 Manzanillo, Col. © **800/448-5028** in the U.S. or 314/333-2000. Fax 314/333-2611. 332 units. High season $342 double, $392–$412 suite; low season $258 double, $248–$308 suite. Rates are all-inclusive. AE, MC, V. **Amenities:** 3 restaurants, 4 bars; grand pool on the beach, children's pool; 4 lighted tennis courts; health club with exercise equipment, aerobics, hot tub, men's and women's sauna and steam rooms; salon with massage; room service; travel agency; 24-hr. currency exchange; laundry service. *In room:* A/C, TV, dataport, minibar, hair dryer.

**Karmina Palace** ★★★ *Value* The quality of rooms and services at this all-inclusive resort makes the newest of Manzanillo's hotels probably one of the area's—and Mexico's—very best values. It's the best choice for families in Manzanillo. The buildings resemble Maya pyramids, and even though the architecture at first might seem a little overdone, somehow it works. Rooms are all very large suites, with rich wood accents, comfortable recessed seating areas with pull-out couches, and two 27-inch TVs in each room. The extra-large bathrooms have marble floors, twin black marble sinks, separate tubs, and glassed-in showers. Most rooms have terraces or balconies with views of the ocean, overlooking the tropical gardens and swimming pools. Master suites have spacious sun terraces with private splash pools, plus a full wet bar, full refrigerator, and a large living room area with 42-inch TV. Two full-size bedrooms close off from the living/dining area.

The Kid Club offers a host of activities, while adults have numerous choices for fun—all included in the price. There's also an exceptionally well-equipped gym and European-style spa. In-room safe-deposit boxes are available for an extra charge of $2, or you can use the safe-deposit box in the reception for free.

Blvd. Miguel de la Madrid s/n, Peninsula de Santiago, Manzanillo, Col. © **314/334-1313.** Fax 314/334-1108. www.karminapalace.com. 324 units. $190 per person. Rates are all-inclusive. 2 children under 12 stay free in parents' room. Ask for seasonal specials. AE, MC, V. **Amenities:** 2 restaurants, snack bar, 5 bars; 8 connected swimming pools; tennis courts; beach volleyball; windsurfing; kids' activity program; health club with treadmills and Cybex equipment; full spa facilities, including men's and women's sauna and steam rooms; 24-hr. concierge; 24-hr. room service; car rental; money exchange. *In room:* A/C, TV, dataport, minibar, hair dryer, iron.

## WHERE TO DINE

### DOWNTOWN

**Roca del Mar** MEXICAN/INTERNATIONAL Join the locals at this informal cafe facing the plaza. The large menu includes club sandwiches, hamburgers, *carne asada a la tampiqueña* (thin grilled steak served with rice, poblano pepper, an enchilada, and refried beans), fajitas, fish, shrimp, and vegetable salads. A specialty is its *paella* (served on Sun and Tues) and the economical *pibíl* tacos are outstanding. This spot is very clean and offers sidewalk dining.

21 de Marzo 204 (across from the plaza). ✆ **314/332-0302.** Main courses $3–$12. No credit cards. Daily 7am–10:30pm.

### LAS BRISAS

The Hotel La Posada (see "Where to Stay," above) offers breakfast to nonguests at its beachside restaurant; it's also a great place to mingle with other tourists and enjoy the sunset and cocktails.

**Willy's** ★★★ *Finds* SEAFOOD/INTERNATIONAL You're in for a treat at Willy's, one of Manzanillo's most popular restaurants. It's homey, casual, and small, with perhaps 13 tables inside and 10 more on the narrow balcony over the bay. The exquisite cuisine belies the atmosphere, with starters that include escargot and salmon carpaccio. Among the grilled specialties are shrimp imperial wrapped in bacon, red snapper tarragon, dorado basil, sea bass with mango and ginger, and tender fresh lobsters (four to a serving). Live guitar jazz plays after 8pm. If you double back left at the Las Brisas crossroads, you'll find Willy's on the right, down a short side street that leads to the ocean.

Las Brisas crossroads. ✆ **314/333-1794.** Reservations required. Main courses $8–$17. MC, V. Daily 7pm–midnight.

### SANTIAGO ROAD

The restaurants below are on the Costera Madrid between downtown and the Santiago Peninsula, including the Salahua area.

**Benedetti's Pizza** PIZZA Since there are several branches in town, you'll probably find a Benedetti's not far from where you are staying. The variety isn't extensive, but the pies are quite good; add some *chimichurri* sauce to enhance the flavor. Benedetti's specializes in seafood pizzas, such as smoked oyster and anchovy. You can also select from pastas, sandwiches, burgers, fajitas, salads, Mexican soups, cheesecake, and apple pie. This branch is on the Costera Madrid, on the left, just after the Las Brisas turn across from the Coca-Cola plant.

Av. del Mar 1, Crucero Las Brisas. ✆ **314/334-0141.** Pizza $9–$12; main courses $2–$5.55. AE, MC, V. Daily 1–11:30pm.

**Bigotes III** *Finds* SEAFOOD Locals flock to this large, breezy restaurant (the name translates as "Mustaches") by the water for the good food and festive atmosphere. Strolling singers serenade diners, who dig into large portions of grilled seafood. To find Bigotes, follow the Costera de la Madrid from downtown past the Las Brisas turnoff. It's behind the Penas Coloradas Social Club across from the beach.

Puesta del Sol 3. ✆ **314/333-1236.** Main courses $9.50–$22.50. MC, V. Daily noon–10pm.

**Manolo's Norteño Campestre** INTERNATIONAL/STEAK/SEAFOOD Owners Manuel and Juanita López and family offer excellent dining in a tropical garden setting. They cater to American tastes: Dinners include a "safe" salad. Among the popular entrees are filet of fish Manolo (on a bed of spinach with melted cheese, Florentine-style), and frog legs in brandy batter. Most people can't leave without being tempted by the fresh coconut or homemade pecan pie. Coming from downtown, Manolo's is on the right, about 3 blocks before the turn to Las Hadas.

Km 11.5, Costera Miguel de la Madrid. ✆ **314/333-0475.** Main courses $5–$20. AE, MC, V. Mon–Sat 5pm–midnight.

### SANTIAGO PENINSULA

**Legazpi** ★★ INTERNATIONAL This is a top choice in Manzanillo for sheer elegance, gracious service, and outstanding food. The candlelit tables are set with silver and flowers. Enormous bell-shaped windows on two sides show off the sparkling bay below. The sophisticated menu includes prosciutto with melon marinated in port wine, crayfish bisque, broiled salmon, roast duck, lobster, veal, and flaming desserts from crêpes to Irish coffee.

In the Camino Real Las Hadas hotel, Santiago Peninsula. ✆ **314/334-0000.** Main courses $8.50–$15.75. AE, MC, V. High season daily 7–11:30pm. Closed low season.

## MANZANILLO AFTER DARK

Nightlife in Manzanillo is much more exuberant than you might expect, but then Manzanillo is not only a resort town—it's a thriving commercial center. Clubs and bars tend to change from year to year, so check with your concierge for current hot spots. Perennial favorites include **Carlos 'n' Charlie's,** Av. Audiencia Cocoteros s/n (✆ **314/334-1272**), always a good choice for food and fun. In the evening during high season, there may be a minimum or cover if you come just to drink and dance, but the cover includes three drinks. **El Bar de Felix,** between Salahua and Las Brisas by the Avis rental-car office (✆ **314/334-1444**), is open Tuesday to Sunday from 9pm to 2am and doesn't charge a cover. **Vog Disco** (✆ **314/333-1875**), km 9.2 Blvd. Costero Miguel de la Madrid, features alternative music in a cavernous setting; it's Manzanillo's current late-night hot spot, open until 5am. It features an early happy hour from 9 to 11pm, and waives the $4 cover for women on Friday night. Also very popular—with a built-in crowd—is the nightclub at the **Club Maeva Hotel & Resort** (✆ **800/523-8450**), on the inland side of the main highway, north of the Santiago Peninsula. It's open Tuesday, Thursday, and Saturday from 10pm to 3am. Couples are given preferential entrance. Nonguests are welcome, but must pay an entrance fee, after which all drinks are included. The fee varies depending on the night of the week and the time of year. Some area clubs have a dress code prohibiting shorts or sandals, principally applying to men.

## A SIDE TRIP TO COLIMA & ITS VOLCANO

The city of Colima makes an interesting and accessible day trip from Manzanillo. It's about an hour's drive along the well-maintained, four-lane Highway 54 to this charming colonial city, the capital of Colima state. Well-preserved colonial buildings, such as the city's 1527 **cathedral** and the **Palacio de Gobierno,** with its murals depicting Mexican history, are key attractions in the city's center.

Colima has several interesting museums, including the **Museo de las Culturas del Occidente,** which displays an impressive permanent collection of pre-Columbian pottery and artifacts. It's open Tuesday to Sunday from 10am to 5pm; admission is free. The **Casa de la Cultura** hosts changing exhibitions of contemporary art and offers free art, music, and dance classes. It's open Tuesday to Sunday from 10:30am to 5:30pm; admission is free.

Two imposing volcanoes (one still active) border the town. The **Volcán de Fuego** is 24km (15 miles) north, next to the taller, extinct **Nevado de Colima.** In 1999, the Volcán de Fuego became active, sometimes blowing smoke and ash up to 5km (3 miles) high, but it has since settled down. Popular tours to Colima often include a visit to two newly opened archaeological sites, El Chanal and La Campana.

9

# Acapulco & the Southern Pacific Coast

The exotic tropical beaches and rich jungle scenery of this part of Mexico first captured the imagination of travelers to this country. Although the geography of southern Pacific Mexico may be uniform, the resorts along this coast couldn't be more varied in personality. They range from high-energy seaside cities to pristine, primitive coves.

Spanish conquistadors came to this coast for its numerous sheltered coves and protected bays, from which they set sail to the Far East. Years later, Mexico's first tourists found the same elements appealing, but for different reasons—they were seeking escape, and stretches of blue coves nicely complemented the tropical landscape of the adjacent mountains.

Over the years, the area developed a diverse selection of resorts. Each is distinct, and together they offer an ideal attraction for almost any type of traveler. The region encompasses the country's oldest resort, **Acapulco;** its newest, the **Bahías de Huatulco;** and a side-by-side pair of opposites, modern **Ixtapa** and the simple fishing village of **Zihuatanejo.** Between Acapulco and Huatulco lie the small, laid-back beach towns of **Puerto Escondido** and **Puerto Angel,** both on picturesque bays.

This chapter covers coastal towns in two Mexican states, Guerrero and Oaxaca. Stunning coastline and tropical mountains grace the whole region. Outside the urban centers, however, few roads are paved, and these two states remain among Mexico's poorest despite decades of tourist dollars (and many other currencies).

## EXPLORING THE SOUTHERN PACIFIC COAST

Time at the beach used to be the top priority for most travelers to this part of Mexico. Today, eco- and adventure tourism, and more culturally oriented travels, are gaining ground. Each of the beach towns in this chapter is capable of satisfying your sand and surf needs for a few days, or even a week or more. You could also combine several coastal resorts into a single trip, or mix the coastal with the colonial—say, Puerto Escondido and Oaxaca City, or Acapulco and Taxco.

The resorts have distinct personalities, but you get the beach wherever you go, whether you choose a city that offers virtually every luxury imaginable or a rustic town providing little more than seaside relaxation.

The largest and most decadent of Mexican resorts, **Acapulco** leapt into the international spotlight in the late 1930s when movie stars made it their playground. Today, though increasingly challenged by other Mexican seaside destinations, Acapulco still lures visitors with its glitzy nightlife and sultry beaches (even if the Hollywood celebrities who made it a household name have long since moved on). Of all the resorts, Acapulco has the best airline connections, the broadest range of late-night entertainment, the most savory dining, and the widest range of accommodations. The beaches are generally wide and clean, and although the ocean itself remains suspect, it's cleaner than in past years.

The resort of **Ixtapa** and its neighboring seaside village, **Zihuatanejo,** offer beach-bound tourist attractions, but on a smaller, less hectic scale than Acapulco. They attract travelers with their complementary contrasts—sophisticated high-rise hotels in one, local color and leisurely pace in the other. Their excellent beaches front clean ocean waters. To get here, many people fly into Acapulco, then make the 4- to 5-hour trip north by rental car or bus.

**Puerto Escondido,** noted for its stellar surf break, laid-back village ambience, attractive and inexpensive inns, and nearby nature excursions, is a worthy travel destination and an exceptional value. It's 6 hours south of Acapulco on coastal Highway 200. Most people fly here from Mexico City or drive up from Huatulco.

The small village of **Puerto Angel,** 80km (50 miles) south of Puerto Escondido and 48km (30 miles) north of the Bahías of Huatulco, is a nice day trip from either of those destinations. It might also serve as a quiet place to relax for several days, providing you care little for any activity beyond the beach.

Farther south of Acapulco, the **Bahías de Huatulco** encompass a total of nine bays—each lovelier than the last—on a pristine portion of Oaxaca's coast. Development of the area has been gradual and well planned, with great ecological sensitivity. The town of **Huatulco,** 128km (80 miles) south of Puerto Escondido, is emerging as Mexico's most authentic adventure tourism haven. Though it has an 18-hole golf course and a handful of resort hotels, it also offers a growing array of soft adventures that range from bay tours to diving, river rafting, and rappelling. Dining and nightlife remain limited, but the setting is beautiful and relaxing.

## 1 Acapulco ★★

366km (229 miles) S of Mexico City; 272km (170 miles) SW of Taxco; 979km (612 miles) SE of Guadalajara; 253km (158 miles) SE of Ixtapa/Zihuatanejo; 752km (470 miles) NW of Huatulco

I like to think of Acapulco as a diva—maybe a little past her prime, perhaps overly made up, but still capable of captivating an audience. It's tempting to dismiss Acapulco as a passé resort, but the town's temptations are hard to resist. Where else do bronzed men dive from cliffs into the sea at sunset, and where else does the sun shine 360 days a year? Though most beach resorts are made for relaxing, Acapulco has a nonstop, 24-hours-a-day energy. Its perfectly sculpted bay is an adult playground filled with water-skiers in *tanga* swimsuits and darkly tanned, mirror-shaded studs on jet skis. Visitors play golf and tennis with intensity, but the real participant sport is the nightlife, which has made this city famous for decades. Back in the days when there was a jet set, they came to Acapulco—filmed it, sang about it, wrote about it, and lived it.

It's not hard to understand why: The view of Acapulco Bay, framed by mountains and beaches, is breathtaking day or night. And I dare anyone to take in the lights of the city and not feel the pull to go out and get lively.

Though a few years ago tourism to Acapulco was in a state of decline, it's now experiencing a renaissance, in a style reminiscent of Miami's South Beach. Classic hotels are being renovated and areas gentrified. Clean-up efforts have put a whole new face on a place that was once aging less than gracefully.

International travelers began to reject Acapulco when it became clear that the cost of development was the pollution of the bay and surrounding areas. The city government responded, and invested over $1 billion in public and private infrastructure improvements. In addition, a program instituted in the early 1990s and has cleaned up the water—whales have even been sighted offshore for the first time in years.

A city that never sleeps, Acapulco tries hard to hold on to its image as the ultimate extravagant party town. It's still the top choice for those who want to have dinner at midnight, dance until dawn, and sleep all day on a sun-soaked beach.

## ESSENTIALS

### GETTING THERE & DEPARTING

**BY PLANE** See chapter 2, "Planning Your Trip to Mexico," for information on flying from the United States or Canada to Acapulco. Local numbers for major airlines with nonstop or direct service to Acapulco are **Aeromexico** (**© 744/ 485-1600** or 744/481-1766), **American** (**© 744/466-9232** or 01-800/ 904-6000 in Mexico for reservations), **Continental** (**© 744/466-9063**), **Mexicana** (**© 744/466-9121** or 744/486-7586), and **America West** (**© 744/466-9257**).

**Aeromexico** flies from Guadalajara, Mexico City, and Tijuana; **Mexicana** flies from Mexico City. Check with a travel agent about **charter flights.**

The airport (airport code: ACA) is 22km (14 miles) southeast of town, over the hills east of the bay. Private **taxis** are the fastest way to get downtown; they cost $33 to $50. The major **rental car** agencies all have booths at the airport. **Transportes Terrestres** has desks at the front of the airport where you can buy tickets for minivan *colectivo* transportation into town ($10). You must reserve return service to the airport through your hotel.

**BY CAR** From Mexico City, take either the curvy toll-free Highway 95D south (6 hr.), or scenic Highway 95, the four- to six-lane toll highway (3½ hr.), which costs around $50 one-way. The free road from Taxco is in good condition; you'll save around $40 in tolls from there through Chilpancingo to Acapulco. From points north or south along the coast, the only choice is Highway 200, where you should (as on all Mexican highways) always try to travel by day. The reason is not so much crime—although this used to be one of the most dangerous roads for car robberies, especially south from Acapulco—but that most roads are unlit and poorly marked.

**BY BUS** The **Ejido/Central Camionera station,** Ejido 47, is on the far northern end of the bay and north of downtown (Old Acapulco). It's far from the hotels; however, it serves more bus lines and routes than any other Acapulco bus station. It also has a hotel-reservation service.

---

***Tips*** **Car & Bus Travel Warning Eases**

Car robberies and bus hijackings on Highway 200 south of Acapulco on the way to Puerto Escondido and Huatulco used to be common, and you may have heard warnings about this road. The trouble has all but disappeared, thanks to military patrols and greater police protection. However, as in most of Mexico, it's most advisable to travel the highways during daylight hours only—not so much for personal safety, but because highways are unlit, and animals can wander on them.

---

# Acapulco Bay Area

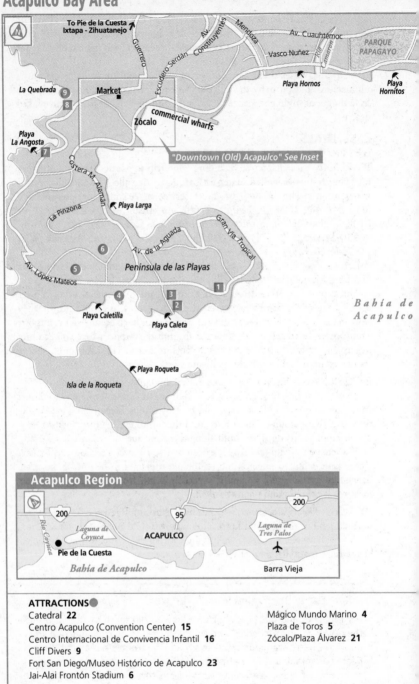

To Pie de la Cuesta
Ixtapa - Zihuatanejo
Guerrero
Av. Constituyentes
Mendoza
Av. Cuauhtémoc
PARQUE PAPAGAYO
Escudero Serdán
Vasco Nuñez
Río Camarón
Playa Hornos
Playa Hornitos
La Quebrada
Market
Zócalo
commercial wharfs
Playa La Angosta
"Downtown (Old) Acapulco" See Inset
Costera M. Alemán
Playa Larga
La Pinzona
Gran Vía Tropical
Av. de la Aguada
Peninsula de las Playas
Av. López Mateos
Playa Caletilla
Playa Caleta
Bahía de Acapulco
Playa Roqueta
Isla de la Roqueta

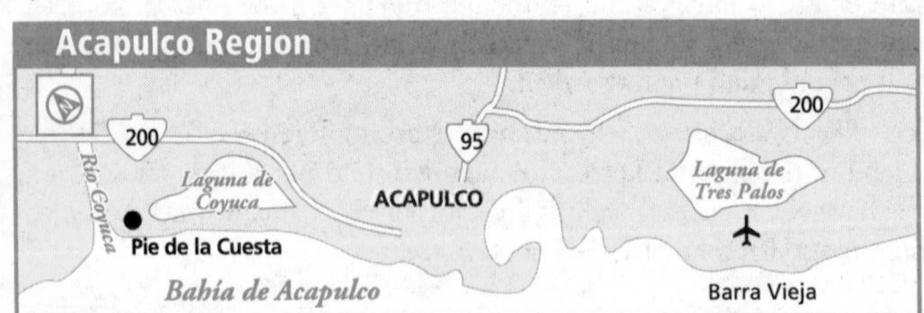


**ATTRACTIONS**

Catedral **22**
Centro Acapulco (Convention Center) **15**
Centro Internacional de Convivencia Infantil **16**
Cliff Divers **9**
Fort San Diego/Museo Histórico de Acapulco **23**
Jai-Alai Frontón Stadium **6**
Mágico Mundo Marino **4**
Plaza de Toros **5**
Zócalo/Plaza Álvarez **21**

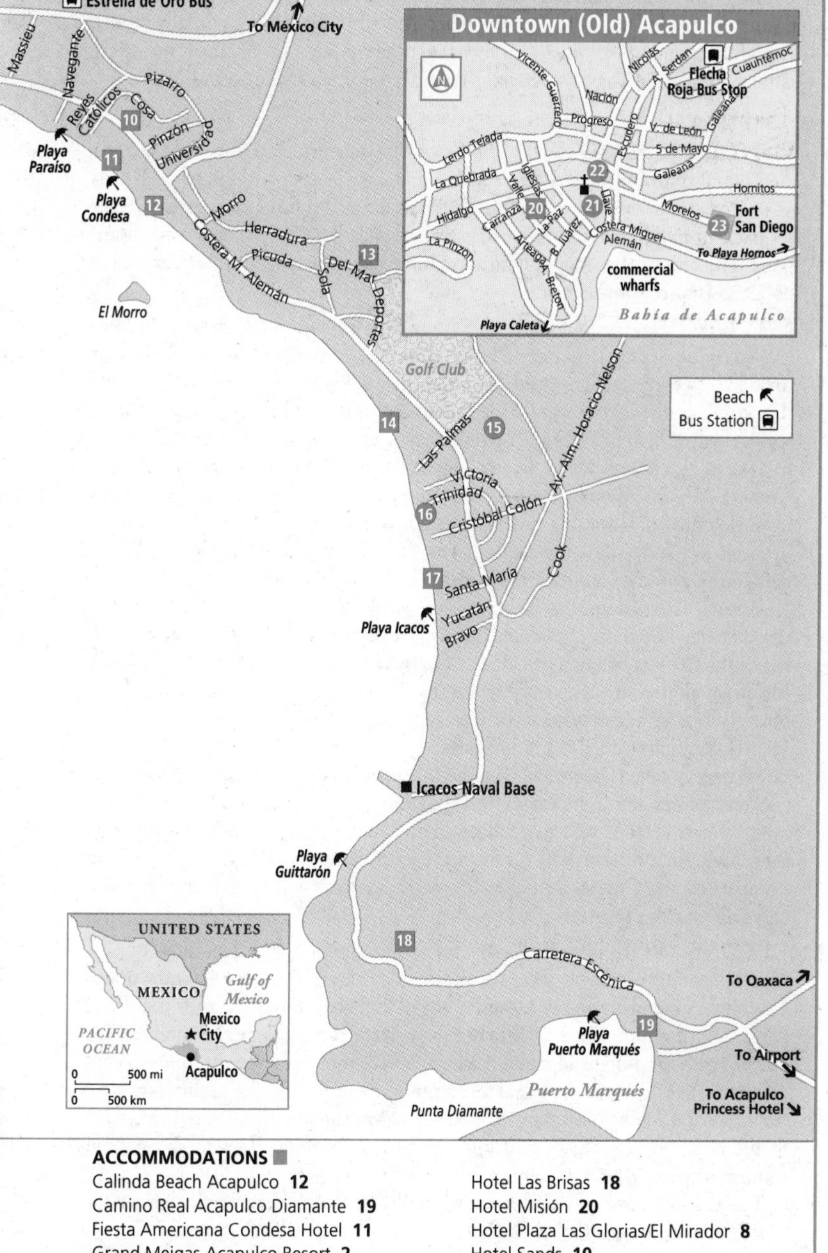


**ACCOMMODATIONS**

Calinda Beach Acapulco **12**
Camino Real Acapulco Diamante **19**
Fiesta Americana Condesa Hotel **11**
Grand Meigas Acapulco Resort **2**
Hotel Costa Linda **3**
Hotel Elcano **14**
Hotel Los Flamingos **1**
Hotel Las Brisas **18**
Hotel Misión **20**
Hotel Plaza Las Glorias/El Mirador **8**
Hotel Sands **10**
Hotel Villa Romana **7**
Hyatt Regency Acapulco **17**
Villa Vera Hotel & Racquet Club **13**

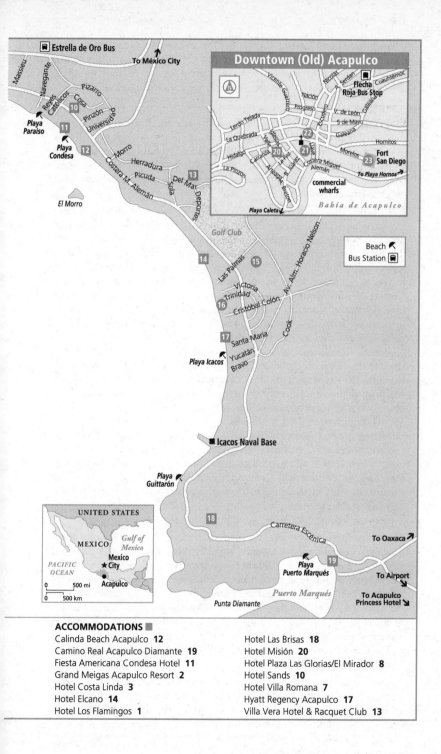

From this station, **Turistar, Estrella de Oro,** and **Estrella Blanca** have almost hourly service for the 5- to 7-hour trip to Mexico City ($42), and daily service to Zihuatanejo ($14). Buses also serve other points in Mexico, including Chilpancingo, Cuernavaca, Iguala, Manzanillo, Puerto Vallarta, and Taxco.

## ORIENTATION

**VISITOR INFORMATION** The **State of Guerrero Tourism Office** operates the **Procuraduría del Turista** (© and fax **744/484-4583** or 744/484-4416), on street level in front of the **International Center,** a convention center set back from the main Costera Alemán, down a lengthy walkway with fountains. The office offers maps and information about the city and state, as well as police assistance for tourists; it's open daily 9am to 10pm.

**CITY LAYOUT** Acapulco stretches more than 6km (4 miles) around the huge bay, so trying to take it all in by foot is impractical. The tourist areas are roughly divided into three sections: **Old Acapulco** (Acapulco Viejo) is the original town that attracted the jet setters of the 1950s and 1960s—and today it looks as if it's still locked in that era, though a renaissance is under way. The second section is known as the **Hotel Zone** (Zona Hotelera); it follows the main boulevard, **Costera Miguel Alemán** (or just "the Costera"), as it runs east along the bay from downtown. Towering hotels, restaurants, shopping centers, and strips of open-air beach bars line the street. At the far eastern end of the Costera lie the golf course and the International Center (a convention center).

**Avenida Cuauhtémoc** is the major artery inland, running roughly parallel to the Costera. The third major area begins just beyond the Hyatt Regency Hotel, where the Costera changes its name to **Carretera Escénica** (Scenic Hwy.), which continues all the way to the airport. Along this section of the road the hotels are most lavish, and extravagant private villas, gourmet restaurants, and flashy nightclubs built into the hillside offer dazzling views. The area fronting the beach here is called **Acapulco Diamante,** Acapulco's most desirable address.

Street names and numbers in Acapulco can be confusing and hard to find—many streets are not well marked or change names unexpectedly. Fortunately, there's seldom a reason to be far from the Costera, so it's hard to get lost. Street numbers on the Costera do not follow logic, so don't assume that similar numbers will be close together.

**GETTING AROUND** **By Taxi** Taxis are more plentiful than tacos in Acapulco—and practically as inexpensive, if you're traveling in the downtown area only. Just remember that you should always establish the price with the driver before starting out. Hotel taxis may charge three times the rate of a taxi hailed on the street, and nighttime taxi rides cost extra, too. Taxis are also more expensive if you're staying in the Diamante section or south. The minimum fare is $2 per ride for a roving VW Bug-style taxi in town; the fare from Puerto Marqués to the hotel zone is $8, or $10 into downtown. *Sitio* taxis are nicer cars, but more expensive, with a minimum fare of $4.

The fashion among Acapulco taxis is flashy, with Las Vegas–style lights—the more colorful and pulsating, the better.

**By Bus** Even though the city has a confusing street layout, using city buses is amazingly easy and inexpensive. Two kinds of buses run along the Costera: pastel color-coded buses and regular "school buses." The difference is the price: New air-conditioned tourist buses (Aca Tur Bus) are 40¢; old buses, 35¢. Covered bus stops are all along the Costera, with handy maps on the walls showing routes to major sights and hotels.

The best place near the *zócalo* to catch a bus is next to Sanborn's, 2 blocks east. CALETA DIRECTO or BASE–CALETA buses will take you to the Hornos, Caleta, and Caletilla beaches along the Costera. Some buses return along the same route; others go around the peninsula and return to the Costera.

For expeditions to more distant destinations, there are buses to **Puerto Marqués** to the east (marked PUERTO MARQUES–BASE) and **Pie de la Cuesta** to the west (marked *zocalo*–PIE DE LA CUESTA). Be sure to verify the time and place of the last bus back if you hop on one of these.

**By Car** Rental cars are available at the airport and at hotel desks along the Costera. Unless you plan on exploring outlying areas, you're better off taking taxis or using the easy and inexpensive public buses.

## *FAST FACTS:* Acapulco

*American Express* The main office is in the Gran Plaza shopping center, Costera Alemán 1628 (✆ **744/469-1100**). It's open Monday to Saturday from 10am to 7pm.

*Area Code* The telephone area code is **744.**

*Climate* Acapulco boasts sunshine 360 days a year, with average daytime temperatures of 80°F (27°C). Humidity varies, with approximately 59 inches of rain per year. June through October is the rainy season, though July and August are relatively dry. Tropical showers are brief and usually occur at night.

*Consular Agents* The **United States** has an agent at the Hotel Club del Sol, Costera Alemán at Reyes Católicos (✆ **744/481-1699** or 744/469-0556), across from the Hotel Acapulco Plaza; the office is open Monday to Friday 10am to 2pm. The **Canadian** office is at the Centro Comercial Marbella, Local 23 (✆ **744/484-1305**). The toll-free emergency number inside Mexico is ✆ 01-800/706-2900. The office is open Monday to Friday 9am to 5pm. The **United Kingdom** office is at the Las Brisas Hotel on Carretera Escénica near the airport (✆ **744/481-2533** or 744/484-1735);. Most other countries in the European Union also have consulate offices in Acapulco.

*Currency Exchange* Numerous banks along the Costera are open Monday to Friday from 9am to 6pm, Saturday from 10am to 1:30pm. Banks and their ATMs generally have the best rates. *Casas de cambio* (currency-exchange booths) along the street may have better exchange rates than hotels.

*Hospital* Try **Hospital Magallanes,** Avenida Wilfrido Massieu 2 Fracc. Magallanes (✆ **744/485-6194** or 744/485-6096), which has an English-speaking staff and doctors, or **Hospital Pacífico,** Calle Fraile y Nao 4, Fracc. La Bocana (✆ **744/487-7180** or 744/487-7161).

*Internet Access* **Acanet,** Costera Alemán 1632 Int., La Gran Plaza, Local D-1, lower floor (✆ **744/486-8182** and 744/486-8184; fax 744/486-9186; www.acanet.com.mx), is open daily from 10am to 9pm. Internet access costs $1.10 per hour. This is a computer shop that also offers Internet access and has a very helpful staff.

*Parking* It is illegal to park on the Costera at any time. Try parking along side streets, or in one of the few covered parking lots, such as in Plaza Bahia and in Plaza Mirabella.

*Pharmacy* One of the largest drugstores in town is **Farmacia Daisy,** Francia 49, across the traffic circle from the convention center (✆ **744/484-7664** or 744/484-5950). Sam's Club and WalMart, both on the Costera, have pharmacy services and lower prices on medicine.

*Post Office* The *correo* is next door to Sears, close to the Fideicomiso office. It's open Monday to Friday from 9am to 5pm, Saturday from 9am to 1pm. Other branches are in the Estrella de Oro bus station on Cuauhtémoc, inland from the Acapulco Qualton Hotel, and on the Costera near Caleta Beach.

*Safety* Riptides claim a few lives every year, so pay close attention to warning flags posted on Acapulco beaches. Red or black flags mean stay out of the water, yellow flags signify caution, and white or green flags mean it's safe to swim.

As is the case anywhere, tourists are vulnerable to thieves. This is especially true when shopping in a market, lying on the beach, wearing jewelry, or visibly carrying a camera, purse, or bulging wallet.

*Telephone* Acapulco phone numbers seem to change frequently. The most reliable source for telephone numbers is the **Procuraduría del Turista** (✆ **744/484-4583**), which has an exceptionally friendly staff.

*Tourist Police* Policemen in white and light blue uniforms belong to a special corps of English-speaking police established to assist tourists.

## ACTIVITIES ON & OFF THE BEACH

Acapulco is known for its great beaches and watersports, and few visitors bother to explore its traditional downtown area. But it's worth a trip there, to the shady ***zócalo*** (also called Plaza Alvarez), to experience a glimpse of local life and color. Inexpensive cafes and shops border the plaza. At its far north end is the **cathedral Nuestra Señora de la Soledad,** with its blue, onion-shaped domes and Byzantine towers. Though reminiscent of a Russian Orthodox church, it was originally (and perhaps appropriately) built as a movie set, then later adapted to be a house of worship. From the church, turn east along the side street going off at a right angle (Calle Carranza, which doesn't have a marker) to find an arcade with newsstands and more shops. The hill behind the cathedral provides an unparalleled view of Acapulco. Take a taxi to the top of the hill from the main plaza, and follow signs to **El Mirador** (lookout point).

Local travel agencies book city tours, day trips to Taxco, cruises, and other excursions and activities. Taxco is about a 3-hour drive inland from Acapulco (see chapter 4 for more information).

**THE BEACHES** Here's a rundown on the beaches, going from west to east around the bay. **Playa la Angosta** is a small, sheltered, often-deserted cove just around the bend from **La Quebrada** (where the cliff divers perform).

South of downtown on the Peninsula de las Playas lie the beaches **Caleta** and **Caletilla.** Separating them is a small outcropping of land that contains the aquarium and water park **Mágico Mundo Marino** (open daily 9am–7pm). You'll find thatched-roofed restaurants, watersports equipment for rent, and brightly painted boats that ferry passengers to **Roqueta Island.** You can rent beach chairs and umbrellas for the day. Mexican families favor these beaches

### *Finds* A Masterpiece of a House

Acapulco is as well known for its exclusive villas as its nightlife, but one house in particular stands out. Though not as impressive as the villas of Las Brisas, the **home of Dolores Olmedo,** Calle Cerro de la Pinzona 6, downtown, is a work of art. In 1956, the renowned Mexican artist Diego Rivera covered its outside wall with a mural of colorful mosaic tiles, shells, and stones. The unique work is one of his last.

Rivera, considered one of Mexico's greatest artists, was one of the founders of the 20th-century Mexican muralist movement. The Olmeda mural, which took him 18 months to complete, features Aztec deities such as Quetzacoatl and Tepezcuincle, the Aztec dog. Rivera and Olmeda were lifelong friends; Rivera once asked Olmeda to marry him, but she refused. He lived in this house for the last 2 years of his life, during which time he also covered the interior with murals. However, since the home is not a museum, you'll have to settle for enjoying the exterior.

The house is a few blocks behind the Casablanca Hotel, a short cab ride from the central plaza. Have the driver wait while you look around—there's not much traffic, and it's a steep climb back to the plaza.

because they're close to several inexpensive hotels. In the late afternoon, fishermen pull their colorful boats up on the sand; you can buy the fresh catch of the day and, occasionally, oysters on the half shell.

Pleasure boats dock at **Playa Manzanillo,** south of the *zócalo.* Charter fishing trips sail from here. In the old days, the downtown beaches—Manzanillo, Honda, Caleta, and Caletilla—were the focal point of Acapulco. Today, beaches and resort developments stretch along the 4-mile length of the shore.

East of the *zócalo,* the major beaches are **Hornos** (near Papagayo Park), **Hornitos, Paraíso, Condesa,** and **Icacos,** followed by the naval base (La Base) and **Punta del Guitarrón.** After Punta del Guitarrón, the road climbs to the legendary Las Brisas hotel. Past Las Brisas, the road continues to the small, clean bay of **Puerto Marqués,** followed by **Punta Diamante,** about 19km (12 miles) from the *zócalo.* The fabulous Acapulco Princess, the new Quinta Real, and the Pierre Marqués hotels dominate the landscape here, which fronts the open Pacific.

**Playa Puerto Marqués,** in the bay of Puerto Marqués, is an attractive area for swimming. The water is calm and the bay sheltered. Water-skiing can also be arranged. Past the bay lies **Revolcadero Beach,** a magnificent wide stretch of beach on the open ocean, where many of Acapulco's grandest resorts are found.

Other beaches are farther north and best reached by car, though buses also make the trip. **Pie de la Cuesta** is 13km (8 miles) west of town. Buses along the Costera leave every 5 or 10 minutes; a taxi costs about $22. The water is too rough to swim here, but it's a great spot for checking out big waves and the spectacular sunset, especially over *coco locos* (drinks served in fresh coconuts with the tops whacked off) at a rustic beachfront restaurant. The area is known for excellent birding and surrounding coconut plantations.

### Tips To Swim or Not to Swim in the Bay?

In the past decade, the city has gone to great lengths (and great expense) to clean up the waters off Acapulco. Nevertheless, this is an industrial port that was once heavily polluted, so many choose to stick to the hotel pool. You may notice the fleet of more than 20 power-sweeper boats that skim the top of the bay each morning to remove debris and oil.

Among the bay beaches that remain popular with visitors and locals are **Caleta and Caletilla beaches,** as well as **Playa Puerto Marqués.**

If you're driving, continue west along the peninsula, passing **Coyuca Lagoon** on your right, until you have almost reached the small air base at the tip. Along the way, various private entrepreneurs, mostly young boys, will invite you to park near different sections of beach. You'll also find *colectivo* boat tours of the lagoon offered for about $10.

**BAY CRUISES & ROQUETA ISLAND** Acapulco has virtually every kind of boat to choose from—yachts, catamarans, and trimarans (single- and double-deckers). Cruises run morning, afternoon, and evening. Some offer buffets, open bars, and live music; others just snacks, drinks, and taped music. Prices range from $24 to $60. Cruise operators come and go, and their phone numbers change so frequently from year to year that it's pointless to list them here; to find out what cruises are currently operating, contact any Acapulco travel agency or your hotel's tour desk, and ask for brochures or recommendations.

Having said that, there is one cruise that stands out—the **Aca Tiki** (**© 744/484-6140** or 744/484-6786), with its heart-shaped strand of red lights visible from the boat's tall masts. The moonlight cruise, known as the "love boat," has live music, dancing, snacks, and an open bar each evening from 10:30pm to 1am. Aca Tiki also offers sunset cruises, with departure times depending upon the time of sunset. Both cruises leave from the *malecón,* across from the central plaza downtown, and cost $22 each.

Boats from Caletilla Beach to **Roqueta Island**—a good place to snorkel, sunbathe, hike to a lighthouse, visit a small zoo, or have lunch—leave every 15 minutes from 7am until the last one returns at 7pm. There are also primitive-style glass-bottom boats that circle the bay as you look down at a few fish and watch a diver swim down to the underwater sanctuary of the Virgin of Guadalupe, patron saint of Mexico. The statue of the Virgin—created by sculptor Castillo Díaz—was placed there in 1959, in memory of a group of divers who lost their lives at the spot. You can purchase tickets ($6) directly from any boat that's loading, or at a discount from the **information booth** on Caletilla Beach (**© 744/482-2389**).

**WATERSPORTS & BOAT RENTALS** An hour of **water-skiing** can cost as little as $35 or as much as $65. Caletilla Beach, Puerto Marqués Bay, and Coyuca Lagoon have facilities. The **Club de Esquis,** Costera Alemán 100 (**© 744/482-2034**), charges $50 per hour.

**Scuba diving** costs $40 for 1½ hours of instruction if you book directly with the instructor on Caleta Beach. It costs $45 to $55 if you book through a hotel or travel agency. Dive trips start at around $40 per person for one dive.

**Boat rentals** are cheapest on Caletilla Beach, where an information booth rents inner tubes, small boats, canoes, paddleboats, and chairs. It also arranges water-skiing and scuba diving (see "Bay Cruises & Roqueta Island," above).

**Tips** **Tide Warning**

Each year, at least one or two unwary swimmers drown in Acapulco because of deadly riptides and undertow (see "Safety" in "Fast Facts," above). Swim only in Acapulco Bay or Puerto Marqués Bay—and be careful of the undertow no matter where you go. If you find yourself caught in the undertow, head back to shore at an angle instead of trying to swim straight back.

For **deep-sea fishing** excursions, go to the boat cooperative's pink building opposite the *zócalo,* or book a day in advance (© **744/482-1099**). Charter trips run from $150 to $200 for 6 hours, tackle and bait included. Credit cards are accepted, and ice, drinks, and lunch are extra. The fishing license is $9. Boats leave at 8am and return at 3pm. If you book through a travel agent or hotel, prices start at around $200 for four people. License, food, and drinks are extra.

**Parasailing,** though not free from risk (the occasional thrill-seeker has collided with a palm tree or even a building), can be brilliant. Floating high over the bay hanging from a parachute towed by a motorboat costs about $37. Most of these rides operate on Condesa Beach, but they also can be found independently operating on the beach in front of most hotels along the Costera.

**GOLF, TENNIS, RIDING & BULLFIGHTS** A round of 18 holes of **golf** at the Acapulco Princess Hotel (© **744/469-1000**) costs $105 for guests, $120 for nonguests; American Express, Visa, and MasterCard are accepted. Tee times begin at 7:35am, and reservations should be made 1 day in advance. Club rental is $31. At the **Club de Golf Acapulco,** off the Costera next to the Convention Center (© **744/484-0781**), you can play 9 holes for $39 and 18 holes for $58, with equipment renting for $17.

The **Club de Tenis Hyatt,** Costera Alemán 1 (© **744/484-1225**), is open daily from 7am to 10pm. Outdoor courts cost $9 during the day, $14.50 per hour at night. Rackets rent for $3.50 and a set of balls for $3.50. Many of the hotels along the Costera have tennis facilities for guests.

You can go **horseback riding** along the beach. Independent operators stroll the Hotel Zone beachfront offering rides for about $20 to $40 for 1 to 2 hours. Horses are also commonly found on the beach in front of the Acapulco Princess Hotel. There is no phone; you go directly to the beach to make arrangements.

Traditionally called *Fiesta Brava,* **bullfights** are held during Acapulco's winter season at a ring up the hill from Caletilla Beach. Tickets purchased through travel agencies cost around $17 to $40 and usually include transportation to and from your hotel. The festivities begin at 5:30pm each Sunday from December to March.

**A MUSEUM & A WATER PARK** The original **Fuerte de San Diego,** Costera Alemán, east of the *zócalo* (© **744/482-3828**), was built in 1616 to protect the town from pirate attacks. At that time, the port reaped considerable income from trade with the Philippine Islands (which, like Mexico, were part of the Spanish Empire). The fort you see today was rebuilt after considerable earthquake damage in 1776, and most recently underwent renovation in 2000. The structure houses the **Museo Histórico de Acapulco** (Acapulco Historical Museum), with exhibits that tell the story of Acapulco from its role as a port in the conquest of the Americas to a center for local Catholic conversion campaigns

### *Moments* Death-Defying Divers

High divers perform at La Quebrada each day at 12:30, 7:15, 8:15, 9:15, and 10:15pm. Admission is $1. From a spotlit ledge on the cliffs, divers (holding torches for the final performance) plunge into the roaring surf 40m (130 ft.) below—after wisely praying at a small shrine nearby. To the applause of the crowd, divers climb up the rocks and accept congratulations and gifts of money from onlookers. This is the quintessential Acapulco experience, and no visit is complete without watching the cliff divers—and that goes for jaded travelers as well. To get there from downtown, take the street called La Quebrada from behind the cathedral for 4 blocks.

The public areas have great views, but arrive early, because performances quickly fill up. Another option is to watch from the lobby bar and restaurant terraces of the **Hotel Plaza Las Glorias/El Mirador.** The bar imposes a $9.50 cover charge, which includes two drinks. You can get around the cover by having dinner at the hotel's **La Perla restaurant.** Reservations (© **744/483-1155**) are recommended during high season.

and for exotic trade with the Orient. Other exhibits chronicle Acapulco's pre-Hispanic past, the coming of the conquistadors (complete with Spanish armor), and Spanish imperial activity. Temporary shows are also held here. Admission is $3.50.

To reach the fort, follow Costera Alemán past old Acapulco and the *zócalo;* the fort is on a hill on the right. The museum is open Tuesday to Sunday from 10am to 5pm, and the best time to go is in the morning, since the air-conditioning is minimal. Admission is $1.60; free on Sunday.

The **Centro Internacional de Convivencia Infantil (CICI),** Costera Alemán at Colón (© **744/484-8033**), is a sea-life and water park east of the Convention Center. It has swimming pools with waves, water slides, and water toboggans. The park is open daily from 10am to 6pm. There are **dolphin shows** (in Spanish) weekdays at 2 and 4pm, and weekends at 2pm. There's also a dolphin swim program, which includes 30 minutes of introduction and 30 minutes of swim time. This park tends to overwork its dolphins. It's an amusement park, and not representative of the more caring and sensitive dolphin swim facilities found in Cancún and Puerto Vallarta. Minimum age is 6 years. Amenities include a cafeteria and restrooms. General admission is $3 weekdays, $7 weekends, and free for children under 2.

## SHOPPING

Acapulco is not among the best places to buy Mexican crafts, but it does have a few interesting shops. The best are the **Mercado Parazal** (often called the Mercado de Artesanías), on Calle Velázquez de León near Cinco de Mayo in the downtown *zócalo* area. When you see Sanborn's, turn right and walk behind it for several blocks, asking directions if you need to. Here you'll find stalls of curios from around the country, including silver, embroidered cotton clothing, rugs, pottery, and papier-mâché. As they wait for patrons, artists paint ceramics with village scenes. The market is a pleasant place to spend a morning or afternoon.

The shopkeepers aren't pushy, but they'll test your bargaining mettle. The starting price will be steep, and dragging it down may take some time. As always, acting uninterested often brings down prices in a hurry. Before buying silver, examine it carefully and look for ".925" stamped on the back (this supposedly signifies that the silver is 92.5% pure, but often, the less expensive silver metal called "alpaca" also bears this stamp). The market is open daily from 9am to 6pm.

For a well-known department store with fixed prices, try **Artesanías Finas de Acapulco** (© **744/484-8039**), called AFA-ACA for short. Tour guides bring groups to this mammoth air-conditioned place, where the merchandise includes mass-produced tacky junk, fairly good folk art, clothes, marble-top furniture, saddles, luggage, jewelry, pottery, papier-mâché, and more. The store is open Monday to Saturday from 9am to 6pm, Sunday from 9am to 2pm. To find it, go east on the Costera until you see the Hotel Romano Days Inn on the seaward side. Then take Avenida Horacio Nelson, across the street; on the right, half a block up, you'll see AFA-ACA. **Sanborn's,** another good department store and drugstore, offers an array of staples, including cosmetics, music, clothing, books, and magazines.

Boutiques selling resort wear crowd the Costera Alemán. These stores carry attractive summer clothing at prices lower than you generally pay in the United States. If there's a sale, you can find incredible bargains. One of the nicest air-conditioned shopping centers on the Costera is **Plaza Bahía,** Costera Alemán 125 (© **744/485-6939** or 744/485-6992), which has four stories of shops, movie theaters, a bowling alley, and small fast-food restaurants. The center is just west of the Costa Club Hotel. The bowling alley, **Bol Bahía** (© **744/485-0970** or 744/485-7464), is open Monday to Saturday from noon to 1:30am, Sunday from 10am to midnight. Another popular shopping strip is the **Plaza Condesa,** adjacent to the Fiesta Americana Condesa, with shops that include Guess, Izod, and Bronce Swimwear. **Olvida Plaza,** near the restaurant of the same name, has Tommy Hilfiger and Aca Joe.

## WHERE TO STAY

The listings below begin with the very expensive resorts south of town (nearest the airport) and continue along Costera Alemán to the less-expensive, more traditional hotels north of town, in the downtown or "Old Acapulco" part of the city. Especially in the "very expensive" and "expensive" categories, inquire about promotional rates or check with the airlines for air-hotel packages. During Christmas and Easter weeks, some hotels double their normal rates.

Private, ultra-secluded **villas** are available for rent all over the hills south of town; staying in one of these palatial homes is an unforgettable experience. **Se Renta** (www.acapulcoluxuryvillas.com) handles some of the most exclusive villas in Acapulco.

### SOUTH OF TOWN

Acapulco's most exclusive and renowned hotels, restaurants, and villas nestle in the steep forested hillsides south of town, between the naval base and Puerto Marqués. This area is several kilometers from the heart of Acapulco; you'll pay a $12 to $20 round-trip taxi fare every time you venture off the property into town.

#### Very Expensive

**Camino Real Acapulco Diamante** ★★★ This relaxing, self-contained resort is an ideal choice for families, or for those who already know Acapulco and don't care to explore much. I consider it one of Acapulco's finest places in

### *Fun Fact* Acapulco, Queen of the Silver Screen

Along with hosting some of the legendary stars of the silver screen, Acapulco has also played a few starring roles. Over 250 films have been shot here, including 1985's *Rambo II,* which used the Pie de la Cuesta lagoon as its backdrop.

terms of contemporary decor, services, and amenities. The Camino Real is tucked in a secluded location on 81 acres; it's part of the enormous Acapulco Diamante project. I like its location on the Playa Puerto Marqués, which is safe for swimming, but you do miss out on compelling views of Acapulco Bay. From Carretera Escénica, you wind down a handsome brick road to the hotel, overlooking Puerto Marqués Bay. The lobby has an enormous terrace facing the water. The spacious rooms have balconies or terraces, small sitting areas, marble floors, ceiling fans (in addition to air conditioning with remote control), and comfortable, classic furnishings.

Km 14 Carretera Escénica, Baja Catita s/n, Pichilingue, 39867 Acapulco, Gro ✆ **744/435-1010.** Fax 744/435-1020. www.caminoreal.com/acapulco. 157 units. High season $429 double, $611 master suite. Rates include American breakfast. Ask about low-season and midweek discounts. AE, MC, V. **Amenities:** 2 restaurants, lobby bar; 3 pools (1 for children); tennis court; health club with aerobics, spa treatments, massage, and complete workout equipment (extra charge); watersports equipment rentals; children's activities; 24-hr. room service; concierge; tour desk; car rental desk; shopping arcade; salon; babysitting; laundry service. *In room:* A/C, TV, dataport, minibar, hair dryer, iron, safe-deposit box.

**Las Brisas** ★★★ *Moments* This is a local landmark, often considered Acapulco's finest hotel. Perched on a hillside overlooking the bay, Las Brisas is known for its tiered pink stucco facade, private pools, and 175 pink Jeeps rented exclusively to guests. If you stay here, you ought to like pink, because the color scheme extends to practically everything.

The hotel is a community unto itself: The simple, marble-floored rooms are like separate villas sculpted from a terraced hillside, with panoramic views of Acapulco Bay from a balcony or terrace. Each room has a private or semiprivate swimming pool. The property has a total of 250 pools. The spacious Regency Club rooms, at the apex of the property, offer the best views. You stay at Las Brisas more for the panache and setting than for the amenities, though rooms have been upgraded. Early each morning, continental breakfast arrives in a cubbyhole. If you tire of your own pool, Las Brisas has a beach club about a half-mile away, on Acapulco Bay; continuous shuttle service departs from the lobby. The club offers casual dining, a large swimming pool, and a natural saltwater pool—actually a rocky inlet. Mandatory service charges cover shuttle service from the hillside rooms to the lobby, from the lobby to the beach club, and all tips. The hotel is on the southern edge of the bay, overlooking the road to the airport and close to the hottest nightclubs.

Apdo. Carretera Escénica 5255, Las Brisas, 39868 Acapulco, Gro. ✆ **800/228-3000** in the U.S., or 744/469-6900. Fax 744/446-5332. 263 units. High season $330 shared pool, $435 private pool, $540 Royal Beach Club; low season $230 shared pool, $345 private pool, $432 Royal Beach Club. $20 per day service charge plus 17% tax. Rates include continental breakfast. AE, DC, MC, V. **Amenities:** 2 restaurants, deli, breakfast delivery; private beach club with fresh- and saltwater pools; 5 tennis courts; guest-only tours and activity program; access to nearby gym; concierge; tour desk; car rental desk; Jeeps for rent; 24-hr. shuttle transportation around the resort; shopping arcade; salon; in-room massage; babysitting; room service; laundry; dry cleaning. *In room:* A/C, minibar, hair dryer, safe-deposit box.

## COSTERA HOTEL ZONE

The following hotels are along the main boulevard, Costera Alemán, extending from the Convention Center (Centro Internacional) in the east to Papagayo Park, just outside Old Acapulco. One of the most familiar images of Acapulco is the twinkling lights of these hotels stretching for miles along the bay.

### Expensive

**Fiesta Americana Condesa Acapulco** ★ Once the Condesa del Mar, the Fiesta Americana Condesa Acapulco is a long-standing favorite deluxe hotel. The 18-story structure towers above Condesa Beach, just east and up the hill from the Glorieta Diana traffic circle. The contemporary, attractive rooms are very comfortable, with marble floors. Each has a private terrace or balcony with ocean view. The more expensive rooms have the best bay views, and all have purified tap water. The hilltop swimming pool has one of the city's finest views. The location is great for enjoying the numerous beach activities, shopping, and more casual nightlife of Acapulco.

Costera Alemán 97, 393690 Acapulco, Gro ✆ **800/FIESTA1** in the U.S., or 744/484-2355. Fax 744/484-1828. www.fiestamericana.com. 500 units. High season $220 double, $315 suite; low season $93–$124 double, $253 suite. Ask about "Fiesta Break" packages, which include meals. AE, DC, MC, V. **Amenities:** 2 restaurants, coffee shop, lobby bar, theme nights with buffet dinner; adults-only hilltop swimming pool, smaller children's pool; sundeck; room service; shopping arcade; pharmacy; salon; travel agency; laundry service. *In room:* A/C, TV, minibar, safe-deposit box.

**Hotel Elcano** ★★★ *Finds* An Acapulco classic, the Elcano is a personal favorite. It offers exceptional service and a prime location—near the convention center, on a broad stretch of beach in the heart of the hotel zone. Rooms are continually upgraded, bright, and very comfortable. They feature classic navy-and-white tile accents, ample oceanfront balconies, and tub/shower combinations. The very large junior suites, all on corners, have two queen-size beds and huge closets. Studios are small but adequate, with king-size beds and small sinks outside the bathroom area. In the studios, a small portion of the TV armoire serves as a closet, and there are no balconies, only large sliding windows. All rooms have purified tap water. This is an ideal place if you're attending a convention or simply want the best of all possible locations, between hillside nightlife and the Costera beach zone. It's an excellent value.

Costera Alemán 75, 39690 Acapulco, Gro. ✆ **800/972-2162** in the U.S., or 744/435-1500. Fax 744/484-2230. http://hotel-elcano.com. 180 units. $176 studio; $208 standard double; $240 jr. suite, $299 master suite. Ask about promotional discounts. AE, DC, MC, V. **Amenities:** 3 restaurants; beachside pool; small workout room; shopping arcade; travel agency; salon; massage; 24-hr. room service; video-game room; babysitting; laundry service. *In room:* A/C, TV, minibar, hair dryer, safe-deposit box.

**Hyatt Regency Acapulco** ★★ The Hyatt is one of the largest and most modern of Acapulco's hotels, a sophisticated oasis. A freeform pool fronts a broad stretch of beautiful beach, one of the most inviting in Acapulco. The sleek lobby encloses a sitting area and bar where there's live music every evening. The stylishly decorated rooms are large, with sizable balconies overlooking the pool and ocean. Some contain kitchenettes. Regency Club guests receive continental breakfast, afternoon *canapés,* and other upgraded amenities. Children are not allowed in Regency Club rooms. This hotel caters to a large Jewish clientele and has a full-service kosher restaurant, synagogue, and Sabbath elevator.

Costera Alemán 1, 39869 Acapulco, Gro. ✆ **800/233-1234** in the U.S. and Canada, 01-800/005-0000 in Mexico, or 744/469-1234. Fax 744/484-3087. www.hyattacapulco.com.mx. 645 units. High season $234 double, $260 Regency Club, $338 suite; low season $208 double, $234 Regency Club, $312 suite. AE, DC, MC, V.

**Amenities:** 3 restaurants, cantina, lobby bar; 2 large, shaded free-form pools; 3 lighted tennis courts; access to a nearby gym; sundeck; children's programs; concierge; business center; tour desk; car rental; shopping arcade; salon; room service; in-room massage; babysitting; safe-deposit box in lobby; car rental desk; laundry; dry cleaning. *In room:* A/C, TV, minibar, robes, hair dryer, iron, safe-deposit box.

**Villa Vera Hotel & Racquet Club** ★★★ *Finds* The legendary Villa Vera started off as a private home with adjacent villas for houseguests. It continues to offer the closest experience to Acapulco villa life that you'll find in a public property. After a while, it became a popular hangout for stars such as Liz Taylor, who married Mike Todd here. This hotel is also where Richard and Pat Nixon celebrated their 25th wedding anniversary and where Elvis's film *Fun in Acapulco* was shot. Lana Turner even made it her home for 3 years.

Now a Starwood Hotels property, Villa Vera has undergone significant renovations and upgrades in facilities that have transformed it into an exclusive boutique-style hotel. The spa offers world-class services 7 days a week. Rooms are tastefully decorated in sophisticated light tones. The complex has 14 pools, including 8 private pools for the six villas and two houses. Most other rooms share pools; guests in standard rooms have the use of the large public pool across from the restaurant. The hotel is a couple of blocks from the Condesa beach.

Lomas del Mar 35, Fracc. Club Deportivo, Acapulco, 39693, Gro. ✆ **800/710-9300** in Mexico, 744/484-0334, or 744/484-0335. Fax 744/484-7479. hotel_villavera_aca@clubregina.com. 69 units, 2 houses. High season $246 studio, $246 double, $340–$405 suite, $481 villa, $1,222 Casa Teddy (4 people), $1,261 Casa Julio (6 people). Ask about low-season rates. AE, MC, V. **Amenities:** Restaurant, pool bar; pool; 2 clay tennis courts; 2 lighted racquetball courts; gym; complete European spa; travel agency; car rental. *In room:* A/C, TV, minibar, safe-deposit box.

## Moderate

**Calinda Beach Acapulco** You'll see this tall cylindrical tower rising at the eastern edge of Condesa Beach. Each room has a view, usually of the bay. Though not exceptionally well furnished, the guest rooms are large and comfortable; most have two double beds. It's the most modern of the reasonably priced lodgings along the strip of hotels facing popular Condesa Beach. Package prices are available; otherwise the hotel is expensive for what it provides.

Costera Alemán 1260, 39300 Acapulco, Gro. ✆ **800/228-5151** in the U.S., or 744/484-0410. Fax 744/484-4676. www.hotelescalinda.com. 357 units. $169 double. AE, DC, MC, V. Limited free parking. **Amenities:** 3 restaurants; poolside snacks; lobby bar with live music; swimming pool; concierge; shopping arcade; room service; travel agency; salon; pharmacy; babysitting; laundry. *In room:* A/C, TV, safe-deposit boxes.

**Hotel Sands** ★ *Value* A great option for budget-minded families, this unpretentious, comfortable hotel is nestled on the inland side, opposite the giant resort hotels and away from the din of Costera traffic. A stand of umbrella palms and a pretty garden restaurant lead into the lobby. The rooms are light and airy in the style of a good modern motel, with basic furnishings and wall-to-wall carpeting. Some units have kitchenettes, and all have a terrace or balcony. The rates here are more than reasonable, the accommodations satisfactory, and the location excellent.

Costera Alemán 178, 39670 Acapulco, Gro. ✆ **744/484-2260.** Fax 744/484-1053. www.sands.com.mx. 93 units. $100 standard double; $76 bungalow. Rates higher during Christmas, Easter, and other major holidays. Rates include coffee in the lobby. AE, MC, V. Limited free parking. **Amenities:** Restaurant; 2 swimming pools (1 for children); squash court; volleyball; Ping-Pong area; concierge; babysitting; laundry and dry cleaning. *In room:* A/C, TV, minibar.

## DOWNTOWN (ON LA QUEBRADA) & OLD ACAPULCO BEACHES

Numerous budget hotels dot the streets fanning out from the *zócalo.* They're among the best values in town, but be sure to check your room first to see that it meets your needs. Several hotels in this area are close to Caleta and Caletilla beaches, or on the backside of the hilly peninsula, at Playa la Angosta. These were the standards of luxury in the 1950s, and many have gorgeous views of the city and bay. Recent renovations are restoring this area's original charm.

### Moderate

**Grand Meigas Acapulco Resort** ★ The all-inclusive Meigas is more familiar to Mexican travelers than to their U.S. counterparts. This high-quality, nine-floor resort, adjacent to one of the liveliest beaches in old Acapulco, offers excellent value. Stay here if you seek the authentic feel of a Mexican holiday, with all its boisterous, family-friendly charms. The Meigas is built into a cliff on the Caleta peninsula, overlooking the beach. Rooms surround a plant-filled courtyard, topped by a glass ceiling. All have large terraces with ocean views, although some lack separation from the neighboring terrace. The simply decorated rooms are very clean and comfortable, with a large closet and desk. Each room has two queen beds, firm mattresses, and cable TV.

A succession of terraces holds tropical gardens, restaurants, and pools. A private beach and boat dock are down a brief flight of stairs. The resort has a changing agenda of theme nights and evening entertainment.

Cerro San Martín 325, Fracc. Las Playas, Acapulco, Gro., 39390. ✆ **744/483-9940** or 744/483-9140. Fax 744/483-9125. meigaca@prodigy.net.mx. 255 units. High season $89 per person; low season $65 per person. Rates are all-inclusive. Room-only prices sometimes available. AE, DC, MC, V. Free private parking. **Amenities:** 3 restaurants, snack bar, bars; large freshwater and saltwater pools; tour desk; car rental desk; shopping arcade. *In room:* A/C, TV, fan.

**Plaza Las Glorias/El Mirador** ★ One of the landmarks of Old Acapulco, the former El Mirador Hotel overlooks the famous cove where the cliff divers perform. Renovated with tropical landscaping and lots of Mexican tile, this hotel offers attractively furnished rooms. Each holds double or queen-size beds, a small kitchenette area with mini-fridge and coffeemaker, and a large bathroom with marble counters. Most have a separate living room, some have a whirlpool tub, and all are accented with colorful Saltillo tile and other Mexican decorative touches. Ask for a room with a balcony or ocean view.

A set-price dinner ($29) offers great views of the cliff-diving show. The large, breezy lobby bar is a favorite spot to relax as day fades into night on the beautiful cove and bay. Nearby is a protected cove with good snorkeling.

Quebrada 74, Acapulco, 39300 Gro. ✆ **800/342-AMIGO** in the U.S., or 744/483-1221, 744/484-0909 for reservations. Fax 744/482-4564. 132 units. High season $185 double, $231 suite with whirlpool; low season $108 double, $135 suite with whirlpool. Add $13 for kitchenette. AE, MC, V. Street parking. **Amenities:** Restaurant, coffee shop, lobby bar; 3 pools, including 1 rather rundown saltwater pool; room service; travel agency; laundry service. *In room:* A/C, TV.

### Inexpensive

**Hotel Costa Linda** Budget-minded American and Mexican couples are drawn to the sunny, well-kept rooms of the Costa Linda, one of the best values in the area. All rooms have individually controlled air-conditioning and a mini-fridge, and some have a small kitchenette (during low season there is a $5 charge for using the kitchenette). Closets and bathrooms are ample in size, and mattresses are firm. Cozy as the Costa Linda is, it is situated adjacent to one of the busier streets in old Acapulco, so traffic noise can be bothersome. It's just a 1-block walk down to lively Caleta beach.

Costera Alemán 1008, Acapulco, Gro, 39390. ✆ **744/482-5277** or 744/482-2549. Fax 744/483-4017. 44 units. High season $89 double; low season $45 double. 2 children under 8 stay free. MC, V. Free parking. **Amenities:** Restaurant and bar; small pool; tennis court; tour desk. *In room:* A/C, TV, minibar.

**Hotel Los Flamingos** ★★★ *Finds* An Acapulco landmark, this hotel, perched on a cliff 152m (500 ft.) above Acapulco Bay, once entertained John Wayne, Cary Grant, Johnny Weissmuller, Fred McMurray, Errol Flynn, Red Skelton, Roy Rogers and others. In fact, the stars liked it so much that at one point they bought it and converted it into a private club. The place is a real find—it's in excellent shape and exceptionally clean, offering visitors a totally different perspective of Acapulco as it maintains all the charm of a grand era. All rooms have dramatic ocean views and a large balcony or terrace, but most of them are not air-conditioned (those that are also have TVs). Still, the constant sea breeze is cooling enough. Rooms are colorful, with mosaic-tile tables and mirrors. Thursdays at Los Flamingos are especially popular, with a weekly *pozole* party and live music by a Mexican band that was probably around in the era of Wayne and Weissmuller—note the seashell-pink bass. Even if you don't stay here, plan to come for a margarita at sunset, and a walk along the dramatic lookout point.

López Matéos s/n, Fracc. Las Playas, Acapulco, Gro. ✆ **744/482-0690.** Fax 744/483-9806. 40 rooms. High season $85 double, $91 double with A/C, $130 jr. suite; low season $65 double, $78 double with A/C, $91 jr. suite. AE, MC, V. **Amenities:** Restaurant, bar; pool; room service; tour desk; car rental; laundry service.

**Hotel Misión** Enter this hotel's plant-filled brick courtyard, shaded by two enormous mango trees, and you'll retreat into an earlier, more peaceful Acapulco. This tranquil 19th-century hotel lies 2 blocks inland from the Costera and the *zócalo.* The original L-shaped building is at least a century old. The rooms have colonial touches, such as colorful tile and wrought iron, and come simply furnished, with a fan and one or two beds with good mattresses. Unfortunately, the promised hot water is not reliable—request a cold-water-only room and receive a discount. Breakfast is served on the patio. The hotel is 2 blocks inland from the fishermen's wharf, main square, and La Quebrada.

Felipe Valle 12, 39300 Acapulco, Gro. ✆ **744/482-3643.** Fax 744/482-2076. 27 units. $56 double. No credit cards. **Amenities:** Restaurant.

**Hotel Villa Romana** This is one of the most comfortable inns in the area for a long stay. Some rooms are tiled and others carpeted; nine have small kitchens with refrigerators. Terraces face Playa la Angosta. The small, plant-filled terrace on the second floor holds tables and chairs; the fourth-floor pool offers a great view of the bay.

Av. López Matéos 185, Fracc. Las Playas, 39300 Acapulco, Gro. ✆ **744/482-3995.** www.aca-novenet.com.mx/villaromana. 9 units. High season $50 double; low season $45 double. MC, V. Street parking. *In room:* A/C, TV.

## WHERE TO DINE

Diners in Acapulco enjoy stunning views and fresh seafood. The quintessential setting is a candlelit table with the glittering bay spread out before you. If you're looking for a romantic spot, Acapulco brims over with such inviting places; most sit along the southern coast, with views of the bay. If you're looking for simple, good food or an authentic local dining experience, you're best off in Old Acapulco.

A deluxe establishment in Acapulco may not be much more expensive than a mass-market restaurant. The proliferation of U.S. franchise restaurants has increased competition, and even more expensive places have reduced prices in response. Trust me—the locally owned restaurants offer the best food and the best value.

## SOUTH OF TOWN: LAS BRISAS AREA

### Very Expensive

**Casa Nova** ★★ GOURMET ITALIAN Enjoy an elegant meal and a fabulous view of glittering Acapulco Bay at this spot east of town. The cliff-side restaurant offers several elegantly appointed dining rooms awash in marble and stone accents, and outdoor terrace dining with a stunning view. If you arrive before your table is ready, have a drink in the comfortable lounge. This is a longstanding favorite of Mexico City's elite; dress tends toward fashionable, tropical attire. The best dishes include veal scaloppini and homemade pastas, such as linguini with fresh clams. A changing tourist menu offers a sampling of the best selections for a fixed price. There's also an ample selection of reasonably priced national and imported wines. And there's live piano music nightly.

Carretera Escénica 5256. ✆ **744/484-6815.** Reservations required. Main courses $12–$22; fixed-price 4-course meal $30. AE, MC, V. Mon–Fri 7–11pm; Sat–Sun 7–11:30pm.

**Mezzanotte Acapulco** ★ ITALIAN/FRENCH/MEXICAN Mezzanotte offers a contemporary blending of classic cuisines, but its strongest asset is the view of the bay. This location has changed hands several times, and the current fare is a mix of trendy international dishes served in an atmosphere that tries a bit too hard to be upscale and chic. Music is loud and hip, so if you're looking for a romantic evening, this is probably not the place. It's a better choice if you want a taste of Mexican urban chic. The view of the bay remains outstanding, though the food still strives for consistency. Dress up a bit for dining here. Mezzanotte is in the La Vista complex near the Las Brisas hotel.

Plaza La Vista, Carretera Escénica a Puerto Marquez 28-1, 39880 Acapulco, Guerrero. ✆ **744/484-7874,** 744/446-5727 or 744/446-5728. Reservations required. Main courses $12–$42. AE, MC, V. Mon–Wed 6pm–midnight; Thurs–Sat 2pm–1:30am; Sun 2pm–midnight. Closed Sun during low season.

**Spicey** ★★★ CREATIVE CUISINE For original food with flair, you can't beat this restaurant in the Las Brisas area, next to Kookaburas. Once considered trendy, it's become a contemporary classic. Seating is in the air-conditioned indoor dining room and on the open rooftop terrace with a sweeping view of the bay. To begin, try the exquisite shrimp Spicey, in fresh coconut batter with orange marmalade and mustard sauce. Among the main courses, grilled veal chop in pineapple and papaya chutney is a winner, as is beef tenderloin, prepared Thai- or Santa Fe–style, or blackened. Chiles rellenos in mango sauce win raves. There's also an exceptional selection of premium tequilas for sipping. Attire is on the dressy side of casual.

---

***Moments*** **Dining with a View**

Restaurants with unparalleled views of Acapulco include **Madeiras, Spicey, Mezzanotte,** and **Casa Nova** in the Las Brisas area, **El Olvido** along the Costera, **Su Casa** on a hill above the Convention Center, and the **Bella Vista Restaurant** at the Las Brisas hotel.

---

Carretera Escénica. ✆ **744/446-6003** or 744/446-5991. Reservations recommended on weekends. Main courses $19–$30. AE, DC, MC, V. Daily 7–11:30pm. Valet parking available.

## COSTERA HOTEL ZONE

### Very Expensive

**El Olvido** ★★ NUEVA COCINA Once in the door of this handsome terrace restaurant, you'll almost forget that it's in a shopping mall. It gives you all the glittering bay-view ambience of the posh Las Brisas restaurants, without the taxi ride. The menu is one of the most sophisticated in the city. It's expensive, but each dish is delightful in both presentation and taste. Start with 1 of the 12 house specialty drinks, such as Olvido, made with tequila, rum, Cointreau, tomato juice, and lime juice. Soups include a delicious cold melon, or a thick black-bean and sausage. Among the innovative entrees are quail with honey and *pasilla* chiles, and thick sea bass with a mild sauce of cilantro and avocado. For dessert, try chocolate fondue or *guanabana* (a tropical fruit) mousse in a rich *zapote negro* (black tropical fruit) sauce. El Olvido is in the same shopping center as La Petite Belgique, below, fronting Diana Circle. Walk into the passage to the right of Aca Joe and bear left; it's at the back.

Diana Circle, Plaza Marbella. ✆ **744/481-0203**, 744/481-0256, 744/481-0214, or 744/481-0240. Reservations recommended. Main courses $14–$33. AE, DC, MC, V. Daily 6pm–2am.

**La Petite Belgique** ★★★ *Finds* SEAFOOD/NORTHERN EUROPEAN An exceptional, intimate restaurant known principally to locals, La Petite Belgique is noted more for its food than its ambience. Although the old-fashioned dining room overlooks Acapulco Bay, an adjacent parking lot dominates the view. But never mind that—you'll be focused on your plate. The European owner was a food and beverage director for a premier hotel chain, but chose to settle in Acapulco years ago and devote his talents to his own restaurant. Although the menu boasts an impressive selection of patés, Continental classics, and fresh fish, I'm hooked on the mussels, flown in fresh daily from a mussel farm the proprietor owns in Baja California. The huge pot of perfectly steamed mussels I enjoyed here may be one of the top five dining experiences of my life. Great espresso drinks, cordials, and sumptuous sweets—there's a full French bakery on site—provide a fitting close to a truly special dinner. The restaurant is in the shopping center fronted by the Aca Joe clothing store on Diana Circle. Walk into the passage to the right of Aca Joe; it's at the back.

Diana Circle, Plaza Marbella. ✆ **744/484-7725**. Fax 744/484-0776. Reservations recommended. Main courses $17–$42. AE, MC, V. Daily 5pm–midnight.

**Su Casa/La Margarita** ★ INTERNATIONAL Relaxed elegance and terrific food at moderate prices are what you get at Su Casa. Owners Shelly and Angel Herrera created this pleasant, breezy open-air restaurant on the patio of their hillside home overlooking the city. Both are experts in the kitchen and are on hand nightly to greet guests on the patio. The menu changes often. Some items are standard, such as shrimp *a la patrona* in garlic; grilled fish, steak, and chicken; and flaming *filet al Madrazo,* a delightful brochette marinated in tropical juices. Most entrees come with garnishes of cooked banana or pineapple. The margaritas are big and delicious. Su Casa is the hot-pink building on the hillside above the Convention Center.

Av. Anahuac 110. ✆ **744/484-4350** or 744/484-1261. Fax 744/484-0803. Reservations recommended. Main courses $14–$50. MC, V. Daily 6pm–midnight.

**Moments** **If There's Pozole, It Must Be Thursday**

If you're visiting Acapulco on a Thursday, indulge in the local custom of eating *pozole,* a bowl of white hominy and meat in broth, garnished with sliced radishes, shredded lettuce, onions, oregano, and lime. The traditional version includes pork, but a newer chicken version has also become a standard. You can also find green *pozole,* which is made by adding a paste of roasted pumpkin seeds to the traditional *pozole* base. Green pozole is also traditionally served with a side of sardines. For a singular Acapulco experience, enjoy your Thursday pozole at the cliffside restaurant of the Hotel Los Flamingos (see above).

### Moderate

**El Cabrito** NORTHERN MEXICAN With its hacienda-inspired entrance, waitresses in white dresses and *charro*-styled neckties, and location in the heart of the Costera, this restaurant targets tourists. But its authentic, well-prepared specialties attract Mexicans in the know—a comforting stamp of approval. Among its specialties are *cabrito al pastor* (roasted goat), *charro* beans, Oaxaca-style *mole,* and *burritos de machaca.* It's on the ocean side of the Costera, south of the Convention Center.

Costera Alemán 1480. ✆ **744/484-7711.** Main courses $5–$15. AE, MC, V. Mon–Sat 2pm–1am; Sun 2–11pm.

### Inexpensive

**Ika Tako** ★★★ *Finds* SEAFOOD/TACOS This is my favorite place to eat in Acapulco, and I never miss it. Perhaps I have simple tastes, but these fresh fish, shrimp, and seafood tacos (served in combinations that include grilled pineapple, fresh spinach, grated cheese, garlic, and bacon) are so tasty that they're addicting. Unlike most inexpensive places to eat, the setting is also lovely, with a handful of tables overlooking tropical trees and the bay below. The lighting may be bright, the atmosphere occasionally hectic, and the service dependably slow, but the tacos are delectable. You can also get beer, wine, soft drinks, and a dessert of the day. This restaurant is along the Costera, next to Beto's lobster restaurant. A second branch is across from the Hyatt Regency hotel, but it lacks the atmosphere of this one.

Costera Aleman 99. No phone. Main courses $2.50–$5. No credit cards. Daily 6pm–5am.

## DOWNTOWN: THE *ZOCALO* AREA

The old downtown area abounds with simple, inexpensive restaurants serving up tasty eats. It's easy to pay more elsewhere and not get food as consistently good as you'll find in this part of town. To explore this area, start at the *zócalo* and stroll west along Juárez. After about 3 blocks, you'll come to Azueta, lined with small seafood cafes and street-side stands.

### Moderate

**El Amigo Miguel** ★★ MEXICAN/SEAFOOD Locals know that El Amigo Miguel is a standout among downtown seafood restaurants—you can easily pay more elsewhere but not eat better. Impeccably fresh seafood reigns here; the large, open-air dining room, 3 blocks west of the *zócalo,* is usually brimming with seafood lovers. When it overflows, head to a branch across the street, with the same menu. Try the delicious *camarones borrachos* (drunken shrimp) in a sauce made with beer, applesauce, ketchup, mustard, and bits of fresh bacon—its whole tastes nothing like the individual ingredients. *Filete Miguel* is red snapper fillet stuffed with seafood and covered in a wonderful *chipotle* pepper sauce. Grilled shrimp with garlic and whole red snapper (*mojo de ajo*) are served at their classic best.

Juárez 31, at Azueta. ✆ **744/483-6981.** Main courses $2.20–$23. AE, MC, V. Daily 10am–11pm.

**Mariscos Pipo** ★ SEAFOOD Check out the photographs of Old Acapulco on the walls while relaxing in this airy dining room decorated with hanging nets, fish, glass buoys, and shell lanterns. The English-language menu lists a wide array of seafood, including *ceviche,* lobster, octopus, crayfish, and baby-shark quesadillas. This local favorite is 2 blocks west of the *zócalo* on Breton, just off the Costera. Another bustling branch, open daily from 1 to 9:30pm, is at Costera Alemán and Canadá (✆ **744/484-0165**).

Almirante Breton 3. ✆ **744/482-2237.** Main courses $5.60–$33.40. AE, MC, V. Daily noon–8pm.

### Inexpensive

**Mi Parri Pollo** MEXICAN/INTERNATIONAL This little restaurant has umbrella-covered tables on one of the coolest and shadiest sections of the *zócalo.* It's especially popular for breakfast; specials include a great fresh fruit salad with mango, pineapple, and cantaloupe. Other specials include fish burgers, *tortas,* a special rotisserie-grilled chicken, and steak *milanesa.* Fruit drinks, including fresh mango juice, come in schooner-size glasses. To find the restaurant, enter the *zócalo* from the Costera and walk toward the kiosk. On the right, you'll see a wide, shady passageway that leads onto Avenida Jesus Carranza.

Jesus Carranza 2B, Zócalo. ✆ **744/483-7427.** Breakfast $1.50–$2.50; sandwiches $1–$2; fresh-fruit drinks $1.25; daily specials $2–$4. No credit cards. Daily 7am–11pm.

## ACAPULCO AFTER DARK

**SPECIAL ATTRACTIONS** The **"Gran Noche Mexicana,"** combines a performance by the Acapulco Ballet Folklórico with one by Los Voladores from Papantla (see chapter 11). It's held in the plaza of the Convention Center Monday, Wednesday, and Friday at 7pm. With dinner and open bar, the show costs $62; general admission (including three drinks) is $42. Call for reservations (✆ **744/484-7046**) or consult a local travel agency. Many major hotels also schedule Mexican fiestas and other theme nights that include dinner and entertainment. Local travel agencies will have information.

**NIGHTCLUBS & DISCOS** Acapulco is even more famous for its nightclubs than for its beaches. Because clubs frequently change ownership—and, often, names—it's difficult to give specific and accurate recommendations. But some general tips will help. Every club seems to have a cover charge of around $20 in high season and $10 in low season; drinks can cost anywhere from $3 to $10. Women can count on paying less or entering free. Don't even think about going out to one of the hillside discos before 11pm, and don't expect much action until after midnight. But it will keep going until 4 or 5am.

Many discos periodically waive their cover charge or offer some other promotion to attract customers. Look for promotional materials in hotel reception areas, at travel desks or concierge booths, in local publications, and on the beach.

The high-rise hotels have their own bars and sometimes discos. Informal lobby or poolside cocktail bars often offer free live entertainment.

**THE BEACH BAR ZONE** Prefer a little fresh air with your nightlife? The young, hip crowd favors the growing number of open-air oceanfront dance clubs along Costera Alemán, most of which feature techno or alternative rock. There's a concentration of them between the Fiesta Americana and Continental Plaza hotels. An earlier and more casual option to the glitzy discos, these clubs include the jamming **Disco Beach, El Sombrero** (you'll know it when you see it), **Tabu,** and the pirate-themed **Barbaroja.** These mainly offer an open bar with cover charge (around $10). Women frequently drink free with a lesser charge (men may pay more, but then, this is where the beach babes are). Most smaller establishments do not accept credit cards; when they do, MasterCard and Visa are more widely accepted than American Express.

If you are brave enough, there's a **bungee jump** in the midst of the beach bar zone at Costera Alemán 107 (✆ **744/484-7529**). For $62 you get one jump, plus a T-shirt, diploma, and membership. Additional jumps are $28, and your fourth jump is free. For $67, you can jump as many times as you like from 4 to 11pm.

**Alebrijes** This high-tech club boasts an exterior of reflection pools, gardens, and flaming torches. Inside, booths and round tables surround the vast dance floor—the disco (capacity 1,200) doubles as a venue for concerts and live performances by some of Mexico's most notable singers. The dress code forbids shorts, T-shirts, tennis shoes, sandals, and jeans. It's open daily from 11pm to 5am. Costera Alemán 3308, across the st. from the Hyatt Regency Acapulco. ✆ **744/484-5902.** Cover (including open bar with national drinks) $5–$27 for women, $8–$35 for men.

**Baby-O** This longtime Acapulco favorite is a throwback to the town's heavy disco days, although the music is exceptionally contemporary now. The mid-to-late-20s crowd dances to everything from swing to hip-hop, techno to rock. Located across from the Romano Days Inn, Baby-O has a small dance floor surrounded by several tiers of tables and sculpted, cave-like walls. Drinks cost $4 to $5. Service is excellent, and it's a great choice for those who shun mammoth clubs in favor of a more intimate setting. It opens at 10:30pm. Costera Alemán. ✆ **744/484-7474.** Cover $5–$17 for women, $10–$28 for men.

**Carlos 'n' Charlie's** For fun, danceable music and good food, you can't go wrong with this branch of the Carlos Anderson chain. It's always packed. Come early and get a seat on the terrace overlooking the Costera. This is a great place to go for late dinner and a few drinks before moving on to a club. It's east of Diana Circle, across the street from the Fiesta Americana Condesa. It's open daily from 1pm to 1am. Costera Alemán 999. ✆ **744/484-1285** or 744/484-0039. No cover.

**Enigma** Venture into this stylish chrome-and-neon extravaganza perched on the side of the mountain for a true Acapulco nightlife experience. The plush, dim club has a sunken dance floor and panoramic view of the lights of Acapulco Bay. The club also has an intimate piano bar and a special champagne menu. Downstairs, there's pumped-in mood smoke, alternating with fresh oxygen to keep you dancing. The late-night weekend floorshow rivals anything in Paris, Milan, or Rio—truly! The door attendants wear tuxedos, indicating that Enigma encourages more sophisticated dress. Tight and slinky is the norm for women; no shorts for men. The club opens nightly at 10:30pm; fireworks rock the usually full house at 3am. Call to find out if you need reservations. Carretera Escénica, between Los Rancheros Restaurant and La Vista Shopping Center. ✆ **744/446-5712.** Cover $15–$28 for women, $15–$32 for men.

**Hard Rock Cafe** If you like your music loud, your food trendy, and your entertainment international, you'll feel at home in Acapulco's branch of this chain bent on world domination. Elvis memorabilia greets you in the entry area, and among other numerous framed or encased mementos is the Beatles' gold record for "Can't Buy Me Love." There's a bandstand for live music—played every night between 10pm and 2am—and a small dance floor. It's on the seaward side toward the southern end of the Costera, south of the Convention Center and opposite El Cabrito. It's open daily from noon to 2am. Costera Alemán 37. ✆ **744/484-0047.** No cover.

**Pepe's Piano Bar** Pepe's has surely been one of the most famous piano bars in the hemisphere, although it appears those days may be over. It has inspired patrons of all ages to sing their hearts out for more than 40 years, and it still draws a crowd, though it now caters to karaoke instead of piano—a big mistake, in my mind. The music ranges from Mexican boleros to English-language love songs. When it was a true piano bar, I witnessed men in the parking lot practicing their lyrics before getting up the nerve to sing before the fun-loving crowd(only in Acapulco. I keep hoping the owners will come to their senses and return to their roots—Pepe's was a true classic, and a pleasure. It's open daily from 10pm to 4am. Carretera Escénica, Comercial La Vista, Local 5. ✆ **744/446-5736.** No cover.

**Salon Q** This place bills itself as "the cathedral of salsa," and it's a fairly accurate claim—Salon Q is the place to get down among the Latin rhythms. Frequently, management raises the cover and features impersonators of top Latin American musical acts. It's open daily from 10pm to 4am. Costera Alemán 3117. ✆ **744/481-0114.** Cover $13–$24.50.

**ZUCCA** This club, formerly called Fantasy, offers a fantastic bay view. It caters to a more mature crowd—it allegedly admits only those over 25, though the attendants seem to bend the rules for women—and is particularly popular with the moneyed Mexico City set. The club periodically projects a laser show across the bay. The dress code prohibits shorts, jeans, T-shirts, or sandals. Reservations are recommended. It's open nightly from 10:30pm to 2:30am, until 4am on weekends and when the crowd demands it. In the La Vista Shopping Center, Carretera Escénica 28. ✆ **744/446-5690** or 744/446-5691. Cover $5–$10.

## 2 Northward to Zihuatanejo & Ixtapa ★

576km (360 miles) SW of Mexico City; 565km (353 miles) SE of Manzanillo; 253km (158 miles) NW of Acapulco

Side-by-side beach resorts, Ixtapa and Zihuatanejo share geography, but they couldn't be more different in character. Ixtapa is a model of modern infrastructure, services, and luxury hotels, while Zihuatanejo—"Zihua," to the locals—is the quintessential Mexican beach village. For travelers, this offers the intriguing possibility of visiting two distinct destinations in one vacation. Those looking for luxury should opt for Ixtapa (eex-*tah*-pah). You can easily and quickly make the 4-mile trip into Zihuatanejo for a sampling of the simple life in a *pueblo* by the sea. Those who prefer a more rustic retreat with real personality, however, should settle in Zihuatanejo (see-wa-tah-*nay*-ho). It's known for its long-standing community of Swiss and Italian immigrants, and its legendary beach playboys. Those who enjoy Zihua seem to return year after year.

The area, with a backdrop of the Sierra Madre mountains and a foreground of Pacific Ocean waters, provides a full range of activities and diversions. Scuba

## Zihuatanejo & Ixtapa Area

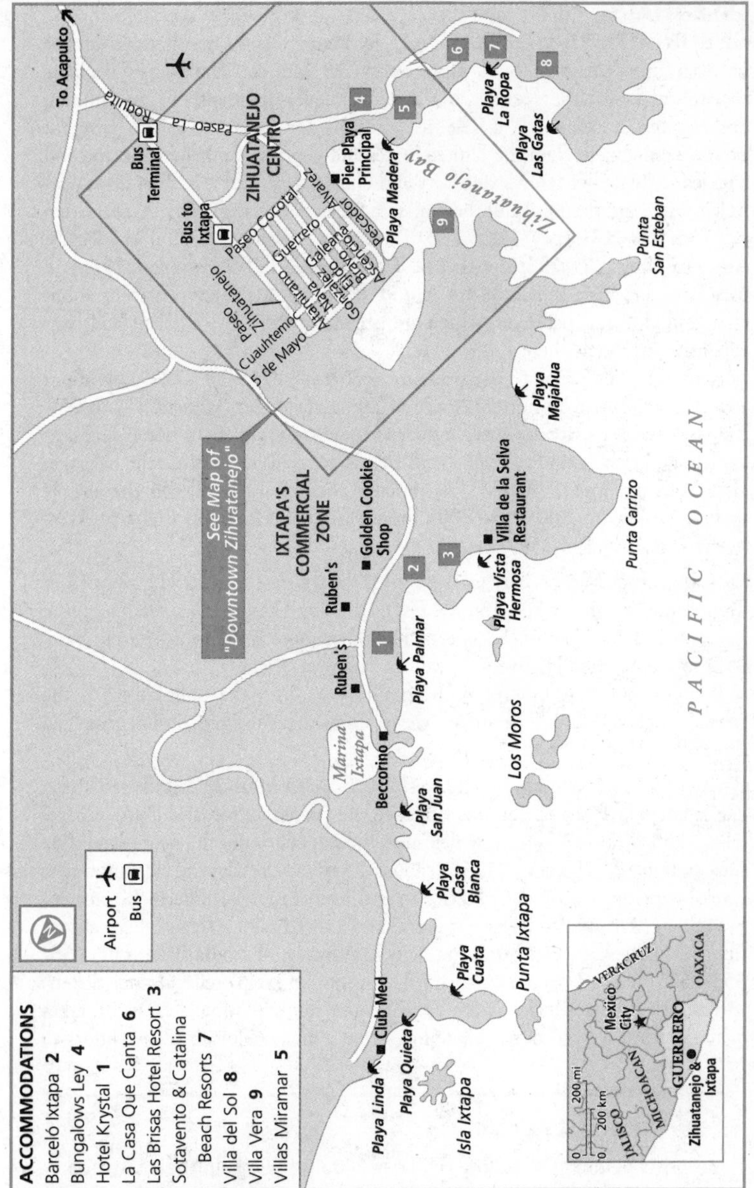


diving, deep-sea fishing, bay cruises to remote beaches, and golf are among the favorites. Nightlife in both towns borders on subdued; Ixtapa is the livelier.

This dual destination is the choice for the traveler looking for a little of everything, from resort-style indulgence to unpretentious simplicity. These two resorts are more welcoming to couples and adults than families, with a number of places that are off-limits to children under 16—something of a rarity in Mexico.

## ESSENTIALS

**GETTING THERE & DEPARTING** **By Plane** These destinations tend to be even more seasonal than most resorts in Mexico. Flights are available year-round from U.S. gateways, but they operate less frequently in the summer. See chapter 2, "Planning a Trip to Mexico," for information on flying to Ixtapa/Zihuatanejo from the United States and Canada. Both **Aeromexico** and **Mexicana** fly daily from Mexico City and Guadalajara, and less often from Acapulco. Here are the local numbers of some international carriers: **Aeromexico** (✆ **755/554-2018,** or 755/554-2019), **Alaska Airlines** (✆ **755/554-8457**), **America West** (✆ **755/554-8634**), **Continental** (✆ **755/554-4219**), and **Mexicana** (✆ **755/554-2208** or 755/554-2209). Ask your travel agent about charter flights and packages, which are becoming the most efficient and least expensive way to get here.

**Arriving:** The **Ixtapa-Zihuatanejo airport** (✆ **755/554-2227**) is about 11km (7 miles) and 15 minutes south of Zihuatanejo. Taxi fares are $12 to $19. **Transportes Terrestres** *colectivo* minivans transport travelers to hotels in Zihuatanejo and Ixtapa, and to Club Med; tickets are sold just outside the baggage-claim area and run $3 to $6. Car-rental agencies with booths in the airport include **Dollar** (✆ **800/800-4000** in the U.S.), and **Hertz** (✆ **800/654-3131** in the U.S., 755/554-2590, or 755/554-2952).

**By Car** From Mexico City (about 7 hr.), the shortest route is Highway 15 to Toluca, then Highway 130/134 the rest of the way. On the latter road, highway gas stations are few and far between. The other route is the four-lane Highway 95D to Iguala, then Highway 51 west to Highway 134.

From Acapulco (2½–3 hr.) or Manzanillo (11 hr.), the only choice is the coastal Highway 200. The ocean views along the winding, mountain-edged drive from Manzanillo can be spectacular.

**By Bus** Zihuatanejo has two bus terminals: the **Central de Autobuses,** Paseo Zihuatanejo at Paseo la Boquita, opposite the Pemex station and IMSS Hospital (✆ **755/554-3477**), from which most lines operate, and the new **Estrella de Oro** station (✆ **755/554-2175**), a block away. At the Central de Autobuses, several companies offer daily service to and from Acapulco, Puerto Escondido, Huatulco, Manzanillo, Puerto Vallarta, and other cities. At the other station, first-class Estrella de Oro buses run daily to Acapulco. **Estrella Blanca** (✆ **755/553-2626**) in the Plaza Ixpamar shopping center in Ixtapa sells advance tickets.

The trip from Mexico City to Zihuatanejo (bypassing Acapulco) takes 5 hours; from Acapulco, 4 to 5 hours. From Zihuatanejo, it's 6 or 7 hours to

---

*Tips* **Motorist Advisory**

Motorists planning to follow Highway 200 northwest up the coast from Ixtapa or Zihuatanejo toward Lázaro Cárdenas and Manzanillo should be aware of reports of car and bus hijackings on that route, especially around Playa Azul, with bus holdups more common than car holdups. Before heading in that direction, ask locals and the tourism office about the status of the route. Don't drive at night. According to tourism officials, police and military patrols of the highway have recently been increased, and the number of incidents has dropped dramatically.

---

Manzanillo, and an additional 6 to Puerto Vallarta, which doesn't include time spent waiting for buses.

**VISITOR INFORMATION** The **State Tourism Office** (✆ **888/248-7037** from the U.S., ✆ and fax 755/553-1967, or 755/553-1968) is in the La Puerta shopping center in Ixtapa, across from the Presidente Inter-Continental Hotel; it's open Monday to Friday from 8am to 8:30pm. This is mainly a self-service office where you may collect brochures; the staff is less helpful than that at other offices in Mexico. The **Zihuatanejo Tourism Office Module** (no phone; www.cdnet.com.mx/turismo/ixtapa_zihuatanejo.html) is on the main square by the basketball court at Alvarez; it's open Monday to Friday from 9am to 8pm and serves basic tourist-information purposes. The administrative office, in City Hall (✆ **755/554-2355**), is open Monday to Friday from 8am to 4pm.

**CITY LAYOUT** The fishing village and resort of **Zihuatanejo** spreads out around the beautiful Bay of Zihuatanejo, framed by downtown to the north, and a beautiful long beach and the Sierra foothills to the east. The heart of Zihuatanejo is the waterfront walkway **Paseo del Pescador** (also called the ***malecón***), bordering the Municipal Beach. Rather than a plaza as in most Mexican villages, the town centerpiece is a **basketball court,** which fronts the beach. It's a point of reference for directions. The main thoroughfare for cars is **Juan Alvarez,** a block behind the *malecón.* Sections of several of the main streets are designated *zona peatonal* (pedestrian zone). The area zigzags, however, and seems to block parts of streets haphazardly.

A cement-and-sand walkway runs from the *malecón* in downtown Zihuatanejo along the water to **Playa Madera.** The walkway is lit at night. Access to Playa La Ropa ("Clothing Beach") is by the main road, **Camino a Playa La Ropa.** Playa La Ropa and Playa Las Gatas ("Cats Beach") are connected only by boat.

A good highway connects Zihua to **Ixtapa,** 6km (4 miles) northwest. The 18-hole **Ixtapa Golf Club** marks the beginning of the inland side of Ixtapa. Tall hotels line Ixtapa's wide beach, **Playa Palmar,** against a backdrop of lush palm groves and mountains. Access is by the main street, **Bulevard Ixtapa.** On the opposite side of the main boulevard lies a large expanse of small shopping plazas (many with air-conditioned shops) and restaurants. At the far end of Bulevard Ixtapa, **Marina Ixtapa** has excellent restaurants, private yacht slips, and an 18-hole golf course. Condominiums and private homes surround the marina and golf course, and more developments of exclusive residential areas are rising in the hillsides past the marina on the road to Playa Quieta and Playa Linda. Ixtapa also has a paved bicycle track that begins at the marina and continues around the golf course and on toward Playa Linda.

**GETTING AROUND** **Taxi** fares are reasonable, but from midnight to 5am, rates increase by 50%. The average fare between Ixtapa and Zihuatanejo is $3.90. A **shuttle bus** runs between Zihuatanejo and Ixtapa every 15 or 20 minutes from 5am to 11pm daily, but is almost always very crowded with commuting workers. In Zihuatanejo, it stops near the corner of Morelos/Paseo Zihuatanejo and Juárez, about 3 blocks north of the market. In Ixtapa, it makes numerous stops along Bulevard Ixtapa.

*Note:* The road from Zihuatanejo to Ixtapa is a broad, four-lane highway, which makes driving between the towns easier and faster than ever. Street signs are becoming more common in Zihuatanejo, and good signs lead in and out of both towns. However, both locations have an area called the "Zona Hotelera" (Hotel Zone), so if you're trying to reach Ixtapa's Hotel Zone, signs in Zihuatanejo pointing to that village's Hotel Zone may be confusing.

## *FAST FACTS:* Zihuatanejo & Ixtapa

*American Express* The main office is in the commercial promenade of the Krystal Ixtapa Hotel (✆ **755/553-0853**; fax 755/553-1206). It's open Monday to Saturday 9am to 6pm.

*Area Code* The telephone area code is **755**.

*Banks* Ixtapa's banks include **Bancomer,** in the La Puerta Centro shopping center. The most centrally located of Zihuatanejo's banks is **Banamex,** Cuauhtémoc 4. Banks change money during normal business hours, which are generally Monday to Friday 9am to 3 or 5pm, Saturday 10am to 1pm. Automatic tellers and currency exchange are available during these and other hours.

*Climate* Summer is hot and humid, though tempered by sea breezes and brief showers; September is the peak of the tropical rainy season, with showers concentrated in the late afternoons.

*Hospital* **Hospital de la Marina Ixtapa** is at Bulevard Ixtapa s/n, in front of the Hotel Aristos (✆ **755/553-0499**).

*Internet Access* Ixtapa has many Internet cafes. Several cybercafes are in the Los Patios Shopping Center in Ixtapa. The cost of Internet access averages $3 per hour. **Comunicación Mundial** is in Local 105 (✆ **755/553-1177**). Go to the back of the shopping center and take the stairs to the second level; Comunicación Mundial is to your right. It's open daily from 9am to 9pm.

*Pharmacy* There's a branch of **Farmacias Coyuca** in each town. They are open 24 hours a day, and will deliver. The Ixtapa branch doesn't have a phone number; in Zihuatanejo, call ✆ **755/554-5390.**

*Post Office* The *correo* is in the SCT building, Edificio SCT, behind El Cacahuate in Zihuatanejo (✆ **755/554-2192**). It's open Monday to Friday from 8am to 3pm, Saturday from 9am to 1pm

## ACTIVITIES ON & OFF THE BEACH

The **Museo de Arqueología de la Costa Grande** (no phone) traces the history of the area from Acapulco to Ixtapa/Zihuatanejo, the Costa Grande, from pre-Hispanic times, when it was known as Cihuatlán, through the colonial era. Most of the museum's pottery and stone artifacts give evidence of extensive trade with far-off cultures and regions, including the Toltec and Teotihuacán near Mexico City, the Olmec on the Pacific and Gulf coasts, and areas known today as the states of Nayarit, Michoacán, and San Luis Potosí. Local indigenous groups gave the Aztec tribute items, including cotton *tilmas* (capes) and *cacao* (chocolate), representations of which can be seen here. This museum, in Zihuatanejo near Guerrero at the east end of Paseo del Pescador, easily merits the half hour or less it takes to stroll through; signs are in Spanish, but an accompanying brochure is available in English. Admission is 50¢, and it's open Tuesday to Sunday from 10am to 6pm.

**THE BEACHES In Zihuatanejo** At Zihuatanejo's town beach, **Playa Municipal,** the local fishermen pull their colorful boats up onto the sand, making for a fine photo op. The small shops and restaurants lining the waterfront are great for people-watching and absorbing the flavor of daily village life. **Playa**

**Madera** ("Wood Beach"), just east of Playa Municipal, is open to the surf but generally peaceful. A number of attractive budget lodgings overlook this area from the hillside.

South of Playa Madera is Zihuatanejo's largest and most beautiful beach, **Playa La Ropa,** a long sweep of sand with a great view of the sunset. Some lovely small hotels and restaurants nestle in the hills; palm groves edge the shoreline. Although it's also open to the Pacific, waves are usually gentle. A taxi from town costs $3. The name *Playa La Ropa* (*ropa* means clothing) comes from an old tale of the sinking of a *galeón* during a storm. The silk clothing that it was carrying back from the Philippines washed ashore on this beach—hence the name.

The nicest beach for swimming, and the best for children, is the secluded **Playa Las Gatas** ("Cats Beach"), across the bay from Playa La Ropa and Zihuatanejo. The small coral reef just offshore is a nice spot for snorkeling and diving, and a little dive shop on the beach rents gear. Shop owner Jean Claude is a local institution—and the only full-time resident of Las Gatas. He claims to offer special rates for female divers and has a collection of bikini tops on display. The waters at Las Gatas are exceptionally clear, without undertow or big waves. Open-air seafood restaurants on the beach make it an appealing lunch spot. Small *pangas* (launches) with shade run to Las Gatas from the Zihuatanejo town pier, a 10-minute trip; the captains will take you across whenever you wish between 8am and 4pm. Usually the last boat back leaves Las Gatas at 6:30pm, but check to be sure.

**Playa Larga** is a beautiful, uncrowded beach between Zihuatanejo and the airport, with several small *palapa* restaurants, hammocks, and wading pools for children.

**In Ixtapa** Ixtapa's main beach, **Playa Palmar,** is a lovely white-sand arc on the edge of the Hotel Zone, with dramatic rock formations silhouetted in the sea. The surf can be rough; use caution, and don't swim when a red flag is posted. Several of the nicest beaches in the area are essentially closed to the public. Although by law all Mexican beaches are open to the public, it is common practice for hotels to create artificial barriers (such as rocks or dunes).

Club Med and Qualton Club have largely claimed **Playa Quieta,** on the mainland across from Isla Ixtapa. The remaining piece of beach was once the launching point for boats to Isla Ixtapa, but it is gradually being taken over by a private development. Isla Ixtapa–bound boats now leave from the jetty on **Playa Linda,** about 13km (8 miles) north of Ixtapa. Inexpensive water taxis ferry passengers to Isla Ixtapa. Playa Linda is the primary out-of-town beach, with watersports equipment and horse rentals available. **Playa las Cuatas,** a pretty beach and cove a few miles north of Ixtapa, and **Playa Majahua,** an isolated beach just west of Zihuatanejo, are both being transformed into resort complexes. Lovely **Playa Vista Hermosa** is framed by striking rock formations

---

*Tips* **Beach Safety**

All beaches in Zihuatanejo are safe for swimming. Undertow is rarely a problem, and the municipal beach is protected from the main surge of the Pacific. Beaches in Ixtapa are more dangerous for swimming, with frequent undertow problems.

---

and bordered by the Las Brisas Hotel high on the hill. All of these are very attractive beaches for sunbathing or a stroll but have heavy surf and strong undertow. Use caution if you swim here.

**WATERSPORTS & BOAT TRIPS** Probably the most popular boat trip is to **Isla Ixtapa** for snorkeling and lunch at the El Marlin restaurant, one of several on the island. You can book this outing as a tour through local travel agencies, or go on your own from Zihuatanejo by following the directions to Playa Linda above and taking a boat from there. Boats leave for Isla Ixtapa every 10 minutes between 11:30am and 5pm, so you can depart and return as you like. The round-trip boat ride is $3. Along the way, you'll pass dramatic rock formations and see in the distance **Los Morros de Los Pericos islands,** where a great variety of birds nest on the rocky points jutting out into the blue Pacific. On Isla Ixtapa, you'll find good snorkeling; snorkeling, diving, and other watersports gear is available for rent on the island. Be sure to catch the last water taxi back at 5pm, and double-check that time upon arrival on the island.

Local travel agencies can usually arrange day trips to Los Morros de Los Pericos islands for **birding,** though it's less expensive to rent a boat with a guide at Playa Linda. The islands are offshore from Ixtapa's main beach.

**Sunset cruises** on the sailboat *Nirvana,* arranged through **Yates del Sol** (© **755/554-2694** or 755/554-8270), depart from the Zihuatanejo town pier at Puerto Mío. The cruises cost $45 per person and include an open bar and hors d'oeuvres. There's also a day trip to **Playa Manzanillo** on the very comfortable, rarely crowded sailboat. It begins at 11am, costs $78 per person, and includes an open bar, lunch, and snorkeling gear. Schedules and special trips vary, so call for current information.

You can arrange **fishing trips** with the **boat cooperative** (© **755/554-2056**) at the Zihuatanejo town pier. They cost $140 to $300, depending on boat size, trip length, and so on. Most trips last about 7 hours. The cooperative accepts Visa and MasterCard; paying cash saves you a 20% tax, but don't expect a receipt. The price includes 10 soft drinks and 10 beers, bait, and fishing gear, but not lunch. You'll pay more for a trip arranged through a local travel agency. The least expensive trips are on small launches called *pangas;* most have shade. Both small-game and deep-sea fishing are offered, and the fishing here is adequate, though not on par with that of Mazatlán or Baja. Other trips combine fishing with a visit to the near-deserted ocean beaches that extend for miles along the coast. Sam Lushinsky at **Ixtapa Sport-fishing Charters,** 19 Depue Lane, Stroudsburg, PA 18360 (© **570/688-9466,** fax 570/688-9554; www.ixtapasportfishing.com) is a noted outfitter.

Boating and fishing expeditions from the new **Marina Ixtapa,** a bit north of the Ixtapa Hotel Zone, can also be arranged. As a rule, everything available in or through the marina is more expensive and more "Americanized."

**Sailboats, Windsurfers,** and other **watersports equipment** rentals are usually available at stands on Playa La Ropa, Playa las Gatas, Isla Ixtapa, and at the main beach, Playa Palmar, in Ixtapa. There's **parasailing** at La Ropa and Palmar. **Kayaks** are available for rent at the **Zihuatanejo Scuba Center** (see below), hotels in Ixtapa, and some watersports operations on Playa La Ropa.

The **Zihuatanejo Scuba Center,** Cuauhtémoc 3 (© and fax **755/554-2147**), arranges **scuba-diving trips.** Fees start at around $84 for two dives, including all equipment and lunch. Marine biologist and dive instructor Juan Barnard speaks excellent English and is very knowledgeable about the area, which has nearly 30 different dive sites, including walls and caves. He's also known as a very fun guide. Diving takes place year-round, though the water is clearest from May through December, when visibility is 30m (100 ft.) or better. The nearest decompression chamber is in Acapulco. Advance reservations for dives are advised during Christmas and Easter.

**Surfing** is particularly good at **Petacalco Beach** north of Ixtapa.

**LAND SPORTS & ACTIVITIES** In **Ixtapa,** the **Club de Golf Ixtapa Palma Real** (**© 755/553-1062** or 755/553-1163), in front of the Sheraton Hotel, has an 18-hole course designed by Robert Trent Jones, Jr. The greens fee is $70; caddies cost $17 for 18 holes, $13 for 9 holes; electric carts are $34; and clubs are $22.50 (AE, MC, V). Tee times begin at 7am, but the course doesn't take reservations. The **Marina Ixtapa Golf Course** (**© 755/553-1410;** fax 755/553-0825), designed by Robert von Hagge, has 18 challenging holes. The greens fee is $75 and includes a cart; caddies cost $20, club rental $30 (AE, MC, V). The first tee time is 7am. Call for reservations 24 hours in advance.

In Ixtapa, the **Club de Golf Ixtapa** (**© 755/553-1062** or 755/553-1163) and the **Marina Ixtapa Golf Course** (**© 755/553-1410;** fax 755/553-0825) both have lighted public **tennis courts,** and both rent equipment. Fees are $6 to $20 an hour during the day, $9 to $30 at night. Call for reservations. In addition, the **Dorado Pacífico** and most of the better hotels on the main beach in Ixtapa have courts.

For **horseback riding, Rancho Playa Linda** (cellular **© 044-755/557-0222**) offers guided trail rides from the Playa Linda beach (about 13km/8 miles north of Ixtapa). Rides begin at 8:30, 9:45, and 11am, and 3, 4, and 5pm. Groups of three or more riders can arrange their own tour, which is especially nice a little later in the evening around sunset (though you'll need mosquito repellent). Riders can choose to trace the beach to the mouth of the river and back through coconut plantations, or hug the beach for the whole ride (which usually lasts 1–1½ hr.). The fee is around $30, cash only. Travel agencies in either town can arrange your trip but will charge a bit more for transportation. Reservations are suggested in high season. Another good place to ride is in Playa Larga. There is a ranch on the first exit coming from Zihuatanejo (no phone, but you can't miss it—it is the first corral to the right as you drive toward the beach). The horses are in excellent shape. The fee is $30 for 45 minutes.

For **off-the-beaten-track tours,** contact Alex León Pineda, the friendly, knowledgeable owner of **Tourismo Incentivos Planificados,** in the Los Patios Center in Ixtapa (**© 755/553-1442;** fax 755/553-2014). His countryside tour ($49) goes to coconut and banana plantations, small villages of traditional brick makers and palm thatch huts, and the beach at La Saladita, where fishermen and visitors together prepare a lunch of fresh lobster, *dorado,* or snapper. His tour to **Petatlán** and the **Laguna de San Valentín** ($49) is also very popular. Highlights include a visit to a small museum, local market, and town church. A stop at the lagoon is next, followed by lunch on a small island. No credit cards.

## SHOPPING

### ZIHUATANEJO

Zihuatanejo has its quota of T-shirt and souvenir shops, but it's becoming a better place to buy crafts, folk art, and jewelry. Shops are generally open Monday to Saturday from 10am to 2pm and 4 to 8pm. Many better shops close Sunday, but some smaller souvenir stands stay open, and hours vary.

The **artisans' market** on Calle Cinco de Mayo is a good place to start shopping before moving on to specialty shops. There's also a **municipal market** on

Avenida Benito Juárez (about 5 blocks inland from the waterfront), but most vendors offer the same things—*huaraches,* hammocks, and baskets. The market sprawls over several blocks. Spreading inland from the waterfront some 3 or 4 blocks are numerous small shops well worth exploring.

Besides the places listed below, check out **Alberto's,** Cuauhtémoc 12 and 15 (no phone), for jewelry. Also on Cuauhtémoc, 2 blocks down from the Nueva Zelanda Coffee Shop, is a small shop that looks like a market stand and sells beautiful tablecloths, napkins, and other linens, all handmade in Aguascalientes.

**Boutique D'Xochitl** Light crinkle-cotton clothing that's perfect for tropical climates. It's open Monday to Saturday from 9am to 9pm, Sunday from 11am to 9pm. Ejido at Cuauhtémoc. ✆ **755/554-2131.**

**Casa Marina** This small complex extends from the waterfront to Alvarez near Cinco de Mayo and houses four shops, each specializing in handcrafted wares from all over Mexico. Items include handsome rugs, textiles, masks, colorful woodcarvings, and silver jewelry. Café Marina, the small coffee shop in the complex, has shelves and shelves of used paperback books in several languages for sale. It's open daily from 9am to 9pm during the high season, 10am to 2pm and 4 to 8pm the rest of the year. Paseo del Pescador 9. ✆ **755/554-2373.** Fax 755/554-3533.

**Coco Cabaña Collectibles** Located next to Coconuts Restaurant, this impressive shop carries carefully selected crafts and folk art from all across the country, including fine Oaxacan woodcarvings. Owner Pat Cummings once ran a gallery in New York, and the inventory reveals her discriminating eye. If you make a purchase, she'll cash your dollars at the going rate. It's open Monday to Saturday from 10am to 2pm and 4 to 8pm; closed August and September. Guerrero and Alvarez, opposite the Hotel Citali. ✆ **755/554-2518.**

**Viva Zapatos** This shop has bathing suits to fit every shape and fashion trend, great casual and not-so-casual resort wear, sunglasses, and everything else for looking good in and out of the water. The store is three doors down from Amueblados Valle. It's open Monday to Saturday from 10am to 2pm and 4 to 9pm. Vicente Guerre 33. ✆ **755/554-4649.**

### IXTAPA

Shopping in Ixtapa is not especially memorable, with T-shirts and Mexican crafts the usual wares. On several plazas, air-conditioned shops carry resort wear as well as T-shirts and jewelry. **Ferroni, Bye-Bye, Aca Joe,** and **Navale** sell brand-name sportswear. All of these shops are in the same area on Bulevard Ixtapa, across from the beachside hotels, and most are open daily 9am to 2pm and 4 to 9pm.

**La Fuente** This terrific shop carries gorgeous Talavera pottery, jaguar-shaped wicker tables, hand-blown glassware, masks, tin mirrors and frames, hand-embroidered clothing from Chiapas, and wood and papier-mâché miniatures. Open daily 9am to 10pm during high season, daily 10am to 2pm and 5 to 9pm in low season. Los Patios Center, Bulevard Ixtapa. ✆ **755/553-0812.**

## WHERE TO STAY

Larger, more expensive hotels, including many well-known chains, dominate accommodations in Ixtapa and on Playa Madera. There are only a few choices in the budget and moderate price ranges. If you're looking for lower-priced rooms, Zihuatanejo offers a better selection and better values. Many long-term guests in Ixtapa and Zihuatanejo search out apartments and condos to rent.

**Lilia Valle** (© **755/554-2084**) is an excellent source for apartment and villa rentals.

## IXTAPA

### Very Expensive

**Las Brisas Resort** ★★★ Set above the high-rise hotels of Ixtapa on its own rocky promontory, Las Brisas (formerly the Westin Brisas) is clearly the most stunning of Ixtapa's hotels, and the most noted for gracious service. The austere but luxurious public areas, all in stone and stucco, exude an air of exclusivity. Minimalist luxury also characterizes the rooms—all redone 3 years ago—which have Mexican-tile floors and private, plant-decked patios with hammocks and lounges. All rooms face the hotel's cove and private beach, which, though attractive, is dangerous for swimming. The six master suites come with private pools, and the 16th floor is reserved for nonsmokers.

Blvd. Ixtapa, 40880 Ixtapa, Gro. © **800/228-3000** in the U.S., or 755/553-2121. Fax 755/553-1091. 423 units. High season $285 deluxe double, $315 Royal Beach Club; low season $196 deluxe double, $230 Royal Beach Club. 3 units are equipped for travelers with disabilities. AE, DC, MC, V. Free parking. **Amenities:** 5 restaurants, 3 bars (including lobby bar with live music at sunset); 4 swimming pools (1 for children); 4 lighted tennis courts with pro on request; elevator to secluded beach; fitness center; travel agency; room service; car rental; shopping arcade; salon; massage; babysitting; laundry service. *In room:* A/C, TV, minibar, hair dryer, safe-deposit box.

### Expensive

**Barceló Ixtapa** ★★ This grand 12-story resort hotel (formerly the Sheraton) has large, handsomely furnished public areas facing the beach; it's an inviting place to sip a drink and people-watch. Most rooms have balconies with views of the ocean or the mountains. Non-smoking rooms are available. Gardens surround the large pool, which has a swim-up bar and separate section for children. It's an excellent value and a great choice for families.

Blvd. Ixtapa, 40880 Ixtapa, Gro. © **800/325-3535** in the U.S. and Canada, or 755/555-2000. Fax 755/553-2438. www.barcelo.com. 331 units. High season $245 double all-inclusive, $180 double with breakfast only; low season $225 double all-inclusive. Rooms equipped for travelers with disabilities are available. AE, DC, MC, V. Free parking. **Amenities:** 4 restaurants, nightclub, lobby bar, weekly Mexican fiesta with buffet and live entertainment; beachside pool; 4 tennis courts; fitness room; concierge; travel agency; car rental; pharmacy/gift shop; salon; room service; laundry service. *In room:* A/C, TV, minibar.

**Krystal** ★★★ *Kids* Krystal hotels are known in Mexico for quality rooms and service, and this was the original hotel in the chain. It upholds its reputation for welcoming, exceptional service. Many staff members have been with the hotel for its 20-some years of operation, and are on hand to greet return guests. It is probably the best hotel in the area for families. This large, V-shaped hotel has ample grounds and a pool area. Each spacious, nicely furnished room has a balcony with an ocean view, game table, and tile bathroom. Master suites have large, furnished, triangular balconies. Some rates include a breakfast buffet. The center of Ixtapa nightlife is here, at Krystal's famed **Christine** disco.

Blvd. Ixtapa s/n, 40880 Ixtapa, Gro. © **800/231-9860** in the U.S., or 755/553-0333. Fax 755/553-0216. 255 units. www.krystal.com. High season $190 double, $280 suite; low season $170 double, $255 suite. 2 children under 12 stay free in parents' room. Ask about special packages. AE, DC, MC, V. Free parking. **Amenities:** 5 restaurants, lobby bar, nightclub; pool; tennis court; racquetball court; gym; kids' club; salon; massage; travel agency; car rental; room service; laundry service. *In room:* A/C, TV, minibar.

## ZIHUATANEJO

Hotels in Zihuatanejo and its nearby beach communities are more economical than those in Ixtapa. The term "bungalow" is used loosely—it may mean an individual unit with a kitchen and bedroom, or just a bedroom. It may also be like a hotel, in a two-story building with multiple units, some of which have kitchens. It may be cozy or rustic, with or without a patio or balcony. Accommodations in town are generally very basic, though clean and comfortable.

Playa Madera and Playa La Ropa, separated by a craggy shoreline, are both accessible by road. Prices tend to be higher here than in town, but the value is much better, and people tend to find that the beautiful, tranquil setting is worth the extra cost. The town is 5 (by taxi) to 20 (on foot) minutes away.

## In Town

**Apartamentos Amueblados Valle** ★★ These well-furnished apartments cost only as much as an inexpensive hotel room. Five one-bedroom apartments accommodate up to three people; the three two-bedroom apartments can fit four comfortably. Units that do not face the street are less noisy than those that do. Each airy apartment is different; all have ceiling fans, private balconies, and kitchenettes. There's daily maid service, and a paperback-book exchange in the office. Owner Guadalupe Rodríguez and her son Luis Valle are good sources of information about cheaper apartments elsewhere, for long-term visitors. Reserve well in advance during high season. It's about 2 blocks from the waterfront.

Vincente Guerrero 33 (between Ejido and N. Bravo), 40880 Zihuatanejo, Gro. ✆ **755/554-2084.** Fax 755/554-3220. 8 units. High season $60 1-bedroom apt, $90 2-bedroom apt; low season $40 1-bedroom apt, $60 2-bedroom apt. Ask about low-season and long-term discounts. No credit cards. *In room:* Fan, kitchenette.

**Hotel Raul 3 Marias** A small hotel known for its guest services, the Raul has small, basic, functional rooms. Nine rooms have a balcony overlooking the street, and the small office handles telephone and fax service. Downstairs is the landmark seafood restaurant **Garrobos,** open for lunch and dinner. The hotel also offers deep-sea fishing and diving charters.

Juan Alvarez 52, 40880 Zihuatanejo, Gro. ✆ **755/554-6706.** www.cdnet.com.mx/r3marias. 17 units. High season $47 double; low season rates vary. AE, MC, V. *In room:* A/C.

**Hotel Susy** Consistently clean, with lots of plants along a shaded walkway set back from the street, this two-story hotel offers small rooms with fans and screened louvered-glass windows. Upper-floor rooms have balconies overlooking the street. Facing away from the water at the basketball court on the *malecón,* turn right and walk 2 blocks; the hotel is on your left.

Juan Alvarez 3 (at Guerrero), 40880 Zihuatanejo, Gro. ✆ **755/554-2339.** 18 units. High season $78 double; low season $34 double. MC, V. *In room:* TV.

**Posada Citlali** In this pleasant, three-story hotel, small rooms with fans surround a shaded, plant-filled courtyard that holds comfortable rockers and chairs. It's a good value for the price. Bottled water is in help-yourself containers on the patio. The stairway to the top two floors is narrow and steep.

Vicente Guerrero 3 (near Alvarez), 40880 Zihuatanejo, Guerrero. ✆ **755/554-2043.** 19 units. $39 double. No credit cards.

## Playa Madera

Madera Beach is a 15-minute walk along the street, a 10-minute walk along the beach pathway, or a cheap taxi ride from Zihuatanejo. Most of the accommodations are on Calle Eva S. de López Matéos, the road overlooking the beach. Most hotels are set against the hill and have steep stairways.

**Bungalows Ley** ★ No two suites are the same at this small complex, one of the nicest on Playa Madera. If you're traveling with a group, you may want to book the most expensive suite (Club Madera); it has a rooftop terrace with a

## Downtown Zihuatanejo

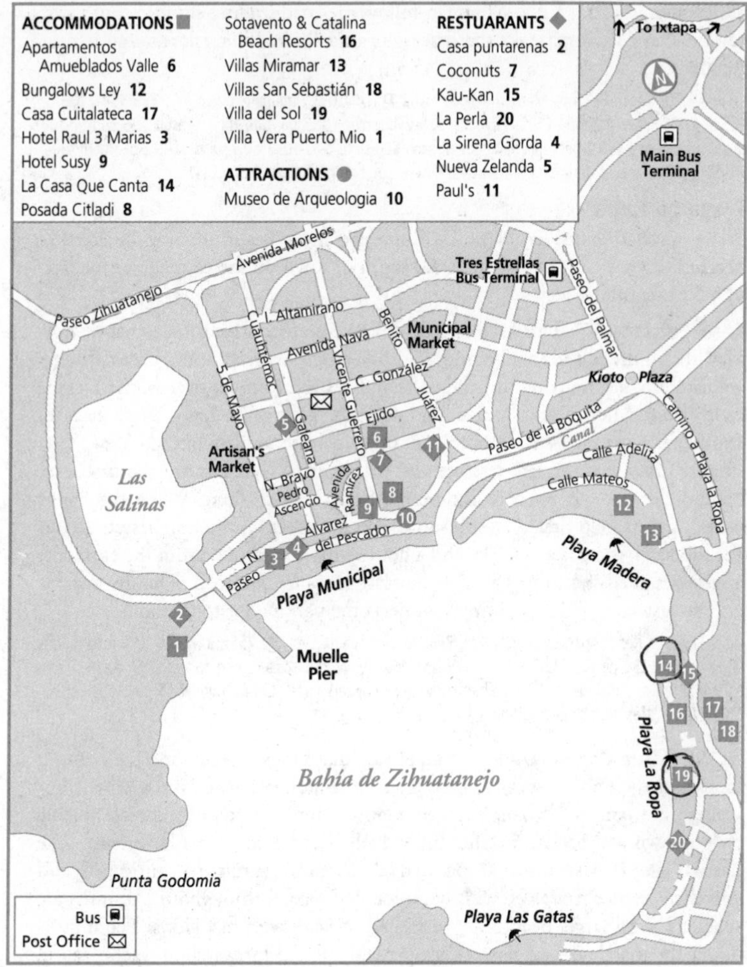


tiled hot tub, outdoor bar and grill, and spectacular view. All the units are immaculate; the simplest are studios with one bed and a kitchen in the same room. All rooms have terraces or balconies just above the beach, and all are decorated in Miami Beach colors. Bathrooms, however, tend to be small and dark. Guests praise the management and the service. To find the complex, follow Matéos to the right up a slight hill; it's on your left.

Calle Eva S. de López Matéos s/n, Playa Madera (Apdo. Postal 466), 40880 Zihuatanejo, Gro. ✆ **755/554-4087.** Fax 755/554-4563. 8 units. $103 double with A/C; $162 2-bedroom suite with kitchen (up to 4 persons) or $212 (up to 6 persons). AE, MC, V. *In room:* TV.

**Villas Miramar** ★★★ This lovely hotel with beautiful gardens offers a welcoming atmosphere, attention to detail, and suburb cleanliness. Some of the elegant suites are around a shady patio that doubles as a restaurant. Those across the street center on a lovely pool and have private balconies and sea views. A terrace with a bay view has a bar that features a daily happy hour (5–7pm). TVs get cable channels, and the restaurant serves a basic menu for breakfast, lunch, and dinner. To find Villas Miramar, follow the road leading south out of town toward Playa La Ropa, take the first right after the traffic circle, and go left on Adelita.

Calle Adelita, Lote 78, Playa Madera (Apdo. Postal 211), 40880 Zihuatanejo, Gro. ✆ **755/554-2106** or 755/554-3350. Fax 755/554-2149. 18 units. www.villasmiramarzihua.com. High season $95 suite, $100 oceanview suite, $135 2-bedroom suite; low season $60 suite, $70 oceanview suite, $106 2-bedroom suite. AE, MC, V. Free enclosed parking. **Amenities:** Restaurant, bar; pool. *In room:* A/C, TV.

### Playa La Ropa

Some travelers consider Playa La Ropa the most beautiful of Zihuatanejo's beaches. It's a 20- to 25-minute walk south of town on the east side of the bay, or a $2 taxi ride.

**Casa Cuitlateca** This exclusive B&B is the perfect place for a romantic holiday. It's on the hillside across from La Ropa beach, with stunning views. Rooms are carefully decorated with handcrafts and textiles from all over Mexico, especially from Michoacán, Puebla, and Oaxaca. One suite has a large terrace, another a very nice sitting area and small private garden but no view. Two smaller units have private terraces and sitting areas. The bar, on the first level behind the pool, is open to the public from 4:30 to 8pm. When the bar is closed, guests help themselves to soft drinks and beer on the honor system. On the top level, there is a sundeck and a hot tub for guests' use. From the entrance, a well-designed yet steep 150-step staircase leads to the B&B. The driveway is also very steep. A hanging bridge connects the parking lot to the house.

Calle Playa La Ropa, Apartado Postal 124, Zihuatanejo, 40880, Gro. ✆ **755/554-2448.** U.S. reservations ✆ 877/541-1234 or 406/252-2834. Fax 406/252-4692. www.cuitlateca.com. 4 suites. $397 double. Extra person $50. Rates include round-trip airport transportation, breakfast. Children under 15 not accepted. AE, MC, V. **Amenities:** Bar; small pool; sun deck; Jacuzzi. *In room:* A/C.

**La Casa Que Canta** ★★★ "The House that Sings" opened in 1992, and in looks alone, it's a very special hotel. It sits on a mountainside overlooking Zihuatanejo Bay, and its striking molded-adobe architecture typifies the rustic-chic style known as Mexican Pacific. Individually decorated rooms have handsome natural-tile floors, unusual painted Michoacán furniture, antiques, and stretched-leather *equipales,* with hand-loomed fabrics throughout. All units are spacious, with large, beautifully furnished terraces with bay views. Hammocks under the thatched-roof terraces are perfectly placed for watching yachts sail in and out of the harbor. Most of the spacious units are suites, and two of them have private pools. Rooms meander up and down the hillside, and while no staircase is terribly long, there are no elevators. La Casa Que Canta is a member of the Small Luxury Hotels of the World. It's on the road leading to Playa La Ropa, but not on any beach. The closest stretch of beach (not Playa La Ropa) is down a steep hill.

Camino Escénico a la Playa La Ropa, 40880 Zihuatanejo, Guerrero. ✆ **888/523-5050** in the U.S., 755/555-7000, 755/555-5730, or 755/554-6529. Fax 755/554-7900. www.lacasaquecanta.com.mx. 24 units. High season $330–$680 double; low season $290–$525 double. AE, MC, V. Children under 16 not accepted. **Amenities:** Small restaurant and bar; freshwater pool on main terrace; saltwater pool on bottom level; laundry service; room service. *In room:* A/C, minibar.

**Sotavento and Catalina Beach Resorts** ★★ Perched on a hill above the beach, these hotels are for people who want to relax near the ocean in a beautiful, simple setting and don't want to be bothered by televisions or closed up in air-conditioned rooms. The Catalina is a collection of bungalows tucked away in the tropical vegetation. The Sotavento consists of two multistory buildings that are situated so as not to intrude on the bungalow dwellers. Between them, the hotels offer quite a variety of rooms: Ask to see a few to find something that suits you. My favorites, the doubles on the upper floors of the Sotavento, are three times the size of normal doubles. They are simply and comfortably furnished. Each has an ocean-view terrace that is half-sheltered, with hammocks, and half-open, with chaises for taking the sun. Screened windows catch the ocean breezes, and ceiling fans keep the rooms airy. One curious feature of the Sotavento is that the floors are slightly slanted—by design. The bungalows in the Catalina are more decoratively furnished, with Mexican tile floors, wrought-iron furniture, and artwork. Some have ocean-view terraces. This hotel is on the side of a hill and is not for people who mind climbing stairs. Take the highway south of Zihuatanejo about a mile, turn right at the hotels' sign, and follow the road.

Playa La Ropa, 40880 Zihuatanejo, Gro. ✆ **755/554-2032.** Fax 755/554-2975. www.giga.com. 126 units (Sotavento) and 85 units (Catalina). $70–$110 standard double, $95 small terrace double; $65–$120 bungalow or terrace suite. AE, DC, MC, V. **Amenities:** Restaurant, lobby bar; pool with whirlpool.

**Villa del Sol** ★★★ This exquisite inn is known as much for its unequivocal attention to luxurious detail as it is for its exacting German owner, Helmut Leins. A tranquil, magnificently designed spot that caters to guests looking for complete privacy and serenity, it sits on a 600-foot-long private beach. Spacious, split-level suites have one or two bedrooms, plus a living area and a large terrace. Some have a private mini-pool, and all have CD players and fax machines. White netting drapes king-size beds, and comfy lounges and hammocks beckon at siesta time. Standard rooms are smaller and lack TV and telephone, but appointed with Mexican artistic details. There are nine beachfront suites, but I prefer the individually designed original rooms. This is one of only two hotels in Mexico that meet the demanding standards of the French Relais and Châteaux, and is a member of the Small Luxury Hotels of the World. Villa del Sol does not accept children under 14 during high season, and generally has a "no children" and "no excess noise" feel. This may make it less enjoyable for travelers who relish a more welcoming ambience. The meal plan (breakfast and dinner) is mandatory during the winter season.

Playa la Ropa (Apdo Postal 84), 40880 Zihuatanejo, Gro. ✆ **888/223-6510** in the U.S., 755/554-2239 or 755/554-3239. Fax 755/554-2758. www.hotelvilladelsol.com. 45 units. High season $475–$1,018 double; low season $305–$702 double. Meal plan $60 per person. AE, MC, V. **Amenities:** Open-air beachfront restaurant and bar; 3 pools (including 60-ft. lap pool); 2 tennis courts; massage; salon; art gallery; tour desk; car rental; room service; doctor on call. *In room:* A/C, TV, minibar, bathrobes, hair dryer.

**Villas San Sebastián** On the mountainside above Playa La Ropa, this nine-villa complex offers great views of Zihuatanejo's bay. The villas surround tropical vegetation and a central swimming pool. Each has a kitchenette and a spacious private terrace. The personalized service is one reason these villas come so highly recommended; owner Luis Valle, whose family has lived in this community for decades, is always available to help guests with any questions or needs.

Blvd. Escénico Playa La Ropa (across from the Dolphins Fountain). ✆ **755/554-4154** Fax 755/554-4154. 9 units. High season $155 1-bedroom villa, $255 2-bedroom villa; low season $105 1-bedroom villa, $165 2-bedroom villa. No credit cards. **Amenities:** Pool. *In room:* A/C.

### Zihuatanejo Beach

**Villa Vera Puerto Mio** ★★ Located on 25 acres of beautifully landscaped grounds, this resort sits apart from the rest of the hotels in Zihuatanejo, at the farthest end of the bay, almost directly across from Las Gatas beach. Casa de

Mar, the cliffside mansion near the main entrance, holds most of the rooms. Other units are in the Peninsula area, on the tip of the bay; a more secluded area holds two suites with ample sitting areas, beautiful views, and no TVs. Three suites between Casa de Mar and the Peninsula have private pools; the upper-level suite is largest. All rooms have just been renovated and are nicely decorated with handcrafted details from around Mexico. They enjoy beautiful views of either Zihuatanejo's bay or the Pacific Ocean. Golf carts provide transportation areas around the property. The resort accepts children under 16 only during the summer, and recommends that you call in advance to check. The private beach can be reached only through the hotel, and the hotel has a sailboat available for charters.

Paseo del Morro 5, 40880 Zihuatanejo, Gro. ✆ **800/021-6566** in Mexico, 755/553-8165, 755/553-8166, 755/553-8167. Fax 755/553-8161. 22 units. High season $291 double, $316 suite, $819 top-level suite with pool, $954 master suite; low season $252 double, $252 suite, $670 top-level suite with pool, $819 master suite. AE, MC, V. **Amenities:** 2 restaurants; small marina with sailboat; concierge; tour desk; car rentals. *In room:* A/C, minibar, bathrobes, safe-deposit box.

## WHERE TO DINE

### IXTAPA

#### Very Expensive

**Villa de la Selva** ★ MEXICAN/CONTINENTAL Clinging to the edge of a cliff overlooking the sea, this elegant, romantic restaurant enjoys the most spectacular sea and sunset view in Ixtapa. The candlelit tables occupy three terraces; try to come early to get one of the best vistas, especially on the lower terrace. The cuisine is delicious, artfully presented, and classically rich. Filet Villa de la Selva is red snapper topped with shrimp and hollandaise sauce. Cold avocado soup or hot lobster bisque makes a good beginning; finish with chocolate mousse or bananas Singapore.

Paseo de la Roca. ✆ **755/553-0362.** Reservations recommended during high season. Main courses $15–$44. AE, MC, V. Daily 6–11pm.

#### Expensive

**Beccofino** ★★★ NORTHERN ITALIAN This restaurant is a standout in Mexico. Owner Angelo Rolly Pavia serves the flavorful northern Italian specialties he grew up knowing and loving. The menu is strong on pasta. Ravioli, a house specialty, comes stuffed with seafood (in season). The garlic bread is terrific, and there's an extensive wine list. A popular place in a breezy marina location, the restaurant tends to be loud when it's crowded, which is often. It's also an increasingly popular breakfast spot.

Marina Ixtapa. ✆ **755/553-1770.** Breakfast $5–$7; main courses $14–$30. AE, MC, V. Daily 9:30am–midnight.

#### Moderate

**Golden Cookie Shop** ★★ PASTRIES/INTERNATIONAL Although the name is misleading—there are more than cookies here—Golden Cookie's freshly baked goods beg for a detour, and the coffee menu is the most extensive in town. Although prices are high for the area, the breakfasts are particularly noteworthy, as are the deli sandwiches. Large sandwiches, made with fresh soft bread, come with a choice of sliced meats. Chicken curry is among the other specialty items. To get to the shop, walk to the rear of the shopping center as you face Mac's Prime Rib; walk up the stairs, turn left, and you'll see the restaurant on your right. An air-conditioned area is reserved for nonsmokers.

Los Patios Center. ✆ **755/553-0310.** Breakfast $4–$6; sandwiches $4–$6; main courses $6–$8.50. No credit cards. Daily 8am–3pm.

**Ruben's** ★★★ *Finds* BURGERS/VEGETABLES The choices are easy here—you can order either a big juicy burger made from top sirloin grilled over mesquite, or a foil-wrapped packet of baked potatoes, chayote, zucchini, or sweet corn. Ice cream, beer, and soda fill out the menu, which is posted on the wall by the kitchen. It's kind of a do-it-yourself place: Patrons snare a waitress and order, grab their own drinks from the cooler, and tally their own tabs. Still, because of the ever-present crowds, it can be a slow process. For years, Ruben's was a popular fixture in the Playa Madera neighborhood; now it's in an expanded, spiffed-up location in Ixtapa, and the food remains as dependable as ever.

Flamboyant Shopping Center, next to Bancomer. ✆ **755/553-0055.** Burgers $4–$5; vegetables $2; ice cream $1.50. No credit cards. Daily 6–11pm.

## ZIHUATANEJO

Zihuatanejo's **central market,** on Avenida Benito Juárez about 5 blocks inland from the waterfront, will whet your appetite for cheap and tasty food. It's best at breakfast and lunch, before the market activity winds down in the afternoon. Look for what's hot and fresh. The market area is one of the best on this coast for shopping and people-watching.

The town has two excellent **bakeries.** At **El Buen Gusto,** Guerrero 4, half a block inland from the museum (✆ **755/554-3231**), you'll find banana bread, French bread, doughnuts, and cakes. It's open daily from 7:30am to 10pm. For more fresh-baked-bread aroma, head for **Panadería Francesa,** González 15, between Cuauhtémoc and Guerrero (✆ **755/554-2742**). You can buy sweet pastries or grab a baguette or whole-wheat loaf for picnicking. It's open daily 7am to 9pm.

### Expensive

**Coconuts** ★★★ *Finds* INTERNATIONAL/SEAFOOD What a find! Not only is the food innovative and delicious, but the restaurant is in a historic building—the oldest in Zihuatanejo. This popular restaurant in a tropical garden was the weigh-in station for Zihua's coconut industry in the late 1800s. *Fresh* is the operative word on this creative, seafood-heavy menu. Chef Patricia Cummings checks what's at the market, then uses only top-quality ingredients in dishes like seafood paté and grilled filet of snapper Coconuts. The bananas flambé has earned a loyal following, with good reason. Expect friendly, efficient service here.

Augustín Ramírez 1 (at Vicente Guerrero). ✆ **755/554-2518** or 755/554-7980. Main courses $11–$34. AE, MC, V. High season daily 6pm–11pm. Closed during rainy season.

**Kau-Kan** ★★★ NUEVA COCINA/SEAFOOD A stunning view of the bay is one of the many attractions of this refined restaurant. Stucco and whitewashed walls frame the simple, understated furniture. Head chef Ricardo Rodriguez supervises every detail, from the ultra-smooth background music that invites after-dinner conversation to the spectacular presentation of all the dishes. Baked potato with baby lobster and mahi-mahi *carpaccio* are two of my favorites, but I recommend you consider the daily specials—Ricardo always uses the freshest seafood and prepares it with great care. For dessert, pecan and chocolate cake served with dark chocolate sauce is simply delicious. On the road to La Ropa, it is on the right-hand side of the road past the first curve coming from downtown.

Camino a Playa La Ropa. ✆ **755/554-8446.** Main courses $13–$25. AE, MC, V. Daily 1–11:30pm.

**Restaurant Paul's** ★ INTERNATIONAL/SEAFOOD This is surely the only place in town that serves fresh artichokes as an appetizer, and the fish filet comes covered with a smooth, delicately flavored shrimp-and-dill sauce. From thick and juicy pork chops and beef medallions to vegetarian main courses such as pasta with fresh artichoke hearts and sun-dried tomatoes, chef Paul's offerings are consistently exceptional. Neither the ambience nor the service quite lives up to the food, but that's okay—what really matters is that you'll enjoy an exceptional meal here. Paul's is half a block from the Bancomer and Serfin banks. Taxi drivers all know how to get here.

Benito Juárez s/n. ✆ **755/554-6528.** Main courses $14–$23. MC, V. Mon–Sat noon–2am.

### Inexpensive

**Casa Puntarenas** MEXICAN/SEAFOOD A modest spot with a tin roof and nine wooden tables, Puntarenas is one of the best places in town for fried whole fish served with toasted *bolillos* (crusty white-bread mini-loaves), sliced tomatoes, onions, and avocado. The place is renowned for chile rellenos, mild and stuffed with plenty of cheese; the meat dishes are less flavorful. Although it may appear a little too rustic for less experienced travelers to Mexico, it is very clean, and the food is known for its freshness. To get to Puntarenas from the pier, turn left on Alvarez and cross the footbridge on your left. Turn right after you cross the bridge; the restaurant is on your left.

Calle Noria, Colonia Lázaro Cárdenas. No phone. Main courses $4.50–$8.50. No credit cards. Daily 6:30–9pm.

**La Sirena Gorda** MEXICAN For one of the most popular breakfasts in town, head to La Sirena Gorda. It serves a variety of eggs and omelets, hotcakes with bacon, and fruit with granola and yogurt. The house specialty is seafood tacos—fish in a variety of sauces, plus lobster—but I consider these overpriced, at $4.50 and $25 respectively. A taco is a taco is a taco. Instead, I'd recommend something from the short list of daily specials, such as blackened red snapper, steak, or fish kebabs. The food is excellent, and patrons enjoy the casual sidewalk-cafe atmosphere. To get here from the basketball court, face the water and walk to the right; La Sirena Gorda is on your right just before the town pier.

Paseo del Pescador. ✆ **755/554-2687.** Breakfast $2–$5.50; main courses $4.50[nd]$12. MC, V. Thurs–Tues 7am–10pm.

**Nueva Zelanda** MEXICAN This clean, open-air snack shop serves rich cappuccino sprinkled with cinnamon, fresh-fruit *liquados* (milkshakes), and pancakes with real maple syrup. The mainstays of the menu are *tortas* and enchiladas, and service is friendly and efficient. Walk 3 blocks inland from the waterfront on Cuauhtémoc; the restaurant is on your right. There's a second location in Ixtapa, in the back section of the Los Patios shopping center (✆ **755/553-0838**).

Cuauhtémoc 23 (at Ejido). ✆ **755/554-2340.** Tortas $3.50; enchiladas $5; *liquados* $2.50; cappuccino $2.50. No credit cards. Daily 8am–10pm.

### Playa Madera & Playa La Ropa

**La Perla** SEAFOOD There are many *palapa*-style restaurants on Playa La Ropa, but La Perla, with tables under the trees and thatched roof, is the most popular. Somehow, the long stretch of pale sand and the group of wooden chairs under *palapas* combine with mediocre food and slow service to make La Perla a local tradition. Rumor has it that it is so hard to get the waiters' attention that you can get take-out food from a competitor and bring it here to eat, and they'll never notice. Still, it's considered the best spot for tanning and socializing. It's near the southern end of La Ropa Beach. Take the right fork in the road; there's a sign in the parking lot.

Playa La Ropa. ✆ **755/554-2700.** Breakfast $4–$6.50; main courses $7.50–$33.50. AE, MC, V. Daily 9am–10pm; breakfast served 10am–noon.

## IXTAPA & ZIHUATANEJO AFTER DARK

With an exception or two, Zihuatanejo nightlife dies down around 11pm or midnight. For a good selection of clubs, discos, hotel fiestas, special events, and fun watering holes with live music and dancing, head for Ixtapa. Just keep in mind that the shuttle bus stops at 11pm, and a taxi to Zihuatanejo after midnight costs 50% more than the regular price. During the off-season (after Easter and before Christmas), hours vary: Some places open only on weekends, while others close completely. In Zihuatanejo, the most popular hangout for local residents and ex-pats is **Paccolo,** around the corner from Amueblados Valle. It's the one place where you can find a lively crowd of locals almost every night.

### THE CLUB & MUSIC SCENE

Many discos and dance clubs stay open until the last customers leave, so closing hours depend upon revelers. Most discos have a "ladies' night" at least once a week—admission and drinks are free for women, making it easy for men to buy them a drink.

**Carlos 'n' Charlie's** Knee-deep in nostalgia, bric-a-brac, silly sayings, and photos from the Mexican Revolution, this restaurant-nightclub offers party ambience and good food. The eclectic menu includes iguana in season (with Alka-Seltzer and aspirin on the house). Out back by the beach is a partly shaded open-air section with a raised wooden platform for "pier dancing" at night. The recorded rock and roll mixes with sounds of the ocean surf. The restaurant is open daily from 10am to midnight; pier dancing is nightly from 9pm to 3am. Blvd. Ixtapa, just north of the Best Western Posada Real, Ixtapa. ✆ **755/553-0085.** Cover (including drink tokens) after 9pm for dancing $10. No cover Sun–Fri during off-season.

**Christine** This glitzy street-side disco is famous for its midnight light show, which features classical music played on a mega sound system. A semicircle of tables in tiers overlooks the dance floor. No tennis shoes, sandals, or shorts are allowed, and reservations are recommended during high season. Open daily at 10pm during high season. Off-season hours vary. In the Hotel Krystal, Blvd. Ixtapa, Ixtapa. ✆ **755/553-0456.** Cover free to $20.

**Señor Frog's** A companion restaurant to Carlos 'n' Charlie's, Señor Frog's has several dining sections and a warehouse-like bar with raised dance floors. Large speakers play rock and roll, sometimes prompting even dinner patrons to shimmy by their tables between courses. The restaurant is open daily from 6pm to midnight; the bar is open until 3am. In the La Puerta Center, Blvd. Ixtapa, Ixtapa. ✆ **755/553-2282.** No cover.

### HOTEL FIESTAS & THEME NIGHTS

Many hotels hold Mexican fiestas and other special events that include dinner, drinks, live music, and entertainment for a fixed price (generally $36). The **Barceló Ixtapa** (✆ **755/555-2000**) stages a popular Wednesday night fiesta; the **Krystal Hotel** (✆ **755/553-0333**) and **Dorado Pacífico** (✆ **755/553-2025**) in Ixtapa also hold good Mexican fiestas. The Barceló Ixtapa is the only one that offers them in the off-season. Call for reservations or visit a travel agency for tickets, and be sure you understand what the fixed price covers (drinks, tax, and tip are not always included).

## 3 Puerto Escondido ★★★

368km (230 miles) SE of Acapulco; 240km (150 miles) NW of Salina Cruz; 80km (50 miles) NW of Puerto Angel

I consider Puerto Escondido (*pwer*-toe es-con-*dee*-do) the best overall beach value in Mexico, from hotels to dining. Although it used to be known only for its ranking as one of the world's top surf sites, today it's broadening its appeal. Think alternative therapies, great vegetarian restaurants, hip nightlife, awesome hotel and dining values, and some of the best coffee shops in Mexico. It's a place for those whose priorities include the dimensions of the surf break (big), the temperature of a beer (cold), the strength of coffee (espresso), and the "OTA" (beach speak for "optimal tanning angle"). The young and very aware crowd that comes here measures time by the tides, and the pace is relaxed.

The location of "Puerto," as the locals call it, makes it an ideal jumping-off point for ecological explorations of neighboring jungle and estuary sanctuaries, as well as indigenous mountain settlements. Increasingly, it attracts those seeking both spiritual and physical renewal, with abundant massage and bodywork services, yoga classes, and exceptional and varied healthful dining options—not to mention seaside tranquility.

People come from the United States, Canada, and Europe to stay for weeks and even months—easily and inexpensively. Ex-pats have migrated here from Los Cabos, Acapulco, and Puerto Vallarta seeking what originally attracted them to their former homes—stellar beaches, friendly locals, and low prices. Added pleasures include an absence of beach vendors and time-share sales, an abundance of English speakers, and terrific, inexpensive dining and nightlife.

This is a real place, not a produced resort. A significant number of visitors are European travelers, and it's common to hear a variety of languages on the beach and in the bars. Solo travelers will probably make new friends within an hour of arriving. There are still scores of surfers here, lured by the best break in Mexico, but espresso cafes and live music are becoming just as ubiquitous, making an intriguing combo.

It's been dismissed as a colony of former hippies and settled backpackers, but it's so much more. I have a theory that those who favor "Puerto" are just trying to keep the place true to its name ("escondido" means "hidden") and undiscovered by tourists. Don't let them trick you—visit, and soon, before it, too, changes.

### ESSENTIALS

**GETTING THERE & DEPARTING** **By Plane** **Aerocaribe** and **Aerovega** (**© 954/582-2023** or 954/582-2024) operate daily flights to and from Oaxaca on small planes. Aerocaribe runs a morning and evening flight during high season; the fare is about $140 each way. Aerovega flies to and from Oaxaca once daily. The price is about $100 each way. **Rodimar Travel** (see below) sells tickets to both.

If flights to Puerto Escondido are booked, you have the (possibly less expensive) option of flying into **Huatulco** on a scheduled or charter flight. This is especially viable if your destination is Puerto Angel, which lies between Puerto Escondido and Huatulco. An airport taxi costs $60 to Puerto Angel, $85 to Puerto Escondido. If you can find a local taxi, rather than a government-chartered cab, you can reduce these fares by about 50%, including the payment of a $5 mandatory airport exit tax. There is frequent bus service between the three

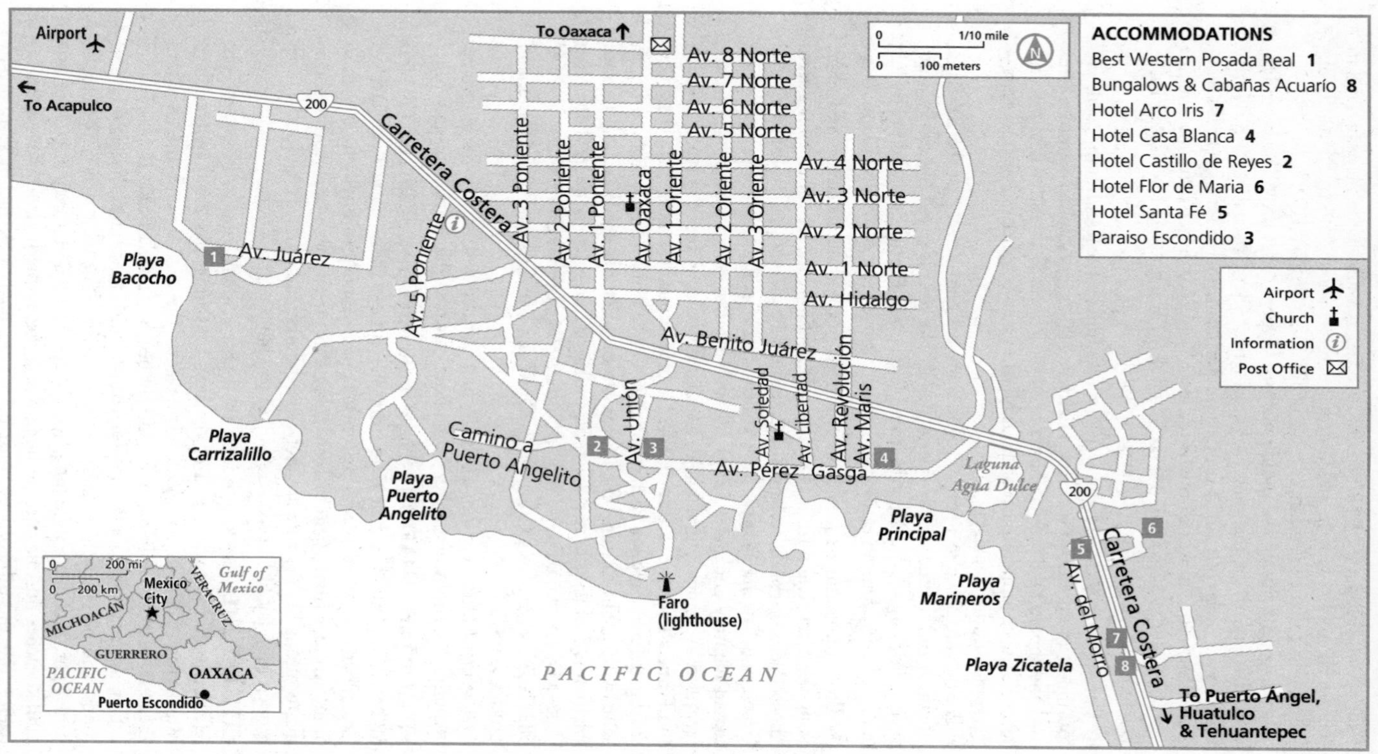
ACCOMMODATIONS
Best Western Posada Real 1
Bungalows & Cabañas Acuarío 8
Hotel Arco Iris 7
Hotel Casa Blanca 4
Hotel Castillo de Reyes 2
Hotel Flor de Maria 6
Hotel Santa Fé 5
Paraiso Escondido 3
Airport
Church
Information
Post Office
0 1/10 mile
0 100 meters
N
To Oaxaca
Airport
To Acapulco
To Puerto Ángel, Huatulco & Tehuantepec
Carretera Costera
200
Av. 8 Norte
Av. 7 Norte
Av. 6 Norte
Av. 5 Norte
Av. 4 Norte
Av. 3 Norte
Av. 2 Norte
Av. 1 Norte
Av. Hidalgo
Av. 3 Oriente
Av. 2 Oriente
Av. 1 Oriente
Av. Oaxaca
Av. 1 Poniente
Av. 2 Poniente
Av. 3 Poniente
Av. 5 Poniente
Av. Benito Juárez
Av. Revolución
Av. Maris
Av. Libertad
Av. Soledad
Av. Pérez Gasga
Av. Unión
Camino a Puerto Angelito
Av. Juárez
Av. del Morro
Laguna Agua Dulce
Playa Principal
Playa Marineros
Playa Zicatela
Playa Puerto Angelito
Playa Carrizalillo
Playa Bacocho
Faro (lighthouse)
PACIFIC OCEAN
Gulf of Mexico
VERACRUZ
Mexico City
MICHOACÁN
GUERRERO
OAXACA
Puerto Escondido
0 200 mi
0 200 km

destinations. **Budget** (✆ **958/581-9004**) has cars available for one-way travel to Puerto Escondido, with an added drop charge of about $10. In Puerto Escondido, Budget is at the entrance to Bacocho (✆ **954/582-0312**).

*Arriving:* The Puerto Escondido **airport** (airport code: PXM) is about 4km (2½ miles) north of the center of town, near Playa Bacocho. The *colectivo* **minibus** to hotels costs $2.25 per person. **Aerotransportes Terrestres** sells *colectivo* tickets to the airport through **Rodimar Travel,** on pedestrian-only Avenida Perez Gasga (✆ **954/582-0734;** fax 954/582-0737), next to Hotel Casa Blanca. The minibus will pick you up at your hotel.

**By Car** From Oaxaca, Highway 175 via Pochutla is the least bumpy road. The 150-mile trip takes 5 to 6 hours. Highway 200 from Acapulco is also a good road and should take about 5 hours to travel. However, this stretch of road has been the site of numerous car and bus hijackings and robberies in recent years—travel only during the day.

From Salina Cruz to Puerto Escondido is a 4-hour drive, past the Bahías de Huatulco and the turnoff for Puerto Angel. The road is paved but can be rutty during the rainy season. The trip from Huatulco to Puerto Escondido takes just under 2 hours; you can easily hire a taxi for a fixed rate of about $50 an hour.

**By Bus** Buses run frequently to and from Acapulco and Oaxaca, and south along the coast to and from Huatulco and Pochutla, the transit hub for Puerto Angel. Puerto Escondido's several bus stations are all within a 3-block area. For **Gacela** and **Estrella Blanca,** the station is just north of the intersection of the coastal highway and Pérez Gasga. First-class buses go from here to Pochutla, Huatulco, Acapulco, Zihuatanejo, and Mexico City. A block north at Hidalgo and Primera Poniente is **Transportes Oaxaca Istmo,** in a small restaurant. Several buses leave daily for Pochutla, Salina Cruz (5 hr.), and Oaxaca (10 hr. via Salina Cruz). The terminal for **Líneas Unidas, Estrella del Valle,** and **Oaxaca Pacífico** is 2 blocks farther down on Hidalgo, just past Oriente 3. They serve Oaxaca via Pochutla. From Primera Norte 207, **Cristóbal Colón** buses (✆ **954/582-1073**) serve Salina Cruz, Tuxtla Gutiérrez, San Cristóbal de las Casas, and Oaxaca.

*Arriving:* Minibuses from Pochutla or Huatulco will let you off anywhere, including the spot where Pérez Gasga leads down to the pedestrians-only zone.

**VISITOR INFORMATION** The **State Tourist Office, SEDETUR** (✆ **954/582-0175**), is about a half mile from the airport at the corner of Carretera Costera and Bulevard Benito Juárez. It's open Monday to Friday from 9am to 5pm, Saturday from 10am to 1pm. A kiosk at the airport is open for incoming flights during high season; another, near the west end of the paved tourist zone, is open Monday to Saturday from 9am to 1pm.

**CITY LAYOUT** Looking out on the Bahía Principal and its beach, to your left you'll see the eastern end of the bay, consisting of a small beach, **Playa Marineros,** followed by rocks jutting into the sea. Beyond this is **Playa Zicatela,** unmistakably the main surfing beach. Zicatela Beach has come into is own as the most popular area for visitors, with restaurants, bungalows, surf shops, and hotels, well back from the shoreline. The west side of the bay, to your right, is about a mile long, with a lighthouse and a long stretch of fine sand. Beaches on this end are not quite as accessible by land, but hotels are overcoming this difficulty by constructing beach clubs reached by steep private roads and Jeep shuttles.

The town of Puerto Escondido has roughly an east-west orientation, with the long Zicatela Beach turning sharply southeast. Residential areas behind (east of) Zicatela Beach tend to have unpaved streets; the older town (with paved streets) is north of the Carretera Costera (Hwy. 200). The streets are numbered; Avenida Oaxaca divides east (*oriente*) from west (*poniente*), and Avenida Hidalgo divides north (*norte*) from south (*sur*).

South of this is the original **tourist zone,** through which Avenida Pérez Gasga makes a loop. Part of this loop is a paved pedestrians-only zone, known locally as the *Adoquín,* after the hexagonal bricks used in its paving. Hotels, shops, restaurants, bars, travel agencies, and other services are all here. In the morning, taxis, delivery trucks, and private vehicles may drive here, but at noon it closes to all but foot traffic.

Avenida Pérez Gasga angles down from the highway at the east end; on the west, where the Adoquín terminates, it climbs in a wide northward curve to cross the highway, after which it becomes Avenida Oaxaca.

The beaches—Playa Principal in the center of town and Marineros and Zicatela, southeast of the town center—are connected. It's easy to walk from one to the other, crossing behind the separating rocks. Puerto Angelito, Carrizalillo, and Bacocho beaches are west of town and accessible by road or water. Playa Bacocho is where you'll find the few more-expensive hotels.

**GETTING AROUND** Almost everything is within walking distance of the Adoquín. **Taxis** around town are inexpensive; call ✆ **954/582-0990** for service. You can rent mountain bikes, motorcycles, and cars at **Arrendadora Express,** Pérez Gasga 605-E (✆ **954/582-1355**), on your right just as you enter the Adoquín on the east. Bikes rentals run about $5 per day, $15 per week.

It's easy to hire a boat, and possible to walk beside the sea from the Playa Principal to the tiny beach of Puerto Angelito, though it's a bit of a hike.

## *FAST FACTS:* Puerto Escondido

*Area Code* The telephone area code is **954.**

*Currency Exchange* Banamex, Bancomer, Bancrear, and Banco Bital all have branches in town, and all will change money during business hours; hours vary, but you can generally find one of the above open Monday to Saturday from 8am to 7pm. Automatic tellers are also available, as are currency-exchange offices.

*Hospital* **Unidad Medico–Quirurgica del Sur,** Av. Oaxaca 113 (✆ **954/582-1288**), offers 24-hour emergency services and has an English-speaking staff and doctors.

*Internet Access* The restaurant Un Tigre Azul, on the Adoquín, has an excellent cybercafe on its second floor (✆ **954/582-1871**). It charges $2 for 30 minutes, $4 per hour for Internet access. It's open Monday to Friday from 11am to 11pm, Saturday and Sunday 3 to 11pm. On Zicatela Beach, **Cyber-café** is a small, extremely busy Internet service at the entrance to the Bungalows & Cabañas Acuario, Calle de Morro s/n (✆ **954/582-0357**). It's open daily from 8am to 9pm. It charges just $1.50 for 15 minutes, $3 for a half-hour, or $5 per hour—but had painfully slow, older computers when I was last there.

*Pharmacy* **Farmacia de Mas Ahorro,** Avenida 1 Norte at Avenida 2 Poniente (✆ **954/582-1911**), is open 24 hours a day.

*Post Office* The *correo,* on Avenida Oaxaca at the corner of Avenida 7 Norte (✆ **954/582-0959**), is open Monday to Friday from 8am to 4pm, Saturday from 8am to 1pm.

*Safety* Depending on whom you talk to, you need to be wary of potential beach muggings, primarily at night. New lighting at Playa Principal has caused the crime rate to drop considerably, and installation of new lighting at Playa Zicatela is planned. Local residents say most incidents happen after tourists overindulge and then go for a midnight stroll along the beach. It's so casual that it's an easy place to let your guard down. Don't carry valuables, and use common sense and normal precautions.

Also, respect the power of the magnificent waves here. Drownings occur all too frequently.

*Seasons* Season designations are somewhat arbitrary, but most consider high season to be mid-December to January, around and during Easter week, July and August, and during other school and business vacations.

*Telephones* Numerous businesses offer long-distance telephone service. Many are along the Adoquín; several accept credit cards. The best bet remains a prepaid Ladatel phone card.

## BEACH TIME

**BEACHES** **Playa Principal,** where small boats are available for fishing and tour services, and **Playa Marineros,** adjacent to the town center on a deep bay, are the best swimming beaches. Beach chairs and sun shades rent for about $2, which may be waived if you order food or drinks from the restaurants that offer them. **Zicatela Beach,** which has lifeguards, adjoins Playa Marineros and extends southeast for several kilometers. The surfing part of Zicatela, with large curling waves, is about 2.5km (1½ miles) from the town center. Due to the size and strength of the waves here, it's not a swimming beach, and only experienced surfers should attempt to ride Zicatela's powerful waves. Stadium-style lighting has been installed in both of these beach areas, in an attempt to crack down on nocturnal beach muggings. It has diminished the appeal of the Playa Principal restaurants—patrons now look into the bright lights rather than at the nighttime sea.

Barter with one of the fishermen on the main beach for a ride to **Playa Manzanillo** and **Puerto Angelito,** two beaches separated by a rocky outcropping. Here, and at other small coves just west of town, swimming is safe and the overall pace is calmer than in town. You'll also find *palapas,* hammock rentals, and snorkeling equipment. The clear blue water is perfect for snorkeling. Enjoy fresh fish, tamales, and other Mexican dishes cooked right at the beach by local entrepreneurs. Puerto Angelito is also accessible by a dirt road that's a short distance from town, so it tends to be busier. **Playa Bacocho** is on a shallow cove farther northwest and is best reached by taxi or boat, rather than on foot. It's also the location of Coco's Beach Club at the Posada Real Hotel. They are open to the public, for a cover charge of $2.50, which gives you access to their pools, food and beverage service, and facilities.

## Ecotours & Other Adventurous Explorations

**Turismo Rodimar Travel Agency,** on the landward side just inside the Adoquín (© **954/582-0734;** fax 954/582-0737; open daily 8am to 10pm), is an excellent source of information and can arrange all types of tours and travel. Manager Gaudencio Díaz speaks English and can arrange individualized tours or more organized ones, such as **Michael Malone's Hidden Voyages Ecotours.** Malone, a Canadian ornithologist, takes you on a dawn or sunset trip to **Manialtepec Lagoon,** a bird-filled mangrove lagoon about 19km (12 miles) northwest of Puerto Escondido. The tour ($32) includes a stop on a secluded beach for a swim.

Another exceptional provider of ecologically oriented tour services is **Ana's Eco Tours** ★★, in Un Tigre Azul restaurant, on the Adoquín (© **954/582-1871** or 954/582-2001; ana@anasecotours.com). "Ana" Marquez was born in the small nearby mountain village of Jamiltepec, and has an intimate knowledge of the customs, people, flora, and fauna of the area. She and her expert guides lead small groups on both eco-adventures and cultural explorations. Tours into the surrounding mountains include a 5-hour horseback excursion up to the jungle region of the Chatino natives' **healing hot springs,** or to **Nopala,** a Chatino mountain village, and a neighboring coffee plantation. An all-day trip to **Jamiltepec** (a small, traditional Mixtex village) offers the opportunity to experience day-to-day life in an authentic village. It includes a stop at a market, church, and cemetery, and visits to the homes of local artisans.

One of the most popular all-day tours offered by both companies is to **Chacahua Lagoon National Park,** about 67km (42 miles) west. It costs $35 with Rodimar, $25 with Ana's. These are true ecotours—small groups treading lightly. You visit a beautiful sandy spit of beach and the lagoon, which has incredible bird life and flowers, including black orchids. Locals provide fresh barbecued fish on the beach. If you know Spanish and get information from the tourism office, it's possible to stay overnight under a small *palapa,* but bring plenty of insect repellent.

An interesting, slightly out-of-the-ordinary excursion is **Aventura Submarina,** Calle del Morro s/n, in the Acuario building near the Cafecito, Zicatela Beach (© **954/582-2353**). Jorge, who speaks fluent English and is a certified scuba instructor, guides individuals or small groups of qualified divers along the Coco trench, just offshore. Price is $62 for a two-tank dive, $39 for a one-tank dive. The company offers a refresher course at no extra charge. Jorge also arranges surface activities such as deep-sea fishing, surfing, and trips to lesser-known nearby swimming beaches. The mailing address is Apdo. Postal 159, Puerto Escondido, 71980 Oax.

Fishermen keep their colorful *pangas* (small boats) on the beach beside the Adoquín. A **fisherman's tour** around the coastline in a *panga* costs about $39, but a ride to Zicatela or Puerto Angelito beaches is only $5. Most hotels offer or will gladly arrange tours to meet your needs.

**SURFING** **Zicatela Beach,** 2.5km (1½ miles) southeast of Puerto Escondido's town center, is a world-class surf spot. A surfing competition in August and Fiesta Puerto Escondido, held for at least 3 days each November, celebrate Puerto Escondido's renowned waves. The tourism office can supply dates and details. Beginning surfers often start out at Playa Marineros before graduating to Zicatela's awesome waves.

**NESTING RIDLEY TURTLES** The beaches around Puerto Escondido and Puerto Angel are nesting grounds for the endangered Ridley turtle. During the summer, tourists can sometimes see the turtles laying eggs or observe the hatchlings trekking to the sea.

**Escobilla Beach** near Puerto Escondido and **Barra de la Cruz Beach** near Puerto Angel seem to be the favored nesting grounds of the Ridley turtle. In 1991, the Mexican government established the Centro Mexicano la Tortuga, known locally as the **Turtle Museum**. On view are examples of all species of marine turtles living in Mexico, plus six species of freshwater turtles and two species of land turtles. The center (no phone) is on **Mazunte Beach,** near the town of the same name. Hours are 10am to 4:30pm Tuesday to Saturday, 10am to 2pm Sunday; admission is $2.50. The museum has a unique shop that sells excellent naturally produced shampoos, bath oils, and other personal-care products. All are made and packaged by the local community as part of a project to replace lost income from turtle poaching. Buses go to Mazunte from Puerto Angel about every half hour, and a taxi ride is around $5.50. You can fit this in with a trip to Zipolite Beach. Buses from Puerto Escondido don't stop in Mazunte; you can cover the 65 km (40 miles) in a taxi or rental car.

## SHOPPING

During high season, businesses and shops are generally open all day. During low season, they close between 2 and 5pm.

The Adoquín holds a row of tourist shops selling straw hats, postcards, and T-shirts, plus a few excellent shops featuring Guatemalan, Oaxacan, and Balinese clothing and art. You can also get a tattoo or rent surfboards and boogie boards. Interspersed among the shops, hotels, restaurants, and bars are pharmacies and mini-markets. The largest of these is **Oh! Mar,** Av. Pérez Gasga 502, (**© 954/582-0286**). It sells anything you'd need for a day at the beach, plus phone (Ladatel) cards, stamps, and Cuban cigars, has a mail drop box, and arranges fishing tours.

Highlights along the Adoquín include **Casa di Bambole,** Av. Pérez Gasga 707 (**© 954/582-1331**), for high-quality clothing, bags, and jewelry from Guatemala and Chiapas; and **La Luna,** Av. Pérez Gasga s/n (no phone), for jewelry, Batik surf wear, and Balinese art. The name of **1000 Hamacas,** Av. Pérez Gasga s/n (no phone), says it all. Custom-made hammocks in all colors—the favored way to take a siesta here—may double as your bedding if you're staying in one of the numerous surfer hangouts on Zicatela Beach. **Central Surf** has a shop on the Adoquín (**© 954/582-0568**) and another on Zicatela Beach, Calle del Morro s/n (**© 954/582-2285**). They rent and sell surfboards, offer surf lessons, and sell related gear. **Un Tigre Azul,** Av. Pérez Gasga s/n (**© 954/582-1871**), is the only true art gallery in town, with quality work and a cafe-bar, plus Internet service upstairs.

Also of interest is **Bazaar Santa Fe,** Hotel Santa Fe lobby, Calle del Morro s/n, Zicatela Beach (**© 954/582-0170**), which sells antiques, including vintage Oaxacan embroidered clothing, jewelry, and religious artifacts. At **Bikini Brazil,**

Calle del Morro s/n (no phone), you'll find the hottest bikinis under the sun, imported from Brazil, land of the *tanga* (string bikini). In front of the Rockaway Resort on Zicatela Beach, there's a 24-hour **mini-super** (no phone) that sells the necessities: beer, suntan lotion, and basic food.

## WHERE TO STAY

### MODERATE

**Best Western Posada Real** *Kids* Set on a clifftop overlooking the beach, the expanse of manicured lawn that backs the hotel is one of the most popular places in town for a sunset cocktail. The smallish standard rooms are less enticing than the hotel grounds. A big plus here is Coco's Beach Club, with a half-mile stretch of soft-sand beach, large swimming pool, playground, and bar with occasional live music. A shuttle ride (or a lengthy walk down a set of stairs) will take you there. This is a great place for families, and it's open to the public ($2.50 cover for nonguests). The hotel is 5 minutes from the airport and about the same from Puerto Escondido's tourist zone, but you'll need a taxi to get to town.

Av. Benito Juárez 1, Fracc. Bacocho, 71980 Puerto Escondido, Oax. ✆ **800/528-1234** in the U.S., 954/582-0133, or 954/582-0237. Fax 954/582-0192. 100 units. High season $130 double; low season $104 double. AE, DC, MC, V. **Amenities:** 2 restaurants, lobby bar, beach club with food service; 2 swimming pools; 1 wading pool; tennis courts; putting green; travel agency; car rental; laundry. *In room:* A/C, TV, hair dryer, safe-deposit box.

**Hotel Santa Fe** ★★★ *Finds* If Puerto Escondido is the best beach value in Mexico, then the Santa Fe is without a doubt one of the best hotel values in Mexico. It boasts a winning combination of unique Spanish-colonial style, a welcoming staff, and comfortable rooms. The hotel has grown up with the surfers who came to Puerto in the 1960s and 1970s—and nostalgically return today. It's a half a mile southeast of the town center, off Highway 200, at the curve in the road where Marineros and Zicatela beaches join—a prime sunset-watching spot. The three-story hacienda-style buildings have clay-tiled stairs, archways, and blooming bougainvillea. They surround two courtyard swimming pools. The ample but simply stylish rooms feature large tile bathrooms, colonial furnishings, handwoven fabrics, Guerrero pottery lamps, and both air-conditioning and ceiling fans. Most have a balcony or terrace, with ocean views from upper floors. Bungalows are next to the hotel; each has a living room, kitchen, and bedroom with two double beds. The restaurant (see "Where to Dine," below) is one of the best on the southern Pacific coast.

Calle del Morro (Apdo. Postal 96), 71980 Puerto Escondido, Oax. ✆ **954/582-0170** or 954/582-0266. Fax 954/582-0260. info@hotelsantafe.com.mx. 69 units, 8 bungalows. High season $100 double, $120 bungalow; low season $78 double, $100 bungalow. AE, MC, V. Free parking. **Amenities:** Restaurant and bar; swimming pool; lap pool; massage; tour service; babysitting; laundry. *In room:* A/C, TV, security box.

**Paraíso Escondido** ★★★ *Finds* This eclectic inn is hidden away on a shady street a couple of short blocks from the Adoquín and Playa Principal. A curious collection of Mexican folk art, masks, religious art, and paintings make this an exercise in Mexican magic realism, in addition to a tranquil place to stay. An inviting pool, surrounded by gardens, Adirondack chairs, and a fountain, affords a commanding view of the bay. The rooms each have one double and one twin bed, built-in desks, and a cozy balcony or terrace with French doors. Each has a different decorative accent, and all are very clean. The suites have much plusher decor than the rooms, with recessed lighting, desks set into bay windows, living areas, and large private balconies. The penthouse suite has a whirlpool tub and kitchenette, a tile chessboard inlaid in the floor, and murals adorning the walls—it is the owners' former apartment.

Calle Union 10, 71980 Puerto Escondido, Oax. ✆ **954/582-0444.** 25 units. $77 double; $150 suite. No credit cards. Limited free parking. **Amenities:** Restaurant, bar; pool; tour desk. *In room:* A/C.

## INEXPENSIVE

**Bungalows & Cabañas Acuario** ★ Facing Zicatela Beach, this surfer's sanctuary offers cheap accommodations plus an on-site gym, surf shop, vegetarian restaurant, and Internet cafe. The two-story hotel and bungalows surround a pool shaded by great palms. Rooms are small and basic; bungalows offer fundamental kitchen facilities but don't have air-conditioning. The *cabañas* are more open and have hammocks. There are public telephones, money exchange, a pharmacy, and a vegetarian restaurant in the adjoining commercial area. The well-equipped gym costs an extra $1 per day, $15 per month. If you're traveling during low season, you can probably negotiate a better deal than the rates listed below once you're there.

Calle del Morro s/n, 71980 Puerto Escondido, Oax. ✆ **954/582-0357** or 954/582-1026. 40 units. High season $53 double, $62 double with A/C, $89 bungalow; low season $28 double, $34 double with A/C, $45 bungalow. No credit cards. **Amenities:** Restaurant; gym.

**Hotel Arco Iris** ★ *Value* Rooms at the Arco Iris are in a three-story colonial style house that faces Zicatela Beach. Each is simple yet comfortable, with a spacious terrace or balcony with hangers for hammocks—all have great views, but the upstairs ones are better. Beds are draped with mosquito nets, and bedspreads are made with beautifully worked Oaxacan textiles. La Galera bar has one of the most popular happy hours in town, daily from 5 to 7pm, with live music during high season. Ample free parking for cars and campers is available.

Calle del Morro s/n, Playa Zicatela, 71980 Puerto Escondido, Oax. ✆ and fax **954/582-0432,** 954/582-1494, and 954582-2344. www.qan.com/Hotels/Arcoiris. 26 rooms, 8 bungalows. $42–$46 double, $46–$50 double with kitchen. Extra person $4. Rates 10%–20% higher at Easter and Christmas. MC, V. **Amenities:** Restaurant, bar; pool; wading pool; TV/game room with foreign channels; drugstore; tour desk; on-call medical services.

**Hotel Casa Blanca** ★ *Value* If you want to be in the heart of the Adoquín, this is your best bet for excellent value and ample accommodations. The courtyard pool and adjacent *palapa* restaurant make a great place to hide away and enjoy a margarita or a book from the hotel's exchange rack. The bright, simply furnished rooms offer a choice of bed combinations, but all have at least two beds and a fan. Some rooms have both air-conditioning and a mini-fridge. The best rooms have a balcony overlooking the action in the street below, but light sleepers should consider a room in the back. Some rooms accommodate up to five ($60). This is an excellent and economical choice for families.

Av. Pérez Gasga 905, 71980 Puerto Escondido, Oax. ✆ **954/582-0168.** 21 units. $29 double, $84 double with A/C. MC, V. **Amenities:** Restaurant; pool; in-room massage; money exchange; tour desk; car rental; room service; safe-deposit boxes. *In room:* TV.

**Hotel Castillo de Reyes** Proprietor Don Fernando has a knack for making his guests feel at home. Guests chat around tables on a shady patio near the office. Most of the bright, white-walled rooms have a special touch—perhaps a gourd mask or carved coconut hanging over the bed, plus over-bed reading lights. The rooms are shaded from the sun by palms and cooled by fans. The "castle" is on your left as you ascend the hill on Pérez Gasga, after leaving the Adoquín (you can also enter Pérez Gasga off Hwy. 200). This hotel is on one of Puerto's busiest streets, so traffic noise is a consideration.

Av. Pérez Gasga s/n, 71980 Puerto Escondido, Oax. ✆ **954/582-0442.** 18 units. High season $25 double; low season $21 double. No credit cards. **Amenities:** Safe-deposit box; money exchange.

**Hotel Flor de María** ★★ Though not right on the beach, this is a real find. Canadians María and Lino Francato own the cheery, three-story hotel facing the ocean, which you can see from the rooftop. Built around a garden courtyard, each room is colorfully decorated with beautiful trompe l'oeil still lifes and landscapes painted by Lino. Two rooms have windows with a view, and the rest face the courtyard. All have double beds with orthopedic mattresses. The roof has a small pool, a shaded hammock terrace, and an open-air bar (open 5–9pm during high season) with a TV that receives American channels—all in all, a great sunset spot. I highly recommend the first-floor restaurant (see "Where to Dine," below). The hotel is a third of a mile from the Adoquín, 60m (200 ft.) up a sandy road from Marineros Beach on an unnamed street at the eastern end of the beach.

Playa Marineros, 71980 Puerto Escondido, Oax. ✆ and fax **954/582-0536.** 24 units. $35–$50 double. Ask about off-season long-term discounts. MC, V. **Amenities:** Restaurant, bar; small pool.

## WHERE TO DINE

In addition to the places listed below, a Puerto Escondido tradition is the *palapa* restaurants on Zicatela Beach, for early-morning surfer breakfasts, or casual dining and drinking at night. One of the most popular is **Los Tíos,** offering economical prices and surfer-sized portions. After dinner, enjoy homemade Italian ice cream from **Gelateria Giardino.** It has two locations, on Calle del Morro at Zicatela Beach, and Pérez Gasga 609, on the Adoquín (✆ **954/582-2243**).

### MODERATE

**Art & Harry's** SEAFOOD/STEAKS About three-quarters of a mile southeast of the Hotel Santa Fe, on the road fronting Zicatela Beach, this robust watering hole is great for taking in the sunset, especially if you're having a giant hamburger or grilled shrimp dinner. Late afternoon and early evening here are like watching a portrait of Puerto Escondido come to life. You sit watching the surfers, tourists, and resident cat as the sun dips into the ocean.

Av. Morro s/n. No phone. Main courses $4.50–$15. No credit cards. Daily 10am–10pm.

**Cabo Blanco** ★★ INTERNATIONAL "Where Legends are Born" is the logo at this beachfront restaurant, and the local crowd craves Gary's special sauces, which top his grilled fish, shrimp, steaks, and ribs. Favorites include dill–Dijon mustard, wine-fennel, and Thai curry sauces. But you can't count on them, because Gary creates based on what's fresh. A bonus is that Cabo Blanco turns into a hot Zicatela Beach bar, with live music Thursday and Saturday after 11pm. Gary's wife, Roxana, and an all-female bartending team keeps the crowd well served and well behaved.

Calle del Morro s/n. ✆ **954/582-0337.** Main courses $7–$45. V. Dec–May daily 6pm–2am. Closed June–Nov.

**Restaurant Santa Fe** ★★★ *Finds* INTERNATIONAL The atmosphere here is classic and casual, with great views of the sunset and Zicatela Beach. Big pots of palms are scattered around and fresh flowers grace the tables, all beneath a lofty *palapa* roof. The shrimp dishes are a bargain for the rest of the world, though, at $15, a little higher-priced than in the rest of town. Perfectly grilled tuna, served with homemade french-fried potatoes and whole-grain bread, is an incredible meal at under $10. A *nopal* (cactus leaf) salad on the side ($2.50) is a perfect complement. Vegetarian dishes are reasonably priced and creatively adapted from traditional Mexican and Italian dishes. A favorite is the house specialty, chiles rellenos. The bar offers an excellent selection of tequilas.

In the Hotel Santa Fe, Calle del Morro s/n. ✆ **954/582-0170.** Breakfast $4.50–$6; main courses $5–$15. AE, MC, V. Daily 7am–11pm.

### INEXPENSIVE

**Arte la Galería** INTERNATIONAL/SEAFOOD At the east end of the Adoquín, La Galería offers a satisfying range of eats in a cool, creative setting. Dark-wood beams tower above, contemporary works by local artists grace the walls, and jazz music plays. Specialties are homemade pastas and brick-oven pizzas, but burgers and steaks are also available. Cappuccino and espresso, plus desserts such as baked pineapples, finish the meal.

Av. Pérez Gasga. ✆ **954/582-2039.** Breakfast $2.50–$3; main courses $4–$12.50. No credit cards. Daily 8am–midnight.

**Carmen's La Patisserie** ★★ FRENCH PASTRY/SANDWICHES/COFFEE This tiny, excellent cafe and bakery has a steady and loyal clientele. Carmen's baked goods are unforgettable and sell quickly, so arrive early for the best selection. She also provides space for an English-speaking AA group. La Patisserie is across the street from the Hotel Flor de María.

Playa Marineros. No phone. Pastries 60¢–$1.50; sandwiches $2.10–$2.70. No credit cards. Mon–Sat 7am–3pm; Sun 7am–noon.

**El Cafecito** ★★ FRENCH PASTRY/SEAFOOD/VEGETARIAN/COFFEE Carmen's second shop opened a few years ago on Zicatela Beach, with the motto "Big waves, strong coffee!" Featuring all the attractions of Carmen's La Patisserie (above), it also serves lunch and dinner. This restaurant spans two facing corners. The northern corner is set up for coffee or a light snack, with oceanfront bistro-style seating. The southern corner, a more relaxed setting, has wicker chairs and Oaxacan cloth–topped tables under a *palapa* roof. Giant shrimp dinners cost less than $6, and creative daily specials are always a sure bet. An oversized mug of cappuccino is $1.20, a fresh and filling fruit smoothie goes for $1.80, and a mango éclair—worth any price—is a steal at $1.20.

Calle del Morro s/n, Playa Zicatela. No phone. Pastries 60¢–$1.50; main courses $2.10–$5.70. No credit cards. Wed–Mon 6am–10pm.

**El Gota de Vida** ★★ *Value* VEGETARIAN/COFFEE Located just in front of the Bungalows Acuario, this popular vegetarian restaurant facing Zicatela Beach is generally packed. It's known for its healthy food, ample portions, and low prices. Under a *palapa* roof, it offers an extensive menu that includes fruit smoothies, espresso drinks, herbal teas, and a complete juice bar. The restaurant makes its own tempeh, tofu, pastas, and whole-grain breads. Creative vegetarian offerings are based on Mexican favorites, like chiles rellenos, cheese enchiladas, and bean tostadas. El Gota de Vida also features fresh seafood.

Calle del Morro s/n, Playa Zicatela. No phone. Main courses $1.80–$5.40. No credit cards. Daily 10am–11pm.

**Herman's Best** MEXICAN/SEAFOOD This small restaurant's atmosphere is about as basic as it comes, but clearly the kitchen is putting all its attention into the simply delicious, home-style cooking. The menu changes daily, but generally includes a fresh fish filet, rotisserie chicken, and Mexican specials like enchiladas—all served with beans, rice, and homemade tortillas. Herman's Best is just outside the pedestrian-only zone at the eastern end of the Adoquín.

Ave. Pez Gasga s/n. No phone. Main entrees $1.80–$4.20. No credit cards. Mon–Sat 5–10pm.

**María's Restaurant** ★★ INTERNATIONAL This open-air hotel dining room near the beach is popular with the locals. The menu changes daily and features specials such as María Francato's fresh homemade pasta dishes. María's is a third of a mile from the Adoquín, 60m (200 ft.) up a sandy road from Marineros Beach on an unnamed street at the eastern end of the beach.

In the Hotel Flor de María, Playa Marineros. ✆ **954/582-0536.** Breakfast $3; main courses $3.60–$6. No credit cards. Daily 8–11:30am, noon–2pm, and 6–10pm.

**Un Tigre Azul** SANDWICHES/COFFEE/MEXICAN This place is primarily known for its lower-level art gallery and Internet access, but climb on up to the third floor and enjoy the view overlooking Playa Principal and the ambience of the casual, colorful cafe. It's near the western entrance to the Adoquín. The light fare includes quesadillas, nachos, fruit smoothies, and sandwiches. There's also excellent coffee and a full bar. Happy hour is every night from 7 to 8pm.

Av. Pérez Gasga s/n. ✆ **954/582-1871.** Breakfast $2–$4; sandwiches $2–$5. AE MC, V. Mon–Fri 11am–11pm; Sat–Sun 3–11pm.

## PUERTO ESCONDIDO AFTER DARK

Sunset-watching is a ritual to plan your days around, and good lookout points abound. Watch the surfers at Zicatela and catch up on local gossip at **La Galera,** on the third floor of the Arco Iris hotel. It has a nightly happy hour (with live music during high season) from 5 to 7pm. Other great sunset spots are the **Hotel Santa Fe,** at the junction of Zicatela and Marineros beaches, and the rooftop bar of **Hotel Flor de María.** For a more tranquil, romantic setting, take a cab or walk half an hour or so west to the **Hotel Posada Real.** The hotel's clifftop lawn is a perfect sunset perch. Or climb down the cliff side (or take the hotel shuttle bus) to Coco's on the beach below.

Puerto Escondido is beginning to develop its cultural side. At **The Library,** on the main street of Zicatela Beach (a few blocks past the Hotel Santa Fe), you can play chess or backgammon, browse through a selection of books for sale, take a Spanish class, or just enjoy an espresso or drink. Farther down the street at the southern end of Calle del Morro, **Surf Papaya** restaurant has an upstairs art gallery. The **Cine Club** at the Rinconada movie theater shows new releases in air-conditioned comfort. Movies are shown Friday through Sunday at 7:30pm. A free shuttle runs from El Cafecito on Zicatela Beach Saturday and Sunday at 7pm.

Puerto's nightlife will satisfy anyone dedicated to late nights and good music. Most nightspots are open until 3am or until the customers leave. **Son y la Rumba** features live jazz, by its house band with Andria Garcia, each night from 8 to 11pm. The cover is $1.20. It's beneath the Un Tigre Azul, on the western end of the Adoquín. Also downtown is **Tequila Sunrise,** a spacious two-story disco overlooking the beach. It plays Latino, reggae, *cumbia,* tropical, and salsa. It's a half a block from the Adoquín on Avenida Marina Nacional. A small cover charge ($1.20–$2.40) generally applies.

The Adoquín offers an ample selection of clubs. Among them is the **Bucanero Bar and Grill,** with a good-sized bar and outdoor patio fronting Playa Principal. **Bar Fly, The Blue Iguana,** and **Rayos X** cater to a younger surf crowd with alternative and techno tunes. **Montezuma's Revenge** has live bands that usually play contemporary Latin American music. **El Tubo** is an open-air beachside disco just west of Restaurant Alicia on the Adoquín.

*Tips* **Important Travel Note**

Although car and bus hijackings along Highway 200 north to Acapulco have greatly decreased, thanks to improved security measures and police patrols, you're still wise to travel this road only during the day.

On Zicatela Beach, don't miss **Cabo Blanco** (see "Where to Dine," above), where local musicians get together and jam Thursdays and Saturdays during high season. **Split Coco,** a few doors down, has live music on Tuesday and Friday, and TV sports on other nights. It has one of the most popular happy hours on the beach, and also serves barbecue.

## A TRIP TO PUERTO ANGEL: BACKPACKING BEACH HAVEN

Eighty kilometers (50 miles) southeast of Puerto Escondido and 48km (30 miles) northwest of the Bays of Huatulco is the tiny fishing port of **Puerto Angel** (*pwer*-toe *ahn*-hel). Puerto Angel, with its beautiful beaches, unpaved streets, and budget hotels, is popular with the international backpacking set and those seeking an inexpensive and restful vacation. Though damage from 1997's Hurricane Paulina was compounded by earthquake damage in 1999, Puerto Angel continues to attract visitors. Its small bay and several inlets offer peaceful swimming and good snorkeling. The village's way of life is slow and simple: Fishermen leave very early in the morning and return with their catch before noon. Taxis make up most of the traffic, and the bus from Pochutla passes every half hour or so.

### ESSENTIALS

**GETTING THERE & DEPARTING** **By Car** North or south from Highway 200, take coastal Highway 175 inland to Puerto Angel. The road is well marked with signs to Puerto Angel. From either Huatulco or Puerto Escondido, the trip should take about an hour.

**By Taxi** Taxis are readily available to take you to Puerto Angel or Zipolite Beach for a reasonable price, or to the Huatulco airport or Puerto Escondido.

**By Bus** There are no direct buses from Puerto Escondido or Huatulco to Puerto Angel; however, numerous buses leave Puerto Escondido and Huatulco for Pochutla, 11km (7 miles) north of Puerto Angel. Take the bus to Pochutla, then switch to a bus going to Puerto Angel. If you arrive in Pochutla from Huatulco or Puerto Escondido, you may be dropped at one of several bus stations that line the main street; walk 1 or 2 blocks toward the large sign reading POSADA DON JOSE. The buses to Puerto Angel are in the lot just before the sign.

**ORIENTATION** The town center is only about 4 blocks long, oriented more or less east-west. There are few signs in the village, and off the main street much of Puerto Angel is a narrow sand-and-dirt path. The navy base is toward the west end of town, just before the creek crossing toward Playa Panteón (Cemetery Beach).

Puerto Angel has several public (Ladatel) telephones that use widely available prepaid phone cards. The closest bank is **Bancomer** in Pochutla, which changes money Monday to Friday from 9am to 6pm, Saturday from 9am to 1pm. The **post office** (*correo*), open Monday to Friday from 9am to 3:30pm, is on the curve as you enter town.

## BEACHES, WATERSPORTS & BOAT TRIPS

The golden sands and peaceful village life of Puerto Angel are all the reasons you'll need to visit. Playa Principal, the main beach, lies between the Mexican navy base and the pier that's home to the local fishing fleet. Near the pier, fishermen pull their colorful boats on the beach and unload their catch in the late morning while trucks wait to haul it off to processing plants in Veracruz. The rest of the beach seems light years from the world of work and purpose. Except on Mexican holidays, it's relatively deserted. It's important to note that Pacific Coast currents deposit trash on Puerto Angel beaches. The locals do a fairly good job of keeping it picked up, but the currents are constant.

**Playa Panteón** is the main swimming and snorkeling beach. "Cemetery Beach," ominous as that sounds, is about a 15-minute walk from the town center, straight through town on the main street that skirts the beach. The *panteón* (cemetery), on the right, is worth a visit—it holds brightly colored tombstones and equally brilliant blooming bougainvillea.

In Playa Panteón, some of the *palapa* restaurants and a few of the hotels rent snorkeling and scuba gear and can arrange boat trips, but they tend to be expensive. Check the quality and condition of gear—particularly scuba gear—that you're renting.

**Playa Zipolite** (*see*-poh-lee-tay) and its village are 6km (4 miles) down a paved road from Puerto Angel. Taxis charge less than $2. You can catch a *colectivo* on the main street in the town center and share the cost.

Zipolite is well known as a good surf break and as a nude beach. Although public nudity (including topless sunbathing) is technically illegal, it's allowed here—this is one of only a handful of beaches in Mexico that permits it. This sort of open-mindedness has attracted an increasing number of young European travelers. Most sunbathers concentrate beyond a large rock outcropping at the far end of the beach. Police will occasionally patrol the area, but they are much more intent on drug users than on sunbathers. The ocean and currents here are quite strong (that's why the surf is so good!), and a number of drownings have occurred over the years—know your limits. There are places to tie up a hammock and a few *palapa* restaurants for a light lunch and a cold beer.

Hotels in Playa Zipolite are basic and rustic; most have rugged walls and palapa roofs. Prices range from $10 to $50 a night, with the highest prices on Mexican holidays.

Traveling north on Highway 175, you'll come to another hot surf break and a beach of spectacular beauty: **Playa San Augustinillo.** One of the pleasures of a stay in Puerto Angel is discovering the many hidden beaches nearby and spending the day. Local boatmen can give details and quote rates for this service, or ask at your hotel.

## A PLACE TO STAY AND DINE

You can stay in Puerto Angel near Playa Principal in the tiny town, or at Playa Panteón. Most accommodations are basic, older, cement-block style hotels, not meriting a full-blown description. Between Playa Panteón and town are several bungalow and guesthouse setups with budget accommodations. The hotel below is the one place in town worth making reservations for.

**Posada Cañon Devata** ★★ *Finds* One of the most inviting places in Puerto Angel, this hotel is a 3-minute walk almost straight up from Playa Panteón. Americans Suzanne and Mateo López and their daughter Kali run this ecologically sound, homey, cool, green-and-wooded oasis in a narrow canyon. Rooms are agreeably rustic chic, with fans, beds covered in Guatemalan tie-dyed cloth, and Mateo's paintings hanging on the walls (the paintings are for sale). Room configurations vary; five of the six bungalows have bathrooms. I love the Sand Room, with its expansive, sunny windows and constant breezes. Don't miss climbing to the rooftop terrace, El Cielo, to see the bay bathed in the light of the setting sun. It holds a small bar that's open each evening during sunset. At other times, the terrace makes a peaceful place for sunbathing or a morning yoga session. The Lopezes can arrange pick-up from the Huatulco airport at rates lower than the Transportes Terrestres charges.

The Restaurant Cañon Devata requires reservations if you're not staying at the hotel. The menu consists of primarily vegetarian dishes, made with organic vegetables grown on-site and served with home-baked bread. It occasionally includes fish. Breakfast averages $3 to $6; sandwiches, $3.50; dinner, $9.50. No credit cards are accepted. The restaurant is open Tuesday to Sunday from 7:30am to 2pm and 7 to 9pm, and is closed in May and June.

Playa del Panteón Apdo. Postal 10, 70902 Puerto Angel, Oax. ✆ and fax **958/584-3048.** www.posadangel.com. 15 units, 6 bungalows. $13–$50 double; $35–$50 bungalow or El Cielo room for 2. No credit cards. Closed May–June. **Amenities:** Restaurant; open-air massage center; safe-deposit boxes; money exchange; laundry service; fishing trip arrangements. Walk past Hotel Cabaña del Puerto Angel, across from Playa Panteón, until road more or less ends; turn right and follow sandy path to small parking area. Cross tiny bridge on right and follow stairs on left to restaurant. Just beyond is the check-in area.

## 4 Bahías de Huatulco

64km (40 miles) SE of Puerto Angel; 680km (425 miles) SE of Acapulco

Huatulco has the same, unspoiled nature and laid-back attitude as its neighbors to the north—Puerto Angel and Puerto Escondido—but with a difference. In the midst of natural splendor, you'll also encounter indulgent hotels and modern roads and facilities.

Pristine beaches and jungle landscapes can make for an idyllic retreat from the stress of daily life—and when viewed from a luxury hotel balcony, even better. Huatulco is for those who want to enjoy the beauty of nature during the day, then retreat to well-appointed comfort by night. Slow-paced and still relatively undiscovered, the Bays of Huatulco enjoy the most modern infrastructure on Mexico's Pacific coast.

Undeveloped stretches of pure white sand and isolated coves await the promised growth of Huatulco, but it's not catching on as rapidly as Cancún, the previous resort planned by FONATUR, Mexico's Tourism Development arm. FONATUR development of the Bahías de Huatulco is an ambitious development project that aims to cover 52,000 acres of land, with over 40,000 acres to remain ecological preserves. The small local communities have been transplanted from the coast into Crucecita. The area consists of three sections: **Santa Cruz, Crucecita,** and **Tangolunda Bay** (see "City Layout," below).

Though Huatulco has increasingly become known for its ecotourism attractions—including river rafting, rappelling, and hiking jungle trails—it has yet to develop a true personality. There's little shopping, nightlife, or even dining outside the hotels, and what is available is expensive for the quality. However, the service in the area shines. Service personnel demonstrate an enthusiasm and willingness to share the treasures of the area with visitors.

If you're drawn to snorkeling, diving, boat cruises, and simple relaxation, Huatulco fits the bill. Nine bays encompass 36 beaches and countless inlets and

## Bahías de Huatulco

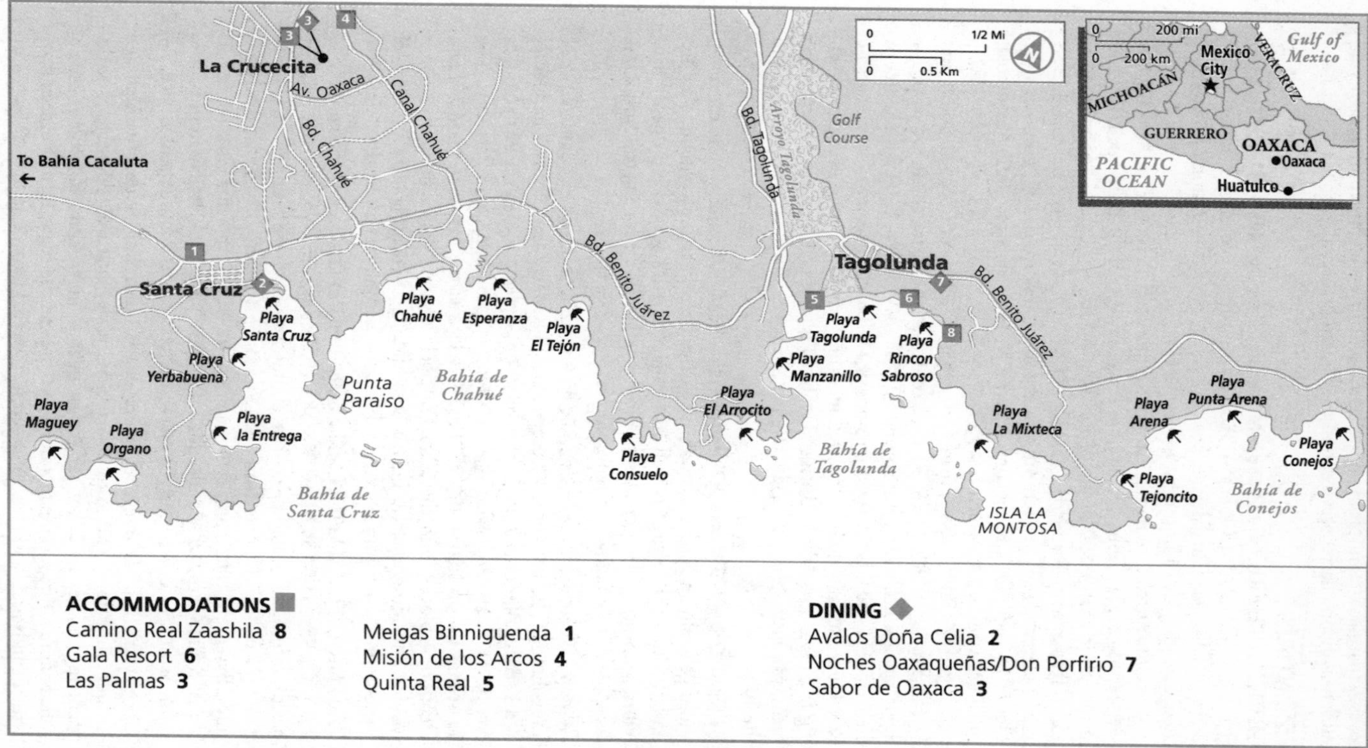


**ACCOMMODATIONS**
Camino Real Zaashila **8**
Gala Resort **6**
Las Palmas **3**
Meigas Binniguenda **1**
Misión de los Arcos **4**
Quinta Real **5**

**DINING**
Avalos Doña Celia **2**
Noches Oaxaqueñas/Don Porfirio **7**
Sabor de Oaxaca **3**

coves. Huatulco's main problem has been securing enough incoming flights. It relies heavily on charter service from the United States and Canada.

## ESSENTIALS

**GETTING THERE** **By Plane** **Mexicana** flights (© **800/531-7921** in the U.S.; 958/587-0223 or 958/587-0260 at the airport) connect Huatulco with Cancún, Chicago, Guadalajara, Los Angeles, Miami, San Antonio, San Francisco, San Jose, and Toronto by way of Mexico City.

From Huatulco's international airport (airport code: HUX; © **958/581-9004** or 958/581-9017), about 19km (12 miles) northwest of the Bahías de Huatulco, private **taxis** charge $39 to Crucecita, $40 to Santa Cruz, and $45 to Tangolunda. **Transportes Terrestres** (© **958/581-9014**) *colectivo* minibus fares are $8 to $10 per person. When returning, make sure to ask for a taxi, unless you have a lot of luggage. Taxis to the airport run $39, but unless specifically requested, you'll get a Suburban, which costs $54.

**Budget** (© **800/322-9976** in U.S., 958/587-0010 or 958/581-9000) and **Advantage** (© **958/587-1379**) have offices at the airport that are open for flight arrivals. Daily rates run around $71 for a VW sedan, $104 for a Sentra or Geo Tracker, and $123 for a Jeep Ranger. **Dollar** also has rental offices at the Royal, Barceló, and downtown, and offers one-way drop service if you're traveling to Puerto Escondido. Because Huatulco is so spread out and has excellent roads, you may want to consider a rental car, at least for a day or two, to explore the area.

**By Car** Coastal Highway 200 leads to Huatulco (via Pochutla) from the north and is generally in good condition. The drive from Puerto Escondido takes just under 2 hours. The road is well maintained, but it's windy and doesn't have lights, so avoid travel after sunset. Allow at least 6 hours for the trip from Oaxaca City on mountainous Highway 175.

**By Bus** There are three bus stations in Crucecita, but none in Santa Cruz or Tangolunda. The stations in Crucecita are all within a few blocks. The **Gacela** and **Estrella Blanca** station, at the corner of Gardenia and Palma Real, handles service to Acapulco, Mexico City, Puerto Escondido, and Pochutla. The **Cristóbal Colón** station (© **958/587-0261**) is at the corner of Gardenia and Ocotillo, 4 blocks from the Plaza Principal. It serves destinations throughout Mexico, including Oaxaca, Puerto Escondido, and Pochutla. The **Estrella del Valle** station, on Jasmin between Sabali and Carrizal, serves Oaxaca.

**VISITOR INFORMATION** The **State Tourism Office,** or Oficina del Turismo (© **958/587-1542;** fax 958/587-1541; sedetur6@oaxaca-travel.gob.mx) has an information module in Tangalundo Bay, near the Grand Pacific hotel. The **Huatulco Convention & Visitors Bureau** (© **958/587-1037;** info@BaysofHuatulco.com) is in the Plaza San Miguel in Santa Cruz at the corner of Santa Cruz and Monte Albán. It's open Monday to Friday from 9am to 6pm, Saturday from 10am to 2pm, and offers very friendly, helpful service.

**CITY LAYOUT** The overall resort area is called **Bahías de Huatulco** and includes nine bays. The town of Santa María de Huatulco, the original settlement in this area, is 27km (17 miles) inland. **Santa Cruz Huatulco,** usually called Santa Cruz, was the first developed area on the coast. It has a central plaza with a bandstand kiosk, which has been converted into a cafe that serves regionally grown coffee. It also has an artisans' market on the edge of the plaza that borders the main road, a few hotels and restaurants, and a marina where bay tours and fishing trips set sail. **Juárez** is Santa Cruz's 4-block-long main street, anchored at one end by the Hotel Castillo Huatulco and at the other by the Meigas Binniguenda hotel. Opposite the Hotel Castillo is the marina, and beyond it are restaurants in new colonial-style buildings facing the beach. The area's banks are on Juárez. It's impossible to get lost; you can take in almost everything at a glance.

About 3km (1½ miles) inland from Santa Cruz is **Crucecita,** a planned city that sprang up in 1985. It centers on a lovely grassy plaza. This is the residential area for the resorts, with neighborhoods of new stucco homes mixed with small apartment complexes. The town has evolved into a lovely, traditional town where you'll find the area's best, and most reasonably priced, restaurants plus some shopping and several clean, less expensive hotels.

Until other bays are developed, **Tangolunda Bay,** 5km (3 miles) east, is the focal point of development. Over time, half the bays will have resorts. For now, Tangolunda has an 18-hole golf course, as well as the Club Med, Quinta Real, Barceló Huatulco, Royal, Casa del Mar, and Camino Real Zaashila hotels, among others. Small strip centers with a few restaurants occupy each end of Tangolunda Bay. **Chahué Bay,** between Tangolunda and Santa Cruz, is a small bay with a beach club.

**GETTING AROUND** Crucecita, Santa Cruz, and Tangolunda are too far apart to walk, but **taxis** are inexpensive and readily available. Crucecita has taxi stands opposite the Hotel Grifer and on the Plaza Principal. Taxis are readily available through hotels in Santa Cruz and Tangolunda. The fare between Santa Cruz and Tangolunda is roughly $2.50; between Santa Cruz and Crucecita, $2; between Crucecita and Tangolunda, $3. To explore the area, you can hire a taxi by the hour (about $15 per hr.) or for the day.

There is **minibus service** between towns; the fare is 30¢. In Santa Cruz, catch the bus across the street from Castillo Huatulco; in Tangolunda, in front of the Grand Pacific; and in Crucecita, cater-corner from the Hotel Grifer.

## *FAST FACTS:* Bahías de Huatulco

*Area Code* The area code is **958.**

*Banks* All three areas have banks with automatic tellers, including the main Mexican banks, Banamex and Bancomer. They change money during business hours, which are Monday to Friday from 9am to 5pm, Saturday from 10am to 1pm. Banks are along Calle Juarez in Santa Cruz, and surrounding the central plaza in Crucecita.

*Doctor* **Dr. Ricardo Carrillo** (**© 958/587-0687** or 958/587-0600) speaks English.

*Hospital* The modern **Centro Medica Huatulco,** Flamboyant 205 La Crucecita (**© 958/587-0104** or 958/587-0435), has English-speaking doctors.

*Pharmacy* **Farmacia del Carmen,** just off the central plaza in Crucecita (**© 958/587-0878**), is one of the largest drugstores in town. **Farmacia La Clinica** (**© 958/587-0591**), Sabalí 1602, Crucecita, offers 24-hour service and delivery.

*Post Office* The *correo,* at Blvd. Chahué 100, Sector R (**© 958/587-0551**), is open Monday to Friday from 9am to 3pm, Saturday from 9am to 1pm.

## BEACHES, WATERSPORTS & OTHER THINGS TO DO

Attractions around Huatulco concentrate on the nine bays and their watersports. The number of ecotours and interesting side trips into the surrounding mountains is growing. Though it isn't a traditional Mexican town, the community of Crucecita is worth visiting. Just off the central plaza is the **Iglesía de Guadalupe,** with a large mural of Mexico's patron saint gracing the entire ceiling of the chapel. The image of the Virgin is set against a deep blue night sky, and includes 52 stars—a modern interpretation of Juan Diego's cloak.

You can dine in Crucecita for a fraction of the price in Tangolunda Bay, with the added benefit of some local color. Considering that shopping in Huatulco is generally poor, you'll find the best choices here, in the shops around the central plaza. They tend to stay open late, and offer a good selection of regional goods and typical tourist take-homes, including *artesania,* silver jewelry, Cuban cigars, and tequila. There's also a small, free trolley train that takes visitors on a short tour of the town.

**BEACHES** A section of the beach at Santa Cruz (away from the small boats) is an inviting sunning spot. Beach clubs for guests at non-oceanfront hotels are here. In addition, several restaurants are on the beach, and *palapa* umbrellas run down to the water's edge. For about $15 one-way, *pangas* from the marina in Santa Cruz will ferry you to **La Entrega Beach,** also in Santa Cruz Bay. There you'll find a row of *palapa* restaurants, all with beach chairs out front. Find an empty one, and use that restaurant for your refreshment needs. A snorkel equipment rental booth is about midway down the beach, and there's some fairly good snorkeling on the end away from where the boats arrive.

Between Santa Cruz and Tangolunda bays is **Chahué Bay.** A beach club has *palapas,* beach volleyball, and refreshments for an entrance fee of about $2. However, a strong undertow makes this a dangerous place for swimming.

**Tangolunda Bay** beach, fronting the best hotels, is wide and beautiful. Theoretically, all beaches in Mexico are public; however, nonguests at Tangolunda hotels may have difficulty entering the hotels to get to the beach.

**BAY CRUISES/TOURS** Huatulco's major attraction is its coastline—a magnificent stretch of pristine bays bordered by an odd blend of cactus and jungle vegetation right at the water's edge. The only way to really grasp its beauty is to take a cruise of the bays, stopping at **Organo** or **Maguey Bay** for a dip in the crystal-clear water and a fish lunch at a *palapa* restaurant on the beach.

One way to arrange a bay tour is to go to the **boat-owners' cooperative** in the red-and-yellow tin shack at the entrance to the marina. Prices are posted, and you can buy tickets for sightseeing, snorkeling, or fishing. Beaches other than La Entrega, including Maguey and San Agustín, are noted for offshore snorkeling. They also have *palapa* restaurants and other facilities. Several of these beaches, however, are completely undeveloped, so you will need to bring your own provisions. Boatmen at the cooperative will arrange return pick-up at an appointed time. Prices run about $15 for 1 to 10 persons at La Entrega, and $35 for a trip to Maguey and Organo bays. The farthest bay is San Agustinillo, and that all-day trip will run $70 in a private *panga.*

Another option is to join an organized daylong bay cruise. Any travel agency can easily make arrangements. Cruises are about $30 per person, with an extra charge of $5 for snorkeling-equipment rental and lunch. One excursion is on the *Tequila,* complete with guide, drinks, and on-board entertainment. Another, more romantic option is the *Luna Azul,* a 44-foot sailboat that also offers bay tours and sunset sails. Call ✆ **958/587-0945** for reservations.

The **Triton** (✆ **958/587-0844**) also offers a variety of day trips. Its popular Beach and Bay Tour costs $20 per person. A snorkeling or fishing trip includes gear and a guide and cost $34 per person. Scuba-diving trips include one basics class, gear, and one dive for noncertified divers for $73; or gear and 2 dives for certified divers for the same price.

In Crucecita, **Shuatur Tours,** Plaza Oaxaca, Local 20 (✆ and fax **958/587-0734**), offers bay tours; tours to Puerto Angel, Puerto Escondido, and associated beaches; an eco-tour on the Río Copalita (7 hr.); and an all-day tour to the coffee plantations in the mountains above Huatulco.

Ecotours are growing in both popularity and number throughout the Bays of Huatulco. **Huatulco Outfitters** (✆ **958/581-0315**) specializes in river-rafting expeditions down the Copalita River. The mountain areas surrounding the Copalita River are also home to other natural treasures worth exploring, including the **Copalitilla Cascades.** Thirty kilometers (19 miles) north of Tangolunda at 400 meters 394m (1,300 ft.) above sea level, this group of waterfalls—averaging 20 to 25m (65–80 ft.) in height—form natural whirlpools and clear pools for swimming. The area is also popular for horseback riding and rappelling.

An especially popular option is a day trip to **Oaxaca City** and **Monte Albán.** The trip includes round-trip airfare on Aerocaribe, lunch, entrance to the archaeological site at Monte Albán, and a tour of the architectural highlights of Oaxaca City, all for $254. It's available through any travel agency or through the **Aerocaribe** office (✆ **958/587-1220**).

**GOLF & TENNIS** The 18-hole, par-72 **Tangolunda Golf Course** (✆ **958/581-0037**) is adjacent to Tangolunda Bay. It has tennis courts as well. The greens fee is $70, and carts cost $40. Tennis courts are also available at the **Barceló** hotel (✆ **958/581-0055**).

**SHOPPING** Shopping in the area is limited and unmemorable. It concentrates in the **Santa Cruz Market,** by the marina in Santa Cruz, and in the **Crucecita Market,** on Guamuchil, half a block from the plaza. Both are open daily 10am to 8pm (no phones). Among the prototypical souvenirs, you may want to search out regional specialties, which include Oaxacan embroidered

---

***Fun Fact*** **Huatulco's Coffee Plantations**

This region of Mexico is known for its rich Pluma coffee, grown in the mountainous areas surrounding Huatulco. Plantations that date back centuries continue to grow and harvest coffee beans, mostly using traditional methods. The majority of the plantations are around the mouth of the Copalita River, in small towns including Pluma Hidalgo, Santa María Huatulco, and Xanica, located roughly 1 to 1½ hours from Tangolunga Bay. Both day tours and overnight stays are available from Huatulco.

**Café Huatulco** (✆ **958/587-0339**) is a unique project of the area coffee producers' association, opened to raise awareness of the region's coffee and to offer an unusual excursion for tourists. It has two outlets that sell whole-bean regional coffee and serve coffee and espresso beverages. One is in the kiosk in the central plaza of Santa Cruz; another is in the Plaza Esmerelda shopping center in Tangolunda Bay. The manager, Salvador López, can arrange coffee tastings for groups of six or more, and provide details about overnight stays at the coffee plantations.

---

blouses and dresses, and *barro negro,* pottery made from dark clay exclusively found in the Oaxaca region. Also in Crucecita is the Plaza Oaxaca, adjacent to the central plaza. Its clothing shops include **Poco Loco Club/Coconut's Boutique** (✆ **958/587-0279**), for casual sportswear; and **Mic Mac** (✆ **958/587-0565**), featuring beachwear and souvenirs. **Coconuts** (✆ **958/587-0057**) has English-language magazines, books, and music.

## WHERE TO STAY

Moderate- and budget-priced hotels in Santa Cruz and Crucecita are generally more expensive than similar hotels in other Mexican beach resorts. The luxury hotels have comparable rates, especially when they're part of a package that includes airfare. The trend here is toward all-inclusive resorts, which in Huatulco are an especially good option, given the lack of memorable dining and nightlife options. Hotels that are not oceanfront generally have an arrangement with a beach club at Santa Cruz or Chahué Bay, and offer shuttle service. Low-season rates apply from August through November only.

### EXPENSIVE

**Camino Real Zaashila** ★★★ One of the original hotels in Tangolunda Bay, the Camino Real Zaashila is on a wide stretch of sandy beach secluded from other beaches by small rock outcroppings. The calm water, perfect for swimming and snorkeling, makes it ideal for families. The white stucco building is Mediterranean in style and washed in colors on the ocean side. Rooms on the lower levels—41 of them—each have their own sizable dipping pool. The boldly decorated rooms are large and have an ocean-view balcony or terrace, marble tub/shower combination, and wicker furnishings. The main pool is a freeform design that spans 121m (400 ft.) of beach, with chaises built into the shallow edges. Well-manicured tropical gardens surround it and the guest rooms.

Blvd. Benito Juárez 5, Bahía de Tangolunda, 70989 Huatulco, Oax. ✆ **800/722-6466** in the U.S., 958/581-0460. Fax 958/581-0461. www.caminoreal.com/zaashila/. 130 units. High season $182 double, $257 Camino Real Club; low season $205 double, $246 Camino Real Club. Low-season rates include breakfast. AE, DC, MC, V. **Amenities:** 3 restaurants (1 Oaxacan), lobby bar with live music; large pool; beachfront watersports center; outdoor whirlpool; lighted tennis court; tour and travel agency services; room service. *In room:* A/C, TV, minibar, safe.

**Quinta Real** ★★★ Double Moorish domes mark this romantic, relaxed hotel, known for its richly appointed cream-and-white decor and complete attention to detail. From the welcoming reception area to the luxurious beach club below, the staff emphasizes excellence in service. The small groupings of suites are built into the sloping hill to Tangolunda Bay and offer spectacular views of the ocean and golf course. Rooms on the eastern edge of the resort sit above the highway, which generates some traffic noise. Interiors are elegant and comfortable, with stylish Mexican furniture, wood-beamed ceilings, marble tub/shower combinations with whirlpool tubs; and original art. Telescopes grace many of the suites. Balconies have overstuffed seating areas and stone-inlay floors. Eight Grand Class Suites and the Presidential Suite have private pools. The Quinta Real is perfect for weddings, honeymoons, or small corporate retreats.

Blvd. Benito Juárez Lt. 2, Bahía de Tangolunda, 70989 Huatulco, Oax. ✆ **888/561-2817** in the U.S., 958/581-0428, or 958/581-0430. Fax 958/581-0429. 28 units. High season $386 Master Suite, $371 Grand Class Suite, $546 suite with private pool; low season $206 Master Suite, $351 Grand Class Suite, $416 suite with private pool. AE, DC, MC, V. **Amenities:** Restaurant (breakfast, dinner), poolside restaurant (lunch), bar with stunning view; beach club with 2 pools (1 for children); beach *palapas;* concierge; tour desk; in-room massage; room service; laundry and dry cleaning. *In room:* A/C, TV, dataport, minibar, bathrobes, hair dryer, safe-deposit box.

## MODERATE

**Gala Resort** ★ With all meals, drinks, entertainment, tips, and a slew of activities included in the price, the Gala is a value-packed experience. It caters to adults of all ages (married and single) who enjoy both activity and relaxation. An excellent kids' activity program makes it probably the best option in the area for families. Rooms have tile floors and Oaxacan wood trim, large tub/shower combinations, and ample balconies, all with views of Tangolunda Bay.

Blvd. Benito Juárez s/n, Bahía de Tangolunda, 70989 Huatulco, Oax. ✆ **800/GO-MAEVA** in the U.S., or 958/581-0000. Fax 958/581-0220. 290 units. $289 double. Extra adult $118; child 12–15 $89; child 7–11 $60. Children under 7 stay free in parents' room. AE, MC, V. **Amenities:** 3 restaurants (buffet and a la carte), theme nights, 4 bars; large free-form pool; 4 lighted tennis courts; full gym; complete beachfront watersports center. *In room:* A/C, TV, minibar, hair dryer, safe-deposit box.

**Hotel Meigas Binniguenda** ★ Huatulco's first hotel retains the charm and comfort that originally made it memorable. A recent addition has more than doubled the hotel's size. Rooms have Mexican-tile floors, foot-loomed bedspreads, and colonial-style furniture; French doors open onto tiny wrought-iron balconies overlooking Juárez or the pool and gardens. The newer rooms have more modern teak furnishings and are generally much nicer—request this section. A nice shady area surrounds the small pool in back of the lobby. The hotel is away from the marina at the far end of Juárez, only a few blocks from the water. It offers free transportation every hour to the beach club at Santa Cruz Bay.

Blvd. Santa Cruz 201, 70989 Santa Cruz de Huatulco, Oax. ✆ **958/587-0077** or 958/587-0078. Fax 958/587-0284. binniguenda@huatulco.net.mx. 165 units. High season $110 per person (all-inclusive), $100 double (room only); low season $75 per person (all-inclusive), $67 double (room only). AE, MC, V. **Amenities:** Large, *palapa*-topped restaurant; small pool; shuttle to beach; travel agency. *In room:* A/C, TV, safe-deposit box.

## INEXPENSIVE

**Hotel Las Palmas** The central location and accommodating staff add to the appeal of the bright, basic rooms at Las Palmas. Located half a block from the main plaza, it's connected to the popular El Sabor de Oaxaca restaurant (see "Where to Dine," below), which offers room service to guests. Rooms have tile floors, cotton textured bedspreads, tile showers, and cable TV.

Av. Guamuchil 206, 70989 Bahías de Huatulco, Oax. ✆ **958/587-0060.** Fax 958/587-0057. www.tomzap.com. 25 units. High season $45 double; low season $28 double. AE, MC, V. Free parking. **Amenities:** Tobacco shop; money exchange; safe-deposit boxes; travel-agency services. *In room:* A/C, TV.

**Misión de los Arcos** ★★ *Finds* This hotel just a block from the central plaza is similar in style to the elegant Quinta Real—at a fraction of the cost. The hotel is completely white, accented with an abundance of greenery, giving it a fresh, inviting feel. Rooms continue the theme, washed in white, with cream and beige bed coverings and upholstery. Built-in desks, French windows, and minimal but interesting decorative accents give this budget hotel a real sense of style. At the entrance level, there is a cafe with Internet access that is open 7:30am to 11:30pm. Guests have the use of a beach club, to which the hotel provides a complimentary shuttle. The hotel is cater-corner from La Crucecita's central plaza, close to all the shops and restaurants.

Gardenia 902, La Crucecita, Huatulco, 70989, Oaxaca. ✆ **958/587-0165.** Fax 958/587-1135. losarcos@huatulco.net.mx. 13 units. High season $66 double without A/C, $91 double with A/C, $117 suite; low season $52 double without A/C, $59 double with A/C, $91 suite. AE, MC, V. **Amenities:** Shuttle to beach club; tour desk; laundry services. *In room:* TV, safe-deposit box.

## WHERE TO DINE

**El Sabor de Oaxaca** ★★★ OAXACAN This is the best place in the area to enjoy authentic, richly flavorful Oaxacan food, among the best of traditional Mexican cuisine. This colorful restaurant is a local favorite that also meets the quality standards of tourists. Among the most popular items are mixed grill for two, with a Oaxacan beef fillet, tender pork tenderloin, *chorizo* (zesty Mexican sausage), and pork ribs; and the Oaxacan special for two, a generous sampling of the best of the menu with tamales, Oaxacan cheese, pork *mole,* and more. Generous breakfasts include eggs, bacon, ham, beans, toast, and fresh orange juice. There's lively music, and the restaurant books special group events.

Av. Guamuchil 206, Crucecita. ✆ **958/587-0060.** Fax 958/587-0057. Breakfast $3.90; main dishes $5–$17. AE, MC, V. Daily 7am–midnight.

**Noches Oaxaqueñas/Don Porfirio** ★ SEAFOOD/OAXACAN This dinner show presents the colorful, traditional folkloric dances of Oaxaca in an open-air courtyard reminiscent of an old hacienda (but in a modern strip mall). The dancers clearly enjoy performing traditional ballet under the direction of owner Celicia Flores Ramirez, wife of Don Willo Porfirio. The menu includes the *plato Oaxaqueño,* a generous, flavorful sampling of traditional Oaxacan fare, with a tamale, a *sope,* Oaxacan cheese, grilled fillet, pork enchilada, and a chile relleno. Other house specialties include shrimp with *mezcal,* and spaghetti marinara with seafood. Meat lovers can enjoy American-style cuts or a juicy *arrachera* (skirt steak). Groups are welcome.

Blvd. Benito Juárez s/n (across from Royal Maeva), Tangolunda Bay. ✆ **958/581-0001.** Show $17. Main courses $16–$43. AE, MC, V. Fri–Sun 8:30–10pm.

**Restaurant Avalos Doña Celia** SEAFOOD Doña Celia, an original Huatulco resident, remains in business in the same area where she started her little thatch-roofed restaurant years ago. In a new building at the end of Santa Cruz's beach, she serves the same good eats. Among her specialties are *filete empapelado* (a foil-wrapped fish baked with tomato, onion, and cilantro) and *filete almendrado* (fish filet covered with hotcake batter, beer, and almonds). The *ceviche* is terrific (one order is plenty for two), as is *platillo a la Huatulqueño* (shrimp and young octopus fried in olive oil with chile and onion, served over white rice). The restaurant is basic, but the food is the reason for its popularity. If you dine here during the day, there are beach chairs and shade, so you can make your own "beach club" in a more traditional and accessible part of Huatulco.

Santa Cruz Bay. ✆ **958/587-0128.** Breakfast $2.50–$3.50; seafood $4–$25. No credit cards. Daily 8:30am–11pm.

## HUATULCO AFTER DARK

The selection of dance clubs is limited—meaning that's where everyone goes. The newest addition is **Ven Aca** (✆ **958/587-1691**), a piano bar and restaurant in Santa Cruz on the main street, Juarez. It's open daily 8pm to midnight (sometimes later) and is a casual, more romantic option than the discos and dance clubs in town. The local branch of the popular Mexican club **Magic Circus** (✆ **958/587-0017**), in Santa Cruz, is the area's most popular disco. It opens at 9pm. **El DexkiteLitros Bar** (✆ **958/587-0971**) is the top late-night spot, with open-air dancing on the Santa Cruz beachfront. Located next to the Marina Hotel on the beach, it plays techno and rock until 5am.

# The Southernmost States: Oaxaca & Chiapas

Oaxaca and Chiapas have the largest populations of Indians in Mexico. The pervasive Indian presence sets these states apart from the rest of the country. It is also the reason they are renowned for the beauty and variety of their crafts.

In **Oaxaca,** most of the native handcrafts come from the central highlands of the state, in the villages surrounding Oaxaca City. This region is a beautiful network of mountains and valleys checkered with cornfields, at its prettiest during the rainy season (June–Oct), when the corn is green. Growing corn is an act of self-realization for the residents of these communities; for many, the production of handcrafts might provide a greater livelihood, but if they didn't grow corn, they wouldn't consider themselves Indians.

Their ancestors established agriculture and civilization in these valleys centuries ago. The same people built and rebuilt the magnificent ceremonial center of **Monte Albán** high on a mountaintop above Oaxaca City. There you'll find an intriguing collection of buildings, ball courts, and plazas whose design is different from those of the Maya to the east and the many cultures of central Mexico to the northwest.

My favorite part of a trip here is visiting the **city of Oaxaca,** a colonial jewel that attaches great value to beautiful urban spaces such as plazas, courtyards, and pedestrian walkways. With the pleasures of elegant surroundings, good food, and warm, welcoming people, it is hard not to find favor with this city.

**Chiapas,** too, has a central highland area that produces many beautiful handcrafts. Its center is the town of **San Cristóbal de las Casas,** which is higher, cooler, and wetter than Oaxaca. It's best to come here during the relatively dry season (late Oct to May). San Cristóbal is much smaller and offers a provincial version of colonial architecture—narrow cobblestone streets, tile roofs, old adobe walls, and wooden balconies. It looks less monumental and more Indian.

Aside from the beauty of the mountains and the many handcrafts, what brings people here are the villages of the highland Maya, a people who cling so tenaciously to their beliefs and traditions that for a long time the area attracted more anthropologists than tourists. These communities have a high degree of autonomy in religious and social practices; a visit to the church in **San Juan Chamula** will bring this home in a way no description can.

North and east of San Cristóbal are the Chiapan lowlands, where you can visit the famous ruins of **Palenque,** a Maya city of the classic age. These ruins look unspeakably old, and the surrounding jungle seems poised to reclaim them should their caretakers ever falter in their duties. Thanks to the deciphering work of epigraphers, we know much about the history of Palenque and its kings. One was King

Pacal, who lay buried for centuries inside his pyramid until an archeological team discovered him in the 1950s.

Eight years ago, Chiapas made headlines when the Zapatista Liberation Army launched an armed rebellion and captured San Cristóbal. This forced the Mexican government to recognize the political and economic problems in Chiapas. Negotiations achieved some results and then stalled. Political violence erupted again in the winter of 1997–1998 with a massacre in Acteal, near San Cristóbal. Sporadic violence occurs in the outlying towns from time to time, but no foreigners have been attacked, and no restrictions have been placed on travel to Palenque or the San Cristóbal region. Social unrest remains latent in the area, but the U.S. State Department has not issued a travel advisory for the region. Before you go, get the most current information by checking the State Department website, **http://travel.state.gov**.

## EXPLORING OAXACA & CHIAPAS

Airline and bus service to this area have improved a lot in the past few years. Most people arrive and depart through Oaxaca, Villahermosa (2 hr. from Palenque), or Tuxtla Gutiérrez (1½ hr. from San Cristóbal). A direct flight daily connects San Cristóbal and Mexico City. If you go through Villahermosa, you might want to check out two attractions. The **Parque–Museo La Venta,** which is half park, half museum, displays artifacts from the mother of all Mesoamerican cultures—the Olmec—including the famous megalithic heads. The **Museo Regional de Antropología Carlos Pellicer** exhibits pre-Columbian artifacts from across Mexico. In Tuxtla, I recommend paying a visit to the beautiful Sumidero Canyon (see "En Route to San Cristóbal de las Casas," at the end of the Oaxaca section of this chapter).

You can see **Palenque** in a day. A couple of worthwhile side trips would add a day or 2. **Oaxaca City** and **San Cristóbal** and their neighborhoods have so much to offer that I would consider 4 days in either place the minimum; a week would be more realistic. Keep in mind, too, that Oaxaca's coastal resorts—including Puerto Escondido and Puerto Angel—are not far away. See chapter 9 for more information.

## 1 Oaxaca City ★★★

520km (325 miles) SE of Mexico City; 230km (144 miles) SE of Tehuacán; 269km (168 miles) NE of Puerto Escondido

What you see today when you walk through the historic district of Oaxaca (wa-*hah*-kah) is largely the product of 3 centuries of colonial society. Beautiful green volcanic stone, for which the city is famous, dresses most of the buildings. Oaxaca has its own style of colonial architecture, characterized by thick, heavily buttressed walls, low arches, and stout churches without lofty bell towers. This was an adaptation to the frequent earthquakes that plagued the region in colonial times.

Before the arrival of the Spanish, the central valley of Oaxaca was an important and populous region. Olmec influence reached the area around 1200 B.C.; by 800 B.C., in the early pre-Classic period, the Zapotec (the original builders of Monte Albán) occupied the valley. Their civilization flourished about the same time as Teotihuacán in central Mexico. Trade between this valley and the valleys of Cholula and Mexico intensified and remained important until the Conquest. There was also trade with the Maya to the east. In early postclassic times, the

# Oaxaca Area

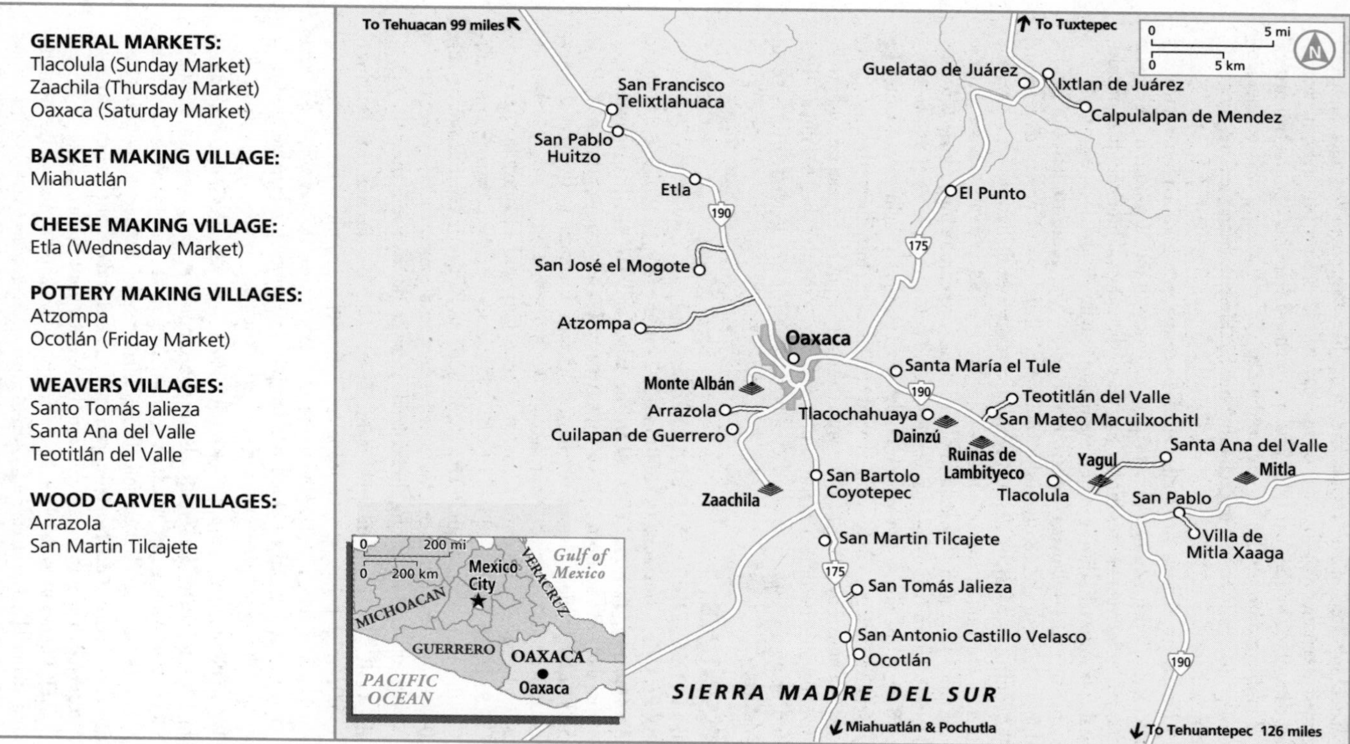
GENERAL MARKETS:
Tlacolula (Sunday Market)
Zaachila (Thursday Market)
Oaxaca (Saturday Market)
BASKET MAKING VILLAGE:
Miahuatlán
CHEESE MAKING VILLAGE:
Etla (Wednesday Market)
POTTERY MAKING VILLAGES:
Atzompa
Ocotlán (Friday Market)
WEAVERS VILLAGES:
Santo Tomás Jalieza
Santa Ana del Valle
Teotitlán del Valle
WOOD CARVER VILLAGES:
Arrazola
San Martin Tilcajete
To Tehuacan 99 miles
To Tuxtepec
0
5 mi
0
5 km
N
Guelatao de Juárez
Ixtlan de Juárez
Calpulalpan de Mendez
San Francisco Telixtlahuaca
San Pablo Huitzo
Etla
190
El Punto
175
San José el Mogote
Atzompa
Oaxaca
Santa María el Tule
Monte Albán
190
Teotitlán del Valle
Arrazola
Tlacochahuaya
San Mateo Macuilxochitl
Cuilapan de Guerrero
Dainzú
Ruinas de Lambityeco
Santa Ana del Valle
Yagul
Mitla
San Bartolo Coyotepec
Tlacolula
San Pablo
Zaachila
Villa de Mitla Xaaga
San Martin Tilcajete
175
San Tomás Jalieza
San Antonio Castillo Velasco
Ocotlán
190
SIERRA MADRE DEL SUR
Miahuatlán & Pochutla
To Tehuantepec 126 miles
0
200 mi
0
200 km
Mexico City
VERACRUZ
Gulf of Mexico
MICHOACAN
GUERRERO
OAXACA
Oaxaca
PACIFIC OCEAN

Mixtec appeared in the region and, most likely through war and conquest, gained ascendancy over much of the Zapotec homeland before both peoples were humbled by the Aztec and later the Spaniards. To this day, the two principal ethnic groups in Oaxaca remain the Zapotec and Mixtec, whose tonal languages are closely related to each other but far different from the Aztec language Nahuatl.

The city of Oaxaca, originally called Antequera, was founded just a few years after the Spanish vanquished the Aztec, and most of the surrounding valley was granted to Hernán Cortés for his services to the crown. Three centuries of colonial rule followed, during which the region remained calm.

In the years following independence, there was more or less continuous upheaval. From the 1830s to the 1860s, the Liberals and Conservatives fought for control of Mexico's destiny, with the French eventually intervening on the side of the Conservatives. One man, a Zapotec Indian from Oaxaca, led the resistance against the French and played the key role in shaping Mexico's future. He was Benito Juárez, and his handiwork is known to history as *La Reforma.*

Born in the village of Guelatao, north of Oaxaca City, Juárez was adopted by a wealthy Oaxacan family who clothed and educated him in return for his services as a houseboy. He fell in love with the daughter of his benefactor and promised he would become rich and famous and return to marry her. He did all three and became president of the Republic in 1861. Juárez is revered throughout Mexico.

## ESSENTIALS

### GETTING THERE & DEPARTING

**BY PLANE** **Mexicana** (© **800/531-7921** in the U.S., or 951/516-8414) and **Aeromexico** (© **800/237-6639** in the U.S., or 951/516-1066) have several flights daily to and from Mexico City. **Aerocaribe,** a Mexicana affiliate © **951/516-0229** or 951/516-0266), flies to Puerto Escondido, Tuxtla Gutiérrez, Huatulco, and Ixtepec. **Aviacsa** (© **01-800/006-2200** inside Mexico, or 951/514-5187) flies once a day to Mexico City and Hermosillo. **AeroVega** (© **951/516-4982** or 951/516-2777) flies a six-passenger twin-engine Aero-Commander to and from Puerto Escondido and Bahías de Huatulco once daily (twice if there are enough passengers). Make arrangements for AeroVega at the Monte Albán Hotel facing the Alameda (next to the *zócalo,* or town square).

**BY CAR** It's a 5-hour drive from Mexico City on the toll road, Highway 135D, which begins at Cuacnoapalan, about 80km (50 miles) east-southeast of Puebla, and runs south, terminating in Oaxaca; the one-way toll is $22. For adventurous souls, the old federal Highway 190 winds through the mountains and offers spectacular views; it takes 9 to 10 hours.

**BY BUS** First-class and better buses to and from Mexico City use the superhighway toll road (*autopista*), which takes 6 hours. A few make a short stop in Nochistlán, which isn't much of a delay. Almost all buses leave from Mexico City's **TAPO** (east) bus station. There is less frequent service to and from Mexico City's **Central del Norte** (north), and the **Central del Sur** (south, also called Taxqueña). There is no service from the Mexico City airport.

**ADO** (Autobuses del Oriente) and its affiliates handle most of the first-class and deluxe bus service. Your options are: *primera clase* (ADO), with almost hourly departures and a one-way fare of $25; *de lujo* (ADO GL) with seven or more departures per day for $33.50 one-way; and *servicio ejecutivo* (UNO), with five-plus departures per day and $46 one-way. *De lujo* has the same seats as first

## Downtown Oaxaca

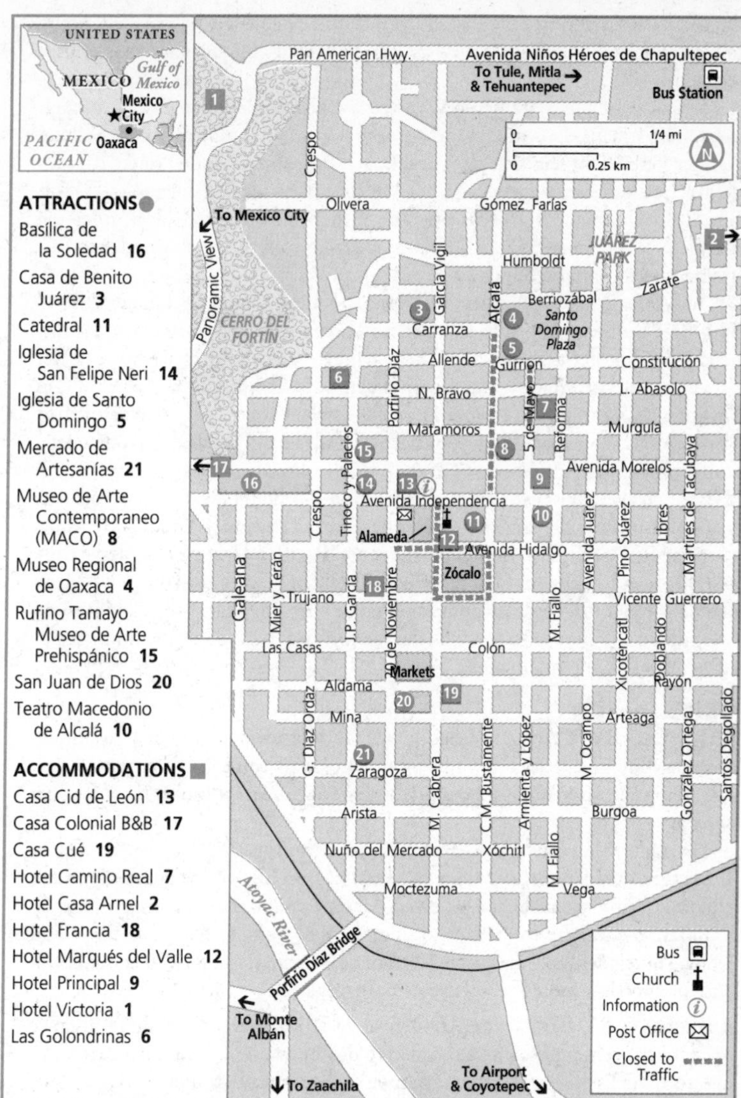


class, but more legroom, free soda and bottled water, and a better bathroom. *Servico ejecutivo* has all this plus super-wide seats that recline far back. During holidays, you need to reserve a seat. Native Oaxaqueños living outside the state fill the buses for the Days of the Dead, Holy Week, and Christmas. It's possible to reserve seats over the Internet for the higher levels of service, and to check departure times and prices (www.adogl.com.mx and www.uno.com.mx).

In Oaxaca, the **ADO station** is on Calzada Niños Héroes. Buses serve Tuxtla Gutiérrez (five a day); San Cristóbal de las Casas (two overnight buses); Puebla (ten a day); Tehuacán (four a day); Tapachula (one a day); Veracruz (three a day); Villahermosa (two a day); and Huatulco, Pochutla, and Puerto Escondido on the coast (two a day, stopping at all three towns). These last buses take 9 hours to reach Puerto Escondido because they go by way of Huatulco; for a faster trip, see below.

Most of these buses are first class; some are deluxe. When you walk through the station's main door, the passage to the buses is in front of you. The long counter to the right sells first-class tickets, and the shorter counter to the left sells deluxe. You can buy your tickets ahead of time at an agency downtown, Ticket Bus, 20 de Noviembre 103-D, near the corner of Hidalgo, 1 block from the *zócalo* (© **951/514-6655**). Office hours are from 9am to 10pm Monday to Saturday, 9am to 4pm on Sunday.

The **Viajes Atlántida** agency, La Noria 101, near Armenta y López (© **951/514-7077**), offers daily service to Puerto Escondido and Pochutla in Suburbans—much faster than the bus. There are seven runs daily to Pochutla (4 hr.; $13.50), four of which continue to Puerto Escondido (5 hr.; $18). From Pochutla you can catch a *colectivo* (inexpensive village taxi) to Huatulco or Puerto Angel. You should buy your tickets in advance. The agency is open daily from 5:30am to 11:30pm.

The speediest buses to **Puerto Escondido**—6 hours away over a tortuous road—leave from the *terminal de segunda clase,* Armenta y López 721, across from the Red Cross. Two lines serve the route. **Pacífico Oaxaca** buses leave daily at 8:30am and 10:30pm. One **Estrella del Valle** bus leaves at 11pm daily. Many people who go to Puerto Escondido on these buses say that if they had it to do over, they'd fly. Motion sickness is the main reason because of the hundreds of curves through the mountains.

## ORIENTATION

**ARRIVING BY PLANE** The airport is south of town; it's about a 20-minute cab ride. Buy a ticket at the window on your left as you exit the airport. A private cab is $8; a *colectivo* is $2 per person for downtown locations, more for outlying areas.

The same company provides service from the town to the airport. Go to **Transportes Aeropuerto Oaxaca** (© **951/514-4350**), on the Alameda, in the building facing the cathedral. It doesn't accept phone reservations, so drop by Monday to Saturday from 9am to 2pm or 5 to 8pm to buy your ticket and arrange hotel pick-up. The cost is $2 from downtown hotels, $4.50 and up from outlying hotels—more if you have extra luggage.

**ARRIVING BY BUS** The ADO first-class bus station is a short distance north of the center of town. A taxi ride to downtown is $2 to $3. If you're coming from the Pacific coast, you may arrive at the Central Camionera de Segunda Clase (second-class bus terminal) next to the Abastos Market. It's 10 long blocks southwest of the *zócalo.*

**VISITOR INFORMATION** The **State Tourist Office** is at Calle Independencia 607, corner of García Vigil, in front of the Alameda (© and fax **951/516-0123**). It's open daily from 8am to 8pm. The information booth at the airport keeps the same hours. The **Municipal Tourist Office** (Oficina de Turismo) is at García Vigil 517; office hours are from 9am to 3pm and 6 to 9pm.

**CITY LAYOUT** Oaxaca's east-west axis is **Independencia.** When streets cross Independencia, their names change. The same is true for the north-south axis, **Alcalá/Bustamante.** The city's center is the ***zócalo,*** a large square surrounded by stone archways, and the **Alameda,** a smaller plaza attached to the northwest part of the *zócalo.* Oaxaca's cathedral faces the Alameda; its Palacio del Gobierno faces the *zócalo.* A few blocks to the north is the **Plaza de Santo Domingo.** The area between these two open spaces holds most of the historic district's shops, hotels, and restaurants. Two of the streets that run from Santo Domingo toward the *zócalo*—**Alcalá** and **Cinco de Mayo**—are partly closed to traffic.

**GETTING AROUND By Car** If you want to reach some of the outlying villages, I recommend hiring a taxi or signing up for a tour. Most taxi drivers have set hourly rates for touring the Oaxacan valleys. A trustworthy and careful taxi driver who speaks English is **Tomás Ramírez** (© **951/511-5061** at home). If you want to rent a car, try **Arrendadora Express,** 20 de Noviembre 103-B (© **951/516-6776**). Rental cars in Oaxaca are expensive, and the process is not exactly streamlined.

**By Bus** Buses to the outlying villages of Guelatao, Teotitlán del Valle, Tlacolula, and Mitla leave from the second-class station just north of the Abastos Market. *Colectivos* leave for nearby villages from Calle Mercaderes, on the south side of the Abastos Market.

## *FAST FACTS:* Oaxaca

*American Express* The office, in **Viajes Micsa,** is at Valdivieso and Hidalgo, at the northeast corner of the *zócalo* (© **951/516-2700;** fax 951/516-7475). American Express office hours are Monday to Friday from 9am to 2pm and 4 to 6pm, Saturday from 9am to 1pm. The travel agency stays open later and doesn't close for lunch.

*Area Code* The telephone area code is **951.**

*Books/Newspapers/Magazines* **Amate Books,** Alcalá 307-2, a few steps from Santo Domingo (© **951/516-6960**), has perhaps the best selection anywhere of books in English about Mexico. It stocks English-language magazines as well as a number of books about Oaxacan handcrafts. Hours are Monday to Saturday from 10:30am to 2:30pm and 3:30 to 7:30pm. A couple of monthly freebies, the English-language *Oaxaca Times* and the trilingual (English, Spanish, and French) *OAXACA,* circulate through the city and have information for tourists.

*Consulates* The **Canadian consulate,** Pino Suárez 700-11B (© **951/513-3777**), is open daily 11am to 2pm. The **U.S. Consular Agency** is at Alcalá 407, Int. 20 (© and fax **951/514-3054**). Hours are Monday to Friday 10am to 3pm.

*Currency Exchange* *Casas de cambio* cluster on the streets at the northeast corner of the *zócalo,* at Alcalá and Valdivieso. These places post their rates, have short lines, and keep better hours than banks. Several exchange Canadian dollars.

*Doctor* Dr. Carlos Arnaud Carreño is a reputable internist at Calle Reforma 905 (© **951/515-4053**). Hours are noon to 2pm and 4 to 8pm Monday to Friday.

*Emergencies* The phone number for emergencies is © **060.**

*Internet Access* In the downtown area, there are more than 20 Internet access services and cybercafes. Most are along Alcalá and around the *zócalo* and the Plaza Santo Domingo.

*Population* Oaxaca has 380,000 residents.

*Post Office* The *correo* is at the corner of Independencia and Alameda Park. It is open Monday to Friday from 8am to 5pm, Saturday from 9am to 1pm.

*Safety* By any standard, Oaxaca is a safe town for tourists. A state government agency, **CEPROTUR,** helps tourists who have been robbed or feel they have been cheated by service providers. It has compiled 6 years' worth of data that show that the incidence of crime against tourists in the city is remarkably low. Most of it is simple theft, which commonly happens in crowded areas such as the markets. One method is to slice open a tourist's backpack; another method is to distract someone who has set down a bag while a partner makes away with it. Should you lose any documents or possessions covered by insurance, contact **CEPROTUR,** in the same building as the state tourism office on the north side of the Alameda (✆ **951/514-2155**). It can document your losses and facilitate paperwork.

*Seasons* April and May are the hottest, driest months. (Also in May, rural teachers invade the *zócalo* and create havoc in the downtown area while they demonstrate for higher wages.) The rains come in June and improve things considerably. From June through March the city is most enjoyable. High seasons for tourists, when you can expect higher hotel rates, are late July and August (especially around the Guelaguetza), early November (around the Days of the Dead), the entire month of December, and during Easter.

*Shipping* The cheapest way to ship is to have your goods packed securely so that you can check them as extra baggage on your flight home. Another way is to ship them. Many stores will pack and ship their own merchandise but not other stores' goods. Recommended shippers are **Corazón del Pueblo** and **ARIPO** (see "Shopping," later).

## SPECIAL EVENTS & FESTIVALS

Oaxaca is famous for its exuberant traditional festivals. The most important ones are **Holy Week,** the **Guelaguetza** in July, **Días de los Muertos** in November, and the **Night of the Radishes** and **Christmas** in December. Make hotel reservations at least 2 months in advance if you plan to visit during these times.

*Note:* If you want to come for Christmas or the Guelaguetza but rooms and transportation are booked, consider using **Sanborn's Tours,** 2015 S. 10th St., McAllen, TX 78502 (✆ **800/395-8482**). **Remarkable Journeys,** P.O. Box 31855, Houston, TX 77231-1855 (✆ **800/856-1993** in the U.S., or 713/721-2517; fax 713/728-8334) also organizes trips that arrive in time for the Night of the Radishes.

At festival time in Oaxaca, sidewalk stands near the cathedral sell *buñuelos,* a thin, crisp, sweet snack food. It is the custom to serve *buñuelos* in cracked or otherwise flawed dishes; after you've finished eating, you smash the crockery on the sidewalk for good luck. Don't be timid! You can wash down the *buñuelos* with hot *ponche* or *atole.*

**HOLY WEEK** During Holy Week, figurines made of palm leaves are sold on the streets. On Palm Sunday (the Sun before Easter) there are colorful parades, and on the following Thursday, Oaxaca residents follow the Procession of the Seven Churches. Hundreds of the pious walk from church to church, praying at each one. The next day, Good Friday, many of the *barrios* (neighborhoods) have *Encuentros,* where groups depart separately from the church, carrying religious figures through the neighborhoods. Then they "encounter" each other back at the church. Throughout the week, each church sponsors concerts, fireworks, fairs, and other entertainment.

**FIESTA GUELAGUETZA** On the last two Mondays in July, Oaxaca holds the Fiesta Guelaguetza. In the villages of central Oaxaca, a *guelaguetza* (literally, a gift) is a celebration by a family in need of assistance to hold a wedding or some other community celebration. Guests bring gifts, which the family repays when they attend other *guelaguetzas.* The Fiesta Guelaguetza, begun in 1974, brings dancers from all the state's various ethnic groups to Oaxaca. For many communities, participation has become a matter of intense civic pride, and an opportunity to show people in the state capital and those from other ethnic groups the beauty of their traditional clothing and dance. Some 350 different *huipils* (women's overblouses) and dresses can be seen during the performances. In the afternoon, there is an interpretive dance of the legend of Princess Donají.

The performances take place in the stadium that crowns the Cerro del Fortín each Monday from 10am to 1pm. Admission ranges from free (in Section C) to $50 to $75 (in Section A). Reserve tickets in advance—no later than May—through the State Tourism Office. A travel agency may be able to help you. I recommend Sections 5 and 6 in Palco (gallery) A for the best seating in the Cerro del Fortín stadium. The ticket color matches the color of your seat. You will be sitting in strong sunlight, so wear a hat and long sleeves.

Even if you don't attend the dances, you can enjoy the festival atmosphere that engulfs the city. There are fairs, exhibits, and a lot of gaiety. On the Sunday nights before the Guelaguetza, university students present an excellent program in the Plaza de la Danza at the Soledad church. The production, the *Bani Stui Gulal,* is an abbreviated history of the Oaxaca valley. The program begins at 9pm; arrive early, because the event is free and seating is limited.

**DIAS DE LOS MUERTOS** This Mexican festival (Nov 1–2) has garnered worldwide attention. It is celebrated across Oaxaca with more enthusiasm than in the rest of Mexico, which says quite a lot. Markets brim with marigolds—the flower of mortality—and every household fills an altar with flowers and the favorite dishes, drinks, and cigarettes of the deceased. People visit relatives and friends, and anyone who visits is offered food. This is also the time to pay one's respects at the graveyard. Try to take one of the nocturnal cemetery tours offered around this time. **Hotel Casa Arnel** (**© 951/515-2856**) runs one. Another common form of celebrating is for young men to dress up in macabre outfits and frolic in the streets in Carnaval-like fashion.

**DECEMBER FESTIVALS** The December Festivals begin on the 12th with the **festival of the Virgin de Guadalupe** and continue on the 16th with a *calenda,* or procession, to many of the older churches in the *barrios,* all accompanied by dancing and costumes. Festivities continue on the 18th with the **Fiesta de la Soledad** in honor of the Virgen de la Soledad, patroness of Oaxaca state. A large fireworks construction known as a *castillo* is erected in Plaza de la Soledad. When it is ignited, look out. December 23 is the **Night of the Radishes,** when Oaxaqueños build fantastic sculptures out of enormous radishes, flowers, and cornhusks. Displays on three sides of the *zócalo* are set up from 3pm on. By 6pm, when the show officially opens, lines to see the figures are 4 blocks long. It's well organized and overseen by a heavy police presence. On December 24, around 8:30pm, each Oaxacan church organizes a procession with music, floats, enormous papier-mâché dancing figures, and crowds bearing candles, all of which converge on the *zócalo.*

## EXPLORING OAXACA

There is so much sightseeing to do inside and outside Oaxaca and so much to claim your attention that you have to be sure to allow some idle time for enjoying the *zócalo.* In the traffic-free square, you can relax while getting a feel for the town and a good glimpse of Oaxacan society. I recommend going in the late afternoon and taking a seat at the outdoor cafe with the best view of the cathedral. You can get a beer or order a bowl of the traditional drink of Oaxaca: chocolate. The afternoon light filters through the shiny green leaves of the laurel trees, heightening the color of the cathedral's green stone. As dusk comes, a small drill corps enters stage left and performs a flag-lowering ceremony with much pomp and circumstance. Then the *marimba* or the municipal band usually strikes up in the central bandstand.

The city contains museums worth visiting, some interesting churches, and colorful markets. Outside town are the famous ruins of Monte Albán and Mitla, and area villages known for their arts and crafts. It is sometimes best to check these out on market day; see "Shopping Splendor: Oaxaca's Market Villages," later in this chapter.

### MUSEUMS

**Museo de Arte Contemporáneo de Oaxaca** The MACO, 2½ blocks north of the *zócalo,* exhibits the work of contemporary artists, primarily from Oaxaca State (which has produced some of Mexico's most famous painters). It also books traveling exhibitions. A small bookstore is to your right as you enter. The 18th-century building housing the museum merits a visit for its own sake. It's called the Casa de Cortés, and some say that it was built by order of Hernán Cortés after he received the title of Marqués of the Valley of Oaxaca (in reality, it was built 2 centuries too late for that).

Alcalá 202, between Murguía and Morelos. ✆ **951/514-2228.** Admission $1. Wed–Mon 10:30am–8pm.

**Museo Regional de Oaxaca** ★★★ Next to the Santo Domingo Church (6 blocks north of the *zócalo*) is the most impressive museum in the city, housed in a former Dominican convent—one of the greatest of colonial Mexico. Construction began early and was largely completed by the early 1600s. The government has spent millions to renovate the former convent, and it shows. The stairs, the arches, the cupolas—everywhere you look, there are lovely details in stone or in the remnants of colonial-era murals. The museum is an ambitious project that displays the course of human development in the Oaxaca valley from earliest times to the 20th century.

The most treasured possessions are the artifacts from Monte Albán's Tomb 7, which were discovered in 1932. The tomb contained 12 to 14 corpses and some 500 pieces of jewelry and art, making use of almost 8 pounds of gold and turquoise, conch shell, amber, and obsidian. This is part of a larger collection of artifacts from Monte Albán, which you would do well to see before going up to the ruins. In the many ceramics and carvings you can see definite Olmec and Teotihuacán influences, yet they display a style distinctly different from either culture. Other rooms are dedicated to the present-day ethnographic make-up of

Oaxaca and a brief history of the efforts of the Dominican order in the region. Attached to the convent is the Santo Domingo Church (see "Churches," below). From some points on the north side of the convent you can look down over the recently opened botanical garden. Admission to the garden is free but by guided tour only (at 1 and 6pm). Sign up at the front desk of the museum the same day of the tour. There are two tours a week in English; ask for info at the front desk.

Gurrión at Alcalá. ✆ **951/516-2991.** Admission $4.50; free Sun and holidays. Tues–Sun 10am–7:45pm.

**Rufino Tamayo Museo de Arte Prehispánico de México** ★★★ The artifacts displayed in this museum were chosen "solely for the aesthetic rank of the works, their beauty, power, and originality." The result is a striking collection of pre-Hispanic art. The famed Oaxacan artist Rufino Tamayo amassed the collection over a 20-year period. The artifacts range from the pre-Classic period up to the Aztec, from far northwest Nayarit to southeastern Chiapas: terracotta figurines, scenes of daily life, lots of female fertility figures, Olmec and Totonac sculpture from the Gulf Coast, and Zapotec long-nosed figures. The beautifully displayed works reveal the great variety of styles of pre-Columbian art in Mexico.

Av. Morelos 503, north of the *zócalo* between Tinoco y Palacios and Porfirio Díaz. ✆ **951/516-4750.** Admission $3. Mon, Wed–Sat 10am–2pm and 4–7pm; Sun 10am–3pm. Closed holidays.

## CHURCHES

**Basílica de la Soledad** ★★ The Basílica is the most important religious center in Oaxaca, and its Virgin is the patroness of the entire state. Adjoining the church is a former convent with a small but charming museum in back. A huge celebration on and around December 18 honors the Virgin, attracting penitents from all over Oaxaca. She is famous for her vestments, which are encrusted with pearls. (Until a few years ago, she was also famous for her crown of silver and jewels, which was stolen.) As with most Virgins, there is a story behind her. The short version is that her figure (actually just her hands and face) was found in a box on the back of a burro that didn't belong to anyone. The burro sat down on an outcropping of rock and refused to get up. This was the spot where the Virgin revealed herself and, consequently, where the basilica (completed in 1690) was constructed. You can still see the outcropping of rock, surrounded by a cage of iron bars, immediately to your right along the wall as you enter the church.

The concave façade of the church projecting forward from the building is unique in Mexico's religious architecture. The way the top is rounded and the tiers are divided suggests an imitation in stone of the traditional carved wooden *retablos* (altarpieces) common in Mexican churches. The interior is most impressive, too, but what I really like is the museum, which contains a curious blend of pieces—some museum-quality, others mere trinkets that might as well have come from my grandmother's attic.

The Basílica's upper plaza is an outdoor patio and theater (Plaza de la Danza) with stone steps that serve as seats. Here, spectators view the famous Bani Stui Gulal (see "Fiesta Guelaguetza" under "Special Events & Festivals," above). When visiting the Basílica, it is traditional to eat ice cream; there are vendors in the lower plaza in front of the church.

Independencia at Galeana. No phone. Museum: Admission 25¢. Mon–Sat 10am–2pm and 4–6pm; Sun 11am–2pm. Basílica: Daily 7am–2pm and 4–9pm.

**Catedral de Oaxaca** ★★ The cathedral was built in 1553 and reconstructed in 1773. Its elaborate 18th-century baroque façade is an excellent example of the

Oaxacan style. The central panel above the door depicts the assumption of the Virgin. Note the heavy, elaborate frame around the picture and the highly stylized wavelike clouds next to the cherubs—these elements, repeated in other churches in the region, are telltale signs of Oaxacan baroque. An uncommon and quite lovely detail is how the Virgin's cape and its folds are depicted in angular lines and facets. The cathedral's interior is not as interesting as its exterior because it was plundered during the Wars of Reform.

Fronting the Parque Alameda. No phone. Free admission. Daily 7am–9pm.

**Iglesia de San Felipe Neri** This church, 2½ blocks northeast of the *zócalo,* was built in 1636 and displays all the architectural opulence of that period: The altar and nave are covered with ornately carved, gilded wood, and the walls are frescoed. In the west transept and chapel is a small figure of St. Martha and the dragon; the faithful have bedecked her with ribbons in hopes of obtaining her assistance.

Tinoco y Palacios at Independencia. No phone. Free admission. Daily 8am–11pm.

**Iglesia de Santo Domingo** ★★★ *Moments* There are 27 churches in Oaxaca, but none can equal the splendor of this one's interior. The church was started in the 1550s by Dominican friars and finished a century later; it contains the work of all the best artists of that period. Ornate plaster statues and flowers cover the extravagantly gilded walls and ceiling. When the sun shines through the yellow stained-glass window, it casts a golden glow over the whole interior and looks like a baroque vision of heaven. If you are there around 11am on Monday through Saturday, you are likely to hear the lovely sound of the gift-shop operator singing her devotions. Just as you enter, look up at the ceiling formed by the choir loft. Notice the beautifully depicted genealogical tree of the Dominican order, which starts with don Domingo de Guzmán, Saint Dominic himself.

Corner of Gurrión and Alcalá. No phone. Free admission. Daily 7am–2pm and 4–11pm.

**San Juan de Dios** This is the oldest church in Oaxaca, originally built in 1521 or 1522 of adobe and thatch. Construction of the present structure started during the mid-1600s and included a convent and hospital (where the 20 de Noviembre Market is now). The exterior is sweetly simple; the interior has an ornate altar and Urbano Olivera paintings on the ceiling. Oaxaqueños especially revere the glass shrine to the Virgin near the entrance, as well as one dedicated to Christ (off to the right). Because it's by the market, 1 block west and 2 blocks south of the *zócalo,* many of the people who visit the church are villagers who have come to Oaxaca to buy and sell.

20 de Noviembre s/n (corner of Aldama and Arteaga). No phone. Free admission. Daily 6am–11pm.

## MORE ATTRACTIONS

Besides visiting the places mentioned below, try to get to the **Casa de Cortés,** which houses the Museo de Arte Contemporáneo (see above), and the former convent of **Santa Catalina,** home of the Hotel Camino Real (see below).

**Casa de Juárez** This modest museum occupies the house where Benito Juárez first lived when he came to the city as a servant boy. It doesn't have any of his personal effects or any furniture belonging to the house, but it shows how a typical 19th-century household would have looked.

García Vigil 609. © **951/516-1860.** Admission $3; free on Sunday. Tues–Sat 10am–7pm; Sun 10am–5pm.

**Cerro del Fortín** To capture Oaxaca in a glance, take a cab to the top of this hill on the west side of town for a panoramic view of the city. It's especially pretty just before sunset. Atop the hill is the statue of Benito Juárez and a stadium built to hold 15,000 spectators. The annual Fiesta Guelaguetza is held here. You can walk to the hill: Head up Díaz Ordaz/Crespo and look for the Escaleras del Fortín (Stairway to the Fortress) shortly after you cross Calle Delmonte; the 218 steps (interrupted by risers) are a challenge, but the view is worth it.

Díaz Ordaz at Calle Delmonte. No phone.

**Teatro Macedonio de Alcalá** This beautiful 1903 Belle Epoque theater, 2 blocks east of the *zócalo,* holds 1,300 people and is still used for concerts and performances in the evening. Peek through the doors to see the marble stairway and Louis XV vestibule. Sometimes, a list of events is posted on the doors.

Independencia at Armenta y López. No phone. Open only for events.

## SHOPPING

Oaxaca and the surrounding villages are wonderful hunting grounds for handcrafted pottery, woodcarvings, and weavings, and the hunt itself may be the best part. Specialties include the shiny **black pottery** for which Oaxaca is famous, **woolen textiles** with the deep reds and purples produced using the natural dye *cochineal,* and highly imaginative **woodcarvings** (*alebrijes*).

For market days in outlying villages and directions to the important crafts villages, see "Shopping Splendor: Oaxaca's Market Villages," later.

### SHOPS AND GALLERIES

Most of the shops, galleries, and boutiques are in the area between **Santo Domingo** and the *zócalo,* comprising the streets of **Alcalá, Cinco de Mayo,** and **García Vigil** and the **cross streets.** Customary store hours are from 10am to 2pm and 4 to 7pm Monday to Saturday.

**Artesanías e Industrias Populares del Estado de Oaxaca** ARIPO is a government store with a broader range of goods than most stores, including masks, baskets, clothing, furniture, and cutlery. The staff speaks English and will ship anywhere. Open Monday to Friday from 9am to 8pm, Saturday from 10am to 6pm, and Sunday from 11am to 4pm. It is 2 blocks above the Benito Juárez house. García Vigil 809 (at Cosijopi). ✆ **951/514-4030.**

**Arte y Tradición** Four blocks north of the *zócalo,* a brightly painted doorway leads into this attractive arcade of shops with an open patio in the center. Each shop functions as a cooperative, with articles on consignment from various villages, such as Teotitlán del Valle and Arrazola. Individuals from the villages are on hand to explain the crafts (weaving, woodcarving, and the like) practiced by their townspeople. You'll also find a restaurant serving Oaxacan food, the Belaguetza Travel Agency, and a small bookstore. The store is open daily from 9am to 8pm; individual shop hours vary. García Vigil 406. ✆ **951/516-3552.**

**Corazón del Pueblo** *Finds* A buyer for museum gift shops recommended this store to me for the sophistication and quality of its wares. The owners, it turned out, used to be wholesale exporters of Mexican folk art and handcrafts. They know what they're doing. You'll find plenty of Oaxacan pottery, woodcarving, and weavings, as well as crafts you won't commonly see elsewhere. Alcalá 307, local 9, 2nd floor. ✆ **951/516-6960.**

**Galería Arte de Oaxaca** This gallery represents some of the state's leading contemporary artists. It's 2 blocks north and 1 block east of the *zócalo.* Murguía 105. ✆ **951/514-0910** or 951/514-1532.

**Galería Quetzalli** A modest-looking art gallery behind the Church of Santo Domingo and next to Los Pacos restaurant, Galería Quetzalli represents some of the big names in Mexican art—Francisco Toledo, José Villalobos—and some up-and-coming artists. Quetzalli has opened a new gallery at Murguía 400. Constitución 104. ✆ **951/514-0030.**

**Indigo** Beautiful and uncommon (and expensive) objects can be found here. The store can really test your resolution not to buy more artwork; go in and take a peek. Allende 104. ✆ **951/514-8338.**

**La Mano Mágica** Come here to see some of the best rug weaving in Oaxaca (by Arnulfo Mendoza) before you head to Teotitlán to see the work of other weavers. In the back rooms you can find well-chosen pieces of regional folk art. Shipping is available. The store is opposite the MACO. Alcalá 203 (between Morelos and Matamoros). ✆ **951/516-4275.**

### MARKETS

There are two market areas: one just south of the *zócalo;* and the newer Abastos Market, about 10 blocks west. Both areas bustle with people and are surrounded by small shops selling anything from hardware to leather goods to fabrics.

A few shops specialize in chocolate (not for eating, but for making hot chocolate) and *mole* paste. The neighboring state of Tabasco grows most of the cacao beans used for the chocolate. They are ground with almonds and cinnamon and pressed into bars or tablets. To prepare the drink, you dissolve the chocolate in hot milk or water (the more traditional drink) and beat until frothy. *Mole* paste, which contains chocolate, is used to make the classic Oaxacan dishes *mole negro* and *mole rojo.* A good place to hunt for chocolate and *mole* paste is along Mina street, on the south side of the 20 de Noviembre market (see listing below). Here you'll find **Chocolate Mayordomo** and **Chocolate La Soledad.** Both offer a variety of preparations to fit American and European tastes, but I like the traditional Mexican best.

**Benito Juárez Market** One block south of the *zócalo,* this covered market is big and busy; stalls sell vegetables, flowers, medicinal preparation, meats, cheeses, and even clothing. Between Calles Las Casas, Cabrera, Aldama, and 20 de Noviembre.

**Mercado Abastos** The Abastos Market is open daily but is most active on Saturday, when Indians from the villages come to town to sell and shop. You'll see dried chiles, herbs, vegetables, crafts, bread, and even burros for sale at this bustling market. Ten blocks west of zócalo, between Calle Mercaderes and the Periférico.

**Mercado de Artesanía** Located 1 block south and 1 block west of the 20 de Noviembre Market, this market sells mostly textiles and articles of clothing at cheap prices. J. P. García and Zaragoza.

**20 de Noviembre Market** This market is just south, across Aldama, from the Benito Juárez market. There are a lot of food stalls, but also some arts and crafts. On the south side, along Mina, are stores selling chocolate and *mole* paste. Between Calles Aldama, Cabrera, Mina, and 20 de Noviembre.

## OTHER THINGS TO DO

**COOKING CLASSES** **Iliana de la Vega** (✆ **951/514-1878;** www.elnaranjo.com.mx.), owner of El Naranjo (see "Where to Dine," below), offers Oaxacan cooking classes. She comes highly recommended. **Susana Trilling** (**© 951/518-7726;** www.seasonsofmyheart.com), author of the cookbook *Seasons of My Heart,* operates a cooking school of the same name just outside Oaxaca.

**SPANISH CLASSES** Oaxaca has about a half dozen language schools. With prior notice, most can arrange home stays with a Mexican family for students looking for total immersion. With little notice, most can arrange a week of classes for visitors who decide to brush up their language skills. The **Instituto Cultural Oaxaca A.C.,** Avenida Juárez 909 (Apdo. Postal 340), 68000 Oaxaca, Oax. (**© 951/515-3404;** www.instculturaloax.com.mx), has the biggest name and, perhaps, the least flexibility. Besides language skill, classes focus on Oaxaca's history, archaeology, anthropology, and botany—a good choice for those who find themselves asking questions about their surroundings. The **Instituto de Comunicación y Cultura,** Alcalá 307–12, 68000 Oaxaca, Oax. (© and fax **951/516-3443;** www.iccoax.com), provides group and private instruction, and uses music, art, and handcrafts to get students into the swing of things. Classes are small. This school has been around for some time and comes recommended by former students. **Becari Language School,** M. Bravo 210, 68000 Oaxaca, Oax. (**© 951/514-6076;** www.becari.com.mx) is about 7 years old, and I'm hearing more and more good things from students.

**HIKING & BIKING** Northwest of the city of Oaxaca is a mountain range known as the Sierra Norte that is cooler and wetter than the valley. The native communities offer guides and simple lodging for active sorts who are interested in seeing yet another side of Mexico. Several ecotourism outfits work with these communities. For information, ask at the State Tourist Office. **Bicicletas Bravo,** García Vigil 409-C, 68000 Oaxaca, Oax. (**© 951/516-0953;** www.bikeoaxaca.com), does bike tours and organizes hiking in the community of Ixtlán de Juárez. This outfit also leads bike tours of the valley, which avoid car traffic and are less challenging than biking the mountains.

## WHERE TO STAY

High season includes Easter, July, August, early November, and most of December. You should have no difficulty finding a room during the rest of the year, and promotional rates are usually available. The prices listed below include the 17% tax. For most of the year, evenings in Oaxaca are cool enough that you don't need air-conditioning, but on about 60 days a year, mostly from April to June, it comes in handy. Plan accordingly.

### VERY EXPENSIVE

**Casa Cid de León** ★★★ A small hotel in a colonial house, Casa Cid de León has easily the four largest suites in the historic district. Each is extravagantly decorated in colonial style, with a few modern touches and fresh-cut flowers. The one that garners the most attention (La Bella Epoca) has three balconies facing the street and a large sitting room. The two-story, two-bathroom suite (El Mio Cid) would be perfect for a family. One of the downstairs suites, La Dominica, is my favorite for its space, comfort, and quiet. Guests have access to a comfortable rooftop terrace. The location, 2 blocks north of the *zócalo,* is excellent, and the owner, Sra. Cid de León, is the most accommodating hotel owner I've ever met, giving new meaning to the phrase "personal service." The hotel offers custom tours of the city and surrounding valley.

Av. Morelos 602, 68000 Oaxaca, Oax. **© 951/514-1893.** Fax 951/514-7013. www.casaciddeleon.com. 4 units. $211–$258 suite. Rates include juice, coffee, newspaper delivery, airport transportation. AE, MC, V. Valet parking $10. **Amenities:** Tour and limo service; business services; in-room salon services; room service until 11pm; in-room massage; babysitting; overnight laundry service. *In room:* TV, hair dryer, bathrobe.

**Hotel Camino Real** ★★★ A magnificent hotel in a 16th-century landmark convent, this is the place to cloister yourself. Several beautiful courtyards with age-old walls bring to mind the original purpose of the building. The rooms, however, do not; nothing in them evokes thoughts of a nunnery. All are comfortable, well furnished, and have the conveniences you would expect in a hotel of this caliber (no small feat given the constraints imposed by the infrastructure). Exterior rooms have triple-glazed windows to reduce noise. Higher prices are for interior rooms with views of the courtyards. The main difference between "deluxe" and "club" is the size of the room. Service is superb. The location—between the *zócalo* and Santo Domingo on a pedestrian-only street—is ideal.

On Friday evenings the hotel holds a *Guelaguetza,* a regional dance show with dinner buffet ($30); on Saturday evenings there's a *mariachi* show with dinner buffet ($15).

Cinco de Mayo 300, 68000 Oaxaca, Oax. ✆ **800/722-6466** in the U.S. and Canada, or 951/516-0611. Fax 951/516-0732. www.caminoreal.com/oaxaca/. 91 units. $246–$270 deluxe; $304–$328 club; $380 jr. suite. Children under 12 stay free in parents' room. AE, DC, MC, V. Valet parking $13. **Amenities:** Restaurant, 2 bars; large outdoor swimming pool; tour desk; car rental; 24-hour room service; babysitting; same-day laundry and dry cleaning; nonsmoking rooms. *In room:* A/C, TV, minibar, hair dryer, safe.

## EXPENSIVE

**Hotel Marqués del Valle** ★ Oaxaca's main square is something special, which makes staying at this hotel right on the square something special, too. Rooms are medium-size and simply appointed, with plain Mexican pine furniture of the '40s and '50s. The beds are comfortable, with ample light for reading, but the lighting in general could be improved. Twenty-five rooms have air-conditioning. The bathrooms vary quite a bit: half contain tub/shower combinations, half just showers. All the exterior rooms have views of the Plaza or the Alameda, and double-glazed windows to keep out the noise; even so, interior rooms are much quieter. And when you step out the front door of the hotel, there you are.

Portal de Clavería s/n, 68000 Oaxaca, Oax. ✆ **951/514-0688** or 951/516-3474. Fax 951/516-9961. hmarques@prodigy.net.mx. 95 units. $120 double; $126 double with A/C. AE, DC, MC, V. **Amenities:** Tour desk; car rental; airport transportation; same-day laundry and dry cleaning; baby-sitting. *In room:* TV, dataport, hair dryer.

**Hotel Victoria** ★★ *Finds* High above the downtown area, the Hotel Victoria offers that rare combination of proximity and the feeling of distance. This place is ideal for those who want a little more peace than staying downtown can offer. And you're only a couple of minutes away on the hotel's shuttle bus. The Victoria also has a lovely view. You can enjoy it from a room or suite in one of the main buildings, or you can stay in one of the villas distributed about the grounds, each with its own terrace. Rooms are large, carpeted, and have modern furnishings. This hotel is not for people who mind climbing stairs.

Lomas del Fortín 1, 68070 Oaxaca, Oax. ✆ **951/515-2633.** Fax 951/515-2411. www.jade.com.mx/victoria. 150 units. $170 standard double; $214 villa; $260 suite. AE, MC, V. Free parking. **Amenities:** Restaurant, bar; large outdoor swimming pool; tennis court; complimentary shuttle to downtown; same-day laundry and dry cleaning; baby-sitting; nonsmoking rooms. *In room:* A/C, TV, minibar, hair dryer, safe.

## MODERATE

**Casa Colonial Bed and Breakfast** The casual and comfortable setting created by attentive hosts Jane and Thornton Robison promptly sets guests at ease.

This is an especially attractive place for first-timers to Oaxaca, who can tap into the owners' knowledge of the area and perhaps even tour some villages with them. The good-size rooms open to a large garden with tall jacaranda trees; they are simply but comfortably furnished. Breakfast is substantial: fresh fruit, yogurt, hot cereal, eggs, bacon, juice, and coffee. The hotel is farther from downtown than most of the others listed here: Walk past La Soledad church on Avenida Morelos, and angle right for a couple of blocks; it will be on your left. There is no sign; just look for a green house with purple trim. Rooms are not available for the Day of the Dead season or Christmas.

División Oriente, corner Negrete (Apdo. Postal 640), 68000 Oaxaca, Oax. ✆ **800/758-1697** in the U.S., or ✆ or fax 951/516-5280. www.mexonline.com/colonial.htm. 15 units. $95 double. Rates include full breakfast and tips. No credit cards. Free parking.

**Casa Cué** A modern, three-story hotel (there's no elevator) 2 blocks from the *zócalo,* Casa Cué has good air-conditioning, good service, and great bathrooms with instant hot water. The lovely terrace on top has comfortable patio furniture and a good view of the mountains. The medium-size standard rooms are attractively furnished and well lit; most contain two twin beds. Junior suites are large and come with a sofa, coffee table, and writing table; most hold two double beds (some have one king and one double). The suites are still larger, and the second bedroom makes them perfect for a family. The hotel is well managed. It's across the street from the market, which can be a little noisy, but the double-glazed windows do a good job of blocking it out. Lower rates are for low season.

Aldama 103, 68000 Oaxaca, Oax. ✆ and fax **951/516-1336.** hcasacue@rnet.com.mx. 23 units. $68–79 double; $96–$110 jr. suite; $136–159 suite. Rates include continental breakfast. AE, MC, V. Free covered, secure parking. **Amenities:** Restaurant, bar; exercise equipment; tour info; car rental; room service until 10pm; same-day laundry and dry cleaning. *In room:* A/C, TV.

**Hotel Aitana** *Value* Offering the most attractive, comfortable rooms in this price range, this stylish hotel is a good choice. The Aitana is only 8 blocks from the *zócalo* and 6 blocks from Santo Domingo, but it is about 30m (100 ft.) uphill on a noisy street. All the rooms are away from the street, however, past a lovely courtyard restaurant. Background noise filters in. Most of the well-lit, beautifully decorated rooms hold two twin beds, or you can get two doubles or a king. Bathrooms are ample, with shower/tub combinations.

Crespo 313, 68000 Oaxaca, Oax. ✆ **951/514-3788.** Fax 951/516-9856. aita@prodigy.net.mx. 23 units. $84–110 double. MC, V. **Amenities:** Restaurant, bar; tour info; room service until 10:30pm; same-day laundry and dry cleaning. *In room:* TV, coffeemaker, hair dryer.

## INEXPENSIVE

**Hotel Casa Arnel** ★ *Kids* Not far from the bus station, this budget hotel is about a mile from the *zócalo* but still within walking distance of most sights. It's a great choice for those traveling with kids: The Cruz family lives here with a couple of their children, and there is a shady garden where parrots hang out. From the rooftop terrace, you can admire the view and soak up some sun. Most rooms are plain but comfortable; some share bathrooms. Across the street in the new wing are three additional rooms with double beds and private bathrooms, plus four furnished, full-service apartments with fully equipped kitchens. Breakfast, at extra cost, is served on the patio. At Christmas, the family involves guests in the traditional Mexican celebrations or *posadas,* which are held during the 12 nights before Christmas. Rates rise about 30% for Christmas, Guelagetza, Easter, and Día de los Muertos.

Aldama 404, Col. Jalatlaco, 68080 Oaxaca, Oax. ✆ and fax **951/515-2856.** www.casaarnel.com.mx. 40 units, 22 with bathroom. $29 double without bathroom; $38 double with bathroom; suite $67. Apartment $380–$450 monthly. No credit cards. Parking $3. **Amenities:** Laundry; tours of local destinations; Internet access.

**Hotel Francia** The most comfortable of the budget hotels in and about the *zócalo,* the Francia has been around long enough to acquire some history of its own: It has housed some famous writers who have passed through the city (D. H. Lawrence, Malcolm Lowry). Rooms are fairly large, with plain furniture, tile floors, and a variety of combinations of double and twin beds. Most bathrooms are large but minimally furnished, with small sinks and mirrors, and simple showers. Interior rooms are quieter, and the ones on the colonial side are a bit better than most on the modern side.

20 de Noviembre 212, 68000 Oaxaca, Oax. ✆ **951/516-4811** or 951/516-4251. 58 units. $54 double. 10%–20% low-season discount. AE, MC, V. **Amenities:** Restaurant; tour info; limited room service. *In room:* TV.

**Hotel Principal** *Value* The Principal, 1 block east and 2½ blocks north of the *zócalo,* is a longtime favorite of budget travelers. The location—near shops, museums, and restaurants—is great. Rooms are simply furnished and not well lit. Three have balconies over the street; the rest are off the interior patio. Most have a double bed with a comfortable mattress. Except for the three rooms with balconies, all the rooms are quiet.

Cinco de Mayo 208, 68000 Oaxaca, Oax. ✆ and fax **951/516-2535.** 16 units. $40 double. No credit cards. Parking on street.

**Las Golondrinas** ★★ This charming one-story hotel sits amid rambling patios with roses, fuchsia, bougainvillea, and mature banana trees. Owned and managed by Guillermina and Jorge Velasco, Las Golondrinas ("The Swallows") is very popular, so make reservations in advance. The simply furnished rooms, with windows and doors opening onto courtyards, all have tile floors and a small desk and chairs. Each holds either one full or two twin beds. Breakfast is served between 8 and 10am in a small tile-covered cafe in a garden setting ($3–$7); nonguests are welcome. The hotel is 6½ blocks north of the *zócalo.*

Tinoco y Palacios 411 (between Allende and Bravo), 68000 Oaxaca, Oax. ✆ **951/514-3298** or ✆ and fax 951/514-2126. lasgolon@prodigy.net.mx. 29 units. $45 double. MC, V. Limited free parking. **Amenities:** Laundry service.

## WHERE TO DINE

Oaxacan cooking has a great reputation in Mexico. It is a highland style that includes more ingredients from the lowlands and southern areas than central Mexican cooking. The state is best known for its *moles,* which are different from the *moles* of central Mexico.

If you're curious to know more about Oaxacan cooking, **Zapotec Tours** (✆ **800/446-2922** in the U.S.) organizes a weeklong trip to the city in early October. The "Food of the Gods Festival" includes dining at different restaurants, cooking classes, a tour of the market, and field trips.

### EXPENSIVE

**El Ché** ★ STEAK Need a break from spicy Mexican food? Have a steak and salad in attractive surroundings, and wash it down with a classic margarita. The restaurant offers both American and Argentine cuts of beef; the rib-eye and the *churrasco* are the most popular. Salads include Caesar and Roquefort prepared at the table.

## *Finds* Oaxacan Street Food

Unless it's during a festival, don't be surprised to find many restaurants empty. Oaxaqueños do not frequent restaurants but do like eating in market and street stalls. They favor foods such as tacos, tamales, *tlayudas* (12-in. tortillas, slightly dried, with a number of toppings), and *quesadillas* (in Oaxaca, large tortillas heated on the *comal* or among the coals, with several types of fillings). For adventurous diners, here are my picks for Oaxacan street food.

Quesadillas are a morning food, and the best place to eat them is in **La Merced** market (on Murguía, about 10 blocks east of Alcalá), where you'll find a number of food stalls. Everyone has a favorite; mine is **La Florecita,** and my favorite quesadilla comes with huitlacoche. The following places open only at night. For tacos, a little *taquería* called **Tacos Sierra** (on Morelos, a half block west of Alcalá) is a Oaxaca institution. It makes simple tacos with pork filling and a spicy salsa, but I can never order enough. It closes when the pork runs out, usually before 10pm. For *tlayudas,* seek out a hole-in-the-wall on Constitución around the corner from Libres, **El Chepil.** They come with a number of toppings, and with *tasajo* or *cecina* on the side. If you don't like lard, say you want yours without *asiento.* For tamales, find the woman who sets up her little stand on Avenida Hidalgo and 20 de Noviembre, in front of the pharmacy. She often doesn't get there until 7:30pm, but when she does, she draws a crowd that buys tamales to go—six flavors, and my favorite is always the last one I've eaten. Since you're in Oaxaca, you might want to ask for a *tamal* made with *mole negro, mole amarillo,* or *chepil* (an herb).

5 de Mayo 413. ✆ **951/514-2122.** Reservations recommended during special festivals. Steaks $13–$20. MC, V. Daily 1–11pm.

### MODERATE

**El Asador Vasco** INTERNATIONAL/MEXICAN Of the restaurants circling the *zócalo,* this is the best bet. It certainly offers the most pleasant dining area: Tables overlook the *zócalo* from a second-floor stone archway. Take your pick of purely Mexican specialties (chiles rellenos, *moles, carne asada*) or dishes with a European twist (snapper filet cooked in olive oil and *chile guajillo*).

Portal de Flores 11. ✆ **951/514-4755.** Main courses $8–$18. MC, V. Daily 1–11:30pm.

**El Naranjo** ★★★ *Moments* OAXACAN/MEXICAN El Naranjo, where the emphasis is on Oaxacan specialties, is my favorite restaurant in the city. The owner and chef, Iliana de la Vega, prepares dishes that she grew up cooking and eating. She has added some others and made alterations, such as reducing the fat, to bring out the flavors of the vegetables, herbs, and chiles. If you have a craving for a salad but have been reluctant, this is your chance—all the greens are dipped in anti-microbial solution. For a main dish, try the featured *mole* of the day. For an especially exotic flavor, try fish cooked in the leaves of *hoja santa* (an herb) with a tangy sauce made from the *guajillo* chile. For something spicier, try the chile *pasilla oxaqueño* stuffed with string cheese. A milder choice is poblano chile stuffed with squash blossoms. The restaurant occupies the roofed courtyard of a colonial house 1½ blocks from the southwest corner of the *zócalo.* El Naranjo also hosts cooking classes (see "Other Things to Do," earlier).

Trujano 203. ✆ **951/514-1878.** Main courses $7.50–$14. Reservations recommended during festivals and holidays. AE, MC, V. Mon–Sat 1–10pm.

**La Olla** OAXACAN/MEXICAN The small dining area, which opens up to the street through three doors, is bright and cheerful. Popular Oaxacan dishes served here include *mole negro, mole coloradito,* or Oaxacan tamales. Soups, salads, and delicious blends of tropical juice are also available. La Olla is 5 blocks north and east of the *zócalo,* facing the rear wall of the Camino Real Hotel.

Reforma 402. ✆ **951/516-6668.** Main courses $6–$10; *comida corrida* $5. MC, V. Mon–Sat 9am–10pm.

**Marco Polo** SEAFOOD Specialties at this small, cheerfully decorated restaurant include filet of red snapper or a chile de agua, stuffed with shellfish. The empanadas *de cazón* (shark) were good, especially with chipotle mayonnaise. The economical *comida corrida* and breakfasts don't include seafood but bring in lots of people just the same.

5 de Mayo 103. ✆ **951/514-4360.** Main courses $6–$10; breakfast $3; *comida corrida* $4.50. AE, MC, V. Mon–Sat 8am–9pm.

### INEXPENSIVE

**Doña Elpidia** ★ *Finds* OAXACAN The phrase "home-style cooking" is bandied about a lot, but in this case it really means something. For the traveler, it means a meal just like the main dinner in a well-run Mexican home. Finding this place is a bit of a trick; it's 5½ blocks south of the *zócalo.* Look for a small sign saying only RESTAURANT. When you enter, a chalkboard in front of you will list the day's meal. You will find some tables behind the overgrown garden. There is also indoor dining. The *comida corrida* includes a basket of bread, an appetizer, vegetable or pasta soup, rice, a meat or enchilada course, and dessert. Beer and other beverages are available.

Miguel Cabrera 413 (between Arista and Nuño del Mercado). ✆ **951/516-4292.** Fixed-price lunch $5. No credit cards. Daily 1–5pm.

**Restaurant El Mesón** *Value* MEXICAN/REGIONAL The mainstays here are an open buffet catering to working folk and the tacos at night. The all-you-can-eat buffet includes fresh fruit and salads plus a variety of main courses—exercise caution, however, because you'll get charged extra if you leave a lot of food on your plate. Avoid the pasta. To order tacos at night, you'll be presented with a slip of paper listing the tacos and other *antojitos* and a pencil. Check off what you want. Taco prices are per order. The restaurant also serves such specialties as *tamal Oaxaqueño* and *pozole.* It's across from the northeast corner of the *zócalo.*

Av. Hidalgo 805 (at Valdivieso). ✆ **951/516-2729.** Breakfast, lunch, and supper buffet $5; Mexican specialties $1.50–$7. AE, MC, V. Daily 8am–1am.

## OAXACA AFTER DARK

If you are interested in seeing the region's traditional dances, you can check out the small-scale **Guelaguetza** performed by professional dancers at the Hotel Camino Real on Friday from 7 to 10pm. The cost ($30) includes a buffet. **La Casa de Cantera,** Murguía 102 (✆ **951/514-7585**), offers something similar. The $11 cover is for the show only, which runs every night from 8:30 to 10:15pm. Drinks and supper cost extra. Call for reservations.

Concerts and dance programs take place all year at the **Teatro Macedonio de Alcalá,** Independencia and Armenta y López. Schedules are often posted by the front doors of the theater. In the early evening, the ***zócalo*** is a happening place, with all sorts of people out and about. The municipal brass band and marimba players perform free concerts on alternating nights. As the night wears on, usually you'll find some mariachis hanging about.

One of my favorite places to hear music is **El Sol y La Luna,** Reforma 502 (**© 951/514-8069**). The owner gets a lot of good bands from Mexico City—jazz and blues acts mainly—and some interesting performers from Veracruz and other neighboring states. You never know what you'll find, but it's usually good. There's often a cover of around $5, and you can order food (mostly pizza). For salsa, go to **La Candela,** Murguía 413 (**© 951/514-2010**), which offers live music Thursday to Saturday from 10:30pm to 2am. The cover is usually $2.50.

## ROAD TRIPS FROM OAXACA

The countryside around Oaxaca is dotted with small archeological sites and villages, and the most important are easy to reach. The landmark ruins in the region are **Monte Albán** (30 min.) and **Mitla** (1 hr.). If you're heading toward Mitla, you can make a number of interesting stops (see "The Road to Mitla: Ruins & Rug Weavers," below). A number of interesting villages in other directions make good day trips from Oaxaca. The State Tourism Office will give you a map that shows nearby villages where beautiful handcrafts are made. The visits are fun excursions by car or bus. If you want to go overland to one of Oaxaca's seaside resorts, see "By Bus," under "Getting There & Departing," in this chapter and chapter 9.

Many villages have, in the past several years, developed fine small municipal museums. **San José El Mogote,** site of one of the earliest pre-Hispanic village-dweller groups, has a display of carvings and statues found in and around the town, and a display model of an old hacienda. **Teotitlán del Valle** also has a municipal museum; it features displays on the weaving process. Ask at the State Tourism Office for more information.

### MONTE ALBAN: RUINS WITH A VIEW

Had I been the priest-king of a large Indian nation in search of the perfect site on which to build a ceremonial center, this would have been it. **Monte Albán** sits on a mountain that rises from the middle of the valley floor—or, rather, divides two valleys. From here you can see all that lies between you and the distant mountains.

Starting around 2000 B.C., village-dwelling peoples of unknown origin inhabited the Oaxaca valleys. Between 800 and 500 B.C., a new ceramic style appeared, indicating an influx of new peoples, now called Zapotec. Around 500 B.C., these peoples began the monumental exercise of leveling the top of a mountain, where they would build Monte Albán (*mohn*-teh ahl-*bahn*).

Very little of the original structures remain; they've either been obscured beneath newer construction or had their stones reused for other buildings. The **Danzantes friezes** (see below) date from this period.

A center of Zapotec culture, Monte Albán was also influenced by contemporary cultures outside the valley of Mexico. You can see Olmec influence in the early sculptures; more recent masks and sculptures reflect contact with the Maya. When Monte Albán was at its zenith in A.D. 300, it borrowed architectural ideas from Teotihuacán. By around A.D. 800, the significance of Monte Albán in Zapotec society began to wane. Although most likely never completely abandoned, it became a shadow of its former grandeur. At the beginning of the 13th century, the Mixtec appropriated Monte Albán. The Mixtec, who had long coexisted in the area with the Zapotec, began expanding their territory. At Monte Albán, they added little to the existing architecture; however, they seem to have considered it an appropriate burial ground for their royalty. They left many tombs, including **Tomb 7,** with its famous treasure.

Monte Albán centers on the **Great Plaza,** a man-made area created by flattening the mountaintop. From this plaza, aligned north to south, you can survey the Oaxacan valley. The excavations at Monte Albán have revealed more than 170 tombs, numerous ceremonial altars, stelae, pyramids, and palaces.

Begin your tour of the ruins on the eastern side of the Great Plaza at the I-shaped **ball court.** This ball court differs slightly from Maya and Toltec ball courts in that there are no goal rings, and the sides of the court slope. Also on the east side of the plaza are several **altars and pyramids** that were once covered with stucco. Note the sloping walls, wide stairs, and ramps; all are typical of Zapotec architecture and reminiscent of the architecture of Teotihuacán. The building, slightly out of line with the plaza (not on the north-south axis), is thought by some to have been an observatory; it was probably aligned with the heavenly bodies rather than with the points of the compass.

The south side of the plaza has a large **platform** that bore several stelae, most of which are now in the National Museum of Anthropology in Mexico City. There's a good view of the surrounding area from the top of this platform.

The west side has more ceremonial platforms and pyramids. On top of the pyramid substructure are four columns that probably supported the roof of the temple at one time.

The famous **Building of the Dancers** (*Danzantes*), on the west side of the plaza, is the earliest known structure at Monte Albán. This building is covered with large stone slabs that have distorted naked figures carved into them (the ones you see are copies; the originals are protected in the site museum). There is speculation about who carved these figures and what they represent, although there is a distinct resemblance to the Olmec *baby faces* at La Venta, in Tabasco State. The distorted bodies and pained expressions might connote disease. Clear examples of figures representing childbirth, dwarfism, and infantilism are visible. Because of the fluid movement represented in the figures, they became known as the *Danzantes*—merely a modern label for these ancient and mysterious carvings.

The **Northern Platform** is a maze of temples and palaces interwoven with subterranean tunnels and sanctuaries. Take time to wander here, for there are numerous reliefs, glyphs, paintings, and friezes along the lintels and jambs as well as the walls. In this section of the ruins, you are likely to see vendors discreetly selling "original" artifacts found at the site. These guys come from the nearby town of Arrazola, where the fabrication of "antiquities" is a long-standing cottage industry. I like to buy a piece from them occasionally and pretend I'm getting the real thing just to get an opportunity to talk with them.

Leaving the Great Plaza, head north to the **cemetery** and **tombs.** If you have a day to spend at Monte Albán, be sure to visit some of the tombs, which contain magnificent glyphs, paintings, and stone carvings of gods, goddesses, birds, and serpents. Lately, the tombs have been closed to the public, but check anyway. Of the tombs so far excavated, the most famous is **Tomb 7,** next to the parking lot. It yielded some 500 pieces of gold, amber, and turquoise jewelry, as

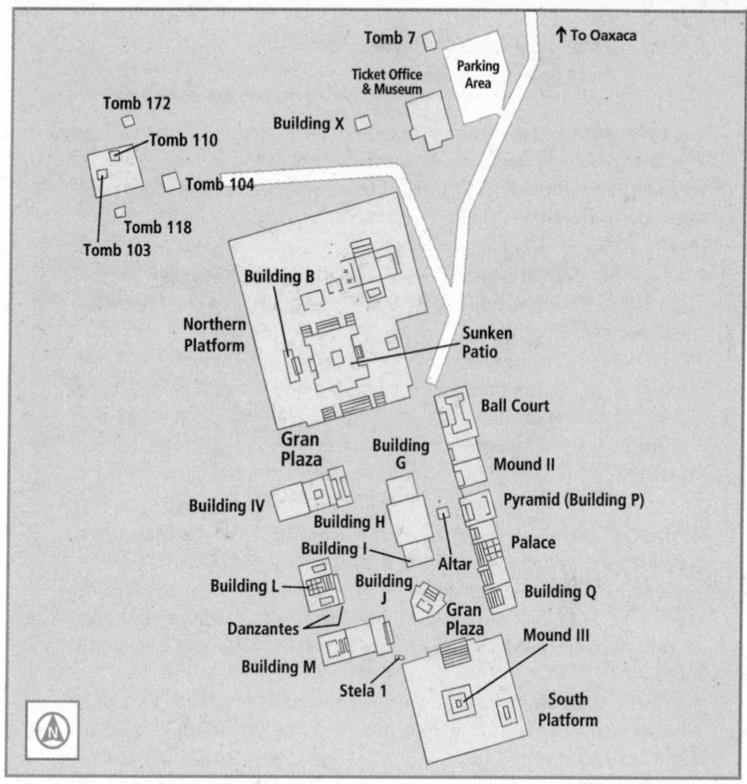


well as silver, alabaster, and bone art objects. This amazing collection is on display at the Regional Museum of Oaxaca.

As you enter the site, you'll see a museum, a shop with guidebooks to the ruins, a cafe, and a craft shop. I recommend purchasing a guidebook. Admission to the ruins is $4 but is free on Sunday and holidays. The site is open daily from 8am to 6pm. Licensed guides charge $15 per person for a walking tour. Video camera permits cost $5.

To get to Monte Albán, take a bus from the Hotel Mesón del Angel, Mina 518, at Mier y Terán. **Autobuses Turísticos** makes seven runs daily, at 8:30, 9:30, 10:30, and 11:30am and 12:30, 1:30, and 3:30pm. Return service leaves the ruins at 11am, noon, 1, 2, 3, 4, and 5:30pm. The round-trip fare is $4. The ride takes half an hour, and your scheduled return time is 2 hours after arrival. It's possible to take a later return for an additional $1 (though you won't be guaranteed a seat); inform the driver of your intent. During high season there are usually additional buses. If you're driving from Oaxaca, take Calle Trujano out of town. It becomes the road to Monte Albán, about 10km (6 miles) away.

## THE ROAD TO MITLA: RUINS & RUG WEAVERS

East of Oaxaca, the Pan American Highway (Hwy. 190) leads to Mitla and passes several important archaeological sites, markets, and craft villages. You can visit the famous El Tule tree, an enormous, ancient cypress; the church at Tlacochahuaya, a lovely example of a 17th-century village church; the ruins at

## *Moments* Shopping Splendor: Oaxaca's Market Villages

You could spend a full week in Oaxaca just visiting the various markets in nearby villages. Each has its specialty—cheese, produce, livestock, weaving, and pottery—and unique character. Market days in the villages are as follows:

| Day | Market |
|---|---|
| Wednesday | **Etla,** known for its cheese; 15 km (9½ miles) north. |
| Thursday | **Zaachila,** ruins and agriculture; 16km (11 miles) southwest. |
| | **Ejutla,** agriculture; 64km (40 miles) south. |
| Friday | **Ocotlán,** pottery, textiles, and food; 30km (19 miles) south. |
| Saturday | **Oaxaca,** Abastos Market. |
| Sunday | **Tlacolula,** agriculture and crafts (visit the chapel as well); 31km (20 miles) southeast. |

You can get to any of these craft villages by bus from the second-class station, 8 blocks west of the *zócalo* on Trujano. On market days, passengers cram these buses. If you get off a bus between destinations—say, at Cuilapan (see below) on the way to Zaachila—but want to continue to the next place, return to the highway and hail a passing bus.

It's also possible to take a *colectivo* taxi to the villages that don't have bus service. To find a *colectivo,* head to the south end of the Abastos Market. On Calle Mercaderes you'll see dozens of maroon-and-white *colectivo* taxis. The town each one serves is written on the door, trunk, or windshield. Posted metal signs also give destinations. Taxis fill up relatively fast and are an economical way to reach the villages. Be sure to go early; by afternoon the *colectivos* don't fill up as fast, and you'll have to wait.

One of the many tour operators in the city can easily arrange tours to all the markets as well as the craft villages and ruins. Go to any travel agent or ask at your hotel.

Dainzú, Lambityeco, and Yagul; the weaver's village of Teotitlán del Valle; and the village of Tlacolula, with its famous Dominican chapel.

There are a lot of little stops on this route, and some are a bit off the highway, so I recommend hiring a taxi, renting a car, or signing up with a small tour rather than using local bus transportation. If you take a tour, ask which sites it includes. To get to the highway, go north from downtown to Calzada Niños Héroes and turn right. This feeds directly on to the highway. All the sites are listed in order of how you would come across them after leaving Oaxaca.

**SANTA MARIA DEL TULE'S 2,000-YEAR-OLD TREE** Santa María del Tule is a small town 8km (5 miles) outside Oaxaca. It's famous for the immense **El Tule Tree,** an *ahuehuete* (Montezuma cypress, akin to the bald cypress) standing in a churchyard just off the main road. Now over 2,000 years old, it looks every bit its age, the way large cypresses do. However, this one is the most impressive tree I've ever seen for the sheer width of its trunk and canopy. It is said to have the broadest trunk of any tree in the world. When the tree was younger, the entire region around Santa María del Tule was marshland; in fact, the word *tule* means "reed." Now, the water table has dropped, so to protect the tree, a private foundation waters and takes care of it. The 25¢ admission fee goes towards these efforts.

The **Iglesia de San Jerónimo Tlacochahuaya,** 6km (4 miles) farther along, is the next stop. You'll see a sign pointing right; go another mile into town. Inside the church is an elaborately carved altar and a crucifix fashioned from a ground paste made from the corn plant. The murals decorating the walls were the work of local artists of the 18th century and are a sweet mix of Spanish and Indian aesthetics. Make a point of seeing the beautifully painted baroque organ in the choir loft. The church is usually open from 10am to 2pm and 4 to 8pm.

**DAINZU'S ZAPOTEC RUINS** Three kilometers (2 miles) farther, visible from the highway (26km/16 miles from Oaxaca), you'll see a sign pointing to the right. It's less than a mile to the ruins, which were first excavated in the 1960s. Dainzú is a pre-Classic site that dates from between 700 and 600 B.C. Increasingly sophisticated building continued until about A.D. 300. The site occupies the western face of a hill, presumably for defense. The main building is a platform structure whose walls were decorated with carvings resembling Monte Albán's *Danzantes.* These carvings are now in a protective shed; a caretaker will unlock it for interested parties. These figures show Olmec influence but differ from the *Danzantes* because they wear the trappings of the "ball game," which make them in all likelihood the earliest representations of the ball game in Mexico. And, in fact, a partially reconstructed ball court sits below the main structure. The site provides an outstanding view of the valley. Admission is $1.50.

**TEOTITLAN DEL VALLE'S BEAUTIFUL RUGS** The next major turnoff you come to is 2km (1½ miles) farther along, 3km (2 miles) from the highway. This is Teotitlán, famous for weaving, and now an obviously prosperous town, to judge by all the current development. This is where you'll want to go for rugs, and you'll find no shortage of weavers and stores. Most weavers sell out of their homes and give demonstrations. The prices are considerably lower than in Oaxaca, and you have the opportunity to visit weavers at home.

The church in town is well worth a visit. The early friars used pre-Hispanic construction stones to build the church and then covered them with adobe. When the townspeople renovated the church, they rediscovered these stones with carved figures, and now proudly display them. You'll see them in odd places in the walls of the church and sacristy. Teotitlán also has a small community museum, opposite the artisans' market and adjacent to the church. The museum has an interesting exhibit on natural dye-making, using herbs, plants, and *cochineal.*

For a bite to eat, consider the **Restaurant Tlamanalli,** Av. Juárez 39 (✆ **951/524-4006**), run by three Zapotec sisters who serve Oaxacan cuisine. Its reputation attracts lots of foreigners. It's on the right on the main street as you approach the main part of town, in a red brick building with black wrought-iron window covers. It's open Monday to Friday from 1 to 4pm. A bit farther on, there's another nice restaurant on the left where the main street intersects with the town center.

**LAMBITYECO'S RAIN GOD** Getting back to the highway and continuing eastward, in 3km (2 miles) you'll see is a turnoff on the right for the small archaeological site of Lambityeco. Of particular interest are the two beautifully executed and preserved **stucco masks** of the rain god Cocijo. At Lambityeco, a major product was salt, distilled from saline groundwaters nearby. Admission is $1.

**TLACOLULA'S FINE MARKET & UNIQUE CHAPEL** Located about 32km (20 miles) from Oaxaca (1.5km/1 mile past Lambityeco), Tlacolula is in *mezcal* country, and along the road from here to Mitla, you'll see a couple of small distilleries and distillery outlets advertising their product. Feel free to stop by any one of them to taste their wares. *Mezcal* is distilled from a species of *agave* different from that of *tequila.* Most *mezcal* has a very strong smell and may or may not come with a worm in the bottle. Many of these small distilleries flavor their *mezcal* much like Russians flavor vodka.

Sunday is market day in Tlacolula, with rows of textiles fluttering in the breeze and aisle after aisle of pottery and baskets. If you don't go on market day, you have the advantage of not competing with crowds. The **Capilla del Mártir** of the parochial church is a stunning display of virtuosity in wrought iron. The doorway, choir screen, and pulpit, with their baroque convolutions, have no equals in Mexico's religious architecture. Also eye-catching are the realistic, almost life-size sculptures of the 12 apostles in their various manners of martyrdom. A few years ago, a secret passage was found in the church, leading to a room that contained valuable silver religious pieces. The silver was hidden during the Revolution of 1916, when there was a tide of anticlerical sentiment; the articles are now back in the church.

**YAGUL'S ZAPOTEC FORTRESS** Yagul, a fortress city on a hill overlooking the valley, is a couple of kilometers farther on down the highway. You'll see the turnoff to the left; it's about half a mile off the road. The setting is spectacular, and because the ruins are not as fully reconstructed as those at Monte Albán, you're likely to have the place to yourself. It's a good place for a picnic lunch.

The city was divided into two sections: the fortress at the top of the hill and the palaces lower down. The center of the palace complex is the plaza, surrounded by four temples. In the center is a ceremonial platform, under which is the **Triple Tomb.** The door of the tomb is a large stone slab decorated on both sides with beautiful hieroglyphs. The tomb may be open for viewing; if there are two guards, one can leave the entrance to escort visitors.

Look for the beautifully restored, typically Zapotec **ball court.** North of the plaza is the **palace** structure built for the chiefs of the city. It's a maze of rooms and patios decorated with painted stucco and stone mosaics. Visible here and there are ceremonial mounds and tombs decorated in the same geometric patterns found in Mitla. The panoramic view of the valley from the fortress is worth the rather exhausting climb.

Admission is $1.50 and is free on Sunday and holidays. Still cameras are free, but use of a video camera costs $3. The site is open daily from 8am to 5:30pm.

It's just a few kilometers farther southeast to Mitla. The turnoff comes at a very obvious fork in the road.

**MITLA'S LARGE ZAPOTEC & MIXTEC SITE** Mitla is 4km (2¾ miles) from the highway; the turnoff terminates at the **ruins** by the church. If you've come here by bus, it's about half a mile up the road from the dusty town square to the ruins; if you want to hire a cab, there are some in the square.

The Zapotec settled Mitla around 600 B.C., and it became a Mixtec bastion in the late 10th century. This city was still flourishing at the time of the Spanish Conquest, and many of the buildings were used through the 16th century.

Tour groups often bypass the **town of Mitla** (pop. 7,000), but it is worth a visit. The University of the Americas maintains the **Museum of Zapotec Art** (previously known as the Frissell collection) in town. It contains some outstanding Zapotec and Mixtec relics. Admission is $3. Be sure to look at the Leigh collection, which contains some real treasures. The museum is in a beautiful old hacienda.

You can easily see the most important buildings in an hour. Mixtec architecture is based on a quadrangle surrounded on three or four sides by patios and chambers, usually rectangular in shape. The chambers have a low roof, which is excellent for defense but makes the rooms dark and close. The stone buildings are inlaid with small cut stones to form geometric patterns.

There are five groups of buildings, divided by the Mitla River. The most important buildings are on the east side of the ravine. The **Group of the Columns** consists of two quadrangles, connected at the corners with palaces. The building to the north has a long chamber with six columns and many rooms decorated with geometric designs. The most common motif is the zigzag pattern, the same one seen repeatedly on Mitla blankets. Human or animal images are rare in Mixtec art. In fact, only one **frieze** has been found (in the Group of the Church, on the north patio). Here, you'll see a series of figures painted with their name glyphs.

Admission to the site is $3. Use of a video camera costs $5. Entrance to the museum is included in the price. It's open daily from 8am to 5pm.

Outside the ruins, vendors will hound you. The moment you step out of a car or taxi, every able-bodied woman and child for 16km (10 miles) around will come charging over with shrill cries and a basket full of bargains—heavily embroidered belts, small pieces of pottery, fake archaeological relics, and cheap earrings. Offer to pay half the price the vendors ask. There's a modern handcrafts market near the ruins, but prices are lower in town.

## SOUTH OF MONTE ALBAN: ARRAZOLA, CUILAPAN & ZAACHILA

**ARRAZOLA: WOODCARVING CAPITAL** Arrazola lies in the foothills of Monte Albán, about 24km (15 miles) southwest of Oaxaca. The tiny town's most famous resident is **Manuel Jiménez,** the septuagenarian grandfather of the resurgence in woodcarving-as-folk-art. Jiménez's polar bears, anteaters, and rabbits carved from copal wood are shown in galleries throughout the world; his home is a mecca for folk-art collectors. Now the town is full of other carvers, all making fanciful creatures painted in bright, festive colors. Little boys will greet you at the outskirts offering to guide you to individual homes for a small tip. Following them is a good way to get to know the town, and after a bit you can take your leave of them.

If you're driving to Arrazola, take the road out of Oaxaca City that goes to Monte Albán, then take the left fork after crossing the Atoyac River and follow the signs for Zaachila. Turn right after the town of Xoxo and you will soon reach Arrazola. You can also take buses from the second-class station near the Abastos Market.

**CUILAPAN'S DOMINICAN MONASTERY** Cuilapan (Kwi-*lap*-an) is about 16km (10 miles) southwest of Oaxaca. The Dominican friars inaugurated their second **monastery** here in 1550. Parts of the convent and church were never completed due to political complications in the late 16th century. The roof of the monastery has fallen in, but the cloister and the church remain. The church, which is still in use, is being restored. There are three naves with lofty arches, large stone columns, and many frescoes. It is open daily from 10am to 6pm; entry is $5.50, plus $4 for a video camera. The monastery is visible on the right a short distance from the main road to Zaachila, and there's a sign as well. The bus from the second-class station stops within a few hundred feet of the church.

**ZAACHILA: MARKET TOWN WITH MIXTEC TOMBS** Farther on from Cuilapan, 24km (15 miles) southwest of Oaxaca, Zaachila (Za-*chee*-la) has a **Thursday market;** baskets and pottery are sold for local household use, and the produce market is always full. Also take note of the interesting livestock section and a ***mercado de madera*** (wood market) just as you enter town.

Behind the church is the entrance to a small **archaeological site** containing several mounds and platforms and two interesting tombs. The artifacts found here now reside in the National Museum of Anthropology in Mexico City, but **Tomb 1** contains carvings that are worth checking out.

At the time of the Spanish Conquest, Zaachila was the last surviving city of the Zapotec rulers. When Cortés marched on the city, the Zapotec offered no resistance, and he formed an alliance with them. This outraged the Mixtec, who invaded Zaachila shortly afterward. The site and tombs are open daily from 9am till 4pm, and the entrance fee is $1.50.

To return to Oaxaca, your best option is to line up with locals to take one of the *colectivo* taxis on the main street across from the market. If you're driving, see the directions for Arrazola, above.

## SOUTH ALONG HIGHWAY 175

**SAN BARTOLO COYOTEPEC'S POTTERY** San Bartolo is the home of the famous **black pottery** sold all over Oaxaca. It's also one of several little villages named Coyotepec in the area. Buses frequently operate between Oaxaca and this village, 16km (10 miles) south on Highway 175. In 1953, a native woman named Doña Rosa invented the technique of smoking the pottery during firing to make it black and rubbing the fired pieces with a piece of quartz to produce a sheen. Doña Rosa died in 1979, and her son, **Valente Nieto Real,** carries on the tradition. Watching Valente change a lump of coarse clay into a work of art with only two crude plates (used as a potter's wheel) is an almost magical experience. The family's home and factory is a few blocks off the main road; you'll see the sign as you enter town. It's open daily from 9am to 5:30pm.

You can buy black pottery at many shops on the little plaza or in the artists' homes. Villagers who make pottery often place a piece of their work near their front door, by the gate, or on the street. It's their way of inviting prospective buyers to come in.

**SAN MARTIN TILCAJETE: WOODCARVING VILLAGE** San Martín Tilcajete, 16km (10 miles) past San Bartolo, is home to **woodcarvers** who produce *alebrijes*—fantastical, brightly painted animals and imaginary beasts—much like those produced in Arrazola. You can wander from house to house viewing the amazing collections of hot-pink rabbits; 4-foot-long, bright-blue twisting snakes; and two-headed Dalmatians.

**SANTO TOMAS JALIETZA** A mile and a half beyond San Martín, you'll see a sign on the left for this village of **weavers** who use backstrap looms. The village cooperative runs a market in the middle of town. Prices are fixed; you'll find the greatest variety of goods on Fridays.

**OCOTLAN** Twenty minutes farther on Highway 175 brings you to this fairly large market town. This city is notable for a few reasons: One is the **Aguilar sisters** (Josefina, Guillermina, Irene, and Concepción) and their families, who produce red clay pottery figures that are colorful, sometimes humorous, and prized by collectors. You'll see their row of home-workshops on the right as you enter. There are pottery figures on the fence and roof. (Don't go around town asking for the Aguilar family. Most of the town's inhabitants are named Aguilar.)

Ocotlán is also the home of **Rodolfo Morales,** a painter who, upon becoming wealthy and famous, took an active role in aiding his hometown with renovation projects. Two projects worth visiting are the parish church and former convent. Inside the convent, you can see some of the original decorations of the Dominicans. The noticeable sheen of the stucco walls is produced using the viscous innards of the *nopal* cactus. The convent is now a community museum.

Friday is market day in Ocotlán, and the town fills up with people and goods. It's a very good small-town market where you can find a variety of things at good prices.

### NORTH OF OAXACA

**GUELATAO: BIRTHPLACE OF BENITO JUAREZ** High in the mountains north of Oaxaca, this lovely town has become a living monument to its favorite son, Benito Juárez. Although usually peaceful, the town comes to life on **Juárez's birthday** (Mar 21). The museum, statues, and plaza all attest to the town's obvious devotion to the patriot.

A second-class bus departs from Oaxaca's first-class station six times daily. There are also several departures from the second-class station. The trip takes at least 2 hours, through gorgeous mountain scenery. Buses return to Oaxaca every 2 hours until 8pm.

## EN ROUTE TO SAN CRISTOBAL DE LAS CASAS

**Tuxtla Gutiérrez,** the boomtown capital of the wild, mountainous state of Chiapas, is about 10 hours from Oaxaca on Highway 190, and about 1½ hours before San Cristóbal. If you need to stop for a night's rest, try the large, comfortable **Hotel Bonampak Tuxtla,** Bulevar Domínguez 180 (✆ **961/613-2050**), on the outskirts of town, or the less expensive but sometimes loud **Gran Hotel Humberto,** Av. Central 180 (✆ **961/612-2080**), downtown. No trip to Tuxtla is complete without a meal at **Las Pichanchas** ★, Av. Central Ote. 837 (✆ **961/612-5351**), a colorful restaurant devoted to the regional food and drink of Chiapas. If you have spare time, check out Tuxtla's fine **zoo** (ZOOMAT), Bulevar Samuel León Brinois s/n (✆ **961/614-4700**).

On the highway to San Cristóbal 10 minutes outside of Tuxtla, you get a good view of majestic canyon walls rising from a wide river. This is the **Sumidero Canyon** ★★, and a boat trip through it makes a fun outing. Boats leave from a dock where Highway 190 crosses the river and from **Chiapa de Corzo,** a pleasant town just off the highway a couple of minutes down the road. A boat leaves when enough people are waiting. Cost per person is about $9; the trip takes 2 hours. You can get to Chiapa de Corzo from Tuxtla by *colectivo* for about $1.50. One leaves every 10 minutes from the corner of Calles 3 Oriente and 3 Sur.

### Tips An Excellent Website for Chiapas

**The Net Traveler** (www.thenettraveler.com) specializes in information about the Yucatán, Quintana Roo (home state of Cancún), Chiapas, and other areas in the old Maya empire. Its information on archaeological sites and on diving in the region's caves and *cenotes* (sinkholes) is especially good.

## 2 San Cristóbal de las Casas ★

229km (143 miles) SW of Palenque; 80km (50 miles) E of Tuxtla Gutiérrez; 74km (46 miles) NW of Comitán; 166km (104 miles) NW of Cuauhtémoc; 451km (282 miles) E of Oaxaca

San Cristóbal is a colonial town of white stucco walls and red-tile roofs, of cobblestone streets and narrow sidewalks, of graceful arcades and open plazas. It lies in a lush valley nearly 2,121km (7,000 ft.) high. The city owes part of its name to the 16th-century cleric Fray Bartolomé de las Casas, who was the town's first bishop and spent the rest of his life waging a political campaign to protect the indigenous peoples of the Americas.

Surrounding the city are many villages of Mayan-speaking Indians who display great variety in their language, dress, and customs, making this area one of the most fascinating in Mexico. San Cristóbal is the principal market town for these Indians, and their point of contact with the outside world. Most of them trek down from the surrounding mountains to sell goods and perform errands; some even live in San Cristóbal because they have been expelled from their villages for religious reasons.

Probably the most visible among the local indigenous groups are the **Chamula.** The men wear baggy thigh-length trousers and white or black *sarapes,* while the women wear blue *rebozos,* gathered white blouses with embroidered trim, and black wool wraparound skirts.

Another local Indian group is the **Zinacantecan,** whose men dress in light-pink overshirts with colorful trim and tassels and, sometimes, short pants. Hat ribbons (now a rare sight) are tied on married men, while ribbons dangle loosely from the hats of bachelors and community leaders. Zinacantecan women wear beautiful, brightly colored woven shawls and black wool skirts. You may also see **Tenejapa** men clad in knee-length black tunics and flat straw hats, and Tenejapa women dressed in beautiful reddish and rust-colored *huipils.* Women of all groups are barefoot, while men wear handmade sandals or cowboy boots.

Several Indian villages lie within reach of San Cristóbal by road: **Chamula,** with its weavers and highly unorthodox church; **Zinacantán,** whose residents practice their own syncretic religion; **Tenejapa, San Andrés,** and **Magdalena,** known for brocaded textiles; **Amatenango del Valle,** a town of potters; and **Aguacatenango,** known for embroidery. Most of these "villages" consist of little more than a church and the municipal government building, with homes scattered for miles around and a general gathering only for church and market days (usually Sun).

Evangelical Protestant missionaries recently have converted large numbers of indigenous peoples, and some villages expel new converts from their homelands; in Chamula, for example, as many as 30,000 people have been expelled. Many of these people, called *expulsados* (expelled ones), have taken up residence in new villages on the outskirts of San Cristóbal de las Casas. They still wear traditional

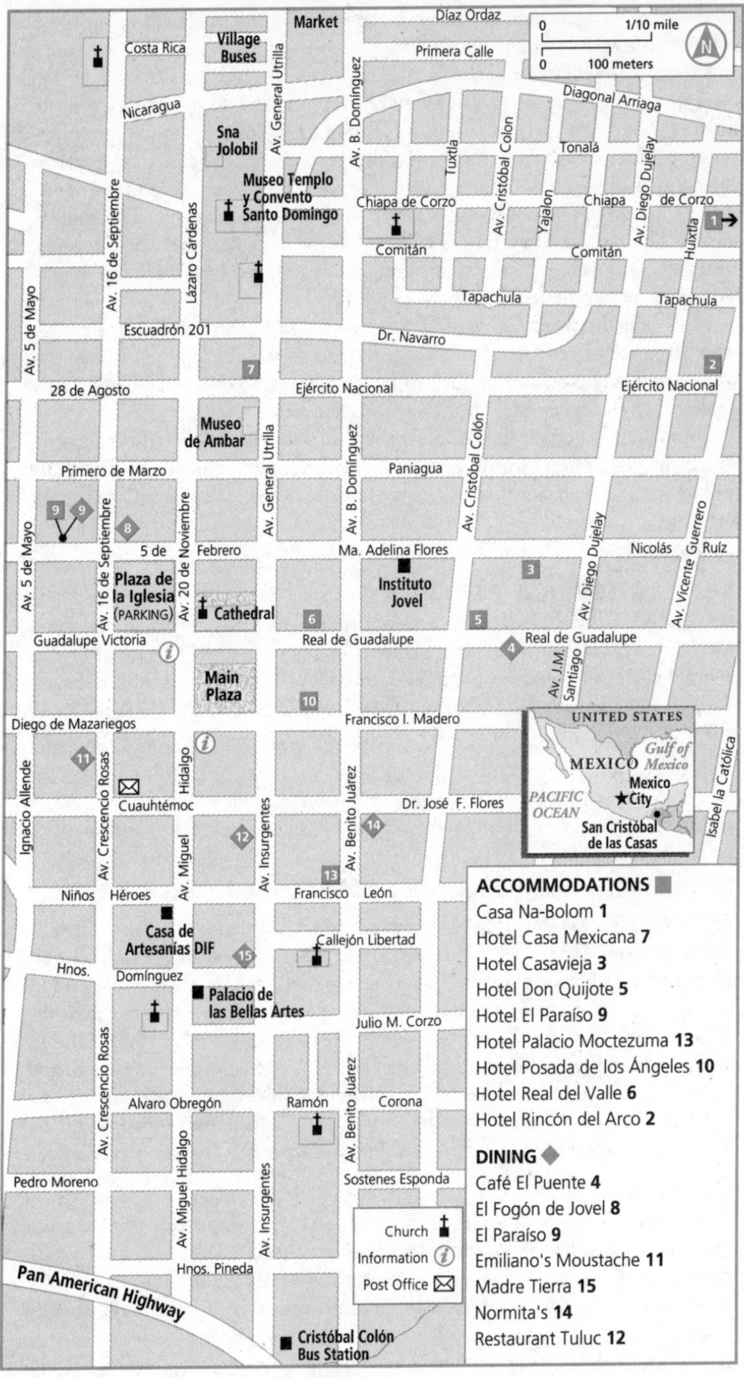

Market
Village Buses
Sna Jolobil
Museo Templo y Convento Santo Domingo
Museo de Ambar
Plaza de la Iglesia (PARKING)
Cathedral
Main Plaza
Instituto Jovel
Casa de Artesanías DIF
Palacio de las Bellas Artes
Cristóbal Colón Bus Station
Pan American Highway
0 1/10 mile
0 100 meters
N
UNITED STATES
Gulf of Mexico
MEXICO
PACIFIC OCEAN
Mexico City
San Cristóbal de las Casas
Church
Information
Post Office
ACCOMMODATIONS
Casa Na-Bolom 1
Hotel Casa Mexicana 7
Hotel Casavieja 3
Hotel Don Quijote 5
Hotel El Paraíso 9
Hotel Palacio Moctezuma 13
Hotel Posada de los Ángeles 10
Hotel Real del Valle 6
Hotel Rincón del Arco 2
DINING
Café El Puente 4
El Fogón de Jovel 8
El Paraíso 9
Emiliano's Moustache 11
Madre Tierra 15
Normita's 14
Restaurant Tuluc 12

dress. Other villages, such as Tenejapa, allow the Protestant church to exist and villagers to attend it without prejudice.

Although the influx of outsiders is nothing new, and in the last 20 years has been increasing, it doesn't seem to make most Indians want to adopt a more modern style of manners and dress. It's interesting to note that the communities closest to San Cristóbal are the most resistant to change. The greatest threat to the cultures in this area comes not from tourism, but from the action of large market forces, population pressures, and environmental damage. The Indians aren't really interested in acting or looking like the foreigners they see. They may steal glances or even stare at tourists, but mainly they pay little attention to outsiders, except as potential buyers for handcrafts.

You'll hear the word *ladino* here; it refers to non-Indian Mexicans or people who have taken up modern ways, changed their dress, dropped their Indian traditions and language, and decided to live in town. It may be used derogatorily or descriptively, depending on who is using the term and how.

Other local lingo you should know about includes *Jovel,* San Cristóbal's original name, used often by businesses, and *coleto,* meaning someone or something from San Cristóbal. You'll see signs for *tamales coletos, coleto* bread, and *coleto* breakfast.

## ESSENTIALS

### GETTING THERE & DEPARTING

**BY PLANE** San Cristóbal has a new airport with daily flights to and from Mexico City. Charter-flight arrangements or flight changes on any airline in another city can be made through **ATC Tours and Travel,** across from El Fogón de Jovel restaurant in San Cristóbal (✆ **967/678-2550;** fax 967/678-3145).

**BY CAR** From Tuxtla, a 1½-hour trip, the road winds through beautiful mountain country. From Palenque, the road is just as beautiful, if somewhat longer (5 hr.), and it provides jungle scenery, but portions of it may be heavily potholed or obstructed during rainy season. Check with the state tourism office before driving.

**BY TAXI** Taxis from Tuxtla Gutiérrez to San Cristóbal cost around $50.

**BY BUS** The two bus stations in town are directly across the Pan American Highway from each other. The smaller one belongs to **Transportes Rodolfo Figueroa,** which provides first-class service to and from Tuxtla (every 40 min.) and Palenque (four buses per day, with a stop in Ocosingo—cheaper than the competition). For other destinations, go to the large station run by **ADO** and its affiliates, Cristóbal Colón and Maya de Oro. This company offers service to and from Tuxtla (twelve buses per day), Palenque (almost every hr.), and several other destinations: Mérida (two buses per day), Villahermosa (two buses per day), Oaxaca (two buses per day), and Puerto Escondido (two buses per day).

### ORIENTATION

**ARRIVING** To get to the main plaza if you're arriving by car from Oaxaca and Tuxtla, turn left on **Avenida Insurgentes** (there's a traffic light); if you're coming from Palenque and Ocosingo, turn right. From the bus station, the main plaza is 9 blocks north up Avenida Insurgentes (a 10-min. walk, slightly uphill). Cabs are cheap and plentiful.

**VISITOR INFORMATION** The **State Tourism Office** is just off the southwest corner of the main plaza, at Avenida Hidalgo 1 (✆ **967/678-6570**); it's

## The Zapatista Uprising & Lingering Tensions

In January 1994, Indians from this area rebelled against the *ladino*-led towns and Mexican government over health care, education, land distribution, and representative government. Their organization, the **Zapatista Liberation Army,** known as EZLN (Ejército Zapatista de Liberación Nacional), and its leader, Subcomandante Marcos, have become world famous. Since the revolt, discussions between government officials and the leadership of the EZLN have stalled. Progress has been made, but the principal issues remain unresolved, and tension remains. In 1997 and 1998 there were more killings, but these have been attributed to local political division rather than the tension between Zapatistas and the national government. We may never know the truth.

When I was in San Cristóbal, I saw no evidence of tension in the town or the valley. The only visible signs I found of the confrontation were the initials EZLN painted on a few walls and Subcomandante Marcos dolls, replete with black ski masks, offered for sale by street vendors (a very hot-selling item, by the way). Locals did not display concern. Tourists were present. Only the newspapers made issue of an impending confrontation.

One of the first actions of President Vicente Fox was to withdraw most of the military forces from the region and offer the olive branch to the Zapatistas. But direct benefits from talks between Zapatistas and members of the national legislature ended in stalemate. President Fox will most likely have to make the next move, but the general mood in Chiapas remains positive. Before traveling to Chiapas, check your news sources and see if the State Department has issued any advisories: **http://travel.state.gov**.

open Monday to Saturday from 9am to 9pm, Sunday from 9am to 2pm. The **Municipal Tourism Office** (✆ and fax **967/678-0665**) is in the town hall, west of the main square. Hours are Monday to Saturday from 9am to 8pm. Check the bulletin board here for apartments, shared rides, cultural events, and local tours. Both offices are helpful, but the state office is open an hour later and is better staffed.

**CITY LAYOUT** San Cristóbal is laid out on a grid; the main north-south axis is **Insurgentes/Utrilla,** and the east-west axis is **Mazariegos/Madero.** All streets change names when they cross either of these streets. **Real de Guadalupe** seems to have become a principal street for tourism-related businesses. The market is 7 blocks north along Utrilla. From the market, minibuses (*colectivos*) trundle to outlying villages.

Take note that this town has at least three streets named Domínguez and two streets named Flores. There's Hermanos Domínguez, Belisario Domínguez, Pantaleón Domínguez, María Adelina Flores, and Dr. José Flores.

**GETTING AROUND** Most of the sights and shopping in San Cristóbal are within walking distance of the plaza.

***Urbano* buses** (minibuses) take passengers between town and the residential neighborhoods. All buses pass by the market and central plaza on their way through town. Utrilla and Avenida 16 de Septiembre are the two main arteries; all buses use the market area as the last stop. Any bus on Utrilla will take you to the market.

***Colectivos*** to outlying villages depart from the public market at Avenida Utrilla. Buses late in the day are usually very crowded. Always check to see when the last or next-to-last bus returns from wherever you're going, and then take the one before that—those last buses sometimes don't materialize, and you might be stranded. I speak from experience!

**Rental cars** come in handy for trips to the outlying villages and may be worth the expense when shared by a group, but keep in mind that insurance is invalid on unpaved roads. There's a **Budget** office at Av. Mazariegos 36 (© **967/678-3100**). Office hours are daily from 8am to 1pm and 5 to 8pm. You'll save money by arranging the rental from your home country; otherwise, a day's rental with insurance will cost $62 for a VW Beetle with manual transmission, the cheapest car available.

**Bikes** are another option for getting around the city; a day's rental is about $8. **Los Pingüinos,** Av. 5 de Mayo 10-B (© **967/678-0202**), offers bike tours to a few out-of-town locations. It's open daily from 10am to 2:30pm and 4 to 7pm.

## *FAST FACTS:* San Cristóbal de las Casas

*Area Code* The telephone area code is **967.**

*Books* ***Living Maya,*** by Walter Morris, with photography by Jeffrey Fox, is the best book to read to understand the culture, art, and traditions surrounding San Cristóbal de las Casas, as well as the unsolved social, economic, and political problems that gave rise to the 1994 Chiapas Indian uprising. ***The People of the Bat: Mayan Tales and Dreams from Zinacantán,*** by Robert M. Laughlin, is a priceless collection of beliefs from that village near San Cristóbal. Another good book with a completely different view of today's Maya is ***The Heart of the Sky,*** by Peter Canby, who traveled among the Maya to chronicle their struggles (and wrote his book before the Zapatista uprising).

*Bookstore* For the best selection of new and used books and reading material in English, go to **La Pared,** Av. Hidalgo 2 (© **967/678-6367**). The owner, Dana Gay Burton, also sells postcards and T-shirts and is a fanatic about amber.

*Bulletin Boards* Because San Cristóbal is a cultural crossroads for travelers from all over the world, several places maintain bulletin boards with information on Spanish classes, local specialty tours, rooms or houses to rent, rides needed, and so on. These include boards at the **Tourism Office, Café El Puente, Madre Tierra,** and **Casa Na-Bolom.**

*Climate* San Cristóbal can be cold day or night year-round, especially during the winter. Most hotels are not heated, although some have fireplaces. There is always a possibility of rain, but I would particularly avoid going to San Cristóbal from late August to late October, during the height of the rainy season.

*Currency Exchange* There are at least five *casas de cambio* on Real de Guadalupe near the main square, and a couple under the colonnade facing the square. Most are open until 8pm, and some are open on Sunday.

*Doctor* The only doctor worth seeing is **Dr. Roberto Lobato,** Av. Belisario Domínguez 17, at Calle Flavio A. Paniagua (✆ **967/678-7777**). Don't be unsettled by the fact that his office is next door to Funerales Canober.

*Internet Access* **The Cyberc@fe** (✆ **967/678-7488**) is in the little concourse that cuts through the block just east of the main square. Look for the entrance on either Real de Guadalupe or Francisco Madero. It is one of the largest Internet cafes I have seen in Mexico, with several well-connected machines and a few other toys.

*Language Classes* The **Instituto Jovel,** María Adelina Flores 21 (Apdo. Postal 62), 29250 San Cristóbal de las Casas, Chi. (✆ and fax **967/678-4069**), gets higher marks for its Spanish courses than the competition. It also offers courses in weaving and cooking. The **Centro Bilingüe,** at the Centro Cultural El Puente, Real de Guadalupe 55, 29250 San Cristóbal de las Casas, Chi. (✆ **800/303-4983** in the U.S., or ✆ and fax 967/678-3723), offers classes in Spanish. Both schools can arrange home stays for their students.

*Parking* If your hotel does not have parking, use the underground public lot (*estacionamiento*) in front of the cathedral, just off the main square on 16 de Septiembre. Entry is from Calle 5 de Febrero.

*Population* San Cristóbal has 90,000 residents.

*Post Office* The *correo* is at Crescencio Rosas and Cuauhtémoc, a block south and west of the main square. It's open Monday to Friday from 8am to 7pm, Saturday from 9am to 1pm.

*Telephone* The best price for long-distance telephone calls and faxing is at **La Pared** bookstore (see "Bookstore," above) at Calle Hidalgo 2, across the street from the State Tourism Office.

## EXPLORING SAN CRISTOBAL

With its beautiful scenery, clean air, and mountain hikes, San Cristóbal draws many visitors. However, the town's biggest attraction is its colorful, centuries-old indigenous culture. The Chiapanecan Maya, attired in their unique native garb, can be seen anywhere in San Cristóbal, but most travelers take at least one trip to the outlying villages to get a close-up of Maya life. Don't neglect to meander through the San Cristóbal market. It's behind the Santo Domingo church (see "Attractions in Town," below), and it's open almost every day but never on Sunday. You can witness scenes of everyday local life, plus some that aren't so everyday.

### ATTRACTIONS IN TOWN

**Casa Na-Bolom** ★★ If you're interested in the anthropology of the region, you'll want to visit this house museum. Stay here, if you can. The house, built as a seminary in 1891, became the headquarters of anthropologists Frans and Trudy Blom in 1951, and the gathering place of outsiders interested in studying the region. Frans Blom led many early archaeological studies in Mexico, and Trudy was noted for her photographs of the Lacandón Indians and her efforts

**Tips** **Photography Warning**

Photographers should be very cautious about when, where, and at whom or what they point their cameras. In San Cristóbal, taking a photograph of even a chile pepper can be a risky undertaking; local people just do not like having people take pictures. Especially in the San Cristóbal market, people who think they or their possessions are being photographed may angrily pelt photographers with whatever object is at hand—rocks or rotten fruit. Be respectful and ask first. Young handcraft vendors will sometimes offer to be photographed for money.

Nearby villages have strict rules about photography. Villages around San Cristóbal, especially Chamula and Zinacantán, require visitors to go to the municipal building upon arrival and sign an agreement (written in Spanish) not to take photographs. The penalty for disobeying these regulations is stiff: confiscation of your camera and perhaps even a lengthy stay in jail. And they mean it!

to save them and their forest homeland. A room at Na-Bolom contains a selection of her Lacandón photographs, and postcards of the photographs are on sale in the gift shop (open daily 9am–2pm and 3–7pm). A tour of the home covers the displays of pre-Hispanic artifacts collected by Frans Blom; the cozy library, with its numerous volumes about the region and the Maya (open weekdays 10am–2pm); and the gardens Trudy Blom started for the ongoing reforestation of the Lacandón jungle. The tour ends with a showing of *La Reina de la Selva,* an excellent 50-minute film on the Bloms, the Lacandón, and Na-Bolom. Trudy Blom died in 1993, but Na-Bolom continues to operate as a nonprofit public trust.

The 12 guest rooms, named for surrounding villages, are decorated with local objects and textiles. All rooms have fireplaces and private bathrooms. Prices for rooms (including breakfast) are $44 single, $55 double.

Even if you're not a guest here, you can come for a meal, usually a delicious assortment of vegetarian and other dishes. Just be sure to make a reservation at least 2½ hours in advance, and be on time. The colorful dining room has one large table, and the eclectic mix of travelers sometimes makes for interesting conversation. Breakfast costs $4; lunch and dinner cost $7 each. Dinner is served at 7:30. Following breakfast (8–10am), a guide not affiliated with the house offers tours to San Juan Chamula and Zinacantán. (See "The Nearby Maya Villages & Countryside," later in this chapter.)

Av. Vicente Guerrero 3, 29200 San Cristóbal de las Casas, Chi. ✆ **967/678-1418.** Fax 967/678-5586. Group tour and film $3. Tours Tues–Sun 11:30am and 4:30pm. Leave the square on Real de Guadalupe, walk 4 blocks to Avenida Vicente Guerrero, and turn left; Na-Bolom is 5½ blocks up Guerrero.

**Catedral** San Cristóbal's main cathedral was built in the 1500s but has little of interest inside besides a lovely, uncommon beam ceiling and a carved wooden pulpit.

Calle 20 de Noviembre at Guadalupe Victoria. No phone. Free admission. Daily 7am–6pm.

**Museo Templo y Convento Santo Domingo** Inside the front door of the carved-stone plateresque façade, there's a beautiful gilded wooden altarpiece built in 1560, walls with saints, and gilt-framed paintings. Attached to the church is the former Convent of Santo Domingo, which houses a small museum about San Cristóbal and Chiapas. The museum has changing exhibits and often shows cultural films. It's 5 blocks north of the *zócalo,* in the market area.

Av. 20 de Noviembre. ✆ **967/678-1609.** Church admission free; museum admission $2. Museum Tues–Sun 10am–5pm.

**Palacio de las Bellas Artes** Be sure to check out this building if you are interested in the arts. It periodically hosts dance events, art shows, and other performances. The schedule of events is usually posted on the door if the Bellas Artes is not open. There's a public library next door. Around the corner, the Centro Cultural holds a number of concerts and other performances; check the posters on the door to see what's scheduled.

Av. Hidalgo, 4 blocks south of the plaza. No phone.

**Templo de San Cristóbal** For the best view of San Cristóbal, climb the seemingly endless steps to this church and *mirador* (lookout point). A visit here requires stamina. By the way, there are 22 more churches in town—some of which also demand strenuous climbs.

At the very end of Calle Hermanos Domínguez.

### *Moments* Special Events in & near San Cristóbal

In nearby Chamula, ***Carnaval,*** the big annual festival that takes place in the days before Lent, is a fascinating mingling of the Christian pre-Lenten ceremonies and the ancient Maya celebration of the 5 "lost days" at the end of the 360-day Maya agricultural cycle. Around noon on Shrove Tuesday, groups of village elders run across patches of burning grass as a purification rite. Macho residents then run through the streets with a bull. During *Carnaval,* roads close in town, and buses drop visitors at the outskirts.

Nearby villages (except Zinacantán) also have celebrations during this time, although perhaps not as dramatic. Visiting these villages, especially on the Sunday before Lent, will round out your impression of *Carnaval* in all its regional varieties. In Tenejapa, the celebration continues during the Thursday market after Ash Wednesday.

During Easter and the week after, for the annual **Feria de Primavera** (Spring Festival), San Cristóbal is ablaze with lights and excitement and gets hordes of visitors. Activities include carnival rides, food stalls, handcraft shops, parades, and band concerts. Hotel rooms are scarce and more expensive.

Another spectacle is staged from July 22 to 25, during the annual **Fiesta de San Cristóbal,** honoring the town's patron saint. The steps up to the San Cristóbal church are lit with torches at night. Pilgrimages to the church begin several days earlier, and on the 24th, there's an all-night vigil.

For the **Día de Guadalupe,** on December 12, honoring Mexico's patron saint, the streets are gaily decorated, and food stalls line the streets leading to the church on a hill where she is honored.

## HORSEBACK RIDING

The **Casa de Huéspedes Margarita,** Real de Guadalupe 34, and **Hotel Real del Valle** (see "Where to Stay," later in this chapter) can arrange horseback rides for around $15 for a day, including a guide. Reserve your steed at least a day in advance. A horseback-riding excursion might go to San Juan Chamula, to nearby caves, or just up into the hills.

## THE NEARBY MAYA VILLAGES & COUNTRYSIDE

The Indian communities around San Cristóbal are fascinating worlds unto themselves. If you are unfamiliar with these indigenous cultures, you will understand and appreciate more of what you see by visiting them with a guide, at least for your first foray out into the villages. Guides are acquainted with members of the communities and are viewed with less suspicion than newcomers. These communities have their own laws and customs—and visitors' ignorance is no excuse. Entering these communities is tantamount to leaving Mexico, and if something happens, the state and federal authorities will not intervene except in case of a serious crime.

The best guided trips are the locally grown ones. Three operators go to the neighboring villages in small groups. They all charge the same price ($10 per person), use minivans for transportation, and speak English. They do, however, have their own interpretations and focus.

**Pepe** leaves from **Casa Na-Bolom** (see "Attractions in Town," above) for daily trips to San Juan Chamula and Zinacantán at 10am, returning to San Cristóbal between 2 and 3pm. Pepe looks at cultural continuities, community relationships, and, of course, religion.

**Mercedes Hernández Gómez,** a very opinionated *mestiza* woman, leads a tour from the main plaza at 9am. She always carries an umbrella by which you can identify her. Mercedes, a largely self-trained ethnographer, is well informed about the history and folkways of the villages, and her opinions make for a good tour.

**Alex and Raul** can be found in front of the cathedral between 9:15 and 9:30am. They are quite personable and get along well with the Indians in the communities. They focus on cultural values and their expression in social behavior, which provides a glimpse of the details and the texture of life in these communities (and, of course, they talk about religion). Their tour is very good.

For excursions farther afield, see "Road Trips from San Cristóbal," later in this chapter. Also, the above-mentioned guides (especially Alex and Raul) can be persuaded to go to other communities besides Chamula and Zinacantán; talk to them.

**CHAMULA & ZINACANTAN** A side trip to the village of San Juan Chamula will really get you into the spirit of life around San Cristóbal. Sunday, when the market is in full swing, is the best day to go for shopping; other days, when you'll be less impeded by eager children selling their crafts, are better for seeing the village and church.

The village, 8km (5 miles) northeast of San Cristóbal, has a large church, a plaza, and a municipal building. Each year, a new group of citizens is chosen to live in the municipal center as caretakers of the saints, settlers of disputes, and enforcers of village rules. As in other nearby villages, on Sunday local leaders wear their leadership costumes, including beautifully woven straw hats loaded with colorful ribbons befitting their high position. They solemnly sit together in a long line somewhere around the central square. Chamula is typical of other villages in that men are often away working in the "hotlands," harvesting coffee or *cacao,* while women stay home to tend the sheep, the children, the cornfields, and the fires. It's almost always the women's and children's work to gather firewood, and you see them along roadsides bent under the weight.

Don't leave Chamula without seeing the **church interior.** As you step from bright sunlight into the candlelit interior, you feel as if you've been transported to another country. Pine needles scattered amid a meandering sea of lighted candles cover the tile floor. Saints line the walls, and before them people are often kneeling and praying aloud while passing around bottles of Pepsi-Cola. Shamans are often on hand, passing eggs over sick people or using live or dead chickens in a curing ritual. The statues of saints are similar to those you might see in any Mexican Catholic church, but beyond sharing the same name, they mean something completely different to the Chamulas. Visitors can walk carefully through the church to see the saints or stand quietly in the background and observe.

***Carnaval,*** which takes place just before Lent, is the big annual festival. The Chamulas are not a wealthy people, but the women are the region's best wool weavers, producing finished pieces for themselves and for other villages.

In Zinacantán, a wealthier village than Chamula, you must sign a rigid form promising *not to take any photographs* before you see the two side-by-side **sanctuaries.** Once permission is granted and you have paid a small fee, an escort will usually show you the church, or you may be allowed to see it on your own. Floors may be covered in pine needles here, too, and the rooms are brightly sunlit. The experience is an altogether different one from that of Chamula.

**AMATENANGO DEL VALLE** About an hour's ride south of San Cristóbal is Amatenango, a town known mostly for its **women potters.** You'll see their work in San Cristóbal—small animals, jars, and large water jugs—but in the village, you can visit the potters in their homes. Just walk down the dirt streets. Villagers will lean over the walls of family compounds and invite you in to select from their inventory. You may even see them firing the pieces under piles of wood in the open courtyard or painting them with color derived from rusty iron water. The women wear beautiful red-and-yellow *huipils,* but if you want to take a photograph, you'll have to pay.

To get here, take a *colectivo* from the market in San Cristóbal. Before it lets you off, be sure to ask about the return-trip schedule.

**AGUACATENANGO** This village 16km (10 miles) south of Amatenango is known for its **embroidery.** If you've visited San Cristóbal's shops, you'll recognize the white-on-white and black-on-black floral patterns on dresses and blouses for sale. The locals' own regional blouses, however, are quite different.

**TENEJAPA** The **weavers** of Tenejapa make some of the most beautiful and expensive work you'll see in the region. The best time to visit is on market day (Sun and Thurs, though Sun is better). The weavers of Tenejapa taught the weavers of San Andrés and Magdalena—which accounts for the similarity in their designs and colors. To get to Tenejapa, try to find a *colectivo* in the very last row by the market, or hire a taxi. On Tenejapa's main street, several stores sell locally woven regional clothing, and you can bargain for the price.

**THE HUITEPEC CLOUD FOREST** Pronatura, Av. Benito Juárez 11-B (© **967/678-5000**), a private, nonprofit, ecological organization, offers environmentally sensitive tours of the cloud forest. The forest is a haven for **migratory birds,** and more than 100 bird species and 600 plant species have been discovered here. Guided tours run from 9am to noon Tuesday to Sunday. They cost $25 per group of up to eight people. Make reservations a day in advance.

To reach the reserve on your own, drive on the road to Chamula; the turn-off is at km 3.5. The reserve is open Tuesday to Sunday from 9am to 4pm.

## SHOPPING

Many Indian villages near San Cristóbal are noted for weaving, embroidery, brocade work, leather, and pottery, making the area one of the best in the country for shopping. You'll see beautiful woolen shawls, indigo-dyed skirts, colorful native shirts, and magnificently woven *huipils,* all of which often come in vivid geometric patterns. Working in leather, the craftspeople are artisans of the highest caliber. Tie-dyed *jaspe* from Guatemala comes in bolts and is made into clothing. The town is also known for amber, sold in several shops and at La Pared bookstore (see "Bookstores," in "Fast Facts," earlier in this chapter). Shops line the streets leading to the market. Calle Real de Guadalupe has more shops than any other street.

### CRAFTS

**Casa de Artesanías DIF** This fine showroom is in one of the city's old houses. Here you'll find such quality products as lined woolen vests and jackets, pillow covers, amber jewelry, and more. In back is a fine little museum showing costumes worn by villagers who live near San Cristóbal. It's open Tuesday to Saturday from 9am to 2pm and 5 to 8pm. Niños Héroes at Hidalgo. © **967/678-1180.**

**Central Market** The market buildings and the surrounding streets offer just about anything you need. The market in San Cristóbal is open every morning except Sunday (when each village has its own local market), and you'll probably enjoy observing the sellers as much as the things they sell. See the earlier photography warning in "Fast Facts" regarding photography here. The *mercado* is north of the Santo Domingo church, about 9 blocks from the *zócalo.* Av. Utrilla. No phone.

**El Encuentro** You should find some of your best bargains here—at a minimum, you'll think that the price is fair. The shop carries many regional ritual items, such as new and used men's ceremonial hats, false saints, and iron rooftop adornments, plus many *huipils* and other textiles. It's open Monday to Saturday from 9am to 8pm. Calle Real de Guadalupe 63-A (between Dujelay and Guerrero). © **967/678-3698.**

**La Alborada, Centro Desarrollo Comunitario DIF** At this government-sponsored school, young men and women from surrounding villages come to learn how to hook Persian-style rugs, weave fabric on foot looms, sew, make furniture, construct a house, cook, make leather shoes and bags, forge iron, and grow vegetables and trees for reforestation. Probably the most interesting crafts for the general tourist are the rugs and woven goods. Artisans from Temoaya in Mexico State learned rugmaking from Persians, who came to teach this skill in the 1970s. The Temoaya artisans, in turn, traveled to San Cristóbal to teach the craft to area students, who have taught others. The beautiful rug designs come from brocaded and woven designs used to decorate regional costumes. Visitors should stop at the entrance and ask for an escort. You can visit the various areas and see students at work or go straight to the weavers. A small outlet at the entrance sells newly loomed fabric by the meter, leather bags, rugs, and baskets made at another school in the highlands. La Alborada is in a far southern suburb of the city off the highway to Comitán, to the right. To get there, take a cab. The school may be closed; midmorning is the likeliest time to find it open. Barrio María Auxiliadora. No phone.

**La Galería** This lovely gallery beneath a cafe shows the work of well-known national and international painters. Also for sale are paintings and greeting cards by Kiki, the owner, a German artist who has found her niche in San Cristóbal. There are some Oaxacan rugs and pottery, plus unusual silver jewelry. It's open daily from 10am to 9pm. In the evenings, the bar opens and a jazz band plays from 9 to 10pm; afterward, another band plays Latin dance music. Hidalgo 3. ✆ **967/678-1547.**

**Taller Leñateros** Papermaking isn't all they do here, but it's done with enough creativity and diversity of materials to warrant mention on that alone. This shop and workshop is a cooperative effort by six women: five Maya Indians and one American. They also make paper creations, silk screens, woodcuts, and binding, and they've put all those talents together to produce their own magazine, which has garnered quite a bit of attention in Mexico City. This shop is open Monday to Friday from 8:30am to 8pm, Saturday from 8:30am to 6pm; if you want to see paper being made, show up before 4pm. Flavio A. Paniagua 54. ✆ **967/678-5174.**

## TEXTILE SHOPS

**Kun Kun SC** The name means "little by little." This cooperative society to aid local native artisans sells mostly ceramic tiles, weavings, and pottery. The weavings are made of locally produced wool that has been spun, dyed, and woven by members. Kun Kun holds workshops for artisans on such things as working with floor looms, which you can watch at the store. The tiles are wonderful. Also, if you're interested, ask about classes in using a backstrap loom. The workshop and store are open Monday to Saturday from 9am to 3pm. Another store, at Real de Guadalupe 55, closer to the plaza, stays open until 8pm. Real de Mexicanos 21. ✆ **967/678-1417.**

**Plaza de Santo Domingo** The plazas around this church and the nearby Templo de Caridad fill with women in native garb selling their wares. Here you'll find women from Chamula weaving belts or embroidering, surrounded by piles of loomed woolen textiles from their village. Their inventory includes Guatemalan shawls, belts, and bags. If you take the time to look and bargain, there are also some excellent buys on Chiapanecan-made wool vests, jackets, rugs, and shawls, which are similar to those in Sna Jolobil (described below). Vendors arrive between 9 and 10am and begin to leave around 3pm. Av. Utrilla. No phone.

**Sna Jolobil** Meaning "weaver's house" in Mayan, this place is in the former convent (monastery) of Santo Domingo, next to the Templo de Santo Domingo. Groups of Tzotzil and Tzeltal craftspeople operate the cooperative store, which has about 3,000 members who contribute products, help run the store, and share in the moderate profits. Their works are simply beautiful; prices are high, as is the quality. Be sure to take a look. It's open Monday to Saturday from 9am to 2pm and 4 to 6pm; credit cards are accepted. Calzada Lázaro Cárdenas 42 (Plaza Santo Domingo, between Navarro and Nicaragua). ✆ **967/678-2646.**

**Unión Regional de Artesanías de los Altos** Also known as J'pas Joloviletic, this cooperative of weavers is smaller than Sna Jolobil (described above) and not as sophisticated in its approach to potential shoppers. It sells blouses, textiles, pillow covers, vests, sashes, napkins, baskets, and purses. It's near the market and worth looking around. It's open Monday to Saturday from 9am to 2pm and 4 to 7pm, Sunday from 9am to 1pm. Av. Utrilla 43. ✆ **967/678-2848.**

## WHERE TO STAY

Among the most interesting places to stay in San Cristóbal is the seminary-turned-hotel-museum **Casa Na-Bolom;** see "Attractions in Town," earlier in this chapter, for details.

Hotels in San Cristóbal are inexpensive by comparison with most of Mexico. You can do pretty well for $20 to 30 per night per double. For really low-cost accommodations, there are hostels known as *hospedajes* and *posadas,* which charge about $8 for a single and $10 to $12 for a double. Usually these places are unadvertised; if you're interested, ask around in a restaurant or cafe or go to the tourist office, which often displays notices of new *hospedajes* on a metal flip rack.

### MODERATE

**Hotel Casa Mexicana** ★ Created from a large mansion, this beautiful hotel with a colonial-style courtyard makes for comfortable lodging. Rooms, courtyards, the restaurant, and the lobby are decorated in modern-traditional Mexican style, with warm tones of yellow and red. The rooms are carpeted and come with one or two double beds or a king bed. They have good lighting, electric heaters, and spacious bathrooms. Guests are welcome to use the sauna, and inexpensive massages can be arranged. The hotel handles a lot of large tour groups; it can be quiet and peaceful one day and full and bustling the next. There is a new addition to the hotel across the street, but I like the doubles in the original section better. This hotel is 3 blocks north of the main plaza.

28 de Agosto 1 (at Utrilla), 29200 San Cristóbal de las Casas, Chi. ✆ **967/678-1348** or 967/678-0698. Fax 967/678-2627. www.hotelcasamexicana.com. 55 units. $78 double. AE, MC, V. Free secured parking 1½ blocks away. **Amenities:** Restaurant, bar; sauna; massage; laundry. In room: TV.

**Hotel Casavieja** ★ The Casavieja is aptly named: It has a charming old feel that is San Cristóbal to a "T." Originally built in 1740, it has undergone restoration and new construction faithful to the original design in essentials such as wood-beam ceilings. One nod toward modernity is carpeted floors, a welcome feature on cold mornings. The rooms also come with electric heaters. Bathrooms vary, depending on what section of the hotel you're in, but all are adequate. The hotel's restaurant, Doña Rita, faces the interior courtyard, with tables on the patio and inside, and offers good food at reasonable prices. I recommend the *molcajete de pollo* (chicken and vegetables baked in a volcanic stone mortar). The hotel is 3½ blocks northeast of the plaza.

Ma. Adelina Flores 27 (between Cristóbal Colón and Diego Dujelay), 29200 San Cristóbal de las Casas, Chi. ✆ and fax **967/678-6868** or 967/678-0385. www.casavieja.com. 40 units. $60 double. AE, MC, V. Free parking. **Amenities:** Restaurant, bar; laundry service. *In room:* TV.

**Hotel El Paraíso** For the independent traveler, this is a safe haven from the busloads of tour groups that can upset the atmosphere and service at other hotels. Rooms are small but beautifully decorated, and they have comfortable beds with soft patchwork bedspreads and reading lights; some rooms even have a ladder to a loft holding a second bed. Bathrooms are small, too, but the plumbing is good. The entire hotel is decorated in terracotta and blue, with beautiful wooden columns and beams supporting the roof. The hotel's restaurant, El Edén (see "Where to Dine," below) may be the best in town.

Av. 5 de Febrero 19, 29200 San Cristóbal de las Casas, Chi. ✆ **967/678-5382** or 967/678-0085. Fax 967/678-5168. hparaiso@prodigy.net.mx. 14 units. $53 double. AE, MC, V. **Amenities:** Restaurant. *In room:* TV.

**Hotel Rincón del Arco** This well-run hotel has comfortable rooms at a good price. The original section of the former colonial-era home surrounds a small interior patio and dates from 1650. Rooms in this part are spacious, with tall ceilings and carpet over hardwood floors. The adjacent new section looks out across a grass yard to the mountains and the valley. These rooms are nicely furnished, and the thick bedspreads come from the family factory, which you can visit next door. Some rooms have small balconies; all have fireplaces. There's a restaurant just behind the lobby. The only downside is that it's a bit of a walk from the main plaza (8 blocks northeast).

Ejército Nacional 66 (at V. Guerrero), 29220 San Cristóbal de las Casas, Chi. © **967/678-1313.** Fax 967/678-1568. hotel_rincon@hotmail.com. 50 units. $62 double. MC, V. Free parking. **Amenities:** Restaurant; room service; laundry. *In room:* TV.

### INEXPENSIVE

**Hotel Don Quijote** Rooms in this three-story hotel (no elevator) are small but quiet, cheerful, carpeted, and well lit. All have two double beds with reading lamps over them, tiled bathrooms, and plenty of hot water. The TVs actually carry English channels (uncommon for hotels in this price range). There's complimentary coffee in the mornings and Internet access. It's 2½ blocks east of the plaza.

Colón 7 (near Real de Guadalupe), 29200 San Cristóbal de las Casas, Chi. © **967/678-0920.** Fax 967/678-0346. 24 units. $25 double. MC, V. Free secured parking 1 block away. *In room:* TV.

**Hotel Palacio de Moctezuma** This three-story hotel is more open and lush with greenery than other hotels in this price range. Fresh-cut flowers tucked around tile fountains are its hallmark. The rooms have carpeting and modern tiled showers; many are quite large but, alas, can be cold in winter. The restaurant looks out on the interior courtyard. On the third floor is a solarium with comfortable tables and chairs and great city views. The hotel is 3½ blocks southeast of the main plaza.

Juárez 16 (at León), 29200 San Cristóbal de las Casas, Chi. © **967/678-0352** or 967/678-1142. Fax 967/678-1536. 42 units. $25 double. No credit cards. Free limited parking. **Amenities:** Restaurant. *In room:* TV.

**Hotel Posada de los Angeles** This well-managed hotel offers good service and tidy rooms and public areas. Guest rooms come with either a single and a double bed or two double beds, and the well-kept bathrooms are modern; windows open onto a pretty courtyard with a fountain. The rooftop sun deck is a great siesta spot.

Calle Francisco Madero 17, 29200 San Cristóbal de las Casas, Chi. © **967/678-1173** or 967/678-4371. Fax 967/678-2581. hmansion@mundomaya.com.mx. 20 units. $40 double. AE, MC, V. *In room:* TV

**Hotel Real del Valle** The Real del Valle is just off the main plaza. The 24 new rooms in the back three-story section have new bathrooms, big closets, and tile floors. In addition to a rooftop solarium, you'll find a small cafeteria and an upstairs dining room with a big double fireplace.

Real de Guadalupe 14, 29200 San Cristóbal de las Casas, Chi. © **967/678-0680.** Fax 967/678-3955. hrvalle@mundomaya.com.mx. 36 units. $27–$32 double. No credit cards. **Amenities:** Cafeteria, dining room.

## WHERE TO DINE

San Cristóbal is not known for its cuisine, but you can eat well at several restaurants. **El Fogón de Jovel** is the place to try typical Chiapanecan fare. Some interesting local dishes include tamales, *butifarra* (a type of sausage), and *pox* (pronounced "posh"—the local firewater). For baked goods, try the **Panadería**

**La Hojaldra,** Mazariegos and 5 de Mayo (✆ **967/678-4286**). It's open daily 8am to 9:30pm. In addition to the restaurants listed below, consider making reservations for dinner at Casa Na-Bolom (see "Attractions in Town," earlier).

### MODERATE

**El Edén** ★★ INTERNATIONAL This is a small, quiet restaurant where it is obvious that somebody who enjoys the taste of good food prepares the meals; just about anything except Swiss rarebit is good. The cuts of meat are especially tender, and the margaritas are especially dangerous (one is all it takes). Specialties include Swiss cheese fondue for two, the Eden salad, and the brochette. This is where locals go for a splurge. It's 2 blocks from the main plaza.

In the Hotel El Paraíso, Av. 5 de Febrero 19. ✆ **967/678-5382.** Breakfast $5; main courses $6–$15. AE, MC, V. Daily 8am–9pm.

**El Fogón de Jovel** CHIAPANECAN The waiters here wear local costumes, and Guatemalan and Chiapanecan prints and folk art hang on the walls. The menu, which is available in English, explains each dish and regional drink. A basket of warm handmade tortillas with six filling condiments arrives before the meal. Among the specialties are corn soup, *mole chiapaneco,* pork or chicken *adobado* in a chile sauce, and *pepián,* a dish of savory chile-and-tomato sauce served over chicken. For a unique dessert, try the *changleta,* which is half of a sweetened, baked *chayote.* Cooking classes for small groups can be arranged, but make reservations well in advance. The restaurant is a block northwest of the plaza.

16 de Septiembre 11 (at Guadalupe Victoria/Real de Guadalupe). ✆ **967/678-1153.** Main courses $4–$9. No credit cards. Daily 12:30–10pm.

**Madre Tierra** INTERNATIONAL/VEGETARIAN For vegetarians and meat-eaters alike, Madre Tierra is a good place for a cappuccino and pastry or an entire meal. The *comida corrida* is very filling; or try the chicken curry, lasagna, and fresh salads. The bakery specializes in whole-wheat breads, pastries, pizza by the slice, quiche, grains, granola, and dried fruit. The restaurant is in an old mansion with wood-plank floors, long windows looking onto the street, and tables covered in colorful Guatemalan *jaspe.* Madre Tierra is 3½ blocks south of the plaza.

Insurgentes 19. ✆ **967/678-4297.** Main courses $4–$8, *comida corrida* (served after noon) $6. No credit cards. Restaurant daily 8am–9:45pm; bakery Mon–Sat 9am–8pm, Sun 9am[nd2pm.

### INEXPENSIVE

**Café el Puente** ★ MEXICAN/AMERICAN El Puente is more than a cafe; it's a center for cultural activities where tourists and locals can converse, take Spanish classes, arrange a home stay, leave a message on the bulletin board, and send and receive faxes. Movies are presented nightly in a back courtyard and meeting room. A pleasant cafe occupies the front courtyard, the kind of place where a Brandenburg concerto accompanies waffles for breakfast and sub sandwiches or brown rice and vegetables for lunch. There is Mexican fare as well. The long bulletin board is well worth checking out if you're looking for a ride, a place to stay, or information on out-of-the-way destinations. It's 2½ blocks east of the plaza.

Real de Guadalupe 55 (between Dujelay and Cristóbal Colón). No phone. Breakfast $2–$3; main courses $3–$7. No credit cards. Mon–Sat 8am–11pm; Sun 3–11pm.

**Emiliano's Moustache** *Finds* MEXICAN/TACOS Like any right-thinking tourist, I initially avoided this place on account of its unpromising name and some cartoonlike *charro* (Mexican cowboy) figures by the door. But a conversation with some local folk tickled my sense of irony, and I overcame my prejudice. Sure enough, the place was crowded with *coletos* enjoying the restaurant's highly popular *comida corrida* and delicious tacos, and there wasn't a foreigner in sight. The daily menu is posted by the door for inspection; if it isn't appealing, you can choose from a menu of taco plates (a mixture of fillings cooked together and served with tortillas and a variety of hot sauces).

Crescencio Rosas 7. ✆ **967/678-7246.** Main courses $3–$6; *comida corrida* $3.50. No credit cards. Daily 8am–midnight.

**Normita's** MEXICAN Normita's is famous for its *pozole,* a hearty chicken and hominy soup to which you add a variety of things. It also offers cheap, dependable, short-order Mexican mainstays. It's an informal "people's" restaurant; the open kitchen takes up one corner of the room, and tables sit in front of a large paper mural of a fall forest scene from some faraway place. It's 2 blocks southeast of the plaza.

Av. Juárez 6 (at Dr. Jose Flores). No phone. Breakfast $2–$2.50; *comida corrida* (served 1:30–7pm) $4; *pozole* $3; tacos $1. No credit cards. Daily 7am–11pm.

**Restaurant Tuluc** *Value* MEXICAN/INTERNATIONAL A real bargain here is the popular *comida corrida*—delicious and filling. Tuluc also has that rarest of rarities in Mexico: a nonsmoking section. Other popular items are the sandwiches and the enchiladas. The house specialty is *filete Tuluc,* a beef filet wrapped around spinach and cheese served with fried potatoes and green beans; while not the best cut of meat, it's certainly priced right. The Chiapaneco breakfast is a filling quartet of juice, toast, two Chiapanecan tamales, and your choice of tea, coffee, cappuccino, or hot chocolate. Tuluc is 1½ blocks south of the plaza.

Insurgentes 5 (between Cuauhtémoc and Francisco León). ✆ **967/678-2090.** Breakfast $2–$3; main courses $4–$5; *comida corrida* (served 2–4pm) $3.75. No credit cards. Daily 7am–10pm.

### COFFEEHOUSES

Because Chiapas-grown coffee is highly regarded, it's natural to find a proliferation of coffeehouses here. Most are concealed in the nooks and crannies of San Cristóbal's side streets. Try **Café La Selva,** Crescencio Rosas 9 (✆ **967/678-7244**), for coffee served in all its varieties and brewed from organic beans. It's well known for its baked goods, and open daily 9am to 11pm. A more traditional-style cafe, where locals meet to talk over the day's news, is **Café San Cristóbal,** Cuauhtémoc 1 (✆ **967/678-3861**). It's open Monday to Saturday from 9am to 10pm, Sunday from 9am to 9pm.

## SAN CRISTOBAL AFTER DARK

San Cristóbal is blessed with a variety of species of nightlife, both resident and migratory. There is a lot of live music, which is surprisingly good and varied. The bars and restaurants are cheap—none charges a cover, and only one imposes a minimum. And they are easy to get to: You can hit all the places mentioned here without setting foot in a cab. Weekends are best, but on any night you'll find something going on.

**El Cocodrilo** El Cocodrilo, on the main plaza, is a good place to start the evening. The musicians cover a lot of Beatles and Santana tunes, but they put their own stamp on the music, such as playing a rock 'n' roll standard to a reggae beat and mixing in some funk riffs. In the Hotel Santa Clara, Plaza 31 de Marzo. ✆ **967/678-0871.** Live music daily 9–11pm.

**La Margarita** You can catch flamenco and Latin guitar music at this popular restaurant and bar 1½ blocks from the plaza. The band consists of two guitarists, congas, and bass. It plays flamenco-style music with a lot of flair, if not all the passion of real flamenco. As the night progresses, you might hear some Latin jazz. You can't go wrong here unless you are in the mood to dance. Real de Guadalupe 34. No phone. Live music daily 9:30pm–12am.

**Las Velas** Bands here play with a rougher edge than those at El Cocodrilo. Some get into Latin beats and "*rock en Español,*" which is increasingly gaining a foothold all over the world. The crowd is mostly *coletos* in their early twenties. The tight space guarantees that it will be crowded. The cost of admission if you are male is to be frisked for weapons, but this is more for setting the ambience than actual security. All the locals I spoke with said that nothing has ever happened there, or at any other of the bars, that would warrant such a practice. Madero 14. ✆ **967/678-7584.** $2.50 minimum. Live music daily 11pm–1am.

**Latino's** A large dance floor and a really impressive nine-piece house band playing salsa and merengue are all the invitation the patrons need to start dancing. This was the best band I heard in San Cristóbal—and, at present, it's the most popular. The place fills on weekends with people of all ages, and everybody dances. Mazariegos 19. ✆ **967/678-2083.** Live music Mon–Sat 10pm–2am.

### ROAD TRIPS FROM SAN CRISTOBAL

For excursions to nearby villages, see "The Nearby Maya Villages & Countryside," earlier in this chapter; for destinations farther away, there are several local travel agencies. I recommend **ATC Travel and Tours,** Calle 5 de Febrero 15, at 16 de Septiembre, across from El Fogón de Jovel restaurant (✆ **967/678-2550;** fax 967/678-3145). The agency has bilingual guides and good vehicles. ATC regional tours focus on birds and orchids, textiles, hiking, and camping.

Strangely, the cost of the trip includes a driver but does not necessarily include either a bilingual guide or guided information of any kind. You pay extra for those services, so when checking prices, be sure to flesh out these details.

## 3 Palenque ★★

142km (89 miles) SE of Villahermosa; 229km (143 miles) NE of San Cristóbal de las Casas

The ruins of Palenque look out over the jungle from a tall ridge that projects from the base of steep, thickly forested mountains. It is a dramatic sight colored by the mysterious feel of the ruins themselves. The temples here are in the Classic style, with tall, high-pitched roofs crowned with elaborate combs. Inside many are representations in stone and plaster of the rulers and their gods, which give evidence of a cosmology that is—and perhaps will remain—impenetrable to our understanding. This is one of the grand archaeological sites of Mexico.

Eight kilometers (5 miles) from the ruins is the town of Palenque. There you can find lodging and food, as well as make travel arrangements. Transportation between the town and ruins is cheap and convenient.

### ESSENTIALS

#### GETTING THERE & DEPARTING

**BY PLANE** The new airport has service to various destinations on **Aerocaribe** (✆ **916/345-0618**): Cancún; Mérida; Tuxtla Gutiérrez; Ciudad Flores,

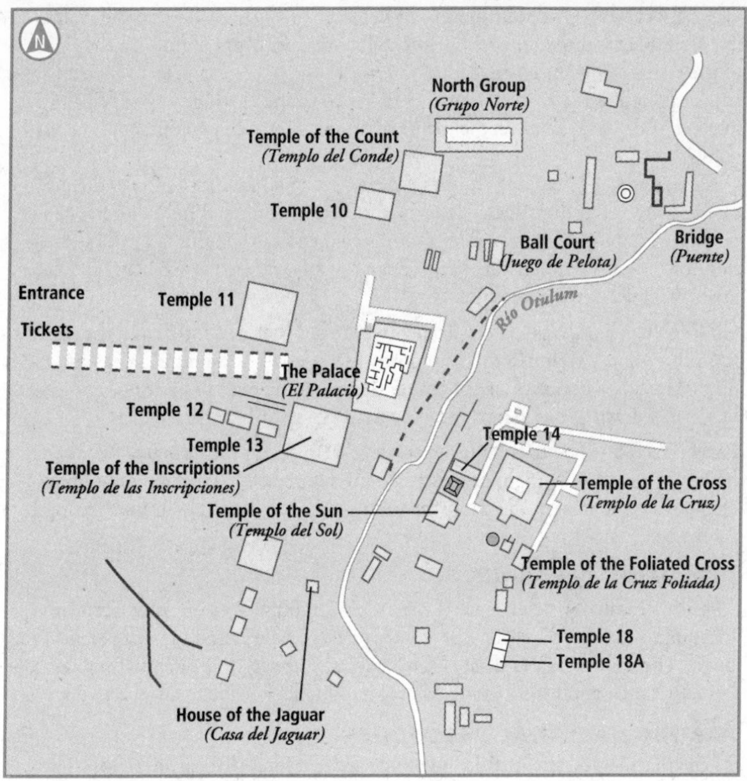


Guatemala (for those visiting Tikal); and Villahermosa. You can book flights on Aerocaribe through **Mexicana** (© **01-800/531-7921**).

**BY CAR** The 143-mile trip from San Cristóbal to Palenque takes 5 hours and passes through lush jungle and mountain scenery. Take it easy, though, and watch out for potholes and other hindrances. Highway 186 from Villahermosa is in good condition, and the trip from there should take about 2 hours. You may encounter military roadblocks that involve a cursory inspection of your travel credentials and perhaps your vehicle.

**BY BUS** The two first-class bus stations are about a block apart. Both are on Palenque's main street between the main square and the turn-off for the ruins. The smaller company, **Transportes Rodolfo Figueroa,** offers good first-class service four times a day to and from San Cristóbal (5 hr.) and Tuxtla (6½ hr.). **Cristóbal Colón** offers service to those destinations and to Campeche (six per day, 5 hr.), Villahermosa (nine per day, 2 hr.), and Mérida (two per day, 9 hr.).

## ORIENTATION

**VISITOR INFORMATION** The **State Tourism Office** (© and fax **916/345-0356**) is a block from the main square, where Avenida Juárez intersects Abasolo. The office is open Monday to Saturday from 9am to 9pm, Sunday from 9am to 1pm.

**CITY LAYOUT** **Avenida Juárez** is Palenque's main street. At one end of it is the **main plaza;** at the other is the impossible-to-miss **Maya statue.** To the right of the statue is the entrance to the Cañada; to the left is the road to the ruins, and straight ahead past the statue are the airport and the highway to Villahermosa. The distance between the town's main square and the monument is about a mile.

**La Cañada,** a restaurant and hotel zone, is a small area tucked into the rain forest. Here you'll find shaded, unpaved streets; a few small hotels and restaurants; and stands of artists. Aside from the main plaza area, this is the best location for travelers without cars because the town is within a few blocks, and the buses that run to the ruins pass right by.

**GETTING AROUND** The cheapest way to get back and forth from the ruins is on the white **VW buses** that run down Juárez every 10 minutes from 6am to 6pm. The buses pass La Cañada and hotels along the road to the ruins and can be flagged down at any point, but they may not stop if they're full.

**FAST FACTS** The telephone area code is **916.** As for the **climate,** Palenque's high humidity is downright oppressive in the summer, especially after rain showers. During the winter, the damp air can occasionally be chilly in the evenings. Rain gear is important any time of year.

## EXPLORING PALENQUE

The real reason for being here is the ruins; although you can tour them in a morning, many people savor Palenque for days. There are no must-see sights in town. The La Cañada area (see "City Layout," above) is a pleasant spot for a leisurely lunch and for browsing Maya reproductions made by local artists.

### PARQUE NACIONAL PALENQUE ★★★

The archaeological site of Palenque underwent several changes in 1994, culminating in the opening of a **museum and visitor center** not far from the entrance to the ruins. The complex includes a large parking lot, a refreshment stand serving snacks and drinks, and several shops. Though it's not large, the museum is worth the time it takes to see; it's open Tuesday to Sunday from 10am to 5pm and is included in the price of admission. It contains well-chosen and artistically displayed exhibits, including the jade contents of recently excavated tombs. (The museum was robbed in 1996, but most of the jade pieces have been recovered.) Explanatory text in Spanish and English explains the life and times of the magnificent city of Palenque. New pieces are always being added as they are uncovered in ongoing excavations.

The **main entrance,** about a half-mile beyond the museum, is at the end of the paved highway. There you'll find a large parking lot, a refreshment stand, a ticket booth, and several shops. Among the vendors selling souvenirs by the parking lot are Lacandón Indians wearing white tunics and hawking bows and arrows.

Admission to the ruins is $5 and is free on Sunday. Bringing in a video camera costs $4. Parking at the main entrance and at the visitor center is free. The site and visitor center shops are open daily from 8am to 4:45pm; King Pacal's crypt is closed for now for restoration and preservation work.

**TOURING THE RUINS** Pottery found during the excavations shows that people lived in this area as early as 300 B.C. During the Classic period (A.D. 300–900), the ancient Maya city of Palenque was a ceremonial center for the high priests; the civilization peaked around A.D. 600 to 700.

When John Stephens visited the site in the 1840s, the cleared ruins that you see today were buried under centuries of accumulated earth and a thick canopy of jungle. The dense jungle surrounding the cleared portion still covers unexplored temples, which are easily discernible in the forest even to the untrained eye. But be careful not to drift too far from the main paths. In the recent past there have been a few incidents where solitary tourists venturing into the rain forest were assaulted.

Of all the ruins in Mexico open to the public, this is the most haunting because of its majesty and sense of the past. Scholars have unearthed names of the rulers and their family histories, putting visitors on a first-name basis with these ancient people etched in stone. You can read about it in *A Forest of Kings,* by Linda Schele and David Freidel.

As you enter the ruins, the building on your right is the **Temple of the Inscriptions,** named for the great stone hieroglyphic panels found inside. (Most of the panels, which contain the family tree of King Pacal, are in the National Anthropological Museum in Mexico City.) This temple is famous for the tomb, or crypt, of King Pacal, which is currently closed for restoration. In exploratory excavations done in 1951 and 1952, archaeologist Alberto Ruz Lhuller discovered a stone stairway leading from the temple deep down into the base of the pyramid. The original builders had carefully filled it in with stone and then concealed the entrance. Excavation took months, but Ruz Lhuller finally uncovered the crypt of King Pacal, which contained several fascinating objects including a magnificent sarcophagus of carved stone. The stairway is closed to visitors, but may be opened in the future. Ruz's own gravesite is opposite the Temple of the Inscriptions, on the left as you enter the park.

Just to your right as you face the Temple of the Inscriptions is **Temple 13,** which is receiving considerable attention from archaeologists. They recently discovered the burial of another richly adorned personage, accompanied in death by an adult female and an adolescent. These remains are still being studied, but the treasures are on display in the museum.

Back on the main pathway, the building directly in front of you is the **Palace,** with its unique watchtower. The explorer John Stephens camped in the Palace when it was completely covered in vegetation, spending sleepless nights fighting off mosquitoes. A pathway between the Palace and the Temple of the Inscriptions leads to the **Temple of the Sun,** the **Temple of the Foliated Cross,** the **Temple of the Cross,** and **Temple 14.** This group of temples, now cleared and in various stages of reconstruction, was built by Pacal's son, Chan-Bahlum, who is usually shown on inscriptions with six toes. Chan-Bahlum's plaster mask was found in Temple 14 next to the Temple of the Sun. Archaeologists have recently begun probing the depths of the Temple of the Sun in search of Chan-Bahlum's tomb. Little remains of this temple's exterior carving. Inside, however, behind a fence, a carving of Chan-Bahlum shows him ascending the throne in A.D. 690. The panels, which are still in place, depict Chan-Bahlum's version of his historic link to the throne.

To the left of the Palace is the North Group, also undergoing restoration. Included in this area are the **Ball Court** and the **Temple of the Count,** where Count Waldeck camped in the 19th century. At least three tombs, complete with offerings for the underworld journey, have been found here, and the lineage of at least 12 kings has been deciphered from inscriptions left at this site.

Just past the North Group is a small building (once a museum) now used for storing the artifacts found during the restorations. It is closed to the public. To the right of the building, a stone bridge crosses the river, leading to a pathway down the hillside to the new museum. The path, lined with rocks and with steps in the steepest areas, leads past the **Cascada Motiepa,** a beautiful waterfall that creates a series of pools perfect for cooling weary feet. Benches are placed along the way as rest areas, and some small temples have been reconstructed near the base of the trail. In the early morning and evening, you may hear monkeys crashing through the thick foliage by the path; if you keep noise to a minimum, you may spot wild parrots as well. Walking downhill (by far the best way to go), it will take you about 20 minutes to reach the main highway. The path ends at the paved road across from the museum. The *colectivos* going back to the village will stop here if you wave them down.

## WHERE TO STAY

The fanciest hotel in town (the Hotel Misión Park Inn Palenque) gets too many complaints for me to recommend it. And with the recent addition of some upscale hotels, it faces stiff competition. English is spoken in most of the good hotels. Transportation to and from the ruins is easy from just about any hotel.

### MODERATE

**Chan-Kah Ruinas** This hotel is a grouping of comfortable, roomy bungalows that offer privacy and quiet in the surroundings of a tropical forest. Most have air-conditioning. The grounds are beautifully tended, and there is an inviting pool made to look like a lagoon. A broad stream runs through the property. The hotel is on the road to the ruins, midway between the ruins and the town. Christmas prices will be higher than those quoted here, and you may be quoted a higher price if you reserve a room in advance from the United States. The outdoor restaurant and bar serves Mexican food.

Km 30 Carretera Palenque, 29960 Palenque, Chi. ✆ **916/345-1100.** Fax 916/345-0820. 78 units. $98 double. AE, MC, V. Free parking. **Amenities:** Restaurant, bar; large pool; game room; tour desk; room service until 10pm; laundry; nonsmoking rooms. *In room:* Hair dryer.

**Hotel Ciudad Real** This is your best bet for creature comforts and modern convenience. The hotel is on the highway to the airport. The rooms are large, quiet, well lit, and comfortably furnished. The bar features live marimba music at night. Also on the premises are a travel agency and a handcrafts store. When making a reservation, be sure that the reservation-taker understands that it's for the hotel in Palenque.

Carretera a Pakal-Na, 29960 Palenque, Chi. ✆ **916/345-1343.** Reservations ✆ **967/678-0187** in San Cristóbal. www.ciudadreal.com.mx. 72 units. $110 double. AE, MC, V. Free secured parking. **Amenities:** Restaurant (international), bar; large pool, baby pool; game room; tour desk; car rental; room service until 11pm. *In room:* A/C, TV.

**Hotel Maya Tucán** Get a room in back, and you will have a view of the hotel's natural pond. The cheerfully decorated rooms are adequate in size and come with double beds. The air-conditioner is quiet and gets the job done. The hotel sometimes operates a discotheque when large tour groups are present (which might bear asking about before checking in). The grounds are well kept in a tropical fashion, and scarlet macaws kept by the hotel fly about the parking lot. The Maya Tucán is a stone's throw from the Ciudad Real on the highway to the airport.

Carretera-Palenque Km 0.5, 29960 Palenque, Chi. ✆ **916/345-0443.** Fax 916/345-0337. Hmtucan@tnet.net.mx. 56 units. $99 double. MC, V. Free secured parking. **Amenities:** Restaurant, bar; room service until 11pm; laundry. *In room:* A/C, TV.

**Hotel Maya Tulipanes** ★ This hotel tries hard to remind you why you have come to Palenque—Maya statues, carvings, and paintings fill the hallways and public areas of the rambling, overgrown, but comfortable two-story hotel. All in all, it's a fun, very Mexican place to stay. Because the hotel is in the Cañada, it has a definite tropical-forest feel; the dark shade is a cool respite from the sun's glare. Most rooms are a little dark, and some are small. They vary from section to section, so ask to see rooms in different parts of the hotel, especially in the 2-year-old new section.

Calle Cañada 6, 29960 Palenque, Chi. ✆ **916/345-0201** or 916/345-0258. Fax 916/345-1004. www.maya tulipanes.com.mx. 72 units. $82 double. AE, MC, V. Free secured parking. **Amenities:** Restaurant, bar; 2 pools; tour desk; room service until 11pm; laundry. *In room:* A/C, TV.

### INEXPENSIVE

**Hotel Casa de Pakal** This bright, relatively new four-story hotel might be the best bargain in town if you don't have a car. The rooms are a little small but far brighter and cleaner than those at nearby choices, and they come with one double and one single bed. The air-conditioning is strong and quiet. The hotel is a half block west of the main plaza. It shares a phone number with the Maya Tucán—make sure that the person taking your reservation understands that you want to stay at Casa de Pakal.

Av. Juárez 10, 29960 Palenque, Chi. ✆ **916/345-0443.** 15 units. $40 double. No credit cards. **Amenities:** Laundry. *In room:* A/C.

**Hotel Kashlan** This is the closest hotel to the bus station and a dependable choice. The tidy rooms have interior windows opening onto the hall, marble floors, soft bedspreads, tile bathrooms, small vanities, and luggage racks. Show owner Ada Luz Navarro your Frommer's book, and you'll receive a discount. Higher prices are for rooms with air-conditioning (there are 27, and some of the new rooms are quite comfortable); the ceiling fans (in 30 rooms) are powerful. The hotel restaurant features vegetarian food. The hotel offers trips to Agua Azul and Misol Ha.

5 de Mayo 105, 29960 Palenque, Chi. ✆ **916/345-0297.** Fax 916/345-0309. www.palenque.com.mx/ kashlan. 59 units. $23–$45 double. Promotional rates often available. Rates include coffee all day. MC, V. **Amenities:** Restaurant, bar; tour desk; Internet service.

## WHERE TO DINE

Many small restaurants, none of which are noteworthy, line Avenida Juárez. I do like a couple in the main plaza, some on the road to the ruins, and a couple in the Cañada.

### MODERATE

**La Chiapaneca** ★ MEXICAN Considered by many to be Palenque's best restaurant, La Chiapaneca serves top-notch regional cuisine in a pleasant tropical setting. The *pollo Palenque* (chicken with potatoes in a tomato-and-onion sauce) is a soothing choice; save room for flan. You can order Mexican wines by the bottle. La Chiapaneca is about a mile toward the ruins from the Maya statue.

Carretera Palenque Ruinas. ✆ **916/345-1711.** Main courses $8–$10. AE, MC, V. Daily 8am–midnight.

**La Selva** ★★ MEXICAN/INTERNATIONAL La Selva (the jungle) offers fine dining in a large, outdoor space under a beautiful thatched roof beside well-tended gardens. The menu includes seafood, freshwater fish, steaks, and enchiladas. The most expensive thing on the menu is Pigua, a freshwater lobster that is caught in the large rivers of southeast Mexico. These can get quite large—the size of small saltwater lobsters. I especially liked fish stuffed with shrimp, and *mole* enchiladas. La Selva is on the highway to the ruins close by the Maya statue.

Km 0.5 Carretera Palenque Ruinas. ✆ **916/345-0363.** Main courses $8.50–$30. MC, V. Daily 11:30am–11:30pm.

### INEXPENSIVE

**La Cañada** MEXICAN This *palapa* restaurant tucked into the jungle is one of the best in town and is usually very peaceful. Though the dining room has a dirt floor, the place is spotless, the service attentive, and the food good, if not outstanding. Try one of the local specialties such as *pollo mexicano* or bean soup.

In the Hotel La Cañada, Prolongación Av. Hidalgo 12. ✆ **916/345-0102.** Main courses $5–$11. No credit cards. Daily 7am–10pm.

**Restaurant Maya** ★ MEXICAN/STEAKS A popular place among tourists and locals, Restaurant Maya faces the main plaza on the northwest corner. The dining area is breezy and open. At breakfast, there are free refills of very good coffee. Try the tamales or any of the other local dishes or traditional Mexican fare. This restaurant was awarded a national prize for quality and service. There's a branch in the Cañada, called Maya Cañada.

Av. Independencia s/n. ✆ **916/345-0042.** Breakfast $4–$5; main courses $4–$7. AE, MC, V. Daily 7am–11pm.

11

# Veracruz & Puebla: On the Heels of Cortez

The region of Veracruz and Puebla, in the east-central part of the country, was, for Hernán Cortez and his conquistadors, the door to Mexico. The region also played this role for most of the visitors who came to the area during colonial and early republic times. But today only a small fraction of the multitudes who flock to Mexico each year pass through.

This is a shame, for the area has much to recommend it to the visitor. For adventure travelers, it offers excellent whitewater river rafting through the Sierra Madre Oriental, challenging climbs that include Mexico's highest mountain—a dormant volcano called the Pico de Orizaba—and scuba diving along Veracruz's coastal reefs to visit shipwrecks. For the culture crowd, the region has three fascinating ruins, some excellent museums and historical sites, and great food. I find the lovely colonial cities of this region particularly enjoyable.

**Veracruz** is a fun town for music and food, and for soaking up the easygoing rhythms of the tropics. **Puebla** has the ideal highland climate, even better food, and a great historic district with museums, former convents and churches everywhere you look. The ruins in the area feature the startlingly vivid pre-Columbian murals of Cacaxltla, the great ceremonial center of El Tajín, and the New World's largest man-made structure, the great pyramid of Cholula.

## 1 Veracruz City

232km (145 miles) E of Mexico City; 109km (68 miles) SE of Xalapa

Veracruz has a reputation as a town with a rich history but little to show for it. True enough—and in my opinion, this has to do with the history: Much of it consisted of sackings by pirates, heavy bombardment by three different foreign powers (including the wonderfully named French Pastry War), and epidemics of malaria, yellow fever, and cholera. One might not necessarily want to preserve such a history even when artifacts weren't destroyed by those same events.

For the visitor, the important thing to note is that Veracruz, unlike Puebla, is more suitable for cafe-goers than for museumgoers. With the exception of the old fort of San Juan de Ulúa and perhaps the aquarium, the museums can be missed. You come here for the feel of the tropics, the balmy air, and the carefree attitude of the locals. Veracruz brings to mind other Gulf and Caribbean port cities—part New Orleans, part Maracaibo. Even more than in the rest of Mexico, things such as schedules are managed rather loosely, and if you expect Veracruzanos to act any differently, you'll just be banging your head against a wall. Here, you relax: you get your coffee in the morning at the Café de la Parroquia, you stroll down *el malecón* (boardwalk) in the evening, you take in the party scene at the *zócalo* (town square) at night.

The tolerance you'll find in Veracruz characterizes, to varying degrees, the rest of the state. Throughout the area, music is very important. Particular to the city of Veracruz are *marimba, danzonera,* and *comparsa* (carnavalesque) music. Just south of the city begins the Jarocha region of the state, whose music is rhythmic, with sexually suggestive lyrics that depend on double meanings. This is the home of "La Bamba," popularized by Ritchie Valens. In the northern part of the state is the Huasteca region. Its music, the *huapango huasteco,* involves a violin, a couple of small strumming guitars, and harmonized singing. In Xalapa, the state's highland capital, you can hear just about anything—it's home to the largest and best music school in the country.

Veracruz's history began with the arrival of Cortez and his army. There was little in the way of Indian settlement here at the time, which is why he chose this point to land in a possibly hostile continent. Within 3 months, the conquistador moved his forces 72km (45 miles) north to Quiauixtlán, a small Indian settlement known today as Villa Rica. Six years later, the Spanish resettled near the mouth of the Río Huitzilapan, at what is now Antigua (about 22km/14 miles north of modern Veracruz). The ruins of several massive stone houses, including the House of Cortez (*La Casa de Cortez*), still stand there. In 1599, the settlement moved south to the original landing site, and Villa Rica de la Vera Cruz ("Rich Town of the True Cross"), Cortez's name for the town, became permanent.

The famous Spanish galleons sailed from the port of Veracruz, loaded with silver and gold. Pirates repeatedly attacked, and on occasion captured, the city. The citizens defended themselves, eventually constructing a high wall around the old town and a massive fort (San Juan de Ulúa) on what was a harbor island (a pier now connects it to the mainland). The walls surrounding the city are gone now, but the fort of San Juan de Ulúa remains intact—an impressive example of Spanish military architecture.

## ESSENTIALS

**GETTING THERE & DEPARTING By Plane Continental** (© **800/231-0856,** or 01-800/900-5000 in Mexico) has nonstop service to and from Houston. **Aeromexico** (© **800/237-6639** from the U.S., 01-800/021-4000, 229/935-0283, or 229/934-1534 at the airport) and **Mexicana** (© **800/531-7921** from the U.S., 229/932-2242, or 229/938-0008 at the airport) operate frequent flights from Mexico City with connecting service to the U.S. The smaller airlines **Aerolitoral** (© **800/237-6639** from the U.S., or 229/935-0142), an Aeromexico affiliate, and **Aerocaribe/Aerocozumel** (© **229/922-5212,** or229/922-5210 at the airport) have direct flights to several Mexican cities.

The **airport** (airport code: VER) is 11km (7 miles) from the town center. Getting there by **taxi** costs about $10. Major car-rental agencies with counters at the airport and locations in downtown hotels include **Avis** (© **800/331-1212** or 229/931-1580), **Dollar** (© **800/800-4000** or 229/935-5231), and **National** (© **800/328-4567** or 229/931-7556).

**By Car** From Mexico City (6 hr.) and Puebla (4 hr.), take the *autopista* (toll Hwy. 150D) into Veracruz. From Xalapa (1½ hr.), take Highway 140 (to the coast) and coastal toll Highway 180 south.

**By Bus** The ADO first-class bus station is 20 blocks south of the town center on Díaz Mirón between Calles Orizaba and Molina. There is frequent bus service to Mexico City, Puebla, Xalapa and other cities. Taxis wait in front of the terminal; the trip to the center costs $2 or less. DIAZ MIRON city buses go to and

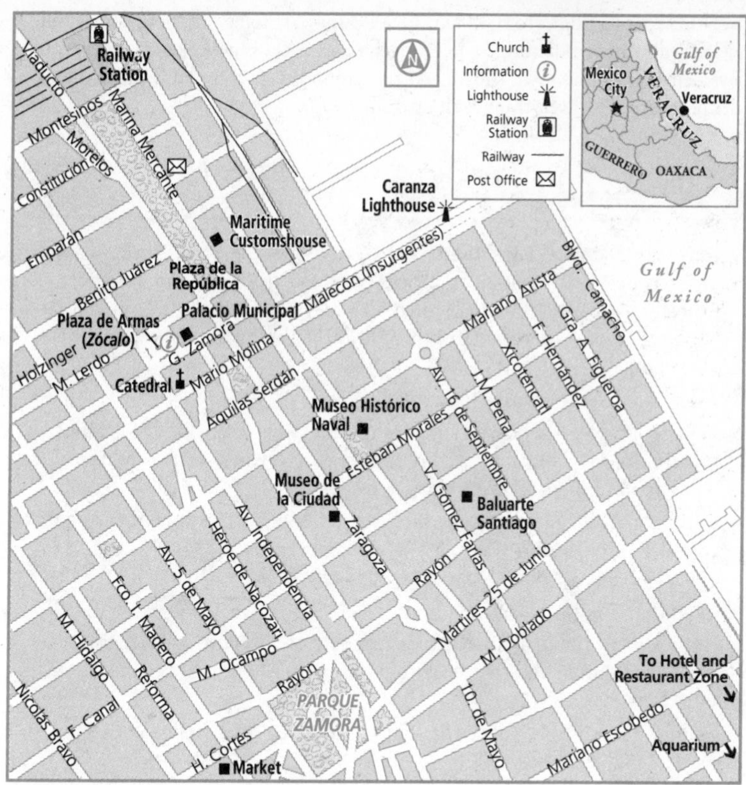


Downtown Veracruz

from the town center. Catch them going outbound on Avenida 5 de Mayo (2 blocks west of the *zócalo*). You can buy a bus ticket downtown at the "Ticket Bus" agency, Allende 1500 (at Zamora). It's open Monday to Saturday from 11am to 2:30pm and 3 to 7pm.

**VISITOR INFORMATION** The **tourism office** (✆ and fax **229/989-8817** and 229/989-8800, ext. 158), is downtown by the *zócalo,* on the ground floor of the Palacio Municipal (City Hall). It is open Monday to Saturday from 8am to 8pm, Sunday from 10am to 6pm.

**CITY LAYOUT** Downtown Veracruz is a jumble of streets. The social center of town is the ***zócalo,*** or town square (formally Plaza de Armas), where you'll find the tourism office. Two short blocks away is another landmark, ***el malecón,*** a long promenade fronting the harbor where Veracruzanos like to stroll in the evenings to catch the cool sea breeze. The city has begun the construction of a plaza to enlarge the promenade. Starting at the *malecón* and running south along the coast is **Bulevard Avila Camacho,** known as *el bulevard.* It connects downtown to Veracruz's hotel and restaurant zone, which stretches along the coast all the way to the one-time village of Boca del Río.

**GETTING AROUND** **Taxis** are plentiful. **City buses** are cheap (25¢–50¢) and not hard to use. There are **sightseeing trolleys**—open-air, rubber-wheeled replicas of the originals that ran in Veracruz until the early 1980s. They leave from the corner of 16 de Septiembre and the *malecón* around every hour (weather permitting) from 10am to 11:30pm, making an hour-long tour ($3.50) down the Bulevard Avila Camacho and back. On weekends other trolleys depart from the town square and run around the main plazas and some of the port facilities. Everything is in Spanish.

## *FAST FACTS:* Veracruz

*American Express* **Viajes Reptur** represents American Express. The main office is at Serdán 690-B, ✆ **229/931-0838.** Office hours for American Express-related business are Monday to Friday from 9am to 1:30pm and 4 to 6pm, Saturday from 9am to 1pm, but you can reach the staff during the lunch hour.

*Area Code* The telephone area code is **229.**

*Climate* Veracruz is hot and humid most of the year, but the hottest months are May and June. In the winter, strong winds known as *nortes* occasionally bring cool, even chilly, weather

*Consulate* The American consulate is closed, and there is no Canadian consulate. The **British Consulate** is at Independencia 1394 (✆ and fax **229/931-6694**). It's open Monday to Friday from 9am to 1pm.

*Emergencies* Dial ✆ **060.**

*High Season* The peak tourist times are July and August, December, Carnaval, and Easter. Veracruz is more popular with Mexican nationals than with foreigners.

*Hospital* The **Hospital de María** is at Alacio Pérez 1004, between Carmen Serdán and 20 de Noviembre (✆ **229/931-3626** or 229/931-3619).

*Pharmacy* **Farmacia Las Torres,** Av. Díaz Mirón 295 between Abasolo and Paso y Toncoso (✆ **229/932-2885**), is open daily 24 hours.

*Police* In Veracruz, ✆ **229/938-0664;** in Boca del Río ✆ **229/986-1997.**

*Post Office* The *correo,* on Avenida de la República near the Maritime Customs House, is open Monday to Saturday from 8am to 4pm.

## EXPLORING VERACRUZ

The ***zócalo*** ★★ is the social hub, where locals hang out in the cafes chatting with friends while the marimbas, Jarocha bands, and mariachis make a lively scene, playing well into the night. Bordering the *zócalo* are the **cathedral** and the **Palacio Municipal** (City Hall). There always seems to be some kind of performance on the square: exhibitions of ***danzón*** (see "Music, Dance & Carnaval," below), clown acts, band concerts, and comedy sketches.

One block east is the **Plaza de la República,** a long plaza where you'll find the **post office,** the old **customs house,** and the civil registry, all built around the turn of the 19th century. On the north side is the old train station, **Estación de Ferrocarriles,** which has a remarkable yellow-and-blue tile facade. From the east side of this plaza, you can board a bus to Veracruz's most famous tourist attraction, the fortress of **San Juan de Ulúa.** Just around the corner from the south side of the plaza is *el malecón,* where you can take a boat ride of the harbor or have coffee at the city's most popular gathering spot, **El Café de la Parroquia.**

## MUSIC, DANCE & CARNAVAL

Hang out in the *zócalo* and you'll be serenaded with *danzonera, marimba, Jarocha, mariachi,* and *norteño* music playing to a large crowd of Veracruzanos who've stopped to drink some coffee or beer and chat with friends. On Tuesday, Thursday, and Saturday a band plays in front of the Palacio Municipal for couples dancing the *danzón.* It's a stately affair: couples alternate between dancing perfectly erect in a slow rumba-like fashion and promenading arm in arm while the women wave their fans. The *danzón* came to Veracruz from Cuba in the 1890s; today you won't often see it elsewhere. On other evenings, there is *danzón* and salsa dancing in **Parque Zamora,** and on Wednesdays at the **Plazuela de la Campana.**

If you would like to see more styles of traditional dance, inquire at the tourist office in the *zócalo* (see above) about performances by the **Ballet Tradiciones de México.** Several times throughout the year, the company appears at the **Teatro Clavijero** (✆ **229/931-0574** or 229/932-6693 for reservations) Tickets cost $5 to $7. The shows are fun and colorful.

In the week before Ash Wednesday, Veracruz explodes with **Carnaval,** one of the best in Mexico. By local tradition, Carnaval begins with the ritual burning of "ill humor" and ends with the funeral of "Juan Carnaval." Visitors flood in from all over the country, packing the streets and hotels; those without rooms are content to live out of their cars. Locals crowd the streets moving to the music, which seems to be coming from everywhere.

Floats (*carros alegóricos*) are made with true Mexican flair—bright colors, papier-mâché figures, flowers, and live entertainment. Groups from neighboring villages dance in peacock- and pheasant-feathered headdresses. Draculas, drag queens, and women in sparkling dresses fill the streets. The parades follow Bulevard Avila Camacho; most of the other activities center in the *zócalo* and begin around noon, lasting well into the night.

On the Sunday before Ash Wednesday, the longest and most lavish of the Carnaval parades takes place on the *malecón.* Parades on Monday and Tuesday are scaled-down versions of the Sunday parade (ask at the tourist office about these routes); by Wednesday, it's all over. Most Mexicans consider Veracruz more uninhibited than the rest of the country. Carnaval attracts hordes of people from cities across Mexico wanting to cut loose. Excess is the norm. If you plan to be in Veracruz for Carnaval, reserve hotel space months in advance.

## THE TOP ATTRACTIONS

**Baluarte Santiago** Built in 1635, this bastion is all that remains of the wall and system of fortifications that encircled the city. It was one of the nine original bastions fortifying the wall. A small collection of pre-Hispanic gold jewelry, recovered several years ago by a fisherman along the coast some kilometers north of Veracruz, is on permanent display here.

Calle Canal, between Gómez Farías and 16 de Septiembre. ✆ **229/931-1059.** Admission $2.50; free Sun and holidays. Tues–Sun 10am–4:30pm.

**El Acuario** ★ *Kids* For most Mexican visitors, the aquarium is one of the city's major attractions. The largest aquarium in Latin America, with 9 freshwater and 15 saltwater tanks, it's an impressive attraction that can hold its own with American public aquariums. The doughnut-shaped *gran pecera* (large tank) gives the illusion of being surrounded by the ocean and its inhabitants. New this year is the even larger shark tank. To reach it, take a cab.

Plaza Acuario Veracruzano, Bulevard M. Avila Camacho. ✆ **229/932-7984.** Admission $4.50 adults, $2.50 children 2–12. Daily 10am–7pm.

**Fun Fact** **A Piece of Film History**

The Fort of San Juan de Ulúa was the site of the spooky "alligator scene" toward the end of the Michael Douglas–Kathleen Turner movie *Romancing the Stone.*

**Fort of San Juan de Ulúa** ★★★ Built to ward off pirates and foreign invasions, the fortress was repeatedly enlarged throughout the colonial period until it became the massive work you see today. After independence, the fort served as a prison noted for its harsh conditions and for the famous people incarcerated there, among them Benito Juárez, who later led the reform movement and became one of Mexico's most revered presidents. It is a formidable example of colonial military architecture, with crenellated walls projecting straight up some 11m (35 ft.) from the water's edge, and bastions at each corner. Inside is a large courtyard, with wide ramps along the inside walls, storehouses, barracks, and old prison cells. English-speaking guides are available at the entrance. A narrow stretch of landfill connects the onetime island to the mainland.

✆ **229/938-5151.** Admission $3.50; free Sun. Tues–Sun 9am–5pm. Bus: "San Juan de Ulúa" (25¢) from Avenida de la República in front of the Customs House (15 min.). A taxi charges $4. By car, cross the bridge that heads north between Avenida de la República and Avenida Morelos, then turn right past the container storage and piers.

**Museo de la Ciudad** On the ground floor of a 19th-century building is this small city museum. The exhibits concern the history of the city and its social evolution from colonial times to the present. Text and audio are in Spanish; most of the exhibits are photos or dioramas.

Zaragoza 397. ✆ **229/989-8872.** Admission $2.50. Wed–Sun 10am–6pm. From the Palacio Municipal, walk 5 blocks south on Zaragoza; it's on the right.

**Museo Histórico Naval** This museum occupies the building that once housed Mexico's naval academy. Exhibits concern the history of navigation, including nautical paraphernalia, the history of the naval academy and Mexico's struggles with other countries. When renovating the courtyard, workmen came upon the foundations of the old wall that used to encircle the city, which has been left exposed. As you enter, look for uniformed guides, who will show you around the place for free.

Calle Arista between Landero y Coss and Gómez Farías. ✆ **229/931-4078.** Free admission. Tues–Sun 9am–5pm.

### MORE ATTRACTIONS

**BOAT TRIPS** Boats tour the harbor (most narration is in Spanish only), around the tankers and ships docked in the port and San Juan de Ulúa fortress, and out to the Isle of Sacrifices. Departures are sporadic (depending on the weather and demand) from *el malecón* in front of the Hotel Emporio. The cost is $6 for adults and $3 for children ages 2 to 8.

**BEACHES** Veracruz has beaches, but they mostly have brown sand, and the Gulf water is a dull green. The nearest true beach is at the **Villa del Mar,** a little down the bulevard, followed by **Costa de Oro** and then **Mocambo** beach.

**EXCURSIONS** Popular day trip destinations include **La Antigua;** the Totonac ruins at **Zempoala; Xalapa,** the state capital and home of an excellent anthropology museum; and the archaeological site at **El Tajín.** For prices and reservations, contact **VIP Tours** (✆ **229/922-3315** or 229/922-1918) or **Centro de Reservaciones de Veracruz** (✆ **229/935-6422**).

For the actively inclined, **river rafting, mountain climbing,** and **diving** are all possible options. River rafting is centered outside Xalapa (see "Xalapa: Museums & White Water," below). **Divers** can explore series of reefs and shipwrecks south of town toward Boca del Río. Contact **Dorado Divers** (✆ **229/931-4305**) for details.

**SHOPPING** Veracruz excels in one category and no other. It has sublimely **tacky souvenirs,** which make perfect payback for coworkers who have burdened you with white elephants. On *el malecón* across from Café de la Parroquia, you'll find a long row of small souvenir shops that are Veracruz's version of Fisherman's Wharf. Another place of interest (not so much for buying as for looking) is the **city market.** It's possible to find just about anything here, from parrots and iguanas to medicinal shrubs, not to mention groceries. It's at the corner of Madero and Cortez.

## WHERE TO STAY

Most hotels have high- and low-season rates. Low season is most of the year, when there are some pretty good deals. High season is July, August, December, Carnaval, and Easter. Prices quoted include the 17% tax.

### VERY EXPENSIVE

**Fiesta Americana Veracruz** ★★ *Kids* Veracruz's most resort-like hotel is six stories high and very long, stretching out across a wide beachfront. Spacious and decorated in muted colors, most rooms have either terraces or balconies, and all have ocean views. Each contains two full beds or one king. Wheelchair-accessible rooms are available. It's on the Playa Costa de Oro, one of Veracruz's nicest beaches, but there is also a large and inviting pool area, with an ample shaded section.

Blvd. Avila Camacho s/n, 94299 Boca del Rio, Ver. ✆ **800/FIESTA-1** in the U.S. and Canada, or 229/989-8989. Fax 229/989-8909. www.fiestaamericana.com. 233 units. $233 double; $310 jr. suite. AE, DC, MC, V. Secured parking $2.50. **Amenities:** 2 restaurants (international, Italian), poolside snack bar, bar; 2 large pools; 2 whirlpools; golf at local club; lighted tennis court; health club and spa; watersports equipment; children's activities (weekends and high season); concierge; tour desk; car rental; business center; salon; 24-hour room service; babysitting; same-day laundry and dry cleaning; nonsmoking rooms; executive-level rooms. *In room:* A/C, TV, dataport, minibar, coffeemaker, hair dryer, iron, safe.

### EXPENSIVE

**Hotel Emporio** ★ Across from *el malecón* by the old lighthouse, the Emporio occupies an excellent location. Most of the rooms in the nine-story building have a view of the harbor. Some have balconies, while others have simply a large window. All are carpeted and have well-equipped bathrooms and double-glazed windows to keep out the noise. The suites are a bit larger and better lit. Rooms are furnished with rattan chairs and tables, with a choice of two double beds or one king-size. Sunday brunch on the top floor of the hotel is a popular event.

Paseo del Malecón s/n, 91700 Veracruz, Ver. ✆ **229/932-0020** or 01-/800-295-3000 in Mexico. Fax 229/931-2261. emporio@ver.megared.net.mx. 203 units. $119 double; $151 jr. suite. Promotional rates available. AE, MC, V. Free guarded parking. **Amenities:** 2 restaurants (regional, international), bar; 2 large outdoor pools; heated indoor pool; health club; game room; activities desk; car rental; business center; executive services; room service until midnight; babysitting; same-day laundry. *In room:* A/C, TV, hair dryer.

**Hotel Lois** ★ Perched on the coast south of town, at the beginning of the hotel zone, this 10-story hotel is something of a monument to frivolity, with outlandish décor that mixes many colors and shapes to create a send-up of modern minimalism. I imagine the aim is to get guests into vacation mode, which makes the lobby bar a popular hangout. Rooms are competitively priced and comfortable, though the standard rooms are staid compared to the rest of the hotel. They are medium size, with two double beds or one king, ample lighting, and good-sized bathrooms with plenty of counter space. The suites are more in character with the rest of the hotel. They're larger, with larger bathrooms, and some contain Jacuzzi tubs. The large, attractive pool area, on the third floor, affords a good view of the coastline.

Calz. Ruiz Cortines 10, 91590 Boca del Río, Ver. ✆ **229/937-8089,** or 01-800/712-9136 in Mexico. 116 units. High season $110–$130 double, $130–$150 suite; low season $85–$95 double, $95–$120 suite. MC, V. Free parking. **Amenities:** Restaurant, cafe, bar; large pool; Jacuzzi; squash court; health club with sauna, massage; game room; travel agency; tour desk; room service until 11:30pm; same-day laundry and dry cleaning. *In room:* A/C, TV, minibar, safe.

**Hotel Mocambo** ★★ *Kids* The Mocambo, built in 1932, was the city's first resort hotel, playing host to presidents and movie stars during the '40s and '50s. It overlooks some of Veracruz's finest beaches in the hotel zone south of downtown. The low buildings spread out over spacious gardens with lots of coconut palms. In marked contrast to the cramped, boxy corridors and hallways of the modern beachfront hotels, the architecture and decor are simple and elegant, with wide, open-air walkways and terraces looking out over the ocean. The hotel shows its age, but it echoes Mexico's *bella época* with stylish touches such as the Art Deco indoor pool. Most of the simply furnished rooms are large, with sea views and tile floors. My favorite rooms are those on the upper floors, which have balconies. Suites are very large and come with many more amenities. The hotel serves good Saturday and Sunday brunches on the restaurant terrace.

Boca del Río (Apdo. Postal 263), 91700 Veracruz, Ver. ✆ **229/922-0205.** Fax 229/922-0212. www.hotelmocambo.com.mx. 105 units. High season $183 double; low season $85. Low-season rates include full breakfast and 4th night free. AE, DC, MC, V. Free guarded parking. **Amenities:** 2 restaurants (Mexican, international), 2 bars; 2 pools (1 indoor); whirlpool; lighted tennis court; gym with sauna and steam room; spa; children's activities (high season); tour desk; car rental; room service until midnight; babysitting; same-day laundry and dry cleaning; nonsmoking rooms. *In room:* A/C, TV.

### MODERATE

**Hotel Colonial** Two hotels sit next door to each other on the *zócalo:* the Hotel Colonial (which isn't so colonial), and the Hotel Imperial (which isn't so imperial). In terms of rooms, services, and price, they are much the same—comfortable, but not fancy. The location is great: you can enjoy the music and party atmosphere in the *zócalo* and then conveniently retire to your room (preferably an interior one). The Colonial has two sections: Rooms in the new section are bright and comfortable, with tile floors and better air-conditioning; rooms in the old section are comfortable but darker and more worn. Outside rooms, which are noisier and more expensive, have small balconies overlooking the plaza. The Imperial's lobby is more impressive, but the pool emits a slight smell of chlorine to parts of the hotel, and the Colonial seems to be better managed. Still, I think of these hotels for the most part as interchangeable. If you can't get a room at the Colonial, try the Imperial (✆ **229/932-1204**).

Miguel Lerdo 117, 91700 Veracruz, Ver. ✆ and fax **229/932-0193.** 174 units. $52–$71 double. AE, MC, V. Covered guarded parking $3. **Amenities:** Sidewalk cafe and bar; indoor pool. *In room:* A/C, TV.

## WHERE TO DINE

The restaurants on the *zócalo* are the best spots for drinking a beverage and taking in the scene. While more expensive than places a few blocks away, their prices are still reasonable. If you want to have seafood with the locals, go to the city fish market on Lendero y Coss around the corner from *el malecón.* Facing the street are several small restaurants. Find the one called **La Cría.**

Seafood and coffee are two readily available commodities in Veracruz. The state of Veracruz is all coastline and well known for the variety of its seafood dishes. You will find *pescado a la veracruzana* (fish cooked in a sauce of tomatoes, onions, olives, garlic, and chiles) on menus across Mexico. And the mountains surrounding the cities of Xalapa, Orizaba, and Córdoba provide the ideal altitude and climate for growing coffee.

### EXPENSIVE

**Restaurant El Cacharrito** ★ STEAKS Midway between downtown and Mocambo beach is this family-run, Argentine-style steakhouse. The steaks are expertly cooked and served on wooden boards (as in Argentina). Order the *bife de chorizo* (rib-eye) and wash it down with some of the good house red wine. Take a taxi here, and be sure to have the address handy.

Blvd. Ruiz Cortines 15. ✆ **229/937-7027.** Reservations recommended during Carnaval. Steaks $18–$23. MC, V. Daily 2–11pm.

### MODERATE

**Gran Café del Portal** MEXICAN In the *portales* that face the front door of the cathedral is this dependable restaurant with good prices and local color. In the evenings a parade of strolling troubadours, harpists, *marimba* players, and shoeshine men passes by. For the midafternoon meal, the *comida del dia* provides lots of food at a reasonable price and a choice of dishes for each course (the price depends on the main course you select). Avoid the overcooked pasta and most beef dishes, which are tough. The exception is the tenderized *milanesa* (breaded and fried beef), done very well in the Mexican style. For seafood, ask the waiter what's freshest. The enchiladas and the soups are good, and the *flan napolitano* could feed a family of four.

Independencia at Zamora. ✆ **229/931-2759.** Main courses $6–$10; *comida del dia* $6–$8. No credit cards. Daily 6am–midnight.

**Mariscos Villa Rica Mocambo** ★★★ SEAFOOD This establishment prides itself on cooking Veracruz style. All the seafood standards are on the menu, plus a few dishes that are harder to come by in Mexico, let alone north of the border. Everything I tried, I enjoyed enormously. For starters, try a classic seafood cocktail. Veracruzano specialties include *pampano al acuyo* (pompano cooked in a sauce of green herbs), conch filet *al ajillo* (with toasted strips of *guajillo* peppers), and *steak de camarón a la naranja* (shrimp pressed together and cooked in an orange sauce). Service is excellent. Look for an open-air thatched structure below the Mocambo hotel.

Calz. Mocambo 527. ✆ **229/922-2113.** Main courses $8–$13. AE, MC, V. Daily noon–10pm.

### INEXPENSIVE

**Gran Café de la Parroquia** ★★ MEXICAN/COFFEE More than a coffeehouse, La Parroquia is an institution. Making the scene here for morning or afternoon coffee is practically mandatory on any trip to Veracruz. The action takes place in a large, bustling dining area facing *el malecón.* There's nothing fancy about it; white tiles cover the floor and walls, and the furniture is simple but comfortable. The thing to order is *café lechero,* which is so good I would pit it against any other coffee-and-milk drink. You'll get two fingers of dark coffee in a glass. Then, to get the attention of the waiter who circulates with the kettle of steaming milk, you tap the glass with your spoon. The sound of clinking glass rings constantly throughout the dining room as the regulars consume coffee upon coffee. The cafe also offers pastries and decent breakfasts, but some of the main courses are disappointments.

Av. Gómez Farías 34. ✆ **229/932-2584.** Breakfast $2–$5; coffee $1–$2; main courses $4–$10. No credit cards. Daily 6am–1am.

**Samborcito** ★ *Finds* REGIONAL No need to say the name twice to any cab driver in town; everybody knows this place. Samborcito is simple eating at its best for either breakfast or lunch. The name pokes fun at Sanborn's, the oldest, best-known chain of restaurants in Mexico (never mind the difference in spelling; Mexicans don't distinguish between certain consonant combinations). Classic dishes include *picadas* (thick masa pancake with cheese and sauce—a Veracruz tradition), and puffy *gordita negra* (masa cooked with black bean paste and flavored with the toasted leaf of the aguacatillo—not spicy). Tamales are available on weekends. All the breakfasts are great. Samborcito is near downtown; a cab will run about $1.50.

16 de Septiembre 727. ✆ **229/931-4388.** Main courses $7–$12; breakfast $2.50–$5; antojitos $1–$5. No credit cards. Daily 6am–6pm.

## 2 Exploring North of Veracruz: Ruins, More Ruins & a Great Museum

### THE RUINS OF ZEMPOALA

On Highway 180, about 22km (14 miles) north of Veracruz, is the village of Antigua (on the river of the same name). It's not very well known today, but for 75 years beginning in 1525, it was a seat of Spanish power. The village is known locally for its seafood restaurants and is especially popular on weekends.

About 40km (25 miles) north of Veracruz, a little past Antigua, are the ruins of **Zempoala** (or Cempoala), surrounded by lush foliage and rich agricultural land. Though not as large as the site of El Tajín, they're still noteworthy. Zempoala was the principal city of the Totonac at the time of the Spanish Conquest. Zempoala means "place of the 20 waters," named for the several rivers that converge near the site. When the conquerors saw Zempoala for the first time, the whitewashed stucco walls glimmered like silver in the tropical sun, which of course brought the Spaniards running. Disappointed at seeing little in the way of precious metals, the Spaniards made allies of the Totonac Indians, who were resentful of Aztec domination.

Most buildings at Zempoala date from the 14th and 15th centuries—late post-Classic. Yet the town was in existence at least 1,500 years earlier. The Great Temple resembles the Temple of the Sun in Tenochtitlán, probably a result of 15th-century Aztec influence. The Temple of the Little Faces is decorated with stuccoed faces in the walls and hieroglyphs painted on the lower sections. The Temple of Quetzalcoatl, the feathered serpent god, is square, and the Temple of Ehecatl, god of the wind, is (as usual) round.

Admission to the archaeological site is $4.50; it's open daily from 9am to 6pm. A video camera permit costs $4. On weekends and during vacation months, you're likely to find a group of the famous *voladores* from Papantla performing their acrobatic ritual (see El Tajín, below). If you're going by car, driving time is 40 minutes north on Highway 180 through Cardel; the ruins of Zempoala are just north of Cardel. **Transportes Regionales Veracruzanas** (TRV) buses run hourly from Veracruz; the trip takes 1½ hours.

## XALAPA: MUSEUMS & WHITE WATER

Xalapa (104km/65 miles northwest of Veracruz; pronounced ha-*lap*-a and sometimes spelled "Jalapa") is a highland city in the middle of Mexico's prime coffee-growing area and the capital of the state of Veracruz. Less than 2 hours from the port of Veracruz, it offers an easy escape from the high temperatures there. It's a hilly city, crisscrossed by narrow, winding streets and alleys. A fine, misty rain known as *chipi chipi* often floats in the air, cloaking the views in a vaporous shroud.

Xalapa is a university town and has the best music school in the country, which is part of the University of Veracruz. Xalapa is also known for its outstanding symphony orchestra. With so many musicians present, there is a tremendous variety of music here. If your interests are more archaeological, Xalapa's anthropology museum is second only to Mexico City's monster of a museum. For active sorts, there's excellent whitewater rafting nearby. More than a dozen companies offer rafting trips. Finally, Xalapa is known as the hometown of Antonio López de Santa Anna, whose eleven terms as president of Mexico spanned 22 years; his hacienda southeast of town is now a museum.

**Tasty Fun Fact**

Xalapa or "Jalapa" lent its name to the famed *jalapeño* pepper.

### ESSENTIALS

**GETTING THERE** Veracruz, less than 2 hours away, has the closest major airport, although some charter flights use the small Xalapa airport. If you're driving from Veracruz, take Highway 180 to Cardel, then turn left (west) onto Highway 140 past the coffee plantations. From Papantla, you can avoid the mountains by taking 180 south to Cardel. From Mexico City and Puebla, there's a turn-off for Highway 140 on the toll highway to Veracruz (150D). Fog is common and dangerous between Perote and Xalapa. The trip by bus to or from Papantla takes 4 hours.

The **bus station** (CAXA) is 2.5km (1½ miles) east of the town center just off Calle 20 de Noviembre. Taxis are downstairs, and prices are controlled. Tickets to the center of town cost around $2. Buses run to Veracruz every 20 to 30 minutes and to Puebla 9 or 10 times a day. You can buy tickets downtown at the "Ticket Bus" Agency, Av. Enríquez 13, a block east of the cathedral (no phone). The office is open Monday to Friday from 10am to 2pm and 4 to 7pm.

**VISITOR INFORMATION** The easiest place to go is the **tourist information booth** at the Ayuntamiento, across from the Plaza Juárez. Hours are Monday to Friday from 9am to 2pm and 4 to 6pm, Saturday from 9am to 1pm. Occasionally it closes for a week. Much more difficult to reach and not worth the effort is the **State Tourism Office** on the first floor of Bulevard Cristóbal Colón 5 Fracc. Jardines de las Animas. (© **228/812-8500,** ext. 133). Hours are Monday to Friday from 8:30am to 9pm, Saturday from 9am to 1pm.

**CITY LAYOUT** Xalapa is a hilly town with streets that defy order. In the center of town is the large **Plaza Juárez,** where on a clear day the Pico de Orizaba is visible to the southwest. Across the street (north) from the plaza is the Ayuntamiento (city hall); just east is the Palacio del Gobierno (state offices). The cathedral is across (north) from this.

**GETTING AROUND** Most of the recommended hotels and restaurants (see "Where to Stay" and "Where to Dine," below) are within easy walking distance of the central Plaza Juárez. Taxis in Xalapa are inexpensive, as are city buses. Because streets are busy and narrow in the center of town, cabs aren't allowed to stop just anywhere. Sometimes you have to look for a TAXI sign.

**FAST FACTS** The telephone **area code** is **228.** The **climate** is humid and cool for most of the year. Year-round, be prepared for the light *chipi chipi* rain that comes and goes. The hardest rains fall from May through July. The **American Express** office is in Viajes Xalapa, Clavijero 311 (© **228/840-6971**). Hours for traveler services are weekdays from 9am to 2 pm and 4 to 7:30pm.

## EXPLORING XALAPA

Walk through the streets and admire the blossoming bougainvillea, fruit trees, and flowers. Halfway between the mountains and the hotlands, Xalapa's gardens can grow just about anything.

For information on cultural events, go to the **Agora,** a cultural center with a coffee shop beneath the Plaza Juárez (reached by steps on the south side of the plaza). The coffee shop offers a view of the city, and an occasional film series. Look for posters announcing upcoming concerts. There's usually something going on. Also, look in the local paper, *Diario de Xalapa.*

**Hacienda El Lencero** Occasionally called the Museo de Muebles (Furniture Museum), this country estate 14km (9 miles) southeast of the town center was for 14 years (1842–56) the home of Antonio López de Santa Anna, the 11-time president of Mexico. Here, he retreated from the world, though on occasion he opened his doors to receive notable visitors.

Furniture from Mexico, Europe, and Asia fills the rooms, illustrating the cosmopolitan tastes of Mexico's upper classes during the 19th century. Among the notable pieces is the leader's bed, embellished with the national emblem (an eagle holding a snake in its beak). The grounds are lovely and shaded by ancient trees. The grand house has a roofed area overlooking a spring-fed pond. A restaurant serves light snacks, pastries, and soft drinks.

Carr. Xalapa-Veracruz Km 10. No phone. Admission $3; free guided tours (in Spanish only) on request. Tues–Sun 10am–5pm. Drive or take a taxi ($10 round-trip) about 10km (6 miles) south of town on Hwy. 140 toward Veracruz, past the country club; watch for the signs on the right. Bus: BANDERILLA–P. CRYSTAL–LENCERO from Av. Lázaro Cárdenas to village of Lencero or nearby spot along the highway.

**Museo de Antropología de Xalapa** ★★★ This museum exhibits excellent examples of the megalithic heads and other monumental sculptures made by the Olmec—better than those in Mexico City or at the museum in Villahermosa. The collection of Totonac pieces, from the highly stylized smiling faces to the unadorned, realistic sculptures of faces and heads, is the best anywhere. The firm of Edward Durrell Stone (the architect of the Kennedy Center in Washington, D.C.) designed the museum. It's laid out in order from earliest to latest cultures, from the Olmec—the mother culture of Mesoamerican civilization—to the post-classic civilizations of Veracruz. Explanatory text is in Spanish. Bilingual museum guides are available.

Av. Xalapa s/n. © **228/815-0920** or 228/815-0708. Admission $3.50. Daily 9am–4:30pm.

## OTHER ATTRACTIONS

**RIVER RAFTING** Close by Xalapa are three popular rivers for rafting and a number of rafting companies that can accommodate you. No experience is necessary. If you're planning ahead, call the highly recommended **Far Flung Adventures** (© **800/359-4138** in the U.S.). If you're in Xalapa already, call the local

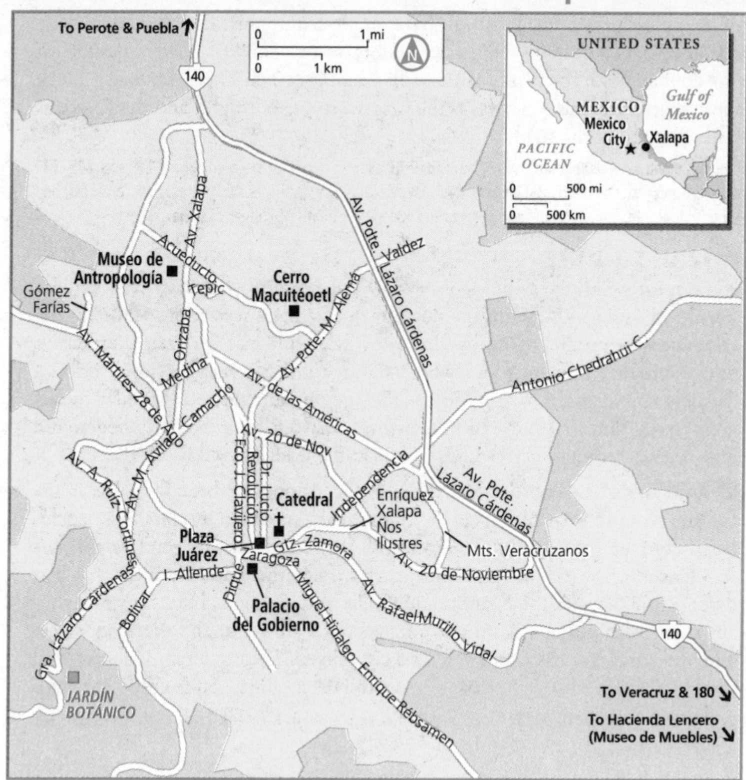


office, **Ecoexpediciones** (✆ **228/817-0600**). Another outfit that I can recommend is **Mexico Verde** (✆ **01-800/362-8800** in Mexico). Either company can do day trips from Xalapa (about $50), but it might not be on the day you want to go.

## WHERE TO STAY

**Mesón del Alférez** ★★ In most other parts of Mexico, rooms such as these, in a beautiful colonial house, would go for much more money. The owners have thoroughly renovated the old house and retained its residential feel. Rooms are spacious and beautifully decorated. Standard rooms and junior suites come with one double bed, suites with a choice of two doubles or one king. Rooms are colonial in style, accented by bright colors and stone. In some, a loft creates extra space. A new addition is around the corner in a modern house, Balcones del Alférez. Rooms there are comfortable, modern, and a little quieter. The hotel faces the back of the Palacio del Gobierno.

Sebastián Camacho 2, esq. Zaragoza, 91000 Xalapa, Ver. ✆ and fax **228/818-0113.** mesonalferez@hotmail.com. 28 units. $55 standard; $66 jr. suite; $77 suite. Rates include continental breakfast. AE, MC, V. Free secured parking 2 blocks away. **Amenities:** Restaurant; tour desk; car rental; room service until 10pm; laundry service. *In room:* TV, coffeemaker, hair dryer.

**Posada del Cafeto** ★ This colorful, comfortable hotel has three stories of rooms surrounding a tidy garden. Furnishings and decor are simple and attractive, with handsome wood furniture and cheerful colors. Each room is slightly different: Some are small, but all have ample bathrooms. Bed choices include one double, two twins, a twin and a double, or two doubles. Lower rates are for one double. From the Plaza Juárez, walk 4 blocks east on Zaragoza, then 1 block south where it bends. Canovas is the first street on your right, and the Posada is farther down on the right.

Canovas 8 and 12, 91000 Xalapa, Ver. ✆ **228/817-0023.** p_cafeto@xal.megared.net.mx. 29 units. $33–$40 double. Rates include continental breakfast. AE, MC, V. No parking available. **Amenities:** Cafe (breakfast and supper); tour info; limited room service; same-day laundry. *In room:* TV, coffeemaker, hair dryer.

### WHERE TO DINE

You can eat well for very little money in Xalapa, probably because it's a student town. Almost every street in the downtown area has a restaurant. **Callejón del Diamante** is an alley close by the cathedral, with half a dozen inexpensive restaurants that cater to office workers and students. One, **La Sopa,** offers a daily blue plate special for $3. Most of these restaurants are open Monday to Saturday from 8am to 10pm. To find them, turn your back to the cathedral and walk left on Enríquez across Lucio 1 block; the Callejón will be on the left.

**Churrería del Recuerdo** MEXICAN For supper or breakfast, this is my favorite place in town. It serves the traditional supper fare of *antojitos*—enchiladas, gorditas, and tamales. You can wash them down with a good *horchata de coco* (coconut) or *tepache* (pineapple) drink. The other specialty is *churros,* best described perhaps as the Spanish equivalent of doughnuts, but crispy and usually eaten with hot chocolate. All the breakfasts are good, and the food is very safe: the restaurant has won awards for cleanliness. The restaurant is across from the Hotel Finca Real de Xalapa; it's best to take a cab ($1.50 from downtown).

Victoria 158. ✆ **228/818-1678.** Order of antojitos $2.50–$4.50. No credit cards. Daily 8am–1pm and 5pm–midnight.

**Restaurant la Casona del Beaterio** MEXICAN This place near the *zócalo* offers good food and service and has a charming atmosphere. Dine on an outdoor patio with a tile roof and a fountain, or indoors under high, beamed ceilings. Specialties include *pastel Azteca* (a casserole of chicken and tortilla) and a platter of traditional dishes called *cazuelitas mexicanas.* You can find La Casona on Zaragoza, 2 blocks east from Parque Juárez on the south side of the street. Live music begins at 9pm from Thursday to Sunday.

Zaragoza 20. ✆ **228/818-2119.** Breakfast $3–$4; main courses $4–$8; *comida corrida* $4. AE, MC, V. Mon–Sat 8am–11pm; Sun 8:30am–10pm.

## EL TAJIN AND THE CITY OF PAPANTLA

El Tajín (el-ta-*heen*) is among the most important archeological sites in Mexico. It has a large ceremonial center with several pyramids, platforms, and ball courts, some in the architectural styles of other cultures (Olmec, Teotihuacán, Maya) and some in the city's own unique style. It was probably built and inhabited (at least in its last stages) by the Totonac Indians who still live in this region. The Totonac culture is most famous for the "dance" of the ***voladores,*** a pre-Columbian religious ritual in which four men are suspended from the top of a tall pole while another manages to beat a drum and play a flute while balancing himself at the top. This "dance" is performed frequently at El Tajín.

The major stopover for seeing these ruins is **Papantla,** a hilly city of 165,000 situated in the coastal lowlands 224km (140 miles) north of Veracruz. In many respects, it's a typical Mexican town with lots of clay tile roofs, a jumble of small shops, and a lively street scene. One of the major products of Papantla, since the time of the Aztec, is vanilla beans. Vanilla is native to Mexico and was used principally to flavor chocolate made from cacao, also indigenous to Mexico. In Papantla you can buy high-quality vanilla extract or vanilla beans.

## ESSENTIALS

**GETTING THERE** **By Car** If you're driving from the south, follow the coastal road, Highway 180, from Veracruz. From Xalapa, it's best to do the same: drive down to the coast and then north.

**By Bus** The quaint ADO station (✆ **784/842-0218**) is at the corner of Venustiano Carranza and Benito Juárez, 4 blocks below the main square. Almost all buses are *de paso* (originating elsewhere), so departure times can be a little earlier or later than the schedule says. Taxis pass in front of the station frequently.

**CITY LAYOUT** Easily visible from many parts of town, the parish church and the Hotel El Tajín are at the top of a hill. This is where you'll find the *zócalo.*

**GETTING AROUND** Taxis are available around the central plaza, and city buses go to the ruins of El Tajín (see below). Almost everything worth seeing is within easy walking distance of the central plaza.

**FAST FACTS** The telephone **area code** is **784.** The **climate** is steamy for most of the year except when the occasional *norther* (strong, sudden north wind) makes it this far south.

**SPECIAL EVENTS** The **Feast of Corpus Christi,** the ninth Sunday after Easter, is part of a very special week in Papantla. Well-known Mexican entertainers perform, and the native *voladores* (see "The Ruins of El Tajín," below) make special appearances. Lodging is scarce during this week, so be sure to book ahead.

## EXPLORING PAPANTLA & EL TAJÍN

In Papantla, the shady *zócalo* built of ceramic tile is where couples and families come in the evenings to sit or stroll. The large wall below the church and facing the zócalo is covered with the image of El Tajín and a modern depiction of Totonac carved reliefs.

**THE RUINS OF EL TAJIN** The ruined city sits among some low hills clothed in thick tropical forest. The views are lovely, but climbing on any of the pyramids is forbidden; your best view is from a high, man-made terrace that supports the Tajín Chico buildings towards the back. The city is divided into old (**Tajín Viejo**) and new (**Tajín Chico**) sections. Of the 150 buildings identified at the site, 20 have been excavated and conserved, resurrecting their forms from what were grass-covered mounds. At least 12 ball courts have been found, of which 6 have been excavated. The most impressive structure, in the old section, is the **Pyramid of the Niches,** which is a unique stone-and-adobe pyramid with 365 recesses extending to all four sides of the building. The pyramid was formerly covered in red-painted stucco, and the niches were painted black. Try to imagine how that must have looked. Near the Pyramid of the Niches is a restored **ball court** with beautiful carved reliefs depicting gods and kings.

The most important building in the Tajín Chico section is the **Temple of the Columns.** A stairway divides the columns, three on either side, each decorated with reliefs of priests and warriors and hieroglyphic dates. Many mounds remain unexcavated, but with the reconstruction that has been done so far, it's increasingly easier to visualize the ruins as a city.

In a clearing near the museum, a group of local Totonac Indians called *voladores* (flyers) performs their acrobatic and symbolic ritual. This is a traditional, solemn ceremony that dates back centuries. The Totonac perform the unusual ritual in honor of the four poles of the earth. There's no set schedule for performances; the sound of a slow-beating drum and flute signals that the *voladores* are preparing to perform. Five flyers, dressed in brightly colored ceremonial garments and cone-shaped hats with ribbons and small round mirrors, climb to a square revolving platform at the top of a 24m (80-ft.) pole. While four flyers perch on the sides of the platform and attach themselves by the waist to a rope, the fifth stands and plays an instrument called a *chirimía,* used in rituals by the Toltec and Olmec. The instrument is a small bamboo flute with a deerskin drum attached. The performer plays the three-holed flute with his left hand and beats the drum with his right hand.

When the time is right, the four fall backward, suspended by the rope, and descend as they revolve around the post.

The small but impressive **museum** is worth seeing as well. A small snack and gift shop and small restaurant are across from the museum. Admission to the site and museum is $5, free on Sunday. The fee to use a personal video camera is $3.50. If you look like a professional photographer, using a tripod and other uncommon gear, the authorities will ask you to get a permit from the **Instituto Nacional de Antropología e Historia** in Mexico City. If you watch a performance of the *voladores,* one of them will collect an additional $2 from each spectator. The site is open daily 9am to 5pm.

To El Tajín from Papantla, taxis charge about $20, but it's easy to take a local bus for 75¢. Look for buses marked CHOTE/TAJIN, which run beside the town church (on the uphill side) every 15 minutes beginning at 7am. Buses marked CHOTE pass more frequently and leave you at the Chote crossroads; from there, take a taxi for around $5. From Veracruz, take Highway 180 to Papantla, then Route 127, a back road to Poza Rica that runs through El Tajín.

**SHOPPING** There are two markets in Papantla, and both are near the central plaza. **Mercado Juárez** is opposite the front door of the church. **Mercado Hidalgo** is 1 block downhill on the same street. The former has more food stalls, where you can order a bowl of *zacahuil,* a typical dish of the region. The latter has locally made baskets, vanilla extract, *Xanath,* a locally produced vanilla liqueur, and whole vanilla beans. You'll also find vanilla beans worked into different shapes, such as a crucifix, for putting in closets and drawers. While they do lend a good smell, they're not terribly attractive.

## WHERE TO STAY

**Hotel Provincia Express** Opened in 1990, this hotel is a good choice in a place with an otherwise meager selection. Rooms are nicely furnished, with tile floors, and hold a king-size or two double beds. The medium-to-small bathrooms have showers, and on occasion it takes a while for water to heat up, but it will. Rooms 1 to 6 have small balconies overlooking the *zócalo.* Others, toward the back, are windowless and quiet, and are reached through a tunnel-like hallway.

Enríquez 103, 93400 Papantla, Ver. ✆ **784/842-1645.** Fax 784/842-4213. hotprovi@prodigy.net.mx. 20 units. $45 double. No credit cards. Free secured parking ½ block away. **Amenities:** Cafe; room service until 3pm; laundry service. *In room:* A/C, TV.

**Hotel Tajín** At the top of the hill toward the back of the church sits this large, easily visible hotel. Rooms are small and tidy. Bed choices include one or two doubles or one king. Thirty-one rooms have air-conditioning, the rest have fans, and some have a view.

Nuñez 104, 93400 Papantla, Ver. © **784/842-0121** or 784/842-1623. Fax 784/842-1062. htajin@hotmail.com. 73 units. $32–$55 double. MC, V. Free secured parking ½ block away. **Amenities:** Overnight laundry. *In room:* TV.

### WHERE TO DINE

Mercado Juárez has numerous shops offering the delicious local specialty, *zacahuil* (a huge tamale cooked in a banana leaf), in the morning. Look around until you see a cook with a line of patrons—that's where you'll get the best *zacahuil.* Outside the market, rolling cart vendors sell steamy hot *atole:* a thick, sweet, cornmeal-based beverage with various flavorings.

Besides *zacahuil,* be sure to try delicious *molotes,* small football-shaped creations of fried dough that are served as appetizers.

**Plaza Pardo** MEXICAN This upstairs restaurant facing the main plaza serves plenty of Mexican standards and a couple of regional dishes. A few tables are on a balcony looking out over the *zócalo,* church, and giant statue of the *volador.* Specialties include *bocales* (small gorditas with different fillings), enchildadas, and *mole.*

Enríquez 105-altos. © **784/842-0059.** Breakfast $2–$4; sandwiches $2–$3; main courses $3–$5. No credit cards. Daily 7:30am–11pm.

## 3 Colonial Puebla

128km (80 miles) E of Mexico City, 285km (178 miles) W of Veracruz

At an elevation of over 2121m (7,000 ft.) in a broad plane between mountain ranges and snow-capped volcanoes, Puebla is blessed with the year-round spring-like climate of the highlands. It's considered the cradle of Mexican cuisine, having produced some of the country's classic dishes—the intricate *mole* and *chiles en nogada,* as well as *tinga* (pork or chicken stew) and *mixiotes* (rabbit, lamb, or chicken cooked in mild chile sauce, wrapped like a *tamal,* and steamed).

Puebla has a larger colonial center than any other city in Mexico. It's home to so many mansions, convents, and churches that it has been named a UNESCO World Heritage Site. This is colonial architecture of grand proportions, different from that of the rest of Mexico in its heavy use of painted tiles, gold leaf, and molded plaster. This is partly because the local building stone is not pretty (like Oaxaca's green *cantera* or Morelia's pink *cantera*). Facades and courtyards are commonly surfaced with clay and Talavera tiles. Early in the city's history, artisans from the Spanish town of Talavera settled here and established their craft of making hand-painted tiles—a tradition the Moors originally brought to Spain in the 8th century. These tiles, along with dishes, pots, and other objects made in the same tradition, are referred to as Talavera. The finest Talavera is still made completely by hand and doesn't come cheap.

Puebla is a very Catholic city, even for Mexico; there are so many churches and former convents that even most Poblanos can't keep them all straight. Churches not to be missed include the **Cathedral,** one of the largest in Mexico, and the **Capilla del Rosario,** with its overpowering baroque design and lavish use of gold leaf. Modern Puebla surrounds the historic district. The principle industry of the city is a large Volkswagen plant on the outskirts. It produces most of the Volkswagens sold in the United States.

## ESSENTIALS

**GETTING THERE & DEPARTING** **By Plane** Puebla's airport is falling into disuse, with fewer and fewer flights. Most people fly into Mexico City and take the bus directly from the airport to Puebla. Exit the door opposite Gate D, and you'll see a ticket booth and buses lined up at the curb. They leave every half hour; the cost is $13.

**By Car** There are two roads to Puebla from the capital: Highway 150, an old, winding two-lane scenic road with limited passing capabilities and the likelihood of slow traffic; and Highway 150D, a four- or six-lane toll road that's faster. From Veracruz, take Highway 150D west. From Xalapa, take Highway 140 west to the intersection with 150, then turn right. Tolls from Mexico City run $12; from Veracruz, $20.

**By Bus** The bus ride from **Veracruz** to Puebla takes 3½ hours and costs $18. From **Mexico City,** it takes 2 hours and costs $12. Several bus lines have regular departures from Mexico City's TAPO bus station, as frequent as every 15 minutes. Also keep in mind that you can catch a bus to Puebla directly from the **Mexico City airport** (see "By Plane," above).

You'll probably arrive at a large **bus station,** known by its acronym, **CAPU.** To get to downtown Puebla, look for one of several booths marked TAXI AUTORIZADO or a city bus marked CAPU CENTRAL CAMIONERA–CENTRO. Many buses to and from the Mexico City airport use the **Estrella Roja** station, 4 Poniente 2110, which is closer to downtown. The "Ticket Bus" agency (✆ **222/232-1952**), downtown, sells bus tickets. Look for a small counter inside the lobby of the office building at the corner of Palafox y Mendoza and 6 Norte. Hours are Monday to Saturday from 9am to 7pm.

**VISITOR INFORMATION** The **State Tourism Office** (✆ **222/246-1615** or 222/246-1285) is your best bet. It's at 5 Oriente 3, across the street from the south side of the cathedral. The office is open Monday to Saturday from 9am to 8:30pm, Sunday from 9am to 2pm. The staff can answer questions, provide a map, and set you up with a guide if you want a private tour of the city. The **City Tourism Office** is across from the *zócalo* in the Portal Hidalgo 14 (✆ **222/246-0429;** fax 222/232-1399). It's not very helpful. Hours are Monday to Friday from 9am to 8pm, Saturday and Sunday from 9am to 3pm.

**CITY LAYOUT** The heart of town is the shady *zócalo,* or **Plaza de la Constitución.** Actually, the intersection at its northwest corner (where Av. Reforma becomes Palafox y Mendoza, and Av. 5 de Mayo becomes 16 de Septiembre) is the center of town. Puebla's streets are laid out in a Cartesian quadrant system, with these two avenues as the x and y axes. Instead of each axis dividing positive from negative numbers, they divide even from odd. Streets north of the **horizontal axis** (Reforma/Palafox y Mendoza) are numbered 2, 4, 6, and so on. Streets to the south are 3, 5, 7, and so forth. The **north-south axis** (5 de Mayo/16 de Septiembre) does the same thing. East of it are even-numbered streets, and west are odd-numbered. Streets also have a direction (*norte, sur, oriente, poniente*). So if someone tells you that a church is on 7 Oriente, then you know what part of town it's in: "Oriente" tells you that it's the eastern portion of an east-west street, and the odd number indicates that it's south of Palafox y Mendoza, thus it's in the southeast quadrant.

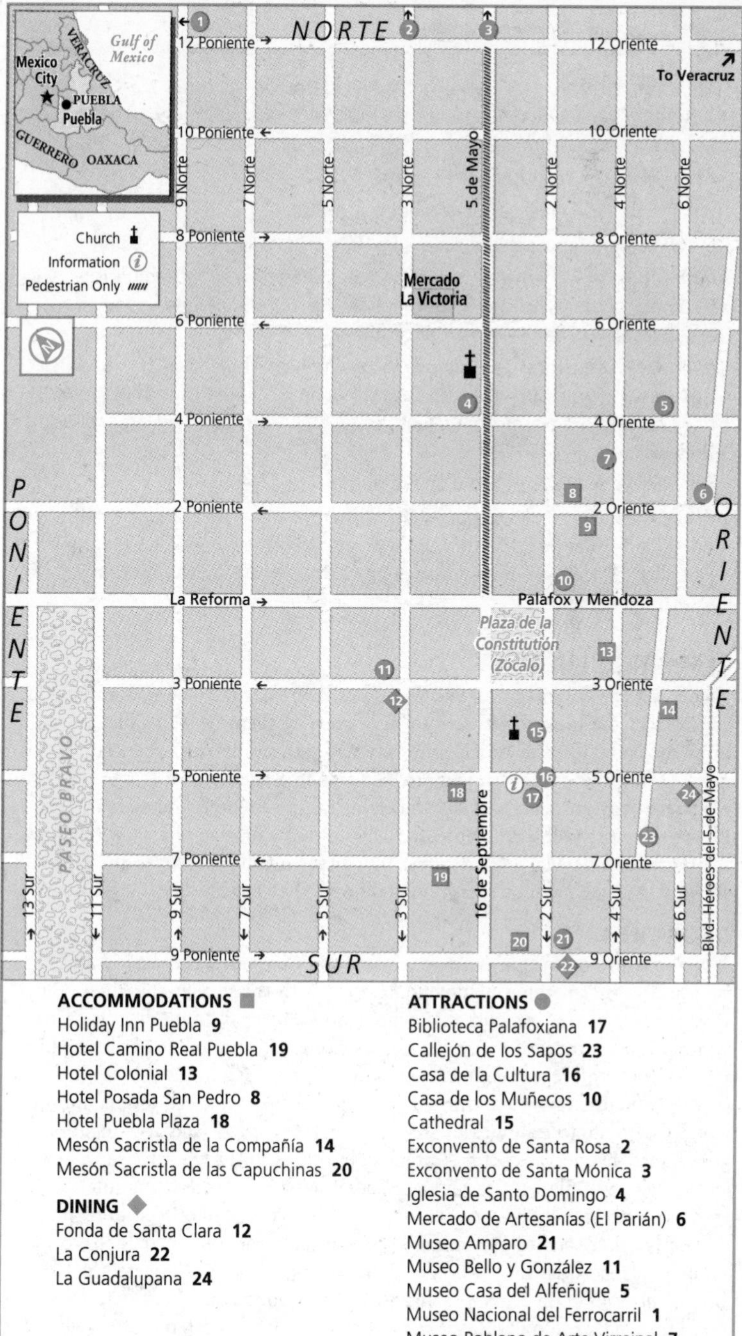

NORTE
SUR
PONIENTE
ORIENTE
Gulf of Mexico
Mexico City
VERACRUZ
PUEBLA
Puebla
GUERRERO
OAXACA
Church
Information
Pedestrian Only
To Veracruz
12 Poniente
12 Oriente
10 Poniente
10 Oriente
8 Poniente
8 Oriente
6 Poniente
6 Oriente
4 Poniente
4 Oriente
2 Poniente
2 Oriente
La Reforma
Palafox y Mendoza
3 Poniente
3 Oriente
5 Poniente
5 Oriente
7 Poniente
7 Oriente
9 Poniente
9 Oriente
9 Norte
7 Norte
5 Norte
3 Norte
5 de Mayo
2 Norte
4 Norte
6 Norte
13 Sur
11 Sur
9 Sur
7 Sur
5 Sur
3 Sur
16 de Septiembre
2 Sur
4 Sur
6 Sur
Blvd. Héroes del 5 de Mayo
PASEO BRAVO
Mercado La Victoria
Plaza de la Constitutión (Zócalo)
ACCOMMODATIONS
Holiday Inn Puebla 9
Hotel Camino Real Puebla 19
Hotel Colonial 13
Hotel Posada San Pedro 8
Hotel Puebla Plaza 18
Mesón Sacristìa de la Compañía 14
Mesón Sacristìa de las Capuchinas 20
DINING
Fonda de Santa Clara 12
La Conjura 22
La Guadalupana 24
ATTRACTIONS
Biblioteca Palafoxiana 17
Callejón de los Sapos 23
Casa de la Cultura 16
Casa de los Muñecos 10
Cathedral 15
Exconvento de Santa Rosa 2
Exconvento de Santa Mónica 3
Iglesia de Santo Domingo 4
Mercado de Artesanías (El Parián) 6
Museo Amparo 21
Museo Bello y González 11
Museo Casa del Alfeñique 5
Museo Nacional del Ferrocarril 1
Museo Poblano de Arte Virreinal 7

## *FAST FACTS:* Puebla

*American Express* The office is at Plaza Dorado 2, local 21, Colonia Ansures (✆ **222/229-1500**). Hours are Monday to Friday from 9am to 6pm, Saturday 9am to 1pm.

*Area Code* The telephone area code is **222.**

*Emergency* The emergency number is ✆ **066.**

*Hospital* **Beneficiencia Española** is at 19 Nte. 1001 (✆ **222/232-0500**).

*Internet Access* There are plenty of shops downtown. The going rate is $1.50 per hour. Try to check your mail in the morning, when connections are quicker. By 2pm there's a noticeable drop in speed.

*Pharmacy* Drugstores are almost as common as churches. They usually close around 9pm but take turns staying open late (*de turno*). Should you need something overnight, **Farmatodo** (✆ **222/237-7133**) delivers around the clock.

*Population* Puebla has 1,800,000 residents.

*Post Office* The *correo* is around the corner from the State Tourism office, on 16 de Septiembre, the third door down from the corner (at 5 Oriente). Hours are Monday to Friday from 9am to 3pm, and Saturday mornings.

## EXPLORING PUEBLA

Puebla is a city full of stories and anecdotes that color the colonial houses and convents of the historic district. To hear some of them, you can hire a guide from the State Tourism office, who can also provide historical context. For a quick (1 hr.) tour of the city, you can hop on one of the little buses that park on the street between the *zócalo* and the cathedral (3 Oriente). Tours are in Spanish, depart every half hour, and cost $3.50. They include a quick view of where the Battle of 5 de Mayo was fought. Your ticket is valid for the entire day and allows you to get off at any location and board the next bus that comes along.

### CHURCHES

If you were to stop to examine every church you pass, you would be in for a long stay. Still, it is something I enjoy doing, even with the smaller churches. Many have simple, austere interiors that express a sweetness and humility that I like without the dour feel of many of Europe's churches. Three churches in the historic district require specific mention.

The **cathedral** ★★★, completed in 1649, has the tallest bell towers in Mexico. Its dark stone exterior and severe *Herrerian* design lend it a lugubrious appearance that perhaps befits a cathedral but takes a little while to warm up to. In the country, only Mexico City's cathedral has a more interesting interior. In front, you can usually find guides (or they'll find you) who offer a short tour.

The **Iglesia de Santo Domingo** ★★★, on the corner of Cinco de Mayo and 4 Poniente, was originally part of a Dominican monastery completed in 1611. Lining the walls of the nave are some exquisite baroque altars. In the left transept you'll find the **Capilla del Rosario,** built in 1690. It is a masterpiece of gold leaf and plaster convolutes dedicated to the Virgin of the Rosary. Note, too, the intricate Talavera wainscoting.

## "Cinco de Mayo" & the Battle of Puebla

In the United States, the Mexican holiday "Cinco de Mayo" is often compared to the Fourth of July—a Mexican Independence Day. In truth, the date commemorates the Battle of Puebla, on May 5, 1862, which resulted in a memorable victory against foreign invaders.

At the time, Napoleon III of France was scheming to occupy Mexico. A well-trained and handsomely uniformed army of 6,000, under the command of General Laurencez, landed in Veracruz with the objective of occupying Mexico City. In its path were 4,000 ill-equipped Mexicans under General Ignacio Zaragoza. Despite the odds, the Mexicans won a resounding victory. The French were humiliated and suffered their first defeat in nearly half a century at the hands of the penniless, war-torn republic of Mexico.

For Mexico, it marked the nation's first victory against foreign attack, and the battle remains a matter of intense national pride. Never mind that by the following year the French were in possession of both Puebla and Mexico City. Today, the Cinco de Mayo holiday is an enduring symbol of Mexico's sense of patriotism.

On a visit to Puebla, you can visit the forts of Guadalupe and Loreto, where the battle took place, just north of the old part of the city.

Last, there is the massive **church of the Compañía,** built by the Jesuits, where "La China Poblana" worshipped and was briefly entombed. Look to the right of the church doorway and you'll see a curious bit of text in Talavera. It marks the date of the execution of a con man whose head was hung from the church's main archway. He arrived in Mexico on a boat from Spain carrying papers identifying him as a *visitador* (Papal emissary and inspector). He was wined and dined by the bishops and lived the good life for several weeks before being discovered and executed. The fact that his head was then hung on the front of a church seems awfully un-Christian. The church authorities may have been sending a message.

### MUSEUMS

A number of museums are closed for renovation; ask at the tourism office to see whether they're open. The **Museo Bello** ★ is a personal collection of art and decorative objects from around the world. The **Biblioteca Palafoxiana** ★, an impressive colonial library built by Palafox y Mendoza, a 17th-century bishop of Puebla, is on the second floor of the Casa de Cultura, next to the state tourism office. The **Casa de Alfeñique** is a colonial mansion and a landmark for its exterior plaster decoration, which is reminiscent of cake icing; the museum collection, a hodgepodge of things Poblano, is fun if you have time. The **Casa de los Muñecos** is more important for its exterior than for the museum collection inside.

**Exconvento de Santa Mónica** After independence, a long political struggle arose between the national government and the Church. It climaxed in the Reform Wars of the 1850s, when the government instituted several anticlerical measures, including the closing of all convents. The nuns here discreetly closed

### *Fun Fact* A Princess . . . and Then Some

If you're in Puebla for any length of time, you will notice that "La China Poblana" appears virtually everywhere. She was a real person with a fascinating life. Originally a princess from India (not China), she was captured by a Portuguese raiding party, sold into slavery, and shipped to Mexico on a Philippine galleon in the 17th century. Somehow, she became the property of a rich family of Puebla. This family, impressed with the woman's simplicity and spirituality, eventually adopted her. Thus freed from domestic chores, she delved into a life of religious devotions, mixing elements of her native beliefs with Catholicism. She became a mystic who led an austere life of prayer, and in time became revered by the population of the city. At her death, she was interred in the church of the Compañía, but church authorities later moved her remains when a cult began to form around them. Her form of dress has become the standard folkloric outfit of the region.

their doors and kept functioning as a religious community with the aid of their neighbors and the blind eye of local officials. They survived with little assistance from the outside as, over the years, the convent slowly crumbled around them. Then, in 1934 (when the Cristero War had again heightened tensions between the government and the Church), a local official "discovered" them. This history makes for an interesting visit: displays include the contents of this and two other clandestine convents confiscated at the same time. These nuns weren't sitting on great treasures—most of the paintings are poor examples of their era (But you will find a rare set of mid-19th-century paintings on velvet that predate Elvis and the dogs playing poker.) Things not to miss are the crypt, the chapel, and the upper and lower *coros.* While you're there, visit the church next door and pay your respects to the much-revered image of Nuestro Señor de las Maravillas, alongside the back of the nave, to the left as you enter.

Av. 18 Pte. 103. ✆ **222/232-0178.** Admission $3; free Sun and holidays. Tues–Sun 9am–6pm.

**Exconvento de Santa Rosa** ★ Unlike its neighbor, this former convent near Santa Mónica was unable to postpone confiscation and served variously as barracks, hospital, and public housing. It is now the home of the **Museo de Arte Popular.** Here you can see the kitchen where *mole* was invented (for this alone it is worth the pilgrimage), and afterward the museum guide will take you upstairs to see displays of the crafts practiced in the state of Puebla. If you enjoy handcrafts, don't miss this place; it has some rare and beautiful examples of artisanship. The main door is usually closed; enter through the public parking lot at 14 Poniente 305.

Calle 3 Nte. (at 14 Pte.). ✆ **222/232-9240.** Admission $1. Tues–Sun 10am–4:30pm.

**Museo Amparo** ★★★ The finest museum in the city, the Museo Amparo (named for the deceased wife of the founder) has a stunning collection of pre-Columbian pieces from across Mexico, beautifully displayed and intelligently organized. Its collections of colonial and modern art are quite good, and the museum frequently gets important traveling exhibitions, which usually don't require an additional admission charge. The collection of colonial art (*arte virreinal*) is on the second floor and includes decorative objects and furniture. It is exhibited in the restored living quarters of the original mansion. The interiors are all from the Porfiriate (1870s), with the elaborate decoration that the period is known for. Audio tours of the pre-Columbian collection are for rent ($1, plus $1 deposit). You can hire an English-speaking guide for the entire museum ($20). Signs are in Spanish and English; no cameras are permitted. The museum has a lovely gift shop and cafe.

Calle 2 Sur 708. © **222/246-4210.** Admission $3 adults; $1.50 children 3–12 and students; free Mon. Wed–Mon 10am–6pm.

**Museo Nacional del Ferrocarril** This is a treat for railroad buffs. It consists of a large open area with several train engines (both steam and diesel), baggage cars, passenger cars, a presidential car, a dining car, Pullman coaches, and a caboose. You can board and inspect the cars. Even those not interested in railroads might enjoy seeing the design and details of some of these—they sketch in microcosm a bygone era. A small gallery exhibits railway landscapes.

11 Norte and 12 Poniente. © **222/232-4988.** Free admission. Tues–Sun 10am–5pm.

**Museo Poblano de Arte Virreinal** Recently opened in the beautifully restored colonial San Pedro Hospital, this museum has only a small permanent collection, but it is the location of choice for traveling expositions. Whether you will come upon something you like is a matter of timing.

Calle 4 Norte 203. © **222/246-6618.** Admission $1.50. Daily 10am–5pm.

## SHOPPING

Puebla is the home of the famous **Talavera dinnerware** ★. Numerous workshops produce this expensive pottery. Operating since 1824, **Uriarte Talavera,** Calle 4 Pte. 911 (© **222/232-1598**), is one of the city's established potters. Behind an unprepossessing doorway, the factory produces exquisite pieces, many examples of which are on display in its showrooms. Some are for sale, while others are samples. Tours of the factory start at 10am, 11am, noon, and 1pm from Monday to Saturday. The factory is open Monday to Saturday from 9am to 6:30pm, Sunday from 11am to 6pm. The factory can ship your purchases; it accepts American Express, MasterCard, and Visa. The **Centro Talavera Poblana,** Calle 6 Ote. 11, between Calle 2 Norte and Avenida 5 de Mayo (© **222/242-0848**), offers a wide range of Talavera from producers in Puebla as well as Tlaxcala. The huge showroom stocks sets of 6 to 12 place settings. It's open Monday to Saturday from 9:30am to 8pm, Sunday from 10am to 7pm. You can ship your purchases; American Express, Diners Club, MasterCard, and Visa are accepted.

The **Mercado de Artesanías,** or **El Parián,** is a pedestrians-only, open-air shopping area just east of Calle 6 Norte between Avenidas 2 and 6 Oriente. You'll see rows of neat brick shops selling crafts and souvenirs. Don't judge all Talavera pottery by what you see here, though: The artists seem to have gone overboard with design. The shops are open daily from 10am to 8pm. Bargain to get a good price. While you're in this area, you can take a look at the **Teatro Principal.**

For antique browsing, go to **Callejón de los Sapos** (Alley of the Frogs), about 3 blocks southeast of the *zócalo* near Calle 4 Sur and Avenida 7 Oriente. Wander in and out; there's good stuff large and small. Shops are generally open daily from 10am to 2pm and 4 to 6pm. On Saturday mornings there's a flea market in the little square. Bargain to get a good price. If you're there between 2:30 and 5:30pm, stop by **La Pasita,** across Calle 5 from the Plaza de los Sapos, to taste homemade cordials and browse through the owner's humorous collection of Mexicana. Start with a *pasita,* then work your way up to a *China Poblana*—a layered cordial of red, white, and green liqueurs. The owner is an inveterate leg-puller.

## WHERE TO STAY

Prices quoted include the 17% tax. All hotels listed here are in the historic district. Puebla's comfortable **Crowne Plaza Hotel** (✆ **800/HOLIDAY** in the U.S. and Canada) is a short taxi ride from the center of town. Room rates are about $215 for a standard double.

### VERY EXPENSIVE

**Hotel Camino Real Puebla** ★★ This hotel, in the 16th-century former convent of the Immaculate Conception, is a colonial gem that has been nicely restored. Courtyards spill into more courtyards, and remnants of polychromed colonial-era frescos are everywhere, even in the rooms. Rooms are decorated in handsome blue-and-yellow schemes inspired by Talavera colors. All have tile floors and original paintings, and some contain antiques. The hotel is 2½ blocks south of the *zócalo.*

Av. 7 Pte. 105 (between Calle 3 Sur and Av. 16 de Septiembre), Centro Histórico, 72000 Puebla, Pue. ✆ **800/722-6466** in the U.S., 222/229-0909, or 222/229-0910. Fax 222/232-9251. www.caminoreal.com/puebla/. 84 units. $205 double; $320 jr. suite. AE, DC, MC, V. **Amenities:** 2 restaurants (Mexican, international), bar; whirlpool; tour desk; car rental; business center; executive business services; room service until midnight; same-day laundry; dry cleaning; babysitting; nonsmoking rooms. *In room:* TV, dataport, minibar, coffeemaker, hair dryer.

**Mesones Sacristía** ★★★ Two small hotels offer different ways to delve into Puebla's colonial past. If you're looking for modern convenience rather than atmosphere, stay at the Holiday Inn or the Crowne Plaza. If you want some colonial flavor mixed with sophistication or gaiety, try one of these unique hotels. Both are elegant adaptations of colonial houses, excellently located, but otherwise very different. The **Capuchinas** offers quiet rooms, lots of privacy, and a smart blend of colonial and modern architecture. The small restaurant has won praise for its modern international cooking. The sister hotel, Mesón de la Sacristía de la **Compañía,** is less quiet and more fun. It offers an experience of the old city in all its antiquity and even quirkiness. For starters, you receive a massive colonial skeleton key to your room. And the rooms feel as colonial as the hotel could get away with. In the courtyard, a great restaurant and popular nightspot serves Poblano specialties. A guitarist performs romantic songs and ballads until about 11pm. Sometimes the entertainment is a guitar trio or some members of a *tuna* (traditional Spanish music sung to the accompaniment of string instruments). This hotel is clearly not for those who like to retire early. The hotels offer packages for those interested in cooking lessons or Talavera.

Calle 6 Sur 304, Callejón de los Sapos, 72000 Puebla, Pue. ✆ and fax **222/232-4513** or 222/242-3554. www.mesones-sacristia.com. 8 and 7 units. $180 double; $200–$220 suite. AE, MC, V. Free secured parking. **Amenities:** Restaurant, bar; access to local health club; tour and activities desk; car rental; room service until 10pm; in-room massage; same-day laundry and dry cleaning. *In room:* TV, coffeemaker, hair dryer.

### EXPENSIVE

**Hotel Holiday Inn Puebla** ★ The lobby here is more fun than that of any Holiday Inn I've ever visited, but the rooms are very much in character with the rest, especially the properties in the Midwest. The resemblance is so strong that it's a little unnerving. Still, the rooms are comfortable and have the best heat and air-conditioning in the downtown area. Rooms are medium size and carpeted. Bathrooms come with showers, good lighting, and good counter space. Avoid the lower rooms near the kitchen, which makes an unbelievable amount of noise.

Av. 2 Ote. 211, 72000 Puebla, Pue. ✆ **800/HOLIDAY** in the U.S. and Canada, or 222/223-6600. www.holiday-inn.com. 79 units. $130 double. AE, DC, MC, V. Free covered parking. **Amenities:** Restaurant, bar; heated pool; room service until 11pm; babysitting; same-day laundry and dry cleaning; nonsmoking rooms. *In room:* A/C, TV, coffeemaker, hair dryer, iron.

**Hotel Posada San Pedro** ★ *Kids* A better bargain than most downtown hotels offering the same level of amenities, especially for families, this place is convenient and comfortable. Spacious rooms come with plain wooden furniture, carpeting, and medium-size bathrooms. One section of the hotel has air-conditioning. There is a well-manicured courtyard with a small pool, surrounded by five stories of rooms. It's a family hotel, with afternoon videos for the kids and child care by prior arrangement.

Av. 2 Ote. 202, 72000 Puebla, Pue. ✆ **222/246-5077.** Fax 222/246-5376. www.hotelposadasanpedro.com.mx. 80 units. $110 double. Low-season rates available. AE, MC, V. Free covered parking. **Amenities:** Restaurant, bar; outdoor heated pool; Jacuzzi; children's activities; travel agency; car rental; business center; room service until 10:30pm; babysitting; same-day laundry and dry cleaning. *In room:* TV, hair dryer.

### MODERATE

**Hotel Colonial** *Value* The four-story hotel (with elevator) is comfortable and in a good location at a great price. The rooms and lobby are attractive, but avoid units along Calle 3. The furnishings are simple; standard rooms usually contain twin beds. Bathrooms are basic but sufficient and have showers. The hotel restaurant is good. The Colonial is 1 block east of the *zócalo,* on a pedestrian way.

Calle 4 Sur 105 (between Palafox y Mendoza and 3 Ote.), 72000 Puebla, Pue. ✆ **222/246-4199.** Fax 222/246-0818. www.colonial.com.mx. 70 units. $62 double. AE, MC, V. Amenities: Restaurant; tour info; room service until 10pm; overnight laundry and dry cleaning. *In room:* TV.

### INEXPENSIVE

**Hotel Puebla Plaza** *Value* The most attractive and comfortable of the budget hotels in the historic district, the Puebla Plaza is almost in the shadow of the cathedral. Rooms are small to medium size, with small bathrooms equipped with showers. Get a room in back to avoid the commotion in the front courtyard and at the restaurant next door.

Calle 5 Pte. 111, 72000 Puebla, Pue. ✆ **222/246-3175.** Fax 222/242-5792. www.hotelpueblaplaza.com 30 units. $35–$43 double. MC, V. Limited parking. Amenities: Tour info; laundry and dry cleaning. *In room:* TV.

## WHERE TO DINE

Puebla is known throughout Mexico for *mole poblano,* a spicy sauce with more than 20 ingredients (including chocolate), as well as *mixiotes* (meesh-*oh*-tehs), a dish of beef, pork, or lamb in a spicy red sauce baked in maguey paper. Another regional specialty, *pipián,* is somewhat like *mole* but based on ground toasted squash seeds. *Dulces* (sweets) shops are scattered about, with display windows brim-full of marzipan crafted into various shapes and designs, candied figs, and guava paste. If you're in the city during the season for *chiles en nogada* (July–Sept), make a point of trying one. It's a dish of elegant contrasts involving a poblano chile (you can guess where this chile got its name), a spicy-sweet filling made of pork, chicken, and sweetmeats, and a walnut cream sauce. The city goes crazy for this dish, and you'll see it everywhere. Besides the restaurants listed below, try those in the **Mesones Sacristía** (see above). I also love the *mole* and traditional *chalupas* at the **Compañía.**

## VERY EXPENSIVE

**La Conjura** ★★★ SPANISH There's little to dislike about this restaurant—except the cost. The highest prices are mostly for hard-to-get Spanish items such as genuine *jamón serrano.* Still, with tapas, soup, a main course, and some wine, even if you do avoid the expensive items, you'll drop quite a bundle. But the food is excellent. The restaurant doesn't strive for purity but plays with combinations of Old and New World ingredients, like a tapa of *chistorra* (sausage) cooked with a small amount of guajillo peppers, or a shrimp dish with mild goat cheese from Oaxaca and passion-fruit sauce. The ambitious menu changes daily, with offerings of seafood, lamb, veal, and beef on any given day. You dine in an attractive brick and stone room with a low, vaulted ceiling that creates the atmosphere of a cellar. The chairs are comfortable, and the tables are well spaced and covered in white tablecloths.

9 Ote. 201. ✆ **222/232-9693.** Reservations recommended. Main courses $10–$28; tapas $2–$10. AE, DC, MC, V. Sun–Tues 2–6pm; Wed–Sat 2–11pm.

## MODERATE

**Fonda de Santa Clara** *Overrated* REGIONAL This is one of those restaurants invariably associated with a particular city. For many people, it is the automatic choice in Puebla, and unfortunately, this has been cause for a decline in quality. Still, many visitors love it, and the main restaurant is a pretty place. The *mole* is worth trying. It's 1½ blocks west of the *zócalo.*

Av. 3 Pte. 307. ✆ **222/242-2659.** Lunch $7–$14; dinner $5–$10. AE, DC, MC, V. Daily 9am–10pm.

**La Guadalupana** REGIONAL/MEXICAN This restaurant off the Callejón de Los Sapos serves good regional specialties, including *mole, mole verde,* and *pipián.* The restaurant has two dining areas—the central front courtyard of a colonial house and the narrow patio of a former working-class *vecindad* (an enclosed grouping of simple apartments that share kitchen and bath areas).

5 Ote. 605. ✆ **222/242-4886.** Main courses $6–$12. AE, MC, V. Daily 8am–9pm.

**Mi Ciudad** ★★ MEXICAN You'll have to take a cab to this restaurant, in the middle of Puebla's restaurant and club district along Avenida Juárez. The dining room is large, with lots of references to Puebla in the decoration. The menu is large as well, with lots of dishes from other parts of Mexico as well as some original numbers. The grilled meats are good. For those who like the taste of poblano chiles, the poblano cream soup is thoroughly satisfying; small cubes of slightly salty, slightly squeaky farmer's cheese provides contrast. Not on the menu, but you can ask for it anyway, is a half-and-half combination of *mole* and *pipián*—two Poblano classics.

Av. Juárez 2507. ✆ **222/231-5326.** Reservations recommended on weekends. Main courses $7–$14. AE, MC, V. Daily 8am–10pm.

# PUEBLA AFTER DARK

***Mariachis*** play daily, beginning at 6pm, on **Plaza de Santa Inés,** Avenida 11 Poniente and Calle 3 Sur. They stroll through the crowds that gather at the sidewalk cafes. Another square where you can hear live music is **Plaza de los Sapos,** Avenida 7 Oriente near Calle 6 Sur. To get there, walk 2 blocks south from the *zócalo* and take a left onto Avenida 7 Oriente, toward the river. The plaza will be on your left, spreading out between Avenida 7 and Avenida 5 Oriente just past Calle 4 Sur. If you take Avenida 5 Oriente from the cathedral to reach the Plaza de los Sapos, you'll pass several local hangouts where students, artists, and others gather for conversation, coffee, drinks, snacks, and live music.

Another place to hear live music is down the block from los Sapos at **Mesón Sacristía de la Compañía,** Calle 6 Sur 304. A singer-guitarist entertains with popular ballads from 9pm to midnight. The restaurant, which fills the inner patio and adjacent rooms, is moderately priced and serves a complete selection of Puebla specialties—you can dine or drink and enjoy the free entertainment without breaking the bank.

**Teorema,** Reforma 540 near Calle 7 Norte (✆ **222/242-1014**), is a good coffee shop and bookstore that features guitarists and folksingers every evening. It's open daily from 9:30am to 2:30pm and 4:30pm to midnight, and accepts MasterCard and Visa.

## SIDE TRIPS FROM PUEBLA

### CHOLULA, TONANTZINTLA & SAN FRANCISCO ACATEPEC

Ten minutes outside of Puebla on the old highway to Mexico City is the small town of Cholula. In pre-Columbian times, this was a large city—the religious capital of highland Mexico. The Spanish razed the hundreds of temples that stood here, and we know little about them. But the **Great Pyramid** still sits there, the largest pyramid in the New World, much larger in volume than the great pyramids of Egypt. At first glimpse, it looks more like a hill crowned by a church (Nuestra Señora de los Remedios, which suffered extensive damage in the 1999 earthquake). But if you climb the unreconstructed pyramid beside it, you will see plainly the geometric outline of the original structure, which rises from the ground in four levels. From this viewpoint, you also get a good look at el Popocatépetl, the majestic snow-capped volcano that separates this valley from the valley of Mexico. The entrance fee for the Cholula pyramid is $2; the site is open Tuesday to Sunday from 9am to 5pm. Archaeologists have reconstructed one side of one of the lower segments of the pyramid and have dug tunnels into the pyramid, which visitors are free to explore.

A perfect complement to this trip is a visit to the church of **Tonantzintla,** just to the south. Leave the town on Blvd. Miguel Alemán, which becomes the road to Tonantzintla. A mile ahead, it's in plain sight of the road. This church is justly famous for its jewel-box interior, executed in an endearing style that people have come to call Indian baroque. It has mesmerized many visitors, including R. Gordon Wasson, who saw in its manifold imagery allusions to a secret mushroom cult. If this visit hasn't quenched your appetite for visiting churches, proceed a bit farther down the road, and you will imperceptibly cross into the neighboring community of San Francisco Acatepec. Its church is also along the road and cannot be missed; it has a stunning tile façade.

### COLONIAL TLAXCALA AND THE CACAXTLA & XOCHITÉCATL RUINS

**Tlaxcala,** 40km (25 miles) north of Puebla and 120km (75 miles) east of Mexico City, is the capital of Mexico's smallest state (also named Tlaxcala) and a colonial-era city with several claims to fame. Tlaxcalan warriors allied with Cortez against the Aztec and were essential in his victory. Tlaxcalan chiefs were the first to be baptized by the Spaniards; the baptismal font is in the **Templo de San Francisco** (2 blocks from the main plaza, just above the bullring). The church is noted for the elaborately inlaid Moorish ceiling below the choir loft. A painting inside the Chapel of the Third Order shows the baptism of the chiefs.

To the right of the Templo is the **Exconvento,** now a museum containing early paintings and artifacts from nearby archaeological sites. The **Government Palace** ★★, on the handsome, tree-shaped central *zócalo,* contains vivid murals by a local artist, Desiderio Hernández Xochitiotzin, that illustrate the city's history. The expanded **Museo de Artesanías,** on Sanchez Piedras between Lardizabal and 1 de Mayo, showcases the state's wide-ranging crafts and customs. Here, local artisans give visitors demonstrations in such crafts as embroidery, weaving, and pulque making. Don't plan to breeze through; tours are mandatory, rather structured, and take an hour or more—but are very interesting. The museum is open Tuesday to Sunday from 10am to 6pm; admission (including tour) is $1.

Tlaxcala's **tourist information office** is at the intersection of Av. Juárez and Av. Lardizábal (© **246/465-0961**). Office hours are Monday to Friday from 9am to 7pm, Saturday and Sunday from 10am to 2pm.

Tlaxcala's main attractions are **Cacaxtla-Xochitécatl** (kah-*kahsh*-tlah soh-she-*teh*-kahtl) ★★★, unique pre-Hispanic hilltop sites 19km (12 miles) southwest of the city. Tlaxcala attracts few tourists and retains its small-town atmosphere and overall low prices. If you are there on a weekend, the State Tourism Office sponsors a Saturday tour of the city and a Sunday tour of the Cacaxtla-Xochitécatl sites. Tours leave from the front of the Posada San Francisco at 10am. Board the bus; the guide will collect the $4 fee.

Just over half a mile from the town center is the famed **Ocotlán Sanctuary** ★, constructed after Juan Diego Bernardino claimed to have seen an apparition of the Virgin Mary on that site in 1541. Baroque inside and out, it has elaborate interior decorations of carved figures and curling gilded wood that date from the 1700s. The carvings are attributed to Francisco Miguel Tlayotehuanitzin, an Indian sculptor who labored for more than 20 years to create them.

Santa Ana, a wool-weaving village, is only 2.5km (1½ miles) east of Tlaxcala. Shops selling large rugs, *serapes,* and locally woven sweaters line the main street. Huamantla, 48km (30 miles) southeast of Tlaxcala, is a small village noted for its commemoration of the Assumption of the Virgin on August 14 and 15.

## Where to Stay & Dine in Tlaxcala

Tlaxcala has several good restaurants beneath the portal on the east side of the *zócalo,* and some schedule live music in the evening. Budget hotels are nearby and along the road to Apizaco.

**Hotel Alifer** The Alifer's rooms, with black-and-red Spanish colonial decor, are carpeted and have tile-and-marble bathrooms with showers. To get there from the Plaza Constitución, with your back to the Posada San Francisco, walk to the right 2 blocks (you'll reach the hotel entrance just before the street turns to the right). The parking lot is next to the lobby entrance. The restaurant is open from 7am to 10pm.

Morelos 11, 90000 Tlaxcala, Tlax. © **246/462-5678.** 40 units. $40 double. MC, V. Free parking. **Amenities:** Restaurant; room service until 10pm; overnight laundry service. *In room:* TV.

**Hotel Posada San Francisco** This *posada* opened in 1992 on Tlaxcala's *zócalo* in a 19th-century mansion known as the Casa de las Piedras (House of Stones) for its gray stone façade. Rooms are in two-story, colonial-style wings that face either the pool or small courtyards. The hotel is attractive because of its modern comforts and its ideal location on the town's central square. Even if you don't stay, stop in for a look around (there is some interesting art on display and for sale in the lobby) or for a meal at La Trasquila, a Mexican restaurant on the second story overlooking the plaza and lobby; it's open daily from 2 to 11pm. There's also a first-floor cafeteria and bar with evening entertainment.

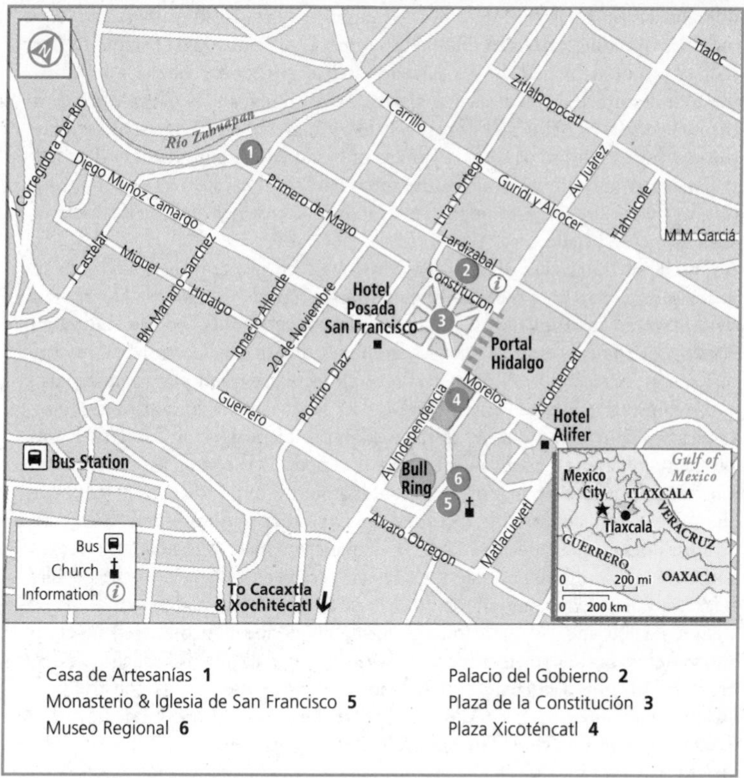


Plaza de la Constitución 17, 90000 Tlaxcala, Tlax. ✆ 246/462-6022. Fax 246/462-6818. 68 units. $92 double; $140 suite. AE, MC, V. Free parking. **Amenities:** Restaurant, bar; tennis court; game room; room service; massage service; overnight laundry and dry cleaning. *In room:* A/C, TV.

### Exploring the Cacaxtla-Xochitécatl Archaeological Site

Scholars were startled by the discovery in 1975 of vivid murals in red, blue, black, yellow, and white, showing Maya warriors (from the Yucatán Peninsula). Since then, more murals, more history, and at least eight construction phases have been uncovered.

Scholars attribute the influence of the site to a little-known tri-ethnic group (Náhuatl, Mixtec, and Chocho-popoloca) known as Olmec-Xicalanca, from Mexico's Gulf Coast. Among the translations of its name, "merchant's trade pack" seems most revealing. Like Casas Grandes north of Chihuahua City and Xochicalco (also with distinctive Maya influence) between Cuernavaca and Taxco, Cacaxtla appears to have been an important crossroads for merchants, astronomers, and others in the Mesoamerican world. Its apogee, between A.D. 650 and 900, corresponds with the abandonment of Teotihuacán (near Mexico City), the beginning of Casas Grandes culture, and, in the final phase, the decline of the classic Maya civilization, the emergence of the Toltec culture at Tula (also near Mexico City), and the spread of Toltec influence to the Yucatán.

How—or even if—those events affected Cacaxtla isn't known. The principal **mural** apparently is a vividly detailed victory scene, with triumphant dark-skinned warriors wearing jaguar skins, and the vanquished dressed in feathers and having their intestines extracted. Numerous symbols of Venus (a half star with five points) found painted at the site have led archaeoastronomy scholar John Carlson to link historical events such as wars, captive-taking, and ritual sacrifice with the appearance of Venus; all of this was likely undertaken in hopes of assuring the continued fertility of crops. Symbols of blood, along with toads and turtles (all water symbols), sacrifice, Venus, corn stalks, and cacao trees (symbolizing fertility) were supposed to appease the gods and ensure a productive cycle of rain, crops, and trade.

The latest mural discoveries show a wall of corn plants from which human heads sprout, next to a merchant whose pack is laden with goods. The murals flank a grand **acropolis** with unusual architectural motifs. For an illustrated account of the site, read "Mural Masterpieces of Ancient Cacaxtla" (*National Geographic,* Sept 1992). A giant steel roof protects the grand plaza and murals.

**Xochitécatl** is a small ceremonial center located on a hilltop overlooking Cacaxtla, about 1km (½ mile) to the east and in plain sight of Cacaxtla. It was probably inhabited, at least in the classical period, by the same people living in Cacaxtla. A curious circular pyramid stands atop this hill, 182km (600 ft.) above the surrounding countryside. Beside it are two other **pyramids** and three massive **boulders** (one about 3m/10 ft. in diameter), which were hollowed out for some reason. Hollowed boulders appear to have been restricted to the Puebla-Tlaxcala valley. Excavation of the Edificio de la Espiral (circular pyramid), dated between 1000 and 800 B.C. (middle formative period), encountered no stairways. Access is thought to have been by its spiral walkway. Rounded boulders from the nearby Zahuapan and Atoyac rivers were used in its construction. Rounded pyramids in this part of Mexico are thought to have been dedicated to Ehécatl, god of the wind. The base diameter exceeds 55m (180 ft.); it rises to a height of 15m (50 ft.).

The stepped and terraced **Pyramid of the Flowers,** made of rounded boulders, was started during the middle formative period. Modifications continued into colonial times, as exemplified by faced-stone and stucco-covered adobe. Of the 30 bodies found during excavations, all but one were children. Little is known about the people who built Xochitécatl, but at least part of the time they were contemporaneous with neighboring Cacaxtla. Evidence suggests that the area was dedicated to Xochitl, goddess of flowers and fertility. The small **museum** on site contains pottery and small sculpture, and a **garden** holds displays of larger sculpture.

To get to Cacaxtla from Tlaxcala, take a *combi* (collective minivan) or city bus to Nativitas (also called San Miguel Milagro), the village nearest the Cacaxtla ruins. Combis depart from behind the Hotel Posada San Francisco. From there, walk the paved road for a mile or take a taxi to the entrance. From the parking lot, the archaeological site is a 100-yard climb.

---

*Tips* **Photo Pointer**

When you purchase admission to Cacaxtla-Xochitécatl, you'll have to pay an extra $4 for bringing in a still or video camera. Keep in mind, though, that at Cacaxtla, neither a flash nor a tripod is allowed, so the site is difficult to photograph from the inside because of dust and low light caused by shading from the giant roof.

---

From Puebla, take Highway 119 north to the crossroads near Zacualpan and turn left, passing Tetlatlahuaca; turn right when you see signs to Nativitas and Cacaxtla. From Mexico City, take Highway 190 to San Martin Texmelucan, where you should ask directions for the road leading directly to the ruins, which are about 10km (6 miles) ahead. (This is the southern road you can use without going through Tlaxcala.)

Admission is $4 (one ticket is good for both sites), plus $4 for a video or still camera; free Sunday and holidays. Both sites are open Tuesday to Sunday 10am to 5pm.

# 12

# Cancún

Simply stated, Cancún is the reason most people travel to Mexico. Mexico's calling card to the world, Cancún perfectly showcases both the country's breathtaking natural beauty and the depth of its thousand-year-old history. The sheer number of annual travelers to Cancún underscores its magnetic appeal, with almost three million people visiting this enticing beach resort annually—most of them on their first trip to the country. The reasons for this are both numerous and obvious.

Cancún offers an unrivaled combination of high-quality accommodations, dreamy beaches, and a wide diversity of shopping, dining, nightlife, and activities nearby—most of them exceptional values—and easy air access. There is also the added lure of ancient cultures evident in all directions and a growing number of eco-oriented theme parks.

No doubt about it—Cancún embodies Caribbean splendor, with translucent turquoise waters and powdery white-sand beaches, coupled with coastal areas of great natural beauty. But Cancún is also a modern megaresort. Even a traveler feeling apprehensive about visiting foreign soil will feel completely at home and at ease here. English is spoken, dollars are accepted, roads are well paved, and lawns are manicured. Malls are the mode for shopping and dining, and you could swear that some hotels are larger than a small town. Travelers feel comfortable in Cancún. You do not need to spend a day getting your bearings because you immediately see familiar names for dining, shopping, nightclubbing, and sleeping.

You may have heard that in 1974 a team of Mexican government computer analysts picked Cancún for tourism development for its ideal mix of elements to attract travelers—and they were right on. It's actually an island, a 14-mile long sliver of land connected to the mainland by two bridges and separated from it by the expansive Nichupté lagoon. (Cancún means "Golden Snake" in Mayan.)

In addition to attractions of its own, Cancún is a convenient distance from the more traditional resorts of Isla Mujeres, Playa del Carmen, and Cozumel, and the Maya ruins at Tulum, Chichén-Itzá, and Cobá. All are within driving distance for a day trip.

You will run out of vacation days before you run out of things to do in Cancún. Snorkeling, jet-skiing, jungle tours, and visits to ancient Maya ruins or modern ecological theme parks are among the most popular diversions. There are a dozen malls with name-brand and duty-free shops (with European goods at prices better than in the U.S.), plus more than 350 restaurants and nightclubs. The more than 24,000 hotel rooms in the area offer something for every taste and every budget.

Cancún's luxury hotels have pools so spectacular that you may find it tempting to remain poolside, but don't. Set aside some time to simply gaze into the ocean and wriggle your toes in the fine, brilliantly white sand. It is, after all, what put Cancún on the map.

## 1 Orientation

### GETTING THERE

**BY PLANE** If this is not your first trip to Cancún, you'll notice that the airport's facilities and services continue to expand. **Aeromexico** (✆ **800/237-6639** in the U.S., 01-800/021-4000 toll-free in Mexico, or 998/884-7005 in Cancún; www.aeromexico.com) offers direct service from Atlanta, Houston, Miami, and New York, plus connecting service via Mexico City from Dallas, Los Angeles, and San Diego. **Mexicana** (✆ **800/531-7921** from the U.S., 01-800/502-2000 toll-free in Mexico, or 998/887-4444 or 998/886-0124 in Cancún; www.mexicana.com.mx) flies from Chicago, Denver, Los Angeles, Oakland, San Antonio, San Francisco, and San Jose via Mexico City, with nonstop service from Miami and New York. In addition to these carriers, many charter companies—such as Apple Vacations, Funjet, and Friendly Holidays—travel to Cancún; these package tours make up as much as 60 percent of the arrivals here by U.S. visitors (see "The Pros & Cons of Package Tours," in chapter 2).

Regional carrier **AeroCaribe,** a Mexicana affiliate (✆ **998/884-2000**) flies from Cozumel, Havana, Mexico City, Mérida, Chetumal, and other points within Mexico. You'll want to confirm departure times for flights to the U.S.; here are the Cancún airport numbers of major international carriers: American (✆ **998/883-4461;** www.im.aa.com), Continental (✆ **998/886-0006;** www.continental.com), and Northwest (✆ **998/886-0044** or 998/886-0046; www.nwa.com).

Most major car-rental firms have outlets at the airport, so if you're renting a car, consider picking it up and dropping it off at the airport to save on airport-transportation costs. Another way to save money is to arrange for the rental before you leave home. If you wait until you arrive, the daily cost of a rental car will be around $65 to $75 for a VW Beetle. Major agencies include Avis (✆ **800/331-1212** in the U.S., or 998/886-0222; www.avis.com); Budget (✆ **800/527-0700** in the U.S., or 998/886-0417; fax 998/884-5011); Dollar (✆ **800/800-4000** or 998/886-0775; www.dollar.com); National (✆ **800/328-4567** in the U.S., or 998/886-0152; www.nationalcar.com); and Hertz (✆ **800/654-3131** in the U.S. and Canada, or 998/887-6634; www.hertz.com). The *Zona Hotelera* (Hotel Zone) is 10km (6½ miles), or about a 20-minute drive, from the airport along wide, well-paved roads.

Rates for a private taxi from the airport are around $20 to downtown Cancún, or $35 to $40 to the Hotel Zone, depending on your destination. Special vans (*colectivos*) run from the airport into town. Buy tickets, which cost about $8, from the booth to the far right as you exit the airport terminal. There's minibus transportation ($9.50) from the airport to the Puerto Juárez passenger ferry to Isla Mujeres. A private taxi can also be hired for about $40. There is no *colectivo* service returning to the airport from Ciudad Cancún or the Hotel Zone, so you'll have to hire a taxi, but the rate will be much less than for the trip from the airport. (Only federally chartered taxis may take fares *from* the airport, but any taxi may bring passengers *to* the airport.) Ask at your hotel what the fare should be, but expect to pay about half what you were charged from the airport to your hotel.

**BY CAR** From Mérida or Campeche, take Highway 180 east to Cancún. This is mostly a winding, two-lane road that branches off into the express toll road 180D between Izamal and Nuevo Xcan. Nuevo Xcan is approximately 42km (26 miles) from Cancún. Mérida is about 83km (52 miles) away, or a 3½-hour drive.

### Tips The Best Websites for Cancún

- **All About Cancún: www.cancunmx.com** This site is a good place to start planning. There's a database of answers to the most common questions, called "The Online Experts." It's slow, but it has input from lots of recent travelers to the region.
- **Cancún Convention & Visitors Bureau: http://gocancun.com** This official site of the Cancún Convention & Visitors Bureau lists excellent information on events and area attractions. Its hotel guide is one of the most complete available, and it offers online booking.
- **Cancún Online: www.cancun.com** This comprehensive guide has lots of information about things to do and see in Cancún, with most details provided by paying advertisers. Highlights include forums, live chat, property swaps, bulletin boards, plus information on local Internet access, news, and events. You can even reserve a tee time or conduct wedding planning online.
- **Cancún Travel Guide: www.go2cancun.com** This group specializing in online information about Mexico has put together an excellent resource for Cancún rentals, hotels, and area attractions. Note that it lists only paying advertisers, but you'll find most of the major players here.
- **Mexico Web Cancún Chat: www.mexicoweb.com/chats/cancun/** This is one of the more active chats online specifically about Cancún. The users share inside information on everything from the cheapest beer to the quality of food at various all-inclusive resorts.

**BY BUS** Cancún's **ADO bus terminal** (© **998/884-4352** or 998/884-4804) is in downtown Ciudad Cancún at the intersection of Avenidas Tulum and Uxmal. All out-of-town buses arrive here. Buses run to Playa del Carmen, Tulum, Chichén-Itzá, other nearby beach and archaeological zones, and other points within Mexico. For package deals to popular destinations, see "Day Trips: Archaeological Sites & Eco-Theme Parks," later in this chapter.

## VISITOR INFORMATION

The **State Tourism Office,** Avenida Tulum 26 (© **998/881-9000**), is centrally located downtown next to Banco Inverlat, immediately left of the Ayuntamiento Benito Juárez building, between Avenidas Cobá and Uxmal. It's open daily from 9am to 9pm. The Convention & Visitors Bureau tourist information office, Avenida Cobá at Avenida Tulum (© **998/884-6531** or 998/884-3438), next to Pizza Rolandi, is open Monday to Friday from 9am to 8pm. Each office lists hotels and their rates, and ferry schedules. For information prior to your arrival in Cancún, call © **800/CANCUN-8** from the U.S., or visit the Convention Bureau's website, **www.gocancun.com**.

Pick up copies of the free monthly ***Cancún Tips*** booklet and a seasonal tabloid of the same name. Both are useful and have fine maps. The publications are owned by the same people who own the Captain's Cove restaurants, a couple of sightseeing boats, and time-share hotels, so the information, though good, is not completely unbiased.

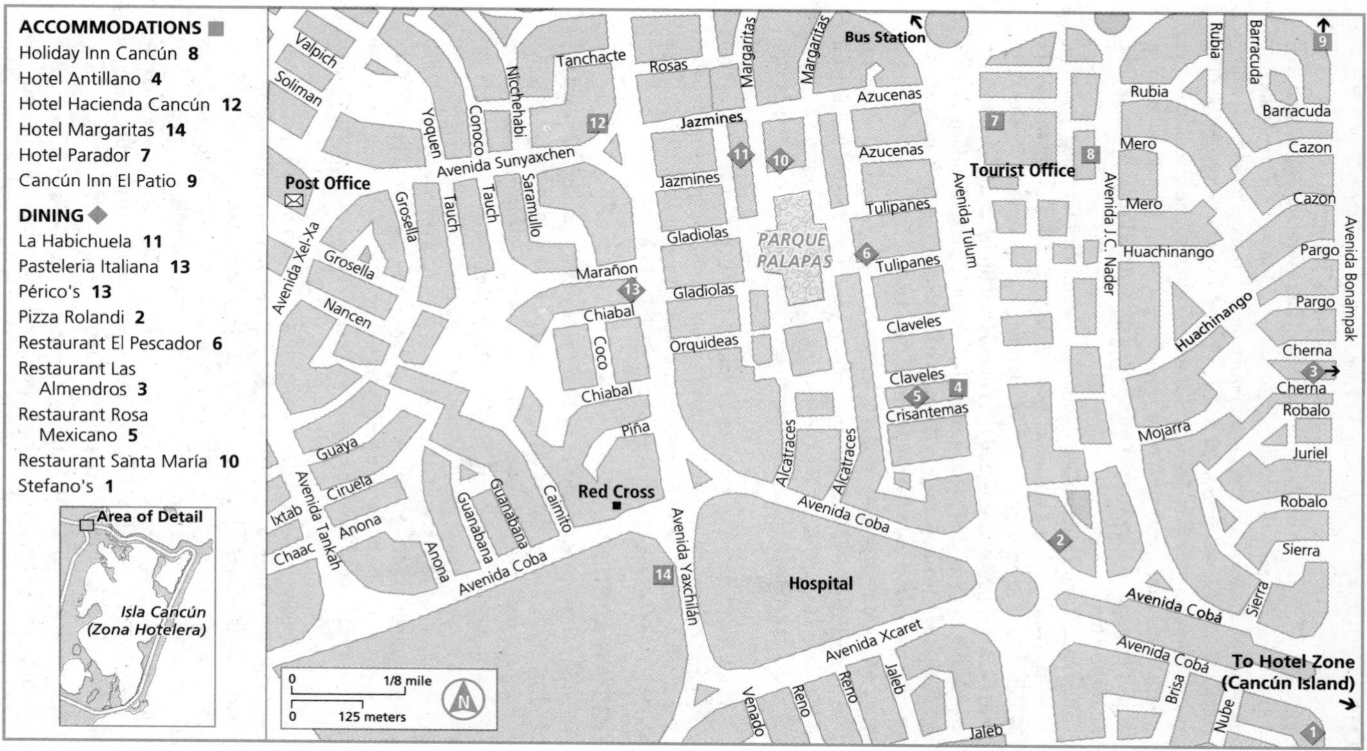
ACCOMMODATIONS ■
Holiday Inn Cancún 8
Hotel Antillano 4
Hotel Hacienda Cancún 12
Hotel Margaritas 14
Hotel Parador 7
Cancún Inn El Patio 9
DINING ◆
La Habichuela 11
Pasteleria Italiana 13
Périco's 13
Pizza Rolandi 2
Restaurant El Pescador 6
Restaurant Las Almendros 3
Restaurant Rosa Mexicano 5
Restaurant Santa María 10
Stefano's 1
Area of Detail
Isla Cancún (Zona Hotelera)
Bus Station
Post Office
Tourist Office
Red Cross
Hospital
PARQUE PALAPAS
To Hotel Zone (Cancún Island)
Avenida Bonampak
Avenida J.C. Nader
Avenida Tulum
Avenida Coba
Avenida Cobá
Avenida Yaxchilán
Avenida Xcaret
Avenida Sunyaxchen
Avenida Tankah
Avenida Xel-Ha
Valpich
Soliman
Yoquen
Conoco
Nicchehabi
Tanchacte
Rosas
Jazmines
Margaritas
Azucenas
Tulipanes
Gladiolas
Orquideas
Claveles
Crisantemas
Alcatraces
Grosella
Tauch
Saramullo
Marañon
Chiabal
Coco
Piña
Nancen
Guaya
Ciruela
Anona
Guanabana
Caimito
Ixtab
Chaac
Venado
Reno
Jaleb
Brisa
Nube
Rubia
Barracuda
Mero
Cazon
Huachinango
Pargo
Cherna
Robalo
Juriel
Mojarra
Sierra
0 1/8 mile
0 125 meters

## CITY LAYOUT

There are really two Cancúns: **Isla Cancún** (Cancún Island) and **Ciudad Cancún** (Cancún City). The latter, on the mainland, has restaurants, shops, and less-expensive hotels, as well as all the other establishments that make life function—pharmacies, dentists, automotive shops, banks, travel and airline agencies, and car-rental firms—all within an area about 9 blocks square. The city's main thoroughfare is **Avenida Tulum.** Heading south, Avenida Tulum becomes the highway to the airport and to Tulum and Chetumal; heading north, it intersects the highway to Mérida and the road to Puerto Juárez and the Isla Mujeres ferries.

The famed **Zona Hotelera** (the Hotel Zone, also called the **Zona Turística,** or Tourist Zone) stretches out along Isla Cancún, which is a sandy strip 22km (14 miles) long, shaped like a "7." It connects to the mainland by the Playa Linda Bridge at the north end and the Punta Nizuc Bridge at the southern end. Between the two areas lies Laguna Nichupté. Avenida Cobá from Cancún City becomes Paseo Kukulkán, the island's main traffic artery. Cancún's international airport is just inland from the south end of the island.

**FINDING AN ADDRESS** Cancún's street-numbering system is a holdover from its early days. Addresses are still given by the number of the building lot and by the *manzana* (block) or *supermanzana* (group of city blocks). The city is still relatively compact, and the downtown commercial section can easily be covered on foot.

On the island, addresses are given by kilometer number on Paseo Kukulkán or by reference to some well-known location. In Cancún, streets are named after famous Maya cities. Chichén-Itzá, Tulum, and Uxmal are the names of the boulevards in Cancún, as well as nearby archeological sites.

## GETTING AROUND

**BY TAXI** Taxi prices in Cancún are clearly set by zone, although keeping track of what's in which zone can take some doing. The minimum fare within the Hotel Zone is $5 per ride, making it one of the most expensive taxis areas in Mexico. In addition, you'll find that the taxis operating in the Hotel Zone feel perfectly justified in having a discriminatory pricing structure: Local residents pay about half of what tourists pay, and prices for guests at higher-priced hotels are about double those for budget hotel guests—these are all established by the taxi union. Rates should be posted outside your hotel; if you have a question, all drivers are required to have an official rate card in their taxis, though it's generally in Spanish.

Within the downtown area, the cost is about $2 per cab ride (not per person); within any other zone, it's $6. Traveling between two zones will also cost $6, and if you cross two zones, that'll cost $8.50. Settle on a price in advance, or check at your hotel. Trips to the airport from most zones cost $15. Taxis can also be rented for $20 per hour for travel around the city and Hotel Zone, but this rate can generally be negotiated down to $12 to $15. If you want to hire a taxi to take you to Chichén-Itzá or along the Riviera Maya, expect to pay about $35 per hour—many taxi drivers feel that they are also providing guide services.

**BY BUS** Bus travel within Cancún continues to improve and is increasingly popular. In town, almost everything is within walking distance. Ruta 1 and Ruta 2 (HOTELES) city buses travel frequently from the mainland to the beaches along Avenida Tulum (the main street) and all the way to Punta Nizuc at the far end of the Hotel Zone on Isla Cancún. Ruta 8 buses go to Puerto Juárez/Punta Sam for ferries to Isla Mujeres. They stop on the east side of Avenida Tulum. All these city buses operate between 6am and 10pm daily. Beware of private buses along the same route; they charge far more than the public ones. Public buses have the fare painted on the front; at press time, the fare was 5 pesos (60¢).

**BY MOPED** Mopeds are a convenient but dangerous way to cruise around through the very congested traffic. Rentals start at $30 for a day, and a credit card voucher is required as security. You should receive a crash helmet (it's the law) and instructions on how to lock the wheels when you park. Read the fine print on the back of the rental agreement regarding liability for repairs or replacement in case of accident, theft, or vandalism.

## *FAST FACTS:* Cancún

*American Express* The local office is at Avenida Tulum 208 and Agua (✆ **998/881-4000** or 998/881-4040; www.americanexpress.com), 1 block past the Plaza México. It's open Monday to Friday from 9am to 6pm, Saturday from 9am to 2pm.

*Area Code* The telephone area code is **998.**

*Climate* It's hot but not overwhelmingly humid. The rainy season is May through October. August through October is the hurricane season, which brings erratic weather. November through February is generally sunny but can also be cloudy, windy, somewhat rainy, and even cool, so a sweater is handy, as is rain protection.

*Consulates* The **U.S. Consular Agent** is in the Plaza Caracol 2, 3rd level, 320–323, Km 8.5 Blvd. Kukulkán (✆ **998/883-0272**). The office is open Monday to Friday from 9am to 1pm. The **Canadian Consulate** is in the Plaza México 312 (✆ **998/883-3360**). The office is open Monday to Friday from 9am to 5pm. The **United Kingdom** has a consular office in Cancún (✆ **998/881-0100,** ext. 65898; fax 998/848-8229; information@british consulatecancun.com). Irish, Australian, and New Zealand citizens should contact their embassies in Mexico City.

*Crime* Car break-ins are just about the only crime here. They happen frequently, especially around the shopping centers in the Hotel Zone. VW Beetles and Golfs are frequent targets.

*Currency Exchange* Most banks are downtown along Avenida Tulum and are usually open Monday to Friday from 9:30am to 5pm. Many have automatic teller machines for after-hours cash withdrawals. In the Hotel Zone, you'll find banks in the Plaza Kukulkán and next to the convention center. There are also many *casas de cambio* (exchange houses). Downtown merchants are eager to change cash dollars, but island stores don't offer very good exchange rates. Avoid changing money at the airport as you arrive, especially at the first exchange booth you see—its rates are less favorable than those of any in town or others farther inside the airport concourse.

*Drugstores* Next to the Hotel Caribe Internacional, **Farmacia Canto,** Avenida Yaxchilán 36, at Sunyaxchen (✆ **998/884-9330**), is open 24 hours. It accepts American Express and Visa.

*Emergencies* To report an emergency, dial ✆ **060,** which is supposed to be similar to 911 emergency service in the United States. For first aid, the **Cruz Roja,** or Red Cross (✆ **998/884-1616;** fax 998/884-7466), is open 24 hours on Avenida Yaxchilán between Avenidas Xcaret and Labná, next to the Telmex building. **Total Assist,** Claveles 5, SM 22, at Avenida Tulum (✆ **998/884-1058** or 998/884-1092; htotal@prodigy.net.mx), is a small (nine-room) emergency hospital with English-speaking doctors. It's open 24 hours and accepts American Express, MasterCard, and Visa. Desk staff may have limited command of English. Air Ambulance service is available by calling ✆ **800/305-9400** (toll-free within Mexico). *Urgencias* means "Emergencies."

*Internet Access* **C@ncunet,** in a kiosk on the second floor of Plaza Kukulkán, Paseo Kukulkán Km 13 (✆ **998/885-0055**), offers Internet access at $4 for 15 minutes, or $16 per hour. It's open daily from 10am to 10pm. In downtown Cancún, **Sybcom,** in the Plaza Alconde, Local 2, at Avenida Náder, in front of Clinica AMAT (✆ **998/884-6807**), offers Internet access for $4 per hour, $2.50 for 30 minutes, or $1.50 for 15 minutes. It is open Monday to Saturday from 9am to 11pm.

*Luggage Storage/Lockers* Hotels will generally tag and store luggage while you travel elsewhere.

*Newspapers/Magazines* For English-language newspapers and books, go to **Fama,** Avenida Tulum between Tulipanes and Claveles (✆ **998/884-6586**). It's open daily from 8am to 10pm and accepts American Express, MasterCard, and Visa. Most hotel gift shops and newsstands carry English-language magazines and English-language Mexican newspapers.

*Police* Cancún has a fleet of English-speaking tourist police to help travelers. To reach the **police** (Seguridad Pública), dial ✆ **998/884-1913** or 998/884-2342. The ***Procuraduría del Consumidor*** (consumer protection agency), Avenida Cobá 9–11 (✆ **998/884-2634** or 998/884-2701), is opposite the Social Security Hospital and upstairs from the Fenix drugstore. It's open Monday to Saturday from 9am to 3pm.

*Post Office* The main ***correo*** is at the intersection of Avenidas Sunyaxchen and Xel-Ha (✆ **998/884-1418**). It's open Monday to Friday from 8am to 5pm, Saturday from 9am to noon.

*Safety* There is very little crime in Cancún. People are generally safe late at night in tourist areas; just use ordinary common sense. As at any other beach resort, don't take money or valuables to the beach. See "Crime," above.

Swimming on the Caribbean side presents a danger because of the undertow. See the information on beaches in "Beaches, Watersports & Boat Tours," later in this chapter, for information about flag warnings

*Seasons* Technically, high season is from December 15 to Easter; low season is from May to July and October 1 to December 15, when prices are reduced 10% to 30%. Some hotels are starting to charge high-season rates between July and September, when Mexican, European, and school-holiday visitors often travel, although rates may still be lower than in winter months. There's a short low season in January just after the Christmas to New Year's Day holiday.

*Special Events* The annual **Cancún Jazz Festival** ★★, featuring internationally known musicians, is held each year over the U.S. Memorial Day weekend, in late May. The Cancún Marathon takes place each December and attracts world-class athletes as well as numerous amateur competitors. Additional information is available through the Convention & Visitors Bureau.

*Telephones* The area code for Cancún is **998** (until 1999, it was 98). All local numbers have seven digits and begin with 8.

## 2 Where to Stay

Island hotels line the beach like dominoes, almost all of them offering clean, modern facilities. Extravagance is the byword in the newer hotels, many of which are awash in a sea of marble and glass. Some hotels, while exclusive, affect a more relaxed attitude. The water on the upper end of the island facing Bahía de Mujeres is placid, while beaches lining the long side of the island facing the Caribbean are subject to choppier water and crashing waves on windy days. (For more information on swimming safety, see "Beaches, Watersports & Boat Tours," later in this chapter.) Be aware that the farther south you go on the island, the longer it takes (20–30 min. in traffic) to get back to the "action spots," which are primarily between the Plaza Flamingo and Punta Cancún on the island and along Avenida Tulum on the mainland.

Almost all major hotel chains are represented on Cancún Island, so this list can be viewed as a representative summary, with a select number of notable places. The reality is that Cancún is so popular as a package destination from the U.S. that prices and special deals are often the deciding factor for those traveling here (see "The Pros & Cons of Package Tours," in chapter 2). Ciudad Cancún offers independently owned, smaller, less expensive lodging. Prices are lower here during the off-season (Apr–Nov). For condo, home, and villa rentals as an alternative to hotel stays, check with **Cancún Hideaways** (www.cancunhideaways.com), a company specializing in luxury properties, downtown apartments, and condos—many at prices much lower than comparable hotel stays. Owner Maggie Rodriguez, a former resident of Cancún, has made this niche market her specialty.

The hotel listings in this chapter begin on Cancún Island and finish in Cancún City, where bargain lodgings are available. Free parking is available at all island hotels.

### CANCUN ISLAND

#### VERY EXPENSIVE

**Fiesta Americana Grand Coral Beach** ★ This is an ideal choice for any type of traveler looking to be at the heart of all that Cancún has to offer. The spectacular hotel, which opened in 1991, has one of the best locations in Cancún, with 303m (1,000 ft.) of prime beachfront and proximity to the main shopping and entertainment centers. The key word here is *big*—everything at the Fiesta Americana seems oversized, from the lobby to the suites. Service is gracious, if cool: The hotel aims for a sophisticated ambience. It's embellished with elegant dark-green granite and an abundance of marble. The large guest rooms are also decorated with marble, and all have balconies facing the ocean. Master suites are enormous, with double vanities, a dressing room, bathrobes, whirlpool tubs, and large terraces. The hotel's great Punta Cancún location (opposite the convention center) has the advantage of facing the beach to the north, meaning that the surf is calm and perfect for swimming.

Km 9.5 Paseo Kukulkán, 77500 Cancún, Q. Roo. ✆ **800/343-7821** in the U.S., or 998/881-3200. Fax 998/881-3263. bcenter1@fiestaamericana.com.mx. 602 units. High season $380–$555 double; $529–$650 Club Floor double; $875 Caribbean Suite. Low season $277–$424 double; $381–$504 Club Floor double; $695 Caribbean Suite. AE, MC, V. **Amenities:** 2 restaurants, poolside snack bar, 5 bars; 660-foot-long free-form swimming pool with swim-up bars; 3 indoor tennis courts with stadium seating; gymnasium with weights, sauna, and massage; watersports rentals on the beach; concierge; travel agency; car rental; business center; salon; room service; babysitting; laundry; 2 concierge floors with complimentary cocktails. 2 jr. suites for travelers with disabilities are available. *In room:* A/C, TV, minibar, hair dryer, iron, safe.

**Hilton Cancún Beach & Golf Resort** ★ *Kids* Grand, expansive, and fully equipped, this is a true resort in every sense of the word and is especially perfect for anyone whose motto is "the bigger the better." The Hilton Cancún, formerly the vintage 1994 Caesar Park Resort, joined the Hilton chain in December 1999. It sits on 250 acres of prime beachfront property, a location that gives every room a sea view (some have both sea and lagoon views), with an 18-hole par-72 golf course across the street. Like the sprawling resort, rooms are grandly spacious and immaculately decorated in minimalist style. Area rugs and pale furnishings soften marble floors and bathrooms throughout. The elegant Beach Club rooms occupy separate two- and three-story buildings (no elevators) and have their own check-in and concierge service, plus nightly complimentary cocktails. The hotel is especially appealing to golfers because it's one of only two in Cancún with an on-site course (the other is the Mélia, with an 18-hole executive course). Greens fees for guests are $77 for 9 holes, $99 for 18 holes, and include the use of a cart.

Km 17 Paseo Kukulkán, Retorno Lacandones, 77500 Cancún, Q. Roo. ✆ **800/228-3000** in the U.S., or 998/881-8000. Fax 998/881-8080. www.hiltoncancun.com.mx. 426 units. High season $350–$415 standard double; $440–$585 Beach Club double; $555–$779 suite. Low season $258–$300 standard; $350–$550 Beach Club; $450–$500 suite. AE, DC, MC, V. **Amenities:** 2 restaurants; 7 interconnected pools with swim-up bar; golf course across the street, golf clinic; 2 lighted tennis courts; large, fully equipped gym with daily aerobics and Kids Club; massage; 2 whirlpools; sauna; watersports center; concierge; tour desk; car rental; salon; room service; babysitting; laundry. *In room:* A/C, TV, minibar, coffeemaker, hair dryer, iron, safe, robes, house shoes.

**Le Méridien Cancún Resort & Spa** ★★★ Of all the luxury properties in Cancún, Le Méridien is the most inviting, with a refined yet welcoming sense of personal service. From the intimate lobby and reception area to the best

---

### *Tips* Important Note on Hotel Prices

Cancún's hotels, in all price categories, generally set their rates in dollars, so they are immune to swings in the peso. Travel agents and wholesalers always have air/hotel packages available, and Sunday papers often advertise inventory-clearing packages at prices much lower than the rates listed here. Cancún also has numerous all-inclusive properties, which allow you to take a fixed-cost vacation. Note that the price quoted when you call a hotel's reservation number from the United States may not include Cancún's 12% tax. Prices can vary considerably throughout the year, so it pays to consult a travel agent or shop around.

---

## Isla Cancún (Zona Hotelera)

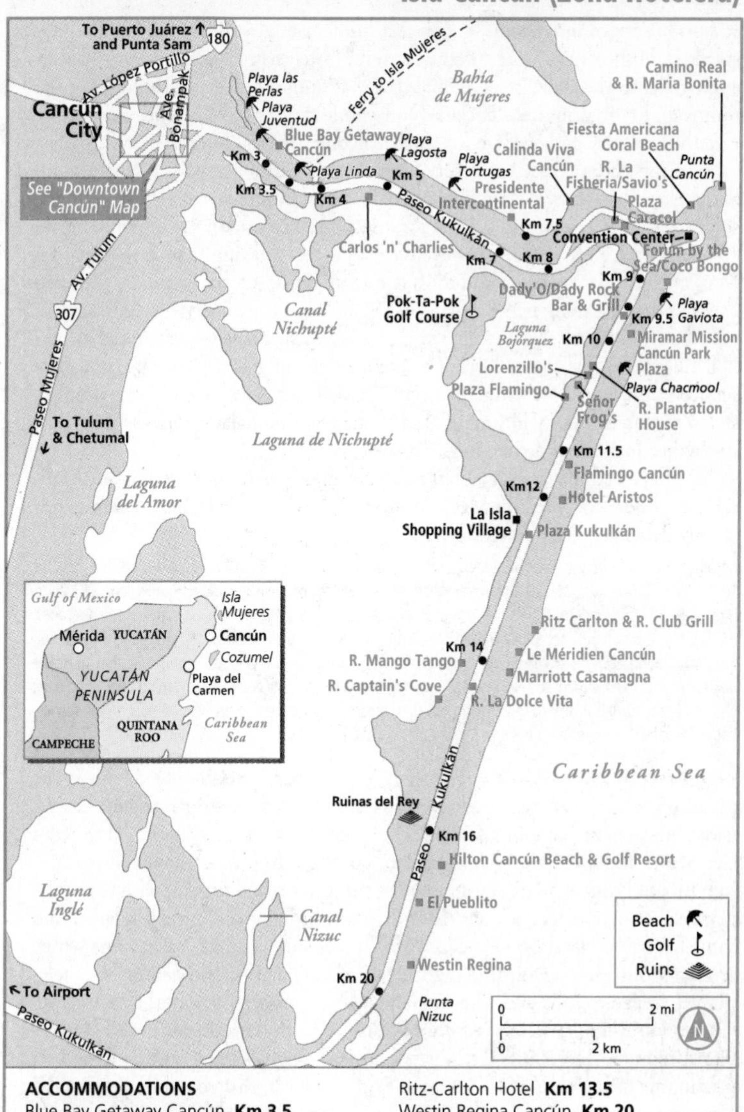


**ACCOMMODATIONS**

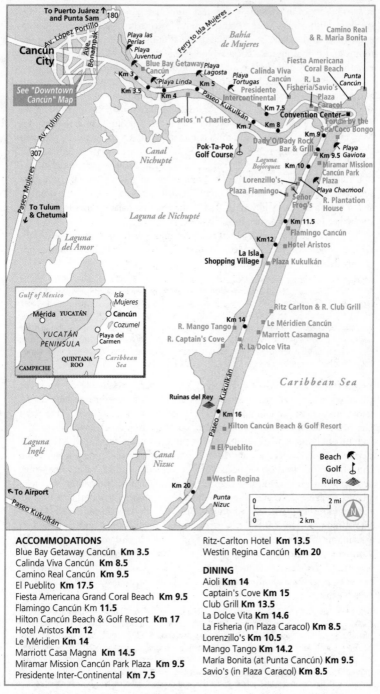

Blue Bay Getaway Cancún **Km 3.5**
Calinda Viva Cancún **Km 8.5**
Camino Real Cancún **Km 9.5**
El Pueblito **Km 17.5**
Fiesta Americana Grand Coral Beach **Km 9.5**
Flamingo Cancún Km **11.5**
Hilton Cancún Beach & Golf Resort **Km 17**
Hotel Aristos **Km 12**
Le Méridien **Km 14**
Marriott Casa Magna **Km 14.5**
Miramar Mission Cancún Park Plaza **Km 9.5**
Presidente Inter-Continental **Km 7.5**
Ritz-Carlton Hotel **Km 13.5**
Westin Regina Cancún **Km 20**

**DINING**

Aioli **Km 14**
Captain's Cove **Km 15**
Club Grill **Km 13.5**
La Dolce Vita **Km 14.6**
La Fisheria (in Plaza Caracol) **Km 8.5**
Lorenzillo's **Km 10.5**
Mango Tango **Km 14.2**
María Bonita (at Punta Cancún) **Km 9.5**
Savio's (in Plaza Caracol) **Km 8.5**

concierge service in Cancún, guests feel immediately pampered. The relatively small establishment is more elegant boutique hotel than immense resort—a welcome relief to those overstressed by activity at home. The decor throughout the rooms and common areas is classy and comforting, not overdone. Rooms are generous in size, and most have small balconies overlooking the pool, with a view to the ocean. Each has a very large marble bathroom with a separate tub and a glassed-in shower. The hotel attracts many Europeans as well as younger, sophisticated travelers, and is ideal for a second honeymoon or romantic break.

Certainly, a highlight of—or even a reason for—staying here is the **Spa del Mar,** one of Mexico's finest and most complete European spa facilities, with two levels and more than 1,394 square m (15,000 sq. ft.) of services dedicated to your body and soul. A complete fitness center with extensive cardio and weight machines is on the upper level. The spa consists of a health snack bar, a full-service salon, and 14 treatment rooms, as well as separate men's and women's steam rooms, saunas, whirlpools, cold plunge pool, inhalation rooms, tranquility rooms, lockers, and changing areas.

You may need that health club if you fully enjoy the gourmet restaurant **Aioli,** with its specialties based on Mediterranean and Provençal cuisines. The menu is simply delicious—not pretentious.

Retorno del Rey Km 14, Zona Hotelera, 77500, Cancún, Q. Roo. ✆ **800/543-4300** in the U.S., or 998/881-2200. Fax 998/881-2201. www.meridiencancun.com.mx or www.lemeridien-hotels.com. 213 units. High season $336 standard; $504 suite. Low season $247 standard; $392 suite. Ask for special spa packages. AE, DC, MC, V. Small pets accepted, with prior reservation. **Amenities:** 2 restaurants, lobby bar; 3 cascading swimming pools; 2 lighted championship tennis courts; whirlpool; watersports equipment and massage *palapa* on the beach; supervised children's program with clubhouse, play equipment, wading pool; concierge; tour desk; car rental; business center with Internet access; small shopping arcade; 24-hour room service; babysitting; laundry; concierge floor. *In room:* A/C, TV, dataport, minibar, hair dryer, iron, safe.

**Ritz-Carlton Hotel** ★★★ For those who want to feel indulged, this is the place to stay. On 7½ acres, the nine-story Ritz-Carlton sets the standard for elegance in Cancún and in Mexico. The hotel fronts a 1,200-foot white-sand beach, and all rooms overlook the ocean, pool, and tropical gardens. The style—in both public areas and guest rooms—is sumptuous and formal, with thick carpets, elaborate chandeliers, and fresh flowers throughout. Suites are large, and some have a private dressing area, two TVs, balconies, and 1½ bathrooms—they are slated for remodeling this year. In all rooms, marble bathrooms have telephones, separate tubs and showers, and lighted makeup mirrors. Ritz-Carlton Club floors offer guests five minimeals a day, private butler service, and Hermès bath products. **The Club Grill,** a fashionable English pub, is one of the best restaurants in the city (See "Where to Dine," later in this chapter). The **Lobby Lounge,** the original home of proper tequila tastings, features one of the world's most extensive menus of fine tequilas, as well as Cuban cigars. The hotel has won countless accolades for service. Special golf, spa, and weekend packages are worth exploring.

Retorno del Rey 36, off Km 13.5 Paseo Kukulkán, 77500 Cancún, Q. Roo. ✆ **800/241-3333** in the U.S. and Canada, or 998/885-0808. Fax 998/881-0815. www.ritzcarlton.com. 365 units. High season $425–$475 double; $537–$850 Club floor, $499–$559 suite. Low season $235–$302 double; $335–$503 Club floor, $335–$447 suite. AE, MC, V. **Amenities:** 5 restaurants; 2 connecting swimming pools (heated in winter); deluxe beach cabañas for 2; 3 lighted tennis courts; fully equipped gym and spa with Universal weight training and cardiovascular equipment, personal trainers; steam, sauna, facial, and massage services; Ritz Kids program with supervised activities; concierge; travel agency; business center; shopping arcade; salon; 24-hour room service; babysitting; laundry; dry cleaning; Club floors. *In room:* A/C, TV, dataport, minibar, hair dryer, iron, safe, robes.

## EXPENSIVE

**Camino Real Cancún** ★★ *Kids* On 4 acres at the tip of Punta Cancún, the Camino Real is among the island's most appealing places to stay. The architecture is trademark Camino Real style—contemporary and sleek, with bright colors and strategic angles. Rooms in the newer 18-story Camino Real Club have extra services and amenities; rates here include full breakfast in the Beach Club lobby. Master suites have expansive views, large dining tables for four, and hot tubs on the balconies. The lower-priced rooms have lagoon views. While the setting is sophisticated, the hotel is also very welcoming to children; it is a favored name in Mexico, where vacations are synonymous with family.

Av. Kukulkán, 77500 Punta Cancún (Apdo. Postal 14), Cancún, Q. Roo. ✆ **800/722-6466** in the U.S., or 998/848-7000. Fax 998/848-7001. www.caminoreal.com/cancun. 389 units. High season $275 standard double; $264–$465 Camino Real Club double; $1,600 suite. Low season $195 standard double; $230 Camino Real Club double; $1,320 suite. AE, DC, MC, V. **Amenities:** 3 restaurants; nightclub; pool; private saltwater lagoon with sea turtles and tropical fish; 3 lighted tennis courts; fitness center with steam bath; beach volleyball; sailing pier; watersports center; travel agency; car rental; salon; 24-hour room service; massage; babysitting (with advance notice). *In room:* A/C, TV, minibar, hair dryer, iron, safe.

**Marriott Casa Magna** ★★ *Kids* This is quintessential Marriott—those who are familiar with the chain's standards will feel at home here and appreciate the hotel's attention to detailed service. Entering through a half circle of Roman columns, you pass through a domed foyer to a wide, lavishly marbled 44-foot-high lobby filled with plants and shallow pools. Guest rooms have contemporary furnishings, tiled floors, and ceiling fans; most have balconies. All suites occupy corners and have enormous terraces, ocean views, and TVs in both the living room and the bedroom. The hotel caters to family travelers with specially priced packages (up to two children can stay free with parents) and the Club Amigos supervised children's program. In 2001 Marriott opened the 450-room luxury **JW Cancún,** Blvd. Kukulkán Km 14.5, 77500 Cancún, Q. Roo (✆ **998/848-9600;** www.marriott.com/cunjw), on the beach next to the Casa Magna.

Km 14.5 Paseo Kukulkán, 77500 Cancún, Q. Roo. ✆ **800/228-9290** in the U.S., or 998/881-2000. Fax 998/881-2071. www.marriott.com. 452 units. High season $260–$285 double; $395 suite. Low season $156–$180 double; $336 suite. Ask about packages. AE, MC, V. **Amenities:** 5 restaurants, lobby bar with live music; swimming pool; 2 lighted tennis courts; health club with saunas, whirlpool, aerobics, and juice bar; salon with massage and facials; concierge; travel agency; car rental; room service; babysitting; laundry. *In room:* A/C, TV, dataport, minibar, coffeemaker, hair dryer, iron, safe.

**Presidente Inter-Continental Cancún** ★ On the island's best beach, facing the placid Bahía de Mujeres, the Presidente's location is reason enough to stay here, and it's just a 2-minute walk to Cancún's public Pok-Ta-Pok Golf Club (Club de Golf Cancún). For its ambience, I consider it an ideal choice for a romantic getaway or for couples who enjoy indulging in the sports of golf, tennis, or even shopping. Cool and spacious, the Presidente sports a postmodern design with lavish marble and wicker accents and a strong use of color. Guests have a choice of two double beds or one king-size bed. All rooms have tastefully simple unfinished pine furniture. Sixteen rooms on the first floor have patios with outdoor whirlpool tubs. The expansive pool has a pyramid-shaped waterfall and is surrounded by cushioned lounge chairs. Coming from Cancún City, you'll reach the Presidente on the left side of the street before you get to Punta Cancún.

Km 7.5 Av. Kukulkán, 77500 Cancún, Q. Roo. ✆ **800/327-0200** in the U.S., or 998/848-8700. Fax 998/883-2602. www.interconti.com. 299 units. High season $280–$336 double. Low season $230–$280 double. Rates include breakfast, coffee with wakeup call, 2 massages on the beach, unlimited golf at Pok-Ta-Pok,

2 bottles of water delivered daily. AE, MC, V. Ask about special packages. **Amenities:** 3 restaurants; 2 swimming pools; lighted tennis courts; fitness center; whirlpool; watersports equipment rental; marina; travel agency; car rental; shopping arcade; 24-hour room service; babysitting; laundry; nonsmoking floors; Club floors; 2 rooms for travelers with disabilities are available. *In room:* A/C, TV, dataport, minibar, hair dryer, safe.

**Westin Regina Cancún** ★★ The strikingly austere architecture of the Westin Regina, impressive with its elegant use of stone and marble, is the stamp of leading Latin American architect Ricardo Legorreta. The hotel consists of two sections, the main building and the more exclusive six-story hot-pink tower section. Standard rooms are unusually large and beautifully furnished with cool, contemporary furniture. Those on the sixth floor have balconies, and first-floor rooms have terraces. Rooms in the tower all have ocean or lagoon views, furniture with Olinalá lacquer accents, Berber area rugs, oak tables and chairs, and terraces with lounge chairs. It's important to note that this hotel is a 15- to 20-minute ride from the lively strip that lies between the Plaza Flamingo and Punta Cancún, so it's a good choice for those who want a little more seclusion than Cancún typically offers. However, it is easy to join the action—buses stop in front, and taxis are readily available.

Km 20 Paseo Kukulkán, 77500 Cancún, Q. Roo. ✆ **800/228-3000** in the U.S., 800/215-7000 in Mexico, or 998/848-7400. Fax 998/885-0296. www.westin.com. 293 units. High season $370–$450 double. Low season $180–$415 double. AE, DC, MC, V. **Amenities:** 2 restaurants, 2 bars; 5 swimming pools; 2 lighted tennis courts; gym with Stairmaster, bicycle, weights, aerobics, sauna, steam, massage; 3 whirlpools; concierge; travel agency; car rental; pharmacy/gift shop; salon; room service; babysitting; laundry. *In room:* A/C, TV, dataport, minibar, coffeemaker, hair dryer, iron, safe.

## MODERATE

**Blue Bay Getaway Cancún** ★★ The adults-only Blue Bay Getaway Cancún is a spirited yet relaxing all-inclusive resort favored by young adults. Surrounded by acres of tropical gardens, it's ideally located at the northern end of the Hotel Zone, close to the major shopping plazas, restaurants, and nightlife. It has a terrific beach with calm waters for swimming. The comfortable, modern rooms are in two sections. The central building features 72 rooms decorated in rustic wood, the main lobby, administrative offices, restaurants, and Tequila Sunrise bar. The remaining nine buildings feature colorful Mexican decor; rooms have lagoon, garden, and ocean views. Safes are available for an extra charge. Blue Bay allows guests to use the amenities and facilities at its sister resort, the family-oriented Blue Bay Club and Marina, located just outside Ciudad Cancún, near the ferry to Isla Mujeres. Free bus and boat shuttle service connects the Blue Bay resorts. During the evenings, guests may enjoy a variety of theme-night dinners, nightly shows, and live entertainment in an outdoor theater.

Km 3.5 Paseo Kukulkán, 77500 Cancún, Q. Roo. ✆ **800/BLUE-BAY** in the U.S., or 998/848-7900. Fax 998/848-7994. www.bluebayresorts.com. 216 units. High season $280 double. Low season $207 double. Rates include food, beverages, and activities. AE, MC, V. **Amenities:** 4 restaurants, 4 bars; 2 swimming pools; tennis court; exercise room with daily aerobics classes; 4 whirlpools; watersports equipment; snorkeling and scuba lessons; marina; bicycles; game room with pool and Ping-Pong tables. Wheelchair-accessible rooms are available. *In room:* A/C, TV, dataport, hair dryer.

**Calinda Viva Cancún** From the street, this hotel looks like a blockhouse; on the ocean side you'll find a small but pretty patio garden and Cancún's best beach for safe swimming. The location is ideal, close to all the shops and restaurants near Punta Cancún and the Convention Center, and you have a choice of lagoon or ocean view. The rooms are large and undistinguished in decor, but they're comfortable, with marble floors and either two double beds or a king-size bed. Several studios have kitchenettes.

Km 8.5 Paseo Kukulkán, 77500 Cancún, Q. Roo. ✆ **800/221-2222** in the U.S., or 998/883-0800. Fax 998/883-2087. 216 units. High season $145–$250 double. Low season $138–$158 double. AE, MC, V. **Amenities:** Restaurant, 2 snack bars, 3 bars; 2 swimming pools (1 for adults, 1 for children); 2 lighted tennis courts; watersports equipment rental; marina; nonsmoking areas; wheelchair access. *In room:* A/C, TV.

**El Pueblito** ★ *Kids* Consistent renovations and upgrades and a changeover to an all-inclusive concept have made this hotel more appealing than ever. It is an exceptional all-inclusive value. Dwarfed by its ostentatious neighbors, the El Pueblito lobby resembles a traditional Mexican hacienda, with several three-story buildings (no elevators) terraced in a V-shape down a gentle hillside toward the sea. A meandering swimming pool with waterfalls runs between the two series of buildings. Rooms are very large, with modern rattan furnishings, travertine marble floors, and large bathrooms. Each has either a balcony or a terrace, facing the pool or sea. In addition to a constant flow of buffet-style meals and snacks, there's also the choice of a nightly theme party, complete with entertainment. Mini-golf and a water slide, plus a full program of kids' activities, make this an ideal place for families with children. Babysitting is available for $10 per hour. The hotel is located toward the southern end of the island past the Hilton Resort.

Km 17.5 Paseo Kukulkán, 77500 Cancún, Q. Roo. ✆ **998/881-8800** or 998/881-8814. Fax 998/885-2066. www.pueblitohotels.com. 349 units. High season $300 double. Low season $240 double. Rates are all-inclusive. AE, MC, V. **Amenities:** 3 restaurants, 2 bars, lobby cafe; large pool; tennis courts; aerobics; volleyball, nonmotorized watersports; cooking classes. *In room:* A/C, TV.

**Flamingo Cancún** ★ The Flamingo seems to have been inspired by the dramatic, slope-sided architecture of the Camino Real, but it's considerably smaller and less expensive. The comfortable, modern guest rooms—all with balconies—border a courtyard facing the interior swimming pools and *palapa* pool bar. A second pool with a sundeck overlooks the ocean. The Flamingo is in the heart of the island hotel district, opposite the Flamingo Shopping Center and close to other hotels, shopping centers, and restaurants. It's a friendly, accommodating choice for families.

Km 11.5 Blvd. Kukulkán, 77500 Cancún, Q. Roo. ✆ **998/883-1544.** Fax 998/883-1029. www.flamingo cancun.com. 221 units. High season $200 double. Low season $180 double. AE, MC, V. **Amenities:** 2 restaurants; 2 pools; small gym; watersports equipment rentals; tour desk; car rental; babysitting; laundry; dry cleaning. *In room:* A/C, TV, minibar.

**Miramar Misión Cancún Park Plaza** Each of the ingeniously designed rooms here has a partial view of both the lagoon and ocean. Public spaces throughout the hotel have lots of dark wood accents, but the most notable feature is the large, rectangular swimming pool that extends through the hotel and down to the beach, with built-in, submerged sun chairs. There's also an oversized whirlpool (the largest in Cancún), a sundeck, and a snack bar on the seventh-floor roof. Rooms are on the small side but are bright and comfortable, with small balconies and bamboo furniture; bathrooms have polished limestone vanities. A popular nightclub, **Batacha,** has live music for dancing from 9pm to 4am Tuesday to Sunday.

Km 9.5 Av. Kukulkán, 77500 Zona Hotelera Cancún, Q. Roo. ✆ **800/215-1333** in the U.S., or 998/883-1755. Fax 998/883-1136. www.hotelesmision.com. 266 units. High season $290 double; low season $190 double. AE, MC, V. **Amenities:** 3 restaurants, 2 bars, rooftop snack bar; swimming pool; whirlpool. *In room:* A/C, TV, minibar, hair dryer, safe.

## INEXPENSIVE

**Hotel Aristos** This was one of the island's first hotels, and it continues to welcome repeat guests, especially European and senior travelers. The recently remodeled rooms have upgraded wood furnishings and decor. Though small, they are very clean and cool, with red tile floors and small balconies. All rooms face either the Caribbean or the *paseo* and lagoon; the best views (and no noise from the *paseo*) face the Caribbean side. A central pool overlooks the ocean and a wide stretch of beach one level below the lobby. Beware of spring break, when the hotel rocks with loud music poolside all day. The hotel wisely books the spring-breakers into their own section, facing the *paseo,* and reserves the beach-facing rooms for other guests.

Km 12, Av. Kukulkán, 77500 Cancún Q. Roo. ✆ **998/883-0011.** Fax 998/883-0078. aristcun@prodigy.net.mx. 245 units. High season $120 double; $156 double with 3 meals and drinks. Low season $100 double; $136 double with 3 meals and drinks. AE, MC, V. **Amenities:** Restaurant, 3 bars; swimming pool; 2 lighted tennis courts; marina with watersports equipment; travel agency; room service; babysitting; laundry. *In room:* A/C, TV.

## CANCUN CITY

### MODERATE

**Holiday Inn Cancún** ★★ *Value* This is the nicest hotel in downtown Cancún, and one of the best values in the area. The Holiday Inn offers all the expected comforts of a chain, yet in an atmosphere of Mexican hospitality. Resembling a hacienda, rooms are set off from a large rotunda-style lobby, lush gardens, and a pleasant pool area. All have Talavera tile inlays and brightly colored fabric accents; views of the garden, the pool, or the street; and a small sitting area and balcony. Bathrooms have a combination tub and shower. Guests of the Holiday Inn have access to the facilities of the Melía Cancún Beach Club, with complimentary shuttle service. The hotel is behind the State Government building, within walking distance of downtown Cancún dining and shopping.

Av. Nader 1, SM2, Centro, 77500 Cancún, Q. Roo. ✆ **998/887-4455.** Fax 998/884-7954. www.holidayinncancun.com. 248 units. High season $145 standard; $175 jr. suite. Low season $125 standard; $140 jr. suite. Ask about special all-inclusive rates. AE, MC, V. **Amenities:** 2 restaurants, lively lobby bar; pool with adjoining bar and separate wading area for children; tennis courts; small gym with sauna; travel agency; car rental; salon. *In room:* A/C, TV, coffeemaker, hair dryer, iron, safe.

### INEXPENSIVE

**Cancún Inn El Patio** ★ *Finds* Many guests at this small hotel stay for up to a month, drawn by its combination of excellent value and warm hospitality. This European-style guesthouse caters to travelers looking for more of the area's culture. You won't find bars, pools, or loud parties; you will find excellent service and impeccable accommodations. Rooms face the plant-filled interior courtyard, dotted with groupings of wrought-iron chairs and tables. Each room has slightly different appointments and amenities, but all have white tile floors and rustic wood furnishings. Some rooms have kitchenettes, and there's also a common kitchen area with purified water and a cooler for stocking your own supplies. There is a public phone in the entranceway, and the staff can arrange for a cellular phone in your room on request. A game and TV room has a large-screen cable TV, a library stocked with books on Mexican culture, backgammon, cards, and board games. The hotel offers special packages with lodging and Spanish lessons.

Av. Bonampak 51 and Cereza, SM2A, Centro, 77500 Cancún, Q. Roo. ✆ **998/884-3500.** Fax 998/884-3540. www.cancun-suites.com. 12 units. $56 double. Ask for discounts for longer stays. AE, MC, V. **Amenities:** Small restaurant (breakfast and dinner). *In room:* A/C, safe.

**Hotel Antillano** A quiet and very clean choice, the Antillano is close to the Ciudad Cancún bus terminal. Rooms overlook Avenida Tulum, the side streets, or the interior lawn and pool. Pool-view rooms are most desirable because they are quietest. The newly remodeled rooms feature coordinated furnishings, one or two double beds, a sink area separate from the bathroom, and red-tile floors. Guests have the use of the hotel's beach club on the island. To find the Antillano from Tulum, walk west on Claveles a half block; it's opposite the Restaurant Rosa Mexicana.

Av. Claveles 1 (corner with Av. Tulum), 77500 Cancún, Q. Roo. ✆ **998/884-1532.** Fax 998/884-1878. www.hotelantillano.com. 48 units. High season $70 double. Low season $61 double. AE, MC, V. Street parking. **Amenities:** Small bar; travel agency; babysitting. *In room:* A/C, TV.

**Hotel Hacienda Cancún** *Value* This extremely pleasing little hotel is a great value. The façade has been remodeled to look like a hacienda, and all rooms were refurbished in 2000, with new floors and rustic Mexican furnishings. The guest rooms are very comfortable; all have two double beds, but no views. There's a nice small pool and cafe under a shaded *palapa* in the back. To find it from Avenida Yaxchilán, turn west on Sunyaxchen; it's on your right next to the Hotel Caribe International, opposite 100% Natural. Parking is on the street

Sunyaxchen 39-40, 77500 Cancún, Q. Roo. ✆ **998/884-3672.** Fax 998/884-1208. hhda@cancun.com.mx. 35 units. High season $45 double. Low season $38 double. MC, V. Street parking. **Amenities:** Restaurant; pool. *In room:* A/C, TV, safe.

**Hotel Margaritas** ★ *Value* Located in downtown Cancún, this four-story hotel (with elevator) is comfortable and unpretentious, offering one of the best values in Cancún. The pleasantly decorated rooms, with white tile floors and small balconies, are exceptionally clean and bright. Lounge chairs surround the attractive pool, which has a wading section for children. The hotel offers complimentary safes at the front desk. New air conditioners were installed last year.

Av. Yaxchilán 41, SM22, Centro, 77500 Cancún, Q. Roo. ✆ **998/884-9333** or 01-800/711-1531. Fax 998/884-1324. 100 units. High season $95 double. Low season $78 double. AE, MC, V. **Amenities:** Restaurant; pool; travel agency; medical service; money exchange; room service; babysitting. *In room:* A/C, TV.

**Hotel Parador** The conveniently located three-story Parador is one of the most popular downtown hotels. Recently remodeled guest rooms are arranged around two long, narrow garden courtyards leading back to a pool (with a separate children's pool) and grassy sunning area. The rooms are modern, each with two double beds and a shower. Guests can help themselves to bottled drinking water in the hall. The hotel is next to Pop's restaurant, almost at the corner of Uxmal.

Av. Tulum 26, 77500 Cancún, Q. Roo. ✆ **998/884-1043** or 998/884-1310. Fax 998/884-9712. 66 units. High season $73 double. Low season $50 double. Ask about promotional rates. MC, V. Limited street parking. **Amenities:** Restaurant and bar; pool. *In room:* A/C, TV.

## 3 Where to Dine

The restaurant scene in Cancún is dominated by U.S.-based franchise chains—which really need no introduction. These include Hard Rock Cafe, Planet Hollywood, Rainforest Cafe, Tony Roma's, TGI Fridays, Ruth's Chris Steak House, and the gamut of fast-food burger places. The establishments listed here are locally owned, one-of-a-kind restaurants or exceptional selections at area hotels. Many schedule live music. Unless otherwise indicated, parking is free.

One unique way to combine dinner with sightseeing is aboard the **Lobster Dinner Cruise** (✆ **998/849-4621**). Cruising around the tranquil, turquoise waters of the lagoon, passengers feast on lobster dinners accompanied by wine. Cost is $69 per person. There are two daily departures from the Royal Mayan

Marina: A sunset cruise leaves at 4pm during the winter and 5pm during the summer; a moonlight cruise leaves at 7pm winter, 8pm summer.

## CANCUN ISLAND

### VERY EXPENSIVE

**Aioli** ★★★ FRENCH For the quality and originality of the cuisine, coupled with excellent service, this is my top pick for the best fine-dining value in Cancún. The Provençal—but definitely not provincial—Aioli offers simply exquisite French and Mediterranean gourmet specialties in a warm and cozy country French setting. Though it offers perhaps the best breakfast buffet in Cancún (for $16), most visitors outside the hotel come here in the evening, when low lighting and superb service make it a top choice for a romantic dinner. Starters include a variety of risottos, as well as a Caesar salad with pan-seared scallops. A specialty is duck breast served in a honey and lavender sauce. Equally scrumptious is rack of lamb, prepared in Moroccan style and served with couscous. Pan-seared grouper is topped with a paste of black olives, crushed potato, and tomato, and bouillabaisse contains an exceptional array of seafood. Desserts are decadent, in true French style; the signature "Fifth Element" is a sinfully delicious temptation rich with chocolate.

In Le Méridien Hotel, Retorno del Rey Km 14. ✆ **998/881-2260.** www.meridiencancun.com.mx. Reservations required. Main courses $22–$36. AE, DC, MC, V. Daily 6:30am–11pm.

**Club Grill** ★★★ INTERNATIONAL This is the place for that truly special night out. Cancún's most elegant and stylish restaurant is also among its most delicious. Even rival restaurateurs give it an envious thumbs up. The gracious service starts as you enter the anteroom, with its comfortable couches and chairs and selection of fine tequilas and Cuban cigars. It continues into a candlelit dining room with shimmering silver and crystal. Elegant plates of peppered scallops, truffles, and potatoes in tequila sauce; grilled lamb; or mixed grill arrive at a leisurely pace. The restaurant has smoking and no-smoking sections. A band plays romantic music for dancing from 8pm on. A dress code is enforced: no sandals or tennis shoes, and men must wear long pants.

In the Ritz-Carlton Hotel, Km 13.5 Blvd. Kukulkán. ✆ **998/885-0808.** Reservations required. Main courses $30–$40. AE, DC, MC, V. Tues–Sun 7–11pm.

**The Plantation House** ★ CARIBBEAN/FRENCH This casually elegant, pale-yellow-and-blue clapboard restaurant overlooking Nichupté lagoon takes you back to the time when the Caribbean first experienced European tastes and culinary talents. The decor combines island-style colonial charm with elegant touches of wood and crystal. For starters, try the signature poached shrimp with lemon juice and olive oil, or creamy crabmeat soup. Move on to the main event, which may consist of classic veal Wellington in puff pastry with duck paté, fish filet crusted in spices and herbs and topped with vanilla sauce, or lobster *medaillons* in mango sauce. The service is excellent, but the food is only mediocre, especially considering the price. Flambéed desserts are a specialty, and the Plantation House has one of the most extensive wine lists in town. It's generally quite crowded, which makes it a bit loud for a truly romantic evening.

Km 10.5 Paseo Kukulkán, Zona Hotelera, 77500, Cancún, Q. Roo. ✆ **998/883-1433** or 998/883-2120. Reservations recommended. Main courses $13–$35. AE, MC, V. Daily 5pm–12:30am.

### EXPENSIVE

**Captain's Cove** ★ INTERNATIONAL/SEAFOOD Though it sits almost at the end of Paseo Kukulkán, far from everything, the Captain's Cove continues to pack in customers with its consistent value. Diners sit on several dining levels, facing big open windows overlooking the lagoon and Royal Yacht Club Marina. For breakfast there's an all-you-can-eat buffet. Main courses of steak and seafood are the norm at lunch and dinner, and there's a children's menu. For dessert there are flaming coffees, crêpes, and Key lime pie. The restaurant is on the lagoon side, opposite the Omni Hotel.

Km 15 Paseo Kukulkán. ✆ **998/885-0016.** Main courses $16–$30; breakfast buffet $11. AE, MC, V. Daily 7am–11pm.

**La Dolce Vita** ★★ ITALIAN/SEAFOOD Casually elegant La Dolce Vita is known as Cancún's favorite Italian restaurant. Appetizers include paté of quail liver and carpaccio in vinaigrette, and mushrooms Provençal. The chef specializes in homemade pastas combined with fresh seafood. You can order green tagliolini with lobster *medaillons,* linguine with clams or seafood, or rigatoni Mexican-style (with *chorizo,* mushrooms, and chives) as a main course, or as an appetizer for half price. Other main courses include veal with morels, fresh salmon with cream sauce, spinach linguini with *medaillons* of lobster and shrimp in white-wine sauce, and fresh fish in a variety of sauces. New choices include vegetarian lasagna and grilled whole lobster. You have a choice of dining in air-conditioned comfort or on an open-air terrace with a view of the lagoon. Live jazz plays from 7 to 11:30pm Monday to Saturday.

Km 14.6 Av. Kukulkán, on the lagoon, opposite the Marriott Casamagna. ✆ **998/885-0150** or 998/885-0161. Fax 998/85-05-90. www.cancun.com/dining/dolce. Reservations required for dinner. Main courses $12–$33. AE, MC, V. Daily noon–midnight.

**La Fisheria** ★ *Kids* SEAFOOD If you're at the mall shopping, this is your best bet. Patrons find a lot to choose from at this restaurant overlooking Bulevard Kukulkán and the lagoon. The expansive menu includes shark fingers with jalapeño dip, grouper fillet stuffed with seafood in lobster sauce, Acapulco-style *ceviche* (in tomato sauce), New England clam chowder, steamed mussels, grilled red snapper with pasta—you get the idea. The menu changes daily, but there's always *tikin xik,* that great Yucatecan grilled fish marinated in *achiote* sauce. For those not inclined toward seafood, a pizza from the wood-burning oven, or perhaps a grilled chicken or beef dish, might do. La Fisheria has a nonsmoking section.

Plaza Caracol shopping center, 2nd floor. ✆ **998/883-1395.** Main courses $7–$30. AE, MC, V. Daily 11am–midnight.

**Lorenzillo's** ★★★ *Kids* SEAFOOD This festive, friendly restaurant is a personal favorite—I never miss a lobster stop here when I'm in Cancún. Live lobster is the overwhelming favorite, and part of the appeal is selecting your dinner out of the giant lobster tank. Lorenzillo's sits on the lagoon under a giant *palapa* roof. A dock leads down to the main dining area, and when that's packed (which is often), a wharf-side bar handles the overflow. In addition to lobster—which comes grilled, steamed, or stuffed—good bets are shrimp stuffed with cheese and wrapped in bacon, the Admiral's filet coated in toasted almonds and light mustard sauce, and seafood-stuffed squid. Desserts include the tempting "Martinique": Belgian chocolate with hazelnuts, almonds, and pecans, served with vanilla ice cream. A new sunset pier offers a lighter menu of cold seafood, sandwiches, and salads. Children are very welcome.

Km 10.5 Paseo Kukulkán. ✆ **998/883-1254.** www.lorenzillos.com.mx. Reservations recommended. Main courses $8–$50. AE, MC, V. Daily noon–midnight. Valet parking available.

**Mango Tango** ★★ INTERNATIONAL The beauty of dining here is that you can stay and enjoy a hot nightspot. Mango Tango has made a name for itself with sizzling floor shows and live reggae music (see "Cancún After Dark," later in this chapter), but its kitchen deserves attention as well. Try the peel-your-own shrimp, Argentine-style grilled meat with *chimichurri* sauce, and other grilled specialties. Mango Tango Salad is shrimp, chicken, avocado, red onion, tomato, and mushrooms served on mango slices. Entrees include rice with seafood and fried bananas. Creole gumbo comes with lobster, shrimp, and squid, and a coconut-and-mango cake is a suitable finish to the meal.

Km 14.2 Paseo Kukulkán, opposite the Ritz-Carlton Hotel. ✆ **998/885-0303.** Reservations recommended. Main courses $12–$57; dinner show $40–$55. AE, MC, V. Daily 2pm–2am.

**María Bonita** ★ Kids REGIONAL/MEXICAN/NOUVELLE MEXICAN In a stylish setting overlooking the water, María Bonita captures the essence of the country through its music and food. Prices are higher and the flavors more institutionalized than at traditional Mexican restaurants in Ciudad Cancún, but this is a good choice for the Hotel Zone. There are three sections: **La Cantina Jalisco,** with an open, colorful Mexican kitchen and tequila bar (with more than 50 different tequilas); the **Salón Michoacán,** which features that state's cuisine; and the **Patio Oaxaca.** The menu also includes the best of Mexico's other cuisines, with a few international dishes. Prix-fixe dinners include appetizer, main course, and dessert. Trios, marimba and jarocho music, and the ever-enchanting mariachis serenade you while you dine. A nice starter is Mitla Salad, with slices of the renowned Oaxaca cheese dribbled with olive oil and coriander dressing. Wonderful stuffed chile La Doña—a mildly hot poblano pepper filled with lobster and *huitlacoche,* in a cream sauce—comes as an appetizer or a main course.

In the Hotel Camino Real, Punta Cancún (enter from the street). ✆ **998/848-7000,** ext. 8060 or 8061. Reservations recommended. Prix-fixe dinner $30–$45; main courses $17–$31. AE, DC, MC, V. Daily 6:30–11:45pm.

**Savio's** ★ ITALIAN Centrally located at the heart of the Hotel Zone, Savio's is a great place to stop for a quick meal or coffee. Its bar is always crowded with patrons sipping everything from cappuccino to imported beer. Repeat diners look forward to large fresh salads and rich, subtly herb-flavored Italian dishes. Ravioli stuffed with ricotta and spinach comes in delicious tomato sauce. Stylish, with black-and-white decor and tile floors, it has two levels and faces Paseo Kukulkán through two stories of awning-shaded windows.

Plaza Caracol. ✆ and fax **998/883-2085.** Main courses $10–$30. AE, MC, V. Daily 10am–midnight.

## CANCUN CITY

### EXPENSIVE

**La Habichuela** ★ GOURMET SEAFOOD/CARIBBEAN/MEXICAN In a garden setting with soft music playing in the background, this restaurant is ideal for a romantic evening. For an all-out culinary adventure, try *habichuela* (string bean) soup; shrimp in any number of sauces, including Jamaican tamarind, tequila, or ginger-and-mushroom; and Maya coffee with *xtabentun* (a strong, sweet, anise-based liqueur). Grilled seafood and steaks are excellent, but this is a good place to try a Mexican specialty such as *enchiladas suizas* or *tampiqueña*-style beef (thinly sliced, marinated, and grilled). For something totally divine, try *Cocobichuela,* which is lobster and shrimp in curry sauce served in a coconut shell and topped with fruit.

Margaritas 25. ✆ **998/884-3158.** habichuela@infosel.net.mx. Reservations recommended in high season. Main courses $12–$35. AE, MC, V. Daily noon–midnight.

**Périco's** ★★★ MEXICAN/SEAFOOD/STEAK Périco's has colorful murals that almost dance off the walls, a bar area with saddles for barstools, colorful leather tables and chairs, and accommodating waiters; it's always booming and festive. The extensive menu offers well-prepared steak, seafood, and traditional Mexican dishes for reasonable rates (except for lobster). This is a place not only to eat and drink, but also to let loose and join in the fun, so don't be surprised if everybody drops their forks and dons huge sombreros to shimmy and snake in a conga dance around the dining room. It's fun whether or not you join in, but it's definitely not the place for a romantic evening alone. There's marimba music from 7:30 to 9:30pm, and mariachis from 9:30pm to midnight. This is a popular spot, so expect a crowd.

Yaxchilán 61. ✆ **998/884-3152.** Reservations recommended. Main courses $11–$25. AE, MC, V. Daily 1pm–1am.

## MODERATE

**Restaurant El Pescador** ★ SEAFOOD Locals all seem to agree: This is the best spot for fresh seafood in Cancún. There's often a line here for the well-prepared fresh seafood served on a street-side patio and in an upstairs space overlooking Tulipanes. Feast on shrimp cocktail, conch, octopus, *camarones à la criolla* (Creole-style shrimp), charcoal-broiled lobster, and stone crabs. *Zarzuela* is a combination seafood plate cooked in white wine and garlic. There's a Mexican specialty menu as well. Another branch, **La Mesa del Pescador,** is in the Plaza Kukulkán on Cancún Island and keeps the same hours, but it's more expensive.

Tulipanes 28, off Av. Tulum. ✆ **998/884-2673.** Fax 998/884-3639. Main courses $10–$55; Mexican plates $7–$12. AE, MC, V. Daily 11am–11pm.

**Restaurant Rosa Mexicano** MEXICAN HAUTE This beautiful little place has candlelit tables and a plant-filled patio in back, and is almost always packed. Colorful paper banners and piñatas hang from the ceiling, efficient waiters wear bow ties and cummerbunds that match the Mexican flag, and a trio plays romantic Mexican music nightly. The menu features "refined" Mexican specialties. Try *pollo almendro* (chicken covered in cream sauce and sprinkled with ground almonds), or pork baked in a banana leaf with a sauce of oranges, lime, ancho chile, and garlic. Steak *tampiqueño* is a huge platter that comes with guacamole salad, quesadillas, beans, salad, and rice.

Claveles 4. ✆ **998/884-6313.** Fax 998/884-2371. Reservations recommended for parties of 6 or more. Main courses $8–$15; lobster $30. AE, MC, V. Daily 5–11pm.

## INEXPENSIVE

**Pizza Rolandi** *Kids* ITALIAN This is an institution in Cancún, and the Rolandi name is synonymous with dining in both Cancún and neighboring Isla Mujeres. Pizza Rolandi and its branch in Isla (see chapter 13) have become standards for dependably good casual fare. At this shaded outdoor patio restaurant, you can choose from almost two dozen wood-oven pizzas and a full selection of spaghetti, calzones, Italian-style chicken and beef, and desserts. There's a full bar as well.

Cobá 12. ✆ **998/884-4047.** Fax 998/884-3994. www.rolandi.com. Pasta $7–$12; pizza and main courses $7–$17. AE, MC, V. Daily 12:30pm–midnight.

**Restaurant Los Almendros** ★ YUCATECAN To steep yourself in Yucatecan cuisine and music, head directly to this large, colorful restaurant opposite the bullring. Readers have written to say they ate here almost exclusively because the food and service are good; the illustrated menu, with color pictures of dishes, makes ordering easy. Regional specialties include lime soup, *poc chuc* (marinated, barbecue-style pork), chicken or pork *pibil* (sweet and spicy shredded meat), and such appetizers as *panuchos* (soft fried tortillas with refried beans and shredded turkey or pork *pibil*). The *combinado* Yucateco is a sampler of four typical main courses: chicken, *poc chuc,* sausage, and *escabeche* (onions marinated in vinegar and sour-orange sauce).

Av. Bonampak and Sayil. ✆ **998/887-1332.** Main courses $6–$10. AE, MC, V. Daily 11am–10pm.

**Restaurant Santa María** MEXICAN The open-air Santa María is a clean, gaily decked-out place to sample authentic Mexican food. It's cool and breezy, with a patio dining area that's open on two sides, and furnished with leather tables and chairs covered in multicolored cloths. A bowl of *frijoles de olla* (beans cooked in a clay pot) and an order of beefsteak tacos will fill you up for a low price. You may want to try tortilla soup or enchiladas, or go for one of the specialty grilled U.S.–cut steaks, fajitas, ribs, or grilled seafood, all of which arrive with a baked potato. New offerings include traditional Yucatecan dishes.

Azucenas at Parque Palapas. ✆ **998/884-3158.** Fax 998/884-0940. Main courses $3.50–$9; tacos 75¢–$5. AE, MC, V. Daily 5pm–1am.

**Stefano's** ITALIAN/PIZZA/PASTA Stefano's began primarily as a local restaurant, serving Italian food with a few Mexican accents, and now it's equally popular with tourists. On the menu you'll find ravioli stuffed with *huitlacoche;* rigatoni in tequila sauce; and seafood with chile peppers. Pizza options include the Stefano special, with fresh tomato, cheese, and pesto, and three-cheese-and-shrimp. Stefano's offers vegetarian pizza, calzones stuffed with spinach, mozzarella, and tomato sauce, and other options for non-meat-eaters. For dessert, ricotta strudel is something out of the ordinary. There are lots of coffees and mixed drinks, plus a wine list.

Bonampak 177. ✆ **998/887-9964.** Main courses $6–$9; pizza $5.75–$9.75. AE, MC, V. Daily noon–1am.

### COFFEE & PASTRIES

**Pastelería Italiana** ★ COFFEE/PASTRIES/ICE CREAM More a casual neighborhood coffeehouse than a place aimed at tourists, this shady little spot has been doing business since 1977. A white awning covers the small outdoor, plant-filled table area. Inside are refrigerated cases of tarts and scrumptious-looking cakes, ready to be carried away whole or by the piece. The coffeehouse is in the same block as Périco's.

Av. Yaxchilán 67-D (between Maraño and Chiabal), SM 25, near Sunyaxchen. ✆ **998/884-0796.** Pastries $1.75–$2.25; ice cream $2; coffee $1–$2. AE. Mon–Sat 9am–11pm; Sun 1–9pm.

## 4 Beaches, Watersports & Boat Tours

**THE BEACHES** Big hotels dominate the best stretches of beach. All of Mexico's beaches are public property, so you can use the beach of any hotel by walking through the lobby or directly onto the sand. Be especially careful on beaches fronting the open Caribbean, where the undertow can be quite strong. By contrast, the waters of Mujeres Bay (Bahía de Mujeres), at the north end of the island, are usually calm and ideal for swimming. Get to know Cancún's water-safety pennant system, and make sure to check the flag at any beach or hotel before entering the water. Here's how it goes:

- **White** Excellent
- **Green** Normal conditions (safe)
- **Yellow** Changeable, uncertain (use caution)
- **Black or red** Unsafe; use the swimming pool instead!

In the Caribbean, storms can arrive and conditions can change from safe to unsafe in a matter of minutes, so be alert: If you see dark clouds heading your way, make for the shore and wait until the storm passes.

**Playa Tortuga** (Turtle Beach), **Playa Langosta** (Lobster Beach), **Playa Linda** (Pretty Beach), and **Playa Las Perlas** (Beach of the Pearls) are some of the public beaches. At most beaches, you can rent a sailboard and take lessons, ride a parasail, or partake in a variety of watersports. There's a small but beautiful portion of public beach on **Playa Caracol,** by the Xcaret Terminal. It faces the calm waters of Bahía de Mujeres and, for that reason, is preferable to those facing the Caribbean.

**WATERSPORTS** Many beachside hotels offer watersports concessions that rent rubber rafts, kayaks, and snorkeling equipment. On the calm Nichupté Lagoon are outlets for renting **sailboats, jet skis, windsurfers,** and **water skis.** Prices vary and are often negotiable, so check around.

For windsurfing, go to the Playa Tortuga public beach, where there's a **Windsurfing School** (no phone) with equipment for rent.

**DEEP-SEA FISHING** You can arrange a day of **deep-sea fishing** at one of the numerous piers or travel agencies for around $200 to $360 for 4 hours, $420 for 6 hours, and $520 for 8 hours for up to four people. Marinas will sometimes assist in putting together a group. Charters include a captain, a first mate, bait, gear, and beverages. Rates are lower if you depart from Isla Mujeres or from Cozumel Island—and frankly, the fishing is better closer to these departure points.

**SNORKELING & SCUBA** Known for its shallow reefs, dazzling color, and diversity of life, Cancún is one of the best places in the world for beginning **scuba diving.** Punta Nizuc is the northern tip of the Great Mesoamerican Reef (Gran Arrecife Maya), the largest reef in the Western Hemisphere and one of the largest in the world. In addition to the sea life along this reef system, several sunken boats add a variety of dive options. Inland, a series of caverns and *cenotes* (wellsprings) are fascinating venues for the more experienced diver. Drift diving is the norm here, with popular dives going to the reefs at **El Garrafón** and the **Cave of the Sleeping Sharks**—although be aware that the famed "sleeping sharks" have long since departed, driven off by too many people watching them snooze.

A variety of hotels offer resort courses that teach the basics of diving—enough to make shallow dives and slowly ease your way into this underwater world of unimaginable beauty. Scuba trips run around $64 for two-tank dives at nearby reefs, and $100 and up for locations farther out. **Scuba Cancún,** Km 5 Paseo Kukulkán (✆ **998/849-7508** or 998/849-4736; www.scubacancun.com.mx), on the lagoon side, offers a 4-hour resort course for $64. Phone reservations are available from 7:30 to 10:30pm using the fax line, 998/884-2336. Full certification takes 4 to 5 days and costs around $368. Scuba Cancún is open daily from 9am to 6pm, and accepts major credit cards. The largest operator is **Aquaworld,** located across from the Meliá Cancún at Km 15.2 Paseo Kukulkán (✆ **998/885-2288** or 998/848-8300; www.aquaworld.com.mx), offers resort courses and diving from a manmade anchored dive platform, Paradise Island. Aquaworld has the

**Sub See Explorer,** a submarine-style boat with picture windows that hang beneath the surface. The boat doesn't submerge—it's an updated version of a glass-bottom-boat concept—but it does provide nondivers with a look at life beneath the sea. This outfit is open 24 hours a day and accepts all major credit cards.

Scuba Cancún also offers diving trips, in good weather only, to 20 nearby reefs, including Cuevones (9m/30 ft.) and the open ocean (9–18m/30–60 ft.). The average dive is around 11m (35 ft.). One-tank dives cost $55, and two-tank dives cost $64. Discounts apply if you bring your own equipment. Dives usually start around 9am and return by 2:15pm. Snorkeling trips cost $35 and leave every afternoon after 2pm for shallow reefs about a 20-minute boat ride away.

Besides **snorkeling** at **El Garrafón National Park** (see "Boating Excursions," below), travel agencies offer an all-day excursion to the natural wildlife habitat of **Isla Contoy,** which usually includes time for snorkeling. This island, 90 minutes past Isla Mujeres, is a major nesting area for birds and a treat for nature lovers. Only two boats hold permits for excursions there, which depart at 9am and return by 5pm. The price ($70) includes drinks and snorkeling equipment.

**JET SKI TOURS** Several companies offer the popular **Jungle Cruise,** which takes you by jet ski or WaveRunner through Cancún's lagoon and mangrove estuaries out into the Caribbean Sea and a shallow reef. The excursion runs about 2½ hours (you drive your own watercraft) and costs $40 to $55, including snorkeling and beverages. Some of the motorized miniboats seat one person behind the other—meaning that the person in back gets a great view of the driver's head; others seat you side by side.

The operators and names of boats offering excursions change often. The popular **Aquaworld,** Km 15.2 Paseo Kukulkán (✆ **998/885-2288**), calls its trip the Jungle Tour and charges $55 for the 2½-hour excursion, which includes 45 minutes of snorkeling time. It even gives you a free snorkel, but has the less-desirable seating configuration of one behind the other. Departures are at 9am, noon, and 2:30pm daily. To find out what's available when you're there, check with a local travel agent or hotel tour desk; you should find a wide range of options.

## BOATING EXCURSIONS

**ISLA MUJERES** The island of **Isla Mujeres,** just 13km (8 miles) offshore, is one of the most pleasant day trips from Cancún. At one end is **El Garrafón National Park,** which is excellent for snorkeling. At the other end is a captivating village with small shops, restaurants, and hotels, and **Playa Norte,** the island's best beach. If you're looking for relaxation and can spare the time, it's worth several days. For complete information about the island, see chapter 13.

There are four ways to get there: **public ferry** from Puerto Juárez, which takes between 15 and 45 minutes; **shuttle boat** from Playa Linda or Playa Tortuga—an hour-long ride, with irregular service; **Watertaxi** (more expensive, but faster), next to the Xcaret Terminal; and a daylong **pleasure-boat trips,** most of which leave from the Playa Linda pier.

The inexpensive Puerto Juárez **public ferries** ★ are just a few kilometers from downtown Cancún. From Cancún City, take the Ruta 8 bus on Avenida Tulum to Puerto Juárez. The fast ferry (20 min.) costs $4 per person. Departures are every half hour, starting between 6 and 7am and ending between 9 and 11pm. The slow boat (45–60 min.) is a bargain at about $2. It departs every 2 hours, or less frequently depending on demand. Upon arrival, the ferry docks in downtown Isla Mujeres near all the shops, restaurants, hotels, and Norte beach. You'll need a taxi to get to El Garrafón Park, at the other end of the island. You can stay as long as you like on the island (even overnight) and return by ferry, but be sure to double-check the time of the last returning ferry—the hours are clearly posted.

**Pleasure-boat cruises** to Isla Mujeres are a favorite pastime. Modern motor yachts, catamarans, trimarans, and even old-time sloops—more than 25 boats a day—take swimmers, sun lovers, snorkelers, and shoppers out into the translucent waters. Some tours include a snorkeling stop at El Garrafón, lunch on the beach, and a short time for shopping in downtown Isla Mujeres. Most leave at 9:30 or 10am, last about 5 or 6 hours, and include continental breakfast, lunch, and rental of snorkel gear. Others, particularly sunset and night cruises, go to beaches away from town for pseudo-pirate shows and include a lobster dinner or Mexican buffet. If you want to actually see Isla Mujeres, go on a morning cruise, or go on your own using the public ferry from Puerto Juárez. Prices for the day cruises run around $55 per person.

In the El Garrafón area is a theme park, **El Garrafón Natural Park** ★★, which is under the same management as Xcaret (✆ **998/883-3143;** see "Eco-Theme Parks and Reserves," later). The basic entrance fee of $25 includes access to the reef and a museum, as well as use of kayaks, inner tubes, life vests, the pool, hammocks, and public facilities and showers. Snorkel gear and lockers can be rented for an extra charge. There are also nature trails as well as several restaurants on-site. An all-inclusive option is available for $50, which includes dining on whatever you choose at any of the restaurants, plus unlimited domestic drinks and use of snorkel gear, locker, and towel. El Garrafón also has full dive facilities and gear rentals, plus an expansive gift shop.

Other excursions go to the **reefs** in glass-bottom boats, so you can have a near-scuba-diving experience and see many colorful fish. However, the reefs are some distance from the shore and are impossible to reach on windy days with choppy seas. They've also suffered from overvisitation, and their condition is far from pristine. The glass-bottomed **Nautibus** (✆ **998/883-3732** or 998/883-2119) has been around for years. Trips begin at 9:30 and 11am, 12:30 and 2pm from the El Embarcadero Pier. The journey to the Chitale coral reef to see colorful fish takes about 1 hour and 20 minutes, with about 50 minutes of transit time back and forth. Tickets cost $35 for adults, $15.50 for children 6 to 12. Nautibus's **Atlantis Submarine** takes you close to the aquatic action. Departures vary, depending on weather conditions. Prices range from $44 to $65, depending on the length of the trip. Reservations are recommended for both. Other boat excursions visit **Isla Contoy,** a **national bird sanctuary** that's well worth the time. If you are planning to spend time in Isla Mujeres, the Contoy trip is easier and more pleasurable to take from there.

---

*Tips* **An All-Terrain Tour**

**Marina Neptuno** (no phone; www.cancunmermaid.com) in Cancún offers all-terrain vehicle (ATV) jungle tours for $38.50 per person. The 4-hour ATV tours travel through the jungles of Cancún and emerge on the beaches of the Riviera Maya. The tour includes equipment, instruction, the services of a tour guide, and bottled water; it departs daily at 8am and 1:30pm; the company picks you up at your hotel. Another ATV option is Rancho Loma Bonita; see "Horseback Riding," below.

---

## 5 Outdoor Activities & Attractions

### OUTDOOR ACTIVITIES

**DOLPHIN SWIMS** On Isla Mujeres, you have the opportunity to swim with dolphins at **Dolphin Discovery** ★ (© **998/849-4757;** fax 998/849-4758; www.dolphindiscovery.com). Each session lasts 1 hour, with an educational introduction followed by 30 minutes of swim time. The price is $119 (MC, V), with transportation to Isla Mujeres an additional $15. Advance reservations are required. Assigned swimming times are 9am, 11am, 1pm, or 3pm, and you must arrive 1 hour before your scheduled swim time. In Cancún, the **Parque Nizuc** (© **998/881-3030**) marine park offers guests a chance to swim with dolphins and view them in their dolphin aquarium, Atlántida. The price of the dolphin swim ($132) includes admission to the park. It's a fun place for a family to spend the day, with its numerous pools, waterslides, and rides. A new attraction lets visitors snorkel with manta rays, tropical fish, and tame sharks. It's at the southern end of Cancún, between the airport and the Hotel Zone. Admission is $31 for adults, $24 for children 3 to 11 (AE, MC, V). Open daily 10am to 5:30pm.

La Isla Shopping Center, Blvd. Kukulkán, Km 12.5, also has an **Interactive Aquarium** (© **998/883-0413,** 998/883-0436, or 998/883-5077), with dolphin swims and the chance to feed a shark. Prices for interactive encounters and swims start at $110.

**GOLF & TENNIS** The 18-hole **Pok-Ta-Pok Club,** or Club de Golf Cancún (© **998/883-0871;** poktapok@sybcom.com), a Robert Trent Jones Sr. design, is on the northern leg of the island. Greens fees run $120 per 18 holes, with clubs renting for $26 and shoes for $15. Hiring a caddy costs $22 per bag. The club is open daily and accepts American Express, MasterCard, and Visa. The club also has tennis courts.

The **Melía Cancún** (© **998/881-1100**) has a 9-hole executive course; the fee is $35. The club is open daily from 8am to 4pm and accepts American Express, MasterCard, and Visa.

The **Hilton Cancún Golf & Beach Resort** (© **998/881-8016;** fax 998/881-8084) has a championship 18-hole, par-72 course designed around the Ruinas Del Rey. Greens fees for the public are $88 for 9 holes, $121 for 18 holes; Hilton Cancún guests $77 and $99, respectively, which includes a golf cart. Golf clubs and shoes are available for rent. The club is open daily from 6am to 6pm.

The **Mini Golf Palace** (© **998/885-0533**), Km 14.5 Paseo Kukulkán, offers a more compact version of the game for all ages. It's open 11am to 10pm daily.

**HORSEBACK RIDING** **Rancho Loma Bonita** (© **998/887-5465** or 998/887-5423), about 30 minutes south of town, is Cancún's most popular option for horseback riding. Five-hour packages include 2 hours of riding through the mangrove swamp to the beach, where you have time to swim and relax. The tour costs $67 for adults, $61 for children 6 to 12. The ranch also offers a four-wheel ATV ride on the same route as the horseback tour. It costs $66 per person if you want to ride on your own, $50 if you double up. Prices for both tours include transportation to the ranch, riding, soft drinks, and lunch, plus a guide and insurance. Visa is accepted, but cash is preferred.

**IN-LINE SKATING** You can rent in-line skates outside Plaza Las Glorias Hotel and in front of Playa Caracol, where the valet parking is located. The jogging track that runs parallel to Paseo Kukulkán along the Hotel Zone is well maintained and safe.

### ATTRACTIONS

**A MUSEUM** To the right side of the entrance to the Cancún Convention Center is the **Museo Arqueológico de Cancún** (✆ **998/883-0305;** mac98@qroo1.telmex.net.mx), a small but interesting museum with relics from archaeological sites around the state. Admission is $3.50; free on Sunday and holidays. It's open Tuesday to Sunday from 9am to 7pm.

**BULLFIGHTS** Cancún has a small bullring (✆ **998/884-8372;** bull@prodigy. net.mx) near the northern (town) end of Paseo Kukulkán opposite the Restaurant Los Almendros. Bullfights take place every Wednesday at 3:30pm during the winter tourist season. There are usually four bulls; the spectacle begins with a folkloric dance exhibition, followed by a performance of the *charros* (Mexico's sombrero-wearing cowboys). Travel agencies in Cancún sell tickets: $35 for adults, free for children; seating is by general admission. American Express, MasterCard, and Visa are accepted.

## 6 Shopping

Despite the surrounding natural splendor, shopping has become a favorite activity. Cancún is known throughout Mexico for its diverse shops and festive malls catering to a large number of international tourists. Tourists arriving from the United States may find apparel more expensive in Cancún, but the selection is much broader than at other Mexican resorts. Numerous duty-free shops offer excellent value on European goods. The largest is **UltraFemme,** Avenida Tulum, Supermanzana 25 (✆ **998/884-1402** or 998/885-0804), specializing in imported cosmetics, perfumes, and fine jewelry and watches. The downtown Cancún location offers lower prices than branches in Plaza Caracol, Kukulkán Plaza, Plaza Mayafair, Flamingo Plaza, and the international airport.

Handcrafts and other *artesanía* works are more limited and more expensive in Cancún than in other regions of Mexico because they are not produced here. They are available, though; several **open-air crafts markets** are on Avenida Tulum in Cancún City and near the convention center in the Hotel Zone. One of the biggest is **Coral Negro,** Km 9.5 Paseo Kukulkán (✆ **998/883-0758;** fax 998/883-0758), open daily 7am to 11pm. A small restaurant inside, Xtabentun, serves Yucatecan food and pizza slices, and metamorphoses into a disco from 9pm to 11pm.

Cancún's main venues are the **malls**—not quite as grand as their U.S. counterparts, but close. All are air-conditioned, sleek, and sophisticated. Most are on Avenida Kukulkán between Km 7 and Km 12. They offer everything from fine crystal and silver to designer clothing and decorative objects can be found, along with numerous restaurants and clubs. Stores are generally open daily from 10am to 10pm, with clubs and restaurants remaining open much later. Here's a brief rundown of the malls and some shops.

The **Plaza Kukulkán** (✆ **998/885-2200;** www.kukulcanplaza.com) offers the largest selection—more than 300—of shops, restaurants, and entertainment. There's a branch of Banco Serfin; OK Maguey Cantina Grill; a theater with U.S. movies; an Internet access kiosk; Tikal, which sells Guatemalan textile clothing; several crafts stores; a liquor store; several bathing-suit specialty stores; record and tape outlets; a leather goods store (including shoes and sandals); and a store specializing in silver from Taxco. The Fashion Gallery features designer clothing. In the food court are a number of U.S. franchise restaurants, including Ruth's Chris Steak House, plus one featuring specialty coffee. For entertainment, there's a bowling alley, Q-Zar laser game pavilion, and video game arcade. There's also a large indoor parking garage. The mall is open daily from 10am to 10pm, until 11pm during high season. Assistance for those with disabilities is available upon request, and wheelchairs, strollers, and lockers are available at the information desk.

Planet Hollywood anchors the **Plaza Flamingo** (© **998/883-2945**), which also has branches of Bancrecer, Subway, and La Casa del Habano (Cuban cigars).

The long-standing **Plaza Caracol** (© **998/883-1038**) holds Cartier jewelry, Guess, Waterford Crystal, Señor Frog clothing, Samsonite luggage, Gucci, and La Fisheria restaurant.

**Maya Fair Plaza/Centro Comercial Maya Fair,** frequently called "Mayfair" (© **998/883-2801**), is the oldest mall. The lively center holds open-air restaurants and bars such as Tequila Sunrise, and several stores sell silver, leather, and crafts.

The entertainment-oriented **Forum by the Sea,** Km 9 Avenida Kukulkán (© **998/883-4425**), has shops including Tommy Hilfiger, Levi's, Diesel, Swatch, and Harley Davidson. Most people come here for the food and fun, choosing from Hard Rock Cafe, Coco Bongo, Rainforest Cafe, Beer Factory, Cambalache, Sushi-ito, Zandunga, and Santa Fe Beer Factory, plus an extensive food court. It's open daily 10am to midnight (bars remain open later).

The newest and most intriguing mall is the **La Isla Shopping Village,** Km 12.5 Paseo Kukulkán (© **998/883-5025;** www.cancunmalls.com), an open-air festival mall that looks like a small village. Walkways lined with shops and restaurants crisscross over little canals. It also has a "riverwalk" alongside the Nichupté Lagoon, and an interactive aquarium and dolphin swim facility. Shops include Zara clothing, Benetton, Guess, Swatch, H. Stern, UltraFemme, and the first **Warner Bros. Studio** store in Mexico. Dining choices include **Johnny Rockets, The Food Court** (actually an Anderson's restaurant), and the beautiful Mexican restaurant **La Casa de las Margaritas.** There's also a first-run movie theater, a video arcade, and several nightclubs, including **Max-O's** and **Alebrejes.** It's across from the Sheraton, on the lagoon side of the street.

## 7 Cancún After Dark

One of Cancún's main draws is its active nightlife. The hottest centers of action are the **Centro Comercial Maya Fair, Forum by the Sea,** and **La Isla Shopping Village.** Hotels also compete, with happy-hour entertainment and special drink prices to entice visitors and guests from other resorts. (Lobby-bar-hopping at sunset is one great way to plan next year's vacation.)

### THE CLUB & MUSIC SCENE

Clubbing in Cancún, still called *discoing,* is a favorite part of the vacation experience and can go on each night until the sun rises over that incredibly blue sea. Several big hotels have nightclubs (usually discos) or schedule live music in their lobby bars. At discos, expect to stand in long lines on weekends, pay a cover charge of $15 to $25 per person, and pay $5.50 to $8.50 for a drink. Some of the higher-priced discos include an open bar or live entertainment. The places listed in this section are air-conditioned and accept credit cards (AE, MC, V).

A great idea to get you started is the **Bar Crawl Tour** ★★ offered by American Express Travel Agency (© **998/881-4050;** fax 998/884-6942). For $49, you'll be taken by bus from bar to club—generally a range of four to five top choices—where you'll bypass any lines and spend about an hour. Entry to the clubs, one welcome drink at each, and transportation by air-conditioned bus is included, allowing you to get a great sampling of the best of Cancún's nightlife.

Numerous restaurants, such as **Carlos 'n' Charlie's, Planet Hollywood, Hard Rock Cafe, Señor Frog's, TGI Friday's,** and **Iguana Wana,** double as nighttime party spots, offering wild-ish fun at a fraction of the price of more costly discos.

The most refined and upscale of all Cancún's nightly gathering spots is the **Lobby Lounge** at the **Ritz-Carlton Hotel** ★ (✆ **998/885-0808**), with live dance music and a list of more than 120 premium tequilas for tasting or sipping.

**La Boom,** Km 3.5 Paseo Kukulkán (✆ **998/883-1152;** fax 998/883-1458; www.laboom.com.mx), has two sections: one side is a video bar, the other a bi-level disco with cranking music. Each night there's a special deal: no cover, free bar, ladies' night, bikini night, and others. Popular with early-20-somethings, it's open nightly from 10pm to 6am. A sound-and-light show begins at 11:30pm in the disco. The cover varies for the disco and the bar depending on the night—most nights women enter free, and men pay $10 to $20, which includes an open bar.

**Carlos 'n' Charlie's,** Km 4.5 Paseo Kukulkán (✆ **998/849-4052**), is a reliable place to find both good food and packed-frat-house entertainment in the evening. There's a dance floor; live music starts nightly around 8:30pm. A cover charge kicks in if you're not planning to eat. It's open daily from 11am to 2am.

With recorded music, **Carlos O'Brian's,** Tulum 107, SM 22 (✆ **998/884-1659**), is only slightly tamer than other Carlos Anderson restaurants and nightspots in town (Señor Frog and Carlos 'n' Charlie's). It's open daily from 9am to midnight.

**Christine's,** at the Hotel Krystal on the island (✆ **998/883-1793**), has been around for years. It has signature laser-light shows, infused oxygen, and large video screens, but has been overtaken by hipper clubs. The dress code forbids shorts or jeans. Open nightly at 9:30pm.

Maintaining its reputation as the hottest spot in town is **Coco Bongo** ★★★ in Forum by the Sea, Km 9.5 Paseo Kukulkán (✆ **998/883-5061;** www.cocobongo.com.mx). Its main appeal is that with no formal dance floor, you can dance anywhere you can find space—and that includes on the tables, on the bar, or even on the stage with the live band! This place can—and regularly does—pack in up to 3,000 people. You have to experience it to believe it. Despite its capacity, lines are long on weekends and in high season. The music alternates between Caribbean, salsa, techno, and classics from the 1970s and '80s. It draws a mixed crowd, but the young and hip dominate. Choose between a $12 cover or $25 with an open bar.

**Dady'O,** Km 9.5 Paseo Kukulkán (✆ **998/883-3333**), is a highly favored rave with frequent long lines. It opens nightly at 9:30pm and generally charges a cover of $15.

**Dady Rock Bar and Grill,** Km 9.5 Paseo Kukulkán (✆ **998/883-1626**), the offspring of Dady'O, opens early (7pm) and goes as long as any other nightspot, offering a new twist on entertainment with a combination of live bands and DJ-orchestrated music, along with an open bar, full meals, a buffet, and dancing.

**Hard Rock Cafe,** in Plaza Lagunas Mall and Forum by the Sea (✆ **998/881-8120** or 998/883-2024; www.hardrock.com), schedules a live band at 10:30pm Thursday through Tuesday night. At other times you get lively recorded music to munch by—the menu combines the most popular foods from American and Mexican cultures. It's open daily from 11am to 2am.

**Planet Hollywood,** Flamingo Shopping Center, Km 11 Paseo Kukulkán (© **998/885-3003;** www.planethollywood.com), is the still-popular brainchild of Sylvester Stallone, Bruce Willis, and Arnold Schwarzenegger. One of the last remaining branches of the chain, it's both a restaurant and a nighttime music and dance spot with mega-decibel live music. It's open daily from 11am to 2am.

### THE PERFORMING ARTS

Several hotels host **Mexican fiesta nights,** including a buffet dinner and a folkloric dance show; admission, including dinner, ranges from $35 to $50. In the Costa Blanca shopping center, **El Mexicano** restaurant (© **998/884-4207**) offers a tropical dinner show every night and has live music for dancing. The entertainment alternates each night, with *mariachis* playing off and on from 7 to 11pm and a folkloric show from 8 to 9:30pm. Cover charge is $5.

You can also get in the party mood at **Mango Tango** ★, Km 14, Paseo Kukulkán (© **998/885-0303**), a lagoon-side restaurant and dinner-show establishment opposite the Ritz-Carlton Hotel. Diners can choose from two levels, one nearer the music and the other overlooking it all. Music is loud and varied but mainly features reggae or salsa. The 80-minute dinner show begins at 8:30pm nightly and costs $55. If you're not dining but come just for the music and drinks, a $10 cover charge applies.

Tourists mingle with locals at the downtown **Parque de las Palapas** (the main park) for *Noches Caribeños,* which involves free live tropical music for anyone who wants to listen and dance. Performances begin at 7:30pm on Sundays, and sometimes there are performances on Fridays and Saturdays.

## 8 Day Trips: Archaeological Sites & Eco-Theme Parks

One of the best ways to spend a vacation day is exploring the nearby archeological ruins or an ecological theme park near Cancún. Within easy driving distance are historical and natural treasures unlike any you've likely encountered before. Cancún can be a perfect base for day or overnight trips, or the starting point for a longer exploration.

Organized day trips are popular and easy to book through any travel agent in town, or you can plan a journey on your own and travel by bus or rental car. **Greenline** (© **998/883-4545**) buses offer packages (*paquetes*) to popular nearby destinations. The package to **Chichén-Itzá** ($68) departs at 8:30am and includes the round-trip air-conditioned bus ride, a video of a current movie that plays during the 3-hour trip, entry to the ruins, 2 hours at the ruins, and lunch. The tour returns to Cancún by 7:30pm.

The Maya ruins to the south at **Tulum** or **Cobá** should be your first goal, and then perhaps the *caleta* (cove) of **Xel-Ha** or the ecological theme park **Xcaret.** If you're going south, consider staying a night or 2 on the island of **Cozumel** or at one of the budget resorts on the **Tulum coast** or **Punta Allen,** south of the Tulum ruins. **Isla Mujeres** is an easy day trip off mainland Cancún. Although I don't recommend it, by driving fast or catching the right buses you can go inland to **Chichén-Itzá,** explore the ruins, and return in a day, but it's much better to spend at least 2 days seeing Chichén-Itzá, Mérida, and Uxmal.

**More Info**

For more information on the destinations covered in this section, see chapters 13 and 14.

## ARCHAEOLOGICAL SITES

**TULUM** A popular excursion combines a visit to the ruins at Tulum with the ecological water park Xel-Ha (discussed below). **Ancient Tulum** ★★★ is a stunning site, and my personal favorite of all the ruins. (For another take on Tulum, see the box "Tulum: A Friendly Difference of Opinion," p. 579.)

A wall surrounds the site on three sides, which explains the name (*tulum* means fence, trench, or wall). Its ancient name is believed to have been *Záma,* a derivative of the Maya word for "morning" or "dawn," and sunrise at Tulum is certainly dramatic. The wall is believed to have been constructed after the original buildings, to protect the interior religious altars from a growing number of invaders. It is considered to have been principally a place of worship, but members of the upper classes later took up residence here. Between the two most dramatic structures—the Castle and the Temple of the Wind—lies Tulum Cove. A small inlet with a beach of fine, white sand, it was a point of departure for Maya trading vessels in ancient times. Today it's a playground for tourists, and you can enjoy a refreshing swim. Admission to the site without a tour is $2. parking costs $1, and use of video camera requires a $4 permit.

**RUINAS DEL REY** Cancún has its own **Maya ruins** (✆ **998/884-8073**)—a small site that's less impressive than the ruins at Tulum, Cobá, or Chichén-Itzá. Maya fishermen built the small ceremonial center and settlement very early in the history of Maya culture. It was then abandoned, to be resettled again near the end of the post-Classic period, not long before the arrival of the conquistadors. The platforms of numerous small temples are visible amid the banana plants, papayas, and wildflowers. The Hilton Cancún hotel golf course surrounds the ruins, which have a separate entrance for sightseers. You'll find the ruins about 21km (13 miles) from town, at the southern reach of the Zona Hotelera, almost to Punta Nizuc. Look for the Hilton hotel on the left (east) and the ruins on the right (west). Admission is $4.50; free on Sunday and holidays. It's open daily from 8am to 5pm.

## ECO-THEME PARKS AND RESERVES

The popularity of Xcaret and Xel-Ha has inspired entrepreneurs to ride the wave of interest in ecological and adventure theme parks. Be aware that "theme park" is the more pertinent part of the phrase. The newer parks of Aktun Chen and Tres Ríos are—so far—less commercial and more focused on nature than their predecessors. Included here are several true reserves, which have less in the way of facilities but offer an authentic encounter with the natural beauty of the region.

**AKTUN CHEN** ★ This park, consisting of a spectacular 5,000-year-old grotto and an abundance of wildlife, is the first above-the-ground cave system in the Yucatán to be open to the public. The name means "cave with an underground river inside," and the main cave (of three) is more than 600 yards long, with a magnificent vault. Discreet illumination and easy walking paths make visiting the caves comfortable, without appearing to alter them much from their natural state. The caves contain thousands of stalactites, stalagmites, and sculpted rock formations, along with a 40-foot-deep *cenote* with clear blue water. Aktun Chen was once underwater, and fossilized shells and fish embedded in the limestone are visible as you walk along the paths. Caves are an integral part of the region's geography and geology, and knowledgeable guides provide explanations of what you see and offer minihistory lessons in the Maya's association with these caves. Tours have no set times—guides are available to take you when you arrive—and the maximum group size is 20. Surrounding the caves are nature trails throughout the 988-acre park, where spottings of deer, spider monkeys, iguanas, and wild turkeys are common. A small informal restaurant and gift shop are also on-site.

It's easy to travel by yourself to Aktun Chen (✆ **998/892-0662** or 998/850-4190; www.aktunchen.com); from Cancún, go south along Highway 307, the road to Tulum. Just past the turn-off for Akumal, a sign on the right side of the highway indicates the turn-off to Aktun-Chen; from there it's a 3km (2-mile) drive west along a smooth but unpaved road. Travel time from Cancún is about an hour The park is open daily from 9am to 5pm; the last tour departs at 4pm. The entry fee of $17 for adults or $9 for children includes the services of a guide.

**EL EDEN RESERVA ECOLOGICA** Established in 1990, this is a privately owned 500,000-acre reserve dedicated to research for biological conservation in Mexico. It takes around 2 hours to reach the center of this reserve deep in the jungle, yet it's only 48km (30 miles) northwest of Cancún. It's intended as an overnight (or more) excursion for people who want to know more about the biological diversity of the peninsula.

Within the reserve, or near it, are marine grasslands, mangrove swamps, rain forests, savannas, wetlands, and sand dunes, as well as evidence of archaeological sites and at least 205 species of birds, plus orchids, bromeliads, and cacti. Among the local animals are the spider monkey, jaguar, cougar, deer, and ocelot. The "eco-scientific" tours include naturalist-led birding, animal tracking, stargazing, spotlight surveys for nocturnal wildlife, and exploration of *cenotes* and Maya ruins. Comfortable, basic accommodations are provided. Tours include transportation from Cancún, 1 or 2 nights of accommodation at La Savanna Research Station, meals, nightly cocktails, guided nature walks, and tours. The tours cost $235 to $380, depending on the length of stay, plus $95 per extra night. American Express is accepted. Contact **Ecocolors,** Camarón 32 SM 27 (✆ **998/884-3667;** fax 998/884-9580; www.cancun.com.mx), which specializes in ecologically oriented tours around the Cancún area.

**SIAN KA'AN BIOSPHERE RESERVE** ★ About 128km (80 miles) south of Cancún, this 1.3-million-acre area was set aside in 1986 to preserve a region of tropical forests, savannas, mangroves, canals, lagoons, bays, *cenotes,* and coral reefs, all of which are home to hundreds of birds and land and marine animals. The Friends of Sian Ka'an, a nonprofit group based in Cancún, offers biologist-escorted day trips, weather permitting, from the **Cabañas Ana y José** (www.anayjose.com), just south of the Tulum ruins. They cost $68 per person in a company vehicle, or $58 per person if you drive yourself. The price includes chips and soft drinks, round-trip van transportation to the reserve, a guided boat and birding trip through one of the reserve's lagoons, and use of binoculars. Tours can accommodate up to 18 people. Trips start from the Cabañas Monday to Saturday at 9am and return there around 3pm. For reservations, contact **Amigos de Sian Ka'an,** Crepúsculo 18, and Amanecer, Supermanzana 44, Manzana 13 Residencial Alborada, Cancún (✆ **998/848-2136,** 998/848-1618, or 998/848-1593; fax 998/848-1618; sian@cancun.com.mx). Office hours are 9am to 5pm.

**TRES RIOS** ★ This eco-adventure park 25 minutes south of Cancún is actually a nature reserve on more than 150 acres of land. Tres Ríos (✆ **998/887-8077** in Cancún; www.tres-rios.com) offers guests a beautiful natural area for kayaking, canoeing, snorkeling, horseback riding, or biking along jungle trails. It's definitely less commercial than the other eco-theme parks and is essentially just a great natural area for participating in these activities. The entrance fee—$21 for adults, $17 for children—includes canoe trips; the use of bikes, kayaks, and snorkeling equipment; and the use of hammocks and beach chairs once you tire yourself out. Extra charges apply for scuba diving, horseback riding, and other extended, guided tours through the preserve and its estuary. You can also opt for an all-inclusive package that covers admission, diving, horseback riding, and all food and beverages. It costs $74 per adult, $58 for children under 12, and reservations are required. Tres Ríos also has bathroom facilities, showers, and a convenience store. Most Cancún travel agencies sell a half-day Kayak Express tour to Tres Ríos. Priced at $45, it includes admission and activities, plus round-trip transportation, lunch, and two nonalcoholic drinks. The park is open daily from 9am to 5pm.

**XCARET: A DEVELOPED NATURE PARK** Eighty kilometers (50 miles) south of Cancún and 10km (6½ miles) south of Playa del Carmen is the turnoff to Xcaret (pronounced ish-car-*et*), an ecological and archaeological theme park that is one of the area's most popular tourist attractions. Xcaret has become almost a reason in itself to visit Cancún. It's the closest thing to Disneyland that you'll find in Mexico, with myriad attractions in one location, most of them participatory. Signs throughout Cancún advertise Xcaret, which has its own bus terminal to take tourists there at regular intervals. Plan to spend a full day.

Xcaret may celebrate Mother Nature, but its builders rearranged quite a bit of her handiwork in completing it. If you're looking for a place to escape the commercialism of Cancún, this may not be it; it's relatively expensive and may be very crowded, diminishing the advertised "natural" experience. Children love it, however, and the jungle setting and palm-lined beaches are beautiful. Once past the entrance booths (built to resemble small Maya temples) you'll find pathways that meander around bathing coves, the snorkeling lagoon, and the remains of a group of real Maya temples. You'll have access to swimming beaches; limestone tunnels to snorkel through; marked palm-lined pathways; a wild-bird breeding aviary; a *charro* exhibition; horseback riding; scuba diving; a botanical garden and nursery; a sea turtle nursery that releases the turtles after their first year; a pavilion showcasing regional butterflies; a tropical aquarium, where visitors can touch underwater creatures such as manta rays, starfish, and octopi; and a "Dolphinarium," where visitors (on a first-come, first-served basis) can swim with the dolphins for an extra charge of $80.

Another attraction at Xcaret is a replica of the ancient Maya game pok-ta-pok, where six "warriors" bounce around a 9-pound ball with their hips. The Seawalker is a watersport designed for nonswimmers. By donning a special suit and helmet with a connected air pump, you can walk on the ocean floor or examine a coral reef in a small bay.

There is also a visitor center with lockers, first aid, and gifts. Visitors aren't allowed to bring in food or drinks, so you're limited to the rather expensive on-site restaurants. No personal radios are allowed, and you must remove all suntan lotion if you swim in the lagoon (to avoid poisoning the habitat).

Xcaret is open Monday to Saturday from 8:30am to 8pm, Sunday from 8:30am to 5:30pm. The admission price of $49 per person entitles you to all the facilities—boats, life jackets, and snorkeling equipment for the underwater tunnel and lagoon, and lounge chairs and other facilities. Other attractions, such as snorkeling ($32), horseback riding ($49), scuba diving ($55 for certified divers;

$75 for a resort course), and the dolphin swim ($80), cost extra. There may be more visitors than equipment (such as beach chairs), so bring a beach towel and your own snorkeling gear. Travel agencies in Cancún offer day trips to Xcaret that include transportation, admission, and a guide. They depart at 8am, return at 6pm, and cost $75 for adults and $55 for children. The "Xcaret Day and Night" package includes round-trip transportation from Cancún, a *charreada* festival, lighted pathways to Maya ruins, dinner, and a folkloric show. It's $89 for adults, $40 for children age 5 to 11, free for children under 5. Buses leave the terminal at 9 and 10am daily, with the "Day and Night" tour returning at 9:30pm. You can also buy tickets to the park at the **Xcaret Terminal** (✆ **998/883-3143**), next to the Fiesta Americana Grand Coral Beach hotel on Cancún Island.

**XEL-HA** The eco-park at Xel-Ha (✆ **998/884-9422;** www.xelha.com.mx), 13km (8 miles) south of Akumal, attracts throngs of snorkelers and divers with its warm waters and brilliant fish. The beautiful, calm cove is a perfect place to bring kids for their first snorkeling experience.

Xel-ha (shell-*hah*) also offers dolphin swims and has food and beverage service, changing rooms, showers, and other facilities. For a complete description, see chapter 13.

Just south of the Xel-Ha turn-off on the west side of the highway, don't miss the ruins of **ancient Xel-Ha** ★. You'll likely be the only one there as you walk over limestone rocks and through the tangle of trees, vines, and palms. There is a huge, deep, dark *cenote* to one side, a temple palace with tumbled-down columns, a jaguar group, and a conserved temple group. A covered *palapa* on one pyramid guards a partially preserved mural. Admission is $3.50.

Xel-Ha is close to the ruins at **Tulum** (discussed earlier in this chapter) and makes a good place for a dip when you've finished climbing these Maya ruins. You can even make the 8-mile hop north from Tulum to Xel-Ha by public bus. When you get off at the junction for Tulum, ask the restaurant owner when the next buses come by; otherwise, you may have to wait as long as 2 hours on the highway.

13

# Isla Mujeres, Cozumel & the Riviera Maya

As tempting and popular as Cancún may be, the region surrounding this popular beach resort is even richer in natural and cultural treasures. Neighboring Isla Mujeres, Cozumel, Tulum, and other sites along the Yucatán coastline also boast lucid waters and white-sand beaches, but they add a dash of mystery, history, or simply local color to the equation. Each also holds remnants of ancient settlements in addition to many modern attractions.

In fact, those who shun the highly stylized, rather Americanized ways of Cancún will find that these and other stops in the Yucatán offer abundant natural pleasures, authentic experiences, and a relaxed charm. They're close to the easy air access of Cancún, yet miles away in mood and matter.

The northern half of the **Quintana Roo** Caribbean coast, commonly known as the "Riviera Maya," stretches south from Cancún to Tulum. The southern half, from Tulum to Chetumal, is the "Costa Maya." Together this area comprises 368km (230 miles) of powdery white-sand beaches, scrubby jungle, and crystal-clear lagoons full of coral and colorful fish. Along this coastline and on the islands off the peninsula are a growing number of stylized resort hotels—mostly of the all-inclusive type—as well as a handful of inexpensive hideaways. Over the past few years, it has attracted a lot of attention from developers and is rapidly evolving into a destination dotted with "eco-tourism resorts"—an oxymoron, perhaps, but a marketable one nonetheless. Some treasured spots on both the Punta Allen Peninsula and the Majahual Peninsula also merit attention.

Many travelers become acquainted with these areas only after an initial stay in Cancún, venturing out on day trips that take them sailing over to Isla Mujeres, down the Caribbean coast to Tulum, or exploring the reefs off Cozumel. Their next trip often concentrates on one or more of these smaller towns.

When I think of this area, I can't help but recall what a Mexican friend of mine once said in reference to it: "You realize that the Mayas never settled in Cancún, and these original inhabitants always chose the best places to live," he reasoned, pointing to the remains of their settlements in Tulum and other places along this coast.

## EXPLORING MEXICO'S CARIBBEAN COAST

**ISLA MUJERES** A day trip to Isla Mujeres on a party boat is one of the most popular excursions from Cancún. This fish-shaped island is just 13km (8 miles) northeast of Cancún, a quick boat ride away, allowing ample time to get a taste of the peaceful pace of life. To fully explore the small village and its shops and cafes, relax at the broad, tranquil Playa Norte, or snorkel or dive El Garrafón

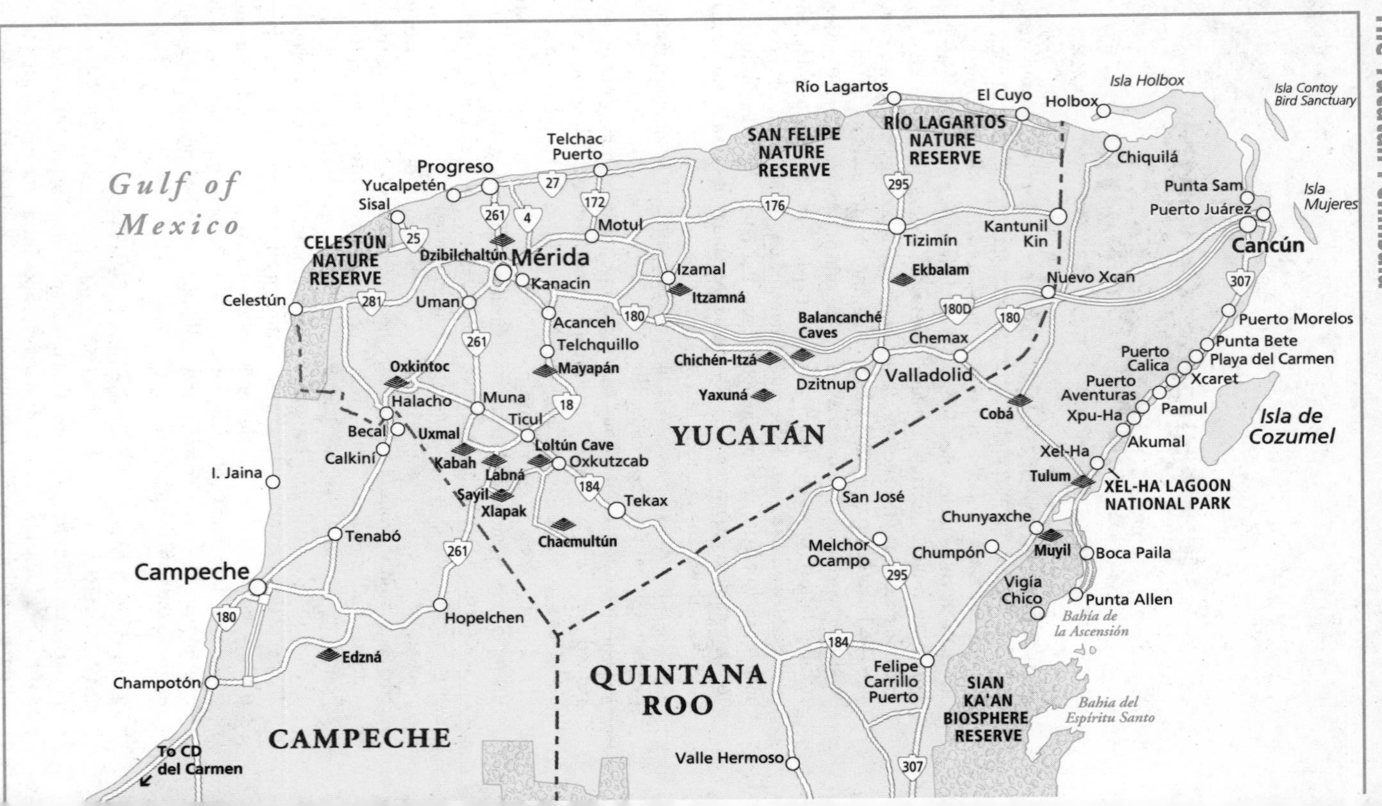

Gulf of Mexico
Río Lagartos
El Cuyo
Holbox
Isla Holbox
Isla Contoy Bird Sanctuary
Isla Mujeres
Chiquilá
Punta Sam
Puerto Juárez
Cancún
307
Puerto Morelos
Punta Bete
Playa del Carmen
Puerto Calica
Xcaret
Puerto Aventuras
Pamul
Xpu-Ha
Akumal
Isla de Cozumel
Xel-Ha
Tulum
XEL-HA LAGOON NATIONAL PARK
Chunyaxche
Muyil
Boca Paila
Chumpón
Vigía Chico
Punta Allen
Bahía de la Ascensión
Bahía del Espíritu Santo
SIAN KA'AN BIOSPHERE RESERVE
RÍO LAGARTOS NATURE RESERVE
SAN FELIPE NATURE RESERVE
Telchac Puerto
Progreso
Yucalpetén
Sisal
27
172
176
295
261
4
25
Motul
Kantunil Kin
Tizimín
Ekbalam
Nuevo Xcan
180D
180
CELESTÚN NATURE RESERVE
Dzibilchaltún
Mérida
Kanacin
Izamal
Itzamná
Celestún
281
Uman
Acanceh
Telchquillo
Mayapán
Balancanché Caves
Chichén-Itzá
Chemax
Valladolid
Dzitnup
Yaxuná
Cobá
Oxkintoc
Halacho
Muna
18
Ticul
Becal
Uxmal
Calkiní
Kabah
Labná
Loltún Cave
Oxkutzcab
Sayil
Xlapak
184
Tekax
Chacmultún
YUCATÁN
San José
Melchor Ocampo
I. Jaina
Tenabó
Campeche
Hopelchen
Edzná
Champotón
Felipe Carrillo Puerto
QUINTANA ROO
CAMPECHE
Valle Hermoso
To CD del Carmen

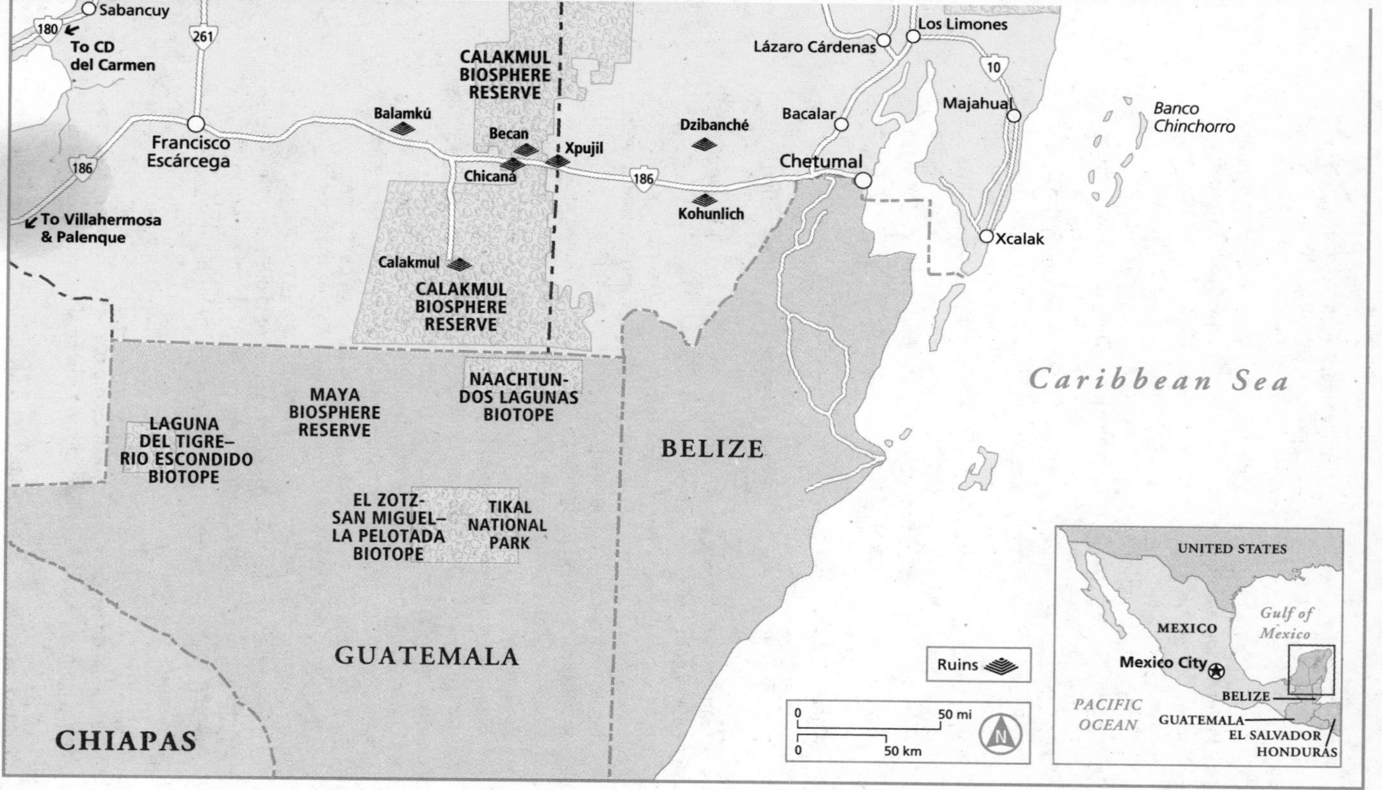
Sabancuy
180
To CD
del Carmen
261
Francisco
Escárcega
186
To Villahermosa
& Palenque
CALAKMUL
BIOSPHERE
RESERVE
Balamkú
Becan
Xpujil
Chicaná
Calakmul
CALAKMUL
BIOSPHERE
RESERVE
186
Dzibanché
Kohunlich
Lázaro Cárdenas
Los Limones
10
Majahual
Bacalar
Chetumal
Xcalak
Banco
Chinchorro
Caribbean Sea
NAACHTUN-
DOS LAGUNAS
BIOTOPE
MAYA
BIOSPHERE
RESERVE
LAGUNA
DEL TIGRE–
RIO ESCONDIDO
BIOTOPE
EL ZOTZ-
SAN MIGUEL–
LA PELOTADA
BIOTOPE
TIKAL
NATIONAL
PARK
BELIZE
GUATEMALA
CHIAPAS
Ruins
0
50 mi
0
50 km
N
UNITED STATES
MEXICO
Gulf of
Mexico
Mexico City
PACIFIC
OCEAN
BELIZE
GUATEMALA
EL SALVADOR
HONDURAS

### Tips The Best Websites for Isla Mujeres, Cozumel & the Caribbean Coast

- **Cozumel.net: www.cozumel.net** This site is a cut above the typical dining/lodging/activities sites. Click on "About Cozumel" to find schedules for ferries, island-hop flights, and to check the latest news. There's also a comprehensive listing of B&Bs and vacation home rentals, plus great info on diving, maps, and a chat room.
- **Cozumel Travel Planner: go2cozumel.com** This is a well-done guide to area businesses and attractions, by an online Mexico specialist.
- **Travel Notes: travelnotes.cc** This site boasts more than 1,000 pages of information and photos on Cozumel island—with an emphasis on diving, deep sea fishing, and other water-bound activities.
- **Viva Cozumel: viva-cozumel.com** With weather forecasts, links to dive shops, and listings of restaurants and hotels, this site can come in handy—just don't expect objectivity; the businesses pay for space to advertise. They do offer some Internet-only deals that can make a visit worthwhile, though.
- **Cancún South: www.cancunsouth.com** Billed as a guide for independent travelers, this site has itineraries and detailed driving instructions, plus tips on lodging and attractions for exploring the areas south of Cancún.
- ***Diario Yucatán:* www.yucatan.com.mx** This is a Spanish-language newspaper serving the Yucatán region.
- **Ecotravels in Mexico: www2.planeta.com/mader/ecotravel/mexico/mexico.html** This site covers the whole country and has a nice section on the Yucatán (about halfway down the page).
- **Kuartos.com: www.kuartos.com** Here's a well-designed and easy-to-use site for finding hotels and making reservations throughout Cancún and the Riviera Maya. Each hotel listing has a photo and detailed description (plus lowest rates) and allows you to check availability and make reservations. It also features super specials for selected properties.
- ***Playa* Magazine Online: www.playadelcarmen.com** This online version of the popular information guide offers plenty of tips, news, and tourist information for those bound for Playa del Carmen.
- **The Net Traveler: www.thenettraveler.com** This site specializes in information about the Yucatán, Quintana Roo (home state of Cancún), and Chiapas, as well as other areas in the old Maya empire. Its information on archeological sites, as well as on diving in the region's caves and *cenotes* (sinkholes), is especially good.

Reef (a national underwater park), you'll need more time. Overnight accommodations range from rustic to offbeat chic on this small island where relaxation rules.

Passenger ferries go to Isla Mujeres from Puerto Juárez, and car ferries leave from Punta Sam, both near Cancún. More expensive passenger ferries, with less frequent departures, leave from the Playa Linda pier on Cancún Island.

**COZUMEL** Cozumel is a large island 19km (12 miles) off the coast, across from Playa del Carmen. Life here turns around two major activities: scuba diving and being a port of call for cruise ships. It is far and away the most popular destination along this coast for either activity. Diving is big because of the fabulous reefs that stretch along the southwestern coast. Why the island became so popular with cruise ships is a more difficult question—probably because it is an island, it has lovely water, and it's impossible to get lost here. Despite the cruise ship traffic and all the stores that have spawned, life on the island moves at a relaxed and comfortable pace. There is just one town, San Miguel de Cozumel, which occupies only a small portion of the land. On the coast north and south of the town are hotels; the rest of the shore is deserted and predominantly rocky, with a scattering of small sandy coves that you can have practically all to yourself.

**THE RIVIERA MAYA** This has become the official designation for the entire stretch of coast from south of Cancún to Tulum and the Sian Ka'an Biosphere Preserve. I know the term smacks of boosterism, but it's too late to come up with anything better. And, of course, it's not the first time that promoters have had their way in naming places—look at Greenland. This part of the coast is 130km (81 miles) long, not including the preserve. It's dotted with small towns, a few hideaways, some nature parks, and a number of large resorts. The largest towns on this coast are Puerto Morelos, Playa del Carmen, Puerto Aventuras, Akumal, and Tulum. Hideaways include Punta Bete, Xpu-Ha, Paamul, and Punta Allen.

**PUERTO MORELOS** This town 30 minutes south of Cancún remains a sleepy little village with a few small hotels and rental houses. The coast is sandy and well protected by an offshore reef, which means good snorkeling and diving nearby, but the lack of surf means lots of seagrass and shallow water. If you're looking for good swimming, you should head farther down the coast. If you're looking for a quiet seaside retreat, this might work for you.

**PLAYA DEL CARMEN** This is the most happening place on the coast—lots of beach (especially when the wind and currents are flowing in the right direction), along with restaurants and nightlife, most of which are on or near the Quinta Avenida, Playa's very popular promenade. In the last few years the town has grown quickly, and local residents and the tourism board are working hard to keep it from becoming a smaller version of Cancún. They have imposed height limits on new construction and hope to encourage builders to use the same kind of tropical, slightly quirky architectural style that characterizes Playa.

**AKUMAL** The community at Akumal and Half-Moon Bay is relatively old and established for this shore and doesn't have the boomtown feel of Playa or Tulum. And Akumal has a strong ecological orientation. The locals are a mix of Americans and Mexicans, who obviously enjoy the unhurried lifestyle of the tropics, making this a good place to relax and work on your hammock technique. There are a few hotels, but mostly rental houses dot this shore. Consequently, you see a lot of vacationing families who save some money by buying groceries and cooking for themselves.

**TULUM** The town of Tulum (close by the ruins of the same name) has a hotel district of about 30 *palapa* hotels, which stretch down the coast of the Punta Allen peninsula. A few years ago it was mainly a destination for backpacker types, but with some of the most beautiful beaches on this coast and many improvements in hotel amenities, it is attracting a greater variety of visitors. Construction is booming, both in the town and along the coast. Here you can enjoy the beach in relative solitude and quiet (unless your hotel is busy building additional rooms). The flip side of this is that Tulum doesn't have the variety of restaurants that Playa and Cancún do.

**COSTA MAYA** South of Tulum lies the large Sian Ka'an Biosphere Preserve and, beyond that, what is known as the Costa Maya, a term that designates the rest of the coast all the way down to Belize. This coast does not have beaches as good as those of the Riviera Maya. Most of the coast is along the Majahual Peninsula, which is very attractive for scuba divers and fly fisherman. Farther south is Lake Bacalar, a large, clear freshwater lake fed by *cenotes* (wells or sinkholes), which makes for an attractive destination. Inland from here are the many fascinating ruins of the Río Bec area.

## 1 Isla Mujeres ★★★

16km (10 miles) north of Cancún

Isla Mujeres (Island of Women) is a casual, laid-back refuge from the conspicuously commercialized action of Cancún, visible across a narrow channel. Just 8km (5 miles) long and 4km (2½ miles) wide, it's known as the best value in the Caribbean, assuming that you favor an easy-going vacation pace and prefer simplicity to pretense.

This is an island of white-sand beaches and turquoise waters, complemented by a town filled with Caribbean-colored clapboard houses and rustic, open-air restaurants specializing in the bounty of the sea. Hotels are clean and comfortable, but if you're looking for lots of action or opulence, you'll be happier in Cancún. A few recent additions on Isla Mujeres provide more luxurious lodging choices, but they still maintain a decidedly casual atmosphere.

Francisco Hernández de Córdoba, seeing figurines of partially clad females along the shore, gave the island its name when he landed there in 1517. These are now believed to have been offerings to the Maya goddess of fertility and the moon, Ixchel. Their presence indicates that the island was probably sacred to the Maya.

At midday, suntanned visitors hang out in open-air cafes and stroll streets lined with frantic souvenir vendors. Calling for attention to their bargain-priced wares, they give a carnival atmosphere to the hours when tour-boat traffic is at its peak. Befitting the size of the island, most of the traffic consists of golf carts, *motos* (mopeds), and bicycles. Once the tour boats leave, however, Isla Mujeres reverts to its more typical, tranquil way of life, where taking a *siesta* in a hammock is a favored pastime.

Days in "Isla"—as the locals call it—can alternate between adventurous activity and absolute repose. Trips to the Isla Contoy bird sanctuary are popular, as are the excellent diving, fishing, and snorkeling—in 1998, the island's coral coast became part of Mexico's new Marine National Park. The island and several of its traditional hotels attract regular gatherings of yoga practitioners. In the evenings, most people find the slow, casual pace one of the island's biggest draws. The cool night breeze is a perfect accompaniment to casual open-air dining and drinking in small street-side restaurants. Most people pack it in as early as 9 or 10pm, when most of the businesses close. Those in search of a party, however, will find kindred souls at the bars on Playa Norte that stay open late.

### ESSENTIALS

**GETTING THERE & DEPARTING** **Puerto Juárez** (**© 998/877-0618**), just north of Cancún, is the dock for the passenger ferries to Isla Mujeres, the

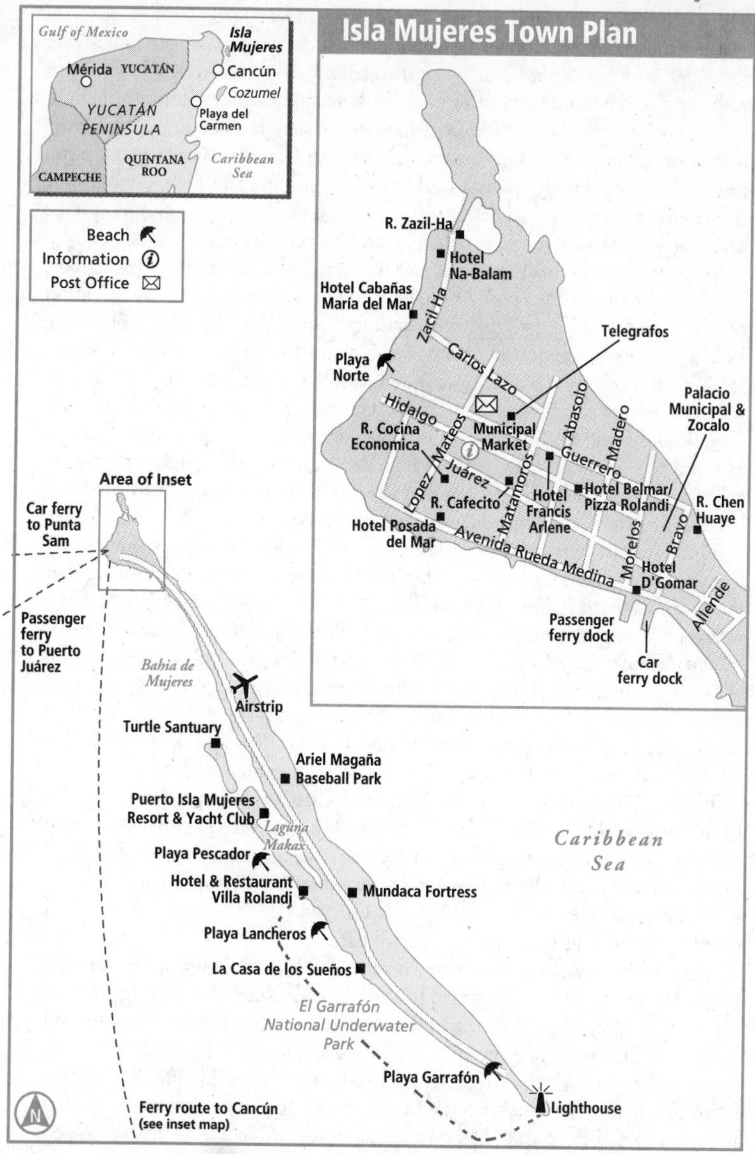


least expensive way to travel to Isla. The *Caribbean Savage* makes the 45-minute trip every 2 hours and costs just $2. The newer, air-conditioned *Caribbean Express* makes the trip in 20 minutes, has storage space for luggage, and costs about $4, every half hour, starting between 6 and 7am and ending between 9 and 11pm. These boats leave early if they're full. Pay at the ticket office—or, if the ferry is about to leave, aboard.

*Note:* Upon arrival by taxi or bus in Puerto Juárez, be wary of pirate "guides" who tell you either that the ferry is cancelled or that it's several hours until the next ferry. They'll offer the services of a private *lancha* (small boat) for about

$40—and it's nothing but a scam. Small boats are available and, on a co-op basis, charge $15 to $25 one-way, based on the number of passengers. They take about 50 minutes and are not recommended on days with rough seas. Check with the clearly visible ticket office—the only accurate source—for information.

Taxi fares are posted by the street where the taxis park, so be sure to check the rate before agreeing to a taxi for the ride back to Cancún. Rates generally run $12 to $15, depending upon your destination. Moped and bicycle rentals are also readily available as you depart the ferry. This small complex also has public bathrooms, luggage storage, a snack bar, and souvenir shops.

Isla Mujeres is so small that a vehicle isn't necessary, but if you're taking one, you'll use the **Punta Sam** port a little beyond Puerto Juárez. The ferry (40 min.) runs five or six times daily between 8am and 8pm, year-round except in bad weather. Times are generally as follows: Cancún to Isla 8am, 11am, 2:45pm, 5:30pm, and 8:15pm; Isla to Cancún 6:30am, 9:30am, 12:45pm, 4:15pm, and 7:15pm. Always check with the tourist office in Cancún to verify this schedule. Cars should arrive an hour before the ferry departure to register for a place in line and pay the posted fee, which varies depending on the weight and type of vehicle. The sole gas pump in Isla is at the intersection of Avenida Rueda Medina and Abasolo Calle, just northwest of the ferry docks.

There are also ferries to Isla Mujeres from the **Playa Linda,** known as the Embarcadero pier in Cancún, but they're less frequent and more expensive than those from Puerto Juárez. A **Water Taxi** (✆ **998/886-4270** or 998/886-4847; asterix1@prodigy.net.mx) to Isla Mujeres operates from **Playa Caracol,** between the Fiesta Americana Coral Beach Hotel and the Xcaret terminal on the island, with prices about the same as those from Playa Linda and about four times the cost of the public ferries from Puerto Juárez. Scheduled departures are 9am, 11am, and 1pm, with returns from Isla Mujeres at noon and 5pm. Adult fares are $17; kids ages 3 to 12 are $8.50; and it's free for those under age 3.

To get to Puerto Juárez or Punta Sam from **Cancún,** take any Ruta 8 city bus from Avenida Tulum. If you're coming from Mérida, you can either fly to Cancún and proceed to Puerto Juárez or take a bus directly from the Mérida bus station to Puerto Juárez. From **Cozumel,** you can either fly to Cancún (there are daily flights) or take a ferry to Playa del Carmen (see "Cozumel," later in this chapter), where you can travel to Puerto Juárez.

*Arriving:* Ferries arrive at the ferry docks (✆ **998/877-0065**) in the center of town. The main road that passes in front is Avenida Rueda Medina. Most hotels are close by. Tricycle taxis are the least expensive and most fun way to get to your hotel; you and your luggage pile in the open carriage compartment and the driver pedals through the streets. Regular taxis are always lined up in a parking lot to the right of the pier, with their rates posted. If someone on the ferry offers to arrange a taxi for you, politely decline, unless you'd like some help with your luggage down the short pier—it just means an extra, unnecessary tip for your helper.

**VISITOR INFORMATION** The **City Tourist Office** (✆ and fax **998/877-0767**) is on Avenida Rueda Medina, in front of the pier. It's open Monday to Friday from 8am to 8pm, Saturday and Sunday from 8am to 2pm. Also look for *Islander,* a free publication with history, local information, advertisements, and event listings.

**ISLAND LAYOUT** Isla Mujeres is about 8km (5 miles) long and 4km (2½ miles) wide, with the town at the northern tip. "Downtown" is a compact

4 blocks by 6 blocks, so it's very easy to get around. The **ferry docks** are at the center of town, within walking distance of most hotels, restaurants, and shops. The street running along the waterfront is **Avenida Rueda Medina,** commonly called the ***malecón*** (boardwalk). The **market** (Mercado Municipal) is by the post office on **Calle Guerrero,** an inland street at the north edge of town, which, like most streets in the town, is unmarked.

**GETTING AROUND** A popular form of transportation on Isla Mujeres is the electric **golf cart,** available for rent at many hotels for $12 per hour or $40 per day. **El Sol Golf Cart Rental,** Avenida Francisco Madero 5 (© **998/877-0068**), will deliver one to you, or you can pick one up. The golf carts don't go more than 20 mph, but they're fun. Anyway, you aren't on Isla Mujeres to hurry. Many people enjoy touring the island by ***moto,*** the local sobriquet for motorized bikes and scooters. Fully automatic versions are available for around $25 per day or $7 per hour. They come with seats for one person, but some are large enough for two. There's only one main road with a couple of offshoots, so you won't get lost. Be aware that the rental price does not include insurance, and any injury to yourself or the vehicle will come out of your pocket. **Bicycles** are also available for rent at some hotels for $3 per hour or $7 per day, including a basket and a lock.

If you prefer to use a taxi, rates are about $2.50 for trips within the downtown area, or $4.50 for a trip to the southern end of Isla. You can also rent them for about $12 per hour.

## *FAST FACTS:* Isla Mujeres

*Area Code* The area code of Isla Mujeres is **998.**

*Consumer Protection* The local branch of **Profeco** consumer protection agency has a local phone number, © **998/877-0106.**

*Currency Exchange* Isla Mujeres has numerous *casas de cambios,* or money exchanges, that you can easily spot along the main streets. Most of the hotels listed here provide this service for their guests, although often at less favorable rates than the commercial enterprises. There is only one bank in Isla, Banco Bital, across from the ferry docks. It's open Monday to Friday from 9am to 5pm.

*Hospital* The **Hospital de la Armada** is on Avenida Rueda Medina at Ojon P. Blanco (© **998/877-0001**). It's half a mile south of the town center.

*Internet Access* **CompuIsla,** Abasolo 11, between Medina and Juárez streets (© **998/877-0898**), offers Internet access for $4 per hour Monday to Friday from 8am to 10pm, Saturday from 9am to 4pm.

*Pharmacy* **Isla Mujeres Farmacía** (© **998/877-0178**) has the best selection of prescription and over-the-counter medicines. It's on Calle Benito Juárez, between Morelos and Bravo, across from Van Cleef & Arpels.

*Post Office/Telegraph Office* The *correo* is at Calle Guerrero 12 (© **998/877-0085**), at the corner of López Matéos, near the market. It's open Monday to Friday from 9am to 4pm.

*Taxis* To call for a taxi, dial © **998/877-0066.**

*Telephone* Ladatel phones accepting coins and prepaid phone cards are at the plaza and throughout town.

*Tourist Seasons* Isla Mujeres's tourist season (when hotel rates are higher) is a bit different from that of other places in Mexico. High season runs December through May, a month longer than in Cancún; some hotels raise their rates in August, and some hotels raise their rates beginning in mid-November. Low season is from June to mid-November.

## BEACHES & OUTDOOR ACTIVITIES

**THE BEACHES** The most popular beach in town used to be called Playa Cocoteros ("Cocos," for short). Then, in 1988, Hurricane Gilbert destroyed the coconut palms on the beach. Gradually, the name has changed to **Playa Norte** ★. The long stretch of beach extends around the northern tip of the island, to your left as you get off the boat. This is a truly splendid beach—a wide stretch of fine white sand and calm, translucent, turquoise-blue water. Topless sunbathing is permitted. The beach is easily reached on foot from the ferry and from all downtown hotels. Watersports equipment, beach umbrellas, and lounge chairs are available for rent. Those in front of restaurants usually cost nothing if you use the restaurant as your headquarters for drinks and food. New palms have sprouted all over Playa Norte, and it won't be long before it deserves its old name.

**El Garrafón National Park** ★★ is known best as a snorkeling area, but there is a nice stretch of beach on either side of the park. **Playa Lancheros** is on the Caribbean side of Laguna Makax. Local buses go to Lancheros, then turn inland and return downtown. The beach at Playa Lancheros is nice, but the few restaurants there are expensive.

**SWIMMING** Wide Playa Norte is the best swimming beach, with Playa Lancheros second. There are no lifeguards on duty on Isla Mujeres, which does not use the system of water-safety flags used in Cancún and Cozumel.

**SNORKELING** By far the most popular place to snorkel is **El Garrafón National Park** ★★. It is at the southern end of the island, where you'll see numerous schools of colorful fish. The well-equipped park has two restaurant-bars, beach chairs, a swimming pool, kayaks, changing rooms, rental lockers, showers, a gift shop, and snack bars. The park is under the same management as Xcaret, south of Cancún. Admission is $25 for adults, $13 for children (AE, MC, V). You can also choose a package ($40) that includes food, beverages, locker rental, and snorkeling gear rental. Day-trip packages from Cancún (✆ **998/884-9422** in Cancún, or 984/875-6000 at the park) are also available. Prices start at $25 and include round-trip transportation. The park is open daily from 8:30am to 6pm.

Also good for snorkeling is the **Manchones Reef,** off the southeastern coast, where a bronze cross was installed in 1994. The reef is just offshore and accessible by boat.

Another excellent location is around the lighthouse (*el faro*) in the **Bahía de Mujeres** at the southern tip of the island, where the water is about 2m (6 ft.) deep. Boatmen will take you for around $25 per person if you have your own snorkeling equipment or $30 if you use theirs.

**DIVING** Most of the dive shops on the island offer the same trips. **Bahía Dive Shop,** Rueda Medina 166, across from the car-ferry dock (✆ **998/877-0340**), is a full-service shop that offers resort and certification classes as well as dive equipment for sale or rent. The shop is open daily from 9am to 7pm, and accepts MasterCard and Visa. Another respected dive shop is **Coral Scuba Center,** at Matamoros 13A and Rueda Medina (© **998/877-0061** or 998/877-0763). It's open daily from 8am to 12:30pm and 3 to 10pm, and accepts American Express, MasterCard, and Visa. It offers discounted prices for those who bring their own gear, and it also has rental bungalows available for short-term and long-term stays.

**Cuevas de los Tiburones** ★ ("Caves of the Sleeping Sharks"), Isla's most famous dive site, costs $70 to $80 for a two-tank dive at a depth of 21 to 24 meters (70–80 ft.), advisable only for experienced divers. The sleeping sharks have mostly been driven off, and a storm collapsed the arch featured in a Jacques Cousteau film showing them, but the caves survive. Other dive sites include a **wreck** 15km (9 miles) offshore; **Banderas** reef, between Isla Mujeres and Cancún, where there's always a strong current; **Tabos** reef on the eastern shore; and **Manchones** reef, 1km (½ mile) off the southeastern tip of the island, where the water is 4.5- to 11m (15–35 ft.) deep. Another underwater site, **The Cross of the Bay,** is close to Manchones reef. A bronze cross, weighing 1 ton and standing 12m (39 ft.) high, was placed in the water between Manchones and Isla in 1994, as a memorial to those who have lost their lives at sea. The best season for diving is June to August, when the water is calm.

In May 1999, a shrimp boat suffering engine failure ran aground on a portion of a large coral reef just north of Isla. A section of the reef suffered significant damage, and officials are trying to place buoys in the area to steer as much traffic as possible away from the damaged area.

**FISHING** To arrange a day of fishing, ask at the **Sociedad Cooperativa Turística** (the boatmen's cooperative), on Avenida Rueda Medina (no phone), next to Mexico Divers and Las Brisas restaurant, or the travel agency mentioned in "A Visit to Isla Contoy, below." The cost can be shared with four to six others and includes lunch and drinks. Captain Tony Martínez (© **998/877-0274**) also arranges fishing trips aboard his *lancha,* ***Marinonis.*** Reservations are recommended. Year-round you'll find bonito, mackerel, kingfish, and amberjack. Sailfish and sharks (hammerhead, bull, nurse, lemon, and tiger) are in good supply in April and May. In winter, larger grouper and jewfish are prevalent. Four hours of fishing close to shore costs around $110; 8 hours farther out goes for $250. The cooperative is open Monday to Saturday from 8am to 1pm and 5 to 8pm, and Sunday 7:30 to 10am and 6 to 8pm.

**YOGA** Increasingly, Isla is becoming known as a great place to combine a relaxing beach vacation with yoga practice and instruction. The trend began at **Hotel Na Balam** (© **998/877-0279;** www.nabalam.com), which offers yoga classes under its large poolside *palapa,* complete with yoga mats and props. The classes, which begin at 9am Monday through Friday, are free to guests, $10 per class to visitors. Na Balam is also the site of frequent yoga instruction vacations featuring respected teachers and a more extensive practice schedule.

The **Casa de la Cultura,** on Avenida Guerrero, between Abasolo and Madero streets (© **998/877-0639**), holds yoga classes on Wednesdays at 9am. Call to confirm the schedule. The center is open Monday to Saturday from 9am to 1pm and 4 to 8pm. It also offers dance classes, drawing classes, and a book exchange that's the closest thing to a library on Isla.

## MORE ATTRACTIONS

**DOLPHIN DISCOVERY** You can swim with live dolphins (© **998/877-0207,** or © 998/849-4757 in Cancún; fax 998/849-4751; www.dolphindiscovery.com) in an enclosure at Treasure Island, on the side of Isla Mujeres that faces Cancún. Groups of six people swim with two dolphins and one trainer. Swimmers listen to an educational video and spend time in the water with the trainer and the dolphins before enjoying 15 minutes of free swimming time with them. Reservations are recommended, and you must arrive an hour before your assigned swimming time, at 9am, 11am, 1pm, or 3pm. The cost is $119 per person, plus $15 if you need round-trip transportation from Cancún.

**A TURTLE SANCTUARY** ★★ This reserve, dedicated to preserving Caribbean sea turtles and to educating the public about them, makes a worthwhile outing.

As recently as 20 years ago, fishermen converged on the island nightly from May to September waiting for the monster-size turtles to lumber ashore to deposit their Ping-Pong-ball-shaped eggs. Totally vulnerable once they begin laying their eggs, and exhausted when they have finished, the turtles were easily captured and slaughtered for their highly prized meat, shell, and eggs. Then a concerned fisherman, Gonzalez Cahle Maldonado, began convincing others to spare at least the eggs, which he protected. It was a start. Following his lead, the fishing secretariat founded the **Centro de Investigaciones** 11 years ago; both the government and private donations fund it. Since then, at least 28,000 turtles have been released, and every year local schoolchildren participate in the event, planting the notion of protecting the turtles for a new generation of islanders.

Six species of sea turtles nest on Isla Mujeres. An adult green turtle, the most abundant species, measures 1- to 1.5m (4–5 ft.) in length and can weigh as much as 450 pounds. At the center, visitors walk through the indoor and outdoor turtle pool areas, where the creatures paddle around. The turtles are separated by age, from newly hatched up to 1 year. Besides protecting the turtles that nest on Isla Mujeres of their own accord, the program also captures turtles at sea, brings them to enclosed compounds to mate, and later frees them to nest on Isla Mujeres after they have been tagged. People who come here usually end up staying at least an hour, especially if they opt for the guided tour, which I recommend. The sanctuary is on a piece of land separated from the island by Bahía de Mujeres and Laguna Makax; you'll need a taxi to get there. Admission is $2.30; the shelter is open daily 9am to 5pm. For more information, call © **998/877-0595.**

**A MAYA RUIN** ★★ Just beyond the lighthouse, at the southern end of the island, are the strikingly beautiful remains of a small Maya temple, believed to have been built to pay homage to the moon and fertility goddess, Ixchel. The location, on a lofty bluff overlooking the sea, is worth seeing and makes a great place for photos. It is believed that Maya women traveled here on annual pilgrimages to seek Ixchel's blessings of fertility. If you're at El Garrafón National Park and want to walk, it's not too far. Turn right from El Garrafón. When you see the lighthouse, turn toward it down the rocky path.

**A PIRATE'S FORTRESS** The Fortress of Mundaca is about 4km (2½ miles) in the same direction as El Garrafón, about half a mile to the left. A slave trader who claimed to have been the pirate Mundaca Marecheaga built the fortress. In the early 19th century, he arrived at Isla Mujeres and set up a blissful paradise in a pretty, shady spot, while making money selling slaves to Cuba and Belize.

According to island lore, he decided to settle down and build this hacienda after being captivated by the charms of an island girl. However, she reputedly spurned his affections and married another islander, leaving him heartbroken and alone on Isla Mujeres. Admission is $2; the fortress is open daily from 10am to 6pm.

**A VISIT TO ISLA CONTOY** ★ If at all possible, plan to visit this pristine uninhabited island, 30km (19 miles) by boat from Isla Mujeres, that was set aside as a national wildlife reserve in 1981. The oddly shaped, 3.8-mile-long island is covered in lush vegetation and harbors 70 species of birds as well as a host of marine and animal life. Bird species that nest on the island include pelicans, brown boobies, frigates, egrets, terns, and cormorants. Flocks of flamingos arrive in April. June, July, and August are good months to spot turtles burying their eggs in the sand at night. Most excursions troll for fish (which will be your lunch), anchor en route for a snorkeling expedition, skirt the island at a leisurely pace for close viewing of the birds without disturbing the habitat, and then pull ashore. While the captain prepares lunch, visitors can swim, sun, follow the nature trails, and visit the fine nature museum. For a while the island was closed to visitors, but it reopened after fishermen and those bringing visitors agreed to rules for its use and safety. The trip from Isla Mujeres takes about 45 minutes each way and can take longer if the waves are choppy. Because of the tight-knit boatmen's cooperative, prices for this excursion are the same everywhere: $40. You can buy a ticket at the **Sociedad Cooperativa Turística** on Avenida Rueda Medina, next to Mexico Divers and Las Brisas restaurant (no phone), or at one of several travel agencies, such as **La Isleña,** on Morelos between Medina and Juárez (✆ **998/877-0578**). La Isleña is open daily from 7:30am to 9:30pm and is a good source for tourist information. Isla Contoy trips leave at 8:30am and return around 4pm. The price (cash only) is $40 for adults, $20 for children. It usually includes snorkeling equipment, but double-check before heading out.

Three types of boats go to Isla Contoy. Small boats have one motor and seat 8 or 9. Medium-size boats have two motors and hold 10. Large boats have a toilet and hold 16. Most boats have a sun cover. The first two types are being phased out in favor of larger, better boats. Boat captains should respect the cooperative's regulations regarding capacity and should have enough life jackets to go around. On the island, there is a small government museum with bathroom facilities.

## SHOPPING

Shopping is a casual activity here. There are only a few shops of any sophistication. Shop owners will bombard you, especially on Hidalgo, selling Saltillo rugs, onyx, silver, Guatemalan clothing, blown glassware, masks, folk art, beach paraphernalia, and T-shirts in abundance. Prices are lower than in Cancún or Cozumel, but with such overeager sellers, bargaining is necessary to avoid paying too much.

The one treasure you're likely to take back is a piece of fine jewelry—Isla is known for its excellent, duty-free prices on gemstones and handcrafted work made to order. Diamonds, emeralds, sapphires, and rubies can be purchased as loose stones and then mounted while you're off exploring the island. The superbly crafted gold, silver, and gems are available at very competitive prices in the workshops near the central plaza. The stones are also available in the rough. **Van Cleef & Arpels** (✆ **998/877-0331**) has a store at the corner of Morelos and Juárez streets, with a broad selection of jewelry at competitive prices. Easily the largest store in Isla, it's open daily from 9am to 9pm and accepts all major credit cards.

## WHERE TO STAY

You'll find plenty of hotels in all price ranges on Isla Mujeres. Rates peak during high season, which is the most expensive and most crowded time to go. Elizabeth Wenger of **Four Seasons Travel** in Montello, Wisconsin (✆ **800/552-4550**), specializes in Mexico travel and books a lot of hotels in Isla Mujeres. Her service is invaluable in the high season when hotel occupancy is high. Those interested in private home rentals or longer-term stays can contact **Mundaca Travel and Real Estate** in Isla Mujeres (✆ **998/877-0025;** fax 998/877-0076; www.mundacatravel.com).

In the last few years, Isla has seen the emergence of several smaller but decidedly upscale places to stay. Anyone wanting the proximity and ease of arrival that Cancún offers—but not its excesses—should seriously consider these new options.

### VERY EXPENSIVE

**Hotel Villa Rolandi Gourmet & Beach Club** ★★★ Isla's newest hotel is adding to the island's options for guests who enjoy its tranquility—but also like being pampered. Villa Rolandi is an exceptional value, with Mediterranean-style rooms that offer every conceivable amenity, as well as its own small, private beach in a sheltered cove. Each of the 20 oversize suites has an ocean view and a large terrace or balcony with a full-size private whirlpool—whose water is changed with each guest's arrival. Floors are made of stone, and ceilings are vaulted. TVs offer satellite music and movies, and rooms all have a sophisticated in-room sound system. There's a recessed seating area that extends out to the balcony or terrace. Bathrooms are large and tastefully decorated in deep-hued Tikal marble. The stained-glassed shower has dual showerheads, stereo speakers, and jet options, and it even converts into a steam room.

Dining is an integral part of a stay at Villa Rolandi. Its owner is a Swiss-born restaurateur who made a name for himself with his family of Rolandi restaurants on Isla Mujeres and in Cancún (see "Where to Dine," below). This intimate hideaway with highly personalized service is ideal for honeymooners, who receive a complimentary bottle of domestic champagne upon arrival, when notified in advance. Only children over age 13 are welcome.

Fracc. Lagunamar SM 7 Mza. 75 L 15 & 16, 77400 Isla Mujeres, Q. Roo, ✆ **998/877-0700.** Fax 998/877-0100. www.rolandi.com. 20 units. High season $318 double; low season $250 double. Rates include round-trip transportation from Playa Linda in Cancún aboard private catamaran yacht; continental breakfast; and a la carte lunch or dinner in the onsite restaurant. AE, MC, V. **Amenities:** Restaurant (see "Where to Dine"); 24-hour room service; breakfast delivery; Infinity pool with waterfall; small fitness room with basic equipment and open-air massage area; concierge; tour desk to arrange diving, snorkeling, or fishing, or other tour services. *In room:* TV/VCR, dataport, minibar, hair dryer, iron, safe.

**La Casa de los Sueños** ★★★ *Finds* This "house of dreams" is easily Isla Mujeres's most intimate, sophisticated, and romantic property, and one of a few luxury B&Bs in Mexico. Originally built as a private residence, luckily for us it became an upscale, adults-only B&B in early 1998. Its location on the southern end of the island, adjacent to El Garrafón National Park, makes it ideal for snorkeling and diving enthusiasts. The captivating design features vivid sherbet-colored walls—think watermelon, lime, and blueberry—and sculpted architecture. The house has a large interior courtyard, tropical gardens, a sunken living area, and an infinity pool that melts into the cool Caribbean waters. All rooms have balconies or terraces and face west, offering stunning views of the sunset over the sea, as well as the lights of Cancún. In addition, the rooms—which have names such as "Serenity," "Passion," and "Love"—have large, marble bathrooms, and luxury amenities. One master suite ideal for honeymooners has an exceptionally spacious bathroom area, complete with whirlpool and steam room shower, plus other deluxe amenities. Geared to a healthful, stress-free vacation, the B&B forbids smoking and encourages casual dress and no shoes. Two large, gentle mastiff dogs provide companionship, if you'd like. Private boat transportation from Cancún to the B&B's dock can be arranged on request. Light lunches (extra charge) are available upon request, and there's an honor-system bar in the courtyard reception area.

Carretera Garrafón s/n, 77400 Isla Mujeres, Q. Roo. ✆ **800/551-2558** in the U.S., or 998/877-0651. Fax 998/877-0708. www.lossuenos.com. 10 units. High season $250–$375 double; low season $215–$335 double. Rates include full American breakfast. MC, V. No children. **Amenities:** Coffee, juice, and fruit delivery; swimming pool; sun terrace; meditation areas; massage; yoga and reiki classes (must be scheduled in advance); free use of bikes and kayaks; boat dock; diving and snorkeling available. *In room:* Fan, TV/VCR, hair dryer, no phone.

**Puerto Isla Mujeres Resort & Yacht Club** ★ The concept here—an exclusive glide-up yachting and sailing resort—is unique not only to Isla Mujeres, but also to most of Mexico. Facing an undeveloped portion of the glass-smooth, mangrove-edged Makax Lagoon, Puerto Isla Mujeres is a collection of modern suites and villas with sloping white-stucco walls and red-tile roofs spread across spacious palm-filled grounds. Beautifully designed with Scandinavian and Mediterranean elements, guest quarters feature tile, wood-beam ceilings, natural teakwood, and marble accents. Suites have a large, comfortable living area with minibar on a lower level, with the bedroom above, loft-style. Villas have two bedrooms upstairs with a full bathroom, and a small bathroom downstairs with a shower. Each villa also holds a small kitchen area with a dishwasher, microwave, refrigerator, and coffeemaker. A whirlpool is on the upper patio off the master bedroom. Nightly turndown service leaves the next day's weather forecast on the pillow beside the requisite chocolate. The beach club, with refreshments, is a water-taxi ride across the lagoon on a beautiful stretch of beach. A staff biologist can answer questions about birds and water life on Isla Mujeres.

Puerto de Abrigo Laguna Macax, 77400 Isla Mujeres, Q. Roo (reservation address Km 4.5 Paseo Kukulkán, 77500 Cancún, Q. Roo). ✆ **800/960-ISLA** in the U.S.; 998/877-0413, 998/877-0330, or 998/883-1228 in Cancún. www.puerto-isla.com. 24 units. High season $290–$350 suite; $550 villa. Low season $280 suite; $350 villa. Rates include boat transportation from office in Playa Linda, continental breakfast. AE, MC, V. **Amenities:** 2 restaurants (1 indoor, 1 poolside); breakfast delivery; free-form swimming pool with swim-up bar; on-site spa with complete massage services; nearby beach club; full-service marina with 60 slips for 30- to 60-foot vessels, fueling station, charter yachts and sailboats, and sailing school; mopeds, golf carts, bikes, and watersports equipment for rent; video and CD library; laundry. *In room:* TV/VCR, stereo with CD, minibar, safe.

### EXPENSIVE

**Hotel Na Balam** ★★ *Finds* Increasingly, Na Balam is becoming known as a haven for yoga students or those interested in an introspective vacation. This popular, two-story hotel near the end of Playa Norte has comfortable rooms on a quiet, ideally located portion of the beach. Rooms are in three sections; some facing the beach, and others are across the street in a garden setting with a swimming pool. All rooms have a terrace or balcony, with hammocks. Each spacious suite contains a king or two double beds, a seating area, and folk-art decorations. Though other rooms are newer, the older section is well kept, with a bottom-floor patio facing the peaceful, palm-filled, sandy inner yard and Playa Norte. Yoga classes (free for guests; $10 per class for nonguests) start at 9am Monday through Friday. The restaurant, **Zazil Ha,** is one of the island's most popular (see

"Where to Dine," below). A beachside bar serves a selection of natural juices and is one of the most popular spots for sunset watching.

Zazil Ha 118, 77400 Isla Mujeres, Q. Roo. ✆ **998/877-0279.** Fax 998/877-0446. www.nabalam.com. 31 units. High season $208–$302 suite; low season $175–$225 suite. Ask about weekly and monthly rates. AE, MC, V. Free unguarded parking. **Amenities:** Restaurant (Mexican/Caribbean), 2 bars; swimming pool; diving and snorkeling trips available; mopeds, golf carts, bikes for rent; library; Internet access; rec room with TV, VCR, and Ping-Pong tables; salon services, including yoga classes; in-room massage; babysitting; laundry. *In room:* Fan.

## MODERATE

**Hotel Cabañas María del Mar** ★ A good choice for simple beach accommodations, the Cabañas María del Mar is on the popular Playa Norte. The older two-story section behind the reception area and beyond the garden offers nicely outfitted rooms facing the beach. All have two single or double beds, refrigerators, and ocean-view balconies strung with hammocks. Eleven single-story *cabañas* closer to the reception area were remodeled in late 1999, in a rustic Mexican style, with new bathroom fixtures and the addition of a minifridge. The newest addition, **El Castillo,** is across the street, over and beside Buho's restaurant. It contains all "deluxe" rooms, but some are larger than others; the five rooms on the ground floor have large patios. Upstairs rooms have small balconies. All have ocean views, blue-and-white tile floors, and tile baths, and contain colonial-style furniture. There's a small pool in the garden.

Av. Arq. Carlos Lazo 1 (on Playa Norte, ½ block from the Hotel Na Balam), 77400 Isla Mujeres, Q. Roo. ✆ **800/223-5695** in the U.S., or 998/877-0179. Fax 998/877-0213 or 998/877-0156. 73 units. High season $100–$130 double; low season $55–$88 double. MC, V. **Amenities:** Standard-size pool; bus for tours and boat for rent; golf-cart and *moto* rentals. From the pier, walk left 1 block and turn right on Matamoros. After 4 blocks, turn left on Lazo (the last street); hotel is at end of block.

## INEXPENSIVE

**Hotel Belmar** ★★ Situated in the center of Isla's small-town activity, this hotel sits above Pizza Rolandi (consider the restaurant noise) and is run by the same people. Each of the simple but stylish tile-accented rooms comes with two twin or double beds. Prices are high considering the lack of views, but the rooms are pleasant. This is one of the few island hotels that have televisions (with U.S. channels) in the room. There is one large colonial-decorated suite with a whirlpool and a patio.

Av. Hidalgo 110 (between Madero and Abasolo, 3½ blocks from the passenger-ferry pier), 77400 Isla Mujeres, Q. Roo. ✆ **998/877-0430.** Fax 998/877-0429. hotel.belmar@mail.caribe.net.mx. 11 units. High season $56–$95 double; low season $28–$90 double. AE, MC, V. **Amenities:** Restaurant/bar (see "Where to Dine," below); room service until 11:30pm; laundry. *In room:* TV.

**Hotel D'Gomar** *Value* This hotel is known for comfort at reasonable prices. You can hardly beat the value for basic accommodations, which were completely remodeled inside and out just a few years ago. Rooms—each with two double beds—have new mattresses, drapes, and tiled bathrooms with new fixtures. A wall of windows offers great breezes and views. The higher prices are for air-conditioning, which is hardly needed with the breezes and ceiling fans. The only drawback is that there are five stories and no elevator. But it's conveniently located cater-corner (look right) from the ferry pier, with exceptional rooftop views. The name of the hotel is the most visible sign on the "skyline."

Rueda Medina 150, 77400 Isla Mujeres, Q. Roo. ✆ **998/877-0541.** 16 units. High season $53 double; low season $37 double. No credit cards. *In room:* Fan.

**Hotel Francis Arlene** ★ The Magaña family operates this neat little two-story inn built around a small, shady courtyard. This hotel is very popular with families and seniors, and it welcomes many repeat guests. You'll notice the tidy cream-and-white façade from the street. Some rooms have ocean views, and all are remodeled or updated each year. They are comfortable, with tile floors, tiled bathrooms, and a very homey feel. Each downstairs room has a coffeemaker, refrigerator, and stove; each upstairs room comes with a refrigerator and toaster. Some have either a balcony or a patio. Higher prices are for the 14 rooms with air-conditioning; other units have fans. Rates are substantially better if quoted in pesos and are reflected below. In dollars they are 15% to 20% higher.

Guerrero 7 (5½ blocks inland from the ferry pier, between Abasolo and Matamoros), 77400 Isla Mujeres, Q. Roo. ✆ and fax **998/877-0310** or 998/877-0861. 26 units. High season $45–$60 double; low season $38–$48 double. No credit cards. **Amenities:** Money exchange (at front desk); in-room massage; safe. *In room:* No phone.

**Hotel Posada del Mar** Kids Simply furnished, quiet, and comfortable, this long-established hotel faces the water and a wide beach 3 blocks north of the ferry pier. It has one of the few swimming pools on the island. This is probably the best choice in Isla for families. The ample rooms are in a three-story building or one-story bungalow units. For the spaciousness of the rooms and the location, this is among the best values on the island and is very popular with readers, though I consistently find the staff to be the least gracious on the island. A wide, seldom-used but appealing stretch of Playa Norte is across the street, where watersports equipment is available for rent. A great, casual *palapa*-style bar and a lovely pool are on the back lawn, and the restaurant **Pinguino** (see "Where to Dine," below) is by the sidewalk at the front of the property.

Av. Rueda Medina 15 A, 77400 Isla Mujeres, Q. Roo. ✆ **800/544-3005** in the U.S., or 998/877-0044. Fax 998/877-0266. www.mexhotels.com/pdm.html. 62 units. High season $78 double; low season $70 double. Children under 12 stay free with paying adults. AE, MC, V. **Amenities:** Restaurant/bar; pool. From the pier, go left for 4 blocks; hotel is on the right.

## WHERE TO DINE

At the **Municipal Market,** next to the telegraph office and post office on Avenida Guerrero, obliging, hard-working women operate several little food stands. At the **Panadería La Reyna** (no phone), at Madero and Juárez, you can pick up inexpensive sweet bread, muffins, cookies, and yogurt. It's open Monday to Saturday from 7am to 9:30pm.

As in the rest of Mexico, a ***cocina económica*** restaurant literally means "economic kitchen." Usually aimed at the local population, these are great places to find good food at rock-bottom prices, and especially so on Isla Mujeres, where you'll find several, most of which feature delicious regional specialties. But be aware that the hygiene is not what you'll find at more established restaurants, so you're dining at your own risk.

### EXPENSIVE

**Casa Rolandi** ★ ITALIAN/SEAFOOD The gourmet Casa Rolandi restaurant and bar has become Isla's favored fine-dining experience. It boasts a view of the Caribbean and the most sophisticated menu in the area. There's a colorful main dining area as well as more casual, open-air terrace seating for drinks or light snacks. Food is the most notable on the island; however, the overall experience falls short—lights are a bit too bright and the music is a bit too close to what you'd hear on an elevator. Along with seafood and northern Italian specialties, the famed wood-burning-oven pizzas are a good bet. Careful—the wood-oven-baked bread, which arrives looking like a puffer fish, is so divine that you're likely to fill up on it. This is a great place to enjoy the sunset, and it offers a selection of more than 80 premium tequilas.

On the pier of Villa Rolandi, Lagunamar SM 7. ✆ **998/877-0430.** Dinner $8–$31. AE, MC, V. Daily 11am–11pm.

### MODERATE

**Las Palapas Chimbo's** ★ SEAFOOD If you're looking for a beachside *palapa*-covered restaurant where you can wiggle your toes in the sand while relishing fresh seafood, this is the best of them. It's the locals' favorite on Playa Norte. Try the delicious fried whole fish, which comes with rice, beans, and tortillas. You'll notice a bandstand and dance floor in the middle of the restaurant, and sex-hunk posters all over the ceiling—that is, when you aren't gazing at the beach and the Caribbean. Chimbo's becomes a lively bar and dance club at night, drawing a crowd of drinkers and dancers (see "Isla Mujeres After Dark," below).

Norte Beach. No phone. Sandwiches and fruit $2.50–$4.50; seafood $6–$9. No credit cards. Daily 8am–midnight. From the pier, walk left to the end of the *malecón,* then right onto the Playa Norte; it's about ½ block on the right.

**Pinguino** MEXICAN/SEAFOOD The best seats on the waterfront are on the deck of this restaurant and bar, especially in late evening, when islanders and tourists arrive to dance and party. This is the place to feast on lobster—you'll get a beautifully presented, large, sublimely fresh lobster tail with a choice of butter, garlic, and secret sauces. The grilled seafood platter is spectacular, and fajitas and barbecued ribs are also popular. Breakfasts include fresh fruit, yogurt, and granola, or sizable platters of eggs, served with homemade wheat bread. Pinguino also has no-smoking areas.

In front of the Hotel Posada del Mar (3 blocks west of the ferry pier), Av. Rueda Medina 15. ✆ **998/877-0044.** Main courses $4–$7; daily special $7; all-you-can-eat buffets $5. AE, MC, V. Daily 7am–10pm; bar closes at midnight.

**Pizza Rolandi** ★★ ITALIAN/SEAFOOD You're bound to dine at least one night at Rolandi's, which is practically an Isla institution. The plate-size pizzas and calzones are likely to lure you with exotic ingredients—including lobster, black mushrooms, pineapple, and Roquefort cheese—as well as more traditional tomatoes, olives, basil, and salami. A wood-burning oven provides the signature flavor of the pizzas, as well as baked chicken, roast beef, and mixed seafood casserole with lobster. The extensive menu also offers a selection of salads and light appetizers, as well as an ample array of pasta dishes, steaks, fish, and scrumptious desserts. The setting is the open courtyard of the Hotel Belmar, with a porch overlooking the action on Avenida Hidalgo.

Av. Hidalgo 10 (3½ blocks inland from the pier, between Madero and Abasolo). ✆ **998/877-0430.** Main courses $3.70–$12.70. AE, MC, V. Daily 11am–11:30pm.

**Zazil Ha** ★★ CARIBBEAN/INTERNATIONAL You can enjoy some of the island's best food at this restaurant while sitting at tables on the sand among palms and gardens. The food—terrific pasta with garlic, shrimp in tequila sauce, fajitas, seafood pasta, and delicious *mole* enchiladas—enhances the serene environment. Caribbean specialties include cracked conch, coconut sailfish, jerk chicken, and stuffed squid. A selection of fresh juices complements the vegetarian menu, and there's even a special menu for those participating in yoga retreats. Between the set hours for meals, you can have all sorts of enticing food, such as vegetable and fruit drinks, tacos and sandwiches, *ceviche,* and terrific nachos. It's likely you'll stake this place out for several meals.

At the Hotel Na Balam (at the end of Playa Norte, almost at the end of Calle Zazil Ha). ✆ **998/877-0279.** Fax 998/877-0446. Main courses $8.50–$15.75. AE, MC, V. Daily 7:30am–10:30am, 12:30–3:30pm, and 7–10pm.

### INEXPENSIVE

**Cafecito** ★ CREPES/ICE CREAM/COFFEE/FRUIT DRINKS Sabina and Luis Rivera own this cute, Caribbean-blue corner restaurant where you can begin the day with flavorful coffee and a croissant and cream cheese, or end it with a hot-fudge sundae. Terrific crêpes come with yogurt, ice cream, fresh fruit, or chocolate sauces, as well as ham and cheese. The two-page ice cream menu satisfies almost any craving, even one for waffles with ice cream and fruit. The three-course fixed-price dinner starts with soup and includes a main course (such as fish or curried shrimp with rice and salad) and dessert.

Calle Matamoros 42, corner of Juárez (4 blocks from the pier). ✆ **998/877-0438.** Crêpes $2.10–$4.50; breakfast $2.50–$4.50; sandwiches $2.80–$2.90. No credit cards. Year-round daily 8am–2pm. High season Fri–Wed 5:30–10:30 or 11:30pm.

**Cocina Económica Carmelita** MEXICAN/HOME COOKING Few tourists find their way to this tiny restaurant, but locals know they can get a filling, inexpensive, home-cooked meal. Carmelita prepares food in the back kitchen, and her husband serves it at the three cloth-covered tables in the front room of their home. Two or three *comida corridas* are available each day until they run out. They begin with the soup of the day and include a fruit water drink (*agua fresca*). Common selections include *paella, cochinita pibil,* and fish-stuffed chiles. Menu specialties include chicken in *mole* sauce, pork cutlet in a spicy sauce, and breaded shrimp. For fancier tastes, there is the least expensive lobster in town—served grilled or in a garlic sauce—at $13 for an ample portion.

Calle Juárez 14 (2 blocks from the pier, between Bravo and Allende). No phone. Main dishes $4–$6; daily lunch special $4. No credit cards. Year-round Mon–Sat 12:30–3pm; Dec–Mar Mon–Sat 4–8pm.

## ISLA MUJERES AFTER DARK

Those in a party mood by day's end might want to start out at the beach bar of the **Hotel Na Balam** on Playa Norte, which draws a crowd until around midnight. On Saturday and Sunday there's live music from 4 to 7pm. **Las Palapas Chimbo's** restaurant on the beach becomes a jammin' dance joint with a live band from 9pm until whenever. Farther along the same stretch of beach, **Buho's,** the restaurant and beach bar of the Cabañas María del Mar, has its moments as a popular, low-key hangout. **Pinguino** in the Hotel Posada del Mar offers a convivial late-night hangout; a band plays nightly during high season from 9pm to midnight. Near Matéos and Hidalgo, **KoKo Nuts** caters to a younger crowd, with alternative music for late-night dancing.

# 2 Cozumel ★★

70km (44 miles) S of Cancún; 19km (12 miles) SE of Playa del Carmen

Cozumel was a well-known diving spot before Cancún ever existed, and it has ranked for years among the top five dive destinations in the world. Tall reefs line the southwest coast, creating towering walls that offer divers a fairy-tale landscape to explore. For nondivers, it has the beautiful water of the Caribbean with all the accompanying watersports and seaside activities. What's more, Cozumel has the feel of a small island—short roads that don't go very far, lots of mopeds, few buses and trucks, and a sense of isolation. The island is 45km (28 miles) long, 18km (11 miles) wide, and is 19km (12 miles) from the mainland. Most of the terrain is flat, undisturbed scrubland. The name comes from the Maya word *Cuzamil,* meaning "land of the swallows." Today, it remains the home of two species of birds found nowhere else: the Cozumel vireo and the Cozumel thrasher.

The only town on the island is San Miguel, which, despite the growth of the last 20 years, can't be called anything more than a small town. It's not particularly attractive, but the place and its inhabitants are agreeable—on Sunday evenings, everybody congregates around the plaza to be sociable and have a good time. Staying in town can be fun and convenient. You get a choice of a number of restaurants and nightspots. Because Cozumel enjoys such popularity with the cruise ships, the waterfront section of town is wall-to-wall jewelry stores (many more than you would think demand could support) and souvenir shops. This and the area around the town's main square are as far as most cruise ship passengers venture into town. Elsewhere you find mainly offices, restaurants, small hotels, and dive shops.

Should you come down with a case of island fever, **Playa del Carmen** and the mainland are a convenient 25-to-45-minute ferry ride away, weather permitting. Some travel agencies on the island can set you up with a tour of the major ruins on the mainland, such as **Tulum** or **Chichén-Itzá,** or a visit to a nature park such as **Xel-Ha** or **Xcaret** (see "Trips to the Mainland," later in this chapter).

The island has its own ruins, but they cannot compare with the major cities of the mainland. During pre-Hispanic times, Maya women traveled by boat to the island to worship the goddess of fertility, Ixchel. More than 40 sites containing shrines remain around the island, and archaeologists still uncover the small dolls customarily offered in the fertility ceremony. Hernán Cortez landed here in 1519 on his way to conquering Mexico. Before his own boat docked, Cortez's men sacked the town. Cortez went on to convert the Indians and replace their idols with a cross and a statue of Mary in the main temple at Cozumel. From then until modern times, the island remained little more than a backwater outpost of little concern to the governing elites in Mérida and Mexico City.

## ESSENTIALS

### GETTING THERE & DEPARTING

**BY PLANE** In recent years, the number of international commercial flights in and out of the island has actually decreased, while charter flights have increased. You might want to inquire about buying a ticket from a packager. Some packagers work with several of Cozumel's hotels, even some of the small ones; others will let you buy a ticket without making it part of a package. **Continental** (✆ **800/231-0856** in the U.S., or 987/872-0487 in Cozumel) flies to and from Houston and Newark. **Aerocozumel** (✆ **987/872-3456,** or 998/884-2002 in Cancún), a Mexicana affiliate, has numerous flights to and from Cancún and Mérida. **Mexicana** (✆ **800/531-7921** in the U.S., or 987/872-0157 or 987/872-2945 at the airport) and **Aeromexico** (✆ **800/237-6639** in the U.S., or 01-800/021-4000 in Cozumel) fly from Mexico City. Vans are available from the airport to the town ($4) and the outlying hotels. (See "Arriving," below).

**BY FERRY** Passenger ferries run to and from Playa del Carmen, and a car and passenger ferry runs to and from Puerto Morelos. **Water Jet Service** (✆ **987/872-1508** or 987/872-1588) ferries make the trip between Cozumel and Playa del Carmen in 25 or 45 minutes, depending on the boat. The trip costs $9

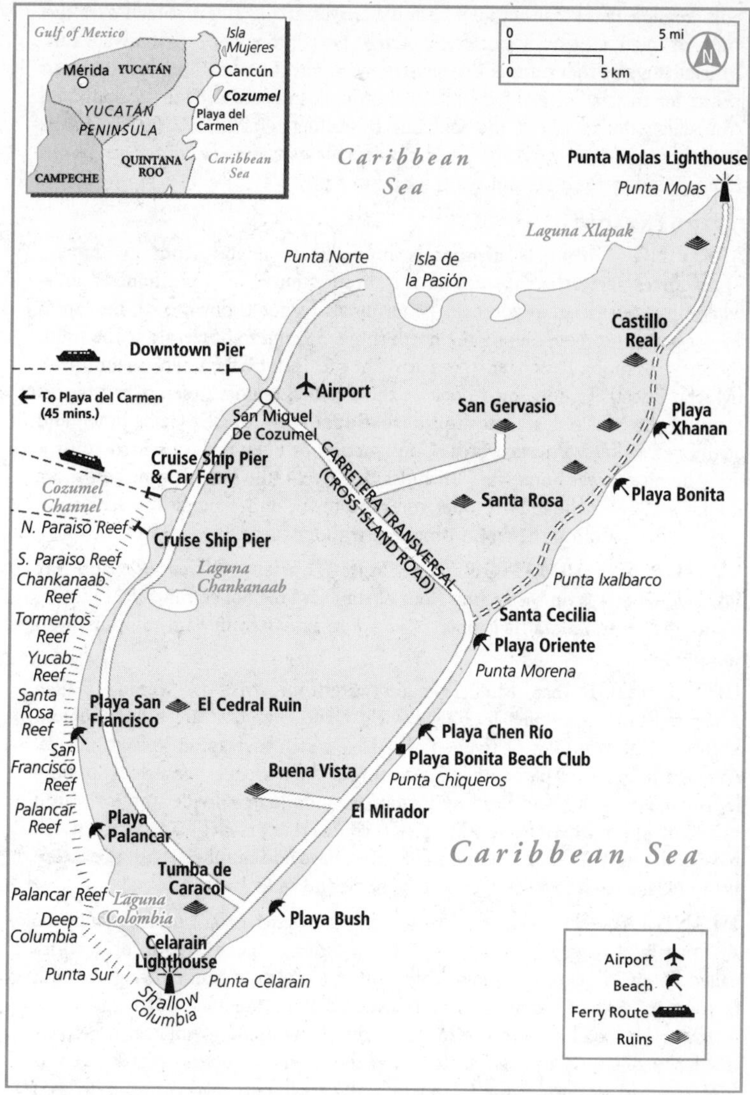


one-way, and the boats are enclosed and air-conditioned. Departures are almost hourly from 5am to midnight. In Playa del Carmen, the ferry dock is 1½ blocks from the main square and the bus station. In Cozumel, the ferries use the town pier (Muelle Fiscal), a block from the main square. Schedules are subject to change, so check at the docks for departure times—especially the time of the last returning ferry, if that's the one you intend to use. Luggage storage at the Cozumel dock costs $2 per day.

The ferry to Cozumel from Puerto Morelos (32km/20 miles north of Playa del Carmen) takes longer and should be avoided if possible. Double-check the schedule, which is usually daily at 5:30am, 10:30am, and 4pm, by calling the **terminal** (© **998/871-0008**). On Sunday the last trips are sometimes canceled.

The crossing takes 2½ hours. The ferry arrives at the International Pier just south of town, near La Ceiba hotel. Cargo takes precedence over private cars. Officials suggest that camper drivers stay overnight in the parking lot to be first in line for tickets. Return trips to Puerto Morelos depart at 8am, 1:30pm, and 7pm daily; double-check the schedule by calling © **987/872-0950.** *Always arrive at least 3 hours before the ferry's departure to purchase a ticket and get in line.* The fare is $55 for a car and $100 for a van.

## ORIENTATION

**ARRIVING** Cozumel's **airport** is immediately inland from downtown. **Transportes Terrestres** provides hotel transportation in air-conditioned Suburbans. Buy your ticket as you exit the terminal. To hotels downtown, the fare is $5 per person; to hotels along the north shore, $8, and to hotels along the south shore, $9 or more. Passenger ferries arrive at the dock by the town's main square (Muelle Fiscal). Cruise ships dock at the **Punta Langosta** pier, a few blocks south of the Muelle Fiscal; at the **International Pier,** near La Ceiba hotel; and at the newest pier, **Puerta Maya.** Construction of Puerta Maya stirred controversy because it was built over North Paradise Reef—the reef with the best shore diving and snorkeling. Dive operators, the town, and ecological-preservation activists from around the world protested without success.

**VISITOR INFORMATION** The **State Tourism Office** (© and fax **987/872-7563**) is on the second floor of the Plaza del Sol commercial building facing the central plaza. It is open Monday to Friday from 9am to 3pm and 6 to 8pm.

**CITY LAYOUT** San Miguel's main waterfront street is **Avenida Rafael Melgar.** Running parallel to Rafael Melgar and the coast are other avenidas numbered in multiples of five—5, 10, 15—which increase as you go inland. **Avenida Juárez** runs perpendicular, starting at the passenger-ferry dock, passing by the main square, and heading inland. Avenida Juárez divides the town into northern and southern halves. The streets (*calles*) that parallel Juárez to the north have even numbers. The ones south of Juárez have odd numbers, with the exception of Calle Rosado Salas, which runs between Calles 1 and 3.

**ISLAND LAYOUT** One road runs along the western coast of the island, the side that faces the Yucatán mainland. It has different names. North of town it's called **Santa Pilar** or **San Juan;** in the city it is **Avenida Rafael Melgar;** south of town it's called **Costera Sur.** Hotels stretch along this road north and south of town. The road runs to the southern tip of the island (Punta Sur). Perpendicular to this road and intersecting it at the town's main ferry pier is Avenida Juárez and its extension, the Carretera Transversal. This road runs east to west across the island, passing the airport and the turn-off to the ruins of San Gervasio before reaching the undeveloped ocean side of the island. It then turns south and follows the coast to the southern tip of the island, where it meets the southern extension of the main road.

The most inexpensive hotels are in the town of San Miguel. Moderate to expensive accommodations are along the coast north and south of town. South of the city is **Chankanaab National Park,** centered on the beautiful lagoon of the same name.

**GETTING AROUND** You can walk to most destinations in town. Getting to outlying hotels and beaches, including the Chankanaab Lagoon, requires a taxi or rental car.

*Tips* **Be Streetwise**

North-south streets—the *avenidas*—have the right of way, and traffic doesn't slow down or stop.

**Car rentals** are roughly the same price as on the mainland, depending on demand. **Avis** (✆ **987/872-0099**) and **Executive** (✆ **987/872-1308**) have counters in the airport. Rentals are easy in town: Arrange them through your hotel or any of the many local rental offices.

**Moped rentals** are available all over the village and cost $15 to $30 for 24 hours, depending upon the season. If you rent a moped, be careful. Riding a moped made a lot more sense when Cozumel had less traffic; now it's a risky activity as taxi drivers and other motorists have become more numerous and pushier. Moped accidents easily rank as the highest cause of injury in Cozumel. Before renting one, give it a careful inspection to see that all the gizmos—horn, light, starter, seat, mirror—are in good shape, and be sure to note all damage to the moped on the rental agreement. Most important, read the fine print on the back of the rental agreement, which states that you are not insured, that you are responsible for paying for any damage to the bike (or for all of it if it's stolen or demolished), and that you must stay on paved roads. It's illegal to ride a moped without a helmet outside of town (subject to a $25 fine).

**Taxis:** Cozumel has lots of taxis and a very strong drivers' union. Fares have been standardized—there's no bargaining. Here are a few sample fares for two people (there is an additional charge for extra passengers): island tour, $60; town to southern hotel zone, $5 to $18; town to northern hotels, $3 to $5; town to Chankanaab, $7; in and around town, $2 to $4.

## *FAST FACTS:* Cozumel

*Area Code* The telephone area code is **987.**

*Climate* From October to December there can be strong winds all over the Yucatán, as well as some rain. May to September is the rainy season.

*Diving* Bring proof of your diver's certification and your log. Underwater currents can be strong, and many of the reef drops are quite steep, so dive operators want to make sure divers are experienced.

*Internet Access* Several cybercafes are in and about the main square. If you go just a bit off Avenida Melgar and the main square, prices are cheaper. **Modutel,** Av. Juárez 15 (at Av. 10), offers good rates. Hours are Monday to Saturday from 10am to 8pm. There are several more in the vicinity.

*Money Exchange* The island has several banks and *casas de cambio,* as well as ATM machines. Most places accept dollars, but you usually get a better deal paying in pesos.

*Post Office* The *correo* is on Avenida Rafael Melgar at Calle 7 Sur (✆ **987/872-0106**), at the southern edge of town. It's open Monday to Friday from 9am to 6pm, Saturday from 9am to noon.

*Recompression Chamber* There are four recompression chambers (*cámaras de recompresión*). **Buceo Médico Mexicano,** staffed 24 hours, is at Calle 5 Sur 21-B, between Avenida Melgar and Avenida 5 Sur (✆ **987/872-2387** or 987/872-1430). The **Hyperbaric Center of Cozumel** (✆ **987/872-3070**) is at Calle 4 Norte, between Avenidas 5 and 10.

*Seasons* High seasons are August and from Christmas to Easter.

## EXPLORING THE ISLAND

For **diving and snorkeling,** there are plenty of dive shops to choose from, including those recommended here. For **island tours, ruins tours** on and off the island, **glass-bottom boat tours, fiesta nights, fishing,** and other activities, go to a travel agency such as **InterMar Cozumel Viajes,** Calle 2 Norte 101-B, between Avenidas 5 and 10 (✆ **987/872-1098;** fax 987/872-0895; intermar@cozumel.com.mx). It's not far from the main plaza.

### WATERSPORTS

**SCUBA DIVING** Cozumel is the number one dive destination in the Western Hemisphere. Don't forget your dive card and dive log. Dive shops will rent you scuba gear but won't take you out on a boat until you show some documentation. If you have a medical condition, bring a letter signed by a doctor stating that you've been cleared to dive. A two-tank morning dive costs around $60; some shops offer an additional afternoon one-tank dive for $9 for those who took the morning dives. A lot of divers save some money by buying a dive package with a hotel. These usually include two dives a day.

Diving in Cozumel is drift diving, which can be a little disconcerting for novices. The current that sweeps along Cozumel's reefs, pulling nutrients into them and making them as large as they are, also dictates how you dive here. The problem is that it pulls at different speeds at different depths and in different places. When it's pulling strong, it can quickly scatter a dive group. The role of the dive master becomes more important, especially with choosing the dive location. Cozumel has a lot of dive locations. To mention but a few: the famous **Palancar Reef,** with its caves and canyons, plentiful fish, and a wide variety of sea coral; the monstrous **Santa Rosa Wall,** famous for its depth, sea life, coral, and sponges; the **San Francisco Reef,** which has a shallower drop-off wall and fascinating sea life; and the **Yucab Reef,** with its beautiful coral.

Finding a dive shop in town is even easier than finding a jewelry store. Of Cozumel's more than 50 dive operators, two that I can recommend are Bill Horn's **Aqua Safari,** on Melgar at Calle 5 (✆ **987/872-0101;** fax 987/872-0661, www.aquasafari.com), which has a PADI five-star instructor center with full equipment and parts in the Hotel Plaza Las Glorias (✆ **987/872-3362** or 987/872-2422); and **Dive House,** on the main plaza (✆ **987/872-1953;** fax 987/872-0368), which offers PADI, NAUI, and SSI instruction.

**Moments** **Mardi Gras**

*Carnaval* (Mardi Gras) is Cozumel's most colorful fiesta. It begins the Thursday before Ash Wednesday, with daytime street dancing and nighttime parades on Thursday, Saturday, and Monday (the best).

## San Miguel de Cozumel

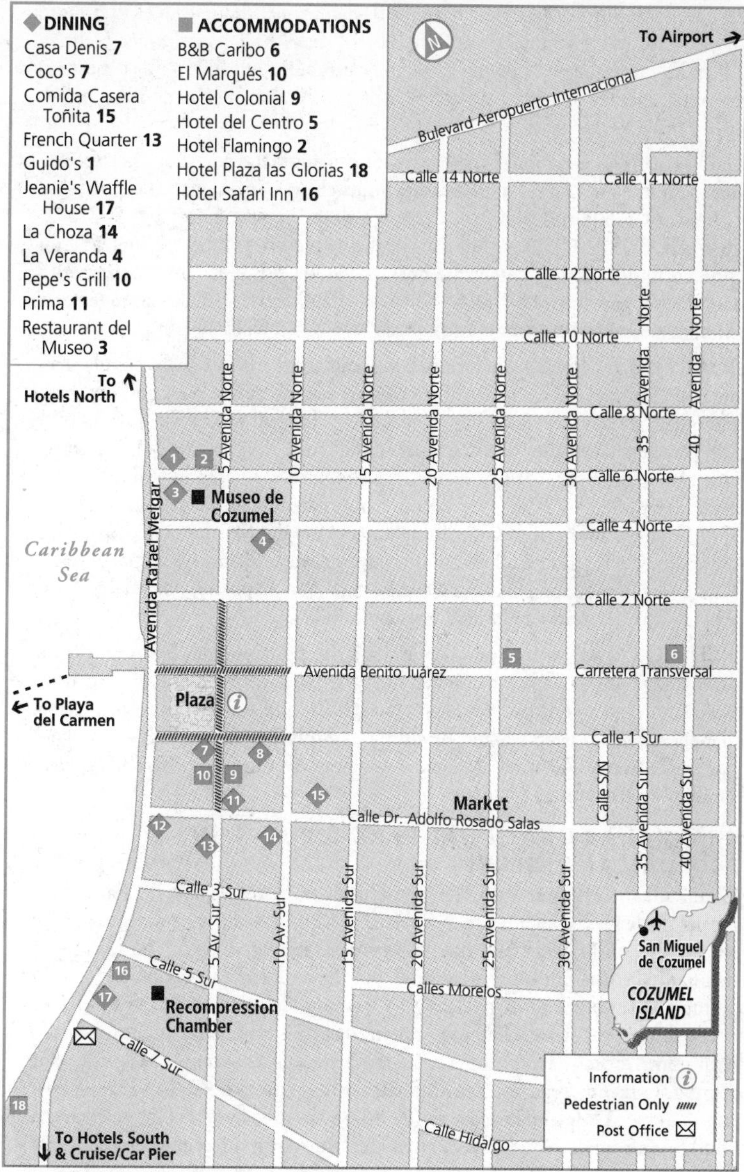


A popular activity in the Yucatán is *cenote* diving. The peninsula's underground ***cenotes*** (say-*noh*-tehs), or sinkholes, lead to a vast system of underground caverns. The gently flowing water is so clear that divers seem to float on air through caves complete with stalactites and stalagmites. If you want to try this but didn't plan a trip to the mainland, contact **Yucatech Expeditions,** 15th Avenida 144, between Calle 1 and Rosado Salas (© and fax **987/872-5659;** yucatech@cozumel.czm.com.mx), which offers a trip five times a week. *Cenotes* are 30 to 45 minutes from Playa del Carmen, and a dive in each *cenote* lasts around 45 minutes. Dives are within the daylight zone, about 40m (130 ft.) into the caverns and no more than 18m (60 ft.) deep. Company owner Germán Yañez Mendoza inspects diving credentials carefully, and divers must meet his list of requirements before cave diving is permitted. For information and prices, call or drop by the office.

**SNORKELING** Anyone who can swim can snorkel. One shop that specializes in snorkeling trips is the **Kuzamil Snorkeling Center,** 50 Av. bis 565 Int. 1, between 5 Sur and Hidalgo, Colonia Adolfo López Matéos (© **987/872-4637** or 987/872-0539). A full-day snorkel trip costs $65 per person; $50 for children under 12. It includes the boat, the guide, a buffet lunch, and snorkel equipment, and it visits 4 reefs. You can call directly or make arrangements through a local travel agency. You can also ask about half-day trips.

**BOAT TRIPS** Travel agencies and hotels can arrange boat trips, a popular pastime on Cozumel. There are evening cruises, cocktail cruises, glass bottom boats, and other options. It's worth inquiring whether the trip will be filled with cruise ship passengers because trips that cater to the cruise ship crowds can be packed. One rather novel boat trip is a ride in a submarine, offered by **Atlantis Submarines** (© **987/872-5671**). The sub can hold 48 people. It operates almost 3km (2 miles) south of town in front of the Casa del Mar hotel and costs $72 per adult; $36 for kids. Call ahead or inquire at one of the travel agents in town. This is a far superior experience to the **Sub See Explorer** offered by **Aqua World,** which is really a glorified glass-bottom boat.

**FISHING** Travel agents can also arrange fishing trips. The best months for fishing are April to September, when the catch includes blue and white marlin, sailfish, tarpon, swordfish, dorado, wahoo, tuna, and red snapper. One agency that specializes in deep sea and fly-fishing is **Aquarius Travel Fishing,** Calle 3 Sur 2 between Avenida Melgar and 5th Avenue (© **987/872-1092;** gabdiaz@hotmail.com).

### CHANKANAAB NATIONAL PARK & PUNTA SUR ECOLOGICAL RESERVE

**Chankanaab National Park** ★★ is the pride of many islanders. Chankanaab means "little sea," which refers to a beautiful land-locked pool connected to the sea through an underground tunnel—a sort of miniature ocean. Snorkeling in this natural aquarium is not permitted, but the park has a lovely beach for sunbathing and snorkeling. Arrive early, to stake out a chair and *palapa* before the cruise ship crowd arrives. Likewise, the snorkeling is best before noon. There are bathrooms, lockers, a gift shop, several snack huts, a restaurant, and a *palapa* for renting snorkeling gear. You can also swim with dolphins here, for $119 per person. Contact **Dolphin Discovery** (© **987/872-6605;** www.dolphindiscovery.com) for information and reservations. The same outfit offers a sea lion show for $5 per person, using rescued sea lions that had been captured illegally. Tickets are available through any travel agency in town. You will also see some scarlet macaws that were confiscated from captors and are in a reproduction and release program.

Surrounding the lagoon is a botanical garden with shady paths and 351 species of tropical and subtropical plants from 22 countries, as well as 451 species from Cozumel. Several Maya structures have been re-created within the gardens to give visitors an idea of Maya life in a jungle setting. There's a small natural history museum as well. Admission to the park costs $10; it's open daily from 8am to 5pm. The park is south of town, just past the Fiesta Americana Hotel. Taxis run constantly between the park, the hotels, and town.

**Punta Sur Ecological Reserve** (admission $15) is a large area encompassing the southern tip of the island, including the large Columbia Lagoon. The only practical way of going there is to rent a car or scooter; there is no taxi stand, and, usually, few people. This is an ecological reserve, not a park, so don't expect much infrastructure. The reserve has an information center, several observation towers, and a snack bar. In addition, there are four boat rides per day around the Colombia Lagoon, where guides point out things of interest about the habitat (bring bug spray). Punta Sur has some interesting snorkeling (bring your own gear), and lovely beaches kept as natural as possible. Regular hours are 9am to 5pm. A special program (© **987/872-2940** for info) allows visitors to observe turtle nests in season, and you can participate as a volunteer in the evenings during the nesting season.

## THE BEACHES

Sixteen kilometers (10 miles) past Chankanaab National Park, you'll come to **Playa San Francisco** ★ and, south of it, **Playa Palancar** ★. Food (usually overpriced) and equipment rentals are available.

Along both coasts you'll see signs advertising beach clubs. A "beach club" in Cozumel usually means a *palapa* hut that's open to the public and serves soft drinks, beer, and fried fish. Some also rent water gear. **Nachi Cocom,** just north of Playa Palancar, is more elaborate than the others, with a swimming pool, a good restaurant, and watersports equipment rental. Other beach clubs include **Paradise Cafe,** on the southern tip of the island across from Punta Sur nature park, and **Playa Bonita, Chen Rio,** and **Punta Morena,** on the eastern side. They are scattered along the coast and do a big business on Sunday, when the locals head for the beaches. Most of the east coast is unsafe for swimming because of the surf. Small beaches occupy the spaces between rocky promontories. Halfway up the east coast, the road turns inland and becomes the transversal road (which passes the ruins of San Gervasio) back to town, 15km (9½ miles) away.

## TOURS OF THE ISLAND

To be frank, the best part of Cozumel isn't on land; it's in the water. Still, you might want to try a tour to do something different. Travel agencies can book you on a group tour of the island for around $40; the price depends on whether it includes lunch and a stop for snorkeling and swimming at Chankanaab Park. (If all you're interested in is Chankanaab, then go by yourself and save money.) A taxi driver charges $60 for a 4-hour tour of the island, which most people would consider only mildly amusing, depending on the driver's personality. Also available are a 4-hour horseback tour of the island's interior jungle, a jungle jeep tour, and a jungle ATV tour. The tours aren't spectacular: Most of the terrain is flat, and the interior is more scrublike than the term "jungle" would indicate. If you're interested in any of these, inquire at one of the local travel agencies.

## OTHER ATTRACTIONS

**MAYA RUINS** One of the most popular island excursions is to **San Gervasio** (100 B.C.–A.D. 1600). Follow the paved transversal road. You'll see the well-marked turn-off about halfway between town and the eastern coast. Stop at the entrance gate and pay the $1 road-use fee. Go straight ahead over the pothole-laden road to the ruins (about 3km/2 miles farther) and pay the $5 fee to enter; still and video camera permits cost $5 each. A small tourist center at the entrance sells cold drinks and snacks.

When it comes to Cozumel's Maya remains, getting there is most of the fun—do it for the mystique and for the trip, not for the size or scale of the ruins. The buildings, though preserved, are crudely made and would not be much of a tourist attraction if they were not the island's principal ruins. More significant than beautiful, this site was once an important ceremonial center where the Maya gathered, coming even from the mainland. The important deity was Ixchel, the goddess of weaving, women, childbirth, pilgrims, the moon, and medicine. Although you won't see any representations of Ixchel at San Gervasio today, Bruce Hunter, in his *Guide to Ancient Maya Ruins,* writes that priests hid behind a large pottery statue of her and became the voice of the goddess, speaking to pilgrims and answering their petitions. Ixchel was the wife of Itzamná, the sun god, and as such, preeminent among all Maya gods.

Tour guides charge $10 for a tour for one to six people. A better option is to find a copy of the green booklet *San Gervasio,* sold at local checkout counters or bookstores, and tour the site on your own. Seeing it takes 30 minutes. Taxi drivers offer a tour to the ruins for about $25; the driver will wait for you outside the ruins.

**A HISTORY MUSEUM** The **Museo de la Isla de Cozumel** ★, on Avenida Melgar between Calles 4 and 6 Norte (✆ **987/872-1475**), is more than just a nice place to spend a rainy hour. On the first floor an excellent exhibit illustrates endangered species, the origin of the island, and its present-day topography and plant and animal life, including an explanation of coral formation. The second-floor galleries feature the history of the town, artifacts from the island's pre-Hispanic sites, and colonial-era cannons, swords, and ship paraphernalia. It's open daily from 9am to 5pm. Admission is $3. The rooftop restaurant serves breakfast and lunch.

**GOLF** Cozumel has a new 18-hole course designed by Jack Nicklaus. It's at the **Cozumel Country Club** (✆ **987/872-9570**), just north of San Miguel. Greens fees are $144, including tax. Tee times can be made 3 days in advance. A few hotels have special memberships with discounts for guests and advance tee times.

## TRIPS TO THE MAINLAND

**PLAYA DEL CARMEN & XCARET** Going on your own to the nearby seaside village of **Playa del Carmen** and the **Xcaret** nature park is as easy as a quick ferry ride from Cozumel (for ferry information, see "Getting There & Departing," earlier in this chapter). Playa del Carmen is covered in detail later in this chapter, Xcaret in chapter 12, "Cancún." Cozumel travel agencies offer an Xcaret tour that includes the ferry fee, transportation to the park, and the admission fee. The price is $80 for adults and $50 for kids.

**CHICHEN-ITZA, TULUM & COBA** Travel agencies can arrange day trips to the fascinating ruins of **Chichén-Itzá** ★★★ by air or bus. The ruins of **Tulum,** overlooking the Caribbean, and **Cobá** ★★, in a dense jungle setting, are closer, so they cost less to visit. These cities are quite a contrast to Chichén-Itzá. Cobá is a grandiose city spread out beside a lake in a remote jungle setting, while Tulum is smaller, more compact, and right on the beach. Neither has been restored to the same extent as Chichén-Itzá. A trip to both Cobá and Tulum begins at 8am and returns around 6pm.

## SHOPPING

If you like shopping for silver jewelry, you can spend a great deal of time examining the wares of all the jewelers along Melgar, which cater to cruise-ship shoppers.

Some duty-free stores sell things such as perfumes and designer wares. If you're interested in Mexican folk art, a number of stores display a wide variety of interesting pieces. Try stores such as **Los Cinco Soles** (✆ **987/872-2040**) and **Indigo** (✆ **987/872-1076**), both on Avenida Melgar. Another is **Santa Fe** (no phone), Rosado Salas 58. Prices for serapes, T-shirts, and the like are lower on the side streets off Melgar.

## WHERE TO STAY

Because Cozumel is such a big destination for divers, all the large hotels and many smaller ones offer dive packages; I don't mention this in the reviews, but you should always ask about them. All the large waterfront hotels have dive shops on the premises and a pier, also making this unnecessary to mention in the reviews. And it's quite okay to stay at one hotel and dive with another operator—any dive boat can pull up to any hotel pier to pick up customers. Most dive shops don't pick up from the hotels north of town, so it's best to dive with the in-house operator at these hotels.

As an alternative to a hotel, you might want to try **Cozumel Vacation Villas and Condos,** Av. Rafael Melgar 685 (between Calles 3 and 5 Sur), 77600 Cozumel, Q. Roo (✆ **800/224-5551** in the U.S., or 987/872-0729; www.cvvmexico.com), which offers accommodations by the week. There are also more than half a dozen all-inclusive resorts. I've listed one of them, **Hotel El Cozumeleño Beach Resort,** which is in a good location on a good stretch of coast. Some of the others in the north are less than ideal, and the large ones to the south are far enough away that it becomes a hassle to go into town, so you end up feeling a little like a prisoner.

Cozumel's hotels are in three locations: along the coast **north** of town, in **town,** and along the coast **south** of town. In the listings below, I discuss them in that order. The hotels in town are the most economical. The prices I've quoted include tax. Expect rates from Christmas to New Year's to be still higher than the regular high-season rates quoted here.

### NORTH OF TOWN

**Carretera Santa Pilar,** or San Juan, is the name of Melgar's northern extension. All the hotels lie in close proximity to each other on the beach side of the road a short distance from town and the airport.

#### Expensive

**Hotel El Cozumeleño Beach Resort** ★★ There are busy hotels and there are quiet ones. This nine-story hotel is a busy one, with lots of people shuffling about, activities coordinators conferring, groups gathering for trips to the ruins, music playing, and more. An all-inclusive resort, El Cozumeleño is for people who want an active vacation with plenty to do. Particular attractions include one of the best bits of beach on this stretch of coast, an extravagant pool and sunning area, and a full array of watersports and equipment rental. The owners have recently more than doubled the number of rooms and have added to the amenities. All rooms are large. Those in the old part are much longer than they are wide; the shape of rooms in the new part allows for a less awkward furniture arrangement. All rooms have balconies with a great ocean view, attractive decor, and large bathrooms. You have a choice of a king bed or two double beds.

Carretera Santa Pilar Km 4.5 (Apdo. Postal 53), 77600 Cozumel, Q. Roo. ✆ **800/437-3923** in the U.S. and Canada, or 987/872-0050. Fax 987/872-0381. www.elcozumeleno.com. 252 units. High season $262 double; low season $178–$220 double. All-inclusive. AE, MC, V. **Amenities:** 2 restaurants, 3 bars (including swim-up bar); 2 large pools (including a very large one with a roofed section), wading pool; tennis court; large whirlpool; extensive watersports equipment/rentals; moped rental; children's programs; game room and miniature golf; activities desk; car rental; limited room service; babysitting; laundry. *In room:* A/C, TV, hair dryer, safe.

**Playa Azul** ★★ This quiet hotel is perhaps the most relaxing of the island's beachfront properties. Its small beach, with shade *palapas,* is one of the best on this side of the island. Service is attentive and personal. Almost all the rooms have balconies and ocean views. The rooms in the original section are all suites—large, with very large bathrooms, painted cool white, and simply decorated. The new wing has mostly standard rooms that are comfortable and large, decorated with light tropical colors and furniture. All rooms contain a king bed or two double beds; suites offer two convertible single sofas in the separate living area. This is an especially good hotel for golfers because guests don't pay greens fees.

Carretera San Juan Km 4, 77600 Cozumel, Q. Roo. ✆ **987/872-0199** or 987/872-0043. Fax 987/872-0110. www.playa-azul.com. 50 units. High season $210 double; $280 suite. Low season $150 double; $180 suite. AE, MC, V. Free parking. **Amenities:** Restaurant, 2 bars; small pool; unlimited golf privileges at local club; watersports equipment/rentals; game room with pool table, TV, and videos; tour info; car rental; room service; massage; babysitting; laundry. *In room:* A/C, TV, fridge, coffeemaker, safe.

## Moderate

**Condumel Condobeach Apartments** If you want some distance from the crowds, consider lodging here. It's not a full-service hotel, but in some ways it's more convenient. The one-bedroom apartments are designed and furnished in a modern, practical fashion. They are large and airy, with large glass sliding doors that face the sea and allow for good cross-ventilation (especially in the upper units). The rooms also have ceiling fans, air-conditioning, and two twin beds or one king. Each apartment has a separate living room and a full kitchen with a partially stocked fridge, so you don't have to run to the store on the first day. There's a small, well-tended beach area (with shade *palapas* and a grill for guests' use) that leads to a low, rocky fall-off into the sea.

Carretera Hotelera Norte s/n, 77600 Cozumel, Q. Roo. ✆ **987/872-0892.** Fax 987/872-0661. www.aquasafari.com. 10 units. High season $133; low season $110. No credit cards. Free parking. *In room:* A/C, kitchen, no phone.

**Hotel Fontán** *Value* This hotel, like the Sol Cabañas, is a relative bargain. The rooms are larger and come with two double beds, but the hotel has fewer services, and I don't find it as much fun. Also, the Fontán is in the timeshare business, so although it's small, a lot of people come and go through the lobby. Forty of the 48 rooms have ocean views. The rooms aren't lit well enough, but the medium-size bathrooms are. There's a small beach and a sunning area by the pool.

Carretera San Juan Km 2.5, 77600 Cozumel, Q. Roo. ✆ **800/221-6509** in the U.S., or 987/872-0300. Fax 987/872-0105. 48 units. High season $110–$125 double; low season $95–$110 double. AE, MC, V. Free parking. **Amenities:** Restaurant, bar; small pool; oceanfront whirlpool; watersports equipment/rentals; room service until 10pm; babysitting. *In room:* A/C, TV.

**Sol Cabañas del Caribe** This hotel offers good rates for an oceanfront lodging. It's quaint and relaxing, and there's a small beach on one side and a nice snorkeling area by the rocky section in front of the restaurant (which is at the water's edge). You have a choice of two types of rooms (for the same price). Rooms in the two-story main section face the water, are medium in size, and are comfortable but a little dark. These units have one double and one single bed, a small sitting area, and a porch or a balcony. I prefer them to the one-story *cabañas,* which are smaller but have patios near the beach. The *cabañas* come with one double bed. Service is friendly. The owners also run the Paradisus, an all-inclusive a little way up the coast.

Carretera Santa Pilar Km 4.5 (Apdo. Postal 9), 77600 Cozumel, Q. Roo. ✆ **800/33MELIA** in the U.S and Canada, or 987/872-0017. Fax 987/872-1599. paradisu@cozumel.com.mx. 48 units. High season $170 double; low season $104–$145 double. Honeymoon packages available. AE, MC, V. Free secured parking. **Amenities:** Restaurant, bar; small pool, wading pool; membership in local golf club; watersports equipment; tour desk; car rental; room service; babysitting; laundry. *In room:* A/C, no phone.

## IN TOWN

### Very Expensive

**Hotel Plaza Las Glorias** ★★ This all-suite five-story hotel combines the top-notch amenities of the expensive hotels farther out with the convenience of being 5 blocks from town. For people who must have a beach, this is not the right hotel. Don't dismiss it out of hand, though; it has a smart terraced sunning area above the water, and easy access to the sea. The split-level rooms are large and have separate sitting areas. The furniture and beds are comfortable, and the bathrooms are large, with stone countertops and tub/shower combinations. Bed choices include two doubles, two twins, or one king. All rooms face out over the water and have a balcony or a terrace. The dive shop comes highly recommended.

Av. Rafael Melgar Km 1.5, 77600 Cozumel, Q. Roo. ✆ **800/342-AMIGO** in the U.S. and Canada, or 987/872-2000. Fax 987/872-1937. www.sidek.com.mx. 174 units. High season $280 double; low season $150 double. AE, MC, V. Free parking. **Amenities:** Restaurant, 2 bars (1 swim-up); large pool; whirlpool; watersports equipment rental; tour desk; car and moped rental; room service until 11pm; babysitting; same-day laundry. *In room:* A/C, TV, fridge, hair dryer, safe, purified tap water.

### Moderate

**Hotel Colonial** Around the corner from the main square, on a pedestrian-only street, you'll find this pleasant four-story hotel. Standard rooms, called "studios," are large and have large bathrooms and attractive red-tile floors, but they could be better lit. These units have one double and one twin bed and are trimmed in yellow pine, which seems oddly out of place here. The suites hold two double beds, a kitchenette, and a sitting and dining area. There's free coffee and sweet bread in the morning. When calling, specify the Colonial.

Av. 5 Sur 9 (Apdo. Postal 286), 77600 Cozumel, Q. Roo. ✆ **987/872-9080.** Fax 987/872-9073. www.casamexicanacozumel.com. 28 units. High season $65 studio; $68 suite. Low season $50–$57 studio; $58–$63 suite. Rates include continental breakfast. AE, MC, V. *In room:* A/C, TV, fridge. From the plaza, walk ½ block south on Av. 5 Sur; the hotel is on the left.

**Hotel del Centro** Although this surprisingly stylish hotel is 5 long blocks from the waterfront, it's a bargain if you want a pool. The rooms are small but modern and extra-clean, and they come with two double beds or one king (which costs $10 less). The rooms surround a garden courtyard with an oval pool framed by comfortable lounge chairs.

Av. Juárez 501, 77600 Cozumel, Q. Roo. ✆ **987/872-5471.** Fax 987/872-0299. hcentro@cozumel.com.mx. 14 units. High season $60–$70 double; low season $50–$60 double. Weekly discounts available. No credit cards. **Amenities:** Medium-size pool. *In room:* A/C, TV, no phone.

**Hotel Flamingo** ★ A small hotel just off Avenida Melgar, the Flamingo offers three stories of attractive, comfortable rooms around a small, plant-filled inner courtyard. Highlights include an inviting rooftop terrace and a comfortable bar and coffee bar that serves breakfast. Second- and third-story rooms, which have air-conditioning and TV, cost more. Rooms are large, with two double beds, white-tile floors, medium-size bathrooms, and ceiling fans. A penthouse suite comes with a full kitchen and sleeps up to six. The English-speaking staff is helpful and friendly.

Calle 6 Norte 81, 77600 Cozumel, Q. Roo. ✆ **800/806-1601** in the U.S., or ✆ and fax 987/872-1264. www.hotelflamingo.com. 22 units. High season $55–$77 double; low season $36–$45 double. Internet specials sometimes available. AE, MC, V. **Amenities:** Cafe and bar; scuba rental; tour info; car rental; overnight laundry. *In room:* A/C. From the plaza, walk 3 blocks north on Melgar and turn right on Calle 6; hotel is on the left.

### Inexpensive

**B&B Caribo** *Value* The American owners of this smartly painted blue-and-white B&B go out of their way to make you feel right at home. The rates are a good deal; they include air-conditioning, breakfast, and several little extras. Six neatly decorated rooms come with cool tile floors, white furniture, and big bottles of purified drinking water; these units share a guest kitchen. The six apartments (minimum 1-week stay) have small kitchens. Most rooms have a double bed and a twin bed. There are a number of common rooms and a rooftop terrace. Breakfasts are full, and the cooking is good. There is also a television and computer room with e-mail service.

Av. Juárez 799, 77600 Cozumel, Q. Roo. ✆ **987/872-3195.** www.visit-caribo.com. 12 units. High season $50 double; $60 apartment. Low season $40 double; $50 apartment. Rates include full breakfast. AE, MC, V. **Amenities:** Massage. *In room:* A/C. From the plaza, walk 6½ blocks inland on Juárez; Caribo is on the left.

**Hotel El Marqués** Step back into the 1960s in these sunny rooms with gold trim and imitation marble countertops. Decorated in French provincial style, they have gray-and-white tile floors and two double beds; some rooms hold a fridge. The location is good, and the price is right.

Av. 5 Sur 180 (near the corner of Salas), 77600 Cozumel, Q. Roo. ✆ **987/872-0677.** Fax 987/872-0537. hotelelmarques@hotmail.com. 39 units. High season $48 double; low season $40 double. Discounts for 3 or more nights if paying cash. MC, V. *In room:* A/C. From the plaza, turn right (south) on Avenida 5 Sur; hotel is on the right, upstairs.

**Hotel Safari Inn** This budget hotel offers a convenient location for divers: directly above the Aqua Safari Dive Shop and across the street from the shop's pier, which means that you don't have to lug your gear very far. The large rooms have little in the way of furniture aside from beds. They have small bathrooms with good hot showers. Some rooms could use better lighting, and in some the air-conditioning is noisy. The hotel becomes a real bargain when four or five people are willing to share a room (some units hold a king and two or three twin beds).

Melgar, between Calles 5 and 7 Sur (Apdo. Postal 41), 77600. Cozumel, Q. Roo. ✆ **987/872-0101.** Fax 987/872-0661. dive@aquasafari.com. 12 units. $45 double. MC, V. *In room:* A/C, no phone. From the pier, turn right (south) and walk 4½ blocks on Melgar.

## SOUTH OF TOWN

The hotels in this area tend to be more spread out and farther from town than hotels to the north. Some hotels are on the inland side of the road and some are on the beach side, which makes for a difference in price. Those farthest from town are all-inclusive properties. The beaches along this part of the coast tend to be slightly better than those to the north; all the hotels have swimming pools and piers from which you can snorkel, and all of them accommodate divers. Head south on Avenida Melgar, which becomes the coastal road **Costera Sur** (also called **Carretera a Chankanaab**).

### Very Expensive

**Presidente Inter-Continental Cozumel** ★★★ This hotel in terms of location, on-site amenities, and service. Pala modern in style, the Presidente spreads across a long stretch of coa distant hotels for neighbors. Rooms come in four categories distribute four buildings (two to five stories tall). "Superior" rooms overlook the gar "deluxe" rooms have a view of the ocean. Most are large, with large, well-lit bathrooms. Deluxe oceanfront rooms (on the second floor) and beachfront rooms (at ground level, with direct access to the beach) are even larger and have spacious balconies or patios. Guests in beachfront rooms can request in-room dining with a serenading trio. Rooms come with a choice of one king-size or two double beds and are furnished in understated modern style. The 17 suites and reef rooms are extremely large and well furnished. A long stretch of sandy beach area dotted with *palapas* and palm trees fronts the entire hotel.

Costera Sur Km 6.5, 77600 Cozumel, Q. Roo. © **800/327-0200** in the U.S., or 987/872-9500. Fax 987/872-9528. www.cozumel.intercontinental.com. 253 units. High season $385–$450 double; low season $336–$400 double. From $800 suite year-round. Discounts and packages available. AE, DC, MC, V. Free parking. **Amenities:** 2 restaurants (international, Mexican), snack bar, 2 bars; large pool, wading pool; 2 lighted tennis courts; access to golf club; fully equipped gym; whirlpool; watersports equipment rental; dive shop; children's activities center; concierge; tour desk; car rental; business center; shopping arcade; salon services; 24-hour room service; in-room massage; babysitting; same-day laundry; dry cleaning; nonsmoking rooms. *In room:* A/C, TV with pay movies, dataport, minibar, hair dryer.

### Expensive

**El Cid La Ceiba** ★★ On the beach side of the road, La Ceiba is always a fun place to stay. It has snorkeling and shore diving to a submerged airplane (the hotel provides unlimited tanks) in front of the hotel. Lots of divers come here: It is the Mares Hub system Center for Cozumel and was voted one of the world's top 15 dive resorts in *Rodale's Scuba Diving* magazine. All rooms have ocean views, balconies, and two doubles or one king bed. Bathrooms are roomy and well lit, with granite countertops and strong water pressure. Superior rooms are larger than standard and have more furniture. Some suites are available for limited periods and only to guests who make direct reservations, not to groups. The emphasis here is on watersports, particularly scuba diving, but nondivers can enjoy the large pool area, tennis court, and seaside restaurant.

Costera Sur Km 4.5 (Apdo. Postal 284), 77600 Cozumel, Q. Roo. © **800/435-3240** in the U.S. and Canada, or 987/872-0844. Fax 987/872-0065. www.elcid.com. 98 units. $105–$152 standard; $126–$187 superior. Ask for the Frommer's discount. AE, MC, V. Free parking. **Amenities:** 2 restaurants, 2 bars; 2 large pools; lighted tennis court; access to golf club; small exercise room with sauna; whirlpool; watersports equipment rental; dive shop; tour desk; car rental; room service until 11pm; in-room massage; babysitting; laundry. *In room:* A/C, TV, fridge, coffeemaker.

## WHERE TO DINE

The island offers a surprising variety of good restaurants. When choosing a restaurant, you should know that taxi drivers will often attempt to take you to restaurants that will pay them commissions. Don't be fooled.

**Zermatt** (© **987/872-1384**), a terrific little bakery, is on Avenida 5 at Calle 4 Norte.

### VERY EXPENSIVE

**Pepe's Grill** ★★ STEAKS/SEAFOOD The chefs at Pepe's were the first to popularize grilling foods on the island and up and down the mainland coast. They seem fascinated with fire; what they don't grill in the kitchen, they flambé

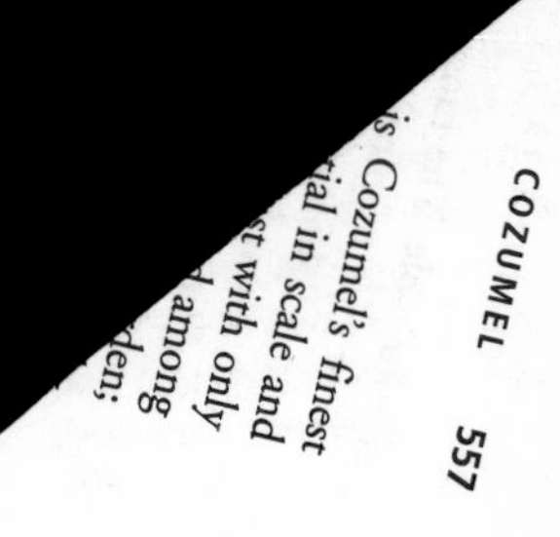

ied items are the good-quality beef (prime
er. For something out of the ordinary, try
little banana and pineapple in a curry sauce
a second-story restaurant with one large air-
massive beamed ceiling. The lighting is soft,
d music. Large windows look out over the har-
readed shrimp and broiled chicken. For dessert
ialties: bananas Foster, crêpe suzette, and café
, and three liqueurs).

872-0213. Reservations recommended. Main courses $18–$35;
1:30pm.

### EXPENSIVE

**French Quarter** ★★ LOUISIANA/SOUTHERN In a pleasant upstairs open-air setting, French Quarter serves Southern and Creole classics. I found the jambalaya and étouffée delicious. The menu also lists blackened fish and fresh lump crabmeat. Filet mignon with red-onion marmalade seems to be a favorite with many customers. There's an air-conditioned dining room and a bar area downstairs.

Av. 5 Sur 18. ✆ **987/872-6321.** Main courses $10–$25. AE, MC, V. Daily 4–11pm.

**La Veranda** ★★★ SEAFOOD/INTERNATIONAL This is the perfect place to go if you're getting tired of fried fish or fish with *achiote* sauce, or if you just want something different. The highly inventive menu emphasizes tropical ingredients and fuses West Indian with European cooking. Every dish I tried here was delicious and artfully presented. The spiced mussel soup had a delicious broth scented with white wine. Veranda mango fish included a mango sauce that was both light and satisfying. And Palancar coconut shrimp consisted of shrimp boiled in a coconut sauce with little bits of raw (not sweet) coconut. The indoor and outdoor dining areas are airy and quite pleasant. You can hear soft jazz and the whirring of ceiling fans in the background. The tables are well separated and attractively set.

Calle 4 Norte (between 5th and 10th Ave.). ✆ **987/872-4132.** Reservations recommended during Carnaval. Main courses $14–$20. MC, V. Daily 4:30pm–midnight.

**Lobster House (Cabaña del Pescador)** ★★★ LOBSTER The thought I often have when I eat a prepared lobster dish is that the cook could have simply boiled the lobster to better effect. The owner of this restaurant seems to agree. The only item on the menu is lobster boiled with a hint of spices and served with melted butter, accompanied by sides of rice, vegetables, and bread. The weight of the lobster tail you select determines the price, with side dishes included. Candles and soft lights illuminate the inviting dining rooms, which sit amid gardens, fountains, and a small duck pond. The owner, Fernando, welcomes you warmly and will even send you next door to his brother's excellent Mexican seafood restaurant, El Guacamayo, if you must have something other than lobster.

Km 4 Carretera Santa Pilar (across from Playa Azul Hotel). No phone. Lobster (by weight) $15–$30. No credit cards. Daily 6–10:30pm.

**Prima** ★★★ NORTHERN ITALIAN Everything at this ever-popular hangout is fresh—pastas, vegetables, and seafood. Owner Albert Domínguez grows most of the vegetables in his local hydroponic garden. The menu changes daily and concentrates on seafood. It might include shrimp scampi, fettuccine with pesto, and lobster and crab ravioli with cream sauce. The fettuccine Alfredo is wonderful, the salads crisp, and the steaks USDA choice. Pizzas are cooked in a wood-burning oven. Desserts include Key lime pie and tiramisu. Dining is upstairs on the breezy terrace.

Calle Rosado Salas 109A (corner of 5th Ave.) ✆ **987/872-4242.** Pizzas $5–$10; pastas $8–$10; steaks $15–$20. AE, MC, V. Daily 4–11pm.

## MODERATE

**El Moro** ★ REGIONAL Crowds flock to El Moro for its good food, service, and prices—but not its decor, which is orange, orange, orange, and Formica. And it's 12 blocks inland, away from everything; a taxi, costing around $2.25, is a must. But all misgivings will disappear as soon as you taste the food (and especially if you sip one of the giant, wallop-packing margaritas). Portions are generous. *Pollo Ticuleño,* a specialty from the town of Ticul, is a rib-sticking, delicious, layered plate of smooth tomato sauce, mashed potatoes, crispy baked corn tortilla, and batter-fried chicken breast, all topped with shredded cheese and green peas. Besides the regional food, other specialties of Mexico include enchiladas and seafood prepared many ways, plus grilled steaks and sandwiches.

75 BIS Norte 124 (between Calles 2 and 4 Norte). ✆ **987/872-3029.** Reservations not accepted. Main courses $6–$15. MC, V. Fri–Wed 1–11pm.

**Guido's** ★ MEDITERRANEAN The inviting interior, with sling chairs and rustic wood tables, makes this a restful place in daytime and a romantic spot at night. The specialty is wood-oven-baked pizzas. Also keep an eye out for the daily specials, which may include an appetizer of sea bass carpaccio, a couple of meat dishes, and usually a fish dish. The other thing that people love here is *pan de ajo*—a house creation of bread made with olive oil, garlic, and rosemary. There's a good, well-priced wine list.

Av. Melgar, between Calles 6 and 8 Nte. ✆ **987/872-0946.** Main courses $8–$13; daily specials $10–$14. AE. Mon–Sat 11am–11pm.

**La Choza** YUCATECAN/MEXICAN Local residents consider this one of the best Mexican restaurants in town. Platters of poblano chiles stuffed with shrimp, mole poblano, and *pollo en relleno negro* (chicken in a sauce of scorched chiles) are among the specialties. The table sauces and guacamole are great, and the daily specials can be good, too. This is an open-air restaurant with well-spaced tables under a tall thatched roof.

Rosado Salas 198 (at Av. 10 Sur). ✆ **987/872-0958.** Reservations not accepted. Breakfast $4; main courses $8–$14. AE, MC, V. Daily 7:30am–11pm.

## INEXPENSIVE

**Casa Denis** REGIONAL/MEXICAN This yellow wooden house, one of the few remaining houses built in the old island style, is a great home-style Mexican restaurant. Small tables are scattered outside on the pedestrian-only street. More tables are in back, on the shady patio. You can make a light meal from empanadas filled with potatoes, cheese, or fish. Better yet, try one of the Yucatecan specialties such as *pollo pibil, panuchos,* or tacos *de cochinita pibil.*

Calle 1 Sur 267 (just off the main plaza). ✆ **987/872-0067.** Reservations not accepted. Breakfast $3–$5; main courses $7–$11. No credit cards. Mon–Sat 7am–11pm; Sun 5–11pm.

**Coco's** MEXICAN/AMERICAN Tended by owners Terri and Daniel Ocejo, Coco's is clean and welcoming to the tourist, right down to the free coffee refills and attentive service. Indulge in stateside favorites like hash browns, corn flakes and bananas, gigantic blueberry muffins, cinnamon rolls, and cream-stuffed rolls. Mexican specialties include *huevos rancheros* and *huevos a la mexicana.*

Av. 5 Sur 180 (down the block from the main plaza). ✆ **987/872-0241.** Breakfast $3–$6. No credit cards. Tues–Sun 6am–noon. Closed Sept–Oct.

**Comida Casera Toñita** HOME-STYLE YUCATECAN The owners have made the living room of their home into a comfortable dining room, complete with filled bookshelves and classical music playing in the background. Whole fried fish, fish filet, and fried chicken are on the regular menu. Daily specials give you a chance to taste authentic regional food, including *pollo a la naranja* (chicken in bitter-orange sauce), chicken *mole, pollo en escabeche* (chicken in vinegar-based sauce), and pork chops with *achiote* seasoning.

Calle Rosado Salas 265 (between Av. 10 and 15). ✆ **987/872-0401.** Breakfast $1.75–$3; main courses $3.75–$7; daily specials $3; fruit drinks $1.75. No credit cards. Mon–Sat 8am–6pm.

**Jeanie's Waffle House** BREAKFAST/DESSERTS The specialty here is crisp, light waffles served in a variety of ways, including waffles *ranchero* with eggs and salsa, waffles Benedict with eggs and hollandaise sauce, and waffles with whipped cream and chocolate. Hash browns, homemade breads, and great coffee are other reasons to drop in for breakfast.

Av. Melgar (between Calles 5 and 7). ✆ **987/872-4145.** Breakfast $4–$7. No credit cards. Mon–Sat 6am–9pm; Sun 6am–3pm.

**Restaurant del Museo** BREAKFAST/MEXICAN The most pleasant place in San Miguel to have breakfast or perhaps an early lunch (weather permitting) is at this rooftop cafe above the island's museum. It offers a serene view of the water, removed from the traffic noise below and sheltered from the sun above. The tables and chairs are comfortable and the food reliable. Your choices are limited to the mainstays of American and Mexican breakfasts and lunch dishes such as enchiladas and guacamole.

Av. Rafael Melgar (corner of Calle 6 Nte.). ✆ **987/872-0838.** Reservations not accepted. Breakfast $4–$5; lunch main courses $5–$9. No credit cards. Daily 7am–2pm.

### COZUMEL AFTER DARK

Cozumel attracts divers and other active visitors who play hard all day and wind down at night. The nightlife scene is often low-key and peaks in the early evening. The exception is the cruise-ship crowd. On Sunday evenings the place to be is the main square, which usually has a free concert and lots of people strolling about and visiting with friends. People sit in outdoor cafes enjoying the cool night breezes until the restaurants close. **Carlos 'n' Charlie's** (✆ **987/872-0191**), the **Hard Rock Cafe** (✆ **987/872-5271**), and a couple of other clubs are along Avenida Melgar on the north side of the main plaza. They are among the liveliest and most predictable places in town.

## 3 Puerto Morelos & Environs

34km (21 miles) S of Cancún

Development has largely passed by Puerto Morelos, and a medium-size resort hotel, **Ceiba del Mar,** recently built on the coast north of town, doesn't look as if it's going to change things. Puerto Morelos remains a quiet place—perfect for a relaxed vacation of lying on the beach and reading a book, with perhaps the occasional foray into a watersport, especially snorkeling, diving, or kayaking.

# The Yucatán's Upper Caribbean Coast

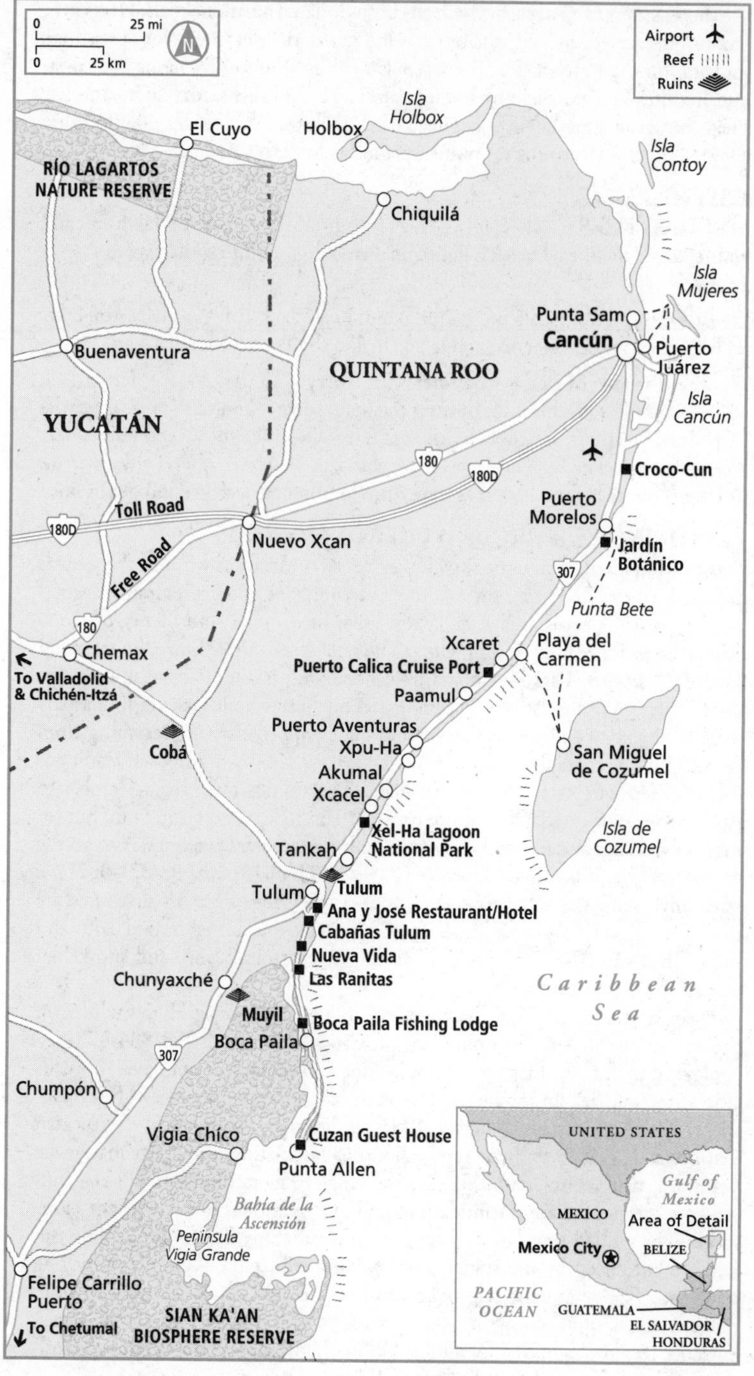

Offshore is a prominent reef, which has been declared a national park for its protection. Because of the reef, the beaches in Puerto Morelos have a lot of sea grass growing on the bottom. But the water is as clear as anywhere along the coast, and if a little sea grass doesn't bother you, you'll find this a cozy spot. Another great thing is a large English-language used bookstore that stocks 30,000 titles. Puerto Morelos is also the terminus for the car ferry to Cozumel.

## ESSENTIALS

**GETTING THERE** **By Car** Drive south from Cancún along Highway 307 to the km 31 marker. There's a light and a large sign pointing the way to Puerto Morelos.

**By Bus** Buses from Cancún to Tulum and Playa del Carmen usually stop here, so be sure to ask in Cancún if your bus makes the Puerto Morelos stop.

**By the Puerto Morelos–Cozumel Car Ferry** To get to the ferry dock (**© 998/871-0008**), head south from the main square. You can't miss it. See the "Cozumel" section for details on the car ferry schedule, but several points bear repeating here: The schedule may change, so double-check it, and always arrive at least 3 hours before the ferry's departure to purchase a ticket and get in line.

## EXPLORING IN & AROUND PUERTO MORELOS

Puerto Morelos attracts visitors who seek seaside relaxation without the crowds and high prices. There are several hotels, a couple of good restaurants, a good pizzeria, an English-language bookstore, two dive shops, and plenty of recreational boats for fishing or snorkeling. The bookstore, **Alma Libre,** on the main square (**© 998/871-0264;** casamaya@yahoo.com), has more English-language books than any other in the Yucatán, and not just whodunits, sci-fi, and spy novels. The owners, Jeanine Kitchel and Paul Zappella, stock everything from philosophy to biography to anthropology; if your idea of good beach reading is *Thus Spake Zarathustra,* this is your place. The store is open from October to April. Hours are Tuesday to Saturday from 10am to 1pm and 6 to 9pm, but for most of October and November it opens only on weekend evenings. Also on the main square is **Sub Aqua Explorers** (**© 998/871-0078;** fax 998/871-0027), a good dive shop that also arranges fishing trips. More than 15 dive sites are nearby, and many are close to shore. A two-tank dive costs around $60, and night dives cost $55. Two hours of fishing costs around $80, and snorkeling excursions run around $5.

If you're traveling by car, there are a couple of stops along Highway 307 on the way to Puerto Morelos from Cancún. **Croco Cun** ★ (**© 998/884-4782**), a zoological park that raises crocodiles, is a lot more than just your average roadside attraction. It's an interactive zoo with crocodiles in all stages of development, as well as animals of nearly all the species that once roamed the Yucatán Peninsula. A visit to the new reptile house is fascinating, though it may make you think twice about venturing into the jungle. The rattlesnakes and boa constrictors are particularly intimidating, and the tarantulas are downright enormous. The guided tour lasts 1½ hours. Children enjoy the guides' enthusiasm and are entranced by the spider monkeys and wild pigs. Wear plenty of bug repellent. The restaurant sells refreshments. Croco Cun is open daily from 8:30am to 5:30pm. As with other attractions of this sort along the coast, entrance fees are high: $15 for adults, $9 for children ages 6 to 12, free for children under 6. The park is at km 31 on Highway 307.

## WHERE TO STAY

**Amar Inn** Simple rooms on the beach, in a home-style setting, make up this small inn. The cordial hostess, Ana Luisa Aguilar, is the daughter of Luis Aguilar, a Mexican singer and movie star of the '40s and '50s. Besides running her little B&B, she keeps busy promoting environmental and equitable-development causes. She can line up snorkeling and fishing trips and jungle tours for guests. There are three *palapas* in back, opposite the main house, and four upstairs rooms with views of the beach. There is something indelibly, unselfconsciously Mexican in the decor. The *palapas* and one of the upstairs rooms have thatched roofs. Bedding choices include one or two doubles, one king-size, or five twin beds. A full Mexican breakfast is served in the garden.

Av. Javier Rojo Gómez (at Lázaro Cardenas), 77580 Puerto Morelos, Q. Roo. ✆ **998/871-0026.** amar_inn@hotmail.com. 7 units. High season $65 double; low season $45 double. Rates include full breakfast. No credit cards. **Amenities:** Tour and rental info. *In room:* Fridge, fan, no phone. From the plaza, turn left; it's ½ mile farther, immediately after the Hotel Ojo de Agua.

**Ceiba del Mar** ★★★ This spa resort is on a slightly isolated part of the coast a bit north of town. It consists of several three-story buildings, each with a rooftop terrace with Jacuzzi. The carefully tended white sand beach with thatched shade umbrellas lies beside a seaside pool with Jacuzzi and bar. Nearby is a native-style steam bath (*temascal*). Rooms are large, with either two doubles or one king-size bed, and have a terrace or balcony. The large, well-appointed bathrooms have shower/tub combinations, marble countertops, and makeup mirrors. Suites are very large, with two bedrooms, two or three full bathrooms and as many TVs and minibars, and separate entryways. Emphasis is on personal service, as exemplified by the delivery of coffee and juice each morning using a closed pass-through.

Av. Niños Héroes s/n, 77580 Puerto Morelos, Q. Roo. ✆ **877/545-6221** from the U.S. or 998/873-8060. Fax 998/872-8061. www.ceibadelmar.com. 126 units. High season $426 deluxe, $708 2-bedroom suite; low season $330 deluxe, $538 2-bedroom suite. Rates include continental breakfast, full breakfast, dinner. AE, MC, V. Free parking. **Amenities:** 2 restaurants (international/Mexican, grill), 2 bars; 2 pools; 1 lighted tennis court; complete spa offering a wide variety of treatments; state-of-the-art gym with sauna, steam room, whirlpool, and Swiss showers; 8 rooftop Jacuzzis; dive shop with watersports equipment; bikes for guests' use; concierge; tour info; car rental; salon; room service until 11pm; babysitting; overnight laundry; non-smoking rooms. *In room:* A/C, TV/VCR, CD player, minibar, hair dryer, bathrobes, safe.

**Hacienda Morelos** This is a small hotel on the water with pleasant rooms and good prices. Simple rooms are spacious and comfortable, and all have ocean views. Most come with a kitchenette and two double beds, and eight have air-conditioning. The hotel has a small pool and a restaurant (Johnny Cairo's; see "Where to Dine," below).

Av. Rafael E. Melgar 2 L. 5, SMZA. 01, 77580 Puerto Morelos, Q. Roo. ✆ and fax **998/871-0448.** 15 units. High season $75 double; low season $56 double. AE, MC. V. Free parking. **Amenities:** Restaurant; bar; pool.

**Hotel Ojo de Agua** *Value* This is a seaside hotel with modern rooms. Two long three-story buildings stand on the beach at a right angle to each other. Most rooms have balconies and glass sliding doors. They are simply furnished and very clean. Most rooms have two double beds or a double and a twin; those with one double bed go for $10 less. Twenty-four rooms have air-conditioning, and 24 have phones. "Studio" units have small kitchenettes. Service is friendly, making one feel very comfortable here.

Supermanzana 2, lote 16, 77580 Puerto Morelos, Q. Roo. ✆ **998/871-0027** or 998/871-0507. Fax 998/871-0202. www.ojo-de-agua.com. 36 units. High season $45–$55 double, $60 studio; low season $30–$40 double, $50 studio. Weekly and monthly rates available. AE, MC, V. **Amenities:** Restaurant, bar; pool; scuba shop; tour info; watersports equipment; room service until 10pm; in-room massage.

## WHERE TO DINE

The pizzeria on the plaza is a popular hangout for much of the community.

**Johnny Cairo's Bar and Grill** ★ ECLECTIC I don't know what to tell you about this restaurant except that you can count on two things: The food will be good, and the next time you go, everything will be totally different. The owner, a onetime Ritz-Carlton chef, seems to get bored easily and is always ready to change things. His ilk is the bane of travel writers, but I can't punish him on that score. His food has been dependably good, and he is careful to get only the freshest seafood. The restaurant is especially popular on Sunday afternoon, when it serves barbecue with all the traditional meats and sides. For the monthly full-moon party, the staff moves the entire restaurant down to the beach, builds a bonfire, and cooks an entirely different menu.

Av. Rafael E. Melgar (in the Hacienda Morelos hotel). ✆ **998/871-0449.** Reservations recommended. Main courses $5–$17. No credit cards. Tues–Sat 6–10pm; Sun 1–6pm.

**Los Pelícanos** SEAFOOD To the right of the plaza, this ocean-view restaurant is quite a pleasant place to dine. Select a table inside under the *palapa* or outside on the terrace (if there's no breeze, wear mosquito repellent in the evenings). The seafood menu has many offerings, mostly prepared in true Mexican fashion, such as *ceviche* and *pescado a la veracruzana.* For those who don't want seafood, there's grilled chicken and steak.

On the ocean side behind the *zócalo* (town square). ✆ **998/871-0014.** Main courses $8–$16; lobster $27. MC, V. Daily 10am–11pm.

## EN ROUTE TO PLAYA DEL CARMEN

From Puerto Morelos, Playa del Carmen is only 32km (20 miles). Before you get there, you'll pass a couple of lodging options and a couple of roadside attractions.

About half a mile from Puerto Morelos is the 150-acre **Jardín Botánico Dr. Alfredo Barrera** (no phone), opened in 1990 and named after the biologist who studied tropical forests. A natural, protected showcase for native plants and animals, it's open Monday to Saturday from 9am to 5pm. Admission is $6. The park has six parts: an **epiphyte area** (plants that grow on others); **Maya ruins;** an **ethnographic area,** with a furnished hut and typical garden; a **chiclero camp** about the once-thriving *chicle* (chewing gum) industry; a **nature park,** where wild vegetation is preserved; and **mangroves.** There's a 3km (2-mile) path, and the dense jungle of plants and trees is named and labeled in English and Spanish. Each sign has the plant's botanical and common names, uses of the plant, and the geographic areas where it is found in the wild. There are about 450 species in the park. The wildlife includes monkeys, but they're wilder (and hence less visible) than at such places as Croco Cun or Aktun-Chen. This park is not frequently visited because it isn't as fun for children as some of the other attractions along the coast. A visit does get you away from the crowds, but will be of most interest to those with a botanical bent.

About midway between Puerto Morelos and Playa del Carmen is **Tres Ríos** (✆ **998/887-8077;** www.tres-rios.com), a nature park along the same lines as Xcaret and Xel-ha. See the "Eco-Theme Parks & Reserves" section of the Cancún chapter.

### WHERE TO STAY & DINE

These establishments lie 24km (15 miles) from Puerto Morelos. On the left side of Highway 307, you'll see a large sign for the entrance to La Posada del Capitán Lafitte. Take the same turn-off and follow the signs to reach KaiLuum II.

**KaiLuum II** ★ This lodging is for those who want an unfiltered beach experience and time off from civilization; KaiLuum is simplicity. The things that matter here are the beach, the water, the stars, the quiet, and the soft light of candles. Things that don't seem to matter are electricity, noise, and bustle. Thirty large tents spread across an immaculately kept beach. Each stands under a thatched roof, and contains chairs, a couple of hammocks, some shelving, and a queen-size bed. A couple of buildings house showers, sinks, and toilets; a tall beach *palapa* serves breakfast, cocktails, and dinner. The food is good. This is the kind of place where you take off your sandals and don't put them on again until it's time to leave.

Carretera Cancún–Tulum Km 62, 77710 Playa del Carmen, Q. Roo. ✆ **800/538-6802** in the U.S. and Canada. ✆ and fax 984/801-3502. www.mexicoholiday.com. 30 units. High season $120–$135 double; low season $100–$120 double. Rates include breakfast and dinner. No credit cards accepted. Children under 17 not accepted. **Amenities:** Restaurant, bar.

**La Posada del Capitán Lafitte** ★ A mile from the highway, down a dirt road, this lovely seaside retreat sits on a solitary stretch of sandy beach. Here you can enjoy being isolated while still having all the amenities of a relaxing vacation. The one- and two-story white stucco bungalows, which hold one to four rooms each, stretch along a powdery white beach. They are smallish but comfortable, with tile floors; small, tiled bathrooms; either two double beds or one king-size bed; and an oceanfront porch. Twenty-nine bungalows have air-conditioning; the rest have fans. Coffee can be served as early as 6:30am in the game room. A dive shop on the premises sees a lot of business because the clientele includes many divers. The hotel offers transportation to and from the Cancún airport for $50 per person (minimum of two passengers).

Carretera Cancún–Tulum Km 62, 77710 Playa del Carmen, Q. Roo. ✆ **800/538-6802** in the U.S. and Canada, or 998/873-0214. Fax 998/873-0212. www.mexicoholiday.com. 62 units. High season $210 double; low season $140 double. Christmas and New Year's rates are higher. Minimum 2–4 nights. Rates include breakfast and dinner. MC, V. Free guarded parking. **Amenities:** Restaurant, poolside grill, bar; medium-size pool; watersports equipment; game/TV room; activities desk; dive shop; car rental; limited room service; laundry. *In room:* Minibar.

**BEACH CABAÑAS** A little over two kilometers farther south are some economical lodgings on a mostly rocky beach just a few kilometers north of Playa del Carmen. A sign that says PUNTA BETE marks the access road. The last time I visited, there was a large warehouse-like structure and a sign advertising a subdivision somewhere that read ARBOLEDAS. The road is rough in places, but in a short time you arrive at the water along a lightly populated stretch of beach. Before you do, the road forks off in a few places, and you'll see signs for different *cabañas.* The word conjures up visions of idyllic native-style dwellings with thatched roofs, but as often as not on the Yucatecan coast, it means simple lodging. This is mostly the case here—Spartan dwellings at $30 to $40 per double. One of these places is **Cabañas Bahía Xcalacoco,** Apdo. Postal 176, 77710 Playa del Carmen, Q. Roo (no phone). Run by a Mexican and American couple, it has six rooms and no electricity. Another is **Paradise Point** (http://paradise-point-resort.com), which has 10 comfortable rooms on a rocky coast right at the water's edge, also without electricity. A Swiss gentleman operates **Coco's Cabañas** (✆ **998/874-7056;** cchr@caribe.net.mx), which has electricity and ceiling fans; a good, inexpensive little restaurant; and a small pool.

## 4 Playa del Carmen ★★★

32km (20 miles) S of Puerto Morelos, 70km (44 miles) S of Cancún, 10.5km (6½ miles) N of Xcaret, 13km (8 miles) N of Puerto Calica

Playa del Carmen is growing quickly. It lies on one of the best stretches of beach on the coast and is perfect for enjoying the simple (and perhaps the best) pleasures of a seaside vacation—taking in the sun and the sea air while working your toes into soft, white sand; cooling down with a swim in clear blue water; and strolling leisurely and aimlessly down the beach while listening to the wash of waves and feeling the light touch of tropical breezes on your skin. The beach grows and shrinks, from broad and sandy to narrower with occasional rocks, depending on the currents and wind.

If solitude is what you're looking for, go elsewhere. Playa draws crowds of visitors with its lively nightlife and burgeoning restaurant scene. South of town, in the Playacar development, are 13 large all-inclusives, and farther south is the cruise-ship pier. Together, these account for a lot of street and beach traffic. The town itself has a casual feel. The local architecture has adopted elements of native building—rustic clapboard walls, thatched roofs, lots of tropical foliage, irregular shapes and angles, and a ramshackle, unplanned look to many structures. All of this reflects the toned-down approach to tourism. Recently, though, slicker architecture has appeared, and chain restaurants and stores have arrived, which detract from Playa's individuality.

Though no longer having the feel of a village, Playa still can provide that rare combination of simplicity (in the form of a small town that can be crossed on foot) and variety (in terms of the many one-of-a-kind hotels, restaurants, and stores). It is this aspect of cosmopolitan counterculture getaway that makes Playa so different from the rest of the coast. And from here it's easy to shoot out to Cozumel on the ferry, to drive south to the nature parks and the ruins at Tulum and Cobá, or to drive north to Cancún. A strong European influence has made topless sunbathing (nominally against the law in Mexico) a nonchalantly accepted practice anywhere there's a beach.

### ESSENTIALS

**GETTING THERE & DEPARTING** **By Air** You can fly into Cancún and take a bus directly from the airport (see "By Bus," below), or fly into Cozumel and take the passenger ferry.

**BY CAR** Highway 307, which connects Cancún with Tulum, is the only highway that passes through Playa. (See "Arriving," below, for more info.)

**BY THE PLAYA DEL CARMEN–COZUMEL PASSENGER FERRY** See the Cozumel section "Getting There & Departing," earlier in this chapter, for details.

**BY TAXI** Taxi fares from the Cancún airport are high—about $70 one-way.

**BY BUS** The **Autobuses Riviera** offers service from the Cancún airport about 12 times a day. Cost is $7 one-way. Buses also connect Playa to Xcaret, Tulum, Chetumal, Chichén-Itzá, and Mérida.

### ORIENTATION

**ARRIVING** As you approach Playa del Carmen from Cancún, Highway 307 divides. Stay left; you'll be able to make a left turn at either of two traffic lights. The first is Avenida Constituyentes, which works well for destinations in

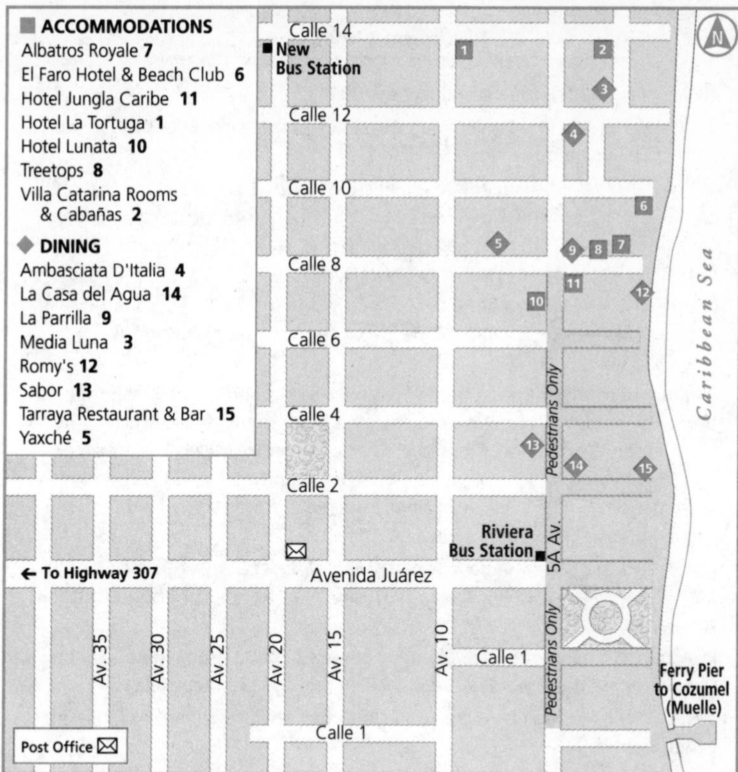


northern Playa. The second is Avenida Juárez, the artery connecting the highway to the town's main square and ferry pier. If you don't get over to the left when the highway divides, you must continue until you get to a turn-around. The **ferry** dock in Playa del Carmen is 1½ blocks from the main square and within walking distance of hotels. Playa has two **bus** stations. Buses coming from Cancún and places along the coast, such as Tulum, arrive at the Riviera station, at the corner of Juárez and Avenida 5, by the town square. Buses coming from destinations in the interior of the peninsula arrive at the new ADO station, on Avenida 20 between 12th and 14th streets. Last time I checked, there was no taxi stand by the new bus station. The Puerto Calica **cruise** pier is almost 13km (8 miles) south of Playa del Carmen; Playa taxis meet each ship.

**CITY LAYOUT** Locals know and use street names, but few street signs exist. The main street, **Avenida Juárez,** leads to the *zócalo* (town square) from Highway 307. As it does so, it crosses several numbered avenues that run parallel to the beach, all of which are multiples of 5. Avenida 5 is closest to the beach; it's closed to traffic from the *zócalo* to Calle 6 (and some blocks beyond, in the evening). On this avenue are many hotels, restaurants and shops. Almost all the town is north and west of the *zócalo.* Immediately south are the ferry pier and the Continental Plaza Playacar Hotel. This is the southern edge of town. Beyond it are the airstrip and the golf course development called Playacar, with lots of private residences and over a dozen resort hotels.

## *FAST FACTS:* Playa del Carmen

*Area Code* The telephone area code is **984.**

*Doctor* Dr. E. Medina Peniche (✆ **984/873-0134**) speaks English and can be reached around the clock.

*Internet Access* The speediest connections are at the **Atomic Internet Café,** Calle 8 between Avenidas 5 and 10. It's open Monday to Saturday 9am to 11pm. But there are so many Internet cafes that you won't have to walk 2 blocks out of your way to find one.

*Money Exchange* Playa has several banks with automatic teller machines, and several *casas de cambio.* Many are close to the pier or along Avenida 5 at Calle 8.

*Parking* Because of Playa's pedestrian-only blocks and increasing population and popularity, parking close to hotels has become more difficult. The most accessible parking lot is the Estacionamiento Mexico, at Avenida Juárez and Avenida 10. It's open daily 24 hours and charges $1.25 per hour or $8 per day. There's also a 24-hour lot a block from the pier, where you can leave your car while you visit Cozumel.

*Pharmacy* The **Farmacia del Carmen,** Avenida Juárez between Avenidas 5 and 10 (✆ **984/873-2330**), states on its sign that it's open 24 hours, but it sometimes closes at midnight.

*Post Office* The *correo* is on Avenida Juárez 3 blocks from the plaza, on the right past the Hotel Playa del Carmen and the launderette.

*Seasons* High season is August and December to Easter. Low season is all other months.

## EXPLORING PLAYA DEL CARMEN

Mainly what you do is hang out on the beach and enjoy the Fifth Avenue nightlife. But, as is the case with just about anywhere on this coast, you can always line up a snorkel or scuba trip. A number of shops, including **Tank-Ha Dive Center** (✆ **984/873-0302;** fax 984/873-1355; www.tankha.com), arrange reef and cavern diving. The owner, Alberto Leonard, came to Playa by way of Madrid and offers reef and *cenote* diving excursions. Snorkeling trips cost around $30 and include soft drinks and equipment. Two-tank dive trips are $65; resort courses with SSI and PADI instructors cost $75.

If golf is your bag, an 18-hole championship **golf course** (✆ **984/873-0624**), designed by Robert Von Hagge, is adjacent to the Continental Plaza Playacar. Greens fees are $120 (includes cart), caddies cost $20, club rental costs $20, and the price includes tax. The club also has two **tennis** courts.

Day-trip possibilities include **Tulum, Xel-Ha,** and **Xcaret.** (See the Tulum section of this chapter, later, and the "Eco-Theme Parks & Reserves" section of the Cancún chapter.) The magnificent ruins of Chichén-Itzá are 2½ hours away. Several agencies offer tours to these and other places. **Cozumel,** a 30-minute ferry ride on one of the new faster boats, can be a day trip, but I don't believe its best side is shown in a short trip. You'll pretty much see exactly what the cruise ship passengers see—lots of duty-free, souvenir, and jewelry shops. To enjoy Cozumel you have to spend at least a couple of nights.

## WHERE TO STAY

One of the small hotels in Playa can be more fun than one of the resorts outside of town. Don't hesitate to book a place that's not on the beach. Town life here is much of the fun, and staying on the beach in Playa has its disadvantages—in particular, the noise of a couple of beachside bars. Beaches are public property in Mexico, and you can lay out your towel anywhere you like without anyone bothering you. If you want a quiet room on the beach, consider the **Shangri-La Caribe,** listed below. It's on the outskirts of town, far from the bars but within walking distance or a short taxi ride of downtown. The rates listed below include the 12% hotel tax and assume double occupancy. High-season rates generally don't include the week between Christmas and New Year's, when rates go still higher.

### VERY EXPENSIVE

**El Faro Hotel and Beach Club** ★ Rooms and suites spread out on a large property graced by tall palms and manicured gardens fronting 75 meters of sandy beachfront. A small but stunning pool (heated in winter) has islands of palms inside and is bordered by cushioned lounges and a *palapa* bar. The entire property has a cool feel to it. The rooms, most of which are in two-story buildings with white-and-cream stucco exteriors, have clay-tile floors, ceiling fans, and marble bathrooms. They hold one king, one queen, or two double beds. Most rooms have a large balcony or terrace. Rates vary according to the dominant view—garden, sea, or beachfront—the size of the room, and the time of year. Five smaller "standard" rooms and three cabañas lack air-conditioning and are cheaper. Also on the property is a working lighthouse.

Calle 10 Norte, 77710 Playa del Carmen, Q. Roo. ✆ **888/243-7413** from the U.S., or 984/873-0970. Fax 984/873-0968. www.hotelelfaro.com. 29 units. High season $190–$240 deluxe with A/C, $110–$150 without A/C. Low season $150–$185 deluxe with A/C, $97–$134 without A/C. Rates include full breakfast. AE, MC, V. Limited free guarded parking available. **Amenities:** Restaurant, bar; pool; tour desk.

**Shangri-La Caribe** ★★ Most of the rooms in this property are in two-story, thatched bungalows spread out across a wide and beautiful beach. Accommodations have a patio (ground floor) or terrace (second floor), complete with hammock. Most come with two double beds, but a few have a king bed. Windows are screened, and a ceiling fan circulates the breeze. The 33 rooms farthest from the sea have air-conditioning, and prices are higher for the bungalows close to the beach. Though you're near Playa del Carmen, the feeling is one of being many comforting miles from civilization. Book well in advance during high season. The turn-off to the hotel is on the north side of the city, by a Volkswagen dealership. A mile of paved road leads to the hotel.

Calle 38 (Apdo. Postal 253), 77710 Playa del Carmen, Q. Roo. ✆ **800/538-6802** in the U.S. or Canada, or 984/873-0611. Fax 984/873-0500. www.shangri-la.com.mx. 107 units. High season $180 garden view with A/C; $200–$240 oceanview or beachfront. Low season $130 garden view; $150–$190 oceanview or beachfront. Rates include breakfast and dinner. AE, MC, V. Free guarded parking. **Amenities:** 2 restaurants, poolside grill, 4 bars; 2 large pools; whirlpool; watersports equipment; dive shop; game room; tour desk; car rental; in-room massage; babysitting; overnight laundry; nonsmoking rooms. *In room:* Hair dryer, no phone.

### MODERATE

**Albatros Royale** The Albatros consists of several two-story buildings occupying a narrow lot facing the beach and one three-story building in back. Deluxe rooms have air-conditioning, microwave, fridge, coffeemaker, and a king-size bed. Other rooms have two double beds or a queen. All have tile floors and bathrooms with marble countertops and showers. Each of the bungalow units has a balcony or terrace with a hammock. Most have two double beds, but seven have queen beds.

Calle 8, between Av. 5 and the beach (Apdo. Postal 31), 77710 Playa del Carmen, Q. Roo. ✆ **800/538-6802** in the U.S. and Canada, or 984/873-0001. 39 units. High season $82 double, $92 deluxe. Low season $51 double, $61 deluxe. AE, MC, V. **Amenities:** Tour info; overnight laundry.

**Hotel Jungla Caribe** ★★ Located right in the heart of the 5th Avenue action, "La Jungla" is an imaginative place, with a highly stylized look that mixes neoclassical with Robinson Crusoe. Its character is perfectly in keeping with the quirkiness of the town. Owner Rolf Albrecht envisioned space and comfort for guests, so all but eight of the standard rooms are large, with gray-and-black marble floors, the occasional Roman column, and large bathrooms. Fifteen of the rooms are suites. Catwalks connect the "tower" section of suites to the hotel. There's an attractive pool in the courtyard beneath a giant *Ramón* tree. Eight small rooms lack air-conditioning and are priced lower than the rates listed here.

Av. 5 Norte (at Calle 8), 77710 Playa del Carmen, Q. Roo. ✆ and fax **984/873-0650.** www.junglacaribe.com. 25 units. High season $95 double; $110–$135 suite. 30% low-season discount. AE, MC, V. **Amenities:** Restaurant, 2 bars; tour info; room service until 11pm. *In room:* A/C, TV, no phone.

**Hotel Lunata** ★★ This hotel offers a combination of location, comfort, attractiveness, and price that no other hotel in this category can beat. It's built in hacienda style, with cut stone, wrought iron, and contemporary Mexican colors. The rooms show a lot of polish, with good air-conditioning and nicely finished bathrooms. The majority of rooms are deluxe, which are medium to large and come with a king or two doubles and good central air. A complimentary continental breakfast is served in the garden, and the third-story terrace makes a nice place to hang out.

Av. 5 (between Calles 6 and 8), 77710 Playa del Carmen, Q. Roo. ✆ **984/873-0884.** Fax 984/873-1240. www.lunata.com. 10 units. $50–$80 standard; $70–$120 deluxe and jr. suite. Promotional low-season rates available. AE, MC, V. **Amenities:** Snorkel and bike rentals; tour desk; babysitting; massage; overnight laundry; nonsmoking rooms. *In room:* A/C, TV, fridge, safe, no phone.

**La Tortuga** This lovely two-story hotel appears tropical, with *palapa* roofs and lots of raw-wood bracing. The rooms, however, offer comfort and polish. They have balconies or terraces facing lovely garden courtyards. Most rooms have a king bed, and some have two queens. The bathrooms are large, and the suites contain whirlpool tubs. The hotel is 3 blocks from the beach. Guests get a voucher for the nearby Tukan Beach Club, which offers some food and drink service on one of the nicest stretches of beach in Playa.

Av. 10 732 (between Calles 12 and 14), 77710 Playa del Carmen, Q. Roo. ✆ and fax **984/873-1484** or 984/873-0626. Fax 984/873-0798. www.hotellatortuga.com. 33 units. High season $95 double; $135 suite. Low season $75 double; $115 suite. AE, MC, V. Rates include continental breakfast. **Amenities:** Restaurant, bar; 2 pools; bike rental; tour info; limited room service; in-room massage; overnight laundry and dry cleaning. *In room:* A/C, TV, minibar, fridge, hair dryer, safe.

### INEXPENSIVE

**Villas Amanecer** Located some distance from the center of town, this hotel offers attractive rooms and apartments near the water at an attractive price. Rooms are modern Mediterranean in style, with lots of built-in counters and sitting areas. Choices of bed include a king or two doubles. There are also some condos, which rent for a week or a month. They're larger and have TVs, and many come with large sitting and dining areas and kitchenettes. Guests get the use of a nearby beach club.

Calle 26 Norte 286, 77710 Playa del Carmen, Q. Roo. ✆ **984/873-2716**; fax 984/873-2717. www.villa-amanecer.com 49 units. High season $90 double; low season $70 double. 1-bedroom condo $420/week; 2-bedroom condo $616/week. Internet specials sometimes available. AE, MC, V. Free guarded parking. **Amenities:** Restaurant; 2 pools; tour info; car rental; room service until 11pm; massage; same-day laundry; nonsmoking rooms. *In room:* A/C, safe.

**Treetops** ★ *Value* The rooms at Treetops encircle a patch of preserved jungle (and a small *cenote*) that shades the hotel and lends it the proper tropical feel. Rooms are large and comfortable and have balconies or patios looking out over the "jungle." Some of the upper rooms, especially the central suite, have the feel of a treehouse. Two suites are large, with fully loaded kitchenettes; and they're great for groups of four. The location is excellent: half a block from the beach, half a block from Avenida 5. That little bit of distance keeps the rooms quiet. There's a small pool.

Calle 8 s/n, 77710 Playa del Carmen, Q. Roo. ✆ and fax **984/873-0351**. www.treetopshotel.com. 18 units. High season $45–$78 double; low season $35–$65 double. Rates include continental breakfast. Dive and honeymoon packages available. MC, V. **Amenities:** Bar; small pool. *In room:* A/C, fridge.

**Villa Catarina Rooms & Cabañas** ★★ Hammocks stretch in front of each of the stylishly rustic rooms and *cabañas* here, nestled in a grove of palms and fruit trees. Each of the well-furnished rooms has one or two double beds on wooden bases, with carpeted or wood floors. Some rooms have a small loft for reading and relaxing; others have *palapa* roofs or terraces. Bathrooms are detailed with colorful tiles, and some of the larger rooms have sitting areas. There's good cross-ventilation through well-screened windows. Coffee is available every morning.

Calle Privada Norte (between Calles 12 and 14), 77710 Playa del Carmen, Q. Roo. ✆ **984/873-2098**. Fax 984/873-2097. 14 units. High season $65–$85 double; low season $45–$60 double. Rates include morning coffee. MC, V.

## WHERE TO DINE

Restaurants in Playa constantly open and close. Most do not take reservations, though there seems to be little trouble getting a table. If you want to try some *comida del pueblo* (people's food) I can recommend a taco restaurant, **El Sarape Grill,** on Avenida Juárez between Avenidas 20 and 25. For something farther off the beaten path, try **Pozolería Mi Abuelita** on Avenida 30, between Calles 20 and 22. It serves good pozole rojo and enchiladas verdes. Across Avenida 30 is a taquería called **El Pastorcito,** which makes great tacos al pastor. All of these places are open at night.

### EXPENSIVE

**Ambasciata D'Italia** ★ NORTHERN ITALIAN The predominantly Italian crowd filling the tables here is a telling sign that the food is authentic and delicious. Entrees cover a range of homemade pasta and northern Italian specialties, with seafood prominently featured. There's an admirable selection of wines, and the espresso is exceptional. The ambience is lively and sophisticated.

Av. 5 (at Calle 12). ✆ **984/873-0553**. Reservations not accepted. Main courses $8–$12. AE, MC, V. Daily 7pm–midnight.

**La Parrilla** ★ MEXICAN/GRILL One of the most popular restaurants in town, this place has an open-air dining area where the aroma of grilling meats permeates the air. The chicken fajitas fill the plate. Grilled lobster is also on the menu. The cooks do a good job with Mexican standards such as tortilla soup, enchiladas, and quesadillas. Mariachis show up around 8pm; if you want to avoid them and dine in relative tranquility, get a table on the upper terrace in back.

Av. 5 (at Calle 8). ✆ **984/873-0687.** Reservations not accepted. Main courses $8–$18. AE, MC, V. Daily noon–1am.

## MODERATE

**La Casa del Agua** ★★★ EUROPEAN/MEXICAN This new arrival to Playa offers some of the best of both Old and New Worlds. What I tried was delicious—chicken in a wonderfully scented sauce of fine herbs accompanied by fettuccine, and a well-made tortilla soup listed as *sopa mexicana.* There are a number of cool and light dishes that would be appetizing for lunch or an afternoon meal; for example, an avocado stuffed with shrimp and flavored with a subtle horseradish sauce on a bed of alfalfa sprouts and julienne carrots—a good mix of tastes and textures. This is an upstairs restaurant under a large and airy *palapa* roof.

Av. 5 (at Calle 2). ✆ **984/803-0232.** Main courses $9–$15. AE, MC, V. Daily 2pm–midnight.

**Media Luna** ★★★ VEGETARIAN/SEAFOOD The owner-chef here has come up with an outstanding, eclectic menu that favors grilled seafood, sautés, and pasta dishes with inventive combinations of ingredients. Everything I had was quite fresh and prepared beautifully, taking inspiration from various culinary traditions—Italian, Mexican, and Japanese. Keep an eye on the daily specials. The open-air restaurant also makes sandwiches and salads, black bean quesadillas, and crêpes. The decor is primitive-tropical chic.

Av. 5 (between Calles 12 and 14). 984/873-0526. Breakfast $4–$8; main courses $8–$14; sandwich with salad $4–$8. No credit cards. Daily 7:30am–11:30pm.

**Ronny's** INTERNATIONAL A beach restaurant where you can wiggle your toes into the sand, sip a beer, and chow down on a large burger and fries—what's not to like? The food is dependably good. Menu items include fajitas, peel-your-own Cajun-flavored shrimp with U.S.–style tartar sauce, hamburgers, hot dogs, quesadillas, beer, wine, and coffee. Daily specials include such dishes as grilled steaks, shrimp *al ajillo,* and pork chops.

On the beach at Calle 6 (in front of the Pelícano Inn). ✆ **984/873-0997.** Reservations not accepted. Daily specials $10–$15; sandwiches $5–$6. No credit cards. Daily 11am–11pm.

**Yaxché** MAYA/YUCATECAN The menu here makes use of many native foods and spices to produce a style of cooking different from what you usually get when ordering Yucatecan food. You find such things as a cream of *chaya* (a native leafy vegetable), or xcatic chile stuffed with cochinita. I also like the classic fruit salad, done Mexican style with lime juice and dried powdered chile. The menu is varied and includes a lot of seafood dishes, and the ones I had were fresh and well prepared.

Calle 8 (between Avenidas 5 and 10). ✆ **984/873-2502.** Main courses $8–$20. AE, MC, V. Daily noon–midnight.

## INEXPENSIVE

**Tarraya Restaurant/Bar** ★ SEAFOOD/BREAKFAST THE RESTAURANT THAT WAS BORN WITH THE TOWN, proclaims the sign. This is also the restaurant locals recommend for seafood. It's right on the beach, with the water practically lapping at the foundations. Because the owners are fishermen, the fish is so fresh it's practically still wiggling. The wood hut doesn't look like much, but you can have your fish prepared in any of several ways. If you haven't tried the Yucatecan specialty *tik-n-xic* fish (with *achiote* and bitter-orange sauce, cooked in a banana leaf), this would be a good place to do so. Tarraya is on the beach opposite the basketball court. It serves a set breakfast menu that includes hot cakes, French toast, and eggs any style.

Calle 2 Norte. ✆ **984/873-2040.** Main courses $4–$7; whole fish $8 per kilo. No credit cards. Daily 7am–9pm.

## PLAYA DEL CARMEN AFTER DARK

It seems as if everyone in town is out on Avenida 5 or on the square until 10 or 11pm; there's pleasant strolling, meals and drinks at streetside cafes, shops to browse, and a few bars with live music. The other nightspot is the beach. The beach bar at the **Blue Parrot** (**✆ 984/873-0083**) is the most popular hangout in town and a classic example of its genre. Down by the ferry dock is a **Señor Frog's** (**✆ 984/873-0930**), which dishes out its patented mix of thumping dance music, Jell-O shots, and frat-house antics. Also on the beach is **Captain Tutiz** (no phone), which is designed like a pirate ship and has a large bar area, dance floor, and live entertainment nightly. Each time I go, the live bands are worse than the ones before. And, finally, there is a new movie theater at Avenida 10 and Calle 8.

# 5 Highway 307 from Xcaret to Xel-Ha

South of Playa del Carmen, after you pass most of the Playacar development, you'll find a succession of commercial nature parks, planned resort communities, and—for now, anyway—a few rustic beach hideaways and unspoiled coves. From north to south, this section covers in the following order: Xcaret, Paamul, Puerto Aventuras, Xpu-Ha, Akumal, and Xel-Ha. The distance from Playa del Carmen to Xel-Ha is 53km (33 miles).

Of the fledgling resorts south of Playa del Carmen, **Akumal** is one of the most attractive and welcoming, with comfortable hotels and bungalows that line two beautiful bays. **Puerto Aventuras** is a privately developed marina community aimed more at condo owners than at travelers. **Paamul** and **Xpu-Ha** offer inexpensive seaside inns. Two water-theme parks offer entertaining ways to spend the day immersed in the beauty of this region. One centers on the crystal-clear *cenotes* and lagoons at **Xel-Ha.** The other is the immensely popular park development of **Xcaret.** Popular day trips from Cancún, they are open to anyone traveling along this coast. There are also a lot of *cenotes* in this region, especially south of Akumal. For *cenote* diving, ask around in the dive shops in Akumal. If you want to snorkel in a *cenote,* the one with the easiest access is Dos Ojos, which you will see advertised on the highway. There is a dive shop on site. There's also a small nature park with a natural cavern called Aktun Chen, just beyond Xel-Ha.

**HEADING SOUTH FROM PLAYA DEL CARMEN** The best way to travel this coast is in a rental car; Playa has many agencies. The wide, well-paved highway to Tulum makes for an easy 1-hour drive. Buses to Chetumal depart fairly regularly from Playa. Most stop several times along the highway; however, from the highway it can be a long walk to the coast and to your final destination. There's also bus service to and from Cobá three times a day. Another option is to hire a car and driver.

### The Caribbean Coast South of Cancún (Riviera Maya & Costa Maya)

Mexico has 384km (240 miles) of Caribbean coast, from Cancún south all the way to the state capital, Chetumal (south of Chetumal lies Belize). The Sian Ka'an biopreserve occupies a large area in the middle. North of this is the Riviera Maya; south is the Costa Maya. A large reef system protects most of this coast, especially the Costa Maya. Where there are gaps in the reef, you find good beaches—Playa del Carmen, Xpuhá, and Tulum. The action of the surf washes away silt and seagrass and erodes rocks, leaving a sandy bottom. Where the reef is prominent, you get good snorkeling and diving with lots of fish and other sea creatures. Here the shoreline is often occupied by mangrove; beaches are sandy up to the water's edge, but shallow, with a silty or rocky floor.

A single road, Highway 307, runs down the coast. From Cancún to Playa del Carmen (51km/32 miles) it is a four-lane divided highway with speed limits up to 110kmph (68 mph). There are a couple of traffic lights and several reduced-speed zones around the major turnoffs. From Playa to Tulum (131km/82 miles from Cancún) the road becomes a smooth two-lane highway with wide shoulders. Speed limits are the same, but more places require you to reduce your speed. It takes around 1½ hours to drive from the Cancún airport to Tulum.

From Tulum, the highway turns inland to skirt the edges of Sian Ka'an. The roadway is narrower, without shoulders, and in some areas the forest crowds in on both sides. The speed limit is mostly 90kmph (56 mph), but you'll need to slow down in several places and must watch for speed bumps (*topes*) where the road passes through villages and towns. To drive from Tulum to Chetumal takes a little more than 3 hours.

## XCARET: A DEVELOPED NATURE PARK

About ten kilometers (6½ miles) south of Playa del Carmen (and 80km/50 miles south of Cancún) is the turn-off to Xcaret (pronounced ish-car-*et*), a specially built **ecological and archaeological theme park** that is one of the area's most popular tourist attractions. It's open Monday to Saturday from 8:30am to 8:30pm, Sunday from 8:30am to 5:30pm. Everywhere you look in Cancún, signs advertise Xcaret or someone hands you a leaflet about it. It even has its own bus terminal to take tourists from Cancún at regular intervals, and it has added an evening extravaganza. For this reason, we've covered it in the Cancún chapter (see chapter 12). **Puerto Calica,** the new cruise-ship pier, is 4km (2½ miles) south of Xcaret and 13km (8 miles) south of Playa del Carmen.

## PAAMUL: SEASIDE GETAWAY

About 16km (10 miles) beyond Xcaret, 26km (16 miles) from Playa del Carmen, and 96km (60 miles) from Cancún is Paamul (also written "Pamul"), which in Maya means "a destroyed ruin." The exit is clearly marked. At Paamul you can enjoy the Caribbean away from the crowds; the water is wonderful, but the beach is rocky. Thirty years ago the Martín family gave up coconut harvesting on this stretch of coast bordering a large, shallow bay, and established this comfortable, out-of-the-way respite. Most of the area is dedicated to trailer and RV spaces, but the family also rents 17 rooms.

**Scubamex** (© **984/873-0667**; fax 984/874-1729; www.scubamex.com) is a fully equipped PADI-, NAUI-, and SSI-certified dive shop next to the *cabañas*. Using two boats, the staff takes guests on dives 8km (5 miles) in either direction. If it's too choppy, the reefs in front of the hotel are also excellent. The night dive in Paamul is considered the best night dive along the Mexican Caribbean. The cost for a two-tank dive is $45, plus $25 if you need to rent gear. Snorkeling is also excellent in this protected bay and the one next to it. The shop offers a great 3-hour snorkeling trip ($25).

## WHERE TO STAY & DINE

**Cabañas Paamul** ★ This complex has eight rooms in a couple of long one-story buildings just steps away from the Caribbean, and 10 new freestanding wood *cabañas*. Despite the number of mobile homes (which are occupied more in winter than at any other time), there's seldom a soul on the beach. Each of the rooms has two double beds, tile floors, rattan furniture, ceiling fans, hot water, and 24-hour electricity. The new *cabañas* have wooden floors and stucco interior walls, *palapa* roofs, two double beds with comfortable mattresses, and a porch on the beach. All rooms come with private bathrooms. A large, breezy *palapa* restaurant serves food at American prices. The trailer park isn't what you might expect—some trailers have decks or patios and thatched *palapa* shade covers. Trailer guests have access to 12 showers and separate bathrooms for men and women. Laundry service is available nearby. Turtles nest here from June to September. Visitors not staying here are welcome to use the beach, though the owners request that they not bring in drinks or food and use the restaurant instead.

Km 85 Carretera Cancún–Tulum. © **984/875-1056.** paamulmx@yahoo.com. 18 units; 190 trailer spaces (all with full hookups). July–Aug and Dec–Feb $75–$85 double. March–June and Sept–Nov $50 double. Ask about discount for stays longer than 1 week. RV space with hookups $18 per day, $395 per month. No credit cards. **Amenities:** Restaurant, bar.

## PUERTO AVENTURAS: A RESORT COMMUNITY

Five kilometers (3 miles) south of Paamul (104km/65 miles from Cancún), you'll come to the large, glitzy development of Puerto Aventuras on Chakalal Bay. It's a marina community with a nine-hole golf course and three expensive hotels. One is the **Omni Puerto Aventuras** (© **800/THE-OMNI** in the U.S., or 984/873-5101). It has only 30 rooms, which is rather odd—I imagine that it was originally intended to be larger. Although Puerto Aventuras is almost as large as a city, the population of permanent residents is surprisingly low, and you get the feeling that most of them are real estate agents wanting to sell you a condo. You might stop here just to see what the place looks like, to swim with dolphins, to eat at a good restaurant, or to see the museum. But I don't think the resort is as interesting a destination as other places along this coast.

The museum is the **Museo CEDAM** (no phone). CEDAM stands for Center for the Study of Aquatic Sports in Mexico, and the museum houses displays on the history of diving on this coast from pre-Hispanic times to the present. Besides dive-related memorabilia, there are displays of pre-Hispanic pottery, figures, copper bells found in the *cenotes* of Chichén-Itzá, shell fossils, and sunken ship contents. It's open daily from 10am to 1pm and 2 to 6pm. Donations are requested. To make reservations to swim with the dolphins, call **Dolphin Discovery** (© **984/883-0779**). A 1-hour session costs $119.

## XPU-HA: BEAUTIFUL BEACH

About three kilometers (2 miles) beyond Puerto Aventuras is **Xpu-Ha** (ish-poo-*hah*) ★★★, a wide bay lined by a broad, beautiful sandy beach, perhaps the best beach on the entire coast. At each end of the bay is an all-inclusive resort (**Xpu-Ha Palace** and **Robinson Club**), and in the middle is the all-inclusive **Hotel Copacabana.** But the beach is long enough that it usually feels empty, except on weekends when a lot of local people come for the day. To get to the beach, turn off when you see the Copacabana and take the road that goes along the south side of the hotel or the next road after that, labeled X-6. Construction work is always changing the signs and road around, so I can't provide definite directions. But no one can close off access, because there are some restaurants and small hotels on the beach. The rooms in these hotels are very simple: two twin or full beds, private bathroom, cement floors, and perhaps a ceiling fan. Most are rented on a first-come, first-served basis. Rates vary from $20 to $50 a night, depending upon how busy they are. The nicest establishment is **Villas del Caribe Xpu-Ha** (✆ **984/873-2194**), which will let you make a reservation. Rates run $35 to $50 for a double. Rooms have private bathrooms with hot water and 24-hour electricity, but no ceiling fans. If you find a good deal in nearby Akumal, you're probably better off staying there and visiting this beach during the day.

## AKUMAL: BEAUTIFUL BAYS AND CAVERN DIVING

Continuing south on Highway 307 for 2.5km (1½ miles), you'll come to the turn-off for Akumal, a small, modern, ecologically oriented community built on the shores of two beautiful bays. This community has been around long enough that it feels more relaxed than other, booming places on the coast, such as Playa and Tulum. Akumal draws a lot of families. From the highway, turn off at the sign that reads PLAYA AKUMAL. (Don't be confused by other signs reading VILLAS AKUMAL or AKUMAL AVENTURAS or AKUMAL BEACH RESORT.) Less than half a mile down the road is a white arch. Just before it are a couple of convenience stores and a laundry service. Just after it (to the right) is the Club Akumal Caribe/Hotel Villas Maya. If you follow the road to the left and keep to the left, you'll come to shallow, rocky Half Moon Bay, lined with two- and three-story condos, and eventually to Yalku Lagoon. Vacationers can rent most of these condos for a week at a time. **Akumal Vacations** (✆ **800/448-7137;** www.akumalvacations.com) and **Caribbean Fantasy** (✆ **800/523-6618;** www.caribbfan.com) rent condos and villas.

You don't have to be a guest to enjoy the beach, swim or snorkel, or eat at one of the restaurants. This is a comfortable place to spend a day on a trip down the coast, but you might consider staying longer if you want to try **technical diving** or **cavern diving.** On Akumal Bay are two dive shops with PADI-certified instructors. The older is the **Akumal Dive Shop** (✆ **984/875-9032;** www.akumal.com), one of the oldest and best dive shops on the coast. Offshore there are almost 30 dive sites to visit (from 9–24m/30–80 ft. deep). Both Akumal Dive Shop and **Akumal Dive Adventures** (✆ **984/875-9157**), the dive shop at the Vista del Mar hotel on Half Moon Bay, offer resort courses as well as complete certification.

A bit beyond Akumal is the turn-off for **Aktun Chen** cavern. It is well lit, with underground pools and large chambers. The tour takes about an hour and requires a good amount of walking. The footing is generally good. There is also a zoo with specimens of the local fauna, some of them running about freely.

Admission is $17 for adults; $9 for children; and it's open from 9am to 5pm daily. The turn-off is to the right, and the cave is 3 to 5km (2–3 miles) from the road.

### WHERE TO STAY

**Club Akumal Caribe/Hotel Villas Maya Club** ★★ Kids The hotel rooms and garden bungalows of this hotel sit along Akumal Bay. Both are large and comfortable, with tile floors and good-size bathrooms. The 40 **Villas Maya Bungalows** are simply and comfortably furnished and have kitchenettes. The 21 rooms in the three-story **beachfront hotel** are more elaborately furnished and come with refrigerators. They have a king or two queen beds, tile floors, and Mexican accents. There is a large pool on the grounds. Other rooms belonging to the hotel are condos and the lovely **Villas Flamingo** on Half Moon Bay. The villas have two or three bedrooms and large living, dining, and kitchen areas, as well as a lovely furnished patio just steps from the beach. The four villas share a pool.

Km 104 Carretera Cancún–Tulum (Hwy. 307). ✆ **984/875-9010.** For reservations: P.O. Box 13326, El Paso, TX 79913. ✆ **800/351-1622** in the U.S., 800/343-1440 in Canada, or 915/584-3552. www.hotelakumalcaribe.com. 70 units. High season $120 bungalow; $145 hotel room; $160–$420 villa/condo. Low season $95 bungalow; $66 hotel room; $100–$300 villa/condo. Reservations with prepayment by check only. AE, MC, V; cash only at restaurants. Low-season packages available. Free parking. **Amenities:** 2 restaurants, bar; large pool; dive shop; tour desk; children's activities (seasonal); in-room massage; babysitting. *In room:* A/C, fridge, coffeemaker; no phone.

**Vista del Mar Hotel and Condos** ★ This beachfront property is a great place to stay for several reasons. It offers hotel rooms at good prices, and large, fully equipped condos that you don't have to rent by the week. The lovely, well-tended beach in front of the hotel has chairs and umbrellas. There's an on-site dive shop with an experienced staff, which eliminates the hassle of organizing dive trips. Hotel rooms contain a queen bed or a double and a twin. The 12 condos are large and though they lack air-conditioning, they have ceiling fans and good cross-ventilation. They consist of a kitchen, a living area, and two or three bedrooms and one or two bathrooms. All have balconies or terraces facing the sea and are equipped with hammocks. Several rooms come with whirlpool tubs.

Half Moon Bay, Akumal. ✆ **877/425-8625.** Fax 505/988-3882 in the U.S. www.akumalinfo.com. 27 units. High season $85 double; $175–$240 condo. Low season $56 double; $84–$125 condo. MC, V. Free parking. **Amenities:** Restaurant, bar; small pool; watersports equipment rental; dive shop. *In room:* TV, CD player, fridge, coffeemaker, no phone.

### WHERE TO DINE

There are about 10 places to eat in Akumal, and a good grocery store, **Super Chomak,** by the archway. The **Turtle Bay Café and Bakery** is good for breakfast or a light lunch; it's by the Akumal Dive Shop. A good dining spot for lunch or dinner is **La Buena Vida,** on Half Moon Bay.

## XEL-HA: SNORKELING & SWIMMING ★★

Eight miles south of Akumal, a beautiful lagoon called **Xel-ha** (shell-*hah*) is the centerpiece of a 10-acre ecological park where you can swim and snorkel in perfectly calm, clear water and view a variety of brilliantly colored tropical fish. The variety is less than what you'll find in the open water along the coastal reefs, but snorkeling here offers a much higher comfort level for those who feel anxious about waves and currents. The park entertains lots of visitors, mainly families.

Signs clearly mark the turn-off to Xel-ha (© **998/884-9422** in Cancún or 984/875-5000 in Playa; www.xelha.com.mx.). A half-mile of paved road leads to the entrance. Xel-Ha is close to the ruins of Tulum. A popular day tour from Cancún combines the two.

Inside the park, you can rent snorkeling equipment and an underwater camera. Platforms allow nonsnorkelers to view the fish. When swimming, be careful to observe the signs directing you where not to swim. (You can see the greatest variety of fish right near the ropes marking the no-swimming areas and near any group of rocks.) Another way to view fish is to use the park's "snuba" gear—a contraption that allows you to breath air through 20-foot tubes connected to scuba tanks floating on the surface. It frees you of the cumbersome tank and weights while allowing you to stay down without having to hold your breath. Rental costs $39 for approximately an hour.

Another attraction is swimming with dolphins. A 1-hour swim costs $90; a 15-minute program costs $35. Make reservations (© **998/887-6840**) at least 24 hours in advance for one of the four daily times: 9:30am, 12:30, 2, and 3:15pm.

Xel-Ha is open daily 8:30am to 5pm. Parking is free. Admission for adults is $25 on weekdays, $19 on weekends; for children age 5 to 11 it's $13 on weekdays, $10 on weekends; children under 5 enter free. Admission includes use of inner tubes, life vest, and shuttle train to the river. Changing rooms and showers are available. An all-inclusive option includes snorkeling equipment rental, locker rental, towels, food, and beverages for $52 for adults and $26 for children (no weekend discounts). The park accepts American Express, MasterCard, and Visa.

About a mile farther south is the **Hidden Worlds Cenotes** center (© **984/877-8535;** www.hiddenworlds.com.mx), which offers an excellent opportunity to snorkel or dive in a couple of nearby caverns. The water is crystalline (and a bit cold) and the rock formations impressive.

## TANKAH AND PUNTA SOLIMAN BAYS

After you pass Hidden Worlds, the next couple of turnoffs to the left lead to Soliman and Tankah bays. On Punta Soliman Bay is a good beach restaurant called **Oscar y Lalo's,** where you can rent kayaks and snorkel equipment and paddle out to the reefs for some snorkeling. A mile or two farther is the turn-off for Tankah. Pull in here and you come to a *cenote* by a lovely bay. Once you get beyond the shallow beach, you'll find great snorkeling—in just a short while I managed to see a number of rays and scores of fish. The *palapa* restaurant next to the *cenote* serves grilled food. If you elect to stay here, a couple from Texas offers lodging and full dive facilities.

**Tankah Dive Inn** ★ This place is an uncommon combination of small hotel and full dive shop (offering PADI instruction). The rooms are spacious and attractive, and the hotel is right on the shore. From the second-story dining area, you have a great view of the entire bay. This is a terrific place to hang out after a dive or a snorkeling trip, and the accommodating owners make you feel very much at home. The kitchen has a small menu, and the food is good. Sometimes the owners will cook the famous pit-baked *cochinita pibil.* The hotel offers dive packages and discounts for extended stays or for renting out the entire place.

Apartado Postal 5, 77780 Tulum, Q. Roo. © **984/874-2188.** Fax 984/871-2092. www.tankahdiveinn.com. 5 units. High season $100 double. Low season $80 double. Rates include continental breakfast. No credit cards. **Amenities:** Restaurant, bar; watersports equipment; dive shop.

## 6 Tulum, Punta Allen & Sian Ka'an

Tulum (130km/81 miles from Cancún) and the Punta Allen Peninsula border the northern edge of the Sian Ka'an biopreserve. The walled Maya city of Tulum is a large post-Classic site overlooking the Caribbean in dramatic fashion. Tour companies and public buses make the trip regularly from Cancún and Playa del Carmen; get there early to avoid the crowds. Tulum also has wonderful, sandy beaches and no large resort hotels. It's a perfect spot for those who like to splash around in the water and lie on the beach away from the resort scene. The town has a half-dozen restaurants and three cybercafes, a bank, and three cash machines.

For those who really want to leave the modern world behind, there's the Punta Allen Peninsula. Getting there from Tulum can take 1½ to 3 hours, depending on the condition of the road. It's a place without crowds, frenetic action, or creature comforts; the generator (if there is one) shuts down at 10pm. You'll find great fishing and snorkeling, the natural riches of the Sian Ka'an Biosphere Reserve, and a chance to rest up at what truly feels like the end of the road. A few beach *cabañas* offer reliable power, telephones, and hot showers.

**ORIENTATION** Highway 307 passes the entrance to the ruins (on your left) before cutting through town. A little bit beyond the entrance to the ruins, it intersects another highway at the edge of Tulum. There is a traffic light. To the right is the highway leading to the ruins of Cobá (see "Cobá Ruins," later in this chapter); to the left is the Tulum hotel zone, which begins about 2.5km (1½ miles) away; straight ahead is the village of Tulum. The same road that goes to

### *Fun Fact* Tulum: A Friendly Difference of Opinion

Two of us cover the entirety of Mexico for Frommer's, and almost without exception we agree on the country's top destinations. However, we have an ongoing dialogue regarding the relative merits and beauty of the ruins at Tulum. Herewith we present our respective cases, and leave it for you to decide with whom you agree.

**Lynne says:** Ancient Tulum is my favorite of all the ruins, poised as it is on a rocky hill overlooking the transparent, turquoise Caribbean. It's not the largest or most important of the Maya ruins in this area, but it's the only one by the sea, which makes it the most visually impressive. Intriguing carvings and reliefs decorate the well-preserved structures, which date back to between the 12th and 16th centuries A.D., in the post-Classic period.

**David says:** Aside from the spectacular setting, Tulum is not as impressive a city as Chichén-Itzá or Uxmal (both discussed in chapter 14). When looking at the ruins of Tulum, it quickly becomes apparent that the city's builders were concerned foremost with security and defense. For this reason they chose the most rugged section on this coast and then built stout walls on the other three sides. This must have absorbed a tremendous amount of energy that might otherwise have been used to build the large ceremonial centers we see in other parts of the Yucatán.

the hotel zone continues south all the way down the narrow **Punta Allen Peninsula,** entering the **Sian Ka'an Biosphere Reserve** and eventually arriving at **Punta Allen,** a lobstering and fishing village at the peninsula's tip.

## EXPLORING THE TULUM ARCHAEOLOGICAL SITE

Thirteen kilometers (8 miles) south of Xel-Ha are the ruins of Tulum, a Maya fortress-city overlooking the Caribbean. The ruins are open to visitors from 7am to 5pm in the winter, 8am to 6pm in the summer. It's always best to go early before the crowds start showing up around 9:30am. The entrance to the ruins is about a 5-minute walk from the archaeological site. There are artisans' stands, a bookstore, a museum, a restaurant, several large bathrooms, and a ticket booth. After walking through the center, visitors pay the admission fee to the ruins ($4; free on Sun), another fee ($1.50) if you choose to ride an open-air shuttle to the ruins, and, if you're driving, another fee ($3) to park. A video camera permit costs $4. Licensed guides have a stand next to the path to the ruins and charge $20 for a 45-minute tour in English, French, or Spanish for up to four persons. They will point out many architectural details that you might otherwise miss.

By A.D. 900, the end of the Classic period, Maya civilization had begun its decline, and the large cities to the south were abandoned. Tulum is one of the small city-states that rose to fill the void. It came to prominence in the 13th century as a seaport, controlling maritime commerce along this section of the coast, and remained inhabited well after the arrival of the Spanish. The primary god here was the diving god, depicted on several buildings as an upside-down figure above doorways. Seen at the Palace at Sayil and Cobá, this curious, almost comical figure is also known as the bee god.

The most imposing building in Tulum is a large stone structure above the cliff called the ***Castillo*** (castle). Actually a temple as well as a fortress, it was once covered with stucco and painted. In front of the Castillo are several unrestored palacelike buildings partially covered with stucco. On the **beach** below, where the Maya once came ashore, tourists swim and sunbathe, combining a visit to the ruins with a dip in the Caribbean.

The **Temple of the Frescoes,** directly in front of the Castillo, contains interesting 13th-century wall paintings, though entrance is no longer permitted. Distinctly Maya, they represent the rain god Chaac and Ixchel, the goddess of weaving, women, the moon, and medicine. On the cornice of this temple is a relief of the head of the rain god. If you pause a slight distance from the building, you'll see the eyes, nose, mouth, and chin. Notice the remains of the red-painted stucco—at one time all the buildings at Tulum were painted bright red.

Much of what we know of Tulum at the time of the Spanish Conquest comes from the writings of Diego de Landa, third bishop of the Yucatán. He wrote that Tulum was a small city inhabited by about 600 people who lived in platform dwellings along a street and who supervised the trade traffic from Honduras to the Yucatán. Though it was a walled city, most of the inhabitants probably lived outside the walls, leaving the interior for the residences of governors and priests and ceremonial structures. Tulum survived about 70 years after the Conquest, when it was finally abandoned. Because of the great number of visitors this site receives, it is no longer possible to climb all of the ruins. In many cases, visitors are asked to remain behind roped-off areas to view them.

### WHERE TO STAY IN & AROUND TULUM

You can stay either on the beach at one of the *cabaña* hotels in the hotel zone, or in town. The seven or eight hotels in town are generally cheaper than all but

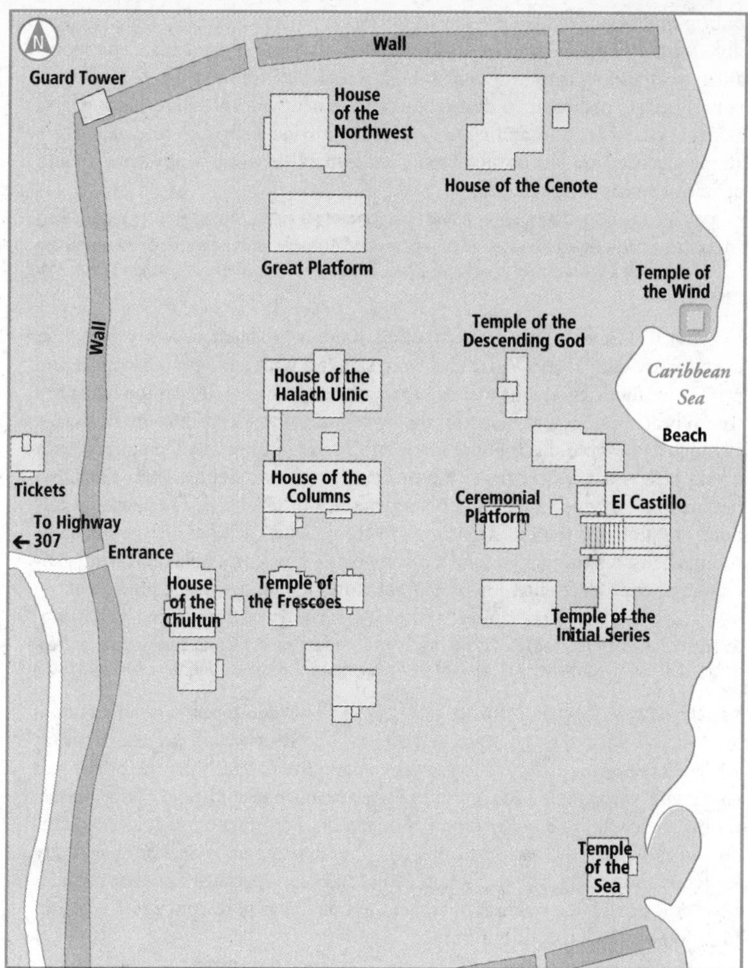


the most basic of beach accommodations, but they aren't as much fun. They offer basic lodging for $20 to $50 a night. I really like staying in the *cabaña* hotels. There are more than 20 of these, and they run the gamut from minimal lodging requirements to refined luxury. To get to the hotels on the beach, turn east at the highway intersection. Two and a half kilometers (1½ miles) ahead, you have to turn either north or south. North are most of the cheap *cabañas.* I would warn against these; I've heard from several sources that travelers have had their possessions stolen. South are the majority of the *cabañas,* including some moderately priced places. The pavement quickly turns into sand, and on both sides of the road you start seeing thatched-roof structures. You can try your luck at one of many places.

## Expensive

**Hotel Nueva Vida de Ramiro** ★ I like this place because it's so different, with few rooms, much space, and an ecological orientation. It's on 150 meters of beautiful beachfront where the vegetation as been preserved as much as possible, with little paths cutting through from the beach to the cabañas. The rooms are in freestanding thatched cabañas built 4m (12 ft.) off the ground. Each contains a private bathroom, a double and a twin bed with mosquito netting, and a ceiling fan (solar cells and wind generators provide energy 24 hr. a day; there are no electrical outlets in the units). The owners are from South America and operate a family-style restaurant.

Km 8.5 Carr. Punta Allen, 77780 Tulum, Q. Roo. ✆ **984/877-8512** in Cancún. Fax 984/871-2092. www.nuevavida.com.mx. 7 units. High season $100 double; low season $70 double. Rates include continental breakfast. MC, V. **Amenities:** Restaurant; tour information; limited room service; massage; limited laundry service; nonsmoking rooms.

**Las Ranitas** ★★ This property offers more solitude than Ana y José, and more luxury than Nueva Vida. The owners built it with ecological principles and privacy in mind. Footpaths through the native vegetation connect the two-story stucco beach houses and look as if they were meant to blend into the landscape as much as possible. Each house holds two rooms: an upstairs ("premier") with a king bed, and a downstairs ("conventional") with two double beds. The hotel has four suites, which are quite a bit larger and a little fancier. The rooms in this hotel are probably the nicest on this stretch of coast; each has a large tile bathroom, chairs, a writing table, and a private patio or balcony. Solar and wind generators provide electricity. The restaurant closes for supper in the off-season.

Punta Allen Peninsula. Km 9 Carr. Punta Allen, 77780 Tulum, Q. Roo. ✆ **984/877-8554.** Fax 984/845-0861. www.lasranitas.com. 17 units. $165–$210 double; $242–$275 suite. No credit cards. Rates include continental breakfast during high season, full breakfast during low season. **Amenities:** Restaurant, bar; small pool.

**Restaurant y Cabañas Ana y José** ★★ This comfortable hotel sits on a great beach with a good beach restaurant. The rock-walled *cabañas* in front (called "oceanfront"), closest to the water, are a little larger than the others and come with two double beds. I also like the attractive second-floor "vista al mar" rooms, which have tall *palapa* roofs. The standard rooms are much like the others but don't face the sea. The hotel has one suite. There is 24-hour electricity for lights and ceiling fans. Sometimes you can book a package deal that includes hotel and a rental car waiting for you at the Cancún airport. Ana y José is 6.5km (4 miles) south of the Tulum ruins.

Punta Allen Peninsula, Km 7 Carretera Punta Allen (Apdo. Postal 15), 77780 Tulum, Q. Roo. ✆ **998/887-5470,** in Cancún. Fax 998/887-5469. www.anayjose.com. 15 units. High season $100–$140 double. Low season $90–$130 double. Rates higher at Christmas and New Year's. Internet specials sometimes available. MC, V. Free parking. **Amenities:** Restaurant; small pool; tour info; car rental.

### Moderate

**Cabañas Tulum** Next to Ana y José's is a row of bungalows facing the same beautiful ocean and beach. This place offers basic accommodations. Rooms are simple yet attractive and large, though poorly lit. The large bathrooms are tiled. All rooms have two double beds (most with new mattresses), screens on the windows, a table, one electric light, and a porch facing the beach. Electricity is available from 7 to 11am and 6 to 11pm. There are billiard and Ping-Pong tables. The *cabañas* are often full between December 15 and Easter, and in July and August.

Punta Allen Peninsula, Km 7 Carretera Punta Allen (Apdo. Postal 63), 77780 Tulum, Q. Roo. ✆ **984/879-7395.** Fax 984/871-2092. www.hotelstulum.com. 32 units. $50–$70 double. No credit cards. **Amenities:** Restaurant; game room.

**Zamas** Zamas is a grouping of stylish beach *cabañas* built on a rocky point on the coast. Each *cabaña* comes with a small porch area and hammocks, a thatched roof, a large bathroom, and electricity. Mosquito netting hangs over each bed. What the *cabañas* don't have are ceiling fans, but they generally don't need them. There is almost always a breeze here. Rooms come with a variety of bed combinations and are ranked in three categories: oceanview, gardenview, and beachfront. Even if you don't stay here, try the restaurant; the seafood is very fresh.

Km 5 Carr. Punta Allen, 77780 Tulum, Q. Roo. ✆ **800/538-6802** in the U.S. or Canada. www.zamas.com. 16 units. High season $125 oceanview double, $80–$105 gardenview or beachfront double; low season $90 oceanview double, $50–$80 gardenview or beachfront double. No credit cards. **Amenities:** Restaurant.

### WHERE TO DINE

A few restaurants in the town of Tulum have reasonable prices and good food. On the main street are **Charlie's** (✆ **984/871-2136**), my favorite for Mexican food, and **Don Cafeto's** (✆ **984/871-2207**). A good Italian-owned Italian restaurant, **Il Giardino di Toni e Simone** (cell phone ✆ **984/804-1316;** closed Wed), is 1 block off the highway—you'll see a large building supply store called ROCA. It's on the opposite side of the road, 1 block away. Also in town are a couple of roadside places that grill chicken and serve it with rice and beans. Out on the coast, you can eat at Zamas or at Ana y José (see above).

## EXPLORING THE PUNTA ALLEN PENINSULA

If you've been captured by an adventurous spirit and have an excessively sanguine opinion of your rental car, you might want to take a trip down the Punta Allen Peninsula, especially if your interests lie in fly-fishing, bird-watching, or simply exploring new country. The far end of the peninsula is only 48km (30 miles) away, but it can be a very slow trip (up to 3 hr., depending on how much water is on the road) due to the poor condition of the road. Not far from the last *cabaña* hotel is the entrance to the 1.3-million-acre **Sian Ka'an Biosphere Reserve** (see below). Halfway down the peninsula, at Boca Paila, a bridge crosses to the lower peninsula (where the Boca Paila Fishing Lodge is). On your right is a large lagoon. Another 24km (15 miles) gets you to the village of **Punta Allen,** where you can arrange a bird-watching expedition (available June–Aug, with July being best) or boat trips (see the entry for Cuzan Guest House in "Where to Stay," below).

*A note about provisions:* Because the Punta Allen Peninsula is remote and there are few stores, handy items to bring along include a flashlight, mosquito repellent, snacks, and bottled water. From October to December, winds may make for nippy nights, so come prepared—some hotels don't have blankets.

### WHERE TO STAY

The peninsula offers simple but comfortable lodgings. One or two have electricity for a few hours in the evening, but it goes off around 10pm. Halfway down the peninsula, the **Boca Paila Fishing Lodge** (✆ **800/245-1950,** or 412/935-1577 in the U.S.) specializes in hosting fly-fishers. Its weeklong packages include everything, even the boat and guide. Prices start at $1,500 per person.

Between Boca Paila and Punta Allen are a couple of small, comfortable, affordable hotels run by Americans. Punta Allen is a lobstering and fishing village on a palm-studded beach. Isolated and rustic, it's the most laid-back end of the line you'll find for a long time. The small town has a lobster cooperative, a few streets with modest homes, and a lighthouse at the very end of the peninsula.

## The Sian Ka'an Biosphere Reserve

Down the peninsula, a few kilometers south of the Tulum ruins, you'll pass the guardhouse of the Sian Ka'an Biosphere Reserve. The reserve is a tract of 1.3 million acres set aside in 1986 to preserve tropical forests, savannas, mangroves, coastal and marine habitats, and 112km (70 miles) of coastal reefs. The area is home to jaguars, pumas, ocelots, margays, jaguarundis, spider and howler monkeys, tapirs, white-lipped and collared peccaries, manatees, brocket and white-tailed deer, crocodiles, and green, loggerhead, hawksbill, and leatherback sea turtles. It also protects 366 species of birds—you might catch a glimpse of an ocellated turkey, a great curassow, a brilliantly colored parrot, a toucan or trogon, a white ibis, a roseate spoonbill, a jabiru (or wood stork), a flamingo, or one of 15 species of herons, egrets, and bitterns.

The park has three parts: a "core zone" restricted to research; a "buffer zone," to which visitors and families already living there have restricted use; and a "cooperation zone," which is outside the reserve but vital to its preservation. Driving south from Tulum on Highway 307, everything on the left side of the highway is part of the reserve, but there's no access to any of it except at the ruins of Muyil/Chunyaxche. At least 22 archaeological sites have been charted within Sian Ka'an. The best place to check out the reserve is on the Punta Allen Peninsula, part of the "buffer zone." The inns were already in place when the reserve was created. Of these, only the Cuzan Guest House (see "Where to Stay," below) offers birding trips. But bring your own binoculars and birding books and have at it—the bird life here is rich. Birding is best just after dawn, especially during the April to July nesting season.

Visitors can arrange day trips in Tulum at **Sian Ka'an Tours** (✆ **984/871-2363,** siankaan_tours@hotmail.com), on the east side of the road, 1 block south of the highway intersection. This outfit offers a general-interest day tour and a sunset tour.

**Cuzan Guest House** ★★ *Finds* This place has a rustic charm perfectly in character with its location at the end of the road, plus the great benefits of hot water, 24-hour solar electricity, comfortable beds, and private bathrooms. You have a choice of Maya-style stucco buildings with thatched roofs, concrete floors, and a combination of twin and king beds with mosquito netting, or raised wooden cabins with thatched roofs and little porches that overlook the water. These have two double beds each. The hotel's restaurant, a large *palapa* with a sand floor, serves three meals a day. Full breakfast and lunch run about $5 each, and dinner costs $12 to $15. The menu sometimes includes lobster in season (July–Apr). The food is good, and, of course, the seafood is fresh. Payment for meals must be in cash or traveler's checks.

Co-owner Sonja Lilvik, a Californian, offers fly-fishing trips for bone, permit, snook, and tarpon to the nearby saltwater flats and lagoons of Ascension Bay. One-week packages (priced per person, double occupancy) include lodging, three meals a day, a boat, and a guide. She also offers a fascinating 3-hour boat tour of the coastline that includes snorkeling, slipping in and out of mangrove-filled canals for birding, and skirting the edge of an island rookery loaded with frigate birds. November to March is frigate mating season, when the male shows off his big, billowy red breast pouch to impress potential mates. You can also go kayaking along the coast or relax in a hammock on the beach.

Punta Allen. Reservations: Apdo. Postal 24, 77200 Felipe Carrillo Puerto, Q. Roo. ✆ **983/834-0358.** Fax 983/834-0292. www.flyfishmx.com. 12 units. High season $40–$80 double. Low-season discounts available. All-inclusive fly-fishing packages $1,899/week. No credit cards. **Amenities:** Restaurant; tours and activities desk.

## 7 Cobá Ruins ★★

168km (105 miles) SW of Cancún

The impressive Maya ruins at Cobá, deep in the jungle, are a worthy detour from the route south. You don't need to stay overnight to see the ruins, but there are a few hotels. The village is small and poor, gaining little from the visitors who pass through to see the ruins. Used clothing (especially for children) would be a welcome gift.

From the turn-off at the Tulum junction, travel inland an hour or so to arrive at the ruins, which jut up from the forest floor.

### ESSENTIALS

#### GETTING THERE & DEPARTING

**BY CAR** The road to Cobá begins in Tulum, across Highway 307 from the turn-off to the Punta Allen Peninsula. Turn right when you see signs for Cobá, and continue on that road for 64km (40 miles). Enter the village, proceed straight until you see the lake, then turn left. The entrance to the ruins is a short distance down the road past some small restaurants. Cobá is also about a 3-hour drive south from Cancún.

**BY BUS** Several buses a day leave Cobá for Tulum and Playa del Carmen.

#### ORIENTATION

The highway into Cobá becomes the one main paved street through town, which passes El Bocadito restaurant and hotel on the right and goes a block to the lake. If you turn right at the lake, you reach the Villas Arqueológicas, another hotel, a block farther.

### EXPLORING THE COBA RUINS

The Maya built many intriguing cities in the Yucatán, but few grander than *Cobá* ("water stirred by the wind"). Much of the 109 square km (42-sq.-mile) site, on the shores of two lakes, is unexcavated. A 96km (60-mile) *sacbé* (a pre-Hispanic raised road or causeway) through the jungle linked Cobá to Yaxuná, once a large, important Maya center 40km (30 miles) south of Chichén-Itzá. It's the Maya's longest known *sacbé,* and at least 50 shorter ones lead from here. An important city-state, Cobá flourished from A.D. 632 (the oldest carved date found here) until after the founding of Chichén-Itzá, around 800. Then Cobá slowly faded in importance and population until it was finally abandoned. Scholars believe Cobá was an important trade link between the Yucatán Caribbean coast and inland cities.

Once at the site, keep your bearings—it's very easy to get lost on the maze of dirt roads in the jungle. If you're into it, bring your bird and butterfly books; this is one of the best places to see both. Branching off from every labeled path, you'll notice unofficial narrow paths into the jungle, used by locals as shortcuts through the ruins. These are good for birding, but be careful to remember the way back.

The **Grupo Cobá** boasts a large, impressive pyramid, the **Temple of the Church** (La Iglesia), which you'll find if you take the path bearing right after the entrance. Walking to it, notice the unexcavated mounds on the left. Though the urge to climb the temple is great, the view is better from El Castillo in the Nohoch Mul group farther back.

From here, return to the main path and turn right. You'll pass a sign pointing right to the ruined ***juego de pelota*** (ball court), but the path is obscure.

Continuing straight ahead on this path for 5 to 10 minutes, you'll come to a fork in the road. To the left and right you'll notice jungle-covered, unexcavated pyramids, and at one point, you'll see a raised portion crossing the pathway—this is the visible remains of the *sacbé* to Yaxuná. Throughout the area, intricately carved stelae stand by pathways or lie forlornly in the jungle underbrush. Although protected by crude thatched roofs, most are weatherworn enough that they're indiscernible.

The left fork leads to the **Nohoch Mul Group,** which contains **El Castillo.** With the exception of Structure 2 in Calakmul, this is the tallest pyramid in the Yucatán (rising even higher than the great El Castillo at Chichén-Itzá and the Pyramid of the Magician at Uxmal). So far, visitors are still permitted to climb to the top. From this magnificent lofty perch, you can see unexcavated jungle-covered pyramidal structures poking up through the forest all around.

The right fork (more or less straight on) goes to the **Conjunto Las Pinturas.** Here, the main attraction is the **Pyramid of the Painted Lintel,** a small structure with traces of its original bright colors above the door. You can climb up to get a close look. Though maps of Cobá show ruins around two lakes, there are really only two excavated groups.

**For Your Comfort at Cobá**

Visit Cobá in the morning or after the heat of the day has passed. Mosquito repellent, drinking water, and comfortable shoes are imperative.

Admission is $4, free for children under age 12; Sunday and holidays it's free to everyone. Parking is $1. A video camera permit costs $4. The site is open daily from 8am to 5pm, sometimes longer.

## WHERE TO STAY & DINE

**El Bocadito** El Bocadito, on the right as you enter town (next to the hotel's restaurant of the same name), offers rooms arranged in two rows facing an open patio. They're simple, with tile floors, two double beds, no bedspreads, a ceiling fan, and a washbasin separate from the toilet and cold-water shower cubicle. The clean, open-air restaurant offers good meals at reasonable prices, served by a friendly, efficient staff.

Calle Principal, Cobá, Q. Roo. No phone. Reservations: Apdo. Postal 56, 97780 Valladolid, Yuc. 8 units. $18–$25 double. No credit cards. Free unguarded parking.

**Villas Arqueológicas Cobá** This lovely lakeside hotel is a 5-minute walk from the ruins. It is laid out like its Club Med counterparts in Chichén-Itzá and Uxmal. The beautiful grounds include a pool and tennis court. The restaurant is top-notch, though expensive, and the rooms are stylish and modern, but small. Beds occupy niches that surround the mattress on three sides and can be

**Tips** **Last Gas**

Felipe Carrillo Puerto is the only place to buy **gasoline** between Tulum and Chetumal. If you're desperate, there is a guy who sells gas in Bacalar; just ask when you get there.

somewhat uncomfortable for those taller than about 6-foot-2. The hotel also has a library on Mesoamerican archaeology (with books in French, English, and Spanish). Make reservations—this hotel fills with touring groups.

Cobá, Q. Roo. ✆ **800/258-2633** in the U.S., or 55/5203-3086 in Mexico City. 41 units. $90 double. Rates include continental breakfast. Half-board (breakfast plus lunch or dinner) $29 per person; full board (3 meals) $58 per person. AE, MC, V. Free guarded parking. **Amenities:** Restaurant, bar; medium-size pool. Drive through town and turn right at lake; hotel is straight ahead on the right.

### EN ROUTE TO THE LOWER CARRIBEAN COAST: FELIPE CARRILLO PUERTO

If you continue south on the main highway from Tulum, note that the road narrows, the speed limit drops, and you begin to see *topes* (speed bumps). Down the road some 24km (15 miles), a sign points to the small but dramatic ruins of **Muyil.** If you stop to see these ruins, take bug repellent. The principal ruins are a small group of buildings and a plaza dominated by the Castillo, a pyramid of medium height but interesting construction. From here, a canal dug by the Maya empties into a lake, with other canals going from there to the saltwater estuary of Boca Paila on the coast. The local community offers a boat ride ($35) through these canals and lakes. The 3½-hour tour includes snorkeling the canal and letting the current carry you along. Soft drinks are also included.

**Felipe Carrillo Puerto** (pop. 60,000) is the first large town you pass on the road to Ciudad Chetumal. It has gas stations, a market, a small ice plant, a bus terminal, and a few modest hotels and restaurants, but no banks or cash machines. The main road intersects the road to Mérida, so Carrillo Puerto is the turning point for those making a "short circuit" of the Yucatán Peninsula. Highway 184 heads west to Ticul, Uxmal, Campeche, and Mérida.

The town is of interest for being a rebel stronghold during the War of the Castes and the center for the millenarian cult of the "Talking Cross." It is still home to a strong community of believers in the cult who practice their own brand of religion and are respected by the whole town.

## 8 Majahual, Xcalak & the Chinchorro Reef

South of Felipe Carrillo Puerto, the speed bumps begin in earnest. In 45 minutes you reach the turn-off for Majahual and Xcalak. This area mainly attracts fishermen and divers who come to visit its coastal reefs and the Chinchorro Reef, 48km (30 miles) offshore. This is not the place to come if all you're looking for is a stretch of pure sandy beach free of seaweed where you can walk out into the surf and swim without feeling anything under your toes but sand. For this purpose, the beaches around Tulum and Playa del Carmen are better suited. But if you want to snorkel or dive among pristine reefs, kayak in calm turquoise water, or perhaps do some fly-fishing away from the crowds, you've come to the right place.

The road to **Majahual** (mah-hah-*wahl*) is often badly pitted, so you'll be forced to drive slowly. This may change because a cruise-ship company has built a large dock in Majahual and is bringing in boats. Because there is nothing to do in Majahual, I can only assume that the company will truck the passengers out to one of the local ruins (quite a haul, even with a good road). And my advice to anyone considering taking a cruise to Majahual is: don't. An old coastal road passes through Majahual and goes all the way down to Xcalak, and a new paved road runs inland directly to Xcalak. Xcalak has better lodging than Majahual, a decent dive shop, and more interesting coastal features. Taking the new road saves you a lot of time; it's 1½ hours to Xcalak from the turn-off point. Less than a third of the way down this road is a turn-off toward the coast for the **Maya-Ha Dive Resort** (see below).

**Xcalak** (eesh-kah-*lahk*) is a depopulated, weather-beaten fishing village with a couple of comfortable places to stay and a couple of barely decent restaurants. From here you work your way back up the coast to get to the main dive shop. There are several small inns just beyond the town. The village of Xcalak once had a population as large as 1,200 before the 1958 hurricane; now it has only 300 permanent residents.

## ORIENTATION

**ARRIVING** **By Car** Driving south from Felipe Carrillo Puerto, you'll come to the turn-off (left) onto Highway 10, 2.5km (1½ miles) after Limones; then it's a 30-mile drive to the coastal settlement of **Majahual.** Before Majahual, there's a military guard station. Tell the guard your destination and turn right to continue to **Xcalak** on the new paved highway for another 56km (35 miles). To orient you further, the turn-off from Highway 307 is 261km (163 miles) southwest of Cancún and 141km (88 miles) southwest of Tulum.

**BY PLANE** A 4,500-foot airstrip opened in 1998, and starting this year, **Aero Ferinco** (✆ **998/873-0636** in Cancún for reservations) will operate a round-trip flight from Cancún to Majahual-Xcalak each Saturday.

## DIVING THE CHINCHORRO REEF

The **Chinchorro Reef Underwater National Park** is a 24-mile-long, 8-mile-wide oval reef. It is as shallow as 1m (3 ft.) on its interior and as deep as 910m (3,000 ft.) on its exterior. It lies 32km (20 miles) offshore. Locals claim it's the last virgin reef system in the Caribbean. It's invisible from the ocean side; hence, one of its diving attractions is the **shipwrecks**—at least 30—that decorate the underwater landscape. One is on top of the reef. Divers have counted 40 cannons at one wreck site. On the west side are walls and coral gardens.

At present, the only outfit making regular trips to the reef is the **Maya-Ha Dive Resort** (✆ **877/443-1600** in the U.S., or 983/831-0065; fax 512/443-2978; www.mayaharesort.com), on the coast between Majahual and Xcalak. Take the new road to Xcalak and look for a sign. The resort caters to divers with a variety dive packages, which can include transportation between the hotel and the Cancún airport. It also offers activities for bad-weather days and for non-divers, including tours of ruins. The 18 rooms are large, with large bathrooms and purified tap water. All have air-conditioning and are well lit, thanks to an on-site generator. There are also a few small rental houses on the property. The restaurant serves inventive Mexican nueva cocina. There is a pool on site.

**Aventuras XTC** (✆ **983/831-0461;** divextc@pocketmail.com) is the fully equipped dive shop for the hotels in the Xcalak area. It does a lot of dives around the local reefs, which offer some good diving.

# The Yucatán's Lower Caribbean Coast

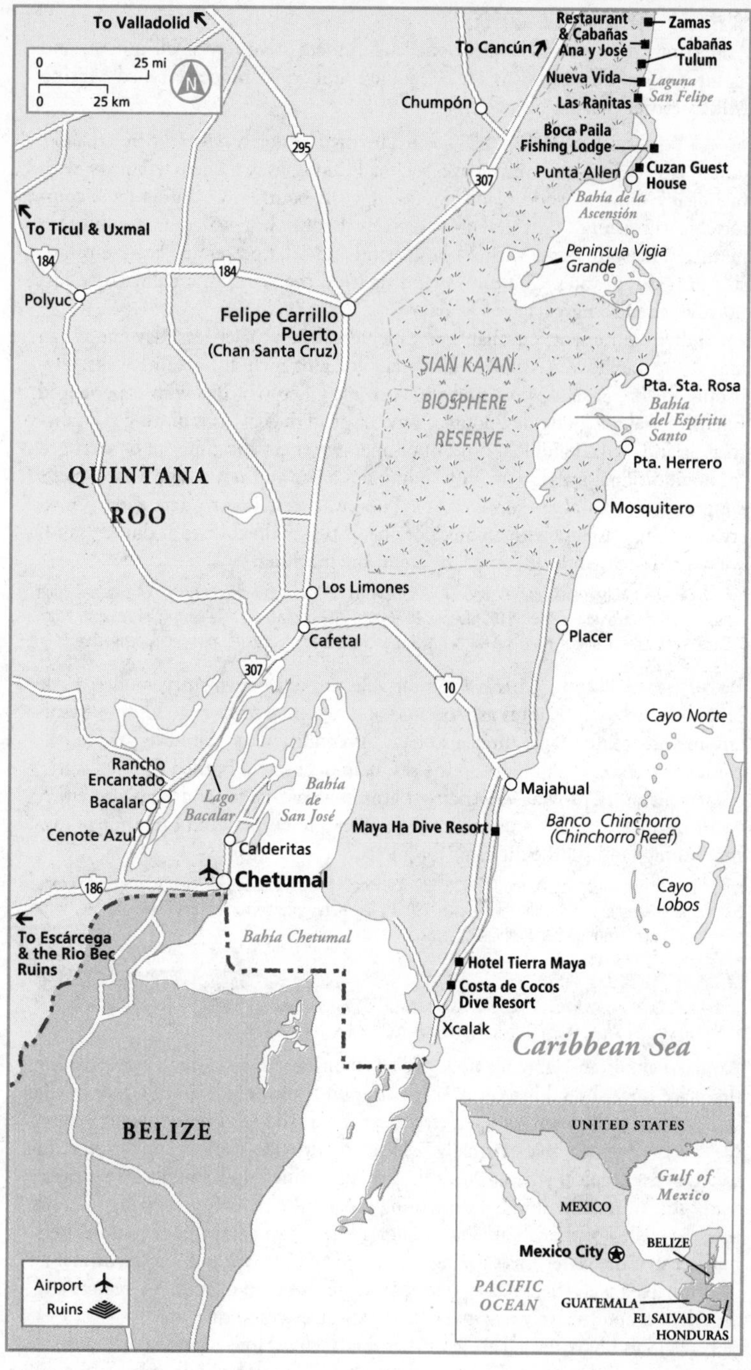

To Valladolid
0 25 mi
0 25 km
N
Restaurant & Cabañas Ana y José
Zamas
Cabañas Tulum
To Cancún
Nueva Vida
Laguna San Felipe
Chumpón
Las Ranitas
Boca Paila Fishing Lodge
Punta Allen
Cuzan Guest House
295
307
Bahía de la Ascensión
To Ticul & Uxmal
Peninsula Vigia Grande
184
184
Polyuc
Felipe Carrillo Puerto
(Chan Santa Cruz)
SIAN KA'AN BIOSPHERE RESERVE
Pta. Sta. Rosa
Bahía del Espíritu Santo
Pta. Herrero
QUINTANA ROO
Mosquitero
Los Limones
Cafetal
Placer
307
10
Cayo Norte
Rancho Encantado
Bacalar
Lago Bacalar
Bahía de San José
Majahual
Cenote Azul
Maya Ha Dive Resort
Banco Chinchorro
(Chinchorro Reef)
Calderitas
Chetumal
186
Cayo Lobos
To Escárcega & the Rio Bec Ruins
Bahía Chetumal
Hotel Tierra Maya
Costa de Cocos Dive Resort
Xcalak
Caribbean Sea
BELIZE
UNITED STATES
Gulf of Mexico
MEXICO
BELIZE
Mexico City
PACIFIC OCEAN
GUATEMALA
EL SALVADOR
HONDURAS
Airport
Ruins

## WHERE TO STAY & DINE

Aside from the two places mentioned here, there are a few small inns in and about Xcalak. The newest is a nice looking four-room property called **Marina Mike's Hotel** (www.xcalak.com).

**Costa de Cocos Dive Resort** ★★ The thatch-roofed *cabañas* here are fashioned after Maya huts but have such additions as screened windows with mahogany louvers, wood plank floors, large tile bathrooms, ceiling fans, comfortable furnishings, shelves of paperback books, hot water, and mosquito netting. They also come with 24-hour wind and solar power and reverse-osmosis purified tap water. The *cabañas* are right on the water in a palm grove just north of the fishing village of Xcalak.

All dive equipment is available and included in dive packages; day guests can rent it separately. Watersports equipment for rent includes ocean kayaks. Fly-fishing for bonefish, tarpon, and snook inside Chetumal Bay with experienced English-speaking guides is a popular way to spend the day, as is birding at a sanctuary island. NAUI and PADI resort or open-water certification can be arranged for an additional fee. The main building has a bar and restaurant where guests congregate for an afternoon cocktail. The casual restaurant offers good home-style cooking, usually with a choice of one or two main courses at dinner, sandwiches at lunch, and full breakfast fare in the morning.

Km 52 Carretera Majahual-Xcalak, Q. Roo. ✆ **983/831-0110.** www.costadecocos.com. 14 *cabañas.* High season $120 double; low season $100 double. Dive rates and packages available; e-mail request. Rates include breakfast and dinner. No credit cards. **Amenities:** Restaurant, bar; watersports equipment; dive shop.

**Hotel Tierra Maya** This is a comfortable, attractive, two-story, modern-style hotel on the beach. Rooms are spacious and designed to have good cross-ventilation, with ceiling fans; three also have air-conditioning. All have private balconies or terraces looking out to the sea, hammocks, and bottled purified water. Solar generators provide electricity. Bathrooms are large, and beds are either twins or queens. The owners recently opened a restaurant and can arrange diving, fishing, and snorkeling trips for guests.

Km 54 Carr. Majahual-Xcalak, Q. Roo. ✆ **800/480-4505** or 941/488-4505, both in the U.S. www.xcalak.com. 6 units. High season $90 double; low season $80 double. Rates include continental breakfast. MC, V for advance payments. **Amenities:** Restaurant.

## 9 Lago Bacalar ★★★

104km (65 miles) SW of Felipe Carrillo Puerto, 37km (23 miles) NW of Chetumal

Bacalar Lake is an elaborate trick played upon the senses. I remember visiting the place once: I couldn't get over the illusion it produced. From a pier in the lake, I could gaze down into perfectly clear water, and as I lifted my eyes I could see several hues of blue normally associated with the Caribbean. Beyond the water, dense tropical vegetation clothed the shoreline. How could a lake of fresh water surrounded by jungle be anything but murky? A breeze blowing in from the sea smelled of the salt air, and though I knew it to be untrue, I couldn't help but feel that the water I was gazing on was, in fact, the sea and not freshwater at all, perhaps a well-sheltered lagoon. My senses rebelled against my reason and experience, and the only way to settle the dispute was to dive in.

Few places I have visited are as enchanting as this. How is it possible that such a large lake, 104km (65 miles) long and several kilometers wide, can be so clear and so blue? The answer is that Bacalar is not the watershed for the surrounding area; it is not fed by surface runoff, but by several *cenotes* that lie beneath its surface. Only in the Yucatán is such a thing possible.

This is the perfect spot for being bone idle. If you prefer, there are plenty of activities, including trips to view the large variety of bird life, the elegant Maya architecture in the nearby Río Bec area, a couple of beautiful *cenotes,* and a wonderful museum in Chetumal. Given the choice, I would rather stay in Bacalar and visit Chetumal than the reverse. In the town of Bacalar is an 18th-century fort with a moat and stout bastions. Inside is a small museum (admission is 50¢) that has several artifacts on display. All text is in Spanish.

**ORIENTATION** Driving south on Highway 307, the town of Bacalar is 1½ hours beyond Felipe Carrillo Puerto, clearly marked by signs. If you're driving north from Chetumal, it takes about a half-hour. Buses going south from Cancún and Playa del Carmen stop here, and there are frequent buses from Chetumal.

## WHERE TO STAY

**Hotel Laguna** The Laguna overlooks the lake from a lovely vantage point, and all the rooms share the view and have little terraces that make enjoyable sitting areas. The medium-size rooms have ceiling fans, and most come with two double beds (the mattresses in the bungalows aren't good). The bathrooms are simple but have no problem delivering hot water. A restaurant that shares the same view is open from 7am to 9pm. The bar makes a credible margarita. The highest occupancy rates are from July to August and December to January, when you should make a reservation. The hotel is easy to spot from the road; look for the sign about a half-mile after you pass through the town of Bacalar.

Bulevard Costera de Bacalar 479, 77010 Lago Bacalar, Q. Roo. ✆ **983/834-2206.** Fax 983/834-2205. 34 units. $45 double; $77–$95 bungalow for 5–8 persons. MC, V. **Amenities:** Restaurant, bar; small pool.

**Rancho Encantado Cottage Resort** ★★ This beautiful, serene lakeside retreat consists of 12 immaculate white stucco cottages scattered over a shady lawn beside the smooth Lago Bacalar. Each is large and has mahogany-louvered windows, a red-tile floor, a dining table and chairs, a living room or sitting area, a porch with chairs, and hammocks strung between trees. Some rooms have cedar ceilings and red-tiled roofs, and others have thatched roofs. All are decorated with folk art and murals inspired by Maya ruins. The newest units are the four waterfront cottages (rooms 9–12). Beds come in different combinations of doubles and twins. Orange, lime, mango, *sapote,* ceiba, banana, palm, and oak trees; wild orchids; and bromeliads on the grounds make great bird shelter, attracting flocks of chattering parrots, turquoise-browed motmots, toucans, and at least 100 more species, many of which are easy to spot outside your room.

The hotel offers almost a dozen excursions. Among them are day trips to the **Río Bec** ruin route, an extended visit to **Calakmul,** outings to the **Majahual Peninsula,** and a riverboat trip to the Maya ruins of **Lamanai,** deep in a Belizian forest. Excursions cost $55 to $115 per person, depending on the length and difficulty of the trip, and several have a three-person minimum. To find the Rancho, look for the hotel's sign on the left about 1 mile before Bacalar.

Km 3 Carretera Felipe Carrillo Puerto–Chetumal, 77000 Chetumal, Q. Roo. ✆ and fax **983/831-0037.** Reservations: P.O. Box 1256, Taos, NM 87571. ✆ **800/505-MAYA** in the U.S. Fax 505/758-9790. www.encantado.com. 13 units. Dec–Apr $150–$180 double. May–Nov $140–$160 double. Rates include continental breakfast and dinner. MC, V. **Amenities:** Restaurant, bar; large outdoor whirlpool; watersports equipment; tour desk; massage service. *In room:* Fridge, coffeemaker.

## WHERE TO EAT

Besides the restaurants at the hotels discussed above, you may enjoy the **Restaurant Cenote Azul,** a comfortable open-air thatched-roof restaurant on the edge of the beautiful Cenote Azul. Main courses cost $5 to $12. To get to Restaurant Cenote Azul, follow the highway to the south edge of town and turn left at the restaurant's sign; follow the road around to the restaurant. At Rancho Encantado you can swim in Lago Bacalar, and at the Restaurant Cenote you can take a dip in placid Cenote Azul—but without skin lotion of any kind, because it poisons the *cenote.*

# 10 Chetumal

251km (156 miles) S of Tulum, 37km (23 miles) S of Lago Bacalar

Quintana Roo became a state in 1974, with Chetumal (pop. 208,000) as its capital. While Quintana Roo was still a territory, Chetumal was made a free-trade zone to encourage trade and immigration between neighboring Guatemala and Belize. The old part of town, down by the river (Río Hondo), has a Caribbean feel, but the newer parts are modern Mexican. Chetumal is really the gateway to Belize or to the Río Bec ruins, and it's not an interesting city for tourists. However, it is worth a detour to see the wonderful **Museo de la Cultural Maya** (© **983/832-6838**), especially if you plan to follow the Río Bec ruin route (see below).

## ESSENTIALS

### GETTING THERE & DEPARTING

**BY PLANE** **Aerocaribe** (© **983/832-6336** or 983/832-6675) has weekday flights to and from Cancún. **Aviacsa** (© **983/872-7698**) has a direct flight to and from Mexico City. The airport is west of town, just north of the entrance from the highway.

**BY CAR** It's a little more than 3 hours from Tulum. If you're heading to Belize, you'll need a passport and special auto insurance, which you can buy at the border. You can't take a rental car over the border. To get to the ruins of Tikal in Guatemala, you must go through Belize to the border crossing at Ciudad Melchor de Mencos.

**BY BUS** The main bus station (© **983/832-5110**) is 20 blocks from the town center on Insurgentes at Niños Héroes. Buses go to Cancún, Tulum, Playa del Carmen, Puerto Morelos, Mérida, Campeche, Villahermosa, and Mexico City. **Omniturs del Caribe** (© **983/832-7889** or 983/832-8001) runs first-class buses to Mérida.

**To Belize:** Buses depart from the Lázaro Cárdenas market. Ask for Autobuses Novelo. Novelos buses are predominantly yellow, but they aren't marked clearly. The company has local service every 45 minutes ($9) and four express buses per day ($12). To see the ruins at Tikal, you have to get off at Benque and get transportation from there.

### VISITOR INFORMATION

The **State Tourism Office** (© **983/835-0860**) is at Avenida Hidalgo 22, at the corner of Carmen Ochoa. Office hours are Monday to Friday from 9am to 4:30pm.

### ORIENTATION

The telephone **area code** is **983.**

All traffic enters the city from the west, following **Obregón** into town. **Héroes** is the main north-south street.

## A MUSEUM NOT TO MISS

**Museo de la Cultura Maya** ★★★ Sophisticated, impressive, and informative, this new museum unlocks the complex world of the Maya. Push a button, and an illustrated description appears, explaining the medicinal and domestic uses of plants with their Mayan and scientific names; another exhibit describes the five social classes of the Maya by the way they dress; yet another shows how the beauty signs of cranial deformation, crossed eyes, and facial scarification were achieved. An enormous screen flashes images taken from an airplane flying over more than a dozen Maya sites from Mexico to Honduras. Another large television shows the architectural variety of Maya pyramids and how they were probably built. Then a walk on a glass floor takes you over representative ruins in the Maya world, clearly depicting the variety of pyramidal shapes. Finally, one of the most impressive sections is the three-story, stylized, sacred ceiba tree, which the Maya believed represented the underworld (Xibalba), Earth, and the 13 heavens. From this you'll have a better idea of the symbolism represented by Maya pyramids. If you can arrange it, see the museum before you tour the Río Bec ruins; it will all make more sense after visiting the museum.

Av. Héroes s/n. ✆ **983/832-6838.** Admission $3 adults, $1 children. Tues–Thurs 9am–7pm; Fri–Sun 9am–8pm. It's on the left between Colón and Gandhi, 8 blocks from Av. Obregón, past the Holiday Inn.

## WHERE TO STAY & DINE

**Hotel Holiday Inn Puerta Maya** This modern hotel (formerly the Hotel Continental) across from the central market was remodeled in 1995. The hotel has the best air-conditioning in town and is only 2 blocks from the Museo de la Cultura Maya. Most rooms are medium in size and come with two double beds or one king. Bathrooms are roomy and well lit. To find the hotel as you enter the town on Obregón, turn left on Avenida Héroes, go 6 blocks, and look for the hotel on the right, opposite the market.

Av. Héroes 171, 77000 Chetumal, Q. Roo. ✆ **800/465-4329** in the U.S., or 983/835-0400. Fax 983/832-1676. 85 units. $110 double. AE, MC, V. Free parking. **Amenities:** Restaurant, bar; medium-size pool; room service; laundry. *In room:* A/C, TV.

**Hotel Nachancán** One block from the new Lázaro Cárdenas market, this hotel offers plain but comfortable rooms, with two double beds. Bathrooms are small. It's relatively convenient to the bus station, but not close enough to walk. However, it is within walking distance of the Museo de la Cultura Maya. To find it from Avenida Obregón, turn left on Calzada Veracruz and follow it for at least 10 blocks; the hotel will be on the right.

Calz. Veracruz 379, 77000 Chetumal, Q. Roo. ✆ **983/832-3232.** 20 units. $25 double, $33 suite. No credit cards. **Amenities:** Restaurant, bar. *In room:* A/C, TV.

## ONWARD FROM CHETUMAL

From Chetumal you have several choices. The Maya ruins of Lamanai, in Belize, are an easy day trip if you have transportation (not a rental car). You can explore the Río Bec ruin route directly west of the city (see below) by heading out on Highway 186. At the Campeche state line there's a military guard post with drug-sniffing dogs; every vehicle is searched. A military guard post at the Reforma intersection just before Bacalar requires motorists to present the identification you used to enter Mexico (birth certificate or passport), plus your tourist permit. Other photo identification may be required, as well as information on where you're staying or where you're headed.

## SIDE TRIPS TO MAYA RUINS FROM CHETUMAL

West of Bacalar and Chetumal is the **Río Bec** area, where you can visit several Maya cities. These are picturesque and quite different architecturally from the large sites in the northern part of the peninsula. From Highway 307, take Highway 186 west. The road, a clearly marked federal highway, heads into the state of Campeche. Along the way are several ruins, some very close to the road, others a bit of a drive. You could fit visits to several of the ruins into a day trip, or you could spend the night in or near Xpujil. It has a few cheap hotels and one upscale place, **Chicanná Eco Village** (**© 981/816-2233** in Campeche for reservations). From there, you can visit the ruins farther west on your way to Palenque or Villahermosa.

The following section lists sites in the order in which you would see them driving from Bacalar or Chetumal. For a map of this area, consult the Yucatán Peninsula map (p. 526). Entry to each site costs $2 to $4, and all are free on Sunday. Informational signs at each building within the sites are in Mayan, Spanish, and English. Keep the mosquito repellent handy.

**Dzibanché** (or Tzibanché) means "place where they write on wood." Two large adjoining plazas have been cleared. Despite centuries of an unforgiving wet climate, a wood lintel in good condition with a date carving still supports a partially preserved corbeled arch on top of this building. Inside the temple, a tomb was discovered. This site is not as impressive as Kohunlich.

**Kohunlich** ★ (koh-*hoon*-leek), 42km (26 miles) from the intersection of highways 186 and 307, dates from around A.D. 100 to 900. The turn-off is well marked on the left. The ruins are only 8km (5 miles) from the highway. You'll find a large, shady ceremonial area flanked by four large pyramids. Continue walking, and just beyond this grouping you'll come to Kohunlich's famous Pyramid of the Masks under a thatched covering.

**Chacán Bacán** ★ (chah-*kahn* bah-*kahn*), which dates from around 200 B.C., was first discovered in 1980. The discovery in the 1990s of large Olmec-style heads on the façade of one of its pyramids caused lots of excitement. The site is about 80km (50 miles) from Bacalar. The turn-off (left) to it is at Caoba, where you follow a paved road for about 2.5km (1½ miles).

**Xpujil, Becán** ★, and **Chicanná** ★ are close to the highway just past the border that separates Quintana Roo from Campeche. Here you'll find the elegant high-pitched roofs and decorative staircases that are a principal feature of the sites in this region. Chicanná was a large walled city; several of its buildings have been restored. Becán has an impressive ceremonial center. This area is a little over 160km (100 miles) from Chetumal.

**Calakmul** ★★★ is another walled city. The site is quite large and beautiful, but it's also a 90 minutes from the highway on a one-lane paved road. Its grand pyramid is the tallest pyramid in the Yucatán, at 54m (178 ft.).

**Balamkú** ★★, close to the highway not far beyond the turn-off for Calakmul, has some buildings in beautiful condition. In one you'll find a chamber with three large sculpted figures descending into the underworld in the gaping mouths of animals.

14

# Mérida, Chichén-Itzá & the Maya Interior

Ask most people about the Yucatán, and they think of Cancún, the Caribbean coast, and Chichén-Itzá. In fact, there's much more to the Yucatán than just those places. With a little exploring, you'll find a great variety of things to do, the kind of variety that can make a trip really fun. One morning you can climb a pyramid and in the afternoon take a dip in the cool, clear water of a *cenote* (deep natural well). The next day may find you strolling along a lonely beach or riding in a small boat through mangroves to pay a visit to a colony of pink flamingos, and by nighttime, dancing in the streets of **Mérida.** This chapter covers the interior of the Yucatán peninsula, including the famous Maya ruins at **Chichén-Itzá** and **Uxmal,** the flamingo sanctuary at **Celestún,** and many less famous spots that can be fun to visit.

## EXPLORING THE YUCATAN'S MAYA HEARTLAND

The best way to see the Yucatán is by car. The terrain is flat, the towns are laid out in a simple manner, there is little traffic, and the main highways are in great shape. If you do drive around the area, one little Spanish word will be etched in your mind for a long time thereafter: *topes* (*toh*-pehs), the ubiquitous speed bumps that come in varying shapes and sizes and with varying degrees of warning. Be on your guard so that they don't catch you by surprise. Off the beaten path, the roads are narrow and rough, but hey—we're talking rental cars. Rentals are, in fact, a little pricey compared with those in the U.S. (due perhaps to wear and tear?), but some promotional deals are available. See "By Car," in "Mérida: Gateway to the Maya Heartland," below.

Plenty of buses ply the roads between the main towns and tourist destinations, and plenty of tour buses circulate, too—but buses to the smaller towns and ruins and the haciendas are infrequent or nonexistent. One bus company, Autobuses del Oriente (ADO), controls most of the first-class bus service and does a good job with the destinations it serves. Second-class buses go to some of the out-of-the-way places, but they can be slow, they stop a lot, and they are not air-conditioned, which is the key to comfortable bus travel.

The Yucatán is ***tierra caliente*** (the hotlands). Don't travel in this region without sunblock, mosquito repellent, and water. The coolest weather is from November to February; the hottest is from April to June, when the air is still. From July to October, during the rainy season, the air can be a little cooler because of winds and thundershowers. For tourism, the high-season/low-season distinction is less important in the interior than on the Caribbean coast, and most hotels have dropped the two-tiered pricing system.

Should you decide to travel into this part of the world, don't miss

## The Best Websites for Mérida, Chichén-Itzá & the Maya Interior

- **Maya: Portraits of a People: www.nationalgeographic.com/explorer/maya/more.html** A fascinating collection of articles from *National Geographic* and other sources.
- **Mexico's Yucatán Directory: www.mexonline.com/yucatan.htm** A nice roundup of vacation rentals, tour operators, and information on the Maya sites. For more information on Mexico's indigenous history, see the links on the pre-Columbian page (www.mexonline.com/precolum.htm).
- **Mysterious Places: Chichén-Itzá: www.mysteriousplaces.com/chichen_itza_page.html** An illuminating photo tour of Chichén-Itzá's temples. See images of the Temple of the Warriors, the Nunnery, and the Observatory, among other ruins.

**Mérida.** It is, and has been for centuries, the cultural and commercial center of the Yucatán. You won't find a more vibrant tropical city anywhere. Every time I visit, there is some festival or celebration to attend, on top of the nightly performances that the city offers its citizens and visitors. It's also the Yucatán's shopping center, where you can buy the area's specialty items, such as hammocks, Panama hats, and the embroidered native blouses known as *huipils.* And Mérida makes the perfect base from which to launch a variety of side trips. Here are some of the essential places to visit:

**CHICHEN-ITZA & VALLADOLID** These destinations are 40km (25 miles) apart from each other, about midway between Mérida and Cancún. It's 2½ hours by car from Mérida to Chichén on the new toll road, or *autopista.* You can spend a day at the beautifully restored ruins and then stay at one of the nearby hotels—or drive 40km (25 miles) to Valladolid, a quiet, charming colonial town with a pleasant central square. Valladolid features two eerie *cenotes,* and the spectacular ruins at Ekbalam are only 40km (25 miles) to the north. Also nearby is the Río Lagartos Nature Reserve, teeming with flamingos and other native birds.

**CELESTUN NATIONAL WILDLIFE REFUGE** These flamingo sanctuary wetlands along the Gulf coast contain a unique shallow-water estuary where freshwater from *cenotes* mixes with saltwater, creating the perfect feeding grounds for flamingos. Touring this area by launch is relaxing and rewarding. Only 1½ hours from Mérida, Celestún makes for an easy day trip.

**DZIBILCHALTUN** This Maya site, now a national park, is 14km (9 miles) north of Mérida along the Progreso road. Here you'll find pre-Hispanic ruins, nature trails, a *cenote,* and the new Museum of the Maya. You can make this the first stop in a day trip to Progreso and other attractions north of Mérida.

**PROGRESO** A modern city and Gulf coast beach escape 34km (21 miles) north of Mérida, Progreso has a wide beach and oceanfront drive that's popular on the weekends and during the summer. The recent arrival of cruise ships might make Progreso even more popular, but with so much beach, if you go on a weekday, you'll easily find a place to yourself. From Progreso you can drive down the coast to **Uaymitún** to see some flamingos and visit the recently excavated ruins of **Xcambó.**

**UXMAL** Smaller than Chichén, but architecturally more striking and mysterious, Uxmal is about 80km (50 miles) to the south of Mérida. You can see it in a day, though it's a good idea to extend that somewhat to see the sound-and-light show and spend the night at one of the hotels by the ruins. Several other nearby sites comprise the Puuc route and can be explored on the following day. It's also possible, though a bit rushed, to see Uxmal and the other ruins on a 1-day trip by special excursion bus from Mérida. Sunday is a good day to go because admission to the archaeological sites is free.

## 1 Mérida: Gateway to the Maya Heartland ★★

1,440km (900 miles) E of Mexico City; 320km (200 miles) W of Cancún

Mérida is the capital of the state of Yucatán and has been the dominant city in the region since the Spanish Conquest. The colonial historic center is large but easy to navigate, and there are abundant activities for the visitor. Mérida's nightlife is more varied and representative of the region than Cancún's. People here know how to have a good time, and they seem driven to organize concerts, theatrical productions, art exhibits, and such. In recent years the city has been in the midst of a cultural explosion.

### ESSENTIALS

**GETTING THERE & DEPARTING** **By Plane** **Aeromexico** (✆ **999/927-9277** or 999/927-9433) and **Mexicana** (✆ **999/924-6633** or 999/924-6910) have nonstop flights to and from Miami. **Continental** (✆ **999/946-1888** and 999/946-1900) has nonstop service to and from Houston. Otherwise, you will most likely have to fly through Cancún, Cozumel, or Mexico City. **Mexicana** flies to and from Mexico City. **Aeromexico** flies to and from Cancún and Mexico City. **Aerocaribe** (✆ **999/928-6786**), a Mexicana affiliate, provides service to and from Cozumel, Cancún, Veracruz, Villahermosa, and points in Central America. **Aviateca** (✆ **999/946-1312**) flies to and from Guatemala City and Flores (Tikal). **Aviacsa** (✆ **999/926-9087**) provides service to and from Cancún, Monterrey, Villahermosa, Tuxtla Gutiérrez, Tapachula, Oaxaca, and Mexico City. Taxis from the airport to the city run $11.

**BY CAR** **Highway 180** is the old federal highway (*carretera federal*) between Mérida and Cancún. The trip takes 6 hours, and the road is in good shape; you will pass through many Maya villages. A four-lane divided **toll road** (the *cuota* or *autopista*) parallels Highway 180 and begins at the town of Kantunil, 56km (35 miles) east of Mérida. By avoiding the tiny villages and their not-so-tiny speed bumps, the *autopista* cuts 2 hours from the journey between Mérida and Cancún; one-way tolls cost $28. Coming from Cancún (or, for that matter, Valladolid or Chichén-Itzá, both of which are en route), Highway 180 enters Mérida by feeding into Calle 65, which passes 1 block south of the main square.

**Tips** **Mapping the Region**

To see a map of the region surrounding Mérida, see "The Yucatán Peninsula" map on p. 526.

If you are coming from the south (Campeche or Uxmal) you will enter the city on Avenida Itzáes. To get to the town center, turn right on Calle 59 (the first street after the zoo).

A traffic loop or *periférico* encircles Mérida, making it possible to skirt the city. Directional signs into the city are generally good, but going around the city on the loop requires constant vigilance.

**BY BUS** There are five bus stations in Mérida, two of which offer first-class buses; the other three provide local service to nearby destinations. The larger of the first-class stations, **CAME,** is on Calle 70, between Calles 69 and 71 (see "City Layout," below). The ADO bus line and its affiliates operate the station. When you get there, you'll see a row of ticket windows. All but the last couple to the right sell first-class tickets. The first window sells tickets to Palenque and San Cristóbal. The other windows sell tickets to other destinations, including Palenque. The last two windows sell tickets for ADO's deluxe services: ADO-GL and UNO. The former is only slightly better than first class; the latter has superwide roomy seats. Unless it's a long trip, I generally choose the bus that has the most convenient departure time. Tickets can be purchased in advance.

The other first-class station is the small **Maya K'iin** used by the bus company **Elite.** It's on Calle 65 no. 548, between Calles 68 and 70.

**To and from Cancún:** You can pick up a bus at the CAME (almost every hr.) or through **Elite** (6 per day). Both bus lines also pick up passengers at the Fiesta Americana Hotel, across from the Hyatt (12 per day). You can buy a ticket there at the "Ticket Bus" agency. Cancún is 4 hours away; a few buses stop in **Valladolid.**

**To and from Chichén-Itzá:** Three buses per day (2½ hr.) depart from the CAME. Also, check out tours operating from the hotels in Mérida if you want to visit in a day.

**To and from Playa del Carmen, Tulum, and Chetumal:** From the CAME, there are eight departures per day for Playa del Carmen (5 hr.), six for Tulum (6 hr.), and eight for Chetumal (7 hr.).

**To and from Campeche:** From the CAME station, there is service every hour between 6am and 10pm. Elite has four departures per day. It's a 2½-hour trip.

**To and from Palenque and San Cristóbal de las Casas:** There is service to San Cristóbal twice daily from the CAME, and once daily on Elite. To Palenque there are 6 and 1, respectively. There have been reports of minor theft on buses to Palenque. You should do three things: Don't take second-class buses to this destination; check your luggage so that it's stowed in the cargo bay; and put your carry-on in the overhead rack, not on the floor.

The main **second-class bus station** is around the corner from the CAME on Calle 69, between Calles 68 and 70.

**To and from Uxmal:** There are four buses per day. (You can also hook up with one of the various tours to Uxmal through most hotels or any travel agent or tour operator in town.) There's also one bus per day that combines Uxmal with the other sites to the south (Kabah, Sayil, Labná, and Xlapak—known as the Puuc route) and does the whole round-trip in a day. It stops for 2 hours at Uxmal and 30 minutes at each of the other sites.

**To and from Progreso and Dzibilchaltún:** The bus station that serves these destinations is the **Estación Progreso,** Calle 62 no. 524, between Calles 65 and 67. The trip to Progreso takes an hour by second class. There are also some *colectivos* (village taxis) to Dzibilchaltún that you can pick up beside the San Juan church, south of the main plaza off of Calle 62.

**To and from Celestún:** The Celestún station is at Calle 71 no. 585 between Calles 64 and 66. The trip takes 1½ to 2 hours, depending on how often the bus stops. There are 10 buses per day.

**ORIENTATION** **Arriving by Plane** Mérida's airport is 13km (8 miles) from the city center on the southwestern outskirts of town, near the entrance of Highway 180. The airport has desks for renting a car, reserving a hotel room, and getting tourist information. Taxi tickets to town are sold outside the airport doors, under the covered walkway, and cost $11.

**VISITOR INFORMATION** There are city tourism offices and state tourism offices, which have different resources; if you don't get the info you need at one, go to the other. The state operates two downtown tourism offices: One is in the **Teatro Peón Contreras,** facing Parque de la Madre (© **999/924-9290**); and the other is on the main plaza, in the **Palacio de Gobierno,** immediately to the left as you enter. These offices are open daily 8am to 8pm. There are also information booths at the airport and the CAME bus station. The city's **visitor information offices** are downtown on Calle 59 between Calles 60 and 62 (© **999/923-0883**) and on the Paseo de Montejo 472 between Calles 37 and 39 (© **999/926-0809**). Hours are 8am to 8pm.

Also keep your eye out for the free monthly magazine *Yucatán Today;* it's a good source of info for Mérida and the rest of the region.

**CITY LAYOUT** Mérida has the standard layout of towns in the Yucatán: Streets running north-south are even numbers; those running east-west are odd numbers. The numbering begins on the north and the east sides of town, so if you are walking on an odd-numbered street and the even numbers of the cross-streets are increasing, then you know that you are heading west; likewise, if you are on an even-numbered street and the odd numbers of the cross streets are increasing, you are going south.

Another useful tip is that address numbers don't tell you anything about what cross street to look for, so you can't be sure of where your destination is on the city grid. This is why, in addition to a street number, you will often see cross-streets listed, usually like this: "Calle 60 no. 549 × 71 y 73." The "×" is a multiplication sign—shorthand for the word *por* (meaning "by")—and "y" means "and." So this place would be on Calle 60 between Calles 71 and 73.

The town's main square is the bright, busy **Plaza Mayor** (referred to simply as *El Centro*). It's bordered by Calles 60, 62, 61, and 63. Calle 60, which runs in front of the cathedral, is an important street to remember; it connects the main square with several smaller plazas, some theaters and lovely churches, and the University of Yucatán, just to the north. Here, too, you'll find a concentration of handcraft shops, restaurants, and hotels. Around Plaza Mayor are the cathedral, the Palacio de Gobierno (state government building), the *Ayuntamiento* (town hall), and the Palacio Montejo. The plaza always has a crowd, and it's full on Sundays, when it holds a large street fair. (See the box, "Festivals & Special Events in Mérida," below.) Within a few blocks are several smaller plazas and the bustling market district.

Mérida's most fashionable district is the broad, tree-lined Bulevard **Paseo de Montejo** and its surrounding neighborhood. The Paseo de Montejo parallels Calle 60 and begins 7 blocks north and a little east of the main square. There are a number of trendy restaurants, modern hotels, offices for various banks and airlines, and a few clubs here, but the bulevard is mostly known for its stately mansions built during the boom times of the *henequen* industry. Near where the

## *Moments* Festivals & Special Events in Mérida

Many Mexican cities offer weekend concerts in the park and such, but Mérida surpasses them all with performances every day of the week. Unless otherwise indicated, admission to the following is free.

**Sunday** Each Sunday from 9am to 9pm, there's a fair called *Mérida en Domingo* (Mérida on Sun). The main plaza and a section of Calle 60 from El Centro to Parque Santa Lucía close to traffic. Parents come with their children to stroll around and take in the scene. There are booths selling food and drink, along with a lively little flea market and used-book fair, children's art classes, and educational booths. At 11am in front of the Palacio del Gobierno, musicians play everything from jazz to classical and folk music. Also at 11am, the police orchestra performs Yucatecan tunes at the Santa Lucía park. At 11:30am, you'll find bawdy comedy acts at the Parque Hidalgo, on Calle 60 at Calle 59. There's a lull in the midafternoon, and then the plaza fills up again as people walk around and visit with friends. Around 7pm in front of the *Ayuntamiento,* a large band starts playing mambos, rumbas, and cha-cha-chas with great enthusiasm; you may see 1,000 people dancing in the street. Afterward, folk ballet dancers reenact a typical Yucatecan wedding inside.

**Monday** *Vaquería Regional*—traditional music and dancing to celebrate the *Vaquerías* feast, associated originally with the branding of cattle on Yucatecan haciendas. Among the featured performers are dancers with trays of bottles or filled glasses on their heads—a sight to see.

**Tuesday** At 9pm in Parque Santiago, Calle 59 at Calle 72, the Municipal Orchestra plays big-band music from the 1940s, both Latin and American.

**Wednesday** At 9pm in the Teatro Peón Contreras, Calle 60 at Calle 57, the University of Yucatán Folklore Ballet presents "Yucatán and Its Roots." Admission is $5.

**Thursday** Yucatecan *trova* music (boleros, baladas) and dance are presented at the *Serenata* in Parque Santa Lucía at 9pm.

**Friday** At 9pm in the courtyard of the University of Yucatán, Calle 60 at Calle 57, the University of Yucatán Ballet Folklórico performs typical regional dances from the Yucatán.

**Saturday** *Noche Mexicana* at the park at the beginning of Paseo de Montejo begins at 9pm. It features several performances of traditional Mexican music and dance. Some of the performers are amateurs who acquit themselves reasonably well; others are professional musicians and dancers who thoroughly know their craft. Food stands sell very good *antojitos,* as well as drinks and ice cream.

Paseo intersects Avenida Colón, you'll find the two fanciest hotels in town: the Hyatt and the Fiesta Americana.

**GETTING AROUND** **By Car** In general, reserve your car in advance from the U.S. to get the best weekly rates during high season (Nov–Feb); in low season, I usually do better renting a car once I get to Mérida. The local rental companies are very competitive and have promotional deals that you can get only if you are there. When comparing, make sure that it's apples to apples; ask if the price quote includes the IVA tax and insurance coverage. (Practically everybody offers free mileage.) For tips on saving money on car rentals, see "Getting Around," in chapter 2. Rental cars are generally a little more expensive (unless you find a promotional rate) than in the U.S. By renting for only a day or two, you can avoid the high cost of parking lots in Mérida. These *estacionamentos* charge one price for the night and double that if you leave your car for the following day. Many hotels offer free parking, but make sure they include daytime parking in the price.

**By Taxi** Taxis are easy to come by and much cheaper than in Cancún.

**By Bus** City buses are a little tricky to figure out but aren't needed very often because almost everything of interest is within walking distance of the main plaza. Still, it's a bit of a walk from the plaza to the Paseo de Montejo, and you can save yourself some work by taking a bus, minibus, or *pesero* (Volkswagen minivan) that is heading north on Calle 60. Most of these will take you to Paseo Montejo or drop you off at Plaza Santa Ana, right by the Paseo. The *peseros* or *combis* (usually painted white) run out in several directions from the main plaza along simple routes. They usually line up along the side streets next to the plaza.

## *FAST FACTS:* Mérida

*American Express* The office is at Paseo de Montejo 492 (© **999/942-8200**). Open for travelers' services weekdays from 9am to 2pm and 4 to 6pm.

*Area Code* The telephone area code is **999.**

*Bookstore* The Librería Dante, Calle 59 between Calles 60 and 62 (© **999/928-3674**), has a small selection of English-language cultural-history books on Mexico. It's open Monday to Saturday from 8am to 9:30pm, Sunday from 10am to 6pm. There is another Libreria Dante on the main plaza.

*Business Hours* Generally, businesses are open Monday to Saturday from 10am to 2pm and 4 to 8pm.

*Climate* From November to February, the weather can be pleasantly cool and windy. In other months, it's just hot, especially during the day. Rain can occur any time of year, especially during the rainy season (July–Oct), and usually comes in the form of afternoon tropical showers.

*Consulates* The **American Consulate** is at Paseo de Montejo 453, at Avenida Colón (© **999/925-6219** or 999/925-5011). Office hours are Monday to Friday from 9am to 1pm. The **British Vice-Consulate** is at Calle 53 no. 498, at Calle 58 (© **999/928-6152**). Office hours are weekdays from 9am to 1pm. The vice-consul fields questions about travel to Belize as well as all matters British.

*Currency Exchange* Most banks in Mérida are a mess to deal with and don't offer outstanding exchange rates to offset the hassle. A *casa de cambio* called **Cambios Portales,** Calle 61 no. 500 (© **999/923-8709**), is on the north side of the plaza in the middle of the block. It's open daily from

8:30am to 8:30pm. There are also many ATMs; one is on the south side of the same plaza.

*Hospitals* The best hospital is **Centro Médico de las Américas,** Calle 54 no. 365 between 33-A and Avenida Pérez Ponce. The main phone number is © **999/926-2619;** for emergencies, call © **999/927-3199.** You can also call the Cruz Roja (Red Cross) at © **999/924-9813.**

*Internet Access* There are so many Internet access providers in town that you hardly have to walk more than a couple of blocks to find one.

*Language Classes* Maya scholars, Spanish teachers, and archaeologists from the United States are among the students at the **Centro de Idiomas del Sureste,** Calle 14 no. 106 at Calle 25, Colonia México, 97000 Mérida, Yuc. (© **999/926-1155;** fax 999/926-9020). The school has two locations: in the Colonia México, a northern residential district, and on Calle 66 at Calle 57, downtown. Students live with local families or in hotels; sessions running 2 weeks or longer are available for all levels of proficiency and areas of interest. For brochures and applications, contact Chloe Conaway de Pacheco, Directora.

*Pharmacy* **Farmacia Yza,** Calle 63 no. 502, between Calles 60 and 62 (© **999/924-9510**), on the south side of the plaza, is open 24 hours.

*Police* Mérida has a special body of police to assist tourists. They patrol the downtown area and the Paseo Montejo, wearing white shirts with the words *Policía Turística.* The phone number for both the tourist police and the regular police is © **999/925-2555.**

*Post Office* The *correo* is near the market at the corner of Calles 65 and 56. A branch office is at the airport. Both are open Monday to Friday from 8am to 7pm, Saturday from 9am to 12pm.

*Seasons* There are two high seasons for tourism, but they aren't as pronounced as on the coast. One is in July and August, when Mexicans take their vacations, and the other is between November 15 and Easter Sunday, when Canadians and Americans flock to the Yucatán to escape winter weather.

*Telephones* There are long-distance phone service centers at the airport and the bus station. In the downtown area is **TelWorld,** Calle 59 no. 495-4 between Calles 56 and 58. To use the public phones, buy a *Ladatel* card from just about any newsstand or store. The cards come in a variety of denominations and work for long distance within Mexico and sometimes even abroad. Also see "Telephone/Fax," in "Fast Facts: Mexico," in chapter 2.

## EXPLORING MERIDA

Most of Mérida's attractions are within walking distance from the downtown area. To see a larger area of the city, a popular **bus tour** is worth taking. The man who operates these tours has bought a few small buses and given them a fancy paint job, pulled out all the windows, raised the roof several inches, and installed wooden benches so that the buses remind you of the traditional buses of coastal Latin America, known as *chivas* in Colombia and Venezuela or as *guaguas* in other places. You can find these buses on the corner of Calles 60 and 55 (next to the church of Santa Lucía) at 10am, 1, 4, and 7pm. The tour costs $9 per person and lasts 2 hours. Another option for seeing the city is via **horse-drawn carriage.** A 45-minute ride around central Mérida costs $17. You can usually find the carriages beside the cathedral or on Calle 60.

**EXPLORING PLAZA MAYOR** Downtown Mérida is a great example of a lowland colonial city. The town has a casual, relaxed feel. Buildings lack the severe baroque and neoclassical features that characterize central Mexico; most are finished in stucco and painted light colors. Mérida's gardens add to this relaxed, tropical atmosphere. Gardeners do not strive for the kind of garden where all is exactly in its place, displaying the gardener's control over nature. Here, natural exuberance is the ideal, with plants growing in a wild profusion that disguises human intervention. A perfect example is the courtyard in the Palacio Montejo. Mérida's plazas are a slightly different version of this aesthetic: Unlike the highland plazas, with their carefully sculpted trees, Mérida's squares are typically built around large trees that are left to grow as tall as possible.

**Plaza Mayor** (often referred to as "El Centro") has this sort of informality. Even when there's no orchestrated event in progress, the park is full of people sitting on the benches talking with friends or taking a casual stroll. A plaza like this is a great advantage for a big city such as Mérida, giving it a personal feel and a sense of community that combat the modern bustle of urban life. Notice the beautiful scale and composition of the major buildings surrounding it. The most prominent of these is the cathedral.

The oldest **cathedral** on the continent, it was built between 1561 and 1598. Much of the stone in the cathedral's walls came from the ruined buildings of Tihó, the former Maya city. The original finish was stucco, and you can see some remnants still clinging to the bare rock. However, people like the way the unfinished walls show the cathedral's age. Notice how the two top levels of the bell towers are built off-center from their bases—an uncommon feature. Inside, decoration is sparse, with altars draped in fabric colorfully embroidered like a Maya woman's shift. The most notable item is a picture of Ah Kukum Tutul Xiú, chief of the Xiú people, visiting the Montejo camp to make peace; it's hanging over the side door on the right.

To the left of the main altar is a small shrine with a curious figure of Christ that is a replica of one recovered from a burned-out church in the town of Ichmul. In the 1500s a local artist carved the original figure from a miraculous tree that was hit by lightning and burst into flames—but did not char. The statue later became blistered in the church fire at Ichmul, but it survived. In 1645 it was moved to the cathedral in Mérida, where the locals attached great powers to the figure, naming it *Cristo de las Ampollas* (Christ of the Blisters). It did not, however, survive the sacking of the cathedral in 1915 by revolutionary forces, so another figure, modeled after the original, was made. Take a look in the side chapel (open daily 8–11am and 4:30–7pm), which contains a life-size diorama of the Last Supper. The Mexican Jesus is covered with prayer crosses brought by supplicants asking for intercession.

Next door to the cathedral is the old bishop's palace, now converted into the city's contemporary art museum, **Museo de Arte Contemporáneo Ateneo de Yucatán** (✆ **999/928-3236**). The palace was confiscated and rebuilt during the Mexican Revolution in 1915. The museum's entrance faces the cathedral from the recently constructed walkway between the two buildings called the Pasaje de la Revolución. There are 17 exhibition rooms displaying work by contemporary artists, mostly from the Yucatán. (The best known are Fernando García Ponce and Fernando Castro Pacheco, whose works also hang in the government palace described below.) Nine of the rooms hold the museum's permanent collection; the rest are for temporary exhibits. It's open Wednesday to Monday 10am to 6pm. Admission is $2.50; free on Sunday.

Across the street, on the south side of the plaza, is the **Palacio Montejo.** Its façade, with heavy decoration around the doorway and windows, is a good example of the Spanish architectural style known as plateresque. But the content of the decoration is very much a New World creation. Conquering the Yucatán was the Montejo family business, begun by the original Francisco Montejo and continued by his son and nephew (both named Francisco Montejo). Construction of the house started in 1542 under the son, Francisco Montejo El Mozo ("The Younger"). Bordering the entrance are politically incorrect figures of conquistadors standing on the heads of vanquished Indians—borrowed, perhaps, from the pre-Hispanic custom of portraying victorious Maya kings treading on their defeated foes. The posture of the conquistadors and their facial expression of wide-eyed dismay make them less imposing than the Montejos might have wished. A bank now occupies the building, but you can enter the courtyard, view the garden, and see for yourself what a charming residence it must have been for the descendants of the Montejos, who lived here as recently as the 1970s. (Curiously enough, not only does Mérida society keep track of who is descended from the Montejos, but it also keeps track of who is descended from the last Maya king Tutul Xiú.)

In stark contrast to the severity of the cathedral and Casa Montejo is the light, unimposing **Palacio Municipal** (town hall) or *Ayuntamiento.* The exterior dates from the mid–19th century, an era when a tropicalist aesthetic tinged with romanticism began asserting itself across coastal Latin America. Inside on the second floor you can see the meeting hall of the city council, and enjoy a lovely view of the plaza from the balcony. Next door to the *Ayuntamiento* is a recently completed building called **El Nuevo Olimpo** (The New Olympus). It took the place of the old Olimpo, which a misguided town council demolished in the 1970s, to the regret of many older Meridanos. The new building tries to incorporate elements of the original while presenting something new. It holds concert and gallery space, a bookstore, and a lovely courtyard. There is a comfortable cafe under the arches, and a bulletin board at the entrance to the courtyard showing upcoming performances.

Cater-corner from the Nuevo Olimpo is the old **Casa del Alguacil** (Magistrate's House). Under its arcades is something of an institution in Mérida: the **Dulcería y Sorbetería Colón,** an ice cream and sweet shop that will appeal to those who prefer less-rich ice creams. A spectacular side doorway on Calle 62 bears viewing, and across the street is the new **Ciné Merida,** with two movie screens showing art films and one stage for live performances. Returning to the main plaza, down a bit from the ice cream store is a **shopping center** of boutiques and convenience food vendors called Pasaje Picheta. At the end of the arcade is the **Palacio de Gobierno,** dating from 1892. Large murals by the Yucatecan artist Fernando Castro Pacheco, executed between 1971 and 1973, decorate the walls of the courtyard. Scenes from Maya and Mexican history abound, and the painting over the stairway depicts the Maya spirit with ears of sacred corn, the "sunbeams of the gods." Nearby is a painting of mustachioed Lázaro Cárdenas, who as president in 1938 expropriated 17 foreign oil companies and was hailed as a Mexican liberator. Upstairs is a long, wide gallery with more of Pacheco's paintings, which achieve their effect by localizing color and imitating the photographic technique of double exposure. The palace is open

Monday to Saturday from 8am to 8pm, Sunday from 9am to 5pm. There is a small tourism office to the left as you enter.

Further down Calle 61 is the **Museo de la Ciudad.** It faces the side of the cathedral and occupies the former church of San Juan de Dios. An exhibit outlining the history of Mérida will be of interest to those curious about the city, and there is explanatory text in English. Hours are Tuesday to Sunday from 10am to 2pm, Tuesday to Friday from 4 to 8pm. Admission is free.

**EXPLORING CALLE 60** Heading north from Plaza Mayor up Calle 60, you'll see many of Mérida's old churches and squares. Several stores along Calle 60 sell gold-filigree jewelry, pottery, clothing, and folk art. A stroll along this street leads to the Parque Santa Ana and continues to the fashionable Bulevard Paseo de Montejo and its Museo Regional de Antropología.

The first place of interest is the Teatro Daniel de Ayala, only because it sometimes schedules interesting performances. Then on your left will be a small park called **Parque Cepeda Peraza** (or Parque Hidalgo). Named for 19th-century General Manuel Cepeda Peraza, the *parque* was part of Montejo's original city plan. Small outdoor restaurants front hotels on the *parque,* making it a popular stopping-off place at any time of day. Across Calle 59 is the **Iglesia de Jesús,** or *El Tercer Orden* (the Third Order). Built by the Jesuit order in 1618, it has the richest interior of any church in Mérida, making it a favorite spot for weddings. The entire block on which the church stands belonged to the Jesuits, who are known as great educators. The school they left behind after their expulsion became the Universidad de Yucatán.

On the other side of the church is the **Parque de la Madre** (or Parque Morelos). The park contains a modern statue of the Madonna and Child, a copy of the work by Renoir. Beyond the Parque de la Madre and across the pedestrian-only street is the **Teatro Peón Contreras,** an opulent theater designed by Italian architect Enrico Deserti a century ago. The theater is noted for its Carrara marble staircase and frescoed dome. Try to get a peek at it, and look at the performance schedule to see if anything of interest will be held during your stay. Great national and international performers appear here frequently. In the southwest corner of the theater, facing the Parque de la Madre, is a **tourist information office.** Across Calle 60 is the main building of the **Universidad de Yucatán.** Inside is a flagstone courtyard where the *ballet folklórico* performs on Friday nights.

A block farther north brings you to Parque Santa Lucía. Bordered by an arcade on the north and west sides, this park was where visitors first alighted in Mérida from the stagecoach. On Sundays, Parque Santa Lucía holds a used-book market, and several evenings a week it hosts popular entertainment. On Thursday nights performers present Yucatecan songs and poems. Facing the park is the **Iglesia de Santa Lucía** (1575).

Four blocks farther up Calle 60 is Parque Santa Ana; if you turn right, you'll come to the beginning of the Paseo in 2 blocks.

**EXPLORING THE PASEO DE MONTEJO** The Paseo de Montejo is a broad, tree-lined bulevard that runs north-south starting at Calle 47, 7 blocks north and 2 blocks east of the main square. In the late 19th century, stalwarts of Mérida's upper crust (mostly plantation owners) decided that the city needed something grander than its traditional narrow streets lined by wall-to-wall townhouses. They built this monumentally proportioned bulevard and lined it with mansions. Things went sour with the henequen bust, but several of these mansions survive—some in private hands, others as offices, restaurants, or consulates.

Today, this is the fashionable part of town, with many fine restaurants, trendy discos, and expensive hotels.

Of the mansions that survive, the most notable is the Palacio Cantón, which now houses the **Museo Regional de Antropología** ★★, or Anthropology Museum (✆ **999/923-0557**). Designed and built by Enrico Deserti, the architect of the Teatro Peón Contreras, it was constructed between 1909 and 1911, during the last years of the Porfiriato. It was the residence of General Francisco Cantón Rosado, who enjoyed his palace for only 6 years before dying in 1917. For a time the mansion served as the official residence of the state's governor.

Viewing the museum also affords you an opportunity to see some of the surviving interior architecture. The museum's main focus is the pre-Columbian cultures of the peninsula, especially the Maya. Topics include cosmology, history, and culture. Captions for the permanent displays are mostly in Spanish. Starting with fossil mastodon teeth, the exhibits take you through the Yucatán's history, paying special attention to the daily life of its inhabitants.

Some exhibits vividly illustrate such strange Maya customs as tying boards to babies' heads to create the oblong shape that they considered so beautiful, and filing teeth or perforating them to inset jewels. There are enlarged photos of several archaeological sites and drawings that illustrate the various styles of Maya dwellings. Even if you know only a little Spanish, this is a worthwhile stop, and it provides good background for explorations of Maya sites. The museum is open Tuesday to Saturday from 8am to 8pm, Sunday from 8am to 2pm. Admission is $3.50; free on Sunday.

## SHOPPING

Mérida is known for **hammocks,** ***guayaberas*** (lightweight men's shirts worn untucked), and **Panama hats. Baskets and pottery** made in the Yucatán and crafts from all over Mexico are sold cheaply in the **central market.** Mérida is also the place to pick up prepared ***achiote,*** a pastelike mixture of ground *achiote* seeds (annatto), oregano, garlic, masa, and other spices used in Yucatecan cuisine. Mixed with sour orange to a soupy consistency, it makes a great marinade, especially for grilled meat and fish. It can be found bottled in this form. It's also the sauce for baked chicken and *cochinita pibil.*

**EXPLORING THE MARKET** Mérida's bustling **market district** is a few blocks southeast of the Plaza Mayor. The area surrounding the market is full of shops, and hordes of pedestrians crowd the sidewalks. Behind the post office (at Calles 65 and 56) is the oldest part of the market, the **Portal de Granos** (Grains Arcade), a row of maroon arches where the grain merchants used to sell their goods. Just east, between Calles 56 and 54, is the new market building, Mercado Lucas de Gálvez. Inside, chaos seems to reign, but after a short while a certain order emerges. Here you can find anything from fresh fish to flowers to leather goods. In the building directly south of the market, you can find more locally manufactured goods; on the second floor of this building is a crafts market (**Bazaar de Artesanías**). Another crafts market, **Bazaar García Rejón,** lies a block west of the market on Calle 65 between Calles 58 and 60.

### CRAFTS

**Casa de las Artesanías** This store occupies the front rooms of a restored monastery. Here you can find a wide selection of crafts, 90% of which come from the Yucatán. For the most part, the quality of work is higher than elsewhere, but so are the prices. The monastery's back courtyard is used as a gallery, with rotating exhibits on folk and fine arts. It's open Monday to Saturday from

9am to 8pm, Sunday from 9am to 1pm. Calle 63 no. 513, between Calles 64 and 66. ✆ 999/928-6676.

**Miniaturas** This fun little store is packed to the rafters with miniatures, a traditional Mexican folk art form that has been evolving in a number of directions, including social and political commentary, pop art, and bawdy humor. Alicia Rivero, the owner, collects them from several parts of Mexico and offers plenty of variety, from traditional miniatures such as furniture for dollhouses, to popular cartoon characters and celebrities. The store also sells other forms of folk art such as masks, games, and traditional crafts. Hours are Monday to Saturday 10am to 8pm. Calle 59 no. 507A-4 (between Calles 60 and 62). ✆ **999/928-6503.**

**Museo de Artes Populares** This isn't a store, but it will be of great interest to crafts collectors. Exhibits show regional costumes, tools, and crafts from various parts of Mexico. Some of the craftwork displayed here has all but disappeared from present-day Mexico. The collection includes jewelry, folk pottery, baskets, lacquer ware, and woodcarvings. It's open Tuesday to Saturday from 8am to 6pm, Sunday from 9am to 2pm. Admission is $1.75 for adults and 50¢ for children under 12. Calle 59 no. 441, between Calles 50 and 48. No phone.

## GUAYABERAS

Business suits are hot and uncomfortable in Mérida's soaking humidity, so businessmen, politicians, bankers, and bus drivers alike wear the *guayabera,* a loose-fitting shirt decorated with narrow tucks, pockets, and sometimes embroidery, worn over the pants rather than tucked in. Mérida is famous as the best place to buy *guayaberas,* which can go for less than $15 at the market or for more than $50 custom-made by a tailor. A *guayabera* made of linen can cost about $80. Most are made of cotton, although other materials are available. The traditional color is white.

Most shops display ready-to-wear shirts in several price ranges. *Guayabera* makers pride themselves on being innovators. I have yet to enter a shirt-maker's shop in Mérida that did not present its own version of the *guayabera.* When looking at *guayaberas,* here are few things to keep in mind: When Yucatecans say *seda,* they mean polyester; *lino* is linen or a linen/polyester combination. Take a close look at the stitching and such details as the way the tucks line up over the pockets; with *guayaberas,* the details are everything.

**Guayaberas Jack** The craftsmanship here is very good, the place has a reputation to maintain, and some of the salespeople speak English. Prices are as marked. This will give you a good basis of comparison if you want to hunt for a bargain elsewhere. If the staff does not have the style and color of shirt you want, they will make it for you in about 3 hours. This shop also sells regular shirts and women's blouses. Hours are Monday to Saturday from 10am to 8pm, Sunday from 10am to 2pm. Calle 59 no. 507A (between Calles 60 and 62). ✆ **999/928-6002.**

## HAMMOCKS

Natives across tropical America used hammocks long before the Europeans arrived in the New World. Our word "hammock" comes from the Spanish *hamaca,* which is a borrowing from Taino, a Caribbean Indian language. Hammocks are still in use throughout Latin America and come in a wide variety of forms, but none is so comfortable as the Yucatecan hammock, which is woven with cotton string in a fine mesh. For most of us, of course, the hammock is lawn furniture, something to relax in for an hour or so on a lazy afternoon. But for the vast majority of Yucatecans, hammocks are the equivalent of beds, and they greatly prefer hammocks to mattresses. I know a hotel owner who has 150 beds in his establishment but won't sleep on them. When he does, he complains of waking up unrested and sore. Many well-to-do Meridanos keep a bed just for show. In hotels that cater to Yucatecans, you will always find hammock hooks in the walls.

My advice to the hammock buyer is this: The woven part should be cotton, it should be made with fine string, and the strings should be so numerous that when you get in it and stretch out diagonally (the way you're supposed to sleep in these hammocks), the gaps between the strings remain small. Don't pay attention to the words used to describe the size of a hammock; they have become practically meaningless. Good hammocks don't cost a lot of money ($15–$30). If you want a superior hammock, ask for one made with fine crochet thread, *hilo de crochet* (the word *crochet* is also sometimes bandied about, but you can readily see the difference). This should run about $100.

Nothing beats a tryout; the two shops mentioned here will gladly hang a hammock for you to test-drive. When it's up, look to see that there are no untied strings. You can also see what street vendors are offering, but you have to know what to look for, or they are likely to take advantage of you.

**Hamacas El Aguacate** El Aguacate sells hammocks wholesale and retail. It has the greatest variety and is the place to go for a really fancy or extra-large hammock. A good hammock is the no. 6 in cotton; it runs $33. The store is open Monday to Friday from 8:30am to 7:30pm, Saturday from 8am to 5pm. It's 6 blocks south of the main square. Calle 58 no. 604 (at Calle 73). ✆ **999/928-6429.**

**Tejidos y Cordeles Nacionales** This place near the municipal market sells only cotton hammocks, priced by weight—a pretty good practice because hammock lengths are standard here. The prices are better than at El Aguacate, but quality control isn't as good. My idea of a good hammock weighs about 1½ kilos and runs about $25. Calle 56 no. 516-B (between Calles 63 and 65). ✆ **999/928-5561.**

### PANAMA HATS

Another useful and popular item is this soft, pliable hat made from the fibers of the *jipijapa* palm in several towns south of Mérida along Highway 180, especially Becal, in the neighboring state of Campeche. The hat makers in these towns work inside caves so that the moist air keeps the palm fibers pliant.

*Jipi* hats come in various grades determined by the quality (pliability, softness, and fineness) of the fibers and closeness of the weave. The difference in weave is easy to see, as a fine weave improves the shape of a hat. It has more body and regains its shape better. I like two places in particular for Panama hats; if you speak Spanish, you can hear two different takes on buying a hat. Expect to pay between $15 and $80. One store is **El Becaleño,** Calle 65 no. 483, across from the post office. The owner can show you differences in qualities and has some very expensive hats. The other store is a short distance away in one of the market buildings: Walk down Calle 56 south past the post office; right before the street ends in the market place, turn left into a passage with hardware stores at the entrance. The fourth or fifth shop is the **Casa de los Jipis.** You can always ask people in the area to point it out to you.

## WHERE TO STAY

Mérida is easier on the budget than the resort cities. The stream of visitors is steadier than on the coast, so most hotels no longer use a high-season/low-season rate structure. Still, you are more likely to find promotional rates

# Mérida Accommodations & Dining

**ACCOMMODATIONS**

Casa Mexilio Guest House **5**
Casa San Juan **18**
Fiesta Americana Mérida **1**
Hotel Caribe **14**
Hotel Casa del Balam **8**
Hotel Dolores Alba **13**
Hotel Mucuy **11**
Hyatt Regency Mérida **2**
Posada Toledo **9**

**DINING**

Alberto's Continental **6**
Café Alameda **10**
Café Amaro **12**
Eladio's **16**
El Pampero **4**
La Casa del Paseo **3**
Pórtico del Peregrino **7**
Restaurant Los Almendros **15**
Vito Corleone **13**

during low season. Mérida has a new convention center, which attracts large trade shows that can fill a lot of hotels, so it's a good idea to make reservations. The rates quoted here include the 17% tax. When inquiring about prices, always ask if the price quoted includes taxes. Most hotels in Mérida offer at least a few air-conditioned rooms, and some also have pools. But many hotels, especially in the inexpensive range, haven't figured out how to provide a comfortable bed. Either the mattresses are bad, or the bottom sheet is too small to tuck in properly. Some hotels here would offer a really good deal if only they would improve their beds. One last thing to note: In Mérida, free parking is a relative concept—for many hotels, free parking means only at night; during the day there may be a charge.

## VERY EXPENSIVE

**Fiesta Americana Mérida** ★★ This six-story hotel on the Paseo Montejo is built in the grand *fin-de-siècle* style of the old mansions along the Paseo. Guest rooms are off the cavernous lobby, so all face outward and have views of one or another of the avenues. The rooms are comfortable and large, with furnishings and decorations aiming for, and achieving, innocuousness in light, tropical colors. The floors are tile and the bathrooms large and well equipped. The suites seem overpriced for what they offer, but they are frequently discounted. Service is quite attentive. There is a shopping center on the ground floor, below the lobby.

Av. Colón 451, Esq. Paseo Montejo, 92127 Mérida, Yuc. ✆ **800/343-7821** in the U.S. and Canada, or 999/942-1111. Fax 999/942-1112. www.fiestaamericana.com.mx. 350 units. $174 double; $195 executive level; $258 jr. suite. AE, DC, MC, V. Free secured parking. **Amenities:** 2 restaurants, bar; medium-size pool; tennis court; health club with saunas, men's steam room, unisex whirlpool, and massage; children's programs; concierge; tour desk; small business center with secretarial services; shopping arcade; room service until midnight; babysitting; same-day laundry and dry cleaning; executive-level rooms. *In room:* A/C, TV with pay movies, Internet connections, minibar, coffeemaker, hair dryer, safe.

**Hyatt Regency Merida** ★★★ This Hyatt is much like Hyatts elsewhere, wherein lies this hotel's chief asset and its one small liability. On the asset side, the rooms are dependably comfortable and quiet, the quietest in an admittedly noisy city. They're carpeted and well furnished, with great bathrooms. In decoration and comfort, I find them superior to those of the Fiesta Americana. The Hyatt's facilities, especially its tennis courts and health club, also rank above the Fiesta Americana's. The pool is more attractive and larger, but its location puts it in the shade for most of the day. On the liability side, the hotel has no local flavor—it could be anywhere in the world. At 17 stories, the Hyatt is not hard to find in Mérida's skyline; it's close by the Paseo de Montejo and across Avenida Colón from the Fiesta Americana.

Calle 60 no. 344 (at Av. Colón), 97000 Mérida, Yuc. ✆ **800/223-1234** in the U.S. and Canada, 999/942-1234. Fax 999/925-7002. www.hyatt.com. 299 units. $220 double. Ask about promotional rates. AE, DC, MC, V. Free guarded parking. **Amenities:** 2 restaurants, 2 bars (1 swim-up, open seasonally); large pool; 2 lighted tennis courts; state-of-the-art health club with men's and women's steam rooms, whirlpool, and massage; children's activities (seasonal); concierge; tour desk; car rental; well-equipped business center with secretarial services; shopping arcade; 24-hour room service; babysitting; same-day laundry and dry cleaning; nonsmoking rooms; executive-level rooms. *In room:* A/C, TV, minibar, hair dryer.

## EXPENSIVE

**Hotel Casa del Balam** ★★ The "House of the Jaguar" has the best downtown location of any large hotel. Most of the rooms are large and bright, with double windows that reduce noise. Even the rooms on lower floors that face the street aren't noisy (if you're a very light sleeper, you might still ask for something on a high floor). Rooms have tile floors and area rugs, comfortable-size bathrooms with tub/shower combinations, and a choice of two double beds or one queen. Three suites are in the original part of the hotel off the courtyard; they are very large and have more character. The courtyard lends the hotel a tropical feel lacking in the more expensive hotels on the Paseo Montejo and is a comfortable setting for cocktails. The owners also operate the hotel **Hacienda Chichén,** at the ruins of Chichén-Itzá.

Calle 60 no. 488 (at Calle 57), 97000 Mérida, Yuc. ✆ **800/624-8451** in the U.S., or 999/924-2150. Fax 999/924-5011. www.yucatanadventure.com.mx. 52 units. $100 double; $130 suite. AE, DC, MC, V. **Amenities:** Restaurant, bar; small pool; free access to health club; tour desk; car rental; room service until 11pm; massage; babysitting; same-day laundry and dry cleaning. *In room:* A/C, TV, minibar, hair dryer.

## MODERATE

**Casa Mexilio Guest House** ★★ *Finds* This bed-and-breakfast is unlike any other I know. The owners are geniuses at playing with space in an unexpected and delightful manner. Rooms are at different levels, creating private spaces joined to each other and to rooftop terraces by stairs and catwalks. Most are spacious and airy, furnished and decorated in an engaging mix of new and old, polished and primitive. Five come with air-conditioning. A small pool with a whirlpool and profuse tropical vegetation take up most of the central patio. Breakfasts are great. The hotel is part of the Turquoise Reef Group, a reservation service for inns on Mexico's Caribbean coast. It's 4 blocks west of the plaza. A small bar serves during happy hour, and, weather permitting, you can have your cocktail on one of the rooftop terraces.

Calle 68 no. 495 (between Calles 57 and 59), 97000 Mérida, Yuc. ✆ **800/538-6802** in the U.S.; ✆ and fax 999/928-2505. www.mexicoholiday.com. 9 units. $55–$83 double. Rates include full breakfast. MC, V. **Amenities:** Bar; small pool; whirlpool. *In room:* No phone.

**Hotel Caribe** ★ This three-story colonial-style hotel (no elevator) is great for a couple of reasons: Its location at the back of Plaza Hidalgo is both central and quiet, and it has a nice little pool and sundeck on the rooftop with a view of the cathedral. The rooms are moderately comfortable, though they aren't well lit, and have only small windows facing the central courtyard. Thirteen "tourist class" rooms don't have air-conditioning, but standard rooms do. Superior rooms (on the top floor) have been remodeled and have safes, hair dryers, larger windows, and quieter air-conditioning. Avoid the rooms on the ground floor. The hotel offers a lot of variety in bedding arrangements, mostly combinations of twins and doubles. Mattresses are often softer than standard. The TVs add little value to the rooms. Nearby parking is free at night but costs extra during the day beginning at 7am. The restaurant serves good Mexican food.

Calle 59 no. 500 (at Calle 60), 97000 Mérida, Yuc. ✆ **888/822-6431** in the U.S. and Canada, or 999/924-9022. Fax 999/924-8733. www.hotelcaribe.com.mx. 53 units. $55–$70 double. AE, MC, V. **Amenities:** Restaurant, bar; small pool; tour desk; room service until 10pm; overnight laundry. *In room:* TV, safe.

## INEXPENSIVE

**Casa San Juan** ★★ *Value* This B&B, in a colonial house, is loaded with character and provides a good glimpse of the old Mérida that lies behind the colonial facades in the historic district. Guest rooms are beautifully decorated, large, and comfortable. Those in the original house have been modernized but maintain the feel of colonial times, with 20-foot ceilings and 18-inch-thick walls. The modern rooms in back look out over the rear patio. The lower rate is for the three rooms without air-conditioning (they have ceiling and floor fans). Choice of beds includes one queen-size, one double, or two twins, all with good mattresses and sheets. Breakfast includes fruit or juice, coffee, bread, and homemade preserves. Casa San Juan is 4 blocks south of the main square.

Calle 62 no. 545a (between Calles 69 and 71), 97000 Mérida, Yuc. ✆ **999/923-6823.** Fax 999/986-2937. www.casasanjuan.com. 8 units (7 with private bathroom). High season $25–$60 double; low season $25–$45 double. No credit cards. Rates include continental breakfast. Parking nearby $2/day. *In room:* No phone.

**Hotel Dolores Alba** ★★ *Value* The Dolores Alba offers attractive, comfortable rooms, air-conditioning, a lovely swimming pool, and free parking, all for a great price. The new addition, a three-story section (with elevator) surrounding the back courtyard, offers large new rooms with good-size bathrooms. Beds (either two doubles or one double and one twin) have supportive foam-core mattresses, usually in a combination of one medium firm and one medium soft. All rooms have windows or balconies looking out over the pool. An old mango tree shades the front courtyard. The older rooms in this section are decorated with local crafts and have small bathrooms. The family that owns the **Hotel Dolores Alba** outside Chichén-Itzá manages this hotel; you can make reservations at one hotel for the other. This hotel is 3½ blocks from Plaza Mayor.

Calle 63 no. 464 (between Calles 52 and 54), 97000 Mérida, Yuc. ✆ **999/928-5650.** Fax 999/928-3163. www.doloresalba.com. 100 units. $30–$40 double. No credit cards. Free guarded sheltered parking. **Amenities:** Restaurant; pool; tour desk; room service until 10pm; overnight laundry. *In room:* A/C, TV.

**Hotel Mucuy** The Mucuy is a simple, quiet, pleasant hotel in a great location. The gracious owners strive to make guests feel welcome, with conveniences such as a communal refrigerator in the lobby and, for a small extra charge, the use of a washer and dryer. Guest rooms are basic; most contain two twin beds (with comfortable mattresses) and some simple furniture. A lovely garden patio with comfortable chairs is the perfect place for sitting and reading. The Mucuy is named for a small dove said to bring good luck to places where it alights.

Calle 57 no. 481 (between Calles 56 and 58), 97000 Mérida, Yuc. ✆ **999/928-5193.** Fax 999/923-7801. 24 units. $22 double. No credit cards.

**Posada Toledo** ★ This hotel's charm lies in the fact that so much of the original domestic architecture survived the conversion from mansion to hotel. Furniture, decoration, paintings, details of design—from all this, you glean an uncontrived view of the past. As is typical in such old *casonas,* some guest rooms were meant to impress, while others were an expression of simple domesticity—make sure you get one you like. Rooms along the street can be noisy. Two of the grandest rooms, with ornate cornices and woodwork, have been converted into a large suite. Those on the third floor (not originally part of the house) are comfortable and have a rooftop terrace. The hotel has a couple of common rooms and a beautiful courtyard lobby. The location is exceptionally good.

Calle 58 no. 487 (at Calle 57), 97000 Mérida, Yuc. ✆ **999/923-1690.** Fax 999/923-2256. hptoledo@finred.com.mx. 23 units. $35–$45 double. MC, V. Free parking next door. **Amenities:** Restaurant (breakfast only); tour info. *In room:* A/C, TV.

## WHERE TO DINE

The people of Mérida have definite ideas and traditions about food. Certain dishes are always associated with a particular day of the week. In households across the city, Sundays would feel incomplete without *puchero* (a kind of stew). On Mondays, at any restaurant that caters to locals, you are sure to find *frijol con puerco.* Likewise, you'll find *potaje* on Thursday; fish, of course, on Friday; and *chocolomo* on Saturday. If you want to sample one of these, try **El Anfitrión,** Calle 62 no. 272, at Calle 27 (✆ **999/925-6190**). These dishes are heavy and slow to digest; they are for the midday meal, and not suitable for supper. What's more, Meridanos don't believe that seafood is a healthy food to eat at night. All seafood restaurants in Mérida close by 6pm unless they cater to tourists.

The preferred supper food is turkey (which, by the way, is said to be high in tryptophan, a soporific), and it's best served in the traditional *antojitos—salbutes* and *panuchos.* The best I've eaten were at a well-known restaurant in the village of Kanasín, on the outskirts of Mérida, **La Susana Internacional.** Practically the entire menu is based on turkey, including a delicious soup. The only way to get there is by taxi, but if you are a fairly large party, it's worth organizing the expedition.

Another thing you will notice about Mérida is the surprising number of Middle Eastern restaurants. The city received a large influx of Lebanese immigrants around 1900. This population has had a strong influence on local society, to the point where Meridanos think of *kibbe* the way Americans think of pizza.

### EXPENSIVE

**Alberto's Continental** ★ LEBANESE/YUCATECAN/ITALIAN There's nothing quite like dining here at night in a softly lit room or on the wonderful old patio framed in Moorish arches. Nothing glitzy; just elegant *mudejar*-patterned tile floors, simple furniture, decoration that's just so, and the gurgling of a fountain creating a romantic mood. I find the prices on the expensive side. For supper, you can choose a sampler plate of four Lebanese favorites, or traditional Yucatecan specialties, such as *pollo pibil* or fish Celestún (bass stuffed with shrimp). Polish off your selections with Turkish coffee.

Calle 64 no. 482 (at Calle 57). ✆ **999/928-5367.** Reservations recommended. Main courses $8–$20. AE, MC, V. Daily 1–11pm.

**El Pampero** ★ ARGENTINE/STEAK If you feel like a steak, I recommend this homey restaurant for its simplicity, prices, and food. Order *bife de chorizo,* and wash it down with a good Chilean wine. The restaurant also offers tasty Argentine empanadas, and delicious homemade ravioli Argentine-style. The owner is a likable sort who believes a restaurant should be welcoming and personal. There are often performances of tango music or something similar.

Calle 47 no. 558-C (between Calles 76 and 78). ✆ **999/928-0594.** Main courses $6–$14. AE, DC, MC, V. Daily 1pm–midnight.

**El Pórtico del Peregrino** ★ REGIONAL/INTERNATIONAL El Pórtico is a favorite among visitors, who enjoy its charm, comfort, and distinctive Mérida flavor. The interior is a lovely garden with three dining areas—two air-conditioned rooms and a patio. One room is nonsmoking, a rarity in Mexico. The menu offers soups (*sopa de tortilla* and *sopa de lima* are both good), seafood (a platter, or grilled gulf shrimp), and Yucatecan specialties (*pollo pibil*). Other favorites include baked eggplant with chicken and cheese, and coconut ice cream topped with Kahlúa. The restaurant is 2 blocks north of the main square.

Calle 57 no. 501 (between Calles 60 and 62). ✆ **999/928-6163.** Reservations recommended. Main courses $6–$15. AE, MC, V. Daily noon–11pm.

**La Casa del Paseo** ★★ INTERNATIONAL Set in one of the mansions on the Paseo de Montejo, this restaurant offers excellent food and service in a lovely setting. You can dine inside or out in a small patio area along the Paseo. The cooking is wonderful. Where to begin? Perhaps with a fresh mozzarella salad, salmon carpaccio, or mushrooms Provençal. For main dishes, consider the daily specials; if you want something light, the stuffed chicken breast, *pechuga suiza,* is good; for something more meaty, try *tres mosquiteros,* three grilled beef filets, each with a different sauce.

Paseo de Montejo 465 (between Calle 35 and Av. Colón, 2 doors down from the American consulate). ✆ **999/920-0528.** Reservations recommended. Main courses $9–$18. AE, MC, V. Daily 1pm–1am.

## MODERATE

**Restaurant Amaro** ★ REGIONAL/VEGETARIAN Customers have the pleasure of dining in a old courtyard beneath the canopy of a large orchid tree. The menu offers many interesting vegetarian dishes, such as *crema de calabacitas* (cream of squash soup), apple salad, and avocado pizza. There is also a limited menu of fish and chicken dishes; you might want to try the Yucatecan chicken. The *agua de chaya* (*chaya* is a leafy vegetable prominent in the Maya diet) is refreshing on a hot afternoon. All desserts are made in-house. The restaurant is a little north of Plaza Mayor.

Calle 59 no. 507 interior 6 (between Calles 60 and 62). ✆ **999/928-2451.** Main courses $5–$9. MC, V. Mon–Sat 11am–2am.

**Restaurant Los Almendros** *Overrated* YUCATECAN Ask where to eat Yucatecan food, and locals will inevitably suggest this place because of its reputation. After all, this was the first place to offer tourists such Yucatecan specialties as *cochinita pibil, salbutes, panuchos papadzules,* and *poc chuc.* The menu even comes with color photographs to facilitate acquaintance with these strange-sounding dishes. The food is okay and not much of a risk, but you can find better elsewhere. Still, it's a safe place to try Yucatecan food for the first time, and it's such a fixture that the idea of a guidebook that doesn't mention this restaurant is unthinkable. It's 5 blocks east of Calle 60, facing the Parque de la Mejorada.

Calle 50A no. 493. ✆ **999/928-5459.** Main courses $4–$9, daily special $5–$9. AE, MC, V. Daily 10am–11pm.

## INEXPENSIVE

**Café Alameda** ★ MIDDLE EASTERN/VEGETARIAN The trappings here are simple and informal (metal tables, plastic chairs), and it's a good place for catching a light meal. The trick is figuring out the Spanish names for popular Middle Eastern dishes. *Kibbe* is *quebbe bola* (not *quebbe cruda*), hummus is *garbanza,* and shish kebab is *alambre.* I leave it to you to figure out what a spinach pie is called (and it's excellent). Café Alameda is a treat for vegetarians, and the umbrella-shaded tables on the patio are perfect for morning coffee and *mamules* (walnut-filled pastries).

Calle 58 no. 474 (between Calles 55 and 57). ✆ **999/928-3635.** Main courses $2–$4. No credit cards. Daily 7:30am–5:30pm.

**Eladio's** ★ YUCATECAN This is where locals come to relax in their off hours, drink very cold beer, and snack or dine on Yucatecan specialties. You have two choices: Order a beer and enjoy *una botana* (a small portion that accompanies a drink, in this case usually a Yucatecan dish), or order from the menu. *Cochinita, poc chuc,* and *longaniza asada* are all good. Or try a *panucho* or *salbute* if you're there in the evening. Often there is live music in this open-air restaurant, which is around the corner from Los Almendros, by Parque la Mejorada.

Calle 59 (at Calle 44). ✆ **999/923-1087.** Main courses $4–$5. AE, MC, V. Daily noon–8pm.

**Vito Corleone** PIZZA Feel like some quick food that you can order to go? Try the pizza here. You can also dine at the restaurant, but the tables by the sidewalk are the only bearable places to sit when it's warm, because the oven generates incredible heat. Another section upstairs in the back might be tolerable. The thin-crust pizzas have a nice smoky taste.

Calle 59 no. 508 (between Calles 60 and 62). ✆ **999/928-5777.** Pizzas $5–$9. No credit cards. Daily 9:30am–11:30pm.

## MERIDA AFTER DARK

For nighttime entertainment, see the box, "Festivals & Special Events in Mérida," earlier in this chapter, or check out the theaters noted here.

**Teatro Peón Contreras,** Calles 60 and 57, and **Teatro Ayala,** Calle 60 at Calle 61, both feature a wide range of performing artists from Mexico and around the world. **El Nuevo Olimpo,** on the main square, schedules frequent concerts; and **Cine Mérida,** a half block north of the Nuevo Olimpo, has two screens for showing classic and art films, and one live stage.

Mérida's club scene offers everything from ubiquitous rock/disco to some one-of-a-kind spots that are nothing like what you find back home. Most of the discos are in the big hotels or on Paseo de Montejo. For dancing, a small cluster of clubs on Calle 60, around the corner from Santa Lucía, offer live rock and salsa music.

**El Trovador Bohemio** *Finds* It's hard to overstate the importance of *música de trio* and *trova* in Mexican popular culture. This music, mainly in the form of songs called *boleros,* may have been at its most popular in the 1940s and '50s, but every new Mexican pop music heartthrob feels compelled to release a new version of the classics. I like the originals best, and so do most Mexicans. If you know something of this music and are curious about it, El Trovador gives you a chance to hear how the music should be played. And if you understand colloquial Spanish, all the better; the language of boleros is vivid, passionate, and quite Mexican—definitely a unique cultural experience. El Trovador is small and dark, and everything is red. It can be smoky. The best days to go are Thursday, Friday, and Saturday. The club faces the Santa Lucía Park.

Calle 55 no. 504. ✆ **999/923-0385.** Daily 9pm–3am. Cover $2.

**Pancho's** If you take this place seriously, you won't like it. Pancho's, which serves Tex-Mex and international food, is a parody of the tourist attraction, a place for drinking beer and loosing the occasional *grito.* Waiters wear bandoliers and oversize sombreros, and blow-ups of Revolution-era photos and assorted emblems of Mexican identity adorn the walls. Live music in the courtyard begins at 9pm on most nights, 10:30pm on Saturday. The five-piece band, with its large repertoire of cover tunes is quite good; it'll crank out salsa, rock, and jazz.

Calle 59 no. 509. ✆ **999/923-0942.** Daily 6pm–3am. 2-drink minimum on weekends if you do not order food.

## ECOTOURS & ADVENTURE TRIPS

The Yucatán Peninsula has seen a recent explosion of companies that organize nature and adventure tours. One well-established outfit with a great track record is **Ecoturismo Yucatán,** Calle 3 no. 235, Col. Pensiones, 97219 Mérida (✆ **999/920-2772;** fax 999/925-9047; www.ecoyuc.com). Alfonso and Roberta Escobedo create itineraries to meet just about any special or general interest you may have for going to the Yucatán or southern Mexico. Alfonso has been creating adventure and nature tours for more than a dozen years. Specialties include archaeology, birding, natural history, and kayaking. The company also offers day trips that explore contemporary Maya culture and life in villages in the Yucatán. Package and customized tours are available.

## SIDE TRIPS FROM MERIDA

### IZAMAL

Izamal is a sleepy town some 80km (50 miles) east of Mérida, an easy day trip by car. You can visit the famous Franciscan convent of San Antonio de Padua and the ruins of four large pyramids that overlook the center of town. One pyramid is partially reconstructed to give the viewer an idea of how they must have appeared before their destruction. Life in Izamal is easygoing in the extreme, as evidenced by the *victorias,* the horse-drawn buggies that serve as taxis here. Even if you come by car, you should make a point of touring the town in one of these.

### HACIENDA HOPPING

Another relaxing trip is to one of the former haciendas that dot the countryside around Mérida. In recent years it has become popular practice to restore these decaying haciendas to their former glory and convert them into attractions, restaurants, and even luxury hotels, usually with an ecological bent. One of the fanciest, and the one that gets the most press, is **Hacienda Katanchel** (✆ **999/920-0997**). It is also one of the most expensive, offering luxury accommodations, Old World service, a pool, 650 acres of forested land, gardens, gourmet food, and excursions. Other haciendas-turned-hotels include **Hacienda Temozón** and **Hacienda Santa Rosa** (✆ **999/944-3637**), and **Hacienda Blanca Flor,** in the area of the Puuc route, southeast of Uxmal (✆ **888/BLANCAF** in the U.S.). **Hacienda Teya** (✆ **999/928-1885** or 999/988-0800), just outside Mérida, has a lovely restaurant and four guest rooms. For information on **Hacienda Yaxcopoil,** which offers tours of the old buildings and grounds, see "En Route to Uxmal, " later in this chapter.

### CELESTUN NATIONAL WILDLIFE REFUGE: FLAMINGOS & OTHER WATERFOWL

On the coast west of Mérida is a large area of marshland that has been declared a biopreserve. It is a long, shallow estuary where freshwater mixes with Gulf saltwater, creating a habitat perfect for flamingos and many other species of waterfowl. This estuary (*ría* in Spanish), unlike other estuaries that are fed by rivers or streams, receives fresh water through about 80 *cenotes,* most of which are underwater. It is very shallow (.5–1m/1–4 ft. deep) and thickly grown with mangrove, with an open channel a quarter of a mile wide and 48km (30 miles) long, sheltered from the open sea by a narrow strip of land. Along this corridor, you can take a launch to see flamingos as they dredge the bottom of these shallows for a species of small crustacean and a particular insect that make up the bulk of their diet.

You can get here by car or bus; it's an easy 90-minute drive. (For information on buses, see "Getting There: By Bus," earlier in this chapter.) To drive, leave downtown Mérida on Calle 57. Shortly after Santiago Church, Calle 57 ends and there's a dogleg onto Calle 59-A. This crosses Avenida Itzáes and changes its name to Jacinto Canek; continue until you see signs for Celestún Highway 178. This will take you through Hunucmá, where the road joins Highway 281, which takes you to Celestún. You'll know you have arrived when you get to the bridge.

In the last few years, the state agency CULTUR has come into Celestún and established order where once there was chaos. Immediately to your left after the bridge, you'll find modern facilities with a snack bar, clean bathrooms, and a ticket window. Prices for tours are fixed. A 75-minute tour costs about $45 and can accommodate up to six people. You can join others or hire a boat by yourself. On the tour you'll definitely see some flamingos; you'll also get to see some mangrove close up, and one of the many underwater springs. Please do not urge the boatmen to get any closer to the flamingos than they are allowed to; if pestered too much, the birds will abandon the area for other, less fitting habitats. The ride is quite pleasant—the water is calm, and CULTUR has supplied the boatmen with wide, flat-bottom skiffs that have canopies for shade.

In addition to flamingos, you will probably see frigate birds, pelicans, spoonbills, egrets, sandpipers, and other waterfowl feeding on shallow sandbars at any time of year. At least 15 duck species have been counted, and I once saw an eagle fishing in the waters. Of the 175 bird species that come here, some 99 are permanent residents. Nonbreeding flamingos remain here year-round; the larger group of breeding flamingoes takes off around April to nest on the upper Yucatán Peninsula east of Río Lagartos, returning to Celestún in October.

After the tour, you might want to visit the fishing town of Celestún, which is a little beyond the bridge, on a wide, sandy beach facing the Gulf. It has several seafood restaurants (all very similar). If you want a quiet night away from Mérida, you can stay at one of the local hotels. My favorite is the **Hotel María del Carmen,** Calle 12 no. 111 (✆ **988/916-2051**), facing the water. The accommodations are simple but comfortable, and all come with small balconies facing the water. Rooms cost $22.

Another option is Eco Paraíso, a big step up from the modest hotels you'll find in Celestun.

**Hotel Eco Paraíso Xixim** ★★ Eco Paraíso is meant to be a refuge from the modern world. It sits on a deserted 3-mile stretch of beach that was once part of a coconut plantation. It attracts much the same clientele as the former-haciendas-turned-luxury-hotels, but in some ways it has more going for it (like the beach). Some guests come here for a week of idleness; others use this as a base of operations for visiting the biopreserve and making trips to the Maya ruins in the interior. The hotel offers its own tours to various places. Rooms are quite private; each is a separate bungalow with palapa roof. Each comes with two comfortable queen-size beds, a sitting area, ceiling fans, and a private porch with hammocks. On my last visit, the food was very good, and the service was great. What's more, the concept is ecologically friendly in more than name only. The hotel composts waste, and treats and uses wastewater.

Km 10 Antigua Carretera a Sisal, 97367 Celestún, Yuc. ✆ **988/916-2100.** Fax 988/916-2111. www.mexonline.com/eco-paraiso.htm. 15 units. High season $192 double; low season $166 double. Rates include 2 meals per person. AE, MC, V. Free parking. **Amenities:** Restaurant, bar; medium-size pool; tour desk. *In room:* Safe.

## DZIBILCHALTUN: MAYA RUINS AND MUSEUM

This destination makes for a quick morning trip that will get you back to Mérida in time for a siesta, or it could be part of a longer trip to Progreso, Uaymitún, and Xcambó. It's part of a national park, located 14km (9 miles) north of Mérida along the Progreso road and 5km (3 miles) east off the highway. To get there, take Calle 60 all the way out of town and follow signs for Progreso and Highway 261. Look for the sign for Dzibilchaltún, which also reads UNIVERSIDAD DEL MAYA; it will point you right. After a few kilometers you'll see a sign for the entrance to the ruins and the museum. If you don't want to drive, take one of the *colectivos* that line up along Parque San Juan.

Dzibilchaltún was founded about 500 B.C., flourished around A.D. 750, and was in decline long before the coming of the conquistadors. It may have been occupied for almost 100 years after their arrival. Since the ruins were discovered in 1941, more than 8,000 buildings have been mapped. The site covers an area of almost 29 square km (10 sq. miles) with a central core of almost 65 acres, but the area of prime interest is limited to the buildings surrounding two plazas next to the *cenote,* and another building, the Temple of the Seven Dolls, connected to these by a *sacbé* (ceremonial road). Dzibilchaltún means "place of the stone writing," and at least 25 stelae have been found, many of them reused in buildings constructed after the original ones were covered or destroyed.

Start at the **Museo del Pueblo Maya,** which is quite good. It's open Tuesday to Sunday from 8am to 4pm. Admission is $6. The museum's collection includes artifacts from various sites in the Yucatán. Explanations are printed in bilingual format and are fairly thorough. Objects include a beautiful example of a plumed serpent from Chichén-Itzá and a finely designed incense vessel from Palenque. From this general view of the Maya civilization, the museum moves on to exhibit specific artifacts found at the site of Dzibilchaltún, including the rather curious dolls that have given one structure its name. Then there's an exhibit on Maya culture in historical and present times, including a lovely collection of *huipils,* the woven blouses that Indian women wear. From here a door leads out to the site.

The first thing you come to is the *sacbé* that connects the two areas of interest. To the left is the **Temple of the Seven Dolls.** The temple's doorways are lined up with the *sacbé* to catch the rising sun at the spring and autumnal equinoxes. To the right are the buildings grouped around the **Cenote Xlacah,** the sacred well, and a complex of buildings around **Structure 38,** the **Central Group** of temples. The Yucatán State Department of Ecology has added nature trails and published a booklet (in Spanish) of birds and plants seen at various points along the mapped trail.

## PROGRESO, UAYMITUN & XCAMBO: GULF COAST CITY, FLAMINGO LOOKOUT & MORE MAYA RUINS

For another beach escape, go to the port of Progreso, Mérida's weekend beach resort. This is where Meridanos have their vacation houses and where they come in large numbers in July and August. At other times the crowds and traffic disappear, and you can enjoy the Gulf waters without fuss. Along the *Malecón* (boardwalk), a wide oceanfront drive that extends the length of a sandy beach, you can pull over and enjoy a swim anywhere you like. The water here is not the blue of the Caribbean, but it is clean. A long pier, or *muelle* (pronounced *mway-*yeh), extends several kilometers into the bay to service oceangoing ships. Progreso is also the part-time home of some Americans and Canadians escaping northern winters.

Along or near the Malecón are several hotels and restaurants, including **Le Saint Bonnet,** Malecón at Calle 78 (**© 969/935-2299**), where locals dine on fresh seafood. It has a large menu with several good dishes; for something very Mexican, I recommend *pescado al ajillo* (fish sautéed with garlic and guajillo chile).

From Mérida, buses to **Progreso** leave the special bus station at Calle 62 no. 524, between Calles 65 and 67, every 15 minutes, starting at 5am. The trip takes almost an hour and costs $2.50.

If you have a car, you might want to drive down the coastal road east toward Telchac Puerto. After about 20 minutes, at the right side of the road you'll see a large, solid-looking wooden observation tower for viewing flamingos. A sign reads UAYMITUN. The state agency CULTUR constructed the tower, operates it, and provides binoculars free of charge. A few years ago, flamingos from Celestún migrated here and established a colony. Your chances of spotting them are good, and you don't have to pay for a boat. Twenty minutes farther down this road, there's a turn-off for the road to Dzemul, and a few minutes after that you'll see a sign for **Xcambó** that points to the right. This city is thought to have been a center for maritime trading, and perhaps it made use of some nearby salt flats to produce salt for trade. The central ceremonial center is completely reconstructed, and archaeologists are finding a number of graves.

After viewing these ruins, you can continue on the same road through the small towns of Dzemul and Baca. At Baca, take Highway 176 back to Mérida.

## EN ROUTE TO UXMAL

Two routes go to Uxmal, about 80km (50 miles) south of Mérida. The most direct is Highway 261 via Uman and Muna. On the way you can stop to see Hacienda Yaxcopoil, which is 32km (20 miles) from Mérida. From downtown, take Calle 65 or 69 to Avenida Itzáes and turn left; this feeds onto the highway.

If you have the time and want a more scenic route, try the meandering State Highway 18. This is sometimes known as the Convent Route, but all tourism hype aside, it makes for a good drive and you'll see some really interesting sights. You could make your trip to Uxmal into a loop by going one way and coming back the other, but with so many stops, it would take the better part of 2 days to complete the trip, especially if you want to see the ruins of the Puuc Route. One way to do this would be to take the long route on Highway 18, arriving in Uxmal in time to see the sound and light show. Stay overnight in Uxmal and see the ruins early in the morning before returning to Mérida. All the attractions on these routes have the same hours: Churches are open from 10am to 2pm and 4 to 6pm; ruins are open from 8am to 5pm.

**HIGHWAY 261: YAXCOPOIL & MUNA** Sixteen kilometers (10 miles) beyond Uman along Highway 261 is **Yaxcopoil** (yash-koh-poe-*eel*), a fascinating 19th-century hacienda on the right side of the road between Mérida and Uxmal. It's difficult to reach by bus.

This hacienda, dating from 1864, was originally a cattle ranch of more than 23,000 acres. Around 1900, it was converted to *henequen* production (for the manufacture of rope). Take a half hour to tour the house, factory, outbuildings, and museum. Haciendas were the administrative, commercial, and social centers of vast private domains; they were almost little principalities carved out of the Yucatecan jungle. It's open Monday to Saturday from 8am to 6pm, Sunday from 9am to 1pm.

Twenty-seven kilometers (17 miles) after Yaxcopoil is the busy little crossroads market town of **Muna** (64km/40 miles from Mérida) where you might run into a traffic slowdown. The typical Yucatecan tricycle taxis are everywhere. Muna offers little for sightseers but may interest those curious about contemporary Maya life. Make sure to stay on Highway 281 as you leave; 16km (10 miles) beyond Muna is Uxmal.

**HIGHWAY 18: KANASIN, ACANCEH, MAYAPAN & TICUL (the Convent Route)** Take Calle 63 east to Circuito Colonias and turn right; then make a left at Calle 69, which at that level is a two-way street. This feeds onto Highway 18 to Kanasín (kahn-ah-*seen*) and then Acanceh (ah-kahn-*keh*). In **Kanasín,** watch for signs that say "Circulación" or "Desviación." As in many Yucatán towns, you're being redirected to follow a one-way street through the urban area. Go past the market, church, and the main square on your left, and continue straight out of town. (On this route you'll be passing through a lot of small villages without any road signs, so get used to poking your head out the window and saying *"Buenos días, ¿dónde está el camino para...?"* which translates as "Good day, where is the road to . . . ?" This is what I do, and I ask more than one person.)

The next village you come to, at km 10, is **San Antonio Tehuit,** an old *henequen* hacienda. At km 13 is **Tepich,** another hacienda village, with funny little *henequen*-cart tracks crisscrossing the main road. After Tepich comes **Petectunich** and finally **Acanceh.**

Across the street from and overlooking Acanceh's church is a restored pyramid. On top of this pyramid under a makeshift roof are some recently discovered large stucco figures of Maya deities. The caretaker, Mario Uicab, will guide you up to see the fascinating figures and give you a little explanation (in Spanish). Admission is $3. There are some other ruins a couple of blocks away called **El Palacio de los Estucos.** In 1908, a stucco mural was found here in mint condition. It was left exposed and has deteriorated somewhat. Now it is sheltered, and you can still easily distinguish the painted figures in their original colors.

From Acanceh's main square, turn right (around the statue of a smiling deer) and head for **Tecoh** on a good road. Tecoh's parish church sits on a massive pre-Columbian raised platform—the remains of a ceremonial complex that was sacrificed to build the church. With its rough stone and simple twin towers that are crumbling around the edges, the church looks ancient. Inside are three carved *retablos,* covered in gold leaf and unmistakably Indian in style. In 1998 they were cleaned and refurbished, and are now quite dazzling.

Continuing on, shortly after the village of Telchaquillo, a sign on the right side of the road points to the entrance to the ruins of Mayapán.

## RUINS OF MAYAPAN

Founded, according to Maya lore, by the man-god Kukulkán (Quetzalcoatl in central Mexico) in about A.D. 1007, Mayapán ranked in importance with Chichén-Itzá and Uxmal. It covered at least 6.5 square km (2½ sq. miles). For more than 2 centuries it was the capital of a Maya confederation of city-states that included Chichén and Uxmal. But before 1200, the rulers of Mayapán ended the confederation by attacking and conquering Chichén and forcing the rulers of Uxmal to live as vassals in Mayapán. Eventually, a successful revolt by the other cities brought down Mayapán, which was abandoned during the mid-1400s.

In the last few years, archaeologists have been very busy excavating and rebuilding the city, and work continues. Several buildings bordering the principal plaza have been reconstructed, including one that is similar to El Castillo in Chichén-Itzá. The scientists have discovered murals and stucco figures that provide more grist for the mill of conjecture: *atlantes,* skeletal soldiers, macaws, entwined snakes, and a stucco jaguar. This place is definitely worth stopping to see.

The site is open daily from 8am to 5pm. Admission is $3.50, free on Sunday. Use of a personal video camera is $4.

**FROM MAYAPAN TO TICUL** The road is a good one, but directional signs through the villages are almost nonexistent, so you'll need to stop and ask directions frequently. The streets in these villages are full of children, bicycles, and livestock, so drive carefully and keep an eye out for unmarked *topes.* From Mayapán, continue along Highway 18 to **Tekit** (8km/5 miles). The road narrows, and then you're on to **Mama,** sometimes called Mamita. Stop to see the recently rescued former convent and the church with its lovely façade. Inside are several fascinating *retablos* sculpted in a native form of baroque. During the restoration of these buildings, colonial murals and designs were uncovered and restored. Make sure to get a peek at them in the sacristy. From Mama you head to Ticul, a large (for this area) market town with a couple of simple hotels and the original Los Almendros restaurant.

### TICUL

Best known for the cottage industry of *huipil* (native blouse) embroidery and for the manufacture of women's dress shoes, Ticul isn't the most exciting stop on the Puuc route, but it's a convenient place to wash up and spend the night. It's also a center for large commercially produced pottery; most of the widely sold sienna-colored pottery painted with Maya designs comes from here. If it's a cloudy, humid day, the potters may not be working (part of the process requires sun drying), but they still welcome visitors to purchase finished pieces.

One place worth a visit is **Arte Maya,** Calle 23 no. 301, Carretera Ticul-Muna (✆ **997/972-1095;** fax 997/972-0334), owned and operated by Luis Echeverría and Lourdes Castillo. This shop and gallery produces museum-quality art in alabaster, stone, jade, and ceramics. Much of the work is done as it was in Maya times; soft stone or ceramic is smoothed with the leaf of the siricote tree, and colors are derived from plant sources. If you buy something, hang on to the written description of your purchase—their work looks so authentic that U.S. Customs has delayed entry of people carrying it, thinking that they're smuggling real Maya artifacts.

Ticul is only 19km (12 miles) northeast of Uxmal, so thrifty tourists stay here instead of at the more expensive hotels at the ruins. I recommend the **Hotel Plaza,** Calle 23 no. 202, on the town square near intersection with Calle 26 (✆ **997/972-0484**). It's a modest hotel, as you would expect in a town of this sort, but it's comfortable and recently remodeled. A double room with air-conditioning costs $31; without air-conditioning, $26. In both cases, there's a 5% charge if you want to pay with a credit card (MC, V). Get an interior room if you're looking for quiet because Ticul has quite a lively plaza. Once in Ticul, you can do one of two things: Head straight for Uxmal via Santa Elena, or loop around the Puuc Route, the long way to Santa Elena. For information on the Puuc route, see "The Puuc Maya Route & Village of Oxkutzcab," below.

**FROM TICUL TO UXMAL** Follow the main street (Calle 23) west through town. Turn left at the sign to Santa Elena. It's 16km (10 miles) to Santa Elena; then, at Highway 261, cut back right for about 3km (2 miles) to Uxmal. In Santa Elena, by the side of Highway 261, is a clean restaurant with good food, **El Chac Mool.**

## 2 The Ruins of Uxmal ★★★

80km (50 miles) SW of Mérida; 19km (12 miles) W of Ticul; 19km (12 miles) S of Muna

One of the highlights of a Yucatán vacation, the ruins of Uxmal—noted for their rich geometric stone façades—are perhaps the most beautiful on the peninsula. Remains of an agricultural society indicate that the area was occupied possibly as early as 800 B.C. The great building period took place more than 1,000 years later, between A.D. 700 and 1000, when the population probably reached 25,000. After 1000, Uxmal fell under the sway of the Xiú princes (who may have come from central Mexico). In the 1440s, the Xiú conquered Mayapán, and not long afterward the glories of the Maya ended when the Spanish conquistadors arrived.

Close to Uxmal, four other sites—**Sayil, Kabah, Xlapak,** and **Labná**—are worth visiting. With Uxmal, these ruins are collectively known as the

**Puuc route,** for the Puuc hills of this part of the Yucatán. See "Puuc Maya Sites," later in this chapter, if you want to explore these sites.

## ESSENTIALS

**GETTING THERE & DEPARTING** **By Car** Two routes to Uxmal from Mérida, Highway 261 and State Highway 18, are described in "En Route to Uxmal," above. *Note:* There's no gasoline at Uxmal.

**BY BUS** See "Getting There & Departing," in "Mérida: Gateway to the Maya Heartland," earlier in this chapter for information about bus service between Mérida and Uxmal. To return, wait for the bus on the highway at the entrance to the ruins. To see the sound-and-light show, don't bother with regular buses; sign up with a tour operator in Mérida.

**ORIENTATION** Uxmal consists of the archaeological site and its visitor center, five hotels, and a highway restaurant. The visitor center, open daily 8am to 9pm, has a restaurant (with good coffee); toilets; a first-aid station; shops selling soft drinks, ice cream, film, batteries, and books; and a state-run Casa de Artesanía. There are no phones except at the hotels. Most public buses pick up and let off passengers on the highway at the entrance to the ruins. The site is open daily from 8am to 5pm. Admission to the archaeological site is $10, which includes admission to the nightly sound-and-light show, but a Sunday visit to Uxmal and other recommended sites nearby is free. Bringing in a video camera costs $4. Parking costs $1.

**Guides** at the entrance of Uxmal give tours in a variety of languages and charge $20 for a single person or a group. The guides frown on unrelated individuals joining a group. As usual, they'd rather charge you as a solo visitor, but you can ask other English speakers if they'd like to join you in a tour and split the cost. As at other sites, the guides vary in quality but will point out areas and architectural details that you might otherwise miss.

Included in the price of admission is a 45-minute **sound-and-light show,** staged each evening at 8pm. It's in Spanish, but headsets are available for rent ($3) for listening to the program in several languages. After the impressive show, the chant *"Chaaac, Chaaac"* will echo in your mind for weeks.

## A TOUR OF THE RUINS

**THE PYRAMID OF THE MAGICIAN** As you enter the ruins, note the *chultún,* or cistern, where Uxmal stored its water. Unlike most of the major Maya sites, Uxmal has no *cenote* to supply fresh water. No wonder the people were so obsessed with Chaac, the rain god.

Just beyond the *chultún,* the remarkable Pyramid of the Magician (also called Pyramid of the Dwarf) looms majestically on the right. The name comes from a legend about a mystical dwarf who reached adulthood in a single day after being hatched from an egg, and who built this pyramid in 1 night. Beneath it are five earlier structures, which is not an uncommon feature of Maya pyramids; the practice was to build new structures atop old ones at regular intervals. The pyramid is unique because of its rounded sides, height, and steepness, and the doorway on the opposite (west) side near the top. The doorway's heavy ornamentation, a characteristic of the Chenes style, features 12 stylized masks of the rain god Chaac.

Next to the Pyramid of the Magician, to the west, is the Nunnery Quadrangle, and left of it is a partially restored ball court. South of that are several large complexes. The biggest building among them is the Governor's Palace, and behind it lies the massive, largely unrestored Great Pyramid. In the distance is the

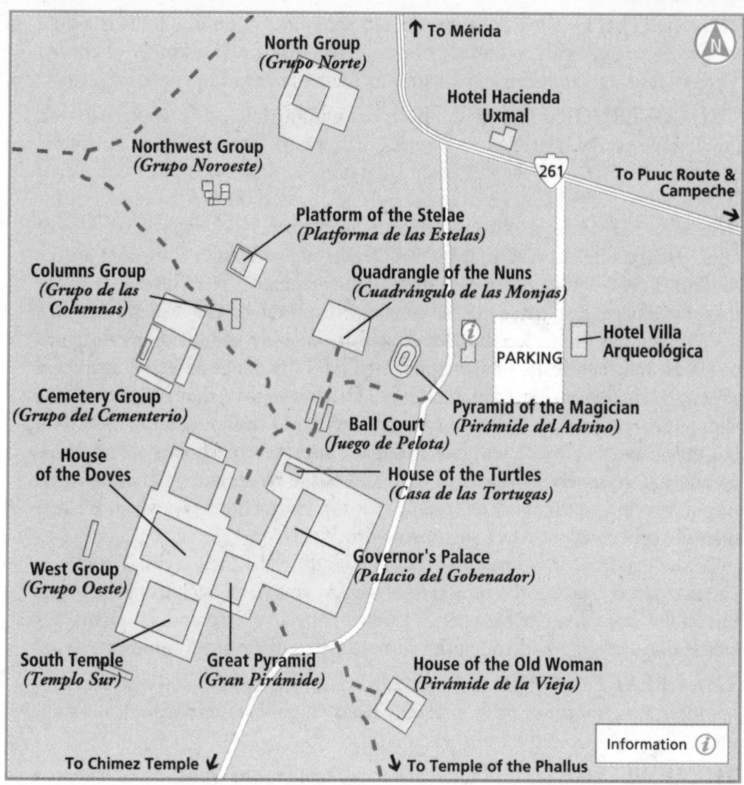


Dovecote (House of the Doves), a small building with a lacy roof comb that looks like the perfect apartment complex for pigeons. From this vantage point, note how Uxmal is unique among Maya sites for its use of huge terraces constructed to support the buildings; look closely and you'll see that the Governor's Palace is not on a natural hill, but rather on a giant platform of packed earth, as is the nearby Nunnery Quadrangle.

**THE NUNNERY QUADRANGLE** The 16th-century Spanish historian Fray Diego López de Cogullado gave the building its name because it resembled a Spanish convent. Possibly it was a military academy or a training school for princes, who may have lived in the 70-odd rooms. The buildings were constructed at different times: The northern one was first; then the southern, eastern, and western buildings. The western building has the most richly decorated façade, composed of intertwined stone snakes and numerous masks of the hook-nosed rain god Chaac.

The corbeled archway to the south was once the main entrance to the Nunnery complex; as you head toward it out of the quadrangle, look above each doorway in that section for the motif of a Maya cottage, or *nah,* still seen throughout the Yucatán today.

**THE BALL COURT** A small ball court is conserved to prevent further decay, but compare it later in your trip to the giant, magnificently restored court at Chichén-Itzá.

**THE TURTLE HOUSE** Up on the terrace south of the ball court is a little temple decorated with colonnade motif on the façade and a border of turtles. Though it's small and simple, its harmony makes it one of the gems of Uxmal.

**THE GOVERNOR'S PALACE** In its size and intricate stonework, this rivals the Temple of the Magician as Uxmal's masterwork—an imposing three-level edifice with a 320-foot-long mosaic façade done in the Puuc style. Puuc means "hilly country," the name given to the hills nearby and thus to the predominant style of pre-Hispanic architecture found here. Uxmal has many examples of Puuc decoration, characterized by elaborate stonework from door tops to the roofline. Fray Cogullado also gave this building its name. The Governor's Palace may have been just that—the administrative center of the Xiú principality, which included the region around Uxmal. It probably had astrological significance as well. For years, scholars pondered why this building was constructed slightly turned from adjacent buildings. Originally they thought the strange alignment was because of the *sacbé* that starts at this building and ends 18km (11 miles) away at the ancient city of Kabah. But recently scholars of archaeoastronomy (a relatively new science that studies the placement of archaeological sites in relation to the stars) discovered that the central doorway, which is larger than the others, is in perfect alignment with Venus.

Before you leave the Governor's Palace, note the elaborately stylized headdress patterned in stone over the central doorway. As you stand back from the building on the east side, note how the 103 stone masks of Chaac undulate across the façade like a serpent and end at the corners, where there are columns of masks.

**THE GREAT PYRAMID** A massive, partially restored nine-level structure, it has interesting motifs of birds, probably macaws, on its façade, as well as a huge mask. The view from the top is wonderful.

**THE DOVECOTE** This building is remarkable in that roof combs weren't a common feature of temples in the Puuc hills, although you'll see one (of a very different style) on El Mirador at Sayil.

## WHERE TO STAY

There are some lovely hotels in Uxmal. If occupancy is low, you might bargain for a room. If you're on a tight budget, consider this a day trip, or stay in nearby Ticul.

**Hotel Hacienda Uxmal** ★★ One of my favorites, this is also the oldest hotel in Uxmal. Located just up the highway from the ruins, it was built as the archaeology staff headquarters. Rooms are large and airy, exuding an impression of a well-kept yesteryear, with patterned tile floors, heavy furniture, and well-screened windows. Guest rooms surround a handsome central garden courtyard with towering royal palms, a bar, and a pool. Other facilities include a dining room, a gift shop, and a second pool. A guitar trio usually plays on the open patio in the evenings. Checkout time is 1pm, so you can spend the morning at the ruins and take a swim before you hit the road.

Mayaland Resorts, owner of the hotel, also runs the striking **Hotel Lodge at Uxmal,** next door. It has lovely rooms, but the restaurant isn't good, and I like the comforting feel of the older hotel better. Mayaland operates transfer service between the hotel and Mérida for about $30 one-way.

Km 80 Carretera Mérida–Uxmal, 97840 Uxmal, Yuc. ✆ **997/976-2011.** Reservations Mayaland Resorts, Robalo 30 SM3, 77500 Cancún, Q. Roo; ✆ 800/235-4079 in the U.S., or 997/887-0870; fax 997/884-4510. 80 units. High season $170 double; low season $150 double. AE, MC, V. Free guarded parking. **Amenities:** Restaurant (see "Where to Dine," below), bar; 2 medium-size pools; tour info; room service until 10pm; overnight laundry. *In room:* A/C, TV.

**Rancho Uxmal** This modest hotel is an exception to the high prices near Uxmal. Ten rooms have air-conditioning, and all have good screens, hot-water showers, and 24-hour electricity. The restaurant is good; a full meal of *poc chuc,* rice, beans, and tortillas costs about $5, and breakfast is $2.25 to $3. It's a long hike to the ruins from here, but the manager may help you flag down a passing bus or *combi*—or even drive you himself, if he has time. A primitive campground out back offers electrical hookups and use of a shower. The hotel is 4km (2¼ miles) north of the ruins on Highway 261.

Km 70 Carretera Mérida–Uxmal, 97840 Uxmal, Yuc. No local phone. (Reservations: Sr. Macario Cach Cabrera, Calle 26 no. 156, Ticul, Yuc., 97860; ✆ **997/949-0526** or 997/923-1576.) 18 units. $27–$32 double; $3 per person campsite. No credit cards. Free guarded parking.

**Villas Arqueológica Uxmal** This hotel is associated with Club Med, but it is just a hotel, not a self-contained vacation village. It offers a beautiful two-story layout around a garden patio and a pool. At guests' disposal are a tennis court, a library, and an audiovisual show on the ruins in English, French, and Spanish. Each of the modern, smallish rooms has two oversize single beds that fit into spaces that are walled on three sides. For this reason, I don't recommend this hotel for tall people. You can also ask for rates that include half or full board.

Ruinas Uxmal, 97844 Uxmal, Yuc. ✆ **800/258-2633** in the U.S., or 55/5203-3086 in Mexico City. 43 units. $90 double. Half-board (breakfast plus lunch or dinner) $29 per person; full board (3 meals) $58 per person. Rates include continental breakfast. AE, MC, V. Free guarded parking. **Amenities:** Restaurant, bar; large pool; tennis court. *In room:* A/C.

## WHERE TO DINE

Besides the restaurants at the Villa Arqueológica and the visitor center, there are a few other dining choices.

**Café-Bar Nicte-Ha** MEXICAN This small restaurant attached to the Hotel Hacienda Uxmal is a lovely place to eat. The food is decent, though prices tend to be high. If you eat here, take full advantage of the experience and spend a few hours by the pool near the cafe: Its use is free to customers. This is a favorite spot for bus tours that fill the place to overcrowding, so come early.

In the Hotel Hacienda Uxmal. ✆ **997/976-2011.** Main courses $5–$8; fixed-price lunch $9. AE, MC, V. Daily 1–8pm.

**Las Palapas** MEXICAN/YUCATECAN Five kilometers (3 miles) north of the ruins on the road to Mérida, you'll find this pleasant open-air restaurant with a large palapa roof. The amiable owner, María Cristina Choy, has the lowest prices around. Individual diners can sometimes become lost in the crowd if a busload of tourists arrives, but otherwise the service is fine and the food quite good. There's also a small gift shop with regional crafts and a few books.

Hwy. 261. No phone. Breakfast $3; *comida corrida* (served 1–4pm) $3.75. No credit cards. Daily 9am–6pm.

## THE PUUC MAYA ROUTE & VILLAGE OF OXKUTZCAB

South and east of Uxmal are several other Maya cities worth exploring. Though smaller in scale than Uxmal or Chichén-Itzá, each contains gems of Maya architecture. The façade of masks on the Palace of Masks at **Kabah,** the enormous palace at **Sayil,** and the fantastic caverns of **Loltún** may be among the high points of your trip. Also along the way are the **Xlapak** and **Labná ruins** and the pretty village of **Oxkutzcab.**

Kabah is 27km (17 miles) southeast of Uxmal. From there it's only a few kilometers to Sayil. Xlapak is almost walking distance (through the jungle) from Sayil, and Labná is just a bit farther east. A short drive beyond Labná brings you

**Tips** **Seeing Puuc Maya Sites**

All of these sites are currently undergoing excavation and reconstruction, and some buildings may be roped off when you visit. Photographers, take note: You'll find afternoon light the best. The sites are open daily from 8am to 5pm. Admission is $3.50 each for Sayil, Kabah, and Labná; $2 for Xlapak; and $5 for Loltún. All except the caves of Loltún are free on Sunday. Loltún has specific hours for tours—9:30 and 11:00am, and 12:30, 2, 3, and 4pm—but if the tour guide is there, a generous tip might persuade him to do a tour and not wait for a tour bus. Use of a video camera at any time costs $4; if you're visiting Uxmal in the same day, you pay only once for video permission and present your receipt as proof at each ruin.

to the caves of Loltún. Oxkutzcab is at the road's intersection with Highway 184, which you can follow west to Ticul or east all the way to Felipe Carrillo Puerto. If you aren't driving, a daily bus from Mérida goes to all these sites, with the exception of Loltún. (See "By Bus," under "Getting There & Departing," earlier in this chapter.)

### PUUC MAYA SITES

**KABAH** From Uxmal to Kabah, head southwest on Highway 261 to Santa Elena (1km/½ mile), then south to Kabah (13km/8 miles). The ancient city of Kabah lies along both sides of the highway. Make a right turn into the parking lot.

The most outstanding building at Kabah is the huge **Palace of Masks,** or *Codz Poop* ("rolled-up mat"), named for its decorative motif. You'll notice it first on the right upon a terrace. Its outstanding feature is the Chenes-style façade, completely covered in a repeated pattern of 250 masks of the rain god Chaac, each one with curling remnants of Chaac's elephant-trunk-like nose. There's nothing else like this façade in all of Maya architecture. For years, stone-carved parts of this building lay lined up in the weeds like pieces of a puzzle awaiting the master puzzle-solver to put them into place. Sculptures from this building are in the anthropology museums in Mérida and Mexico City.

Just behind and to the left of the *Codz Poop* is the **Palace Group** (also called the East Group), with a fine Puuc-style colonnaded façade. Originally it had 32 rooms. On the front are seven doors, two divided by columns, a common feature of Puuc architecture. Across the highway a large, conical dirt-and-rubble mound (on your right) was once the **Great Temple.** Past it is a **great arch,** which was much wider at one time and may have been a monumental gate into the city. A *sacbé* linked this arch to a point at Uxmal. Compare this corbeled arch to the one at Labná (see below), which is in much better shape.

**SAYIL** About 5km (3 miles) south of Kabah is the turn-off (left, which is east) to Sayil, Xlapak, Labná, Loltún, and Oxkutzcab. The ruins of ***Sayil*** ("place of the ants") are 4km (2½ miles) along this road.

Sayil is famous for **El Palacio** ★★. This tremendous palace of more than 90 rooms is impressive for its size alone, but what makes it a masterpiece of Maya architecture is the façade, which stretches across three terraced levels. Its rows of columns give it a Minoan appearance. On the second level, notice the upside-down stone figure known to archaeologists as the Diving God, or Descending God, over the doorway; the same motif was used at Tulum several centuries later. The top of El Palacio affords a great view of the Puuc hills. Sometimes it's difficult to tell which are hills and which are unrestored pyramids, because little temples peep out from the jungle at unlikely places. The large circular basin on the ground below the palace is an artificial catch basin for a *chultún* (cistern); this region has no natural *cenotes* (wells) to catch rainwater.

In the jungle past El Palacio is **El Mirador,** a small temple with an oddly slotted roof comb. Beyond El Mirador, a crude *stele* (tall, carved stone) has a phallic idol carved on it in greatly exaggerated proportions. There is another cluster of buildings called the Southern Group, which are about a quarter of a mile down a trail that branches off from the one heading to El Mirador.

**XLAPAK** Xlapak (*shla*-pahk) is a small site with one building; it's 6km (3½ miles) down the road from Sayil. The Palace at Xlapak bears the masks of the rain god Chaac. You won't miss much if you skip this place.

**LABNA** Labná, which dates from between A.D. 600 and 900, is 29km (18 miles) from Uxmal and only 3km (1¾ miles) past Xlapak. Descriptive placards fronting the main buildings are in Spanish, English, and German. The first thing you see on the left as you enter is **El Palacio,** a magnificent Puuc-style building much like the one at Sayil, but in poorer condition. Over a doorway is a large, well-conserved mask of Chaac with eyes, a huge snout nose, and jagged teeth around a small mouth that seems on the verge of speaking. Jutting out on one corner is a highly stylized serpent's mouth from which pops a human head with an unexpectedly serene expression. From the front, you can gaze out to the enormous grassy interior grounds flanked by vestiges of unrestored buildings and jungle.

From El Palacio, you can walk across the interior grounds on a reconstructed *sacbé* leading to Labná's **corbeled arch,** famed for its beauty and for its representation of what many such arches must have looked like at other sites. This one has been extensively restored, although only remnants of the roof comb can be seen. It was once part of a more elaborate structure that is completely gone. Chaac's face is on the corners of one façade, and stylized Maya huts are fashioned in stone above the two small doorways.

You pass through the arch to **El Mirador,** or El Castillo, as the rubble-formed, pyramid-shaped structure is called. Towering on top is a singular room crowned with a roof comb etched against the sky.

There's a snack stand with toilets at the entrance.

**LOLTUN** The caverns of Loltún are 30km (19 miles) past Labná on the way to Oxkutzcab, on the left side of the road. These fascinating caves, home of ancient Maya, were also used as a refuge during the War of the Castes (1847–1901). Inside are statuary, wall carvings and paintings, *chultúns* (cisterns), and other signs of Maya habitation. Guides will explain much of what you see. When I was there, the guide spoke English but was a little difficult to understand.

**Tours** lasting 1½ hours begin daily at 9:30 and 11am and 12:30, 2, 3 and 4pm, and are included in the admission price. The floor of the cavern can be slippery in places; if you have a flashlight, take it with you. Admission is $4. What you see is quite interesting.

To return to Mérida from Loltún, drive the 7km (4½ miles) to Oxkutzcab. From there, head northwest on Highway 184. It's 19km (12 miles) to Ticul and (turning north onto Hwy. 261 at Muna) 104km (65 miles) to Mérida.

## OXKUTZCAB

Oxkutzcab (ohsh-kootz-*kahb*), 11km (7 miles) from Loltún, is the heartland of the Yucatán's fruit-growing region. Oranges abound. The tidy village of 21,000 centers on a beautiful 16th-century church and the market. **Su Cabaña Suiza** (no phone) is a good restaurant in town. The last week of October and first week of November is the **Orange Festival,** when the village turns exuberant, with a carnival and orange displays in and around the central plaza.

## 3 The Ruins of Chichén-Itzá ★★★

179km (112 miles) W of Cancún; 120km (75 miles) E of Mérida

The fabled pyramids and temples of Chichén-Itzá (no, it doesn't rhyme with "chicken pizza"; the accents are on the last syllables: chee-*chin* eat-*zah*) are the Yucatán's best-known ancient monuments. The ruins are plenty hyped, but Chichén is truly worth seeing. Walking among these stone platforms, pyramids, and ball courts gives you an appreciation for this ancient civilization that cannot be had from reading books. The city is built on a scale that evokes a sense of wonder: To fill the plazas during one of the mass rituals that occurred here a millennium ago would have required an enormous number of celebrants. Even today, with the mass flow of tourists through these plazas, the ruins feel empty.

When visiting this old city, remember that much of what is said about the Maya (especially by tour guides, who speak in tones of utter certainty) is merely educated guessing—or just plain guessing. Itzáes established this post-Classic Maya city perhaps sometime during the 9th century A.D. Linda Schele and David Freidel, in *A Forest of Kings* (Morrow, 1990), have cast doubt on the legend of its founding. It says that the Toltec, led by Kukulkán (Quetzalcoatl), came here from the Toltec capital of Tula, in north-central Mexico. Along with Putún Maya coastal traders, they built a magnificent metropolis that combined the Maya Puuc style with Toltec motifs (the feathered serpent, warriors, eagles, and jaguars). Not so, say Schele and Freidel. According to them, readings of Chichén's bas-reliefs and hieroglyphs fail to support that legend and, instead, show that Chichén-Itzá was a continuous Maya site influenced by association with the Toltec but not by an invasion. Not all scholars embrace this thinking, so the idea of a Toltec invasion still holds sway.

Though it's possible to make a round-trip from Mérida to Chichén-Itzá in a day, it will be a long, tiring, and very rushed day. Try to spend at least a night at Chichén-Itzá (you will already have paid for the sound-and-light ticket) or the nearby town of Valladolid.

### ESSENTIALS

**GETTING THERE & DEPARTING By Plane** Travel agents in the United States, Cancún, and Cozumel can arrange day trips from Cancún and Cozumel.

**BY CAR** Chichén-Itzá is on the main Highway 180 between Mérida (2½ hr.) and Cancún (1½ hr.). Take the *autopista* from either city, and you'll enter the village of Pisté from the north. When you come to the old Highway 180, turn left. Signs point the way.

**BY BUS** From Mérida, there are three first-class **ADO** buses per day, and a couple that go to Valladolid stop here. Also, there are several second-class buses per day. If you want to take a day trip from Mérida, go with a tour company. From Cancún, there are any number of tourist buses, and regular first-class buses leave for Chichén every hour

**AREA LAYOUT** The village of **Pisté,** where most hotels and restaurants are located, is about 2.5km (1½ miles) from the ruins of Chichén-Itzá. Public buses from Mérida, Cancún, Valladolid, and elsewhere discharge passengers here.

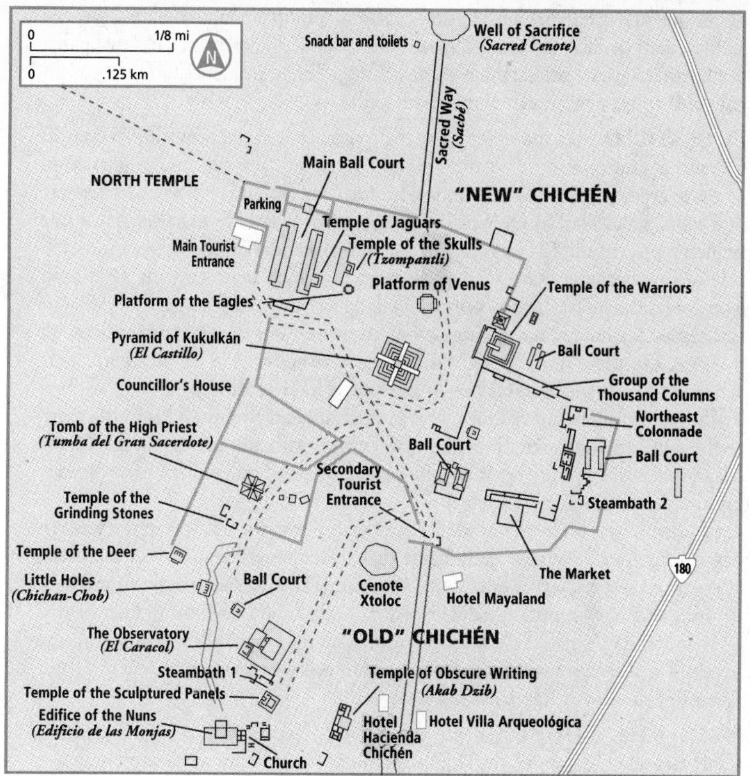


A few hotels are at the edge of the ruins, and one, the Hotel Dolores Alba (see "Where to Stay," below), is out of town about 2.5km (1½ miles) from the ruins on the road to Valladolid.

## EXPLORING THE RUINS

The site occupies 10 square km (4 sq. miles), and it takes most of a day to see all the ruins, which are open daily from 8am to 5pm. Service areas are open from 8am to 10pm. Admission is $11, free for children under age 12, and free for all on Sunday and holidays. A video camera permit costs $4. Parking is extra. *Note:* You can use your ticket to reenter on the same day, but you'll have to pay again for an additional day. Chichén-Itzá's **sound-and-light** show is worth seeing and is included in the cost of admission. The show, held at 7 or 8pm depending on the season, is in Spanish, but headsets are available for rent ($4.50) in several languages.

The large, modern visitor center, at the main entrance where you pay the admission charge, is beside the parking lot and consists of a museum, an auditorium, a restaurant, a bookstore, and bathrooms. You can see the site on your own or with a licensed guide who speaks English or Spanish. Guides usually wait at the entrance and charge around $40 for one to six people. Although the guides frown on it, there's nothing wrong with approaching a group of people who speak the same language and asking if they want to share a guide. Be wary of the history-spouting guides—some of it is just plain out-of-date—but the architectural details they point out are enlightening. Chichén-Itzá has two parts: the northern (new) zone, which shows distinct Toltec influence, and the southern (old) zone, with mostly Puuc architecture.

**EL CASTILLO** As you enter from the tourist center, the beautiful 75-foot El Castillo pyramid (also called the Pyramid of Kukulkán) will be straight ahead across a large open area. It was built with the Maya calendar in mind. There are 364 stairs plus a platform to equal 365 (days of the year), 52 panels on each side (which represent the 52-year cycle of the Maya calendar), and 9 terraces on each side of the stairways (for a total of 18 terraces, which represents the 18-month Maya solar calendar). If this isn't proof enough of the mathematical precision of this temple, come for the **spring** or **fall equinox** (Mar 21 or Sept 21, between 3–5pm). On those days, sunlight touches the seven stairs of the northern stairway and the serpent-head carving at the base, which become a "serpent" formed by the play of light and shadow. This serpent appears to descend into the earth as the sun hits each stair from the top, ending with the serpent head. To the Maya this was a fertility symbol: The golden sun had entered the earth, meaning that it was time to plant corn.

El Castillo was built over an earlier structure. A narrow stairway at the western edge of the north staircase leads inside that structure, where there is a sacrificial altar-throne—a red jaguar encrusted with jade. The stairway is open from 11am to 3pm and is cramped, usually crowded, humid, and uncomfortable. A visit early in the day is best. In addition, visitors are no longer allowed to climb the pyramid as they were in years past—too many fell off and were injured or killed. Photos of the jaguar figure are not allowed.

**MAIN BALL COURT (Juego de Pelota)** Northwest of El Castillo is Chichén's main ball court, the largest and best preserved anywhere, and only one of nine ball courts built in this city. Carved on both walls of the ball court are scenes showing Maya figures dressed as ball players and decked out in heavy protective padding. The carved scene also shows a headless player kneeling with blood shooting from his neck; another player holding the head looks on.

Players on two teams tried to knock a hard rubber ball through one of the two stone rings placed high on either wall, using only their elbows, knees, and hips (no hands). According to legend, the losing players paid for defeat with their lives. However, some experts say the victors were the only appropriate sacrifices for the gods. One can only guess what the incentive for winning might be in that case. Either way, the game must have been riveting, heightened by the wonderful acoustics of the ball court.

**THE NORTH TEMPLE** Temples are at both ends of the ball court. The North Temple has sculptured pillars and more sculptures inside, as well as badly ruined murals. The acoustics of the ball court are so good that from the North Temple, a person speaking can be heard clearly at the opposite end, about 136m (450 ft.) away.

**TEMPLE OF JAGUARS** Near the southeastern corner of the main ball court is a small temple with serpent columns and carved panels showing warriors and jaguars. Up the flight of steps and inside the temple, a mural was found that chronicles a battle in a Maya village.

**TEMPLE OF THE SKULLS (Tzompantli)** To the right of the ball court is the Temple of the Skulls, an obvious borrowing from the post-Classic cities of central Mexico. Notice the rows of skulls carved into the stone platform. When a sacrificial victim's head was cut off, it was impaled on a pole and displayed in a tidy row with others. Also carved into the stone are pictures of eagles tearing hearts from human victims. The word *Tzompantli* is not Mayan but comes from central Mexico. Reconstruction using scattered fragments may add a level to this platform and change the look of this structure by the time you visit.

**PLATFORM OF THE EAGLES** Next to the Tzompantli, this small platform has reliefs showing eagles and jaguars clutching human hearts in their talons and claws, as well as a human head emerging from the mouth of a serpent.

**PLATFORM OF VENUS** East of the Tzompantli and north of El Castillo, near the road to the Sacred Cenote, is the Platform of Venus. In Maya and Toltec lore, Venus was represented by a feathered monster or a feathered serpent with a human head in its mouth. This is also called the tomb of Chaac-Mool because a Chaac-Mool figure was discovered "buried" within the structure.

**SACRED CENOTE** Follow the dirt road (actually an ancient *sacbé,* or causeway) that heads north from the Platform of Venus; after 5 minutes you'll come to the great natural well that may have given Chichén-Itzá (the Well of the Itzáes) its name. This well was used for ceremonial purposes, not for drinking water—according to legend, sacrificial victims were drowned in this pool to honor the rain god Chaac. Anatomical research done early in the 20th century by Ernest A. Hooten showed that bones of both children and adults were found in the well. Judging from Hooten's evidence, they may have been outcasts or diseased or feeble-minded persons.

Edward Thompson, who was the American consul in Mérida and a Harvard professor, purchased the ruins of Chichén early in the 20th century and explored the *cenote* with dredges and divers. His explorations exposed a fortune in gold and jade. Most of the riches wound up in Harvard's Peabody Museum of Archaeology and Ethnology—a matter that continues to disconcert Mexican classicists today. Excavations in the 1960s unearthed more treasure, and studies of the recovered objects detail offerings from throughout the Yucatán and even farther away.

**TEMPLE OF THE WARRIORS (Templo de los Guerreros)** Due east of El Castillo is one of the most impressive structures at Chichén: the Temple of the Warriors, named for the carvings of warriors marching along its walls. It's also called the Group of the Thousand Columns for the rows of broken pillars that flank it. During the recent restoration, hundreds more of the columns were rescued from the rubble and put in place, setting off the temple more magnificently than ever. A figure of Chaac-Mool sits at the top of the temple, surrounded by impressive columns carved in relief to look like enormous feathered serpents. South of the temple was a square building that archaeologists called the **Market** (*mercado*); a colonnade surrounds its central court. Beyond the temple and the market in the jungle are mounds of rubble, parts of which are being reconstructed.

The main Mérida–Cancún highway once ran straight through the ruins of Chichén, and though it has been diverted, you can still see the great swath it cut. South and west of the old highway's path are more impressive ruined buildings.

**TOMB OF THE HIGH PRIEST (Tumba del Gran Sacerdote)** Past the refreshment stand to the right of the path is the Tomb of the High Priest, which stood atop a natural limestone cave in which skeletons and offerings were found, giving the temple its name.

**TEMPLE OF THE GRINDING STONES (Casa de los Metates)** This building, the next one on your right, is named after the concave corn-grinding stones the Maya used.

**TEMPLE OF THE DEER (Templo del Venado)** Past Casa de los Metates is this fairly tall though ruined building. The relief of a stag that gave the temple its name is long gone.

**LITTLE HOLES (Chichan-chob)** This next temple has a roof comb with little holes, three masks of the rain god Chaac, three rooms, and a good view of the surrounding structures. It's one of the oldest buildings at Chichén, built in the Puuc style during the Late Classic period.

**OBSERVATORY (El Caracol)** Construction of the Observatory, a complex building with a circular tower, was carried out over centuries; the additions and modifications reflected the Maya's careful observation of celestial movements and their need for increasingly exact measurements. Through slits in the tower's walls, astronomers could observe the cardinal directions and the approach of the all-important spring and autumn equinoxes, as well as the summer solstice. The temple's name, which means "snail," comes from a spiral staircase within the structure.

On the east side of El Caracol, a path leads north into the bush to the **Cenote Xtoloc,** a natural limestone well that provided the city's daily water supply. If you see any lizards sunning there, they may well be *xtoloc,* the lizard for which this *cenote* is named.

**TEMPLE OF PANELS (Templo de los Tableros)** Just south of El Caracol are the ruins of a steam bath (*temazcalli*) and the Temple of Panels, named for the carved panels on top. This temple was once covered by a much larger structure, only traces of which remain.

**EDIFICE OF THE NUNS (Edificio de las Monjas)** If you've visited the Puuc sites of Kabah, Sayil, Labná, or Xlapak, the enormous nunnery here will remind you of the palaces at those sites. Built in the late Classic period, the new edifice was constructed over an older one. Suspecting that this was so, Le Plongeon, an archaeologist working early in the 20th century, put dynamite between the two and blew away part of the exterior, revealing the older structures within. You can still see the results of Le Plongeon's indelicate exploratory methods.

On the east side of the Edifice of the Nuns is an **annex (Anexo Este)** constructed in highly ornate Chenes style with Chaac masks and serpents.

**THE CHURCH (La Iglesia)** Next to the annex is one of the oldest buildings at Chichén, the Church. Masks of Chaac decorate two upper stories. Look closely, and you'll see other pagan symbols among the crowd of Chaacs: an armadillo, a crab, a snail, and a tortoise. These represent the Maya gods, called *bacah,* whose job it was to hold up the sky.

**TEMPLE OF OBSCURE WRITING (Akab Dzib)** Beloved of travel writers, this temple lies east of the Edifice of the Nuns. Above a door in one of the rooms are some Maya glyphs, which gave the temple its name because the writings have yet to be deciphered. In other rooms, traces of red handprints are still visible. Reconstructed and expanded over the centuries, Akab Dzib may be the oldest building at Chichén.

## WHERE TO STAY

The expensive hotels in Chichén all occupy beautiful grounds, are close to the ruins, and have good food. All have toll-free reservations numbers, which I recommend using. Some of these hotels do a lot of business with tour operators—they can be empty one day and full the next. The inexpensive hotels are in the village of Pisté, 2.5km (1½ miles) away. There is little to do in Pisté at night. Another option is to go on to the colonial town of Valladolid, 30 minutes away, but you'll want reservations because a lot of tour-bus companies use the hotels there (see below).

### EXPENSIVE

**Hacienda Chichén** ★★ This is the smallest and most private of the hotels at the ruins. It is also the quietest and the least likely to have bus tour groups. As a hacienda in 1923, it served as the headquarters for the Carnegie Institute's excavations. Several bungalows were built to house the staff; these have been modernized and are now the guest rooms. Each is simply and comfortably furnished (with a dehumidifier and ceiling fan in addition to air-conditioning) and is a short distance from the others. Each bungalow has a private porch from which you can enjoy the beautiful grounds. Standard rooms come with two twin or double beds. Suites are larger and have larger bathrooms and double or queen beds. The main building belonged to the hacienda; it houses the terrace restaurant, with dining outside by the pool or inside.

Zona Arqueológica, 97751 Chichén-Itzá, Yuc. ✆ and fax **985/851-0045.** www.yucatanadventure.com.mx. (Reservations: Casa del Balam, Calle 60 no. 488, 97000 Mérida, Yuc. ✆ **800/624-8451** in the U.S., or 999/924-2150; fax 999/924-5011.) 28 units. $117 double; $140 suite. AE, DC, MC, V. Free guarded parking. **Amenities:** Restaurant, bar; large pool. *In room:* A/C, minibar, hair dryer.

**Hotel Mayaland** ★★ The main doorway frames El Caracol (the observatory) in a stunning view—that's how close this hotel is to the ruins. If there's a drawback, it's that the hotel books large bus tours, but this isn't so bad because the hotel is on a large piece of property that uses space liberally. The main building is long and three stories high. The rooms are large, with comfortable beds and large tiled bathrooms. Bungalows, scattered about the rest of the grounds, are built native style, with thatched roofs and stucco walls; they're a good deal larger than the rooms. The grounds are gorgeous, with huge trees and lush foliage—the hotel has had 75 years to get them in shape. Mayaland operates a shuttle service between the hotel and Mérida for about $35 each way.

Zona Arqueológica, 97751 Chichén-Itzá, Yuc. ✆ **985/851-0127.** (Reservations: Mayaland Resorts, Robalo 30 SM3, 77500 Cancún, Q. Roo; ✆ 800/235-4079 in the U.S., or 998/887-0870; fax 998/884-4510.) 101 units. High season $150 double, $200 bungalow. 10% low-season discount. AE, MC, V. Free guarded parking. **Amenities:** 2 restaurants, bar; 3 pools; tour desk; room service until 10pm; overnight laundry; babysitting. *In room:* A/C, TV, minibar, coffeemaker, hair dryer.

**Villas Arqueológica Chichén-Itzá** ★ This lovely hotel is built around a courtyard and a pool. Two massive royal poinciana trees tower above the grounds, and bougainvillea drapes from the walls. This chain has similar hotels at Cobá and Uxmal, and is connected with Club Med. The rooms are modern and small but comfortable, unless you're 6-foot-2 or taller—each bed is in a niche, with walls at the head and foot. Most rooms have one double bed and an oversize single bed. You can also book a half-board or full-board plan.

Zona Arqueológica, 97751 Chichén-Itzá, Yuc. ✆ **800/258-2633** in the U.S., 55/5203-3086 in Mexico City, 985/851-0034, or 985/856-2830. 40 units. High season $110 double; low season $90 double. Rates include continental breakfast. Half-board (breakfast plus lunch or dinner) $29 per person; full board (3 meals) $58 per person. AE, MC, V. Free parking. **Amenities:** Restaurant, bar; large pool; tennis court; tour desk. *In room:* A/C.

### MODERATE

**Pirámide Inn** Less than a mile from the ruins at the edge of Pisté, this hotel has simple rooms, most with two double beds, some with three twins or one king. The bathrooms are nice, with counter space and tub/shower combinations. The air-conditioning is quiet and effective. Hot water comes on between 5 and 10am and 5 and 10pm. A well-kept pool and a *temascal* (a native form of steam bath) occupy a small part of the landscaped grounds, which include the remains of a Maya wall. Try to get a room in the back. The hotel is right on the highway.

Calle 15 no. 30, 97751 Pisté, Yuc. ✆ **985/851-0115.** Fax 985/851-0114. www.piramideinn.com. 44 units. $47 double. MC, V. **Amenities:** Restaurant, bar; medium-size pool; steam room; room service. *In room:* A/C.

### INEXPENSIVE

**Hotel Dolores Alba** ★ *Value* This place is of the motel variety, perfect if you come by car. It is a bargain for what you get: two pools (one really special), palapas and hammocks around the place, and large, comfortable rooms. The restaurant serves good meals at moderate prices. The hotel provides free transportation to the ruins and the Caves of Balankanché during visiting hours, though you will have to take a taxi back. The hotel is on the highway 2.5km (1½ miles) east of the ruins (toward Valladolid). You can make reservations here for the Dolores Alba in Mérida.

Km 122 Carretera Mérida–Valladolid, Yuc. ✆ **985/858-1555.** (Reservations: Hotel Dolores Alba, Calle 63 no. 464, 97000 Mérida, Yuc. ✆ 985/928-5650; fax 985/928-3163; www.doloresalba.com.) 40 units. $35 double. No credit cards. Free parking. **Amenities:** Restaurant, bar; 2 pools; room service until midnight; laundry. *In room:* A/C.

## WHERE TO DINE

Reasonably priced meals are available at the restaurant in the visitor center at the ruins and at hotels in Pisté. Prices jump quite a bit at hotel restaurants near the ruins. In Pisté, however, many places cater to large groups, which descend on them after 1pm.

**Cafetería Ruinas** INTERNATIONAL Though it has the monopoly on food at the ruins, this cafeteria actually does a good job with such basic meals as enchiladas, pizza, and baked chicken. It even offers some Yucatecan dishes. Eggs and burgers are cooked to order, and the coffee is very good. You can also get fruit smoothies and vegetarian dishes. Sit outside at the tables farthest from the crowd, and relax.

In the Chichén-Itzá visitor center. ✆ **985/851-0111.** Breakfast $4; sandwiches $4–$5; main courses $5–$8. AE, MC, V. Daily 9am–6pm.

**Fiesta** YUCATECAN/MEXICAN Though relatively expensive, the food here is dependable and good. You can dine inside or out, but make a point of going for supper or early lunch when the tours buses are gone. The buffet is quite complete, and the menu has many Yucatecan classics. Fiesta is on the west end of town.

Carretera Mérida–Valladolid, Pisté. ✆ **985/851-0038.** Main courses $4–$6; buffet (served 12:30–5pm) $8.50. No credit cards. Daily 7am–9pm.

**Restaurant Bar "Poxil"** YUCATECAN A *poxil* is a Maya fruit somewhat akin to a *guanábana.* Although this place doesn't serve them, what is on the simple menu is good, though not gourmet, and the price is right. You will find the Poxil near the west entrance to town on the south side of the street.

Calle 15 no. 52, Pisté. ✆ **985/851-0123.** Main courses $4–$5, breakfast $3. No credit cards. Daily 8am–9pm.

### A SIDE TRIP TO THE GRUTA (CAVE) DE BALANKANCHE

The Gruta de Balankanché is 6km (3½ miles) from Chichén-Itzá on the road to Valladolid and Cancún. Taxis will make the trip and wait. The entire excursion takes about a half-hour, but the walk inside is hot and humid. Of the cave tours in the Yucatan, this is the tamest. It includes a cheesy and uninformative recorded tour. The highlight is a round chamber with a central column the size of a large tree trunk (impressive, but not so much as Loltún or Aktun Chen). You come up the same way you go down. The cave became a hideaway during the War of the Castes. You can still see traces of carving and incense burning, as well as an underground stream that served as the sanctuary's water supply. Outside, take time to meander through the botanical gardens, where most of the plants and trees are labeled with their common and scientific names.

The caves are open daily. Admission is $6, free for children 6 to 12. Children under age 6 are not admitted. Use of a video camera costs $4 (free if you've already bought a video permit in Chichén the same day). Tours in English are at 11am and 1 and 3pm, and, in Spanish, at 9am, noon, and 2 and 4pm. Double-check these hours at the main entrance to the Chichén ruins.

## 4 Valladolid

40km (25 miles) E of Chichén-Itzá; 160km (100 miles) SW of Cancún

Valladolid (pronounced *bye*-ah-doh-*leed*) is a small, pleasant colonial city halfway between Mérida and Cancún. The people are friendly and informal, and, except for the heat, life is easy. The city's economy is based on commerce and small-scale manufacture. There is a large *cenote* is in the center of town and a couple more 5km (3 miles) down the road to Chichén. A restoration project has reconstructed several rows of colonial housing in the neighborhood surrounding the convent of San Bernardino de Siena. Valladolid can also be the starting point for several interesting side trips.

### ESSENTIALS

**GETTING THERE & DEPARTING** **By Car** From Mérida or Cancún, you have two choices: the toll road (*cuota*) and Highway 180. The ***cuota*** passes a few kilometers north of the city, and the exit is at the crossing of **Highway 295** to Tizimín. **Highway 180** takes significantly longer because it passes through a number of villages (with their requisite speed bumps). Both 180 and 295 lead directly to downtown. Leaving is just as easy: from the main square, Calle 41 turns into 180 east to Cancún; Calle 39 heads to 180 west to Chichén-Itzá and Mérida. To take the *cuota* to Mérida or Cancún, take Calle 40. (See "City Layout," below.)

**BY BUS** **Expresso de Oriente** runs eight first-class buses per day to and from Mérida, nine buses to and from Cancún, three to and from Tulum, and three to and from Playa del Carmen. To secure a seat, you can buy a ticket a day in advance. In addition, first-class buses stop in Valladolid while passing through (*de paso*) on the way to Cancún. To get to Chichén-Itzá, you must take a second-class bus, which leaves every hour and sometimes on the half hour. Valladolid has two bus stations, the corner of Calles 39 and 46, and at 37 and 54. For all practical purposes, they are interchangeable; buses pass by both stations to pick up passengers. Passengers going first-class to Mérida or Cancún are dropped off at another station (Isleta) on the *autopista,* where they pick up the bus.

**ORIENTATION** **Visitor Information** At the small **tourism office** in the Palacio Municipal, you can get a map but little else. It's open daily from 10am to 2pm and 4 to 8pm.

**CITY LAYOUT** Valladolid has the standard layout for towns in the Yucatán: Streets running north-south are even numbers; those running east-west are odd numbers. The main plaza is bordered by Calle 39 on the north, 41 on the south, 40 on the east, and 42 on the west. The plaza is named Parque Francisco Cantón Rosado, but everyone calls it **El Centro.** Taxis are easy to come by.

## EXPLORING VALLADOLID

Before it became Valladolid, the city was a Maya settlement called Zací (zah-*kee*), which means "white hawk." There are two *cenotes* in the area. **Cenote Zací** is at the intersection of Calles 39 and 36, in a small park in the middle of town. The walls and part of the roof of the *cenote* have been opened up, and a trail leads down close to the water. Caves, stalactites, and hanging vines contribute to a wild, prehistoric atmosphere. The park has a large palapa restaurant that is popular with local residents, plus three traditional Maya dwellings that house a small photograph collection and some historical materials on Valladolid. Admission is $1.50.

Southwest of El Centro is the Franciscan monastery of **San Bernardino de Siena** (1552). Most of the compound was built in the early 1600s; a large underground river is believed to pass under the convent and surrounding neighborhood, which is called Barrio Sisal. "Sisal," is in this case, a corruption of the Mayan phrase *sis-ha,* meaning "cold water." The *barrio* (neighborhood) has undergone extensive restoration and is a delight to behold.

Valladolid's main square is the social center of town and a thriving market for the prettiest Yucatecan dresses anywhere. On its south side is the principal church, **La Parroquia de San Servacio.** *Vallesoletanos,* as the locals call themselves, believe that almost all cathedrals in Mexico point east, and they cherish a local legend to explain why theirs points north—but don't believe a word of it. On the east side of the plaza is the municipal building known modestly as *El Ayuntamiento.* Be sure to see the four dramatic paintings outlining the history of the peninsula. In particular, note the first panel, featuring a horrified Maya priest as he foresees the arrival of Spanish galleons. On Sunday nights, beneath the stone arches of the *Ayuntamiento,* the municipal band plays *jaranas* and other traditional music of the region.

## SHOPPING

The **Mercado de Artesanías de Valladolid,** at the corner of Calles 39 and 44, gives you a good idea of the local merchandise. Perhaps the main handicraft of the town is embroidered Maya dresses, which can be purchased here or from women around the main square. The latter also sell, of all things, Barbie-doll-size Maya dresses! Just ask, "*¿Vestidos para Barbie?*" and out they come. The area around Valladolid is cattle country; the local leather goods are plentiful, and some of the best sandals (*huaraches*) and leather goods are made on the main plaza in a small shop run by **Adalberto Silva,** above the municipal bazaar. Another good sandal maker has a shop called **Elio's,** Calle 37 no. 202, between streets 42 and 44 (no phone). An Indian named **Juan Mac** makes *alpargatas,* the traditional everyday footwear of the Maya, in his shop on Calle 39, near the intersection with Calle 38, 1 block from the main plaza, before the store Cielito Lindo. Most of his output is for locals, but he's happy to knock out a pair for visitors.

Valladolid also produces a highly prized **honey** made from the *tzi-tzi-ché* flower. You can find it and other goods at the **town market,** Calle 32 between Calles 35 and 37. The best time to see the market is Sunday morning.

## WHERE TO STAY

Hotels (and restaurants) here are less expensive than the competition in Chichén. Occupancy rates are very high, so you should make reservations. If you arrive without reservations and there is no room in either of these hotels, **Hotel Zací,** Calle 44 between Calles 37 and 39, is your next-best bet.

**Hotel El Mesón del Marqués** The Mesón del Marqués is a comfortable, gracious hotel. The first courtyard surrounds a fountain and abounds with hanging plants and bougainvillea. This, the original house, holds a good restaurant (see "Where to Dine," below). In back is another courtyard with plenty of greenery and a pool. Most of the rooms are sheltered from city noise and are large and comfortable. Most have two double beds. The hotel is on the north side of El Centro, opposite the church.

Calle 39 no. 203, 97780 Valladolid, Yuc. ✆ **985/856-3042** or 985/856-2073. Fax 985/856-2280. www.elmesondelmarques.com 90 units. $48 double; $58 jr. suite. AE. Free secured parking. **Amenities:** Restaurant, bar; pool; room service until 11pm; same-day laundry. *In room:* A/C, TV.

**Hotel María de la Luz** The three-story María de la Luz is built around an inner swimming pool. The guest rooms have been refurbished, with new tile floors and bathrooms and new mattresses; three have balconies overlooking the main square. The wide interior space holds a restaurant that is quite comfortable and airy for most of the day—it's a popular place for breakfast. The hotel is on the west side of the main square.

Calle 42 no. 193, 97780 Valladolid, Yuc. ✆ and fax **985/856-2071** or 985/856-2071. www.mariadelaluz.com.mx. 70 units. $34 double. MC, V. Rates include breakfast. Free secured parking. **Amenities:** Restaurant, bar; medium-size pool; tour desk. *In room:* A/C, TV.

## WHERE TO DINE

Valladolid is not a center for haute cuisine, but you should try some of the regional specialties. The lowest prices are in the **Bazar Municipal,** a little arcade of shops beside the Hotel El Mesón del Marqués right on the main square.

**Hostería del Marqués** MEXICAN/YUCATECAN This is part of the Hotel El Mesón del Marqués, facing the main square. The patio is calm and cool for most of the day. The extensive menu features local specialties. If you are hungry, try the Yucatecan sampler. Any of the enchiladas are good, and the guacamole was a hit on my last visit.

Calle 39 no. 203. ✆ **985/856-2073.** Breakfast $3–$5; main courses $3.50–$7. AE. Daily 7am–11:30pm.

## SIDE TRIPS FROM VALLADOLID

### CENOTES DZITNUP AND SAMMULA

The **Cenote Dzitnup** (also known as Cenote Xkekén) ★, 4km (2½ miles) west of Valladolid off Highway 180, is worth a side trip, especially if you have time for a dip. You can take the bike trail there. Antonio Aguilar, who owns a sporting goods store at Calle 41 no. 225, between Calles 48 and 50, rents bikes. Descend a short flight of rather perilous stone steps, and at the bottom, inside a beautiful cavern, is a natural pool of water so clear and blue that it seems plucked from a dream. If you decide to swim, be sure that you don't have creams or other chemicals on your skin—they damage the habitat of the small fish and other organisms living there. Also, no alcohol, food, or smoking is allowed in the cavern. Admission is $2. The *cenote* is open daily from 7am to 7pm. About 100 yards down the road on the opposite side is another recently discovered *cenote,* Sammulá, where you can also swim. Admission is $2.

## EKBALAM: RECENTLY EXCAVATED MAYA RUINS ★★★

About 18km (11 miles) north of Valladolid, off the highway to Río Lagartos, is the spectacular site at **Ekbalam,** which means "dark jaguar" or "star jaguar" in Mayan. Relatively unvisited by tourists, the Ekbalam ruins have been undergoing extensive renovation; they are a must-see for travelers who have access to a rental car. Take Calle 40 north out of Valladolid to Highway 295; go 18km (11 miles) to the sign marking the Ekbalam turn-off. Follow a narrow, winding road through a small village. Ekbalam is 13km (8 miles) from the highway; the entrance fee is $2.50, plus $4 for each video camera. The site is open daily 8am to 5pm.

Built between 100 B.C. and A.D. 1200, the smaller buildings are architecturally unique—especially the large, perfectly restored **Caracol.** The principal buildings in the main group have been reconstructed beautifully. Flanked by two smaller pyramids, the imposing central pyramid is 157m (517 ft.) long and 61m (200 ft.) wide. At more than 30m (100 ft.) high, it is easily taller than the highest pyramids in Chichén-Itzá and Uxmal. On the left side of the main stairway, archaeologists recently uncovered a large, perfectly preserved stucco and stone figure of the gaping mouth of the god Itzamná forming a doorway. Around it are several beautifully detailed human figures. If you climb to the top of the pyramid, in the middle distance you can see unrestored ruins looming to the north. To the southeast, you can spot the tallest structures at **Cobá,** 48km (30 miles) away.

Also plainly visible are the **raised causeways** of the Maya—the *sacbé* appear as raised lines in the forest vegetation. More than any of the better-known sites, Ekbalam excites a sense of mystery and awe at the scale of Maya civilization and the utter ruin to which it came.

## RIO LAGARTOS NATURE RESERVE

Some 80km (50 miles) north of Valladolid (40km/25 miles north of Tizimín) on Highway 295 is Río Lagartos, a 118,000-acre refuge established in 1979 to protect the largest nesting population of flamingos in North America. Generally, it's best to see flamingos at the sites near Mérida. According to biologists, flamingoes should never be approached when nesting. This said, you may still want to visit the reserve to see natural habitats and many other species of animals and birds.

To get to Río Lagartos, you pass through Tizimín, which is about 30 minutes away. The best place to stay there is **Hotel 49,** Calle 49 373-A (**© 986/863-2136**), by the main square. The owner can give you good advice about going to the nature preserve. There is not much to do in Tizimín unless you are there during the first 2 weeks of January, when it holds the largest fair in the Yucatán. The prime fiesta day is January 6.

**SEEING THE RIO LAGARTOS REFUGE** Río Lagartos is a small fishing village of around 3,000 people who make their living from the sea and from the occasional tourist who shows up to see the flamingos. Colorfully painted homes face the *Malecón* (the oceanfront street), and brightly painted boats dock along the same half-moon-shaped port.

Río Lagartos has a dock area where you can hire a boat to the large flamingo colony for $75, which can be split among up to six people; the trip takes 4 to 6 hours. A shorter trip to a closer colony costs $20.

Although thousands of flamingos nest near here from April to August, the law prohibits visiting their nesting grounds. Flamingos need mud with particular ingredients (including a high salt content) to multiply, and this area's mud does the trick. Flamingos use their bills to suck up the mud, and they have the unique ability to screen the ingredients they need from it. What you see on the boat trip is a mixture of flamingos, frigates, pelicans, herons in several colors, and ducks. Don't allow the boatman to frighten the birds into flight for your photographs, or the birds will eventually leave the habitat permanently.

15

# The Copper Canyon

When I first went to the Copper Canyon, I didn't have a clear idea of what to expect. In the back of my mind, I had a vision of the Grand Canyon, because I had read many remarks comparing the two. This turned out to be nonsense! Comparing the two does neither place justice. The canyons are not alike; they have different topography, geology, climate, flora, and fauna, and a different local culture, too. And as far as canyons go, if you've seen one, you definitely have *not* seen them all.

If you are interested in seeing a rugged and beautiful land; if you're interested in taking one of the most remarkable train trips in the world; if you're interested in hiking or riding horseback through remote areas to see an astonishing variety of flora and fauna; or if you're curious about a land still populated by indigenous people living pretty much the way they have for centuries, the Copper Canyon is the place to go.

Most often, when people say **Copper Canyon,** they are referring to a section of the Sierra Madre of northwestern Mexico, known commonly in Mexico as the **Sierra Tarahumara** (after the Indians who live there). The area was formed through violent volcanic uplifting, followed by a slow, quiet process of erosion that carved a vast network of canyons into the soft volcanic stone.

Crossing the Sierra Tarahumara is the famed *Chihuahua al Pacífico* (Chihuahua to the Pacific) railway. Acclaimed as an engineering marvel, the 624km (390-mile) railroad has 39 bridges (the highest is more than 303m/1,000 ft. above the Chinipas River; the longest is a third of a mile) and 86 tunnels (one over a mile long). It climbs from **Los Mochis,** at sea level, up nearly 2,424m (8,000 ft.) through some of Mexico's most magnificent scenery—thick pine forests, jagged peaks, and shadowy canyons—before descending again to its destination, the city of **Chihuahua.**

## EXPLORING THE COPPER CANYON

The principal points of entry for the region are Los Mochis and Chihuahua City, the two terminal points of the railroad. These cities, and how to get to them, are covered later in this chapter. Most people prefer to enter through Los Mochis and take the train to Chihuahua rather than the reverse.

It's easier than ever to get to the region, but it's **trickier than ever to travel through it on your own.** The Mexican government promotes the Copper Canyon heavily, and tour companies buy large blocks of train tickets and hotel rooms, especially during the high seasons. In some parts of the canyon, the number of hotel rooms is limited, making it important to get reservations. Also, there have been numerous changes in the operation of the train, with more to follow.

Consequently, this is not the place to do casual, unplanned, follow-your-nose traveling. You should plan your trip and have an itinerary, train tickets, and hotel reservations *in hand* when you arrive in the region. Either work out the arrangements on your own or go through a travel agent or tour operator. (For tips, see "Choosing a Package or Tour Operator," below.) If you're the adventurous sort and don't mind some inconvenience, it is possible (albeit not advisable) to play it by ear and show up without tickets or reservations. If you do so, I recommend you avoid the high season, begin the trip in Chihuahua (rather than Los Mochis), and make **Creel** your base of operations. It has many more hotel rooms, and some of the cheaper hotels don't take reservations anyway.

**WHEN TO GO** There are two high seasons for the Sierra: October to early November, and March to April. These months are the most popular (and the most crowded) because of the likelihood of moderate temperatures—but even in these months, temperatures in the bottom of the canyon will be warm. (Most canyon visitors stay up in the rim country.) To avoid the crowds and get cheaper prices, I suggest **going in July, August,** or **September** (the rainy season). During that time, barring drought, you'll find afternoon thundershowers (very pretty in the canyon land), green vegetation, flowing water, and comfortable temperatures up along the rim. If you plan to do some serious hikes into the canyon, consider going in the winter, when temperatures will be the least tropical down inside the canyons. **Avoid the Sierra from late April through June.** This is the driest part of the year, with chronic water shortages in many of the towns and hotels; the vegetation is brown, and the canyons can be hazy.

## 1 The Copper Canyon Train & Stops Along the Way

### TRAIN ESSENTIALS

First-class service between Chihuahua and Los Mochis operates daily in both directions. Departure times are listed below. Second-class trains also run daily. They stop more frequently than the first-class trains and are slower. First-class service has undergone major improvements. The passenger cars have been thoroughly revamped, with clean bathrooms that work and improved seating and windows. (They already were air-conditioned in summer and heated in winter.) The train now hauls both a dining car and a club car. In addition, it makes fewer stops than before. The new owner, Ferromex, has also invested heavily in improving the tracks, making delays due to landslides less frequent. It has also spruced up some of the local stations.

The train makes seven stops; the five of principal interest to travelers are described in detail below. The schedule is a word problem that would gratify any high school algebra teacher: two trains depart from opposite ends of the line (Chihuahua and Los Mochis) at the same time (6am) to meet at point *x*

#### *Tips* In Which Direction Should I Travel?

For sightseeing, **Los Mochis,** the western terminus, is the better starting place: The most scenic part of the 12- to 15-hour journey comes between **El Fuerte** and **Bahuichivo/Cerocahui,** which you are guaranteed to see in daylight if you come from Los Mochis. The train that starts in Chihuahua often gets to this area in darkness. This chapter lists the stops in order from Los Mochis to Chihuahua.

(Divisadero). So that you don't have to solve for *y*, I've included the "official" schedule below.

**Train Departure Times**

| From Los Mochis | | From Chihuahua | |
|---|---|---|---|
| Los Mochis | 6am | Chihuahua | 6am |
| El Fuerte | 7:25am | Creel | 11:25am |
| Bahuichivo/Cerocahui | 11:15pm | El Divisadero | 12:45pm |
| Barrancas | 11:25pm | Barrancas | 1:05pm |
| El Divisadero | 12:35pm | Bahuichivo/Cerocahui | 2:30pm |
| Creel | 2:15pm | El Fuerte | 6:15pm |
| Chihuahua (arrives) | 7:50pm | Los Mochis (arrives) | 7:50pm |

The stops are very short except at **Divisadero,** where you have 15 minutes to get out and walk down the steps to the overlook for a spectacular panorama of the canyon, and perhaps time to buy a trinket or a taco from one of the many vendors.

**DELAYS** Due to the severe terrain and the many tunnels and bridges, travelers may have to contend with delays as a result of landslides, derailments, or maintenance projects. Traveling in this region requires some flexibility and patience. In case of a major service interruption, you can travel on a highway that parallels the railway from Chihuahua as far as Divisadero. A rougher road goes all the way to Cerocahui, but the final stretch from Cerocahui to El Fuerte is not much of an option because it requires four-wheel drive.

**BUYING A TICKET** The train offers no kind of rail pass; you must buy a ticket for a particular day, point of departure, and destination—so you must know how long you plan to stay at which stops. You'll have a reserved seat only for the first leg of your trip. After that, you'll have to take the seat the conductor finds for you. Should you deviate from your itinerary, you can buy a new ticket at the local station; if it's not during the high season, you'll most likely have a seat. The cost of a ticket for the entire trip one-way is $115.

Outside Mexico, the only way to buy train tickets by themselves, not as part of a package, is to call a specialized travel agency in Chihuahua or Los Mochis. It's easy; you can order over the phone and pay when you get there. To start out in Chihuahua, contact **Turismo al Mar** (✆ **614/410-9232** or 614/416-5950; www.copper-canyon.net); from Los Mochis, contact **Viajes Araceli** (✆ **668/815-5780;** fax 668/815-8787; ventasaracely@viajearacely.com) or **Viajes Flamingo** (✆ **668/812-1613;** fax 668/812-0046; www.mexicoscoppercanyon.com). Travel agencies outside of Mexico sell tickets only as part of a package that includes transportation to the region and hotel accommodations.

---

**Tips** **Going Solo: Not a Good Idea**

Whether you go by foot, horseback, bus, or guided tour, if you're planning to do any strenuous hiking, rock climbing, or adventuring in the Copper Canyon, I strongly recommend that you take along someone who knows the area. You'll be in the wilderness, and you can't count on anyone to come along and rescue you should an accident occur.

---

## The Copper Canyon

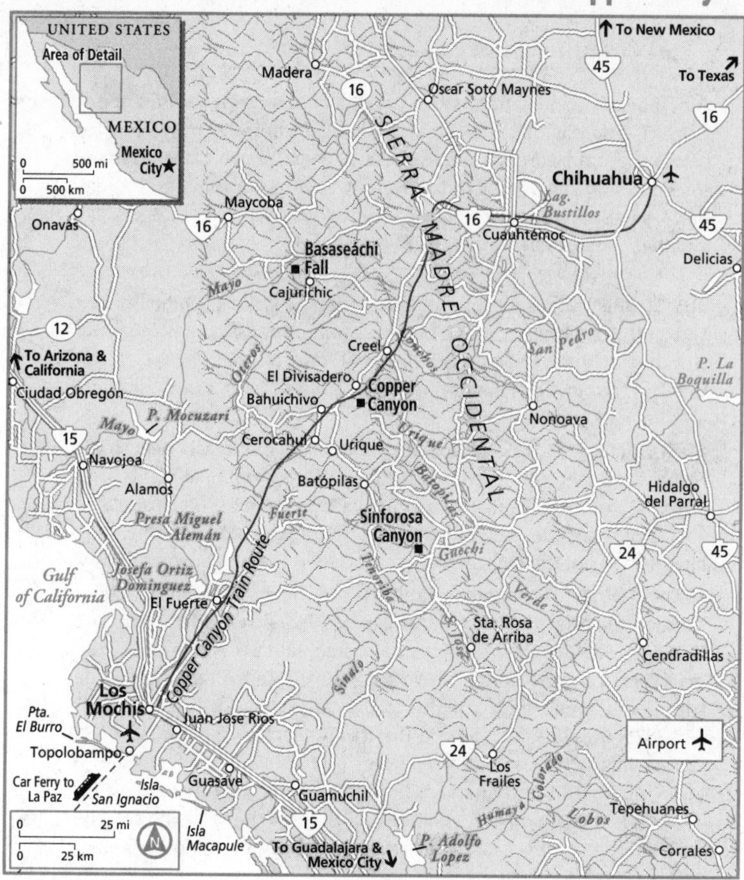


A wide variety of packages and custom trips are available. Look into these carefully before you book (see "Choosing a Package or Tour Operator," below).

**LODGING** If you spend a night at any spot en route, you'll have roughly 24 hours to explore, unless you're heading back in the direction you came. Drivers from all canyon hotels wait for the trains to come in; if you don't have a reservation, ask a driver about room availability. Standard accommodations in the canyon are getting more expensive, especially in Divisadero and Cerocahui. In high season, I wouldn't arrive at either place without reservations. Rates for hotels in both of these towns usually include meals. The number of rooms is limited, and with groups of 40 or 50 people going through the Sierra, a hotel can be empty one day and full the next. When hotels are full, you'll notice a decline in service in the dining room, or you'll have to wait in line at the buffet even if you're not part of the group. Overbooking rooms also seems to be a problem with some of the large hotels, though it's not common enough that you should worry about it.

In Creel, you find the greatest variety of accommodations and restaurants. This is where most of the economical hotels are.

## Tips Choosing a Package or Tour Operator

A number of tour operators and packagers book trips to the Copper Canyon. You can purchase your package through a travel agency (those that do frequent business with Copper Canyon trips have better knowledge of what's out there). Keep in mind the travel agent may try to steer you toward one package over another because it pays a higher commission.

The industry breaks down into the following categories:

**BUS TOURS** Some outfits run buses from El Paso to Chihuahua or Tucson to Los Mochis, then put their customers on the train. The usual length of stay in the Sierra is 2 nights before returning by bus to the U.S. This tour involves a lot of sitting on a bus or train, but these tours are the least expensive.

**BOAT/CANYON TOURS** Cruise ships dock at Topolobampo, next to Los Mochis, and send customers into the canyon for a couple of nights, usually to Barrancas/Divisadero. There have been some problems with a couple of the cruise lines; talk to your travel agent about whether they have ironed out the bugs before you decide to see the canyon this way.

**TRAIN TOURS** A couple of outfits run their own deluxe trains through the canyon. **Sierra Madre Express,** P.O. Box 26381, Tucson, AZ 85726 (✆ **800/666-0346**), runs its train, complete with dining and Pullman cars, from the border down through the canyon and back. The trip takes a week, with 2 nights in the canyon. **Tauck Tours** (✆ **800/468-2825**) uses this train as well. **The Train Collection** (✆ **281/866-9200;** www.thetraincollection.com) operates a private train a few times a year. You board the train in Los Mochis, and it stops in Divisadero for 2 nights before going on to Chihuahua. The train has a dining car. The Train Collection also schedules trips using the regular train service.

**CLIMATE** Los Mochis and El Fuerte are warm year round. Chihuahua can be warm in summer, windy at almost any time, and freezing in winter. The canyon rim may experience freezes from November through March; the bottom of the canyon may get cool enough for a sweater. In the other half of the year, it's hot below and cool above.

## STOP 1: EL FUERTE ★

Though not in the Sierra, El Fuerte has charming cobblestone streets and handsome colonial mansions. It is also a place where ***chupacabras*** seem to be most active. The chupacabras, you might recall, made headlines a few years back when people in Puerto Rico and then in this part of Sinaloa started talking about a werewolf-like monster that attacked *cabras* (goats) and other wildlife. Guides have great fun with leg-pulling about the chupacabras, and the phenomenon has sparked the creation of some very ugly T-shirts.

El Fuerte is the prettiest town along the train route, well worth visiting for at least a night. Only 79m (260 ft.) above sea level, it is most comfortable in winter. The town owes its origin to silver mining, and its existence in recent times to successful agriculture. From the late 18th century onward, the town has been under the control of a few families, and to this day, much of the real estate in

**STANDARD PACKAGES** This option merely bundles airfare, train tickets, and lodging. Hotels in the canyon send drivers to meet the train, so getting to your hotel is not hard once you're in the canyon. With these tours, you can have more time in the canyon, but once you're there, it's up to you to line up activities.

**CUSTOM TOUR OPERATORS** These outfits sell fixed package tours through travel agents only because it simplifies the agent's job. If you eliminate the middle person and call any of the outfits directly, you might be able to arrange a custom trip. Travel through these companies generally allows you more time in the canyon and a better experience. Some assemble small groups with a guide; some allow you to travel by yourself and supply you with contacts in different locations. As the number of people visiting the Sierra increases, these companies are taking people deeper into the mountains to get away from the effects of mass tourism. The best of the bunch is **Columbus Travel,** 900 Ridge Creek Lane, Bulverde, TX 78163-2872 (✆ **800/843-1060;** www.canyontravel.com). Columbus is pretty much in a class by itself. It has lined up some beautiful small lodges in the canyons and in El Fuerte and staffed them with talented local guides. Columbus also offers a lot of flexibility, and it takes responsibility for the people it sends into the Sierra, responding quickly to problems.

Other operators that provide good service are **The California Native,** 6701 W. 87th Place, Los Angeles, CA 90045 (✆ **800/926-1140;** www.calnative.com), and **Native Trails,** 613 Queretaro, El Paso, TX 79912-2210 (✆ **800/884-3107;** www.nativetrails.com).

and about the center of town remains in their hands. The town has a beautiful plaza with a bandstand, and historic houses. One way to see the town is to take a taxi from Los Mochis and pick up the train the next day. An added advantage to this plan is that it allows you an extra hour in bed. The train station is a few kilometers from town.

**EXPLORING THE TOWN** Possible activities include visiting nearby villages, birding, fishing for black bass and trout, and hunting for duck and dove. Hotels can arrange guides and all equipment if notified in advance.

### WHERE TO STAY & DINE

Besides the restaurants at the hotels mentioned here, there are inexpensive restaurants on and near the central plaza.

**El Fuerte Lodge** ★ Owner Robert Brand and his wife have taken one of the oldest homes in El Fuerte and turned it into a charming inn loaded with character. All 31 rooms have double or king beds, tiled bathrooms, and colonial furnishings. It usually books up with large tour groups for most of the high season. The restaurant menu includes plenty of dishes for those not yet accustomed to Mexican food, and is said to be the best in town. The gift shop and gallery has

*Tips* **Money Changing: Be Prepared**

Be sure to start the journey with adequate funds, since exchanging money outside of Creel is almost impossible; even credit cards are only good at the expensive hotels. (I won't use a credit card at some of the hotels listed in this chapter because they use radio communication to the main office to confirm a card—hardly a secure system.)

a wonderful display of paintings of the area and a great selection of *Casas Grandes* pottery.

Montesclaro 37, 81820 El Fuerte, Sin. ✆ **698/893-0226.** 31 units. $110 double. MC, V. **Amenities:** Restaurant, bar; tour info. *In room:* A/C.

**Hotel Posada Hidalgo** This is another good-looking hotel in the middle of town that has largely been taken over by tour groups for most of the year. The mansion section, with open arcades around a central patio, belonged to silver barons in the 18th century; there's even a steep carriage ramp from its days as a stagecoach stop. These rooms have high ceilings and hardwood floors, and they're less affected by the hotel's late-night disco. In the newer section, rooms are similarly decorated and have two double beds; all open onto a shady courtyard with covered walkway. Meals at the hotel restaurant are expensive.

Hidalgo 101, 81820 El Fuerte, Sin. ✆ **800/896-8196** from the U.S. (to the Hotel Santa Anita in Los Mochis) or ✆ and fax 698/893-1194 in El Fuerte. 51 units. $140 double. AE, MC, V. **Amenities:** Restaurant, bar; tour info. *In room:* A/C.

**Rio Vista Lodge** *Finds* Owner Chal Gámez has done it his way in this small hotel on a hill atop the town. The common areas and rooms are decorated with fanciful murals, artifacts of Yaqui and Maya Indians, decorations from southern Mexico, and a few things reminiscent of the Old West, making it a fun place to stay. The outdoor dining area is a lovely place to gaze out over the river or watch the swarms of hummingbirds that feast at Chal's feeders. These birds seem little bothered by the proximity of humans—you can even put your hand under the feeder and be fanned by their wings. Meals are simple but good. Chal is the best guide in the area and very knowledgeable about the local wildlife.

Cerro de la Pilas s/n, 81820 El Fuerte, Sin. ✆ and fax **698/893-0413.** 8 units. $55 double. No credit cards. *In room:* A/C.

## STOP 2: BAHUICHIVO & CEROCAHUI ★★★

This is the first train stop in canyon country. **Bahuichivo** is merely the train depot and did not exist before the train's construction. The village of **Cerocahui** (elevation 1,667m/5,550 ft.) was around before and during the colonial period. It's home to 600 people and is in a valley about 10km (6 miles) from the train stop. The road is unpaved, so the trip takes about 30 minutes.

**EXPLORING CEROCAHUI** Built around a sweet-looking mission church, Cerocahui consists of little more than rambling unpaved streets and 100 or so houses. There is a wonderful view of the mountains, but you have to take an excursion to get real canyon vistas. All three hotels can arrange horseback rides to the falls and other spots, as well as trips by Suburban to **Cerro Gallego,** a famous lookout point with a beautiful vista of Urique canyon. It's possible to see the waterfall on arrival, schedule the Gallego trip for the next morning, have lunch, and still make the train, but I like the quiet of Cerocahui and recommend staying here as long as you can, provided you like hiking or horseback riding. There are a number of secluded places, both near and far, to visit. One possible trip is a hike down to the mining town of **Urique** at the bottom of the Urique Canyon (one of several canyons that make up the Copper Canyon), then a car ride back up. The **Paraíso del Oso** offers a horseback ride to Urique; you overnight en route and ride back in a Suburban the next day.

### WHERE TO STAY & DINE

Rates for doubles in the two hotels listed below include all meals for two people and transportation to and from the train station. The Paraíso del Oso is about a mile short of the village. The Misión is in Cerocahui proper. In the town, you can find some simple lodging, but options are limited.

**Hotel Misión Cerocahui** Established years ago in the village of Cerocahui, the Hotel Misión is right on the town's little plaza. Guest rooms have hot water and electricity until 11pm. The lobby and restaurant area surrounds a large rock fireplace where a local guitarist and singer sometimes entertain in the evenings. The food is usually good, and the ranch-style rooms (with tile floors, wood-burning stoves, and kerosene lanterns) are comfortable. The hotel's generator provides electricity for a couple of hours in the mornings and evenings. Like the others, this hotel offers several tours, including rides to Cerro Gallego, Urique, and the local waterfalls. There are also hiking, mountain biking, and horseback riding trips.

Cerocahui. Dom. Conocido. No phone. (Reservations: Hotel Santa Anita, Apdo. Postal 159, 81200 Los Mochis, Sin.; ✆ **800/896-8196** from the U.S.) 38 units. $270 double. Rates include meals. AE, MC, V. **Amenities:** Restaurant; transportation to and from train station.

**Paraíso del Oso** ★ *Moments* Opened in 1990, Paraíso del Oso sits in a sheltered hollow with a backdrop of impressive stone palisades a mile from the town. Owner Doug Rhodes is an avid horseman and takes guests for rides that can last anywhere from 3 hours to more than a week. Rooms come with two double beds and ranch furniture. They are comfortable, kept warm with wood-burning stoves, and there's plenty of hot water. Solar-generated electricity fuels such vital services as refrigeration, while lanterns provide light. This and the utter solitude of the area are charming traits that make you feel more in touch with the Sierra than the big canyon hotels along the railroad tracks do. There is a cash bar, a small but good library (with both novels and books on Mexican history), and topographical maps of the area.

Cerocahui. ✆ **800/884-3107** or 915/833-3107 (both in the U.S.), or ✆ and fax 614/421-3372 in Chihuahua. www.mexicohorse.com. (Reservations: Paraíso del Oso, P.O. Box 31089, El Paso, TX 79931.) 21 units. $155 double. Rates include meals. MC, V. **Amenities:** Bar; transportation to and from train station.

## STOPS 3 & 4: BARRANCAS/EL DIVISADERO ★★

Between Bahuichivo and here, the train stops at San Rafael to change crews. By the time it arrives in this area, it is at the highest part of its journey. Almost all packages include at least a night here for soaking up the great views of the canyons. Two nights would be better if you want to do some hiking or horseback riding.

Barrancas and Divisadero are less than 3km (2 miles) apart. Coming from Los Mochis, you'll arrive at Barrancas first. At this stop, drivers from the **Posada Barrancas Mirador,** the **Posada Barrancas Rancho,** and the **Mansión Tarahumara** meet passengers. Then the train takes you to **El Divisadero** (elevation 2,242m/7,400 ft.), where you'll find the **Hotel Cabañas Divisadero-Barrancas,** taco stands (at train time), and the most **spectacular view of the canyon** that you'll get if you are making no overnight stops. The train stops for 15 minutes—time enough to walk down the steps to the lookout to enjoy the view and purchase one or two mementos from the Tarahumara Indians who sell sweet-smelling pine needle baskets, homemade violins, and wood and cloth dolls. Hotels arrange various excursions, including a visit to a cave-dwelling Tarahumara family, hiking, and horseback riding.

## WHERE TO STAY & DINE

**Hotel Cabañas Divisadero-Barrancas** ★ This location, on the edge of the canyon overlook, provides the most spectacular view of any hotel in the canyon. As might be expected, the hotel often fills with tour groups. The restaurant has a large picture window, perfect for hours of sitting and gazing at the canyon. The rustic rooms are well appointed, with foot-loomed, brightly colored bedspreads and matching curtains, two double beds, a fireplace, and 24-hour electricity. About half of the rooms offer a view of the canyon.

El Divisadero. ✆ **635/578-3060.** www.hoteldivisadero.com.mx. (Reservations: Av. Mirador 4516, Apdo. Postal 661, Col. Residencial Campestre, 31238 Chihuahua, Chih.; ✆ **614/415-1199;** fax 614/415-6575.) 48 units. $210 double. Rates include meals. Ask about low-season discounts. AE, MC, V (in Chihuahua). **Amenities:** Restaurant, bar; tour info; transportation to and from train station.

**Hotel Posada Barrancas Mirador** ★ *Moments* The Mirador sits on the edge of the canyon 5 minutes up the mountain from its sister hotel, the Rancho (see below). Every room has a dramatic balcony that seems to hang right over the cliff's edge. The views are beautiful. Rooms have attractive decorations and furniture, with bold Mexican color combinations, and most come with two double beds. Each room has its own heater. The common areas are also comfortable and attractive.

El Divisadero. ✆ **635/578-3020.** (Reservations: Hotel Santa Anita, Apdo. Postal 159, 81200 Los Mochis, Sin.; ✆ **800/896-8196** from the U.S.) 50 units. $270 double. Rates include meals. AE, MC, V. **Amenities:** Restaurant, bar; tour info; transportation to and from train station.

**Hotel Posada Barrancas Rancho** The train stops right in front of this inn. Rooms are comfortable, with two double beds and a wood-burning iron stove. Like those in other lodges, meals are a communal affair in the cozy living and restaurant area, and the food is good. You can rent horses or hike to the Tarahumara caves and to the rim of the canyon, where a more expensive sister hotel, the Barrancas Mirador (see above), has a beautiful restaurant and bar with a magnificent view. This hotel sometimes accommodates overbooking at its sister hotel.

El Divisadero. ✆ **635/578-3020.** (Reservations: Hotel Santa Anita, Apdo. Postal 159, 81200 Los Mochis, Sin.; ✆ **800/896-8196** from the U.S.) 33 units. $250 double. Rates include meals. AE, MC, V. **Amenities:** Restaurant, bar; transportation to and from train station.

**Mansión Tarahumara** The Mansión Tarahumara spreads across a mountainside above the train stop at Posada Barrancas. The setting is lovely. The cabin rooms offer more privacy and space than the hotel rooms, but not direct views of the canyon. Made of stone and wood, each room has a big fireplace, a wall heater, and two double beds. The castle-like structure, which is the first thing that catches the guest's eye, houses the restaurant and bar. It offers lovely views from its big windows and good food from its kitchen.

El Divisadero. ✆ **635/578-3030.** (Reservations: Mansion Tarahumara, Calle Juárez 1602-A, Col. Centro, 31000 Chihuahua, Chih.; ✆ **614/415-4721;** fax 614/416-5444; www.online.com.mx/plaza/mansion.) 48 units. $170 double. Rates include meals. AE, MC, V. **Amenities:** Restaurant, bar; heated pool; Jacuzzi; tours; transportation to and from train station.

## STOP 5: CREEL ★★

This rustic logging town with a handful of paved streets offers the most economical lodgings in the canyon, as well as some of the best side trips, especially hiking and overnight camping.

### ESSENTIALS

**GETTING THERE & DEPARTING** **By Train** See the chart on p. 642 for "official" arrival and departure times.

**By Car** From Chihuahua, follow the signs to La Junta until you see signs for Hermosillo. Follow those signs until you see signs to Creel (left). The trip takes about 4 hours on a paved road.

**By Bus** **Estrella Blanca** (© **635/456-0073**), next to the Hotel Korachi, has six trips to Chihuahua per day. The trip takes 4 hours and costs $15.

**ORIENTATION** The train station, around the corner from the Mission Store and the main plaza, is in the heart of the village and within walking distance of all lodgings except the Copper Canyon Sierra Lodge. Look for your hotel's van waiting at the station (unless you're staying at the Casa de Huéspedes Margarita, which is only 2 blocks away). There's one main street, **López Mateos,** and almost everything is within a couple of blocks.

**FAST FACTS** The telephone **area code** is **635. Electricity** is available 24 hours daily in all Creel hotels. Creel has one ATM, one bank, and one *casa de cambio.* The best sources of **information** are the Mission Store and the hotels. Several businesses and many of the hotels offer long-distance **telephone** service; look for LARGA DISTANCIA signs or ask at your hotel. Creel sits at an **elevation** of 2,212m (7,300 ft.) and has a **population** of around 6,000. It's the largest town in the canyon area.

### EXPLORING CREEL

You'll occasionally see the Tarahumara as you walk around town, but mostly, you'll see rugged logging types and tourists from around the world.

Several stores around Creel sell Tarahumara arts and crafts. The best is **Artesanías Misión** (Mission Crafts), which sells quality merchandise at reasonable prices; all profits go to the Mission Hospital run by Father Verplancken, a Jesuit, and benefit the Tarahumara. Here you'll find dolls, pottery, woven purses and belts, drums, violins (an instrument borrowed from the Spanish), bamboo flutes, bead necklaces, bows and arrows, cassettes of Tarahumara music, woodcarvings, baskets, and heavy wool rugs, as well as an excellent supply of books and maps relating to the Tarahumara and the region. Open daily from 9:30am to 1pm, and Monday through Saturday from 3 to 6pm. It's beside the railroad tracks on the main plaza.

### NEARBY EXCURSIONS

Close by are several canyons, waterfalls, a lake, hot springs, Tarahumara villages and cave dwellings, and an old Jesuit mission. Ten kilometers (6 miles) north of town is an ecotourism complex, **San Ignacio de Arareko** (© **635/456-0126**). It has a lake, hiking and biking trails, horses, cabins, and a craft shop, all run by indigenous peoples of the *ejido* (cooperative)—a change from the *mestizo* population's almost total control of tourism in Mexico. **Batopilas,** a fascinating 18th-century silver-mining village at the bottom of the canyon, requires an overnight jaunt. You can ask for information about these and other things to do at your hotel.

**Tips** **Caution: Don't Be a Dope**

It's no secret that marijuana farmers use clandestine farmlands in the Copper Canyon, and that prominent names in the state are rumored to be linked to their activities. This has never affected any of my trips to the region. If you are hiking the backwoods and happen upon a field of marijuana, simply leave the area.

From Creel, you can drive to **El Divisadero** (see "Stops 3 & 4: Barrancas/El Divisadero," above, for details) on the newly paved road. The trip takes about an hour.

**ORGANIZED TOURS** Hotels offer 2- to 10-hour organized tours that cost $15 to $90 per person (four people minimum). The **Hotel Nuevo** and **Casa de Huéspedes Margarita** offer the most economical tours in town but not always the most available. All tour availability depends on whether a group can be assembled; your best chance is at the **Plaza Mexicana** or the **Parador de la Montaña.**

**BASASEACHIC FALLS** This is an exhausting day tour to what is billed as the tallest single cascade in North America. The best time to go is during the rainy season, from July to September. The tour costs around $30 per person and takes about 11 hours. Driving time is 4 hours one-way, and the strenuous hike to the bottom and back up takes 3 hours—not a lot of time to be by the falls. Another option is to stay in one of the simple accommodations that have opened near the falls, if you can get transportation back the next day. Ask around Creel.

**BATOPILAS** You can make an overnight side trip from Creel to the old silver-mining town of Batopilas, founded in 1708. It's 7 to 9 hours from Creel by town bus, 5 hours by sport utility vehicle, along a narrow, winding dirt road through some of the most spectacular scenery in the Copper Canyon. In Batopilas, which lies beside a river at the bottom of a deep canyon, the weather is tropical, though it can get cool in the evenings. You can visit a beautiful little church and do several walks, including one to **Misión Satevó** (a ruined mission church that dates from the early 18th c.). The place has many colorful little details: The dry-goods store has the original shelving and cash register, cobblestone streets twist past whitewashed homes, miners and ranchers come and go on horseback, and the Tarahumara frequently visit. A considerable number of pigs, dogs, and flocks of goats roam at will—this is, after all, Chihuahua's goat-raising capital.

**Getting to Batopilas** From Creel, take the **bus** from the Restaurant Herradero, López Mateos s/n, three doors past the turnoff to Hotel Plaza Mexicana. It goes to Batopilas on Tuesday, Thursday, and Saturday, leaving Creel at 7am and arriving midafternoon. Tickets are sold at the restaurant. Several Suburban-type **vans** offer transportation. One leaves on Monday, Wednesday, and Friday at 10:30am and arrives midafternoon. Both bus and van return the following day. There are no bathrooms, restaurants, or other conveniences of civilization along the way, but the bus may stop to allow passengers to stretch and find a bush.

**Where to Stay & Dine in Batopilas** Batopilas has a few little restaurants and inns. There are no telephones, though, so don't expect to make firm reservations. One night probably isn't enough for a stay here, since you arrive midafternoon and must leave at 7am or 10:30am the next day.

The staff at the Parador de la Montaña in Creel provides information about vacancies at the basic, comfortable, 10-room **Hotel Mary** (formerly Parador Batopilas). All rooms have private bathrooms and cost around $16 double per night. There are also the rustic **Hotel Batopilas** and **Hotel Las Palmeras,** with five or six rooms each; if all else fails, you can probably find a family willing to let you stay in an extra room. There are two fancy hotels in town. One is operated by **Copper Canyon Lodges,** which takes you to Batopilas for a few nights' stay in a beautiful old mansion and returns you to their great lodge outside of Creel (see "Where to Stay," below). The other is **Hacienda San Miguel,** a completely refurbished house that belonged to the son of the owner of the mine in Batopilas. It has only recently opened and was still being rebuilt the last time I was there, but it looked very interesting. It's by the mouth of the mine, right on the river. **Columbus Travel** (see the box "Choosing a Package or Tour Operator," earlier) uses it for some of its tours. If you're not traveling with Columbus but you're interested in staying at this place, inquire at the **Plaza Mexicana Hotel** in Creel (see, "Where to Stay," below).

Restaurants in Batopilas are informal, so bring along some snacks and bottled water to tide you over; some snacks are available at the general store. The place to eat in Batopilas is **Doña Mica's,** facing a little plaza tucked behind the main square. Ask anyone for directions (everyone knows her). She serves meals on her front porch surrounded by plants, but it's best to let her know in advance when to expect you. On short notice, she can probably rustle up some scrambled eggs.

## WHERE TO STAY

Though a small town, Creel has several places to stay. A lot of these cater to backpackers. It's advisable to make reservations during high season.

### Expensive

**Best Western The Lodge at Creel** Each of the hotel's cheerfully decorated cabins holds four units, built completely of pine—flooring, wall paneling, ceiling, and furniture. Some have their own porches. Their construction, decor, and layout remind me of old-style motels that you might find on the fringes of a U.S. national park. The lobby, next to the dining area, has a phone for guests' use and a small gift shop. The hotel offers 3-night backpacking trips to the bottom of the canyon, among other tours, for 4 to 10 people. The on-site restaurant serves all three meals. The van meets all trains.

Av. López Mateos 61, 33200 Creel, Chih. ✆ **888/879-4071** in the U.S.; 635/456-0071. Fax 635/456-0082. 29 units. $122 double. AE, MC, V. **Amenities:** Restaurant, bar; room service; laundry service; tours to various sites. *In room:* TV, coffeemaker.

### Moderate

**Copper Canyon Sierra Lodge** ★★ *Finds* About 20 minutes (22km/14 miles) southwest of Creel, the Sierra Lodge has everything you hope for in a mountain lodge—rock walls, beamed ceilings, lantern lights, and wood-burning stoves; in other words, rustic charm and no electricity. Its out-of-town location is a great starting point for guided or self-guided hikes and walks in the mountains to the Cusárare Waterfalls, cave paintings, and the present-day Tarahumara cave dwellings.

Apdo. Postal 3, 33200 Creel, Chih. ✆ **800/776-3942** in the U.S. Fax (in Creel) 635/456-0036. www.sierratrail.com. 18 units. $50 per person. Rates include meals. No credit cards.

**Hotel Nuevo** The Nuevo has two sections: the older one, across the tracks from the train station and next to the restaurant and variety store, and newer log cabañas in back. Rooms are small to medium size and not as attractive as the higher-priced (and carpeted) cabañas. Half the rooms have TVs. The nice hotel restaurant is open from 8:30am to 8pm, and the small general store carries local crafts as well as basic supplies. Ask at the store about rooms.

Francisco Villa 121, 33200 Creel, Chih. ✆ **635/456-0022.** Fax 635/456-0043. 27 units. $35–$85 double. MC, V. Free parking. **Amenities:** Restaurant; general store. *In room:* Heater or fireplace.

**Motel Parador de la Montaña** This is the largest hotel in town, located 4 blocks west of the plaza. The comfortable rooms have two double beds, high wood-beamed ceilings, central heating, tiled bathroom, and thin walls. Guests congregate in the restaurant, bar, and lobby, which has a roaring fireplace. The hotel caters to groups and offers some 10 overland tours, priced from **$10 to** $60.

Av. López Mateos s/n, 33200 Creel, Chih. ✆ **635/456-0075.** Fax 635/456-0085. (Reservations: **Calle** Allende 1414, 31300 Chihuahua, Chih.; ✆ **614/410-4580**; fax 635/415-3468.) 50 units. $75 double. AE, MC, V. Free secured parking. **Amenities:** Restaurant, bar; tours to various sites.

### Inexpensive

**Casa de Huéspedes Margarita** With its youth-hostel atmosphere, this white house (with no sign) between the two churches on the main plaza is the most popular spot in town with international backpacking, student, and minimal-budget travelers. Yet it's also one of the cleanest hotels in the region. Rooms have pine details and tile floors, and are decorated with frilly curtains and spreads. There is plenty of hot water and gas heat in each room. Breakfasts and suppers are taken family-style around a big dining table. Non-guests can eat here, too, for $2.50—just let the staff know in advance. Margarita is a good source of information about the area and does all she can to help budget travelers enjoy their stays.

Av. López Mateos 11, 33200 Creel, Chih. ✆ and fax **635/456-0045.** 27 units (17 with bathroom). $5 sleeping bag space (10 spaces); $8 share in 4-bed dormitory; $32 private double or cabaña. Rates include breakfast and dinner. No credit cards.

**Margarita's Plaza Mexicana** This is a slightly upscale version of the Casa de Huéspedes Margarita. The rooms are gaily furnished with wood chairs, dressers from Michoacán, and paintings of Tarahumara scenes. Gas wall heaters and carpeting make the rooms comfortable in the cold. A mural depicting Semana Santa celebrations covers one wall of the large dining room, where guests take breakfast and dinner. The food is good. Vegetables and salads are prepared with purified water.

Calle Chapultepec s/n, 33200 Creel, Chih. ✆ and fax **635/456-0245.** 26 units. $50 double. Rates include any 2 meals. No credit cards. Free parking. **Amenities:** Restaurant, bar; tour information. From the plaza, go 2 blocks west on López Mateos, then ½ block south on Chapultepec. Or just ask anyone.

### WHERE TO DINE

There are several eating establishments in Creel, but none stand out particularly. Aside from the restaurants at Margarita's Casa de Huéspedes and the Parador de la Montaña, you might want to try one of the restaurants on López Mateos, such as the **Caballo Bayo, Tio Molcas,** or **Verónica's.**

## 2 Los Mochis: The Western Terminus

202km (126 miles) SW of Alamos; 80km (50 miles) SW of El Fuerte; 309km (193 miles) SE of Guaymas; 416km (260 miles) NW of Mazatlán

Los Mochis, in Sinaloa State, is a coastal city of 350,000 founded in 1893 by Benjamin Johnson of Pennsylvania. It is a wealthy city in a fertile agricultural area but holds little of interest for the visitor. The most important aspects of the city are that it is a boarding point for the train, it has an airport, and it is connected to La Paz, Baja California, by ferry, and to the U.S. border by highway.

## ESSENTIALS

**GETTING THERE & DEPARTING** **By Plane** **Aeromexico/Aerolitoral** (© **800/237-6639** in the U.S., or 668/815-2570 for reservations) has direct service from Phoenix, Chihuahua, Hermosillo, Mazatlán, and La Paz. **Aero California** (© **800/237-6225** in the U.S., or 668/815-2250) flies to and from Tucson, Los Angeles, La Paz, Guadalajara, Mexico City, Culiacán, and Tijuana.

*Arriving:* The airport is 21km (13 miles) north of town; transportation is by *combi* (collective minivan) or airport taxi ($10).

**By Train** The **Chihuahua al Pacífico** (Copper Canyon train) runs between Los Mochis and Chihuahua once daily, departing at 6am. First-class fare is $115.

**By Car** **Coastal Highway 15** is well maintained in both directions leading into Los Mochis.

**By Ferry** The **SEMATUR ferry** from La Paz, Baja California Sur, to Los Mochis (actually the port of Topolobampo) leaves at 10pm and arrives at 8am (except Sun, when it travels from 1–11pm). The ferry in the other direction has the same schedule. Transporting a car costs $180, plus $20 per person. Your ticket reserves a seat for you; during the busiest times, cabins may be available. For reservations and tickets, call **Viajes Ahome,** Morelos 329 Pte., at Gabriel Leyva (© **668/815-6120** or 668/818-6382).

**By Bus** Buses serve Los Mochis, however marginally. Most are *de paso*—passing through. All bus stations are downtown, within walking distance of the hotels. The first-class station is near Juárez at Degollado 200. From here, **Elite** buses go to and from Tijuana, Monterrey, Nogales, and Ciudad Juárez. **Autotransportes Transpacíficos,** in the same station, serves Nogales, Tijuana, Mazatlán, Guadalajara, Querétaro, and Mexico City. A lot of travelers who arrive in Los Mochis prefer to go directly to El Fuerte, spend the night there, then catch the train. There are two places to catch the bus to El Fuerte (1½–2 hr.). The first is at the **Mercado Independencia;** the bus stops at the corner of Independencia and Degollado. The other is at the corner of Cuauhtémoc and Prieto, close to the Hotel America. Ask hotel desk clerks or the tourism office for a schedule. These are second-class buses, which stop frequently, prolonging the trip well beyond the normal 1-hour travel time.

**CITY LAYOUT** Los Mochis contains no central plaza, and streets run northwest to southeast and southwest to northeast. The **Hotel Santa Anita** (Av. Leyva at Av. Obregón) is the reference point for giving directions to restaurants and hotels, which are all within a few blocks.

**FAST FACTS** The local **American Express** representative is **Viajes Araceli,** Avenida Alvaro Obregón 471-A Pte. (© **668/815-5780;** fax 668/815-8787). The telephone **area code** for Los Mochis is **668. Changing money** outside of Los Mochis is difficult, so stock up on pesos before boarding the train. Most places in the canyons do not accept credit cards.

## EXPLORING LOS MOCHIS

For most travelers, Los Mochis is a stopover en route to somewhere else. There isn't much here, but the town is pleasant, and you can enjoy some of the best seafood in Mexico.

The **Viajes Flamingo** travel agency, on the ground floor of the Hotel Santa Anita (✆ **668/812-1613** or 668/812-1929), arranges a city tour, hunting and fishing trips, and boat rides around **Topolobampo Bay.** It's open Monday through Saturday from 8:30am to 1pm and 3 to 6:30pm. The boat ride is really just a spin in the bay and not especially noteworthy, although the bay is pretty and dolphins have been known to surface.

## WHERE TO STAY

**Hotel América** Rooms here have tile floors and large windows facing the street (get one that doesn't face Allende, a very noisy street). On the second floor, there's a sitting area, purified water, and an ice-making machine. To get here from the Hotel Santa Anita, turn right out the front door. Turn left on Obregón, continue 3 blocks and go right on Allende for 2 blocks; the hotel is just past Cuauhtémoc on your left.

Allende 655 Sur, 81200 Los Mochis, Sin. ✆ **668/812-1355** or 668/812-1356. Fax 668/812-5983. 48 units. $40 double. MC, V. Free enclosed parking. **Amenities:** Restaurant. *In room:* A/C, TV.

**Hotel Corintios** Behind a campy entrance with Greek columns are two stories of rooms with ample light, carpeted floors, and adequate space for two comfortable double beds and luggage. The bathrooms have marble tub/showers, large towels, and purified tap water. The small restaurant (open from 7am–10pm) serves the continental breakfast included in the room rate. For those catching the train to Chihuahua, fruit, juice, and coffee are available before you catch your cab at 5:15am.

Obregón 580 Pte., 81200 Los Mochis, Sin. ✆ **668/818-2300** or 01-800-690-3000 in Mexico. Fax 668/818-2277. 42 units. $80 double. Rates include continental breakfast. AE, MC, V. Free parking. **Amenities:** Restaurant; room service; laundry service. *In room:* A/C, TV.

**Hotel Santa Anita** The Santa Anita is the choice of most going to the canyon; not only is it a comfortable, quiet hotel, but it offers reliable transportation to and from the train station, so you don't have to bother with taxis. The rooms are modern and well furnished but vary a good deal in size. All are carpeted and have comfortable beds, color TVs with U.S. channels, and tap water purified for drinking. The hotel's popular restaurant is just off the lobby. There are two bars, one with live music at least1day a week.

Leyva, at the corner of Hidalgo (Apdo. Postal 159), 81200 Los Mochis, Sin. ✆ **800/896-8196** from the U.S. ✆ and fax 668/818-7046. 119 units. $140 double. AE, MC, V. Free parking. **Amenities:** Restaurant, bar; transportation to and from the train station; business center; room service; same-day laundry service; non-smoking rooms. *In room:* A/C, TV.

## WHERE TO DINE

**El Farallón** ★★ SEAFOOD If you like seafood, there's no reason to eat anywhere else in Los Mochis. But don't be put off by the menu, which is confusing—to put it simply, you can order seafood cooked any way you want. Try a Mexican style such as *al ajillo,* which uses mild guajillo chiles. If you're hungry, I recommend the *mariscada* for two or more, which comes with a cold and a hot platter of a variety of fish and shellfish. Try the *calamares* (squid), the cheapest thing on the platter. Forget about those rubbery rings fried up in other restaurants; because the squid get to be giant-size in this region's waters, the meat comes in big, tender chunks. One of my favorites is *machaca,* made with either shrimp or smoked marlin (cooked in a reduced fish stock, which is mild and satisfying at the same time.) The atmosphere is casual, the air-conditioning functions with gusto, and the white-tiled dining area is simply furnished. To get here from the

Santa Anita, turn right on Leyva and right again for 1 block on Obregón. It's on your left.

Obregón, at Angel Flores. ✆ **668/812-1428.** Main courses $5–$12. AE, MC, V. Daily 8am–midnight.

**El Taquito** *Value* MEXICAN Any time of the day or night, El Taquito serves standard Mexican fare at a good price. With orange booths and Formica tables, the cafe looks like an American fast-food place. The tortilla soup comes in a large bowl, and both breakfast and main-course portions are quite generous. From the Hotel Santa Anita, turn left on Leyva, cross Hidalgo and go 1 block. It's on your right.

Leyva at Barrera. ✆ **668/812-8119.** Breakfast $3–$5; main courses $4–$8. AE, DC, MC, V. Daily 24 hr.

**Restaurante España** STEAK/SEAFOOD This Spanish-style restaurant is a favorite among downtown professionals, who feast on large plates of paella at midday. The decor is upscale for Los Mochis, with a splashing cascade fountain in the dining room and heavy, carved-wood tables and chairs. From the Hotel Santa Anita, turn right out the front door to Obregón, then right on Obregón for 1½ blocks. The restaurant is on your right.

Obregón 525 Pte. ✆ **668/812-2221.** Breakfast $4–$6; main courses $8–$10. AE, MC, V. Daily 7am–11pm.

## 3 Chihuahua: The Eastern Terminus ★

341km (213 miles) S of El Paso; 440km (275 miles) NW of Torreón

Chihuahua, a city of wide boulevards and handsome buildings, is the capital of the state of Chihuahua, the largest and richest in Mexico. The wealth comes from mining, timber, cattle raising, *maquiladoras* (assembly plants for export goods), and tourism. The city has grown a lot in the last 30 years, thanks mainly to an increase in manufacturing plants. Consequently, the city has lost its frontier feeling. But the historic center of Chihuahua retains much of its character and holds a few museums and buildings worth visiting, including the house where Pancho Villa once lived.

### ESSENTIALS

**GETTING THERE & DEPARTING** **By Plane** Continental (✆ **800/525-0280,** or 01-800/900-5000 in Mexico) has nonstop service between Houston and Chihuahua on a 50-seat jet. **Aeromexico/Aerolitoral** (✆ **614/415-6303**) fly direct from El Paso, Phoenix, Guadalajara, Hermosillo, Mexico City, Monterrey, Torreón, Tijuana, Culiacán, La Paz, and Los Mochis, with connecting flights from Los Angeles and San Antonio. **Transportes Aeropuerto** (✆ **614/420-3366**) controls minivan service from the airport ($6 per person, $10 if it's an early flight). Taxis from town charge $15 for up to four people.

**By Train** The ***Chihuahua al Pacífico*** (✆ **614/410-9059;** fax 614/416-9059) leaves Chihuahua daily for Los Mochis by way of the Copper Canyon country. (The complete train schedule and the train route appear in section 1 of this chapter.) The train is scheduled to leave at 6am daily. To get to the station in time, it's best to arrange transportation through one of the travel agencies recommended under "Canyon Arrangements" in "Fast Facts: Chihuahua," below. They pick up clients taking the train each morning.

**By Car** **Highway 45** leads south from Ciudad Juárez; **Highway 16** south from Ojinaga; and **Highway 49** north from Torreón. For the drive to Creel, see "Getting There & Departing" under "Stop 5: Creel," earlier.

**By Bus** The Central Camionera **bus station** (also called the Terminal de Autobuses) is on Avenida Juan Pablo II, 8km (5 miles) northeast of town en route to the airport. Buses leave hourly for major points inland and north and south on the coast. **Transportes Chihuahuenses,** the big local line, offers first-class service to Ciudad Juárez every half-hour; the trip takes 4 hours. **Transportes del Norte** and **Autobuses Estrella Blanca** also run buses hourly from the border through Chihuahua to points south. **Omnibus de México** has *real ejecutivo* (deluxe) service from Juárez, Mexico City, and Monterrey. **Futura/Turistar** also has deluxe service to Monterrey and Durango.

For travel to Creel, look for the **Estrella Blanca** line. Buses leave every 2 hours from 6am to 6pm. Direct buses make the trip in 4 hours.

**VISITOR INFORMATION** For basic tourist information, visit the **tourist information center** (✆ **614/410-1077** or 614/429-3300, ext. 4515 or 1061), on Libertad at Carranza in the Government Palace, just left of the altar and murals dedicated to Father Hidalgo. It's open Monday through Friday from 9am to 7pm, Saturday and Sunday from 10am to 2pm.

**CITY LAYOUT** The town center is laid out around the **Plaza Principal,** bounded by Avenidas Libertad and Victoria (which run northeast-southwest) and Avenida Independencia and Calle 4 (which run northwest-southeast). The **cathedral** is at the southwest end of the plaza, and the city offices are on the northeast end. Standing on Independencia with the cathedral on your left, odd-numbered streets and blocks will be to your right, and even-numbered streets and blocks to your left.

**GETTING AROUND** Local buses run along main arteries beginning at the central plaza. Taxis are readily available. If you want to see the sights and have only1day, take a tour (see "Exploring Chihuahua," below).

## *FAST FACTS:* Chihuahua

*American Express* The local representative is **Viajes Rojo y Casavantes,** with one agent in the Hotel San Francisco and a full office at Vicente Guerrero 1207 (✆ **614/415-4636;** fax 614/415-5384).

*Area Code* The telephone area code is **614.**

*Canyon Arrangements* If you have waited to purchase train tickets and make canyon hotel reservations, contact **Turismo al Mar,** Calle Berna 2202, Colonia Mirador, 31270 Chihuahua, Chih. (✆ **614/410-9232** or 614/416-5950; fax 614/416-6589).

*Elevation* Chihuahua sits at 1,424m (4,700 ft.).

*Emergencies* Call ✆ **060.**

*Hospital* **Clinica del Parque** is at Pedro Leal del Rosal and de la Llave ✆ **614/415-7411**). For medical emergencies, call ✆ **614/411-8141.**

*Population* Chihuahua has some 670,000 residents.

## EXPLORING CHIHUAHUA

To see all Chihuahua's sights in1day, consider taking a 3-hour city tour; English-speaking guides are available. Three recommended agencies are **Torre del Sol,** Independencia 116-2 (✆ **614/415-7380**), in the Hotel Palacio del Sol;

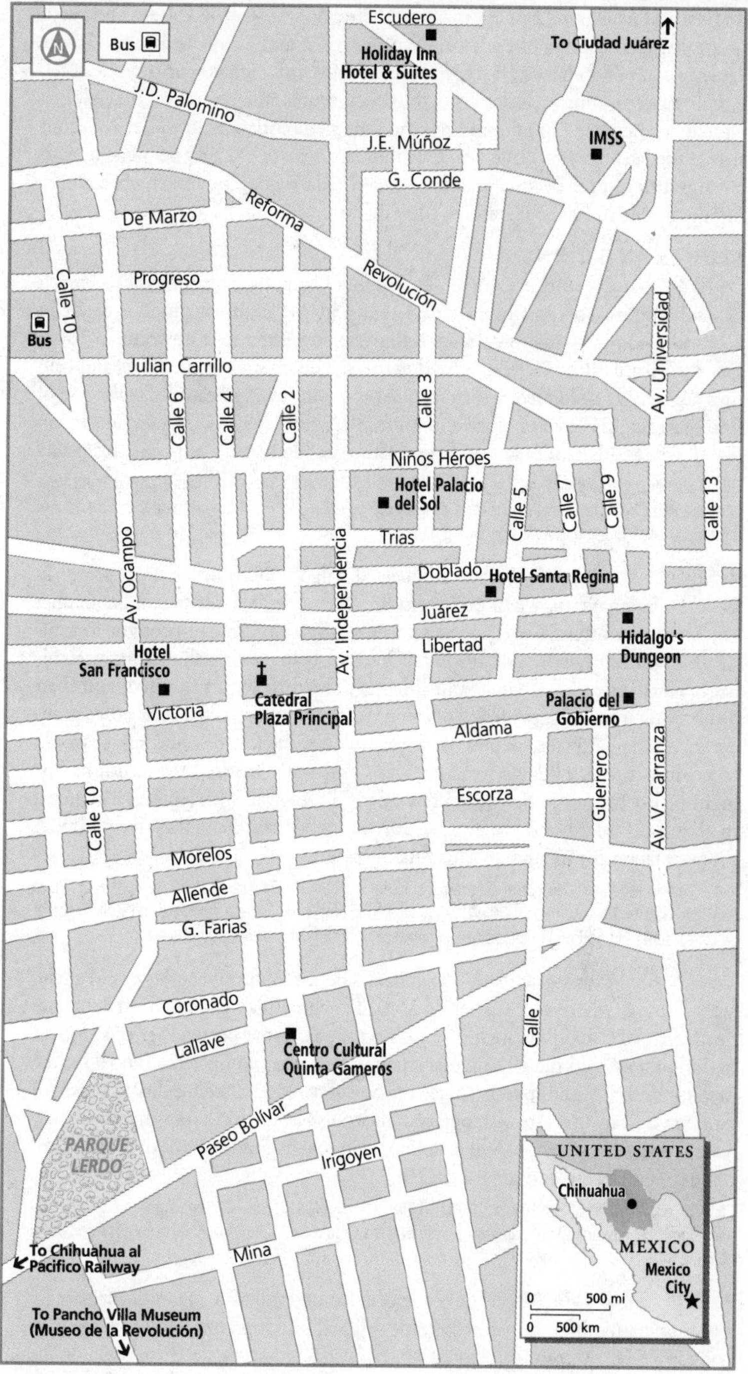
Bus
Escudero
Holiday Inn
Hotel & Suites
To Ciudad Juárez
J.D. Palomino
J.E. Múñoz
IMSS
G. Conde
De Marzo
Reforma
Revolución
Progreso
Calle 10
Bus
Av. Universidad
Julian Carrillo
Calle 6
Calle 4
Calle 2
Calle 3
Niños Héroes
Hotel Palacio
del Sol
Calle 5
Calle 7
Calle 9
Calle 13
Av. Ocampo
Av. Independencia
Trias
Doblado
Hotel Santa Regina
Juárez
Libertad
Hidalgo's
Dungeon
Hotel
San Francisco
Catedral
Plaza Principal
Victoria
Palacio del
Gobierno
Aldama
Escorza
Guerrero
Av. V. Carranza
Calle 10
Morelos
Allende
G. Farias
Coronado
Lallave
Centro Cultural
Quinta Gameros
Calle 7
Paseo Bolívar
PARQUE
LERDO
Irigoyen
Mina
To Chihuahua al
Pacifico Railway
To Pancho Villa Museum
(Museo de la Revolución)
UNITED STATES
Chihuahua
MEXICO
Mexico
City
0
500 mi
0
500 km

**Turismo al Mar** (see "Fast Facts," above); and **Viajes Rojo y Casavantes,** with one agent in the lobby of the Hotel San Francisco and a larger office at Vicente Guerrero 1207 (✆ **614/415-4636**). Any of these will pick you up at your hotel. A half-day city tour includes visits to the museums, the churches, the colonial aqueduct, the state capital building, the state penitentiary, and more. A 7-hour trip to the Mennonite village near Cuauhtémoc costs about $35 per person, with a minimum of four people. Unless you have a particular interest in cheesemaking or the Mennonites, it's not worth your time.

## SIGHTS IN TOWN

**Centro Cultural Universitaria** ★ Quinta Gameros is a neoclassical, French Second Empire–style mansion with a beautiful Art Nouveau interior. Built in 1910 for Manuel Gameros, the mansion was converted to a museum in 1961. Pancho Villa used it briefly as a headquarters. The interior walls, floors and ceilings are lavishly decorated, which inspired the transfer of a beautiful collection of fine Mexican Art Nouveau furnishings from Mexico City to this museum. If you like design and beautiful antiques, especially Art Nouveau, don't miss this place.

Quinta Gameros, Paseo Bolívar 401. ✆ **614/416-6684.** Admission $3. Tues–Sun 10am–7pm. Heading away from the Plaza Principal with the cathedral on your right, walk 7 blocks on Independencia to Bolívar, turn right, and walk 1 block; museum is on the right.

**Hidalgo's Dungeon** Father Miguel Hidalgo y Costilla was a priest in Dolores, Guanajuato, when he started the War of Independence on September 15, 1810. Six months later, he was captured by the Spanish, brought to Chihuahua, and thrown in a dungeon for 98 days, before being shot along with his lieutenants, Allende, Aldama, and Jiménez. The four were beheaded, and their heads hung in iron cages for 9½ years on the four corners of the Alhóndiga granary in Guanajuato (see chapter 5), as examples of the fate revolutionaries would meet. In this cell, Hidalgo lived on bread and water before his execution. The night before his death, he wrote a few words on the wall with a piece of charcoal to thank his guard and the warden for the good treatment they gave him. A bronze plaque commemorates his final message.

In the Palacio Federal, Av. Juárez at Guerrero. No phone. Admission 50¢. Tues–Sun 10am–6pm. From Plaza Principal, walk on pedestrian-only Calle Libertad for 3 long blocks to Guerrero, turn left, and walk to corner of Juárez. Turn right and go ½ block; museum entrance is on the right, below post office.

**Museo de la Revolución** ★★ *Finds* The Revolution Museum is Pancho Villa's house, where Luz Corral de Villa, Pancho Villa's widow, lived until her death in 1981. Exhibits include Villa's weapons, some personal effects, lots of period photos, and the 1922 Dodge in which he was shot in 1923 (you'll see the bullet holes). I found it very interesting and recommend seeing the place with a guide, who can add lots of biographical details about this larger-than-life character. Be sure to ask about Villa's opinions on marriage and about the total number of his offspring and grandchildren.

Calle 10 no. 3014 (at Méndez). ✆ **614/416-2958.** Admission $1. Mon–Sat 9am–1pm and 3–7pm; Sun 9am–5pm. Bus: "Colonia Dale" (runs west on Juárez, then south on Ocampo); exit at corner of Ocampo and Méndez.

**Palacio del Gobierno** The Palacio del Gobierno is a magnificent, ornate structure dating in part from 1890; the original building, the Jesuit College, was built in 1718. A colorful, expressive mural encompasses the first floor of the large central courtyard and tells the history of the area around Chihuahua from the time of the first European visitation through the Revolution. In the far right corner, note the scene depicting Benito Juárez flanked by Abraham Lincoln and Simón Bolívar, liberator of South America. In the far left rear courtyard are a plaque and altar commemorating the execution of Miguel Hidalgo, the father of Mexican independence, at 7am on July 30, 1811; the plaque marks the spot where the hero was executed in the old building, and the mural portrays the scene.

Av. Aldama (between Guerrero and Carranza). ✆ **614/410-6324.** Free admission. Daily 8am–10pm. With the cathedral on your right, walk along Independencia 1 block, turn left on Aldama, continue 2 long blocks, and cross Guerrero; entrance is on the left.

## WHERE TO STAY

### EXPENSIVE

**Holiday Inn Hotel and Suites** ★ This is unlike any Holiday Inn I am familiar with. It offers the most comfortable rooms in Chihuahua. All units are large suites, with a kitchenette including stove, refrigerator, and coffeemaker. The restaurant and room service provide very good food. The hotel staff is helpful and efficient. Guests have the use of a video library. The hotel can provide continental breakfast for people heading off on the train, a box lunch, or both. The hotel is a 5-minute walk from downtown.

Escudero 702 (between Av. Universidad and Av. de Montes), 31240 Chihuahua, Chih. ✆ **800/465-4329** in the U.S., or 614/439-0000. Fax 614/414-3313. 74 units. $185 double. Rates include continental breakfast. AE, MC, V. Free secured parking. **Amenities:** Restaurant, bar; indoor heated pool; outdoor pool; fitness room; room service; laundry service. *In room:* A/C, TV, kitchenette.

**Hotel Palacio del Sol** ★ Well located near the main square, the Palacio del Sol has 17 stories of rooms. They are carpeted and have king-size beds, writing tables, and purified tap water, but can be musty. Decoration is nothing too special. The suites are substantially better than standard rooms in both size and furnishings. The lobby and bar area of the hotel are quite popular with locals, so it's usually a pretty active scene. Leaving the cathedral, it is 3½ blocks to your left on Independencia.

Independencia 116, 31000 Chihuahua, Chih. ✆ **800/852-4049** in the U.S. or 614/416-6000. Fax 614/415-9947. 180 units. $150 double; $180 suite. AE, DC, MC, V. Free valet parking. **Amenities:** 2 restaurants, 2 bars; tour desk; car rental; 24-hour room service; same-day laundry service; nonsmoking rooms. Rooms for travelers with disabilities are available. *In room:* A/C, TV.

**Hotel San Francisco** ★ The good location and comfortable rooms attract many visitors to this hotel. Locals and tourists alike use the lobby bar and restaurant, Degá, as a meeting place, and the atmosphere is always convivial (see "Where to Dine," below). The rooms are attractively furnished but dimly lit. From the cathedral, walk to Victoria and turn right; the hotel is 1½ blocks down on your right, before Avenida Ocampo.

Victoria 409, 31000 Chihuahua, Chih. ✆ **800/847-2546** in the U.S., or 614/416-7550. Fax 614/415-3538. 131 units. $140 double. AE, MC, V. Free covered parking. **Amenities:** Restaurant, bar; fitness room; business center; room service until 10pm; laundry service. *In room:* A/C, TV.

### INEXPENSIVE

**Hotel Santa Regina** The three-story Santa Regina (no elevator) has carpeted rooms that are heated in winter. More than half the rooms have windows facing outside; others have windows on the hall. Make sure to ask for a remodeled room. With the cathedral on your left, walk 2 blocks on Independencia to Doblado. Turn right for 2 more blocks, then left; the hotel is between Juárez and Doblado.

Calle 3 no. 102, 31000 Chihuahua, Chih. ✆ **614/415-3889.** Fax 614/410-1411. 100 units. $45 double. AE, MC, V. Free parking. **Amenities:** Restaurant; laundry service. *In room:* A/C, TV.

## WHERE TO DINE

Dining in Chihuahua is fine so long as you don't rely too heavily on the city's cosmopolitanism. Stick with steaks and Mexican food.

**Degá** MEXICAN/INTERNATIONAL The restaurant/cafeteria/bar at this popular hotel draws both downtown workers and travelers. The breakfast buffet features superb made-to-order omelets. The *plato mexicano* comes with a tamal, chile relleno, beans, chips, and guacamole. Fish, charcoal-grilled chicken, barbecue, and salads are all reasonably priced. The extensive menu includes American breakfasts and burgers. From the cathedral, walk to Victoria and turn right; it's 1 block down on your right, before Avenida Ocampo.

In the Hotel San Francisco, Calle Victoria 409. ✆ **614/416-7550.** Breakfast $5–$7; breakfast buffet $8; main courses $7–$17; Sun buffet $9. DC, MC, V. Daily 7am–11pm.

**Rincón Mexicano** ★ MEXICAN The Rincón serves great Mexican food and offers a substantial number of choices. Good appetizers include *quesadillas de huitlacoche* for the adventurous, and *chile con asadero.* For a main dish that gives you a little of everything, try *enchiladas tres moles.* As you would expect of a restaurant in Chihuahua, the emphasis is on beef, prepared in very Mexican ways such as *puntas en chile pasado* or *molcajete de res.* The interior is easy on the eyes, with muted tones of yellow and orange, good lighting, and tablecloths. A guitar trio occasionally performs soft music in the evenings. The restaurant is a short taxi ride from downtown.

Av. Cuauhtémoc 2224. ✆ **614/411-1510** or 614/411-1427. Main courses $8–$15. AE, MC, V. Daily noon–midnight.

**Tony's** ★★ MEXICAN/STEAK Opened by the wealthy cattle rancher Tony Vega in the 1950s, this club once hosted rugged, rich ranchers who needed a place to drink and dine casually. The restaurant is filled with photos of important historical figures from Chihuahua, including the actor Anthony Quinn, a local boy who hit the big time in Hollywood. The adobe-style building houses a large dining room with a wood-burning fireplace and a separate private dining room. As might be expected, the big draw here is beef, especially the hefty steaks. *Carne asada* comes with superb guacamole. Attached is a small, interesting bar decorated "ranch-style."

Av. Juárez 3901. ✆ **614/410-2988.** Steak dinners $12–$26. AE, MC, V. Mon–Sat 1–9:30pm.

## CHIHUAHUA AFTER DARK

Most nighttime action takes place in hotel lobby bars (see "Where to Stay," above). At the **Hotel San Francisco,** there's live music Monday through Saturday, with happy hour from 5 to 8pm. The lobby bar at the **Hotel Palacio del Sol** schedules live entertainment nightly.

# 16

# Los Cabos & Baja California

Baja California is a place of complementary contrasts: hot desert and cool ocean, manicured golf greens and craggy mountains. Baja lays claim to a striking and peculiar blend of Mexican and American cultures.

The Baja Peninsula is and is not part of Mexico. Attached mostly to the United States and separated from all but a sliver of Mexico by the Sea of Cortez (Gulf of California), the peninsula consists of one long granite ridge extending almost 1,600km (1,000 miles)—longer than Italy—from Mexico's northernmost city of **Tijuana** to **Cabo San Lucas** at its southern tip. Desert terrain rises from both coasts; forests of cardon cactus, spiky Joshua trees, and spindly ocotillo bushes populate the raw landscape.

Baja is legendary as a haven for sportfishing and rugged adventure activities.

For more in-depth coverage of this region, consult *Frommer's Portable Los Cabos & Baja.*

## EXPLORING THE REGION

The weather in this land of extremes can be sizzling hot in summer and cold and windy in winter. Though winter is often warm enough for watersports, bring a wetsuit if you're a serious diver or snorkeler, as well as warmer clothes for chilly weather. Though Baja's weather varies greatly by season, it is predictable—an important quality for the increasing number of golfers looking for sunny skies. Rainy days are few and far between, with most showers concentrated in September.

**THE TWO CABOS** The majority of visitors to Baja Sur are lured by the popularity of the twin towns at the peninsula's tip—**Cabo San Lucas** and **San José del Cabo**—and the stretch of coastline that connects them, known as **the Corridor.** Collectively, they are known as *Los Cabos* (The Capes). "The end of the line," "the last resort," and "no man's land" are all terms used in the past to describe remote Baja Sur.

Cabo San Lucas and the Corridor are an extension of Southern California, with luxury accommodations, golf courses, shopping, franchise restaurants, and spirited nightlife. San José del Cabo, however, remains rooted in the traditions of a quaint Mexican town, though it, too, is becoming gentrified.

Thirty kilometers (18 miles) of smooth highway (the Corridor) lie between the two Cabos. The major new resorts and residential communities, including some of the world's finest golf courses, have been developed along this stretch.

Baja can seem like one of the least crowded corners of Mexico. **Todos Santos,** an artistic community on the Pacific side of the coastal curve (just north of the tip), draws travelers who find that Cabo San Lucas has outgrown them. **La Paz,** capital of Baja Sur, remains an easygoing maritime port.

**MID-BAJA** Among the highlights of the mid-Baja region are the East Coast towns of **Loreto, Bahía Magdalena, Mulegé,** and **Santa Rosalía.** Although they have a much richer cultural heritage than Baja Sur's towns, the tourism boom in the two Cabos has eclipsed them.

These mid-Baja towns were the center of the 18th-century Jesuit Mission movement. Today, they attract travelers who are drawn to Baja's wild natural beauty but find the popularity of Los Cabos a bit overwhelming. This area's natural attractions have made it a center for sea kayaking, sportfishing, and hiking—including excursions to view indigenous cave paintings.

This is the area to visit if you're interested in whale-watching; many tour companies operate out of Loreto and the smaller neighboring towns (see "Whale-watching in Baja," later).

**BAJA NORTE** **Tijuana** has the dubious distinction of being the most visited and perhaps most misunderstood town in all of Mexico. New cultural and sporting attractions, extensive shopping, and strong business growth—of the reputable kind—are brightening Tijuana's image.

Tranquil **Rosarito Beach** has also reemerged as a resort town; it got a boost after the movie *Titanic* was filmed here. Farther south on the Pacific Coast is the lovely port town of **Ensenada,** also known for its surfing and sportfishing. Tours of nearby inland vineyards (Mexico's wine country) are growing in popularity.

## 1 Los Cabos: Resorts, Watersports & Golf ★★

The two towns at the tip of the rugged Baja Peninsula are commonly grouped together and referred to as Los Cabos, although they couldn't be more different. San José del Cabo and Cabo San Lucas are separated not just by 35km (22 miles), but by distinct attitudes and ways of life. Where Cabo San Lucas mirrors a Los Angeles lifestyle, San José del Cabo remains a traditional, tranquil Mexican small town, although recent gentrification is turning it into the more sophisticated of the two resorts.

Great sportfishing originally brought attention to Los Cabos, which were once accessible only by water. It remains a lure today, although golf has overtaken it as the principle attraction. As early as the 1940s, the area attracted a hearty community of cruisers, fishermen, divers, and adventurers. By the early 1980s, the Mexican government realized the growth potential of Los Cabos and invested in new highways, airport facilities, golf courses, and modern marine facilities. The increase in air access and the opening of Transpeninsular Highway 1 in 1973 paved the way for its spectacular growth.

The road that connects Cabo San Lucas and San José del Cabo is the centerpiece of resort growth. Known as "the Corridor," this well-paved four-lane stretch offers clifftop vistas but still has no nighttime lighting. The area's deluxe resorts and renowned golf courses are here, along with a collection of dramatic beaches and coves. The view is especially outstanding in January and February, when gray whales often spout close to shore.

The Los Cabos area is more expensive than other Mexican resorts, as the boom in new hotel construction has been limited to luxury resorts. Unfortunately, prices have not adjusted downward with the added supply of rooms.

You should consider renting a car, even if only for a day. The two Cabos lie over 32km (20 miles) apart, with numerous attractions in between, and taxis are expensive. If you are at all interested in exploring, a rental car is your most economical option.

Because of the distinctive character and attractions of each of the Cabos and the Corridor, they are treated separately here. It is common to stay in one and make day trips to the other two.

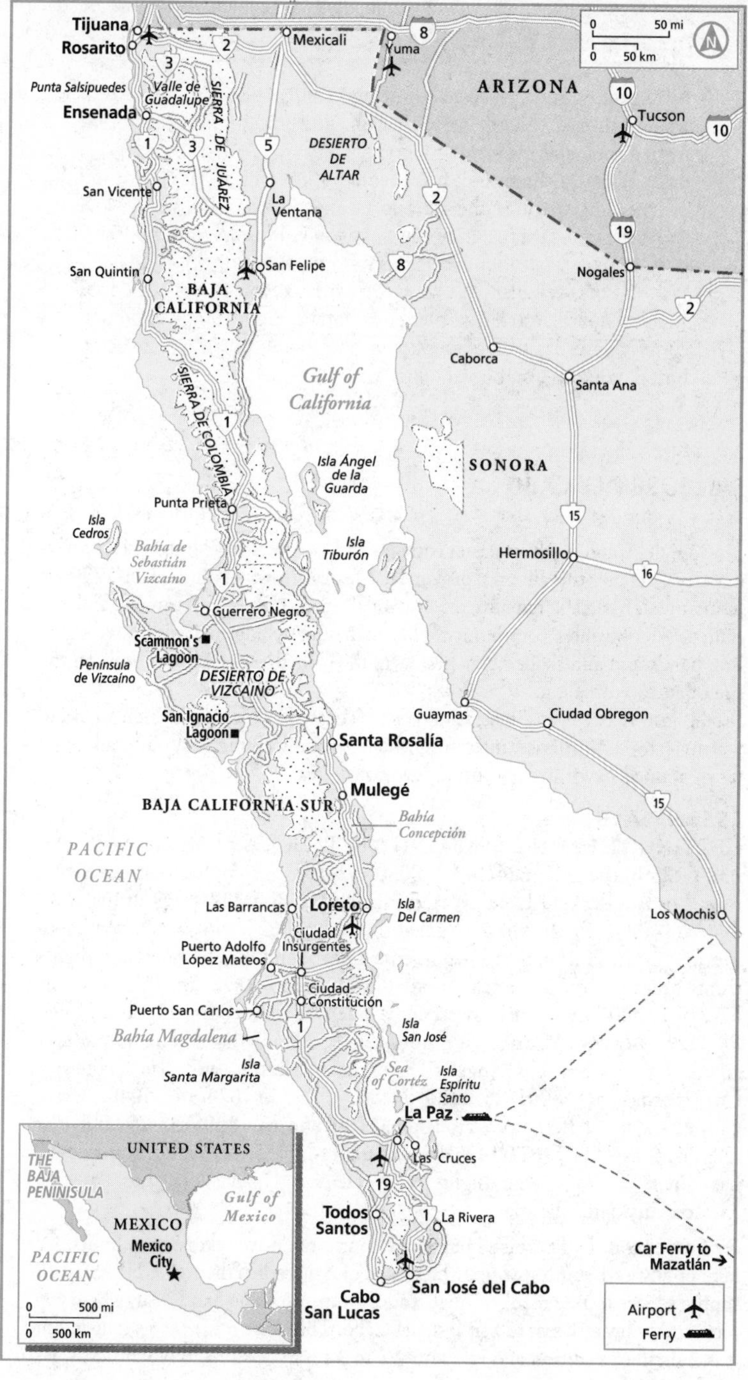
Tijuana
Rosarito
Mexicali
Yuma
ARIZONA
Tucson
Punta Salsipuedes
Valle de Guadalupe
SIERRA DE JUÁREZ
Ensenada
DESIERTO DE ALTAR
San Vicente
La Ventana
Nogales
San Quintín
San Felipe
BAJA CALIFORNIA
Caborca
Santa Ana
Gulf of California
SIERRA DE COLOMBIA
SONORA
Isla Ángel de la Guarda
Punta Prieta
Isla Cedros
Bahía de Sebastián Vizcaíno
Isla Tiburón
Hermosillo
Guerrero Negro
Scammon's Lagoon
Península de Vizcaíno
DESIERTO DE VIZCAÍNO
San Ignacio Lagoon
Guaymas
Ciudad Obregon
Santa Rosalía
Mulegé
BAJA CALIFORNIA SUR
Bahía Concepción
PACIFIC OCEAN
Las Barrancas
Loreto
Isla Del Carmen
Los Mochis
Ciudad Insurgentes
Puerto Adolfo López Mateos
Ciudad Constitución
Puerto San Carlos
Bahía Magdalena
Isla San José
Isla Santa Margarita
Sea of Cortéz
Isla Espíritu Santo
La Paz
Las Cruces
UNITED STATES
THE BAJA PENINSULA
Gulf of Mexico
MEXICO
Mexico City
PACIFIC OCEAN
Todos Santos
La Rivera
Car Ferry to Mazatlán
San José del Cabo
Cabo San Lucas
Airport
Ferry
0 50 mi
0 50 km
0 500 mi
0 500 km

*Tips* **The Best Websites for Los Cabos & Baja**

- **All About Cabo: www.allaboutcabo.com** This site features a weekly fishing report, live golf cam, and information on hotels, restaurants, golf courses, and more.
- **Baja Travel Guide: bajatravel.com** Here you'll find a good overview of activities and transportation, but the extensive Yellow Pages are most useful. They can help you with tours, ground transportation, and outdoor excursions before you go.
- **Visit Cabo: www.visitcabo.com** The official site of the Los Cabos Tourism Board. You'll find plenty of details about things to do and current news, as well as a lodging and dining guide. For selected hotels, you can also book online.

## SAN JOSE DEL CABO

180km (113 miles) SE of La Paz; 33km (21 miles) NE of Cabo San Lucas; 1,760km (1,100 miles) SE of Tijuana

San José del Cabo, with its pastel cottages and narrow streets lined with flowering trees, retains the air of a provincial Mexican town. Founded in 1730 by Jesuit missionaries, it remains the seat of the Los Cabos government and the center of its business community. The main square, adorned with a wrought-iron bandstand and shaded benches, faces the cathedral, which was built on the site of an early mission.

San José is becoming increasingly sophisticated, with a collection of noteworthy cafes, art galleries, interesting shops, and intriguing small inns adding a newly refined flavor to the central downtown area.

### ESSENTIALS

**GETTING THERE & DEPARTING** **By Plane** **Aerocalifornia** (✆ **800/237-6225** in the U.S., 624/143-3700, or 624/143-3915), has nonstop flights from Los Angeles and Phoenix; **Aeromexico** (✆ **800/237-6639** in the U.S., 800/021-4000 in Mexico, 624/146-5098, or 624/146-5097; www.aeromexico.com), flies nonstop from San Diego and has connecting flights from other cities. **America West** (✆ **800/235-9292** in the U.S., or 624/146-5380; www.americawest.com) operates connecting flights through Phoenix; **Alaska Airlines** (✆ **800/426-0333** in the U.S.; www.alaskaair.com) flies from Los Angeles, San Diego, Seattle, and San Francisco; **Continental** (✆ **800/525-0280** in the U.S. or 624/146-5040; www.continental.com) flies from Houston; **Mexicana** (✆ **800/531-7921** in the U.S., 624/146-5001, 624/143-5352, or 624/143-5353; www.mexicana.com), has direct or connecting flights from Denver, Guadalajara, Los Angeles, Mexico City, and Mazatlán.

**By Car** From La Paz, take Highway 1 south; the drive takes 3 to 4 hours. Or take Highway 1 south just past the village of San Pedro, then take Highway 19 south (a less winding road) through Todos Santos to Cabo San Lucas, where you pick up Highway 1 east to San José del Cabo. The latter route seems longer, but it is in better condition and takes only 2 to 3 hours. From Cabo San Lucas, it's a half-hour drive to San José.

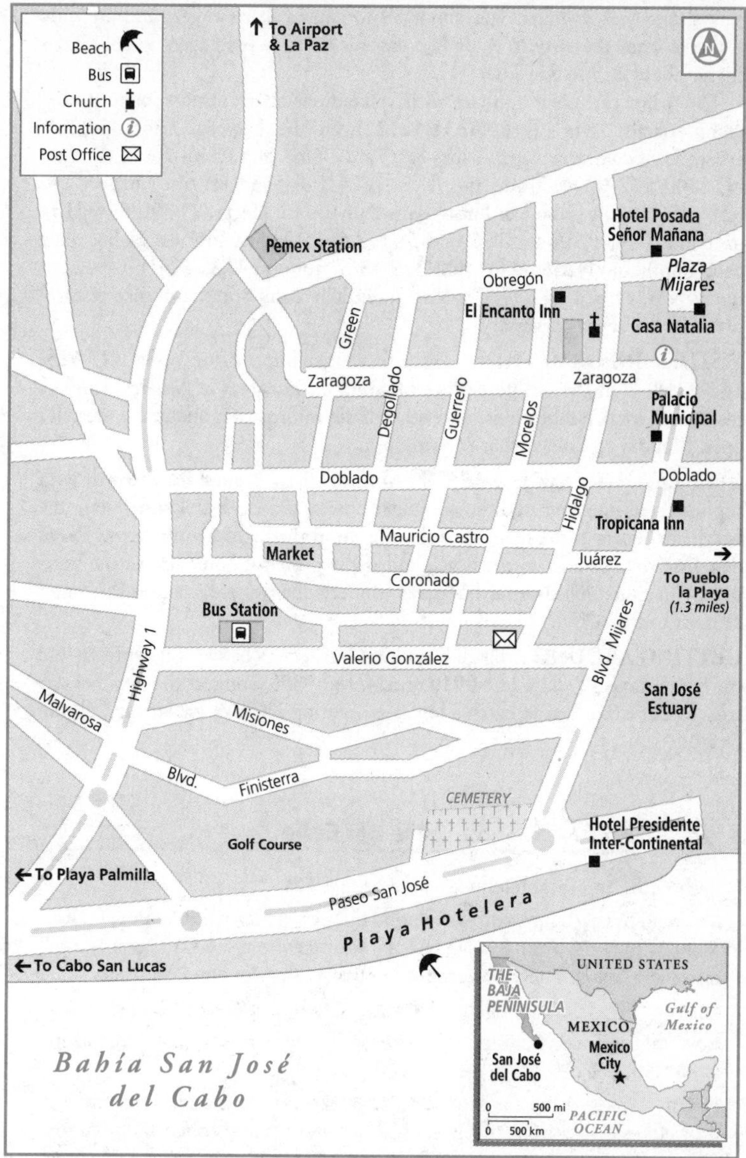


**By Bus** The **bus station** (Terminal de Autobuses), on Valerio González, a block east of Highway 1 (✆ **624/142-1100**), is open daily from 5:30am to 7pm.

## Orientation

**ARRIVING** The **airport** (✆ **624/146-5111**) that serves both Cabos and the connecting Corridor is 12km (7½ miles) northwest of San José del Cabo and 35km (22 miles) northeast of Cabo San Lucas. Upon arrival at the airport, buy a ticket inside the building for a *colectivo* or a taxi, which up to four passengers may share. *Colectivo* fares run about $9 for up to 8 passengers and are only available from the airport. A private van for up to 5 passengers is $60. Taxis charge about $13 to San José.

The major car-rental agencies all have counters at the airport, open during flight arrivals: **Avis** (© **800/331-1212** from the U.S., or 624/146-0201; avissjd@avis.com.mx; open Mon–Sat 7am–9pm, Sun 6am–9pm); **Budget** (© **800/527-0700** from the U.S., 624/146-5333 at the airport, or 624/143-4190 in Cabo San Lucas; daily 8am–6pm); **Hertz** (© **800/654-3131** from the U.S., 624/146-5088 or 624/142-0375 in San José del Cabo; daily 8am–8pm); and **National** (© **800/328-4567** from the U.S., 624/146-5022 at the airport, or 624/142-2424 in San José; daily 8am–8pm). Advance reservations are not always necessary.

**VISITOR INFORMATION** The city tourist information office (© **624/142-3310**) is in the old post office building on Zaragoza at Mijares. It offers maps, free local publications, and other basic information about the area. It's open Monday to Friday from 8am to 3pm.

**CITY LAYOUT** San José del Cabo consists of two zones: **downtown,** with sophisticated inns and traditional budget hotels, and the **hotel zone** along the beach. **Zaragoza** is the main street leading from the highway into town; **Paseo San José** runs parallel to the beach and is the principal boulevard of the hotel zone. The mile-long **Bulevard Mijares** connects the two areas, and is the center of most tourist activity in San Jose.

**GETTING AROUND** There is no local bus service between downtown and the beach; **taxis** (© **624/142-0910** or 624/142-0580) connect the two. For day trips to **Cabo San Lucas,** catch a **bus** (see "Getting There & Departing," above) or a cab.

## *FAST FACTS:* San José Del Cabo

*Area Code* The local telephone area code is **624.**

*Banks* Banks exchange currency during business hours, which are generally Monday to Friday from 8:30am to 6pm, Saturday from 10am to 2pm. There are several major banks on Zaragoza between Morelos and Degollado.

*Emergencies* The local police number at City Hall is © **624/142-0361.**

*Hospital* **Hospital General** is at Retorno Atunero s/n, Col. Chamizal (© **624/142-0013**).

*Internet Access* **Web Land** (© **624/142-5282;** www.webland-cabo.com), is on Mijares across from the Tropicana Bar and Grill. It's open Monday to Saturday from 9am to 8pm and charges $3.50 for 10 minutes or $7.50 per hour. In addition to high-speed access, it has scanners, printers, CD burners, webcams, and joysticks. Serves coffee, too!

*Pharmacy* **Farmacia ISSSTE,** Carretera Transpeninsular, Km 34 Plaza California Local 7, San José del Cabo (© **624/142-2645**), is open daily from 8am to 8pm.

*Post Office* The *correo,* Blvd. Mijares 1924, at Valerio González (© **624/142-0911**), is open Monday to Friday from 8am to 3pm, Saturday from 9am to 1pm.

## BEACHES & SPORTS OUTINGS

The relaxed pace of San José del Cabo makes it an ideal place to unwind and absorb authentic Mexican flavor. Beach aficionados who want to explore the beautiful coves and beaches along the 22-mile coast between the two Cabos should consider renting a car for a day or so. Expect to pay at least $50 per day.

**BEACHES** The nearest beach safe for swimming is **Pueblo la Playa** (also called "La Playita"), about 3km (2 miles) east of town. From Bulevard Mijares, turn east at the small PUEBLO LA PLAYA sign and follow the dusty dirt road through the cane fields and palms. You'll arrive at a small village and beautiful beach where a number of *pangas* (skiffs) that belong to local fishermen are pulled ashore. The La Playita resort's restaurant (see "Where to Stay," below) offers the only formal sustenance on the beach. There are no shade *palapas.*

**Estero San José,** a nature reserve with at least 270 species of birds, is between Pueblo la Playa and the Hotel Presidente Inter-Continental. The estuary is a protected ecological reserve.

A beach with beautiful rock formations, **Playa Palmilla,** 8km (5 miles) west of San José, is near the Hotel Palmilla, an elegant place to stay or to eat lunch or dinner. To reach Playa Palmilla, take a taxi to the road that leads to the Hotel Palmilla grounds, then take the fork to the left (without entering the hotel grounds) and follow signs to Pepe's restaurant on the beach.

For a list of other nearby beaches worth exploring if you have a rental car, see "Outdoor Activities: Fishing, Golf & More," under "Cabo San Lucas."

**LAND SPORTS** **Golf** Los Cabos is rapidly becoming a major golf destination, with several new courses and others under construction. The lowest greens fees in the area ($44) are at the 9-hole **Club Campo de Golf San José** (**© 624/142-0901** or 624/142-0905), on Paseo Finisterra across from the Howard Johnson Hotel. Cart rentals are an additional $30 and club rentals are $16.50. The course doesn't take reservations for tee times. It is open daily from 6:30am to 4pm (to 4:30pm in summer).

**Adventure Tours** **Tio Sports** (**© 624/143-3399;** www.tiosports.com) arranges a variety of land- and water-based adventure and nature tours, including popular ATV tours to Candelaria, parasailing, kayak, catamaran, snorkeling, and diving trips. The website gives current prices.

**Horseback Riding** Horses can be rented near the Presidente Inter-Continental, Fiesta Inn, and Palmilla hotels for $15 to $20 per hour. Most people choose to ride on the beach. You can also arrange horseback riding through **Xplora Adventours** (**© 624/142-9135**). It deals with a good ranch that has a stable of healthy, well-groomed horses (the horses on the beaches are often on the thin side). Xplora offers tours on the beach and down a mountain trail. One-hour rides are $30.

---

**Tips** **Swimming Safety**

Although this area is ideal for watersports, occasional strong currents and undertows can make swimming dangerous at **Playa Hotelera,** the town beach—check conditions before entering the surf. Swimming is generally safe at **Pueblo la Playa** (see "Beaches," above), though it, too, can occasionally be subject to a strong undertow. The safest area beach for swimming is **Medano Beach** in Cabo San Lucas.

---

**Tennis** The two courts at the **Club Campo de Golf Los Cabos,** Paseo Finisterra 1 (✆ **624/142-0905**), rent for $11 an hour during the day, $22 an hour at night. Call the club to reserve. Club guests can also use the swimming pool. You can also play at the Hotel Palmilla; its two lighted courts cost $15 per hour.

**WATERSPORTS Fishing** The least expensive way to enjoy deep-sea fishing is to pair up with another angler and charter a *panga,* a 22-foot skiff used by local fishermen from Pueblo la Playa. Several *panga* fleets offer 6-hour sportfishing trips, usually from 6am to noon, for $25 per hour (3-hr. minimum). Two or three people can split the cost. For information, contact the fishermen's cooperative in Pueblo la Playa. You can also book through **Victor's Aquatics,** at the Hotel Posada Real (✆ **949/496-0960** in the U.S., or 624/142-1092; fax 624/142-1093; victor@1cabonet.com.mx), though note that the price will be higher, as it includes a commission. Victor has a full fishing fleet with both *pangas* ($185 for 6 hr.) and cruisers ($310–$395). Larger boats, up to 10m (33 ft.), are available for $450 to $550. Outfitters supply the boat and tackle, and the client buys the bait, drinks, and snacks.

**Sea Kayaking** Fully guided, ecologically oriented **Ocean Kayak Tours** are available through **Baja's Moto Rent** (✆ **624/143-2050**), **Cabo Expeditions** (✆ **624/143-2700**), and **Aqua Deportes** (✆ **624/143-0117**). Most ocean kayaking tours depart from Cabo San Lucas.

**Snorkeling/Diving Xplora Adventours** (✆ **624/142-9135;** open 8:30am–8:30pm) and **Amigos del Mar** in Cabo San Lucas (✆ **624/143-0505**) arrange trips, which cost $50 per person and up. Among the area's best dive sites are **Cabo Pulmo** and **Gordo Banks.** Cabo Pulmo has seven sites geared for divers of all experience levels, so it never feels crowded. It also offers the possibility to snorkel with sea lions, depending on the currents and the sea lions' behavior. Gordo Banks is an advanced dive site where you can see whale sharks and hammerhead sharks. It's a deep dive—between 27 and 30m (90–110 ft.)—with limited visibility (9–12m/30–40 ft.). Most dives are drift dives, and wetsuits are highly recommended.

**Surfing Playa Costa Azul,** at Km 29 on Highway 1 just south of San José, is the most popular surfing beach in the area. A few bungalows are available for rent, or surfers can camp on the beach. The **Costa Azul Surf Shop,** Km 28, Playa Costa Azul (✆ **624/142-2771,** www.costa-azul.com.mx), rents surfboards by the day. It charges $20 a day for a short or long board, leash, and rack for your rental car. Spectators can watch from the highway lookout point at the top of the hill south of Costa Azul.

**Whale-watching** From January through March, migrating gray whales congregate offshore. Fishermen at Pueblo la Playa take small groups out to see them; a 4-hour trip runs about $45 per person. Organized half-day tours on sportfishing boats, glass-bottom boats, and cruise catamarans depart from Plaza las Glorias in Cabo San Lucas and cost $35 to $50, depending on the type of boat. The price includes snacks and beverages. The ultimate whale excursion is a trip to **Magdalena Bay.** Tours from San José take you by plane—a 75-minute flight—to Magdalena, where you board a *panga* (skiff) and spend 3 hours watching gray whales and humpbacks loll around the coastal lagoons. This tour is $377, including air transportation, and can be arranged through **Xplora Adventours** (✆ **624/142-9135**). You can also spot the whales from shore; good spots include the beach by the Solmar Suites hotel on the Pacific and the beaches and cliffs along the Corridor.

## SHOPPING

The town has a growing selection of unique design shops, hip boutiques, and collections of fine Mexican *artesanía.* They cluster around **Bulevard Mijares** and **Zaragoza,** the main street. A municipal **market** on Mauricio Castro and Green sells edibles and utilitarian wares. The following businesses accept credit cards (AE, MC, V).

**ADD (Arte, Diseño y Decoracion)** This shop sells creative home accessories, fine arts and crafts, pewter, and authentic Talavera ceramics. Shipping is available. Open weekdays from 9am to 8pm, Saturday from 10am to 8pm. Zaragoza at Hidalgo. ✆ **624/142-2777.**

**Copal** Traditional and contemporary Mexican *artesanía* and silver jewelry are the specialties in this former residence, tastefully converted into a contemporary shop. Open weekdays from 9am to 10:30pm, weekends 10am to 2pm and 4 to 10:30pm. Plaza Mijares 10. ✆ **624/142-3070.**

**Escape** This shop sells designer and casual sportswear and accessories, including designer jeans, leather bags, belts, and a trendy selection of sunglasses. There's also a new interior decor shop by the same name next door. A small cafe and espresso bar, **Café Florentina** (daily 11am–11pm), is in the connecting courtyard. Open daily from 9am to 9pm. Plaza Florentine, Zaragoza 20, across from the cathedral. ✆ **624/142-2799.**

**GALLERIES** A growing number of art galleries (mainly artists' studios) are open to the public. Though I've listed the most notable here, there are others.

**Galeria Wentworth Porter** This gallery features a selection of original fine art, along with prints and art cards by local artists. It prominently features the work of the locally popular Dennis Wentworth Porter. It's open weekdays from 10am to 1pm and 4 to 7pm, Saturday from 10am to 2pm. A. Obregon 20. ✆ **624/142-3141.**

## WHERE TO STAY

There's more demand than supply in Baja Sur, so prices tend to be higher than those for equivalent accommodations in other parts of Mexico. San José has only a handful of budget hotels. It's best to call ahead for reservations. A new trend is toward smaller inns or bed-and-breakfasts, which offer stylish accommodations in town. Properties in the beachfront hotel zone often offer package deals that bring room rates down to the moderate range, especially during summer months. Check with your travel agent.

### Expensive

**Casa Natalia** ★★★ *Finds* This exquisite boutique hotel is a real novelty in San José. Owners Nathalie and Loic have transformed a former residence into a beautiful amalgam of palms, waterfalls, and flowers. The inn is a completely renovated historic home that combines modern architecture with traditional Mexican touches. Each of the rooms has a name that reflects the decor, such as *Conchas* (seashells), *Azul* (blue), or *Talavera* (ceramics); all have sliding glass doors that open onto small private terraces or balconies with hammocks and chairs, shaded by bougainvillea and bamboo. The two spa suites each have a private terrace with a whirlpool and hammock. Tall California palms surround a small courtyard pool, and the terraces face onto it. Casa Natalia is in the heart of the Bulevard Mijares action, just off the central plaza.

Blvd. Mijares 4, 23400 San José del Cabo, B.C.S. ✆ **888/277-3814** in the U.S. or 624/142-5100. Fax 624/142-5110. www.casanatalia.com. 20 units. High season $220 standard; $345 spa suite. Low season $180 standard; $295 spa suite. AE, MC, V. Children under 13 not accepted. **Amenities:** Gourmet restaurant (see "Where to Dine," below), bar; heated swimming pool with waterfall and swim-up bar; concierge; room service; massage; laundry service. *In room:* A/C, TV, fan, robes, hairdryer, safe deposit box.

**Hotel Presidente Inter-Continental** ★ Serenity, seclusion, and luxury are the hallmarks of the Presidente, set on a long stretch of beach next to the Estero San José. Low-rise, Mediterranean-style buildings frame the beach and San José's largest swimming pool, which has a swim-up bar. If possible, select a ground-floor oceanfront room; the lower level offers spacious terraces, while upper-level units have tiny balconies. The recently renovated rooms have light-wood furnishings and brightly colored accents, with satellite TV and large bathrooms; suites include a separate sitting area. The all-inclusive resort is a good choice for those who primarily want to stay in one place and enjoy it; it's also popular with families.

Blvd. Mijares s/n, 23400 San José del Cabo, B.C.S. ✆ **800/327-0200** in the U.S., or 624/142-0211. Fax 624/142-0232. http://loscabos.interconti.com/. 395 units. High season $347–$477 standard double; $477 oceanfront double; $511–$693 double suite. Low season rates from $250 double. Rates include all meals, beverages, and many sports. AE, DC, MC, V. **Amenities:** 5 restaurants, garden cafe; 4 swimming pools (2 heated, with swim-up bars), children's pool; golf clinics; tennis; gym; bicycles; horseback riding; tour desk; twice-daily shuttle to Cabo San Lucas (fee); room service; laundry service; safe deposit (in reception area). *In room:* A/C, TV, hair dryers, makeup mirrors.

### Moderate

**El Encanto Inn** ★ *Value* Located on a quiet street in the historic downtown district, this charming inn borders a grassy courtyard with a fountain. It offers a relaxing alternative to busy hotels, as well as excellent value. Rooms are decorated with rustic wood and contemporary iron furniture. Nice-size bathrooms have colorful tile accents. Rooms have two double beds, while suites have king-size beds and a sitting room. The owners, Cliff and Blanca (a lifelong resident of San José), can help arrange fishing packages and golf and diving outings. The property just gained a small outdoor pool. Twelve suites and a *palapa* bar are scheduled to open next door to the original structure in mid-2002. Jazmin's restaurant, half a block away, serves the continental breakfast included in the room rate. The inn is half a block from the church.

Morelos 133 (between Obregón and Comonfort), 23400 San José del Cabo, B.C.S. ✆ **624/142-0388.** www.elencantoinn.com. 19 units. $69 double; $79 jr. suite; $89 suite. AE (payment only), MC, V (payment and reservations). Rates include continental breakfast. Limited street parking available. **Amenities:** Small outdoor pool. *In room:* A/C, TV, coffeemaker, fan.

**La Playita Inn** Removed from even the slow pace of San José, this courtyard hotel is older yet impeccably clean and friendly. It's ideal for fishermen and those looking for something different from a traditional vacation. At the edge of the tiny village of Pueblo la Playa, it's the only hotel on the only beach in San José that's considered safe for swimming. Just steps from the water and the lineup of fishing *pangas,* the two stories of sunlit rooms frame a patio with a pool just large enough to allow you to swim laps. Each room is spacious, with high-quality basic furnishings, screened windows, nicely tiled bathrooms, and cable TV. Two large suites on the second floor have full kitchens. There's a golf-cart shuttle to the beach. Next door, the hotel's La Playita Restaurant (open 11am–10pm) offers a great mix of seafood and standard favorites, plus occasional live jazz or tropical music.

Pueblo la Playa, Apdo. Postal 437, 23400 San José del Cabo, B.C.S. ✆ and fax **624/142-4166.** www.laplayitahotel.com. 26 units. $70 double. Rate includes continental breakfast. MC, V. Free parking. **Amenities:**

Restaurant; outdoor pool. *In room:* A/C, TV. From Blvd. Mijares, follow sign pointing to Pueblo la Playa (dirt road) for about 3km (2 miles). Hotel is on the left.

### Inexpensive

**Hotel Posada Señor Mañana** This comfortable two-story guesthouse, set in a grove of tropical fruit trees, offers basic rooms with tile floors and funky furniture. An abundance of hammocks are strewn about the property. Guests have cooking privileges in a large, fully equipped common kitchen. Upstairs rooms have queen-size beds; downstairs, two double beds or a double and a single. The hotel is next to the Casa de la Cultura, behind the main square.

Alvaro Obregón 1, 23400 San José del Cabo, B.C.S. ✆ and fax **624/142-1372.** Fax 624/142-5761. www.srmanana.com. 8 units. $39–$42 double. No credit cards. **Amenities:** Kitchen; pool table; half-court basketball; Ping-Pong. *In room:* Fan.

## WHERE TO DINE

### Expensive

**Damiana** ★ SEAFOOD/MEXICAN This casually elegant restaurant in an 18th-century hacienda is decorated in the colors of a Mexican sunset: deep-orange walls, and tables and chairs clad in bright rose, lavender, and orange cloth. The favored tables are in the tropical courtyard, where candles flicker under trees and bougainvillea. For an appetizer, try zesty mushrooms *diablo.* For a main course, *ranchero* shrimp in cactus sauce and grilled lobster tail are flavorful choices. You can also enjoy brunch almost until the dinner hour. There is an interior dining room, but the courtyard is the most romantic dining spot in San José. It's on the east side of the town plaza.

San José town plaza. ✆ **624/142-0499** or 624/142-2899. Fax 624/142-5603. damiana@1cabonet.com.mx. Reservations recommended during Christmas and Easter holidays. Lunch $9–$15; main courses $10–$50. AE, MC, V. Daily 11am–10:30pm.

**Mi Cocina** ★ NOUVELLE MEXICAN-EURO Without a doubt, this is currently the best dining choice in the entire Los Cabos area. From the setting to the service, a dinner at Mi Cocina ranks among the most memorable of experiences. The plant-filled courtyard, with its towering palms and exposed brick walls, accommodates al fresco dining. However, this restaurant doesn't rely solely on the romance of its setting—the food is superb, creative, and consistently tasteful. Notable starters include *chile relleno de camarones* (an ancho chile stuffed with baby shrimp and cooked with cream cheese, Brie, and cilantro). Main courses include pasta, seafood, poultry, and beef, with such favorites as Natalia-style filet, served on creamy chile sauce with mushrooms and broccoli, and jumbo shrimp sautéed with rosemary, olive oil, and sun-dried tomatoes. Save room for dessert; choices range from chocolate fondant to fresh-fruit-filled meringue discs topped with Chantilly cream. A full-service *palapa* bar offers an excellent selection of wines, premium tequilas, and single-malt scotches, as well as an extensive array of specialty drinks.

In the Casa Natalia hotel, Blvd. Mijares. ✆ **624/142-5100.** www.mi-cocina.com. Main courses $18–$32. AE, V, MC. Daily 6:30–10pm (to hotel guests only 7am–4pm).

**Tequila** ★ MEDITERRANEAN/ASIAN Contemporary Mexican cuisine with a light and flavorful touch is the star attraction here, although the garden setting is lovely, with rustic *equipal* furniture and lanterns scattered among palms and giant mango trees. Try the specialty, shrimp in tequila sauce. Other enjoyable options include perfectly seared tuna with cilantro and ginger, ribs topped with tamarind sauce, and baked lobster with tequila sauce. Vegetarians

## The Two Cabos & The Corridor

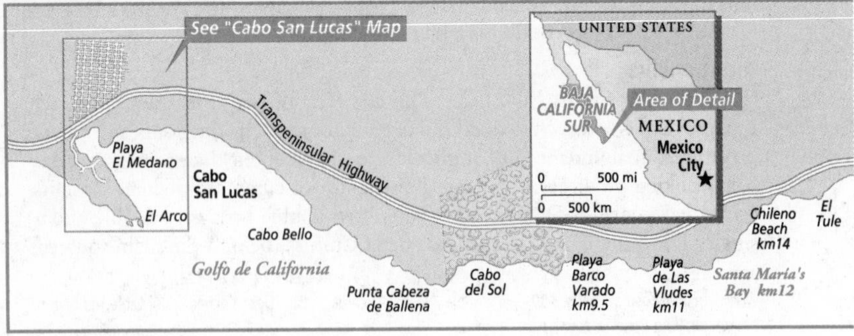


can enjoy bell peppers stuffed with ricotta in tomato sauce, or one of several pasta dishes. The accompanying whole-grain bread arrives fresh and hot, and attentive service complements the fine meal. Cuban cigars and an excellent selection of tequilas are available.

M. Doblado s/n. ✆ **624/142-1155.** Lunch $9–$22; main courses $15–$45. AE. Daily 11:30am–3pm and 6–10:30pm.

### Moderate

**Tropicana Bar and Grill** SEAFOOD/MEAT The Tropicana remains a popular mainstay, especially for tourists. The bar has a steady clientele day and night and often features special sporting events on satellite TV. The dining area is in a garden (candlelit in the evening) with a tiled mural at one end. Cafe-style sidewalk dining is also available, but it's less romantic because of a twirling, brightly lit dessert display. The menu is too extensive to lay claim to any specialty; it aims to please everyone. All meats and cheeses are imported; dinners include thick steaks and shrimp fajitas. *Paella* is the Sunday special. The restaurant is 1 block south of the Plaza Mijares.

Blvd. Mijares 30. ✆ **624/142-1580.** Breakfast $4–$6; main courses $10–$25. AE, MC, V. Daily 8am–midnight.

**Zipper's** BURGERS/MEXICAN/SEAFOOD At the far south end of the beach heading toward Cabo San Lucas and fronting the best surfing waters, this casual hangout owned by Mike Posey and Tony Magdaleno has become popular with gringos in search of American food and TV sports. Burgers have that back-home flavor—order one with a side of spicy curly fries. Steaks, lobster, beer-battered shrimp, deli sandwiches, and Mexican combination plates round out the menu, which is printed with dollar prices.

Playa Costa Azul just south of San José. No phone. Burgers and sandwiches $7–$10; main courses $7–$18. MC, V. Daily 8am–10pm.

### SAN JOSE AFTER DARK

San José's nightlife is non-existent outside of the restaurant and hotel bars. Those intent on real nightlife will find it in Cabo San Lucas. Of particular note here are the bars at **Casa Natalia** and **Tropicana**—the former caters to sophisticated romantics, the latter to those in search of rowdier good times. On some weekends, Tropicana even brings in a live Cuban band for dancing. Several of the larger hotels along the beach have Mexican fiestas and other weekly theme nights that include a buffet (usually all-you-can-eat), drinks, live music, and entertainment for $25 to $35 per person. There's also a large disco on Mijares

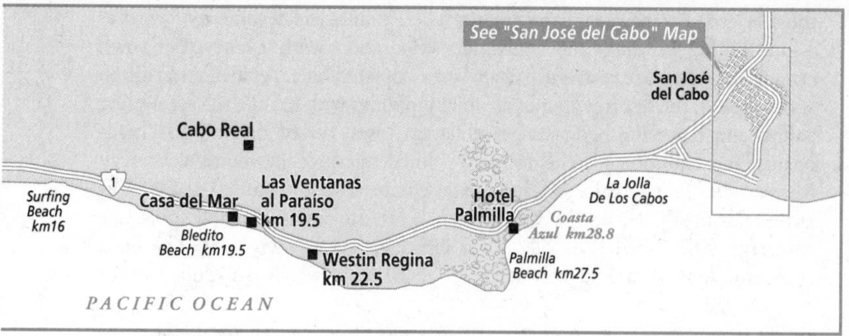


that seems to be under different ownership each year—it was closed at press time, with a RE-OPENING SOON sign on its door.

## THE CORRIDOR: BETWEEN THE TWO CABOS

The Corridor between the towns of San José del Cabo and Cabo San Lucas contains some of Mexico's most lavish resorts. Most growth at the tip of the peninsula is occurring along the Corridor, which has already become a major locale for championship golf. The four major resort areas are **Palmilla, Querencia, Cabo Real,** and **Cabo del Sol,** each a self-enclosed community with golf courses, elegant hotels, and million-dollar homes (or the promise of them).

If you plan to explore the region while staying at a Corridor hotel, you'll need a rental car (available at the hotels) for at least a day or 2. Even if you're not staying here, the beaches and dining options are worth investigating. Hotels—all of which qualify as very expensive—are listed in the order in which you'll encounter them as you drive from San José to Cabo San Lucas. Rates listed are for the high season (winter); typically they'll be 20% lower in the summer. Most resorts offer golf and fishing packages.

### WHERE TO STAY

**Casa del Mar** *Finds* A little-known treasure, this intimate resort is one of the best values along the Corridor. The hacienda-style building offers luxury accommodations in an intimate setting, as well as an on-site spa and nearby golf facilities. It's convenient to the 18-hole championship Cabo Real golf course.

Guest rooms have a clean, bright feel, with white marble floors, light wicker furnishings, a separate sitting area, and a large whirlpool tub plus separate shower. Balconies have oversize chairs with a view of the ocean beyond the pool. It's a romantic hotel for couples and honeymooners, known for welcoming, personalized service.

Km 19.5 on Hwy. 1, 23410 Cabo San Lucas, B.C.S. ✆ **800/221-8808** in the U.S., or 624/144-0030. Fax 624/144-0034. www.casadelmarresort.com. 56 units. High season $475 double; $530 suite. Low season $230 double; $280 suite. AE, MC, V. **Amenities:** Restaurant, lobby bar; beach club (adults only) with pool, hot tub, pool bar, open-air restaurant; 6 other pools (2 with whirlpools and swim-up bars); 2 lighted tennis courts; privileges at Cabo Real and El Dorado golf clubs; full-service spa; small workout room; tour desk; room service; in-room massage; babysitting; laundry and dry cleaning. *In room:* A/C, cable TV, minibar, dataport, bathrobes, hairdryers, Jacuzzi, safe-deposit box.

**Hotel Palmilla** ★★★ One of the most luxurious hotels in Mexico, the Palmilla is the grand dame of Los Cabos resorts. Though it is the oldest property along the Corridor, constant upgrades mean the rooms and facilities surpass those at even the newest luxury resorts. The Palmilla has become renowned as a location for weddings and anniversary celebrations with a renewal of vows; ceremonies take place in its small chapel on a sloped hillside. Perched on a clifftop above the sea, the resort is a series of white buildings with red-tile roofs, towering palms, and flowering bougainvillea. Talavera vases, carved dressers and headboards, and bathrooms walled in hand-painted tiles give the rooms a colonial-Mexico feel. Private balconies have extra-comfortable overstuffed chairs. TVs have built-in VCRs, and a wide selection of movies is available from the concierge. The 5-bedroom villa, Casa Cristina, has its own pool. The hotel automatically adds a 15% service charge to all rates, which is included in the rates quoted below.

Km 27.5 on Hwy. 1, 23400 San José del Cabo, B.C.S. ✆ **800/637-2226** in the U.S., or 624/144-5000. Fax 624/144-5100. www.palmillaresort.com. 114 units, 1 villa. High season $450 double; $690–$2,750 suite or villa. Low season $230–$260 double; $435–$2,000 suite or villa. AE, MC, V. **Amenities:** Restaurant, pool lunch and snack service, Fri night Mexican fiestas, bar; swimming pool; championship golf course designed by Jack Nicklaus; 2 lighted tennis courts; small fitness center; croquet court; 2 volleyball courts; horseback riding; fishing boats; tour desk; car rental; salon; room service; in-room massage; babysitting; laundry. *In room:* A/C, TV/VCR, dataport, minibar, bathrobes, hair dryer, safe deposit box.

**Las Ventanas al Paraíso** ★★★ Las Ventanas is known for its luxury accommodations and attention to detail. The architecture, with adobe structures and rough-hewn wood accents, provides a soothing complement to the desert landscape. The only color comes from the dazzling windows (*ventanas*) of pebbled rainbow glass handmade by regional artisans. Richly furnished, Mediterranean-style rooms are large (starting at 93 sq. m/1,000 sq. ft.) and appointed with every conceivable amenity, from wood-burning fireplaces to computerized telescopes for star- or whale-gazing. Rooms contain satellite TV with VCRs, stereos with CD players, and dual-line phones. Sizable whirlpool tubs overlook the room but may be closed off for privacy. Larger suites offer extras like rooftop terraces, sunken whirlpools on a private patio, or a personal pool. The spa is among the best in Mexico. With a staff that outnumbers guests by four to one, this is the place for those who want (and can afford) to be seriously spoiled. The 15% service charge is not included in the prices below, which do include taxes.

Km 19.5 on Hwy. 1, 23410 San José del Cabo, B.C.S. ✆ **888/525-0483** in the U.S., or 624/144-0300. Fax 624/144-0301. www.lasventanas.com. 61 suites. $644 garden-view double; $784 ocean-view double; $896 split-level ocean-view suite with rooftop terrace; $1,120 split-level ocean-front suite with rooftop terrace. Luxury suites (1 and 3 bedrooms) $2,464–$3,920. Spa and golf packages and inclusive meal plans available. AE, DC, MC, V. Free valet parking. **Amenities:** Ocean-view restaurant, terrace bar with live music, seaside grill, fresh-juice bar; access to adjoining championship Cabo Real golf course; deluxe European spa with complete treatment and exercise facilities; watersports; sportfishing and luxury yachts available; tour services; car rental; shuttle services; 24-hour room service; laundry. *In room:* A/C, TV, dataport, minibar, bathrobes, hairdryer, iron, safe deposit box.

### WHERE TO DINE

**Pitahayas** ★ PACIFIC RIM In a beachfront setting in the Hacienda del Mar resort, Pitahayas offers gourmet dining under a grand *palapa* or on open-air terraces under a starlit sky. Master chef Volker Romeike has assembled a creative menu that blends Pacific Rim cuisine with Mexican herbs and seasonings. Notable sauces include mango, black bean, and curry. Rotisserie barbecued duck is a house specialty, as are mesquite grill and wok cooking. A dessert pizza with fresh fruit, chocolate, and marzipan makes a fitting finish to a stunning meal. Formal resort attire is requested, and reservations are a must during high season.

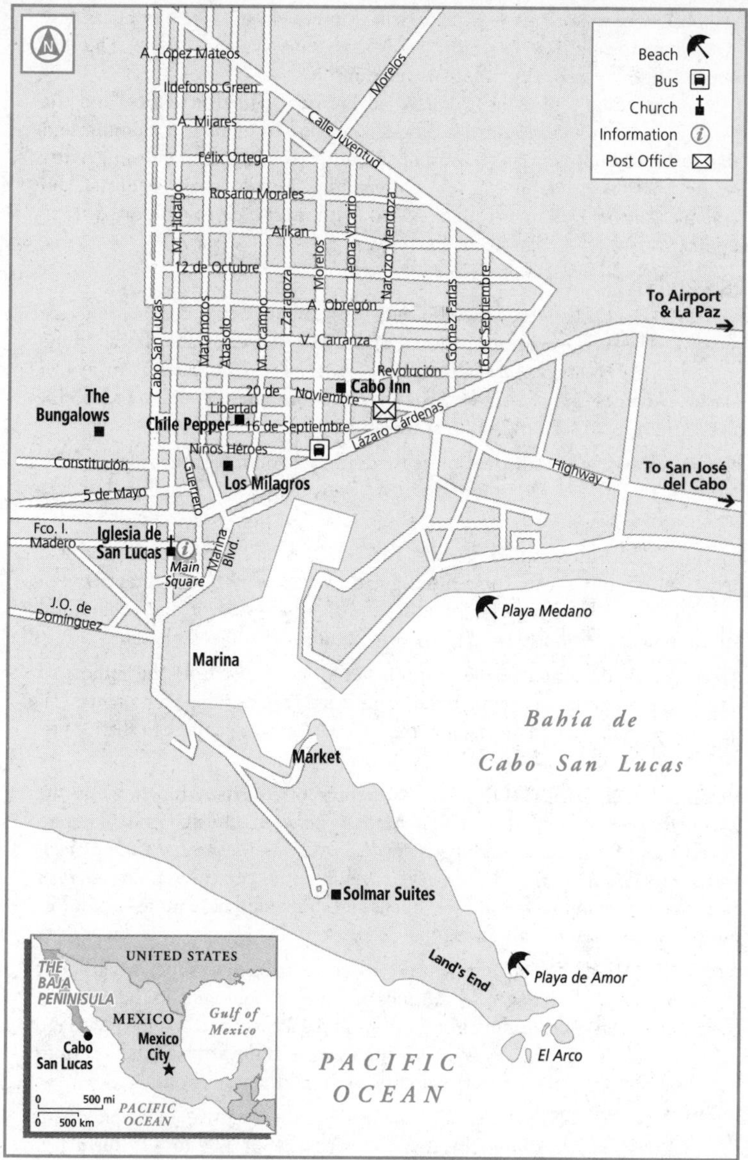


At Hacienda del Mar, Km 10 on Hwy. 1, Cabo del Sol. ✆ **624/145-8010.** Main courses $12–$30. AE, MC, V. Daily 5–10:30pm.

## CABO SAN LUCAS

183km (114 miles) S of La Paz; 35km (22 miles) W of San José del Cabo; 1,792km (1,120 miles) SE of Tijuana

The hundreds of luxury hotel rooms along the Corridor north of Cabo San Lucas have transformed this formerly rustic and rowdy outpost. Although it retains boisterous nightlife, Cabo San Lucas is no longer the simple town

Steinbeck wrote about. Once legendary for big-game fish, Cabo San Lucas now draws more people for its nearby world-class fairways and greens. This has become Mexico's most elite resort destination.

Travelers enjoy a growing roster of adventure-oriented activities, and the nightlife is as hot as the desert in July. A collection of popular restaurants and bars along Cabo's main street stay open and active until the morning's first fishing charters head out to sea. Despite the growth in diversions, Cabo remains more or less a one-stoplight town, with most everything located along the main strip.

## ESSENTIALS

**GETTING THERE & DEPARTING** **By Plane** For information, see "Getting There & Departing," earlier, under San José del Cabo. Local airline numbers are as follows: **Aerocalifornia** (✆ **624/143-3700** or 624/143-3915); **Alaska Airlines** (✆ **624/146-5166**); and **Mexicana** (✆ **624/143-5353,** 624/146-5001, or 624/142-0606 at the airport).

**By Car** From La Paz, the best route is Highway 1 south past the village of San Pedro, then Highway 19 south through Todos Santos to Cabo San Lucas, a 2-hour drive.

**By Bus** The **bus terminal** (✆ **624/143-5020**) is on Héroes at Morelos; it is open daily from 6am to 7pm. Buses go to La Paz every 90 minutes between 6am and 6pm. To and from San José, the more convenient and economical **Suburcabos** public bus service runs every 20 minutes and costs $2.50.

**Arriving** At the airport, either buy a ticket for a *colectivo* from the authorized transportation booth inside the building (about $13) or arrange for a rental car, the most economical way to explore the area. Up to four people can share a private taxi, which costs about $60.

**VISITOR INFORMATION** The **Secretary of Tourism** functions as the information office in Cabo. It's on Madero between Hidalgo and Guerrero (✆ **624/142-0446**). The English-language ***Los Cabos Guide, Los Cabos News, Cabo Life, Baja Sun,*** and the irreverent and extremely entertaining ***Gringo Gazette*** are distributed free at most hotels and shops, and have up-to-date information on new restaurants and clubs.

**CITY LAYOUT** The small town spreads out north and west of the harbor of **Cabo San Lucas Bay,** edged by foothills and desert mountains to the west and south. The main street leading into town from the airport and San José del Cabo is **Lázaro Cárdenas;** as it nears the harbor, **Marina Bulevard** branches off from it and becomes the main artery that curves around the waterfront.

**GETTING AROUND** Taxis are easy to find but expensive, in keeping with the high cost of everything else. Expect to pay about $15 to $25 for a taxi between Cabo and the Corridor hotels.

For day trips to San José del Cabo, take the Suburcabos (see "Getting There & Departing," above) or a cab. You'll see car-rental specials advertised in town, but before signing on, be sure you understand the total price after insurance and taxes are added. Rates can run between $40 and $75 per day, with insurance an extra $10 per day.

## *FAST FACTS:* Cabo San Lucas

*Area Code* The telephone area code is **624.**

*Beach Safety* Before swimming in the open water, *check if conditions are safe.* Undertows and large waves are common. **Medano Beach,** close to the marina and town, is the principal beach that's safe for swimming. The Hotel Melia Cabo San Lucas, on Medano Beach, has a roped-off swimming area to protect swimmers from personal watercraft and boats. Colored flags to signal swimming safety aren't generally found in Cabo, and neither are lifeguards.

*Currency Exchange* Banks exchange currency during normal business hours, generally Monday to Friday from 9am to 6pm, Saturday from 10am to 2pm. Currency-exchange booths, throughout Cabo's main tourist areas, aren't as competitive, but they're more convenient. ATMs are widely available and even more convenient, dispensing pesos—and in some cases dollars—at bank exchange rates.

*Emergencies/Hospital* See "Fast Facts: San José Del Cabo," earlier.

*Internet Access* **Dr. Z's Internet Café & Bar,** L. Cárdenas 7, edificio Posada, across from the Pemex gas station (✆ **624/143-5390**), charges $3 for 10 minutes, $7 for 40 minutes, or $8.50 for an hour. It's open Monday to Saturday from 9am to 6pm.

*Pharmacy* A drugstore with a wide selection of toiletries as well as medicine is **Farmacia Aramburo,** in Plaza Aramburo, on Cárdenas at Zaragoza (✆ **624/143-1489**). It's open daily from 7am to 9pm.

*Post Office* The *correo* is at Cárdenas and Francisco Villa (✆ **624/143-0048**), on the highway to San José del Cabo, east of the bar El Squid Roe. It's open Monday to Friday from 9am to 4pm, Saturday from 9am to noon.

## OUTDOOR ACTIVITIES: FISHING, GOLF & MORE

Although superb sportfishing put Cabo San Lucas on the map, there's more to do than dropping your line and waiting for the Big One. For most cruises and excursions, try to make fishing reservations at least a day in advance; keep in mind that some trips require a minimum number of people. Most sports and outings can be arranged through a travel agency; fishing can also be arranged directly at one of the fishing-fleet offices at the far south end of the marina.

Besides fishing, there's kayaking ($60 for a sunset trip around the Arch rock formation; $40 for morning trips) and boat trips to Los Arcos or uninhabited beaches. All-inclusive daytime or sunset cruises are available on a variety of boats, including a restored pirate ship. Many of these trips include snorkeling; serious divers have great underwater venues to explore.

Between January and March, whale-watching is one of the most popular local activities. Guided ATV tours take you down dirt roads and through desert landscape to the old Cabo Lighthouse or an ancient Indian village. And then there's the challenge of world-class golf, a major attraction of Los Cabos.

*Tips* **Information, Please**

The many "visitor information" booths along the street in Cabo are actually time-share sales booths, and their staffs will pitch a visit to their resort in exchange for discounted tours, rental cars, or other giveaways.

For a complete rundown of what's available, contact **Xplora Adventours** (**© 624/142-9135**). It offers tours from any local company, rather than working with only a select few. Xplora has tour desks in the Westin Regina hotel and at the Sierra Madre store on Lázaro Cárdenas. Most businesses in this section are open from 10am to 2pm and 4 to 7pm.

**ATV TRIPS** Travel agencies book expeditions on all-terrain vehicles to Cabo Falso (an 1890 lighthouse) and La Candelaria (an Indian pueblo in the mountains). A 440-pound weight limit per two-person vehicle applies to both tours. The 3-hour tour to **Cabo Falso** includes a stop at the beach, a look at some sea-turtle nests (without disturbing them) and the remains of a 1912 shipwreck, a ride over 500-foot sand dunes, and a visit to the lighthouse. Guided tours cost around $45 per person on a single bike or $60 for two riding on one ATV. The vehicles are also available for rent at $35 for 3 hours.

**La Candelaria** is an isolated Indian village in the mountains 40km (25 miles) north of Cabo San Lucas. The old pueblo is known for the white and black witchcraft that is still practiced here. Lush with palms, mango trees, and bamboo, the settlement gets its water from an underground river that emerges at the pueblo. Retuning, you'll travel down a steep canyon, along a beach (giving you time to swim), and past giant sea turtle nesting grounds. The La Candelaria tour, which begins at 9am, costs around $80 per person or $100 for two people on the same ATV.

**BEACHES** All along the curving sweep of sand known as Medano Beach, on the east side of the bay, you can rent snorkeling gear, boats, WaveRunners, kayaks, and windsurf boards. You can also take windsurfing lessons. This is the town's main beach and is a great place for safe swimming as well as people-watching from one of the many outdoor restaurants along its shore.

Beach aficionados may want to rent a car (see "Getting Around," above) and explore the five more remote beaches and coves between the two Cabos: Playa Palmilla, Chileno, Santa María, Barco Varado, and Vista del Arco. Beaches other than Medano are not considered safe for swimming, though many people don't heed the warning. Experienced snorkelers may wish to check them out, but other visitors should go for the view only. Always check at a hotel or travel agency for directions and swimming conditions. Although a few travel agencies run snorkeling tours to some of these beaches, there's no public transportation: Your only option for beach exploring is to rent a car.

**CRUISES** **Glass-bottom boats** leave from the town marina daily every 45 minutes between 9am and 4pm. They cost $13.50 for a 1-hour tour, which passes sea lions and pelicans on its way to the famous "El Arco" (Rock Arch) at Land's End, where the Pacific and the Sea of Cortez meet. Boats drop you off at Playa de Amor; make sure you understand which boat will pick you up—it's usually a smaller one run by the same company that ferries people back at regular intervals. Check the timing to make sure you have the correct boat, or expect an additional $10 charge for boarding a competitor's boat.

There are a number of **daylong** and **sunset cruises** on a variety of boats and catamarans. They cost $30 to $45, depending on the boat, duration of cruise, and amenities. A sunset cruise on the 42-foot catamaran ***Pez Gato*** (© **624/143-3797** or 624/143-5297; pezgato@cabotel.com.mx) departs from the Plaza las Glorias Hotel dock at 5pm. A 2-hour cruise costs $35 and includes margaritas, beer, and sodas. The seasonal (winter) whale-watching tour leaves at 10:30am and returns at 1:30pm. It costs $35, and includes open bar and snacks. Similar boats leave from the marina and the Plaza las Glorias Hotel. Check with travel agencies or hotel tour desks.

**GOLF** Los Cabos has become the golf mecca of Mexico, and though most courses are along the Corridor, people look to Cabo San Lucas for information about this sport in Baja Sur. The master plan for Los Cabos golf calls for a future total of 207 holes. Fees listed below are for 18 holes, including golf cart, water, club service, and tax. Summer rates are about 25% lower, and many hotels offer golf packages. (For specifics on the various courses, see the box "The Lowdown on Golf in Cabo.")

The 27-hole course at the **Palmilla Golf Club,** at the Palmilla resort (© **800/386-2465** in the U.S., or 624/144-5250; open 7am–7pm) was the first Jack Nicklaus Signature layout in Mexico, on 900 acres of dramatic oceanfront desert. The course offers your choice of two back-nine options, with high-season greens fees of $235.75 (lower after 2pm). Guests at some hotels pay discounted rates.

Just a few kilometers away is another Jack Nicklaus Signature course, the 18-hole Ocean Course at **Cabo del Sol,** at the Cabo del Sol resort development in the Corridor (© **800/386-2465** in the U.S., or 624/145-8200). The 7,100-yard Ocean Course is known for its challenging three finishing holes. Greens fees are $240 to $262. Tom Weiskopf designed the new 18-hole Desert Course.

The 18-hole, 6,945-yard course at **Cabo Real,** by the Melia Cabo Real Hotel in the Corridor (© **624/144-0232;** caborealgolf@1cabonet.com.mx; 6:30am–6pm) was designed by Robert Trent Jones, Jr., and features holes that sit high on mesas overlooking the Sea of Cortez. Fees run $220 for 18 holes.

**El Dorado Golf Course** (© **624/144-5451;** www.caboreal.com) is a Jack Nicklaus Signature course next to the Westin Regina hotel at Cabo Real. The course is open daily 7am to dusk. Greens fees are $246 (after 2pm, $168). Carts are included; caddies are $50.

An 18-hole course designed by Roy Dye is at the **Cabo San Lucas Country Club** (© **800/854-2314** in the U.S., or 624/143-4653; fax 624/143-5809). The entire course overlooks the juncture of the Pacific Ocean and Sea of Cortez, including the famous Land's End rocks. It includes the 607-yard, par-5 7th hole—the longest hole in Mexico. Greens fees are $90 for 9 holes, $126 for 18 holes.

The lowest greens fees in the area are at the public 9-hole **Club Campo de Golf San José** (© **624/142-0900** or 624/142-0905) in San José del Cabo (see earlier). Greens fees are just $44 for 9 holes, $77 for 18 holes, with carts an additional $30 and $45, respectively.

**SNORKELING/DIVING** Several companies offer snorkeling; a 2-hour cruise to sites around El Arco costs $30, and a 4-hour trip to Santa María costs $55, including gear rental. Among the beaches visited on different trips are Playa de Amor, Santa María, Chileno, and Barco Varado. Snorkeling gear rents for $10 to $15. Contact **Xplora Adventours** (© **624/142-9135**). For scuba diving,

## The Lowdown on Golf in Cabo

Los Cabos, one of the world's finest golf destinations, offers an ample and intriguing variety of courses to challenge golfers of all levels.

The reason so many choose to play here is not just the selection, quality, and beauty of the courses, but the very reliable weather. The courses highlighted below compare to the great ones in Palm Springs and Scottsdale, with the added beauty of ocean views and a wider variety of desert cacti and flowering plants.

Course fees are high in Cabo—generally over $200 per round. But these are true world-class courses, worth the world-class price. Courses generally offer 20% to 30% off rates if you play after 2 or 2:30pm. This is actually a great time to play, as the temperature is cooler and play is generally faster. The golf offerings in Los Cabos will only continue to expand; four courses are in various phases of construction.

**PALMILLA GOLF CLUB** The original Cabo course is now a 27-hole course. The original 18 holes are known as the Arroyo; the new holes are the Ocean 9. It's a bit of a misnomer—although the newer holes lie closer to the water, only one has a true ocean view, with a spectacular play directly down to the beach. You must play the Arroyo for your first nine holes, then you choose between Mountain and Ocean for your back nine. If you play this course only once, choose the Mountain, which offers better ocean views. The signature hole is the Mountain 5; you hit over a canyon, then down to the green below over a forced carry. This is target golf, on a Jack Nicklaus course that was constructed with strategy in mind. A mountaintop clubhouse provides spectacular views. Although it is currently a semiprivate club, most Corridor hotels have membership benefits. The eventual plan is for guests of the Palmilla Hotel and residents of the adjacent real estate development to have exclusive use of this course.

**CABO DEL SOL** The Ocean Course was the second Jack Nicklaus course constructed in Los Cabos. Its dramatic finishing oceanside holes make it the "Pebble Beach of Baja." It is much more difficult than the Palmilla course, with less room for error.

Don't be fooled by the wide, welcoming first hole. This is challenging target golf, with numerous forced carries—even from the red tees.

contact **Amigos del Mar** (© **800/344-3349** or 310/459-9861, fax 310/454-1686 in the U.S.; © 624/143-0505, fax 624/143-0887 in Mexico; www.amigosdelmar.com; open 8am–4:30pm) at the marina, near the Solmar hotel. Dives are along the wall of a canyon in San Lucas Bay, where you can see the "sandfalls" that even Jacques Cousteau couldn't figure out—no one knows their source or cause. There are also scuba trips to Santa María Beach and more distant places, including the Gordo Banks and Cabo Pulmo. Prices start at $45 for a one-tank dive, $66 for two tanks; trips to the coral outcropping at Cabo Pulmo start at $120. You'll need a wetsuit for winter dives. A 5-hour resort course is available for $100.

Seven holes are along the water. The signature hole is 17, which runs by the water with a forced carry. Cabo del Sol offers another option, the newly opened Desert Course.

**CABO REAL** This Robert Trent Jones, Jr., design is known for its holes along the Sea of Cortez, which sit high on mesas overlooking the sea; exceptional among these is the frequently photographed 12th. Jones designed the course to test low handicappers, but multiple tees make it enjoyable for average players as well. The par-72 layout is 6,945 yards long, and was designed with professional tournament play in mind. The most famous hole is the 14th, right on the beach near the Melia resort.

**THE CABO SAN LUCAS COUNTRY CLUB** The front and back nines are the work of members of the Dye family, so the course plays like two different courses. Characteristic of Dye designs, it has deep waste bunkers, subtle terracing up hillsides, and holes built into the natural desert terrain. The most challenging hole is the 607-yard, par-5 7th hole, around a lake; it's the longest hole in Mexico. The course is designed to offer a variety of play options, from a short course played on front tees to a super-long course with numerous bunkers and hazards.

**EL DORADO GOLF COURSE** A Jack Nicklaus Signature course at Cabo Real, El Dorado is a links-style course in the Scottish tradition. The layout is challenging—7 holes border the Sea of Cortez, and 12 are carved out of two pristine canyons. The ocean-view holes are not the only water; manmade lakes are also a part of the scenery. El Dorado bills itself as the "Pebble Beach of Baja"—but then again, so does Cabo del Sol. You decide.

*Note:* The recently opened **Querencia** (**© 624/145-6670;** www.loscabosquerencia.com) is a Tom Fazio design. This is a private club, with play limited to property owners and members. If you take a property tour with a sales rep, you can play for $345. Be aware that the screening process is strict; they want to determine if you are a qualified prospect or simply a passionate golfer.

**SPORTFISHING** Many larger hotels, like the Solmar, have their own fleets. To make your own arrangements, go to the town marina on the south side of the harbor, where you'll find several fleet operators with offices near the docks. ***Panga* fleets** offer the best deals; 5 hours of fishing for two or three people costs $200 to $450. But stroll around the marina and talk with the captains—you may make a better deal. Try **ABY Charters** (**© 624/143-0831;** abcabo@prodigy.net.mx; 10% surcharge for paying with MC, V), or the **Picante/Blue Water Sportfishing Fleet** (**© 624/143-2474;** open 6:30am–8pm; AE, MC, V). Both have booths (with bathrooms) at the sportfishing dock at the far south end of the marina. A day on a fully equipped cruiser with captain

**Fun Fact Don't Sweat the One That Got Away**

"Catch and release" is strongly encouraged in Los Cabos. Anglers reel in their fish, which are then tagged and released unharmed into the sea. The angler gets a certificate and the knowledge that there will still be fish in the sea when he or she returns.

and guide starts at around $700 for up to four people. For deluxe trips with everything included aboard a 40-foot boat, you'll have to budget $1,400. (See also "Active Vacations in Mexico," in chapter 2, for companies that arrange fishing in advance.) If you've traveled in your own vessel, you'll need a fishing permit. Depending on the size of the boat, it will cost $15 to $45 per month. Daily permits ($4–$10) and annual permits are also available.

The fishing here lives up to its reputation: Bringing in a 100-pound marlin is routine. Angling is good all year, though the catch varies with the season. Sailfish and wahoo are best from June through November; yellowfin tuna, May through December; yellowtail, January through April; black and blue marlin, July through December. Striped marlin are prevalent year-round.

**SURFING** Good surfing can be found from March through November all along the beaches west of town, and there's a famous right break at **Chileno Beach,** near the Cabo San Lucas Hotel east of town. (See "Surfing," in "San José," earlier, for details on Playa Azul and Zippers.)

**WHALE-WATCHING** Whale-watching cruises are not to be missed. See "Whale-watching," on p. 668, for information on the excursions, which operate between January and March.

**OTHER SPORTS** **Bicycles, boogie boards, snorkels, surfboards,** and **golf clubs** are available for rent at **Cabo Sports Center** in the Plaza Náutica on Bulevard Marina (© **624/143-4272**). The center is open Monday to Saturday from 9am to 9pm, Sunday from 9am to 5pm.

You can rent **horses** through **Rancho Colin** (© **624/143-3652**) for around $20 per hour. Guided beach rides and sunset tours to El Faro Viejo (the Old Lighthouse) cost $60 per person; tours to the Pacific for sunset riding on the beach cost $30 per person per hour. It's open from 8am to 6pm.

## A BREAK FROM SPORTS: EXPLORING CABO SAN LUCAS

**FESTIVALS & EVENTS** **October 12** is the festival of the patron saint of Todos Santos, a town about 104km (65 miles) north. **October 18** is the feast of the patron saint of Cabo San Lucas, celebrated with a fair, feasting, music, dancing, and other special events.

**HISTORIC CABO SAN LUCAS** Sports and partying are Cabo's main attractions, but there are also a few cultural and historical points of interest. The stone **Iglesia de San Lucas** (Church of San Lucas) on Calle Cabo San Lucas, close to the main plaza, was established in 1730 by the Spanish missionary Nicolás Tamaral. A large bell in a stone archway commemorates the completion of the church in 1746. The Pericúe Indians, who resisted Tamaral's demands that they practice monogamy, eventually killed him. Buildings on the streets facing the main plaza are gradually being renovated to house restaurants and shops, and the picturesque neighborhood has the most Mexican ambience in town.

**DAY TRIPS** Most local and hotel travel agencies book day trips to the city of La Paz; they cost around $60, including beverages and a tour of the countryside along the way. Usually there's a stop at the weaving shop of Fortunato Silva, who spins his own cotton and weaves it into wonderfully textured rugs and textiles. Day trips are also available to **Todos Santos** ($60), with a guided walking tour of the Cathedral Mission, museum, Hotel California, and various artists' homes.

## SHOPPING

Most shops are on or within a block or two of Bulevard Marina and the plaza. A new shopping mall, Puerto Paraiso, is scheduled to open in 2002. Facing the marina, it will combine dining, entertainment, and shopping.

**Cuca's Blanket Factory** This open-air stand sells the usual Mexican cotton and wool blankets, with an added attraction—you can design your own and have it ready the next day. It's open daily from 9am to 9pm. No credit cards. Cárdenas at Matamoros. No phone.

**El Callejon** ★ The most eclectic shop in Los Cabos features antiques, unique gifts, paintings, and home furnishings. The one-of-a-kind items are mostly the work of local artists. It's open Monday to Saturday from 9:30am to 8pm. AE, MC, V. Vicente Guerrero s/n, between Cárdenas and Madero. ✆ **624/143-1139**; fax 624/143-3188.

**Rostros de México** ★ Walls of wooden masks and carved religious statues are the draw at this gallery, whose name means "Faces of Mexico." It's open Monday to Saturday from 10am to 7pm, Sunday 10am to 2pm. No credit cards. Cárdenas at Matamoros. ✆ **624/143-0558.**

## WHERE TO STAY

All hotel prices listed here are for the high season, in effect from November through Easter; summer rates are about 20% less. Several hotels offer package deals that significantly lower the nightly rate; ask your travel agent for information.

Budget accommodations are scarce, but there is a growing number of small inns and B&Bs. Several notable ones have opened in recent years. As most of the larger hotels are well maintained and offer packages though travel agents, I will focus on smaller, unique accommodations.

### Very Expensive

**Solmar Suites** ★ Set against sandstone cliffs at the very tip of the Baja Peninsula, the Solmar is beloved by those seeking seclusion, comfort, and easy access to Cabo's diversions. The suites are in two-story white stucco buildings along the edge of a broad beach. They have either a king or two double beds, satellite TV, separate seating areas, and private balconies or patios on the sand. Guests gather by the pool and on the beach at sunset and all day long during the winter whale migration. The Solmar has one of the best sportfishing fleets in Los Cabos, including the deluxe *Solmar V,* for long-range diving, fishing, and whale-watching expeditions. A small time-share complex adjoins the Solmar; some units are available for nightly stays. Rates below include the hotel's mandatory 10% service charge.

Av. Solmar 1, 23410 Cabo San Lucas, B.C.S. ✆ **624/143-3535.** Fax 624/143-0410. www.solmar.com. (Reservations: Box 383, Pacific Palisades, CA 90272; ✆ **800/344-3349** or 310/459-9861; fax 310/454-1686.) 194 units. High season $219–$402; low season $201–$366. AE, MC, V. **Amenities:** Restaurant (with Sat Mexican fiesta), 2 bars (1 beach, 1 swim-up); 3 pools; Jacuzzi; sportfishing; concierge; tour desk; car-rental desk; salon; room service; laundry and dry cleaning. *In room:* A/C, TV, dataport, minibar, coffeemaker, hairdryer, safe deposit box.

## Moderate

**The Bungalows** ★ This is one of the most special places to stay in Los Cabos. Each "bungalow" is a charming retreat decorated with authentic Mexican furnishings. Terra-cotta tiles, hand-painted sinks, wooded chests, blown glass, and other creative touches make you feel as if you're a guest at a friend's home rather than a hotel. Each room has a mini-kitchenette, purified water, TV with VCR, and designer bedding. Rooms surround a lovely heated pool with cushioned lounges and tropical gardens. A brick-paved breakfast nook serves a gourmet breakfast with fresh-ground coffee and fresh juices. Under owner Steve's warm and welcoming management, this is Cabo's most spacious, comfortable, full-service inn. A 100% smoke-free environment, it is 5 blocks from downtown Cabo.

Miguel A. Herrera s/n, in front of Lienzo Charro, 23410 Cabo San Lucas, B.C.S. ✆ and fax **624/143-5035** or 624/143-0585. www.cabobungalows.com. 16 units. $90 double; $106–$128 suite. Extra person $15. Rates include full breakfast. Ask about summer promotions. AE. Street parking available. **Amenities:** Breakfast room; pool; tour desk; concierge. *In room:* A/C, TV/VCR, dataport, mini-fridge, coffeemaker.

**Los Milagros** The elegant white two-level buildings containing the 11 suites and rooms of Los Milagros (the Miracles) border either a grassy garden area or the small pool. Rooms contain contemporary iron beds with straw headboards, buff-colored tile floors, and artistic details. Some units have kitchenettes, and the master suite has a sunken tub. E-mail, fax, and telephone service are available through the office, and there's coffee service in the mornings on the patio. Evenings are romantic: Candles light the garden and classical music plays. Request a room in one of the back buildings, where conversational noise is less intrusive. It's located just a block and a half from the Giggling Marlin and Cabo Wabo.

Matamoros 116, 23410 Cabo San Lucas, B.C.S. ✆ and fax **624/143-4566.** www.losmilagroshotel.com. 11 units. $84 double. Ask about summer discounts, group rates, long-term discounts. No credit cards. Limited street parking. **Amenities:** Small pool. *In room:* A/C.

## Inexpensive

**Cabo Inn** ★★ *Finds* This three-story hotel on a quiet street is a real find, and it keeps getting better. It offers a rare combination of low rates, extra-friendly management, and great, funky style. Rooms are basic and very small, with either two twin beds or one queen; although this was a bordello in a prior incarnation, everything is new, from the mattresses to the mini-refrigerators. Muted desert colors add a spark of personality. The rooms surround a courtyard where you can enjoy satellite TV, a barbecue grill, and free coffee. The third floor has a rooftop terrace with *palapa* and a small swimming pool. Also on this floor is "Juan's Love Palace," a.k.a. the honeymoon suite. It's a colorful, *palapa*-topped, open-air room with hanging *tapetes* (woven palm mats) for additional privacy. A large fish freezer is available, and most rooms have kitchenettes. The hotel's just 2 blocks from downtown and the marina. A lively restaurant next door will even deliver pitchers of margaritas and dinner to your room.

20 de Noviembre and Leona Vicario, 23410 Cabo San Lucas, B.C.S. ✆ and fax **624/143-0819.** www.mexonline.com/caboinn.htm. 23 units. $58 double. $330 double weekly (low season only). No credit cards. Street parking. **Amenities:** Communal TV and barbecue; small rooftop pool and sunning area. *In room:* A/C.

**Chile Pepper Inn** *Value* This bright yellow stucco building contains simple but tasteful rooms surrounding a common courtyard. Light wood furnishings are of the hand-carved, rustic variety so popular in Mexico. Palm mats line the floors, and muslin curtains cover the windows that open onto the courtyard.

The beds have top-quality mattresses and colorful cotton linens; the small bathrooms, although small are decorated in painted tiles with Talavera sinks. Individual air-conditioning units are new and quiet, local calls are free, and the TV has a large variety of U.S. channels. The one suite has two queen beds in an L-shaped room. It's 4 blocks from the Hard Rock Cafe on a quiet street, but still close to Cabo's nightlife action.

16 de Septiembre and Abasolo, 23410 Cabo San Lucas, B.C.S. ✆ **877/708-1918** from the U.S. and Canada, or 624/143-8611. ✆ and fax **624/143-0510.** www.chilepepperinn.com. 9 units. $73 double; $106.50 suite. AE, MC, V. Street parking. *In room:* A/C, TV.

## WHERE TO DINE

It's not uncommon to pay a lot for mediocre food in Cabo, so try to get a couple of unbiased recommendations. If people are only drinking and not dining, take that as a clue, since many seemingly popular places are long on party atmosphere but short on food. Prices decrease the farther you walk inland. The absolute local favorite is **Manuel's Tamales,** a street stand selling traditional treats of corn meal stuffed with meat or cheese, then steamed in a cornhusk. Look for him on weekend nights on the corner of Cárdenas and Zaragoza. Streets to explore for other good restaurants include Hidalgo and Cárdenas, plus the Marina at the Plaza Bonita. Note that many restaurants automatically add the tip (15%) to the bill.

### Very Expensive

**Casa Rafael's** ★ INTERNATIONAL Looking for a little romance? Casa Rafael's, though overpriced, is among the most romantic places in Cabo. Dine in one of the large house's candlelit rooms and alcoves (which are air-conditioned), or outside beside the small swimming pool. Piano music plays in the background while you enjoy a leisurely meal. To start, try sublime smoked *dorado* paté, or perhaps hearts of palm with a raspberry-vinaigrette dressing. House specialties—a tasty combination of selections from the meat, seafood, and pasta menus—include Cornish game hen in champagne sauce. Black Angus steaks are imported from the United States; the lamb comes from New Zealand. To find it, follow the Hacienda Road toward the ocean; when you top the hill, turn left and drive until you find the rosy-pink château with an arched front and a patio with caged birds and fountain.

Calle Medano and Camino el Pescador. ✆ **624/143-0739.** Fax 624/143-1679. www.allaboutcabo.com. Reservations strongly recommended. Main courses $20–$58. AE, MC, V. Daily 6–10pm.

### Expensive

**Nick-San** ★ JAPANESE/SUSHI Exceptional Japanese cuisine and sushi are the specialties in this air-conditioned restaurant with clean, minimalist decor. A rosewood sushi bar with royal blue tile accents welcomes diners to watch the master sushi chef at work. An exhibition kitchen behind him demonstrates why this place has been honored with a special award for cleanliness.

Blvd. Marina, Plaza de la Danza, Local 2. ✆ **624/143-4484.** Reservations recommended. Main courses $15–$30; sushi from $3.50. MC, V. Tues–Sun 11:30am–10:30pm.

### Moderate

**La Dolce** ITALIAN This restaurant is the offspring of Puerto Vallarta's La Dolce Vita, with authentic Italian thin-crust, brick-oven pizzas and other specialties. The food is some of the best in the Baja Peninsula, and the fact that 80% of the business is from local customers underscores the point. Partner Stefano (a dead ringer for Michelangelo's *David,* albeit with pants) keeps the service attentive and welcoming, and the food up to high standards. The simple menu also features sumptuous pastas and calzones, plus great salads. This is the best late-night dining option.

M. Hidalgo y Zapata s/n. ✆ **624/143-4122.** Main courses $8–$18. MC, V. Mon–Sat 5pm–midnight. Closed Sept.

**Mi Casa** ★ MEXICAN The building's vivid cobalt-blue façade is your first clue that this place celebrates Mexico, and the menu confirms that impression. This is one of Cabo's most renowned gourmet Mexican restaurants. Traditional specialties such as *manchamanteles* (literally, "tablecloth stainers"), *cochinita pibil,* and *chiles en nogada* are menu staples. Fresh fish is prepared with delicious seasonings from throughout Mexico. Especially pleasant at night, the restaurant's tables, scattered around a large patio, are set with colorful cloths, traditional pottery, and glassware. It's across from the main plaza.

Calle Cabo San Lucas (at Madero). ✆ **624/143-1933.** Reservations recommended. Main courses $11–$23. AE, MC, V. Daily noon–3pm and 5:30–10:30pm.

### Inexpensive

**Felix's** ★ MEXICAN This colorful, friendly family-run place has grown up since opening in 1958, going from just serving tacos to offering a full array of tasty Mexican and seafood dishes. Everything's fresh and homemade, including the corn tortillas and the numerous and varied salsas—more than 30! Fish tacos made with fresh *dorado* are superb, as are any of the shrimp dishes—the honey mustard version is especially tasty. Don't leave without sampling the original Mexican bouillabaisse, a rich stew of shrimp, crab, sea bass, scallops, Italian sausage, and savory seasonings. Mexican specialties include *carne asada* (grilled beef) with chile verde sauce, and chimichangas. There is full bar service; the specialties are fresh fruit margaritas and daiquiris. At breakfast time, this is Mama's Royale Café (see below).

Hidalgo and Zapata s/n. ✆ **624/143-4290.** Main courses $8–$15. MC, V. Daily 2:30–10pm.

**Mama's Royale Café** BREAKFAST What a great place to start the day! The shady patio decked with cloth-covered tables and the bright, inviting interior dining room are both comfortable places to settle in. And the food's just as appetizing. Effrain and Pedro preside over this dining mecca with breakfast selections that include grilled sausage, French toast stuffed with cream cheese and topped with pecans, strawberries, and orange liqueur; several variations of eggs Benedict, home fries, fruit crepes, and, of course, traditional breakfasts, plus free coffee refills. The orange juice is fresh squeezed, and there usually is live *bolero* music to get your morning off to a lively start.

Hidalgo at Zapata. ✆ **624/143-4290.** Breakfast special $2.50; a la carte $2.50–$10. MC, V. Daily 7:30am–1pm.

**Mocambo's** ★ SEAFOOD The new location of this longstanding Cabo favorite is not inspiring—it's basically a large cement building—but the food obviously is. The place is always packed, generally with locals tired of high prices and small portions. Ocean-fresh seafood is the order of the day, and the specialty platter can easily serve four people. The restaurant is 1½ blocks inland from Lázaro Cárdenas.

Av. Leona Vicario and 20 de Noviembre. ✆ **624/143-6070.** Main courses $5–$23. MC, V. Daily noon–10pm.

## CABO SAN LUCAS AFTER DARK

Cabo San Lucas is the nightlife capital of Baja. After-dark fun centers around the casual bars and restaurants on Bulevard Marina or facing the marina, rather than a flashy disco scene. You can easily find a happy hour with live music and a place to dance, or a Mexican fiesta with *mariachis.*

**MEXICAN FIESTAS & THEME NIGHTS** Some larger hotels have weekly fiesta nights, Italian nights, and other buffet-plus-entertainment theme nights that can be fun as well as a good buy. Check travel agencies and the following hotels: the **Solmar** (© **624/143-3535**), the **Finisterra** (© **624/143-3333**), and the **Melia San Lucas** (© **624/143-4444**). Prices range from $22 (not including drinks, tax, and tips) to $35 (which covers everything, including an open bar with national drinks).

**SUNSET WATCHING** Come twilight, check out Land's End, where the two seas meet. At **Whale Watcher's Bar,** in the Hotel Finisterra (© **624/143-3333**), you'll get a world-class view of the sun sinking into the Pacific. The high terrace offers vistas of both sea and beach, as well as magical glimpses of whales from January to March. *Mariachis* play on Friday from 6:30 to 9pm. The bar is open daily 10am to 11pm.

**HAPPY HOURS, CLUBS & HANGOUTS** If you shop around, you can usually find an *hora alegre* (happy hour) somewhere in town between noon and 7pm. The most popular places to drink and carouse until all hours are long-standing favorites like the Giggling Marlin, El Squid Roe, and the Cabo Wabo Cantina.

Two places to enjoy live music in a more adult setting are the **Sancho Panza Wine Bar and Bistro** (see below) and the **El Bistro** restaurant and live jazz bar, Zaragoza, at Niños Héroes (© **624/143-8999**). Both offer classic jazz in more of a club-style atmosphere, accommodating conversation.

**Cabo Wabo Cantina** Owned by Sammy Hagar (formerly of Van Halen) and his Mexican and American partners, this "cantina" packs in youthful crowds, especially when rumors (frequent, and frequently false, just to draw a crowd) fly that a surprise appearance by a vacationing musician is imminent. Live rock bands from the United States, Mexico, Europe, and Australia perform. When there isn't a band, a disco-type sound system plays mostly rock and some alternative and techno. Overstuffed furniture frames the dance floor. Beer goes for $3, margaritas for $5. For snacks, the "Taco-Wabo," just outside the club's entrance, stays up late, too. The cantina is open from 11am to 4am. Vicente Guerrero at Cárdenas. © **624/143-1188.** No cover.

**El Squid Roe** El Squid Roe is one of the late Carlos Anderson's inspirations, and it still attracts wild, fun-loving crowds of all ages with its two stories of nostalgic decor. The eclectic food is far better than you'd expect from such a party place. As fashionable as blue jeans, this is a place to see—women's tops are known to be discarded with regularity, as the dancing on tables moves into high gear. There's also a patio out back for dancing when the tables, chairs, and bar spots are taken. It's open daily from noon to 2am. Blvd. Marina, opposite Plaza Bonita. © **624/143-0655.** No cover.

**Latitude 22+** This raffish restaurant and bar never closes. License plates, signs, sports caps, and a 959-pound blue marlin are the backdrop for U.S. sports events that play on six TVs scattered among pool tables, dart boards, and assorted games. You can order dishes from hamburgers to chicken-fried steak, or breakfast anytime. Happy hour is from 4 to 6pm. Latitude 22+ is 1 block north of the town's only traffic light. Blvd. Cárdenas s/n. © **624/143-1516.** No cover.

**Sancho Panza Wine Bar and Bistro** Finally, an alternative to beer bars. Sancho Panza combines a gourmet food market with a wine bar that features live jazz music plus an intriguing menu of Nuevo Latino cuisine. The place has a cozy neighborhood feeling, with tourists and locals taking advantage of the selection of more than 150 wines, plus espresso drinks. During high season, make reservations. It's open Monday to Saturday from 3pm to midnight. Plaza Las Glorias boardwalk, next to the Lighthouse. ✆ **624/143-3212**. www.sanchopanza.com. No cover.

**MEN'S CLUBS** Or should they be called "ladies' clubs," since that's who's doing the dancing? In any event, Cabo has a selection of places that offer so-called exotic dancing. **Lord Black,** on Bulevard Marina in the Plaza Náutica (no phone), features not only showgirls, but sushi, too. **Showgirls 20** (✆ **624/143-5380**) at the corner of Lázaro Cárdenas and Francisco Villa, calls itself a world-class cabaret. It also offers pool tables, satellite TVs, and private dancers. It's open from 8:30pm to 3am, has a cover charge of $7, and accepts major credit cards. It's located across the street from McDonald's.

## 2 Todos Santos: A Creative Oasis ★★★

68km (42 miles) N of Cabo San Lucas, on Hwy. 19

Todos Santos is known as "Bohemian Baja" among those looking for the latest, the trendiest, and the hippest of artist outposts—and among those simply weary of the L.A.-ization of Cabo San Lucas.

The art and artistry created here—from the kitchen to the canvas—is of an evolved type that seems to care less about commercial appeal than quality. In doing so, it becomes more of a draw. Not to be overlooked are the arts of agriculture, masonry, and weaving created by some of the town's original residents. From superb meals at **Café Santa Fe** to an afternoon browsing at **El Tecolote Libros,** the best bookstore I've come across in Mexico, Todos Santos is intriguing to its core.

Not only is the town a cultural oasis in Baja, it's an oasis in the true sense of the word—in this desert landscape, Todos Santos enjoys an almost continuous water supply from the peaks of the Sierra de la Laguna mountains. It's just over an hour's drive up the Pacific coast from Cabo San Lucas; you'll know you've arrived when the arid coastal scenery suddenly gives way to verdant groves of palms, mangos, avocados, and papayas.

During the Mission Period of Baja, this oasis valley was deemed the only area south and west of La Paz worth settling, as it had the only reliable water supply. In 1723, an outpost mission was established, followed by the full-fledged Misión Santa Rosa de Las Palmas in 1733. At the time, the town was known as Santa Rosa de Todos Santos, eventually shortened to its current name, which translates as "All Saints."

Over the next 200 years, the town alternated between prosperity and difficulty. Its most recent boom lasted from the mid-19th century until the 1950s, when the town flourished as a sugarcane production center and began to develop a strong cultural core. Many of the buildings now being restored and converted into galleries, studios, shops, and restaurants were built during this era. It wasn't until the 1980s that a paved road connected Todos Santos with La Paz, and tourism began to draw new attention to this tranquil town.

The demand for the town's older colonial-style structures by artists, entrepreneurs, and foreign residents has resulted in a real-estate boom. New shops,

**Fun Fact** **You Can Check Out Any Time You Like . . .**

In Todos Santos, the most renowned accommodation is the **Hotel California,** alleged namesake of the famous Eagles song. The hotel was originally constructed in 1928, in part from planks salvaged from a shipwrecked Norwegian vessel. Currently closed for a complete renovation, it's still worth walking past—you'll find it on Calle Juárez Colonia Centro between Morelos and Marquez de León.

galleries, and cafes crop up continuously. The coastal strip south of Todos Santos is in the process of being developed, with its first luxury hotel and spa slated to open during 2002. For the casual visitor, Todos Santos can easily be explored in a day, but a few tranquil inns welcome guests who want to stay a little longer.

## WHAT TO SEE & DO

During the **Festival Fundador** (Oct. 10–14), which celebrates the founding of the town in 1723, streets around the main plaza fill with food, games, and wandering troubadours. Many of the shops and the Café Santa Fe close from the end of September through the festival.

There are at least half a dozen galleries, including the noted **Galería de Todos Santos,** corner of Topete and Legaspi (✆ **612/145-0500**), which features a changing collection of works by regional artists. It's open daily 11am to 4pm (closed Sun May–Nov) and doesn't accept credit cards. The **Galería Santa Fé,** Centenario, across from the plaza (✆ **612/145-0340**), is an eclectic collection of original and creative Mexican folk art and *artesanía* treasures that include Frida-adorned frames, and "shrines"—kid-size chairs decorated in bottle caps, Virgin of Guadalupe images, *milagros,* and more. It's open Wednesday to Monday 10am to 5pm, and accepts Visa and MasterCard.

## WHERE TO STAY & DINE

Consider the **Todos Santos Inn,** Calle Legaspi 33, between Topete and Obregón (✆ **612/145-0040**). An elegant place to stay, it is in a historic house that has served as a general store, cantina, school, and private residence. Details include luxurious white bed linens, netting draped romantically over the beds, Talavera tile bathrooms, antique furniture, and high, wood-beamed ceilings. Two rooms and two suites border a courtyard terrace and garden. Rates run $95 to $135 per night. The suites are air-conditioned, but have neither television nor telephone. Currently, no credit cards are accepted. Seasonal discounts are available, but the inn closes for the month of September.

For myself—and I would suspect many others—a meal at the **Café Santa Fe** ★, Calle Centenario 4 (✆ **612/145-0340**), is reason enough to visit Todos Santos. Much of the attention the town has received in recent years can be directly attributed to this outstanding cafe, and it continues to live up to its lofty reputation. Owners Ezio and Paula Colombo refurbished a large stucco house across from the plaza, creating an exhibition kitchen, several dining rooms, and a lovely courtyard adjacent to a garden of hibiscus, bougainvillea, papaya trees, and herbs. My favorite interior room is the one in homage to Frida Kahlo, with reproductions of her work on grand canvases that flatter her more than her originals.

The excellent Northern Italian cuisine emphasizes local produce and seafood; try the ravioli stuffed with spinach and ricotta in a Gorgonzola sauce, or ravioli with lobster and shrimp, accompanied by an organic salad. In high season, the wait for a table at lunch can be long. Everything is prepared to order, and reservations are recommended. Main courses run $10 to $15. It's open Wednesday to Monday noon to 9pm; closed September and October, and accepts MasterCard and Visa.

A more casual option, and a magical place to start the day, is the garden setting of the **Café Todos Santos,** Centenario 33, across from the Todos Santos Inn (© **612/145-0300**). Among the espresso drinks is the bowl-size café latte, accompanied by a freshly baked croissant or one of the signature cinnamon buns. Lunch or a light meal may include a *frittata,* a filling sandwich on home-baked bread, or fish filet wrapped in banana leaves with coconut milk. Main courses average $3 to $6. The cafe is open 7am to 9pm Tuesday through Sunday, 7am to 2pm Monday. No credit cards.

## 3 La Paz: Peaceful Port Town ★★

176km (110 miles) N of Cabo San Lucas; 195km (122 miles) NW of San José del Cabo; 1,544 km (968 miles) SE of Tijuana

La Paz means "peace," and the feeling seems to float on the ocean breezes of this provincial town. Despite being an important port, home to almost 200,000 inhabitants, and the capital of the state of Baja California Sur, it remains slow-paced and relaxed. It's an easygoing yet sophisticated city and the guardian of "old Baja" atmosphere. Beautiful deserted beaches just minutes away complement the lively beach and palm-fringed *malecón* that front the town center.

The presence of the University of South Baja California adds a unique cultural presence that includes museums, and a theater and arts center. The surrounding tropical desert diversity and uncommon wildlife are also compelling reasons to visit. Adventurous travelers enjoy countless options, including hiking, rock climbing, diving, fishing, and sea kayaking. Islands and islets sit just offshore, once hiding places for looting pirates but now magnets for kayakers and beachcombers. At Espíritu Santo and Los Islotes, it's possible to swim with sea lions.

Despite its name, La Paz has historically been a place of conflict between explorers and indigenous populations. Beginning in 1535, Spanish conquistadors and Jesuit missionaries arrived and exerted their influence on the town's architecture and traditions. This was the center of pearl harvesting from the time conquistadors saw local Indians wearing pearl ornaments through the late 1930s, when an unknown disease killed off the oysters in the Bay of La Paz. John Steinbeck immortalized a local legend in his novella *The Pearl.*

La Paz is ideal for anyone nostalgic for Los Cabos the way it used to be. From accommodations to taxis, it's also one of Mexico's most outstanding beach vacation values and a great place for family travelers.

### ESSENTIALS

**GETTING THERE & DEPARTING** **By Plane** **Aerocalifornia** (© **800/237-6225** in the U.S., or 612/125-1023) has flights from Los Angeles, Tijuana, and Mexico City. **Aeromexico** (© **800/237-6639** in the U.S., 612/122-0091, 612/122-0093, or 612/122-1636) connects through Tucson and Los Angeles in the United States, and flies from Mexico City and other points within Mexico.

**By Car** From San José del Cabo, Highway 1 north is the longer, more scenic route; a flatter and faster route is Highway 1 east to Cabo San Lucas, then Highway 19 north through Todos Santos. A little before San Pedro, Highway 19

rejoins Highway 1 and runs north into La Paz; the trip takes 2 to 3 hours. From to the north, Highway 1 south is the only choice; the trip takes 4 to 5 hours.

**By Bus** The *Central Camionera* (main bus station) is at Jalisco and Héroes de la Independencia, about 25 blocks southwest of the center of town. It's open daily 6am to 10pm.

**By Ferry** Two SEMATUR car ferries serve La Paz from Topolobampo (the port for Los Mochis) Monday to Saturday at 10pm (10 hr.), and from Mazatlán Sunday to Friday at 3pm (18 hr.). The dock is at Pichilingue, 18km (11 miles) north of La Paz. Passengers pay one fee for themselves and another for their vehicles; prices for cars vary, depending on size. The office at Cinco de Mayo 502, at Guillermo Prieto, 23000 La Paz, B.C.S. (✆ **612/125-8899** ext. 109, or 612/122-5005), sells ferry tickets. The office is open daily 8am to 6pm. For information, call ✆ **01-800/696-9600** toll-free within Mexico.

**Buses** ($1.80 one-way) to Pichilingue depart from the beach bus terminal (✆ **612/122-7898**), on the *malecón* at Independencia, 10 times a day from 7am to 6pm.

**ORIENTATION** **Arriving by Plane** The airport is 18km (11 miles) northwest of town along the highway to Ciudad Constitución and Tijuana. Airport ***colectivos*** (around $11) run only from the airport to town, not vice versa. **Taxi** service (around $17) is available as well. Most major rental car agencies have booths inside the airport. **Budget's** local number is ✆ **612/124-6433.**

**By Bus** Buses arrive at the *Central Camionera,* about 25 blocks southwest of downtown, or at the beach station, along the *malecón.* Taxis line up out front of both.

**By Ferry** Buses line up in front of the ferry dock at Pichilingue to meet every arriving ferry. They stop at the beach bus station, on the *malecón* at Independencia; it's within walking distance of many downtown hotels if you're not encumbered with luggage. Taxis meet each ferry as well, and cost about $8 to downtown La Paz.

**VISITOR INFORMATION** The most accessible visitor information office is on Alvaro Obregón across from the intersection with Calle 16 de Septiembre (✆ **612/122-5939;** turismo@lapaz.cromwell.com.mx). It's open daily 9am to 8pm. The extremely helpful staff speaks English and can supply information on La Paz, Los Cabos, and the rest of the region.

**CITY LAYOUT** Although La Paz sprawls well inland from the ***malecón*** (the seaside blvd., Paseo Alvaro Obregón), you'll probably spend most of your time in the older, more congenial downtown section within a few blocks of the waterfront. The main plaza, **Plaza Pública,** or Jardín Velasco, is bounded by Madero, Independencia, Revolución, and Cinco de Mayo.

**GETTING AROUND** Because most of what you'll need in town is on the *malecón* between the tourist information office and the Hotel Los Arcos, or a few blocks inland from the waterfront, it's easy to get around La Paz on foot. Public buses go to some of the beaches north of town (see "Beaches & Sports," below). To explore the many beaches within 80km (50 miles) of La Paz, your best bet is to rent a car or hire a taxi. There are several car-rental agencies on the *malecón.*

**FESTIVALS & EVENTS** February features the biggest and best **Carnaval/ Mardi Gras** in Baja, as well as a 4- to 5-week **Festival of the Grey Whale** (starting in late Jan or early Feb, sometimes extending through early Mar). On **May 3,** a festival celebrates the city's founding by Cortez in 1535, and features *artesanía* exhibitions from throughout southern Baja. An annual marlin-fishing tournament is in **August,** with other fishing tournaments scheduled in **September** and **November.** On **November 1 and 2,** the Days of the Dead, altars are on display at the Anthropology Museum.

## *FAST FACTS:* La Paz

*Area Code* The telephone area code is **612.**

*Banks* Banks generally exchange currency during normal business hours: Monday to Friday from 9am to 6pm, Saturday from 10am to 2pm. ATMs are readily available and offer bank exchange rates on withdrawals.

*Emergencies* Dial ✆ **060.**

*Hospitals* You can choose between **Hospital Especialidades Medicas,** in Fidepaz (✆ **612/124-0400**), and **Hospital Juan Maria de Salvatierra** (✆ **612/122-1496**), Nicolas Bravo 1010, Col. Centro.

*Internet Access* **BajaNet,** Madero 430 (✆ **612/125-9380**), charges **$1.10** for each 10 minutes. It's open Monday to Saturday from 8am to 10pm, Sunday from 9am to 9pm.

*Pharmacy* One of the largest pharmacies is **Farmacia Baja California,** Independencia y Madero (✆ **612/122-0240** and 612/123-4408).

*Post Office* The *correo,* 3 blocks inland at Constitución and Revolución de 1910 (✆ **612/122-0388**), is open Monday to Friday from 8am to 2pm, Saturday from 9am to 1pm.

*Tourism Office* The office is at Km. 5.5 Carretera al Norte, Edificio Fidepaz, Col. Fidepaz, 23090, La Paz, B.C.S. (✆ **612/124-0199**). It's open daily from 10am to 2pm and 4 to 8pm.

## BEACHES & SPORTS

La Paz combines the unselfconscious bustle of a small capital port city with beautiful, isolated beaches not far from town. Well on its way to becoming the undisputed adventure tourism capital of Baja, it's the starting point for whale-watching, diving, sea kayaking, climbing, and hiking tours throughout the peninsula. For those interested in day adventures, travel agencies in major hotels or along the *malecón* can usually arrange all of the above, plus beach tours, sunset cruises, and visits to the sea-lion colony. Agencies in the United States that specialize in Baja's natural history also book excursions (see "Active Vacations in Mexico," in chapter 2).

**BEACHES** Within a 10- to 45-minute drive from La Paz lie some of the loveliest beaches in Baja. Many rival those of the Caribbean with their clear, turquoise water.

The ***malecón*** is the most convenient beach in town. Although the sand is soft and white and the water appears crystal clear and gentle, locals don't generally swim there. Because of the commercial port, the water is not considered as clean as that at the very accessible outlying beaches. With colorful playgrounds dotting the central beachfront and numerous open-air restaurants that front the water, it's best for a casual afternoon of post-sightseeing lunch and play.

The best beach in town is the one immediately north of town at **La Concha Beach Resort;** nonguests may use the hotel restaurant and bar and rent equipment for snorkeling, diving, skiing, and sailing. It's 10km (6 miles) north of town on the Pichilingue Highway at Km 5.5. The other beaches are all farther north of town, but midweek you may have these distant beaches to yourself.

For more information about beaches and maps, check at the tourist information office on the *malecón.* For a general tour of all of the beaches before deciding where to spend your precious vacation days, **Viajes Lybs** (© **612/122-4680**) offers a 4-hour beach tour for $22 per person, with stops at Balandra and El Tecolote beaches.

**CRUISES** A popular and very worthwhile cruise is to **Isla Espíritu Santo** and **Los Islotes.** You visit the largest sea-lion colony in Baja, stunning rock formations, and remote beaches, with stops for snorkeling, swimming, and lunch. If conditions permit, you may even be able to snorkel beside the sea lions. Both boat and bus tours are available to **Puerto Balandra,** where bold rock formations rising up like humpback whales frame pristine coves of crystal-blue water and ivory sand. **Viajes Palmira** (© **612/122-4030**), on the *malecón* across from Hotel Los Arcos, and other travel agencies can arrange these all-day trips, weather permitting. Price is $67 per person.

**SCUBA DIVING** Scuba-diving trips are best from June through September. **Fernando Aguilar's Baja Diving and Services,** Obregón 1665-2 (© **612/122-1826;** fax 612/122-8644; bajadiving@lapaz.cromwell.com.mx) arranges them. Rates start at $80 per person for an all-day outing and two-tank dive.

**SEA KAYAKING** Kayaking in the many bays and coves near La Paz has become extremely popular. Many enthusiasts bring their own equipment. Several companies in the United States (see "Active Vacations in Mexico," in chapter 2) can book trips in advance. Locally, **Mar y Aventuras** (© **612/122-7039,** or 612/122-27039; fax 612/122-3559; www.kayakbaja.com) arranges trips.

**SPORTFISHING** La Paz, justly famous for its sportfishing, attracts anglers from all over the world. Its waters are home to more than 850 species of fish. The most economical approach is to rent a *panga* (skiff) with guide and equipment. It costs $125 for 3 hours, but you don't go very far out. Super *pangas,* which have a shade cover and comfortable seats, start at around $180 for two persons. Larger cruisers with bathrooms start at $240. Local hotels and tour agencies arrange sportfishing trips.

**WHALE-WATCHING** Between January and March, and sometimes as early as December, 3,000 to 5,000 gray whales migrate from the Bering Strait to the Pacific coast of Baja. The main whale-watching spots are **Laguna San Ignacio** (on the Pacific near San Ignacio), **Magdalena Bay** (on the Pacific near Puerto López Mateos—about a 2-hr. drive from La Paz), and **Scammon's Lagoon** (near Guerrero Negro).

Most tours originating in La Paz go to Magdalena Bay, where the whales give birth to their calves in calm waters. Several companies arrange whale-watching tours that originate in La Paz or other Baja towns or in the United States; 12-hour tours from La Paz start at around $105.50 per person, including breakfast, lunch, transportation, and an English-speaking guide. Make reservations at **Viajes Lybs,** 16 de Septiembre 408, between Revolución and Serdán (© **612/122-4680;** fax 612/125-9600).

## A BREAK FROM THE BEACHES: EXPLORING LA PAZ

Most tour agencies offer city tours of all the major sights. Tours last 2 to 3 hours, include time for shopping, and cost around $15 per person.

**HISTORIC LA PAZ** When Cortez landed here on May 3, 1535, he named it Bahía Santa Cruz. It didn't stick. In April 1683, Eusebio Kino, a Spanish Jesuit, arrived and dubbed the place Nuestra Señora de la Paz (Our Lady of Peace). It wasn't until November 1, 1720, however, that Jaime Bravo, another Jesuit, set up a permanent mission. He used the same name as his predecessor, calling it the Misión de Nuestra Señora de la Paz. The mission church stands on La Paz's main square, on Revolución between Cinco de Mayo and Independencia.

**The Anthropology Museum** The museum features large, though faded, color photos of Baja's prehistoric cave paintings. There are also exhibits on various topics, including the geological history of the peninsula, fossils, missions, colonial history, and daily life. All information is in Spanish.

Altamirano and Cinco de Mayo. ✆ and fax **612/122-0162** or ✆ 612/125-6424. Free admission (donations encouraged). Mon–Fri 8am–6pm, Sat 9am–2pm.

**Biblioteca de las Californias** The small collection of historical documents and books at the Library of the Californias is the most comprehensive in Baja. Free international films are sometimes shown in the evenings.

In the Casa de Gobierno, Madero between Cinco de Mayo and Independencia, across the plaza from the mission church. No phone; for information call the tourism office (✆ **612/124-0199**). Mon–Fri 8am–8pm.

**El Teatro de la Ciudad** The city theater is the cultural center, with performances by visiting and local artists. Bookings include small ballet companies, experimental and popular theater, popular music, and an occasional classical concert or symphony.

Av. Navarro 700. ✆ **612/125-0486.**

## SHOPPING

La Paz has little in the way of folk art or other treasures from mainland Mexico. The dense cluster of streets behind the **Hotel Perla,** between 16 de Septiembre and Degollado, is full of small shops, some tacky, others quite upscale. In this area, there is also a very small but authentic **Chinatown,** dating to the time when Chinese laborers were brought to settle in Baja. Serdán from Degollado south is home to dozens of sellers of dried spices, piñatas, and candy. Stores selling crafts, folk art, clothing, and handmade furniture and accessories lie mostly along the *malecón* (Paseo Obregón) or within a block or 2.

**Antigua California** This shop manages to stay in business as others come and go. It carries a good selection of folk art from throughout Mexico. It's open Monday to Saturday from 9:30am to 8:30pm, Sunday from 10am to 5pm. AE, MC, V. Paseo Alvaro Obregón 220, at Arreola. ✆ **612/125-5230.**

**Artesanías Cuauhtémoc (The Weaver)** If you like beautiful hand-woven tablecloths, place mats, rugs, and other textiles, it's worth the long walk or taxi ride to this unique shop. Fortunato Silva, an elderly gentleman, weaves wonderfully textured cotton textiles from yarn he spins and dyes himself. He charges far less than you'd pay for equivalent artistry in the United States. It's open Monday to Saturday from 10am to 3pm and 5 to 7pm, Sunday from 10am to 1pm. No credit cards. Abasolo 3315, between Jalisco and Nayarit. ✆ **612/122-4575.**

**Dorian's** If you've forgotten any essentials or want to stock up on perfume and cosmetics, head for Dorian's, La Paz's major department store. La Paz is a duty-free port city, so prices are excellent. Dorian's also carries a wide selection of stylish clothing, shoes, lingerie, jewelry, and accessories. It's open daily from 9am to 9pm. AE, MC, V. 16 de Septiembre, between Esquerro and 21 de Agosto. No phone.

**Ibarra's Pottery** Here you not only shop for tableware, hand-painted tiles, and decorative pottery, you can watch people make it. Each piece is individually hand-painted or glazed and then fired. It's open Monday to Friday from 8am to 4pm, Saturday from 8am to 2pm. No credit cards. Guillermo Prieto 625, between Torre Iglesias and Republica. ✆ **612/122-0404.**

**SENI Jewelry** In addition to exceptionally priced, exquisitely stylish jewelry, you'll also find a good selection of Cuban and Veracruz cigars stored in a humidor. It's open Monday to Saturday from 11am to 2pm and 4 to 8pm. MC, V. Parque Cuauhtémoc, at Paseo Alvaro Obregón. ✆ **612/122-2604.**

## WHERE TO STAY

### EXPENSIVE

**La Concha Beach Resort** ★ Ten kilometers (6 miles) north of downtown La Paz, this resort's setting is perfect: on a curved beach ideal for swimming and watersports. All rooms face the water and have double beds, balconies or patios, and small tables and chairs. Condos with full kitchens and one or three bedrooms are available on a nightly basis in the high-rise complex next door. If available, they're worth the extra price for a perfect family vacation stay. The hotel offers scuba, fishing, and whale-watching packages.

Km 5 Carretera Pichilingue, 23000 La Paz, B.C.S. ✆ **800/999-2252**, 612/121-6161 or 612/121-6344. www.laconcha.com. 113 units. $106.50 double; $140 jr. suite; $125.50–$241 condo. AE, DC, MC, V. Free guarded parking. **Amenities:** Restaurant (with theme nights), 2 bars; beachside pool; Jacuzzi; complete aquatic-sports center with WaveRunners, kayaks, and paddleboats; beach club with scuba program; tour desk; free twice-daily shuttle to town; room service; laundry service. *In room:* A/C, TV.

### MODERATE

**Hotel Los Arcos** This three-story neocolonial-style hotel at the west end of the *malecón* is the best place for downtown accommodations with a touch of tranquility. Los Arcos has functional furnishings and amenities, and the hotel is filled with fountains, plants, and even rocking chairs. Most of the recently remodeled rooms and suites come with two double beds. Each has a balcony overlooking the pool in the inner courtyard or the waterfront, plus a whirlpool tub. I prefer the South Pacific–style bungalows with thatched roofs and fireplaces located in the back part of the property. Satellite TVs carry U.S. channels.

Av. Alvaro Obregón 498, between Rosales and Allende (Apdo. Postal 112), 23000 La Paz, B.C.S. ✆ **800/347-2252** or 714/450-9000 in the U.S., or 612/122-2744. Fax 612/125-4313. www.losarcos.com. 130 units; 52 bungalows. $75–$85 double; $85 suite; $60–$84 bungalow. AE, MC, V. Free guarded parking. **Amenities:** Cafeteria, restaurant, bar with live music; 2 pools (1 heated); sauna; travel agency; desk for fishing information; room service; laundry; Ping-Pong tables. *In room:* A/C, TV, minibar.

**Posada Santa Fe** ★ Gracious owners Ed and Raquel Rose make this elegant B&B La Paz's most romantic place to stay. Each room is individually decorated with high-quality rustic Mexican furniture and antiques, hand-loomed fabrics, and exquisite artisan details. Bathrooms are especially welcoming, with marble tubs and thick towels. Breakfast is served from 8 to 11am daily. Telephone, fax, and Internet service are available through the office. It's at the northern end of the *malecón.*

Alvaro Obregón 440, 23000 La Paz, B.C.S. ✆ **612/125-5871.** www.quintasol.com/posadasantafe/. 8 units. $85 double; $105 suite; $125 master suite. Rates include full breakfast. No credit cards. **Amenities:** Small pool. *In room:* A/C.

#### INEXPENSIVE

**Hotel Mediterrane** ★ Simple yet stylish, this unique inn mixes Mediterranean with Mexican, creating a cozy place for couples or friends to share. All rooms face an interior courtyard and are decorated with white tile floors and *equipal* furniture, with colorful Mexican *sarapes* draped over the beds. Some rooms have mini-fridges. All have VCRs. Its location is great—just a block from the *malecón.* The adjacent La Pazta restaurant (see "Where to Dine," below) is one of La Paz's best, and there is an Internet cafe next door. Rates include use of kayaks, bicycles for exploring the town, and 1 hour of Internet service.

Allende 36, 23000 La Paz, B.C.S. ✆ and fax **612/125-1195.** www.hotelmed.com. 8 units. $65–75 double; $80 suite. AE, MC, V. Weekly discounts available. *In room:* A/C, TV/VCR.

### WHERE TO DINE

Although La Paz is not known for culinary achievements, it has a growing assortment of small, pleasant restaurants that are good and reasonably priced. In addition to the usual seafood and Mexican dishes, you can find Italian, French, Spanish, Chinese, and a growing selection of vegetarian offerings. Restaurants along the seaside *malecón* tend to be more expensive than those a few blocks inland.

#### MODERATE

**Trattoria La Pazta** ★ ITALIAN/SWISS The trendiest restaurant in town, La Pazta gleams with black lacquered tables and white tile; the aromas of garlic and espresso float in the air. The menu features local fresh seafood in items such as pasta with squid in wine and cream sauce, and crispy fried calamari. There's also homemade lasagna, baked in a wood-fired oven. La Pazta is appealing for breakfast, too. The restaurant is in front of the Hotel Mediterrane, 1 block inland from the *malecón.*

Allende 36. ✆ **612/125-1195.** Breakfasts $2–$4; main courses $8–$11. AE, MC, V. Wed–Mon 7am–11pm.

#### INEXPENSIVE

**Caffé Gourmet** FRENCH/CAFE You'll feel as if you've suddenly been transported across the Atlantic in this incongruous but welcome addition to La Paz. Indulge in any number of espresso coffee drinks, plus French and Austrian pastries, while sitting at marble-topped bistro tables. Jazz music plays in the background.

Ave. Esquerro and 16 de Septiembre. No phone. Coffees and pastries $1–$3. No credit cards. Mon–Sat 7am–8pm; Sun 9am to 3pm.

**El Quinto Sol** VEGETARIAN Not only is this La Paz's principal health food market, it's a cheerful, excellent cafe for fresh fruit *liquados* (shakes), *tortas,* and vegetarian dishes. Tables sit beside oversize wood-framed windows with flowering planters in the sills. Sandwiches are served on whole-grain bread—also available for sale—and the potato tacos are an excellent way for vegetarians to indulge in a Mexican staple.

Ave. Independencia and B. Domínguez. ✆ **612/122-1692.** Main courses $1.50–$6.50. No credit cards. Mon–Sat 7am–9:30pm; Sun 8am to 3pm.

### LA PAZ AFTER DARK

A night in La Paz logically begins at a cafe along the *malecón* as the sun sinks into the sea—have your camera ready.

A favorite ringside seat at dusk is a table at **La Terraza,** next to the Hotel Perla (✆ **612/122-0777**). La Terraza makes good schooner-size margaritas.

## Exploring Northern Baja: Cruising the Sea of Cortez

John Steinbeck made this journey famous, collecting marine specimens and recording his observations, philosophies, and beliefs in the 1951 classic *The Log From the Sea of Cortez.* Now, even less adventurous souls can experience the magic of Steinbeck's 4,000-mile expedition in a more concentrated version. A few companies offer small-ship cruises from Cabo San Lucas north to the French colonial town of Santa Rosalía. Any travel agent can assist in pricing and booking these cruises. The following companies were among the first and are still considered the best.

**Cruise West** ★ (✆ **800/888-9378** or 206/441-8687 in the U.S.; fax 206/441-4757; www.cruisewest.com) offers an exceptional voyage that explores the interior Baja coast, spends time in a few key towns, and offers relaxed time for indulging in light adventure activities. The 217-foot *Spirit of Endeavor* has 51 cabins, all with double accommodations and full facilities. The spacious, comfortable cabins are considered among the best in small-ship cruising, with large picture windows, TV/VCRs, individually controlled air-conditioning, desk, twin bunks, and ample closet space. The common lounge area has a good selection of books, games, and videos, and features nature talks nightly. Prices for the 7-night cruise range from $1,695 to $3,195 per person (based on double occupancy), including all meals and activities. Prices vary depending on the dates. This cruise is oriented toward a slightly older passenger; educational and photography-themed cruises are also available, as are trip extensions to the Copper Canyon (see chapter 15).

**Voyager Cruise Line** (✆ **800/451-5952** in the U.S.; www.voyagercruiseline.com), offers a similar cruise program and itinerary, with a more active, adventurous traveler in mind. Its two ships offer 43 staterooms in four categories. Prices for a 7-night cruise start at $2,399 per person (based on double occupancy), including all meals and activities.

**Baja Expeditions,** 2625 Garnet Ave., San Diego, CA 92109 (✆ **800/843-6967** or 619/581-3311; www.bajaex.com), offers natural-history cruises, whale-watching, sea kayaking, and scuba-diving trips out of La Paz.

**Pelicanos Bar,** in the second story of the Hotel Los Arcos (✆ **612/122-2744**), has a good view of the waterfront and a clubby, cozy feel. **Carlos 'n' Charlie's La Paz–Lapa** (✆ **612/122-9290**) has live music on weekends. **La Cabaña** nightclub in the Hotel Perla (✆ **612/122-0777**) features Latin rhythms. It opens at 9:30pm, and there's an $11 minimum.

For dancing, a few of the hottest clubs are **Laser Disco** Obregón and Degollado (no phone), which plays dance music from the '70s to '90s; **Xtasis,** Arreola and Zaragoza (no phone), spinning techno and alternative dance tunes; and the locally hip **Las Varitas,** Independencia and Dominguez (✆ **612/125-2025**), where you'll hear Latin rock, ranchero, and salsa. All three are open from 9pm to 3 or 4am, with cover charges around $5.50. Note that covers may rise or fall depending on the crowd.

The poolside bar overlooking the beach at **La Concha Beach Resort,** Km 5.5 Pichilingue Highway (© **612/121-6161,** or 612/121-6344), is the setting for the ubiquitous Mexican fiesta at 7pm on Friday. The price is $18, including tax and tips.

## 4 Mid-Baja: Loreto, Mulegé & Santa Rosalía

Halfway between the resort sophistication of Los Cabos and the frontier exuberance of Tijuana lies Baja's midsection, an area rich in history and culture. The indigenous cave paintings here are a UNESCO World Heritage Site, and the area was home to numerous Jesuit missions in the 1700s. These days, mid-Baja is known for its excellent sea kayaking, sportfishing, and hiking.

Overlooked by many travelers (except avid informed sportfishermen), **Loreto** is a rare gem that sparkles under the desert sky. The purple hues of the Giganta Mountains meet the indigo waters of the Sea of Cortez, providing a spectacular backdrop of natural contrasts for the historic town. **Mulegé** is, literally, an oasis in the Baja desert. The only freshwater river (Río Mulegé) in the peninsula flows through town. And the port town of **Santa Rosalía,** while slightly past its prime, makes a worthy detour, with its pastel clapboard houses and unusual steel-and-stained-glass church, designed by Gustave Eiffel (of Eiffel Tower fame).

The region is also a popular jumping-off point for whale-watching tours. To find out when, where, and how to view these gentle giants, consult the **whale-watching primer** at the end of this section.

### LORETO & THE OFFSHORE ISLANDS

389km (243 miles) NW of La Paz; 533km (333 miles) N of Cabo San Lucas; 1,125km (703 miles) SE of Tijuana

The center of the Spanish mission effort during colonial times, Loreto was the first capital of the Californias and the first European settlement in the peninsula. Founded on October 25, 1697, it was selected by Father Juan Maria Salvatierra as the site of the first mission in the Californias. (California, at the time, extended from Cabo San Lucas to the Oregon border.) He held mass beneath a figure of the Virgin of Loreto, brought from a town in Italy bearing the same name. For 132 years, Loreto served as the state capital, until an 1829 hurricane destroyed most of the town. The state capital moved to La Paz the following year.

During the late '70s and early '80s, the Mexican government saw in Loreto the possibility for another mega-development along the lines of Cancún, Ixtapa, or Huatulco. It invested in a golf course and championship tennis facility, modernized the infrastructure, and built an international airport and marina facilities at Puerto Loreto, several kilometers south of town. The economics, however, didn't make sense, and few hotel investors and even fewer tourists came. Today, Loreto remains the wonderfully funky fishing village and well-kept secret that it has been for decades. The recent celebration of its 300-year anniversary had the added benefit of updating the streets, plaza, and mission in Loreto.

#### ESSENTIALS

The **Loreto International Airport** (© **613/135-0499;** airport code: LTO) is 6km (4 miles) southwest of town. Taxis (© **613/135-1255**) are readily available and charge about $11 for the 10-minute ride to Loreto. Loreto's Terminal de Autobuses, or **bus station** (© **613/135-0767**) is on Salvatierra and Paseo Tamaral, a 10-minute walk from downtown. It's open 7am to midnight. The trip from La Paz takes 5 hours and costs $15.

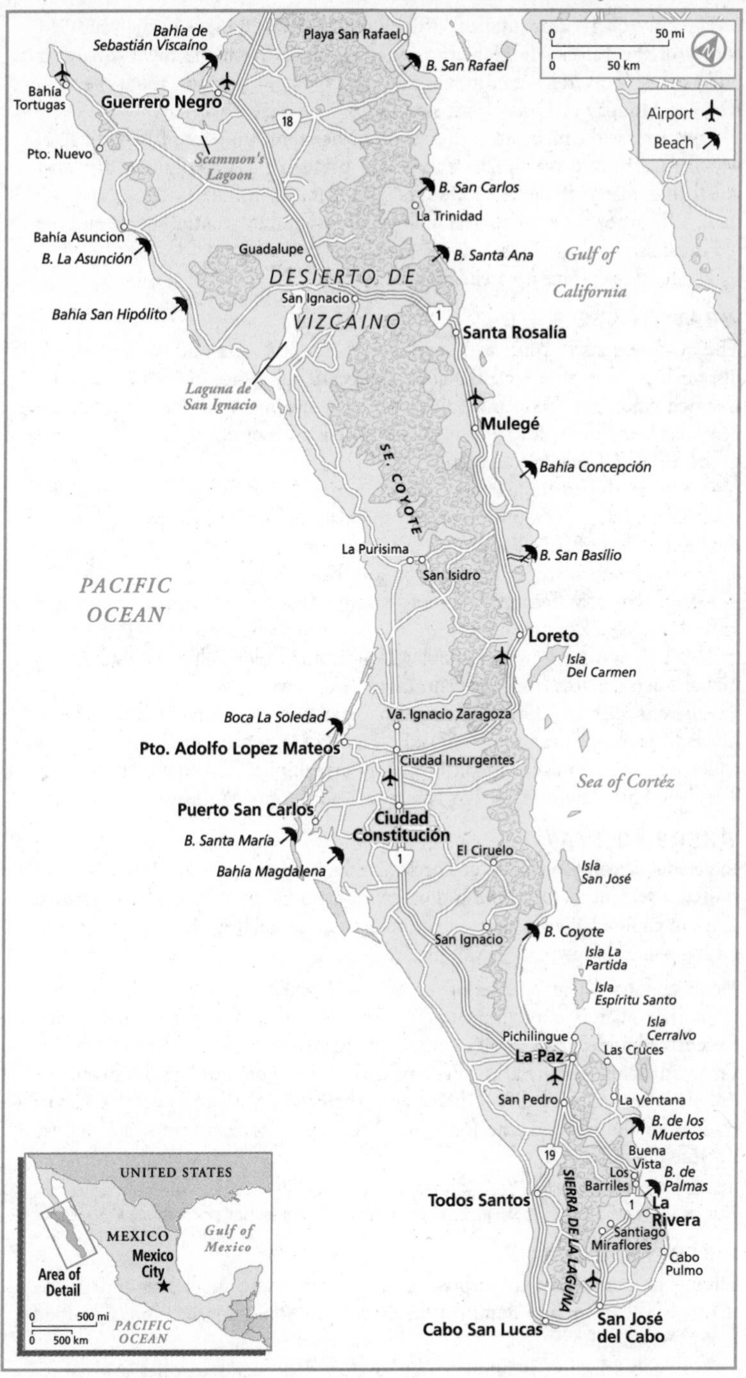
Bahía de
Sebastián Viscaíno
Playa San Rafael
B. San Rafael
0
50 mi
0
50 km
Bahía
Tortugas
Guerrero Negro
18
Airport
Beach
Pto. Nuevo
Scammon's
Lagoon
B. San Carlos
La Trinidad
Bahía Asuncion
B. La Asunción
Guadalupe
B. Santa Ana
Gulf of
California
DESIERTO DE
VIZCAINO
San Ignacio
1
Santa Rosalía
Bahía San Hipólito
Laguna de
San Ignacio
Mulegé
SE. COYOTE
Bahía Concepción
La Purisima
B. San Basílio
San Isidro
PACIFIC
OCEAN
Loreto
Isla
Del Carmen
Boca La Soledad
Va. Ignacio Zaragoza
Pto. Adolfo Lopez Mateos
Ciudad Insurgentes
Sea of Cortéz
Puerto San Carlos
Ciudad
Constitución
B. Santa María
Bahía Magdalena
El Ciruelo
Isla
San José
San Ignacio
B. Coyote
Isla La
Partida
Isla
Espíritu Santo
Isla
Cerralvo
Pichilingue
La Paz
Las Cruces
San Pedro
La Ventana
B. de los
Muertos
Buena
Vista
19
Los
Barriles
B. de
Palmas
SIERRA DE LA LAGUNA
Todos Santos
La
Rivera
Santiago
Miraflores
Cabo
Pulmo
San José
del Cabo
Cabo San Lucas
UNITED STATES
MEXICO
Gulf of
Mexico
Mexico
City
Area of
Detail
0
500 mi
0
500 km
PACIFIC
OCEAN

The city **tourist information office** (✆ **613/135-0036**) is in the southeast corner of the Palacio de Gobierno building, across from the town square. It offers maps, local free publications, and other basic information about the area. It's open Monday to Friday from 8am to 3pm.

Salvatierra is the main street that runs northeast, merging into Paseo Hidalgo, which runs toward the beach. Calle Playa parallels the water; along this road you'll find many of the hotels, seafood restaurants, fishing charters, and the marina. Most of the town's social life revolves around the central square and the old mission.

The local telephone **area code** is **613.**

## WHAT TO SEE & DO

The main reasons to come to Loreto are the Sea of Cortez and the five islands just offshore; they offer exceptional kayaking, sailing, diving and fishing. **Isla del Carmen** and **Isla Danzante** are wonderful overnight sailing destinations. Kayakers launch here for trips to the offshore islands or down the remote coast of the Sierra la Giganta to La Paz.

Loreto is the nearest major airport and city to **Bahía de Magdalena** (Magdalena Bay), the southernmost of the major gray whale calving lagoons on the Pacific coast of Baja. For more information on popular whale-watching spots and tour operators, see "Whale-watching in Baja," below.

**Misión Nuestra Señora de Loreto** was the first mission in the Californias, started in 1699. The original Virgen de Loreto, brought to shore by Padre Kino in 1697, is on display in the church's 18th-century gilded altar. The mission is on Salvatierra, across from the central square of town.

Adjacent to the mission church and of equal or greater interest is the **Museo de las Misiones,** Salvatierra 16 (✆ **613/135-0441**). It has a small but complete collection of historical and anthropological exhibits. The museum is open Tuesday to Sunday from 9am to 1pm and 1:45 to 6pm. Admission is $3.

## WHERE TO STAY

In general, accommodations in Loreto are the kind travelers to Mexico used to find all over: inexpensive and unique, with genuine, friendly owner-operators. You can choose between a secluded resort, more casual beachfront inns, or even greater values in town.

**Plaza Loreto** The location of the well-established Plaza Loreto, just 1 block from the mission church, makes it easy to find and a perennial favorite. Recently remodeled and well maintained, this two-story motel frames a courtyard with shady seating areas. Each of the basic rooms comes with one or two double beds, a table and two chairs, and a bathroom with a shower. It's a short walk from the mission, the museum, several favorite restaurants, and all the notable nightlife.

Hidalgo 2, Centro, 23880 Loreto, B.C.S. ✆ **613/135-0280.** Fax 613/135-0855. www.hotelplazaloreto.com. 25 units. $44 single; $52 double; $60 triple. AE, MC, V. **Amenities:** Restaurant; tour desk. *In room:* A/C, TV.

## WHERE TO DINE

Dining in Loreto affords surprising variety, given the small size and simple nature of the town. The dominant menu features some combination of seafood and Mexican cuisine.

Although selection is limited, Loreto after dark seems to offer a place for almost every nightlife preference, from rowdy beach pubs to an elegant billiard bar. Generally, though, closing time is around midnight. In addition, as is the tradition throughout Mexico, Loreto's central plaza offers a **free concert** in the bandstand every Sunday evening.

**Café Ole** LIGHT FARE Along with specialty coffees, this breezy cafe is a good option for breakfast; try eggs with *nopal* cactus, hotcakes, or a not-so-light lunch of a burger and fries. Tacos and some Mexican standards are also on the menu, as are the fresh fruit shakes, *liquados.*

Madero 14. © **613/135-0495.** Breakfast $2–$5; sandwiches $2–$3.50. No credit cards. Mon–Sat 7am–10pm; Sun 7am–2pm.

**El Chile Willie** ★ SEAFOOD/MEXICAN Chile Willie serves a seafood menu in an attractive and appropriate setting—right at the water's edge. The extensive menu features Choco Clams (a local type of clam, not as bizarre as it sounds), clams Rockefeller, lobster served many different ways, and a succulent fish fillet baked in foil with tamarind herb sauce. There is also chicken breast stuffed with *nopal* cactus, beef burger in BBQ sauce, and (the restaurant claims) the largest Mexican combo for two. The place is lively, and its location on the main beach in town makes it great for people-watching, especially during weekend breakfast and lunch. From 4 to 6pm, it features a 2-for-1 happy hour with free appetizers.

López Mateos s/n. © **613/135-0677.** Main courses $4–$16. AE, MC, V. Daily noon–11pm.

## MULEGE: OASIS IN THE DESERT

989km (618 miles) SE of Tijuana; 136km (85 miles) N of Loreto; 493km (308 miles) NW of La Paz; 706km (441 miles) NW of Cabo San Lucas

Verdant Mulegé offers shady coolness in an otherwise scorching part of the world. Founded in 1705, it is home to one of the best preserved and most beautifully situated Jesuit missions in Baja.

Mulegé (pronounced moo-leh-*hay*), at the mouth of beautiful Bahía de Concepción, has great diving, kayaking, and fishing. There are also several well-preserved Indian caves with stunning paintings that can be reached by guided hikes into the mountains. Accommodations are limited and basic. Good beach camping is available just south of town along the Bahía de Concepción.

### ESSENTIALS

The closest international airport is in Loreto, 136km (85 miles) south. From Loreto, you'll need to rent a car or hire a taxi; taxis average $75 each way, for the 90-minute trip. There is no formal **bus station** in Mulegé; buses pick up and drop passengers on the main highway at the fork in the road that marks the entrance leading into town (at the La Cabaña restaurant).

Essentially, Mulegé has an east-west orientation, running from the Transpeninsular Highway in the west to the Sea of Cortez. The Mulegé River (also known as Río Santa Rosalía) borders the town to the south, with a few hotels and RV parks along its southern shore. It's easy to find the principle sights downtown; two main streets take you either east or west, and both border the town's central plaza. There is no local bus service in town or to the beach, but you can easily walk or take a **taxi.** Taxis line up around the central plaza, or you can call the taxi dispatch at © **615/153-0420.** They usually charge about $2 to $4 for a trip anywhere in town.

Tourist information is available at the office of the centrally located **Hotel Las Casitas,** Calle Madero 50 (© **615/153-0019**). You won't find banks in Mulegé, but you can exchange currency at **El Pez de Oro Casa de Cambio,** Prol.

Moctezuma 17, close to the main square (© **615/153-0525**). It's open Monday to Friday from 9am to 1pm and 3 to 7pm.

## WHAT TO SEE & DO

Mulegé has long been a favorite destination for adventurous travelers looking for a place to relax and enjoy the diversity of nature. Divers, sportfishermen, kayakers, history buffs, and admirers of beautiful beaches all find reasons to linger.

To the north are the mostly secluded beaches of **Bahía Santa Inés** and **Punta Chivato,** both known for their beauty and tranquility. You can reach Santa Inez by way of a long dirt road that turns off from Highway 1 at Km 151. A few kilometers south is the majestic **Bahía Concepción,** a 30-mile-long body of water that's dotted with islands and protected on three sides by over 80km (50 miles) of beach. Along with fantastic landscapes, the bay has numerous soft, white-sand beaches such as **Santispac, Concepción, Los Cocos, El Burro, El Coyote, Buenaventura, El Requesón,** and **Armenta.** You can enjoy swimming, diving, windsurfing, kayaking, and other watersports; local equipment rentals are available.

One of the big attractions in this region is the large **cave paintings** in the Sierra de Guadalupe. UNESCO has declared the cave paintings a World Heritage Site, and the locals take great pride in protecting them. Unlike many typical cave paintings, these are huge, complex murals. Legally, you are only allowed to visit the caves with a licensed guide.

Although **scuba diving** is very popular, be aware that Mulegé is not an ideal destination. Fresh water and the not-so-fresh water that flows into the sea from the numerous septic tanks in the area mar visibility. But as you head south into Bahía de Concepción, there is excellent snorkeling at the numerous shallow coves and tiny offshore islands. Bahía de Concepción is also a **kayaker**'s dream—clear, calm waters, fascinating shorelines, and lots of tempting coves with white sandy beaches. Rent a kayak at El Candil restaurant for $29 per day and explore on your own. **Baja Tropicales,** Las Casitas Hotel Office, Fco. Madero 50 (© **615/153-0409;** fax 615/153-0190), Mulegé's undisputed kayak expert, rents kayaks and offers fully guided tours.

**Misión Santa Rosalía de Mulegé,** founded in 1706 by Father Juan de Ugarte and Juan María Basaldúa, is just upstream from the bridge where Highway 1 crosses the Mulegé River. The original mission building was completed in 1766, to serve a local Indian population of about 2,000. In 1770, a flood destroyed nearly all of the common buildings, and the mission was rebuilt on the site it occupies today, on a bluff overlooking the river.

## WHERE TO STAY & DINE

Accommodations in Mulegé are basic but clean and comfortable. The must-have meal is the traditional **pig roast.** It's an event—the pig is roasted Polynesian-style in a palm-lined open pit for hours, while guests enjoy a few beers or other beverages. When it's done, homemade tortillas, salsas, an assortment of toppings, and the ubiquitous rice and beans accompany the succulent pork. The perennially popular pig roast happens each Saturday night at both the **Las Casitas** Restaurant and at the **Hotel Serenidad,** and costs about $10.

Mulegé's nightlife pretty much centers on the bars of the Hacienda Hotel and Las Casitas, in town. In addition, **La Jungla Bambú,** corner of Gnl. Martinez and Zaragoza (no phone) is an American-style sports bar gone tropical. The other nightlife alternative, **Super Disco,** on the corner of Gnl. Martinez and

Zaragoza, 2nd floor (no phone), is upstairs from La Jungla Bambú; on Friday, Saturday, and Sunday nights starting at 9pm, it features predominantly dance music that packs in people.

**Las Casitas Hotel** *Value* This longtime favorite welcomes many repeat visitors, along with the local literati—it was the birthplace of Mexican poet Alan Gorosave. Rooms are in a courtyard just behind (and adjacent to) Las Casitas Restaurant, one of Mulegé's most popular. The basic accommodations all have tile baths and rustic decor. The bar has a steady clientele day and night and often features special sporting events on satellite TV.

You can dine in the stone-walled dining area or on its adjoining plant-filled patio. Live music plays from 6pm on, and the place really livens up during the Saturday night pig roast. Fridays feature a Mexican fiesta and buffet with *mariachi*. If you're dining off the menu, how can you resist fresh lobster for $10? Menu offerings are standard fare with an emphasis on fresh seafood, but the quality is good. Expect to pay about $2 to $4 for breakfast, with main courses priced from $3.50 to $11. MasterCard and Visa are accepted. The restaurant is open daily from 7am to 10pm. The inn and restaurant are on the main east-west street in Mulegé, 1 block from the central plaza.

Madero 50, Col. Centro 23900 Mulegé, B.C.S. ✆ **615/153-0019.** 8 units. $28 single; $33 double; $38 triple. MC, V. Limited street parking. *In room:* A/C.

## SANTA ROSALIA

61km (38 miles) N of Mulegé

Located in an *arroyo* (dry streambed) north of Mulegé, Santa Rosalía is a mining town that dates to 1855. Founded by the French, the town has a European ambience and a distinctly Mexican culture. Pastel clapboard houses surrounded by picket fences line the streets, giving the town its nickname—*ciudad de madera* (city of wood). The large harbor and rusted ghost of its copper smelting facility dominate the central part of town bordering the waterfront.

The town was a copper-mining center for years. A French outfit began operations in 1885 and continued until 1954, when the Mexicans regained the use of the land. But problems plagued the facility, which closed permanently in 1985.

Today, Santa Rosalía (pop. 14,000) is known for its manmade harbor—the recently constructed Marina Santa Rosalía, complete with concrete piers, floating docks, and full docking accommodations for up to a dozen ocean liners. Because this is the prime entry point of manufactured goods into Baja, the town abounds with auto-parts and electronics stores, along with shops selling Nikes and sunglasses.

The town has no real beach to speak of and few recreational attractions.

### EXPLORING SANTA ROSALIA

The principal attraction in Santa Rosalía is the **Iglesia de Santa Barbara,** a structure of galvanized steel designed by Gustave Eiffel (of Eiffel Tower fame) in 1884. It was created for the 1889 Paris World Expo, then transported here section by section and reassembled in 1897. Its somber gray exterior belies the beauty of the intricate stained-glass windows as viewed from inside.

The other obligatory sight to see is the former Fundacíon del Pacifico, or **Museo Histórico Minero de Santa Rosalía.** Located in a landmark wooden building, it houses a permanent display of artifacts from the days of Santa Rosalía's mining operations. It's open Monday to Saturday from 8:30am to 2pm and 5 to 7pm. Admission is $1.50.

### *Moments* Whale-watching in Baja

Few sights inspire as much reverence as close contact with a whale in its natural habitat. The various protected bays and lagoons on Baja's Pacific coast are the preferred winter waters for migrating gray whales as they journey south to mate and give birth to their calves. These whales are known to be so friendly and curious that they frequently come up to the boats and stay close by, and sometimes even allow people to pet them.

The experience is particularly rewarding in the protected areas of the **El Vizcaino Biosphere Reserve,** where you can easily see many whales. This area encompasses the famous **Laguna Ojo de Liebre**—also known as **Scammon's Lagoon**—close to Guerrero Negro, Laguna San Ignacio, and Bahía Magdalena.

Because these protected waters offer ideal conditions for gray whales during the winter, the neighboring towns have developed the infrastructure and services to accommodate whale-watchers. Whale-watching season generally runs from January to March. But remember that the colder the water, the farther south the whales migrate, so check on water temperatures and whale sightings before you plan your expedition. The temperature on the boat can be quite cool; bring a light jacket.

**Loreto** is the best place to launch a whale-watching journey; it has a well-developed tourist infrastructure and a number of lovely resort hotels. Trips take you by road to Bahía Magdalena, where you board a skiff to get up close to the gentle giants. Locally based **Loreto Center** (✆ **613/135-0798**) and **Las Parras Tours** (✆ **613/135-1010**) offer excellent tours. Among the many groups that run expeditions is U.S.-based **Baja Expeditions,** 2625 Garnet Ave., San Diego, CA 92109 (✆ **800/843-6967,** or 612/125-3828 in La Paz). Prices for package trips from Loreto run around $90 to $100 per person for a daylong trip.

Bordering the museum are the most attractive of the **clapboard houses,** painted in a rainbow of colors—mango, lemon, blueberry, and cherry. The wood used to construct these houses was the return cargo on ships that transported copper to refineries in Oregon and British Columbia during the 1800s.

The **Plaza Benito Juarez,** or *zócalo* (town square), which fronts the **Palacio Municipal** (City Hall), is an intriguing structure of French Colonial architecture.

## WHERE TO STAY & DINE

Santa Rosalía claims to have the best bakery in all of Baja—**El Boleo,** Avenida Obregón at Calle 4 (✆ **615/152-0310**), which has been baking French baguettes since the late 1800s. It's 3 blocks west of the church, and is open 8am to 9pm.

**Hotel Francés** Founded in 1886, the Hotel Francés once set the standard of hospitality in Baja Sur, welcoming European dignitaries and hosting the French administrators and businessmen of the mining operations. Today it has a worn air of elegance but retains its position as the most welcoming accommodation in

**Tips** **Exploring Northern Baja by Car**

If you have a car, it's easy to venture into Baja Norte from Southern California for a getaway of a few days. Whether you drive your own car or a rented one, you'll need Mexican auto insurance in addition to your own. It's available at the border in San Ysidro or through the car-rental companies (see "Getting Around by Car," in chapter 2).

It takes relatively little time to cross the international border in Tijuana, but be prepared for a delay of an hour or more on your return.

Santa Rosalía. Rooms are in the back, with wooden porches and balconies overlooking a small courtyard pool. Each room has individually controlled air-conditioning, plus windows that open for ventilation. Floors are wood-planked, and the small baths are beautifully tiled. You have a choice of two double beds or one king. Telephone service is available in the lobby. The popular restaurant serves Mexican cuisine and seafood from 6am to 10pm.

Calle Jean Michel Cousteau s/n 23920, Santa Rosalía B.C.S. ✆ and fax **615/152-2052.** 17 units. $50 single or double. No credit cards. Free parking. **Amenities:** Restaurant and bar; small courtyard pool; tour desk. *In room:* A/C, TV.

## 5 Tijuana & Rosarito Beach

Northern Baja California is not only Mexico's most infamous border crossing, it also claims to be the birthplace of the original Caesar salad and the Margarita. Along the Pacific coastline south of the border, the towns of Tijuana and Rosarito Beach combine to make one of the country's most important entry points.

Long notorious as a hard-partying 10-block border town, **Tijuana** has cleaned up its act a bit on its way to becoming a full-scale city. A growing number of sports and cultural attractions now augment the legendary shopping experience and wild nightlife. **Rosarito Beach,** of recent *Titanic*-inspired fame, remains a more tranquil resort town; the decidedly laid-back atmosphere makes enjoying its miles of beachfront easy.

### TIJUANA: BAWDY BORDER TOWN

In northern Baja, 26km (16 miles) south of San Diego, the first point of entry from the West Coast of the U.S. is infamous Tijuana—a town that continues to delude travelers into thinking that a visit there means they've been to Mexico.

Tijuana's "sin city" image is gradually morphing into that of a shopper's mecca and a nocturnal playground. Vineyards associated with the growing wine industry are nearby, and an increasing number of cultural offerings have joined the traditional sporting attractions of greyhound racing, jai alai, and bullfights.

You are less likely to find the Mexico you may be expecting here—no charming town squares and churches, no women in colorful embroidered skirts and blouses, no bougainvillea spilling out of every crevice here. Tijuana has an urban culture, a profusion of U.S.-inspired goods and services, and relentless hawkers playing to the thousands of tourists.

#### ESSENTIALS

A visit to Tijuana requires little in the way of formalities—people who stay less than 72 hours in the border zone do not need a passport or tourist card. If you plan to stay longer, a tourist card is required. They're available free of charge from the border crossing station, or from any immigration office.

From downtown San Diego, you also have the option of taking the **bright-red trolley** headed for San Ysidro and getting off at the last, or San Ysidro, stop (it's nicknamed the Tijuana Trolley for good reason). From here, follow the signs to walk across the border. It's simple, quick, and inexpensive; the one-way fare is $2. The last trolley leaving for San Ysidro departs downtown around midnight; the last returning trolley from San Ysidro is at 1am. On Saturdays, the trolley runs 24 hours.

Once you're in Tijuana, it's easy to get around by taxi. Cab fares from the border to downtown average $5. You can also hire a taxi to Rosarito for about $20 one-way.

The Tijuana airport is about 8km (5 miles) east of the city. To drive to Tijuana from the U.S., take I-5 south to the Mexican border at San Ysidro. The drive from downtown San Diego takes about half an hour.

For **tourist information,** visit the Centro Cultural Tijuana, Paseo de los Héroes and Mina (**© 664/687-9600**). It's in the Zona Río, the principal shopping and dining district, adjacent to the Tijuana River.

There are major banks with ATMs and *casas de cambio* (money exchange houses) all over Tijuana, but you can easily come here (or to Rosarito and Ensenada, for that matter) without changing money because dollars are accepted everywhere.

## EXPLORING TIJUANA

For many visitors, Tijuana's main event is the bustling **Avenida Revolución.** Beginning in the 1920s, American college students, servicemen, and hedonistic tourists discovered this street as a bawdy center for illicit fun. Some of the original attractions—gambling, back-alley cockfights (now illegal), and girlie shows—have fallen by the wayside, with drinking and shopping the main order of business these days. You'll find the action between Calles 1 and 9; the landmark jai alai palace anchors the southern portion.

If you're looking to see a different side of Tijuana, the best place to start is the **Centro Cultural Tijuana,** Paseo de los Héroes and Mina Rio Zone (**© 664/687-9600,** ext. 9650). You'll easily spot the ultramodern Tijuana Cultural Center complex, which houses an Omnimax theater, the museum's permanent collection of Mexican artifacts, and a gallery of visiting exhibits. The center is open daily from 9am to 9pm. Admission to the permanent exhibits is free, there's a $2 charge for the special event gallery, and tickets for Omnimax films are $4 for adults and $2.50 for children.

In the Zona Río, you'll find some classier shopping and a colorful local marketplace, plus the ultimate kid destination, **Mundo Divertido,** Paseo de los Héroes at Calle José Maria Velasco (**© 664/634-3213**). The park is open daily from noon to 8:30pm. Admission is free, and several booths inside sell tickets for the various rides.

The fertile valleys of Northern Baja produce most of Mexico's finest wines and export many high-quality vintages to Europe. For an introduction to Mexican wines, stop into **Cava de Vinos L. A. Cetto** (L. A. Cetto Winery), Av. Cañón Johnson 2108, at Av. Constitución Sur (**© 664/685-3031;** lacetto@compuserve.com). Shaped like a wine barrel, this building's striking façade is made from old oak aging barrels—call it inspired recycling. It's open Monday to Friday from 10:30am to 2pm and 3:30 to 6:30pm, Saturday from 10:30am to 4pm.

Tijuana's biggest attraction is shopping. People come to take advantage of low prices on a variety of merchandise—terra-cotta and colorfully glazed pottery,

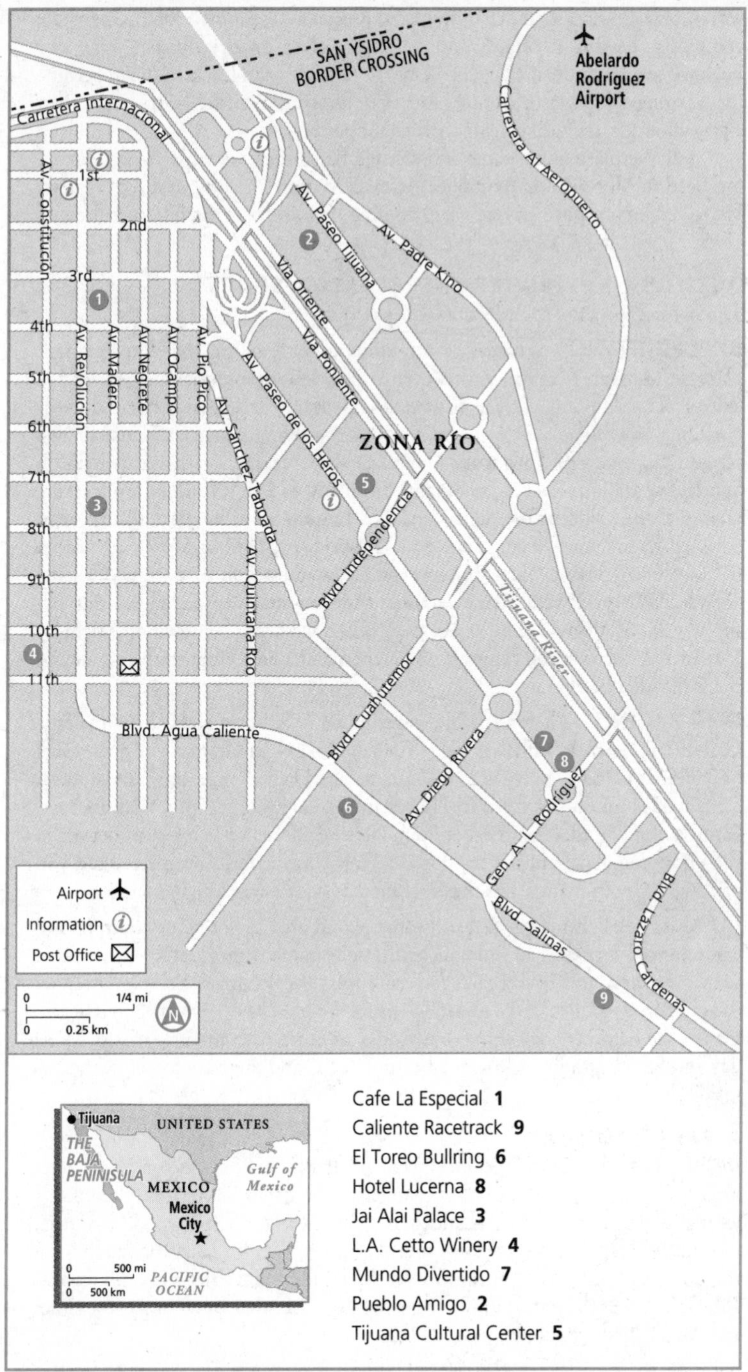


Cafe La Especial **1**
Caliente Racetrack **9**
El Toreo Bullring **6**
Hotel Lucerna **8**
Jai Alai Palace **3**
L.A. Cetto Winery **4**
Mundo Divertido **7**
Pueblo Amigo **2**
Tijuana Cultural Center **5**

woven blankets and serapes, embroidered dresses and sequined sombreros, onyx chess sets, beaded necklaces and bracelets, silver jewelry, leather bags and *huarache* sandals, rain sticks, Cuban cigars, and Mexican liquors. You're permitted to bring $400 worth of purchases back across the border (sorry, no Cuban cigars allowed), including 1 liter of alcohol per person.

If a marketplace atmosphere and spirited bargaining are what you're looking for, head to **Mercado de Artesanías (Crafts Market),** Calle 2 and Av. Negrete. Here, vendors of pottery, clayware, clothing, and other crafts fill an entire city block.

## OUTDOOR ACTIVITIES & SPECTATOR SPORTS

Tijuana is a spectator's (and gambler's) paradise.

**BULLFIGHTING** Whatever your opinion, bullfighting has a prominent place in Mexican heritage, and is even considered an essential element of the culture. The skill and bravery of matadors is closely linked with cultural ideals regarding *machismo,* and some of the world's best perform at Tijuana's two stadiums. The season runs from May through September, with events held on Sundays at 4:30pm. Ticket prices range from $10 to $42 (the premium seats are on the shaded side of the arena) and can be purchased at the bullring or in advance from San Diego's **Five Star Tours** (© **619/232-5049**). **El Toreo** (© **664/686-1510**) is 3km (2 miles) east of downtown on Blvd. Agua Caliente at Avenida Diego Rivera. **Plaza de Toros Monumental,** also called Bullring-by-the-Sea (© **664/680-1808**), is 10km (6 miles) west of downtown on Highway 1-D (before the first toll station); it's perched at the edge of both the ocean and the California border.

**DOG RACING** There's satellite wagering on U.S. horse races at the majestic **Caliente Racetrack,** off Blvd. Agua Caliente, 5km (3 miles) east of downtown (© **664/681-7811,** or 619/231-1910 in San Diego.), but only greyhounds actually kick up dust at the track. Races are held daily at 7:45pm, with Tuesday, Saturday, and Sunday matinees at 2pm. General admission is free, but bettors in the know congregate in the comfortable Turf Club; admission is free, and you pay $10 for your drinks, but that's refundable with a wagering voucher.

**JAI ALAI** A lightning-paced ball game played on a slick indoor court, jai alai (pronounced *high*-ah-lye) is an ancient Basque game incorporating elements of tennis, hockey, and basketball. You can't miss the **Frontón Palacio,** Avenida Revolución at Calle 7 (© **664/638-4308,** or 619/231-1910 in San Diego). Games are held Monday through Saturday at 8pm, with matinee events Monday and Friday at noon. General admission is $2, and there are betting windows inside the arena.

## A PLACE TO STAY

**Hotel Lucerna** Once the most chic hotel in Tijuana, Lucerna now feels slightly worn, though it still has personality. The flavor is Mexican Colonial—wrought-iron railings and chandeliers, rough-hewn heavy wood furniture, brocade wallpaper, and traditional tiles. The hotel is in the Zona Río, away from the noise and congestion of downtown, so a quiet night's sleep is easily attainable here. All of the rooms in the five-story hotel have balconies or patios. Hotel rates in Tijuana are subject to a 12% tax.

Av. Paseo de los Héroes, 10902 Zona Río, Tijuana. © **664/633-3900.** www.hotel-lucerna.com.mx. 165 units. $175 double; $190 suite. AE, DC, MC, V. **Amenities:** Coffee shop; swimming pool; room service. *In room:* A/C, TV.

### Finds A Northern Baja Spa Sanctuary

One of Mexico's best-known spas is in Northern Baja, just 58km (36 miles) south of San Diego. The **Rancho La Puerta** ★★, opened in 1940 as a "health camp," was among the pioneers of the modern spa and fitness movement. The location was chosen for its perfect climate. The rates at the time were $17.50 a week—but you had to bring your own tent.

Much has changed. Today, the ranch occupies 3,000 acres of lush oasis surrounded by pristine countryside, which includes a 6-acre organic garden. Cottages can accommodate up to 150 guests per week, and the ranch has a staff of 300. Each cottage has its own patio garden and is decorated with Mexican folk art.

Three swimming pools, four tennis courts, four whirlpools, saunas, steam rooms, and nine gyms for aerobic and restorative classes make up the common facilities. Separate men's and women's health centers offer the full range of spa services. Hiking trails surround the resort.

Rancho La Puerta runs weeklong programs—Saturday to Saturday—emphasizing a mind/body/spirit philosophy. Prices begin at $1,430 for the week during the summer, and at $1,645 for the week from mid-September through June. Included in the rates are three modified vegetarian meals per day, use of facilities, exercise classes, evening educational programs, and round-trip airport transfers.

Reservations: Rancho La Puerta, Carretera a Tijuana Km 5 "A," 21440, Tecate, B.C.N., or P.O. Box 69, Tecate, CA 91980 (✆ **800-443-7565** in the U.S., or 665/654-1155 at the ranch; fax 665/654-1108; www.rancholapuerta.com). MasterCard and Visa are accepted.

## WHERE TO DINE

**Cafe La Especial** MEXICAN Tucked away in a shopping *pasaje* at the bottom of some stairs (turn in at the taco stand of the same name), this restaurant is a well-known purveyor of home-style Mexican cooking at reasonable prices. The gruff, efficient waitstaff carries out platter after platter of *carne asada* (grilled marinated beef served with fresh tortillas, beans, and rice). Traditional dishes like tacos, enchiladas, and burritos round out the menu, augmented by frosty cold Mexican beers.

Av. Revolución 718 (between Calles 3 and 4), Zona Centro. ✆ **664/685-6654.** Menu items $3–$12. MC, V. Daily 9am–10pm.

**Cien Años** MEXICAN This elegant and gracious Zona Río restaurant offers artfully blended Mexican flavors (tamarind, poblano chile, mango) in stylish presentations. If you're interested in haute cuisine, the buzz around Tijuana is all about this place.

Jose Maria Velazco 1407. ✆ **664/634-3039** or 664/634-7262. Main courses $10–$15. AE, MC, V. Mon–Thurs 8am–11pm; Fri–Sat 8am–midnight; Sun 8am–8pm.

## TIJUANA AFTER DARK

**Avenida Revolución** is the center of the city's nightlife; many compare it with Bourbon Street in New Orleans during Mardi Gras—except here it's a regular occurrence, not a once-a-year blowout.

A recent addition to Tijuana's nightlife has been the proliferation of sports bars. The most popular cluster in **Pueblo Amigo,** Via Oriente and Paseo Tijuana, in the Zona Río. Two of the town's hottest discos, **Rodeo de Media Noche** (**© 664/682-4967**) and **Señor Frogs** (**© 664/682-4962**), are also in Pueblo Amigo. Pueblo Amigo is less than 3km (2 miles) from the border, a short taxi ride or—during daylight hours—a pleasant walk away.

## ROSARITO BEACH: BAJA'S FIRST BEACH RESORT

Just 29km (18 miles) south of Tijuana and a complete departure in ambience, Rosarito Beach is a tranquil, friendly beach town. Hollywood has played a major part in Rosarito's recent renaissance—it was the location for the sound stage and filming of the Academy Award–winning *Titanic.* The Titanic Museum continues to draw the fans of the film. The beaches between Tijuana and Rosarito are also known for excellent surf breaks.

**GETTING THERE** Two roads run between Tijuana and Ensenada (the largest and third-largest cities in Baja)—the scenic, coast-hugging toll road (marked *cuota,* or 1-D), and the free but slower public road (marked *libre,* or 1).

### WHAT TO SEE & DO

A few kilometers south of Rosarito proper lies the **seaside production site** of 1997's mega-blockbuster *Titanic.* Rosarito officials are eager to attract more films to the state-of-the-art facility; in the meantime, a makeshift "museum" has sprung up on the site. Originally filled with *Titanic* memorabilia, it has become a movie-making theme park, complete with rides. Admission is a hefty $12 for adults, $9 for children 3 to 11. The ***Titanic* Museum** (**© 661/614-0110**) is open Thursday to Monday from 10am to 6pm (often also holidays and during busy seasons).

If you have only a few hours to spend in Rosarito Beach, that's still enough time to have a swim or a horseback ride at the beach, shop for souvenirs, and dine on fish tacos or tamales from one of the family-run stands along **Bulevard Benito Juárez,** the town's main (and only) drag. The dozen or so blocks of Rosarito north of the Rosarito Beach Hotel are packed with stores typical of Mexican border towns: curio shops, cigar and *licores* (liquor) stores, and *farmacias* (where drugs like Viagra, Retin-A, Prozac, Rogaine, and many more are available at low cost and without a prescription).

Because the legal drinking age in Baja is 18, the under-21 crowd from Southern California tends to flock across the border on Friday and Saturday nights. The most popular spot in town is **Papas & Beer** (**© 661/612-0444**). It's a relaxed come-as-you-are-type club on the beach, just a block north of the hotel. Even for those young in spirit only, it's great fun, with outdoor tables and a bar surrounding a sand volleyball court. The **Salón Mexicano** (**© 661/612-0144**), in the Rosarito Beach Hotel, attracts a slightly more mature evening crowd, with live music on Friday, Saturday, and Sunday.

### WHERE TO STAY & DINE

**Rosarito Beach Hotel & Spa** Although this once-glamorous resort has been holding steady since its heyday, it's currently defined by glaring nighttime neon and party-mania. Despite the resort's changed personality, its unique artistic construction and lavish decoration remain. It has a wide, family-friendly stretch of beach. The stately home of the original owners has been transformed into the full-service **Casa Playa Spa,** where massages and other treatments are only slightly less costly than in the U.S.

## The Upper Baja Peninsula

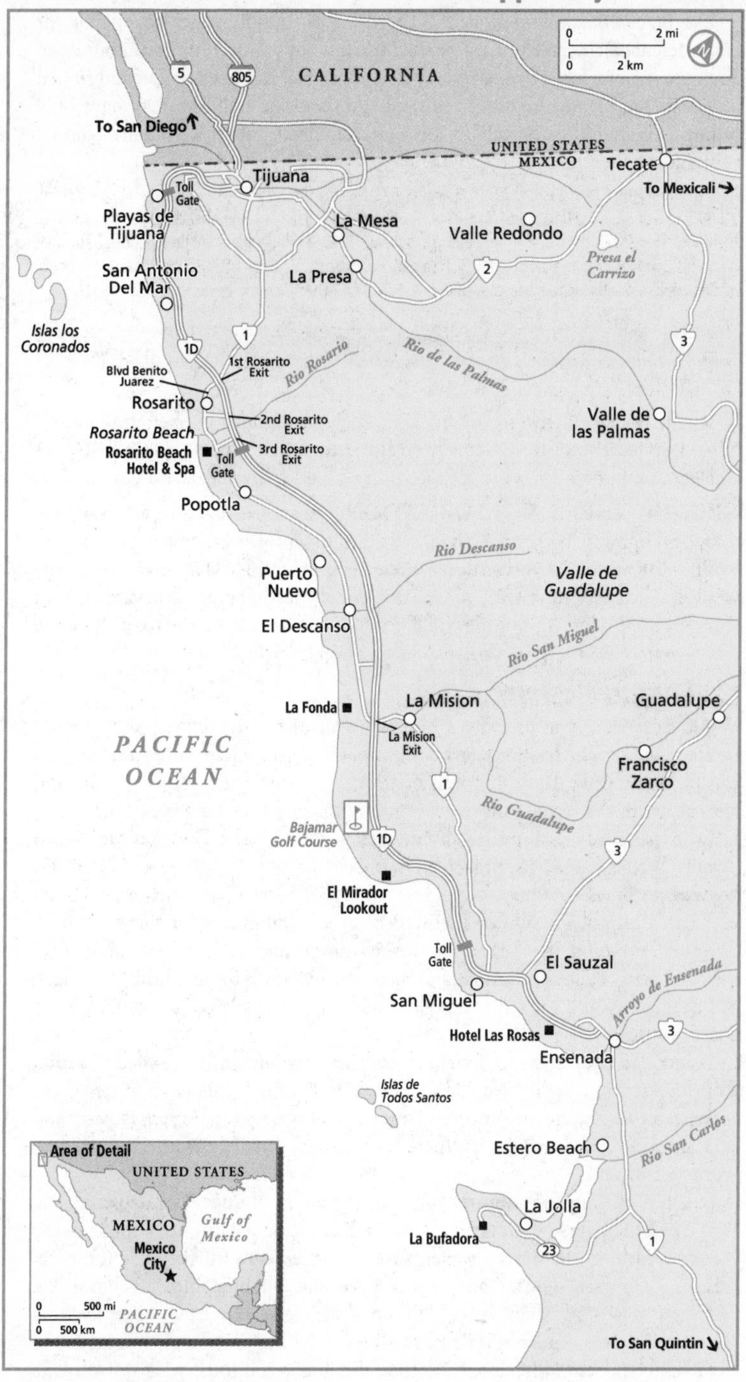

0
2 mi
0
2 km
CALIFORNIA
5
805
To San Diego
UNITED STATES
MEXICO
Tecate
To Mexicali
Tijuana
Toll Gate
Playas de Tijuana
La Mesa
Valle Redondo
Presa el Carrizo
La Presa
2
San Antonio Del Mar
Islas los Coronados
1
1D
3
Rio de las Palmas
Rio Rosario
1st Rosarito Exit
Blvd Benito Juarez
Rosarito
2nd Rosarito Exit
Valle de las Palmas
Rosarito Beach
Rosarito Beach Hotel & Spa
Toll Gate
3rd Rosarito Exit
Popotla
Rio Descanso
Puerto Nuevo
Valle de Guadalupe
El Descanso
Rio San Miguel
La Fonda
La Mision
Guadalupe
La Mision Exit
PACIFIC OCEAN
Francisco Zarco
1
Rio Guadalupe
Bajamar Golf Course
1D
3
El Mirador Lookout
Toll Gate
El Sauzal
San Miguel
Arroyo de Ensenada
Hotel Las Rosas
3
Ensenada
Islas de Todos Santos
Estero Beach
Rio San Carlos
La Jolla
La Bufadora
23
1
To San Quintin
Area of Detail
UNITED STATES
MEXICO
Gulf of Mexico
Mexico City
0
500 mi
0
500 km
PACIFIC OCEAN

The mansion's dining room (Chabert's Steakhouse) charges top dollar for Continental cuisine; Azteca is a casual Mexican restaurant in the main building. You'll pay more for an ocean view, and more for the newer, air-conditioned rooms in the tower; the older rooms in the poolside building may have only ceiling fans, but they prevail in the character department, with hand-painted trim and original tile.

Blvd. Benito Juárez, Zona Centro, 22710 Rosarito, B.C. Mexico (P.O. Box 430145, San Diego, CA 92143). ✆ **800/343-8582** in the U.S., or 661/612-0144. Fax 661/612-1125. www.rosaritobeachhotel.com. 278 units. Sept–June $133–$222 double; July–Aug and U.S. holidays $110–$179 double. 2 children under 12 stay free in parents' room. Packages available. MC, V. Free parking. **Amenities:** 2 restaurants, bar; 2 swimming pools, wading pool; racquetball court; spa; playground. *In room:* A/C, TV.

## 6 Ensenada: Port of Call

134km (84 miles) S of San Diego; 109km (68 miles) S of Tijuana

Ensenada is an attractive town on a lovely bay, surrounded by sheltering mountains. Located about 40 minutes from Rosarito, it's the kind of place that loves a celebration—be it for a bicycle race or a seafood festival.

**GETTING THERE & INFORMATION** After passing through the final tollgate, Highway 1-D curves sharply toward downtown Ensenada.

The **Tourist and Convention Bureau booth** (✆ **646/178-2411**) is at the western entrance to town, where the waterfront-hugging Bulevard Lázaro Cárdenas—also known as Bulevard Costero—curves away to the right. It's open daily from 10am to 6pm. Taxis park along López Mateos.

### EXPLORING ENSENADA

While Ensenada is technically a border town, one of its appeals is its multilayered vitality. The bustling port consumes the entire waterfront—beach access can be found only north or south of town—and the Pacific fishing trade and agriculture in the fertile valleys surrounding the city dominate the economy.

Even part-time oenophiles should pay a visit to the **Bodegas de Santo Tomás Winery** ★★, Avenida Miramar 666, at Calle 7 (✆ **646/178-2509;** www.santotomas.com.mx), the oldest winery in Mexico, and the largest in all of Baja. It uses old-fashioned methods of processing grapes, first cultivated by Dominican monks in 1791 in the lush Santo Tomás Valley. Tours in English are conducted daily at 11am, 1, and 3pm. Admission is $2 (including tastings), $3 more gets you a souvenir wineglass, and wines for sale range from $3.50 to $10 a bottle.

Ensenada's equivalent of Tijuana's Avenida Revolución is crowded **Avenida López Mateos,** roughly parallel to Bulevard Lázaro Cárdenas (Costero); the highest concentration of shops and restaurants is between Avenidas Ruiz and Castillo. Compared to Tijuana, there is more authentic Mexican art- and craftwork in Ensenada.

South of the city, 45 minutes by car along the rural Punta Banda peninsula, is one of Ensenada's major attractions: **La Bufadora,** a natural sea spout in the rocks. With each incoming wave, water is forced upward through the rock, creating a geyser whose loud grunt gave the phenomenon its name (*la bufadora* means "buffalo snort"). From downtown Ensenada, take Avenida Reforma (Hwy. 1) south to Highway 23 west. La Bufadora is at the end of the road. Once parked ($1 per car in crude dirt lots), you must walk downhill to the viewing platform, at the end of a 600-yard pathway lined with souvenir stands.

## WHERE TO STAY

**Hotel Las Rosas** Modern and comfortable, this pink oceanfront hotel 3km (2 miles) outside of Ensenada is the favorite of many Baja aficionados. It offers all the comforts of an American hotel. The atrium lobby is awash with pale pink and sea-foam green (including a back-lit, green-glass ceiling), a color scheme that pervades the hotel—including the guest rooms, which are sparsely appointed with quasi-tropical hotel furniture. Some of the 32 rooms have fireplaces, in-room whirlpools, or both. One of the resort's main photo ops is the spectacular swimming pool—it overlooks the Pacific and features a vanishing edge that appears to merge with the ocean beyond. If you're looking to maintain the highest comfort level possible in Ensenada, this is the hotel of choice.

Hwy 1, 3km (2 miles) north of Ensenada. Mail: Apdo. Postal 316, Ensenada, BC, Mexico. ✆ **646/174-4310.** www.lasrosas.com. 48 units. $148–$213 double. Children under 12 $16; extra adult $22. MC, V. **Amenities:** Restaurant, cocktail lounge; swimming pool; clifftop hot tub; small workout room; tennis and racquetball courts. *In room:* TV.

## WHERE TO DINE

**La Embottelladora Vieja** ★ FRENCH/MEXICAN/MEDITERRANEAN Hidden on an industrial side street, and attached to the Bodegas de Santo Tomás winery, this looks more like a chapel than the elegant restaurant it is. Sophisticated diners will feel right at home in this stylish setting, a former aging room for the winery. It's now resplendent with red oak furniture (constructed from old wine casks), high brick walls, and crystal goblets and candlesticks on linen tablecloths. It goes without saying that the wine list is exemplary, featuring bottles from Santo Tomás and other Baja vintners. Look for appetizers like abalone *ceviche* or cream of garlic soup, followed by grilled swordfish in cilantro sauce, filet mignon in port wine–gorgonzola sauce, or quail with a tart sauvignon blanc sauce.

Avenida Miramar 666 (at Calle 7). ✆ **646/174-0807.** Reservations recommended for weekends. Main courses $9–$25. MC, V. Lunch and dinner; call for seasonal hours.

## ENSENADA AFTER DARK

Just like in *Casablanca,* where "everyone goes to Rick's," everyone's been going to **Hussong's Cantina,** Av. Ruiz 113, near Av. López Mateos (✆ **646/178-3210**), since the bar opened in 1892. Nothing much has changed—the place still sports Wild West–style swinging saloon doors, a long bar to slide beers along, and strolling *mariachis* bellowing above the din. Be aware that hygiene and privacy are low priorities in the restrooms. While the crowd (a pleasant mix of tourists and locals) at Hussong's can really whoop it up, they're amateurs compared to those who frequent **Papas & Beer,** Av. Ruiz near Av. López Mateos, across the street. A tiny entrance leads to the upstairs bar and disco. The music is loud and the hip young crowd is definitely here to party. Papas & Beer has quite a reputation with the Southern California college crowd, and has opened a branch in Rosarito Beach (see above).

# Appendix A: Mexico in Depth

The fact that Mexico is so close to the United States and yet so strikingly different amazes many first-time visitors. Flying into Mexico City, you'll immediately see evidence: From the window, you catch a glimpse of majestic snow-capped volcanoes with the strange-sounding names Popocatépetl and Ixtaccihuatl. You are entering an exotic land of volcanoes and pyramids, mountains and jungles, where ancient civilizations have left more than just ruins and strange-sounding place names. Millions of Mexicans still speak their languages—Náhuatl (Aztec), Maya, Zapotec, and others—and their customs and beliefs have shaped a national culture, different from any other in the Spanish-speaking world.

## 1 The Land & Its People

Mexico stretches nearly 2,000 miles from east to west and more than 1,000 miles north to south. Only one-fifth the size of the United States, its territory includes trackless deserts in the north, dense jungles in the south, thousands of miles of lush seacoast and beaches along the Pacific and Caribbean, and the central highlands, where the weather is as close to perfect as anywhere on the planet.

### THE MEXICAN PEOPLE

There are 97 million Mexicans, and 22 million of them live in the capital, Mexico City. Over the last few decades, the rate of population growth has been steadily declining, from 3.2% per year in the 1970s to 1.6% at present. Mexico City has the slowest growth rate, at less than 1% per year.

Today, close to 5 centuries after the Conquest, five million Mexicans speak a native language; of these, 800,000 do not speak Spanish at all. The states with the highest populations of Indians are Oaxaca, Chiapas, Yucatán, Michoacán, and Puebla.

By most measurements, the disparity between rich and poor has increased in the last 30 years. Cycles of boom and bust weigh heavier on the poor than on the rich. But in the face of all of this, Mexican society shows great resilience, due in measure to the values Mexicans live by. For them, family and friends, social gatherings, and living in the present remain eminently important. In Mexico, there is always time to meet relatives or friends for a drink, a cup of coffee, or a special occasion.

**SOCIAL MORES** American and English travelers have often observed that Mexicans have a different conception of time, that life in Mexico obeys slower rhythms. This is true, and yet few observers go on to explain what the consequences of this are for the visitor to Mexico. This is a shame, because an imperfect appreciation of this difference causes a good deal of misunderstanding between the tourist and the native Mexican.

On several occasions, Mexican acquaintances have asked me why Americans grin all the time. At first, I wasn't sure what to make of the question, and only gradually came to appreciate what was at issue. As the pace of life for Americans,

Canadians, and others has quickened, they have come to skip some of the niceties of social interaction. When walking into a store, many Americans simply smile at a clerk and launch right into a question or request. The smile, in effect, replaces the greeting. In Mexico, it doesn't work that way. Mexicans misinterpret this American manner of greeting. After all, a smile when there is no context can be ambiguous; it can convey amusement, smugness, or superiority.

One of the most important pieces of advice I can offer travelers is this: Always give a proper greeting when addressing Mexicans. Don't try to abbreviate social intercourse. Mexican culture places a higher value on proper social form than on saving time. A Mexican must at least say *"¡Buenos días!"* or a quick *"¿Qué pasó?"* (or its equivalent), even to total strangers—a show of proper respect. When an individual meets a group of people, he will greet each person separately, which can take quite a while. For us, the polite thing would be to keep our interruption to a minimum and give a general greeting to all.

Mexicans, like most people, will consciously or subconsciously make quick judgments about individuals they meet. Most divide the world into the well raised and cultured (*bien educado*), and the poorly raised (*mal educado*). Unfortunately, many visitors are reluctant to try out their Spanish, preferring to keep exchanges to a minimum. Don't do this. To be categorized as a foreigner isn't a big deal. What's important in Mexico is to be categorized as one of the cultured foreigners and not one of the barbarians. This makes it easier to get the attention of waiters, hotel desk clerks, and people on the street.

## 2 A Look at the Past

### PRE-HISPANIC CIVILIZATIONS

The earliest "Mexicans" were Stone Age hunter-gatherers from the north, descendants of a race that had probably crossed the Bering Strait and reached North America around 12,000 B.C. They arrived in what is now Mexico by 10,000 B.C. Sometime between 5200 and 1500 B.C., in what is known as the **Archaic period,** they began practicing agriculture and domesticating animals.

**THE PRE-CLASSIC PERIOD (1500 B.C.–A.D. 300)** Eventually, agriculture improved to the point that it could support large communities and free some of the population from agricultural work. A civilization emerged that we call the **Olmec**—an enigmatic people who settled the lower Gulf Coast in what is now Tabasco and Veracruz. Anthropologists regard them as the mother culture of Mesoamerica because they established a pattern for later civilizations in a

### Dateline

- 10,000–1500 B.C. Archaic period: Hunting and gathering; later, the dawn of agriculture. Domestication of chiles, corn, beans, avocado, amaranth, and pumpkin. Mortars and pestles in use. Stone bowls and jars, obsidian knives, and open-weave basketry developed.
- 1500 B.C.–A.D. 300 Pre-Classic period: Olmec culture develops large-scale settlements. Olmec influence spreads. Several cities in central and southern Mexico develop irrigation systems and build ceremonial centers and pyramids. The Maya develop city-states in Chiapas and Central America.
- 300–900 Classic period: The rise of the city of Teotihuacán, which develops a truly cosmopolitan urbanism. Its culture greatly influences the Maya and Zapotec civilizations. The Maya perfect the calendar round, improve astronomical calculations, and build grandiose cities at Palenque, Calakmul, Cobá,

*continues*

wide area stretching from northern Mexico into Central America. The Olmec developed the basic calendar used throughout the region, established a 52-year cycle—which they used to schedule the construction of pyramids—established principles of urban layout and architecture, and originated the cult of the jaguar and the sacredness of jade. They may also have initiated the sacred ritual of "the ball game"—a universal element of Mesoamerican culture.

One intriguing feature of the Olmec was the carving of colossal stone heads. We still don't know what purposes these heads served, but they were immense projects; the basalt stone from which they were sculpted was mined miles inland and transported to Olmec cities on the coast, probably by river rafts. The heads share a rounded, baby-faced look, marked by the peculiar "jaguar mouth"—a high-arched lip that is an identifying mark of Olmec sculpture.

The Maya civilization began developing in the late pre-Classic period, around 500 B.C. Our understanding of this period is sketchy, but Olmec influences are apparent everywhere. The Maya perfected the Olmec calendar and, somewhere along the way, developed an ornate system of hieroglyphic writing and early architectural concepts. Two other civilizations began the rise to prominence around this time: the people of Teotihuacán, just north of present-day Mexico City, and the Zapotec of Monte Albán in the valley of Oaxaca.

**THE CLASSIC PERIOD (A.D. 300–900)** The flourishing of these three civilizations marks the boundaries of this period—the heyday of pre-Columbian Mesoamerican artistic and cultural achievements. These include the pyramids and palaces in Teotihuacán; the ceremonial center of Monte Albán; and the stelae and temples of Palenque, Bonampak, and

and in Central America. The Zapotec construct the religious center on Monte Albán.

- 650–800 Teotihuacán suffers violent attack and is abandoned. Several minor cities in the area reach their zenith as centers of culture and learning.
- 900 Post-Classic period begins: More emphasis is placed on warfare in central Mexico. The Toltec culture emerges at Tula and replaces Teotihuacán as the dominant city of central Mexico. Toltec influence spreads to the Yucatán, forming the culture of the Itzáes, who become the rulers of Chichén-Itzá.
- 1156–1230 Tula, the Toltec capital, is abandoned.
- 1325–1470 Aztec capital Tenochtitlán founded; Aztecs begin military campaigns in the Valley of Mexico and farther out, subjugating the civilizations of the Gulf Coast and southern Mexico.
- 1519 Conquest of Mexico begins: Hernán Cortez and troops make their way along the Mexican coast to present-day Veracruz.
- 1521 Conquest is complete after Aztec defeat at Tlatelolco.
- 1521–24 Cortez begins the creation of the colony of New Spain. He later returns to Europe.
- 1535 The first viceroy of "New Spain" arrives. Sixty viceroys will succeed him before Mexico gains its independence.
- 1767 Jesuits expelled from New Spain.
- 1810–21 War of Independence: Miguel Hidalgo starts movement for Mexico's independence from Spain but is executed within a year. Eventually, Agustín de Iturbide declares Mexico independent.
- 1822 First Empire: Iturbide ascends throne as Emperor of Mexico, loses power after a year, and loses life in an attempt to reclaim throne.
- 1824–64 Early Republic period, characterized by almost perpetual civil war between federalists and centralists, conservatives and liberals, culminating in the victory of the liberals under Juárez.
- 1847–66 War of the Castes in the Yucatán: Degrading segregationist policies against the Maya cause revolt,

the Tikal site in Guatemala. Beyond these achievements, the Maya made significant discoveries in science, including the use of zero in mathematics and a complex calendar with which the priests could predict eclipses and the movements of the stars for centuries to come.

The inhabitants of **Teotihuacán** (100 B.C.–A.D. 700), near present-day Mexico City, built a city that, at its zenith, is thought to have had 100,000 or more inhabitants. It was a well-organized city, covering 9 square miles, and built on a grid with streams channeled to follow the city's plan. Different social classes, such as artisans and merchants, were assigned to specific neighborhoods. Teotihuacán was the greatest cultural center in Mexico, with tremendous influence as far away as Guatemala and the Yucatán. The ceremonial center is so large that the Aztec thought gods had built it. Its feathered serpent god, later known as **Quetzalcoatl,** became part of the pantheon of many succeeding cultures. The ruling classes were industrious, literate, and cosmopolitan. The beautiful sculpture and ceramics of Teotihuacán display a highly stylized and refined aesthetic whose influences can be seen clearly in objects of Maya and Zapotec origin. Around the 7th century, the city was abandoned for unknown reasons. Who these people were and where they went remains a mystery.

Farther south, the **Zapotec,** influenced by the Olmec, raised an impressive civilization in the region of Oaxaca. Their two principal cities were **Monte Albán,** inhabited by an elite of merchants and artisans, and **Mitla,** reserved for the high priests.

**THE POST-CLASSIC PERIOD (A.D. 900–1521)** Warfare was a more conspicuous activity of the civilizations that flourished in this period. Social development was impressive but not as cosmopolitan as the Maya,

upheaval, and decimation of half the Maya population. Strife lasts well into 20th century.

- 1864–67 Second Empire: The French invade Mexico in the name of Maximilian of Austria, who is appointed Emperor of Mexico. Juárez and liberal government retreat to the north and wage war. The French finally abandon Mexico, leaving Maximilian to be defeated and executed by the Mexicans.
- 1872–76 Juárez dies, and political struggles for the presidency ensue.
- 1877–1911 Porfiriato: Porfirio Díaz is president/dictator of Mexico for 35 years, leads country to modernization by encouraging foreign investment in mines, oil, and railroads. Modern economy and a growing disparity between rich and poor develop. Social conditions, especially in rural areas, become desperate.
- 1911–17 Mexican Revolution: Francisco Madero drafts revolutionary plan. Díaz resigns. Leaders jockey for power during period of great violence, national upheaval, and tremendous loss of life.
- 1917–40 Reconstruction: Present constitution of Mexico signed; land and education reforms initiated, and labor unions strengthened; Mexico expropriates oil companies and railroads. Pancho Villa, Zapata, and presidents Obregón and Carranza are assassinated.
- 1940–90 Years of considerable economic development without significant moves towards democratization. From 1976 onward, Mexico suffers periodic severe recessions, which put in doubt the government's economic policies.
- 1994–97 Mexico, Canada, and the United States sign the North American Free Trade Agreement. In an unrelated incident, PRI candidate Luis Donaldo Colosio is assassinated; replacement candidate Ernesto Zedillo becomes Mexico's next president, vowing to be a reformer. Within weeks, the peso is devalued, throwing the nation into turmoil. The middle and lower classes are hurt the most as interest rates soar. Indian uprising in

*continues*

Teotihuacán, and Zapotec societies. In central Mexico, a people known as the **Toltec** established their capital at Tula in the 10th century. They were originally one of the barbarous hordes of Indians that periodically migrated from the north. At some stage in their development, they were influenced by remnants of Teotihuacán culture and adopted the feathered serpent Quetzalcoatl as their god. They also revered a god known as **Tezcatlipoca,** or "smoking mirror," who later became an Aztec god. The Toltec maintained a large military class divided into orders symbolized by animals. At its height, Tula may have had 40,000 people, and it spread its influence across Mesoamerica. By the 13th century, however, the Toltec had exhausted themselves, probably in civil wars and in battles with the invaders from the north.

Chiapas sparks countrywide protests over government policies concerning land distribution, bank loans, health, education, and voting and human rights.

- 1998 Economy improves. Cuauhtémoc Cárdenas becomes the first opposition candidate to become mayor of Mexico City, the second most powerful office in the country.
- 2000 Mexico elects Vicente Fox of the PAN party as president.
- 2002 Federal government struggles with complex reform of the tax code.

Of those northern invaders, the **Aztec** were the most warlike. At first they served as mercenaries for established cities in the valley of Mexico—one of which allotted them an unwanted, marshy piece of land in the middle of Lake Texcoco for their settlement. It eventually grew into the island city of Tenochtitlán. Through aggressive diplomacy and military action, the Aztec soon conquered central Mexico and extended their rule east to the Gulf Coast and south to the valley of Oaxaca.

During this period, the Maya built beautiful cities near the Yucatán's Puuc hills. The regional architecture, called **Puuc style,** is characterized by elaborate exterior stonework appearing above doorframes and extending to the roofline. Examples of this architecture, such as the Codz Poop at Kabah and the palaces at Uxmal, Sayil, and Labná, are beautiful and quite impressive. Associated with the cities of the Puuc region was Chichén-Itzá, ruled by the Itzáes. This metropolis evidences strong Toltec influence in its architectural style and its religion, which incorporated a plumed-serpent god called Kukulkán, obviously the god Quetzalcoatl of central Mexico.

The precise nature of this Toltec influence is a subject of debate. But an intriguing myth in central Mexico tells how Quetzalcoatl quarrels with Tezcatlipoca and, through trickery, is shamed by his rival into leaving Tula, the capital of the Toltec empire. He heads east toward the morning star, vowing someday to return. In the language of myth, this could be an account of an actual civil war between two factions in Tula, each led by the priesthood of a particular god. Could the losing faction have migrated to the Yucatán and formed the ruling class of Chichén-Itzá? Perhaps, but what we do know is that this myth of the eventual return of Quetzalcoatl became, in the hands of the Spanish, a powerful weapon of conquest.

## THE CONQUEST

In 1517, the first Spaniards arrived in what is today known as Mexico and skirmished with Maya Indians off the coast of the Yucatán Peninsula. One of the fledgling expeditions ended in shipwreck, leaving several Spaniards stranded as prisoners of the Maya. The Spanish sent out another expedition, under the command of **Hernán Cortez,** which landed on Cozumel in February of 1519. Cortez inquired about the gold and riches of the interior, and the coastal Maya were happy to describe the wealth and splendor of the Aztec empire in central Mexico. Cortez promptly disobeyed all orders of his superior, the governor of Cuba, and sailed to the mainland.

Cortez arrived when the Aztec empire was at the height of its wealth and power. **Moctezuma II** ruled over the central and southern highlands and extracted tribute from lowland peoples. His greatest temples were literally plated with gold and encrusted with the blood of sacrificial captives. Moctezuma was a fool, a mystic, and something of a coward. Despite his wealth and military power, he dithered in his capital at Tenochtitlán, sending messengers with gifts and suggestions that Cortez leave. Meanwhile, Cortez blustered and negotiated his way into the highlands, always cloaking his real intentions. Moctezuma, terrified by the military tactics and technology of the Spaniard, convinced himself that Cortez was in fact the god Quetzalcoatl making his long-awaited return. By the time the Spaniards arrived in the Aztec capital, Cortez had gained some ascendancy over the lesser Indian states that were resentful tributaries to the Aztec. In November 1519, Cortez confronted Moctezuma and took him hostage in an effort to leverage control of the empire.

In the middle of Cortez's dangerous game of manipulation, another Spanish expedition arrived with orders to end Cortez's authority over the mission. Cortez hastened to meet the rival's force and persuade them to join his own. In the meantime, the Aztec chased the garrison out of Tenochtitlán, and either they or the Spaniards killed Moctezuma. For the next year and a half, Cortez laid siege to Tenochtitlán, with the help of rival Indians and a decimating epidemic of smallpox, to which the Indians had no resistance. In the end, the Aztec capital fell, and when it did, all of central Mexico lay at the feet of the conquistadors.

The Spanish Conquest started as a pirate expedition by Cortez and his men, unauthorized by the Spanish crown or its governor in Cuba. The Spanish king legitimized Cortez following his victory over the Aztec and ordered the forced conversion to Christianity of this new colony, to be called **New Spain.** Guatemala and Honduras were explored and conquered, and by 1540, the territory of New Spain included possessions from Vancouver to Panama. In the 2 centuries that followed, Franciscan and Augustinian friars converted millions of Indians to Christianity, and the Spanish lords built huge feudal estates on which the Indian farmers were little more than serfs. The silver and gold that Cortez looted made Spain the richest country in Europe.

## THE COLONIAL PERIOD

Hernán Cortez set about building a new city, the seat of government of New Spain, upon the ruins of the old Aztec capital. For indigenous peoples (besides the Tlaxcaltecans, Cortez's Indian allies), heavy tributes once paid to the Aztec were now rendered in forced labor to the Spanish. Diseases the Spaniards carried, against which the Indians had no immunity, wiped out most of the native population.

Over the 3 centuries of the colonial period, 61 viceroys appointed by the king of Spain governed Mexico. Spain became rich from New World gold and silver, chiseled out by backbreaking Indian labor. The colonial elite built lavish homes in Mexico City and in the countryside. They filled their homes with ornate furniture, had many servants, and adorned themselves in imported velvets, satins, and jewels. A new class system developed. Those born in Spain considered themselves superior to the *criollos* (Spaniards born in Mexico). Those of other races and the *castas* (mixtures of Spanish and Indian, Spanish and Black, or Indian and Black) occupied the bottom rung of society.

It took great cunning to stay a step ahead of the avaricious Crown, which demanded increasing taxes and contributions from its fabled foreign conquests. Still, wealthy colonists prospered enough to develop an extravagant society.

However, discontent with the mother country simmered for years over social and political issues: taxes, the royal bureaucracy, Spanish-born citizens' advantages over Mexican-born subjects, and restrictions on commerce with Spain and other countries. In 1808, Napoleon invaded Spain and crowned his brother Joseph king in place of Charles IV. To many in Mexico, allegiance to France was out of the question; discontent reached the level of revolt.

## INDEPENDENCE

The rebellion began in 1810, when **Father Miguel Hidalgo** gave the *grito,* a cry for independence, from his church in the town of Dolores, Guanajuato. The uprising soon became a full-fledged revolution, as Hidalgo and Ignacio Allende gathered an "army" of citizens and threatened Mexico City. Although Hidalgo ultimately failed and was executed, he is honored as "the Father of Mexican Independence." Another priest, José María Morelos, kept the revolt alive with several successful campaigns through 1815, when he, too, was captured and executed.

After the death of Morelos, prospects for independence were rather dim until the Spanish king who replaced Joseph Bonaparte decided to make social reforms in the colonies, which convinced the conservative powers in Mexico that they didn't need Spain after all. With their tacit approval, Agustín de Iturbide, then commander of royalist forces, declared Mexico independent and himself emperor. Before long, however, internal dissension brought about the fall of the emperor, and Mexico was proclaimed a republic.

Political instability inflamed the young Mexican republic, which ran through a dizzying succession of presidents and dictators as struggles between federalists and centralists, and conservatives and liberals, divided the country. Moreover, Mexico waged a disastrous war with the United States and lost half its territory. A central figure was **Antonio López de Santa Anna,** who assumed the leadership of his country no fewer than 11 times and was flexible enough in those volatile times to portray himself variously as a liberal, a conservative, a federalist, and a centralist. He probably holds the record for frequency of exile; by 1855 he was finally left without a political comeback and ended his days in Venezuela.

Political instability persisted, and the conservative forces, with some encouragement from Napoleon III, hit upon the idea of inviting in a Hapsburg to regain control (as if that strategy had ever worked for Spain). They found a willing volunteer in Archduke Maximilian of Austria, who accepted the position of Mexican emperor with the support of French troops. The rag-tag Mexican forces defeated the French force—a modern, well-equipped army—in a battle near Puebla (now celebrated annually as **Cinco de Mayo**). A second attempt was more successful, and Ferdinand Maximilian Joseph of Hapsburg became emperor. After 3 years of civil war, the French were finally induced to abandon the emperor's cause; Maximilian was captured and executed by a firing squad near Querétaro in 1867. His adversary and successor (as president of Mexico) was **Benito Juárez,** a Zapotec Indian lawyer and one of the great heroes of Mexican history. Juárez did his best to unify and strengthen his country before dying of a heart attack in 1872; his impact on Mexico's future was profound, and his plans and visions bore fruit for decades.

## THE PORFIRIATO & THE REVOLUTION

A few years after Juárez's death, one of his generals, **Porfirio Díaz,** assumed power in a coup. He ruled Mexico from 1877 to 1911, a period now called the "Porfiriato." He stayed in power through brutal repression of the opposition and by courting the favor of powerful nations. Generous in his dealings with foreign investors, Díaz became, in the eyes of most Mexicans, the archetypal *entreguista* (one who sells out his country for private gain). With foreign investment came the concentration of great wealth in few hands, and social conditions worsened.

In 1910, Francisco Madero called for an armed rebellion that became the **Mexican Revolution** ("La Revolución" in Mexico; the revolution against Spain is the "Guerra de Independencia"). Díaz was sent into exile; while in London, he became a celebrity at the age of 81, when he jumped into the Thames to save a drowning boy. Díaz is buried in Paris. Madero became president but was promptly betrayed and executed by a straight-out-of-the-movies group of villains—the despicable **Victoriano Huerta.** Those who had answered Madero's call responded again—the great peasant hero **Emiliano Zapata** in the south, and the seemingly invincible **Pancho Villa** in the central north, flanked by Alvaro Obregón and Venustiano Carranza. They eventually put Huerta to flight and began hashing out a new constitution.

For the next few years, the revolutionaries Carranza, Obregón, and Villa fought among themselves; Zapata did not seek national power, though he fought tenaciously for land for the peasants. Carranza, who was president at the time, betrayed and assassinated Zapata. Obregón finally consolidated power and probably had Carranza assassinated. He, in turn, was assassinated when he tried to break one of the tenets of the Revolution—no reelection. His successor, Plutarco Elias Calles, learned this lesson well, installing one puppet president after another, until **Lázaro Cárdenas** severed the puppeteer's strings and banished him to exile.

Until Cárdenas's election in 1934, the outcome of the Revolution remained in doubt. There had been some land redistribution, but other measures took a back seat to political expediency. Cárdenas changed all that. He implemented massive redistribution of land and nationalized the oil industry. He instituted many reforms and gave shape to the ruling political party (now the **Partido Revolucionario Institucional,** or PRI) by bringing a broad representation of Mexican society under its banner and establishing mechanisms for consensus building. Most Mexicans practically canonize Cárdenas.

## MODERN MEXICO

The presidents who followed were noted more for graft than for leadership. The party's base narrowed as many of the reform-minded elements were marginalized. Economic progress, a lot of it in the form of large development projects, became the PRI's main basis for legitimacy. In 1968, the government violently repressed a democratic student movement. Police forces shot and killed an unknown number of civilians in the Tlatelolco section of Mexico City. Though the PRI maintained its grip on power, it lost all semblance of being a progressive party. In 1985, a devastating **earthquake in Mexico City** brought down many of the government's new, supposedly earthquake-proof buildings, exposing shoddy construction and the widespread government corruption that fostered it. There was heavy criticism, too, for the government's handling of the relief efforts. In 1994, a political and military **uprising in Chiapas** focused world attention on Mexico's great social problems. A new political force, the Zapatista National

Liberation Army (EZLN for Ejército Zapatista de Liberación Nacional), has skillfully publicized the plight of the peasant in today's Mexico.

In recent years, opposition political parties have grown in power and legitimacy. Facing enormous pressure and scrutiny from national and international organizations, and widespread public discontent, the PRI has had to concede defeat in state governor and congressperson elections. Elements of the PRI have been trying to reform the party from within, creating internal crises as manifested in several political assassinations. In 1998, for the first time ever, the PRI conceded the mayoralty of Mexico City, the second most powerful position in the country, to a leader of the opposition, **Cuauhtémoc Cárdenas,** son of the PRI's brightest star, Lázaro. In 2000 Vicente Fox, of the opposition party PAN, won the presidential election.

## 3 Food & Drink

Authentic Mexican food differs dramatically from what is frequently served in the United States under that name. For many travelers, Mexico will be new and exciting culinary territory. Even grizzled veterans will be pleasantly surprised by the wide variation in specialties and traditions from region to region.

Despite regional differences, some generalizations can be made. Mexican food usually isn't pepper-hot when it arrives at the table (though many dishes have a certain amount of piquancy, and some home cooking can be very spicy). The *picante* flavor is added with chiles and sauces after the food is served; you'll never see a table in Mexico without one or both of these condiments. Mexicans don't drown their food in cheese and sour cream, a la Tex-Mex, and they use a greater variety of ingredients than most people expect. But the basis of Mexican food is simple—tortillas, beans, chiles, squash, and tomatoes, the same as it was centuries ago before the arrival of the Europeans.

### THE BASICS

**TORTILLAS** Traditional tortillas are made from corn that's been cooked in water and lime, then ground into *masa* (a grainy dough), patted and pressed into thin cakes, and cooked on a hot griddle known as a *comal.* In many households, the tortilla takes the place of fork and spoon; Mexicans tear them into wedge-shaped pieces, which they use to scoop up their food. Restaurants often serve bread rather than tortillas because it's easier, but you can always ask for tortillas. A more recent invention from northern Mexico is the flour tortilla, which is seen less frequently in the rest of Mexico.

**ENCHILADAS** The tortilla is the basis of several Mexican dishes, the most famous of which is the enchilada. The original name would have been *tortilla enchilada,* which simply means a tortilla dipped in chile sauce. The enchilada began as a very simple dish: A tortilla dipped in chile (usually ancho) sauce and then into very hot oil, quickly folded or rolled on a plate. It's sprinkled with chopped onions and a little *queso cotija* (crumbly white cheese) and served with a little fried potatoes and carrots. You can get this basic enchilada in food stands across the country. I love them, and if you come across them in your travels, give them a try. In restaurants you get more elaborate enchiladas, filled with cheese, chicken, pork, or even seafood, and sometimes prepared as a casserole.

**TACOS** A taco is anything folded or rolled into a tortilla, and sometimes a double tortilla. The tortilla can be served soft or fried. *Flautas* and quesadillas (except in Mexico City, where they are something quite different) are species of tacos. For Mexicans, the taco is the quintessential fast food, and the ubiquitous taco stand (*taquería*) is a great place to get a filling meal. See the section below, "Eating Out: Restaurants, *Taquerías* & Tipping," for information on *taquerías.*

**FRIJOLES** An invisible "bean line" divides Mexico: It starts at the Gulf Coast in the southern part of the state of Tamaulipas and moves inland through the eastern quarter of San Luis Potosí and most of the state of Hidalgo, then straight through Mexico City and Morelos and into Guerrero, where it curves slightly west to the Pacific. North and west of this line, the pink bean known as the *flor de mayo* is the staple food; to the south and east, the standard is the black bean.

Private households serve beans at least once a day, and the working class and peasantry serve them with every meal if the family can afford it. Mexicans almost always prepare beans with a minimum of condiments, usually just a little onion and garlic and perhaps a pinch of herbs. Beans are meant to be a contrast to the heavily spiced foods in a meal. Sometimes they are served at the end of a meal with a little Mexican-style sour cream.

Mexicans often fry leftover beans and serve them on the side as *frijoles refritos.* "Refried beans" is a misnomer—the beans are fried only once. The prefix "re" actually means "well" (as in "thoroughly"), and what Mexicans actually mean is that the beans are well fried.

**TAMALES** You make a *tamal* by mixing corn masa with a little lard, adding one of several fillings—or no filling at all—then wrapping it in a corn husk or in the leaf of a banana or other plant, and steaming it. Every region in Mexico has a traditional way of making tamales. In some places, a single tamal can feed a family; in others, they are barely 3 inches long.

**CHILES** There are many kinds of chile peppers, and Mexicans call each by one name when they're fresh and another when they're dried. Some are blazing hot, with little flavor; some are mild but have a rich, complex flavor. They can be pickled, smoked, stuffed, and stewed.

## EATING OUT: RESTAURANTS, *TAQUERIAS* & TIPPING

I feel compelled to debunk the prevailing myth that the cheapest place to eat in Mexico is in the market. Actually, this is almost never the case. You can usually find better food at a better price without going more than 2 blocks out of your way. Why? Food stalls in the marketplace pay high rents; they have a near-captive clientele of vendors and truckers; and they get a lot of business from Mexicans for whom eating in the market is a traditional way of confirming their culture.

On the other side of the spectrum, avoid eating at the inviting sidewalk restaurants you see beneath the stone archways that border the main plazas. These places usually cater to tourists and don't need to count on return business. But they are great for getting a coffee or beer and watching the world turn.

You'll see many *taquerías* (**taco joints**). These are generally small places with a counter or a few tables around the cooking area. Find one that seems popular with the locals and where the cook performs with brio (a good sign of pride in the product). Sometimes, a woman will be making the tortillas right there (or working the masa into *gorditas, sopes,* or *panuchos*). You will never see men doing this—this is perhaps the strictest gender division in Mexican society. Men do all other kitchen tasks, and work with already-made tortillas, but will never be found working masa.

For the main meal of the day, many restaurants offer a multicourse blue-plate special called ***comida corrida*** or ***menú del día.*** This is the least expensive way to get a full dinner. In Mexico you need to ask for your check; it is generally considered inhospitable to present a check to someone who hasn't requested it. If you're in a hurry to get somewhere, ask for the check when your food arrives.

**Tips** are about the same as in the United States. You'll sometimes find a 15% **value-added tax** on restaurant meals, which shows up on the bill as "IVA."

To summon the waiter, wave or raise your hand, but don't motion with your index finger, which is a demeaning gesture that may cause the waiter to ignore you. If you want the check, you can motion to the waiter from across the room using the universal pretend-you're-writing gesture.

Most restaurants do not have **nonsmoking sections;** when they do, we mention it in the reviews. But Mexico's wonderful climate allows for many open-air restaurants, usually inside a courtyard of a colonial house, or in rooms with tall ceilings and plenty of open windows.

## DRINKS

All over Mexico, you'll find shops selling **juices** and **smoothies** made from several kinds of tropical fruit. They're excellent and refreshing; while traveling, I take full advantage of them. You'll also come across *aguas frescas*—water flavored with hibiscus, melon, tamarind, or lime. Soft drinks come in more flavors than in any other country I know. Pepsi and Coca-Cola taste the way they did in the United States years ago, before the makers started adding corn syrup. The coffee is generally good, and **hot chocolate** is a traditional drink, as is *atole*—a hot, corn-based beverage that can be sweet or bitter.

Of course, Mexico has a proud and lucrative **beer**-brewing tradition. A less-known brewed beverage is *pulque,* a pre-Hispanic drink made of the fermented juice of a few species of maguey or agave. Mostly you find it for sale in *pulquerías* in central Mexico. It is an acquired taste, and not every gringo acquires it. **Mezcal** and **tequila** also come from the agave. Tequila is a variety of mezcal produced from the *a. tequilana* species of agave in and around the area of Tequila, in the state of Jalisco. Mezcal comes from various parts of Mexico and from different varieties of agave. The distilling process is usually much less sophisticated than that of tequila, and, with its stronger smell and taste, mezcal is much more easily detected on the drinker's breath. In some places like Oaxaca it comes with a worm in the bottle; you are supposed to eat the worm after polishing off the mezcal. But for those teetotalers out there who are interested in just the worm, I have good news—you can find these worms for sale in Mexican markets when in season. *¡Salud!*

# Appendix B: Useful Terms & Phrases

## 1 Telephones & Mail

### USING THE TELEPHONES

All phone numbers listed in this book have a total of 10 digits—the number plus the area code within Mexico. To call a local number, dial the last 7 or 8 digits. Local numbers in Mexico City, Guadalajara, and Monterrey are 8 digits; everywhere else, local numbers have 7 digits. As this book went to press, some regional area codes continued to change. If you try to place a call and the number does not go through, consult the website for Telmex, Mexico's primary long-distance carrier (www.telmex.com/english/areacode/areacode.html), to see if the area code you are calling has changed.

To call long distance within Mexico, dial the national long-distance code **01** before dialing the 2- or 3-digit area code and then the number. Mexico's area codes (*claves*) are listed in the front of telephone directories. Area codes are listed before all phone numbers in this book. For long-distance dialing, you will often see the term "LADA," which is the automatic long-distance service offered by Telmex, Mexico's former telephone monopoly and its largest phone company. To make a person-to-person or collect call inside Mexico, dial ✆ **020.**

To make a long-distance call to the United States or Canada, dial ✆ **001,** then the area code and 7-digit number. For international long-distance numbers in Europe, Africa, and Asia, dial ✆ **00,** then the country code, the city code, and the number. To make a person-to-person or collect call to outside Mexico, to obtain other international dialing codes, or for further assistance, dial ✆ **090.**

For additional details on making calls in Mexico and to Mexico, see chapter 2 and the inside front cover of this book.

### POSTAL GLOSSARY

Airmail **Correo Aéreo**
Customs **Aduana**
General delivery **Lista de correos**
Insurance (insured mail) **Seguro (correo asegurado)**
Mailbox **Buzón**
Money order **Giro postal**
Parcel **Paquete**
Post office **Oficina de correos**
Post office box (abbreviation) **Apdo. Postal**
Postal service **Correos**
Registered mail **Registrado**
Rubber stamp **Sello**
Special delivery, express **Entrega inmediata**
Stamp **Estampilla** or **timbre**

## 2 Basic Vocabulary

Most Mexicans are very patient with foreigners who try to speak their language; it helps a lot to know a few basic phrases. I've included simple phrases for expressing basic needs, followed by some common menu items.

### ENGLISH-SPANISH PHRASES

| English | Spanish | Pronunciation |
|---|---|---|
| Good day | **Buen día** | bwayn *dee*-ah |
| Good morning | **Buenos días** | *bway*-nohss *dee*-ahss |
| How are you? | **¿Cómo está?** | *koh*-moh ess-*tah*? |
| Very well | **Muy bien** | mwee byen |
| Thank you | **Gracias** | *grah*-see-ahss |
| You're welcome | **De nada** | day *nah*-dah |
| Good-bye | **Adiós** | ah-*dyohss* |
| Please | **Por favor** | pohr fah-*vohr* |
| Yes | **Sí** | see |
| No | **No** | noh |
| Excuse me | **Perdóneme** | pehr-*doh*-ney-may |
| Give me | **Déme** | *day*-may |
| Where is . . . ? | **¿Dónde está . . . ?** | *dohn*-day ess-*tah*? |
| the station | **la estación** | lah ess-tah-*seown* |
| a hotel | **un hotel** | oon oh-*tel* |
| a gas station | **una gasolinera** | *oon*-ah gah-so-lee-*nay*-rah |
| a restaurant | **un restaurante** | oon res-tow-*rahn*-tay |
| the toilet | **el baño** | el *bahn*-yoh |
| a good doctor | **un buen médico** | oon bwayn *may*-dee-co |
| the road to . . . | **el camino a/hacia . . .** | el cah-*mee*-noh ah/*ah*-see-ah |
| To the right | **A la derecha** | ah lah day-*reh*-chuh |
| To the left | **A la izquierda** | ah lah ees-ky-*ehr*-thah |
| Straight ahead | **Derecho** | day-*reh*-cho |
| I would like | **Quisiera** | key-see-*ehr*-ah |
| I want | **Quiero** | *kyehr*-oh |
| to eat | **comer** | ko-*mayr* |
| a room | **una habitación** | *oon*-nah ha-bee-tah-*seown* |
| Do you have . . . ? | **¿Tiene usted . . . ?** | tyah-nay oos-*ted*? |
| a book | **un libro** | oon *lee*-bro |
| a dictionary | **un diccionario** | oon deek-seown-*ar*-eo |
| How much is it? | **¿Cuánto cuesta?** | *kwahn*-to *kwess*-tah? |
| When? | **¿Cuándo?** | *kwahn*-doh? |
| What? | **¿Qué?** | kay? |
| There is (Is there . . . ?) | **(¿)Hay ( . . . ?)** | eye? |
| What is there? | **¿Qué hay?** | kay eye? |
| Yesterday | **Ayer** | ah-*yer* |
| Today | **Hoy** | oy |
| Tomorrow | **Mañana** | mahn-*yahn*-ah |
| Good | **Bueno** | *bway*-no |
| Bad | **Malo** | *mah*-lo |

| | | |
|---|---|---|
| Better (best) | **(Lo) Mejor** | (loh) meh-*hor* |
| More | **Más** | mahs |
| Less | **Menos** | *may*-noss |
| No smoking | **Se prohibe fumar** | say pro-*hee*-bay foo-*mahr* |
| Postcard | **Tarjeta postal** | tar-*heh*-ta pohs-*tahl* |
| Insect repellent | **Repelente contra insectos** | reh-peh-*lehn*-te *cohn*-trah een-*sehk*-tos |

## MORE USEFUL PHRASES

| English | Spanish | Pronunciation |
|---|---|---|
| Do you speak English? | **¿Habla usted inglés?** | *ah*-blah oo-*sted* een-*glays*? |
| Is there anyone here who speaks English? | **¿Hay alguien aquí que hable inglés?** | eye *ahl*-gyen ah-*key* kay *ah*-blay een-*glays*? |
| I speak a little Spanish. | **Hablo un poco de español.** | *ah*-blow oon *poh*-koh day ess-pah-*nyol* |
| I don't understand Spanish very well. | **No (lo) entiendo muy bien el español.** | noh (loh) ehn-tee-*ehn*-do moo-ee bee-ayn el ess-pah-*nyol* |
| The meal is good. | **Me gusta la comida.** | may *goo*-sta lah koh-*mee*-dah |
| What time is it? | **¿Qué hora es?** | kay *oar*-ah ess? |
| May I see your menu? | **¿Puedo ver el menú (la carta)?** | *puay*-tho veyr el may-*noo* (lah *car*-tah)? |
| The check, please. | **La cuenta, por favor.** | lah *quayn*-tah pohr fa-*vorh* |
| What do I owe you? | **¿Cuánto le debo?** | *Kwahn*-toh leh *day*-boh? |
| What did you say? | **¿Mande?** (formal) | *Mahn*-day? |
| | **¿Cómo?** (informal) | *Koh*-moh? |
| I want (to see) . . . | **Quiero (ver) . . .** | Key-*yehr*-oh vehr |
| a room | **un cuarto** or **una habitación** | oon *kwar*-toh, *oon*-nah ah-bee-tah-*seown* |
| for two persons | **para dos personas** | *pahr*-ah doss pehr-*sohn*-as |
| with (without) bathroom | **con (sin) baño.** | kohn (seen) *bah*-nyoh |
| We are staying here only | **Nos quedamos aquí solamente** | nohs kay-*dahm*-ohss ah-*key* sohl-ah-*mayn*-tay |
| one night | **una noche** | oon-ah *noh*-chay |
| one week | **una semana** | oon-ah say-*mahn*-ah |
| We are leaving tomorrow | **Partimos (Salimos) mañana** | Pahr-*tee*-mohss; sah-*lee*-mohss mahn-*nyan*-ah |
| Do you accept . . . ? | **¿Acepta usted . . . ?** | Ah-*sayp*-tah oo-*sted* |
| . . . traveler's checks? | **. . . cheques de viajero?** | *chay* kays day bee-ah-*hehr*-oh |
| Is there a Laundromat? | **¿Hay una lavandería?** | Eye *oon*-ah lah-*vahn*-day-*ree*-ah |
| . . . near here? | **. . . cerca de aquí?** | *sehr*-ka day ah-*key* |
| Please send these clothes to the laundry | **Hágame el favor de mandar esta ropa a la lavandería.** | *Ah*-ga-may el fah-*vhor* day mahn-*dahr ays*-tah *rho*-pah a lah lah-*vahn*-day-*ree*-ah |

### NUMBERS

1 **uno** (*ooh*-noh)
2 **dos** (dohs)
3 **tres** (trayss)
4 **cuatro** (*kwah*-troh)
5 **cinco** (*seen*-koh)
6 **seis** (sayss)
7 **siete** (*syeh*-tay)
8 **ocho** (*oh*-choh)
9 **nueve** (*nway*-bay)
10 **diez** (dee-ess)
11 **once** (*ohn*-say)
12 **doce** (*doh*-say)
13 **trece** (*tray*-say)
14 **catorce** (kah-*tor*-say)
15 **quince** (*keen*-say)
16 **dieciseis** (de-*ess*-ee-sayss)
17 **diecisiete** (de-*ess*-ee-*syeh*-tay)
18 **dieciocho** (dee-*ess*-ee-*oh*-choh)
19 **diecinueve** (dee-*ess*-ee-*nway*-bay)
20 **veinte** (*bayn*-tay)
30 **treinta** (*trayn*-tah)
40 **cuarenta** (kwah-*ren*-tah)
50 **cincuenta** (seen-*kwen*-tah)
60 **sesenta** (say-*sen*-tah)
70 **setenta** (say-*ten*-tah)
80 **ochenta** (oh-*chen*-tah)
90 **noventa** (noh-*ben*-tah)
100 **cien** (see-*en*)
200 **doscientos** (*dos*-se-en-tos)
500 **quinientos** (keen-ee-*ehn*-tos)
1,000 **mil** (meal)

### TRANSPORTATION TERMS

| English | Spanish | Pronunciation |
|---|---|---|
| Airport | **Aeropuerto** | Ah-eh-row-*poo-ehr*-tow |
| Flight | **Vuelo** | Bw*ay*-low |
| Rental car | **Arrendadora de autos** | Ah-rain-da-dow-rah day ah-oo-tohs |
| Bus | **Autobús** | ow-toh-*boos* |
| Bus or truck | **Camión** | ka-mee-*ohn* |
| Lane | **Carril** | kah-*rreal* |
| Nonstop | **Directo** | dee-*reck*-toh |
| Baggage (claim area) | **Equipajes** | eh-key-*pah*-hays |
| Intercity | **Foraneo** | fohr-ah-*nay*-oh |
| Luggage storage area | **Guarda equipaje** | gwar-dah eh-key-*pah*-hay |
| Arrival gates | **Llegadas** | yay-*gah*-dahs |
| Originates at this station | **Local** | loh-*kahl* |
| Originates elsewhere | **De paso** | day *pah*-soh |
| Stops if seats available | **Para si hay lugares** | *pah-rah -see -aye loo-gahr-ays* |
| First class | **Primera** | pree-*mehr*-ah |
| Second class | **Segunda** | say-*goon*-dah |
| Nonstop | **Sin escala** | seen ess-*kah*-lah |
| Baggage claim area | **Recibo de equipajes** | ray-see-boh day eh-key-*pah*-hay |
| Waiting room | **Sala de espera** | *Sah*-lah day ess-*pehr*-ah |
| Toilets | **Sanitarios** | Sahn-ee-tahr-*ee*-oss |
| Ticket window | **Taquilla** | tah-*key*-yah |

## 3 Menu Glossary

**Achiote** Small red seed of the *annatto* tree.

**Achiote preparado** A Yucatecan prepared paste made of ground *achiote,* wheat and corn flour, cumin, cinnamon, salt, onion, garlic, and oregano.

**Agua fresca** Fruit-flavored water, usually watermelon, cantaloupe, chia seed with lemon, hibiscus flour, rice, or ground melon-seed mixture.

**Antojito** Typical Mexican supper foods, usually made with *masa* or tortillas and having a filling or topping such as sausage, cheese, beans, and onions; includes such things as *tacos tostadas, sopes,* and *garnachas.*
**Atole** A thick, lightly sweet, hot drink made with finely ground corn and usually flavored with vanilla, pecan, strawberry, pineapple, or chocolate.
**Botana** An appetizer.
**Buñuelos** Round, thin, deep-fried crispy fritters dipped in sugar.
**Carnitas** Pork deep-cooked (not fried) in lard, and then simmered and served with corn tortillas for tacos.
**Ceviche** Fresh raw seafood marinated in fresh lime juice and garnished with chopped tomatoes, onions, chiles, and sometimes cilantro.
**Chayote** A vegetable pear or merleton, a type of spiny squash boiled and served as an accompaniment to meat dishes.
**Chiles en nogada** Poblano peppers stuffed with a mixture of ground pork and beef, spices, fruits, raisins, and almonds, fried in a light batter and covered in walnut-and-cream sauce.
**Chiles rellenos** Usually poblano peppers stuffed with cheese or spicy ground meat with raisins, rolled in a batter, and fried.
**Churro** Tube-shaped, breadlike fritter, dipped in sugar and sometimes filled with *cajeta* (milk based caramel) or chocolate.
**Cochinita pibil** Pork wrapped in banana leaves, pit-baked in a *pibil* sauce of *achiote,* sour orange, and spices; common in the Yucatán.
**Enchilada** A tortilla dipped in sauce, usually filled with chicken or white cheese, and sometimes topped with *mole* (*enchiladas rojas* or *de mole*), or with tomato sauce and sour cream (*enchiladas suizas*—Swiss enchiladas), or covered in a green sauce (*enchiladas verdes*), or topped with onions, sour cream, and guacamole (*enchiladas potosinas*).
**Escabeche** A lightly pickled sauce used in Yucatecan chicken stew.
**Frijoles refritos** Pinto beans mashed and cooked with lard.
**Gorditas** Thick, fried corn tortillas, slit and stuffed with choice of cheese, beans, beef, chicken, with or without lettuce, tomato, and onion garnish.
**Horchata** Refreshing drink made of ground rice or melon seeds, ground almonds, and lightly sweetened.
**Huevos Mexicanos** Scrambled eggs with chopped onions, hot green peppers, and tomatoes.
**Huitlacoche** Sometimes spelled "cuitlacoche." A mushroom-flavored black fungus that appears on corn in the rainy season; considered a delicacy.
**Manchamantel** Translated, means "tablecloth stainer." A stew of chicken or pork with chiles, tomatoes, pineapple, bananas, and jícama.
**Masa** Ground corn soaked in lime; the basis for tamales, corn tortillas, and soups.
**Mixiote** Rabbit, lamb, or chicken cooked in a mild chili sauce (usually chile *ancho* or *pasilla*), and then wrapped like a tamal and steamed. It is generally served with tortillas for tacos, with traditional garnishes of pickled onions, hot sauce, and lime wedges.
**Pan de Muerto** Sweet bread made around the Days of the Dead (Nov 1–2), in the form of mummies or dolls, or round with bone designs.
**Pan dulce** Lightly sweetened bread in many configurations, usually served at breakfast or bought in any bakery.
**Papadzules** Tortillas stuffed with hard-boiled eggs and seeds (pumpkin or sunflower) in a tomato sauce.

**Pibil** Pit-baked pork or chicken in a sauce of tomato, onion, mild red pepper, cilantro, and vinegar.
**Pipián** A sauce made with ground pumpkin seeds, nuts, and mild peppers.
**Poc chuc** Slices of pork with onion marinated in a tangy sour orange sauce and charcoal-broiled; a Yucatecan specialty.
**Pulque** A drink made of fermented juice of the maguey plant; best in the state of Hidalgo and around Mexico City.
**Quesadilla** Corn or flour tortillas stuffed with melted white cheese and lightly fried.
**Queso relleno** "Stuffed cheese," a mild yellow cheese stuffed with minced meat and spices; a Yucatecan specialty.
**Rompope** Delicious Mexican eggnog, invented in Puebla, made with eggs, vanilla, sugar, and rum.
**Salsa verde** A cooked sauce using the green tomatillo and puréed with spicy or mild hot peppers, onions, garlic, and cilantro; on tables countrywide.
**Sopa de calabaza** A soup made of chopped squash or pumpkin blossoms.
**Sopa de lima** A tangy soup made with chicken broth and accented with fresh lime; popular in Yucatán.
**Sopa Tlalpeña** A hearty soup made with chunks of chicken, chopped carrots, zucchini, corn, onions, garlic, and cilantro.
**Sopa Tlaxcalteca** A hearty tomato-based soup filled with cooked nopal cactus, cheese, cream, and avocado, with crispy tortilla strips floating on top.
**Sopa de Tortilla** A traditional chicken broth–based soup, seasoned with chilies, tomatoes, onion, and garlic, with crispy fried strips of corn tortillas.
**Sope** Pronounced "*soh*-pay." An *antojito* similar to a *garnacha,* except spread with refried beans and topped with crumbled cheese and onions.
**Tacos al pastor** Thin slices of flavored pork roasted on a revolving cylinder dripping with onion slices and juice of fresh pineapple slices. Served in small corn tortillas, topped with chopped onion and cilantro.
**Tamal** Incorrectly called a tamale (*tamal* singular, *tamales* plural). A meat or sweet filling rolled with fresh *masa,* wrapped in a corn husk or banana leaf, and steamed.
**Tikin xic** Also seen on menus as "tik-n-xic" and "tikik chick." Charbroiled fish brushed with *achiote* sauce.
**Torta** A sandwich, usually on *bolillo* bread, typically with sliced avocado, onions, tomatoes, with a choice of meat and often cheese.
**Xtabentun** Pronounced shtah-ben-*toon.* A Yucatán liquor made of fermented honey and flavored with anise. It comes *seco* (dry) or *crema* (sweet).
**Zacahuil** Pork leg tamal, packed in thick *masa,* wrapped in banana leaves, and pit-baked, sometimes pot-made with tomato and *masa;* a specialty of mid- to upper Veracruz.

# Index

# Wickedly honest guides for sophisticated travelers—and those who want to be.

**Irreverent Guide to Amsterdam**
**Irreverent Guide to Boston**
**Irreverent Guide to Chicago**
**Irreverent Guide to Las Vegas**
**Irreverent Guide to London**
**Irreverent Guide to Los Angeles**
**Irreverent Guide to Manhattan**
**Irreverent Guide to New Orleans**
**Irreverent Guide to Paris**
**Irreverent Guide to Rome**
**Irreverent Guide to San Francisco**
**Irreverent Guide to Seattle & Portland**
**Irreverent Guide to Vancouver**
**Irreverent Guide to Walt Disney World®**
**Irreverent Guide to Washington, D.C.**

**Available at bookstores everywhere.**

## Frommer's® Complete Travel Guides

Alaska
Alaska Cruises & Ports of Call
Amsterdam
Argentina & Chile
Arizona
Atlanta
Australia
Austria
Bahamas
Barcelona, Madrid & Seville
Beijing
Belgium, Holland & Luxembourg
Bermuda
Boston
Brazil
British Columbia & the Canadian Rockies
Budapest & the Best of Hungary
California
Canada
Cancún, Cozumel & the Yucatán
Cape Cod, Nantucket & Martha's Vineyard
Caribbean
Caribbean Cruises & Ports of Call
Caribbean Ports of Call
Carolinas & Georgia
Chicago
China
Colorado
Costa Rica
Denmark
Denver, Boulder & Colorado Springs
England
Europe
European Cruises & Ports of Call
Florida
France
Germany
Great Britain
Greece
Greek Islands
Hawaii
Hong Kong
Honolulu, Waikiki & Oahu
Ireland
Israel
Italy
Jamaica
Japan
Las Vegas
London
Los Angeles
Maryland & Delaware
Maui
Mexico
Montana & Wyoming
Montréal & Québec City
Munich & the Bavarian Alps
Nashville & Memphis
Nepal
New England
New Mexico
New Orleans
New York City
New Zealand
Northern Italy
Nova Scotia, New Brunswick & Prince Edward Island
Oregon
Paris
Philadelphia & the Amish Country
Portugal
Prague & the Best of the Czech Republic
Provence & the Riviera
Puerto Rico
Rome
San Antonio & Austin
San Diego
San Francisco
Santa Fe, Taos & Albuquerque
Scandinavia
Scotland
Seattle & Portland
Shanghai
Singapore & Malaysia
South Africa
South America
South Florida
South Pacific
Southeast Asia
Spain
Sweden
Switzerland
Texas
Thailand
Tokyo
Toronto
Tuscany & Umbria
USA
Utah
Vancouver & Victoria
Vermont, New Hampshire & Maine
Vienna & the Danube Valley
Virgin Islands
Virginia
Walt Disney World® & Orlando
Washington, D.C.
Washington State

## Frommer's® Dollar-a-Day Guides

Australia from $50 a Day
California from $70 a Day
Caribbean from $70 a Day
England from $75 a Day
Europe from $70 a Day
Florida from $70 a Day
Hawaii from $80 a Day
Ireland from $60 a Day
Italy from $70 a Day
London from $85 a Day
New York from $90 a Day
Paris from $80 a Day
San Francisco from $70 a Day
Washington, D.C. from $80 a Day

## Frommer's® Portable Guides

Acapulco, Ixtapa & Zihuatanejo
Amsterdam
Aruba
Australia's Great Barrier Reef
Bahamas
Berlin
Big Island of Hawaii
Boston
California Wine Country
Cancún
Charleston & Savannah
Chicago
Disneyland®
Dublin
Florence
Frankfurt
Hong Kong
Houston
Las Vegas
London
Los Angeles
Los Cabos & Baja
Maine Coast
Maui
Miami
New Orleans
New York City
Paris
Phoenix & Scottsdale
Portland
Puerto Rico
Puerto Vallarta, Manzanillo & Guadalajara
Rio de Janeiro
San Diego
San Francisco
Seattle
Sydney
Tampa & St. Petersburg
Vancouver
Venice
Virgin Islands
Washington, D.C.

## Frommer's® National Park Guides

Banff & Jasper
Family Vacations in the National Parks
Grand Canyon
National Parks of the American West
Rocky Mountain
Yellowstone & Grand Teton
Yosemite & Sequoia/ Kings Canyon
Zion & Bryce Canyon

## Frommer's® Memorable Walks

Chicago
London
New York
Paris
San Francisco
Washington, D.C.

## Frommer's® Great Outdoor Guides

Arizona & New Mexico
New England
Northern California
Southern New England
Vermont & New Hampshire

## Suzy Gershman's Born to Shop Guides

Born to Shop: France
Born to Shop: Hong Kong, Shanghai & Beijing
Born to Shop: Italy
Born to Shop: London
Born to Shop: New York
Born to Shop: Paris

## Frommer's® Irreverent Guides

Amsterdam
Boston
Chicago
Las Vegas
London
Los Angeles
Manhattan
New Orleans
Paris
Rome
San Francisco
Seattle & Portland
Vancouver
Walt Disney World®
Washington, D.C.

## Frommer's® Best-Loved Driving Tours

Britain
California
Florida
France
Germany
Ireland
Italy
New England
Northern Italy
Scotland
Spain
Tuscany & Umbria

## Hanging Out™ Guides

Hanging Out in England
Hanging Out in Europe
Hanging Out in France
Hanging Out in Ireland
Hanging Out in Italy
Hanging Out in Spain

## The Unofficial Guides®

Bed & Breakfasts and Country Inns in:
- California
- Great Lakes States
- Mid-Atlantic
- New England
- Northwest
- Rockies
- Southeast
- Southwest

Best RV & Tent Campgrounds in:
- California & the West
- Florida & the Southeast
- Great Lakes States
- Mid-Atlantic
- Northeast
- Northwest & Central Plains
- Southwest & South Central Plains
- U.S.A.

Beyond Disney
Branson, Missouri
California with Kids
Chicago
Cruises
Disneyland®
Florida with Kids
Golf Vacations in the Eastern U.S.
Great Smoky & Blue Ridge Region
Inside Disney
Hawaii
Las Vegas
London
Mid-Atlantic with Kids
Mini Las Vegas
Mini-Mickey
New England and New York with Kids
New Orleans
New York City
Paris
San Francisco
Skiing in the West
Southeast with Kids
Walt Disney World®
Walt Disney World® for Grown-ups
Walt Disney World® with Kids
Washington, D.C.
World's Best Diving Vacations

## Special-Interest Titles

Frommer's Adventure Guide to Australia & New Zealand
Frommer's Adventure Guide to Central America
Frommer's Adventure Guide to India & Pakistan
Frommer's Adventure Guide to South America
Frommer's Adventure Guide to Southeast Asia
Frommer's Adventure Guide to Southern Africa
Frommer's Britain's Best Bed & Breakfasts and Country Inns
Frommer's Caribbean Hideaways
Frommer's Exploring America by RV
Frommer's Fly Safe, Fly Smart
Frommer's France's Best Bed & Breakfasts and Country Inns
Frommer's Gay & Lesbian Europe
Frommer's Italy's Best Bed & Breakfasts and Country Inns
Frommer's New York City with Kids
Frommer's Ottawa with Kids
Frommer's Road Atlas Britain
Frommer's Road Atlas Europe
Frommer's Road Atlas France
Frommer's Toronto with Kids
Frommer's Vancouver with Kids
Frommer's Washington, D.C., with Kids
Israel Past & Present
The New York Times' Guide to Unforgettable Weekends
Places Rated Almanac
Retirement Places Rated